Henry William Bristow

A Glossary of Mineralogy

Henry William Bristow

A Glossary of Mineralogy

ISBN/EAN: 9783743325135

Manufactured in Europe, USA, Canada, Australia, Japa

Cover: Foto ©ninafisch / pixelio.de

Manufactured and distributed by brebook publishing software
(www.brebook.com)

Henry William Bristow

A Glossary of Mineralogy

A

GLOSSARY OF MINERALOGY.

BY

HENRY WILLIAM BRISTOW, F.G.S.

OF THE GEOLOGICAL SURVEY OF GREAT BRITAIN.

LONDON:

LONGMAN, GREEN, LONGMAN, AND ROBERTS.

1861.

PREFACE.

———✦———

THIS little work was undertaken to supply a want which the Author had frequently experienced. In compiling it he has endeavoured to produce a handy book, combining facility of reference with a concise and familiar account of all the known minerals.

In carrying this object into execution, the various names used by different authors have been introduced, as well as certain terms, which, though now obsolete, are, nevertheless, of common occurrence in the works of older mineralogists.

To assist those persons who may wish to know something more about minerals than can be learned from books, and who may be desirous of studying our national collections by comparing the printed descriptions with the specimens themselves, references have (when practicable) been made to the Cases in which they will be found both in the British Museum and in the Museum of Practical Geology.

The copious list of synonyms used by German and French mineralogists, will, it is to be hoped, prove of great assistance to the student in reading the works of foreign authors, as well as in studying mineral collections in continental museums, or in private cabinets at home, according to whatever system they may happen to be arranged.

The names of the authors printed in Italics are those of the persons by whom the minerals to which they are appended were originally examined and named, or they are those of the authors in whose works the mineral will be found described under the name which they follow in the Glossary.

The greater part of the work has been written in the country, in moments snatched from the out-door duties of a field-geologist—and is the result either of wet days when field-work was impracticable, of long winter evenings after a hard day's work in the open air, or of early hours stolen from the morning before the regular labours of the day began.

It only now remains for the author to express his grateful thanks to his friends, Mr. Robert Hunt (Keeper of Mining Records), and, especially, to Mr. Warington Smyth, for their valuable aid in revising the proofs in passing through the press, and for enabling him to avoid many errors, which, but for their advice, would otherwise unavoidably have occurred.

The figures of crystals have all been carefully drawn on the wood by Mr. J. B. Jordan of the Mining Record Office, and the whole of the wood-cuts have been executed by Mr. S. J. Mackie. For the tail-piece the author is indebted to Miss Kennedy, by whom it was drawn on the wood; and for the following *jeu d'esprit* to his colleague, Mr. J. W. Salter, of the Geological Survey.

1st September, 1861.   HENRY W. BRISTOW.

ΘΕΟΦΡΑΣΤΟΣ ΠΕΡΙ ΤΩΝ ΛΙΘΩΝ

The following is a list of the principal books which have been referred to in compiling this work.

System of Mineralogy, by Robert Jameson, 3 vols., 1805.
Manual of the Mineralogy of Great Britain and Ireland, by R. P. Greg and W. G. Lettsom, 1858.
System of Mineralogy, by James D. Dana, 4th edition, 2 vols., 1854.
W. Phillips's Elementary Introduction to Mineralogy, by R. Allan, 4th edition, 1837.
Hand-book of Chemistry, by Leopold Gmelin, translated by Henry Watts for the Cavendish Society.
Elementary Treatise on Mineralogy for the use of Beginners, by D. Varley, 1849.
W. Phillips's Elementary Introduction to Mineralogy, by H. J. Brooke and W. H. Miller, 1852.
Manual of Mineralogy, by James Nicol, 1849.
Traité de Minéralogie, par A. Dufrénoy, 5 vols.   Paris, 1856-9.
Mineralogy and Crystallography, by J. Tennant and W. Mitchell, 1856.
Descriptive Guide to the Museum of Practical Geology, by Robert Hunt, F.R.S.; 2nd edition, 1859.
Descriptive Catalogue of the Rock Specimens in the Museum of Practical Geology, by A. C. Ramsay, H. W. Bristow, H. Bauerman, and A. Geikie; 2nd edition, 1859.
Elements of Mineralogy, by Richard Kirwan; 2nd edition, 2 vols., 1794.
A Treatise on Diamonds and Pearls, by David Jeffries, 1751.
Traité élémentaire de Minéralogie, par F. S. Beudant; 2nd edition, 2 vols., 1852.
Traité complet des Pierres précieuses, par Charles Barbot.   Paris, 1858.
Pliny translated into English, by Philemon Holland, Doctor of Phisicke, 1601.
Theophrastus's History of Stones, with an English version by Sir John Hill, 2nd edition, 1774.
The American Journal of Science and Arts.   New Haven, U.S.
Annales des Mines.   Paris.
Edinburgh Philosophical Journal.
Philosophical Magazine, or Annals of Chemistry.
Annales de Chimie et de Physique.   Paris.
Outlines of Mineralogy, by Dr. Th. Thomson, 2 vols., 1836.
Reports on the Geology of Canada, by Sir William Logan.   Montreal.
Quarterly Journal of the Geological Society of London.

TABLE OF CONTENTS.

INTRODUCTION.

TʜɪS book is not intended, in the strict sense of the term, to be a Manual of Mineralogy, but, believing that a concise description of the modes in use for distinguishing between different minerals will assist the student in recognising them, the plan of a mere Glossary has been departed from, and brief hints on the nature of minerals have been introduced.

It must be remembered, however, that there is no short cut to a knowledge of minerals. Mineralogy, like the other sciences, demands industry and attention; and to become an accomplished mineralogist much and careful study must be devoted to the subject; an acquaintance with various other branches of science must be brought to bear on it, while, above all, the eye should be rendered familiar by constant inspection with the forms and appearances of minerals, and with their physical properties. This eye-knowledge (as it may be termed) can only be acquired by long and diligent practice, — by actual examination — and by handling the specimens themselves, no opportunities of doing which should be neglected.

To become well versed in mineralogy involves also a knowledge of Physics and Chemistry. By means of the first we make ourselves acquainted with the physical properties of minerals; while the second teaches us the nature of their chemical composition. It appears necessary, therefore, to refer to the bearings of these sciences on mineralogy; but in the limited space to which these remarks must be confined, it is only possible to do so in a very brief manner.

GENERAL CHARACTERS.

EXTERNAL FORM AND STRUCTURE.
CHARACTERS DEPENDING ON LIGHT.

Colour.
Transparency.
Lustre.

Optical Properties.
Refraction.
Double Refraction.
Dichroism.
Polarization.

Physical Properties.
Specific Gravity.
Phosphorescence.
Fluorescence.
Electricity.
Magnetism.

OTHER CHARACTERS.

Stain.
Streak.
Taste.
Odour.
Adhesion to the tongue.
Feel.

CHARACTERS DEPENDENT ON COHESION.

Frangibility, or Tenacity.
Fracture.
Hardness.
Toughness.

CHEMICAL CHARACTERS.

Action of the Blowpipe.
Action of Acids.

1. OF THE PHYSICAL CHARACTERS OF MINERALS.

External Form and Structure.

Crystallography, or a knowledge of the crystalline forms of minerals, is of the highest importance. It is true minerals frequently occur in an *amorphous* state; in which case, the particles of which they are composed are arranged according to no definite law; but they very often are crystallized, *i. e.* assume certain regular and determinate forms called *crystals*.

To one ignorant of the subject the shapes of these seem to be innumerable; but on closer examination such does not prove to be the case. On the contrary, it is found that all these numerous and sometimes complex varieties of crystals may be reduced to some five or six simple types, of which the others are only modifications or variations — and even that the complicated forms of crystals may be sometimes actually converted into the typical form by the mechanical process of *cleavage*.

This simple or elementary form to which each particular crystal is capable of being ultimately reduced, has been called, therefore, its *primary form*.

Various systems of crystallography have been proposed by different authors. The classification adopted here is nearly the same as that employed by Brooke and Miller in their admirable edition of Phillips's Manual, and is a modification of the systems of various other crystallographers. These systems, six in number, are called respectively, the *Cubical, Pyramidal, Rhombic, Oblique, Anorthic,* and *Hexagonal* or *Rhombohedral.**

1. *The Cubical System* — has three equal axes, intersecting one another at at right angles.

Thus, in the cube, the regular octahedron and the rhombic dodecahedron, which belong to this system, the height, and the length, and the breadth of the axes are all equal, and are at right angles to each other. In the cube the axes are drawn from the centres of opposite faces; in the regular octahedron they connect the opposite solid angles; and similarly in the rhombic dodecahedron.

2. *Pyramidal System.*—In the pyramidal system there are, also, three axes intersecting each other at right angles; but one of these, called the vertical axis, differs in length from the other two, or lateral axes, which are equal.

The right square prism, and the octahedron with a square base, belong to this system.

In the first the axes connect the centres of opposite faces, and are at right angles to one another.

In the octahedron with a square base, which bears the same relation to the right square prism as the regular octahedron does to the cube, the axes connect the opposite solid angles.

3. *Rhombic System.*—In this system there are three unequal axes intersecting one another at right angles. It includes the right rectangular prism, the right rhombic prism, and the octahedron with a rhombic base.

---

* These correspond respectively with the following systems employed in Dana's Manual of Mineralogy, 4th edition :—1. Monometric, or Tesseral. 2. Dimetric. 3. Trimetric. 4. Monoclinic. 5. Triclinic. 6. Hexagonal.

In the first the axes connect the centres of opposite faces.

In the second the vertical axis connects the centres of the basal faces, and the lateral axes connect the centres of the opposite lateral edges.

In the octahedron with a rhombic base the axes, as before, connect the opposite solid angles.

4. *Oblique System.*—This has three unequal axes. The vertical axis is inclined to one of the lateral axes, and at right angles to the other—the two lateral axes being also at right angles to each other.

It comprises the right rhomboidal and the oblique rhomboidal prisms.

In the first the axes connect the centres of opposite faces.

In the second the vertical axis connects the centres of the bases, and the lateral axes the centres of the opposite lateral edges.

5. *Anorthic System.*—In the Anorthic System there are three unequal axes, all intersecting each other obliquely.

It comprises the oblique rhomboidal prism.

6. *Hexagonal*, or *Rhombohedral.*—In this system there are three equal lateral axes, intersecting at an angle of 60°, and one vertical axis at right angles to them.

It comprises the hexagonal prism and the rhombohedron.

In the former the vertical axis connects the centres of the bases, and the lateral axes the centres of the opposite lateral edges, or of the lateral faces.

In the latter the vertical axis connects two of the solid angles diagonally opposite, and the lateral axes opposite lateral edges.

The student will derive great assistance in investigating the primary forms of crystals and their modifications if he make a series of models for himself. Drawings of these, which can be cut out in one piece, and after being stuck on cardboard admit of being fastened together with a very slight degree of trouble, answer the purpose extremely well, and are sold in Germany at a very cheap rate.

Besides occurring singly, crystals are sometimes found in *twins* or in *macles*. In that case they are divided into two groups. 1st. Those in which the crystals are united in such a way that the axes of the two separate crystals, so united, are *parallel* to each other; and 2nd, those in which the axes are *oblique* or inclined to one another.

In other instances minerals, instead of crystallizing in the forms which are properly their own, assume *pseudomorphous forms;* that is to say, forms belonging to some other kind of mineral. This may have happened in several ways. Either the original mineral may have been entirely removed and the newer one deposited in the cast (or the mould) of that which has disappeared, or the original mineral may have been gradually removed atom by atom, and for every particle so carried away portions of another mineral substituted.

" Pseudomorphous crystals are distinguished, generally, by their rounded angles, dull surfaces, and often granular composition. They either have no cleavage, or the cleavage is wholly different in direction from that of the mineral imitated. Their surfaces are frequently drusy, or covered with minute crystals. Occasionally the resemblance to real crystals is so perfect, that they are distinguished with difficulty."*

* Dana's Mineralogy, vol. i. p. 136.

There are other physical characters which furnish extremely useful aids in the identification of minerals. The most important of them will, therefore, now be briefly noticed, nearly in the order in which they are alluded to in the pages of the Glossary, that is as follows :—

Colour.

The colour of a mineral is not, in general, so much to be relied on as some of the other characters. Certain peculiarities in the arrangement of the colours are of importance, thus :—

Play of Colours is said to take place when a mineral, on being turned, presents the appearance of several prismatic colours in rapid succession. Examples of this property are afforded by the Diamond, and in a less degree by the Precious Opal.

A *Change of Colours* is of a somewhat similar nature to the play of colours, only the succession of colours is less rapid, and each particular one is spread over a larger surface. Labradorite furnishes a very good example of this.

Iridescence is when the prismatic colours appear to be reflected from the interior of a crystal.

Opalescence is when a milky or pearly reflection is displayed from the interior of a mineral, as is the case in some kinds of Opal and Cat's-Eye.

Tarnish signifies that the colour of the mineral is different from that exhibited by a newly fractured surface. It is, consequently, merely superficial. When the surface of a mineral (as, for example, Columbite) displays the superficial blue colour of tempered steel, it is said to possess the *steel-tarnish ;* when, as in the Specular Iron Ore of Elba, it exhibits fixed prismatic colours, it is said to be *irised.*

Diaphaneity, or Transparency.

The following terms are made use of to express the different degrees in which minerals possess the capacity of transmitting light.

1. *Transparent :* when the object seen through it appears perfectly distinct, as in Quartz and Gypsum.

2. *Subtransparent,* or *semitransparent :* when the outlines of objects seen through it do not appear distinct.

3. *Translucent :* when only light is transmitted, and objects are not seen, as in Oriental Alabaster.

4. *Subtranslucent :* when light is only transmitted at the edges.

5. *Opaque :* when no light is transmittted.

Lustre.

The kinds of Lustre depending upon the nature of the reflecting surface are six in number, viz. :—

1. *Metallic,* or the lustre of metals ; *Sub-metallic,* denoting that the mineral only possesses the lustre imperfectly.

In the determination of minerals it is very important to distinguish the metallic from the non-metallic lustre.

2. *Vitreous,* or the lustre of broken glass, of which the lustre of Rock Crystal is a good example ; Calc Spar, on the other hand, presenting a *sub-vitreous* or imperfectly vitreous lustre.

3. *Resinous,* or the lustre of common rosin; of which Opal and some kinds of Blende are examples.

4. *Pearly,* or like the lustre of a pearl; as in Talc, Steatite, Brucite, &c. The term *metallic-pearly* is used to denote when the pearly and sub-metallic lustre are displayed in the same mineral, as in Hypersthene.

5. *Silky,* or like silk. It is generally the result of a fibrous structure, as is apparent in fibrous Gypsum and Satin Spar.

6. *Adamantine,* or like Diamond. When combined in the same mineral with sub-metallic it is called *metallic-adamantine,* of which Cerusite and Pyrargyrite are examples.

The different degrees of intensity of lustre produced by a variation in the quantity of light reflected from the surface are four in number :—

(1.) *Splendent:* when the surface of the mineral reflects with sufficient brilliancy to give well-defined images, as is the case with Oxide of Tin and Specular Iron.

(2.) *Shining :* when the image produced by reflection from the surface is not well defined, as in Celestine.

(3.) *Glistening :* when the surface reflects the light, but without producing an image, as in Talc, Copper Pyrites, &c.

(4.) *Glimmering :* when the reflection of the light is imperfect, and apparently proceeding from points on the surface, as in Flint, Chalcedony, &c.

Optical and Physical Properties.

The former of these belong, properly, to the science of Optics, and can be only alluded to here.

The principal properties dependent on light, besides those already noticed, employed in the determination of minerals are *Refraction, Polarization,* and *Dichroism.*

1. *Refraction.*—It is frequently of importance to know the index of refraction, or the ratio between the sine of the angle of incidence, and that of the angle of refraction; for although there is often some variation in the ratio in the same species (frequently corresponding to a change of colour), yet, as a general rule, each mineral refracting the light in an equal degree has its own index of refraction. Those minerals which refract light most powerfully, or in which the rays passing through them deviate the most from their straight path, afford the most brilliant gems. It is to its high refracting power (2·439 to 2·755) that the Diamond owes its brilliancy.

Double Refraction.—Calc Spar and some other minerals present a double image of a point or line seen through them, in every position but one. This is called double-refraction, and a knowledge of whether a mineral possesses this property will enable the observer to refer it at once to its proper crystallographic system. All forms exhibit double refraction, except those belonging to the Cubical System, which have three axes equal to one another. In the Pyramidal and Hexagonal (or Rhombohedral) Systems, in which the horizontal axes are equal, there is *one* axis of double refraction, or one direction in which double refraction is not observable; but in the Rhombic and Anorthic Systems, in which the horizontal axes are unequal, there are *two* axes of double refraction.

2. *Polarization* has the same relation to crystalline form as double refraction, and is displayed by many minerals, of which Tourmaline is a well-known example.

3. *Dichroism* is when crystals present different colours when viewed by transmitted light in two different directions, of which examples are afforded by Iolite and Mica. *Pleochroism* is when the above property is exhibited in more than two directions.

Phosphorescence.

When minerals appear more or less luminous they are said to be phosphorescent. That property may be produced either, 1st, *by friction*, as in Quartz; 2nd, *by heat*, as in Fluor Spar; 3rd, *by electricity*, as in Diamond, Calc Spar, Apatite, and some other kinds of Fluor Spar; and 4th, as in the case of some Diamonds, *by exposure to the light of the sun.*

Fluorescence.

This name has been given to the peculiar phenomenon exhibited by Fluor Spar, of transmitting one colour and reflecting another (according to Sir J. Herschel) from a stratum of small but finite thickness, adjacent to the surface by which the light enters.

After passing through this stratum, the incident light, though not sensibly enfeebled or coloured, has lost the power of producing the same effect, and therefore may be considered as in some way or other qualitatively different from the original light.

This dispersion of the rays, which takes place near the surface, has been called, by Professor Stokes, *Fluorescence.* It is exhibited by Green and Yellow Uranite and by Chalcolite; as well as by certain specimens of Apatite, Aragonite, Chrysoberyl, Kyanite and Topaz, but in these latter cases (as in Fluor Spar) the phenomenon is due to the presence of some substance accidentally present in small quantity.*

Streak.

This is a test of considerable importance, as the colour of the powder of a mineral is more constant and to be depended on than the colour of the mineral itself, which is liable to be altered by the accidental admixture of foreign substances. The streak is produced either by scratching the mineral or by drawing it across a piece of white unglazed porcelain; and observing the colour of the powder or of the trace it leaves behind.

Stain.

This character consists in leaving a mark on paper or linen, and is confined to a few soft minerals. Graphite may be distinguished from sulphide of Molybdenum, which it much resembles in other respects, by the mark which it leaves behind when drawn across paper.

* Phil. Trans. 1852; part ii. 1853: part i.

Frangibility, or Tenacity.

The following terms are employed to denote the relative degrees of *tenacity* in minerals.

1. *Brittle:* when the parts of a mineral separate in grains or powder on attempting to cut it with a knife, as in Calc Spar.

2. *Sectile.* This character is intermediate between brittle and malleable, and is used to denote when pieces may be cut off with a knife without falling to powder, although the mineral, nevertheless, admits of being pulverized under the hammer.

3. *Malleable:* when slices may be cut off and then flattened out under the blows of a hammer, as is the case with native Gold and Native Silver.

4. *Flexible:* when the mineral admits of being bent without breaking, and retains the position given to it, as in Talc.

5. *Elastic:* when, after being bent, the mineral flies back to its original position on the removal of the force, as in Mica.

Fracture.

Minerals are said to possess three kinds of fracture, viz. :—

1. *Conchoidal,* or *Shelly:* when the fractured surface displays curved concavities bearing more or less resemblance to those in the inside of a bivalve shell. Flint and glass are good examples of this kind of fracture.

2. *Even:* when the fractured surface is not rendered rough by the presence of any minute elevations or depressions.

3. *Hackly:* when the elevations are sharp or jagged, as in broken iron.

The *Cleavage* of a mineral is altogether distinct from the *Fracture*, with which it must, in no manner, be confounded. Cleavage denotes that a mineral can be cleaved or divided mechanically in certain directions, yielding smooth surfaces of fracture (called the *cleavage-planes*), parallel with the faces or planes of the primary crystal.

This may be effected by placing a knife or other sharp edge in a direction parallel with the natural joints, and then giving it a smart blow with a hammer. The minerals which yield to cleavage in one direction only, are said to have a lamellar structure.

Hardness.

The manner of testing the hardness of a mineral is by scratching it with one of those named in the following list; or (which is preferable) by trying each with a file, passing it three or four times, with a rather heavy pressure, over the mineral.

The following scale of hardness, by Mohs, is that generally adopted :—

1. *Talc:* the common laminated green variety.
2. *Gypsum:* a crystallized variety.
3. *Calc Spar:* a transparent variety.
4. *Fluor Spar:* a crystalline variety.
5. *Apatite:* a transparent variety.
6. *Felspar (Orthoclase):* white cleavable variety.

7. *Quartz :* a transparent variety.
8. *Topaz :* a transparent variety.
9. *Sapphire :* cleavable variety.
10. *Diamond.*

Toughness.

This quality (which expresses the resistance which a body offers to being broken or torn) must not be considered identical with Hardness. Some soft minerals may be tough, such as sulphate of lime; others, as Flint, though hard, may be easily broken; while others, of which Jade is an instance, are at the same time both hard and tough.

Specific Gravity.

The specific gravity of a mineral is a test of very great importance in the identification of minerals, and in some cases (as in those of polished gems for instance) it is almost the only one which can be had recourse to without occasioning injury to the specimen. In such cases the test of hardness does not admit of being applied, and, for the same reason, chemical analysis is out of the question. When, therefore, the test of colour cannot be relied upon, the determination of the specific gravity will almost always solve the difficulty. The mistakes that have been, and are constantly being, made by not determining the specific gravity of polished stones (even by those whose business it is to buy and sell such articles) are remarkable. It will be seen in the body of the work that colourless Jargoons are often sold in the East, and even in Europe, for inferior Diamonds, and similar substitutions are frequently made by dealers and jewellers in this country, not from any wilful intention to deceive, but in consequence of their relying solely on colour, lustre, and general appearance in the identification of gems.

These mistakes might generally be avoided by ascertaining the specific gravity. The process is very simple, all that is required being an accurately adjusted balance, and care in the use of it.

The determination of the specific gravity is effected by first weighing the mineral in the usual manner, and then, in water, suspended by a fine thread or horsehair. As the mineral will be buoyed up by the water in a degree proportionate to the surface it presents, its weight in water will be less than in air, and the difference between the weight in water and the weight in air, or the loss in weight it has sustained by immersion, will represent the weight of a quantity of water equal in bulk to the substance operated on. Now, as the specific gravity of a body is the proportion which its weight bears to that of an equal bulk of water, the weight in air divided by the loss of weight (or the difference of the weight obtained in and out of water) which it has sustained in water, will give the desired relation and be the required specific gravity.

Taste.

This test is, of course, only applicable in the case of minerals which are soluble in water. It is of seven kinds, viz. :—

1. *Astringent :* as in Sulphate of Iron.
2. *Sweetish astringent :* as in Alum.

3. *Saline* : as in Common Salt.
4. *Alkaline* : as in Soda.
5. *Cooling* : as in Saltpetre.
6. *Bitter* : as in Epsom Salts.
7. *Sour* : as in Sulphuric Acid.

Odour.

The odours of minerals may be tested by breathing strongly upon them or by friction. They are of six kinds, as follows, viz. :—

1. *Alliaceous*, like garlic. Arsenical Iron emits this odour by friction. It may be obtained by heat from all the arsenical ores or salts, and is a sure indication of the presence of arsenic in the substance from which it is evolved.

2. *Horse-radish odour*. The odour of decaying horse-radish is very perceptible on heating the ores of Selenium.

3. *Sulphureous*. Sulphureous odours are given off by Pyrites when it is rubbed, and by many sulphides when heated.

4. *Bituminous*, or the odour of Bitumen.

5. *Fetid*. The odour of sulphuretted hydrogen or rotten eggs is elicited by friction from Quartz and some kinds of Limestone, Anthraconite, &c.

6. *Argillaceous*. The smell of moistened clay may be detected in Serpentine, Clayslate, and some other minerals, by breathing strongly upon them ; and from some, as Pyrargillite, it may be elicited by heat.

Adhesion to the tongue

Is in some cases a useful character, dependent on the capacity of the mineral to imbibe moisture. Lithomarge adheres strongly to the tongue, and is a good example of this character, which is also generally sufficient for distinguishing argillaceous from pure limestones.

Cold.

The cold feel caused by some minerals when taken into the naked hand. Thus various kinds of Rock Crystal and gems may be distinguished from glass, which may be made to imitate them closely, by their relative coolness.

Electricity.

This property may be produced in certain minerals by friction or by heat, the latter being called *Pyro-electricity*. Tourmaline, Calamine, and Boracite are examples of pyro-electric minerals, as are also Topaz, Axinite, Scolecite, Prehnite, Electric Calamine, Sphene, Rhodizite, Rock Crystal, and Barytes.

Magnetism.

The property of attracting the magnetic needle is most strongly exhibited by Iron and some of its compounds ; but Nickel, Cobalt, Platinum, Titanium and Palladium, have also been proved, by the experiments of Faraday, to be magnetic in the sense of iron.

a 2

The following is a list of metals arranged in the order of their magnetic powers, as approximatively determined by Faraday:—Iron, Nickel, Cobalt, Manganese, Chromium, Cerium, Titanium, Palladium, Platinum, Osmium—to which may be added Aluminium.

Chemical Composition.

Mineralogy is daily becoming a science more and more based on Chemistry; as it is only by means of the chemical analysis of minerals that we can arrive at a true knowledge of their composition;—that is to say, of the simple substances of which they are composed, and of the manner in which those substances are combined.

It is quite beyond the scope of a work of this kind to do more than allude to the subject, except so far as to point out that the blowpipe offers a simple and ready means of testing minerals, and of determining the species to which they belong.

For the way of using this useful little instrument, the student may consult, with advantage, several treatises. A brief, but extremely clear and well-written notice of the mode of using the blowpipe, by Mr. Warington Smyth, Professor of Mineralogy and Mining in the Government School of Mines, is contained at p. 259 of the Manual of Scientific Inquiry, published by the Lords of the Admiralty. This notice is drawn up in so comprehensive and masterly a manner that it has been introduced here (by the kind permission of Mr. Smyth, who has allowed it to be made use of).

"The ordinary blowpipe is so well known as scarcely to need description. Various forms have been recommended by their inventors, but for common

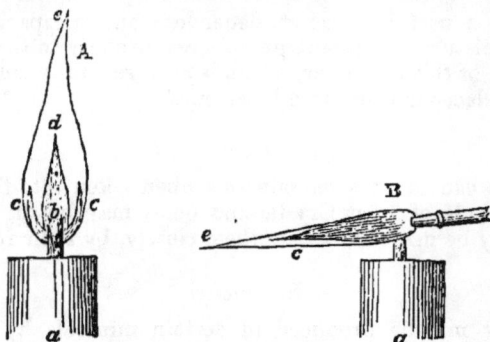

purposes it is only important that the orifice be not too large, and that the tube be provided with a reservoir for the reception of the moisture which is carried into it with the breath. The flame of a neatly-trimmed lamp is, undoubtedly, the most convenient, but that of a common candle is quite applicable to the qualitative tests with which we shall have occasion to deal.

"In looking at the flame of a candle, we may observe two principal divisions which it is necessary by the assistance of the blowpipe to use separately, since their action on the same substances is so different, as, on the one hand, greatly to facilitate certain processes of analysis, and, on the other, to cause much perplexity unless clearly understood.

" The outer and larger part of the flame e, d, c, which is the source of its light, is caused by the full combustion of the gases derived from the oil, wax, or tallow which rises into the wick, and is called the *reducing flame*, because, when concentrated upon the substance to be tested, it tends to abstract oxygen from it and thus to reduce it. In the lower part of the flame a narrow stripe of deep blue may be observed, b, c, which when acted on by the current of air from the blowpipe forms a cone, b, c, (B). This is technically called the *oxidizing flame*, from its property of imparting oxygen to the substance upon which it is directed. To produce the latter, the point or jet of the blowpipe should be inserted into about a third of the flame, and the assay is then to be held at the extremity of the cone of blue flame. For reduction the point of the tube should scarcely penetrate the flame, and the assay should be so placed as to be completely enveloped in it, and thus prevented from receiving oxygen.

" A little practice is sufficient to overcome the slight difficulty which at first is felt in keeping up a continual and even stream of air. The tyro may begin by accustoming himself to breathe through the nostrils whilst his cheeks are inflated, and will soon find it easy to maintain an uninterrupted supply for several minutes.

" Of the instruments used in experimenting by the blowpipe the following are the most necessary : — 1st. A pair of fine-pointed forceps, tipped with platinum. 2nd. A small spoon of platinum. 3rd. An agate pestle and mortar. 4th. Thin platinum wire and holder. 5th. A magnet. 6th. A few small tubes of thin glass. 7th. Some small porcelain capsules or saucers.

" Charcoal is required as a support in many cases, particularly in the reduction of ores ; and the following re-agents are also indispensable, the three first being fluxes applicable under different circumstances : —

" 1st. Soda, or carbonate of soda.

" 2nd. Borax, or borate of soda.

" 3rd. Microcosmic salt, or phosphate of soda and ammonia.

" 4th. Saltpetre, to increase the degree of oxidation of certain metallic oxides.

" 5th. Borax-glass, for the determination of phosphoric acid and of small quantities of lead in copper.

" 6th. Nitrate of cobalt, in solution, to distinguish alumina, magnesia, and oxide of zinc.

" 7th. Oxide of copper for determining small quantities of chlorine in compounds.

" 8th. Fluor-spar for the recognition of lithia, boracic acid, and gypsum.

" 9th. Lead in a pure metallic state.

" 10th Bone-ashes (9th and 10th are used for separating the silver from certain argentiferous ores).

" 11th, 12th, and 13th. Hydrochloric, sulphuric, and nitric acids.

" 14th. Litmus-paper, blue and red, for detecting the presence of acids and alkalies.

" The experiments on an unknown mineral must be made systematically, and referred for comparison to some list or table of minerals in which their behaviour before the blowpipe is described, as Von Kobell's tables.*

* Von Kobel, " Tafeln zur Bestimmung der Mineralien, München ;" and the same translated into English by R. Campbell.

" The first point to examine is, whether it be fusible ; and, if so, in what degree. The various grades of fusibility may be conveniently divided into six ; as representatives of which it is convenient to take the following minerals, species which are everywhere easy to obtain, and which may therefore be often practised upon :—

" 1. Antimony-Glance, or sulphide of antimony, which melts at the candle.

" 2. Natrolite or Mesotype, fine splinters of which may be rounded by the candle-flame.

" 3. Almandine or Precious Garnet, which fuses in large pieces before the blowpipe.

" 4. Actinolite (Hornblende), fusible only in smaller portions.

" 5. Orthoclase (Felspar) offers some difficulty ; and

" 6. Bronzite can only be rounded by the flame in the finest splinters.

" According to this scale, the mineral in question may be referred to either of the above numbers, or placed half-way between any two of them ; as, for instance, Apophyllite, being more easily fused than Natrolite, and yet more refractory than Antimony-Glance, will have its comparative fusibility represented by 1·5.

" The fragment to be experimented upon is generally held in the platinum forceps, but it is necessary to guard against the melting of the test upon the points, since the platinum, though infusible, is by that means rendered brittle.

" In other cases the mineral may be supported upon charcoal ; but whatever be the means of holding it, the phenomena exhibited by the action of the flame must be noted, as —

" 1st. The manner in which it fuses, whether quietly, or with decrepitation, exfoliation, intumescence, or phosphorescence ; whether it loses or retains colour and transparency.

" 2nd. The appearance of the product, whether a *glass,* an *enamel,* or *a slag;* or, as in the case of ores reduced upon charcoal, a metallic bead or *regulus.*

" 3rd. The separation of volatile substances, and the colour of the deposit on the charcoal, by which we may recognise —

" *a.* Lead, giving a greenish yellow deposit.

" *b.* Zinc, having a white crust, which, when heated, becomes yellowish and difficult to volatilize.

" *c.* Antimony, a white deposit, easy to volatilize.

" *d.* Bismuth, a crust partly white, partly orange-yellow, without colouring the flame.

" *e.* Sulphur, with the well-known odour of sulphuric acid.

" *f.* Selenium, in an open glass tube, gives a red deposit of selenium.

" *g.* Tellurium, in a similar glass tube, gives a greyish-white crust of oxide.

" *h.* Arsenic, gives off a greyish-white vapour, which smells like garlic.

" *i.* Quicksilver, in a glass tube, will be precipitated in minute metallic globules.

" *k.* Water, from hydrous minerals, deposited by condensation in the same manner.

" 4th. The colour of the flame when the tip of the blue part is neatly directed upon the mineral ; whence may be distinguished —

" *a.* Red tint, given by several minerals containing strontia and (?) lithium.

" *b.* Green, produced by some phosphates and borates, sulphate of baryta, some copper ores and tellurium ores.

" *c.* Blue, given by chloride of copper, chloride of lead, &c.

" 5th. The development of magnetic properties after treatment in the reducing-flame, as in ores of iron, nickel, and cobalt.

" So far the assay has been considered by itself, but it is frequently necessary to mix it with fluxes, either to render it fusible or to produce a glassy compound of a characteristic colour.

" Thus if borax or microcosmic salt be fused into a glass at the end of a platinum wire bent into an eye, and a little powder of the unknown mineral be added to it, we shall obtain by the use of the oxidizing flame the following results : —

" Manganese, in all its compounds, gives a beautiful violet or amethyst colour.

" Cobalt causes a sapphire-blue colour ; chromium an emerald-green·

" Oxide of iron produces a yellowish-red glass, which becomes paler as it cools, and at length grows yellow or disappears.

" Oxide of cerium gives a red or dark-yellow colour, which also grows paler as it cools.

" Oxide of nickel renders the glass a brown or violet tint, which after cooling becomes reddish-brown.

" Oxide of copper in very small quantity gives a green tint, which grows blue on cooling.

" Oxide of uranium renders the glass bright yellow, which in cooling takes a greenish tint.

" Oxide of antimony gives a pale yellow colour, which soon disappears.

" When soda is used as a flux it is generally upon charcoal, and by this aid the metals may be obtained from most of their combinations in a pure state. For this purpose the powdered ore is either mixed with the moistened soda into a paste, or is enveloped in a piece of thin paper which has been dipped in a solution of soda. After fusion, that portion of the charcoal which has absorbed any of the fluid substance is to be cut off and ground down with it in the mortar, when the metal, if malleable, will at once be recognised. If several metals are combined, of which one is more easily oxidized than another, as, for instance, lead when combined with silver and copper, the latter may be separated by adding metallic lead or boracic acid, according to circumstances, and maintaining a continued oxidizing flame, till the whole of the lead has passed into the state of litharge. By means of more complete apparatus and extended operations, the most exact assays may be undertaken with the blowpipe ; and those who desire a further insight into the subject may consult Plattner's 'Art of Assaying by the Blowpipe ;' Berzelius 'On the Blowpipe ;' and the before-mentioned work by Von Kobell of Münich, — all of which are translated into English."

It is almost impossible, merely by means of books, to teach the student how to recognise minerals. Still, *something* may be effected in that way; and the following brief hints (chiefly compiled from Dana's Mineralogy) may be of use, by enabling him, in the first instance, to ascertain to what particular *class* a specimen may belong; when a few essays with the blowpipe will aid him in finding out the particular *species*.

Thus—*Carbonates* may be distinguished as a class by means of Acids. Muriatic acid, generally diluted with an equal quantity of water, is the acid most frequently made use of for this purpose; but sulphuric or nitric acids, diluted in a similar manner, afford the same results. Such a solution, dropped on a *carbonate* (as, for instance, carbonate of lime) produces an effervescence or disengagement of bubbles of carbonic acid, which gives place to the stronger acid, for which the lime has greater affinity.

Sulphates, on the contrary, afford no effervescence with acids. When in solution, they may be tested with a solution of a salt of baryta, when they throw down a white precipitate of sulphate of baryta, which is insoluble in water. None of the sulphates possess a metallic lustre, and they are often colourless.

Nitrates, when treated with strong sulphuric acid, give off white corrosive vapours of nitric acid.

Phosphates may generally be dissolved, without change, in muriatic and nitric acids, and are decomposed by sulphuric acid. The phosphates which are soluble produce a characteristic yellow precipitate on the addition of nitrate of silver, as also do the neutral nitric solutions of the insoluble phosphates.

All the phosphates have an unmetallic lustre. None of them are soluble in water, or have any taste, except one single phosphate of ammonia. The pure phosphates also give off no odour before the blowpipe.

Silicates, in many cases, gelatinize with acids, the silica forming a jelly or separating in a gelatinous state. Sometimes this may be effected with cold acid, but, generally, the mineral, previously reduced to a finely-powdered state, is placed in strong acid, and then gently heated. After a short time, as the solution cools, the jelly appears, or, in some cases, partial evaporation is required before the jelly makes its appearance.

Borates, when reduced to powder, and heated with sulphuric acid, impart a green colour to the flame, on the addition of alcohol.

Sulphides have a metallic lustre, or an unmetallic lustre with a coloured streak; the only exceptions being Blende and Voltzite, which have an unmetallic lustre and an uncoloured streak.

Chlorides all afford a white curdy precipitate with nitrate of silver, which becomes dark or violet-coloured on exposure to the atmosphere.

Fluorides, when pulverised and heated with strong sulphuric acid in a platinum crucible, give off fumes of hydro-fluoric acid, which will corrode a plate of glass placed over the crucible.

Salts of Lime, in solution (even in a diluted state), on the addition of oxalic acid or oxalate of ammonia, afford a white precipitate of oxalate of lime, which is insoluble in water, but is very soluble in any of the stronger acids.

Iron.—The protoxide salts afford a greenish-white precipitate with potash or soda, which becomes green in the first instance, and then yellow on exposure. The peroxide salts, with the same tests, afford a brown precipitate of hydrated peroxide of iron.

Compounds of Copper are, for the most part, soluble in nitric acid. Metallic iron, dipped in such a solution, becomes coated with a precipitate of metallic copper. Compounds of copper in solution, on the addition of potash or soda, yield a precipitate, which is blue at first, but turns black on being boiled; with ammonia they give a green precipitate, which is re-dissolved in excess of ammonia, and becomes of a fine blue colour.

Compounds of Lead, when dissolved in nitric acid, give a black precipitate with sulphuretted hydrogen (which is insoluble in excess), and a yellow precipitate with iodide of potassium or chromate of potash. Neutral solutions of lead precipitate metallic lead on metallic zinc.

Compounds of Zinc.—The sulphates afford no precipitate with sulphuretted hydrogen, but give a white precipitate with potash soluble in excess of that reagent. Acetate of Zinc affords an abundant precipitate with sulphuretted hydrogen.

Compounds of Manganese.—The salts, when heated with potash or nitrate of potash, afford manganate of potash, which gives a green solution in water, and with dilute acids a rose tint, which is destroyed by sulphurous acid or organic matters. The oxides give off chlorine when heated with muriatic acid.

Compounds of Tin form chlorides when dissolved in muriatic acid, which afford a purple colour with chloride of Gold; or if strong, a brown precipitate.

Compounds of Silver.—When dissolved in nitric acid, the addition of a chloride or muriatic acid throws down a dense white curdy precipitate of chloride of silver, which turns black on exposure, and is soluble in ammonia. A slip of copper dipped in a solution of silver becomes coated with a deposit of metallic silver.

Gold is not soluble in any of the acids singly, but is dissolved by a mixture of nitric and muriatic acid (or *aqua regia*). The solution gives a purple precipitate on the addition of protochloride of tin, and metallic gold with protosulphate of Iron.

Platinum is not dissolved either by nitric or muriatic acid, but is dissolved in a mixture of the two. Muriate of ammonia throws down a yellow precipitate from such a solution, and the precipitate, heated in a platinum crucible, yields metallic platinum in the state of powder.

Compounds of Mercury afford a white precipitate with muriatic acid. Solutions of the protosalts give a black precipitate with potash, which is insoluble in excess of that reagent; and a black insoluble precipitate with sulphuretted hydrogen. A precipitate of metallic mercury is deposited on a slip of copper when immersed in the above solutions, and is dissipated by heat.

The various members of the *Quartz* family, though one of the most abundant in nature, and presenting a great diversity of colours, yet possess certain characters in common which render them easily recognisable after a little practice. The most important of these characters is the total absence of cleavage, and the degree of hardness which is No. 7 in the table given at

p. xvii. It cannot be scratched with a file, but itself is hard enough to scratch glass easily. It is infusible before the blowpipe; is not acted on by acids, whether cold or hot; and, with the addition of carbonate of soda, is easily dissolved to a glass before the blowpipe. None of the members of the Quartz family have a specific gravity exceeding 2·84.

Calc Spar or *Calcite*, the next mineral to Quartz as regards its abundance, also assumes a variety of aspects. They may all be scratched with the point of a knife; they all effervesce on the addition of a drop of dilute muriatic acid, and are infusible before the blowpipe, but shine with an intense light, and are rendered alkaline by being converted into quick lime, when the carbonic acid is expelled by heat. When not compact massive, the cleavage is very perfect rhombohedral, and the specific gravity does not exceed 2·8.

The *Felspars* rarely assume granular forms, and never occur fibrous or columnar, but either in tabular crystals or in cleavable masses. They are commonly colourless, or varying in tint from white to flesh-red, sometimes bluish-green and brown, and have a vitreous lustre, which, in some instances, inclines to pearly. The cleavage of Felspar is highly characteristic: one face of cleavage is perfectly smooth, and another, nearly at right angles to it, is somewhat less perfect. Orthoclase may be recognised from the other varieties of Felspar, by having the two cleavage-planes at right angles to each other.

The *Zeolites* are most frequently associated together in cavities or cracks in amygdaloidal rocks, though they are sometimes found in granite and other rocks. The various members of the Stilbite group are distinguishable by the pearly lustre of their cleavage. They are likewise remarkable for often assuming laminato-radiated forms, and are frequently acicular or in radiated masses consisting of slender fibres.

Hornblende and Pyroxene are often not easily distinguishable when not in crystals, except by chemical analysis. When crystallized, Hornblende often occurs in six-sided prisms, while Pyroxene has commonly four-sided prisms. They both vary in colour, from white to black through grass-green and olive-green shades. Both are distinctly cleavable, with the exception of Epidote, which has no very distinct cleavage. The crystals and the columnar forms of the latter variety have also a more solid appearance, and present a smoother surface; and, when broken longitudinally, the prisms do not show the cleavage-plane and that splintery look which are observable in Pyroxene and Hornblende under similar circumstances.

Micaceous Minerals consist of every thin and easily separable laminæ. Of these, Muscovite, Phlogopite, Biotite, and Lepidolite are closely related, and possess in common the characters of having their laminæ elastic; of yielding no water (or very little) in a tube; of fusing only at the edges before the blowpipe; of not being acted on by acids; and of affording, with a cobalt solution, sometimes a clear blue, but generally a dull blue tint. The specific gravity of this group varies from 2·75 to 3·3, and the hardness from 1·5 to 2.

Pyrophyllite, Margarite, Euphyllite.— With the exception of the former mineral, the laminæ are rather brittle, and the colours are white, or of a pale tint. They all afford water in a tube; are fusible before the blowpipe at their edges (Pyrophyllite swells out); afford little or no action with acids, and give a blue colour with a cobalt solution. The specific gravity varies from 2·7 to 3·1. The hardness ranges between 3·5 and 4·5, except in Pyrophyllite, in which it is only 1·5.

Chlorite, Ripidolite, Clinochlore, and Pyrosclerite.—In these minerals the laminæ are flexible, but not elastic, and they often have a slightly greasy feel.

They afford no water in a tube ; fuse at the edges more easily, before the blowpipe, than the preceding group, but give no blue colour to cobalt solutions. They are slightly acted on by acids, giving mostly dark green solutions, except in the case of Pyrosclerite, which is often reddish.

Talc resembles the preceding group in most characters, but the laminæ are much softer and more greasy, but are not so thin, and the colour is generally pale green. It is infusible before the blowpipe, and insoluble in acids. With cobalt solution it gives a reddish colour, with some difficulty.

Brucite bears some resemblance to Talc in its whitish and greenish colour, and in being infusible before the blowpipe. When heated in a tube, it gives off water, and is entirely dissolved in acids without effervescence.

Diallage, Bronzite, Hypersthene, Clintonite, Chloritoid, though sometimes approaching to micaceous in structure, are, more correctly speaking, foliated. The laminæ are brittle, and not easily separated. Marmolite differs from the above in having a greasy feel, and in bearing some resemblance to Talc.

Gypsum, or sulphate of lime, is very soft, and may be scratched with the nail. It differs from the carbonate (or Calc Spar) in not effervescing with acids. It turns white before the blowpipe and crumbles, but is fused only with difficulty. When crystallized it is generally colourless, often transparent, and separable into thin laminæ, which can scarcely be bent without breaking.

Uranite, Red Zinc Ore, and Copper Mica.—The first is of a bright green or yellow colour, and crystallizes in square tabular crystals ; the second (an oxide of zinc) is bright or deep red ; and the third, a deep green, crystallizing in hexagonal crystals, which give the reaction of copper.

In the following work, under the head of *Comp.* (*Composition*), is represented, by means of a formula, the chemical composition of each mineral, supposing it to be perfectly pure or free from foreign admixtures. The meaning of the symbols employed to denote the simple substances forming the components is explained further on, at p. xliv. The chemical formula is (in most cases) followed by the per-centage amount of each ingredient present, on the above-mentioned supposition of their being altogether free from extraneous matter.

Perhaps, however, it should be stated here that each equivalent of oxygen is represented by a dot placed over the symbol of the substance with which it is combined : thus Fe represents the metal Iron ; $\dot{F}e$, the protoxide of that metal (or the combination of one atom of the metal with one atom of oxygen); and $\ddot{F}e$, the sesquioxide, or peroxide of the same metal, in which *three* atoms of oxygen are present.

The bar drawn through some of the symbols, as in the above, $\overset{...}{Fe}$, $\overset{...}{Al}$, $\overset{...}{Mn}$, $\overset{...}{R}$, &c., indicate that the substances they represent are in the state of a sesquioxide; or, in other words, that two atoms of the base (represented by the letters) are combined with three atoms of oxygen (represented by the dots). By using the above form of expression, the symbols are rendered much simpler than would be the case if figures and letters were employed to represent the oxygen.

The letters R and R are used to denote one or all of those simple substances which can be substituted for each other in a mineral without effecting any essential change in the outward form of the crystal, and which are, therefore, said to be *isomorphous* with each other (*i. e.* to possess similar forms). These substances are Iron, Manganese, Lime, and Magnesia.

Sulphur has, in a few instances, been represented by a dash placed above the symbol; thus Iron Pyrites, or Bisulphide of Iron, may be represented either by FeS^2, or by $\overset{'}{Fe}$.

The small figures in the formulæ imply that they only refer to the symbol which they immediately follow: thus, in $3\overset{...}{Al}\overset{..}{Si}^2$, the small figure ^{2} placed after $\overset{..}{Si}$ means that it applies only to the Silica; while the figure 3 placed *before* the formula denotes that it has reference to all the succeeding symbols, which, written in full, would then become $3\overset{...}{Al} + 3\overset{..}{Si}^2$, or $3\overset{...}{Al} + 6\overset{..}{Si}$. When symbols are joined, it means that they are in a state of chemical combination: thus $\overset{..}{Si}\overset{...}{Al}$ denotes that the silica and alumina are combined in the form of silicate of alumina.

CLASSIFICATION OF MINERALS.

WHEN the first difficulties of the science have been overcome, and the student has acquired a sufficient knowledge of minerals to be able to recognise them by their characters and properties—the next step is that of classification—or their arrangement into classes, families, and species.

To accomplish this in a satisfactory manner is a task of considerable difficulty. Each author, in consequence, seems to consider himself at liberty to recommend a system of his own—the result of which is that numerous modes have been proposed by different writers, of various degree of merit; some natural, others artificial, and some, again, partaking of a sort of compromise between these two extremes.

This has led to much confusion, and a highly unsatisfactory state of things. It is partly in consequence of the want of agreement between the various authors who have treated on this branch of the subject, and the practical inconvenience of a purely chemical arrangement (combined with some other motives relating more especially to facility of reference), that the author has been led to the adoption of an alphabetical form for the present work.

But although it has now become a recognised principle, that chemical composition must constitute the basis of any really perfect system of classification, an arrangement founded solely on chemistry is practically attended with much inconvenience. In some instances, the adoption of an artificial system, or some modification of one, may be found useful. For example, in a collection of minerals intended to illustrate some special purpose, as the application and use of minerals in the arts and in jewelry, what are commonly known by the name of *gems* and *precious stones* might with propriety be allowed to occupy a prominent position, and be formed into a group by themselves, as was proposed by Allan. On a similar principle, collections illustrative of the mineral resources of our own and Foreign Countries (such as those which will form a part of the proposed International Exhibition of 1862) will convey more information to the mind, and be of much more use as objects of comparison, if each metal be made to form a separate group; the ores of iron, of copper, and of lead, for instance, being all placed by themselves.

On the same principle, other modifications of previous systems may be devised to suit particular cases, or as necessity may require.

The system of classification proposed originally by Berzelius, and adopted at the British Museum, is founded upon the Electro-Chemical theory. This, in many cases, leads to a great amount of inconvenience in practice. The minerals of the various metals, for instance, are by this means, dispersed and widely separated from each other—occasioning much confusion to the student, and involving considerable loss of time in tracking the ores of each particular metal through the various Cases amongst which they are distributed.

A far more generally useful mode of arrangement, and one recommended by its greater comparative simplicity for working purposes, is that according to which the following List of Minerals has been drawn up. It is based on chemical composition, with the introduction of such modifications only as have been considered likely to increase its practical utility. At the outset it commences by making a broad distinction between the metallic and non-metallic minerals; thus dividing minerals into two sufficiently well marked groups. The former, again, are subdivided into four subordinate classes, and the latter into five; the different members composing each of which are allied to one another by mutual affinities. Thus it will be perceived that each metal, with its Ores and Salts, constitutes a group by itself; the latter being formed with reference to the component bases of the Minerals, and not to the Acids.

The general principle of the classification here laid down is that followed by Mr. Warington Smyth in his Lectures on Mineralogy at the School of Mines.

NON-METALLIC MINERALS.

CLASS I.
Carbon and Boron.

Carbon and its natural Compounds.

Diamond.
  Boort.

Graphite.
  Tremenheerite.

Coals.
  Anthracite.
  Common Coal.
  Cannel Coal. }
  Torbanite. }
  Brown Coal or Lignite. }
  Jet. }
Dysodile.

Mineral Oils and Resins.

Naphtha.
Petroleum.
Bitumen.
Asphalt.
Elaterite.

Amber.
Scleretinite.
Retinite.
Piauzite.
Walchowite.
Copaline.
  Highgate Resin.
Krantzite.
Berengelite.

Middletonite.
Anthracoxene.
Pyropissite.
Phylloretine.
Ozokerite.
Hatchettine.
Idrialine.
Tekoretine.
Scheererite.
Könlite.
  Könleinite.
Baikerite.
Fichtelite.
Guyaquillite.
Hartite.
  Hartine.
  Ixolyte.
  Bog Butter.

Inflammable Salts.

Dinite.
Dopplerite.
Mellite.

Boron.

Boracic Acid, or Sassolin.
Borate of Ammonia, or Larderellite.
Borate of Soda, or Borax.
Borate of Lime, or Hayesine.
Borate of Magnesia, or Boracite.
  Stassfurthite.

Rhodizite.
Hydroboracite.
Lagonite.
Warwickite.

CLASS II.
Sulphur and Selenium.

Sulphur.

Native Sulphur.
Selen-Sulphur.

Selenium.

Clausthalite.
  Selenbleikupfer.
  Selenkobaltblei, or Tilkerodite
Onofrite.
Lehrbachite.
Berzelianite.
Naumannite.
Selenkupferblei.
Eukairite.

CLASS III.
Haloids and Salts.

Ammonia.

Ammonia Alum, or
  Tschermigite.
Bicarbonate of Ammonia.

Sulphate of Ammonia, or Mascagnine.
Muriate of Ammonia, or Sal Ammoniac.

Potash.

Nitrate of Potash, or Nitre.
Sulphate of Potash, or Glaserite.
Misenite.
Muriate of Potash, or Sylvine.
Jarosite.
Polyhalite.

Soda.

Carbonate of Soda, or Trona.
Urao.
Natrolite.
Thermonatrite.
Thenardite.
Glauber Salt.
Exanthalose.
Lecontite.
Glauberite.
Nitrate of Soda, or Nitratine.
Loweïte.
Common or Rock Salt.
Martinsite.
Reussite.
Stercorite.

Baryta.

Witherite.
Baryto-calcite.
Barytes.
Bolognese Stone.
Hepatite.
Allomorphite.
Cawk.

Strontia.

Strontianite.
Emmonite.
Barystrontianite.
Celestine.

Lime.

Calc Spar, or Calcite.
Stalactite.
Stalagmite. ⎱
Oriental Alabaster. ⎰
Eye Stone.
Travertine.
Ostreocolla.
Calcareous Tufa.
Kunkur.
Marble.

Lumachello, or Fire Marble.
Cotham, Ruin, or Landscape Marble.
Stinkstone, or Swinestone.
Agaric Mineral.
Aphrite.
Fontainebleau Sandstone.
Natro-calcite.
Plumbo-calcite.
Strontiano-calcite.

Conistonite.
Whewellite.
Aragonite.
Mossotite.
Flos Ferri.
Satin Spar.
Tarnowitzite.
Dolomite.
Conite.
Brossite.
Rauchkalk.
Pearl Spar.
Bitter Spar, or Rhomb Spar ⎱
Miemite. ⎰
Predazzite.
Brown Spar.
Ankerite.
Pennite.
Gurhofite.
Apatite.
Asparagus Stone.
Moroxite.
Phosphorite.
Francolite.
Odontolite.
Osteolite.
Talc-Apatite.
Herderite.
Anhydrite.
Tripe Stone.
Vulpinite.
Selenite.
Alabaster.
Gypsum.
Satin Spar.
Schaumkalk.
Dreelite.
Polyhalite.
Datholite.
Nitro-calcite.
Gay-Lussite.
Pharmacolite.
Haidingerite.
Kühnite.
Romeine.

Scheelite.

Perowskite.
Rutherfordite.

Azorite.

Fluor Spar.
Blue John.

Magnesia.

Magnesite.
Giobertite.

Nitro-magnesite.

Magnesia Alum.
Epsomite.

Breunnerite.

Tachydrite.

Struvite.
Wagnerite.

Hoernesite.

Alumina.

Alunogene.
Kapnicite.
Keramohalite.
Websterite.
Hallite.
Paraluminite.
Potash Alum.
Pissophane.
Svanbergite.
Amblygonite.

Wavellite.
Lasionite.
Turquois.
Fischerite.
Peganite.
Lazulite.
Childrenite.

Yttria.

Phosphate of Yttria, or Xenotime.

Zirconia

Wöhlerite.
Pyrrhite.

Ceria.

Fergusonite.

CLASS IV.

EARTHS.

SILICA, ALUMINA, MAG-
NESIA, AND THEIR HY-
DRATES.

Silica.

Vitreous Quartz.

Rock Crystal.
Rock Crystal with inclu-
ded capillary crystals of
Titanium.
Epidote.
Amphibole.
Scales of Mica.
Chlorite.
Bitumen.
Enhydros, or Crystals con-
taining Water and other
liquids; also Brewster-
line,   Amethystotine,
Cryptotine, &c.
Amethyst.
False Topaz, or Citrine.
Smoky Quartz, or Cairngorm.
Morion.
Rose Quartz.
Siderite.
Greasy Quartz.
Fœtid Quartz.
Milk Quartz.
Ferruginous Quartz.
Aventurine.
Hacked Quartz.
Potato Stone, or Geode.
Fulgurite.

Chalcedonic Quartz.

Chalcedony.
Saphirine.
Haytorite.
Carnelian.
Stygmite.
Sard.
Cat's Eye.
Chrysoprase.
Agate.
Moss Agate.
Ribbon Agate.
Circle Agate.
Eye Agate.
Fortification Agate.
Zoned or Banded Agate.
Variegated Agate.
Brecciated Agate.
Mocha-stone.
Agate Jasper.
Plasma.
Onyx.

Sardonyx.
Silicified Wood.
Flint.
Chert.
Hornstone.
Bombite.

Jaspery Quartz.

Jasper.
Red Jasper.
Yellow Jasper.
Egyptian Pebble.
Ribbon or Banded Jasper.
Bloodstone, or Heliotrope.
Porcellanite, or Porcelain
Jasper.
Touchstone, Lydian Stone,
or Basanite.
Cellular Quartz, or Float-
stone.
Siliceous Sinter.
Pearl Sinter, or Fiorite.
Geyserite.
Tripoli.
Sandstone.
Flexible Sandstone.
Randanite.

Hydrous Silica.

Opal.
Noble or Precious Opal.
Harlequin Opal.
Golden Opal.
Fire Opal.
Common Opal.
Wax Opal.
Semi-Opal.
Hyalite, or Muller's Glass.
Hydrophane.
Pyrophane.
Cacholong.
Tabasheer.
Wood Opal.
Menilite.
Michaelite.
Opal Jasper.
Alumocalcite.

Alumina.

Corundum.
Sapphire.
Oriental Ruby.
Asteria, or Star Stone.
Star Sapphire.
Star Ruby.
Emery.
Rotten Stone.

Diaspore.
Gibbsite.
Hydrargillite }

Aluminate of Magnesia.

Völknerite.
Houghite.
Spinel.
Automolite.
Candite.
Ceylanite.
Dysluite.
Chlorospinel.
Gahnite.
Hercinite.
Zeilanite.
Spinel Ruby.
Balas Ruby.
Rubicelle.

Aluminate of Zinc and Iron.

Kreittonite.

Aluminate of Glucina.

Chrysoberyl.
Cymophane.
Alexandrite.

Aluminate of Lime.

Prosopite.

*Aluminate of Lime, Mag-
nesia, and Iron.*

Turnerite.

Magnesia.

Native Magnesia, or Pe-
riclase.
Hydrate of Magnesia, or
Brucite

CLASS V.

SILICATES.

Silicates and Alumi-
nates.

*Hydrous Silicates and Bo-
rate of Lime.*

Datholite.
Botryolite.

Silicates of Lime.

Anhydrous.

Wollastonite, or Tabular
Spar.

Hydrous.

Plombierite.
Cryolite.
Okenite.
Dysclasite.
Ædelforsite.

Hydrous Silicates of Lime and Soda.

Pectolite.
Soda Table-Spar.
Ratholite.
Stellite.

Anhydrous Silicates of Iron and Soda.

Arfvedsonite.
Achmite.

Hydrous Silicates of Lime and Potash.

Apophyllite.
Tesselite.
Albin.
Oxhaverite.

Anhydrous Silicate of Lime, Soda, and Potash.

Osmelite.

Anhydrous Silicates of Lime and Iron.

Babingtonite.

Iron-lime Garnet.
Black Garnet, or Melanite.
Aplome.
Colophonite.
Pyreneite.

Silicates of Magnesia.

A n h y d r o u s.

Chrysolite, or Peridot.
Monticellite.
Olivine.
Boltonite.

H y d r o u s.

Hydrated Olivine, or Villarsite.
Noble Serpentine.
Common Serpentine :—
Bowenite.
Williamsite.
Verde di Prato.
Verde di Susa.
Fibrous Serpentine :—
Baltimorite.
Chrysotile.
Metaxite.
Picrolite.
Foliated Serpentine :—
Antigorite.
Marmolite.

Deweylite.
Hydrophite.
Schiller Spar.
Aphrodite.
Quincite.

Spadaite.
Asbestos of Koruk.
Kerolite.
Picrosmine.
Talc.
Neolite.
Steatite, or Soapstone.
Potstone.
Rensselaerite.
Meerschaum.

Anhydrous Silicate of Magnesia and Fluoride of Magnesium.

Chondrodite.

Anhydrous Silicates of Magnesia and Lime.

Batrachite.
Jade, Nephrite, or Axe Stone.

Pyroxene.
Augite.
Ægyrine.
Hedenbergite.
Polylite.
Green Coccolite.
Diopside.
White Coccolite.
Alalite.
Fassaite.
Sahlite.
Baikalite.
Pyrgom.
Malacolite.
Breislackite.
Acanthoide.
Jeffersonite.
Aluminous Augite, or Diallage.
Bronzite.
Hypersthene.
Schiller Spar (G. Rose).
Smaragdite.

Uralite.

Pargasite, or Noble Hornblende.
Common Hornblende.
Diastatite.
Edenite.
Tremolite.
Peponite.
Grammatite.
Raphilite.
Calamite.
Glassy Actynolite.

Asbestiform Actynolite.
Byssolite.
Rock Wood.
Mountain Paper.
Mountain Leather.
Mountain Cork.
'Asbestos.
Amianthus.
Green Diallage.
Anthophyllite.
Cummingtonite.
Gedrite.
Ferruginous and Aluminous Hornblende, or Carinthine.

Hydrous Silicates of Magnesia and Iron.

Cummingtonite (variety of Anthophyllite).
Monradite.
Dermatin.
Picrophyll.

Silicate of Magnesia, Lime, and Iron

Diaclasite.

Hydrous Silicate of Soda, Magnesia, and Iron.

Crocidolite.

Hydrous Silicate of Cerous Oxide.

Cererite.

Anhydrous Silicate of Yttria.

Gadolinite.

Anhydrous Silicate of Glucina.

Phenakite.

Anhydrous Silicate of Glucina and Lime.

Leucophane.

Silicates of Alumina.

A n h y d r o u s.

Staurolite.

Andalusite.
Chiastolite.

Kyanite.
Rhœtizite.
Bamlite.
Monrolite.

b

Sillimanite.
Bucholzite.
Fibrolite.
Wörthite.
Xenolite.
Talcite, or Nacrite.

Hydrous.

Scarbroïte.
Opal Allophane, or Schröt-
terite.
Miloschine.
Allophane.
Bole of Sinope.
Porcelain Clays.
Kaolin.
Smelite.
Pholerite.
Rock Marrow, or Litho-
marge.
Carnat.
Melopsite.
Myelin.
Halloysite.
Severite.
Smectite.
Bole.
Ochran.
Lenzinite.
Razoumoffskin.
Salt Clay.
Figure Stone, or Agalmato-
lite.
Catlinite.
Lardite.
Dysyntribite.
Pyrophyllite.
Collyrite.
Dillnite.
Cimolite.
Tuesite.
Montmorillonite.
Lemnian Earth.
Malthacite.
Rock Soap.
Fullers' Earth.

*Anhydrous Silicates of Alu-
mina and Fluorine*

Topaz.
Yellow Topaz.
Blue Topaz, or Brazilian Sap-
phire.
White Topaz.
Minas Novas.
Pingos d'agua, or Water Drops.
Pycnite.
Pyrophysalite.

*Compounds of Silicate of
Alumina with Silicates of
Potash, Soda, Lithia, Ba-
ryta, Strontia, Magnesia,
Protoxide of Cerium, Yt-*

*tria, Glucina, Manganese,
and Protoxide of Iron.*

*Anhydrous Silicates of Alu-
mina, Potash, and Soda.*

Sodalite.
Lapis Lazuli.
Haüyne.
Noseane
Leucite.
Nepheline.
Elæolite.
Davyne.
Cancrinite.

FELSPAR SECTION.

Potash Felspar, or Ortho-
clase.
Adularia.
Moonstone.
Sunstone.
Amazon Stone.
Glassy Felspar.
Rhyacolite.
Valencianite.
Unionite.
Amanzite.
Loxoclase.
Microcline.
Murchisonite.
Necronite.
Chesterlite.
Erythrite.
Leelite.
Ice Spar.
Perthite.
Variolite.

Soda Felspar, or Albite.
Pericline.
Peristerite.
Oligoclase-Albite.

*Anhydrous Silicates of Alu-
mina, Lime, Soda, &c.*

Anorthite.
Indianite.
Amphodelite.
Biotina.
Latrobite.
Lepolite.
Thiosaurite.
Polyargite.
Rosellane.
Oligoclase.
Labradorite.
Paralogite.
Paulite.
Mauilite.
Vosgite.
Silicite.
Andesine.
Saccharite.

Obsidian, or Volcanic Glass.
Pitchstone.
Cantalite.
Pearlstone.
Sphærulite.
Pumice.
Krablite.
Baulite.

*Anhydrous Silicates of Alu-
mina, Lime, &c.*

GARNET SECTION.

Common Garnet.
Almandine, or Precious
Garnet.
Allochroite.
Lime-Garnet, or Grossular.
Cinnamon Stone, or Essonite.
Grossular, or Wiluite.
Romanzowite.
Topazolite.
Succinite.
Iron-Lime Garnet.
Black Garnet, or Melanite
Pyreneite.
Aplome.
Colophonite.
Manganese Garnet, or Spes-
sartine.
Polyadelphite.
Lime-Chrome Garnet, or
Uwarowite.
Pyrope, or Fire-Garnet.
Carbuncle.

Meionite.
Sarcolite.
Scapolite.
Ekebergite.
Gabronite.
Glaucolite.
Nuttallite.
Algerite.
Palagonite.
Paranthine.
Prehnite.
Edelite.
Pufflerite.
Koupholite.
Porcelain Spar.
Unionite, or White Lime-
Epidote.
Zoisite.
Dipyre.

*Hydrous Silicates of Alu-
mina, Potash, Soda, &c.*

Pollux.
Damourite.
Herschelite.

ZEOLITE SECTION.

Analcime.

Eudnophite.
Glottalite.
Cluthalite.
Doranite.
Natrolite or Soda Meso-
  type.
Bergmannite.
Lehuntite.
Radiolite.
Savite.
Galactite.
Iron Natrolite.

Alumina, Lime, &c.

Okenite.
  Dysclasite.
Ædelforsite.
Scolezite, Lime Mesotype,
  or Needlestone.
  Stellite.
  Poonahlite.
  Scolexerose.
Mesolite.
  Antrimolite.
  Farbelite.
  Harringtonite.
Mesole.
Brevicite.
Thomsonite.
  Picrothomsonite.
  Chalilite.
  Scoulerite.
  Ozarkite.
  Carphostilbite.
Stilbite, or Radiated Zeo-
  lite.
  Hypostilbite.
Sphærostilbite.
Heulandite, or Foliated
  Zeolite.
  Beaumontite.
Laumontite, or Efflorescing
  Zeolite.
Caporcianite.
  Retzite.
Ittnerite.
Epistilbite.
  Ehrenbergite.
Leonhardite.
Faujasite.
Phillipsite, or Lime Har-
  motome.
Gismondine, or Zeagonite.
Pectolite.
  Soda Table-Spar.
  Ratholite.
  Stellite.
Apophyllite, or Pyramidal
  Zeolite.
  Tesselite.
  Albin.
  Oxhaverite.

Chabazite.
  Acadialite.
  Haydenite.
  Phacolite.
Gmelinite, or Soda Chaba-
  zite.

Ledererite.
Levyne.

Alumina, Baryta, &c.

Harmotome, or Cross-stone.
  Morvenite.

Brewsterite.
Edingtonite.

*Alumina, Lime, and Mag-
  nesia.*

Sloanite.
Portite.
  End of Zeolite Section.

Pyrallolite.

Alumina, Lime, &c.

Ellagite.
Beaumontite.
Neurolite.
Thulite.
Margarite.
Diphanite.
Uigite.
Euphyllite.

*Silicates of Alumina, Iron,
  and Lime.*

A n h y d r o u s.

Isopyre.
  Tachylite.
Cyclopite.

H y d r o u s.

Plinthite.
Melanolite.

*Hydrous Silicates of Alu-
  mina and Magnesia.*

Soapstone, or Saponite.
  Piotine.
  Thalite.

Pyrosclerite.
  Loganite.
  Chonikrite.
  Vermiculite.

Anauxite.

*Anhydrous Silicates of Alu-
  mina and Iron.*

Almandine, or Precious
  Garnet.
Allochroite.
Common Garnet.

*Silicates of Alumina, Lime,
  Iron, Cerium, &c.*

A n h y d r o u s.

Cerium Epidote.
Allanite.

b 2

H y d r o u s.

Thulite.

*Anhydrous Silicates of Alu-
  mina, Lime, and Chrome.*

Uwarowite.
Pyrope, or Fire-Garnet.
Carbuncle.

*Silicates of Alumina, Lime,
  Magnesia, and Alkalies.*

A n h y d r o u s.

Couzeranite.

H y d r o u s.

Wilsonite.
Pipestone.
Gieseckite.

*Silicates of Alumina, Mag-
  nesia, and Iron.*

A n h y d r o u s.

Magnesia-Garnet.
Iolite.
  Aspasiolite.
  Bonsdorffite.
  Peliom.
  Steinheilite.
  Fahlunite.
  Hard Fahlunite.
  Gigantolite.
  Liebenerite.
  Pinite.
  Praseolite
  Pyrargillite.

H y d r o u s.

Chlorite.
  Pennine.

Clinochlore.

  Ripidolite.
  Kämmererite.
  Rhodochrome.
  Lophoite.
  Ogcoïte.
  Aphrosiderite.

Leuchtenbergite.

Green Earth.
Epichlorite.
Schiller Spar.

Pimelite.
Polychroilite.
Chloritoid.
  Masonite.

*Silicates of Alumina, Lime,
  Magnesia, and Iron.*

A n h y d r o u s.

Gehlenite.
Glauconite.

Idocrase.
  Egeran.
  Frugardite.
  Jeffreinowite.
  Protherite.
  Xanthite.

Hydrous.

Teratolite.
Delessite.
  Grengesite.
Baralite.

Silicates of Alumina, Lime, Magnesia, Iron, and Alkalies.

Anhydrous.

Mellilite.
  Somervillite.
  Zurlite.
  Humboldtilite.
Wichtisite.
  Sordawalite.

Biaxial or Potash Mica.
Muscovite, or Muscovy Glass.
  Margarodite.
  Damourite.
  Paragonite.

Uniaxial Mica, or Biotite.
  Meroxene.
  Rubellane.
  Voigtite.
Lepidomelane.

Phlogopite, or Rhombic Mica.

Hydrous.

Clintonite.
  Disterrite.
  Brandisite.
  Seybertite.
  Xanthophyllite.
Palagonite, or Hydrous Scapolite.
  Notite.
Skolopsite.
Green Earth.
  Kirwanite.

Anhydrous Silicates of Alumina, Lime, and Yttria.

Pistacite, or Lime and Iron-Epidote.
  Arendalite.
  Bucklandite.

Puschkinite.
Achmatite.
Thallite.
Rosstrevorite.

Zygadite.

Anhydrous Silicates of Alumina, Potash, Lithia, &c.

Lithia-Mica, or Lepidolite.
  Zinnwaldite.
Weissigite.

Anhydrous Silicate of Alumina and Manganese.

Manganese Garnet, or Spessartine.

Hydrous Silicate of Alumina, Manganese, and Iron.

Carpholite.

Anhydrous Silicates of Alumina, &c. with Boracic Acid.

Tourmaline.
Rubellane.
  Aphrizite.
Schorl.
Zeuxite.

Anhydrous Silicates of Alumina, Lime, and Boracic Acid.

Axinite.
Danburite.

Anhydrous Silicate of Alumina, Titanic Acid, Yttria, Lime, &c.

Keilhauite.

Hydrous Silicate of Alumina, Chromium, &c.

Chrome Ochre.

Anhydrous Silicate of Alumina, Magnesia, and Alkalies.

Pegmatolite.

Anhydrous Silicates of Alumina and Lithia.

Spodumene.
  Killinite.
Castor.

Anhydrous Silicate of Alumina, Lithia, and Soda.

Petalite.

Anhydrous Silicates of Alumina and Glucina.

Emerald.
Beryl.
  Aquamarine.
  Davidsonite.
  Goshenite.
Euclase.

Anhydrous Silicate of Glucina and Lime.

Leucophane.

Silicates of Zirconia, &c.

Anhydrous.

Zircon.
  Jargoon.
  Jacynth, or Hyacinth.
  Zirconite.
  Ostranite.
  Erdmannite.
  Malacone.
  Tachyaphaltite.
  Calyptolite.
Auerbachite.
Eudyalite.
  Eukolite.

Hydrous.

Catapleiite.

Hydrous Silicate of Thoria.

Thorite.

Hydrous Silicate of Cerium, Lanthanium, Didymium, &c.

Mosandrite.

METALLIC MINERALS.

CLASS I.

BRITTLE AND DIFFICULTLY FUSIBLE.

Titanium.

Rutile.
Sagenite.
Anatase.
Brookite.
Nigrine.
Gallicinite.
Iserine.
Ilmenite.
Hystatite.
Washingtonite.
Crichtonite.
Ilmenorutile.
Menaccanite.
Mohsite.

Warwickite.

Perowskite.
Polymignite.
Polycrase.
Æschynite.

Sphene.
Greenovite.
Guarinite.
Lederite.
Séméline.
Spinthère.
Ligurite.

Keilhauite.
Oerstedtite.
Mosandrite.
Tschewkinite.

Tantalum.

Fergusonite.
Tyrite.
Tantalite.
Cassiterotantalite.
Ixiolite.
Dianite.
Yttrotantalite.
Euxenite.
Pyrochlore.
Microlite.

Niobium and Pelopium.

Samarskite.
Adelpholite.

Tungsten.

Wolframine.

Scheelite.

Wolfram.

Scheelitine.

Molybdenum.

Molybdine.

Molybdenite.

Vanadium.

Vanadinite.

Volborthite.

Chromium.

Oxide of Chrome, or Chrome Ochre.

Wolchonskoite.
Chrome Garnet, or Uwarowite.
Chromic Iron.

Uranium.

Uranochre, or Zippeite.
Pitchblende.
Coracite.
Pittinerz.
Gummierz.

Eliasite.

Liebigite.
Urankalk-carbonat.
Voglite.

Johannite.
Zippeite.
Medjidite.

Uranite.
Yellow Uranite, or Autunite.
Chalcolite.
Urangreen.

Manganese.

Psilomelane.
Varvicite.
Wad.
Pyrolusite.
Polianite.
Manganite.
Braunite.
Marceline.
Hausmannite.
Rancierite.

Diallogite.
Wiserite.
Manganocalcite.

Manganese Spar, or Rhodonite.
Allagite.
Bustamite.
Fowlerite.
Dyssnite.
Opsimose.
Paisbergite.
Strutopeite.
Photizite.
Troostite.
Tephroite.
Knebelite.
Helvine.
Carpholite.
Manganese Blende.
Hauerite.

Manganesian Alum.

Triplite.
Hureaulite.

Kaneite.

Greenovite.

Crednerite.
Peokonite.
Lampadite.

b 3

CLASS II.

BBITTLE, EASILY FUSIBLE, AND VOLATILE.

Arsenic.

Native Arsenic.

Arsenolite.

Orpiment.
Realgar.
Dimorphine.
Arsenical Pyrites, or Leu-
copyrite.

Skutterudite.

Gersdorffite.
Amoibite.

Antimony.

Native Antimony.
Senarmontite.
Valentinite.
Antimonphyllite.
Antimonial Ochre.
Stibiconise.
Cervantite.
Volgerite.

Red Antimony, or Kermes-
ite.

Stibnite.

Zinkenite.
Jamesonite.
Plagionite.

Arsenical Antimony.

Ullmannite.

Tellurium.

Native Tellurium.

Tellurite, or Telluric Ochre.

Hessite.
Petzite.
Graphic Tellurium, or Syl-
vanite.
Yellow Tellurium, or Mül-
lerine.
Aurotellurite.
Black Tellurium, or Na-
gyagite.

Bismuth.

Native Bismuth.

Bismuth Ochre.
Agnesite.
Bismutite.

Bismuth Blende, or Euly-
tine.

Karelinite.

Bismuthine.
Cupreous Bismuth, or Wit-
tichite.
Tannenite.

Needle Ore, or Aikenite.

Telluric Bismuth, or Tetradymite.

CLASS III.

MALLEABLE — NOT REDU-
CIBLE BY HEAT ALONE.

Zinc.

Red Oxide of Zinc, or
Zincite.

Zinc Spar, or Calamine.
Zinc Bloom.
Herrerite.
Aurichalcite.
Buratite.
Kapnite.
Zinc-Iron Spar.

Zinc Glance, or Smith-
sonite.
Willemite.
Troostite (Shepard).
Automolite.

Hopeite.

Voltzite.
Blende.
Cleiophane.
Mariatite.
Sulphate of Zinc, or Gos-
larite.
Almagrerite.

Cadmium.

Greenockite.

Cadmiferous Blende from
Przibram, or Przibra-
mite (Huot).

Tin.

Oxide of Tin, or Cassiterite.
Sparable Tin.
Stream Tin.
Wood Tin.
Toads-eye Tin. }
Rosin Tin.

Tin Pyrites.

Lead.

Native Lead.

Plumbic Ochre.
Native Minium.
Plattnerite.

White Lead Ore, or Ce-
rusite.

Galena.
Blue Lead.
Johnstonite.

Anglesite.

Lanarkite.
Leadhillite.
Susannite.

Cotunnite.
Matlockite.
Mendipite.

Horn Lead, or Cromfordite.

Pyromorphite.
Polysphærite.
Miesite.
Nussierite.

Clausthalite.
Raphanosmite.
Tilkerodite.

Plumbocalcite.

Scheeletine.

Yellow Lead Ore, or Wul-
fenite.
Vanadinite.

Descloizite.

Dechenite.
Crocoisite.
Melanochroite.

Mimetite.
 Hedyphane.
 Kampylite.
Dufrenoysite.

Bleinierite.
 Moffrasite.

Kilbrickenite.
Geocronite.
 Schulzite.
Boulangerite.
Feather Ore, or Heteromor-
 phite.
 Meneghinite.
Jamesonite.
Plagionite.
Zinkenite.

Altaite.

Kobellite.

Bournonite.
Percylite.
Caledonite.
Linarite.
Cuproplumbite.
Wölchite.
Vauquelinite.

Iron.

Native Iron.
 Meteoric Iron.
Magnetite.
 Iron Earth.
Martite.

Goethite.
 Lepidokrokite.
 Onegite.
 Przibramite.
 Rubinglimmer,
 Sammetblende.
 Stilpnosiderite.
 Pyrosiderite.

Brown Iron Ore, or Limon-
 ite.
 Brown Hematite.
 Quellerz.
 Bohn-erz, or Bean Ore.
 Pea Iron Ore.
 Xanthosiderite.
 Wood Hematite.
 Brown Ochre, or Ochry Brown
  Iron Ore.
 Yellow Ochre.
 Umber.
 Terra di Sienna.

Hematite.
Specular Iron.
Micaceous Iron.
Red Hematite, or Fibrous
 Red Iron Ore.
 Red Ochre.
 Reddle.
 Red Chalk.
 Scaly Red Iron Ore, or Red-
  Iron Froth.
 Turgite ?

Sparry Iron, or Chalybite.
 Sphærosiderite.
 Oligon Spar.
 Junckerite.
 Clay Iron Stone
 Black Band.
 Septaria.

Vivianite.
 Mullicite.
 Anglarite.
 Blue Iron Earth.
 Dufrenite.
 Calciferrite.
 Delvauxene
 Beraunite
 Carphosiderite.
 Triplite.
 Zwiselite.
Triplite.
 Hureaulite.
Triphyline.
 Heteposite.
Tetraphyline.
 Alluaudite.

Magnetic Pyrites, or Pyr-
 rhotine.
Pyrites.
White Iron Pyrites, or Mar-
 casite.
 Radiated Pyrites.
 Spear Pyrites.
 Cellular Pyrites.
 Cockscomb Pyrites,
 Hepatic Pyrites.
 Wasserkies.
 Kyrosite.
Copperas.
Copiapite.
Coquimbite.
 Blakeite.
Halotrichite.
Halotrichine.
Jarosite.
Botryogene.
Voltaite.
Misy.
Diadochite.

Zeilanite.

Karphosiderite.
Sideroschisolite.
Hyalosiderite.
Chlorophæite.
b 4

Fayalite.
Pyrosmalite.
Hisingerite.
 Thraulite.
Nontronite.
Chamoisite.
Stilpnomelane.
Lievrite.
 Wehrlite.
Cronstedtite.
Pinguite.
Gramenite.
Chloropal.

Iron Apatite.

Mispickel.
 Plinian.
 Danaite.
 Glaucodote.
 Leucopyrite.
 Satersbergite.
Symplesite.
Cube Ore, or Pharmaco-
 siderite.
Scorodite.
Pitchy Iron Ore, or Pitti-
 cite.
Arsenosiderite.
Franklinite.

Cobalt.

Earthy Cobalt, or Asbolan.

Remingtonite.

Syepoorite.
Cobalt Pyrites, or Linnæite.
Carrollite.

Bright White Cobalt, Co-
 balt Glance, or Cobaltine.
Tin-White Cobalt, or Smaltine.
 Safflorite.

Cobalt Bloom, or Erythrine.
Köttigite.
Cobalt Coating.
Cobalt Crust.
Roselite.

Cobalt Vitriol or Bieberite.

Nickel.

Annabergite.

Emerald Nickel.

xl INTRODUCTION.

Capillary Pyrites, or Millerite.
Placodine.

Antimonial Nickel, or
Breithauptite.
Allmannite.

Arsenical Nickel, or Chlo-
anthite.
White Nickel Pyrites, or
Rammelsbergite.
Nickel Glance, or Gers-
dorffite.
Tombazite.

Copper Nickel.

Nickel Ochre.

Nickel-Bismuth Glance, or
Grünauite.

Meteoric Iron, or Meteo-
rites.
Meteoric Minerals, viz.:
Apatoid.
Chantonnite.
Chladnite.
Dyslytite.
Iodilite.
Howardite.
Olivenoid.
Partschite.
Schreibersite, or She-
pardite.
Sphenomite.
Iron-nickel Pyrites, or Ei-
sennickelkies.

Pimelite.

Nickel Vitriol, or Pyromeline.

Copper.

Native Copper.
Red Copper.
Chalcotrichite.
Tile-Ore, or Ziegelerz.
Black Copper, or Melaco-
nite.
Tenorite.

Mysorine.
Malachite.
Chessylite.

Phosphorochalcite.
Ehlite.

Thrombolite.
Libethenite.
Tagilite.

Copper Glance.
Nail-headed Copper Ore.
Covelline.
Purple Copper, Erubescite,
or Bornite.
Copper Pyrites, Towanite,
or Chalcopyrite.
Peacock Copper.
Blistered Copper Ore.
Barnhardtite.
Grey Copper, Fahlerz, or
Tetrahedrite.
Annivite.
Polytelite.
Freibergite.
Fournelite.
Spaniolite,
Schwarzerz. }
Wolfsbergite.
Bournonite.

Brochantite.
Königite.
Krusivite.
Cyanosite.
Lettsomite.
Vitriolite.

Atacamite

Emerald Copper, or Diop-
tase.
Chrysocolla.
Kupferpecherz.
Chalkolite.
Crednerite.
Darwinite.
Algodonite.
Domeykite.
Cornwallite.
Condurrite.
Erinite.
Clinoclase.
Tyrolite.
Olivenite.
Wood Arseniate.
Euchroite.
Liroconite.
Chalcophyllite.
Lindackerite.
Whitneyite.

Alisonite.

Berzelianite.
Selenkupferblei.
Selenbleikupfer.
Vauquelinite.

CLASS IV.

NOBLE METALS — REDUCI-
BLE BY HEAT ALONE.

Mercury.

Native Quicksilver.

Native Amalgam.

Cinnabar.

Horn Quicksilver, or Calomel.

Coccinite.

Ammiolite.

Silver.

Native Silver.

Selbite.

Horn Silver, or Kerargyr-
ite.
Butter-milk Silver.

Silver Glance.
Silver Black.
Flexible Sulphide of Silver.

Antimonial Silver, or Dis-
crasite.
Brittle sulphide of Silver,
or Stephanite.
Polybasite.
Psaturose.
Fireblende.
Sternbergite.
Freieslebenite.

Red Silver Ore:
a. Dark Red Silver Ore,
or Pyrargyrite.
b. Light Red Silver Ore,
or Proustite.
Xanthocone.
Miargyrite.

Argentiferous Copper
Glance, or Stromyerite.
Jalpaite.

Bismuthic Silver.

Selenide of Silver, or Naumannite.
Riolite.

INTRODUCTION.

Eucairite.

Telluric Silver, or Hessite.
Bromide of Silver, or Bromyrite.
Embolite.
Megabromite.

Mikrobromite.

Iodic Silver, or Iodyrite.

Gold.
Native Gold.

Electrum.

Gold Amalgam.

Auriferous Pyrites.

Aurotellurite.

Platinum.
Native Platinum.

Palladium.
Native Palladium.

Oro Pudre, or Porpezite.

Rhodium.
Rhodium Gold.

Iridium.
Native Iridium.

Iridosmine.

Irite.

Osmium.
Irid-Osmine.

Irite.

Lanthanium.
Lanthanite.

Lanthanium, Cerium, and Didymium.
Parisite.

Lanthanium, Cerium, Didymium, and Titanic Acid.
Tschewkinite.

Columbium.
Microlite.
Torrelite.
Pyrorthite.

Columbic and Titanic Acid, and Lanthanium.
Pyrochlore.

Cerium.
Cererite.
Allanite.
  Orthite.
  Uralorthite. }
  Xanthorthite. }
  Bodenite.
  Cerine.
Tritomite.

Cryptolite.
  Phosphocerite.
Monazite.
  Edwardsite.

Yttro-cerite.

Fluocerine.

Note.—A few of the names in the preceding list have been purposely inserted twice. By that means, the varities of Garnet can either be kept together as a distinct group; or they can be inserted in the places they would more properly occupy, if arranged strictly according to the chemical composition of each individual member.

The names printed in smaller type are those of varieties of the mineral which they immediately follow.

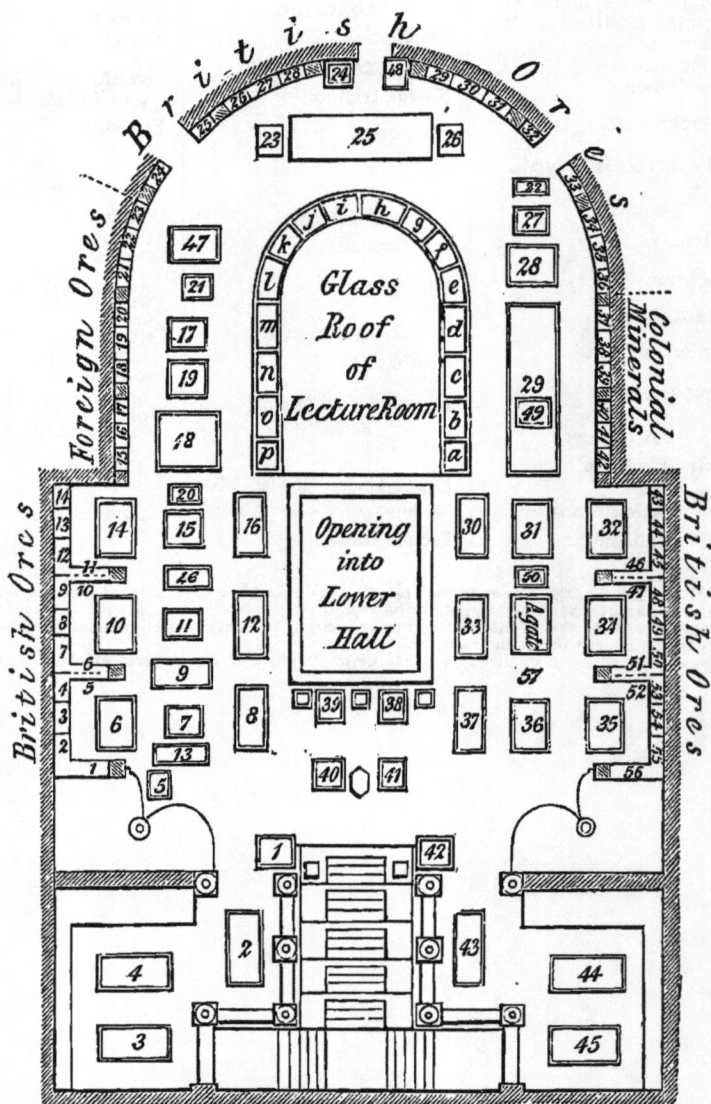

GROUND PLAN OF PRINCIPAL FLOOR OF THE MUSEUM OF PRACTICAL GEOLOGY, LONDON.

The plan of the Museum of Practical Geology, on the opposite page, is borrowed, with some alterations, from that published in Mr. Hunt's Descriptive Guide. It will be of use by indicating the position and numbers of the Cases referred to in the Glossary. The Wall-cases which contain the collections of British and Foreign ores and metallic minerals, are those situated at the outer margin of the Plan, and the Horse-shoe Case is that surrounding the central area, which forms the glass roof of the Lecture Room.

The following is a general list of the contents of the various compartments into which the Horse-shoe Case is divided, commencing at the southeast end.

a. CARBON (and its natural compounds) : — *Diamond, Graphite.*

b.   „   *Coal, Coke, Bitumen, Lignite, Mellite, Amber, Ozocerite, Hatchettine, &c.*

c. SULPHUR, and its compounds.

d. HALOIDS and SALTS. — *Common or Rock Salt, Boracic acid, Alum, Cryolite, Nitrate of potash.*

e.   „   „   *Barytes, Strontia, Witherite.*

f.   „   „   *Gypsum, Selenite, Apatite, Vivianite, &c.*

g.   „   „   *Fluor.*

h.   „   „   *Calc Spar.*

i.   „   „   *Calc Spar, Marble, Stalagmite, or Oriental Alabaster, Aragonite, Dolomite, Fire Marble, &c.*

j. EARTHS: — *Rock Crystal* (and its varieties) :—*Amethyst, Cairngorm, False Topaz, Citrine, Morion, Rose Quartz, Ferruginous Quartz, Aventurine, Cat's-Eye, Chrysoprase, &c.*

k.   „   Amorphous Silica — *Quartz, Chalcedony, Carnelian, Mocha-stone, Agate, Sard, Sardonyx, Onyx, Jasper, Heliotrope or Bloodstone.*

l.   „   Amorphous Silica — *Flint, Sandstone, Silicified Wood, &c.* Hydrous Silica — *Opal, Hyalite, &c.*

m. ALUMINA, ALUMINATES, and SILICATES.   *Ruby, Sapphire, Schorl, Tourmaline, Emerald, Chrysoberyl, Cymophane, Zircon (Jacinth, Hyacinth), &c.* *Garnets (Almandine, Cinnamon stone, Romanzowite, Uwarowite, Grossular, Dimanthoid), &c.* *Idocrase, Topaz, Pycnite, Chrysolite or Peridot, Chondrodite, Spinel.*

n. ALUMINATES and SILICATES.   *Felspar (Adularia, Orthoclase, Labradorite), Lapis Lazuli, Mica, Lepidolite, Gilbertite, Haüyne, Jade, Leucite, Rhodonite, Anthophyllite, Augite, Epidote, Hornblende, Chlorite, Tremolite, &c.*

o. HYDROUS SILICATES.   *Serpentine, Steatite, Diallage, Websterite, Cimolite, Bole, Turquois, Asbestos, Amianthus, Prehnite, Chabazite, &c.*

p. HYDROUS SILICATES (continued).   *Harmotome, Poonahlite, Heulandite, Apophyllite, Phacolite, Thomsonite, Cluthalite, Analcime, Pectolite, Stilbite, Talc, Meerschaum, &c.*

The British Ores are contained in the Wall-cases numbered 1 to 14, 24 to 36, and 43 to 56; the Colonial Minerals in Wall-cases 37 to 42, and the Foreign Ores in Wall-cases 15 to 23.

The remaining numbers in the square compartments indicate the positions of Table-Cases, Models, and other objects.

LIST OF SYMBOLS AND SIGNS

MADE USE OF IN THE FOLLOWING WORK.

—◆—

Al	Aluminium
Äl	Alumina
Ag (*Argentum*)	Silver
Am	Ammonia
As	Arsenic
Äs	Arsenious acid
Äs	Arsenic acid
Au (*Aurum*)	Gold
B	Boron
B̈	Boracic acid
Ba	Barium
Ḃa	Baryta
Be (*Beryllium*)	Glucinum
Be or B̈e	Glucina
Bi	Bismuth
Ḃi	Oxide of Bismuth
Br	Bromine
C	Carbon
C̈	Carbonic acid
Ca	Calcium
Ċa	Lime
Cb	Columbium (Tantalum) or Niobium
C̈b	Columbic acid
Cd	Cadmium
Ce	Cerium
Ċe	Protoxide of Cerium
C̈e	Peroxide of Cerium
Cl	Chlorine
Co	Cobalt
Ċo	Oxide of Cobalt
Cr	Chromium
C̈r	Oxide of Chrome
C̈r	Chromic acid
Cu (*Cuprum*)	Copper
Ċu	} Oxide of Copper
Ċu	}
D	Didymium
F	Fluorine
Fe (*Ferrum*)	Iron
Ḟe	Protoxide of Iron
F̈e	Peroxide of Iron
H	Hydrogen
Ḣ	Water
H Cl	Hydrochloric or muriatic acid
HF	Hydro-fluoric acid
Hg (*Hydrargyrum*)	Quicksilver or Mercury
I	Iodine
Ir	Iridium
K (*Kalium*)	Potassium
K̇	Potash
La	Lanthanium
Ḷa	Protoxide of Lanthanium
L̈a	Peroxide of Lanthanium
Li	Lithium
Lı̇	Lithia
Ṁ	Mellitic acid
Mg	Magnesium
Ṁg	Magnesia
Mn	Manganese
Ṁn	Protoxide of Manganese
M̈n	Peroxide of Manganese

Mo	.	.	.	Molybdenum		Sr	.	.	.	Strontium
M̈o	.	.	.	Molybdic acid		Ṡr	.	.	.	Strontia
N	.	.	.	Nitrogen		Ta	.	.	.	Tantalum
N̈	.	.	.	Nitric acid		T̈a	.	.	.	Tantalic acid
Na (*Natrium*)	.	.	Sodium		Te	.	.	.	Tellurium
						Th	.	.	.	Thorinum
Ṅa	.	.	.	Soda		Ṫh	.	.	.	Thoria
NH⁴O	.	.	.	Ammonia		Ti	.	.	.	Titanium
O	.	.	.	Oxygen						
Os	.	.	.	Osmium		T̈i	.	.	.	Titanic acid
P	.	.	.	Phosphorus						
P̈	.	.	.	Phosphoric acid		Ṫ̈i	.	.	.	Oxide of Titanium
Pb	.	.	.	Lead		V	.	.	.	Vanadium
						U	.	.	.	Uranium
Ṗb	.	.	.	Oxide of Lead						
Pd	.	.	.	Palladium		U̇	.	.	.	Protoxide of Uranium
Pt	.	.	.	Platinum						
Rh	.	.	.	Rhodium		Ü	.	.	.	Peroxide of Uranium
Ru	.	.	.	Ruthenium		W (*Wolframium*)	.	Tungsten
S	.	.	.	Sulphur						
S̈	.	.	.	Sulphuric acid		Ẅ	.	.	.	Tungstic acid
Sb (*Stibium*)	.	Antimony		Y	.	.	.	Yttrium
Se	.	.	.	Selenium						
Si	.	.	.	Silicium		Ẏ	.	.	.	Yttria
						Zn	.	.	.	Zinc
S̈i	.	.	.	Silica						
Sn (*Stannum*)	.	Tin		Żn	.	.	.	Oxide of Zinc
						Zr	.	.	.	Zirconium
S̈n	.	.	.	Oxide of Tin		Z̈r	.	.	.	Zirconia

Signs and Abbreviations.

=	.	.	.	Sign of equality, or equal to		*Comp.*	.	.	Chemical Composition
+	.	.	.	plus, or sign of addition		*BB*	.	.	Before the blowpipe
						Brit. Mus.	.	.	British Museum
H.	.	.	.	Hardness		*M.P.G.*	.	.	Museum of Practical Geology
S.G.	.	.	.	Specific Gravity					

TECHNICAL TERMS

USED BY JEWELLERS AND LAPIDARIES.

Bezils. — The upper sides and corners (*d d*) of the *Brilliant*, lying between the edge of the Table and the Girdle.

Cabochon. — The smooth convex elliptical form used for cutting Precious Garnet, Turquois, Opal, &c. *Fig. e*, side view. *Fig. f*, plan.

Collet. — The small horizontal plane, or face (*h*) at the bottom of the *Brilliant.*

Crown. — The upper work of the *Rose*, which all centres in the work at the top, and is bounded by the horizontal ribs.

Facets. — Small triangular faces or planes, both in *Brilliants* and *Roses.*

In *Brilliants* there are two sorts, *Skew-* and *Skill-*facets, and *Star-*facets. Skill-facets are divided into *upper* and *under*. Upper Skill-facets (*c c*) are wrought on the lower part of the Bezil, and terminate in the Girdle; Under Skill-facets (*f f*) are wrought on the Pavilions, and terminate in the Girdle. Star-facets (*b b*) are wrought on the upper part

of the Bezil, and terminate in the Table.

Girdle. — The line (*e e*) which encompasses the stone, parallel to the horizon; or which determines the greatest horizontal expansion of the stone.

Goutte de suif is similar to Cabochon, only the relief is not so great, and, consequently, the form of the stone is flatter.

Lozenges are common to *Brilliants* and *Roses*. In Brilliants they are formed by the meeting of the Skill-, and Star-facets on the Bezil: in *Roses*, by the meeting of the Facets in the horizontal Ribs of the Crown.

Pavilions are the undersides and corners (*g g*) of the *Brilliants*, and lie between the Girdle and the Collet.

Ribs. — The lines or ridges which distinguish the several parts of the work, both of *Brilliants* and *Roses.*

Table. — The large horizontal planes or faces (*a*) at the top of the *Brilliant.*

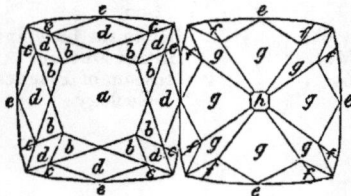
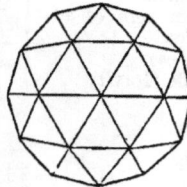
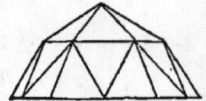

Fig. *d.*

Fig. *a.*   Fig. *b.*   Fig. *c.*   Fig. *e.*

Fig. *f.*

Fig. *a.*	Plan of the upper side of a *Brilliant.*
Fig. *b.*	Plan of the under side of a *Brilliant.*
Fig. *c.*	Plan of the upper side of a *Rose.*
Fig. *d.*	Side view of a *Rose.*
Fig. *e.*	Side view of a stone cut *en cabochon.*
Fig. *f.*	Plan of a stone cut *en cabochon*, or *en goutte de suif.*

Note.—The horizontal line beneath the figures *a b*, is the distance between the Table and the Collet, or the depth which should be given to a stone of such a size as that in the figure, to insure the greatest amount of lustre.

ERRATA AND ADDENDA.

Page 1, column 1, line 10 from bottom: *for* "See GREY OXIDE OF MANGANESE" *read* "GREY OXIDE OF MANGANESE. See MANGANITE."

9, column 2, line 10 from bottom: *for* "Bromley" *read* "Brownley."

10, column 2, bottom line: *for* "rhomboid" *read* "rhombohedron."

line 13: *for* 99·10 *read* 99·10.

12, column 1, line 26 from top: *dele* "now."
line 29: *for* "with coal and lignite" *read* "with Brown Coal and Lignite."

14, column 2, line 25 from bottom: *for* "potash" *read* "alumina."

21, column 1, line 10 from top: *for* "Sb" *read* "S̈b."

26, column 2, line 7 from bottom: *for* "Elæotite" *read* "Elæolite."

41, column 1, line 26 from bottom: *for* "Selenite" *read* "Selenide."

54, column 1, line 15 from top: *for* "Ċa" *read* "Ċa."

58, column 1: transfer the *Analysis* of BYSSOLITE, and the two following lines, to article on "BURATITE."

64, column 1: transfer the paragraphs headed "*Analysis*," "*Locality*," and "*Name*," from article "CARNALLITE" to "CARNAT."

78, column 1, line 24 from bottom: *for* "Aluminum" *read* "Aluminium."

79, column 2, line 32 from top: *for* "H" *read* "Ḣ."

82, column 1, line 4 from top: *after* "Si²" *add* "+6Ḣ."

89, column 2, last line: *for* "Copper" *read* "Cobalt."

134, column 2, line 25 from bottom: *for* "T̈i" *read* "T̈i."

Pa. 152, column 1, line 9 from bottom: *after* "*Nicol*" *add* "A native hydrate of alumina."

176, column 2, line 15 from top: *for* "Statoust" *read* "Slatoust."

192, column 2, line 20 from bottom: *for* "T̈i" *read* "T̈i.²"

193, column 2, line 22 from bottom: *for* "T̈T̈²" *read* "T̈i F̈i."

195, column 1, line 24 from bottom: *for* "S" *read* "S̈."

197, column 2, line 7 from bottom: *after* "*Dufrénoy*" *add* "A kind of Sparry Iron."

217, column 1, line 5 from top: *for* "Ċ" *read* "Ċa."

220, column 2, line 17 from bottom: *for* "Alumina" *read* "Arsenious acid."
line 19 from bottom: *for* "Ä̈s" *read* "Ä̈s."

241, column 2, line 5 from bottom: *for* "alumina" *read* "potash."

248, column 2, line 7 from top: *for* "100" *read* "1·00."

252, column 2, line 22 from top: *for* "BRUCITE" *read* "PERICLASE."

341, column 1, last line: *for* "NATE" *read* "NITE."

348, column 2, line 2 from top: *for* "Tantalit" *read* "Tantalite."

389, column 1, line 1 from top: *after* A, *add* "(ferruginous silicate of manganese (Thomson))."
line 3 from top: *for* "oxide of manganese" *read* "carbonate of protoxide of manganese: (See Dana, vol. ii. p. 189, Analysis 7, from Stirling.)"
line 18 from top: *after* "*Locality*" *add*, "Stirling,".

GLOSSARY OF MINERALOGY.

ABICHITE.

ABICHITE, *Haidinger*. See CLINOCLASE.

ABRAZITE, *Breislak, Brocchi*. See GIS-MONDINE.

ACADIALITE or ACADIOLITE. A variety of Chabazite, probably containing an admixture of Quartz. The colour (wine-yellow or flesh-red passing into white) is arranged in a tesselated manner in some crystals, the angles being almost colourless.

Analysis by Hayes:

Silica .	.	.	.	. 52·02
Alumina	.	.	.	. 17·88
Lime .	.	.	.	. 4·24
Soda .	.	.	.	. 4·07
Potash .	.	.	.	. 3·03
Water .	.	.	.	. 18·30

99·54

The word Acadialite is derived from a former name of Nova Scotia, where the mineral is found.

ACANTHOÏDE, *Dufrénoy* (from ἄκανθα, *a spine*). A mineral apparently related to Breislakite occurring in dark brown fibres passing into reddish-brown, disseminated in lava; and in very slender and silky, whitish needles in a Vesuvian lava erupted in 1821.

ACANTICONITE, *Dandrada*. See ARENDALITE. This name is derived from ἀκανθίς, *a goldfinch*, and κόνις, *powder*, because the yellow colour of the powdered mineral resembles that of the plume of a goldfinch.

ACERDÈSE, *Beudant*. See GREY OXIDE OF MANGANESE. From ἀκερδὴς, *unprofitable*, because it is of but little use in the arts, compared with Pyrolusite, which it greatly resembles.

ACHATES or Ἀχάτης: the name by which the Agate was known to the ancient Greeks. According to Theophrastus (LVIII.) it was so called after the river Achates in Sicily, where probably it was first discovered.

ACHMITE.

ACHIRITE, the name given by Werner to Dioptase after Achir Mamed, a Bucharian merchant, who first brought the stone from Siberia, and endeavoured to sell it for Emerald.

ACHMATIT, *Hermann*. A variety of lime-and-iron-Epidote, from Achmatowsk. See BUCKLANDITE.

ACHMITE, *Berzelius, Beudant, Dana, Nicol, Phillips*.

Oblique · primary form an oblique rhombic prism. Isomorphous with Augite. Colour brownish, or reddish-brown. Opaque; translucent in thin fragments, which exhibit a yellowish-brown tint by transmitted light. Lustre vitreous, inclining to resinous. Streak pale yellowish-grey. Brittle. Fracture imperfect conchoidal. H. 6 to 6·5. S. G. 3·5 to 3·6.

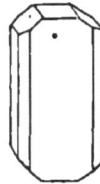

Fig. 1.   Fig. 2.

Comp. N̈a S̈i + F̈e S̈i² = Silica 55·07, Peroxide of iron, 32·4, Soda, 12·6 = 100.

Analysis by Lehunt:

Silica .	.	.	.	. 56·02
Peroxide of iron .	.	.	. 28·08
Protoxide of manganese	.	3·49
Soda .	.	.	.	. 13·33
Lime .	.	.	.	. 0·89
Magnesia .	.	.	. 0·50
Alumina .	.	.	. 0·69

103·00

BB fuses readily to a black magnetic globule.

Locality. This somewhat rare mineral occurs imbedded in Felspar and Quartz at Rundemyr, near Kongsberg in Norway, in crystals nearly a foot long. They are often macled and bent, and quite fragile.

Name. From άκμή, *a point;* in allusion to the pointed form of the crystals.

G. Rose suggests that Achmite is an altered form of Pyroxene (the *Ægirine* of Brevig).

Brit. Mus., Case 34.

ACHRENSTEIN. See BARYTES.

ACHROITE (from *α priv.* and χρόα, *colour*) the name proposed by Rammelsberg for colourless varieties of Tourmaline. They are found at St. Gotthard, in Elba, and Siberia.

ACICULAR ARSENIATE OF COPPER, *Allan.* See OLIVENITE.

ACICULAR BISMUTH; or ACICULAR BISMUTH-GLANCE, Needle-ore. See AIKENITE.

ACICULAR-ORE, *Jameson.* See AIKENITE.

ACICULAR STONE, *Jameson.* See SCOLECITE.

ACICULITE, *Nicol.* See AIKENITE.

ACIDE ARSENIEUX, *Beudant.* See ARSENOLITE.

ACMITE. See ACHMITE.

ACORITE, *Dufrénoy.* See AZORITE.

ACTINOLITE, *Dana, Nicol;* ACTINOTE; ACTYNOLITE, *Phillips, Jameson,* comprehends the glassy and fibrous varieties of Hornblende, and has been subdivided into *glassy, asbestiform,* and *granular. Glassy Actinolite* includes the bright-green bladed crystals or columnar forms, with a vitreous or pearly lustre. The crystals are long slender prisms, which are easily broken. The fibrous crystallizations of a green or greenish-grey colour, disposed in wedge-shaped masses or in radii, sometimes promiscuously aggregated, are often termed *asbestiform Actinolite. Granular Actinolite* includes such grass-green varieties as have a granular composition. The green colour is owing to a small quantity of iron and chromium.

Comp. $\dot{M}g^3 \ddot{S}i^2 + (\dot{C}a, \dot{F}e, \dot{M}n,) \ddot{S}i.$

Analysis by *Bonsdorff,* from Taberg:

Silica . . . . 59·75
Lime . . . . 14·25
Magnesia . . . 21·10
Protoxide of iron . 5·95
Protoxide of manganese . 0·31
Fluoric acid . . 0·76
                        _____
                        102·12

Localities.—English. Cornwall; the Lizard; the Cheesewring; Cadgwith Point;

Cape Cornwall; Huel Unity, Botallack, Huel Owls, and several other mines. Near the Bowder-stone, in Borrowdale, Cumberland.—*Welsh.* Caer Caradoc, Caernarvonshire; in amygdaloid. Anglesea.—*Scotch.* Glen Tilt in Perthshire. Eilan Reach, Glenelg, Inverness-shire. The Hebrides. Hillswickness Point and elsewhere in the Shetlands.—*Foreign.* Saltzburg and Greiner in the Zillerthal, Tyrol. St. Gotthard. Sweden. Norway. Finland. Greenland. Piedmont.

Name. From άκτινωτός, *radiated.*

Brit. Mus., Case 33.

M. P. G. Horse-shoe Case, 1048 to 1051.

ADAMANT, *Kirwan:* ADAMANTINE SPAR, *Phillips:* from *α priv:* and δαμάω, *to subdue.* Names given to Corundum from its hardness or from the peculiar lustre which it occasionally displays, resembling that of the Adamant or Diamond. The term Adamantine-spar is sometimes applied to Sapphire of a hair-brown colour.

ADELPHOLITE, *Nordenskiöld.* A niobate or tantalate of iron and manganese, with 9·7 per cent of water. Colour brownish-yellow to brown and black. Subtranslucent. Lustre greasy. Streak white or yellowish-white. H. 3·5 to 4·5. S.G. 3·8.

Locality. Rajamaki in Tamela, Finland.

ADIAPHANE SPAR, *Mohs.* See GEHLENITE and NEPHRITE.

ADINOLE, *Beudant.* See PETROSILEX.

ADULAIRE, *La Metherie;* ADULAR, *Werner, Haidinger;* ADULARIA, *Jameson.* A transparent or translucent variety of potash-Felspar (Orthoclase), found in granitic rocks. It occurs both massive and crystallized in forms which are sometimes extremely complicated. Colour commonly greenish-white, greyish. or milk-white. Frequently iridescent. Lustre vitreous inclining to pearly on the faces of perfect cleavage. Brittle. Fracture uneven to conchoidal. H. 6. S.G. 2·575.

Analysis by *Abich,* from St. Gotthard:

Silica . . . . 65·69
Alumina . . . 17·97
Peroxide of iron . . trace
Potash . . . 13·99
Lime . . . . 1·34
Soda . . . . 1·01
                        _____
                        100·00

Localities.—English. Tintagel, Cornwall; in slate.—*Welsh.* Snowdon; with Quartz. —*Scotch.* Island of Arran, Buteshire. — *Irish.* Slieve Corra, Mourne Mountains, co. Down.—*Foreign.* St. Gotthard in Switzerland, and particularly on one of the highest peaks named Adula, whence has been derived the name Adularia.

"Adularia is distinguished from common Felspar by its greenish-white colour, particular colour reflection, complete conchoidal cross-fracture, lamellar distinct concretions, its higher degree of transparency, and by the want of those rents which cross the cleavage obliquely in common Felspar."—*Jameson*, vol. i. p. 289.

For varieties of Adularia, see MOONSTONE, SUNSTONE, VALENCIANITE.

Brit. Mus., Case 30.

M. P. G. Horse-shoe Case, Nos. 955 to 959, 1039.

ÆDELFORSITE, *Dana*, *v. Kobell.* Occurs massive, and fibrous or feathery. Colour white or greyish. Transparent or translucent at the edges. Lustre shining. H. 6. S.G. 2·58.

Comp. Neutral silicate of lime, or $\overset{..}{\mathrm{Ca}}\,\overset{...}{\mathrm{Si}}$ = lime 37·8, silica 62·2 = 100. *BB* fuses to a white translucent glass. Forms a jelly with acids.

Localities. Ædelfors in Smaoland, Sweden; Cjelleback in Norway; Cziklowa, in the Bannat.

Brit. Mus., Case 25.

ÆDELFORSITE, *Retzius*, *Nicol*: ÆDILITE, *Kirwan*: or Red Zeolite of Ædelfors; see RETZITE.

ÆDILITE: a variety of Prehnite from Ædelfors, in Sweden.

ÆGIRINE; or ÆGYRINE. A black or greenish-black to leek-green variety of Pyroxene, allied to Arfvedsonite. Resembles Hornblende in outward appearance. H. 5·5 to 5·75. S.G. 3·432 to 3·504.

Comp. 5($\overset{.}{\mathrm{K}}$, Na, $\overset{..}{\mathrm{Ca}}$, Mg, Mn, Fe) $\overset{...}{\mathrm{Si}}^{4}$.

Analysis by *Plantamour*, from Esmark:

Silica	46·57
Alumina	3·41
Protoxide of manganese .	2·07
Protoxide of iron . .	24·38
Titanic acid	2·02
Soda	7·79
Potash	2·96
Lime	5·91
Magnesia	5·81
Fluorine	trace
	100·92

BB fuses to a black globule; with a large quantity of borax forms a green transparent globule, with a still larger quantity a black globule.

Locality. Brevig in Norway.

Brit. Mus., Case 33.

ÆROSITE. See PYRARGYRITE.

ÆSCHYNITE, *Berzelius, Phillips.* Rhombic: primary form an oblique rhombic prism. Occurs in oblique rhombic prisms, terminated by four-sided pyramids, which are generally striated and imperfect. Colour nearly black, inclining to brownish-yellow when translucent. Opaque or translucent only at thin edges. Lustre resinous. Fracture imperfect small conchoidal. H. 5 to 6. S.G. 5·14 to 1·5.

Fig. 3.

Fig. 4.

Comp. Titanate of zirconia, and cerium.

Analysis by *Hartwall* :

Titanic acid . . .	25·9
Zirconia	20·0
Peroxide of cerium . .	15·0
Lime	3·8
Peroxide of iron . . .	2·6
Oxide of tin	0·5
	97·8

When heated evolves water and traces of hydrofluoric acid.

BB swells up and fuses, at the edges only, to a black slag. With borax fuses readily to a dark yellow glass, which is colourless when cool. With salt of phosphorus forms a transparent colourless globule.

Locality. The Ilmen range, near Miask, in Siberia; imbedded in Felspar, and associated with Mica and Zircon.

Name. The name (derived from αἰσχύνη, *disgrace*) given to this mineral by Berzelius, is in allusion to the inability of chemists, at the time of its discovery, to separate the two substances titanic acid and zirconia, which enter into its composition.

Brit. Mus., Case 37.

ÆTITES, *Pliny.* Stones composed commonly of several crusts one within another, and having in them cavities containing loose and moveable matter; either, first, solid and stony, called a *Callimus*, or secondly, loose, as sand, ochre, chalk, earth, &c., *Geode*; or thirdly, liquid, *Enhydros*. (J. Woodward.)

AFTONITE. See APHTHONITE.

AGALMATOLITE, *Phillips*, is a clay or clay-slate altered by heat, and by the action and addition of alkalies contained in infiltrating waters holding in solution alkaline silicates, or carbonates derived from the decomposi-

tion of Felspar on a large scale. H. 2 to 3.
S.G. 2·8 to 2·9. Occurs massive of various
shades of greenish-grey, passing into yellow-
ish-grey and yellowish-brown. Translucent.
Feels rather greasy. Yields to the nail.
Sectile. Fracture splintery.

Comp. $4 \ddot{A}l \ddot{S}i + \dot{K} \ddot{S}i^2 + 3 \dot{H}.$

Analysis by *Klaproth*, from China:

Silica	. . .	54·50
Alumina	. . .	34·00
Potash	. . .	6·25
Water	. . .	4·00
Oxide of iron	. .	0·75

                99·50

Localities.—*English.* Restormel Royal iron
mines, Cornwall; of a pale flesh-colour.—
Welsh. Glyder Bach, Caernarvonshire.—
Irish. Lugganure lead-mines, co. Wicklow,
(pale green).—*Foreign.* Norway. Nagyag
in Transylvania.

Name. From ἄγαλμα, *an image*, and λίθος,
stone.

Agalmatolite is brought from China,
carved into grotesque figures and chimney-
ornaments. It is distinguished by its chemical composition from Steatite, which always contains magnesia, but no potash.

Brit. Mus., Case 26.

M. P. G. Horse-shoe Case, Nos. 1102,
1109, 1112.

AGAPHITE. See TURQUOIS.

AGATE. A variegated variety of chalcedonic Quartz, the colours of which are
arranged in clouds, spots, or bands. The
latter consist of parallel or concentric layers,
either straight (ribbon agate), circular, or
in zigzag forms, the latter receiving the
name of fortification agate from the fancied
resemblance of the bands to the angular
outline of a fortification.

Agates are found in Scotland, Saxony,
Arabia, India, Surinam, &c. in amygdaloid,
mostly in the form of hollow balls or geodes,
coated inside with Quartz or Amethyst.

Immense quantities of Agate are cut and
polished at Oberstein in Rhenish Bavaria,
and at Galgernberg in the north of Germany,
whence they are exported to all parts of the
world.* There is also a manufactory at
Katherinenberg in Siberia.

Agates are used for burnishers, and are
made into mortars for chemical purposes.
They are also much employed in a polished
state for ornamental articles, as brooches,
bracelets, beads, the handles of seals, paper-
knives, daggers, &c. The brooch-stones
sold by the name of Scotch pebbles are true
Agates, found in the amygdaloid of Dunbar,
and of the Hill of Kinnoul, near Perth; but
the stones found in the Isle of Wight and
sold in a polished state under the name of
Agates, are merely flints from the Upper
Chalk, much of the beauty of which is derived from the silicified remains of sponges
and other marine bodies.

The colours of Agate, when indistinct,
may be increased by boiling first in oil,
and afterwards in sulphuric acid; the latter
process carbonising the oil which has been
absorbed between the layers, heightens the
contrast between their different tints.

The imperial treasury of France possesses
some beautiful works in Agate, consisting of
a service valued at 500,000 francs (20,000*l.*)
Several very beautiful articles were exhibited at the Exhibition of 1851, from
Oberstein, and obtained prize medals.

The name is derived from that of the river
Achates, whence, according to Theophrastus,
agates were first brought.

Brit. Mus., Case 23.

M. P. G. A 11 in Hall; inlaid slab of
Agates, Jaspers, &c., from Aberystwith in
North Wales. Principal floor, Case 51,—a
suite of 87 specimens, illustrative of the formation and mode of occurrence of Agates.
Horse-shoe Case, Nos. 571, 572, 583, 585,
657.

AGARIC MINERAL, *Kirwan, Phillips*, is
nearly pure carbonate of lime, deposited at
the bottom of and around lakes, the waters
of which are impregnated with lime; also
in fissures of calcareous rocks, and in limestone caverns. It is loose and friable, of a
white or greyish-white colour, dull and
meagre to the touch, soils the fingers, and is
so light as to float for a time on water.

---

* "The agate trade at Oberstein and Idal has
lately undergone a singular change in consequence
of a falling off in the supply of the agate nodules.
The agates now worked in that district, and sold
as native productions, are chiefly obtained from
the Brazils, where, on the Paraguay, brought
down from the interior by the Rio de la Plata,
they are in such abundance as to be shipped for
ballast. Notwithstanding the source of supply is

so remote, agate articles are sold in Germany at
prices astonishingly low. One other fact, in connection with the agate frauds may be worth re-
cording. Upper Egypt is known to yield agates,
though different from those of South America,
and much less abundant. Travellers from Europe in passing through that country enquire for
these; and, to meet the demand, Brazilian agates
are now sent to Egypt, and there sold for Egyptian agates. At Cairo, especially, numbers are
thus disposed of to English and other travellers,
who purchase them as souvenirs of the country."
— *Handbook to the Geology of Weymouth and
Portland, by R. Damon; Stanford*, 1860.

Localities.—English. Banner Down, near Bath. Chipping Norton, Oxfordshire. Near Sunderland.— *Welsh.* Llyn Savaddan, on the river Llynvi, in Brecknockshire. Trevor, near Llangollen, Merionethshire. — *Scotch.* Near Edinburgh. — *Irish.* Aghanloo and Curly Burn, in New Red Sandstone. Slieve Gallion, coating flint balls.—*Foreign.* Near Ratisbon. Switzerland, where it is used for whitewashing houses. The United States, covering the sides of a cave at Watertown.

Name. From its resemblance to agaric (*a fungus*) in colour and texture.

AGATE-JASPER. A variety of Jasper found in agate-veins.

Brit. Mus., Case 23.

AGATE MOUSSEUSE. Moss Agate.

AGATE PÉRIGONE. Fortification Agate.

AGATE TERREUSE. See CACHOLONG, FLOATSTONE, &c.

AGATE VERSICÒLORE. Variegated Agate.

AGATE ZONAIRE. Agate, the layers of which are arranged in concentric curvilinear bands.

AGATHE CORNALINE, *La Metherie.* See CARNELIAN.

AGNESITE: an earthy steatitic mineral from Huel Coates, near St. Agnes, in Cornwall. It is, probably, an impure Bismuth-ochre, according to Greg & Lettsom.

AIGUE MARINE. See AQUA-MARINE.

AIGUE MARINE DE SIBERIE, *Romé de L'Isle.* See BERYL.

AIKENITE, *Chapman, Dana.* Rhombic: occurs in imbedded acicular four or six-sided prisms, indistinctly terminated, and striated longitudinally; also massive.

Colour. When fresh broken dark steel-grey, but soon acquiring a yellowish or pale copper-red tarnish. Opaque. Lustre metallic. Streak blackish-grey. Structure lamellar. Fracture small-grained, uneven; sometimes approaching to conchoidal. H. 2 to 2·5. S.G. 6·1 to 6.8.

Comp. Sulphide of Bismuth, Copper and Lead, or $(Cu, Pb) S + 3 Bi S^3$.

Analysis by *Hermann*, from Beresowsk:

Bismuth	.	.	.	34·87
Lead	.	.	.	36·31
Copper	.	.	.	10·97
Sulphur	.	.	.	16·50
Nickel	.	.	.	0 36
Gold	.	.	.	0·09
			99·00

BB gives off fumes of sulphur, fuses and emits numerous burning globules, and finally yields a globule of lead containing copper, which colours glass of borax greenish-blue. Dissolves in nitric acid with separation of lead-sulphate and a small quantity of sulphur.

Localities. Beresowsk near Ekatherinenberg, in Siberia, imbedded in white Quartz, and accompanying Gold, Malachite, and Galena.

Names. Named by Chapman after Aiken the chemist.

Brit. Mus., Case 9.

M.P.G. Principal Floor, Wall-cases 9, No. 465 ; 20 (Russia).

AIMANT, *Beudant.* See MAGNETITE.

AIMANT DE CEYLON. See TOURMALINE.

AKANTHITE, *Dufrénoy :* (from ἄκανθα, a *spine,*) a variety of Epidote from Achmatowsk.

AKANTICONE. See EPIDOTE.

AKMIT, *Haidinger.* See ACHMITE.

ALABANDICUS, a stone " Called after the name of the countrey that yieldeth it, it is black : Howbeit, there is of it to be found growing in Miletus, but not altogether so blacke, for it enclineth or declineth rather to a purple colour. This stone of Miletus will resolve in the fire, and commonly they use to melt it for drinking cups, in manner of glasses."—*Pliny,* book XXXVIII. ch. 7.

ALABANDINE, *Beudant, Brooke & Miller.* See MANGANBLENDE.

ALABANDINE, *Pliny :* those carbuncles which were cut and polished at Alabanda, and were called in consequence Alabandine or Alamandine. " Æthiopian Rubies and the Alexandrian, which are found, indeed, among the cliffs of the hill Orthosia, but trimmed and brought to their perfection by the Alabandians. . . . Many authors have written . . that the Alabandines be more darke and blackish than others, and withal rough in hand." — *Pliny,* book XXXVIII. ch. 7.

ALABASTER : is the name by which the fine massive varieties of Gypsum are called. It is a sulphate of lime, composed of sulphuric acid, 46·51 ; lime, 32 56 ; water, 20·93. At Volterra and Castellina, in Tuscany, it occurs extremely pure and compact, and is conveyed thence in large blocks to Florence, where it is manufactured into figures, vases, and other works of art, which are exported to all parts of Europe. Twenty years ago there was a great taste for such objects in France, and the material was then obtained from quarries at Lagny, near Paris. In England it occurs in New Red Marl, principally at Ashton-on-Trent, and Chellaston Hill, near Ashbourne, in Derbyshire, at both of which places it is extensively worked for ornamental purposes " The principal demand for this material usually slightly streaked with red, is by the potters in Staffordshire, who form their moulds of plaster of Paris from it. It is therefore called 'Potter's stone,' and sells at about 9s. per ton of 2,400 lbs. (the long ton). In working the Potter's stone, the fine blocks are selected, and sold to the turners of alabaster ornaments."—(*Robert Hunt.*) It is also found in large quantities at Penarth, Cardiff, Leckwith, and Lavenock, in Glamorganshire; at Newark, in Nottinghamshire; at Fauld Hill, in Staffordshire; at Old Chine, in Somerset; between Penrith and Carlisle, in Cumberland; and in Monaghan co., Ireland. Alabaster is soluble in 400 to 500 parts of water. When heated it parts with its water of composition, and becomes *Plaster of Paris*, for which see GYPSUM. This stone is the Alabastrum of the ancients, by whom it was carved into statues and other objects. The name is derived from Alabastron, a village of Egypt. (See ORIENTAL ALABASTER).

Brit. Mus., Case 57.

M. P. G. Sides of vestibule, Derbyshire. Large tazza and pedestal, on the eastern side of the hall, from Fauld Hill, Staffordshire. Column against east wall. Column supporting serpentine vase, west side of the hall. Horse-shoe Case, Nos. 303 and 304.

ALABASTRA AGATATO. A yellow variety of Alabaster found at Sienna.

ALABASTRITES, *Pliny*. See ORIENTAL ALABASTER. "This Onyx stone, or Onychites aforesaid, some name Alabastrites; whereof they use for to make hollow boxes and pots to receive sweet perfumes and ointments, because it is thought that they will keepe and preserve them excellently well, without corruption. The same being burnt and calcined, is very good for diverse plastres."—*Pliny*, book xxxvi. ch. 8.

ALALITE. A variety of Diopside from Ala, in Piedmont.

M. P. G. Horse-shoe Case, Nos. 1032, 1033.

ALAUNSTEIN, *Werner*. See ALUMSTONE.

ALBERT COAL, or ALBERTITE. A bituminous kind of Coal found in Nova Scotia, and at Hillsborough, in New Brunswick.

Analysis by Stessor:

Volatile matters.	.	.	54·39
Fixed carbon	.	.	45·44
Ash .	.	.	0·17
			100·00
Carbon	.	.	87·25
Hydrogen	.	.	9·62
Nitrogen	.	.	1·75

Oxygen and Sulphur.	.	1·21
Ash .	. . .	0·17
		100·00

It yields, on distillation, 100 gallons of crude oil per ton. See MELANASPHALT.

ALBIN, *Werner*. A white, opaque variety of Apophyllite, found, associated with Natrolite, at Aussig, in Bohemia.

Brit Mus., Case 27.

ALBITE, *Beudant, Brooke & Miller, Dana, Phillips, Greg & Lettsom*. Anorthic. Primary form a doubly-oblique prism. Occurs generally in flat twin crystals.

Colour. Usually white; sometimes grey, green, or brown. Translucent to opaque. Lustre vitreous, pearly on cleavage planes. Streak white. Brittle. Fracture uneven. H. 6. S.G. 2·59 to 2·65.

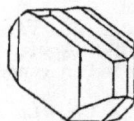

Fig. 5.

Comp. $\ddot{N}a\ \ddot{S}i + \ddot{A}l\ \ddot{S}i^3$ = silica 68·7, alumina 19.5, soda 11·8 = 100.

Analysis by Abich, from Miask:

Silica .	.	.	.	68·45
Alumina	.	.	.	18·71
Peroxide of iron	.	.	0·27
Soda .	.	.	.	11·24
Potash	.	.	.	0·65
Lime .	.	.	.	0·50
Magnesia	.	.	.	0·18
Protoxide of manganese	.	trace
				100,00

BB behaves like Felspar, but imparts a more distinct yellow colour to the flame. Not acted on by hot acids.

Localities.— *English.* Cornwall; at Huel Friendship on Quartz, and in white translucent crystals at Tintagel, near Camelford, *Fig.* 5; Beverley, Yorkshire; in greenstone.— *Welsh:* Tremadoc, Caernarvonshire—*Scotch.* Near Edinburgh, in greenstone.—*Ireland.* In very perfect, white translucent twin-crystals at Ross, and in the granite of Slieve Corra, one of the Mourne Mountains. The forms found in the United Kingdom are represented in Fig. 5.— *Foreign:* The Tyrol, in large transparent, colourless crystals, with Pearl-spar; St. Gotthard, in white translucent twins; Arendal, in Norway, with

Epidote and Garnet; Greenland,with Eudy-alite and Hornblende; Massachusetts, U. S., with Tourmaline; Siberia; Norway; Sweden; Bohemia; Oisans, in Dauphiny; and elsewhere.

Name. From *albus* (*white*), in allusion to its colour.

Brit. Mus., Case 30.

M. P. G. Horse-shoe Case, No. 953.

Albite is a soda Felspar, a small portion of the soda being sometimes replaced by potash and lime. It is frequently a constituent of granite, and, more frequently than common Felspar, of syenite and greenstone (as in the rocks round Edinburgh); but it often occurs associated with the latter in the same granite, when it may be distinguished by its greater whiteness and translucency. Thus, in the granite of Pompey's Pillar, and the block on which the statue of Peter the Great in St. Petersburg is placed, the Albite presents a greenish-white colour, while the Felspar is flesh-red.

ALEXANDRITE. A variety of Chryso-beryl found in mica-slate with Beryl and Phenacite, 85 wersts from Ekatherinenberg in the Ural. It is of an emerald-green colour by reflected light and columbine-red by transmitted light. The colour is supposed to be produced by the presence of oxide of chrome. Named after Alexander I., Emperor of Russia.

Brit. Mus., Case 19.

ALGERITE. An altered form of Scapolite. Occurs in slender square prisms imbedded in Calc-spar. Colour yellowish to grey. Usually dull. Brittle. H. 3 to 3·5: of more altered crystals 2·5. S.G. 2·7 to 2·78.

Analysis by T. S. Hunt:

Silica	49·82
Alumina	24·91
Magnesia	1·15
Potash	10·21
Carbonate of lime	3.94
Water	7·57
	97·60

Locality. Franklin, Sussex co., New Jersey.

Name. After Alger, the American mineralogist.

ALGODONITE. A new mineral found in small white lumps and veins, (at first supposed to be native silver,) in the silvermine of Alogodes (whence the name Algodonite) near Coquimbo in Chili.

Comp. A compound of arsenic and copper in which the proportion of copper is twice that in Domeykite, or Cu^{12} AS, or copper 83·66, arsenic 16·34 = 100.

Analysis by F. Field:

Copper	83·30
Arsenic	16·23
Silver	0.31
	99·84

Colour brilliant silver-white; also white, but quickly tarnishes on exposure to the air. Fracture strong granular. Soluble in dilute nitric acid.

ALISONITE, *F. Field.* Massive. Colour deep indigo-blue, quickly tarnishing on exposure. Fracture slightly conchoidal. H. 2·5 to 3. S.G. 6·1.

Comp. Double sulphide of copper and lead or 3 Cu^2S + Pb S = copper 53·33, lead 28·80, sulphur 17·77 = 100.

Analysis by Frederick Field:

Copper	53·63
Lead	28·25
Sulphur	17·00
	98·88

Violently acted on by nitric acid with the formation of sulphate of lead and liberation of free sulphur.

Locality. Mina Grande, near Coquimbo, Chili, associated with carbonate of lead and carbonate of copper.

Name. After R. E. Alison.

ALIZITE, *Glocker.* See PIMELITE.

ALKALI MINERALE, *Brochant.* See NATRON.

ALLAGITE. A compact variety of Rhodonite, altered through the tendency of protoxide of manganese to pass to a higher state of oxidation, accompanied with the absorption of water. It is of a greenish-grey colour, verging upon black, and is somewhat fibrous, resembling altered Bustamite.

Analysis by Du Menil:

Peroxide of manganese	75·0
Silica	16·0
Lime	7·5
	98·5

Locality. The vicinity of Rubeland in the Harz.

Name. From ἀλλαγή, *change;* in allusion to its change on exposure.

Brit. Mus., Case 26.

ALLANITE. *Phillips, Thomson, Nicol, Dana.* Oblique. Isomorphous with Epidote. Occurs in long and slender, or flat tabular crystals, or in masses and grains. Colour black, passing into reddish- or greenish-brown. Opaque; feebly translucent and of a yellowish-brown colour in thin splinters. Lustre submetallic, inclining to vitreous or resinous. Streak greenish-grey.

Brittle. Fracture uneven, passing into small conchoidal. H. 6. S.G. 2·86 to 2·9.

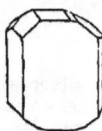

Fig. 6.

Comp. $3\ddot{R}^3 \ddot{S}i + 2\ddot{\ddot{H}} \ddot{S}i + 10 \dot{H}$.

Analysis by *D. Forbes*, from Naes Mine:

Silica . . .	31·03
Alumina . . .	9·29
Glucina . . .	3·71
Protoxide of iron . .	20·68
Protoxide of manganese .	0·07
Protoxide of cerium .	6·74
Oxide of lanthanium .	4·35
Yttria . . .	1·02
Lime	6·68
Magnesia . . .	2·06
Potash . . .	0·90
Soda	0·56
Oxide of copper . .	trace
Water	12·24
	99·33

BB on charcoal swells up, becomes brownish-yellow and fuses to a black (somewhat magnetic) glass.

Localities.—Scotch. 1 mile west of New Abbey, near Criffel, E. Kirkcudbrightshire; in syenite.—*Foreign. Norway;* at Naes Mine about 10 miles east of Arendal; Jotun Fjeld, in porphyry: Snarum, with Albite. Greenland, in granite. Plauensche Grund, near Dresden, in Saxony. Near Suhl in the Thuringerwald, in granite. Moriah, Essex co., New York, with Lanthanite, at the junction of the Sanford magnetic iron with the granite walls.

Name. After Thomas Allan, of Edinburgh, by whom it was first noticed as a distinct species.

Brit. Mus., Case 38.

ALLEMONTITE. A name given to arsenical antimony, found at Allemont in Dauphiny.

Analysis by. *Rammelsberg:*

Arsenic	62·15
Antimony . . .	37·85
	100·00

ALLEY STONE. See WEBSTERITE.

ALLOCHROITE, a fine-grained, massive variety of iron-Garnet of a greyish, dingy yellow, or reddish colour. Opaque. Fracture uneven. H. not so hard as Quartz, but strikes fire with steel. S.G. 3·7 to 4·21.

BB behaves like Melanite.

Locality. Norway; principally in an iron-mine near Drammen.

Name. From ἄλλος *other*, and χροία, *colour ;* in allusion to its variety of colours.

Brit. Mus., Case 36.

ALLOGONITE, *Breithaupt.* See HERDE-RITE.

ALLOMORPHITE, *Breithaupt.* (From ἄλλος, *other,* and μορφή, *form*), A variety of Barytes found in scaly masses in Unterwirbach near Rudolstadt in Schwarzburg. According to Gerngross it contains 1·9 per cent. of sulphate of lime, as impurity.

ALLOPHANE. Occurs reniform, massive, encrusting; occasionally almost pulverulent. Colour pale blue, sometimes green, brown, yellow or colourless. Translucent. Lustre, vitreous or resinous; internally splendent and waxy. Streak white. Very brittle. Fracture flat conchoidal and shining. Adheres to the tongue. H. 3. S.G. 1·76 to 1·89.

Comp. Hydrated silicate of alumina, or

$\ddot{A}l^3 \ddot{S}i^2 + 15\dot{H}$. = silica 24·22, alumina 40·39, water 35·39=100.

Analysis by *A. B. Northcote*, from Woolwich:

Silica . . .	20·50
Alumina . . .	31·34
Protoxide of iron . .	0·31
Lime	1·92
Carbonic acid . .	2·73
Water . . .	42·91
	99·71

BB soon loses colour, and becomes pulverulent, causing some intumescence and tinging the flame green. Alone infusible; with borax fuses readily to a transparent colourless glass. Dissolves perfectly in dilute acids; when digested in concentrated acids, leaves a silicious jelly.

Localities. Allophane has been lately observed at the chalk-pits at New Charlton, near Woolwich, Kent, by the students of the Government School of Mines, and determined by them in the laboratory of Dr. Percy. It occurs abundantly, of a honey-yellow colour, in the chalk of Beauvais in France; also lining irregular cavities in a kind of marl at Saalfield in Thuringia, Schneeberg in Saxony, Visé in Belgium and elsewhere. At Richmond, Massachusetts, U.S., it occurs with Gibbsite, forming a hyaline crust, scaly or compact in structure, and brittle; also, at the Bristol copper mine, Connecticut, U.S.

Name. From ἄλλος, *other*, and φαίνω, *to appear ;* in allusion to its change of appearance under the blowpipe.

Brit. Mus., Case 26.

Allophane usually occurs lining small cavities, and in veins in marl or chalk; sometimes in little reniform masses with a resinous or waxy lustre.

ALLOPHANE OPAL. See SCHRÖTTERITE.

ALLOY OF IRIDIUM AND OSMIUM, *Wollaston, Phillips.* See IRIDOSMINE.

ALLUAUDITE, *Damour, Nicol.* Occurs massive, with a triple cleavage at right angles to each other. Colour clove-brown. Subtranslucent or opaque. Lustre dull. Streak yellowish. Fracture scaly, shining. H. above 4. S.G. 3·468.

Comp. ($\ddot{M}n \ \dot{N}a$) $\ddot{P} + \ddot{F}e \ \ddot{P} + \dot{H}$.

Analysis (mean of several) by *Damour* :

Phosphoric acid	41·25
Peroxide of iron	25·62
Protoxide of manganese	23·08
Peroxide of manganese	1·06
Soda	5·47
Silica	0·60
Water	2·65
	99·73

BB on platina wire fuses to a black magnetic globule. Forms a solution in muriatic acid which is black when cold, and yellowish-brown when heated.

Locality. Chanteloupe, near Limoges in France, associated with Vivianite and Dufrénite.

Name. After Mons. Alluaud of Limoges.

ALMAGRERITE, *Breithaupt.* An anhydrous sulphate of zinc occurring in crystals isomorphous with Anglesite and Heavy Spar, at the Barranca Jaroso Mine, in the Sierra Almagrera, Spain. S.G. 4·53.

ALMANDINE, or ALMANDINE GARNET, is the name given to red transparent varieties of Garnet. It is an *alumina-iron* Garnet, the composition of which is represented by the formula $\ddot{F}e^3 \ \ddot{S}i + \ddot{A}l \ \ddot{S}i$ =silica 36·3, alumina 20·5, protoxide of iron 43·2 = 100. Cubical : occurs in rhombic dodecahedrons, and, in the same with all the edges replaced by six-sided planes. Lustre vitreous, shining. Streak white. Fracture subconchoidal, uneven. H. 6·5 to 7·5. S.G. 3·7 to 4·21.

Analysis by *Hisinger*, from Fahlun :

Silica	39·66
Alumina	19·66
Protoxide of iron	39·68
Protoxide of manganese	1·80
	100·80

BB fuses rather readily to a black magnetic globule: with borax more slowly to a dark glass, affording an iron reaction. Insoluble in acid.

Localities. This stone is found in sand, alluvial soil, and gneiss, in Ceylon, Pegu, Hindostan, Brazil, Greenland; also at Elie in Fifeshire, at Ala in Piedmont, and in various parts of Bohemia.

When of good size, finely coloured, transparent, and free from flaws it is used as a gem. It should be cut quite thin on account of its depth of colour; with a pavilion on the under side and a broad table above, bordered with small facets. An octagonal Garnet, measuring 8½ lines by 6½, has sold for near 700 dollars. Almandine may be distinguished from Corundum or Spinel by its duller colour.

Brit. Mus., Case 36.

M. P. G. Horse-shoe Case, Nos. 889 to 893, 897, 898.

ALMANDINE RUBY. The name given to violet-coloured varieties of Spinel.

ALMANDINE SPAR, *Mohs.* See EUDIALITE.

ALSTONITE, *Breithaupt, Nicol, Greg & Lettsom.* Rhombic. Primary form a right rhombic prism. Colour snow-white or greyish-yellow. Translucent. Lustre vitreous, on surfaces of fracture resinous. Fracture conchoidal, uneven. H. 4 to 4·5. S.G. 3·65 to 3·7.

Fig. 7.

Comp. Identical with Barytocalcite. $\ddot{B}a$ $\ddot{C} + \dot{C}a \ \ddot{C}$, or carbonate of baryta 66·1, carbonate of lime 33·9 = 100.

Analysis by *Thomson*, from Fallowfield :

Carbonate of baryta	60·63
Carbonate of lime	30·09
Carbonate of manganese	9·18
	99·90

BB decrepitates and phosphoresces. Dissolves in acids with effervescence.

Localities. Fallowfield, near Hexham, Northumberland ; in small six-sided pyramidal crystals, of a pinkish tinge. Bromley Hill, near Alston (whence the name Alstonite) Cumberland ; of a white or grey colour, in veins with Galena.

ALTAITE, *Dana, Haidinger, Nicol.* Cubical. Usually occurs massive in granular aggregates ; rarely in cubes. Colour tin-white, with a yellow tarnish. Lustre metallic. Sectile. Fracture uneven. H. 3 to 3·5. S.G. 8·10.

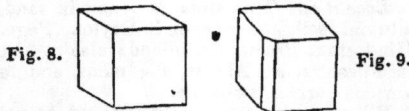

Fig. 8.   Fig. 9.

Comp. Telluride of lead or Pb Te = lead 61·7, tellurium 38·3 = 100.

Analysis by G. Rose.

Lead . . . . 60·35
Tellurium . . . 38·37
Silver . . . . 1·28

               100·00

BB colours the flame blue: in the inner flame volatilizes, except a minute globule of silver. Soluble in nitric acid.

Locality. The Savodinsky mine, near Barnaoul, in the Altai; mixed with telluric silver.

ALVITE, *David Forbes & F. Dahll.* Crystallizes like Zircon. Colour reddish-brown, becoming greyish-brown on alteration. Opaque; translucent at the edges. Lustre greasy. Fracture conchoidal. H. 5·5. S.G. 3·40 to 3·6.

BB in the platina forceps infusible: becomes paler by heat. With borax yields a yellow glass, which becomes colourless on cooling.

Comp. An approximative analysis shows it to consist chiefly of silica, yttria, thorina (?), alumina, and glucina, peroxide of iron and water.

Localities. Helle and Naröstö in Norway.

ALUM. Under this name are comprised several compounds which have the general formula $\ddot{R}\,\ddot{S} + \ddot{Al}\,\dot{S}^3 + 24\,\dot{H}$, ($\ddot{R}$ representing different bases, as potash, soda, magnesia, protoxide of manganese, &c.) which are described under their respective names. All these compounds crystallize in octahedrons, but they usually occur in nature in fibrous masses, or as a mealy efflorescence, with a sweetish astringent taste, more or less resembling that of common alum. It is soluble in from 16 to 20 times its weight of cold water, and in little more than its own weight of boiling water. On exposure to heat, it melts easily in its own water of crystallization, and froths up in a remarkable way, and by continuance of heat it is converted into a white spongy mass. Alum is used largely in the manufacture of leather and paper, as a mordant in dyeing, in medicine, for preserving animal substances from putrefaction, and for various other purposes. The alum of commerce is made either from clay or from alum-slate or shale. Much of

the Dorsetshire pipe-clay, which is not of sufficiently good quality for use in the potteries, is converted into alum by being treated with sulphuric acid. The sulphate of alumina which is thus formed, being lixiviated with water, potash salts are added, and crystals of alum are ultimately obtained by evaporation. At Whitby, in Yorkshire, the alum-shale is mixed with fuel and set on fire; the residue is lixiviated with water, and purified by subsequent evaporation; potash salts are added, and crystallized alum is finally formed. The best alum is made from the Alum-stone of Tolfa, near Civita Vecchia.

ALUM, *Nicol, Phillips.* Native alum. See POTASH-ALUM.

ALUMINE FLUATÉE ALCALINE, *Haüy.* See CRYOLITE.

ALUMINE FLUATÉE SILICEUSE, *Haüy.* See TOPAZ.

ALUMINE HYDRATÉE SILICIFÈRE, *Levy.* Siliciferous hydrate of alumina.

ALUMINE-HYDRO-PHOSPHATÉE, *Haüy.* See WAVELLITE.

ALUMINE MAGNÉSIÉE. *Haüy.* See SPINEL.

ALUMINE SOUS-SULFATÉE. See WEBSTERITE.

ALUMINE SOUS-SULFATÉE ALCALINE, *Haüy.* See ALUMSTONE.

ALUMINE SULFATÉE, *Haüy.* ⎫ See
ALUMINE SULFATÉE ALCA- ⎬ ALUNO-
LINE, *Haüy.* ⎭ GENE.

ALUMINILITE, *La Metherie.* See ALUMSTONE.

ALUMINITE, *Jameson.* See WEBSTERITE.

ALUMOCALCITE, *Phillips, Breithaupt.* An impure Opal of a milk-white colour inclining to blue, and containing six per cent. of lime. Streak white. Fracture conchoidal. Adheres strongly to the moistened lip. May be crushed between the fingers. S.G. 2·174.

Analysis by Kersten:

Silica . . . . 86·60
Alumina . . . 2·25
Lime . . . . 6·25
Water . . . . 4·00

            99·10

BB in the platina forceps becomes opaque and grey-coloured. With borax forms a colourless glass. Forms a transparent jelly in concentrated muriatic acid.

Locality. Eibenstock, in Saxony; in clefts in veins of ironstone.

Alumocalcite was formerly considered to be a decomposed Opal.

Brit. Mus., Case 25.

ALUMSTONE, *Phillips,* occurs massive and crystallized in modifications of an obtuse rhomboid. The crystals are minute, shining, and sometimes brownish externally. Colour white, also greyish or reddish. Transparent to subtranslucent. Lustre vitreous or pearly. Streak white. Brittle. Fracture flat conchoidal, uneven ; of massive varieties, splintery, occasionally earthy. H. 3·5 to 4. S.G. 2·58 to 2·78.

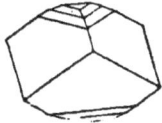 

Fig. 10.   Fig. 11.

Comp. $\ddot{K}\ddot{S} + 3\ddot{Al}\ddot{S} + 9\ddot{H}$.

Analysis by *Cordier*, of crystals from Tolfa :

Alumina	. . .	. 39·65
Sulphuric acid	. .	. 35·50
Potash .	. . .	. 10·02
Water .	. . .	. 14·83

100·00

BB decrepitates and is infusible alone and with soda : with borax forms a colourless glass.

Soluble in sulphuric acid, when reduced to powder. Insoluble in water, but after gentle ignition, gives up alum to it, the excess of alumina remaining undissolved.

Localities. Tolfa, near Civita Vecchia, in the Papal States. Musay and Bereghszasz, in Hungary. Milo, Argentiera, in the Grecian Archipelago. The Island of Nevis. Pic de Sancy, in France. Elizabethpol, in Georgia. Silesia, in a coal-bed.

Much of the best alum of commerce is procured from Alumstone by repeated roastings, washings, and finally crystallizing by evaporation. Some of the Hungarian varieties are so hard and compact as to be used for millstones.

Brit. Mus., Case 55.

M. P. G. Upper gallery, table-case B, in recess 6, Nos. 179 to 186.

ALUN-AMMONIACAL, *Dufrénoy.* See AMMONIA-ALUM.

ALUN DE PLUME, *Dufrénoy.* See HALOTRICHITE.

ALUN DE ROME, the commercial name for alum made at Tolfa. See ALUM-STONE.

ALUN-MAGNESIEN, *Dufrénoy.* See MAGNESIA-ALUM.

ALUN SODIFÈRE, *Dufrénoy.* See SODA ALUM.

ALUNITE, *Necker.* See ALUMSTONE.

ALUNOGENE, *Beudant, Dana*, is a hydrous sulphate of alumina, composed, when pure, of alumina 15·42, sulphuric acid 35·99, water 48·59 = 100·00, corresponding

to the formula $\ddot{Al}\ddot{S}^3 + 18\ddot{H}$. It occurs generally in delicate fibrous masses or crusts, either white or tinged with yellow or red, when impure. Translucent. Lustre silky. Taste like that of common alum. H. 1·5 to 2. S.G. 1·6 to 1·8.

BB intumesces and fuses easily. Very soluble.

Localities. It occurs at Araya near Cumana ; Socono ; Copiapo, in Chili, and other parts of South America ; in numerous places in the United States ; at Adelaide, in New South Wales, &c. &c.

Alunogen results from volcanic action, and the decomposition of Pyrites in shales.

AMALGAM, *Dana.*

AMALGAME, *Necker.*

AMALGAME NATIF D'ARGENT, *La Metherie.*

See NATIVE AMALGAM.

AMALGAME D'OR. See ELECTRUM.

AMANSITE   •

AMANTICE

AMAUSITE, *Dufrénoy*

AMAUTITE

AMAUZITE

A variety of compact Felspar (Orthoclase) from Ædelfors in Sweden. Colour clear grey passing into greyish-white. Fracture perfect conchoidal.

AMAZON STONE. A bluish-green variety of Felspar (Orthoclase). It is slightly translucent at the edges, and possesses a considerable amount of varying lustre. The stone brought from Lake Baikal in Siberia is sometimes, though rarely, in pieces sufficiently large to be made into small vases and other ornaments ; and, when well cut, it forms an Aventurine composed of silvery spangles in a green base. The verdigris-green variety found on the east side of Lake Ilmen is coloured by copper.

Brit. Mus., Case 30.

M. P. G. Horse-shoe Case, No. 955.

AMBER is found in irregular masses of all shades of yellow, from the palest primrose to the deepest orange, sometimes brown. It is brittle, yields readily to the knife, affording a white streak, and breaks with a fracture which is more or less perfectly conchoidal. It varies from perfect transparency to complete opacity, sometimes, but rarely, being nearly as white as ivory, and has a vitreous or resinous lustre. H. 2 to 2·5 S.G. 1·08.

Comp. $C^{10} H^8 O$ = carbon 78·96, hydrogen 10·51, oxygen 10·52. Burns readily with a yellow flame, emitting an agreeable odour, and leaves a black, shining, light, carbonaceous residue. Becomes negatively electric by friction. Soluble in alcohol.

Considerable quantities of Amber are cast ashore during autumnal storms on the coasts of Pomerania and Prussia Proper, and are carefully collected. Amber is also found along the whole line of the Baltic coast, but the largest specimens are procured from the Prussian shores, and the search for it is an industry exercised from Dantzic to Memel. This is distinguished as marine Amber. The other description, called terrestial Amber, is dug in mines and is generally found in alluvial deposits of sand and clay, associated with fossil wood, Iron Pyrites, and alum-shale. It is also found on the Sicilian coast, near Catania ; at Hasen Island in Greenland ; in clay at Auteuil, near Paris; but more plentifully in certain lignite deposits of the Aisne, and occasionally on the sea-coasts of Norfolk, Essex, Sussex, and Kent. It occurs in sand at Kensington, near London ; in Ireland on the coast at Howth, near Dublin ; at Craignashoke, in Ulster ; and at Rathlin Island, Antrim. Amber, to a considerable amount, is also said to be taken to China from a northerly part of Upper Burmah.

The vegetable origin of Amber is now fully ascertained, by the experiments of Sir David Brewster on its optical properties, as well as from its association with coal, and lignite, and the occurrence in it of the remains of insects and plants. According to Goeppert, Amber is the mineralised resin of extinct Coniferæ, one of which he has named *Pinites succinifer*, or Amber-bearing Pinetree. The insects inclosed in it, which are mostly, if not all, of extinct species, appear to have been entangled in the then viscous substance while alive, and, in many cases, to have struggled hard to escape, as is evident from the legs and wings which are frequently found separated from the bodies to which they once belonged.

Yellow amber, cut in facets, or simply in beads for bracelets and necklaces, was long in fashion, and is sometimes worn at the present day. It is used in the East by Turks, Egyptians, Arabs, Persians, and the natives of India, to ornament their pipes, arms, the saddles and bridles of their horses, and even of their camels ; and in the West it is made into beads, necklaces, brooches, earrings, boxes, and small works of art, cane-handles, mouth-pieces of pipes, and occasionally into candlesticks, salvers, pipe-tubes, and other larger articles. Four amber mouth-pieces, set with brilliants, exhibited in the Turkish Section of the Great Exhibition of 1851 were valued together at £1,000. The estimation in which Amber is held in Turkey for the mouth-pieces of pipes, may be in some measure accounted for by the current belief entertained in that country, where it is a great mark of politeness to offer the pipe to a stranger, that Amber is incapable of transmitting infection. The straw-yellow, slightly clouded, translucent variety is the rarest, and that preferred to all others by the Orientals, who purchase it at extravagant prices. In other countries the orange-yellow transparent variety is decidedly preferred.

"Sir Plume, of amber snuff-box justly vain,
And the nice conduct of a clouded * cane :"
              POPE, *Rape of the Lock.*

In the Museum of Mineralogy in Paris there is the handle of a cane made of Amber, the colour of which is of so pure a yellow, and so limpid, that it might almost be mistaken for a Brazilian Topaz.

The principal use of Amber in the Arts is for obtaining, by distillation, succinic acid and oil of amber, which it affords at a low temperature, leaving an extremely black, shining residue, which is employed as the basis of the finest black varnishes.

Amber was known to the ancients, and made by them into various ornamental articles. It was said by the common fable to consist of the tears of those poplars into which Phaeton's sisters were transformed. Pliny says, because our ancestors believed that it was the juice of a tree (*succum*) they called it (in Latin) *succinum.* The Greeks called it "Ηλεκτρον, (either from its resemblance in colour to the alloy of gold and silver of that name, or from 'Ηλίκτωρ, a name of the sun), and whence, on account of its electrical properties, the derivation of the word electricity. By some of the ancients Amber was called Lyncurion, and believed to be produced from the urine of the lynx ; from that of the males when of a deep and fiery tint ; but when of a pale hue from that

* These clouded canes were made of fine marbles, richly mounted with gold, silver, amber, &c. In the early part of the eighteenth century the most fashionable sorts of walking-sticks were made of certain fine marbles and agates, exhibiting either a splendid variety of colour, or a rich semi-opaque plain tint, which was most expressively described by the English term *"clouded."* These wands were made of the most slender proportions, both on account of their specific gravity, and the quality of the persons by whom they were to be carried ; and they were often richly mounted with silver, gold, amber, or precious stones. Such were the "clouded canes" of the age of Pope and Gay, which were frequently so greatly valued, as to be preserved in cases of shagreen or sheaths of leather.—(See the *Tatler* No. 103, 6th December, 1709.)

of the other sex. In common with other stones the ancients attributed particular properties to Amber. Pliny states that it is useful in medicine, and that a collar of Amber worn round the neck of a young infant was considered in his time a singular preservative against secret poisoning, and a countercharm to witchcraft and sorcery. " Callistratus saith, that such collars are very good for all ages, and namely, to preserve as many as weare them against fantasticall illusions and frights that drive folke out of their wits: yea and amber, whether it be taken in drinke or hung about one, cureth the difficultie of voiding urine."— Pliny, book xxxvii. cap. 3.

The modern name Amber is probably derived from that by which this substance is known in the East; anbar or anabar (*Persian*), anbaron (*Arabic*).

Amber is imitated by mixing by degrees, at a moderate and gradually raised heat, rectified oil of asphalt with turpentine in a yellow copper vessel. When, after two or three boilings, it has become sufficiently thick, it is poured into moulds.

Amber may be distinguished from Mellite and copal, which are often substituted for it, by spitting and frothing when burning, and when its liquefied particles drop, by their rebounding from the surface on which they fall; while Mellite does not fuse in the same manner when heated, and copal, when heated at the end of a knife, takes fire and melts into drops which flatten as they fall.

Amber ornaments, when broken, may be mended with cement composed of linseed oil, gum mastic, and litharge, or by warming the fractured surfaces and pressing them together, after they have been moistened with a solution of potash, or soluble glass,—the pieces being tied round with string for a few days.

Brit. Mus., Case 60.

M. P. G. Horse-shoe Case, No. 92.

AMBLYGONIC AUGITE SPAR,*Haidinger*; or AMBLYGONITE, *Breithaupt, Dana.* Rhombic. This mineral occurs massive and in oblique rhombic prisms, which are rough externally and of a greenish-white, a mountain- or sea-green colour. Lustre vitreous, inclining to pearly. Translucent. Streak white. Fracture uneven. H. 6. S.G. 3.0 to 3·11.

Comp. Phosphate of alumina and lithia, in combination with double fluoride of aluminum and lithium; represented by the formula $(\ddot{A}l^5 \ddot{P}^3 + \dot{R}^5 \ddot{P}^3) + (Al^2 F^3 + RF)$ where R stands for lithium, sodium, and potassium.

Analysis by *Rammelsberg*, from Camsdorf:

Phosphoric acid	. . . 47·15
Alumina	. . . 38·43
Lithia	. . . . 7.03
Soda	. . . . 3·29
Potash	. . . . 0·43
Fluorine	. . . 8·11
	104·44

BB fuses readily with intumescence, and becomes opaque white on cooling. Forms a transparent colourless glass with borax. Easily soluble in sulphuric acid. Occurs in granite at Chursdorf and Arnsdorf near Penig, in Saxony, associated with Tourmaline and Garnet: also at Arendal, in Norway.

The name is derived from ἀμβλυγώνιος, having an obtuse angle; (ἀμβλύς, *blunt,* and γωνία, *angle*).

Brit. Mus., Case 54.

AMETHYST. A variety of Quartz of a clear purple or violet-blue, of various degrees of intensity; the colour not unfrequently passing, in the same specimen, from the richest tint to almost colourless. The colour is supposed to be produced by the presence of a small per centage of manganese. Heintz, however, on analysing a very deep purple specimen from the Brazils, obtained in addition to silica, 0·0187 protoxide of iron, 0·6236 lime, 0·0133 magnesia, and 0·0418 soda ; whence he infers that the colour is due to a compound of iron and soda. The finest Amethysts are brought from India, Brazil, Ceylon, Persia, Morocco, and Siberia; but inferior, though beautiful specimens are found in Transylvania, Hungary, Saxony, the Harz, Brioude in Auvergne, Murcia and Catalonia in Spain. A vein of Amethyst of a very beautiful colour is said to exist at Kerry Head, in Ireland, and many years ago it was used for jewelry. (*F. J. Foot.*) It occurs massive, in rolled pieces, and in hexagonal crystals, which are rarely so distinct as those of Quartz, being generally united together for the entire length of the prisms, so that only the pyramidal terminations are separated from each other. For this reason, when broken in the direction of the prisms, the fracture presents a coarsely fibrous or wrinkled appearance, somewhat resembling that of the skin on the palm of the hand. All the varieties of Rock Crystal having this peculiar wrinkled fracture are classed by Sir David Brewster under the head of Amethyst, of whatever colour they may happen to be. It is also found in veins, or forming the interior coatings of Agates in trap-rocks. The Amethyst varies considerably in transparency. It has always been esteemed, on account of its beauty, as a gem, and possesses the advantage of being almost the only coloured stone that can be worn with mourning. It appears to the greatest advantage when set in gold and surrounded with pearls; but when of a vivid tinge it will sustain the presence of the diamond, and may, in consequence, be set round with brilliants. The less gold that is employed in making it up the better.

The name Amethyst is derived from the word ἀμέθυστος, which the Greeks supposed to be formed of α, neg., and μεθύω, to inebriate, from some supposed quality of the stone in resisting intoxication. Pliny mentions an opinion that it takes its name from its colour approaching that of wine, but not reaching it.

"The reason of the name, Amethyst, is generally thought to be this, that notwithstanding it approach very neare to the colour of wine, yet before it throughly tast thereof, it turneth into a March violet colour: and that purple lustre which it hath is not altogether fix, but declineth in the end to the colour of wine."—*Pliny*, book xxxvii. ch. 9.

Brit. Mus., Case 20.

M. P. G. Horse-shoe Case, Nos. 501 to 504.

AMETHYSTOLINE. The name given to the volatile fluid observed by Brewster in cavities of Amethyst.

AMIANTH, *Jameson, Werner.* } See AMI-
AMIANTHE, *Brochant.* } ANTHUS.

AMIANTHOIDE, *Haüy.* A variety of Amianthus from Oisans, in Dauphiny, the fibres of which are somewhat elastic.

Brit. Mus., Case 34.

AMIANTHOID MAGNESITE, *Nuttall.* See BRUCITE.

AMIANTHUS. The name given to the whiter and more delicate varieties of Asbestos, which possess a satin-like lustre, owing to the greater separation of the fibres of which they are composed. Amianthus usually occurs in Serpentine. It is found in the Tarantaise in Savoy, in Corsica, Dauphiny, St. Gotthard, Saltzburg, the Tyrol, United States, &c. It is also met with in Cornwall, near Liskeard, and at the Lizard Point; in Scotland, at Portsoy, in Banffshire; at Towenrieff in Aberdeenshire; at Glenelg in Inverness-shire; and on the east coast of Balta Island in the Shetlands. The word Amianthus (from ἀμίαντος, undefiled,) is expressive of the simple manner by which, when soiled, it may be cleansed and restored to its original purity. "From its flexibility, and its resisting the effects of fire, it is said to have been, by the ancients, wove into a kind of cloth, in which they wrapped the

bodies of persons of distinction before they were placed on the funeral pile, that their ashes might be collected free from admixture; it was also used for incombustible wicks," * a purpose to which it is applied at the present day.

Brit. Mus., Case 34.

M. P. G. Horse-shoe Case, No. 1151.

AMIOLITE, *Dana.* Antimonite of quicksilver mixed with clay and oxide of iron, forming a red powder, found at the quicksilver mines in Chili, accompanied by ores of antimony, copper, and mercury; also at Silbe, near Olpe, in Westphalia.

Analysis by *Domeyko:*

Antimonious acid . .	12·5
Protoxide of mercury .	14·0
Silica . .	26·5
Peroxide of iron . .	22·3
Water and loss . .	24·7
	100·0

Name. From ἀμμιον, *vermilion.*

AMMONALUM, *Beudant, Necker;* AMMONIA-ALUM; AMMONIAK ALAUN, *v. Kobell.* Occurs in thin fibrous layers and in octahedrons, in Brown Coal, at Tschermig in Bohemia. H. 1 to 2. S.G. 1·56.

Comp. Sulphate of alumina and ammonia, or $N\,H^4\,O\,\ddot{S} + \ddot{Al}\,\ddot{S} + 24\,\dot{H} =$ sulphate of ammonia 14·6, sulphate of potash 37·8, water 47·6 = 100.

Analysis by *Pfaff:*

Sulphuric acid . .	36·00
Alumina . . .	12·14
Ammonia . . .	6·58
Magnesia . . .	0·28
Water . . .	45·00
	100·00

This salt is manufactured and used in France instead of potash-alum. It is prepared by mixing the sulphate of alumina obtained from alum-shale, lignite containing Iron-pyrites, or any other aluminous mineral impregnated with sulphide of iron, or by treating clay with sulphuric acid with decomposing urine (which contains ammoniacal salts). The ammonia-alum then separates, and may be purified by repeated solution and recrystallization.

AMMONIAQUE MURIATÉE, *Haüy.* See SAL-AMMONIAC.

AMMONIAQUE SULFATÉE, *Haüy.* See MASCAGNINE.

AMOIBITE, *v. Kobell.* A variety of Gers-

---

* Jameson's Mineralogy, vol. i. p. 445.

dorffite, occurring in small octahedrons of a pale steel-grey colour at Lichtenberg in the Fitchtelbirge. H. 4. S.G. 6·08.

Analysis by *Von Kobell* :

Arsenic	.	.	.	. 45·34
Nickel .	.	.	.	. 37·34
Sulphur	.	.	.	. 14·00
Iron	.	.	.	. 2·50
Lead	.	.	.	. 0·82
Cobalt .	.	.	.	. trace

　　　　　　　　　　100·00

AMPELITIS, *Dioscorides.* Cannel Coal.
AMPHIBOLE, *Haüy.* See HORNBLENDE. The name is derived from ἀμφίϐολος, *ambiguous ;* because it had been confounded with Tourmaline.
AMPHIBOLE BLANC, *Haüy.* See TREMO-LITE.
AMPHIGÈNE, *Haüy,* (from ἀμφὶ, *double,* and γίνος, *origin.*) See LEUCITE.
AMPHILOGITE. See DIDRIMITE.
AMPHODELITE, *Nordenskiöld, Phillips.* A reddish-grey or dingy peach-blossom-red variety of Anorthite, occurring both crystallized and massive at Lojo in Finland and at Tunaberg in Sweden. It resembles Felspar in crystalline form, and Scapolite in fracture. H. 4·5. S.G. 2·763.

Analysis by *Nordenskiöld,* from Finland :

Silica .	.	.	.	. 45·80
Alumina	.	.	.	. 35·45
Lime .	.	.	.	. 10·15
Magnesia	.	.	.	. 5·05
Protoxide of iron		.	.	1·70
Water .	.	.	.	. 1·85

　　　　　　　　　　100.00

Name. From ἀμφω, *both,* and ὁδελὸς, a *spit* or pointed pillar.
Brit. Mus., Case 31.
ANAGENITE. See CHROME OCHRE.
ANALCIME, *Haüy, Dana, Nicol, Phillips.* Cubical. Primary form a cube. Occurs generally in icositetrahedral (or 24-sided) crystals.
Colourless and transparent; or white, grey, red and opaque. Lustre shining, between pearly and vitreous. Streak white. Brittle. Fracture imperfect conchoidal. Becomes feebly electric by friction. H. 5 to 5·5. S.G. 2·068 to 2·2.

Fig. 12.

Fig. 13.

Comp. Na³ S̈i + 3Äl S̈i² + 6Ḧ = silica 54·6, alumina 23·2, soda 14·0, water 8·1 = 100.

Analysis by *Connel,* from Old Kirkpatrick :

Silica .	.	.	.	. 55·07
Alumina	.	.	.	. 22·23
Soda	.	.	.	. 13·71
Water .	.	.	.	. 8·22

　　　　　　　　　　99·23

BB loses water and becomes milk-white ; but when the heat is increased it again becomes clear, and then fuses quietly to a transparent glass. Readily decomposed by muriatic acid, with separation of viscid silica ; after ignition the decomposition is effected with more difficulty than before.

Analcime usually occurs in the cavities of amygdaloidal rocks, and is common in the trap rocks of Ireland and Scotland.

Localities. — *Scotch.* Dumbartonshire ; Bowling and Long Craig, above Old Kirkpatrick ; Salisbury Craig, Calton Hill, Batho quarry, Edinburghshire ; Elie, Fifeshire ; Campsie Hills, Stirlingshire ; Canna, Eig, Mull and Staffa ; Waas in Hoy, Orkney. — *Irish.* Giant's Causeway, in small transparent crystals ; O'Hara's Rocks, near Port Stewart ; Gweedore, Donegal, in dolomite ; Craignashoke, Derry.—*Foreign.* The most perfectly pellucid crystals are found in the dolerite of the Cyclopean Isles, near Catania, in Sicily ; also from the Seisser Alpe and Fassa in the Tyrol. It is also found in the Faroe Isles, Iceland, the Vicentine, Arendal in Norway, Andreasberg in the Harz, Nova Scotia, &c.

Name. From ἄναλχις, *weak ;* in allusion to its weak electric power, when heated or rubbed.
Brit. Mus., Case 29.
M.P.G. Horse-shoe Case, Nos. 1175, 1176. Upper Gallery, Table-case A in recess 4, No. 130.
ANALCIME CARNEA, the name given by Monticelli to Sarcolite, from its flesh-red colour.
ANALZIM, *Haidinger.* See ANALCIME.
ANATASE. *Dana, Haüy, Greg & Lettsom, Nicol, Phillips.* Pyramidal ; primary form an octahedron with a square base. Occurs in small octahedral crystals of various shades of brown, passing into indigo-blue, which appear greenish-yellow by transmitted light. Semi-transparent to opaque. Lustre splendent and adamantine. Structure lamellar. Streak white. Brittle. Fracture sub-conchoidal. Becomes negatively electric by friction. Exhibits a reddish-

yellow phosphorescent light when heated. H. 5·5 to 6.   S.G. 3·83 to 3·95.

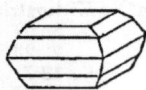   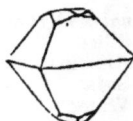

Fig. 14.   Fig. 15.

Comp. Pure titanic acid or $\ddot{T}i$=titanium 60·29, oxygen 39·71=100.

BB alone infusible.   With soda forms a dull yellow globule, which becomes white on cooling.   Dissolves in warm concentrated sulphuric acid.

Localities.—English. Cornwall; at Looe Mills Hill quarry, near Liskeard; and at Tintagel Cliffs. Devonshire; Virtuous Lady mine, near Tavistock, *fig.* 14.—*Welsh.* Tremadoc, Snowdon, *fig.* 15, with Brookite and Cleavelandite. — *Foreign.* Bourg d'Oisans in Dauphiny; Brazil, in Quartz, and at Minas Geraes, in detached crystals, which are so splendent as to be sometimes mistaken for Diamonds. Tavatsch in the Tyrol. The Grisons in mica-slate. Slidre in Norway. The Ural. Spain.

Name. From ἀνατασις, *extension*, in allusion to the height of the pyramids of the octahedral crystals.

Brit. Mus., Case 37.

ANAUXITE, *Breithaupt.* Occurs massive and granular. Colour greenish-white. Translucent at the edges. Lustre pearly. H. 2 to 3. S.G. 2·26.

Comp. According to Plattner it is composed of silica 55·7, with much alumina, a little magnesia and protoxide of iron, and 11·5 per cent. of water.

BB becomes white and fuses at thin edges. *Locality.* Bilin in Bohemia.

Name. From ἀναύξητος, *without augmentation.*

ANDALUSITE, *Phillips, Jameson, Dana, Nicol, Haüy.* Rhombic. Occurs in slightly rhombic, four-sided prisms; also massive, when it is exceedingly tough. Structure lamellar. Colour pearl-grey or flesh-red, sometimes purplish-red. Translucent at the edges or opaque. Lustre vitreous, often weak. Streak white. Tough. Fracture uneven. H. 7·5. S.G. 3·1 to 3·2.

Fig. 16.

Comp. Anhydrous silicate of alumina or $\ddot{\overset{...}{Al}}^4\,\ddot{\overset{...}{Si}}^3$=alumina 59·7, silica 40·3=100.

Analysis by *Hubert*, from the Tyrol:

Alumina	. . .	59·49
Silica .	. . .	39.24
Peroxide of iron	. .	0·63
Magnesia	. . .	0·25
Lime .	. . .	0·51
		100.12

BB infusible alone: with borax fuses with difficulty, when reduced to powder, to a transparent colourless glass; and with still greater difficulty and less perfectly in microcosmic salt. With soda swells up, but does not fuse. Insoluble in acids.

Localities.—Scotch. Auchindoir, Aberdeenshire; Botriphny, Banffshire; Unst, Shetlands.—*Irish.* Scalp mountain, Donegal; Douce mountain, co. Wicklow; also at Lugganure, Glendalough and Glen Malure.— *Foreign.* Lisenz valley above Innspruck, in the Tyrol, in very large crystals. Near Braunsdorf in Saxony; Guldenstein, in Moravia; Bavaria; Siberia.

Andalusite occurs in crystalline schists, principally in gneiss, in mica and clay-slate. It may be distinguished from Felspar by its greater hardness and infusibility; from Corundum by its structure and lower specific gravity.

Name. It is named after the province of Andalusia, in Spain, where it was first observed. See CHIASTOLITE.

Brit. Mus., Case 26.

ANDESINE, *Dana.* Anorthic. Resembles Albite. Colour white, grey, greenish, yellowish, flesh-red. Lustre subvitreous, inclining to pearly. H. 6. S.G. 2·65 to 2·74.

Comp. $\dot{R}^3\,\ddot{Si}+3\ddot{Al}\,\ddot{Si}$ or $(\dot{K},\dot{Na},\dot{Ca},\dot{Mg})^3$ $\ddot{Si}+3\ddot{Al}\,\ddot{Si}^2$.

Analysis by *Abich*, from Marmato:

Silica .	. . .	59·60
Alumina	. . .	24·18
Peroxide of iron	. .	1·58
Lime .	. . .	5·77
Magnesia	. . .	1·08
Potash .	. . .	1·08
Soda .	. . .	6·53
		99·82

BB fuses much more readily than Albite, and yields a turbid glass. Imperfectly soluble in acids.

Localities. Andesine is one of the components of the rock Andesite, which occurs in the Andes (hence the names Andesine and Andesite) of South America. It is also met with in the syenite of Alsace, in the Vosges, and at Vapnefiord, Iceland, in honey-yellow transparent crystals.

ANDREASBERGOLITE: ANDREOLITE, or ANDREOLITHE, La Metherie, names for Harmotome; after that of the place where it was first discovered, Andreasberg (in the Harz) and λίθος, stone.

ANGLARITE. A fibrous and compact variety of phosphate of iron, of a grey colour inclining to blue. Translucent.

Comp. $\ddot{F}e^4 \overset{..}{P} + 4\ddot{H}$.

Analysis by Berthier :

Phosphoric acid	. .	27·3
Protoxide of iron	. .	56·0
Water	. . .	16·5
		99·8

BB fuses to a black globule.

Locality. Anglar (whence the name Anglarite) in the Haute Vienne, France.

ANGLÉSINE, *Beudant ;* ANGLESIT, *Haidinger, v. Kobell ;* ANGLESITE, *Beudant : Greg & Lettsom, Nicol, Dana.* Rhombic : is a sulphate of lead, occurring in rhombic prisms with dihedral terminations, but the crystals, when short, assume the general form of the octahedron. Colour white, grey, or yellowish ; frequently tinged blue or green by oxide of copper. Lustre adamantine, inclining to resinous. Transparent, opaque. Very brittle, and yields to the nail. Fracture conchoidal. H. 3. S. G. 6·2 to 6·3.

Fig. 17.　　　　Fig. 18.

Comp. Pb $\overset{..}{S}$=sulphuric acid 26·4, oxide of lead 73·6 =100.

Analysis by Klaproth, from Anglesea :

Oxide of lead	. .	71·0
Peroxide of iron	. .	1·0
Sulphuric acid	. .	24·8
Water	. . .	2·0
		98·8

BB decrepitates and melts to a globule, which becomes milk-white when cool : in the inner flame effervesces and is soon reduced to the metallic state.

This ore of lead is derived from the decomposition of Galena, with which it generally occurs.

Localities.—Anglesite was first observed as a distinct species at Pary's mine in Anglesea (whence the name). It is found in brilliant crystals at Rent Tor, near Wirksworth ; and in small yellow crystals at Cromford in Derbyshire ; in Cumberland, at the Mexico mine, near Hesket Newmarket (*fig.* 17.) In Scotland, large and beautiful crystals were formerly found at Leadhills in Lanarkshire, and at Wanlock Head in Dumfriesshire, sometimes two inches long and with perfect terminations. Small but extremely perfect transparent crystals have been brought from Fondon, in Granada.

Brit. Mus. Case 55.

M.P.G. Principal Floor, Wall-case 44, No. 72 (British).

ANHYDRITE *Dana, Greg & Lettsom, Phillips, Jameson, Nicol* : Rhombic : occurs (but rarely) crystallized in the form of a rectangular prism, of which the lateral edges are sometimes, though rarely, replaced. Chiefly in granular, or almost compact aggregates, or with a columnar structure. Colour white, sometimes tinged with grey, blue, violet, or red ; also brick-red. Translucent, sometimes transparent. Lustre vitreous, inclining to pearly. Streak greyish-white. Fracture uneven : of finely lamellar and fibrous varieties, splintery. Exhibits double refraction. H. 3 to 3·5. S. G. 2.899.

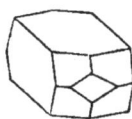　

Fig. 19.　　　　Fig. 20.

Comp. Anhydrous sulphate of lime, or $\overset{...}{C}$a $\overset{...}{S}$=lime 41·18, sulphuric acid 58·82=100. BB becomes white and is finally covered with a friable enamel. With borax dissolves, with effervescence, to a transparent glass, which becomes yellow or brownish-yellow on cooling.

Slightly soluble in water and muriatic acid.

Localities.—*English.* Granular and of a pale blue colour, in the gypsum-pits at Aston-on-Trent, near Derby ; Newark, Notts ; with Gypsum.—*Irish.* Cave Hill, near Belfast ; in trap.—*Foreign.* Bex, in Switzerland ; Salzburg, in the Tyrol ; Wurtemberg ; the Harz ; Hungary ; Bavaria ; Aussee, in Upper Austria, of a brick-red colour, in Rock Salt.

Anhydrite may be distinguished from Gypsum by its greater hardness and specific gravity. By absorbing water, which it does very slowly, it becomes changed to Gypsum. At Bex extensive beds are altered in this manner, but by digging to a depth of 60 to 100 feet, the Anhydrite is found unaltered. See also GEKROSSTEIN, MURIACITE, VULPI-NITE.

Name. From *a, priv.,* and *ὕδωρ, water.*
Brit. Mus., Case 54.

ANHYDROUS BINOXIDE OF MANGANESE, *Turner.* See PYROLUSITE.

ANHYDROUS SCOLEZITE : anhydrous lime-Labradorite from Pargas, in Finland.

ANHYDROUS SILICATE OF IRON, *Phillips, Thomson.* See FAYALITE.

ANHYDROUS SILICATE OF MANGANESE. See TEPHRONITE.

ANHYDROUS SILICATE OF ZINC. See HEBETINE, TROOSTITE, WILLELMINE, WILLEMITE, WILLIAMSITE.

ANHYDROUS SULPHATE OF ALUMINA. See THENARDITE.

ANHYDROUS SULPHATE OF LIME. See ANHYDRITE.

ANHYDROUS SULPHATE OF SODA AND LIME, *Cleaveland.* See GLAUBERITE.

ANKERITE, *Dana, Nicol, Phillips, Haidinger, Greg & Lettsom.* A crystallized variety of Dolomite, containing a large proportion of iron.

Hexagonal. Yellowish, or reddish-white; becoming brown on exposure. Translucent at the edges. Lustre vitreous, inclining to pearly. Brittle. Fracture uneven. H. 3·5 to 4. S.G. 2·95 to 3·1.

Comp. $\ddot{C}a \ddot{C} + (\dot{F}e, \dot{M}g, \dot{M}n) \ddot{C}$.
Analysis by *Berthier,* from Gollrath :

Carbonate of lime	. 51·1
Carbonate of iron .	. 20·0
Carbonate of magnesia	. 25·7
Carbonate of manganese	. 3·0

99·8

BB becomes black and magnetic; with borax gives the colour of iron; with soda gives indications of manganese.

Dissolves with effervescence in nitric acid.

Localities. Near Torness, in the Orkneys, massive and in curved crystals, in amygdaloid; Golrath, Eisenerz, and the Nieder Alp in Styria, with Siderite; Rathhausberg, in the valley of Gastein, in Salzburg, in mica-slate. See also ROHWAND.

Name. After Prof. Anker, of Grätz.
Brit. Mus., Case 47.

ANNABERGITE, *Dana, Haidinger.* Oblique. Occurs in capillary crystals of a fine apple-green colour, adhering to, or coating, Arsenical Nickel, of the decomposition of

which it is a result. It is soft, and has a greenish-white streak, and an uneven or earthy fracture. H 2·5 to 3. G. 3·078 to 3·131.

Comp. $\dot{N}i^5 \ddot{A}s + 8\dot{H} =$ oxide of nickel 37·59, arsenic acid 38·41, water 24·00 = 100.

Analysis by *Kersten :*

Arsenic acid	. .	38·30
Oxide of nickel .	. .	36·20
Oxide of cobalt .	. .	1·53
Water	. . .	23·91
Protoxide of iron	. .	trace

99·94

BB on charcoal, gives out an odour of arsenic, and, in the inner flame, fuses to a metallic globule.

Dissolves in nitric acid.

Annabergite occurs, with White Nickel, at Allemont, in Dauphiny, at Annaberg*, and elsewhere.

M. P. G. Principal Floor, Wall-case 20.

ANNIVITE, *Dufrénoy.* A mineral analogous to Grey Copper, and according to Kenngott, an impure variety of that ore. It is found in the valley of Annivier with Copper Pyrites.

ANORTHITE, *Rose, Dana.* Anorthic. Primary form an oblique rhombic prism. Occurs in white translucent or transparent crystals, with a vitreous lustre inclining to pearly on the planes of cleavage. Streak white. Fracture conchoidal. H. 6 to 7. S.G. 2·66 to 2·78.

Fig. 21.

Comp. $\ddot{C}a^3 \ddot{S}i + 3 \ddot{A}l \ddot{S}i$ or like Scapolite, except that small portions of the lime are replaced by magnesia, potash, and soda.

Analysis by *Abich,* from Somma :

Silica .	. .	44·12
Alumina	. .	35·12
Peroxide of iron .	.	0·70
Lime .	. .	19·02
Magnesia	. .	0·56
Soda .	. .	0·27
Potash .	. .	0·25

100·04

---

* Whence the name Annabergite.

ANTHOPHYLLITE.

BB like Felspar, except that with carbonate of soda, in every proportion, it yields a white enamel, never a transparent glass. Is entirely decomposed by muriatic acid.

Localities.—Irish. Carlingford Mountain, co. Down, with Hornblende and syenite, in greenstone dykes, traversing limestone.— *Foreign.*—Principally at Vesuvius, among the old lavas of Monte Somma, generally occupying the cavities of chloritic masses, and associated with Ice-spar, Augite, Mica, and Idocrase; Island of Procida; Faroë Islands; Java; the Konchêkowskoi Kamen in the Ural.

Anorthite may be distinguished from all the zeolites, as well as from Nepheline and Leucite, by its infusibility before the blowpipe; from Topaz by inferior hardness and specific gravity; and from Chrysolite by lower degrees of specific gravity. Nitric acid has no effect on Chondrodite, while Anorthite is partly dissolved in it; the former, too, is always yellow or brownish-yellow, the latter is invariably white.

Name From ἄνοϱθος, *oblique.*
Brit. Mus., Case 30.
ANORTHITIC MELANE ORE, *Haidinger.* See ALLANITE.
ANORTHOTOMOUS FELSPAR, *Mohs.* See ANORTHITE.

ANTHOPHYLLITE, *Phillips.* A variety of Hornblende (Tremolite) occurring in masses consisting of acicular fibres, which are often disposed in a radiating form. It has a grey or clove-brown colour, with an occasional blue tinge and a glistening, pearly, pseudo-metallic lustre. Translucent at the edges. H. 5 to 5·5. S.G. 2·94 to 3·16.

Comp. Fe S̈i + M̈g³ S̈i = protoxide of iron 15·5, magnesia 25·9, silica 58·6 = 100.
Analysis by *Thomson*, from Perth in Canada E.:

Silica	57·60
Alumina	3·20
Magnesia	29·30
Lime	3·55
Protoxide of iron . .	2·10
Water	3·55
	99·80

BB fusible with great difficulty, alone to a blackish-grey glass; with borax to a transparent glass coloured grass-green by iron. Not decomposed by acids.

Localities. Kongsberg and Snarum, in Norway; Ujordlesoak, in Greenland; Haddam, Connecticut, U. S.
The name has reference to the resem-

ANTHRACONITE. 19

blance of its colour to that of the flower anthophyllum.
Brit. Mus., Case 34.
M. P. G. Horse-shoe Case, 1007.

ANTHOSIDERITE, *Dana, Hausmann, Nicol.* A mineral resembling Cacoxene, occurring in fine fibrous, flower-like aggregates, of an ochreous-yellow, and yellowish-brown colour. Opaque or slightly subtranslucent. Lustre silky. Tough. Gives sparks with steel. H. 6·5. S.G. 3·6.

Comp. Fe S̈i³ + Ḧ = silica 60·4, peroxide of iron 35·6, water 4·0 = 100·0.
BB becomes reddish-brown, then black, and fuses with difficulty to a black, magnetic slag.
Soluble in muriatic acid.
Locality. Minas Geraes in Brazil, associated with Magnetic Iron.
Name. From ἄνθος, *a flower*, and σίδηϱος, *iron*; in allusion to its occurrence in fibrous tufts, which are sometimes aggregated into feathery flowers.
Brit. Mus., Case 14.

ANTHRACITE. A non-bituminous variety of Coal, with a bright and often iridescent lustre, and a sharp-edged, shining, conchoidal fracture. H. 2 to 2·5. S.G. 1·3 to 1·75.
The Anthracite of South Wales contains from 88 to 95 per cent. of carbon, 4 to 7 of water, with some earthy impurities.
*Analysis** from Glamorganshire. S.G. 1·375:

Carbon	.	.	.	91·44
Hydrogen	.	.	.	3·46
Nitrogen	.	.	.	0·21
Sulphur	.	.	.	0·79
Oxygen	.	.	.	2·58
Ash	.	.	.	1·52
				100·00

Coke left by the Coal 92·9 per cent.
This variety of Coal is not easily ignited but when burning it gives out an intense heat, unaccompanied by smoke, and with little flame. It occurs in Carmarthenshire and Pembrokeshire in S. Wales; Bideford in Devon; Binney Craig, Linlithgowshire; Kilkenny, in Ireland; largely in Pennsylvania, U.S., &c.
Brit. Mus., Case 4.
M. P. G. Upper Gallery, Wall-case 41, No. 164.
See also COAL.
ANTHRACONITE. Limestone, which emits

---

* Report on the Coal suited to the Steam Navy, by Sir H. T. De la Beche and Dr. Lyon Playfair.

c 2

a fetid odour when scraped or struck with a hammer, owing, probably, to its containing sulphuretted hydrogen. It occurs columnar, granular, and compact, of various shades of grey, brown and black. The harder varieties, which take a good polish, are used for chimney-pièces, and in ornamental architecture. It is found in Sweden, Carinthia, &c.; also, in the mountain limestone on the banks of the Avon, near Clifton; and near Castleton and Matlock in Derbyshire. Most of the Purbeck and Portland Limestones of Dorsetshire and Wiltshire belong to this class, and may be recognised when used for mending the roads, by the strong fetid odour they give out when crushed by the passage of heavy vehicles. See also SWINESTONE.

Brit. Mus., Case 46.

M.P.G. Upper Gallery, Wall-case, 43.

ANTHRACOXENE. A mineral resin of a brownish-black colour from the coal-beds of Brandeisl, in Bohemia. In thin splinters it is hyacinth-red. H. 2·5. S.G. 1·181. It melts easily with intumescence and burns to a slag, giving off much smoke and an odour which is not disagreeable.

It is partly soluble in ether, but not at all so in alcohol, except after exposure, when it absorbs oxygen, and then alcohol takes up a little of it.

ANTIEDRIT, *Breithaupt.* See EDINGTONITE.

ANTIGORITE, *Schweizer.* Rhombic. Occurs in foliated masses of a brownish-green colour by reflected light, and leek-green by transmitted light. Transparent in thin laminæ. Lustre weak. Streak white. Feel smooth but not greasy. H. 2·5. S.G. 2·6.

Comp. Hydrated silicate of magnesia,

$\dot{M}g^4 \ddot{S}i^2 + \dot{H}$, or more correctly $(\dot{M}g^5 \dot{F}e) \ddot{S}i^3$

$+ \dot{H}.$

Analysis by *Schweizer :*

Silica	46·18
Magnesia . .	35·19
Protoxide of iron .	12·68
Alumina . . .	1·89
Water . . .	3·70
	99·64

BB fuses at the edges to a yellowish-brown enamel. With borax forms a glass coloured by iron.

Locality. The Antigorio* Valley to the N.W. of Domo d'Ossola, in Piedmont.

Antigorite has been shown by Professor G. J. Brush to be slaty serpentine in which,

---

* Whence the name Antigorite.

according to Stockar-Escher, alumina replaces the silica.

ANTIMOINE BLANC, *Brochant.* See VALENTINITE.

ANTIMOINE GRIS, *Brochant.* Grey Antimony. See STIBNITE.

ANTIMOINE HYDRO-SULFURÉ, *Haüy.* See KERMESITE.

ANTIMOINE MURIATIQUE, *La Metherie.* See VALENTINITE.

ANTIMOINE NATIF, *Haüy.* See NATIVE ANTIMONY.

ANTIMOINE OXIDÉ, *Haüy.* See VALENTINITE.

ANTIMOINE OXIDÉ SULFURÉ, *Haüy.* See KERMESITE.

ANTIMOINE OXIDÉ TERREUX, *Haüy.* See STIBICONISE.

ANTIMOINE ROUGE, *Brochant.* See KERMESITE.

ANTIMOINE SULFURÉ, *Haüy.* See STIBNITE.

ANTIMOINE SULFURÉ CAPILLAIRE, *Haüy.* A fibrous variety of Stibnite, occasionally presenting a plumose, woolly, or felt-like appearance.

ANTIMOINE SULFURÉ NICKELIFÈRE, *Haüy.* See ULLMANNITE.

ANTIMOINE SULFURÉ PLOMBIFÈRE. See ZINKENITE.

ANTIMOINE SULFURÉ PLUMBO-CUPRIFÈRE, *Haüy.* See BOURNONITE.

ANTIMON-ARSEN, *Naumann.* See ARSENICAL ANTIMONY.

ANTIMONATE OF LEAD. See BLEINIERITE.

ANTIMONBLENDE, *v. Leonhard.* See KERMESITE.

ANTIMONBLÜTHE, *v. Leonhard.* See VALENTINITE.

ANTIMONGLANZ, *Naumann, v. Leonhard.* See STIBNITE.

ANTIMONIAL COPPER. See WOLFSBERGITE.

ANTIMONIAL COPPER GLANCE. See WOLCHITE.

ANTIMONIAL GREY COPPER, *Phillips.* Is merely a variety of Grey Copper. It rarely occurs crystallized and is of a dark lead-grey colour, with no appearance of any regular structure. Not very brittle. Fracture conchoidal. The principal locality is Schwatz in the Tyrol, but it is also found at Kapnik in Transylvania, Clausthal in the Harz, Siberia, &c. It is the Schwarzerz of German miners.

M. P. G. Principal floor, Wall-case 16 (Spain).

ANTIMONIAL NICKEL, *Phillips.* See ULLMANNITE.

ANTIMONIAL NICKEL. See BREITHAUP-TITE.

ANTIMONIAL OCHRE, *Phillips.* Occurs in earthy masses, and as a pulverulent crust; also in pseudomorphs after Stibnite. Colour yellow, yellowish grey, or brownish opaque. Dull. Streak grey or yellowish-white and glistening. Soft and friable. Fracture uneven or earthy. S.G. 3·7 to 3·8.

Comp. Probably antimonious acid or Sb with water.

BB does not fuse, but forms a slight stain on the charcoal: with soda is reduced.

Localities. Associated with Stibnite and other ores of antimony at Bruck in Rhenish Prussia, Nassau, Wolfsberg in the Harz, Kremnitz in Hungary, Saxony, Gallicia in Spain, France &c.

Brit. Mus., Case 38.

ANTIMONIAL SILVER, *Jameson, Phillips.* See DISCRASITE.

ANTIMONIAL SILVER BLENDE, *Naumann.* See PYRARGYRITE.

ANTIMONIAL SULPHIDE OF IRON. See BERTHIERITE.

ANTIMONIATED NATIVE SILVER, *Kirwan.* See DISCRASITE.

ANTIMONIAL SULPHURET OF SILVER. See PYRARGYRITE & FREISLEBENITE.

ANTIMONIATE OF LEAD. See BLEINIE-RITE.

ANTIMONIGSAURES BLEIOXYD. See AM-MIOLITE.

ANTIMONIT, *Haidinger,* ⎫
v. Kobell.   ⎬ See STIBNITE.
ANTIMONITE, *Brooke &*
Miller, Greg & Lettsom. ⎭

ANTIMONITE OF LEAD. See BLEINIERITE.

ANTIMONITE OF LIME. See ROMEINE.

ANTIMONITE OF QUICKSILVER, *Domeyko.* See AMMIOLITE.

ANTIMONKUPFERGLANZ, *Breithaupt.* See WOLCHITE.

ANTIMONNICKEL. See BREITHAUPTITE.

ANTIMONNICKELGLANZ, *Hausmann.* See ULLMANNITE.

ANTIMONOCHRE   ⎫ See CERVAN-
ANTIMONOKER, *v. Leon-* ⎬ TITE, STIBI-
hard.   ⎮ CONITE, VOL-
                  ⎭ GERITE.

ANTIMONOXYD. See VALENTINITE AND CERVANTITE.

ANTIMONPHYLLITE, *Breithaupt, Phillips.* A mineral containing oxide of antimony, and occurring in thin inequiangular six-sided prisms. The locality is not known.

ANTIMONSILBER, *v. Leonhard.* See DIS-CRASITE.

ANTIMONSILBERBLENDE. See PYRAR-GYRITE.

ANTIMONY, *Dana, Nicol.* See NATIVE ANTIMONY.

ANTIMONY BLENDE. See KERMESITE.

ANTIMONY BLOOM. See VALENTINITE.

ANTIMONY GLANCE. See STIBNITE.

ANTIMONY OCHRE, *Jameson, Nicol.* See ANTIMONIAL OCHRE.

ANTIMONY SILVER, *Nicol.* See DISCRA-SITE.

ANTRIMOLITE, *Thomson.* A variety of Mesolite occurring in white, silky, fibrous stalactites, about the size of a finger, in cavities of amygdaloid, at Ballintoy, co. Antrim, in Ireland. The fibres radiate from the axes. H. 3·7. S.G. 2·1.

Analysis by Heddle :

Silica	.	.	.	. 47·04
Alumina	.	.	.	. 26·26
Lime	.	.	.	. 9·88
Soda	.	.	.	. 4·88
Water	.	.	.	. 12·24
				100·30

B B melts quietly to a white enamel. Gelatinizes with muriatic acid.

Brit. Mus., Case 29.

APATELITE. *Meillet.* A mineral resembling Copiapite, occurring in small friable nodules of a clear yellow colour, disseminated in an argillaceous bed connected with the Plastic Clay, at Meudon and Auteuil, in France.

Comp. $2 \ddot{F}e^2 \ddot{S}^3 + 3 \dot{H}.$

Analysis by Meillet :

Sulphuric acid	.	.	. 42·90
Peroxide of iron	.	.	. 53·30
Water .	.	.	. 3·96
			100·16

APATITE. *Werner, Dana, Phillips.* Crystalline phosphate lime. Hexagonal, often hemihedral, occurs in six-sided prisms,

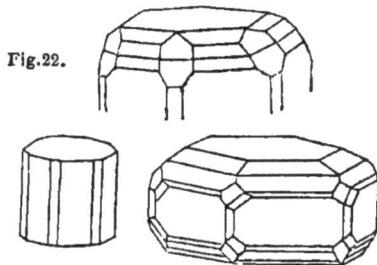

Fig.22.

Fig. 23.   Fig. 24.

terminated by one or more planes, or the prism is terminated by a six-sided pyramid, and the lateral edges are sometimes replaced. Colours, usually pale and most commonly white, yellowish-white, wine-yellow, green, blue, or bluish-green, and red, which are sometimes intermixed in the same crystal. Externally it is splendent; internally the lustre is shining and resinous approaching to vitreous. Transparent to opaque. A bluish opalescence is sometimes displayed in the direction of the vertical axis. Brittle. Cross fracture uneven, approaching to small-conchoidal. H. 5. S.G. 3·25.

Comp. 3 $\ddot{C}a^3 \ddot{P}$ + Ca (Cl, F) = phosphoric acid 42·26, lime 50·0, fluorine 3·77, calcium 3·97; or phosphate of lime 92·26 and fluoride of calcium 7·74, with part of the fluoride sometimes replaced by chloride.

Analysis by *G. Rose,* from Cabo de Gata, Spain: S.G. 3·235.

Phosphate of lime	.	. 92·066
Chloride of calcium	.	. 0·885
Fluoride of calcium	.	. 7·049
		100·000

BB fusible with difficulty on thin edges: with borax forms a clear globule, and in salt of phosphorus dissolves in great quantity, affording a transparent glass, which when nearly saturated becomes opaque on cooling, and presents crystalline faces. Some varieties are phosphorescent when placed on ignited charcoal, and before the blowpipe.

Localities.—English. Cornwall, of a greyish blue at Stenna Gwynn near St. Austell; St. Michael's Mount; Huel Kind, near St. Agnes; Fowey Consols and Huel Franco (*Francolite*), near Tavistock. Cumberland at the foot of Brandygill, Carrock Fells, of the form of *figs.* 22 and 23. Devonshire at Bovey Tracey, in crystals sometimes two inches long, associated with black Tourmaline.—*Scotch.* Dee side in Aberdeenshire.—*Irish.* Near Kilroot, co. Antrim, in granite; near Hilltown, Dublin; and at Killiney Hill, in limestone.—*Foreign.* Ehrenfriedersdorf and Schneeberg in Saxony; Schlackenwald in Bohemia, Pfitsch-Thal in Tyrol, St. Gotthard in Switzerland, Krageröe and Snarum in Norway, and (according to Nordenskiöld) in Bucharia in Asia, in crystals of a blue colour, (*Lazur-apatite*) associated with Lapis Lazuli. An hexagonal prism of a pale amethyst colour, in the Brit. Mus. (Case 57 B.), said to be from the neighbourhood of St. Petersburg, was purchased by Mr. Greville for 78*l.* Professor Voelcker states that all the specimens of Apatite which he obtained from Krageröe, were

perfectly free from fluorine and contained variable quantities of chloride of calcium. In Spain, at Logrosan in Estremadura, the massive varieties are used for building-stone. Losacio, province of Zamora, near Portugal.

Apatite usually occurs in crystalline rocks, especially in those containing tin veins and iron ore: it is also found in granular limestone, and sometimes in serpentine.

The name, derived from ἀπάταω (to deceive), was given to this mineral by Werner, in consequence of the fallacious resemblance it bears to other minerals. For varieties, see ASPARAGUS STONE, MOROXITE and PHOSPHORITE.

Brit. Mus., Case 57 B.
M. P. G. Horse-shoe Case, Nos. 312 to 317: Wall Case, 25.

APATOID, one of the minerals found in meteorites, which have been named by Prof. C. U. Shepard. It occurs in very minute quantity, in small, yellow, semitransparent grains in the Richmond stone, and sparingly in that of Bishopsville. H. 5·5. It is so named from its resemblance in appearance to Apatite, but chemically it differs from the latter in not containing phosphoric acid.

APHANÈSE, *Beudant.*
APHANESITE, *Dana.*
} A name for Clinoclase; from ἀφανής, *unmanifest;* in allusion to the extremely minute crystals in which it occurs.

APHÉRÈSE, *Beudant.* See LIBETHENITE. From ἀφαίρεσις, *subtraction;* in allusion to its being only a variety of an already recognised species.

APHRITE, *Phillips,* is a nearly pure carbonate of lime, differing from Schiefer-spar in being less coherent. It has a very pale yellowish, nearly silver-white colour, sometimes approaching to greyish-white. Occurs massive and disseminated, sometimes solid, more often in a loose or friable state, and composed of fine scaly particles, with a shining lustre intermediate between semi-metallic and pearly. It is opaque and very soft. It is usually found in veins or cavities in limestone rocks. It occurs in Hessia, and in the neighbourhood of Gera, in the forest of Thuringia.

Brit. Mus., Case 46.

APHRIZITE: APHRYSITE: APHRYZITE, *Dufrénoy.* A subvariety of Tourmaline, occuring in small, brilliant, black crystals, bearing a resemblance at first sight to those of tin-ore. It is found in white Quartz, in

Norway; in decomposed Felspar at Andreasberg in the Harz; and at St. Just in Cornwall. (*Fig. 25.*)

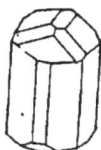

Fig. 25.

APHRODITE. A soft and earthy mineral like Meerschaum, of a white or yellowish colour, and with a waxy lustre. Translucent. S.G. 2·21.

Comp. $\ddot{M}g^3 \ddot{S}i^2 + 3 \dot{H}$.

Analysis by *Berlin:*

Silica . . . . . 51·55
Magnesia . . . . 33·72
Protoxide of manganese . 1·62
Protoxide of iron . . . 0·59
Alumina . . . . 0·20
Water . . . . . 12·32
_____
100·00

Locality. Longbanshytta, in Sweden.

APHROSIDERITE, *Sandberger.* A ferruginous Ripidolite, occurring in fine scaly grains in the Duchy of Nassau and Weilburg, composed of

Silica . . . . . 26·45
Alumina . . . . 21·25
Protoxide of iron . . . 44·24
Magnesia . . . . 1·06
Water . . . . . 7·74
_____
100·74

Comp. $3 \dot{R}^3 \ddot{S}i + 3 \ddot{A}l \ddot{S}i + 6 \dot{H}$ (Genth.) See OWENITE and THURINGITE.

APHTHALOSE, *Beudant.* From ἄφθιτος, unalterable, and ἅλος, salt. See GLASERITE.

APHTHITALITE, *Shepard.* See GLASERITE.

APHTHONITE, *Svanberg.* A mineral resembling an argentiferous Tetrahedrite (Grey Copper). It occurs massive, of a steel-grey colour and with a black streak, at Wermland. H. 3. S.G. 4·87.

Analysis by *Svanberg:*

Sulphur . . . . 30·05
Antimony . . . . 24·77
Copper . . . . . 32·91
Zinc . . . . . 6·40
Silver . . . . . 3·09
Iron . . . . . 1·31
Lead . . . . . 0·04
Cobalt . . . . . 0·49
Arsenic . . . . . trace

Gangue . . . . 1·29
_____
100·37

APJOHNITE, *Glocker.* A manganesian alum occurring in acicular crystallizations with a silky lustre, like Asbestos, near Lagoa Bay, in S. Africa.

Comp. $\ddot{M}n \dot{S} + \ddot{A}l \ddot{S}^3 + 24 \dot{H}$, or sulphate of manganese 16·3, sulphate of alumina 37·0, water 46·7 = 100.

The name Apjohnite has also been given to a metallic ore of a brownish-leaden colour, found in Ireland, mixed with Iron Pyrites. The composition, according to *Heddle*, is represented by the formula 5 Fe S² + 2 Pb S + 12 Zn S, or bisulphide of iron 26·75, sulphide of lead 21·32, sulphide of zinc 51·93 = 100.

APLOME, *Haüy, Phillips.* A variety of iron-lime Garnet, commonly occurring in rhombic dodecahedrons, having their planes striated parallel to the shorter diagonal. Colour deep-brown, or orange-brown. Opaque. Harder than quartz. S.G. 3·44.

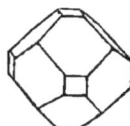

Fig. 26.

Localities. The banks of the river Lena, in Siberia; the Banat; and Schwarzenberg, in Saxony.

Name. From ἁπλόος, *simple;* from the supposed derivation of the dodecahedron from a cube, by one of the most simple laws of decrement, viz., by replacement parallel to all its edges.

APOPHYLLITE, *Dana, Haüy, Phillips, Nicol.* Pyramidal. Occurring in square prisms, whose solid angles are sometimes replaced by triangular planes, which, by a deeper replacement, assume the form of rhombic planes. Cleavage highly perfect, parallel to all the planes of the primary form, but most

Fig. 27.

Fig. 29.

Fig. 28.

readily perpendicular to its axis. Structure lamellar. Colour white or greyish, sometimes with a green, yellow, or reddish tinge.

c 4

Transparent to opaque. Lustre shining on the lateral planes of the prism, pearly on the terminal. Becomes feebly electric by friction. Streak white. Brittle. Fracture uneven. H 4·5 to 5. S.G. 2·3.

Comp. Silica 52·7, lime 26·0, potash 4·4, water 16·7 = 100.

Analysis by *Berzelius*, from Faroe :

Silica	52·38
Lime	24·70
Potash	5·37
Fluorine . . .	1·20
Water	16·20
	99·85

BB exfoliates, intumesces, and ultimately fuses to a white vesicular glass; with borax melts readily to a transparent globule. In nitric acid it separates into flakes, and in powder becomes gelatinous and translucent. *Localities.—Scotch.* It is found in Old Kilpatrick(*fig.* 29), in Dumbartonshire; in Fifeshire, at the Chapel Quarries, near Raith; at Talisker, in Invernesshire (*fig.* 28); and in very transparent crystals at Ratho, near Edinburgh.—*Irish.* At Ballintoy, in Antrim, it is met with of a white colour upon Stilbite (*fig.* 29); in small transparent crystals, and in large white crystals like *fig.* 27, at Portrush, and at Agnew's Mountain.—*Foreign.* Fine specimens of Apophyllite, coating cavities in amygdaloid, occur in Greenland, Iceland, Poonah, and Ahmednuggar, in Hindostan. It is also found in Sweden and Norway, and in perfect, well-defined crystals at Plombières, in an ancient crust of cement, which was formerly spread over the valley where the hot springs rise.

The name Apophyllite is derived from ἀποφυλλίζω, to *exfoliate*, alluding to its behaviour before the blowpipe.

Brit. Mus., Case 27.

M. P. G. Horse-shoe Case, No. 1177.

APOSTLE GEMS. In the middle ages the apostles were sometimes symbolised under the names of various gems, as follows :

St. Peter . .	Jasper.
St. Andrew . .	Sapphire.
St. James . .	Chalcedony.
St. John . .	Emerald.
St. Philip . .	Sardonyx.
St. Bartholomew .	Carnelian.
St. Matthew . .	Chrysolite.
St. Thomas . .	Beryl.
St. Thaddeus . .	Chrysoprase.
St. James the Less	Topaz.
St. Simeon . .	Hyacinth.
St Matthias .	Amethyst.

APYROTI (from ἀ *priv.*, and πῦς *fire*). A

name given by some of the ancients to Rubies, because "fire hath no power of them."

AQUAMARINE, comprises the varieties of Beryl which are of clear tints of sky-blue or mountain-green. (See BERYL.)

It is made into bracelets, necklaces, brooches, and other articles of jewelry, as well as into seals and intaglios. The larger prisms are valued by the Turks for forming the handles of daggers, sword-hilts, &c. It is a pleasant stone for lapidaries to work, as it bears cutting and polishing without risk. Want of lustre, paleness and weakness of colour, being the principal defects to which it is liable, a good stone should have a sufficient depth in proportion to its spread surface, and it should be formed with a small table, a high bizel, with the under-part cut into delicate steps. The only stone with which the Aquamarine is likely to be confounded is the blue Topaz, from which it may be distinguished by its inferior specific gravity and hardness, and inferior lustre.

It is found in Hindostan, Brazil, Siberia, in the granite district of Nertschinsk, and in the Uralian and Altai Mountains. The prisms are commonly striated longitudinally, and they have been obtained exceeding a foot in length.

The most splendid specimen of which we have any account belonged to Dom Pedro. It approaches, both in size and shape, the head of a calf, and exhibits a crystalline structure only on one side, the rest being water-worn. It weighs 225 ozs. Troy, or more than 18½ lbs. The specimen is transparent and without a flaw.

The name is derived from *aqua*, water, and *marina*, of the sea, in allusion to its limpid, pale green colour, like that of sea-water.

The Aquamarine is the stone known to the ancients as the Beryl.

Brit. Mus., Case 37.

M. P. G. Horse-shoe Case, Nos. 816a, 836 to 838.

ARÆOXENE. A mineral resembling Crocoisite, only darker. It occurs massive, or imperfectly crystalline, with traces of a columnar structure, of a deep red colour, with a brownish tinge, and a pale yellowish streak. H. 3. S.G. 5·79.

Analysis by *Bergemann* :

Vanadic acid . .	16·81
Arsenic acid . .	10·52
Oxide of lead . .	52·55
Oxide of zinc . .	18·11
Alumina and peroxide of iron	1·34
Phosphoric acid . . .	trace
	99·33

BB on charcoal fuses with intumescence, yielding an arsenical odour, and a globule of lead.

Locality. Dahn, in Bavaria.

Dr. Krantz suggests that Aræoxene and Dechenite are identical.

ARAGONITE, *Dana, Brooke & Miller*; ARAGONSPATH. Rhombic. Primary form a right rhombic prism. Occurs in hexagonal prisms, very frequently in twin crystals, also in globular, reniform, dendritic, and coralloid shapes; sometimes fibrous and in compact masses. (See FLOS FERRI and SATIN SPAR). Colour generally white, but sometimes tinged yellow, blue, and green. Lustre vitreous, inclining to resinous on fractured surfaces. Translucent, the small crystals sometimes colourless and transparent, and refracting doubly in certain directions. Brittle. Fracture subconchoidal. Yields to the knife, but scratches Calc-spar easily. H. 3·5 to 4. S.G. 2·93 to 2·94.

Fig. 30.

Comp. Ċa C̈ like Calcite=carbonic acid 44·00, lime 56·0 = 100.

Analysis, by *Stromeyer*, from Aragon:

Carbonate of lime . . .	94·82
Carbonate of strontia . .	4·08
Water	0·98
	99·88

Thin fragments of transparent crystals decrepitate in the flame of a candle; other varieties lose their translucency and fall to powder. Becomes phosphorescent on red-hot iron.

Dissolves with effervescence in nitric and muriatic acids, and paper dipped into a mixture of the solution and alcohol burns with a purple flame.

Name. This mineral is named after Aragon, the province in Spain where it was first discovered in large detached twin hexagonal crystals, imbedded with Gypsum in ferruginous clay.

Localities.—English. Various parts of the United Kingdom; in Devonshire, at Torbay, in aggregations of acicular crystals with a fibrous structure, and at Ilfracombe, in a spicular form. In fine radiating crystals, of a reddish-brown colour, at Cleator Moor, in Cumberland.—*Scotch.* At Lead-

hills, in long, radiating, transparent crystals, terminated as in *fig.* 30.—*Foreign.* The most transparent and perfectly defined prisms have been found in a vein traversing basalt, at Bilin, in Bohemia. Radiated and minute white crystals occur in the recent lavas of Vesuvius. In radiated columnar forms, of a fine green colour, near Gerfalco, in Tuscany.

Aragonite differs from Calcite in its greater hardness and specific gravity, and in containing generally from $\frac{1}{2}$ to 4 per cent. of carbonate of strontia, and more rarely from 2 to 4 per cent. of carbonate of lead. It may be readily distinguished from Calcite by at once flying to powder when exposed to heat, while Calc-spar placed by its side remains unchanged, and does not lose even its transparency. The cleavage planes of Calc-spar are, moreover, always inclined, while those of Aragonite are in a longitudinal direction. The calcareous concretions formed in the boilers of steam-engines are, in cases where the incrustations are composed of carbonate of lime, almost always Aragonite.

Brit. Mus., Case 41.

M. P. G. Slabs A 14—21, in Hall, from Beni-Souef in Egypt.

ARCANITE, *Haidinger.* See GLASERITE.

ARCTIZITE, *Jameson*; WERNERITE. See SCAPOLITE.

ARENDALITE. A variety of lime-and-iron-Epidote from Arendal, in Norway. The fine crystals from this locality often consist of concentric coats, the exterior of which can be removed, by which means, out of a large and imperfect crystal, one smaller but of a more perfect form can be obtained. S.G. 3·4.

Analysis by *Geffken* :

Silica	36·14
Alumina . . .	22·24
Peroxide of iron . .	14·29
Lime	22·86
Magnesia . . .	2·38
Protoxide of manganese .	2·12
	100·03

Brit. Mus., Case 35.

ARFVEDSONITE, *Dana, Nicol*; ARFVEDSONITE, *Brooke, Phillips, Allan.* A variety of Hornblende containing a large proportion of iron, and also soda. Colour black and opaque. Lustre vitreous, inclining to resinous. Streak greyish-green. H. 6. S.G. 3·4 to 3·5.

Comp. N̈a³ S̈i + F̈e S̈i = silica 49·4, soda 11·3, protoxide of iron 39·3 = 100.

Analysis by *v. Kobell*, from Greenland :

Silica	. 49·27
Alumina . . .	. 2·00
Protoxide of iron . .	. 36·12
Soda	. 8·00
Lime	. 1·50
Magnesia . . .	. 0·42
Protoxide of manganese	. 0·62
Chlorine . . .	. 0·24
	98·17

Fuses even in the flame of a candle. *BB* boils up strongly, and yields a black magnetic globule.

Not soluble in acids or in caustic potash.

Localities. Kangerdluarsuk, in Greenland, associated with Sodalite and Eudialite. Frederickshaven, in Norway.

Name. After Professor Arfvedson, of Sweden.

Brit. Mus., Case 33.

ARGENT AMALGAME, *Dufrénoy.* See NATIVE AMALGAM.

ARGENT ANTIMONIAL, *Haüy.* See DISCRASITE.

ARGENT ANTIMONIAL FERRO-ARSENIFÈRE, *Haüy.* See ARSENIC-SILVER.

ARGENT ANTIMONIÉ SULFURÉ, *Haüy.* See PYRARGYRITE.

ARGENT ANTIMONIÉ SULFURÉ NOIR, *Haüy.* See STEPHANITE.

ARGENT ARSENICAL, *Brochant.* See ARSENIC-SILVER.

ARGENT CARBONATÉ, *Haüy.* See SELBITE.

ARGENT CORNÉ, *Brochant, La Metherie.* See STEPHANITE.

ARGENT ET CUIVRE SULFURÉ, *Bournon.* See STROMEYERITE.

ARGENT FRAGILE, *De Born.* See STEPHANITE.

ARGENT GRIS ANTIMONIAL, *De L'Isle.* See FREISLEBENITE.

ARGENT IODURÉ, *Dufrénoy.* See IODYRITE.

ARGENT MURIATÉ, *Brochant, Haüy.* See KERARGYRITE.

ARGENT NATIF, *Haüy.* See NATIVE SILVER.

ARGENT NOIR, *Haüy.* See STEPHANITE.

ARGENT ROUGE ANTIMONIÉ, *Necker.* See PYRARGYRITE.

ARGENT ROUGE ARSENIÉ, *Necker.* See PROUSTITE.

ARGENT SULFURÉ, *Haüy.* See SILVER GLANCE.

ARGENT SULFURÉ ANTIMONIFÈRE ET CUPRIFÈRE, *Levy.* See FREISLEBENITE.

ARGENT SULFURÉ FLEXIBLE, *Bournon.* See FLEXIBLE SILVER-ORE.

ARGENT SULFURÉ FRAGILE, *Haüy, Dufrénoy.* See STEPHANITE.

ARGENT TELLURÉ, *Necker.* See HESSITE.

ARGENT VITREUSE, *La Metherie.* See SILVER GLANCE.

ARGENT VITREUX AIGRE, *Brochant.* See STEPHANITE.

ARGENTIFEROUS COPPER GLANCE, *Jameson.* See STROMEYERITE.

ARGENTIFEROUS GOLD, *Phillips.* See ELECTRUM.

ARGENTIFEROUS SELENIET OF COPPER. See EUKAIRITE.

ARGENTIFEROUS SULPHURET OF COPPER, *Allan.* See STROMEYERITE.

ARGENTINE, *Kirwan.* See SLATE-CLAY.

ARGENTINE, *Dana.* A form of carbonate of lime with a silvery-white lustre, a slaty structure, and containing a little silica. It is found in the United States, near Williamsberg and Southampton, in Massachusetts; and at the iron mines of Franconia, New Hampshire.

ARGENTITE, *Greg & Lettsom, Haidinger, Nicol.* See SILVER-GLANCE.

M. G. P. Principal Floor, Wall-case 14 (British).

ARGILE FIGUELINE. A name often given to common plastic clay in France. It occurs at the base of the Paris basin, as at Auteuil and Vauves, near Paris, and makes into a red ware requiring a glaze.

ARGILE LITHOMARGE, *Haüy.* See LITHOMARGE.

ARGILE MARTIALE ROUGE, *De Born.*　⎫
ARGILE OCHREUSE GRAPHIQUE, *Haüy*　⎬ See RED CHALK.

ARGILE OCHREUSE JAUNE, *Haüy.* See YELLOW IRON-OCHRE.

ARGILE SCHISTEUSE, *Brochant.* See SLATE-CLAY.

ARGILE SMECTIQUE, *Haüy.* See FULLERS' EARTH.

ARGILLACEOUS IRONSTONE. See CLAY IRONSTONE and BLACKBAND.

ARGYROSE, *Beudant.* See SILVER GLANCE.

ARGYRYTHROSE, *Beudant.* Sulphide of silver and antimony. See PYRARGYRITE.

ARKANSITE. The name given by Shepard to the thick black crystals of Brookite which occur, with Elæotite and Schorlamite, at Magnet Cove, in Arkansas, U. S.

Brit. Mus., Case 37.

ARMENIAN STONE. A commercial name for Lapis Lazuli.

ARPIDELITE. See SPHENE.

ARQUERITE, *Domeyko.* A silver amalgam

occurring in small octahedral crystals, and in arborescent forms, at the mines of Arqueros, near Coquimbo, in Chili. Ductile and malleable. H. 2 to 2·5. S.G. 10·8.

Comp. 'Native Amalgam or Hg Ag^6= silver 86·5, mercury 13·5 = 100.

ARRAGON, *Werner.*
ARRAGONE, *Jameson.*
ARRAGONIT, *Haidinger, Hausmann.*
ARRAGONITE, *Brochant, Nicol, Phillips, Haüy :*
ARRAGON SPAR, *Kirwan.*

} See ARRAGONITE.

ARSEN, *Naumann.* See NATIVE ARSENIC.
ARSENATE OF LEAD. See MIMETITE.
ARSENATE OF LIME. See PHARMACOLITE.
ARSENATE OF ZINC. See KÖTTIGITE.
ARSENEISEN. See LEUCOPYRITE.
ARSENEISENSINTER, *Naumann.* See PITTICITE.
ARSENGLANZ, *Breithaupt.* An impure native arsenic, containing 3 per cent. of bismuth, from Marienberg. H. 2. S.G. 5·36 to 5·39.
ARSENIATE OF COBALT. See ERYTHRINE.
ARSENIATE OF COPPER, *Phillips.* See SCORODITE, EUCHROITE, ERINITE, LIROCONITE.
ARSENIATE OF IRON, *Phillips.* See PHARMACOSIDERITE.
ARSENIATE OF LEAD, *Phillips.* See MIMETITE.
ARSENIATE OF LIME. See PHARMACOLITE.
ARSENIATE OF NICKEL. See ANNABERGITE.
ARSENIC, *Dana, Nicol.* See NATIVE ARSENIC.
ARSENIC-ANTIMONY, *Nicol.* See ARSENICAL ANTIMONY.
ARSENIC BLOOM. See ARSENOLITE.
ARSENIC NATIF, *Haüy.* See NATIVE ARSENIC.
ARSENIC OXYDÉ, *Haüy.* See ARSENOLITE.
ARSENIC PYRITES, *Jameson.* See MISPICKEL.
ARSENIC-SILVER. A mixture of Mispickel, Arsenical Iron, and Discrasite, found at Andreasberg, in the Harz.
M. P. G. Principal Floor, Wall-case 14, No. 683, from Dolcoath mine, Cornwall.
ARSENIC SULFURÉ JAUNE, *Haüy.* See ORPIMENT.
ARSENIC SULFURÉ ROUGE, *Haüy.* See REALGAR.
ARSENICAL ANTIMONIAL SILVER, *Phillips.* See ARSENIC-SILVER.
ARSENICAL ANTIMONY, *Dana, Phillips.*

Occurs in kidney-shaped masses and amorphous; with a granular or almost compact texture. Colour tin-white or reddish-grey, with a brownish-black tarnish. Lustre metallic, occasionally splendent, sometimes dull. Structure curved, lamellar. H. 3·5. S.G. 6·2.
B B emits fumes of arsenic and antimony, and fuses to a metallic globule, which burns away, leaving oxide of antimony on the charcoal.
Comp. SbAs^3, or antimony 36·38, arsenic 63·62 = 100·00.
Localities. Przibram, in Bohemia; Schladming, in Styria; Andreasberg, in the Harz; sparingly at Allemont, in Dauphiny.
ARSENICAL BISMUTH, *Allan.* See EULYTINE.
ARSENICAL COPPER PYRITES, *Levy.* See DOMEYKITE.
ARSENICAL IRON, *Phillips.* See MISPICKEL.
ARSENICAL MANGANESE. See KANEITE.
ARSENICAL MUNDIC. See MISPICKEL.
ARSENICAL PYRITES, *Allan, Phillips, Kirwan.* See LEUCOPYRITE.
ARSENICAL SILVER, *Allan.* See ARSENIC SILVER.
ARSENICAL SILVER BLENDE, *Naumann.* See PROUSTITE.
ARSENICITE. See PHARMACOLITE.
ARSENICUM SANDARACA, *Linnæus.* See REALGAR.
ARSENIDE OF MANGANESE. See KANEITE.
ARSENIET OF NICKEL, *Thomson.* See COPPER NICKEL.
ARSENIKALKIES. See LEUCOPYRITE.
ARSENIKANTIMON. See ARSENICAL ANTIMONY.
ARSENIKBLEISPATH. See MIMETENE.
ARSENIKBISMUTH. See EULYTINE.
ARSENIKBLÜTHE, *Karsten.* See ARSENOLITE; The Arsenikblüthe of Werner is, in part, Pharmacolite; which see.
ARSENIKEISEN. See LEUCOPYRITE.
ARSENIKGLANZ. See ARSENGLANZ.
ARSENIKKIES, *Werner.* See MISPICKEL.
ARSENIKKODALTKIES. See SKUTTERUDITE.
ARSENIKMANGAN. See KANEITE.
ARSENIKKUPFER. See DOMEYKITE.
ARSENIKNICKEL. See COPPER NICKEL, AND SMALTINE.
ARSENIKSILBER. See ARSENIC SILVER.
ARSENIKSILBERBLENDE. See PROUSTITE.
ARSENIK-SINTER. See IRON-SINTER.
ARSENIK-WISMUTH, *Werner.* See EULYTINE.
ARSENIOSIDERITE, *Dufrénoy, Dana.* Occurs in fibrous concretions of a yellowish-brown or golden colour, resembling Caco-

xene. The fibres are large and easily separated by the fingers; when rubbed in a mortar, the powder, which is yellowish-brown, and rather darker than yellow-ochre, adheres to the pestle. Lustre silky. H. 1 to 2. S.G. 3·52 to 3·88.

Comp. $\ddot{C}a^6 \ddot{A}s + 4 \ddot{F}e^2 \ddot{A}s + 15 \dot{H}$, or arsenic 37·86, peroxide of iron 42·14, lime 11·11, water 8·89 = 100.

Analysis by *Dufrénoy:*

Arsenic acid	. .	34·26
Peroxide of iron	.	41·31
Peroxide of manganese	.	1.29
Lime .	. . .	8·43
Potash	. . .	0·76
Silica .	. . .	4·04
Water .	. . .	8·75
		98·84

BB fuses to a black enamel, and gives off a slight odour of arsenic on adding soda.

Dissolves readily in hot nitric or muriatic acid.

This mineral seems to vary much in constitution; it occurs in a manganese bed at Romanèche (Dep. Saone et Loire), in France.

ARSENIOUS ACID. See ARSENOLITE.

ARSENITE, *Haidinger, Brooke & Miller, Greg & Lettsom, Nicol.* See ARSENOLITE.

ARSENIURET OF MANGANESE, *Kane, Phillips.* See KANEITE.

ARSENOCROCITE. See ARSENIOSIDERITE.

ARSENOLITE, *Dana.* White arsenic, or arsenious acid, is formed from the decomposition of other ores, and (when pure) is composed of arsenic 65·76, oxygen 24·24. It occurs either in minute radiating capillary crystals and crusts investing other minerals, or in a stalactitic or botryoidal form. It is white, sometimes with a yellowish or reddish tinge, and has a silky or vitreous lustre. It possesses an astringent and sweetish taste, and is highly poisonous. H. 1·5. S.G. 3·69.

BB volatilizes in white fumes; in the inner flame blackens and gives off an alliaceous odour. It differs from Pharmacolite in being slightly soluble in hot water.

Localities. Huel Sparnon, in Cornwall, in acicular crystals, filling cavities in Arsenical Cobalt; Andreasberg, in the Harz; Bohemia; Hungary; Hanau.

In an interesting paper on the arsenic-eaters of Styria, by Charles Heisch, F.C S., in the *Pharmaceutical Journal,* it is stated that "Arsenic is commonly taken by the peasants in Styria, the Tyrol, and the Salz Kammergut, principally by huntsmen and woodcutters, to improve their wind and prevent fatigue. The following particulars in reference to this subject were communicated to Mr. Heisch by Dr. Lorenz, Imperial Professor of Natural History, formerly of Salzburg:—' The arsenic is taken pure in some warm liquid, as coffee, fasting, beginning with a bit the size of a pin's head, and increasing to that of a pea. The complexion and general appearance are much improved, and the parties using it seldom look so old as they really are, but he has never heard of any case in which it was used to improve personal beauty, though he cannot say that it never is so used. The first dose is always followed by slight symptoms of poisoning, such as burning pain in the stomach, and sickness, but not very severe. Once begun, it can only be left off by very gradually diminishing the daily dose, as a sudden cessation causes sickness, burning pain in the stomach, and other symptoms of poisoning, very speedily followed by death. As a rule, arsenic-eaters are very long lived, and are peculiarly exempt from infectious diseases, fevers, &c., but unless they gradually give up the practice, invariably die suddenly at last. In some arsenic works near Salzburg with which he is acquainted, he says the only men who can stand the work for any time are those who swallow daily doses of arsenic, the fumes, &c., soon killing the others.' "

Brit. Mus., Case 56.

M. P. G. Table-case 14, on principal floor.

ARSENOPYRITE, *Glocker.* See MISPICKEL.

ARSENOUS ACID. See ARSENOLITE.

ARSENPHYLLITE, *Breithaupt.* A mineral similar in composition to Arsenolite, but homœomorphous with Valentinite.

ARSEN-SILBER BLENDE, *Breithaupt.* See PROUSTITE.

ASBEST, *Werner.* ASBESTE, *Haüy, Brochant.* See ASBESTOS.

ASBESTE LIGNIFORME, *Haüy.* See ROCK WOOD.

ASBESTOS, ASBESTUS, *Kirwan, Dana, Phillips, Nicol.* A hornblendic mineral: a fibrous variety of Actinolite or Tremolite. In the process of decomposition, these minerals assume a paler colour, and separate into fibres, which are sometimes as fine as those of flax. When heated to redness all extraneous matter is destroyed, while the fibres themselves remain uninjured. In that form it may be woven into cloth, which, from its incombustibility, has been employed for various purposes. By the ancients it was used to wrap up the bodies of the dead before placing them on the funeral pile, by which means the ashes and unconsumed bones were preserved separately for subsequent preservation in vases. They also made napkins of it, which, when soiled, were cleansed by being thrown into the fire; and used it for wicks of lamps, which maintained perpetual fire in their temples; which lamps were called ἀσβέστα, *unextinguished* or *perpetual.* The people of Greenland make wicks of lamps of it at the present day. It is said that certain tribes of Indians used to make dresses of Asbestos, which, when dirty, had only to be thrown into the fire to be rendered clean again. At the present day it is chiefly used for wicks of lamps, and for making fire-proof safes. It is from the property of resisting the action of fire that it has received the name of ἀσβέστος (Asbestos) or unconsumable.

Localities.—*English.* Cornwall, at the Lizard, St. Cleer, Goonhilly Downs, and near Liskeard.—*Scotch.* Portsoy, in Banffshire, Glenelg, Inverness-shire, and Swinaness, Batta and Fetla, in the Shetland Islands.—*Irish.* Near Strabane, and at Bloomfield, co. Wexford. — *Foreign.* Savoy, the Tyrol, Saltzburg, and in Corsica in such abundance as to have been used by Dolomieu for packing minerals. The Corsicans mix it with clay, which they make into pots, which, though light, are less fragile than if made of clay alone, at the same time that they bear sudden changes of temperature better.

Brit. Mus., Case 34.

ASBOLAN, *Breithaupt*; ASBOLANE, *Brooke & Miller.* See EARTHY COBALT. The name is derived from ἀσβόλη, soot.

ASPARAGUS STONE. A translucent wine-yellow coloured variety of Apatite, found imbedded in Talc at Zillerthal in the Tyrol, and Villa Rica in Spain.

Brit. Mus., Case 57 B.

ASPASIOLITE. A variety of Iolite, occurring in six-sided and twelve-sided prisms, like Fahlunite, but with a less perfect cleavage. It is of greenish-grey to a whitish colour, with a weak lustre. H. 3·5. S.G. 2·76.

Comp. Iolite + A̶l S̶i + 5 H̶.

Analysis by Scheerer :

Silica	50·40
Alumina	32·38
Peroxide of iron	2·34
Magnesia	8·01
Water	6·73
	99·86

BB infusible.

Locality. Krageroe in Norway, associated with Quartz and Iolite.

Name. From α *priv.* and σβεννύω, *to extinguish.*

Brit. Mus., Case 32.

M. P. G. Horse-shoe Case, Nos. 1148 to 1150.

ASPHALTIC OIL. See ASPHALTUM—SENECA OIL.

ASPHALT, *Kirwan, Phillips,* ASPHALTUM, *Hatchett,* ἄσφαλτος, Dioscorides. A compact species of Bitumen. Solid and opaque, of a velvet-black colour, sometimes approaching to brownish-black; with a shining resinous lustre, and a brilliant conchoidal fracture. Sectile. Feels greasy, and emits a bituminous odour when rubbed. Soft. S.G. 1 to 1·2. Fuses at 100° C. (212° Fahr.). Burns with a bright light and a smoky flame, leaving a small quantity of ashes. An Asphaltum from the island of Brazza, in Dalmatia, consists, according to Kersten, of petrolene (volatile oil) 5·0, brown resin, soluble in ether, 20·0, asphaltene (bitumen soluble in alcohol and ether) 74·0, yellow resin, soluble in alcohol, 1·0 = 100·0. (Dana).

Asphaltum is the most common variety of Bitumen. It is found in great abundance of a black colour, with a fracture like ordinary pitch, on the shores, or floating on the surface of the Dead Sea; in the islands of Barbadoes and Trinidad; and a large deposit of it occurs in Tschetschna, between Terek and Argun. " The Pitch Lake in Trinidad, three miles in circumference, covers an area of 99 square miles, and is of unknown thickness. The Bitumen is solid and cold near the shores, but gradually increases in temperature and softness towards the centre, where it is boiling. The solidified bitumen appears as if it had cooled as the surface boiled, in large bubbles. The ascent to the lake from the sea, a distance of three-quarters of a mile, is covered with a hardened pitch, on which trees and vegetables flourish; and about Point La Braye, the masses of pitch look like black rocks among the foliage. The lake is underlaid by a bed of mineral coal." (Manross, quoted by Dana). The Pitch Lake of Trinidad, according to Mr. G. P. Wall, yields three kinds of Asphaltum, viz. :—

1. *Asphaltum Glance,* which is hard and brittle, of an intensely black brilliant lustre, and eminent conchoidal fracture. It contains but a small proportion of earthy impurity, and only a little water. This is the rarest and most valuable kind.

2. *Ordinary Asphaltum,* of a brownish-black colour, dull, and generally with an even fracture. It contains 20 to 35 per cent. of earthy admixture, a considerable propor-

tion of water, and possesses the property of plasticity, which it gradually loses on long exposure to the sun and atmosphere.

3. *Asphaltic Oil*, occurring associated and diluted with water, but when concentrated it appears as a dense black fluid, with a powerful bituminous odour. If collected in an open vessel, the more volatile part evaporates after a few months, leaving a solid black substance of similar appearance, and with properties analogous to those of Asphaltum Glance.

Asphaltum is also found near Matlock, and in the Odin mine, near Castleton, in Derbyshire, and occasionally in the Freestone Quarries at Binney, near Edinburgh, where it is so abundant, that the workmen make candles of it. In Cuba it is very extensively diffused (*Chapapote*). It is also found along the margin of the Magdalena Valley, in New Grenada, Coxitambo, in Peru, of great purity, with a high lustre, and a perfect conchoidal fracture. In Texas, within 100 miles of Houston, there is a small lake about a quarter of a mile in circumference, filled with Bitumen or Asphaltum. In France at Aniches (Department du Nord); near Alcobaca, in Portugal; Avlona in Albania; Mount Lebanon; Arabia; Persia; in the countries on the borders of the Tigris; and the Lower Euphrates; and in Koordistan; Birmah; Ava; Pegu; &c.

Asphaltum was employed by the ancient Egyptians in the process of embalming the dead, either alone, or in combination with other substances. The ancients also used it as an ingredient in mortar, and the walls of Babylon are said to have been built of a mortar of this kind. The people of Arabia still use a solution of it, in oil, to besmear their horse-harness, to preserve it from insects, and in Albania it is used for paying the bottoms of ships. Two ship-loads of Asphalt were sent to this country from the Pitch Lake of Trinidad, by Admiral Cochrane; but it was found that the cost of the oil necessary to render it fit for use exceeded the price of pitch in England, and the project was therefore abandoned. Asphalt is used for lining cisterns, and for pavements. It is also a constituent of Japan varnish.

Brit Mus., Case 60.

M. P. G. A 28 in Hall, large mass from the Pitch-Lake, Trinidad. Horse-shoe Case, Nos. 111 to 116.

ASTERIA. The name used by Pliny to denote the asteriated crystals of Sapphire, or those displaying diverging rays of light. It

is an opalescent variety of Sapphire, which, when cut *en cabochon*, displays a silvery star with six rays. It is semi-transparent, and has often a reddish-purple tinge. The summits of the primary rhombohedron are replaced by secondary planes, that present a varying chatoyant lustre. If these crystals are cut *en cabochon*, or in the form of an ellipse, taking care that the summit of the ellipse shall be situated exactly over the point corresponding with the summit of the rhombohedron, there will be produced the appearance of a star with six rays, from which, when held in the sunshine, a bright yellowish-white light streams forth in beautiful contrast to the rich purplish blue of the other parts of the stone. The flatter the ellipse the more varying is the lustre displayed over the surface of the stone; as on the other hand, with a high ellipse it is condensed on a single spot."—(*Mawe*).

" The jewellers appraise the value of the $\hat{A}yn$-ul-$hireh$ according to the number or perfection of the threads (*zanár*) visible in it, which should give the stone, when turned about, the appearance of a drop of floating water. This description accords with the quartz Cat's-eye rather than with the asteria; but there is some difficulty in reconciling the uncertainties regarding this mineral. The $\hat{A}yn$-ul-$hireh$, probably comprises both of the above minerals; in the same manner as the *turmali* apparently embraces both the tourmaline and zircon families."—*Prinsep*: " *Oriental Account of the Precious Minerals.*"

ASTRAKANITE, *Rose.* A mineral occurring in whitish, transparent or translucent, imperfect prismatic crystals, in the salt lakes east of the mouth of the Volga. S.G. 2·251.

Comp. Mg. $\ddot{S}$ + Na $\ddot{S}$ + 4 $\dot{H}$, or sulphate of magnesia 35·9, sulphate of soda 42·5, water 21·6 = 100.

ASTRAPHYALITE, from ἀστραπὴ, *a flash of lightning.* See FULGURITE.

ASPHALTUM GLANCE. See ASPHALT.

ATACAMITE, *Dana, Jameson, Nicol.* Rhombic; usually occurs in minute rectangular octahedrons, or in modified rectangular

Fig. 31.

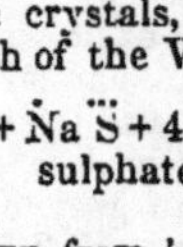

prisms; also massive lamellar. Colour various shades of bright green, rather darker than emerald, sometimes blackish-green. Translucent or nearly transparent, soft and brittle, with an apple-green streak. Lustre vitreous. H. 3 to 3·5. S.G. 4 to 4·3.

Comp. Muriate of Copper, or $CuCl + 3Cu$

$\dot{H}$ = oxide of copper 55·8, chloride of copper 31·5, water 12·7 = 100.

Analysis by Bibra, from Algodan Bay, in Bolivia:

Oxide of copper	56·00
Copper	14·54
Chlorine	16·12
Water	12·13
Silica	0·91
	99·70

BB tinges the flame bright green or blue, and gives off fumes of muriatic acid; yields a bead of copper on charcoal.

Soluble without effervescence in nitric acid, and communicates instantaneously a fine blue colour to ammonia.

Localities. Chiefly at Los Remolinos and Solidad, in Chili; in Bolivia, in the district of Tarapaca; and at Tocopilla, 16 leagues north of Cobija. Also in the iron mines of Schwartzenberg, in Saxony; on some of the lavas of Vesuvius; in South Australia, and in small rhombic prisms on Malachite and Quartz, at the Malachite mines in the Serra do Bembe, near Ambriz, on the West Coast of Africa.

What was originally called "Peruvian green sand," or Atacamite, from its being obtained from the Atacama Desert, between Chili and Peru, is produced artificially by pounding the crystallized and laminar varieties for the purpose of using it as sand for letters (Arsenillo), instead of blotting paper.

Atacamite is distinguished from Malachite by its solubility in nitric acid without effervescence; the colour it communicates to flame, and the rapidity with which it turns ammonia blue. It differs from arseniates of copper by not exhaling arsenical fumes BB.

Brit. Mus., Case 59.

M. P. G. Principal Floor, Wall-case 16.

ATELESITE. The name given by Breithaupt to small oblique crystals containing bismuth.

ATHEREASTITE. An altered Scapolite, which it resembles both in form and appearance. Colour green and opaque.

Locality. The mines of Arendal, in Norway.

ATLASERZ. See MALACHITE.
ATRAMENSTEIN. See MISY.
AVANTURINE, AVANTURINO-QUARTZ, or AVENTURINE. A vitreous variety of Quartz, generally translucent, and of a grey, green, brown, or reddish-brown colour, and containing minute yellow spangles. These are most frequently produced by scales of Mica, but sometimes, according to Gahn, by metallic copper crystallized in the form of flat segments of a regular octahedron. Aventurine was formerly found on the north shores of the White Sea; it is now found tolerably abundantly in Silesia, Bohemia, France, Cape de Gata in Spain, India, but chiefly in the neighbourhood of Ekaterinenburg in Siberia. It is used for ringstones, shirt-studs, ear-rings, snuff-boxes, and other ornamental articles of a similar kind. By far the finest specimen of the Siberian variety in this country is a highly polished vase, four feet high and six feet in circumference, which, with its pedestal of polished grey porphyry, was presented to Sir Roderick I. Murchison as "the explorer of the geology of Russia" by the late Emperor Nicholas I. The prevailing tint of this magnificent work of art is French-white or pearl-grey, clouded with delicate rose-coloured tints, and it is equally remarkable for the beauty of the material, and the elegance of its form, as for its excessive rarity; the difficulty of procuring a stone of such large dimensions, and of polishing so hard a substance being so great, that only one other similar vase (presented to the late Baron Humboldt, and now in the Royal Museum, Berlin), has been made. The materials of the base and pedestal were obtained in the Kourgon mountains in the province of Tomsk, and were cut and polished in Siberia. According to Frèmy & Clemandole, beautiful specimens of artificial Aventurine may be obtained by heating together for twelve hours a mixture of 300 parts of pounded glass, 40 of protoxide of copper, and 80 of oxide of iron, and afterwards allowing the mixture to cool very slowly. In fact the name for the natural substance has been borrowed from that of the artificial gold-spangled glass, which in its turn, originated in the circumstance of a workman having accidentally (par aventure) let fall some brass filings into a pot of melted glass, which he thereupon called Aventurine; and mineralogists subsequently adopted the term, and applied it to the natural substance, an imitation of which had been thus obtained by accident.

Brit. Mus., Case 21.

M. P. G. Horse-shoe Case, Nos. 535 to 542.

AVENTURINE FELSPAR. See SUNSTONE.

AVENTURINE QUARTZ. See AVENTURINE.

AUGITE, *Dana, Nicol, Phillips, Werner.* Oblique: a sub-species of Pyroxene, confined to the opaque and black or greenish-black varieties common in basaltic and volcanic rocks. It occurs crystallized, but mostly in indeterminately angular pieces and roundish grains. The crystals are generally small and imbedded, and have a vitreous lustre inclining to resinous. Streak varying from white to grey. Fracture uneven, conchoidal. Brittle. H. 5 to 6. S.G. 3·33 to 3·36.

Fig. 32.

Comp. ($\dot{C}a$, $\dot{F}e$, $\dot{M}g$)^3 ($\ddot{S}i$, $\ddot{A}l$)^2.

Analysis by *Von Waltershausen*, from Etna (*black*):

Silica	47·63
Alumina	6·74
Magnesia	12·90
Lime	20·87
Protoxide of iron	11·39
Protoxide of manganese	0·21
Water	0·28
	100·02

BB fuses, emits a few bubbles, and finally yields a glassy globule, more or less tinged by iron: readily soluble with borax.

Localities.—*Scotch.* Arthur's Seat, Edinburgh in basalt; Inchkeith, and in the Isle of Skye.—*Irish.* Portrush, in Antrim, in large, perfect, black crystals; also at Fairhead in larger but less perfect crystals.— *Foreign.* In very fine crystals imbedded in basalt, at Aussig and Töplitz in Bohemia, and in some of the scoriæ of Monti Rossi, on Etna; also in the volcanic regions of Vesuvius (in small brilliant crystals), Stromboli, Auvergne, the Eifel, Teneriffe, Bourbon, and numerous other localities.

Name. From αυγή, *brilliancy.*

Augite forms an important constituent in basaltic and volcanic rocks, but it is never found in granite rocks. The crystals met with in basalt are generally larger than those found in lava.

Brit. Mus., Case 34.

M. P. G. Horse-shoe Case, Nos. 1034 to 1038, 1042: Upper Gallery; Wall-case 1, Nos. 37 to 41: Table-cases A. and B.

AUINA, *Monticelli.* See HAÜYNE.

AUERBACHITE. A mineral nearly allied to Zircon in form and composition, but differing from it in inferior hardness and specific gravity, and greater fusibility with potash. Probably it is altered Zircon, in which a portion of the zirconia is removed. Pyramidal. Colour brownish-grey. Lustre weak, greasy. H. 6·5. S.G. 4·06.

BB alone infusible: fuses with hydrated potash.

Comp:

Silica	42·91
Zirconia	55·18
Oxide of iron	0·93
Unknown and loss	0·95
	99·97

It was named by Hermann after Dr. Auerbach.

AURICHALCITE, *Böttger, Dana.* A carbonate of zinc and copper, occurring in acicular crystals, forming drusy incrustations, or in fibrous, silky, and divergent groups; also, laminated, or columnar and granular. It is translucent, with a pearly lustre, and varies in colour from pale green to verdigris-green. H.2.

Comp. 2($\dot{Z}n$, $\dot{C}u$) $\ddot{C}$+3($\dot{Z}n$, $\dot{C}u$,) $\dot{H}$, or oxide of copper 29 2, oxide of zinc 44·7, carbonic acid 19·2, water 9·9=100.

Analysis by *Böttger*, from the Altai:

Oxide of zinc	45·62
Oxide of copper	28·35
Carbonic acid	16·07
Water	9·93
	99·97

BB gives out water in a matrass, and green crystals become brownish-black. In the outer flame does not fuse, but in the inner flame forms a slag, which is yellow while hot, but white on cooling. Yields a green glass with borax and salt of phosphorus. Soluble with effervescence in muriatic acid.

Localities.—*English:* in small groups of a pale-green colour and laminated structure, at the Rutland mine, near Matlock, in Derbyshire, and at Roughten Gill, in Cumberland. — *Foreign.* Loktefskoi, a copper-mine in the Altai, forming a drusy covering on Calc-spar and Brown Iron-ore; and at Reszbanya, in Hungary. The *Green Calamine* of Patrin is a variety of Aurichalcite, found in cavities, near Cleopinski.

AURIFEROUS PYRITES. Iron Pyrites containing minute quantities of gold. It occurs in most gold regions.

AURIFEROUS QUARTZ. Veins chiefly composed of Quartz containing Native Gold are found in North Wales, Spain, Portugal, California, Australia, and other countries. Several veins of this character occur near Dolgelly, in Merionethshirre.

Specimens of gold-bearing Quartz from the Grass Valley, Nevada county, California, will be found in the entrance-hall of the Museum of Practical Geology. See also Case 11, Principal Floor (Australia).

AUROTELLURITE. *Haidinger*. A variety of Sylvanite from Nagyag in Transylvania, where it is associated with Blende, Grey Copper ore, and Copper Pyrites, with Quartz and Brown Spar. Colour silver-white, inclining to brass-yellow, and sometimes to grey. Occurs disseminated and crystallized in very small, rather broad, four-sided prisms. Sectile. S. G. 7·99 to 8·33.

Analysis of yellow crystals, by *Petz*:

Tellurium	.	.	.	51·52
Antimony	.	.	.	5·75
Gold	.	.	.	27·10
Silver	.	.	.	7·47
Lead	.	.	.	8·16
				100·00

Affords a grass-green solution in nitric acid, with the evolution of much nitrogen. As it contains a considerable quantity both of gold and silver, Aurotellurite is worked on account of both those metals.

Brit. Mus., Case 49.

AURUM PARADOXUM, AURUM PROBLEMATICUM. } Names for Native Tellurium, used in older works on Mineralogy.

AUTOMALITE, *Nicol, Phillips*. AUTOMALITH, *Werner*. AUTOMOLITE, *Dana*. A Zinc-Spinel. Occurs in octahedrons and in tetrahedrons, of which the angles are replaced: also macled. Colour dark green or black; dark bluish-green by transmitted light. Nearly opaque. Lustre vitreous, inclining to resinous. Streak grey. Brittle. Fracture splintery or conchoidal. H. 8. S.G. 4·1 to 4·6.

Comp. Žn Äl.

Analysis from Fahlun, by *Ekeberg*:

Alumina	.	.	60·00
Oxide of zinc	.	.	24·25
Peroxide of iron	.	.	9·25
Silica	.	.	4·75
Protoxide of manganese	.	trace
			98·25

BB alone, unaltered; and nearly so with borax and salt of phosphorus. Not acted on by acids or alkalis.

Localities. Fahlun in Sweden, in talcose slate. Near Säther and Garpenberg in Sweden, compact. Franklin, New Jersey, with Quartz, Felspar, and Jeffersonite. Haddam, Connecticut; in Granite associated with Chrysoberyl, Garnet and Tantalite.

Name. From αὐτόμολος, *a deserter;* in allusion to the presence of oxide of zinc in a mineral not resembling an ore.

Brit. Mus., Case 19.

AUTUNITE, *Brooke & Miller, Greg & Lettsom*. A name given to the yellow phosphate of Uranium and Lime (Uranite) from its occurrence in the neighbourhood of Autun in France.

It has also been found in Cornwall at South Basset, Tolcarne mine, and Huel Edwards.

Fig. 33.

AXESTONE, (*Jameson*), a name for Jade; in consequence of its being used by the New Zealanders for axes and offensive weapons. See NEPHRITE.

AXINITE, *Dana, Haüy, Nicol, Phillips*. Anorthic. This mineral is seldom found massive, oftener disseminated, but most frequently crystallized in very oblique rhomboidal prisms, which are often so flat as to appear tabular. Its most common colour is violet or clove-brown of various shades, passing into plum-blue or pearl-grey, and greyish-black. Lustre brilliant externally, of fractured surface vitreous. Transparent to translucent. Streak uncoloured. Easily frangible. Fracture in transparent varieties, small and imperfectly conchoidal. Be-

  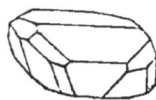

Fig. 34.   Fig. 35.   Fig. 36.

comes electric by heat or friction. Exhibits trichroism; different colours, as cinnamon-brown, violet-blue, olive-green being seen in different directions, while "on looking through a crystal in the direction of the optic axis, a dark-violet stripe is seen, which is interrupted at the point occupied by the axis." H. 6·5 to 7. S. G. 3·27.

Comp. $\ddot{R}^3 (\ddot{S}i, \ddot{B})^2 + 2 \ddot{H} (\ddot{S}i, \ddot{B})$ *Rammelsberg & Rose:* or $(\dot{C}a \ \dot{M}g \ \dot{M}n \ \dot{F}e) \ \ddot{S}i^2 + 2(\ddot{F}e \ \ddot{A}l) \ \ddot{S}i + 2 \ \dot{C}a \ \ddot{B}.$ *L. Gmelin.*

Analysis from Dauphiny, by *Rammelsberg:*

Silica	. . .	43·68
Boracic acid	. .	5·61
Alumina	. . .	15·63
Peroxide of iron	. .	9·45
Peroxide of manganese	.	3·05
Lime	. . .	20·67
Magnesia	. .	1·70
Potash	. . .	0·64
		100·43

BB melts easily, with intumescence, to a greenish-white semitransparent glass, which becomes black in the outer flame, in consequence of the manganese passing to a higher degree of oxidation. With borax dissolves readily, yielding an iron-coloured glass, which assumes a violet tint after long heating in the outer flame.

Not acted on by acid, except after fusion, and pulverisation, when it is completely dissolved in muriatic acid, with the formation of a jelly of silica.

Localities.—English. In very perfect crystals of a clove-brown colour (*figs.* 35 and 36) in Cornwall, at Botallack and Trewellard, near St. Just; also lately at Lostwithiel and St. Columb. Brent Tor, four miles north of Tavistock in Devonshire. Pseudomorphous crystals of Chlorite, with the form of the Crystals from St. Just, are found on Dartmoor.—*Foreign.* Axinite was first found at Thum, in Saxony, whence its name of Thumite or Thumerstone; it is also found at St. Christophe, near Bourg d'Oisans in Dauphiné; near Barèges in the Pyrenees; at Santa Maria in Switzerland; at the silver mines of Kongsberg in Norway, at Arendal; in Savoy; in the Harz; Coquimbo in Chili; Cold Spring in New York, &c.

Name. The name is derived from ἀξίνη, *an axe*, in allusion to the form of the crystals, which are sharp like the edge of an axe.

M.P.G. Horse-shoe Case, No. 1010.

Brit. Mus., Case 40.

AXOTOMOUS ARSE- | NIC PYRITES, *Jameson.* | See LEUCOPYRITE. | AXOTOMOUS ARSE- | NICAL PYRITES, *Mohs.* |

AXOTOMOUS IRON, *v. Kobell.* See KIBDELOPHANE.

AXOTOMOUS IRON-ORE, *Mohs.* See ILMENITE.

AZORITE, *Teschemacher, Dana.* Pyramidal. Columbate of lime, occurring in minute square pyramids, somewhat shorter proportionally than the regular octahedron. Colourless, or white with a faint greenish-yellow tinge. Translucent to opaque. Vitreous in fracture. H. 4.4 to 4·5

BB infusible; smaller crystals become opaque white, the larger become reddish in the outer flame, and pale yellow in the inner.

It is found in an albitic rock, associated with black Tourmaline and Pyrrhite in the Azores, whence the name Azorite.

AZURE COPPER-ORE, *Jameson.* Blue carbonate of copper; See CHESSYLITE.

AZURE-SPAR. AZURESTONE, *Jameson.* AZURITE, *Phillips, Jameson.* See LAZULITE. Beudant uses the term Azurite for Blue Carbonate of Copper. See CHESSYLITE.

B.

BABEL QUARTZ. A variety of Rock Crystal. Instead of tapering gradually

Fig. 37.

towards their extremities, as is the case with many crystals of Quartz, these diminish suddenly at intervals, and are built up as it were of a series of short steps, which, from their fanciful resemblance to the successive storeys of the Tower of Babel, have caused the name of Babel-Quartz to be given to this variety.

Locality. Tamar mines, Devonshire.

M. P. G. Horse-shoe Case, No. 528.

BABINGTONITE, *Levy, Dana, Nicol, Phillips.* Anorthic. Colour dark greenish-black. Lustre vitreous. Surface brilliant. Faintly translucent in splinters: appearing greenish parallel to the axis, and brown transversely

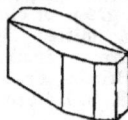 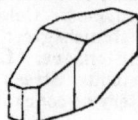

Fig. 38.   Fig. 39.

to it. Fracture imperfect conchoidal. H. 5·5. to 6. S.G. 3·35 to 3·5.

Comp. $(\dot{C}a \ \dot{F}e)^6 \ \ddot{S}i^5.$

Analysis from Arendal, by *Arppe:*

Silica	. . .	54·4
Lime	. . .	19·6

Protoxide of iron	.	.	21·3
Protoxide of manganese	.		1·8
Magnesia	.	.	2·2
Alumina	.	.	0·3
Loss by ignition	.	.	0·9

100·5

BB fuses easily on the surface to a black magnetic enamel. With borax gives a transparent amethystine-coloured bead, which becomes bluish-green in the reducing flame.

Dissolves slowly in boiling muriatic acid. Babingtonite resembles certain dark varieties of Augite. It occurs in very distinct crystals at Arendal in Norway, and in large irregular laminated crystals, imbedded in white Quartz in one of the Shetlands.

Name. After Dr. Babington.

Brit. Mus., Case 35.

BAGRATIONITE, *Kokscharow.* A variety of Allanite, having the same angles as Uralorthite.

BAIERINE, *Beudant.* The name proposed by Damour for varieties of Columbite from Limoges, which give a streak like those from Bavaria. S.G. 5·6 to 5·7.

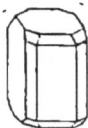

Fig. 40.

Analysis by Damour :

Columbic acid	.	.	78·44
Protoxide of iron	.		14·96
Protoxide of manganese		.	6·52

99·92

Name from Baiern, *Bavaria.*

BAIKALITE, a dingy-green coloured crystalline variety of Sahlite (Augite) found in Granite at the mouth of the Sljumanka river, which falls into lake Baikal in Siberia: hence the name Baikalite.

BAIKERITE, a chocolate-brown coloured mineral wax. It has the hardness of ordinary wax, but becomes soft with the warmth of the hand; at 52° C. (125·6° F.) it melts to an oily liquid, and at a higher temperature distils over, leaving a little carbonaceous residue. Soluble in hot ether, naphtha, and turpentine.

Analysis :

Wax-like substance insoluble in alcohol.	.	.	.	7·02
Wax-like substance soluble in do.				60 18

Thick fluid resin	.	.	32·41
Earthy impurities	.	.	0·39

100·00

Locality. The vicinity of Lake Baikal in Siberia.

Brit. Mus., Case 34.

BALAIS RUBY, BALAS RUBY: BALASS RUBY, *Kirwan.* The name given to the rose-red varieties of Spinel. The Balas Ruby is held in much less estimation than either Oriental or Spinel Ruby, and is often confounded with burnt Topaz. Nevertheless it is sometimes employed in jewelry, and fetches a high price; a fine stone of 24 to 30 carats, being worth from 8*l.* to 16*l.* In an oriental work on jewels, entitled *Khawās-ul-hejar,* the stone is treated of under the name of *Balaksh* (Balakshan being synonomous with Badakshan). Hence the European name— Balas Ruby, or Ruby of Badakshan.

The Rubinus Balassius or Pallacius, was one of the gems included by the ancients under the general name Carbuncle: probably it is the *Carbunculus amethystizontes* of Pliny.

BALLESTEROSITE, a variety of Pyrites from Gallicia, containing traces of zinc and tin.

BALTIMORITE, *Thomson.* A mineral of a greyish-green colour, composed of longitudinal fibres adhering to each other. It is opaque, but translucent at very thin edges. Lustre silky. Hardness very little less than Calc-spar, or nearly 3.

Analysis :

Silica	.	.	.	.	40·95
Magnesia	.	.	.	34·70
Oxide of iron	.	.	.	10·05
Alumina	.	.	.	1·50
Water	.	.	.	12·60

99 80

BB infusible, but turns brown: with soda melts to an opaque, with borax to a transparent bead.

This mineral bears considerable resemblance to Asbestos, but the latter contains more silica and much lime, which is absent in Baltimorite.

The name was given by Dr. Thomson, who first examined it, from its being found at Baltimore, U.S. It also occurs dark green and fibrous at Killin in Perthshire.

Brit. Mus., Case 25.

BAMLITE, *Erdmann.* A mineral with the structure and appearance of some kinds of Kyanite. Occurs in oblique and generally strongly striated, four-sided prisms: also massive and radiated plumose. Colour greyish or greenish-white, or bluish-green. Translucent. Lustre silky. Fracture uneven and splintery. H. 6 to 7. S. G. 2·984.

Comp. $\ddot{A}l^4 \ddot{S}i^6$, or alumina 42·4, silica 57·6 = 100.

Analysis by Erdmann :

Silica . . . . . 56·90
Alumina . . . . 40·73
Peroxide of iron . . . 1·04
Lime . . . . . 1·04
Fluorine . . . . trace
———
99·71

BB infusible.'
Localities. Bamle (whence the name *Bamlite*) and Brakka in Norway, in gneiss.
BAND JASPIS, *Werner.* See RIBBON JASPER.

BARALITE, *Dana.* Occurs massive and cellular. Colour greenish-black. Opaque. Lustre glimmering. Streak greyish-green. H. 4.
Comp. Silica, alumina, peroxide of iron, lime, magnesia and water.
BB alone infusible. Wholly soluble in muriatic acid.
Locality. Baralon, Côte-du-Nord,'France.
BARBADOES TAR. See PETROLEUM.
BARNHARDTITE. Occurs massive, of a pale bronze-yellow colour, resembling that of Pyrites, but with a less bright lustre. Tarnishes readily to pinchbeck and iridescent tints. Streak black, and slightly shining.

Comp. 2 Cu S + Fe² S³.
Analysis by Taylor.

Sulphur . . . . 29·40
Copper . . . . 47·61
Iron . . . . 22·23
Silver . . . . trace
———
99·24

BB gives off fumes of sulphur, and melts to an iron-black magnetic globule.
Localities. United States, in a mine on the land of Dan Barnhard (whence the name Barnhardtite), Cabarras co., North Carolina; near Pioneer Mills, and at the Phœnix and Vanderberg mines, and near Charlotte in Mecklenburg co.
BAROLITE, *Kirwan.* Witherite; the name derived from βαρύς, *heavy,* and λίθος, *stone,* has reference to its high specific gravity.
BAROSELENITE. The name used by Kirwan for Barytes; derived from βαρύς, *heavy,* and *Selenite,* in allusion to its high specific gravity, and the resemblance some of its crystals bear to those of Selenite.
Brit. Mus., Case 52.

BARSOWITE, *Brook & Miller.* A Felspathic mineral occurring in boulders in the auriferous sand of Barsowkoi, near Kyschtimsk, in the Ural, as the gangue of the blue Corundum. It is found massive, of a snow-white colour, and a more or less pearly lustre. Texture granular, with a nearly perfect cleavage in one direction. Fracture granular, or splintery. H. 5·5 to 6. S.G. 2·74 to 2·75.

Comp. $\dot{C}a^3 \ddot{S}i^2 + 3 \ddot{A}l \ddot{S}i = (\dot{C}a + \ddot{A}l) \ddot{S}i\frac{3}{4}$.
Analysis by *Varrentrapp :*

Silica . . . . 49·01
Alumina 33.85
Lime . . . . 15·46
Magnesia . . . . 1·55
———
99·87

BB alone fuses to a vesicular glass at the edges: with borax melts slowly to a colourless glass.
Gelatinises easily on being heated with muriatic acid.
BARYSTRONTIANITE, *Traill.* The mineral to which this name has been given is not a distinct species, but a mechanical mixture found at an old lead mine two miles west of Stromness, on Pomona, or Mainland, one of the Orkneys; and on the beach at the Point of Ness. It occurs in yellowish-white aggregations, with a dull pearly lustre. It consists of

Strontianite . . . 68·6
Barytes . . . 27·5
Carbonate of lime . . 2·6
Oxide of iron . . . 0·1
———
100·0

BARYTA, CARBONATE OF. See WITHERITE.
BARYTA, BICALCAREO-CARBONATE OF. See ALSTONITE and BROMLITE.
BARYTA, SULPHATE OF. See BARYTES.
BARYTA, SULPHATO-CARBONATE OF. See SULPHATO-CARBONATE OF BARYTA.
BARYTA HARMOTOME. See HARMOTOME.
BARYTE CARBONATÉE. See WITHERITE.
BARYTE, *Brooke & Miller.* BARYTE SULFATÉE, *Haüy.* BARYTES, *Dana, Greg & Lettsom, Phillips.* Rhombic. Occurs massive and crystallized, with a lamellar structure, which in the massive varieties is sometimes curved; also fibrous or granular. Colourless, or inclining to yellow, blue, red, grey, or brown. Transparent to opaque. Lustre vitreous, inclining to resinous. Streak white. Possesses double refraction when held in a particular direc-

tion. Sometimes fetid when rubbed. II.
2·5 to 3·5. S.G. 4·3 to 4·7.

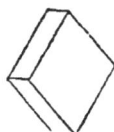   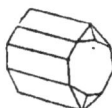   

Fig. 41.   Fig. 42.   Fig. 43.

Comp. Ba S̈. = sulphuric acid 24·33, baryta 65·67; but, part of the baryta is frequently replaced by strontia, and oxide of iron, silica, carbonate of lime and alumina occur sometimes as impurities.

BB decrepitates violently, and melts with great difficulty or only at the edges, imparting a yellowish-green colour to the flame. In the inner flame reduced to a sulphide, which when moistened, smells slightly hepatic. Not acted on by acids.

May be distinguished from Strontia by not tinging the flame red when tested with muriatic acid and alcohol.

Localities.—British. The finest crystallized specimens found in the United Kingdom have been procured from Dufton in Cumberland, see *fig.* 41. Very large and perfect detached crystals occur in the mud at the bottom of a cave at Silverband near Dufton; one of them has been found weighing 1 cwt. Fine translucent dagger-shaped crystals of a yellowish-white tint occur at the iron mines at Cleator moor in Cumberland; *fig.* 43.' *Figs.* 42 and 43 represent Cornish forms. Other British localities are the Fullers' Earth pits at Nutfield, near Reigate in Surrey; Leadhills in Lanarkshire, *figs.* 41 and 42; Breidden Hills, Shropshire; Wotherton in Derbyshire; Co. Cork; &c.—*Foreign.* Pzzibram and Mies in Bohemia; Felsobanya and Kremnitz in Hungary; Freiberg, Marienberg, Clausthal; Roya, and Raure, in Auvergne.

Name. From βαϱὺς, heavy.

Barytes is a very widely diffused mineral, and commonly occurs in beds or veins of metallic ores; when associated with ores of iron it exercises an injurious influence on the process of smelting. It sometimes forms veins in secondary limestone.

The following have been described as subspecies, though differing only in appearance: 1. *Granular Heavy Spar*: 2. *Columnar Heavy Spar*: 3. *Radiated Heavy Spar, or Bolognese Stone*: 4. *Hepatite*: 5. *Cawk.*

The white varieties of Barytes are ground, after having been heated and thrown into water, and used as a pigment, either alone or mixed with white-lead. It has, also, lately been proposed to employ Barytes in sugar-refining. Most of its salts are highly poisonous. The nitrate is used in pyrotechny for making *green fire*, in the following proportion: Nitrate of Barytes 77, Flowers of Sulphur 13, Chlorate of Potash 5, Metallic Arsenic 2, Charcoal 3. In the year 1847, 10,320 tons of Barytes, worth about 1*l.* per ton, for grinding, were raised in the United Kingdom, principally in Shropshire and Derbyshire.

Brit. Mus., Case 52.

M.P.G. The largest crystal of Barytes ever found in the United Kingdom is placed on the floor at the S.E. end of the Horseshoe Case. It weighs 100lbs. See also Horseshoe Case Nos. 241 to 254.

BARYTINE, *Beudant.* See BARYTES.

BARYTOCALCITE, *Brooke.* Oblique. Primary form an oblique rhombic prism. Occurs massive and crystallized. White, yellowish, greyish or greenish. Transparent or translucent, with a vitreous lustre inclining to resinous. Streak white. Brittle. Fracture imperfect conchoidal. H. 4. S.G. 3·6 to 3·7.

Fig. 44.   Fig. 45

Comp. Ba C̈ + Ca C̈=carbonate of baryta 66·3, carbonate of lime 33·7 = 100·0.

Analyses; *a.* by *Children,* *b.* by *Delesse:*

	a.	*b.*
Carbonate of baryta	65·9	66·20
Carbonate of lime .	33·6	31·89
Silica . .	„	0·27
	99·5	98·36

BB infusible alone, becomes cloudy, and gives a yellowish-green colour to the flame. With borax fuses to a transparent glass, in the oxidating flame of a pale amethystine tinge, which becomes colourless in the inner flame.

Soluble with effervescence in muriatic acid.

Localities. It occurs plentifully, both crystallized and massive, in veins in Mountain Limestone, at Bleagill, Alston Moor, Cumberland. The crystals are greyish-white, and semi-transparent. Sometimes crystals two inches long are met with, but in gene ral they do not exceed half an inch to an inch in length. The larger crystals are frequently decomposed, and converted into a white mealy-looking substance like Barytes. Brit. Mus., Case 41.

BARYTO-CALCITE, *Thomson*. See LEEDSITE.

BARYTO-CELESTINE, *Thomson*. The mineral from Kingston and Sydenham, Canada W., so called by Thomson, is pure Celestine.

BARYTOPHYLLIT, *Breithaupt*. See CHLORITOID.

BASALT-JASPER, a name given to semi-vitrified on porcellanic shales.

BASALTINE, the name given by Kirwan to crystallized Hornblende, because it is "mostly found in basalts and lava."

BASANITE. See LYDIAN STONE.

BASANOMELANE, *Kobell*. Titaniferous Iron; according to Breithaupt, a variety of Hystatite.

Analysis from Gastein in Switzerland, by v. *Kobell* :

Protoxide of iron	5·01
Peroxide of iron	85·33
Titanic acid	9·66
	100·00

Name. From βάσανος, *touchstone*, and μίλας, *black*.

BASIC FLUCERIEN. See FLUCERINE.

BASICERINE, *Beudant*. See FLUOCERINE.

BASISCHES SCHWEFELSAURES EISENOXYD. See COPIAPITE.

BASTITE, *Brooke & Miller*. A name given to Schiller Spar from its occurrence at Baste in the Harz.

BATRACHITE, *Breithaupt*. A variety of Chrysolite in which a great part of the Magnesia is replaced by lime. ($\dot{C}a^5 \ddot{M}g^2$) $\ddot{S}i$. It occurs massive, exhibiting traces of a rhombic prism. Colour pale greenish-grey to nearly white. Lustre resinous inclining to vitreous. Streak white. Fracture small conchoidal. H. 5. S.G. 3·03.

BB infusible alone; slowly soluble in salt of phosphorus leaving a silica residue; with soda fuses with difficulty to a dark-coloured pearl.

Not acted on by acids.

Locality. Rinzoniberg, a mountain in Southern Tyrol.

Name. From βάτραχος, *a frog*, from its resemblance to the colour of that animal. Brit. Mus., Case 25.

BAVALITE, *Dufrénoy*. A silico-aluminate of oolitic iron, analogous to the Chamoisite and Berthierine of Hayanges, but of a some-

what deeper colour. It is found at Bavalon (Côtes-du-Nord).

BAUDISSERITE. A name given to Magnesite, from its occurrence at Baudissero in Piedmont.

BAULITE. A variety of Krablite, resembling pitchstone and pearlstone; formerly ejected abundantly from the volcanoes of Iceland and Faroe. Occurs in globular masses sometimes with a radiated and concentric fracture. S.G. 2·623.

Soluble in muriatic acid.

Name. After the mountain of Baula in Iceland.

Brit. Mus., Case 30.

BEAUME DE MOMIE. See ASPHALT. The colour *momie*, made from Asphalt, received its name from the circumstance of the material being sometimes taken from Egyptian mummies, that being supposed to be of the finest quality.

BEAUMONTITE. The minute crystals, seldom exceeding a line in length, occurring on syenite-schist with Haydenite, at Jones's Falls, near Baltimore, U. S., have been described by Levy, under the name of Beaumontite, as modified square prisms. Dana has shown that the form cannot be a square prism. In physical and other characters the crystals resemble Heulandite. S.G. 2·24. An analysis by Delesse afforded

Silica	64·2
Alumina	14·1
Protoxide of iron	1·2
Lime	4·8
Magnesia	1·7
Loss and soda	0·6
Water	13·4
	100·0

Name. After Élie de Beaumont, Professor of Geology at the École des Mines, Paris.

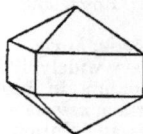

Fig. 46.

BEEKITE, *Kengott, W. Pengelly*. This is not, strictly speaking, a distinct mineral species, but merely a particular form of Chalcedony deposited on fossils, either sponges, corals, or shells—generally spiral univalves. It occurs in New Red Conglomerate in rounded masses, resembling the pebbles with which they are associated, and similar to them both in form and dimensions. The Beekites, as these rounded masses are called, vary in diameter from half an inch to a foot, but they rarely exceed from three to six inches in diameter. Their surfaces are composed of Chalcedony, generally arranged in tubercles varying in size from a pin's head to a pea, each of which is not unfrequently surrounded by one or more rings, and occasionally the same ring invests two or even more tubercles.

When broken the interior is most commonly found to be calcareous, and in a decomposing state. Occasionally the nucleus has entirely decomposed; in which case only a few grains of matter remain within the crust, and the Beekite will float in water.

Localities.—British. A very few specimens have been found in Carboniferous Limestone, near Sidcot, in Somersetshire, and in the north of Scotland. They are, however, found in every part of the Conglomerate of Torbay, in Devonshire, from Goodrington Sands on the south, to Tor-Abbey Sands on the north; but they are considerably more abundant at Livermead Head, and at and near Paignton Harbour than elsewhere in the district. — *Foreign.* Beekites have also been found in Australia, in Triassic Conglomerates, and on the banks of the Nerbuddah in India.

Name. After Dr. Beeke, dean of Bristol, by whom they were first publicly noticed.

BEETLE OR BETTLE-STONES. Names sometimes given in S. Wales to septarian nodules of Clay Ironstone from the Coalmeasures.

BEILSTEIN, *Werner.* See NEPHRITE.

BELL-METAL ORE. A name given to Tin Pyrites, from its resemblance in appearance to bronze, or bell-metal.

BELONIT, *Glocker.* See AIKENITE.

BERAUNITE, *Breithaupt.* A variety of Delvauxene, resulting from the decomposition of Vivianite. It occurs foliated and radiated, with one perfect and one imperfect cleavage. Colour hyacinth-red, or reddish-brown. Streak reddish, ochreous-yellow.

Comp. Hydrous phosphate of peroxide of iron.

BB fuses and colours the flame bluish-green.

Soluble in muriatic acid.

Localities.— English. Huel Jane, near Truro in Cornwall, in scaly and brittle masses, associated with Vivianite on Eisen-nickel-kies.—*Foreign.* Near Beraun (whence the name *Beraunite*) in Bohemia, in Limonite. Near Kertch in the Crimea.

Brit. Mus., Case 57.

BERENGELITE. A mineral near Guayquillite, described by Prof. Johnston. Colour dark brown with a green tinge. Lustre and fracture resinous. Powder yellow. Odour resinous and disagreeable. Taste slightly bitter.

Comp. $C^{40} H^{31} O^{8}$.

Analysis :

Carbon	.	.	.	72·472
Hydrogen	.	.	.	9·198
Oxygen	.	.	.	18·330
				100·000

Forms a bitter solution with cold alcohol. A resin of a clear red colour is obtained by evaporation, and remains soft and viscid at the ordinary temperature.

Locality. It forms a lake like the Pitch-lake of Trinidad (*see* Asphaltum) in the province of St. Juan de Berengela (whence the name *Berengelite*), about one hundred miles from Arica in Peru, and is used instead of pitch for paying boats and vessels.

BERGBUTTER, *Werner.* Rock-Butter. See PETROLEUM.

BERGCRYSTAL, *German.* See Rock-Crystal.

BERGHOLZ, *Sterzing.* Probably an altered Chrysotile. See XYLOLITE.

BERGHOLZ, *Werner.* See ROCKWOOD.

BERGMANNITE. A brick-red or greyish-white Natrolite, occurring massive in Zircon-syenite, near Brevig and Stavern in Norway; and shown by R. Blum to result from the alteration of Elæolite.

Analyses by Scheerer :

		Red.	White.
Silica	. .	47·97	48·12
Alumina	. .	26·62	26·96
Peroxide of iron	.	0·73	0·22
Soda	. .	14·07	14·23
Lime	. .	0·68	0·69
Potash	. .	trace	trace
Water	. .	9·77	10·48
		99·88	100·7

Brit. Mus., Case 31.

BERGMEHL, *Fabbroni, Widenman.* See MOUNTAIN-MEAL.

BERGMILCH, *Werner.* See AGARIC-MINERAL.

BERGPECH. See ASPHALT.

BERGSEIFE, *Werner.* See ROCK-SOAP.

BERGTHEER, *Hausmann.* See ASPHALT.

BERIL NOBLE, *Brochant.* BERILI, *Werner.* BERILLUS, *Wallerius.* See BERYL.

BERNERDE. See RETINITE.

BERNSTEIN, *Werner.* See AMBER.

BERTHIERITE, *Phillips, Nicol, Dana.* Is

not found crystallized, but in indistinct elongated prisms or confusedly lamellar masses, with a longitudinal cleavage parallel to the axis of the prism. Colour dark steel-grey, inclining to pinchbeck-brown; surface often covered with iridescent spots. Lustre metallic. H. 2 to 3. S.G. 4 to 4·3.

Comp. Fe S + Sb² S³ = Sulphur 28·9, antimony 58·4, iron 12·7.

Analysis of specimens from the Neue Hoffnung Gottes, near Freiberg, by *C. v. Hauer* :

Sulphur	. . .	30·53
Iron	. . .	10·16
Antimony	. . .	59·30
		99·99

BB fuses readily, emits vapours of antimony, and forms a black magnetic slag. Gives an iron reaction with fluxes.

Dissolves readily in muriatic acid, giving out sulphuretted hydrogen.

Localities. Chazelles and Martourel in Auvergne, associated with Quartz, Calc-spar, and Iron Pyrites; Commune of Lalaye, in the Vosges; Braunsdorf in Saxony; Arany Idka in Hungary; the neighbourhood of Padstow in Cornwall, of a steel-grey colour, and with a fibro-crystalline structure.

Name. This mineral was first discovered and described by M. Berthier, who called it Haidingerite, after his friend Mr. Haidinger; but his name being already associated with another species, Mr. Haidinger proposed the present name in compliment to the original discoverer.

Berthierite yields antimony of such inferior quality, as to be worthless as an ore of that metal.

Brit. Mus., Case 11.

BERYL. A variety of Emerald, possessing the same crystalline form, hardness and specific gravity, and differing from it only in colour. H. 7·5 to 8. S.G. 2·67 to 2·732.

Fig. 47.   Fig. 47*.

Comp. ($\ddot{Be}$ + $\ddot{Al}$) $\dddot{Si}$² = $\ddot{Be}$ + $\ddot{Al}$ + 4$\dddot{Si}$ = Glucina 14·1, alumina 19·0, silica 66·9 = 100·0.

Analyses : *a.* from Siberia, by *Du Menil*; *b.* from Hirschgasse by *Bornträger* :

			a.	b.
Silica	.	.	67·00	66·90
Alumina	.	.	16·50	18·15
Glucina	.	.	14·50	12·20

Peroxide of iron	.	1·00	2·95
Lime	. . .	0·50	„
		99·50	100·20

From these analyses it appears that the colouring matter is oxide of iron. Sometimes the same crystal is of two or even more colours, and occasionally it is iridescent. Some Beryls are quite colourless, but the colours are generally blue or yellow. The crystals (six-sided prisms) are of very variable dimensions, from mere threads to a foot or more in length, and 4 inches in thickness; but the latter are never sufficiently perfect or transparent to be used in jewelry. The finest Beryls are described by Pliny as those " qui viridatem puri maris imitantur," which are of a clear sea-green colour, hence, crystals of clear tints of sea-green or sky-blue are called Aqua-marinas, or Aquamarines. The Beryl when of good colour is best cut into facets. The greenish-yellow variety is sometimes mistaken for Chrysoberyl, but may be distinguished from it by its inferior lustre, hardness and specific gravity. Pebbles of Quartz are sometimes taken for Beryls, and *vice versâ*. The two may be distinguished by observing that the crystals of Beryl are striated longitudinally, while those of Quartz are striated transversely, or at right angles to the axis of the prism. Moreover the fracture of the two minerals is widely different, for the Beryl breaks in smooth planes, the faces of which are at right angles to the axis of the crystals, whereas the fractured surface of Quartz is invariably conchoidal.

Localities.—English. Beryls are found in Cornwall, at St. Michael's Mount, in small bluish crystals in Mabe parish, 3 miles west of Falmouth, and in the parish of Constantine; also amorphous at Huel Castle near St. Just.—*Scotch.* Kinloch Rannoch. Mount Baltoch, in diverging prisms of a pale green in Granite. With Topaz, near Braemar, in the alluvium of the Don and Dee. In the granite and gneiss of Cairngorm, Banffshire, and in primary limestone at Portsoy.—*Irish.* Very fine specimens, mostly of a fine blue, sometimes quite transparent and of considerable size, in the Mourne mountains, of co. Down. On the north-west side of the small lake on Binion Hill. In fine radiating crystals on Slieve Havila, and on the Chimney Rock mountain. Also in Dublin co., in the neighbourhood of Killiney and Dalkey; at the Three Rock mountain, and at Stillorgan. Near Round Wood, in Glen Malure, and also in Glen Macnass, Wicklow.—*Foreign.* Siberia, in the granite district of

Nertschinsk, and in the Uralian and Altai mountains. Limoges in France; Finbo and Broddbo in Sweden; Pfitscher Joch in the Tyrol. Bodenmais and Rabenstein in Bavaria; the island of Elba; the mines of Schlackenwald; Australia and the East Indies.

Beryls of gigantic dimensions have been found in the United States, at Acworth and Grafton, N.H., and Royalston, Mass. One Beryl from Grafton, N.H., weighs 2900 lbs.; it is 32 inches through in one direction and 22 in another, transverse, and is 4 feet 3 inches long. Another crystal from this locality, according to Prof. Hubbard, measures 45 inches by 24 in its diameters, and a single foot in length; by calculation it weighs 1076 lbs. At Royalston one crystal exceeded a foot in length. A gigantic opaque Beryl from North America, unfit for jewelry, weighing 80 lbs., was in the Great Exhibition of 1851. There is also one of about the same size, but of more perfect form, in the British Museum. It is also found in Siberia, Hindostan and Brazil.

In Mr. Turner's collection there is a crystal of Beryl, exhibiting decided opalescence, and showing a six-rayed star like some varieties of Corundum.

The name is derived from the Persian *belur*, changed by the Romans into *beryllus*.

Brit. Mus., Case 37.

M.P.G. Horse-shoe Case, Nos. 810 to 817, 823, 825.

BERZELIANITE, or Selenite of Copper. Occurs in thin dendritic crusts, having an impalpable composition. Colour silver-white, with a metallic lustre, and a shining streak. Soft, and when rubbed down and polished, assumes the colour of tin.

Comp. Cu Se = Selenium 38·4, copper 61·6.

BB emits fumes of Selenium, and fuses to a grey bead, which is slightly malleable. With soda, slowly reduced.

This mineral is generally found in minute seams traversing Calc-spar, or as dendritic delineations of a black colour, owing to the decomposition it undergoes from exposure to the air. It comes from the copper mine of Scrickerum, in Smaland, Sweden, and near Lehrbach in the Harz.

BERZELIIT, *Kuhn.* See KUHNITE.

BERZELIN, *Necker.* See HAÜYNE.

BERZELINE. The name given by Beudant to Selenide of Copper. See BERZELIANITE.

BERZELINE, *Necker, Phillips.* A mineral near Leucite in composition, found in Peperino at Monte Albano and San Marino near Rome; and also at Galloro, near La Riccia, in the drusy cavities of an augitic

rock. It occurs in extremely minute white octahedrons and cubo-octahedrons, as well as in twin crystals, the faces of which are often uneven and rounded, and dull superficially: also massive. It is colourless, white or grey, with a vitreous lustre, and is slightly translucent and very brittle. H. 5. S.G. 2·727, to 2·428.

BB in the forceps, fuses with difficulty to a pale glass.

With heated muriatic acid forms a greenish jelly.

Name. After Berzelius, the Swedish chemist.

Brit. Mus., Case 4.

BEUDANITE, *Covelli.* See NEPHELINE.

BEUDANTITE, occurs in aggregations of small slightly obtuse rhombs, with the summits truncated. Colours black and brown. Opaque. Translucent in thin fragments, and of a deep brown colour by transmitted light. Lustre resinous, streak greenish-grey. H. 4 to 4·5. S.G. 4·295.

Comp. $2\dot{P}b \ \ddot{S} + \ddot{F}e \ \ddot{S} + \ddot{F}e^3 \ \dddot{P} + 9 \dot{H}$ or $2\dot{P}b^3 \ \dddot{P} + \ddot{F}e^3 \ \dddot{P} + 9\ddot{F}e \ \ddot{S} + 27\dot{H}.$

Analysis by Dr. John Percy:

Arsenic acid	9·68
Phosphoric acid	1·46
Silica	12·31
Peroxide of iron	42·46
Oxide of lead	24·47
Water	8·49
	98·19

BB infusible, but gives off odours of sulphurous acid, and deposits a yellow coating on the charcoal. With fluxes gives the reaction of iron and some copper.

Muriatic acid attacks the powder slowly when boiled, forming a reddish-yellow solution.

Beudantite has been referred to Pharmacosiderite (Cube Ore), but the above analysis shows that it must be a distinct mineral.

Localities. Associated with Brown Iron-ore at Horrhausen and Montabaur (Dernbach) in the district of Nassau, on the Rhine; also found by Dr. Krantz, in 1856, at the Glendore iron mine near Cork. The crystals from this locality are small but very brilliant and distinct, resembling Pharmacosiderite of a brown colour and translucent. The crystals from Dernbach and Cork contain little or no arsenic, while in those from Horrhausen arsenic acid almost entirely replaces the phosphoric.

Name. After Beudant, the French mineralogist.

BEURRE DE MONTAGNE, *Dufrénoy.*
Mountain Butter. See PETROLEUM.

BEZOAR MINERALE, *J. Woodward.* Stones
composed commonly of several crusts one
within another, and having the crusts close
and cohering without any internal cavity.

BICARBONATE OF AMMONIA. Occurs in
yellowish to white crystals in the guano deposits on the coasts of Africa and Patagonia
and the Chinca Islands. H. 1·5.   S.G. 1·45.

Comp. $NH^4O\ddot{C}^2 + \dot{H}$ = ammonia 32·91,
carbonic acid 55·69, water 11·40 = 100.

BILDSTEIN, *Werner.* See AGALMATOLITE.

BIMSTEIN, *German.* See PUMICE.

BIOTINA, or BIOTINE. The name given by
Monticelli to the Anorthite found by him
among the old lavas at Mount Vesuvius. It
is easily distinguished from other species
with which it is associated by its superior
brilliancy.   Colour white or yellowish.
Transparent.   Fracture vitreous, inclined to
conchoidal.   Presents double refraction.
BB unchanged.
Partly soluble in nitric acid.
Name. In honour of M. Biot.

BIEBRITE.   Oblique.   Usually occurs
in stalactites and crusts investing other
minerals. Colour flesh- and rose-red. Lustre
vitreous.   Translucent.   Friable.   Taste astringent.

Comp. $(\dot{C}o, \dot{M}g)\,\ddot{S} + 7\,\dot{H}.$

Analysis by *Winkelblech:*

Sulphuric acid	29·05
Oxide of cobalt	19·90
Magnesia	3·86
Water	46·83
	99·65

BB imparts a blue colour to glass of borax.
This mineral is found in the rubbish of old
mines at Bieber (whence the name *Biebrite*)
near Hanau; at Leogang in Saltzburg, and
at Tres Puntos, near Copiapo, in Chili.

BIEGSAMER SILBERGLANZ. See FLEXIBLE
SILVER ORE.

BINNITE, *Heusser.* A mineral identical
with Enargite except in crystallization. It
occurs in longitudinally striated, right rhombic prisms.   Colour steel-grey to black.
Streak a little darker than Dufrenoysite.
Brittle.   Fracture conchoidal.

Locality.—Found with Dufrenoysite in
the Dolomite of Binnen Valley, in Valais.

BIOTITE, *Brooke & Miller, Dana, Greg &
Lettsom, Hausmann.* Rhombic. Occurs
in six-sided tabular prisms, with a highly
perfect basal cleavage. Sectile; thin laminæ

flexible and elastic. Sometimes white or
colourless, but generally dark-green or
brown or nearly black. Lustre vitreous.
Transparent to opaque.   Streak uncoloured.
Optically uniaxial.   H. 2·5 to 3.   S.G. 2·7
to 3·1.

Fig. 48.

Comp. $(\dot{M}g, \dot{F}e, \dot{K})^3\,\ddot{S}i + (\ddot{A}l\,\ddot{F}e)\,\ddot{S}i.$
Analysis of a black Mica from Pfitsch in
Tyrol, by *F. Bukeisen:*

Silica	38·43
Alumina	15·71
Protoxide of iron	13·04
Magnesia	17·28
Potash	11·42
Lime, manganese, and fluorine	trace
Water	2·76
	99·64

BB fuses with difficulty to a grey or black
glass.
Biotite may be distinguished from biaxial
Mica by being completely decomposed by
concentrated sulphuric acid, leaving a residue of pearly scales of silica.

Localities. Inverness in Scotland; Skye,
fig. 48; Vesuvius (see MEROXENE).

Name. After Professor Biot, who first
pointed out the optical differences between
various kinds of Mica.

Brit. Mus., Case 32.

BIROUSA. The Persian name for Turquois.

BISMUTH-BLENDE, *Phillips.* See EULY-
TINE.

BISMUTH-GLANCE, *Jameson.*   See BIS-
MUTHINE.

BISMUTH-NICKEL. See GRÜNAUITE.

BISMUTH-OCHRE, *Jameson, Kirwan.*
Crystalline form, according to Von Born,
that of cubes or quadrangular lamellæ. Occurs massive or disseminated; pulverulent,
earthy.   Colour straw-yellow, sometimes
passing into pale yellowish-grey and ash-
grey, or verging on apple-green. Lustre
glimmering, dull in earthy specimens.
Opaque. Easily frangible. Fracture small-
grained, uneven or earthy. S.G. 4·36.

Comp. $\ddot{B}i$ = oxygen 10·35, bismuth 89·65,
= 100, with iron and other impurities.

Analysis by *Lampadius:*

Oxide of bismuth	86·4
„ „ iron	5·1
Carbonic acid	4·1
Water	3·4
	99·0

BB on charcoal, easily reduced to the metallic state, and is volatilized if the heat be continued. Soluble with effervescence in acid.

Localities. — *English.* Cornwall at Cost-all-lost Mine, St. Roach, and at the Royal Iron Mine near Lostwithiel. — *Foreign.* Pulverulent at Schneeberg and Johanngeorgenstadt in Saxony; Joachimstahl in Bohemia; with plumbo-cupriferous sulphide of bismuth and native gold at Beresof in Siberia.

Bismuth-ochre has been often mistaken for Green Iron-ore, from which it may be distinguished by its external aspect, and by the minerals which accompany it.

It occurs with Native Bismuth, and is also accompanied by Quartz and Brown Spar.

BISMUTH GLANCE. See BISMUTHINE.

BISMUTH SILVER, *Dana*; BISMUTHIC SILVER, *Phillips*; BISMUTHIC SILVER-ORE, *Kirwan.* Probably either cubical or hexagonal. Generally in amorphous masses; rarely in acicular or capillary crystals. Colour tin-white or greyish, subject to tarnish. Lustre metallic. Opaque. Fracture uneven. Sectile. Soft.

Analysis by *Klaproth:*

Bismuth	.	.	.	. 27·0
Lead	.	.	.	. 33·0
Silver	.	.	.	. 15·0
Iron	.	.	.	. 4·3
Copper	.	.	.	. 0·9
Sulphur	.	.	.	. 16·3

96·5

BB melts readily to a silvery bead, covering the charcoal with the oxides of lead and bismuth, and giving off fumes of sulphur.

Soluble in nitric acid.

Localities. With Copper Pyrites, in small amorphous masses, at Schapbach, in the Valley of Kinzig in Baden; in the cupreous shale of Mansfeld in Thuringia, and at the mine of S. Antonio, near Copiapo, Chili. It was formerly worked as an ore of silver.

BISMUTH OXIDÉ, *Haüy.* See BISMUTH OCHRE.

BISMUTH SULFURÉ, *Haüy.* See BISMUTHINE.

BISMUTH SULFURÉ PLOMBO-ARGENTIFÈRE, *Levy.* See BISMUTH SILVER.

BISMUTH SULFURÉ PLOMBO-CUPRIFÈRE, *Haüy.* See AIKENITE.

BISMUTHINE, *Brooke & Miller, Beudant, Greg & Lettsom.* Rhombic. Primary

form a right rhombic prism. Occurs in acicular prisms, and in minute crystals deeply striated longitudinally; also massive or coarsely disseminated with a foliated structure like that of Galena, or a fibrous one like Antimony. Colour and streak tin-white or lead-grey, sometimes yellowish-white, with an iridescent tarnish. Lustre metallic. Opaque. Soft and brittle. H. 2 to 2·5. S.G. 6·4 to 6·5.

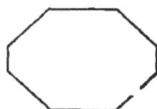

Fig. 49.　　　　Fig. 50.

Comp. Bi^2 S^3 = sulphur 18·4, bismuth 81·6.
Analysis from Cornwall, by *Rammelsberg:*

Sulphur	.	.	.	. 18·42
Bismuth	.	.	.	. 78·00
Iron	.	.	.	. 1·04
Copper	.	.	.	. 2·42

99·88

Melts in the flame of a candle. *BB* melts easily with a blue flame and sulphurous smell; if the heat be continued it is for the most part volatilized, emitting numerous small drops in an incandescent state, covering the charcoal with yellow, and leaving a residue which is reducible with difficulty to the metallic state.

Readily soluble in hot nitric acid; and yields a white precipitate on dilution with water.

Localities.—English. In Cornwall (*fig.* 49) at Dolcoath, near Camborne; St. Just, Botallack; Fowey Consols mine; Huel Arthur; George and Charlotte mine near Callington; near Tavistock; also in Cumberland at Brandy Gill, Carrock Fells, &c.—*Foreign.* Joachimsthal, and Schlackenwald in Bohemia; Johanngeorgenstadt, Schwarzenberg, Altenberg and Schneeberg in Saxony; foliated with Cerite at Bastnäs near Riddarhytta in Sweden; with Chrysoberyl at Haddam, Connecticut, U.S. Tal-ca in Chili.

M. P. G. Principal Floor, Wall-case 9 (British).

BISMUTITE, *Breithaupt, Dana.* Occurs in pseudomorphous acicular crystals; also incrusting and amorphous. Colour white, and dull mountain-green, occasionally straw-yellow and yellowish-grey. Lustre vitreous when pure, sometimes dull. Streak greenish-grey or colourless. Subtranslucent to opaque. Brittle. H. 4 to 4·5 S.G. 6·86 to 7·67.

Comp. $\ddot{B}i^4\,\ddot{C}^3H^4$=oxide of bismuth 90·28, carbonic acid 6.29, water 3·43=100.

Analysis, from South Carolina, by *Rammelsberg*:

Bismuth	90·00
Carbonic acid . . .	6·56
Water	3·44
	100·00

Melts on a burning coal, and is reduced with effervescence to a metallic globule, covering the coal with white oxide of bismuth.

Soluble in muriatic acid, affording a deep yellow solution.

Localities. In small amorphous pieces at Joachimsthal in Bohemia, with small longish prisms of what are considered to be a new carbonate of bismuth; Johanngeorgenstadt and Schneeberg in Saxony, with Native Bismuth; near Hirschberg in Reuss Voigtland, with Brown Iron Ore, Native Bismuth, and Bismuth Glance; also, in the gold district of Chesterfield, S. Carolina. Brit. Mus., Case 49.

BISULPHURET OF COPPER, *Covelli.* See COVELLINE.

BISULPHURET OF IRON, *Thomson.* See IRON PYRITES.

BITELLURET OF LEAD, *Thomson.* See NAGYAGITE.

BITELLURET OF SILVER, *Thomson.* See HESSITE.

BITTERKALK, *Hausmann.* See DOLOMITE.

BITTERSALZ, *Werner.* See EPSOMITE.

BITTER SPAR, *Phillips*, or RHOMBSPAR. The crystallized or large grained and easily cleavable kinds of Dolomite.

Hexagonal. Usually occurring in the form of its primary crystal, an obtuse rhombohedron, very nearly allied to that of carbonate of lime. Colour greyish or yellow. Lustre somewhat pearly. Semitransparent. Very brittle: harder than Calc-spar. Cleaves readily into rhombohedrons of the same form as the crystals. H. 3·5 to 4. S.G. 2·85 to 2·9.

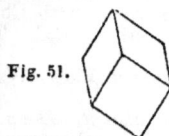

Fig. 51.

Comp. $\dot{C}a\,\ddot{C}+\dot{M}g\,\ddot{C}$=carbonate of lime 54·35, carbonate of magnesia 45·65 = 10, but the latter is sometimes replaced by a small proportion of carbonate of iron.

BB not distinguishable from Calc-spar, but it is more slowly soluble in acids, with a very slight effervescence.

Localities.—The finest and most transparent crystals are found at Traversella in Piedmont, at St. Gotthard; and near Gap in France. In England it is a common mineral at many localities.

BITTER SPATH. See BITTER SPAR.

BITUME ASPHALTE, *Brochant.* BITUME DE JUDÉE, *Romé de l'Isle.* See ASPHALT.

BITUME ELASTIQUE, *Haüy.* See ELATERITE.

BITUME GLUTINEUX, *Haüy.* See EARTHY BITUMEN.

BITUME LIQUIDE] BLANCHATRE, *Haüy.* See NAPHTHA.

BITUME LIQUIDE BRUN OU NOIRATRE, *Haüy.* See PETROLEUM.

BITUMEN. Includes several distinct varieties, as Earthy Bitumen, Compact Bitumen or Asphaltum, Elastic Bitumen, Maltha or Mineral Tar, Naphtha, Petroleum, including Seneca or Genessee oil, &c. Brit. Mus., Case 60.

M. P. G. Horse-shoe Case, Nos. 101, 102, 111 to 116.

BITUMINITE, *Traill.* See TORBANITE. See also CANNEL COAL.

BITUMINÖSES HOLZ. Bituminous Wood.

BITUMINOUS COAL. Softer than Anthracite, less lustrous, and of a more purely black or brownish-black colour. S.G. varies from 1·14 to 1·5. The proportion of Bitumen is very inconstant, varying from 10 to 60 per cent., and the coal is termed *Dry* or *Fat* according to the amount of Bitumen it contains. There are several varieties of Bituminous Coal, viz. Pitch or Caking Coal; Cherry Coal, Splint Coal, Flint Coal, Parrot or Cannel Coal, Coking Coal, Brown Coal, &c.

BLACK AMBER. The name given by the Prussian Amber-diggers to Jet, because it is found accompanying Amber, and, when rubbed, becomes faintly electric. It is cut into various ornamental articles by the Amber-diggers.

BLACK BAND. The most valuable kind of Clay Ironstone, from which the greater part of the Scotch iron has been made, since its discovery by Mr. Mushet in 1801. Black-band ironstone is distinguished from ordinary Clay Ironstone by the large proportion of carbonaceous matter which it contains. It is found in the Upper Coal-measures of Lanarkshire; also in those of South Wales; Staffordshire; and in Ireland, at Roscommon and Clonmore.

M. P. G. Principal Floor, Wall-cases, 51

and 52. Upper Gallery, Wall-case, 48. No. 154.

BLACK CHALK. A kind of clay containing a large amount of carbon. Colour black. Opaque. Sectile. Soils the fingers and leaves a mark on paper. Streak black and shining. H. 1 to 1·5. S.G. 2·1 to 2·2.

Becomes red or white in the fire.

Black Chalk is found in England, France, Portugal, Spain and Italy.

The finer kinds are made into artists' crayons, and used for drawing on paper.

BLACK COBALT OCHRE, *Allan, Jameson, Kirwan*. See EARTHY COBALT.

BLACK COPPER, *Phillips*, BLACK OXIDE OF COPPER. An impure, earthy, black oxide of copper, resulting from the decomposition of other ores; being mixed with more or less sulphide of copper, Pyrites, and other impurities. See MELACONITE.

M. P. G., Principal Floor, Wall-cases 1 (British); 15 (Foreign).

BLACK GARNET; BLACK GARNET OF FRASCATI. See MELANITE.

BLACK HEMATITE. See PSILOMELANE.

BLACK IRON ORE. See PSILOMELANE.

BLACK JACK. The name for Blende among English miners.

BLACK LEAD. See GRAPHITE.

BLACK MANGANESE-ORE, *Jameson*. See HAUSMANNITE.

BLACK SILICATE OF MANGANESE. See OPSIMOSE.

BLACK SILVER. See STEPHANITE.

BLACK SULPHIDE OF SILVER. The name given to an earthy form of Silver Glance found in some of the Cornish mines.

BLACK TELLURIUM, *Phillips*. See NAGYAGITE.

BLACK WAD. See WAD.

BLAKEITE. The name given to octahedral crystals, possibly of iron-alum (Coquimbite) from Coquimbo, analysed by J. H. Blake.

Analysis:

Sulphuric acid	41·87
Peroxide of iron	26·79
Alumina	1·05
Magnesia	0·30
Silica	0·82
Water	29·40
	99·73

BLÄTTERERZ, BLÄTTERTELLUR. See NAGYAGITE.

BLATTERKIES. See MARCASITE.

BLATTERZEOLITE, *Werner*. See HEULANDITE.

BLATTRIGER STILBIT, *Hausmann*. See HEULANDITE.

BLAU-BLEIERZ, *Werner*. See GALENA.

BLAUE EISENERZ, *Werner*. See VIVIANITE.

BLAUEISENSTEIN, *Klaproth*. See CROCIDOLITE.

BLAUSPATH, *Werner*. See LAZULITE.

BLEICARBONAT, *Naumann*. See CERUSITE.

BLEIERDE, *Werner*. See CERUSITE.

BLEIFAHLERZ. See BOURNONITE.

BLEIGELB, *Hausmann*. See WULFENITE.

BLEIGLANZ. See GALENA.

BLEIGLÄTTE. See PLUMBIC OCHRE.

BLEIGUMMI. See PLUMBO-RESINITE.

BLEILASUR. See LINARITE.

BLEIHORNERZ, *Naumann, v. Leonhard*. See CROMFORDITE.

BLEIMOLYBDAT. See WULFENITE.

BLEINIÈRE, *Hausmann*. BLEINIERITE, *Nicol*. Amorphous, reniform, spheroidal; also earthy and incrusting. Structure often curved lamellar. Colour white, grey, yellow, brown. Lustre resinous. Dull or earthy. Opaque to translucent. Streak white, greyish or yellowish. H. 4. S. G. 3·93 to 5·05.

Comp. Antimoniate of lead.

Analysis from Cornwall, by *Dr. J. Percy*.

Antimonious acid	47·36
Oxide of lead	40·73
Water	11·91
	100·00

BB on charcoal fuses to a metallic globule, gives out fumes of antimony, and finally yields a bead of lead.

This mineral is, probably, a mechanical mixture of Lead and Antimony Ochres. It occurs at Nertschinsk, in Siberia, where it is supposed to result from the decomposition of other ores of antimony. Also, in large detached masses near the surface of the ground, at Trevinnick mine, near Endellyon, in Cornwall, with Jamesonite and Antimony Ochre; and is the result of the decomposition of the former mineral.

M. P. G. Principal floor, Wall-case 20.

BLEIMULM, a black, powdery, sulphide of lead.

BLEISCHEELAT. See SCHEELETINE.

BLEISCHIMMER. See JAMESONITE.

BLEISULPHOTRICARBONAT, *Rammelsberg*. See LEADHILLITE.

BLEISCHWEIF. The name given by Werner to compact Galena, in contradistinction to the crystalline and granular forms of that mineral. It occurs in veins, and is generally accompanied by common Galena. When that is the case, the Bleischweif always forms the sides of the vein.

BLEIVITRIOL. See ANGLESITE.

BLENDE. Cubical, tetrahedral. Primary form the rhombic dodecahedron. Occurs crystallized and amorphous, in macles, and massive, fibrous, and botryoidal. The forms of its crystals are very numerous. Structure perfectly lamellar, and mechanically divisible with facility into the dodecahedron, octahedron, obtuse rhombohedron, acute rhombohedron, and irregular tetrahedron. Lustre splendent to adamantine. Colour brown, yellow, red, blackish-brown, rarely green; white or yellow when pure. Translucent or opaque. Streak varying with the colour, from white to reddish-brown. Yields to the knife, is moderately brittle, and easily frangible in the direction of the laminæ. H. 3·5 to 4. S. G. 3·9 to 4·2.

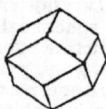 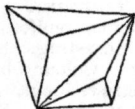 

Fig. 52.   Fig. 53.   Fig. 54.

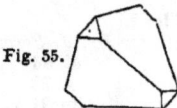 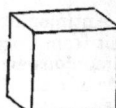

Fig. 55.   Fig. 56.

Comp. Sulphide of zinc, or Zn S = sulphur 33, zinc 67=100; but part of the zinc is often replaced by iron and cadmium.

BB infusible both alone and with borax, when strongly heated in the outer flame it emits vapours of zinc, which coat the charcoal.

Soluble in nitric acid with the evolution of sulphuretted hydrogen.

This mineral (the Black Jack or Mock Ore of the English miners) is of very frequent occurrence, being met with in beds and veins accompanying most of the ores of silver, lead, and copper. It was divided by Werner into three subspecies, Yellow Blende, Brown Blende, and Black Blende. Of these the brown was considered to be the most common, and of intermediate age between the other subspecies, of which the yellow is the newest. The value of this ore has considerably increased of late years, but formerly large heaps of refuse were frequently formed in the Cornish mines of the Blende extracted in working for Copper and Tin ores. Although thus looked upon in itself as a worthless substance, it was considered a favourable indication as regarded future prospects; the saying

being that " Jack rode a good horse;" by which was meant that a rich deposit of the ore in request might be expected to occur below it.

Localities. — *English.* In Cornwall at mines near St. Agnes (*figs.* 54, 55, and 56.) Huel Crofty, Camborne; and white, mammillated, with a fibrous structure, at Huel Unity and Fowey Consols. Alston, and other places in Cumberland.— *Scotch.* Of the form of *fig.* 54, with Galena, in the Edinburgh coal-fields.— *Foreign.* The black varieties are found in Transylvania, Hungary, and the Harz. Fine black and brown crystals are met with at Sahla in Sweden, Ratieborzitz, in Bohemia, and many Saxon localities.

Name. From the German blendena, *brilliant;* from blenden, *to dazzle.*

Brit. Mus., Case 5.

M. P. G. Principal Floor, Wall-cases 12, 27 to 29 (British); 21 (Foreign).

BLISTERED COPPER-ORE. The name given in Cornwall to botryoidal and reniform varieties of Copper Pyrites (Chalcopyrite). It is found at Cook's Kitchen, Huel Basset, &c.

BLOODSTONE. A jaspery variety of Quartz of a deep green colour, interspersed with red spots like drops of blood. On account of its beautiful colour and great hardness, it is much used for seals, rings, and such other ornaments as are commonly made of Agate. That which possesses the most translucency, and has the most numerous red spots is the most highly esteemed.

In the middle ages, the red spots were supposed to be the blood of Christ.

Bloodstone is also made into burnishers.

It is found massive in Bucharia, Tartary, Persia, Siberia; also in Upper Saxony, Iceland, and the Hebrides.

The name Heliotrope (from ἥλιος, *the sun*, and τρέπω, *to turn*) was given to it because, when immersed in a vessel of water, it was said to make the image of the sun to appear in it of the colour of blood. The Ethiopian Heliotrope especially produced this phenomenon. "Out of the water the sun is seen in it as in a mirror, the eclipses of the sun become visible, and the moon is beheld to pass under the great star." (Pliny.)

Brit. Mus., Case 23.

M. P. G. Horse-shoe Case, Nos. 551, 552.

BLŒDITE, a mineral occurring on Anhydrite at Ischl, and proved by analyses of Von Hauer to be identical with Astrakanite. Colour, orange-yellow. Translucent. Compact. S. G. 2·251.

BLUE ASBESTOS. See CROCIDOLITE.

BLUE CARBONATE OF COPPER, BLUE COPPER, *Phillips, Jameson.* See AZURITE.

BLUE COPPER. See COVELLINE.

BLUE FELSPAR. See LAZULITE.

BLUE IRON EARTH, an earthy variety of Vivianite, found in Cornwall, Greenland, Syria, Carinthia, &c. It is frequently white when first dug up, and becomes blue on exposure to the atmosphere.
Analysis from Kertsch, by *Segeth*:

Phosphoric acid	. .	24.95
Protoxide of iron	. .	48·79
Water	. . .	26·26
		100·00

BLUE IRONSTONE. See CROCIDOLITE.

BLUE JOHN. The name by which the compact and granular varieties of Fluorspar are known by the miners of Derbyshire. It is turned in a lathe and made into vases, tazzas, and other ornamental articles, the finest varieties for which purposes are found at Tray Cliff, near Castleton. The red and some other tints of the ornaments into which it is converted are not those natural to the stone, but are brought out by exposing it to heat.

M. P. G. Entrance Hall. A beautiful vase of Derbyshire Fluor-spar stands on pedestal 35. See also Horse-shoe Case on the Principal Floor.

BLUE LEAD, or BLUE ORE. Names often given by miners to distinguish Galena from Cerussite, Anglesite, &c.

BLUE LEAD. A variety of Galena pseudomorphous after Pyromorphite. It occurs massive, and likewise in long, irregular, six-sided prisms, which are superficially dull and rough, and of a colour between lead-grey and indigo-blue. Soft, sectile, and easily frangible. S.G. 5·4.

Localities. It has been found in Cornwall, at Herodsfoot Mine, near Liskeard, and at Huel Hope; at Zschopau in Saxony; and at Huelgöet and Poullaouen, in France, accompanying carbonates of lead and copper. The specimens from Huel Hope, when held in the flame of a candle, burn like the supersulphuret of lead of Johnston.

BLUE MALACHITE. See AZURITE.

BLUE SPAR. See LAZULITE.

BLUE TALC OF TABERG, in Wermland, *Werner.* See TABERGITE.

BLUE VITRIOL, *Allan.* See CYANOSITE.

BLUTSTEIN, *Hausmann.* See HEMATITE.

BODENITE. Probably a variety of Allanite. It occurs in long prismatic crystals of a rhombic form. Colour brown, reddish-brown, to nearly black, with a somewhat greasy lustre. H. 6 to 6·5. S. G. 2·53.

Analysis by *Kerndt* :

Silica	.	.	.	26·12
Alumina		.	.	10·34
Protoxide of iron		.	.	12·05
Yttria	.	.	.	17·43
Oxide of cerium		.	.	10·46
Oxide of lanthanium		.	7·57
Lime	.	.	.	6·32
Magnesia		.	.	2·34
Protoxide of manganese		.	1·62
Potash	.	.	.	1·21
Soda	.	.	.	0·84
Water	.	.	.	3·82
			100·00

BB glows like Gadolinite; in platinum forceps fuses at the edges after long heating. and gives to the flame the yellow colour of soda in the outer flame.

Locality. Occurs with Oligoclase at Boden, near Marienberg, in the Saxon Erzgebirge.

BOG-BUTTER, *Williamson.* A variety of Hartite or Guayaquillite, occurring in Irish peat-swamps. It melts at 51° C (124° F.), and dissolves easily in alcohol.

Comp. $C^{33}\ H^{32}\ O^5 + \dot{H} =$ carbon 75·05, hydrogen 12·56, oxygen 12·39.

BOGHEAD CANNEL COAL, BOGHEAD COAL, BOGHEAD MINERAL. See TORBANITE.

BOG-IRON-ORE is a loosely aggregated form of peroxide of iron (Limonite) occurring in low marshy grounds, and frequently found in the peat-bogs of Ireland and the Shetlands. It is of recent formation, resulting from the decomposition of other varieties of iron, and often takes the form of the leaves, nuts, or stems found in the marshy soil. It varies in composition, containing from 20 to 78 per cent. of peroxide of iron; the protoxides of iron and manganese, from a mere trace to 9 or 10 per cent. of phosphoric and organic acids, from 7 to 30 per cent. of water, with almost always silica in a state of chemical combination. When it occurs in small globular concretions, it is termed *Pea-iron-ore*.

Bog-iron-ore was subdivided by Werner into three species, having reference rather to the conditions under which they are formed than to any particular difference in their characters or composition, viz. 1. Morasterz or Morass-Ore; 2. Sumpferz or Swamp-Ore; and, 3. Wiesenerz or Meadow-Ore, which have been formed, according to that author, in the following manner. "The water which flows into marshy places is impregnated with a vegetable acid, formed

from decaying vegetables, which enables it
to dissolve the iron in the rocks over which
it flows, or over which it stands. The water
having reached the lower points of the country, or being poured into hollows, becomes
stagnant, by degrees evaporates; and the
dissolved iron being accumulated in quantity by fresh additions of water, then follow
successive depositions, which at first are yellowish, earthy, and of little consistence, and
this is Morass-Ore; but in course of time
they become harder, their colour passes to
brown, and thus Swamp-ore is formed. After
the water has completely evaporated, and
the swamp is dried up, the swamp-ore becomes much harder, and at length passes
into Meadow-ore, which is already covered
with soil and grass."—*Jameson's Min.*, vol.
ii. pp. 338-9.

Brit. Mus., Case 16.

M. P. G. Principal Floor, Wall-case 19
(Foreign).

BOG-MANGANESE or WAD chiefly consists
of oxides of manganese and water, with some
oxide of iron, and often silica, alumina,
lime or baryta. See WAD.

BOHEMIAN DIAMOND. A name sometimes
given to limpid and transparent Rock-crystal,
when cut and polished.

BOHEMIAN GARNET. See PYROPE and
CARBUNCLE.

BOHEMIAN TOPAZ. See CITRINE.

BOHNERZ, BEAN-ORE. A variety of Limonite, or hydrous oxide of iron, occurring
in spherical or ellipsoidal concretions, which
have a concentric lamellar structure.

M. P. G. Wall-case, 18.

BOIS DE MONTAGNE, *Brochant.* See
MOUNTAIN WOOD.

BOIS PETRIFIÉ. *Brochant.* WOOD-STONE.
See WOOD-OPAL.

BOLE. This substance is closely related to
Halloysite in appearance, and particularly
so in the large amount of water which it contains; but it is more variable in character. It
probably results from the alteration of some
felspathic or aluminous mineral, and consists
chiefly of hydrated bisilicate of alumina, in
which a portion of the alumina is replaced
by sesquioxide of iron. From the analysis
of Wackenroder it appears to contain either
2 or 4 atoms of water, according to the way
in which it is dried. It occurs in solid
amorphous masses of a brownish, yellowish,
or reddish colour, inclining to blackish-
brown, has a greasy feel, and adheres strongly to the tongue. It yields to the nail, breaks
with a conchoidal fracture, and has a shining streak; subtranslucent to opaque. In
water it emits a crackling noise, and sepa-

rates into small pieces with the evolution of
air-bubbles. H. 1·5. S. G. 1·4 to 2.

BB fuses easily to a yellow or green
enamel.

Analysis, from Capo di Bove, by *C. Von
Hauer :*

Silica	.	.	45·64
Alumina	.	.	29·33
Peroxide of iron	.	.	8·88
Lime	.	.	0·60
Magnesia	.	.	trace
Water	.	.	14·27
			98·72

Localities. Bole is found in irregular beds
or disseminated masses in clayslate and
basalt. It occurs at Striegau in Silesia, the
Habichtswald in Hessia, near Sienna in
Italy.

Bole is distinguished from Lithomarge
by its fusibility and physical characters. It
was formerly employed in medicine as an
astringent, and is now used as a pigment.

Name. From βῶλος, *a clod of earth.*

M. P. G. Horse-shoe Case, No. 1121,
Upper Gallery, Table-case B in recess 6, Nos.
202 to 204.

BOLOGNESE STONE. A grey or yellowish-
grey variety of Barytes forming rounded
masses, composed of minute fibrous crystals,
diverging from the centre. It becomes
phosphorescent when heated, and remains so
for some time even after cooling. Bolognese phosphorus is made by mixing the
powder of this stone with a little gum, and
exposing the mixture to a slight red heat,
and afterwards for some time to the light of
the sun, when it is found to be phosphorescent in the dark. It is found in clay at
Monte Paterno, near Bologna, whence the
name.

Brit. Mus.. Case 52.

BOLTONITE, *Shepard, Geo. J. Brush.* A
variety of Chrysolite. It occurs disseminated
in irregular masses, seldom showing any
traces of crystalline form. Colour ash-grey
to yellowish-white, the darker colours changing to yellow on exposure to the weather.
Lustre vitreous. Fracture uneven or small
conchoidal. Fragments colourless and
nearly transparent. H. 6 to 6·5. S.G. 3·21.

Comp. Magnesia-chrysolite, or R̈³ S̈i.

Analysis by J. L. Smith :

Silica	.	.	42·82
Alumina	.	.	trace
Magnesia	.	.	54·44
Protoxide of iron	.	.	1·47

Lime . . . . . 0·85
Loss by ignition . . . 0·76
                                        ————
                                        100·34

BB in the platinum forceps does not fuse, but becomes pale yellow. With salt of phosphorus gives a reaction for silica and iron. Partially decomposed by very dilute muriatic acid, when reduced to powder.

Locality. Bolton, Massachusetts, U. S.

Boltonite differs from other varieties of Chrysolite in being a silicate of magnesia, and not of magnesia and iron.

BOLUS, or BOLE OF SINOPE. A variety of Bole, the composition of which, according to the following analysis of Klaproth, is nearly $(\ddot{\text{F}}\text{e}, \ddot{\text{A}}\text{l}) \ddot{\text{S}}\text{i} + 2\ddot{\text{H}}$.

Analysis :

Silica	. . . .	32·0
Alumina	. . .	26·5
Peroxide of iron	. .	21·0
Chloride of sodium	. .	1·5
Water	. . . .	17·0

                                        ————
                                        98·0

BOMBITE, *Leschenault.* A mineral considered by Laugier to be a variety of Touchstone, of which it possesses all the characters. It has no definite chemical composition or form, but occurs in rounded fragments or amorphous masses, derived apparently from some old formation. Colour bluish-black. Very finely granular. Scratches Quartz. S.G. 2·21.

Analysis by Laugier :

Silica	. . . .	50·00
Alumina	. . .	10·50
Peroxide of iron	. .	25·00
Magnesia	. . .	3·50
Lime	. . . .	8·50
Carbon	. . .	3·00
Sulphur	. . .	0·30

                                        ————
                                        100·80

Locality. The environs of Bombay.

BONSDORFFITE. A hydrated variety of Iolite, of a dark olive-green or greenish-brown colour, found at Abo.

Comp. Iolite + 6$\ddot{\text{H}}$.

Analysis by Bonsdorff :

Silica	. . .	45·05
Alumina	. . .	30·05
Peroxide of iron	. .	5·30
Magnesia	. . .	9·00
Water,with some protoxide of manganese and magnesia.		10·60

                                        ————
                                        100·00

Brit. Mus., Case 32.

BOORT, BORT, or BOWR. A kind of Diamond, forming from two to ten per cent. of the rough diamonds imported from the Brazils. It is generally of a spherical shape, and appears to be formed of a confused mass of interlaced and twisted parts, like the knots in a piece of wood. For this reason it cannot be cleaved like ordinary Diamonds, and is only of use as a material for polishing other stones, for which purpose it is broken and reduced to powder in a mortar. Although usually round, it sometimes presents crystalline forms, in which case they are generally badly defined, at the same time that the stone itself has a more uneven outside than ordinary rough Diamonds. Its colour is mostly greyish-white, or blackish, and it is less frequently found coloured than the more regularly crystallized stones of the same class. Its specific gravity is also somewhat greater than that of ordinary Diamonds.

M. P. G. Horse-shoe Case, No. 3 (under glass shade); No. 4.

BORACIC ACID, *Phillips.* See SASSOLIN.

BORACITE. Cubical, tetrahedral. Occurs in transparent and colourless cubes, with dodecahedral and tetrahedral surfaces: also amorphous. Colour white, inclining to grey, yellow, or green. The opaque white crystals are not so hard, and contain a proportion of carbonate of lime. Lustre vitreous, more or less translucent. Streak white. Fracture conchoidal, uneven. Pyroelectric. Harder than Felspar. H. 4·5. S.G. 2·95.

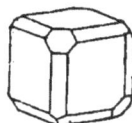

Fig. 57.

Comp. $2(\dot{\text{M}}\text{g}^3 \ddot{\text{B}}^4) + \text{Mg Cl}$, or boracic acid 62·50, magnesia 36·86, chloride of magnesium 10·64 = 100.

Analysis by Siewert :

Chloride of magnesium	.	11.14
Boracic acid	. .	61·34
Magnesia	. . .	26·00
Protoxide of iron.	.	1·52

                                        ————
                                        100·00

BB on charcoal, fuses with difficulty, and forms a clear yellowish bead, which, on cooling, solidifies to a crystalline enamellike mass, covered with needles.

Slightly soluble in hot water, and slowly dissolved by acids.

E

Localities. In beds of Anhydrite, Gypsum, or Salt, in small but very perfect isolated crystals at Kalkberg and Schildstein, near Lüneberg, in Hanover; Segeberg, near Kiel, in Holstein; Luneville, La Meurthe, in France; massive or as part of the rock at the salt-mine of Stassfurth, in Prussia.

Brit. Mus., Case 39.

BORATE OF LIME, *Hayes.* See HAYESINE.

BORATE OF LIME, *Phillips.* See DATHOLITE.

BORATE OF MAGNESIA, *Phillips.* See BORACITE.

BORATE OF SODA, *Phillips*; BORAX, *Dana.* Oblique. Occurs in prismatic crystals variously terminated, and yielding to mechanical division parallel to the lateral planes of the primary form — an oblique rhombic prism of 86° 30′ and 93° 30′ — and both its diagonals. Colour whitish, sometimes with tinges of blue, green, or grey. Lustre vitreous, sometimes earthy. Translucent or nearly transparent to opaque. Streak white. Soft and brittle. Fracture conchoidal. Taste sweetish-alkaline. H. 2 to 2·5. S.G. 1·74.

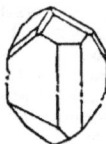

Fig. 58.

Comp. Ṅa B̈² + 10 Ḣ = boracic acid 36·58, soda 16·25, water 47·17 = 100.

BB swells and then fuses to a transparent globule.

Soluble in eighteen parts of water at temp. 60° F., and in six parts of boiling water; and the solution changes vegetable blues to greens.

Localities. Thibet, where it is dug in large lumps on the borders of lakes, when the heats of summer have rendered the waters shallow; or the water of the lakes is admitted into reservoirs, at the bottom of which the salt is found after the water has evaporated. From Thibet it is carried to the East Indies, whence, after being purified, it is exported under the name of Tincal. In Persia, the water of certain wells being conducted into reservoirs and evaporated, deposits the Borax, or Borech, as they call it. It is now made in large quantities from the boracic acid of the Tuscan lagoons. It is also found in the province of Potosi, in

Peru; in Ceylon, and in the mineral springs of Chambly, St. Ours, Canada W.

This salt is used as a flux in several metallurgical processes, and is highly valuable in aiding the process of soldering. It is also used in the manufacture of glass and artificial gems. See TINCAL.

Brit. Mus., Case 39.

BORAZIT. See BORACITE.

BORNINE, *Beudant.* See TETRADYMITE. Named after De Born.

BORNITE, *Brooke & Miller. Nicol.* See ERUBESCITE. This name has also been given by one or two authors to a variety of Telluric Bismuth (see TETRADYMITE), which occurs in thick foliated masses, with a crystalline structure, and from half an inch to an inch in diameter, splitting into thin plates like Talc and Mica. Colour and lustre like those of highly polished steel. Flexible. Sectile. Soils the fingers like Plumbago or Molybdenite. Streak metallic, and nearly the colour of the pulverised mineral. H. 2·25. S.G. 7·866.

Comp. 2 Bi Te + Bi S².

Analysis by *C. T. Jackson:*

Bismuth	.	.	.	79·08
Tellurium	.	.	.	18·00
Selenium	.	.	.	1·18
Gold	.	.	.	0·06
Loss	.	.	.	1·14
				100·00

BB on charcoal, fuses giving off white fumes, which have the odour of Selenium; leaves a white deposit on the charcoal, and a yellow ring near the globule, and a little metallic Bismuth is obtained. This, cupelled, gives a little gold.

Localities. Field's gold mine, in Dahlonga, Georgia; in a vein of Quartz, in hornblende-slate rocks, associated with Native Gold and some Auriferous Iron Pyrites. Jose, in Brazil, in marble.

Name. After De Born.

Brit. Mus., Case 7.

BÖRNSTEIN or BERNSTEIN. See AMBER.

BOROCALCITE. } See HAYESINE.
BORONATROCALCITE. }

BOROSILICATE OF LIME, *Thomson.* See DATHOLITE.

BORSAURERKALK. See HAYESINE.

BOTRYOGENE, *Nicol, Haidinger, Phillips.* Oblique: Primary form an oblique rhombic prism of 119° 66′ and 60° 4′. Occurs in small crystals, which are often aggregated in reniform and botryoidal shapes, consisting of globules with a crystalline surface, sometimes like a bunch of grapes;

whence its name from βότρυς, *a grape.* Colour deep hyacinth-red, passing into ochreyellow in massive varieties. Lustre vitreous. Translucent. Streak ochre-yellow. Taste slightly astringent. H. 2·25 to 2·5. S.G. 2·04.

Fig. 59.

Comp. $\ddot{F}e^3 \ddot{S}^2 + 3 \ddot{F}e \ddot{S}^2 + 36 \dot{H}$ = sulphate of protoxide of iron 19·0, sulphate of peroxide of iron 48·3, water 32·7 = 100·0.

Becomes covered with a dirty yellow powder when exposed to a moist atmosphere, but remains unaltered if kept dry. *BB* intumesces and gives off water, leaving a reddish-yellow earth.

Partly soluble in boiling water, leaving an ochreous residue.

Locality. The Mellanrumsort level in the great copper mine of Fahlun in Sweden, forming a coating on Gypsum or Pyrites. Brit. Mus., Case 55.

BOTRYOLITE, *Hausmann.* A variety of Datholite occuring in mammillary concretions, formed of concentric layers, having a splintery or fibrous texture. Colour externally pearl- or yellowish-grey; internally white, greyish and red in concentric circles. Translucent at the edges. Brittle. It differs from Datholite in containing two atoms of water instead of one.

Comp. $\dot{C}a \ddot{B} + \dot{C}a \ddot{S}i + 2 \dot{H}.$

Analysis by *Rammelsberg:*

Lime	34·27
Silica . . .	36·39
Boracic acid . .	18·34
Water	10·22
Alumina and peroxide of iron	0·78
	100·00

BB melts into a white glass.

Locality. Arendal in Norway, in gneiss, accompanied by Schorl, Magnetic Iron ore and Iron Pyrites.

Name. From βότρυς, *a grape,* and λίθος, *stone;* from its occurring sometimes in small botryoidal masses, which are white and have an earthy texture.

Brit. Mus., Case 39.

BOTTLE STONE OF MORAVIA. A kind of Chrysolite of a dirty green and greyishgreen colour, found in flat pieces about an inch in size.

BOULANGERITE, *Thaulow.* Generally occurs massive, in plumose masses which exhibit a crystalline structure when fractured; also granular and compact. Colour bluish, lead-grey, often covered with yellow spots from oxidation. Lustre metallic. H. 2·5 to 3. S.G. 5·75 to 6.

Comp. Pb S + ⅛ Sb² S³ = sulphur 17·9, antimony 24·1, lead 58·0 = 100.

Analysis from Molières, by *Boulanger:*

Sulphur	18·5
Antimony . . .	25·5
Lead	53·9
Iron	1·2
Copper	0·9
	100·0

BB fuses readily, giving off sulphurous acid, and fumes of oxide of antimony; on charcoal the presence of lead is indicated by a yellow circle.

Localities. Abundantly at Molières (Gard) in France; Nasafjeld in Lapland; Wolfsberg; massive, acicular, and fibrous near Bottino in Tuscany.

Name. After M. Boulanger, Engineer. Brit. Mus., Case 11.

M. P. G. Principal Floor, Wall-case 21.

BOURNONITE, *Jameson, Phillips, Nicol.* Rhombic: occurs crystallized in a right rhomboidal prism (the primary form) variously modified. Crystals often cruciform; also massive, granular, and compact. Colour and streak steel-grey, inclining to dull leadgrey with a tinge of black. Opaque. Fracture uneven, or flat conchoidal, with a brilliant metallic lustre. Brittle; yields to the pressure of the nail. H. 2·5 to 3. S.G. 5·7 to 5·9.

 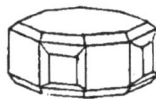

Fig. 60.　　　　　Fig. 61.

Fig. 62.

Comp. $\dot{P}b^4 \ddot{S}b + \dot{C}u^2 \ddot{S}b.$

Analysis from Wolfsberg by *Rammelsberg:*

Sulphur	19·76
Antimony . . .	24·34

E 2

Lead . . . . . 42·88
Copper . . . . . 13·06

                        100·00

BB decrepitates and melts, giving off sulphur and fumes of antimony, after which a crust of sulphide of lead remains, inclosing a globule of copper. Readily dissolves in nitric acid, forming a blue solution.

Localities.— English. In Cornwall at Huel Boys, in the parish of St. Endellion (where it was first noticed), *figs.* 60 and 61; also at St. Merryn, near Padstow; Nansloe, near Helstone; Budock Vean, near Falmouth; and in very fine, sometimes compound crystals (*wheel-ore*) at Herodsfoot mine, near Liskeard, *fig.* 62.— *Irish.* Cahirglissawn lead mine, between Gort and Kenmare, Kerry.— *Foreign.* Very large crystals of Bournonite are found in the mines of Neudorf, in the Harz, where they occasionally exceed an inch in diameter. Good crystals occur at Kapnik in Transylvania, and at Servoz in Piedmont. Other localities are Braunsdorf and Gersdorf in Saxony. Clausthal and Andreasberg in the Harz. France, at Cransac, Dept. of l'Aveyron. Mexico.

Named in honour of Count de Bournon, who first described this mineral, and who gave it the name of Endellione, after the parish of Endellion, in Cornwall, where it was first found.

Brit. Mus., Case 11.

M. P. G. Principal Floor, Case 15, Wall-cases 7 and 14 (British); 21 (Foreign).

BOURNONIT-NICKELGLANZ. An ore from Wolfsberg, in the Harz, which is considered by Rammelsberg to be a compound of Ullmannite and Bournonite. It occurs in cubes. H. 4·5.   S.G. 5·63 to 5·7.

Analysis:

Arsenic . . . . 28·00
Antimony . . . . 19·53
Nickel . . . . 27·04
Cobalt . . . . 1·60
Lead . . . . 5·13
Copper . . . . 1·33
Iron . . . . 0·51

                        100·00

BOVEY COAL. A kind of Lignite occurring in deposits of pipe-clay in the neighbourhood of Bovey-Tracey, in Devonshire. It burns with a weak, often bluish flame, and gives off an offensive smell. S.G. 1·4 to 1·558.

BOWENITE. A bright apple-green variety of Serpentine, resembling Nephrite. Structure granular. Very tough. H. 5. S.G. 2·57.

Comp. $2 \dot{M}g^3 \ddot{S}i^2 + \dot{M}g \dot{H}$.

Analysis by *Smith & Brush:*

Silica . . . . 42·29
Magnesia . . . 42·29
Protoxide of iron . . . 1·21
Lime · . . . 1·90
Water . . . . 12·96

                        99·65

Locality. Smithfield, Rhode Island, U. S.

Name. After Bowen, by whom it was first described (as a variety of Nephrite).

BOWR. See BOORT.

BRACHYTYPOUS LEAD BARYTE, *Mohs.* See CROMFORDITE.

BRACHYTYPOUS ZINC BARYTE, *Mohs.* See WILLIAMSITE.

BRANCHITE, *Savi.* A colourless, translucent mineral, resembling Scheererite, from the Brown Coal of Mount Vaso, in Tuscany. It fuses at 75° C. (167° F.), but does not crystallize on cooling. S.G. 1. Soluble in alcohol.

BRANDISITE. A variety of Clintonite, occurring in crystals, lining cavities in a rock chiefly composed of Pyroxene, at Toal de la Faja de Monzani, in the valley of Fassa, Tyrol.

It was named by Von Kobell after Count de Brandi. See DISTERITE.

Brit. Mus., Case 25.

BRASS ORE, *Kirwan.* A mixture of Copper Pyrites and Blende.

BRAUNBLEIERZ, *Werner;* or BROWN LEAD ORE. See PYROMORPHITE.

BRAUN EISENSTEIN, *Werner.* See LIMONITE.

BRAUNITE. Pyramidal. General form a pyramid very like the regular octahedron. Occurs both crystalline and massive, or fibrous and divergent, of a dark brownish-black colour, with a submetallic lustre. Streak black, or slightly brownish. Brittle. Fracture even. H. 6 to 6·5. S.G. 4·75 to 4·81.

Comp. $\ddot{M}n = (\dot{M}n \ \ddot{M}n) =$ manganese 69·68, oxygen 30·32.

Analysis from Vizianagram, by *A. J. Scott,* (S.G. 4·5):

Binoxide of manganese . 73·79
Oxygen . . . . 1·86
Magnesia . . . . 2·34
Water . . . . 0·54
Silica . . . . 8·30
Peroxide of iron . . . 12·91

                        99·74

BB alone on charcoal infusible, but with

borax it melts with a slight effervescence. Soluble in muriatic acid, with the evolution of chlorine, leaving a trace of silicious matter.

Localities. Forms veins in porphyry at Œhrenstock, near Ilmenau; Elgersburg and Friedrichsroda in Thuringia; Leimbach in Mansfeld; St. Marcel (see MARCELINE) in Piedmont; Vizianagram in India, &c.

Named by Turner and Haidinger in honour of M. Braun, of Gotha.

Brit. Mus., Case 13.

Braunite may be distinguished from other ores of Manganese by its greater hardness, and from Hausmannite by the direction of its cleavage being parallel to the faces of the pyramid, instead of being parallel with the bases, as is always the case with the latter mineral.

BRAUNSPATH. See BROWN SPAR.

BRAUNSTEIN, *Hausmann.* See HAUSMANNITE.

BRAUNSTEINKIESEL, *Werner.* See GARNET.

BRAZILIAN RUBY. The name given by lapidaries to light rose-coloured Spinelle, and pink-coloured Topaz.

BRAZILIAN SAPPHIRE. The name given by some authors to light-blue Topaz, and by lapidaries to Indicolite.

BRAZILIAN TOPAZ. The name given by lapidaries to gold-yellow Topaz, with a tinge of red.

BRAZILIAN TOURMALINE. The name sometimes given by lapidaries to Brazilian Emerald.

BRECCIATED AGATE. Agates consisting of fragments of Jasper, Bloodstone, Carnelian, &c., cemented by a paste of Chalcedony.

M. P. G. Horse-shoe Case, No. 557.

BREISLACKITE, *Nicol*; BREISLAKITE, *Brocchi, Phillips.* A variety of Augite occurring in wool-like flexible fibres, of a chestnut-brown colour, at Capo di Bove, amongst the older lavas of Vesuvius.

BB alone, fuses to a brilliant and magnetic black scoria; with borax forms a green glass, which becomes colourless on cooling.

Not apparently acted on by boiling muriatic acid.

Name. After Breislak, the Italian geologist.

M.P.G. Upper Gallery, Table-case B in recess 6; Nos. 88 to 135.

BREITHAUPTITE, *Haidinger*; or ANTIMONIAL NICKEL. A mineral formerly found in the Andreasberg mountains, but long since exhausted. Hexagonal. Occurs in thin hexagonal plates; also arborescent and disseminated. Colour light copper-red, in-

clining to violet when fresh fractured. Lustre metallic. Opaque. Streak reddish-brown. Fracture uneven. Brittle. H. 5·5. S.G. 7·54.

Comp. Ni Sb = antimony 68·6, nickel 31·4.

Analysis by *Stromeyer*:

Antimony	.	.	.	. 63·73
Nickel .	.	.	.	. 28·94
Iron .	.	.	.	. 0·86
Galena .	.	.	.	. 6·43

                 99·98

BB on charcoal the antimony sublimes.

Locality. The Pyrenees, especially in the neighbourhood of the Pic du Midi d'Ossau.

Name. After Breithaupt, Professor of Mineralogy at Freyberg.

Breithauptite has been observed in a crystallized form amongst the products of blast furnaces.

BREUNNERITE, *Dana, Phillips, Brooke & Miller.* Hexagonal, with a perfect rhombohedral cleavage. Primary form a rhomb of about 107° 30'. Occurs crystallized, also massive, granular, and fibrous. Colourless, yellowish, or brown. Lustre vitreous, sometimes inclining to pearly on cleavage surfaces. Streak greyish-white. Brittle. Fracture flat conchoidal. H. 4 to 4·5. S.G. 3 to 3·6.

Fig. 63.

Comp. $(\dot{M}g, \dot{F}e, \dot{M}n) \ddot{C}. \dot{M}g \ddot{C} + \dot{F}e \ddot{C} =$ carbonate of magnesia 42·0, carbonate of iron 58 0 = 100.

Analysis from Zillerthal, by *Stromeyer*:

Carbonate of magnesia	.	84·79
Carbonate of iron .	.	13·82
Carbonate of manganese	.	0·69

                 99·30

BB infusible; gives an iron re-action, becomes black, and sometimes magnetic. Slowly soluble in muriatic acid when pulverised.

Breunnerite usually occurs in detached imbedded crystals, of the primary form, in Chlorite-slate, and Serpentine. It may be distinguished by its brown or yellow colour from the crystals of Bitter Spar, with which it is accompanied, the latter being white or translucent.

Localities. St. Gotthard; the Zillerthal, and Hall in the Tyrol. The only British locality where it has been met with is in the Island of Unst, in Shetland, where it occurs in small yellowish-brown crystals, imbedded in green foliated Talc, at the head of Norwick Bay.

Named by Haidinger, in compliment to Count Breunner.

Brit. Mus., Case 49.

BREUNNERIT, *Haidinger, Hausmann;* or BREUNNERITE, *Nicol.* Native carbonate of Magnesia. See MAGNESITE.

BREVICITE occurs in transparent colourless prisms, and white, laminar, radiated masses, which are sometimes marked with striæ of a dark-red hue.

Comp. $2 \dot{N}a \dot{C}a, 2 \ddot{A}l, 5 \ddot{S}i, 4 \dot{H}.$

Analysis from Ströni, by *Souden :*

Soda	.	.	.	.	10·32
Lime	.	.	.	.	6·88
Magnesia	.	.	.	0·21
Alumina	.	.	.	28·39
Silica	.	.	.	.	43·88
Water	.	.	.	.	9·63
					99·31

Locality. Brevig in Norway (whence the name Brevicite).

Brit. Mus., Case 28.

BREWSTERIT, *Haidinger, Hausmann, Naumann, v. Kobell;* BREWSTERITE, *Greg & Lettsom, Phillips, Beudant.* Oblique. Primary form an oblique rectangular prism. In small, greyish-white, or yellowish crystals, with a vitreous lustre, except on the faces of cleavage, which are pearly. Transparent to translucent. Streak uncoloured. Brittle. Fracture uneven. H. 3·5 to 4. S.G. 2·09 to 2·16.

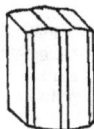

Fig. 64.

Comp. $(\dot{S}r, \dot{B}a, \dot{C}a) \ddot{S}i + \ddot{A}l \ddot{S}i^3 + 5\dot{H}.$

Analysis by *Thomson :*

Silica	.	.	.	53·04
Alumina	.	.	.	16·54
Baryta	.	.	.	6·05
Strontia	.	.	.	9·01
Lime	.	.	.	0·80
Water	.	.	.	14·78
				100·17

BB loses its water, becomes opaque, and then froths and swells, but does not fuse.

With salt of phosphorus melte easily, leaving a skeleton of silica.

Soluble in acids, leaving a residue of silica.

Brewsterite was first discovered at Strontian in Argyleshire, where it occurs in small translucent crystals, both colourless, and of a brownish tinge, generally associated with Calcite. It is found, also, at the Giant's Causeway, lining cavities in amygdaloidal rocks; in the lead mines of St. Turpet; near Freiburg in the Brisgau; in the department of the Isère in France, and in the Pyrenees.

Named after Sir David Brewster.

Brit. Mus., Case 28.

BREWSTOLINE, *Dana,* a transparent, colourless fluid detected by Sir David Brewster in Siberian Amethyst. It also occurs in minute cavities in crystals of Topaz, Chrysoberyl, Quartz crystals from Quebec, and in blue Topaz from Aberdeenshire. The fluid expands one-fourth its size by an increment of 30° F., or is nearly thirty-two times more expansible than water, by a change of temperature from 50° to 80°

Brewstoline is stated by R. T. Simmlen to be liquid carbonic acid.

Name. After Sir David Brewster, by whom the first accurate researches were made into the nature of the liquids and gases which occur in the cavities of Quartz, &c.

BRICK-RED COPPER ORE, *Kirwan.* See TILE-ORE.

BRIGHT WHITE COBALT, *Kirwan, Phillips.* See COBALTINE.

BRITTLE SILVERGLANCE, *Jameson.* ⎱
BRITTLE SILVER ORE, *Allen.* ⎰ See STEPHANITE.
BRITTLE SULPHURET OF SILVER, *Phillips.*

BROAD FOLLIATED GYPSUM, *Kirwan.* See SELENITE.

BROCHANTITE, *Greg & Lettsom.* Rhombic. Primary form a right rhomboidal

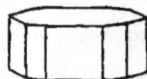   

Fig. 65.   Fig. 66.

prism. Occurs in small, well-defined, transparent crystals of an emerald-green to a blackish-green colour, having a vitreous lustre. Crystals striated vertically. Streak bright green. Brittle. Fracture conchoidal scarcely observable. H. 3·5 to 4. S.G. 3·8 to 3·9.

Comp. $\dot{C}u \ddot{S} + 3 \dot{C}u\ddot{H} = \dot{C}u^4 \ddot{S} \ddot{H}^3 =$ sulphuric acid 17·7, protoxide of copper 70·3, water 12·0 = 100.

Analysis by *Magnus*, from Rezbanya:

Sulphuric acid	17·13
Protoxide of copper	62·62
Oxide of zinc	8·18
Oxide of lead	0·03
Water	11·88
	99·85

BB on charcoal, fuses and yields a bead of copper.

Localities. Associated with Malachite and Native Copper at Ekatherinenburg, in Siberia. Nassau. Also in small brilliant crystals on a white quartzose rock, associated with fibrous Malachite, at Roughten Gill, in Cumberland.

Named by Levy after Brochant de Villiers, the French Mineralogist.

Brit. Mus., Case 28.

BROMIC SILVER. } See BROMY-
BROMITE, *Haidinger.* } RITE.

BROMLITE. The name given by Thomson to Alstonite. It occurs at *Brownley* Hill mine near Alston, which appears to have been mistaken for *Bromley* Hill.

BROMSILBER. } See BROMYR-
BROMURE D'ARGENT. } ITE.

BROMYRITE. Cubical: in cubo-octahedrons. Colour, when pure, bright yellow, with a slightly greenish tinge; often grass-green or olive-green externally. Lustre splendent. Sectile. H. 1 to 2. S.G. 5·8 to 6.

Comp. Bromide of silver or Ag Br = bromine 42·6, silver 57·4 = 100.

BB fuses easily.

Imperfectly soluble in acids: soluble in heated concentrated Ammonia.

Localities. Accompanying other silver-ores in Mexico, in the district of Plateros, and at the mine of San Onofre, seventeen leagues from Zacatecas; also at Chânarcillo, in Chili, with Chloride of Silver; and with Horn Silver, at Huelgoet, in Brittany.

Brit. Mus., Case 59.

BRONGNIARDITE, *Damour.* A mineral near Schilfglaserz (*Dufrénoy*). Lustre metallic. Streak greyish-black. Fracture uneven. H. scratches Calc-spar, and yields to the knife. S.G. 5.95.

Comp. PbS + Ag S + Sb² S³ or (Pb, Ag) S + ½Sb² S³ = sulphur 19·0, antimony 30·7, silver 25·7, lead 24·6 = 100.

Analysis by *Damour:*

Sulphur	19·14
Antimony	29·75
Silver	24·81
Lead	24·94
Copper	0·70
Iron	0·22
Zinc	0·37
	99·93

BB on charcoal decrepitates, fuses easily, giving off sulphurous odours and white vapours; after roasting, yields a globule of silver, surrounded with a yellow areola of lead.

Locality. The mines of Mexico, with Iron Pyrites.

Name. After M. Brongniart.

BRONGNIARTIN, *Von Leonhard.* See GLAUBERITE.

BRONZITE: a variety of Diallage. Oblique; isomorphous with Augite: primary form an oblique four-sided prism with a very distinct cleavage parallel to the lateral planes. Colour greenish-brown, brown, or ash-grey, with a pseudo-metallic lustre, frequently approaching that of bronze. Structure lamellar. Surface striated. Opaque in mass, translucent in thin laminæ. H. 5·5. S.G. 3·4.

Analysis from Ultenthal by *Regnault:*

Silica	55·84
Magnesia	30·37
Protoxide of iron	10·78
Alumina	1·09
Water	1·80
	99·98

BB melts with great difficulty.

Is not acted upon by acids.

Localities. In crystalline masses imbedded in serpentine, near Kraubat in Upper Styria; very abundantly on Monte Bracco, near Sestri, in Piedmont; Baste in the Harz, imbedded in greenstone; near Hoff in Bayreuth; Ulten-Thal, Tyrol; also in Serpentine at Coverack Cove, near the Lizard, in Cornwall; in syenite at Glen Tilt, in Perthshire; In greenstone in the Isle of Skye; and at Benenagh in Londonderry.

Brit. Mus., Case 25.

BROOKITE, *Phillips, Beudant.* Rhombic: primary form a right rhombic prism. Occurs in more or less translucent crystals of a hair-brown, yellowish, or reddish colour, with a brilliant lustre inclining to metallic: the opaque, iron-black crystals with a sub-metallic lustre from Arkansas have been

E 4

named by Shepard, Arkansite. Streak yellowish-white. Brittle. H. 6 to 6·5. S.G. 4·12 to 4·17.

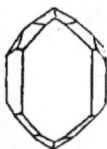

Fig. 67.

Comp. Ti or pure titanic acid, like Anatase.

Analysis, from the Urals, by *Hermann:*

Titanic acid	. .	94·09
Peroxide of iron	. .	4·50
Alumina	. .	trace
Loss	. . .	1·41
		100·00

BB alone on charcoal infusible, but with salt of phosphorus is entirely soluble and forms a brownish-yellow glass.

Insoluble in all acids except boiling oil of vitriol.

Localities. — British. Fine crystals have been found near Tremadoc, in Caernarvonshire, in a vein of white Quartz at Fronlen; in microscopic crystals imbedded in Siderite at Virtuous Lady mine, Tavistock; and rarely in small crystals on titanic iron, at Craig Cailleach, in Perthshire. *Foreign.* Bourg d'Oisans in Dauphiny, with Anatase and Crichtonite; the Tête-noir in Savoy; the Urals, district of Slatoust, and near Miask; and in extremely minute crystals at the Val del Bove, Etna, with Rutile. This mineral was first observed by Soret of Geneva, accompanying Anatase from Dauphiny, and described by Levy who named it after Brooke, the crystallographer.

Brit. Mus., Case 37.

BROSSITE. A name given to the Dolomite of Traversella.

BROWN COAL is of more recent formation than that associated with the true carboniferous rocks, and is found in Miocene tertiary strata. It generally occurs in beds of comparatively small extent, but often of great thickness, and is usually less free from Pyrites than true Coal. Sometimes it retains much of the appearance of the plants from which it is derived, and not only shows distinctly the structure of the wood, but retains its outward form also; while sometimes it can scarcely be distinguished from ordinary coal, breaking with a conchoidal fracture. See LIGNITE, SURTURBRAND.

Brit. Mus., Case 60.

M. P. G. Principal Floor, Wall-case 40, (Jamaica); Horse-shoe Case, Nos. 84 to 87.

BROWN HEMATITE, the name given to compact mammillary and stalactitic varieties of Limonite. See LIMONITE.

BROWN IRON-CINDER. See PITTICITE.

BROWN IRON-ORE. See LIMONITE.

BROWN LEAD-ORE, *Jameson, Kirwan.* See PYROMORPHITE.

BROWN OCHRE includes the soft and earthy, decomposed varieties of Limonite, or Brown Iron-ore.

BROWN QUARTZ, *Phillips.* See SMOKY QUARTZ.

BROWN SPAR. This name has been given both to the brown crystallized varieties of Dolomite, and especially to those varieties which contain a percentage of carbonate of iron.

M. P. G. Principal Floor, Wall-case 50 (British).

BRUCITE. The name given by Cleaveland to Chondlodrite, in honour of Professor Bruce, of New York.

BRUCITE. Hexagonal. Usually foliated, massive, or in fibres which are separable and elastic (Nemalite). Colour white, inclining to grey, blue, or green. Lustre pearly. Translucent, subtranslucent. Streak white. Sectile, thin laminæ flexible. H. 1·5. S.G. 2·35.

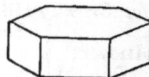

Fig. 68.

Comp. Hydrate of magnesia, or $\overset{\cdot\cdot}{Mg}\overset{\cdot}{H}$ = magnesia 68·97, water 31·03 = 100.

Analysis from Swinaness, by *Thomson:*

Magnesia	. .	66·67
Protoxide of manganese	.	1·57
Protoxide of iron	.	1·18
Lime	. . .	0·19
Water	. . .	30·39
		100·00

BB becomes opaque and friable, but does not fuse.

Entirely soluble in acids without effervescence.

Brucite accompanies other magnesian minerals in Serpentine.

Localities. Pyschminsk in the Urals; Goujot in France; Hoboken, N.J., opposite the city of New York, in veins which are sometimes an inch in width, rarely in minute polished crystals as in *fig.* 68; Wood's mine,

Chester Co., Pennsylvania, in Serpentine, in veins from one to four inches in width, which are coated on the outside with a layer of a greenish mineral resembling Chlorite. The mineral is broad-foliated; folia several inches square being easily obtainable, and either opaque silvery white, or translucent to transparent. Occasionally it has a fine roseate tint. Brucite, also, forms veins in Serpentine at Swinaness, in Unst, one of the Shetlands, where it is found in aggregated, foliated plates of silvery white colour, and translucent. On exposure it absorbs carbonic acid from the air and becomes white.

This mineral was discovered and described by Dr. Bruce of New York.

Brit. Mus., Case 58A.

BUCHOLZITE, *Brandes.* A variety of Sillimanite of a whitish, greyish, or pale brown colour, and with a lustre approaching to adamantine. Both Bucholzite and the Fibrolite of Bournon are generally in fibrous masses, sometimes approaching distinct prisms, like those of Sillimanite. H. 6 to 7·25. S.G. 3·24.

Fig. 69.

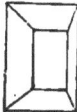

Comp. Sesquisilicate of alumina, or ½Äl

3 S̈i = silica 37, alumina 63 = 100.

Analysis from Faltigl, by *Brandes:*

Alumina	50·0
Silica	46·0
Peroxide of iron	2·5
Potash	1·5
	100·0

Localities. Bucholzite was originally obtained from the Fassa-thal, in the Tyrol, and described by Dr Brandes. It is also found near the Queensbury forge at Chester on the Delaware, and at other places in the United States.

Name. After Bucholz, the German chemist.

Brit. Mus., Case 26.

BUCKLANDITE, *Dufrénoy.* A variety of Pistacite or Epidote-proper, with much general resemblance to Augite. Primary form an oblique rhombic prism. Colour, dark brown, nearly black. Lustre vitreous. Opaque. Fracture uneven. Harder than Augite. S.G. 3·51.

Analysis by *Hermann:*

Silica	36·97
Alumina	21·84
Peroxide of iron	10·19
Protoxide of iron	9·19
Lime	21·14
Carbonate of lime	0·32
Water	0·68
	100·33

Localities. Arendal, in Norway, with black Hornblende, Felspar, and Apatite; and differing from Thallite only in colour, higher specific gravity 3·5 to 3·9, and by dissolving in muriatic acid; in minute but very brilliant crystals in the lavas of the Laacher-See on the Rhine; Achmatowsk.

This rare mineral was distinguished and described by Levy, who named it after Dr. Buckland.

Brit. Mus., Case 36.

BUNTBLEIERZ. See PYROMORPHITE.

BUNTER KUPFERKIES, *Hausmann.* See ERUBESCITE.

BUNTKUPFERERZ, *Werner.* See ERUBESCITE.

BURATITE, *Brongniart.* A mineral closely allied to, if not identical with, Aurichalcite: perhaps a mechanical mixture. Occurs in radiated acicular crystals, or plumose aggregations of a verdigris-green colour. G. 3·32.

Analysis by *Delesse:*

Carbonic acid	21·45
Oxide of zinc	32·02
Oxide of copper	29·46
Lime	8·62
Water	8·45
	100·00

Localities. Lining small cavities in Calamine, at Loktefskoi, in the Altai mountains; Chessy near Lyons; the copper mine of Temperino in Tuscany; Framont in the Tyrol.

Name. Named by Delesse after M. Burat.

Brit. Mus., Case 49.

BURNING GALENA. See JOHNSTONITE.

BUSTAMITE, *Brongniart.* A greyish-red variety of Rhodonite, occurring in irregularly disposed prismatic crystals, having at times a somewhat fibrous structure; almost opaque. H. 7. S.G. 3·1 to 3·35.

Analysis by *Dumas:*

Silica	48·90
Protoxide of manganese	36·06
Lime	14·57
Protoxide of iron	0·81
	100·34

Localities. Real de Minas de Tetala, de Jonotla, in the intendance of Puebla, in Mexico, associated with Iron Pyrites.

BUTTERMILCHERZ, or BUTTERMILK SILVER. An earthy variety of Horn Silver (Kerargyrite), met with at Andreasberg in the Harz. According to Klaproth it is composed of silver 24·64, muriatic acid 8·28, alumina 67·08=100.

Name. After Mons. Bustamente, the discoverer.

Brit. Mus., Case 26.

BUTYRITE, *Glocker.* See BOGBUTTER.

BYSSOLITE or BYSSOLITH, *Hausmann.* A variety of Actinolite, composed of fibres, which are as many small elongated prisms, terminating at their fine extremity in a point. Colour azure-blue. Transparent. Lustre pearly. S.G. 3·32.

Analysis by *Dufrénoy:*

Oxide of zinc . . .	26·98
Oxide of copper . .	4·17
Lime	29·69
Water and carbonic acid	39·16
	100·00

BB on charcoal gives the reaction of zinc. Effervesces briskly in acids.

Name. From βύσσος, *flax,* and λίθος, *stone.*

C.

CABOCLE. The name in Brazil for a compact brick-red mineral found in the diamond-sand of the province of Bahia. It resembles Jasper, but contains phosphoric acid, alumina, lime, and water. Slightly scratches glass. S.G. 3·194.

BB whitens but does not fuse.

Dissolves in concentrated warm sulphuric acid, leaving a white earthy residue, which is soluble in excess of boiling acid, and precipitated by the addition of water.

CACHOLONG. A variety of Opal, closely allied to Hydrophane, with which it is often associated. It is nearly opaque, of a milk- or bluish-white colour, dull externally, but with a somewhat pearly lustre within. Adheres to the tongue. S.G. 2·2.

Analysis by *Forchammer,* from Faröe:

Silica	95·32
Potash	0·07
Soda	0·06
Lime	0·06

Alumina	0 20
Magnesia	0·40
Water	3·47
	99·58

BB infusible.

It occurs in loose masses on the banks of the river Cach, in Bucharia, whence the name Cacholong is said to be derived; also in the trap rocks of Iceland; in the Faröe Islands, and in Greenland. It is also found in Ireland, at Smulgedon, in Ulster; in felspathic porphyry in the parish of Clogher, Tyrone co.; and at Barrack Mountain, in the parish of Pomeroy.

CACOXENE. See KAKOXENE. Occurs in extremely minute fibrous tufts, radiating from a point. Colour yellow or brownish-yellow. Lustre silky. Adheres to the tongue, has an astringent taste, and an argillaceous odour. H. 3 to 4. S.G. 3·38.

It is supposed to be an Iron-Wavellite.

Analysis by *Steinmann,* from Zbirow :

Alumina	10·01
Peroxide of iron . .	36·32
Phosphoric acid . .	17·86
Lime	0·15
Silica	8·90
Water and fluoric acid	25·95
	99·19

BB acts like Wavellite, except that it yields an iron reaction.

Localities. On brown Iron-ore in the iron mines of Hrbeck, near Zbirow, in Bohemia, and may be distinguished from Karpholite, which is found under similar circumstances, by its deeper tint.

Name. The name is derived from κακός, *bad,* ξένος, *guest,* in allusion to the injurious influence exercised by the phosphoric acid it contains upon the iron extracted from the ore with which it is found.

CADMIUM SULFURÉ, *Dufrénoy.* See GREENOCKITE.

CAHOUTCHOU FOSSILE, *La Metherie.* See ELATERITE.

CAILLOUX DU RHIN—DE MÉDOC. Polished rolled pebbles of Rock Crystal.

CAIRNGORM or CAIRNGORUM. The pellucid wine-yellow varieties of smoky Quartz are called Cairngorm, or Cairngorum-stone, after the name of the mountain in Inverness-shire, where they are found. It is also common throughout the central group of the Grampian Hills; the crystals met with on the east side of Loch Aven being pale and very clear, while those from the west side are of a dark brown colour.

The Cairngorm is frequently manufactured into jewelry, and is the stone generally used for ornamenting the handles of dirks, powder-horns, snuff-mulls, and other articles of a similar kind which form part of the Highland costume. (See SMOKY QUARTZ.) Brit. Mus., Case 20.

M.P.G. Horse-shoe Case, No. 507.

CAKING COAL. The name given to those kinds of bituminous coals which burn readily with a yellow flame and have a tendency to cake, or to run together, in the fire. The Newcastle coals are of this description.

CALAMINE, *Dana.* See SMITHSONITE.

CALAMINE, *Jameson, Nicol.* Hexagonal. It is found in obtuse rhombohedrons, and in long quadrilateral tables, which are sometimes modified; also compact, mammillated, *fibrous*, and incrusting other minerals, and occasionally earthy and friable. Colour greyish-white, or yellowish-grey, sometimes inclining to various shades of green and brown. Lustre vitreous, inclining to pearly. Translucent or opaque. Streak white. Yields easily to the knife. Brittle. Fracture uneven. H. 5. S.G. 4 to 4·5.

Fig. 70.

Comp. Zn C̈=carbonic acid 35·19, oxide of zinc 64·81=100, but frequently containing carbonates of iron, manganese, or lime. *BB* flies to pieces and becomes white, but is infusible either alone or with borax. Dissolves with effervescence in nitric acid. *Localities.—English.* Huel Mary, Cornwall; botryoidal at Roughten Gill, in Cumberland; mammillated and in crusts at Alston Moor; radiated, of a bluish-green colour, near Matlock, in Derbyshire; the Mendip Hills, in Somersetshire, sometimes in large pseudomorphous crystals after Calcite; crystallized in obtuse rhombohedrons near Holywell, in Flintshire.—*Scotch.* Leadhills. — *Irish.* Donegal and Galway. — *Foreign.* A dark brown variety, containing Cadmium, and another of a beautiful bright green, are found at Nertschinsk, in Siberia. Other localities are Dognatzka, in the Bannat of Temeswar, in Hungary; Raibel and Bleiberg, in Carinthia; Tarnowitz, in Silesia; Altenberg, near Aix-la-Chapelle; near Santander in Spain; &c.

Name. The name is derived from *calamus*, a reed, because during the process of smelting it adheres to the bottom of the furnace in the form of reeds.

This ore of Zinc is the Smithsonite of Haidinger and Von Kobell. It does not occur crystallized so often as the silicious oxide (see SMITHSONITE), being more frequently stalactitic, reniform, mammillated, cellular, and amorphous, and frequently assuming the aspect of Chalcedony.

Brit. Mus., Case 49.

M.P.G. A 33 in Hall; large cube, from the Vieille Montagne Mines. Principal floor, Wall-cases 12 and 33 (British), 21 (Foreign).

CALAMITE (from *calamus*, a reed). A soft, asparagus-green, translucent variety of Tremolite, from Normarken, in Sweden, where it occurs in longitudinally striated rhombic prisms imbedded in Serpentine.

CALC TUFF, *Jameson.* See CALCAREOUS TUFA.

CALCAREOUS EPIDOTE. See ZOISITE.

CALCAREOUS IRON-ORE, *Kirwan.* See CHALYBITE.

CALCAREOUS MESOTYPE. See SCOLEZITE.

CALCAREOUS OPHIOLITE. The name proposed by T. Sterry Hunt for the varieties of Serpentine containing intimate admixtures of Calcite.

CALCAREOUS SPAR. See CALCITE.

CALCAREOUS TUFA. A loose and friable variety of carbonate of lime, deposited in and about waters which are charged with lime. These sometimes form extensive beds, and are well adapted for building purposes, from their softness when first quarried and the hardness they subsequently acquire on exposure to the atmosphere. Some of the beds at the base of the Purbeck formation appear to have been formed after the manner of Tufas, and the tertiary fluvio-marine Limestones of the Isle of Wight also afford other examples of Calcareous Tufas, having evidently been deposited at the bottom of lakes impregnated with lime, or, in some cases, subaerially. Calcareous Tufa is frequently formed on the leaves and stems of plants, which are then said to be petrified or converted into stone, and the waters which possess this property are called petrifying springs. At Matlock there are springs of this description, where objects speedily become incrusted with carbonate of lime; but in Italy there are very extensive deposits of Calcareous Tufa, as at Terni, and on the banks of the river Anio, near Tivoli. (See TRAVERTINE.) The temples of Pæstum are built of Tufa, which has become hardened by time and exposure; to which circum-

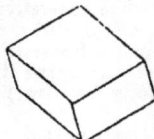

Fig. 71.

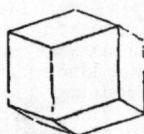

Fig. 72.

stance their preservation is probably owing, as it was found to be less laborious to go to the quarries in the neighbourhood from which the stone was originally raised, and procure the soft stone there, than to break up those of which the temples are constructed.

Brit. Mus., Case 46.

M.P.G. Upper Gallery, Wall-case 40, Table-case B, in recess 6, Nos. 207 to 223.

CALCAREOUS URAN-MICA, or CALCAREOUS URANITE. See URANITE.

CALCEDONY. See CHALCEDONY.

CALCEDONYX. The name given to those varieties of Agates in which opaque white Chalcedony or Cacholong alternates with translucent greyish Chalcedony.

CALCIFERRITE, *J. R. Blum.* A mineral related to Vivianite. Occurs crystalline foliated. Colour sulphur-yellow to siskin green and yellowish-white. Translucent in thin lamellæ. H. 2·5. S.G. 2·523 to 2·529.

Fig. 73

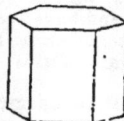

Fig. 74.

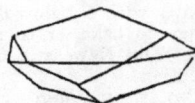

Analysis by Reissig :

Phosphoric acid	.	34·01
Alumina	.	2·90
Peroxide of iron	.	24·34
Lime	.	14·81
Magnesia	.	2·65
Water	.	20·56

99·27

Fig. 75.

Fig. 76.

BB yields a black shining magnetic globule.

Easily decomposed by muriatic acid.

Locality. Battenberg, in Rhenish Bavaria, forming nodules in clay. The exterior of the nodules is massive, and consists of impure or altered Calciferrite of a yellowish-brown or reddish-brown colour.

CALCIFORM COPPER ORE. The name under which Kirwan comprised the different varieties of carbonate of copper.

CALCITE. Hexagonal, rhombohedral: occurs crystallized in upwards of 800 varieties of form, nearly 700 of which have been figured by Count Bournon, in his treatise on Carbonate of Lime. The primary form is an obtuse rhombohedron, which may readily be obtained by cleavage, and may itself be occasionally cleaved parallel to a plane passing through the greater diagonals in one direction. Colour usually white, but sometimes of various shades of grey, red, green, or yellow, owing to the presence of iron, magnesia, bitumen, or other impurities. Lustre vitreous to earthy. Transparent to opaque. Streak white or greyish. Cross fracture conchoidal, but not easily obtained where

Fig. 77.

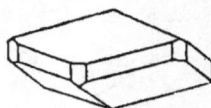

Fig. 78.

Fig. 79.

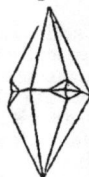

Fig. 80.

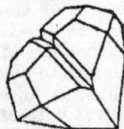

Fig. 81.

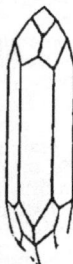

Fig. 82.

Fig. 83.

the specimen is crystallized. H. 2·5 to 3·5. S.G. 2·5 to 2·7.

Comp. Ċa C̈=carbonic acid 44, and lime 56 = 100; often with some carbonate of magnesia or iron.

BB infusible; alone on charcoal it shines with intense brightness when all the carbonic acid is expelled, and becomes converted into pure lime or quicklime. With fluxes behaves like Aragonite. Some varieties, as that accompanying Garnet in Wermeland, Laumonite in Brittany, shine with a yellow phosphorescent light when laid on a hot coal, or struck in the dark.

Effervesces violently with acids.

The purest form of Calcite is Iceland Spar, which in common with other transparent varieties is doubly refractive in a high degree. The different species will be described under their proper names.

Localities. This mineral is so universally distributed, that it is only possible to give a list of its most remarkable localities. Six-sided prisms of great beauty have been found at Andreasberg in the Harz. In England fine specimens are chiefly found in Cornwall, Devonshire and Derbyshire; in Wales, in Flintshire; in Scotland, at Strontian, Argyleshire; and in Ireland, at Kingston Cave, near Cahir, co. Clare. In Cornwall low hexagonal prisms and tabular forms prevail, like *figs.* 74 and 76. *Fig.* 82, represents the crystals from the Breakwater quarries at Plymouth. This *fig.* and *figs.* 79, 80, and 83, are the forms most common in Derbyshire, and at Alston Moor; *fig.* 79, being that called by the Derbyshire miner "Dog's-tooth Spar." In the neighbourhood of Alston, and at Garrigill in Cumberland, the crystals have commonly a hexagonal character, as represented in *figs.* 71, 73, 74, 77, 78, and 81. *Fig.* 77 represents a form met with at Dufton and Patterdale in Westmoreland.

Name. From the Latin calx, *lime.*

Brit. Mus., Cases 42 to 47.

M. P. G. Principal Floor, Wall-cases 27, 28, and 30: Horse-shoe Case, Nos. 367 to 391.

CALDERITE. A massive variety of Garnet from Nepal.

CALEDONITE, *Beudant, Greg & Lettsom.*

Fig. 84.

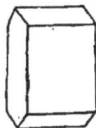

Fig. 85.

Rhombic. Primary form a right rhombic prism. Colour bluish-green, inclining to

mountain-green if the crystals are delicate. Lustre resinous. Translucent. Streak greenish-white. Rather brittle. Fracture uneven. H. 2·5 to 3. S.G. 6·4.

Comp. Cupreous sulphato-carbonate of Lead, or 6 Ṗb S̈ + 4 PḃC̈ + 3 ĊuC̈.

Analysis by Brooke:

Sulphate of lead . . .	55·8
Carbonate of lead . . .	32·8
Carbonate of copper . .	11·4
	100·0

BB on charcoal, easily reduced. Partially soluble, with slight effervescence, in nitric acid.

Localities. Found in flattish crystals accompanied by other ores of lead, at Lead-hills in Lanarkshire, and with Cerussite and Leadbillite at Roughten Gill in Cumberland: also said to occur at T'anné in the Harz, and at Mine la Motte in Missouri. The crystals are generally very minute, and appear sometimes in small bunches radiating from their common point of attachment to the matrix.

Brit Mus., Case 55.

CALLAIS. See TURQUOIS.

CALLAITE, *Allan, Fischer, Phillips, Nicol.* See TURQUOIS.

CALLIMUS, *J. Woodward.* The name given to the stony matter contained in the cavities of Ætites, when it is loose and moveable.

CALOMEL, *Beudant.* Pyramidal. Sometimes occurs crystallized in distinct quadrangular prisms terminated by pyramids: also in tubercular crusts; sometimes fibrous, rarely compact. Colour greyish-white grey, yellowish, greenish-grey, brown: occasionally translucent, with an adamantine lustre. Sectile. Fracture conchoidal. H. 1 to 2. S.G. 6·48

Fig. 86.

Comp. Hg^2 Cl = chlorine 15·1, mercury 84·9=100.

BB on charcoal, it is entirely volatilized if pure.

Localities. Large and well-defined crystals of this rare mineral are found at Moschellandsberg in Deux Ponts (Bavaria), coating the cavities of a ferruginous gangue, and associated with Cinnabar; it is also met with at the quicksilver mines of Idria in Carniola, at Almaden in Spain, and Horzowitz in Bohemia.

CALSTRONBARYTE, *Shepard.* This mineral, found at Schoharie, New York, has been proved by Shepard to be merely a mechanical mixture of Heavy Spar, Strontianite, and Calcite, and not a distinct species. The trivial name alludes to the three bases which enter into its composition.

CALYPTOLITE, *Shepard.* A Zircon, probably somewhat altered, occurring in minute short, square prisms of a dark brown or greenish-brown colour, at Haddam in Connecticut, U.S., with Chrysoberyl. H. 6·5. S.G. 4·34.

CANAANITE, *S. L Dana.* A greyish scapolitic rock from Canaan, Connecticut.

It is composed of

Silica	. .	53·36
Peroxide of iron	. .	4·09
Alumina	. .	10·38
Lime	. .	25·80
Magnesia	. .	1·62
Carbonic acid	. .	4·00
		99·67

CANCRINITE. Hexagonal. Occurs in six and twelve-sided prisms, sometimes with the basal edges replaced: also thin columnar and massive. Colour white, yellow, green, blue, grey, reddish. Lustre vitreous at the fractured surfaces, greasy in other parts. Transparent or translucent. H. 5·5 to 6. S.G. 2·42 to 2·62.

Comp. According to *Breithaupt,* this mineral is identical with Davyne. $2\,[\mathrm{Na^2}$ $\ddot{\mathrm{S}}\mathrm{i}+2\,\ddot{\mathrm{A}}\mathrm{l}\ \ddot{\mathrm{S}}\mathrm{i}+(\dot{\mathrm{N}}\mathrm{a}\ \dot{\mathrm{C}}\mathrm{a})\ \ddot{\mathrm{C}}]\ +3\dot{\mathrm{H}}.$ *P. v. Pusirewsky.*

Analysis, by *Whitney,* from Litchfield, U.S.:

	Yellow.	Green.
Potash . .	0·67	0·50
Soda . .	20·98	20·46
Alumina . .	27·70	27·56
Peroxide of iron . trace		
Peroxide of manganese .	}	0·27
. . 0·86		
Silica . .	37·42	37·20
Lime . .	3·91	5·26
Carbonic acid .	5·95	5·92
Water · .	2·82	3·28
Chlorine .	trace	trace
	100·31	100·45

B B loses colour and fuses easily to a transparent, colourless, blistered glass.

Dissolves in muriatic acid with violent effervescence, and forms a jelly on heating but not before.

Localities. Of a light rose-red colour in the Ilmen mountains (S.G. 2·489); of a citron-yellow colour at Marünskaja, in the Tunkinsk mountains, 400 wersts from Irkutsk, in coarse granite (S.G. 2·454); and crystallized and massive in the United States at Litchfield, in the State of Maine.

Name. After Cancrin, a Russian minister of finance.

CANDITE, *Bournon.* Pleonaste found associated with Tourmaline, &c., loose in the rivers and alluvial district around Kandy, (whence the name Candite,) in Ceylon.

CANEHLSTEIN, from Cannel (Dutch). See CINNAMON STONE.

CANNEL COAL. Cannel is a corruption of the word *Candle,* which has been applied to a particular description of Coal, either because in burning it gives out a bright flame like that of a candle, or because, in some places, poor people use it instead of lights.

It is a bituminous substance, and is supposed to have been formed from decomposed vegetable matter in water, in the finest state of division. It differs from the purer kinds of ordinary Coal and Jet, in containing extraneous earthy matters, which render it specifically heavier than water; Jet, on the contrary, being lighter. It is hard enough to take a fine polish, and is made into inkstands, snuff-boxes, beads, and other ornamental articles. (See also PARROT COAL.) S.G. 1·23. Cannel Coal has a resinous glistening lustre, and a dark greyish-black colour. It is very compact, breaking with a conchoidal fracture, into irregular or cubical fragments. The Cannel Coal of Lesmahagow on distillation yields 40 gallons of crude oil, and 30 gallons of rectified oil per ton.

It is found in England near Whitehaven, at Wigan in Lancashire, Brosely in Shropshire, and Athercliff, near Sheffield; and in Scotland at Lesmahagow in Lanarkshire, Boghead in Linlithgowshire, Gilmerton near Edinburgh, West Wemyss in Fife, and Muirkirk in Clydesdale.

M.P.G. Horse-shoe Case, Nos. 70 and 78. Upper Gallery, Wall-cases 41, No. 161, and 43, Nos 149, 150.

CANOXINITE, *Bischof.* A mineral consisting of the silicates of soda and alumina, and carbonate of lime, from the Miasget in the Ural. There are three varieties found in the granite of Litchfield (Maine, U.S.), consisting of the silicates of soda and alumina, with carbonates of lime and soda.

CANTALITE. A variety of Pitchstone containing crystals of Glassy Felspar. Colour green. Lustre resinous inclining to vitreous. Slightly translucent (most Pitchstones being opaque). Fracture tending to conchoidal. S.G. 2·36.

Comp. 3Äl S̈i + K̇ S̈i⁵ + 3Ḣ.

Analysis by *Berthier* :

Silica	64·45
Alumina . . .	15·64
Lime	1·20
Oxide of iron . .	4·30
Magnesia . . .	1·20
Potash . .	5·40
Water	7·10
	99·24

BB fuses to a white enamel.
Locality. Cantal.

CANTONITE, *N. A. Pratt. Jun.* Is met with crystallized in well-formed cubes diffused through large masses of rock made up of small cubic Pyrites, and in an impalpable state disseminated through a veinstone of granular Quartz and Staurotide. Colour and streak bluish-black. Lustre sub-metallic and shining. H. 1·5 to 2. S.G. 4·18.

In physical properties (except in streak) and in composition, Cantonite is identical with Covelline; being, however, cubical instead of hexagonal, and exactly similar to Harrisite and Galena.

It is named after the locality where it occurs, the Canton mine, Georgia, U.S.

CAPILLARY OBSIDIAN. See PÉLÉ'S HAIR.

CAPILLARY PYRITES, *Jameson, Kirwan.* See MILLERITE.

CAPILLARY RED OXIDE OF COPPER. *Phillips.* See CHALCOTRICHITE.

CAPORCIANITE. Oblique. A flesh-red coloured mineral, with a pearly lustre, probably related to Laumonite.

Comp. Ċa, Äl, 4S̈i, 3Ḣ=lime 12·15, alumina 22·31, silica 53·82, water 11·72=100.

Analysis by *Anderson* :

Silica	52·8
Alumina . . .	21·7
Lime	11·3
Magnesia . . .	0·4
Soda . . .	0·2
Potash . . .	1·1
Peroxide of iron . .	0·1
Water	13·1
	100·7

BB swells up slightly and fuses immediately to a white enamel.
Dissolves easily in acids.
Localities. In geodes in the Gabbro rosso

of Monte de Caporciano, at L'Impruneta and other places in Tuscany; with Calcite, and sometimes with Native Copper.
Brit. Mus., Case 28.

CAPPED QUARTZ. A variety of Quartz Crystal, found in Cornwall, imbedded in compact Quartz. When the investing matrix is broken the crystals are revealed, and at the same time a cast or impression in intaglio of their pyramidal terminations is obtained, forming the capping from which this variety of Quartz derives its name.

In this instance the crystals were formed first and then a deposit of compact Quartz has been deposited over them subsequently, a slight film intervening between the crystals and the Quartz which invests them.

M.P.G. Horse-shoe Case, No. 478. From Tintagel Slate Quarries.

CARBOCERINE, *Beudant.* See LANTHANITE.

CARBONATE OF BARYTES, *Phillips.* See WITHERITE.

CARBONATE OF BISMUTH. See BISMUTITE.

CARBONATE OF CERIUM, *Phillips.* See LANTHANITE.

CARBONATE OF COPPER. See MALACHITE: also MYSORIN, LIME-MALACHITE, AZURITE.

CARBONATE OF IRON. *Phillips.* See CHALYBITE: also CLAY-IRONSTONE, JUNKERITE, SPHÆROSIDERITE.

CARBONATE OF LEAD, *Phillips.* See CERUSITE.

CARBONATE OF LIME, *Phillips.* See CALCITE: also SCHIEFER-SPAR, STALACTITE, STALAGMITE, ORIENTAL ALABASTER, AGARIC-MINERAL, APHRITE, STINKSTONE, TRAVERTINE, TUFA, ARAGONITE, &c.

CARBONATE OF MAGNESIA, *Phillips.* See MAGNESITE.

CARBONATE OF MAGNESIA AND IRON. See BREUNNERITE.

CARBONATE OF MANGANESE, *Phillips.* See DIALLOGITE: also MANGANOCALCITE.

CARBONATE OF NATRON, *La Metherie.* See TRONA.

CARBONATE OF SILVER, *Phillips.* See SELBITE.

CARBONATE OF SODA, *Phillips.* See TRONA.

CARBONATE DE SOUDE, *Brochant.* See NATRON.

CARBONATE OF STRONTIAN. See STRONTIANITE.

CARBONATE OF URANIUM. See VOGLITE and ZIPPEITE.

CARBONATE OF ZINC, *Phillips.* See CALAMINE.

CARBUNCLE. The name given by jewellers to the variety of precious Garnet (Pyrope) which is cut *en cabochon.* It is also one of the stones to which the ancients gave the same name, the Carbunculus Garamanticus, or Carthaginian Carbuncle, being the Garnet of the moderns.

M.P.G. Horse-shoe Case, Nos. 894 to 896.

CARBURET OF IRON. See GRAPHITE.

CARINTHINE. A ferruginous and aluminous Hornblende from Carinthia. S.G. 3·127.

Brit. Mus., Case 33.

CARINTHITE. See WULFENITE.

CARMINE SPAR, CARMINITE, CARMINSPATH, *Sandberger.* An anhydrous arsenate of Lead and Iron, occuring in fine needles, and in spheroidal forms with a columnar structure. Colour carmine to tile-red, translucent, with a vitreous lustre, which is pearly on the planes of cleavage. Brittle. Affords a reddish-yellow powder. S.G. 4·1.

Analysis by *Sandberger :*

Arsenic acid	. .	. 49·11
Peroxide of iron	. .	. 30·29
Oxide of lead	. .	. 24·55

103·95

BB on charcoal fuses readily to a steel-grey globule, giving off arsenical fumes; with soda yields a globule of lead; and an iron reaction with borax.

Locality. Horhausen in Saxony, in Quartz and Brown Iron-ore.

CARNALLITE, *H. Rose.* A salt more soluble than common salt, found crystallized in the mother-water of salt-works at Stassfurth, in Prussia. It occurs in coarsely granular masses, slightly coloured red by oxide of iron. Deliquescent. Lustre very greasy. Fracture conchoidal.

Comp. $2Mg\ Cl + K\ Cl + 12\overset{..}{H}$.

Analysis by *Klaproth :*

Silica	. . .	. 45·25
Alumina	. . .	. 36·50
Peroxide of iron	. .	. 2·75
Potash	. .	trace
Water	. .	. 14·00

98·50

Locality. Rochlitz in Saxony.

Name. From Caro (carnis) *flesh.*

CARNAT, *Breithaupt.* A red variety of Lithomarge.

CARNELIAN. A variety of Chalcedony, generally of a clear bright red tint, and passing into common Chalcedony through greyish-red gradations. The colour is due

to the presence of iron, Heintz having found, by analysis, Carnelian to contain per cent

Peroxide of iron	. .	. 0·050
Alumina	. . .	. 0·081
Magnesia	. . .	. 0·028
Potash	. . .	. 0·0043
Soda	. . . .	. 0·075

The gradation from red to white Carnelian is, insensibly, through flesh-red and blood-red more or less mixed with brown to orange and various tints of yellow. The best specimens are of a perfectly uniform colour, free from undulations and the muddiness to which European specimens are liable.

Carnelian is susceptible of a high polish, and, for that reason, and the brightness of its colour, it has always been a favourite substance, much used for seals, brooches, rings, necklaces, &c., both in ancient and modern times.

" Generally, all Rubies be verie hard for to be cut, & this ill qualitie they have, That they never doe seale cleane, but ordinarily plucke some of the wax away with the signet: contrariwise, the Cornalline or Sarda, signeth verie faire without any of the wax sticking to it.

" In old time, there was not a pretious stone in greater request, than the Cornalline: and in truth, *Menander* and *Philemon* have named this stone in their Comœdies, for a brave and proud gem: neither can we find a pretious stone that maintaineth the lustre longer than it, against any humour wherein it is drenched; and yet oile is more contrarie unto it than any other liquor. To conclude, those that ●be of the colour of honey are rejected for nought; howbeit, if they resemble the colour of earthen pots, they be worse than those." — *Pliny*, book xxxviii. chap. 7.

Forbes states that Carnelians, Agates, and the beautifully variegated stones improperly called Mocha-stones, form a valuable part of the trade of Cambay, to which place the art of cutting and polishing these stones seems to be exclusively confined.

" The best Agates and Carnelians," he adds, " are found in peculiar strata, thirty feet under the surface of the earth, in a small tract among the Rajpipla hills, on the banks of the Nerbudda: they are not to be met with in any other part of Guzerat, and are generally cut and polished in Cambay.* On being taken from their native bed, they are exposed to the heat of the sun for two years: the longer they remain in that situa-

* The revenue derived from these mines has greatly fallen off of late years, and they scarcely yield now 1000 rupees per annum.

tion the brighter and deeper will be the colour of the stone; fire is sometimes substituted for the solar ray, but with less effect, as the stones frequently crack and seldom acquire a brilliant lustre. After having undergone this process, they are boiled for two days and sent to the manufacturers at Cambay. The Agates are of different hues:.those generally called Car·nelians are black, white, and red, in shades from the palest yellow to the deepest scarlet."—*Oriental Mems.*, vol. ii. p. 20.

From the circumstance of the lustre of the stones being inferior when artificial heat has been substituted for that of the solar rays, it may be inferred that the change of colour is not produced by the sun's heat alone, but that light, or the actinic rays, exercise considerable influence in producing the effect described. It may here be observed that the chalk-flints, which form the superficial gravel in many parts of this country, are very frequently of a bright red and yellowish-brown colour, in fact, converted into Agates and imperfect Carnelians by long exposure to the sun's heat and light, and the consequent peroxidation of the iron contained in them.

Localities. The finest specimens of Carnelian are procured from Arabia, and from Cambay and Surat in India; it is also found in the province of Auckland, in New Zealand, in trachytic rocks, in numerous places on the shores of Coromandel; in Saxony, Scotland, &c.

Name. The name is derived from *carneus* (from *caro*, flesh), in allusion to its colour. Brit. Mus., Case 23.

M.P.G. Horse-shoe Case, Nos. 609, 610, 619, 621.

CAROLATHINE, *Sonnenschein.* A mineral somewhat resembling Mellite, found in rounded globular or massive, of a honey-yellow to wine-yellow colour. Subtranslucent. Fracture conchoidal. H. 2·5. S.G. 1·5.

Analysis afforded a volatile part, the composition of which (including water) was

Hydrogen	.	.	. 2·41
Oxygen	.	.	. 19·39
Carbon	.	.	. 1·33

And a fixèd mass composed of

Alumina	.	.	. 47·25
Silica	.	.	. 29·62

100·00

Locality. Near Gleiwitz in Upper Silesia, in a bed of Mineral Coal.

Named after the Prince of Carolath. Brit. Mus., Case 26.

CARPHOLITE, *Werner.* Occurs in tufts of minute, fibrous, imperfectly formed crystals; also massive, with a fibrous and frequently radiated structure, which is rather incoherent; also in an earthy state. Colour pure straw-yellow, sometimes approaching to wax-yellow. Opaque, with a silky lustre. Very brittle. H. 5 to 5·5. S. G. 2·93.

Comp. Hydrated silicate of alumina and

protoxide of manganese, or $(\dot{F}e\ \dot{M}n)^5\ \ddot{S}i +$

$\ddot{A}l\ \ddot{S}i + 2\dot{H}.$

Analysis by *Steinmann:*

Silica	.	.	. 37·53
Alumina	.	.	.. 26·47
Oxide of manganese	.		. 18·33
Peroxide of iron	.	.	. 6·27
Water	.	.	. 11·36

·· 99·96

BB on charcoal intumesces, whitens, and fuses slowly to a turbid brownish glass, which becomes darker in the outer flame. Scarcely attacked by muriatic acid.

Localities. In the tin mines of Schlackenwald in Bohemia, on granite, with Fluor and Quartz.

Named by Werner from κάρφος, *straw,* and λίθος, *stone,* in allusion to its colour.

CARPHOSIDERITE. A straw - coloured mineral, resembling oxalate of iron, from Labrador, where it occurs in reniform masses and incrustations, in fissures in mica-slate. It has a resinous lustre and a greasy feel. Streak yellowish. H. 4 to 4·5. S.G. 2·49 to 5.

Comp. It is composed of oxide of iron, phosphoric acid, and water, with small quantities of manganese and zinc.

BB turns red, and yields a magnetic bead.

Name. From κάρφος, *straw,* and σίδηρος, *iron.*

CARPHOSTILBITE. A straw-yellow and columnar variety of Thomsonite, from Berufiord, in Iceland.

Analysis by *Waltershausen:*

Silica	.	.	. 39·28
Alumina	.	.	. 29·50
Lime	.	.	. 12·38
Soda	.	.	. 4·09
Potash	.	.	. 0·38
Magnesia	.	.	. 0·13
Peroxide of iron	.	.	. 1·49
Water	.	.	. 13·23

100·48

Name. From ϰάϱϕος, *straw*, in allusion to its colour.

CARROLLITE. *Faber.* A copper-Linnæite, composed of $Cu\ S + Co^2\ S^3$. Colour tin-white, inclining to steel-grey. Lustre metallic, tarnished in some places. Streak iron-black. Brittle. Fracture uneven; subconchoidal in small fragments. H. 5·5. S.G. 4·58.

Analysis by *Smith & Brush:*

Sulphur	.	.	.	40·94
Cobalt	.	.	.	38·21
Copper	.	.	.	17·79
Iron	.	.	.	1·55
Nickel	.	.	.	1·54
Arsenic	.	.	.	a trace
				100.03

BB on charcoal emits strong odours of sulphurous acid and arsenic, intumesces and swells to a white, brittle, and magnetic globule.

Locality. Finksburg, Carroll Co., Maryland, U.S., in a vein of Copper Pyrites.

Name. After the locality, Carroll Co.

CARTON DE MONTAGNE, or MOUNTAIN PASTEBOARD. A kind of Mountain Leather.

CARYAT. A synonym for Chalcedony.

CASCHOLONG, *Brooke & Miller.* See CACHOLONG.

CASSITERITE, *Beudant, Dana.* Oxide of Tin. Pyramidal: primary form an obtuse pyramid with a square base. It is found in quadrangular prisms, terminated by four-sided pyramids, and in many more complex forms. Colour most commonly blackish-brown, passing into black; also hair-brown or reddish-brown, yellowish-green, yellowish or greenish-white, and colourless. It varies

Fig. 87.   Fig. 88.

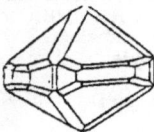   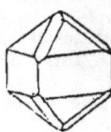

Fig. 89.   Fig. 90.

from semi-transparent to opaque, the darker varieties being opaque, while the lighter are translucent and semi-transparent. Occurs massive, disseminated, in rolled pieces, in grains as sand, but most frequently in crystals, which are generally very indistinct. Externally they are splendent. Brittle. Fracture uneven or imperfect conchoidal, with a shining resinous lustre. Structure lamellar. Streak greyish-white. H. 6 to 7. S.G. 6·8 to 7.

Comp. Sn = tin 78·38, oxygen 21·62 = 100.

Sometimes with small quantities of iron, oxide of manganese, and tantalic acid.

Analysis from Finbo, by *Berzelius:*

Oxide of tin	.	.	93·6
Tantalic acid	.	.	2·4
Peroxide of iron	.	.	1·4
Peroxide of manganese	.	0·8
			98·2

BB decrepitates, becomes pale, and is reduced where it rests on the charcoal. When roasted it is converted into a grey oxide. Insoluble in acids.

Localities.—English. This ore is principally found in Cornwall, where it has been worked from a very remote period. In general, the Cornish crystals, though extremely perfect in form, are not of large size, neither are they so often macled as those of Bohemia. Very fine crystals have been found in the parish of St. Agnes, at Trevaunance (*figs.* 87 and 88), at Polberro Consols, and Huel Pye; fine twinned crystals at Beam, and other mines near St. Austell; and in large macled crystals at Huel Gwinear. Beautiful crystals were met with some years ago at the Wherry Mine, near Penzance, and at St. Just. *Foreign.* Galicia, in Spain: the Granite-hill of Puy les Vignes, Haute Vienne, in France, and near Roc St. André, in Brittany; Pitkaranta, in Finland, in fine crystals; Greenland, at Evigtok, near Arksut, associated with Cryolite and Tantalite; Sweden; United States; Asia, on the east coast of Sumatra; in the island of Banca, and on the peninsula of Malacca; Chili; Xeres, in Mexico; Los Angelos, in California: Australia, in the form of black sand. The compound crystals come mostly from Bohemia and Saxony. Some of the twin forms from Zinnwald and Schlackenwald often weigh several pounds. Splendid crystals are procured from Limoges.

Name. From ϰασσίτεϱος, *tin.*

Most of the tin of commerce is obtained from this ore.

Brit. Mus., Case 18.

CASSITEROTANTALITE.

M.P.G. Principal floor, Wall-cases, 8 and 25 to 27 (British); 20 (Foreign); 39 (E. Indies); 37 (Victoria and Australia).

Cassiterite may be distinguished from Wolfram by its greater hardness, by its giving sparks with steel and by its streak, which is greyish-white, but reddish-brown in Wolfram. From Blende it may be known by its greater hardness and uneven fracture.

Tin Ore is met with in veins traversing granite, gneiss, mica- or clay-slate and porphyry.

CASSITEROTANTALITE. *Hausmann.* A variety of Tantalite from Finbo and Broddbo, in Sweden, containing much oxide of tin, as a mechanical mixture. S.G. 6·2 to 6·5.

Analysis from Broddbo, by *Berzelius;*

Tantalic acid	66·35
Peroxide of iron	11·07
Peroxide of manganese	6·60
Oxide of tin	8·40
Tungstic acid	6·12
Lime	1·50
	100·19

CASTELNAUDITE, *Damour.* A variety of Xenotime, found in imperfect crystals, and irregular grains, in the diamond-sands of Bahia, in the Brazils. It varies in colour from greyish-white to pale yellow, and has a greasy adamantine lustre. Hardness greater than Fluor, but scratched by a steel point.

CASTOR. A mineral discovered by Breithaupt; probably a variety of Petalite, which it resembles in hardness, density, and the direction of its two planes of cleavage. Primary form a modified rhombic prism. Colourless, and transparent, with a high glossy lustre. H. 8·25 to 8·5. S.G. 2·39.

Comp. Li Ṡi + 2(Äl 2Ṡi).

Analysis by *Plattner:*

Silica	78·01
Alumina	18·86
Lithia	2·76
Peroxide of iron	0·61
	100·24

BB in thin laminæ, fuses with difficulty to a transparent, colourless globule; imparts an intense carmine colour to the outer flame.

Locality. Elba, in attached crystals in granite with an allied mineral, which has been named Pollux.

Brit. Mus., Case 30.

CAT'S EYE. 67

CAT SAPPHIRE. Blackish or greenish-blue varieties of Oriental Sapphire; often not transparent.

CAT SILVER. An old German mining term for Mica.

CATAPLEIITE. A mineral of a pale yellowish-brown colour, occurring in imperfect hexagonal crystals, with a perfect basal cleavage. Lustre nearly dull. Slightly vitreous on fractured surfaces. Opaque. Streak Isabella-yellow. H. near 6. S.G. 2·8.

Comp. $\ddot{R}^2 \ddot{Si}^2 + 2\ddot{Z}r \ddot{Si}^2 + 6\dot{H}.$

Analysis by *Sjögren:*

Silica	46·83
Zirconia	29·81
Alumina	0·45
Soda	10·83
Lime	3·61
Peroxide of iron	0·63
Water	8·86
	101·02

BB in the platinum forceps, fuses easily to a white enamel; with borax forms a clear colourless glass.

Locality. The island of Lamö, near Brevig, in Norway.

CAT'S EYE. A variety of Chalcedonic Quartz, usually of a yellowish, greenish, ash-grey, or yellowish-brown colour; also, hair-brown and hyacinth-red; sometimes olive-green and blackish. It occurs massive and in roundish pieces, rarely exceeding a hazel-nut in size, generally much smaller. Commonly more or less translucent, but sometimes perfectly transparent. Easily broken. Fracture small, and imperfectly conchoidal, with a shining lustre between vitreous and resinous.

BB it loses lustre and transparency on exposure to a strong heat, and in small fragments is fusible, though with difficulty.

Localities. Ceylon; the coast of Malabar; the Harz; Bavaria; Sanzawa, in Bohemia. A pale green variety occurs with Epidote in the vale of Llanberis, Caernarvonshire; also in Scotland.

Brit. Mus., Case 22.

M.P.G. Horse-shoe Case, No. 514.

When cut in high *cabochon*, in which state it is generally brought to this country, it displays a peculiar opalescence or floating lustre (resembling the contracted pupil of a cat's eye when held towards the light), which is supposed to be caused by the presence of small parallel fibres of Asbestos. It is mostly used as a ring-stone. Of the opaque varieties the red and almost white

F 2

are preferred, but the value of the stone depends more upon its play of colour than upon the greater or less amount of its transparency.

CATLINITE. A reddish variety of claystone from the Côteau des Prairies, west of the Mississippi, which is carved into tobaccopipes by the North American Indians. It is named by Dr. Jackson after Catlin, the American traveller, who was the first white man allowed by the Indians to visit the quarry where it is found.

Brit. Mus., Case 26.

M.P.G. Horse-shoe Case, No. 4.

CAULIFLOWER. The name given by the quarrymen in the Isle of Portland to stalagmitic carbonate of lime, found in the joints of Portland Stone.

CAVOLINITE, *Monticelli.* See NEPHELINE.

CAWK. An opaque, massive, earthy-looking variety of Barytes, of a dirty-white or reddish colour, very common in Derbyshire with Galena. It is also found at Grassington, in Yorkshire, and in Staffordshire.

Brit. Mus., Case 52.

CELESTIN, *Werner.* CELESTINE, *Jameson, Werner.* Rhombic. It occurs massive, fibrous, stellated, and crystallized; the primary form being a right rhombic prism. Colour white, grey, seldom yellow or reddish, but sometimes of a delicate blue, sometimes approaching to sky-blue, whence the name Celestine. Lustre shining. Transparent to subtranslucent. Streak white. Very brittle. H. 3 to 3·5. S.G. 3·95.

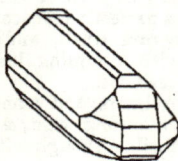

Fig. 91.

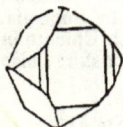 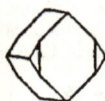 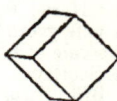

Fig. 92.   Fig. 93.   Fig. 94.

Comp. Sr S̈ = sulphuric acid 43·6, strontia 56·4 = 100, often mixed with carbonate of lime, barytes, or oxide of iron.

BB decrepitates and melts into a white, opaque, friable enamel. When reduced to powder, it phosphoresces on red-hot iron.

Localities. Fine transparent prismatic crystals are found associated with Sulphur and Gypsum in the sulphur mines of Sicily; it is also met with at Bex, in Switzerland; in the Green Marls of Montmartre and Beaumont (Dordogne), and in Chalk Flints at Meudon, in France; Conil, in Spain; Pschow, in Upper Silesia; and in straight fibrous concretions, of a blue colour, imbedded in clay at Dornberg near Jena; and at Frankstown, in Pennsylvania. It occurs in considerable quantities in New Red Marl, in the neighbourhood of Bristol, where it is made into Nitrate of Strontia, which forms the basis of the red fire used in pyrotechny.

Brit. Mus., Case 53..

M. P. G. Horse-shoe Case, Nos. 266 to 280; also No. 147. Upper Gallery, Wallcase 40, No. 45.

CELLULAR PYRITES. Iron Pyrites (Marcasite) which has been deposited in thin films between layers of Galena, on the removal of which a honeycomb appearance is produced.

Locality. Johanngeorgenstadt, in Saxony.

CELLULAR QUARTZ. A cellular variety of Quartz, which is sometimes so porous as to float in water till the air contained in its pores escapes. (See FLOAT STONE.)

It is found in Cornwall, at Relistian mine, Cardrew mine, Huel Alfred, Pednandrea, &c. The curious brownish-grey variety met with at Alston Moor, in Cumberland, is probably the skeleton or the divisions of Septaria which have been left after the removal of the other portions of the stone.

CEMENT COPPER, *Kirwan.* Metallic Copper, produced by the precipitation of copper by iron, from waters which held it in solution.

CENDRES NOIRES. Friable and pulverulent Lignite, from alluvial beds, containing a considerable quantity of Sperkise, or Iron Pyrites, and used by the agriculturalists of Picardy as a manure.

After being burnt, either by spontaneous combustion or calcination, it is called *Cendres rouges.*

CENTRALASSITE, *H. How.* A mineral occurring between the external coating and the central portion of a reniform nodule, partly imbedded in crystalline trap. Structure lamellar. Consists of plates radiating from a centre, and forming truly spherical concretions. Colour white, sometimes yellowish. Translucent; perfectly transparent in thin plates, which are easily obtained and readily broken across. Lustre subresinous; highly pearly on cleavage planes. H. 3·5. S.G. 2·45 to 2·46.

CERASINE.

Comp. $\dot{C}a^4 \overset{...}{Si}^5 + 5\dot{H} = $ lime 29·20, silica 50·06, water 11·74 = 100.

Analysis:

Silica	.	.	.	. 58·86
Alumina	.	.	.	. 1·14
Lime	.	.	.	. 27·91
Magnesia	.	.	.	. 0 16
Potash	.	.	.	. 0·59
Water	.	.	.	. 11·41
				100·07

In matrass yields water, becoming opaque and silvery-white.

BB alone fuses readily, with continued spirting, to an opaque glassy bead.

Decomposed by muriatic acid without gelatinising.

Locality. The Bay of Fundy, on the shore of Annapolis Co., two miles E. of Black Rock.

Name. From κέντρον, *a centre,* and ἀλάσσω, *to change,* in allusion to the passage of the mineral into opaque white, a change of condition which commences uniformly at the centre.

Centralasite differs from Cyanolite, in having 5 equivalents less Silica. See CYANOLITE and CERINITE.

CERASINE or CERASITE; names given by *Beudant,* both to Mendipite and Cromfordite.

CERASITE, *Dana.* See MENDIPITE.

CERAUNIAN SINTER, from κεραύνιος, *struck with lightning.* See FULGURITE.

CERERIT, *Haidinger, Hausmann.* CERERITE, *Brooke & Miller.* CERINSTEIN, *Werner.* Hexagonal. Occurs in short six-sided prisms, also massive and granular. Colour between dark peach-red and clove-brown, passing into grey. Slightly translucent at the edges. Lustre dull adamantine or resinous. Streak greyish white. Scratches glass, and gives sparks with steel. Fracture splintery and more or less shining. H. 5·5. S.G. 4·93.

Comp. Disilicate of Cerous Oxide, or

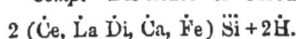

$$2 (\dot{C}e, \dot{L}a \dot{D}i, \dot{C}a, \dot{F}e) \overset{...}{Si} + 2\dot{H}.$$

Analysis (mean) by *Rammelsberg:*

Silica	.	.	.	. 19·18
Protoxide of cerium	.	.	64·55
Protoxides of lanthanum and didymium	.	.	7·28
Protoxide of iron	.	.	1·54
Lime	.	.	.	. 1·35
Water	.	.	.	. 5·71
				99·61

BB on charcoal it splits, but does not fuse: dissolves slowly with borax in the outer

CERITE.   69

flame, forming a dark yellow glass, which becomes colourless as it cools; in the inner flame gives a feeble tint of iron.

Partially decomposed by muriatic acid, leaving an insoluble residue of a different composition from that contained in the solution.

Localities. The Copper mine of Bastnäs, near Riddarhyttan in Sweden, where it forms a bed in gneiss, and is associated with Copper, Molybdena, Bismuth, Mica and Hornblende.

Brit. Mus., Case 26.

CERINE, *Hisinger & Berzelius.* A variety of Allanite. The Cerine of *Berzelius* is found associated with Cerite, Hornblende and Copper Pyrites, at Bastnäs, near Riddarhyttan, in Sweden. It occurs both in crystals and in crystalline masses, of a brownish-black colour, with a weak greasy lustre. Subtranslucent in thin splinters.

H. 6. S.G. 3·77 to 3·8.

Analysis from Bastnäs, by *Hisinger:*

Silica	.	.	.	. 30·17
Alumina	.	.	.	11·31
Protoxide of iron	.		20·72
Protoxide of cerium	.		28·19
Lime	.	.	.	. 9·12
Oxide of copper	.	.	0·87
				100·28

Brit. Mus., Case 38.

CERINITE, *H. How.* A mineral forming the coating or exterior portion of a reniform nodule, about half the size of a fist, partly imbedded in crystalline trap. Amorphous, looking very like white or yellowish-white wax. Lustre subresinous. Subtranslucent, in very thin fragments. H. 3·5.

Comp. $3\dot{C}a \overset{...}{Si} + 2\ddot{A}l \overset{...}{Si}^5 + 12\dot{H}.$

Analysis:

Silica	.	.	.	. 57·57
Alumina	.	.	.	12·65
Peroxide of iron	.	.	1·14
Lime	.	.	.	. 9·82
Magnesia	.	.	.	1·87
Potash	.	.	.	. 0·37
Water	.	.	.	. 15·69
				99·11

BB fuses readily without intumescence.

Locality. The Bay of Fundy, on the shore of Annapolis Co., N. S.; a couple of miles E. of a headland called Black Rock.

Name. From κηρίνος, *waxy;* from its wax-like appearance. See also CENTRALASITE and CYANOLITE.

CERITE, *Phillips.* See CERERITE.

F 3

Cerium Oxidé Silicifère, *Haüy.* See Cerite.

Cerium Oxidé Yttrifère, *Beudant.* See Yttrocerite.

Cerium Phosphaté, *Dufrénoy.* See Edwardsite.

Cerolite. See Kerolite.

Ceroxydul-kohlensaures, *Berzelius, Rammelsberg.* See Lanthanite.

Céruse, *Beudant.* Cerusite, *Haidinger.* Cerussit, *v. Kobell..* Cerussite, *Brooke & Miller.* Rhombic: primary form a right rhombic prism. It occurs in tabular crystals, in six-sided prisms variously terminated, and in other macled crystals of different

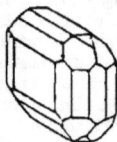

Fig. 95.

forms: also massive and compact, rarely fibrous. Colour white, passing into grey and greyish-black; sometimes tinged green or blue by some of the salts of Copper. Lustre resinous on fractured surfaces, adamantine on planes of cleavage. Transparent to translucent: when transparent, it is doubly refractive in a high degree. Streak white. Brittle: fracture commonly small conchoidal. H. 3 to 3·5. S.G. 6·46 to 6·48.

Fig. 96.

Comp. Monocarbonate of lead or $\dot{P}b$, $\ddot{C}$ =carbonic acid 16·42, oxide of lead 83·58.

Analysis from Leadhills, by *Klaproth:*

Carbonic acid	16
Oxygen	5
Lead	77
Water	2
	100

BB decrepitates, becomes first red, then yellow, and lastly melts into a globule of metallic lead, the charcoal being covered with yellow fumes. It dissolves readily and with effervescence, in dilute nitric acid. Its powder thrown on hot coals emits a phosphorescent light.

Localities.—British. Leadhills in Lanark-

shire, and Wanlock Head in Dumfriesshire (*fig.* 95): also in magnificent tabular crystals at Logylas, near Aberystwith, in Cardiganshire. Cornwall, in exceedingly delicate snow-white acicular crystals, at Pentire Glaze and St. Minver Consols. Derbyshire, principally in mines in the neighbourhood of Matlock (*fig.* 96) and Wirksworth. Cumberland, Devonshire, Durham, Shropshire, Northumberland, Yorkshire, Westmoreland, and at the Sark mine in the Channel Islands. *Ireland,* in heart-shaped macles at Sevenchurches, Wicklow co. — *Foreign.* Very beautiful crystals are found in the mining districts of Saxony, especially at Johanngeorgenstadt; Nertschinsk, and Beresof in Siberia; near Bonn on the Rhine, Clausthal in the Harz; Tarnowitz and Janowitz in Silesia; Bleiberg in Carinthia; Alsace and Croix-aux-Mines (Vosges) in France; the Crimea; Gazimour in Daouria, &c. In the United States, at Phenixville, in Pennsylvania; Perkiomen lead mines, near Philadelphia; Austin's Mines, Wythe co., Virginia, and especially at King's Mine in Davidson co., N. C.

Brit. Mus., Case 49.

M. P. G. Principal Floor, Wall-case 45, and Case 15 (British). Wall case 21 (Foreign).

Next to Galena, Cerusite is the most common ore of lead, but it does not occur so abundantly or in such quantity as often to be an object of consequence to the metallurgist. It may be distinguished from Barytes by the blackening of its surface when exposed to the vapour of sulphide of ammonia.

Cervantite, occurs in acicular crystals; also massive, and as a crust or a powder. Colour nearly white, Isabella-yellow, or sulphur-yellow, with a greasy, bright or earthy lustre.

Comp. $\ddot{S}b + \ddot{S}b$ = oxygen 19·9, antimony 80·1 = 100.

Analysis by *Dufrénoy:*

Oxygen	16·85
Antimony	67·50
Carbonate of lime	11·45
Peroxide of iron	1·50
Loss	2·70
	99·80

BB infusible, but on charcoal easily reduced.

Soluble in muriatic acid.

Localities. Chazelles in Auvergne; Felsobanya, and elsewhere in Hungary.

Cervantite results from the alteration of Grey Antimony (with which it is associated) at Cervantes in Spain: whence the name Cervantite.

CEYLANITE, *Jameson.* An iron-and-magnesia Spinel, named after the locality Ceylon. See PLEONASTE.

CEYLON TOURMALINE. The name given by lapidaries to Chrysolite from Ceylon.

CEYLONESE GARNET. See BOHEMIAN GARNET.

CEYLONIAN ZIRCON. The name given by jewellers to the fire-red, yellow, yellowish-green and grey varieties.

CHABACIT, *Hausmann, Haidinger.* CHABASIE, *Haüy, Phillips, Brooke & Miller.* CHABASIN, *Haidinger.* CHABASIT, *Naumann. v. Kobell, Rose.* CHABASITE, *Bosc d'Antic, Jameson, Nicol.* CHABAZITE, *Dana.* Hexagonal. Found crystallized in the form of an obtuse rhombohedron. Colour white or greyish, sometimes pale red superficially. Lustre vitreous. Transparent, translucent. Brittle; fracture uneven. H. 4 to 4·5. S.G. 2·08 to 2·17.

Fig. 97.　　　　　　Fig. 98.

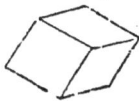 

Fig. 99.　　　　　Fig. 100.

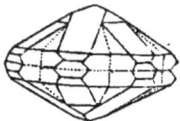 

Comp. (Ċa, Ṅa, K̇) S̈i + 3Ä̶l S̈i² + 6Ḣ.

Analysis from Faröe, by *Berzelius:*

Potash	0·41
Soda	2·75
Lime	8·35
Magnesia	0·40
Alumina	20·00
Silica	48·00
Water	19·30

99·21

BB shrinks up and fuses easily to a blistered slightly translucent white enamel. Soluble in the state of powder in muriatic acid.

Chabazite is met with in fissures and cavities of some basaltic rocks, or within geodes of Quartz and Agate disseminated in those rocks.

Localities. In large and very beautiful crystals in the amygdaloids of Faröe, Iceland and Greenland, often associated with Stilbite and Green Earth. The Giant's Causeway, in Basalt; Portrush, in fine transparent crystals. — *Scotch.* In Trap at Kilmalcolm; Grainger's Quarry, 2½ miles S.W. of Kilmalcolm; Glen Farg in Fifeshire; Eig on the coast of Argyleshire; the Islands of Mull and Skye, &c. Splendid specimens occur in a kind of Greenstone (the *Grau-stein* of Werner) at Aussig in Bohemia; Aunerode near Giessen, of a wine-yellow colour; in Nova Scotia, associated with Heulandite, Analcime, &c. Perfect and well-defined crystals are also found at Plombières, deposited in cavities in the bricks composing the ancient Roman channel through which the thermal waters flow.

Name. From χαϛάξιος, the name of the last of the twenty stones celebrated for their virtues, and mentioned in the poem πεϱὶ λίθων, ascribed to Orpheus.

Brit. Mus., Case 27.

M. P. G. Horse-shoe Case, No. 1144.

CHALCANTHIL, *Glocker.* (From χαλκὸς, *copper,* and ἄνθος, *a flower*). See CYANOSITE.

CHALCEDONY. A variety of Quartz occurring in mammillated and botryoidal forms, and as Stalactites in cavities lined or roofed with Chalcedony, but never in a crystallized state. According to Fuchs, Chalcedony is true Quartz with some Opal disseminated through it. It is usually milk-white, approaching more or less to smalt-blue; the latter varieties are the rarest and most esteemed, and are called Sapphirine by French lapidaries. Many varieties, especially oriental ones, are of a yellowish, instead of a bluish colour, and are known in commerce as white Carnelians: the red and brown varieties are called red Carnelians, and the brown approaching to orange or yellow are termed by the lapidaries Sard.

Chalcedony is more or less semi-transparent, and often exhibits parallel or concentric bands or laminæ of two or more colours, when it is called Agate. It equals Quartz in hardness, and is not very easily broken, but when broken it presents an even fracture passing into finely splintery and flat conchoidal, with little or no lustre.

BB it becomes dead opaque white.

Chalcedony from its hardness and toughness forms an excellent material for the engraver, by whom those varieties are preferred which are of a perfectly uniform tint, unbroken by bands or stripes or other accidental markings; the last are better adapted for small vases, brooches, &c.

F 4

Fine specimens are procured north of Monte Verdi, in Tuscany, and from the amygdaloids of Iceland, and the Faröe Isles; it is also found in Cornwall, Devon, Cumberland, in England; at the Pentland Hills, in Fifeshire and other places in Scotland; and at Antrim, near the Giant's Causeway, and in other parts of Ireland.

Cubical crystals and very fine botryoidal and stalactitic specimens are found in flints at Houghton Chalk-pit, near Arundel in Sussex; and beautiful specimens of sponges of the Cretaceous period, converted into Chalcedony, may be picked up on the shore at Worthing, Littlehampton, Bognor, Selsey, &c.

Name. Chalcedony is named after Chalcedon in Asia Minor, where it is said to have been originally obtained.

Brit. Mus., Case 22 and 23.

M. P. G. Horse-shoe Case, Nos. 661, 662, 654, 666 to 671, 674.

CHALCEDONYX. A variety of Chalcedony, with alternating stripes of white and grey.

CHALCODITE. The name proposed in 1851, by Professor C. U. Shepard, for a mineral which had previously been referred to Cacoxene. It occurs in minute flexible scales, grouped into drusy concretionary crusts, coating Hematite. Colour greenish, bronze, and brass-yellow. H. 1 to 1·5. S.G. 2·76.

Comp. $2\dot{R}\ \ddot{S}i + \ddot{R}\ \ddot{S}i + 2\dot{H}$ (approaching Stilpnomelane, *Brush*).

Analysis (mean) of green variety, by *Brush:*

Silica	45·29
Alumina	3·62
Peroxide of iron	20·47
Protoxide of iron	16·47
Protoxide of manganese	trace
Lime	0·28
Magnesia	4·56
Soda and potash	traces
Water	9·22
	99·91

Dissolves readily in hot muriatic acid.

Locality. The Stirling iron mine, Antwerp, Jefferson co., U.S.

Name. From χαλκώδος, *like brass;* from its bronze-like lustre.

Brit. Mus., Case 26.

CHALCOLITE, *Beudant.* CHALCOLITH, *Werner, Haidinger, Hausmann, v. Kobell.* A variety of Uranite in which copper takes the place of lime. Pyramidal; the crystals generally assuming a tabular form. Colour emerald-, and grass-green, sometimes leek-,

and apple-, and verdigris-green, with a streak somewhat paler than the colour. H. 2 to 2·5. S.G. 3·5 to 3·6.

Comp. $(\dot{C}u,\ 2\ddot{U})\ \ddot{P} + 8\dot{H}$ = phosphoric acid 15·1, oxide of uranium 61·2, oxide of copper 8·4, water 15·3=100.

Analysis by Phillips:

Oxide of uranium	60·0
Phosphoric acid	16·0
Oxide of copper	9·0
Water	15·0
	100·0

BB fuses to a black mass, colouring the flame bluish-green.

In nitric acid gives a yellowish-green solution; in ammonia a blue solution.

Localities.—English. Magnificent specimens have been found at Gunnis Lake, near Callington in Cornwall: other Cornish localities are Huel Buller, and South Huel Basset, Redruth: Tin-croft mine, Illogan; Huel James, Withiel; Stenna Gwynn, near St. Austell; Devonshire, at Bedford United mines near Tavistock. — *Foreign.* Johanngeorgenstadt, Eibenstock and Schneeberg in Saxony; Joachimstahl and Zinnwald in Bohemia; Vielsalm in Belgium, &c.

Name. From χαλκός, *copper,* and λίθος, *stone.*

Brit. Mus., Case 57.

This species may be distinguished from Green Mica by the brittleness of its laminæ, which do not bend, and are not flexible and elastic like those of Mica. Mica, also, is not soluble in nitric acid.

M. P. G. Wall-case 13 on Principal Floor (British).

CHALCOPHACITE, *Glocker.* See LIROCONITE.

CHALCOPHYLLITE. Hexagonal. Occurs in six-sided tabular crystals, of which the lateral planes are trapeziums, inclining alternately in contrary directions; also in foliated masses and druses. Colour emerald-, grass-, or verdigris-green, with a vitreous lustre except on the cleavage planes, where it is pearly. Transparent, or translucent. Streak rather paler than the colour. Sectile. H. 2. S.G. 2·4 to 2·66.

Comp. $\ddot{A}s,\ 6\dot{C}u + 12\dot{H}$ = arsenic acid 24·9, oxide of copper 51·7, water 23·4 (*Damour*).

Analysis from Cornwall, by *Damour:*

Arsenic acid	21·27
Oxide of copper	52·30
Alumina	2·13
Phosphoric acid	1·56

Water . . . . 22·58

      99·84

BB decrepitates strongly, the flame being coloured green by the detached particles; in powder emits arsenical fumes, and passes into a spongy slag, after which it melts quietly into a black, brittle, slightly vitreous globule; which, by a second fusion with soda, affords a globule of metallic copper.

Soluble in acids and ammonia.

Localities.—English. Associated with Cuprite, Copper Pyrites, and Malachite, at Ting-Tang and at Huels Gorland, Muttrell and Unity, in Gwennap; Huel Tamar, and Gunnis Lake near Callington. — *Foreign.* Crystallized in Iron-ore at Sayda in Saxony; in minute crystals at Herrengrund in Hungary; Moldava in the Bannat.

Name. From χαλκός, *copper*, and φύλλον, *a leaf*, in allusion to the ease with which the crystals may be separated into laminæ like Mica.

Brit. Mus., Case 56.

M. P. G. Principal Floor, Wall-case 2 (British).

CHALCOPYRITE, *Beudant, Greg & Lettsom.* Copper Pyrites. Pyramidal; tetrahedral. The crystals present the general form of the tetrahedron or spheroid, having the solid angles always replaced. Their structure is perfectly lamellar, affording brilliant surfaces parallel to the planes of a somewhat acute octahedron with a square base. It also occurs stalactitic, botryoidal, mammillated, and amorphous; these are all harder than the crystallized varieties. Colour brass-yellow, often with a variegated tarnish. Lustre metallic. Streak greenish-black. Fracture most commonly uneven. Opaque. H. 3·5 to 4. S.G. 4·1 to 4·3.

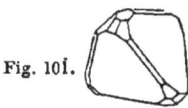

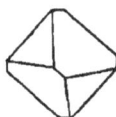

Fig. 101.   Fig. 102.

Comp. CuS FeS = copper 34·78, iron 30·47, sulphur 34·78 = 100.

Analysis from Ramberg, in Sayn, by *H. Rose*:

Sulphur . . . . 35·87
Copper . . . . 34·40
Iron . . . . 30·47
Quartz matrix . . 0·27

      101·01

BB on charcoal emits sulphurous fumes, and melts in a brittle, black globule, which is magnetic. With borax yields pure copper.

Forms a green solution in nitric acid, leaving a residue of sulphur.

Localities. British.—Cornwall, associated with Erubescite, Grey Copper, Galena, and Blende; Devonshire, at Huel Friendship, near Tavistock; Staffordshire, at the Ecton mine; Lancashire, at Bole Gap and Coniston United mines (*fig.* 101); Alston Moor, in Cumberland (*fig.* 102); in many places in Wales and Scotland, and in several counties in Ireland. *Auriferous* Copper Pyrites has been met with at Goldscope mine, near Keswick, in Cumberland, and *argentiferous*, containing 27 ounces of silver to the ton, at Gurtnadyne mines, in Tipperary.— *Foreign.* Pyrenees; Canada, south side of Echo Lake, and north of the mouth of the Root River.

Name. From χαλκός, *copper*, and *pyrites.* Brit. Mus., Case 7.

M.P.G. Principal Floor, Case 15, Wall-cases 3 to 7, and 25 to 27 (British); 16 and 17 (Foreign); 40 (Jamaica).

Chalcopyrite may be distinguished from gold by its brittleness and want of malleability, as well as by its fracture, which is uneven or imperfectly foliated, whereas gold has a hackly fracture. It differs from Iron Pyrites, which it often greatly resembles, by inferior hardness, and by yielding to the knife, whereas Iron Pyrites gives fire with steel; its colour is also generally of a deeper yellow than that of Iron Pyrites, which is more like brass in appearance; hence its richness may be judged of by the colour. The softer varieties, of a fine yellow colour, which yield readily to the hammer, contain the largest quantity of copper; while the harder and paler varieties are poor, from the admixture of Iron Pyrites.

Though a poor ore, it is the most abundant, nearly one-third of all the copper obtained by metallurgical operations being extracted from it.

CHALCOSINE, *Greg & Lettsom*; CHALKOSINE, *Beudant, v. Kobell.* From χαλκός, *copper.* See COPPER GLANCE.

CHALCOSTIBITE, *Glocker.* See WOLFSBERGITE.

CHALCOTRICHITE, *Glocker.* A fibrous variety of Cuprite, or Red Copper, which generally occurs in grouped or reticulated, fine capillary crystals. These have been referred by Brooke to the cubical system, the slender fibres being elongated cubes; while Kengott attributes them to the rhombic system, the fibres, in his opinion, being rhombic prisms, with the obtuse and acute edges truncated. The colour of this mineral is cochineal- and crimson-red. S.G. 5·8.

Comp. Identical with Cuprite.

Localities. English.—It is known by the name of *plush copper* in Cornwall, and has been found at Huel Gorland, the Consolidated mines, Carharrack, Huel Prosper, and Owen Vean; also at the Bedford United mines, near Tavistock. The present localities are South Huel Francis, and the Phœnix mines. *Irish.* — Coosheen mine, Skull, Cork. *Foreign.*—Rheinbreitenbach, on the Rhine; Moldawa; and N. Tagilsk, in Siberia.

Name. From χαλκός, copper, and θρὶξ, hair. Brit. Mus., Case 17.

Chalcotrichite is distinguished from Red Silver-ore by its crystallization and accompanying minerals; from Cinnabar by its colour, weight, and accompanying minerals; from Red Antimony by its colour, that of the latter being cherry-red.

CHALILITE, *Thomson.* Probably an impure massive Thomsonite. According to Kengott there are two species of Chalilite, one of a deep reddish-brown, the other flesh-red, and fusing *BB* with more difficulty than the preceding to a white blebby glass. The first is compact, with a slightly resinous lustre, and a splintery fracture. Subtranslucent to opaque. Streak yellowish, and a little greasy. H. 4·5. S.G. 2·252.

Analysis by *Thomson:*

Silica . . . . . 36·56
Alumina . . . . 26·20
Peroxide of iron . . . 9·28
Lime . . . . . 10·28
Soda . . . . . 2·72
Water . . . . . 16·66
                        _____
                        101·70

BB fuses with intumescence.

Localities. In irregular veins passing through trap, where it rests on the porphyry of the Sandy Brae district, in Antrim; also at Tudree Hill.

Name. From χάλιξ, *a flint*, from its great resemblance in appearance to flint.

CHALK. An earthy variety of carbonate of lime, generally white, soft, and pulverulent, but varying much in hardness.

CHALKANTHIT, *v. Kobell.* See CYANOSITE.

CHALKOLITE. See CHALCOLITE.

CHALKOSINE, *Beudant.* See COPPER GLANCE.

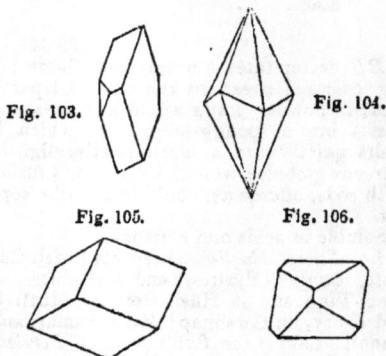
Fig. 103.   Fig. 104.

Fig. 105.   Fig. 106.

CHALYBITE, *Glocker.* SPARRY or SPATHOSE IRON, CARBONATE OF IRON, or SIDERITE. Hexagonal; occurs in obtuse rhombohedrons (whose faces are occasionally curvilinear); in acute rhombohedrons, sometimes perfect, or having the terminal angles replaced; in six-sided prisms, in octahedrons, and in lenticular crystals; also striated and massive. Colour various shades of yellow, passing into brown and brownish-black on exposure to the atmosphere or to heat. Externally shining, internally with a brilliant or pearly lustre. Transparent, translucent, or opaque. Streak yellowish-brown. Structure lamellar. Brittle. Fracture uneven. Affects the magnetic needle. H. 3·5 to 4·5. S.G. 3·7 to 3·9.

Comp. $Fe\ddot{C}$=carbonic acid 37·93, protoxide of iron 62·07,=100. As however it often contains oxide of manganese, magnesia, and lime, its composition is better expressed by the formula $(\dot{F}e\ \dot{M}n\ \dot{M}g\ \dot{C}a)\ \ddot{C}$.

Analysis from Durham, by *Thomson:*
Carbonic acid . . 35·90
Protoxide of iron . . 54·57
Protoxide of manganese . 1·15
Lime . . . . . 3·18
Water . . . . . 2·63
                        _____
                        97·43

BB alone infusible; blackens, becomes more magnetic. Colours borax bottle-green in the reducing flame, and in the oxidating flame yellow. Soluble with difficulty in nitric acid, and scarcely effervesces, unless previously pulverised.

Localities. Nearly all the Styrian and Carinthian Iron is manufactured from Chalybite. In those and the adjoining countries it forms extensive tracts, traversing gneiss, extending along the chain of the Alps on one side into Austria, and on the other into Saltzburg. The Erzberg, between Eisenerz and Vordernberg, in Styria, is composed of gneiss, upon which rests, on the north and west sides, an immense bed of Sparry Iron. This is the great depôt of the ore which is used in the manufacture of the Styrian steel. Fine crystals of Sparry Iron are met with in veins of considerable size, traversing Clay-slate, at Harzgerode, in the Harz. At Freiberg it is found in silver veins. At Somorostro, in the province of Biscay, in Spain, there is a whole hill composed of this ore, which has been worked for several thousand years. In the United Kingdom it occurs chiefly in Cornwall, and in the N. W. of Devonshire and Somersetshire, where considerable quantities are raised on Exmoor and the Brendon Hills. *Fig.* 103 represents crystals found at Fowey Consols, and *fig.* 104 the small brilliant crystals presenting the form of Dog's-tooth Spar, met with at Buckler's Mine, near St. Austell. It affords an iron which is admirably suited for making steel. The black variety is said to afford the best kind of iron.

Brit. Mus., Case 48.

M. P. G. Principal Floor, Wall-case 50 (British).

CHAMOISITE. Probably a mixture of Magnetic Iron and a hydrous silicate of alumina. It has a dark greenish-grey earthy appearance, with a granular, uneven, or earthy fracture. Magnetic. S.G. 3·0 to 3·4.

Comp. Near to Siderochisolite, 2 (5Fe, Si) + Al, 3Si + 13H.

Analysis from Chamoisin, by *Berthier*:

Protoxide of iron	. . . 60·5
Alumina	. . . . 7·8
Silica	. . . . 14·3
Water	. . . . 17·4
	100·0

When heated, gives off water, becomes more strongly magnetic, and turns black, or, if the air has access to it, reddish.

Locality. In beds, of small extent, in a limestone abounding in Ammonites, at Chamoisin in the Valais.

Brit. Mus., Case 26.

CHANTONNITE, *Shepard.* A meteoric mineral, forming compact black veins and angular-shaped masses. Fracture subconchoidal. H. 6·5 to 7. S.G. 3·48.

BB fuses at the edges to a dark black slag.

Named after the Chantonnay stone, in which it is found.

CHATHAMITE, *Shepard.* A variety of Chloanthite occurring in mica-slate, and generally associated with Mispickel, and sometimes with Copper Nickel, at Chatham, Connecticut, U.S. (See SAFFLORITE).

Analysis by *Genth:*

Arsenic	. . . . 70·11
Sulphur	. . . . 4·78
Iron	. . . . 11·85
Cobalt	. . . . 3·82
Nickel	. . . . 9·44
	100·00

Brit. Mus., Case 4.

CHAUX ARSENIATÉE, *Haüy.* See PHARMACOLITE.

CHAUX ARSENIATÉE ANHYDRE, *Dufrénoy.* See KUHNITE.

CHAUX BORATÉE SILICEUSE, *Haüy.* See DATHOLITE.

CHAUX CARBONATÉE, *Haüy.* See CALCITE.

CHAUX CARBONATÉE CONCRETIONNÉE, *Haüy.* See STALAGMITE.

CHAUX CARBONATÉE FERRIFÈRE, *Haüy.* BITTER SPAR coloured black by Bitumen, and found crystallized in acute rhombohedrons in the Gypsum of SALZBURG.

CHAUX CARBONATÉE FERRIFÈRE PERLÉE, *Haüy.* See PEARL-SPAR.

CHAUX CARBONATÉE FETIDE, *Haüy.* See STINKSTONE.

CHAUX CARBONATÉE MAGNÉSIFÈRE, *Haüy.* See DOLOMITE.

CHAUX CARBONATÉE NACRÉE, *Haüy.* See SLATE-SPAR.

CHAUX CARBONATÉE NACRÉE LAMELLAIRE, *Haüy.* See APHRITE.

CHAUX CARBONATÉE SACCHAROÏDE, *Haüy.* See GRANULAR LIMESTONE.

CHAUX CARBONATÉE SPONGIEUSE, *Haüy.* See AGARIC MINERAL.

CHAUX DATOLIT, *Brochant.* See DATHOLITE.

CHAUX FLUATÉE, *Haüy.* See FLUOR.

CHAUX NITRATÉE, *Haüy.* See NITRO-CALCITE.

CHAUX PHOSPHATÉE, *Haüy.* See APATITE.

CHAUX PHOSPHATÉE VERTE, *Haüy.* See ASPARAGUS-STONE.

CHAUX SULFATÉE, *Haüy.* See GYPSUM.

CHAUX SULFATÉE ANHYDRE, *Haüy.* See ANHYDRITE.

CHAUX SULFATÉE CRYSTALLISÉE, *Haüy.* See SELENITE.

CHENOCOPROLITE. Formerly called Gänseköthigerz, or Goose-dung-ore, has been shown to be an impure Iron Sinter (Pitticite), containing Silver and Arseniate of Cobalt. It is the result of decomposition, and not a distinct mineral. It occurs in irregularly mammillated, translucent masses of a yellowish green or olive colour. Shining, with a resinous lustre, white streak and conchoidal fracture. H. 2 to 3. S.G. 2·3.

Localities. Cornwall. Allemont in Dauphiné, chiefly at the mines of Clausthal in the Harz, where, when obtained in sufficient quantity, it is highly prized as an ore of Silver.

Name. From χηνοκόπρος, *goosedung*, and λίθος, *stone*.

CHEROKINE. The mineral so called by Professor Shepard has been proved by the analysis of T. Sterry Hunt, to be Phosphate of Lead (Pyromorphite), containing less than 1 per cent. of a whitish precipitate, which may have been phosphate of lime or alumina.

CHERRY COAL. Resembles Caking Coal, but does not cake when burnt.

CHERT. The name frequently applied to Hornstone, and to any impure flinty rock, including the Jaspers. From its great toughness, which exceeds that of Flint, Chert forms a good road material, and it is used largely in the potteries. It occurs in the uppermost beds of the Upper Greensand of the south of England; also in the Purbeck and Portland formations of Dorsetshire; in the Carboniferous Limestone of Derbyshire and Flintshire, and in Ireland.

It differs from Flint in breaking with a square splintery fracture, instead of a conchoidal fracture.

Brit. Mus., Case 22.

M.P.G. Horse-shoe Case, Nos. 733, 734: Upper Gallery, Wall-case, 42, Nos. 17 to 35A.

CHESSYLITE, *Brooke & Miller, Greg & Lettsom.* Oblique. Primary form an oblique rhombic prism. Colour azure-blue passing into Berlin-blue, in earthy varieties smalt-blue. Transparent to opaque. Lustre vitreous. Yields easily to the knife. Streak paler than the colour. Structure lamellar. Brittle. Fracture conchoidal. H. 3·5 to 4·0. S.G. 3·5 to 3·8.

Fig. 107.　　　　　　　Fig. 108.

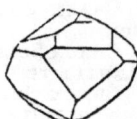

Comp. Carbonate of copper, or $2\dot{C}u\ddot{C}+\dot{C}u\dot{H}$=oxide of copper 69·37, carbonic acid 25·43, water 5·20=100.

Analysis from Chessy, by *Phillips*:

Carbonic acid . . . 25·46
Oxide of copper . . . 69·08
Water . . . . . 5·46
　　　　　　　　　　 ———
　　　　　　　　　　 100·00

BB decrepitates, turns black and yields a globule of copper.

Dissolves with effervescence in nitric acid. Soluble in ammonia.

Localities.—English. Cornwall, at Huel Buller, *fig.* 108, and at many other mines. East Tamar mine, Devonshire. Matlock, &c., Derbyshire. Alston Moor, Cumberland.—*Scotch.* Wanlock Head, Dumfriesshire. Leadhills, Lanarkshire.—*Irish.* Audley mines, Cork co. Killarney.—*Foreign.* Chessy near Lyons, in considerable abundance, and in very beautiful crystals.* Siberia. Moldawa in the Bannat. Thuringia.

Brit. Mus., Case 50.

M.P.G. Principal Floor, Wall-cases 2 (British); 16 (Foreign); 38 (Australian); Case 11, (Burra Burra).

Chessylite is probably a result of the decomposition of other ores of Copper. It generally occurs lining cavities in primary and secondary rocks, and associated with Malachite and Red Copper. Chessylite forms a valuable ore of copper when abundant. It is also used when pulverized, as a pigment under the name of Mineral-blue, or Mountain-blue; but it is not of much value, from its liability to turn green.

CHESTERLITE. A variety of Felspar with the constitution of Orthoclase.

Analysis by *Smith & Brush*:

Silica . . . . 65·17
Alumina . . . 17·70
Peroxide of iron . . 0·50
Lime . . . . 0·56
Potash . . . 13·86
Soda . . . . 1·64
Magnesia . . . 0·25
Loss by ignition . . 0·65
　　　　　　　　　 ———
　　　　　　　　　 100·33

Locality. Chester, Delaware co., U.S. in crystals, often on Dolomite.

Brit. Mus., Case 30.

CHEVEUX DE VENUS. See VENUS' HAIR-STONE.

———————————

* Hence the name Chessylite.

CHIASTOLITE, *Phillips.*   Rhombic.   A variety of Andalusite, occurring crystallized in white or grey right rhombic prisms, which present a black or bluish-black cross in their transverse section.   Lustre vitreous.   Translucent.   Streak white.   Fracture splintery.   H. 3 to 7·5.   S.G. 2·94 to 3·09.

Fig. 109.

Comp. Anhydrous silicate of alumina, or

$\ddot{A}l\ \ddot{S}i$ = alumina 63, silica 37 = 100.

Analysis from Lancaster, by *Bunsen*:

Alumina	.	.	.	. 58·56
Silica	.	.	.	. 39·09
Peroxide of manganese		.		0·53
Lime	.	.	.	. 0·21
Loss by ignition	.		.	0·99

99·38

BB alone infusible, with borax difficultly fusible, forming a clear glass, and with still greater difficulty and less perfectly in microcosmic salt.

Localities.—English. Cumberland, at the top of Skiddaw, and at Carrock Fells, in Slate; Saddleback; Dacre Castle, near Ullswater. Devonshire; Ivy Bridge, and near Okehampton. *Fig.* 109.—*Irish.* Agnavanagh in Wicklow; in mica-slate, near Killiney Bay; Baltinglass Hill, on the borders of Carlow.—*Foreign.* Near Barèges in the Pyrenees; St. Jago de Compostella in Spain; near Santa Elena in the Sierra Morena; St. Brieux in Basse Bretagne; abundantly in the townships of Lancaster and Sterling, Massachusetts, U.S.

Name. From χιαστὸς, *decussated.* The name Chiastolite was given by Karsten, on account of the resemblance of the dark lines on the summits of the crystals to the Greek letter χ.

Brit. Mus., Case 26.

M. P. G. Horse-shoe Case, No. 1005.

CHILDRENITE, *Levy, Greg & Lettsom.* Rhombic.   Primary form a right rhombic prism.   Occurs in yellow or brownish-yellow crystals or crystalline coats on Siderite, Pyrites or Quartz.   Lustre vitreous inclining to resinous.   Translucent.   Streak paler than the colour.   Fracture uneven.   H. 4·5 to 5.   S.G. 3·2.

Fig. 110.

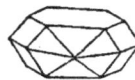

Fig. 111.

Fig. 112.

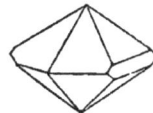

Fig. 113.

Comp. $(\ddot{R}^3, \ddot{A}l)^5 \ddot{P}^3 + 15\dot{H}$, or $2(\dot{F}e, \dot{M}n)^4 \ddot{P} + \ddot{A}l\ \ddot{P} + 15\dot{H}$.

Analysis by *Rammelsberg*:

Phosphoric acid	.	.		. 28·92
Alumina	.	.	.	. 14·44
Protoxide of iron	.	.		. 30·68
Protoxide of manganese		.		9·07
Magnesia	.	.	.	. 0·14
Water	.	.	.	. 16·98

100·28

BB colours the flame bluish-green; with the fluxes affords reaction of iron and manganese.

Localities. This mineral is nearly a Cornish species: it has been found at Crinnis Mine near St. Austell, and at the George and Charlotte Mine, and in the vicinity of Tavistock, at Huel Crebor.

Name. It was first distinguished by Levy, by whom it was named after Mr. Children of the British Museum.

Brit. Mus., Case 57.

M. P. G. Horse-shoe Case, No. 1125.

Childrenite may be distinguished from Siderite by the superior hardness and lustre of its crystals.

CHILEIT. The name given by Breithaupt to a variety of Göthite from Chile.

Analysis by *Breithaupt*:

Peroxide of iron	.	.		. 83·5
Oxide of copper	.	.		. 1·9
Silica	.	.	.	. 4·3
Water	.	.	.	. 10·3

100·0

CHILEITE. The name proposed by Kengott for a Vanadate of Lead and Copper described by Domeyko, and worked for Copper and Silver at the Silver mine, Mina Grande, or Mina de la Marqueza, in Chili, where it occurs in cavities in Arseno-phosphate of Lead, with amorphous Carbonates of Lead and Copper. It has a dark-brown, or brownish-black colour, and an earthy appearance resembling that of a ferruginous clay or earth.

Comp. $\dot{P}b^6 \ddot{V} + \dot{C}u^6 \ddot{V}$.

Analysis by Domeyko:

Vanadic acid	. .	13·33
Arsenic acid .	. .	4·68
Phosphoric acid .	.	0·68
Oxide of copper	.	16·97
Oxide of lead	. .	51·97
Chloride of lead ,	.	0·37
Lime . . .	.	0·58
Peroxide of iron and alumina		3·42
Silica . . .	.	1·33
Clay . . .	.	1·52
Water . . .	.	2·70
		97·55

CHILI SALTPETRE. See NITRATINE.
CHILTONITE, *Emmons.* See PREHNITE.
CHIMBORAZITE. See ARAGONITE.
CHIOLITE, *Hermann & Auerbach.* Pyramidal; occurs crystallized, but generally compact like Cryolite, with a crystalline structure. Colour snow-white. Lustre vitreous, slightly resinous. Translucent. H. 4. S.G. 2·72.

Comp. $3\mathrm{Na}\,\mathrm{F} + 2\,\mathrm{\ddot{A}l}^2\,\mathrm{F}^3$.

Analysis by Hermann:

Sodium	. .	23 78
Aluminum	. .	18·69
Fluorine	. .	57·53
		100·00

BB fuses easily, and affords the re-action of fluorine.

Effervesces and gives off hydrofluoric acid in sulphuric acid.

Locality. Miask, in the Topaz mine No. 5, forming a vein in graphic granite.

Brit. Mus., Case 58.

CHIVIALITE, *Rammelsberg.* A mineral resembling Bismuth-glance, found accompanying Pyrites and Barytes at Chiviato, in Peru. Colour lead-grey. Lustre metallic. S.G. 6·92.

Comp. $(\mathrm{\dot{C}u}, \mathrm{Pb})\,\mathrm{S} + \tfrac{1}{2}\,\mathrm{Bi}^2\,\mathrm{S}^3,\ \mathrm{R}.$

Analysis by Rammelsberg:

Sulphur	. .	18·00
Bismuth	. .	60·95
Lead	. .	16·73
Copper .	. .	2·42
Iron	. .	1·02
Silver .	. .	trace
Insol. .	. .	0·59
		100·00

BB like Aikenite, to which it is near in composition.

CHLADNITE, *Shepard.* A meteoric mineral, forming more than two-thirds (90 per cent.) of the Bishopville stone, in which it occurs in imperfect crystals, very closely approaching, in external form, some of the most common forms of Felspar and Albite. These crystals, whose primary form is a doubly oblique prism, are sometimes nearly an inch in diameter. Colour snow-white, rarely with a tinge of grey. Translucent (in undecomposed fragments semi-transparent). Lustre pearly to vitreous. Very brittle, masses half an inch in diameter, being easily crushed between the fingers. H. 6 to 6·5. S.G. 3·116.

Comp. Ter-silicate of Magnesia.

BB alone, on charcoal, fuses without difficulty and with phosphorescence to a white enamel; with borax, very slowly, to a transparent glass.

It is named after Chladni, the scientific founder of Astrolithology.*

CHLOANTHITE, *Breithaupt.* The term under which is comprised the Nickel varieties of Smaltine, the latter term being restricted to the Cobaltic varieties.

Comp. Ni, As² = arsenic 72·1, nickel 28·3 = 100·0.

CHLORAPATITE. *Voelcker.* A variety of Apatite from Krageröe, in Norway, distinguished by the entire absence of fluorine, and a very small but variable quantity of chloride of calcium, varying from 1·61 to 1·71 in some specimens, to 6·41 to 6·70 in others.

Comp. $3\,(\mathrm{\dot{C}a^3\,\ddot{P}}) + \mathrm{Ce}\,\mathrm{Cl}.$

CHLORASTROLITE, *C. J. Jackson.* A pale bluish-green mineral occurring on the shores of Isle Royale, Lake Superior, in small water-worn pebbles, which have been derived from trap. It is finely radiated or stellate in structure, with a pearly lustre, and is slightly chatoyant on the rounded sides. H. 5·5 to 6. S.G. 3·18.

Comp. $(\mathrm{\dot{C}a}, \mathrm{\dot{N}a})^3\,\ddot{\mathrm{Si}} + 2\,(\mathrm{\ddot{A}l}, \mathrm{\ddot{F}e})\,\ddot{\mathrm{Si}} + 3\,\dot{\mathrm{H}}$

$= (\tfrac{1}{3}\,\dot{\mathrm{R}}^3 + \tfrac{2}{3}\,\mathrm{\ddot{A}l})\,\ddot{\mathrm{Si}} + \dot{\mathrm{H}}.$

Analysis by Whitney:

Silica .	. .	36·99
Alumina	.	25·49
Peroxide of iron (a little protóx.)		6·48
Lime .	. .	19·90
Soda .	. .	3·70

* From ἀστήρ, *a meteor*, λίθος, *a stone*, λόγος, *a treatise*.

Potash 0 40
Water . . . . . 7·22

              100·18

BB fuses readily, with intumescence, to a greyish blebby glass.

Soluble in muriatic acid, giving a flocculent precipitate of silica.

Name. From χλωρὸς, *green,* ἀστερὸν, *a star,* and λίθος, *a stone.*

CHLORIDE OF LEAD, *Thomson.* See COTUNNITE.

CHLORIDE OF POTASSIUM. See SYLVINE.

CHLORIDE OF SILVER, *Allan.* See KERARGYRITE.

CHLORITE, *Werner.* Hexagonal; occurs in tabular six-sided prisms. Colour various shades of dull emerald green in the direction of the axis, and yellowish or hyacinth-red at right angles to it; also pure white or yellowish. Massive varieties olive-green. Semitransparent to subtranslucent. Lustre pearly. Yields to the nail, and, when in powder, is unctuous to the touch. Streak corresponding to the colour. H. 1 to 1·5. S.G. 2·7 to 2·85.

Fig. 114.

Compact Chlorite is amorphous. Chlorite slate possesses a slaty structure, and frequently contains imbedded octahedral crystals of Magnetic Iron, Hornblende and Garnets. Earthy Chlorite is composed of small, pearly, glimmering, scaly particles. It has a somewhat greasy feel, and bears a striking resemblance to Green Earth.

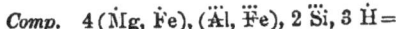

Comp. 4 (Ṁg, Ḟe), (Äl, F̈e), 2 S̈i, 3 Ḣ = 4 Ṁg S̈i + Äl S̈i + 3 Ḣ.

Analysis from the Pyrenees, by *Delesse*:

Silica . . . . . 32·1
Alumina . . . . 18·5
Magnesia . . . . 36·7
Protoxide of iron . . 0·6
Water . . . . . 12·1

              100·0

Chlorite frequently contains as much as 8 or 9 per cent. of protoxide of iron; those kinds which have more (up to 28 or 29 per cent.) are classed with Ripidolite.

BB some lose their colour, and fuse at the edges; with borax affords an iron reaction.

Localities. The tin mines of Cornwall, where it is known by the name of *peach.* Also in Cumberland and Westmoreland, and near Llanberis, in Caernarvonshire. At Port-

soy, in Banffshire, it is mixed with Serpentine, and is frequently cut and polished.

Name. From χλωρὸς, *green.*

This mineral may be distinguished from Mica by its laminæ being flexible, but not elastic, while those of Mica are very elastic.

It has been proposed by Descloiseaux to divide Chlorite into three groups, Pennine, Clinochlore, and Ripidolite; to which may be added Leuchtenbergite.

Brit. Mus., Case 32.

M.P.G. Horse-shoe Case Nos. 1039–1043, 1047.

CHLORITE FERRUGINEUSE, *Delesse.* See DELESSITE.

CHLORITE SPAR. A variety of Chloritoid from Katharinenburg, analysed by Erdmann, who considered it to be a distinct species, in consequence of the absence of water. It was subsequently analysed by Hermann and Von Kobell, by the former of whom it is suggested that the absence of water, in the specimen analysed by Erdmann, might be accounted for by its having been burnt at the mine, where the stone is roasted to separate the Emery.

CHLORITOID. Occurs massive, in coarse folia which are often curved or bent. It has a dark grey or greenish-grey colour, and a weak pearly lustre. Streak uncoloured, or slightly greenish. H. 5·5 to 6. S.G. 3·55.

Comp. Ṙ S̈i + 2 Äl S̈i + 3 Ḣ = (⅓ Ṙ + ⅔ Äl) S̈i + Ḣ = silica 27·6, alumina 31·3, protoxide of iron 32·9, water 8·2 = 100·0.

Analysis from Katharinenberg, by *Hermann:*

Silica . . . . . 24·54
Alumina . . . . 30·72
Protoxide of iron . . 17·30
Magnesia . . . . 3·75
Peroxide of iron . . 17·28
Water . . . . . 6·38

              99·97

BB infusible, but becomes darker and magnetic. Soluble in sulphuric acid.

Localities. Koroibrod, near Katharinenberg, in the Ural; Bregatten in the Tyrol.

CHLORITSPATH, *Fiedler.* See CHLORITOID.

CHLORMERCUR. See CALOMEL.

CHLOROBROMID OF SILVER, *Domeyko.* See EMBOLITE.

CHLOROCARBONATE OF LEAD, *Thomson.* See CROMFORDITE.

CHLOROMELAN, *Naumann.* See CRONSTEDTITE.

CHLOROPAL, *Bernhardi & Brandes.* An

amorphous mineral related to Halloysite, of a greenish-yellow colour, and with a weak waxy lustre. Opaque to subtransparent. Streak greenish-white. Brittle. Fracture splintery and conchoidal. H. 2·5 to 3. S.G. 2·1 to 2·15.

Comp. $\ddot{F}e \ddot{S}i^2 + 3\dot{H}$ = Silica 45·9, peroxide of iron 40·5, water 13·7 = 100·0.

Analysis of compact specimen from Hungary, by *Bernhardi & Brandes :*

Silica	46
Peroxide of iron . .	33
Alumina . . .	1
Magnesia . . .	2
Water	18
	100

BB infusible, but becomes black and then brown.

Partially soluble in muriatic acid, which takes up the hydrate of iron.

Locality. Hungary.

Name. From χλωρὸς *green* and *Opal.*

Brit. Mus., Case 26.

CHLOROPHÆITE. A mineral discovered by D. Macculloch in the amygdaloid of Scuir More in Rum. It occurs foliated, or granular, massive, incrusting or disseminated in small grains or nodules, in basalt or amygdaloid. Colour translucent pistachio- or olive-green, which soon changes to opaque dark-brown or black, with the aspect of Jet or black chalk, according to the degree of lustre or transparency. Lustre dull subresinous. H. 1·5 to 2. S.G. 2·02.

Comp. $\ddot{F}e \ddot{S}i + 6\dot{H}$ = Silica 33·5, protoxide of iron 26 6, water 39 9 = 100·0

Analysis from Faröe, by *Forchammer :*

Silica	32·85
Protoxide of iron . .	22·08
Magnesia . . .	3·44
Water	41·63
	100·00

BB fuses to a black glass.

Localities. The Faröe Islands; Isle of Rum, in Fife; Antrim, Down Hill, in vesicular greenstone.

Name. From χλωρὸς, *green*, and φαιὸς, *brown*, in allusion to the change of colour which takes place in the course of a few hours.

Brit. Mus., Case 26.

CHLOROPHANE. The name given to those varieties of Fluor which, when heated, shine with a phosphorescent light of a peculiarly bright emerald-green colour. This they will exhibit repeatedly, if not subjected to too great a heat. This property is observ-

able in some Cornish specimens, but in a remarkable degree in a violet-coloured Fluor from Nertschinsk in Siberia. In the United States Chlorophane forms two veins in gneiss at Turnbull, Connecticut, accompanied by Topaz and Magnetic Pyrites.

Name. From χλωρὸς, *green,* and φαίνω, *to seem.*

CHLOROPHYLLITE, *Jackson.* Probably an altered or hydrated variety of Iolite. Colour green or brownish. Lustre of basal plane, pearly ; of lateral planes, pearly or greasy to imperfectly vitreous. Translucent to subtranslucent. Highly foliated parallel to the base of the prism. Brittle. H. 0·5 at the edges; of the basal planes 1·5 to 2. S. G. 2·705.

Comp. $\dot{R}^3 \ddot{S}i^2 + 3\ddot{R} \ddot{S}i + 2\dot{H}$ or Iolite + 2$\dot{H}$.

Localities. The United States, at Neal's Mine in Unity, Maine, and at Haddam, Connecticut, in large four-, six-, eight- or twelve-sided prisms, or in foliated masses — usually associated with Iolite in granite.

Name. From χλωρὸς *green,* and φύλλον, a leaf; in allusion to its colour and structure.

Brit. Mus., Case 32.

CHLORQUECKSILBER, *Berzelius.* See CALOMEL.

CHLORSILBER, *Berzelius.* See KERARGYRITE.

CHLOROSPINEL, *G. Rose.* A grass-green Spinel from Slatoust in the Ural, in which a part of the alumina is replaced by peroxide of iron. Streak yellowish-white. H. 8. S.G. 3·591 to 3·594.

Comp. $\dot{M}g$ ($\ddot{A}l$ $\ddot{F}e$).

Analysis by *G. Rose :*

Alumina	64·13
Magnesia	26·77
Peroxide of iron . .	8·70
Lime	0·27
Oxide of copper . .	0·27
	100·14

Becomes brownish-green when heated.

BB with borax fuses easily to a light-green glass, which is colourless when cold.

Brit. Mus., Case 19.

CHODNEFFITE. See CRYOLITE.

CHONDRODITE, *d'Ohsson.* Rhombic; occurs in indistinct crystalline masses, or imbedded grains of a wax-yellow or brown colour, having occasional but not very decided appearances of regular crystalline form. Lustre vitreous—resinous. Translucent. Yields to the knife with difficulty. Streak white, or slightly yellowish or greyish. Fracture sub-conchoidal, uneven. Acquires resinous electricity by friction. H. 6 to 6·5. S.G. 3·12 to 3·19.

Comp. $Mg^4 \ddot{S}i$ with part of the oxygen replaced by fluorine, and part of the magnesia by protoxide of iron.

Analysis of a reddish-yellow variety from Eden, near New York, by *Thomson*:

Magnesia	.	.	.	54·64
Silica	.	.	.	36·00
Protoxide of iron		.	.	3·75
Fluorine	.	.	.	3·97
Water	.	.	.	1·62

99·98

BB when strongly heated yields hydrofluoric acid, loses its colour and fuses at the edges: with borax it fuses slowly but completely, to a clear glass, tinged by iron; but by interrupted blowing or *flaming*, the glass becomes opaque and crystalline.

Soluble in muriatic acid, with separation of gelatinous silica.

Localities.— Scotch. Loch Ness, in granular carbonate of lime, with Magnetic and Arsenical Pyrites.— *Irish.* Near Gweedore, co. Donegal, in crystalline Dolomite.—*Foreign.* The largest and most crystalline masses occur a mile north of Sparta in New Jersey, and near Edenville in New York; it is also met with massive and in grains, associated with Pargasite near Abö, in Pargas, Finland. Aker and Galsjo in Sweden. Tabu in Wermland. Saxony. Achmatowsk in the Ural, and at the mines of Schisminsk with red Spartite.

Name. From χόνδρος *a grain,* in allusion to its granular structure.

Brit. Mus., Case 58.

M. P. G. Horse-shoe Case, Nos. 921, 921.*

CHONIKRITE, *v. Kobell.* A variety of Pyrosclerite, with which it is associated, in Elba. Massive. Colour white with shades of yellow and grey. Lustre glimmering or dull. Translucent: often only at the edges. Fracture conchoidal. H. 2 to 4. S.G. 2·91.

Comp. Hydrosilicate of alumina, magnesia, and lime. $5(\overset{..}{C}a \ \overset{.}{M}g \ \overset{...}{F}e)^2 \ \ddot{S}i + 2\overset{...}{A}l$ $\overset{...}{S}i + 6\overset{.}{H}$. = lime 12·85, magnesia 23·35, protoxide of iron 1·47, alumina 17·14, silica 35·19, water 9·00 = 100·10.

Analysis, by *v. Kobell*:

Lime	.	.	.	12·60
Magnesia		.	.	22·50
Protoxide of iron		.	.	1·46
Alumina	.	.	.	17·12

Silica	.	.	.	.	35·69
Water	.	.	.	.	9·00

98·37

BB fuses with tolerable facility to a greyish-white glass, with the evolution of bubbles of gas; with borax melts slowly to a globule covered with iron.

Soluble in muriatic acid without gelatinising.

Locality. Elba, in irregular masses in Serpentine.

Name. From χώνια, *fusion,* and κριτός, *test,* in allusion to its difference from some allied minerals with regard to fusibility.

Brit. Mus., Cases 27—31.

CHRISMATINE, *Germar.* A mineral allied to Ozocerite, from a red argillaceous sandstone in the coal formation at Wettin, near Halle. It is of an oil-green or yellowish colour, shining and translucent to transparent. It becomes soft at 55° to 60° R. (156° to 167° F.) Burns with flame without smell.

CHRISTIANITE, *Descloiseaux.* The name given by Descloiseaux to the Harmotome from Stempel near Marburg, and small, colourless, translucent crystals from Iceland, referrible to a right rhomboidal prism. The crystals never occur detached, but always pressed closely together, forming mammillary groups or radiating crests like certain varieties of Prehnite. Fragile. Easily scratches glass. S.G. 2·2.

Analysis, from Stempel, by *Genth*:

Silica	.	.	.	48·17
Alumina	.	.	.	21·11
Peroxide of iron	.	.	0·24
Lime	.	.	.	6·97
Potash	.	.	.	6·61
Soda	.	.	.	0·63
Water	.	.	.	16·62

100·35

Localities. The Bay of Dyrefiord on the west coast of Iceland, in cavities in amygdaloid.

The name Christianite was also given by Monticelli to the Anorthite of Vesuvius, in compliment to Prince Christian of Denmark.

CHROMATE OF IRON, *Phillips.* See CHROMIC IRON.

CHROMATE OF LEAD, *Phillips.* See CROCOISITE.

CHROMATE OF LEAD AND COPPER, *Phillips.* See VAUQUELINITE.

CHROME OCHRE, *Hausmann, Nicol.* A clayey substance, occurring in a pulverulent

G

state, and in loose earthy masses of a bright green or yellowish-green colour. Opaque, dull. S.G. 2·7.

Comp. ($\ddot{A}$l, $\ddot{C}$r, $\ddot{F}$e) $\ddot{S}i^2$; but rarely found pure.

Analysis from Silesia, by *Zellner*:

Silica . . . . . 58·50
Oxide of chromium . . 2·00
Alumina . . . 30·00
Peroxide of iron . . . 3·00
Water . . . 6·25
                        ——
                        99·75

BB infusible alone, but becomes paler in colour: with borax forms an emerald-green globule.

Localities. In Unst, one of the Shetlands, in a nearly pure state, in small fissures in Chromate of Iron.—*Foreign.* Creuzot (Saone-et-Loire) in France. Silesia. Mortenberg in Sweden. Savoy and Piedmont in Serpentine. See also CHROME-STONE.

Name. From χεῶμα, *colour.*

Brit. Mus., Case 39.

CHROME - STONE. The name sometimes given to oxide of chrome or Chrome-ochre, when it is so intimately mixed with the rock in which it is contained as only to be separated from it by chemical means. Such mixtures are met with at Creuzot in France, Waldenberg in Silesia, Mortenberg in Sweden and elsewhere.

CHROMEISENERZ, *Naumann, G. Rose.* See CHROMIC IRON.

CHROMEISENSTEIN. See CHROMIC IRON.

CHROMIC IRON, or CHROME-IRON-ORE. Cubical. Occurs crystallized in octahedrons, the primary form, but commonly massive and disseminated in grains. Colour iron-black to brownish-black, with a shining submetallic lustre. Opaque. Streak brown. Brittle. Fracture imperfect conchoidal, and uneven. Sometimes slightly magnetic. H. 5·5. S.G. 4·3.

Comp. $\ddot{F}$e $\ddot{C}$r, or ($\ddot{F}$e Mg) ($\ddot{A}$l, $\ddot{C}$r) part of the protoxide of iron being replaced by magnesia, and part of the oxide of chromium by alumina, and perhaps also by peroxide of iron.

Analysis of crystallized Chrome-iron-ore from Baltimore, by *Abich:*

Magnesia . . . 7·52
Protoxide of iron . . 20·13
Oxide of chromium . 60·04
Alumina . . . 11·77
Silica . . . . 0·36
                        ——
                        99·82

BB alone, infusible; but becomes magnetic in the inner flame. With borax fuses with difficulty, but completely, to a globule which, on cooling, exhibits the emerald-green of oxide of chromium, which becomes most apparent after heating the bead in the inner flame, especially with the addition of tin.

Localities. Scotch.—Massive and crystallized in Unst, one of the Shetland Islands, at Swinaness, Haroldswick, Balta Sound, Buness House, &c., and also in Fetlar, and some of the other smaller islands. Near Portsoy, Banffshire. *Foreign.*—Forms irregular veins, in Serpentine, at Cassin, Departement du Var, in France. Gulsen Mountains, near Kraubat, in Styria. Silesia and Bohemia. In the Eastern Urals.

This ore is highly valuable as affording a pigment which is used in oil, porcelain, and water-colour painting. The ore used for this purpose is chiefly procured from Baltimore (in the Bare Hills), in the United States, Drontheim, and the Shetland Islands.

Brit. Mus., Case 39.

M. P. G. Principal floor, Wall-cases 13 (British); 19 (Foreign); 39 (Madras).

CHROMIT, *Haidinger, v. Kobell.* CHROMITE, *Brooke & Miller.* See CHROMIC IRON.

CHROMSAURES BLEI, *v. Leonhard.* See CROCOISITE.

CHRYSOBERYL. Rhombic. Colour asparagus-green, grass-green, oil-green, greenish-white, and yellowish-green; sometimes with a bluish opalescence internally. Lustre vitreous. Streak white. Fracture conchoidal, uneven. Transparent to translucent. H. 8·5. S.G. 3·5 to 3·8.

Fig. 115.

BB unaltered alone; with borax, or salt of phosphorus, fuses with great difficulty; with soda, the surface is merely rendered dull.

Not acted upon by acids.

Comp. ($\ddot{B}$e + $\ddot{A}$l³) or glucina 19·8, alumina 80·2 = 100.

Analysis from Brazil, by *Awdejew.* (S.G. 3·7837):

Alumina . . . 78·10
Glucina . . . 17·91
Protoxide of iron . . 4·47
                        ——
                        100·15

Analysis from the Ural, by *Awdejew*:

Alumina	78·92
Glucina	18·02
Protoxide of iron	3·12
Oxide of chrome	0·36
Oxides of copper and lead	0·29
	100·71

Analysis from Haddam, Conn., U. S., by *Damour* :

Alumina	76·02
Glucina	18·41
Protoxide of iron	4·51
Quartz	0·49
	99·43

Localities. Irish.—Mourne Mountains, in granite. *Foreign.*—Brazil and Ceylon, in rolled pebbles in the alluvial deposits of rivers. The Ural (*Alexandrite*); Marchensdorf, in Moravia. Haddam, Connecticut; and at Greenfield, near Saratoga, New York, U.S.

Though not much worn in jewelry, the Chrysoberyl, when transparent and of sufficient size to be cut in facets, forms a beautiful yellowish - green stone, which may almost vie with the yellow diamond in lustre, polish, and colour. It is, however, very difficult to work. The finest stones, if sufficiently deep, should be cut in pavilion facets, like a brilliant, and be made into rings, necklaces, &c., with or without diamonds. The smaller stones appear to the greatest advantage set round highly coloured gems, in circular ear-drops, &c. The thinner specimens should be cut in delicate steps.

The name Cymophane is applied to those semi-transparent varieties which exhibit a peculiar bluish-white or milky opalescence floating in the interior of the stone. These Opalescent Chrysolites (as they are sometimes termed), though less prized by jewellers than the more transparent varieties, often possess a very good colour, and when cut *en cabochon* make beautiful ring-stones. Chrysoberyl may be distinguished from Chrysolite, Moonstone, and opalescent Quartz (Cat's-eye) by its superior hardness, and from yellow Topaz by not being rendered electric by heat.

The name Chrysoberyl is derived from χρυσός, *golden*, βήρυλλος, *beryl*; Cymophane from κῦμα, *a wave*, and φαίνω, *to appear*, in allusion to its floating light.

The Chrysoberyl of the ancients was a different stone, probably the Chrysoprase of the moderns.

Brit. Mus., Case 19.

M. P. G. Horse-shoe Case, 859 to 864.

CHRYSOCOLLA, *Phillips, Haidinger.* Occurs kidney-shaped, globular, stalactitic, massive, but oftener investing Malachite and other ores of copper. Colour verdigris- and emerald-green, passing into sky-blue, and inclining to brown when impure. Lustre resinous, shining or dull. Opaque or slightly transparent. Streak white. Fracture small conchoidal. H. very variable, 2 to 3. S.G. 2·2.

Comp. Cu S̈i + 2Ḧ, or oxide of copper 44·94, silica 34·83, water 20·23 = 100·00, oftener mixed with carbonate and oxide of copper.

Analysis from Chili, by *Kittridge* :

Silica	40·09
Oxide of copper	27·97
Protoxide of iron	4·94
Lime	1·49
Magnesia	0·78
Water	24·73
	100·00

BB on charcoal does not fuse, but blackens in the outer and reddens in the inner flame. With borax melts to a green glassy globule, and is partly reduced. Soluble in muriatic acid, with separation of gelatinous silica.

Localities. English.—Cornwall; near the Lizard, in serpentine, associated with Native Copper. Cumberland. Westmoreland. Brada Head Mines, in the Isle of Man. *Scotch.*—Leadhills, in Lanarkshire. *Irish.*—Knockmahon Mines; Audley Mine, co. Cork. *Foreign.* — The Kupferhügel, near Kupferberg, in Bohemia. Spitz, in Austria. Libethen and Herrngrund, in Hungary. The Bannat. Ober and Nieder-Rochlitz, in Transylvania, in crystalline slates. Falkenstein and Schwatz, in the Tyrol. Saxony. Andreasberg, in the Harz. Siberia. Chili. South Australia, &c.

Name. From χρυσός, *gold*, and κόλλα, *glue*.

Chrysocolla may be distinguished from Malachite by colour, conchoidal fracture, transparency, as well as by its very slight effervescence with acids.

Brit. Mus., Case 26.

M. P. G. Principal floor, Wall-case 2 (British).

CHRYSOLITE, *Phillips.* The name given to the paler and more transparent crystals of Olivine; the latter name being restricted to imbedded masses or grains of inferior colour and clearness. Rhombic. Occurs massive and compact, or granular, usually in imbedded grains. Colour greenish-yellow. Lustre brilliantly vitreous. Streak

G 2

white. Transparent. Fracture conchoidal. H. 6·5 to 7. S.G. 3·3514 to 3·441.

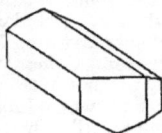

Fig. 116.

Comp. R³ S̈i in which R̈ may be M̈g F̈e M̈n C̈a alone or in combination.

Analysis by *Stromeyer* (Oriental Chrysolite):

Silica	39·73
Magnesia . . .	50·13
Protoxide of iron . .	9·19
Alumina	0·22
Protoxide of manganese .	0·09
Oxide of nickel . .	0·32
	99·68

Localities. Chrysolite occurs near Constantinople, at Vesuvius, and the Isle of Bourbon, in lava. Imbedded in Obsidian at Real del Monte, in Mexico. In pale green transparent crystals among sand at Expailly, in Auvergne. It is also found in Upper Egypt.

It is usually found in angular or rolled pieces, rarely crystallized. The crystals (usually 8, 10, or 12-sided prisms) are variously terminated, and often so compressed as to become almost tabular. They are generally very fragile, and therefore unfit for ornamental stones.

As a gem, the Chrysolite is deficient in hardness and play of colours, but when the stones are large, of good colour, and well matched, free from flaws, and well cut and polished, it is made into necklaces, hair-ornaments. &c., with good effect. From its softness, which is not much greater than that of glass, it requires to be worn with care, or it will lose its polish, and wear off at the edges. The best mode of displaying the colours to the greatest advantage is to cut it in small steps. To give it the highest polish, a copper wheel is used, on which a a little sulphuric acid is dropped.` During the process, a highly suffocating smell is given out, produced probably by the action of the acid on the copper and the gem.

The Chrysolite or Peridot has been confounded not only with the Chrysoberyl but with the greenish-yellow varieties both of Sapphire, Topaz, Aquamarine, and even of Apatite and Idocrase. It is softer than Chrysoberyl, Sapphire, Topaz, or Aquama-

rine, but harder and heavier than Apatite, while its infusibility and non-electrical properties. when heated, distinguish it from green Tourmaline.

The Chrysolite is supposed to have been the Topaz of the ancients.

The name is derived from χρυσὸς, *gold*, and λίθος, *stone*, in allusion to its colour.

Brit. Mus., Case 25.

M. P. G. Horse-shoe Case, Nos. 925 to 928.

CHRYSOLITE COMMUNE. See OLIVINE.

CHRYSOLITE DU CAP. See PREHNITE.

CHRYSOPHANE, *Breithaupt.* A name given to Holmesite or Clintonite, the composition of which may be represented by the formula

$$2(\ddot{A}l\ \ddot{M}g) + \ddot{C}a\ \ddot{S}i + \dot{H}.$$

Analysis by *Richardson :*

Silica	19·35
Alumina	44·75
Magnesia . . .	9·05
Lime	11·45
Peroxide of iron . .	4·80
Protoxide of manganese .	1·35
Zirconia . . .	2·05
Fluorine . . .	0·90
Water	4·55
	98·25

Name. From χρυσὸς, *gold*, and φαίνω, *to seem.*

CHRYSOPRASE (from χρυσὸς, *gold*, and πράσον, *a leek*), an apple-green or leek-green variety of Chalcedony, passing into Hornstone and Chalcedony, and differing from the latter, apparently, in little more than colour. It occurs massive, in thick plates; never crystallized. Fracture even, or finely splintery, or flat-conchoidal, with a slight degree of lustre. H. slightly less than that of Quartz.

Analysis by *Klaproth :*

Silica	96·16
Oxide of nickel . .	1·00
Lime	0·83
	97·99

This stone is not held in much esteem as an article of jewelry in this country, but on the continent it is more highly valued, and is made into brooches, rings, bracelets, seals, ·&c., the larger pieces being converted into snuff-boxes, cane-heads, &c. The apple-green variety is the most valuable. It should be cut *en cabochon*, as it is spoiled if cut in facets, and appears to most advantage by candle-light. Chrysoprase is apt to lose its colour and to become dark and clouded if kept in a dry warm situation, or if it be long exposed to the light of the sun; but the colour may be restored by keeping the stone in a damp place, or in wet cotton or sponge, or even by dipping it into a solution of nitrate of nickel, which also improves the tints of inferior kinds.

The kings of Prussia used only to allow the works where it is found to be opened once in three years, and monopolised most of the finest specimens; consequently, semi-transparent stones of a delicate colour, fit for setting in rings, formerly fetched very high prices in Berlin and Vienna.

The common people of Silesia wear Chrysoprase round the neck as a charm against pains.

It is found at Kosemütz, in Lower Silesia, imbedded in Serpentine, and associated with Opal, Quartz, and Chalcedony; also at Belmont's lead mine, St. Lawrence co., U.S., &c.

Chrysoprase was probably the stone called Chrysoberyl by the ancients.

Brit. Mus., Case 23.

M. P. G. Upper Gallery, Table-case A, in recess No. 138.

CHRYSOPRASE EARTH. An earthy form of Pimelite, from Silesia.

Analysis, by *Klaproth :*

Silica	. 35·00
Protoxide of nickel .	. 15·63
Magnesia . . .	. 1·25
Peroxide of iron . .	. 4·58
Lime	. 0·42
Alumina . . .	. 5·00
Water	. 38··2

               100·00

Name. From χρυσὸς, *gold,* and πράσον, a *leek.*

CHRYSOTIL, *v. Kobel.* An asbestion variety of Serpentine, allied to Picrolite, of olive-oil, yellowish or brownish colour, and metallic or silky lustre. S.G. 2·2 to 2·49.

Analysis from New Haven, U.S., by *Brush :*

Silica	. 44·05
Magnesia . . .	. 39·24
Protoxide of iron .	. 2·53
Water . . .	. 13·49

               99·31

Localities. Anglesey. Reichenstein, in Silesia. Montville, Morris co., and New Haven, Connecticut, U.S.

CHUSITE, *Werner.* An altered form of Chrysolite, occurring in small, uncrystalline, wax-, or honey-yellow masses in the basalt of Limbourg.

The name is derived from χέω, *to pour ;* in allusion to its fusibility.

CIMOLITE. A very soft, massive variety of Pyroxene, of a white or greyish colour. It is opaque, dull, and has an earthy fracture. Lustre of streak greasy. Yields to the nail and adheres to the tongue. Absorbs water but does not fall to pieces. Often incloses small grains of Quartz. S.G. 2·18 to 2·3.

Comp. $\ddot{A}l, 4\ddot{S}i + 3\ddot{H}$, or hydrated quadrosilicate of alumina.

Analysis from Argentiera, by *Klaproth :*

Silica	. 63·00
Alumina . . .	. 23·00
Peroxide of iron .	. 1·25
Water	. 12·00

               99·25

Locality. Very abundant in the island of Cimolos (now called Argentiera) in the Grecian Archipelago, by the inhabitants of which it is used as a substitute for Fuller's earth.

Name. From Cimolos, and λίθος, *stone.*

M. P. G. Horse-shoe Case, No. 1119.

CINNABAR. Hexagonal. Primary form an acute rhombohedron, in which it also occurs crystallized; but the crystals are mostly modified by secondary planes: also granular, massive and forming superficial coatings. Colour passing from carmine, through cochineal-red to lead-grey. The red specimens are more or less translucent, and exhibit an adamantine lustre, but when grey it is opaque and has a metallic lustre. Streak bright scarlet. Structure lamellar. Fracture subconchoidal, uneven. M. Descloiseaux has observed circular polarization in Cinnabar; which previously to this discovery was supposed to be peculiar to Quartz. H. 2 to 2·5. S.G. 8·99.

Fig. 117.

Comp. Protosulphide of mercury, or HgS = mercury 86·21, sulphur 13·79 = 100, but it is sometimes rendered impure by the presence of clay, bitumen, iron, &c.

BB melts and is volatilized with a blue flame and sulphureous fumes.

Localities.—The principal localities of this mineral are Idria in Carniola, and Almaden near Cordova, in Spain, where it is usually massive. Cinnabar, associated with

Realgar, forms the chief produce of the Eugenia mine, near Pola de Lena, in Asturia. The vein of ore is in Carboniferous Limestone. The tetrahedral pseudomorphous crystals afford on analysis,

Mercury . . . . 85·12
Sulphur . . . . 11·35
——————
100·00

(See REALGAR). It is also abundant in China, and forms extensive mines at New Almaden in California, in a mountain south of San José, between Monterey and the Bay of San Francisco.

Cinnabar is the ore from which the Mercury of commerce is obtained, by sublimation. The pigment vermilion is an artificial Cinnabar, which is also prepared from the crude ore.

The name is taken from the ancient Greek term used to denote the same substance, Κινναβαρι; a word itself derived from βαρυς, *heavy*. The ancients derived their supplies from Spain and Colchis.

Brit. Mus., Case 9.
M. P. G. Principal floor, Wall-case 23 (Spain), and 25 (Tuscany).

CINNAMON-STONE, *Phillips.* A variety of lime-Garnet of a clear cinnamon-brown tint, commonly occurring in masses which are full of fissures. Translucent, seldom transparent. Lustre vitreo-resinous. Fracture flat-conchoidal. H. scratches Quartz with difficulty. S.G. 3·5 to 3·6.

Analysis from Ceylon, by *Gmelin :*

Silica . . . . 40·01
Alumina . . . 23·00
Peroxide of iron . . 3·67
Lime . . . . 30·57
Potash . . . . 0·59
Loss by heat . . 0·33
——————
98·17

BB fuses with ebullition to a darkish-green glass: with borax fuses very readily to a transparent glass, more or less feebly coloured by iron.

Localities. — *Scotch.* At the limestone Quarries at Glen Gairn in Aberdeenshire.— *Irish.* In large dodecahedral crystals of a rich cinnamon colour in a coarse crystalline Dolomite at Bun Beg near Gweedore; at Kilranelagh, Wicklow, &c. *Foreign.*— In masses of considerable size in Ceylon, at Malsjö in Wermland, and at St. Gotthard; also in the United States, in beautiful yellow crystals (with Idocrase) at Parsonsfield, Phippsburg, and Rumford in Maine; in trapezohedrons at Dixon's Quarry, Wilmington, Delaware; crystallized and massive, at Amity, and on the Croton aqueduct, near Yonkers, in small rounded crystals and a massive variety, the latter when polished forming a beautiful gem.

Name. From its resemblance in colour to the spice called cinnamon.

When transparent and of good colour and size the Cinnamon-stone from Ceylon is used as a gem: most of the Hyacinths of commerce are in reality Cinnamon-stones.

Brit. Mus., Case 35.
M. P. G. Horse-shoe Case, Nos. 903 and 904.

CIRCLE AGATE. Those kinds of Agate in which the stripes are arranged concentrically round a central point.

CITRINE, OR CITRON. A name sometimes given by lapidaries to limpid and transparent Rock Crystal of a lemon, golden, or wine-yellow colour.

Brit. Mus., Case 20.
M. P. G. Horse-shoe Case, No. 509.

CLAUSSENITE. A variety of Hydrargylite, from Mariana in Brazil.

CLAUSTHALITE, *Beudant.* Cubical. Generally occurs in masses resembling a fine granular Galena, with a slight but peculiar tinge of blue. Lustre metallic. Opaque. Streak darker than the colour. Fracture granular and shining. H. 2·5 to 3. S.G. 7 to 8·8.

Comp. Selenide of lead, or Pb Se=selenium 27·6, lead 72·4=100; with part of the lead frequently replaced by silver.

Analysis from Clausthal, by *Stromeyer :*

Selenium . . . 28·11
Lead . . . . 70·98
Cobalt . . . . 0·83
——————
99·92

BB on charcoal it is quickly decomposed, and besides the usual phenomena arising from the presence of lead, it affords the odour of decayed *horse-radish*, and a reddish-brown substance is deposited on the charcoal. Heated over a spirit lamp in a glass tube, closed at one end, the selenium almost instantly sublimes, and forms a red ring within the tube, at the open end of which its odour is very perceptible. On heating the tube to redness, the ore fuses and the red ring partially disappears, a white crystalline deposit remaining.

Localities. This is a rare mineral, occurring massive in veins of Hæmatite at Hartzgerode, in the Harz; at Clausthal, Tilkerode, Zorge and Lehrbach; at Reinsberg, near Freiberg in Saxony; and at the Rio Tinto mines, near Seville, in Spain.

Brit. Mus., Case 4.

CLAY IRON-STONE. A massive form of Siderite rendered impure by an admixture of clay. Most of the iron of this country is extracted from this ore, which derives an additional value from its occurrence in layers and nodules in the Coal-measure strata. See BLACK BAND.

M. P. G. Principal floor, Wall-cases 50 to 52 (British); 18 and 19 (Foreign); 41 (Vancouver's Island); Upper Gallery, Wall-case 43, Nos. 134 to 169, 179 to 182; Wall-case 44.

CLAYITE, *W. J. Taylor.* A variety of Galena with about 25 per cent. of Arsenic, Copper, and Antimony, and apparently analogous with Steinmannite. Occurs in small cubical crystals, a combination of the tetrahedron with the dodecahedron; also amorphous as a thin coating on a layer of Quartz. Colour and streak blackish-grey. Sectile. H. about 2·5.

Comp. (Pb, Cu) (S, As, Sb).

Analysis.

Lead	68·51
Sulphur . . .	8·22
Arsenic . . .	9·78
Antimony . . .	6·54
Copper . . .	7·67
Silver . . .	trace

100·72

BB on charcoal fuses easily, giving reactions for lead, arsenic, and antimony, and with soda a brilliant metallic globule which becomes lustreless on cooling.

Locality. Peru.

Name. After the Hon. J. R. Clay, U.S. Minister in Peru, and J. A. Clay, of Philadelphia.

CLEAVELANDITE, *Brooke & Levy.* See ALBITE. Named after Parker Cleaveland, Lecturer on Chemistry and Mineralogy, Bowdoin College, U.S.

Brit. Mus., Case 30.

CLEIOPHANE, *Nuttall.* A white transparent variety of Blende. It has been found at Fowey Consol Mines, in Cornwall.

CLINGMANITE, *Silliman.* See MARGARITE. The name was proposed (after that of the Hon. T. L. Clingman) for a distinct species in consequence of an incorrect determination of the silica in the analysis.

CLINOCHLORE, *W. P. Blake.* Rhombic and hemihedral. Occurs in large crystals, having generally a rhombohedral aspect, and in plates with a micaceous structure. Colour olive-green with a somewhat pearly lustre. Transparent in thin plates. Somewhat elastic. Optically biaxial; in compound crystals there is a second pair of

optical axes making 60° with the other. H. 2 to 2·25. S.G. 2·7.

Comp. $5\ddot{R}^3 \ddot{S}i + 3\ddot{A}l \ddot{S}i + 12\dot{H} = (\frac{5}{8}\ddot{R}^3 + \frac{3}{8}\ddot{H}) \ddot{S}i + 1·5 \dot{H}$ = silica 32·6, alumina 17·9, magnesia 36·6, water 12·9=100.

Analysis from Bavaria, by *v. Kobell:*

Silica	33·49
Alumina . . .	15·37
Peroxide of iron . .	2·80
Oxide of chrome . .	0·55
Magnesia . . .	32·94
Protoxide of iron .	4·25
Water	11·50

100·40

BB like Chlorite: exhibits traces of fusion at the edges.

Localities. Lengast in Bavaria, in large crystals and plates, with Serpentine. Achmatowsk in Siberia; and in the United States near Westchester, and Unionville, Chester co., Pennsylvania.

M. Descloiseaux refers to this species Tabergite, and the hexagonal Chlorite of Pfitsch, Pfunders, and Zillerthal in the Tyrol, which occurs in bipyramidal hexagonal compound crystals; and the Chlorite of Traversella is also, according to him, a talcose Clinochlore.

CLINOCLASE. *Greg & Lettsom.* Arseniate of copper. Oblique. Rarely occurs distinctly crystallized in small oblique rhombic prisms. Colour ·dark verdigris-green inclining to blue; also dark-blue. Lustre pearly on cleavage planes, elsewhere vitreous to resinous. Streak verdigris-green. Translucent at the edges. H. 2·5 to 3. S.G. 4·2 to 4·36.

Fig. 118.

Fig. 119.

Comp. $\dot{C}u^5 \ddot{A}s + 3\dot{C}u \dot{H}$ = oxide of copper 62·7, arsenic acid 30·2, water 7·1=100.

Analysis from Cornwall, by *Rammelsberg:*

Arsenic acid . . .	29·71
Phosphoric acid . .	0·64
Oxide of copper . .	60·00
Silica	1·12
Peroxide of iron . .	0·39
Lime	0·50
Water	7·64

100·00

BB deflagrates, emits arsenical fumes, ànd fuses readily, yielding a globule of copper.

Soluble in acids and ammonia.

Localities. Near St. Day, Cornwall, at Ting Tang Mine, Huel Unity and Huel Gorland, and at Bedford United Mines, near Tavistock. The crystals usually present a very dark blue colour and a brilliant lustre, but are rarely recognisable, being aggregated in diverging groups, or disposed in extremely minute individuals in cavities of Quartz (Allan).

Name. From κλίνω, *to incline,* and κλάω, *to break,* in allusion to the oblique cleavage.

Brit. Mus., Case 56.

M. P. G. Principal floor, Wall-case 2 (British).

CLINTONITE, *Mather.* Generally occurs in tabular crystals, or in thinly foliated masses which are micaceous parallel to the base. Colour yellowish, reddish-brown or copper-red, with a pearly submetallic lustre. Streak white, or slightly yellowish or greyish. Brittle. H. 4 to 5. S.G. 3 to 3·1.

Comp. $(\frac{1}{2}\ddot{R}^5 + \frac{1}{2}\ddot{R})$ Si $\ddot{A}l\frac{4}{3} + \frac{1}{2}H.$

Analysis, by *G. H. Brush:*

Silica	.	20·24
Alumina	.	39·13
Zirconia	.	0·75
Lime	.	13·69
Magnesia	.	20·34
Soda	.	1·14
Potash	.	0·29
Peroxide of iron	.	3·27
Water	.	1·04
		100·39

BB alone infusible; but whitens, and with borax or soda forms a transparent pearl.

Locality. Amity, New York, U.S.; in limestone with Serpentine, associated with Hornblende, Spinel, Pyroxene and Graphite.

Name. After the Hon. De Witt Clinton.

CLOUDY CHALCEDONY. Chalcedony displaying dark and clouded spots in a pale grey transparent base.

CLUTHALITE, *Thomson.* The mineral named Cluthalite by Thomson, which occurs in flesh-red, vitreous crystals in amygdaloid at the Kilpatrick Hills, is Analcime, with half of the soda replaced by protoxide of iron, and with a larger amount of water. H. 3·5. S.G. 2·166.

Analysis, by *Thomson:*

Silica	.	51·266
Alumina	.	23·560

Protoxide of iron	.	7·306
Soda	.	5·130
Magnesia	.	1·233
Water	.	10·553
		99·048

Name. After *Clutha,* a name by which the valley of the Clyde has been sometimes distinguished.

M.P.G. Horse-shoe Case, No. 1185.

COAL is vegetable matter which has become mineralized by certain chemical changes which it has undergone, and by subsequent solidification by compression under the weight of the strata which have been accumulated above it since it was originally deposited. It appears to be composed of terrestrial and aquatic plants and trees, (the decay of which probably reduced them to peat,) which grew in a warm and moist climate of equable temperature, on the areas it now occupies, close to, or perhaps in, the margin of a shallow sea; and the clay (*Underclay*) with the roots of plants (*Stigmaria, &c.*) supporting each bed of coal, is the soil on which the vegetation grew of which it is formed. Each separate bed of coal, on this supposition, denotes the former existence of an adjoining surface of land, on the depression of which beneath a sea of moderate depth, the vegetable matter growing upon it became covered up by a deposit of sediment which in its turn, by the further deposit of sediment and oscillation of level, supported a fresh growth of vegetation. In this manner, by a series of depressions of moderate amount, each bed of coal was formed in succession, while its interstratification with beds of limestone, shale, clay, sandstone and ironstone indicates alternations of marine, estuary and lagoon conditions. Although coal for the most part appears to have been formed in the above-mentioned manner, it is probable that other conditions may have occasionally prevailed, as for instance in the north of England and in the south of Russia, where some of the coal beds are stated to be apparently composed of the remains of broken and drifted plants carried into the sea by inundations, and the freshets of rivers.

Coal is composed of Carbon, Hydrogen, Nitrogen, Oxygen, Sulphur, and earthy matter or Ash, in variable proportions. The greater the proportions of Carbon and Hydrogen the better is the coal, while sulphur and ash tend to render the coal both unpleasant to use, and prejudicial in its effects, especially in the smelting of iron and steel.

Coals may be divided into two classes—bituminous and nonbituminous or Anthracite. These change gradually, and merge one into the other, and in the South Wales coalfield the bituminous coal passes into anthracite in a westerly direction. The conversion of the vegetable matter into coal was apparently produced by a kind of moist putrefaction, accompanied by the exclusion of all access of air. Under those circumstances the oxygen escaped in the form of carbonic acid, while the hydrogen, being disengaged in the form of carburetted hydrogen, the carbon became in consequence more concentrated. In this manner by the removal of all the hydrogen, bituminous coal becomes converted into anthracite. S.G. 1·20 to 1·59; mean S.G. of 31 samples 1·3.

Analysis [*] from Graigola in S. Wales (S.G. 1·3):

Carbon	84·87
Hydrogen	3·84
Nitrogen	0·41
Sulphur	0·45
Oxygen	7·19
Ash	3·24
	100·00

Coke left by the Coal 85·5 per cent.

The specific gravity of Coal varies from 1·2 to 1·6. Thirty-one varieties examined by Sir Henry De la Beche and Dr. Lyon Playfair gave an average specific gravity of 1·3. See ALBERT COAL, ANTHRACITE, COKING COAL, CANNEL COAL, TORBANITE, &c.

COBALT ARSENIATÉ, *Haüy*. See ERYTHRINE.

COBALT ARSENICAL, *Haüy*. See SMALTINE.

COBALT BLOOM. See ERYTHRINE.

COBALT-COATING is Cobalt-bloom containing some free arsenous acid. It is produced by the weathering of Cobaltine on which it immediately rests, and may be regarded as a mixture of Cobalt-bloom and arsenious acid, often with the addition of a small quantity of Cobalt-sulphate. Occurs botryoidal, reniform or massive; scaly or earthy. Colour varying from peach-blossom-red to pale-rose. Opaque.

Analysis by *Kersten*, from the Wolfgang-Maassen mine at Schneeberg:

Arsenous acid	51·00
Arsenic acid	19·10
Oxide of cobalt	16·60
Protoxide of iron	2·10

* Report on the Coals suited to the Steam Navy, by Sir Henry T. De la Beche and Dr. Lyon Playfair; Memoirs of the Geological Survey of Great Britain, vol. ii. part 2.

Water	11·90
Nickel, lime,	} traces.
Sulphuric acid	}
	100·70

Localities. Schneeberg, and Annaberg, in Saxony.

Brit. Mus., Case 56.

COBALT CRUST. A name for earthy varieties of Erythrine (Arseniate of Cobalt).

COBALT ÉCLATANT. *Brochant.* } See CO-
COBALT GLANCE, *Jameson.* } BALTINE.

COBALT-GRIS, *Haüy*. See COBALTINE.

COBALT KIES, *v. Leonhard.* See LINNÆITE.

COBALT MICA. See ERYTHRINE.

COBALT OCHRE, *Nicol.* } See WAD,
COBALT OXIDÉ NOIR, *Haüy*. } or EARTHY COBALT.

COBALT PYRITEUX, *Necker;* COBALT PYRITES. See LINNÆITE.

COBALT-SCORODITE. The name given by Lippmann to a mineral occurring in small bluish crystals, with Hypochlorite and Quartz, at Schneeberg in Saxony.

COBALT SULFURÉ, *Lucas.* See LINNÆITE.

COBALT TERREUX RAYONNÉ ROUGE, *Brochant.* See ERYTHRINE.

COBALT VITRIOL. See BIEBERITE.

COBALTIC GERMINATIONS, *Kirwan.* See ERYTHRINE.

COBALTIDE, *Leymerie.* See WAD, or EARTHY COBALT.

COBALTINE, *Beudant, Haidinger.* Cubical. Occurs in the cube and its varieties; its crystalline forms resembling those of Iron Pyrites; the planes of the cube are generally striated, those of the modifications smooth. It also occurs arborescent, stalactitic, botryoidal, and amorphous. Colour silver- or yellowish-white, with a tinge of red; inclining to steel-grey, or greyish-black when much iron is present. Lustre metallic. Streak greyish-black. Brittle. Fracture uneven and lamellar. Yields with difficulty to the knife. H. 5·5. S.G. 6 to 6·3.

 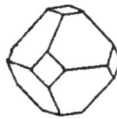 

Fig. 120.   Fig. 121.   Fig. 122.

Comp. (Co, Fe, Ni) As.

Analysis of massive Cobaltine from Schneeberg, by *Hofmann:*

Iron	11·71
Copper	13·95

Nickel	.	.	.	.	1·79
Copper	.	.	.	.	1·39
Arsenic	.	.	.	.	70·37
Bismuth	.	.	.	.	0·01
Sulphur	.	.	.	.	0·66

$$99·88$$

BB on charcoal, it gives off copious arsenical fumes,-and fuses to a white, brittle, metallic globule, which, after being roasted, imparts a blue colour to glass.

Soluble in hot nitric acid, with separation of arsenious acid.

Localities. Cornwall: Botallack Mine, in small particles, interspersed in reddish Quartz and Chlorite. Has been found at Dolcoath Mine, and was formerly worked at Huel Sparnon and the Wherry Mine. It is now worked at St. Austell Consols. *Foreign.*—In large, well-defined crystals at Tunaberg, Riddarhyttan and Hokensbö in Sweden. Modum and Skutterud in Norway in mica-slate. Wehna in Sweden. Querbach in Silesia. Siegen in Westphalia, &c.

This ore of Cobalt and Smaltine furnish the greater portion of the *Smalt* of commerce, which is employed in glass and porcelain painting, and for imparting a blue tint to paper or linen. It is prepared by roasting the ore, and then melting the oxide of cobalt so produced, in certain proportions, with pure potash and pounded quartz, which is afterwards ground to powder and carefully washed: for the most delicate purposes the oxide of cobalt is employed as a pigment.

Name. Kobolds in German are malicious spirits haunting mines, and delighting in mischief. The metal was named after them, because its occurrence is unfavourable to the ores more particularly sought for.

Brit. Mus., Case 12.

M. P. G. Principal Floor, Wall-cases 9 (British); 20 (Foreign).

COCCINITE, *Haidinger*, is found in reddish-brown coloured particles on selenide of mercury, at Casas Viejas, in Mexico. It has an adamantine lustre, and resembles Cinnabar, but the streak is paler than in the latter mineral.

Comp. Protiodide of mercury or Hg,I =mercury 44·1, iodine 55·9=100·0.

BB fuses and easily sublimes.

"It forms a magnificent water-colour, known by the name of *Scarlet*, which, however, fades very quickly when exposed to light, and at the same time destroys the colour of vermilion which may be mixed with it. It is likewise used in calico-printing."—*Gmelin.*

COCCOLITE, *Jameson*, is of two kinds, *white* and *green*. Both are granular, friable varieties of Pyroxene, the former of which may be referred to the sub-species Diopside. Coccolite consists of small, translucent granules of irregular shapes, and of various shades of green, which are very slightly coherent, but sufficiently hard to scratch glass. Lustre vitreous. Fracture lamellar. S.G. 3·3.

BB infusible alone. With carbonate of soda it melts to an olive-green, vesicular, slaggy glass; and with borax, to a pale yellow semitransparent glass.

It is chiefly found at the iron mines of Sudermannland and Nerika in Sweden, and of Arendal in Norway.

Name from χίχχος, *a grain.*

Brit. Mus., Case 34.

COCHINEAL RED COPPER ORE, *Kirwan.* See RED COPPER, TILE ORE, &c.

COCKLE, *Dufrénoy.* See TOURMALINE.

COCK's-COMB BARYTES. A variety of Barytes formed of an aggregation of small greyish-white and opaque crystals. It is found in Cumberland, crystallized at Carrock Fells, and in curved plates at Patterdale: also in Derbyshire and Lancashire.

COCK's-COMB PYRITES. A form of Marcasite composed of a comb-like aggregation of crystals similar in shape to *fig.* 123. Occurs in heaps of refuse (attle-heaps) at Huel Crebor, near Tavistock, in Devonshire; the Harz, &c.

Brit. Mus. Case 6.

Fig. 123.

M. P. G. Horse-shoe Case, No. 151.

COG-WHEEL-ORE, *Nicol.* See RADELERZ.

COKING COAL. The name given to those kinds of Coal which can be used for making Coke. For that purpose they should contain little or no sulphur.

CÖLESTIN, *Haidinger, Hausmann, Naumann, v. Kobell.* See CELESTINE.

COLLYRITE is a very soft, and white clay-like compound, with a glimmering lustre, unctuous to the touch, and adhering strongly to the tongue. H. 1 to 2. S.G. 2 to 2·15.

Comp. Hydrated Disilicate of Alumina, or $\ddot{Al}^2 \ddot{Si} + 10 \dot{H}$.

COLOPHONITE.

Analysis, from Ezquerra, by *Berthier* :

Alumina	. . . . 44·5
Silica	. . . . 15·0
Water	. . . . 40·5
	100·0

BB infusible. In water becomes transparent, and crumbles to pieces: dissolves in acids, and the solution yields a jelly on evaporation.

Localities. Near Schemnitz in Hungary, and Wissenfels in Saxony, in porphyry. Ezquerra in the Pyrenees.

Name. From χόλλη, *glue;* from its gelatinous appearance.

Brit. Mus., Case 26.

COLOPHONITE. The varieties of iron-lime Garnet which have a resinous lustre. S.G. 3·896.

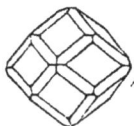

Fig. 124.

Localities. Arendal in Norway. United States; in New York, at Roger's Rock ; and at Willsboro', Essex co., forming a large vein in gneiss, associated with Tabular Spar and green Coccolite: also at Lewis.

Name. From Κόλοφων, a city of Ionia whence resin was obtained ; in allusion to the resinous aspect of the mineral.

Brit. Mus., Case 36.

COLUBRINE, *French.* See POTSTONE.

COLUMBATE OF IRON. See TANTALITE.

COLUMBITE, *Hatchett.* Rhombic: it occurs in single crystals and in small crystalline masses ; the crystals are mostly incomplete, but possess the general form of right rhombic prisms, striated longitudinally, with the lateral edges truncated, and variously modified. Colour greyish or brownish-black, often iridescent, with a dark brown streak. Opaque with metallic lustre. Scratches glass, and gives sparks with steel. Brittle. Fracture sub-conchoidal, and imperfectly laminar. H. 6. S.G. 5·4 to 6·4.

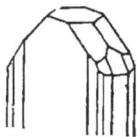

Fig. 125.

Comp. Columbate of protoxide of iron and of manganese or (Fe, Mn) $\ddot{\theta}b^2$.

Analysis, from Evigtok :

Columbic acid (Niobic acid)	78·74
Protoxide of iron	. . 16·40
Protoxide of manganese	. 5·12
Oxide of tin and tungstic acid	0·16
	100·42

This analysis is almost identical with those of specimens from Middletown, U.S., by H. Rose.

BB alone, on charcoal, infusible ; but it becomes somewhat rounded at the corners: dissolves slowly in borax, to which it imparts a blackish-green colour.

Localities. The finest crystals have been found in a felspar-quarry at Middletown ; one of them, described by Professor Johnston, weighed 14 lbs., another 6¾ lbs. It has also been met with at Chesterfield and Beverly in Massachusetts, in granite; and at Haddam in Connecticut, where it was first discovered, it occurs in a granite-vein, with Beryl, Chrysoberyl and Automolite. The Columbite of Bodenmais in Bavaria is also found in granite associated with Beryl. The most beautiful variety of this mineral hitherto procured, remarkable for its well-developed and highly-modified crystallization, is that from Evigtok, in the fiord of Arksut in Greenland. At first it appears to resemble certain kinds of Tinstone, the crystals being either loose or enveloping pieces of decomposed Felspar, or covering the sides of small cavities in the latter mineral. It does not exhibit the beautiful iridescence of the American Columbite.

Name. The name Columbite was bestowed on this mineral from its having been first discovered in America.

Brit. Mus., Case 38.

COLUMNAR HEAVY SPAR. This mineral (which is the Stangenspath of Werner) occurs crystallized in yellowish, milk-, greyish- and greenish-white, acicular, oblique rhombic prisms, which are generally ill-defined and aggregated laterally into columns, and intersect one another. It has a shining pearly lustre, is translucent, and easily frangible—breaking with a straight foliated fracture. It is found in metallic veins at Freiberg in Saxony. It may be distinguished from white-lead ore (Cerusite), to which it bears a resemblance, by its pearly lustre, foliated fracture and specific gravity, which is not above 4·5, while that of white-lead ore is 6·55, its small conchoidal fracture, and its lustre adamantine.

COMBUSTIBLE COPPER ORE, *Kirwan.* Bituminous Shale or Coal impregnated with Copper.

COMMON FELSPAR. See ORTHOCLASE.

COMMON JADE. See NEPHRITE.

COMMON MICA. See MUSCOVITE.

COMMON OPAL. The name applied to the common varieties of Opal which do not exhibit the peculiar play of colours termed opalescence.

Localities. Cornwall: at Huels Stennack, Spinster, Buller, Damsel, Poligine, Rosewarne, &c., and at Botallack Mine, St. Just. Abundantly at the Giant's Causeway in Ireland, the Hebrides, Faröe, Iceland and Hungary. A wax-yellow or greyish-green variety, sometimes white, occurs in Smyrna Harbour, (within half a mile, in a S.W. direction, of the watering-place at Vourla), with yellow Jasper and Hornstone, imbedded in a low ridge of compact pale yellow or greyish-white lime-stone.

Common Opal is sometimes made into pins, cane-heads and other ornaments.

COMMON SALT, *Dana.* See ROCK SALT.

COMMON SERPENTINE. See SERPENTINE.

COMMON SPAR, *Kirwan.* CALCAREOUS SPAR.

COMPACT BITUMEN, *Phillips.* See ASPHALT.

COMPACT MINERAL PITCH, *Kirwan.* See ASPHALT.

COMPOSTELLA HYACINTH. Quartz crystals coloured red by an admixture of ferruginous clay found at Compostella.

COMPTONITE, *Brewster.* Rhombic: is found in white translucent crystals, the primary form of which is a right rectangular prism, of which the base is not square. Lustre vitreous. Streak white. Fracture small-conchoidal and uneven. H. 5 to 5·5. S.G. 2·35 to 2·4.

Fig. 126.

Analysis, from Seeberg, by *Rammelsberg :*

Silica	.	.	.	. 38·74
Alumina	.	.	. 30·84
Lime	.	.	. . 13·43
Soda	.	.	.	. 3·85
Potash	.	.	.	0·54
Water	.	.	.	. 13·10

100·50

BB froths up slightly, becomes opaque, and fuses imperfectly to a vesicular glass.

Comptonite is merely a variety of Thomsonite, and the name was originally given to the specimens of the latter mineral which occur in the vesicular lavas of Vesuvius.

Localities. Renfrewshire, at Kilmalcolm and Port Glasgow. In basalt at the Pflaster Kante, near Eisenach, in Saxe Weimar. Bohemia in Clinkstone at Seeberg and Hauenstein. The Cyclopean Isles, in Sicily, with Analcime and Phillipsite.

Name. After Lord Compton, by whom it was first distinguished.

Brit. Mus., Case 27.

COMPTONITIC KOUPHONE SPAR, *Haidinger.* See COMPTONITE.

CONARITE, *Breithaupt.* Occurs in small grains and crystals, with one perfect cleavage. Colour yellowish, pistachio- and siskin-green; also olive-green. Translucent in thin lamellæ. Streak siskin-green. H. 2·5 to 3. S.G. 2·459 to 2·49.

Locality. Röttis in Voigtland, with Rottisite.

Name. From κόναρος, *evergreen.*

CONDRODITE, *Haüy.* See CHONDRODITE.

CONDURRITE, *Faraday.* Is an arsenite of copper derived from the oxidation or weathering of the arsenide Cu^6 As (*Domeykite*). It occurs mostly in nodular masses, externally of a brownish-black colour (sometimes with a tinge of blue), and earthy; internally on a fresh surface exhibiting a tin-white tarnish. Also black and soft, soiling the fingers. Yields to the knife, producing a metallic-looking surface, nearly of a lead-grey colour. Brittle. Fracture flat-conchoidal. H. 3 to 3·5. S.G. 4·5.

Comp. $6Cu \overset{...}{As} + 4\overset{..}{H}$ = copper 70·11, arsenic 29·88 = 100.

Analysis, by *J. Blyth :*

Copper	.	.	.	. 60·21
Arsenic	.	.	.	. 19·51
Iron	.	.	.	. 0·25
Sulphur	.	.	.	2·33
Oxygen	.	.	.	13·17
Carbon	.	.	.	1·62
Hydrogen	.	.	.	2·41
Nitrogen	.	.	.	0·06
Water	.	.	.	2·41

100·00

BB on charcoal gives off fumes of arsenious acid, and yields a metallic globule of the colour of copper. In a tube affords fumes of arsenious acid and water, and with soda and borax yields a globule of copper.

Not soluble in muriatic acid.

Localities.—English. Cornwall at Condurrow Mine, and at Carn Brea Mines, near Redruth.—*Foreign.* The Cordilleras of Copiapo, Chili, S. America.

Brit. Mus., Case 4.

M. P. G. Principal Floor, Wall-case 2 (British).

CONFETTI DI TIVOLI. See DRAGÉES DE TIVOLI.

CONFOLENSITE. A variety of Halloysite from Confolens, Dept. of the Charente.

CONICHALCITE. A reniform and massive mineral, nearly allied to Olivenite and Volborthite, of a pistachio-green colour, inclining to emerald-green. Subtranslucent. Streak same as the colour. Brittle. Fracture splintery. H. 4·5. S.G. 4·12.

Comp. $(\ddot{C}u, \dot{C}a)^4 (\ddot{P}, \ddot{A}s) + 1·5 \dot{H}$, with part of the phosphoric acid replaced by vanadic acid.

Analysis by *Fritzsche*:

Arsenic acid	.	.	.	30·68
Phosphoric acid	.	.	.	8·81
Vanadic acid	.	.	.	1·78
Oxide of copper	.	.	.	31·76
Lime	.	.	.	.	21·36
Water	.	.	.	.	5·61

100·00

Locality. Probably Hinajosa de Cordova, in Andalusia, Spain.

CONISTONITE, *Greg.* Rhombic. Colourless. Transparent to translucent. Lustre vitreous. Slightly sectile. Fracture small-conchoidal, uneven. S.G. 2·052.

Comp. Hydrated oxalate of lime, $\dot{C}a \ddot{C} + 7\dot{H}$.

Analysis:

Oxalic acid	.	.	28·017
Lime	.	.	.	21·055
Soda and magnesia	.	0·822
Water	.	.	49·155

99·049

Locality. Coniston in Cumberland. Conistonite has been shown to be a result of accidental admixture.

CONITE, *Friesleben.* A variety of Dolomite, of a flesh-red colour, coated externally with Iron-ochre. Opaque. Brittle. Fracture fine-grained or imperfect conchoidal. Scratches glass. S.G. 3.

Comp. $\ddot{C} \dot{C}a + 3\dot{M}g \ddot{C}$.

Analysis from Meissner, by *John*:

Carbonate of lime	.	28·0
Carbonate of magnesia	.	67·4
Carbonate of iron	.	3·5
Water	.	.	.	1·0

98·9

Localities. It occurs amorphous, massive,

and in crusts at Down Hill, co. Derry, in Ireland; in Iceland; on the Meissner in Hessia, and in Saxony.

Brit. Mus., Case 49.

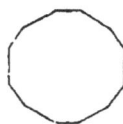

Fig. 127.

CONNELLITE, *Brooke & Miller.* Hexagonal. Occurs in smalt-blue to deep Berlin-blue hexagonal prisms with truncated edges. Lustre vitreous. Translucent.

Comp. Supposed, according to Connell, to be a compound of chloride and sulphate of copper, and a little water.

This is an extremely rare mineral, stated to have been found in Cornwall at Huel Providence, and at Carharrack in St. Day.

Brit. Mus., Case 56.

COPALE FOSSILE, *Dufrénoy*; or COPALINE, *Hausmann, Nicol.* A fossil resin. Is found in irregular pieces of a pale yellowish and dirty-brown colour, resembling the resin copal in colour, lustre, transparency, hardness, and difficult solubility in alcohol. Yields easily to the knife. Brittle. H. 2·5. S.G. 1·04.

Comp. 40C, 32H, O.

Analysis, from Highgate, by *Johnson*:

Carbon	.	.	.	85·408
Hydrogen	.	.	.	11·787
Oxygen	.	.	.	2·669
Ashes	.	.	.	0·136

100·000

Emits an aromatic and resinous odour when broken and heated. Melts easily to a limpid fluid. Volatilizes in the air by a gentle heat, and burns with a clear yellow flame and much smoke, leaving very little residue. Slightly soluble in alcohol.

Locality. Highgate Hill, N. of London, in London Clay.

Another resin (from the walls of a trap-dyke, at an old lead mine in Northumberland, called Settling Stones), has been described by Johnston as resembling Copaline in external appearance, but consisting of carbon 85·133, hydrogen 10·853, ashes 3·256 = 99·242, or nearly 4C, 3H.

COPIAPITE, *Haidinger.* Occurs in small yellow grains, sometimes composed of delicate hexagonal tables; also fibrous and incrusting. Translucent, with a pearly lustre.

Comp. $\ddot{F}e^2 \ddot{S}^5 + 18 \dot{H}$.

Analysis of foliated specimen, by *H. Rose*:

Sulphuric acid	.	.	. 39·60
Peroxide of iron	.	.	. 26·11
Alumina	.	.	. 1·95
Magnesia	.	.	. 2·64
Silica	.	.	. 1·37
Water	.	.	. 29·67

101·34

Locality. Incrusting Coquimbite in the district of Copiapo, in Chili.

COPPER-BLACK, *Jameson.* See BLACK COPPER.

COPPERDIASPORE. See KUPFERDIASPORE.

COPPER EMERALD, *Jameson.* See DIOPTASE.

COPPER FROTH, *Dana.* See TYROLITE.

COPPER GLANCE, *Jameson.* Rhombic: Occurs crystallized in regular six-sided prisms, mostly modified on the terminal edges, sometimes on the lateral; and in acute and obtuse double six-sided pyramids, with triangular planes; massive, and occasionally in pseudomorphous crystals. Colour and streak blackish lead-grey, often tarnished black, and occasionally iridescent. Lustre metallic. Structure perfectly lamellar, sometimes sectile and soft. Fracture conchoidal. Slightly malleable, and much more easily fusible than copper. H. 2·5 to 3. S.G. 5·5 to 5·8. See NAIL-HEADED COPPER-ORE.

 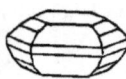 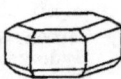

Fig. 128.   Fig. 129.   Fig. 130.

Comp. Disulphide of copper or ©u S= sulphur 20, copper 80=100.

Analysis from the United Mines of Cornwall, by *Thomson :*

Copper	.	.	. 77·16
Sulphur	.	.	. 20·62
Iron	.	.	. 1·45

99·23

BB on charcoal melts very easily after the sulphur is driven off, and yields a globule of copper covered with a blackish scoria. Forms a blue solution in ammonia.

Found in Cornwall, the finest specimens in the neighbourhood of St. Just; also in Ayrshire; in the porphyritic district of Barrack Mountain, in Ulster, and massive at Kenmare Mines, Kerry. The compact and massive varieties occur in Siberia, Hessia, Saxony, and the Bannat, and at the mines near Angina, in Tuscany.

Copper Glance is met with in veins and beds accompanied by other ores of copper, and is highly prized by the miner; but it is rather a scarce ore of copper, and does not occur in very great abundance, although it is found in many different places.

It may be distinguished from Red Silverore (Pyrargyrite) by the colour of its streak, which resembles that of the mineral, while the streak of Pyrargyrite is a fine cochineal-red. From Silver Glance it may be distinguished by many characters, especially by its inferior tenacity; from Bournonite and Grey Copper by its comportment before the blow-pipe, and the green solution it affords with nitric acid. Copper Glance is sectile, but Grey Copper is brittle.

Brit. Mus., Case 7.

M. P. G. Principal Floor, Wall-cases 2 and 7 (British); 17 (Foreign).

COPPER GREEN, *Jameson.* See CHRYSOCOLLA.

COPPER MICA, *Jameson.* See CHALCOPHYLLITE.

COPPER NICKEL, *Allan, Jameson.* Hexagonal, and isomorphous with Breithauptite. It rarely occurs crystallized, but reticulated, dendritic, and botryoidal; most commonly massive. Colour copper-red, acquiring a grey or blackish tarnish by exposure. Lustre metallic. Streak pale brownish-black. Emits an arsenical odour when struck with steel. Yields to the knife with difficulty, and is brittle. Fracture imperfect conchoidal, or fine-grained uneven. H. 5 to 5·5. S.G. 6·6 to 7·6.

Comp. Di-arsenide of nickel or Ni², As= nickel 44·1, arsenic 55·9 = 100; with small quantities of Sb, Co, Pb, Fe, and S.

Analysis from Balen, in the Pyrenees, by *Berthier :*

Nickel	.	.	. 33·67
Iron	.	.	. 1·43
Antimony	.	.	. 28·37
Arsenic	.	.	. 33·67
Sulphur	.	.	. 2·86

100·00

BB on charcoal emits strong arsenical fumes, and fuses to a silver-white, brittle globule.

Soluble in nitric acid, with separation of arsenious acid; more readily in nitro-muriatic acid.

Copper Nickel generally accompanies ores of cobalt, bismuth, silver, and copper. It is found in Cornwall, at Pengelly Mine, St. Teath; at Huel Chance, St. Austell, and at Fowey Consols Mine; also in Norway and Sweden; Koliwan, in Siberia; Andreasberg, in the Harz; Schneeberg, Annaberg,

Freiberg, in Saxony; Querbach, in Silesia; Joachimstahl, in Bohemia; Saalfield, in Thuringia; in Swabia, Styria, Hessia. Allemont, in Dauphiné; and Aragon, in Spain.

Copper Nickel may be distinguished from copper, to which it bears a striking resemblance, by its brittleness. The name is derived from its copper-red colour, and its constituent parts.

Brit. Mus., Case 4.

M. P. G. Principal Floor, Wall-cases 9 (British); 20 (Foreign).

COPPER PYRITES, *Jameson, Phillips.* See CHALCOPYRITE.

COPPER VITRIOL, *Jameson.* See CYANOSITE.

COPPER URANITE, *Naumann.* See CHALCOLITE.

COPPERAS, *Dana.* Oblique: primary form an oblique rhombic prism. It occurs massive, pulverulent, botryoidal, reniform, stalactitic, and crystallized. Colour various shades of green, but generally of a yellow or yellowish-brown colour externally. Translucent. Lustre vitreous. Streak white. Taste metallic and astringent. Brittle. Fracture conchoidal. H. 2. S.G. 1·83.

Fig. 131.

Comp. Heptahydrated protosulphate of iron or $\ddot{\text{F}}\text{e} \ddot{\text{S}} + 7 \dot{\text{H}} =$ sulphuric acid 28·9, protoxide of iron 25·7, water 45·4 = 100·0.

BB on charcoal, becomes magnetic; with borax affords a green glass. On exposure to the air, becomes covered with a yellow powder, which is sulphate of peroxide of iron.

Soluble in 1·6 parts of cold, and 0·3 of boiling water, and the solution turns black on the addition of tincture of galls.

This salt is generally produced by the decomposition of Iron Pyrites; and in Great Britain is found in Lower Bagshot Clays in Branksea Island, in Dorsetshire; in Fuller's Earth at Widcombe, near Bath; in Alumshale at Whitby, in Yorkshire; and Hurlet, near Paisley; at Castleton, in Derbyshire, in small crystals: and in some of the Gwennap Mines in Cornwall. It also occurs in the Rammelsberg Mine, near Goslar, in the Harz; at Gieshübl; near Bodenmais, in Bavaria; at Schwartzenberg, in Saxony; and Schemnitz, in Hungary, and in the United States at Copperas Mount, a few miles east of Bainbridge, Ohio.

Copperas is employed in dyeing and tan-

ning, in the manufacture of writing-ink, of Prussian blue, and sulphuric acid The residue of the latter process (colcothar of iron) is used as a red paint, and, when washed, for polishing glass, steel, &c. (See VITRIOLITE.)

Brit. Mus., Case 55.

M. P. G. Horse-shoe Case, No. 233.

COPPERASINE. The name proposed by Prof. C. U. Shepard for a hydrated ferrous cuprous, and ferric sulphate from Ducktown copper mine, in Eastern Tennessee.

COQUIMBITE, *Brooke & Miller, Dufrénoy.* Hexagonal: occurs in prisms, with the terminal edges deeply replaced, and in fine granular masses. Colour violet-white, yellowish, or brownish. Fracture conchoidal. Taste astringent. H. 2 to 2·5. S.G. 2 to 2·1.

Comp. Tersulphate of iron, or $\ddot{\text{F}}\text{e} \ddot{\text{S}}^3 + 9$ $\dot{\text{H}} =$ peroxide of iron 28·5, sulphuric acid 42·7, water 28·8 = 100·0.

Analysis by H. Rose:

Peroxide of iron	.	.	24·11
Alumina	.	.	0·92
Sulphuric acid	.	.	43·55
Lime	.	.	0·73
Magnesia	.	.	0·32
Silica	.	.	0·31
Water	.	.	30·10

100·04

Dissolves in muriatic acid or in cold water, with the exception of the silica; the latter solution deposits a large quantity of peroxide of iron on boiling.

Coquimbite appears to have been produced by the weathering of Iron Pyrites. It is found in crystals, and massive, with other ores of iron, in a felspathic rock, in the province of Coquimbo, about half a day's journey from Copiapo, in Chili. It also forms the greater part of a large hill near Calama in Bolivia.

CORACITE, *Leconte.* An amorphous mineral, resembling Pitch-blende, of a pitch-black colour. H. 3.

Analysis by J. D. Whitney:

Peroxide of uranium	.	.	72·60
Oxide of lead	.	.	6·56
Lime	.	.	5·99
Peroxide of iron	.	.	2·74
Alumina	.	.	1·10
Silica	.	.	5·33
Water	.	.	5·68

100·00

BB gives the action of uranium with the fluxes. On account of the ready solubility in acid, the uranium is supposed by Mr. Whitney to be in the state of peroxide instead of protoxide as in Pitch-blende.

CORAL ORE. A variety of Hepatic Cinnabar, from Idria, in Carniola, composed of curved lamellar concretions, with the form and apparent structure of fossilized shells. Brit. Mus., Case 9.

CORALINERZ, *Werner.*

CORDIERITE, *Dufrénoy.* The name given by Haüy to Iolite, in honour of Cordier, the geologist.

CORINDON, *Haüy.* See CORUNDUM.

CORNALINE, *Brochant.* CARNELIAN.

CORNALINES DE VIEILLE ROCHE. The name given by lapidaries to clear transparent varieties of Carnelian of a dark red colour, and held in most esteem in consequence of the richness of their colour, and their hardness, which renders them susceptible of a high polish. They are found in the older rocks, and are chiefly brought from Surat, in India.

CORNEOUS LEAD ORE, *Jameson.* See CROMFORDITE.

CORNEOUS MANGANESE, *v. Leonhard.* See RHODONITE.

CORNEOUS MERCURY, *Jameson.* See CALOMEL.

CORNEOUS SILVER-ORE, *Kirwan.* See KERARGYRITE.

CORNISH DIAMOND. The true *Cornish Diamond* is a peculiar variety of Quartz, differing in some respects in its crystalline form; it is usually covered with an opaque coating of silica. These crystals were found abundantly some years since in St. Just, and at some of the mines in St. Agnes; they are now very rarely found: but Rock Crystals are sold as Cornish Diamonds. These, De la Beche says, which are "commonly known as *Cornish diamonds,* are sufficiently transparent to be cut and set in brooches, seals, and other personal ornaments, though far more rarely now than formerly, when, judging from old jewelry preserved in some Cornish families, they would appear to have been very often employed for these purposes. We have seen very clear crystals from thence of the usual form (a hexagonal prism terminated by a hexagonal pyramid), about three inches high and one inch and a half thick. Cornish diamonds would appear to have been esteemed and used for personal ornaments in the time of Queen Elizabeth, for Carew notices them, and observes that, though 'in blacknesse and in hardnesse they come behind the right ones, yet I have knowne some of them set on so good a foile, as at first sight they might ap-

pose a not unskilfull lapidarie.' (Survey of Cornwall, 1602, reprint of 1769, p. 7.) The violet Rock Crystal, or Amethyst, seems scarce; we have, however, seen a few Cornish specimens, and among them some which might have been advantageously employed for personal ornaments if they had not been more precious as mineralogical specimens." (Report on Cornwall, Devon, and W. Somerset, by Sir H. T. De la Beche, p. 496.)

CORNISH TIN-ORE, *Jameson.* See WOOD TIN.

CORNWALLITE, *Zippe.* Amorphous. Colour blackish or verdigris-green. Fracture conchoidal, H. 4·5. S.G. 4·16.

Comp. Arsenate of copper, or $Cu^5 \ddot{As}+$ $5\bar{1}1=$oxide of copper 55·37, arsenic acid 32·07, water 12·56=100.

Analysis, mean of two, by *Lerch :*

Arsenic acid . . .	30·21
Phosphoric acid . .	2·16
Oxide of copper . .	54·61
Water	13·02
	100·00

BB on charcoal gives off fumes of arsenic, and yields a globule of copper enveloped in a brittle crust.

Locality. Cornwall: in small botryoidal or disseminated masses of Olivenite. It may be readily distinguished from Malachite, by not efferverscing with acids.

CORUNDELLITE, *Silliman.* A name given to a supposed variety of Margarite, founded on an incorrect determination of the silica in the analyses of that mineral.

CORUNDITE. See CORUNDUM.

CORUNDOPHILLITE, *Shepard.* Oblique. Colour and streak dark leek-green passing into grey and greenish black, with a pearly lustre. Lamellar; thin laminæ flexible, but less so than Talc. Brittle.

Analysis, by *Shepard :*

Silica	34·75
Protoxide of iron . .	31·25
Alumina	8·55
Alkalies and loss . .	20·00
Water	5·47
	100·00

BB alone, instantly blackens and melts at the extremity to a shining black globule: with borax effervesces and forms a clear bottle-green glass.

Localities. Near Asheville, Buncombe county, North Carolina, in imperfectly stellate groups, and also spreading out into laminæ between layers of Corundum; also frequently with the Corundum of Asia Minor.

Name. From Corund (*Corundum*), and φίλος, *a friend.*

Brit. Mus, Case 32.

CORUNDUM, *Phillips.* CORUNDUM-STONE. Hexagonal: commonly occurs crystallized in six-sided prisms, which rarely exhibit a tendency to flat triedral terminations; also in obtuse and acute hexahedral pyramids. It is likewise found granular or compact. Sometimes nearly colourless and slightly translucent, but more frequently with a greyish, greenish or reddish tint, or brown with a chatoyant lustre. Fracture conchoidal, uneven. Extremely tough when compact. H. 9. S.G. 3·9 to 4·1.

Fig. 132.　　　　　　　　　　Fig. 133.

Comp. A̤l or oxide of aluminium, when pure.—Aluminium 53·19, oxygen 46·81 = 100·00.

Analysis of Corundum of India, by *J. Lawrence Smith:*

Alumina	93·12
Magnesia	0·91
Lime	1·02
Silica	0·96
Water	2·86
	98·87

BB like sapphire.

Localities. In hexagonal crystals at Carrock Fells in Cumberland, and in small rolled fragments in the bed of a stream in the county of Wicklow. *Foreign.*—In granite rocks in China, Ava, on the coast of Malabar and in the Carnatic: also less abundantly at Gellivara, in Sweden, in Magnetic Iron; near Mozzo in Piedmont, and at St. Gotthard. Largely in Asia Minor.

Name. From the Indian, *Korund.*

This is the hardest of all known bodies, except the Diamond. The name Corundum is commonly confined to the opaque rough crystals and cleaveable masses, generally of dingy colours and often dark; while the term Emery embraces the more or less im-

pure, massive, granular and compact kinds, and Sapphire and Ruby comprise the transparent, brightly-tinted varieties. It is used extensively for polishing steel and cutting gems. See EMERY.

Brit. Mus, Case 19.

M. P. G. Horse-shoe Case, Nos. 783 to 785; Wall-case 41.

COTHAM, RUIN, or LANDSCAPE MARBLE. A light grey argillaceous limestone, occurring in thin irregular layers, from two to six inches thick, at Cotham and other places in the neighbourhood of Bristol. Slices of the stone cut at right angles to the bedding exhibit, when polished, fanciful representations of landscapes, and ruins, which have caused it to be called, also, *Ruin* or *landscape marble.*

According to Charles Moore this stone forms the lowest bed of the "White Lias" at Pylle Hill, on the Bristol and Exeter Railway, near Bristol. It is also stated by Phillips to be of common occurrence in the Val d'Arno, near Florence.

COTTONSTONE. The name given to Mesolite in Skye.

COTUNNIA, *Monticelli & Covelli.* COTUNNITE, *v. Kobell.* Rhombic. In extremely minute, white acicular crystals, with an adamantine lustre inclining to silky or pearly. Streak white. May be scratched with the nail. S.G. 5·23.

Comp. Chloride of lead, or Pb Cl = lead 74·5 chlorine 25·5 = 100·0.

BB fuses easily, colouring the flame blue, and emitting a white smoke which is condensed on the charcoal. With soda yields a globule of lead.

Soluble in about twenty-seven times its weight of cold water.

Locality. This mineral was observed by Monticelli and Covelli, in the higher crater of Vesuvius, after the eruption of 1822; next in 1840, soon after the eruption of 1839, in the upper crater, near the Punta del Mauro; and lately in the lava of 1855, which ran into the Fosso della Vetrana.

Name. After a medical man in Naples.

Brit. Mus., Case 59.

M.P.G. Upper Gallery, Table-case A, in recess 4, No. 148.

COUPEROSE BLANCHE. See GOSLARITE.
COUPEROSE BLEUE. See CYANOSE.
COUPEROSE JAUNE. See COPIAPITE.
COUPEROSE VERTE. See COPPERAS.

COUZERANITE, *Charpentier.* Occurs in small, but perfect, square prisms imbedded in limestone. Colour greyish-black to indigo-blue. Lustre vitreous or resinous. Opaque, but in fragments transparent and brilliant. Fragile. Fracture slightly lamellar. H. under 5. S.G. 2·69.

Comp. According to *Dufrénoy:* Silica 52·37; alumina 24·02, lime 11·85, magnesia 1·40, potash 5·52, soda 3·96 = 98·55.

BB fuses to a white enamel.

Not affected by acids.

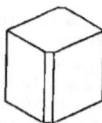

Fig. 134.

Localities. This mineral was noticed by Charpentier, in the defiles of the valley of Seix in the Pyrenees, called "Des Couzerans," whence the name *Couzeranite.* It has been referred to Labradorite; but R. P. Greg suggests that it is a variety of Dipyre.

Brit. Mus., Case 30.

COVELLINE, *Beudant:* or COVELLINITE. Hexagonal. Colour indigo-blue; with submetallic, somewhat greasy lustre, a little pearly on the cleavage-face. Streak black, shining. Opaque. Sectile: thin leaves flexible. H. 1·5 to 2. S.G. 3·8 to 3·85.

Comp. $Cu\,S^2$ = copper 66·5, sulphur 33·5 = 100.

Analysis from Vesuvius, by *Covelli:*

Sulphur	. . .	32
Copper	. . .	66

                 98

BB before becoming red-hot, burns with a blue flame, and melts with ebullition to a globule, which, with soda, yields a button of copper.

Soluble in nitric acid.

Localities.—English. Huel Maudlin in Cornwall: investing Copper Pyrites.—*Foreign.* Leogang in Salzburg. Keilee in Poland. Sangerhausen in Saxony. Mansfeld in Thuringia. In black or greenish-blue incrustations around the fumaroles of the crater of Vesuvius, in the form of a sooty deposit, or net-work like a spider's web.

Name. After its discoverer, Signor Covelli of Naples.

M.P.G. Principal Floor, Wall-case 17.

CRAIE DE BRIANÇON. A subschistous kind of Talc, of a whitish colour and with a scaly texture. It is composed of an intimate mixture of scaly Talc and Steatite; and is met with in the neighbourhood of Briançon, Dept. of the Hautes-Alpes, in France.

CRAITONITE. See CRICHTONITE.

CRAYON ROUGE, *Brochant.* See RED CHALK.

CREDNERITE, *Rammelsberg.* Oblique. Occurs foliated-crystalline. Colour steel-grey to iron-black. Lustre metallic. Streak brownish-black. H. 4·5. S.G. 4·9 to 5·1.

Comp. $Cu^3\,Mn^2$ = oxide of copper 42·9. peroxide of manganese 57·1 = 100.

Analysis from Friederichsrode, by *Rammelsberg:*

Protoxide of manganese	.	64·24
Oxide of copper . .	.	23·73
Baryta . . .	.	2·01
Oxygen . . .	.	8·83

                98·81

BB infusible, except on thin edges: with borax gives a dull-violet coloured glass.

Locality. Friederichsrode.

Name. After Charles Auguste Credner, professor of theology at Giessen.

Brit. Mus., Case 13.

CRICHTONITE, *Bournon, Haidinger.* A Titaniferous Iron occurring in small acute rhombohedrons, having their summits replaced, and being otherwise variously modified by secondary planes. Colour bluish-black, with a brilliant metallic lustre. Opaque. Streak deep black. Fracture conchoidal. H. 6. S.G. 4·79.

Fig. 135.

Comp. $Ti\,Fe.$

Analysis by *Marignac:*

Titanic acid . .	.	52·27
Peroxide of iron .	.	1·20
Protoxide of iron .	.	46·53

                100·00

BB alone infusible; with salt of phosphorus affords a glass, which becomes red on cooling.

Locality. This variety of Ilmenite is found at St. Christophe, near Oisans, in Dauphiné, on Rock Crystal, and associated with Anatase.

Name. In honour of Dr. Crichton.

Brit. Mus., Case 37.

CRISPITE, *Saussure.* See RUTILE.

CRISTATED QUARTZ. Cellular Quartz with the plates arranged in a cristated manner, like the comb of a cock.

CROCIDOLITE. Occurs both compact and in long and easily separable fibres, which are flexible and elastic, like those of Asbestos. Colour and streak lavender-blue and leek-green. Lustre silky. Opaque. H. 4. S.G. 3·2.

Comp. (N̈a, M̈g) 2S̈i + 3(F̈e, S̈i) + 5Ḧ.
Analysis by *Stromeyer*:

Silica	. 51·64
Protoxide of iron . .	. 34·38
Soda	. 7·11
Lime	. 0·05
Magnesia . . .	. 2·64
Peroxide of manganese	. 0·02
Water	. 4·01

                   99·85

BB at a strong red heat, even in the flame of a spirit-lamp, fuses to a black, swollen, strongly magnetic glass. With borax forms a transparent green glass.
Localities. The Grigna country, beyond the Great Orange River, in South Africa, with Magnetite. Stavärn, in Norway, in Zircon-syenite. Greenland. Golling, in Salzburg, in Gypsum.
Name. From κροκίς, *wool*, in allusion to its woolly, fibrous structure.
Brit. Mus., Case 34.

CROCOISK, *Beudant;* CROCOISITE, *v. Kobell.* Oblique: primary or cleavage form an oblique rhombic prism. Occurs in very distinct crystals; also massive. Colour various tints of hyacinth-red. Translucent, with strong refracting power and adamantine lustre. Streak orange-yellow. H. 2·5 to 3. S.G. 5·9 to 6·1.

Fig 136.

Comp. Monochromate of lead, or P̈b C̈r= oxide of lead, 68·7, chromic acid 31 3= 100 0.
Analysis by *Berzelius*:

Oxide of lead . . .	. 68·5
Chromic acid . . .	. 31·5

                 100·0

BB decrepitates when heated, assuming for the time a darker colour; but it may be fused to a black shining slag, containing globules of metallic lead. Colours glass of borax green.

Soluble in nitric acid, forming a yellow solution.
Localities. In narrow veins, traversing decomposed gneiss, at Nischne Tagilsk, near Beresow, in Siberia; and in fine crystals in decomposed granite at Conghonas do Campo, in the Brazils. Rezbanya, in Hungary. The Bannat. Luzon, one of the Philippine Islands.
Crocoisite is used as a pigment, but the colour is not permanent.
Name. From κροκόεις, *aurora-yellow.*
Brit. Mus., Case 39.
M. P. G. Principal Floor, Wall-case 21.

CROISETTE. See STAUROTIDE.

CROMFORDITE, *Greg & Lettsom.* Pyramidal. Primary form a rectangular four-sided prism; in which it also occurs either perfect, or having the lateral and also the terminal edges replaced. Colour white, greyish or yell w. Transparent or translucent. Streak snow-white. Rather sectile, and easily frangible. Fracture conchoidal, with a splendent adamantine lustre. H. 2·75 to 3. S.G. 6 to 6·3.

Fig. 137.

Comp. Chlorocarbonate of lead, or Pb Cl + P̈b C̈=chloride of lead 51, carbonate of lead 49=100.
Analysis, by *Klaproth,* recalculated by *Berzelius*:

Oxide of lead . .	. 85·5
Muriatic acid . .	. 14·0
Carbonic acid . .	. 6·0

                105·5

BB melts readily in the outer flame to a yellow globule, which on cooling becomes white, and somewhat crystalline; on charcoal yields a globule of lead.
Soluble with effervescence in nitric acid.
Localities. The finest crystals of this rare mineral were obtained many years ago, in the air-shaft of a mine between Cromford and Wirksworth, in Derbyshire; many of these specimens are deposited in case 57 B, at the British Museum. It has lately been found by Mr. Brice Wright, in minute crystals, at Lossiemouth lead-mine, at Elgin, in Scotland, and has also been met with at Huel Confidence, in Cornwall.

Name. After that of the locality, Cromford.

The name Hornblei (Corneous Lead-ore) was not given to this mineral by Karsten in consequence of its resemblance in certain external characters to Kerargyrite or Horn Silver, but from its chemical composition.

Cromfordite is principally distinguished from Cerusite or white lead ore, by its colour, crystallization, fracture, inferior hardness, and less specific gravity.

Brit. Mus., Case 57 B.

CRONSTEDTITE, *Steinmann.* Hexagonal. Occurs in regular six-sided prisms, tapering towards their summits, and generally adhering laterally; also massive in opaque jet-black fibres, having a brilliant lustre. Streak dark leek-green. Thin laminæ, somewhat elastic. H. 2·5. S.G. 3·35.

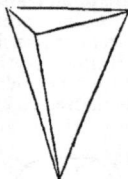

Fig. 138.

Comp. $(\dot{\text{Fe}}\,\dot{\text{Mg}}\,\dot{\text{Mn}})^6\,\ddot{\text{Si}} + \ddot{\text{Fe}}^2\,\ddot{\text{Si}} + 6\dot{\text{H}}$, or more simply $\dot{\text{Fe}}^3\,\ddot{\text{Fe}}\,\ddot{\text{Si}} + 3\dot{\text{H}} =$ silica 17·68, peroxide of iron 30·63, protoxide of iron 41·36, water 10·33 = 100.

Analysis from Przibram, by *Damour :*

Silica . . . . . 21·39
Peroxide of iron . . . 29·08
Protoxide of iron . . . 33·52
Magnesia . . . . 4·02
Protoxide of manganese . 1·01
Water . . . . . 9·06
                          ⎯⎯⎯
                          98·78

BB froths a little, and in the reducing flame fuses to a highly magnetic black slag; with borax gives an iron reaction. Wholly soluble in salt of phosphorus: on the addition of a little nitre gives an iron reaction, and a feeble rose tint, indicating the presence of manganese.

In powder dissolves readily in dilute sulphuric or muriatic acid, forming a solution which becomes gelatinous.

Localities. English.—Huel Maudlin, near Lostwithiel, in Cornwall, on Pharmacosiderite and decomposed Pyrites. *Foreign.*— Mines of Przibram, in Bohemia, in veins containing silver ores; and associated with Quartz and Magnetic Pyrites at the mines of Conghonas do Campo, in the Brazils.

Name. In honour of Cronstedt, the Swedish mineralogist.

Brit. Mus., Case 26.

CROSS-COURSE SPAR. The name given to radiated Quartz by Cornish miners, from its frequent occurrence in cross-courses.

CROSS-STONE, *Jameson.* See HARMOTOME.

CROW COAL. A kind of coal containing only a very small quantity of Bitumen. It is found at Alston Moor, in Cumberland.

CRUCITE, *La Metherie.* See CHIASTOLITE.

CRUMBLING FELSPAR. See ALBITE.

CRYOLITE, *Phillips, J. W. Tayler.* Massive. Structure lamellar. Colour white; yellow or brown when associated with iron. Lustre vitreous. Translucent, becoming transparent when immersed in water. Brittle. H. 2·5 to 3. S.G. 2·96.

Comp. Fluoride of aluminium and sodium, or $3\text{Na F} + \ddot{\text{Al}}^2\,\text{F}^3 =$ aluminium 13·10, sodium 33·27, fluorine 53·63 = 100.

Fuses below a red heat (in the flame of a candle).

BB on charcoal fuses to a globule, which is transparent while hot, but opaque on cooling.

Soluble in sulphuric acid with evolution of fluorine.

Locality. Evigtok, in W. Greenland,12 miles from the Danish settlement of Arksut, forming a vein in gneiss, about 80 feet thick and 300 feet long, running parallel with the strata, in a direction nearly E. and W.

Name. From κρύος, ice, and λίθος, stone, because it melts like *ice* when held in the flame of a candle.

Probably the original colour of the mineral was black or very dark, as the white Cryolite only occurs at the surface, and bears evidence of partial disintegration, becoming more translucent and compact, and of a darker colour in proportion to the depth from the surface. The black Cryolite parts with about 1 per cent. of acid and moisture when heated to redness, and loses the whole of its colour, and some of its transparency, becoming perfectly white like the Cryolite at the surface.

Cryolite was first turned to account by the Greenlanders in the manufacture of snuff. They grind the tobacco-leaf between two pieces of Cryolite, and the snuff so prepared, which contains about half its weight of cryolite powder, they prefer to any other.

Brit. Mus , Case 58.

M. P. G. Horse-shoe Case, No. 200.

CRYPTOLINE. A fluid detected by Sir David Brewster in minute cavities of Topaz,

Chrysoberyl, Quartz-crystals from Quebec, and Siberian Amethyst. It quickly hardens on exposure into a yellow, transparent, resin-like substance, not volatilizable by heat, nor soluble in water or alcohol, but rapidly dissolving, with effervescence, in sulphuric acid. It is also soluble in nitric and muriatic acids.

CRYPTOLITE, *Wöhler.* Occurs in acicular hexagonal prisms, about a line in length, and of a wine-yellow colour. Transparent. S.G. 4·6.

Comp. $\overset{...}{Ce}^3 \overset{...}{P}$, in which the cerium is in part replaced by didymium.

Analysis by *Wöhler :*

Oxide of cerium .	. . 73·70
Protoxide of iron .	. . 1·51
Phosphoric acid .	. . 27·37
	102·58

The excess arises from the protoxide of cerium contained in the mineral being converted by ignition into sesquioxide.

Decomposed by strong sulphuric acid, the whole being reduced to a dry earthy mass.

Locality. Arendal, in Norway, imbedded in greenish and rose-coloured Apatite, from which it is separated by dissolving the Apatite in nitric acid.

Name. From κρυπτὸς, *concealed.*

It has been suggested that Cryptolite is a Cerium-Apatite.

Brit. Mus., Case 57.

CUBAN, *Breithaupt.* A variety of octahedral Pyrites. Cubical. Occurs in cubes or massive. Colour between bronze and brass-yellow. Streak dark reddish bronze to black. H. 4. S.G. 4·1.

Comp. $Cu\,S + Fe^2\,S^3$.

Analysis by *Eastwick :*

Sulphur .	. . . 39·01
Copper .	. . . 19·80
Iron .	. . . 38·01
Silica .	. . . 2·30
	99·12

BB fuses readily, giving off fumes of sulphur.

Locality. Barracanao, Cuba (whence the name *Cuban*).

CUBE–ORE, *Jameson ;* CUBE-ORE OF IRON. See PHARMACOSIDERITE.

CUBE-SPAR, *Jameson.* See ANHYDRITE.

CUBIC NITRE. See NITRATINE.

CUBIC PYRITES. See IRON PYRITES.

CUBIZIT, *Werner.* See ANALCIME.

CUBOITE, *Breithaupt.* See ANALCIME.

CUIR DE MONTAGNE. See MOUNTAIN LEATHER.

CUIVRE ARSENIATÉ, *Haüy.* See PHARMACOSIDERITE.

CUIVRE ARSENIATÉ EN PRISME RHOMBOIDAL OBLIQUE, *Levy.* See APHANESITE.

CUIVRE ARSENIATÉ FERRIFÈRE, *Haüy,* See APHANESITE.

CUIVRE ARSENIATÉ OCTAÈDRE AIGU, *Haüy.* See OLIVENITE.

CUIVRE ARSENIATÉ HEXAGONAL LAMELLIFORME, *Haüy.* See CHALCOPHYLLITE.

CUIVRE ARSENIATÉ OCTAÈDRE OBTUSE. *Haüy.* See LIROCONITE.

CUIVRE ARSENICAL, *Dufrénoy.* See DOMEYKITE.

CUIVRE CARBONATÉ BLEU, *Haüy.* See AZURITE.

CUIVRE CARBONATÉ TERREUX, *Haüy.* See CHRYSOCOLLA.

CUIVRE CARBONATÉ VERT, *Haüy.* See MALACHITE.

CUIVRE CARBONATÉ VERT PULVERULENT, *Haüy.* See CHRYSOCOLLA.

CUIVRE DIOPTASE, *Haüy, Breithaupt.* See DIOPTASE.

CUIVRE GRIS, *Haüy.* See TETRAHEDRITE.

CUIVRE HYDROPHOSPHATÉ. See PHOSPHOROCHALCITE.

CUIVRE HYDROSILICIEUX, *Haüy.* See CHRYSOCOLLA.

CUIVRE MURIATÉ, *Haüy, Breithaupt.* See ATACAMITE.

CUIVRE NATIF, *Haüy.* See NATIVE COPPER.

CUIVRE OXIDÉ NOIR, *Haüy.* See MELACONITE.

CUIVRE OXIDÉ ROUGE, *Haüy.* ⎱ See RED
CUIVRE OXIDULÉ, *Haüy.* ⎰ COPPER.

CUIVRE PHOSPHATÉ, *Haüy, Dufrénoy.* See LIBETHENITE.

CUIVRE PYRITEUX, *Haüy.* See CHALCOPYRITE.

CUIVRE PYRITEUX HÉPATIQUE, *Haüy.* See ERUBESCITE.

CUIVRE SÉLÉNIÉ, *Haüy.* See BERZELIANITE.

CUIVRE SÉLÉNIÉ ARGENTAL, *Haüy.* See EUKAIRITE.

CUIVRE SPICIFORME, or ARGENT EN EPIS, *Haüy.* Vegetable matter impregnated with black sulphide of copper (Copper Glance). It is found at Frankenberg, in Hessia, and at Mahoopeny, Pennsylvania, U. S.

CUIVRE SULFATÉ, *Haüy.* See CYANOSITE,

CUIVRE SULFURÉ, *Haüy.* See COPPER GLANCE.

CUIVRE SULFURÉ ARGENTIFÈRE, *Levy.* See STROMEYERITE.

CUIVRE SULFURÉ HÉPATIQUE, *Haüy.* See VARIEGATED VITREOUS COPPER.

CUIVRE SULFURÉ VIOLET, *De Born.* See EROBESCITE.

CUIVRE VANADATÉ. Soe VOLBORTHITE.

CUIVRE VELOUTÉ, *Levy.* See LETTSOMITE.

CUIVRE VITREUX, *Brochant.* See COPPER GLANCE.

CUMENGITE. The name given by Kengott to a White Antimony from the province of Constantine, in Algiers, after C. Cumenge, by whom it was analysed.

CUMMINGTONITE, *Dewey.* A variety of Anthophyllite, containing a large quantity of oxide of iron. It is often scopiformly arranged, and resembles an asbestiform Tremolite. Colour ash-grey. Lustre silky.

Comp. $(\frac{2}{3}\ddot{F}e + \frac{1}{3}\ddot{M}g)^4 \ddot{S}i^3$.

Analysis (mean of two) by *Smith & Brush :*

Silica	.	.	.	50·91
Magnesia	.	.	.	10·30
Lime	.	.	.	trace
Protoxide of iron	.	.	32·60
Protoxide of manganese	.	1·63
Alumina	.	.	.	0·92
Soda	.	.	.	0·64
Potash	.	.	.	trace
Water	.	.	.	3·04•

100 04

BB alone, fuses with great difficulty.

Localities. Cummington and Plainfield, Massachusetts, U. S.

Brit. Mus., Case 35.

CUPREOUS ANGLESITE. See LINARITE.

CUPREOUS ARSENIATE OF IRON, *Bournon.* See SCORODITE.

CUPREOUS BISMUTH, *Phillips.* See WITTICHITE; also TANNENITE.

CUPREOUS MANGANESE, *Phillips.* Occurs massive; reniform, botryoidal, stalactitic, or earthy. Colour and streak bluish-black. Lustre resinous. Opaque. H. 1·5. S.G. 3·1 to 3·2.

Comp. Hydrous oxides of manganese, containing from 14 to 25 per cent. of black oxide of copper, 4 to 18 per cent. of oxide of cobalt, with various other impurities.

BB infusible, but becomes brown ; with a mixture of soda and borax yields reduced copper.

Localities. Schlackenwald, in Bohemia. Camsdorf. Lauterberg, in the Harz.

CUPREOUS SULPHATE OF LEAD, *Brooke, Phillips.* See LINARITE.

CUPREOUS SULPHATO-CARBONATE OF LEAD, *Brooke.* See CALEDONITE.

CUPREOUS SULPHURET OF SILVER. See STROMEYERITE.

CUPRIFEROUS CALAMINE. See TYROLITE.

CUPRIFEROUS MARLITE, *Kirwan.* Bituminous Schist (*Kupfer Schiefer*), accidentally impregnated with Copper Pyrites, or Purple or Vitreous Copper Ore.

M. P. G. Wall-case 17, Nos. 745 to 748, from Eisleben.

CUPRIFEROUS SULPHURET OF BISMUTH, *Phillips.* See WITTICHITE; also TANNENITE.

CUPRITE, *Haidinger.* See RED COPPER.

CUPROPLUMBITE, *Breithaupt.* Cubical: occurs massive-granular, with a cubic cleavage. Colour blackish lead-grey, with a metallic lustre. Streak black. Rather sectile and brittle. H. 2·5. S.G. 6·4 to 6 42.

Comp. $\mathrm{Cu\ S} + 2\mathrm{Pb\ S}$, or $(\mathrm{Cu, Pb})\ S$ = sulphur 15·1, lead 65·0, copper 19·9 = 100·0.

Analysis by *Plattner :*

Lead	.	.	.	64·9
Copper	.	.	.	19·3
Silver	.	.	.	0·5
Sulphur and loss	.	.	15·1

100·0

BB on charcoal, surrounds the assay with an areola of oxide of lead and sulphate of lead ; with soda affords a globule of metal.

Locality. Chili.

CYANIT, *G. Rose.* CYANITE, *Brochant, Kirwan.* See KYANITE.

CYANOLITE. *H. How.* A mineral forming the central part of a reniform nodule, partly imbedded in crystalline trap. No crystalline structure. Colour bluish-grey. Subtranslucent in very thin pieces; translucent at the edges. Lustre dull. Streak white. Rather brittle. Fracture flat conchoidal, even. H. 4·5. S.G. 2·495.

Comp. $\dot{C}a^4 \ddot{S}i^{10} + 5\dot{H}$, being by far the most highly silicated combination of lime yet met with.

Analysis :

Silica	.	.	.	74·15
Alumina	.	.	.	0·84
Lime	.	.	.	17·52
Magnesia	.	.	.	trace
Potash	.	.	.	0·53
Water	.	.	.	7·39

100·43

In matrass gives off water and becomes white.

BB in platina forceps becomes rounded at the edges. With borax and soda affords transparent globules. Decomposed by muriatic acid, affording slimy silica.

Locality —The Bay of Fundy, on the shore of Annapolis Co., two miles E. of Black Rock.

Name.—From κύανος, *sky blue;* and λίθος, *stone,* in allusion to the blue tint which distinguishes it from its associates, Cerinite and Centralassite (which see).

CYANOSE, *Beudant.* CYANOSITE, *Dana.* Sulphate of copper. Anorthic; but rarely found in distinct crystals; generally occurs stalactitic, reniform, and amorphous or pulverulent. Colour dark sky-blue of various shades, sometimes passing into bluish-green. Lustre vitreous. Translucent. Streak white. Taste metallic and very nauseous. Rather brittle. Fracture conchoidal. H. 2·5. S.G. 2·27.

Fig. 139.

Comp. Sulphate of copper or $\dot{C}u\,\ddot{S}+5\dot{H}$. =sulphuric acid 32, oxide of copper 32, water 36=100. (Thomson.)

BB on charcoal with soda, yields metallic copper.

Soluble in three parts of cold and $\frac{1}{2}$ part of boiling water; affording a blue solution, which deposits a film of pure copper on a polished surface of iron.

Localities. English. — Crystallized, in Cornwall, at Ting Tang and other mines in Gwennap; and at Trevarthen near Marazion: crystallized and fibrous at Gunnis Lake near Callington, in attle-heaps. *Welsh.* — Pary's mine, Anglesea. *Irish.* — Various copper mines in the county of Wicklow. *Foreign.* — Herrngrund, near Neusohl, in Lower Hungary. The Rammelsberg Mine, near Goslar in the Harz. Fahlun in Sweden. Zalathna in Transylvania. Rio Tinto Mines in Spain, &c.

Cyanosite exists in the water issuing from mines, and is derived principally from the decomposition of Iron Pyrites containing small quantities of copper.

When purified it is employed in cotton and linen printing, in dyeing, &c.

"Throughout all the mines (of the Vale of Avoca) the juxtaposition of large quantities of pyrites with clays and soft slates, combined with their exposure to air and the percolation of water, produce various decompositions, which exhibit their effects abundantly in the old workings, under the forms of blue and green vitriol, and other sulphates: The water, trickling through old excavations, continually dissolves a portion of these salts, and at its exit from the mine is carefully led into inclined troughs or 'launders,' in which fragments of scrap iron are laid. At the expense of the sulphate of copper, sulphate of iron is then formed, and the metallic copper is precipitated, and from time to time collected." * This method of extracting a large quantity of valuable metal, which would otherwise run to waste, is also now in use in Gwennap, and at Perranzabuloe in Cornwall. At Alderley Edge, in Cheshire, the copper, being dissolved out of the sandstone by an acid, is precipitated on a large scale by the above process. The same mode of treating cupriferous water is also practised at the mine of Herrngrund, near Neusohl, in Hungary.

Name. The names Cyanose and Cyanite are derived from κύανος, *dark blue.*

Brit. Mus., Case 55.

CYANOTRICHITE. See LETTSOMITE.

CYCLOPITE, *von Waltershausen.* Anorthic. Occurs in small white crystals resembling those of Anorthite and Labradorite. Lustre vitreous. Transparent. H. 6.

Comp. $\ddot{R}^5\,\ddot{S}i+2\ddot{H}\,\ddot{S}i=(\frac{1}{3}\dot{R}^3+\frac{2}{3}\ddot{H})\,\ddot{S}i.$

Analysis by *v. Waltershausen;*

Silica	41·45
Alumina . . .	29·83
Peroxide of iron . .	2·20
Lime	20·83
Magnesia . . .	0·66
Soda	2·32
Potash	1·72
Water	1·91
	100·92

Locality. The Cyclopean Islands near Catania, in Sicily, in dolerite.

CYMATINE. See KYMATIN.

CYMOLITE. See CIMOLITE.

CYMOPHANE (from κύμα, *a wave;* and φαίνω, *to appear*), the name given to those semitransparent varieties of Chrysoberyl which display a peculiar milky or opalescent appearance. When cut *en cabochon* it shows a white floating band of light, and is much prized as a ring-stone. See also CHRYSOBERYL.

Brit. Mus., Case 19.

M. P. G. Horse-shoe Case, Nos. 860 to 863.

CYPRINE. A blue variety of Idocrase, the colour of which is supposed to be produced by a minute portion of copper. S.G. 3·228.

---

* "On the Mines of Wicklow and Wexford," by W. Warrington Smyth, M.A. "Records of the School of Mines," vol. i. part iii. p. 385.

H 4

Analysis by *Richardson* :

Silica	. 38·80
Alumina . . .	. 20·40
Protoxide of iron . .	. 8 35
Lime	. 32·0
	99·55

Locality. The neighbourhood of Telle-marken in Norway.

Brit. Mus., Case 35.

CYPRONICA, *Necker.* See CHALCOPHYLLITE.

D.

DAMOURITE, *Delesse.* A variety of Margarodite; perhaps a hydrous Muscovite. Colour yellow or yellowish-white with a pearly lustre and a scaly texture.

Comp. $(\frac{1}{10}\ddot{R}^3 \times \frac{9}{10}\ddot{H}) \ddot{S}i + \dot{H}$.

Locality. Pontivy in Brittany, associated with Kyanite.

Name. After Damour, the French chemist.

Brit. Mus., Case 26.

DANAITE. A cobaltic variety of Mispickel.

Comp. (Fe, Co) (As, S)².

Analysis by *Hayes:*

Arsenic . . .	. 41·44
Sulphur . . .	. 17·84
Iron	. 32·94
Cobalt	. 6·45
	98·67

Name. After Professor Dana, of Yale College, U.S.

DANBURITE, *Shepard.*

Anorthic : occurs in imbedded crystals, also disseminated massive, without regular form. Colour whitish or pale yellow, with a weak vitreous lustre. Translucent. Very brittle. H. 7. S.G. 2·95.

Comp. $\dot{C}a^3 \ddot{S}i + 3\dot{B} \ddot{S}i =$ silica 48·9, boracic acid 28·4, lime 22·7 = 100·0.

Analysis by *Smith & Brush* :

Silica	. 48·10
Alumina and peroxide of iron . . .	. 0·30
Peroxide of manganese	. 0·56
Lime . . .	. 22·45
Magnesia . . .	. 0·40
Boracic acid . .	. 27·73
Undetermined . .	. 0·50
	100·00

BB fuses rather easily. In the dark colours the flame green, especially after the assay has been moistened and heated with sulphuric acid.

Locality. In dolomite with Oligoclase at Danbury, Connecticut, U.S.

Danburite may be distinguished from Chondrodite, which it resembles in colour, lustre, and brittleness, by being distinctly (though often irregularly) cleavable.

DANNEMORITE, *Kennyott, Erdmann,* a variety of Hornblende, consisting of strongly consolidated fibres, of a greenish, greyish, or yellowish-brown colour. S.G. 3·516.

Comp. $R^4 \ddot{S}i^3$.

Locality. The iron mines of Dannemora, in Sweden.

DAOURIT. See RUBELLITE.

DAPÊCHE. See ELASTIC BITUMEN.

DARK RED SILVER ORE. See PYRARGYRITE.

DARWINITE, *David Forbes.* A new mineral, supposed, when first discovered, to be native silver. Massive, without traces of cleavage. Colour of freshly-fractured surface dark silver-grey, tarnishing on exposure to dirty bronze-yellow. Opaque. Lustre metallic. Streak metallic, dark silver-grey. Rather brittle and easily broken ; receives an indentation from the hammer before yielding. Fracture even. H. 3·5. S.G. 8·57 to 8·69.

Comp. Cu^{18} As = copper 88·37, arsenic 11·63 = 100.

Analysis by *David Forbes* :

Copper	. 88·07
Silver	. 0·24
Arsenic . . .	. 11·69
	100·00

Heated in a close tube does not alter, or at most a faint trace of arsenious acid sublimes on to the side of the tube. In an open tube a distinct white sublimate of arsenious acid is obtained.

BB on charcoal in reducing flame fuses readily to a silver-white globule, which in the act of cooling evolves arsenical fumes, and becomes slightly red on the surface ; in the oxidizing flame on charcoal evolves abundant arsenical fumes, rotates, and ultimately leaves a globule of metallic copper, malleable, but still retaining some arsenic : on cupelling this button of copper with lead, a minute globule of silver is obtained : with fluxes gives the reactions of copper only.

Locality. Potrero Grande, S.E. of the town of Copiapo, in Northern Chili, where it is said to occur in small veins or strings, seldom attaining a breadth of more than two inches across, cutting through the porphyritic claystones which form the mountain range at that place.

Name. Named by David Forbes after Charles Darwin, in honour of his geological examination of the part of South America where the mineral occurs.

DATHOLITE, *Phillips, Dana, Brooke & Miller;* DATHOLITH, *Werner;* DATOLITE; DATOLITH, *Haidinger, Hausmann, v. Kobell.* Oblique ; primary or cleavage-form an oblique rhombic prism (Senarmont). Occurs crystallized in rhombic prisms, of which the lateral edges and solid angles are commonly replaced by planes; also massive. Colourless, or inclining to greyish, greenish-white, or yellowish-grey. Translucent. Lustre vitreous. Streak white. Brittle. Fracture uneven to imperfectly conchoidal. H. 5. to 5·5. S.G. 2·9 to 3·4.

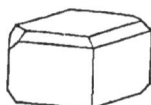 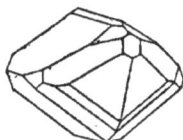

Fig. 140.   Fig. 141.

Comp. Borate and silicate of lime, with one atom of water, or $\dot{C}a\,\ddot{B} + \dot{C}a\,2\ddot{S}i + \dot{H}$.

Analysis from Andreasberg, by *Rammelsberg :*

Silica .	. 38·477
Lime .	. 35·640
Boracic acid	. 20·815
Water	. 5·568

100·000

In a matrass yields water. Becomes opaque and friable in the flame of a candle.

BB swells up and melts readily to a colourless glass, imparting at the same time a green tint to the flame.

Dissolves readily in nitric acid, leaving a jelly of silica.

Localities.—Scotch. In basaltic greenstone, on the Kilpatrick Hills, in Dumbartonshire. In the trap of Salisbury Craigs, Edinburgh. Costorphine Hill, ~~Lanarkshire.~~ Glen Fay Perthshire, *fig.* 141. — *Foreign.* Arendal in Norway. Utö in Sweden. Andreasberg ; near Wolfstein, in Rhenish Bavaria. In large, transparent crystals at Monte Catini, in Tuscany, and Toggiana, in Modena. In large, pellucid crystals at Roaring Brook, 14 miles from New Haven, Connecticut ; in nodules, like the most close-grained

marble at Minnesota Mine, Lake Superior, U.S., &c.

Name. From δαθός, *turbid*, in allusion to its want of transparency.

The synonym Datolite is derived from δατίομαι, *to divide* ; because of its division into granular portions.

Brit. Mus., Case 39.

M. P. G. Horse-shoe Case, No. 1095.

DAURITE. See TOURMALINE.

DAVIDSONITE, *Richardson, Thomson.* A variety of Beryl, occurring in greenish-yellow crystals, near Aberdeen at the granite quarry of Rubislaw, and at Tory, on the south side of the Dee. Texture foliated.

Analysis by *Heddle :*

Silica .	. 67·70
Alumina	. 15·64
Glucina	. 12·52
Magnesia	. 3·10
Protoxide of iron .	. 0·25
Water .	. 0·16

99·27

Name. After the discoverer, Dr. Davidson, Professor of Natural History in the Marischal College, Aberdeen.

DAVINA, *Monticelli & Covelli.* See DAVYNE.

DAVITE, *Mill.* Occurs massive of a white, green, or yellow colour, the changes of colour indicating some changes in the composition. The yellow variety contains sulphate of iron, the green sulphate of copper also, but the white is solely sulphate of alumina. The fracture under the lens exhibits a multitude of fine silky crystals, resembling those of sulphate of quinine. Taste nauseous and highly astringent.

Comp. Native sulphate of alumina.

Analysis :

Extraneous substances .	. 3·2
Sulphate of alumina	. 38·0
Sulphate of iron .	. 2·4
Free sulphuric acid	. 4·6
Water .	. 51·8

100·0

BB on charcoal gives off water, sulphurous and sulphuric acids, and ultimately becomes a white powder Very soluble in water, leaving a little impurity undissolved.

Locality. Near a thermal spring, which contains free sulphuric acid, at Chiwachi, an Indian village in the Andes, one day's journey from Bogotá, in Columbia.

Name. In honour of Sir Humphry Davy.

DAVYNE, *Allan, Phillips* ; DAVYTIC KOUPHONE SPAR, *Haidinger.* A variety of Nepheline occurring in the older lavas of Vesuvius, accompanied by Garnet, Mica, Wollastonite, &c. Colour white or yellowish; inclining to grey when transparent, to whitish when opaque. Lustre inclining to opalescent in transparent, to pearly in opaque specimens. Fracture conchoidal. H. 5 to 5·5. S.G. 2·4.

Fig. 142.

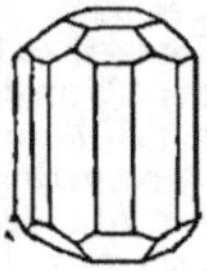

Analysis by *Monticelli & Covelli*:

Silica	42·91
Alumina . . .	33·28
Peroxide of iron . .	1·25
Lime	2·02
Potash . . .	7·43
Loss . . .	3·11
	100·09

BB alone, fuses with effervescence to a somewhat porous, opaque, white globule. Gelatinises by the nitric acid, with effervescence.

Name. By Monticelli and Covelli in honour of Sir Humphry Davy.

Davyne may be distinguished from Nepheline by the length of its crystals exceeding their breadth, the reverse of which is the case with the latter mineral. Its specific gravity is also much lower.

Brit. Mus., Case 31.

DECHENITE, *C. Bergemann.* Occurs in small botryoidal masses, with a crystalline texture, and some appearance of a rhombohedral cleavage. Colour dull-red; sometimes yellowish. Lustre of fresh fracture greasy. Streak yellow. H. 4. S.G. 5·81.

Comp, Pb V̈, or vanadate of lead.

Analysis by *Bergemann*:

Vanadic acid . .	46·101
Oxide of lead . .	53·717
	99·818

BB alone, fuses easily to a yellowish glass; with soda forms a white enamel containing grains of lead.

Locality. The Lauter Valley, near Nieder-Schlettenbach, in Rhenish Bavaria, in variegated sandstone.

Name. After Dr. H. von Dechen, of Bonn. Brit. Mus., Case 38.

DELANOVITE, *Kenngott.* A reddish, amorphous, earthy mineral; a variety of Halloysite, placed by Kenngott near Montmoril-lonite. Coloured by silicate of manganese. Streak reddish, somewhat shining. Adheres to the tongue. Fracture splintery to earthy. H. 1 to 1·5.

Comp. ($\frac{1}{4}$R̈³ + $\frac{3}{4}$Ḧ) S̈i² + 15Ḧ.

Analysis by *Von Hauer*:

Silica	50·55
Alumina	19·15
Lime	0·63
Protoxide of manganese .	4·40
Water	24·05
	98·78

BB infusible.

Locality. Environs of Nontron, department of Dordogne in France.

DELESSITE, *Naumann.* Occurs massive, with a short fibrous or scaly feathery texture, in the amygdaloidal porphyry of Oberstein and Zwickau, in Saxony. The fibres are very delicate, and arranged nearly perpendicular to the surface on which they are implanted. Colour olive-green to blackish-green. In powder always clear green. H. 2·5. S.G. 2·89.

Comp. ($\frac{1}{2}$Ṙ + $\frac{1}{2}$Ḧ̈) S̈i$\frac{3}{4}$ + 1·5 Ḧ.

Analysis from Planitz, near Zwickau, by *Delesse*:

Silica	29·45
Alumina . . .	18·25
Peroxide of iron . .	8·17
Protoxide of iron . .	15·12
Magnesia . . .	15·82
Lime	0·45
Water	12·57
	99·83

BB fuses with difficulty at the edges. Soluble in acids, yielding a deposit of silica. The variety from Planitz, near Zwickau, contains much more iron than that from Oberstein.

DELISLITE, *Leymerie.* A name for Freislebenite after Romé de Lisle, who made it a species, as "Argent gris antimonial."

DELPHINITE. A variety of Epidote from Dauphiny. Colour olive-green. Clear and transparent. Lustre very brilliant. Takes a fine polish.

DELVAUXENE, DELVAUXIT, *Dumont.* Is supposed to be a mechanical mixture. It occurs massive and earthy, with a yellowish-brown, brownish-black, or reddish colour, and a waxy, dull lustre. Opaque to translucent at the edges. H. 2·5. S.G. 1·85.

Comp. F̈e² P̈ + 24Ḧ (Dumont), or F̈e² P̈ + 18Ḧ (Delvaux).

DEMANT.

Analysis, of reddish-brown specimen, by *Dumont*:

Phosphoric acid	. .	. 16·04
Peroxide of iron	. .	. 34·20
Water .	. . .	. 48·30
		100·00

BB changes colour, decrepitates, and fuses to a grey magnetic globule.
Locality. Berneau, near Visé, in Belgium.
Name. After Mons. Delvaux.
Brit. Mus., Case 57.
DEMANT, *Werner.* See DIAMOND.
DEMANT SPATH, *Emerling.* See CORUNDUM.
DEMIDOFFITE, DEMIDOVITE, *Nordenskiöld.* A mineral mixed with the Malachite of Nischne Tagilsk, which it covers in delicate layers. Surface splendent. Slightly earthy. Colour sky-blue, sometimes with a tinge of green. Translucent at the edges. H. 2. S.G. 2·25.

Analysis :

Silica .	. . .	. 31·53
Alumina	. . .	. 0·53
Oxide of copper	. .	. 33·14
Magnesia	. . .	. 3·15
Phosphoric acid	. .	. 10·22
Water .	. . .	. 23·03
		101·62

Localities. Cumberland and Cornwall with quartzose rock and Malachite. Valparaiso, S. America.
Name. After Prince Anatole de Demidov.
DENDRACHATES (from δενδρὸν, *a tree;* and ᾽Αχατης, *Agate*), the name given by the ancients to Moss-agate.
DENT DE COCHON, *De Lisle.* See DOG'S-TOOTH SPAR.
DERMATIN, *Breithaupt.* Occurs in reniform masses, rarely globular, and in thin coatings or crusts on Serpentine. Colour dark olive-green or liver-brown, with a resinous lustre. Translucent at the edges. Feels greasy. Odour, when breathed upon, argillaceous. Streak yellow, inclining to grey. Fracture conchoidal. H. 2·0. S.G. 2·136.

Comp. (Mg, Fe)³ Si² + 6H ?
Analysis by *Ficinus* :

Silica .	. . .	. 35·80
Magnesia	. . .	. 23·70
Protoxide of iron .	.	. 11·33
Peroxide of manganese		. 2·25
Alumina	. . .	. 0·42
Lime .	. . .	. 0·83
Soda .	. . .	. 0·50
Water and carbonic acid		. 25·20
		100·03

· DEWEYLITE. 107

BB splits and becomes somewhat friable, and assumes a darker hue.
Locality. The serpentine quarry at Waldheim in Saxony.
The name is derived from δέρμα, *skin,* in allusion to its occurrence as an incrustation.
DESCLOIZITE, *A. Damour.* Rhombic: no cleavage. Colour mostly deep black; smaller crystals olive, with a chatoyant, bronze lustre. Light brown inclining to red at the edges by transmitted light. The colours are zoned with straw-yellow, reddish-brown and black on surfaces of fracture. H. 3·5. S.G. 5·84.

Fig. 143.

Comp. Pb² V̈ = oxide of lead 7·07, vanadic acid 29·3 = 100·0.

Analysis (mean of two) by *A. Damour* :

Vanadic acid	. .	. 22·46
Oxide of lead	. •	. 54·70
Oxide of zinc	. .	. 2·04
Oxide of copper	. .	. 0·90
Protoxide of manganese		. 5·32
Chlorine	. . .	. 0·32
Peroxide of manganese		. 6·00
Peroxide of iron .	.	. 1·50
Sand .	. . .	. 3·44
Water .	·. . .	. ·2·20
		98·88

The zinc, copper, manganese, and iron are considered impurities.
BB fuses and is partially reduced to a black slag investing a globule of metallic lead.
Soluble in cold dilute nitric acid.
Locality. S. America, in small crystals, on a siliceous and ferruginous gangue.
Name. After Descloiseaux, Crystallographer.
DESMIN, *Breithaupt,*
Hausmann, Naumann, } See STILBITE.
DESMINE, *Dufrénoy.*
DEUTO-FLUATE OF CERIUM. See FLUOCERITE or FLUCERINE.
DEVONITE, *Fuchs.* A name given to Wavellite, in allusion to its having been first discovered in the county of Devon.
DEWEYLITE, *Emmons.* An amorphous mineral, bearing some resemblance to gumarabic. Colour whitish, yellowish, greenish, reddish. Lustre greasy. Translucent. Brit-

tle and often much cracked. H. 2 to 3·5. S.G. 2 to 2·3.

Comp. $\dot{M}g^2 \ddot{S}i + 3\dot{H}$ = magnesia 35·6, silica 40·3, water 24·1 = 100·0.

Analysis, from Fleims, by *von Widtermann*:

Silica	40·82
Magnesia	36·06
Peroxide of iron	0·42
Carbonic acid	0·59
Water	21·72
	99·61

BB decrepitates, becomes opaque, and fuses with great difficulty at the edges: in powder, with borax, forms a transparent colourless glass.

Localities. The Tyrol, with serpentine. United States at Middlefield; Texas, Pennsylvania; and at Bare Hills, Maryland.

Name. After Professor Chester Dewey.

DIACLASITE, *Hausmann.* A mineral with the pale colours of Diallage, passing into brass-yellow, but in composition between Diallage and Hypersthene Streak greenish-grey. H. 3·5 to 4. S.G. 3·32.

Analysis, from Baste, by *Kühler*:

Silica	53·74
Magnesia	25 09
Lime	4·73
Protoxide of iron	11·51
Protoxide of manganese	0·23
Alumina	1·34
Water	3·76
	100·40

Locality. Würlitz in Bavaria. Guadarrama mountains in Spain, in gneiss.

Name. From διὰ κλάω, *to cleave through.*

DIADOCHITE, *Breithaupt.* A variety of Pitticite in which sulphuric acid is associated with the phosphoric acid. Resembles Iron Cinder in outward appearance; reniform or stalactitic, with a curved lamellar structure. Colour yellow or yellowish-brown, with a resinous lustre inclining to vitreous. Somewhat translucent. Streak uncoloured. Fragile. Fracture conchoidal. H. 3. S.G. 2·03.

Comp. Phosphosulphate of iron, or ($\ddot{F}e$ $\overset{...}{P}^2 + 8\dot{H}) + 4$ ($\ddot{F}e \ddot{S} + 6\dot{H}$.)

Analysis by *Plattner*:

Peroxide of iron	39·69
Phosphoric acid	14·81
Sulphuric acid	15·15
Water	30·35
	100·00

BB colours the flame green, and fuses at the edges, with intumescence, to a black, slightly magnetic enamel. With the fluxes gives the reaction of iron.

Boiling water extracts 12·6 per cent. of sulphuric acid without any peroxide of iron, leaving 2·3 per cent.

Localities. Near Gräfenthal and Saalfield in Thuringia; in alum-slate. ·

Brit. Mus., Case 56.

DIAGONITE, *Breithaupt.* See BREWSTERITE.

DIAKLASE. See DIACLASITE.

DIALLAGE, *Haüy.* A variety of Augite, including Bronzite and Schiller-spar (in part). Oblique. The crystals are usually thick and stout. Colour various shades of green, grey and brown. Lustre vitreous, sometimes pearly. Transparent at the edges, or opaque. Streak white-grey. Structure laminated, with cleavage parallel to the sides and diagonals of a slightly rhombic prism. Brittle. Fracture conchoidal — uneven. Yields to the knife. H. 5 to 6. S.G. 3·11 to 3·22.

Comp. $\dot{R} \ddot{S}i$, or one atom of silica to each atom of base, $\dot{R}$ consisting of lime, magnesia, protoxide of iron, protoxide of manganese, or even soda in variable proportions. There is also generally present from 1 to 4 per cent. of alumina, which usually replaces silica, and enters into the composition without changing essentially the crystallization; and ¼ to 4 per cent. of water.

Analysis, from the Gabbro of Prato, near Florence, by *Kühler*:

Silica	53·20
Lime	19·09
Magnesia	14·91
Protoxide of iron	8·67
Protoxide of manganese	0·38
Alumina	2·47
Water	1·77
	100·49

This gives nearly the formulæ 30($\dot{C}a \dot{M}g \ddot{F}e) \ddot{S}i + \ddot{A}l \ddot{S}i^2 + 2\dot{H}$.

BB on charcoal, fuses with difficulty at the edges to a grey slag; with borax forms a glass coloured with iron.

Localities. Generally occurs with serpentine, or forming a constituent of diallage rock. It is found in the serpentine of the Lizard district in Cornwall, and in the serpentine of Portsoy in Banffshire. Landlefoot, near Ballantrae, in Ayrshire. The Alic Hills of Aberdeenshire. Baste in the Forest of

Harzburg in the Harz. Massive or disseminated near Geneva, and on Monte Rosa in Switzerland.

Name. From διαλλαγή, *difference*, alluding to the dissimilar cleavage.

Brit. Mus., Case 25.

M. P. G., Horse-shoe Case, 1088. Upper Gallery, Wall-case 5, Nos. 10 to 37.

DIALLAGE CHATOYANTE. See SCHILLER-SPAR.

DIALLAGE FIBRO LAMINAIRE MÉTALLOIDE, *Haüy*. See BRONZITE.

DIALLAGE MÉTALLOIDE, *Haüy*. See DIALLAGE and HYPERSTHENE.

DIALLAGE VERTE, *Haüy*. See SMARAGDITE.

DIALLOGITE, *Beudant*. Hexagonal: primary form a rhomb. Occurs very commonly in saddle-shaped lenticular crystals; also massive. Colour rose-red and flesh-red. Lustre vitreous inclining to pearly. Translucent. Streak white. Structure lamellar. Scarcely scratches glass, and yields to the knife. Brittle. Fracture uneven. H. 3·5 to 4·5. S.G. 3·4 to 3·6.

Fig. 144.

Comp. Mn C̈ = carbonic acid 38·2, protoxide of manganese, 61·8 = 100·0. The Mn is usually replaced partially by Ċa, Ḟe, and Ṁg; so that the composition may be represented generally by the formula (Ṁn, Ċa, Ḟe, Ṁg) C̈.

Analysis, from Freiberg, by *Stromeyer :*

Carbonate of manganese	73·70
Carbonate of lime	13·08
Carbonate of iron	5·76
Carbonate of magnesia	7·26
Water	0·05
	99·85

Decrepitates when heated.

BB becomes brown or greyish-black, but is infusible without addition.

Very slowly soluble in cold, and rapidly in warm muriatic acid.

On exposure to the air assumes a brown tint, and the bright rose-red varieties become paler.

Localities.—*English.* The mines near Oswestry, in Shropshire. Hartshill, Warwickshire.—*Irish.* Glendree, near Tulla, co.

Clare, &c.—*Foreign.* Freyberg and other mines in Saxony. Those of Kapnik, Nagyag, and Offenbanya in Transylvania. Near Elbingerode in the Harz. In a pulverulent form, coating Triplite, at Washington, Connecticut, U.S. Placentia Bay, Newfoundland; of a fawn or chestnut-brown colour in Silurian slates.

Diallogite may be distinguished from Rhodonite, or Manganese Spar, by its inferior hardness. It generally occurs in metalliferous veins with ores of silver, lead, and copper, as well as with other ores of manganese, both massive and in botryoidal concretions lining cavities.

Brit. Mus., Case 34.

M. P. G. Principal Floor, Wall-case 13 (British).

DIAMANT. *French* for DIAMOND.

DIAMANT D'ALENCON. See SMOKY QUARTZ.

DIAMOND. Cubical. Frequently in twin crystals, with faces often convex. Plane of composition octahedral. Cleavage highly perfect. Rarely massive. Lustre brilliant adamantine. Colour white or colourless, occasionally with tints of yellow, red, orange, green, brown, or black. Transparent to translucent when dark coloured. Fracture conchoidal. H. 10. S.G. 3·5295 to 3·55.

Exhibits vitreous electricity when rubbed.

Index of refraction 2·439, being often irregular, owing probably to the same cause which has produced the convexity of its forms.

Becomes phosphorescent on exposure to the light, and the smaller Diamonds become phosphorescent by a much shorter exposure than those of larger size.

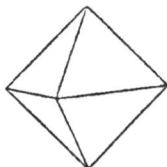

Fig. 145

Fig. 146.

Fig. 147.

Comp. Pure carbon crystallized. Burns

at a temperature of 14° Wedgwood, and is wholly consumed, producing carbonic acid gas; also combustible in oxygen gas and in the oxyhydrogen flame, and in the electric arc is converted into coke and graphite.

The Diamond has in all ages been held in the highest estimation.

The most valuable are perfectly colourless. There is rarely more than one tinge of colour in the same stone, but, while it is considerably deteriorated by a dull or faint tint, its commercial value, on the other hand, is greatly enhanced by a well-defined tint of pink, green, or blue.

Diamonds are weighed in carats (151½ of which make one ounce troy) of 3·16 or 3⅛ grains each. The medium value of a Diamond, when rough, is £2, and the value of rough Diamonds of greater weight is estimated by multiplying the square of their weight in carats by 2, which gives the value in pounds. Example:—To find the value of a rough Diamond 2 carats in weight. The square of the weight $2 \times 2 = 4$, this multiplied by $2 = 4 \times 2 = £8$, the value of a Diamond of two carats.

The price of polished Diamonds is much greater, for, amongst other reasons, the process of polishing is so uncertain, that the cutters think themselves fortunate in retaining one half the original weight, and the greater number of the Diamonds found are very small in size, their rarity increasing at a rapid rate in proportion to their weight. The average weight and size of Diamonds may be learned from the results of an examination of 1000 stones by Professor Tennant, who found that, out of the entire number, one half weighed less than half a carat, 300 less than 1 carat, 80 weighed 1½ carats, 119 varied from 2 to 20 carats, and 1 weighed 24 carats.

A polished Diamond, of the purest water, well cut, and free from flaws, is worth £8; above that weight the value is calculated by multiplying the square of the weight in carats by 8. Thus: the value of a polished Diamond of 2 carats $= 2 \times 2 \times 8 = £32$: the value of a polished stone of 3 carats $3 \times 3 \times 8 = £72$, and so on.

Above 10 carats the price increases in such a rapid ratio, that few persons can afford to purchase the larger stones, and it therefore becomes difficult to sell them at their calculated value.

The natural cleavage is taken advantage of by the native jewellers in the East, who form table Diamonds by adroitly striking the stone placed between two sharp-edged tools.

The art of cutting and polishing Diamonds was discovered by Louis van Berquen, a citizen of Bruges, in 1456, previously to which time the Diamond was only known in its rough, or in its cleaved state.

The cutting is effected (chiefly by Jews at Amsterdam), by means of a scharf or mill, consisting of an iron wheel about 10 inches in diameter, which is made to revolve horizontally with great rapidity, from 2000 to 3000 times in a minute. The stone, imbedded in pewter at one end of an arm, is pressed on the wheel, smeared with diamond-dust and oil, by means of weights varying from 2 to 30 lbs., and regulated according to the amount of pressure it may be considered necessary to produce.

The ancients did not possess the art of polishing the Diamond, but its extreme hardness, and the regularity of its form, coupled with its rarity and supposed indestructibility, caused them to attach a high value to it, and to endue it with many supposed virtues.

Although Diamonds do not appear to have been so much in request with the Romans as pearls, the former are, nevertheless, described by Pliny as amongst the most valuable of human possessions.

From its extreme hardness, which was believed to be sufficient to shiver both the hammer with which it was struck, as well as the anvil on which it was placed, and the impossibility of rendering it red hot by the most violent heat, it was called ἄδαμας, (or unconquerable), by the Greeks, a name which has been adopted by the moderns, though applied indifferently to the loadstone as well as the Diamond. It was also imagined to destroy the effect of poisons, and to cure insanity.

In the East it is still supposed by the credulous to act as a preservative against lightning, and to cause the teeth to fall out when placed in the mouth; but the last bad quality has been disputed by one author, who supports his objection (with some show of reason), by stating that diamond-powder has been used as a dentifrice without producing such injurious effects upon the teeth.

Owing to the general resemblance between Rock Crystal and Diamond, the former is called in the East kacha, or unripe, and the latter pakka, or ripe Diamond.

In addition to its value as a precious stone, the Diamond is employed for engraving and cutting glass, in splinters for drilling, and, reduced to powder, for polishing and cutting other gems. Diamond-powder, being worth £50 per ounce, is too expensive to be used alone; and it is, therefore, generally mixed with emery, and applied to the mill with oil. Diamonds have, also, been made into lenses for microscopes, but the advantage resulting from its slight chromatic aberration, and the large field of view it consequently affords, is counterbalanced by an irregularity of internal structure which renders it unfit for the purpose, even when sufficiently clear.

The largest Diamond of which there is any record is that described by Tavernier as belonging to the Great Mogul. It was found in 1550 in the mine of Colone, and, in its original state, weighed 900 carats or 2844 grains, but was reduced in cutting to 272·46 carats, or 861 grains.

The following are the names and weights of some celebrated Diamonds:—*

Russian diamond, 194 carats, sold for £90,000 and an annuity of £4,000.

Austrian diamond, 139 carats, valued at £9,250.

Regent or Pitt diamond, 186¼ carats (430·55 grains), sold for £125,000.

Pigott diamond, 49 carats, valued at £40,000.

Blue diamond, 44½ carats, valued at £30,000.

Nassuck diamond, 11·23 carats (35½ grains), purchased by the Marquis of Westminster for £7,200.

The most celebrated Diamond of modern times is the Koh-i-noor †, which became the property of the Queen of England on the annexation of the Punjaub by the E. I. Company in 1850. In addition to its intrinsic value, this Diamond is highly interesting from its great antiquity and the historical associations connected with it. It is reputed to be 4,000 years old by Indian traditions; certainly 50 B. C. it is said to have belonged to the Rajah of Mjayin, and to have remained in the possession of his successors until India was subdued by the Mahomedans.

It is mentioned by Tavernier in 1665, as the property of the Mogul Emperor. He says it weighed 279,9/16 carats, and was estimated to be worth half a million sterling. The original weight is variously stated at 787½ and 793 carats. It was called Koh-i-noor, or "the hill of lustre," in allusion to Mount Sinai in Arabia, where God appeared in glory to man.

When brought to this country it measured about 1⅝ inch in its greatest diameter and above ⅞ of an inch in thickness, and weighed 186 1/16 carats. The beauty of the stone being greatly marred by its irregularity of form and the imperfect manner in which it had been cut (the principal face and one or the largest sides having been discovered by Mr. Tennant to be merely cleavage-planes, one, to all appearance, not polished), it was determined to recut it. This was skilfully and successfully accomplished by the Messrs. Garrard in 38 days, each of 12 hours' uninterrupted labour. Although the weight of the stone has been reduced from 186 1/16 to 103¾ carats, its brilliancy and general appearance have been greatly improved.

From a careful examination of the stone before it was recut, Prof. Tennant arrived at the conclusion that it had originally formed a portion of a larger Diamond, the form of which was a rhombic dodecahedron. He also suggested that the great Russian Diamond, and another slab weighing 130 carats, had been taken from it. This division of the original dodecahedron into three, was, most likely, the result of accident, as a very slight blow inadvertently struck in the direction of the planes of cleavage, in setting the stone, or a fall, would have the effect of causing it to split in the manner pointed out. Possibly the slab alluded to above may have formed the diamond, with a flat surface, nearly as valuable as the Koh-i-noor, which Forbes, in his Oriental Memoirs*, describes as being with it in the royal treasury at Ispahan, and called the Doriainoor, "the ocean of lustre."

Both these jewels formed part of the plunder seized by Nadir Shah at the taking of Delhi in 1739, when the riches he carried off exceeded £70,000,000 in value.†

The most celebrated mines of India were those of Golconda, in the territory of the Nizam; and at Raolcondal, near Visiapoor, in the Mahratta empire. The Koh-i-noor was found in the former district at Purteal, between Hyderabad and Masulipatam, but now there are only one or two places of exploration, and the mines have gradually become all but valueless, since the discovery of the diamond mines of Brazil in 1728. Diamonds also occur in Bundelcund, near Panna, and on the Mahanuddy, near Ellore.

* Models of these and other celebrated Diamonds are exhibited at the Museum of Practical Geology. See Horse-shoe Case on the Principal Floor, Nos. 5 to 16.

† See M. P G. Horse-shoe Case, No. 11, for models of the Koh-i noor (and pendants), both in its original and in its present state.

* Vol. ii. p. 84.

† An interesting history of the Koh-i-noor will be found in R. Hunt's Handbook of the Great Exhibition of 1851. See also Ure's Dictionary of Arts, &c. 5th Edition, vol. ii., p. 17, art. Diamond.

Diamonds, when cut, are called Brilliants, rose Diamonds or rosettes, and table Diamonds. Of these the brilliant displays the lustre of the stone to the greatest advanage, and is the most esteemed.

The following figures (148 to 164) showing the different forms and sizes of polished Diamonds, will render intelligible the various modes of cutting them better than a mere verbal description.

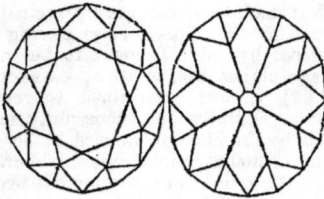

Fig. 148.   Fig. 149.

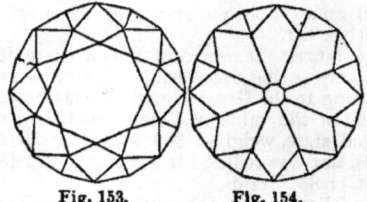

Fig. 153.   Fig. 154.

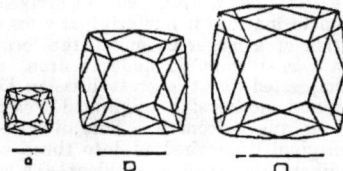

Fig. 150.   Fig. 151.   Fig. 152.

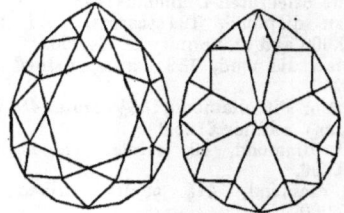

Fig. 155.   Fig. 156.

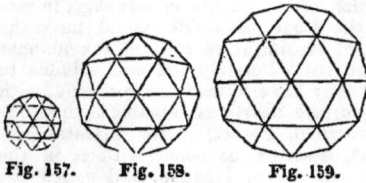

Fig. 157.   Fig. 158.   Fig. 159.

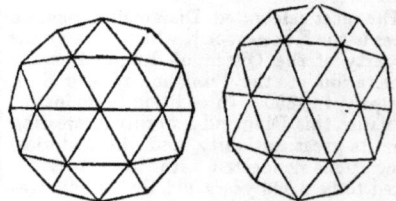

Fig. 160.   Fig. 161.

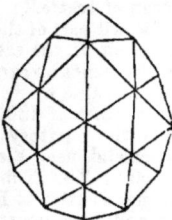

Fig. 162.

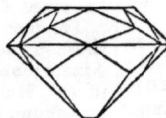

Fig. 163.

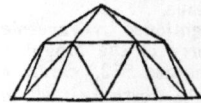

Fig. 164.

Fig. 148. Oval Brilliant.
Fig. 149. Oval Brilliant, under side.
Fig. 150. Brilliant of 1 carat.
Fig. 151. Brilliant of 10 carats.
Fig. 152. Brilliant of 20 carats.
Fig. 153. Round Brilliant.
Fig. 154. Round Brilliant, under side.
Fig. 155. Drop Brilliant.
Fig. 156. Drop Brilliant, under side.

Fig. 157. Rose Diamond of 1 carat.
Fig. 158. Rose Diamond of 10 carats.
Fig. 159. Rose Diamond of 20 carats.
Fig. 160. Round Rose Diamond.
Fig. 161. Oval Rose Diamond.
Fig. 162. Drop Rose Diamond.
Fig. 163. Side view of Brilliant.
Fig. 164. Side view of Rose Diamond.

In *figs* 148 to 152 the horizontal lines beneath each figure represent the depth of the stone, and the small facets below the horizontal lines in figs. 150 to 152 the size of the collet.

Diamonds appear to occur generally in countries where there is a laminated rock called Itacolumite. They are procured by washing, either from the soil or from superficial deposits. At Minas Geraes in the Brazils, there are two of these Diamond-bearing deposits; the one a gravel composed of broken fragments of Quartz covered with a thin layer of sand or earth—which is called *gurgulho*, the other called *cascalhô*, (See *M. P. G.* Horse-shoe Case, No. 1) made up of rolled pebbles of Quartz in a base of ferruginous clays—the whole, as well as the talcose clay on which it rests, being the debris of talcose rocks. The finest Diamonds are found in the gurgulho.

There are also mines called Bagugem in the province of Minas Geraes, on the banks of the river Patrocinho, which have produced some large stones: one in 1851 weighing 117 carats, and another more recently of 247½ carats.

The most celebrated mines are situated to the north of Rio Janeiro, on the rivers Jequetinhonha and Pardo: it has lately, also, been found in Bahia, at the mines of Surua and Cincora on the river Cachoeira, but the quality of the Cincora Diamonds is inferior to those of Minas Geraes or Cuyaba.

The Uralian Diamonds occur in the detritus along the Adolfskoi rivulet, where it is worked for Gold, and also at other places. A few Diamonds have also been found in Georgia and N. Carolina, also in Rutherford co., N. C, and Hull co. Ga., in the United States; in Australia, on the banks of the Turon; at Pontiana in Borneo, on the west side of the Ratoos mountain, and on the river Gunil in the province of Constantine in Algiers.

Brit. Mus., Case 4.

M.P.G. Horse-shoe Case, Nos. 1 to 9.

Case 11. (The first diamond brought to this country from Australia.)

DIAMOND SPAR. See CORUNDUM.

DIANIUM. A new metallic acid, belonging to the same group with tantalic and niobic acids, discovered by Von Kobell in Euxenite, Æschynite, Samarskite, and in a Tantalite from Tammela. It also exists, though in a less pure state, in the Tantalite of Greenland, in the Pyrochlore of the Ilmengebirge, and in the brown Wöhlerite.

The Tantalite from Tammela, which Von Kobell calls Dianite, has a dark, brownish-red streak and a specific gravity of 5·5, while other Tantalites vary in density from 7·06 to 7·3, and have a dark grey streak.

Titanic acid is easily distinguished from other acids of the same group, by boiling it with muriatic acid and tin, and diluting the solution with water. The blue colour then passes to rose-red, and the solution retains this colour several days. When Dianic acid is present, the blue colour predominates, but, after standing some hours, the rose colour of Titanic acid appears.

BB Dianic acid behaves like the Tantalite of Kimito.

DIAPHORITE. See ALLAGITE.

DIASPORE, *Haüy, Philips, Nicol.* Rhombic: usually crystallized in thin flattened prisms, sometimes acicular. Also occurs massive, in slightly curved laminæ, which may be easily separated, of a greenish-grey colour, with a shining pearly lustre: also in cellular masses, with a pearly lustre, intercepting each other in all directions, and of a brown hue externally, but perfectly colourless and transparent when reduced to thin laminæ. Very brittle. Scratches glass. H. 6·5 to 7. S.G. 3·43.

Fig. 165.

Comp. Hydrate of alumina, or $\overset{...}{Al} \overset{.}{H}$ = alumina 85·1, water 14·9 = 100·0.

Analysis from Siberia by *Dufrénoy:*

Alumina	74·66
Water	14·58
Peroxide of iron	4·51
Silica	2·90
Lime and magnesia	1·64
	98·29

Heated in a glass tube decrepitates violently, and crumbles into small, white, brilliant scales, which evolve water when more strongly heated.

BB infusible, alone.

Not soluble in boiling muriatic acid, which only extracts the oxide of iron mechanically mixed with it.

Localities. Near Kosoibrod, district of Katherinenburg, in the Ural. Schemnitz, Broddbo, near Fahlun, in Sweden. St. Gotthard, in dolomite. The Grecian archipelago, with Emery.

Name. From διασπειω, to disperse; from decrepitating and being dispersed when placed in the flame of a candle or *BB.*

Diaspore may be distinguished from Kyanite, to some varieties of which it bears a close resemblance, by its superior lustre.

I

Brit. Mus., Case 19.

DIASTALITE. A variety of Hornblende, from Wermland. According to Breithaupt, the angle of the prism differs one degree from that of Hornblende. S.G $3·09$ to $3·1$.

DIATOMOUS EUKLAS HALOID, *Haidinger.* See COBALT BLOOM.

DIATOMOUS GYPSUM HALOID, *Haidinger.* See HAIDINGERITE.

DIATOMOUS HABRONEM MALACHIT, *Mohs.* See APHANESITE.

DICHROMATIC EUKLAS HALOID, *Haidinger.* See VIVIANITE.

DICHLORID OF MERCURY, *Thomson.* See CALOMEL.

DICHROITE, *Cordier.* (From δίς, *double*, and χϱοία, *colour*). A name for Iolite, in allusion to its dichroism, or exhibition of different colours when viewed in different directions.

DIGENITE, *Breithaupt.* A variety of Copper-glance from Chili and Sangerhausen in Thuringia. S.G. $4·56$ to $4·68$.

Comp. (1 of Copper-glance and 3 of Covelline). $Cu S + 3Cu S = Cu^5 S^4$.

Brit. Mus., Case 7.

DIHYDRATE OF ALUMINA, *Thomson.* See DIASPORE.

DIHYDRITE, *Hermann.* See PHOSPHO-CALCITE.

DILLNITE. A substance allied to Collyrite, found in the gangue of the Diaspore of Schemnitz, in Hungary. It is white and firm (H. $3·5$), or earthy (H. $1·8$ to 2); S.G. $2·57$ to $2·83$.

Comp. $\ddot{Al}^2 \ddot{Si} + 4\frac{1}{2} \dot{H}$ = silica $24·39$, alumina $54·23$, water $21·38 = 100$.

Analysis by Karafiat :

Silica	23·53
Alumina	53·00
Lime	0·88
Magnesia	1·76
Water	20 05
	99·22

Name. After the village of Dilln, near which it is found.

Brit. Mus., Case 26.

DIMAGNETITE, *Shepard.* A pseudomorph of Magnetite, found in slender rhombic prisms, at Monroe, Orange co., New York, U. S. Dana considers that the mineral imitated is probably Lievrite; but Heddle ascertaining certain needle-crystals, usually considered to be Göthite, which occur in drusy cavities in the porphyritic trap of Gourock in Renfrewshire, to be Magnetite, supposes them to be Dimagnetite, and infers that mineral to be a pseudo-

morphous form after Göthite instead of Lievrite.

Brit. Mus., Case 14.

DIMANTHOID. Rolled Garnets somewhat resembling Diamonds in form. From Nigny Tagilsk, in the Uralian Mountains of Siberia. *M. P. G.* Horse-shoe Case, No. 902.

DIMORPHINE. Orpiment found with Realgar, so named by Scacchi, because he considered it to be a particular sulphide of arsenic susceptible of assuming incompatible forms.

Rhombic. Crystals not exceeding half a millimetre ($·018$ inch) in their longest diameter. Colour orange-yellow; powder saffron-yellow. Lustre adamantine. Translucent and transparent. Fragile. H. $1·5$. S.G. $3·58$

Comp. As^4,S^3 = arsenic $75·45$, sulphur $24·55 = 100 00$.

Heated in a porcelain crucible affords an agreeable odour and t rns red; with more heat becomes brown, gives off yellow fumes, and entirely evaporates: with soda gives out an odour of garlic.

Soluble in nitric acid.

Locality. Vesuvius; in the fumaroles of the Solfatara, Phlegræan fields, near Naples.

M. P. G. Upper Gallery, Table-case A in recess 4, No. 147.

DINITE, *Meneghini.* An organic compound resembling ice in appearance, but with a tinge of yellow due to a foreign substance. It is met with forming aggregations or druses of crystals, in a lignite deposit at Lunigiana, in Tuscany. It is inodorous and tasteless. Fragile and easily reduced to powde Insoluble in water; slightly soluble in alcohol, but very soluble in ether, and in sulphide of carbon. Fuses with the warmth of the hand to a yellowish oily-looking liquid; which, on cooling, forms large transparent crystals.

Name. After Professor Dini, by whom it was first found.

DIOPSIDE, *Phillips, Nicol, Dana.* A variety of Augite. Oblique: primary form an oblique rhombic prism, like that of Augite. Occurs in prismatic crystals, which are colourless or various shades of green; and translucent or transparent. They are generally striated longitudinally, have a shining lustre, and may be cleaved parallel with the planes of the primary prism. Scarcely scratches glass. H. 5 to 6. S.G. $3 31$.

Comp. Monosilicate of lime and magnesia, or $\dot{C}a \ddot{Si} + \dot{M}g \ddot{Si} =$ lime $25·46$, magnesia $18·18$, silica $56·36 = 100·00$.

DIOPSIDE BACCILLAIRE.

Analysis, from Fassa, by *Wackenroder* :

Lime	24·74
Magnesia . . . ' .	18·22
Protoxide of manganese	0·18
Protoxide of iron. . .	2·50
Silica	45·16
Alumina . . .	0·20
	100·00

BB alone fuses to a colourless, almost transparent glass.

Localities. In translucent crystals, in veins traversing Serpentine at Ala, in Piedmont, accompanied by Epidote, Hyaciuth, red Garnet, and green Talc. The more transparent crystals from this locality are sometimes cut and worn as gems.

Name. From δια, *through*, and ὄψις, *appearance*; in allusion to its occasional transparency.

Brit. Mus., Case 34.

M. P. G. Horse-shoe Case, No. 1033.

DIOPSIDE BACCILLAIRE, *Dufrénoy.* See MUSSITE, BREISLAKITE.

DIOPSIDE COMPACTE, *Dufrénoy.* See SHERZOLITE, KARLIBINITE.

DIOPSIDE GRANULIFORME, *Dufrénoy.* See COCCOLITE, FUNKITE.

DIOPTASE, *Haüy, Nicol, Dana.* Silicate of Copper. Hexagonal. Colour emerald-green. Lustre vitreous. Transparent to translucent Streak green. Brittle. Fracture conchoidal. H. 5. S.G. 3·27 to 3·84.

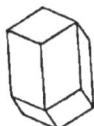

Fig. 165*.

Comp. Silicate of copper or $\overset{...}{Cu^3} \overset{...}{Si^2} + 3H$ = silica, 38·3, oxide of copper 50·3, water 11·4 = 100·0.

Analysis by *Hess* :

Oxide of copper . .	45·10
Silica	36·85
Alumina . . .	2·36
Lime	3·39
Magnesia . . .	0·22
Water	11·52
	99·44

BB decrepitates, tinging the flame yellowish green; becomes black in the outer —red in the inner flame, but does not fuse. With borax fuses to a green globule, and is finally reduced.

Dissolves in heated nitric or muriatic acid, with the formation of a jelly of silica.

Localities. This scarce mineral occurs disposed on Quartz in small but well-defined crystals, at Altyn Tübé, in the Kirghese steppes of Siberia. It is also found between Oberlahnstein and Braubach in the Duchy of Nassau.

Name. From διόπτομαι, *to see through*, in allusion to the natural joints being visible by transmitted light.

It may be distinguished from Emerald by inferior hardness, higher specific gravity, and by becoming negatively electric by friction.

Brit. Mus., Case 26.

DIOXYLITE, *Shepard.* See LANARKITE.

DIPHANITE, *Nordenshiöld.* A mineral allied to Margarite, found in the emerald mines of the Uralian mountains, together with Emerald, Cymophane, and Phenakite, on a brown micaceous slate. It forms regular six-sided prisms with a perfect cleavage at right angles to the principal axes. The crystals appear blue and transparent on one side, and have a vitreous lustre; but on the cleavage-faces the mineral appears white and opaque when in tolerably thick laminæ, and has a mother-of-pearl lustre. Very brittle. H. 5 to 5·5. S.G. 3·04 to 3·07.

Comp. $2(\overset{..}{R^2}\overset{..}{Si}) + 3\overset{..}{Al^2}\overset{..}{Si}) + 4\overset{..}{H}$.

Analysis by *Jewreinow* :

Lime	13·11
Protoxide of iron .	3·02
Protoxide of manganese	1·05
Alumina . . .	48·33
Silica	34·02
Water	5·34
	99·87

BB becomes opaque, swells up, exfoliates, and fuses in the inner flame to a smooth enamel, with borax and microcosmic salt, readily yields a clear glass which becomes yellowish on cooling; whence the name Diphanite—from δι, *double*, and φανὴς, *appearance.*

DIPLOGENIC KOUPHONE SPAR, *Mohs.* See EPISTILBITE.

DIPLOÏTE, *Breithaupt.* A variety of Anorthite. See LATROBITE.

DIPRISMATIC COPPER GLANCE, *Mohs.* See BOURNONITE.

DIPRISMATIC EUCLAS HALOID, *Haidinger.* See HAIDINGERITE.

DIPRISMATIC IRON ORE, *Mohs.* See LICORITE.

DIPRISMATIC HAL BARYT, *Mohs.* See WITHERITE.

DIPRISMATIC LEAD BARYT, *Mohs.* See CERUSITE.

I 2

DIPRISMATIC OLIVE MALACHIT, *Moh* ⚲ See LIBETHENITE.

DIPYRE, *Haüy.* Occurs in slender, indistinctly formed, four-sided prisms, rounded at the ends, and resembling grains of wheat; also in small fascicular masses. Colour greyish-white or reddish-white. Lustre vitreous. Translucent to transparent. Opaque in weathered specimens. Easily frangible, longitudinal fracture foliated. Scratches glass. H. above 4 when fresh. S.G. 2·64.

Comp. 4 (Ċa, Ṅa) S̈i + 3 Äl,S̈i = silica 53·8, alumina 26·2, lime 9·5, soda 10·5 = 100·0.

Analysis by Delesse:

Silica	55·5
Alumina	24·8
Lime	9·0
Soda	9·4
Potash	0·7
	99·4

BB fuses with effervescence to a white blebby glass.

Attacked with much difficulty by the strongest acids.

Localities. A torrent near Mauléon, in the Western Pyrenees, with Talc or Chlorite, in a soft clay-slate; Valley of Castillon, especially at Angomer.

Name. From δὶς, *double,* and πῦς, *fire;* in allusion to the double effect of fire upon it, by fusing it, and rendering it slightly phosphorescent.

Brit. Mus., Case 31.

DIRHOMBOHEDRAL EUTOME GLANCE, *Mohs.* See MOLYBDENITE.

DISCRASE, *Leymerie;* DISCRASITE, *Frobel.* Rhombic: occurs in hexagonal prisms and stellate forms; also massive, disseminated, or in grains. The surfaces of the prisms are usually deeply striated longitudinally; but those of other forms are smooth. Colour and streak between silver-white and tin-white, generally inclining to the former, often tarnished yellow or reddish. Lustre metallic. Opaque. Structure lamellar. Easily frangible. Fracture flat conchoidal. Soft. Slightly malleable. H. 3·5 to 4·0. S.G. 9·44 to 9·8.

Comp. Antimonide of silver, or Ag⁴, Sb = silver 77·01, antimony 22·99=100.

Analysis, of a coarse-grained specimen from Wolfach, by *Klaproth:*

Silver	76
Antimony	24
	100

BB on charcoal, fuses readily, giving off antimonial fumes, which stain the charcoal,

and is reduced to a grey, brittle, metallic globule, which becomes white on continuing the heat, and solidifies, with incandescence, to a crystalline globule on cooling, which, by further blowing, is converted into pure metallic silver.

Soluble in nitric acid, leaving oxide of antimony.

Localities. Altwolfach in Baden, and Wittichen in Swabia, in veins, with Galena, Native Silver, Iron Pyrites, Blende, and other ores, in granite. In clay-slate, at Andreasberg, in the Harz. Allemont, in Dauphiné. Casalla, near Guadalcanal, in Spain. The Goldberg, in Rauris, Salzburg. Near Coquimbo, S. America, &c.

If this mineral were less rare, it would be a valuable ore of silver. It may be distinguished from Native Silver by its brittleness and foliated fracture; from Smaltine by its fracture, which is foliated instead of granular and uneven; from Arsenical Pyrites by fracture and hardness, the Pyrites having a fine-grained, uneven fracture, and giving sparks with steel. (*Jameson.*)

Name. From δὶς, *two-fold,* and χράσις, *mixture,* in allusion to its composition.

DISOMOSE, *Beudant.* See GERSDORFFITE. The name is derived from δὶς, *twice,* and ὁμοῖος, *like,* because the formula is the same as for Grey Cobalt, where cobalt replaces nickel, and as for Antimonickel where antimony replaces arsenic.

DISTÉRITE, *Dufrénoy;* DISTERRITE. A variety of Clintonite, occurring in hexagonal prisms, in the valley of Fassa, Tyrol. H. of base 5; of sides 6 to 6·5. S.G. 3·04 to 3·05.

Analysis by v. Kobell:

Silica	20·00
Alumina	43·22
Magnesia	25·01
Lime	4·00
Potash	0·57
Peroxide of iron	3·60
Water	3·60
	100·00

See BRANDISITE.

DISTHÈNE, *Haüy.* (from δὶς, *double,* and σθένος, *strength.*) A name given by Haüy to Kyanite, on account of its double electric powers; some crystals acquiring negative, others positive electricity by friction.

DODECAHEDRAL CORUNDUM, *Mohs.* See SPINEL.

DODECAHEDRAL DYSTOME GLANCE, *Mohs.* See TENNANTITE.

DODECAHEDRAL GARNET, *Mohs.* See GARNET.

DODECAHEDRAL GARNET BLENDE, *Mohs.* See BLENDE.

DODECAHEDRAL IRON ORE, *Mohs.* See FRANKLINITE.

DODECAHEDRAL KOUPHONE SPAR, *Mohs.* See SODALITE.

DODECAHEDRAL MERCURY, *Mohs.* See NATIVE AMALGAM.

DOG'S-TOOTH SPAR. The name given to certain crystals of Calcite, from their fancied resemblance to the tooth of a dog. They have been found principally at Ecton, in Staffordshire, and in Derbyshire. Fig. 166.

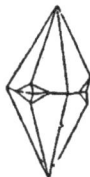

Fig. 166.

DOLOMIE, *Leymerie.* DOLOMITE. The name applied to white crystals and granular varieties of carbonate of lime and carbonate of magnesia. H. 3·5 to 4. S.G. 2·95 to 3·1.

Fig. 167.   Fig. 168.

Fig. 169.

Comp. Ċa C̈ + Ṁg C̈ = carbonate of lime 54·35, carbonate of magnesia 45·65 = 100·00, but carbonate of iron or carbonate of manganese, or both together, are generally present.

BB like Calcite; some varieties become darker and harder.

· Soluble in acid, but more slowly than Calcite.

Localities. Crystallized at Leadhills, in Lanarkshire (*fig.* 167). Jena, &c.; also in the United States, at Richmond co., New York, and at Hoboken, New Jersey. Matea, a coral island near Tahiti. Granular Dolomite or magnesian limestone is found in the Pyrenees, Saxony, France, Sweden, and in Somersetshire, Yorkshire, Nottinghamshire,

&c.; at Building Hill, near Sunderland, it forms globular and radiated earthy-like concretions; and at Marsden, in the same neighbourhood, a schistose Dolomite, of a pale brownish-yellow colour is found, which, when split into thin pieces, is very flexible. This quality is supposed to be owing to the water it contains, as it is nearly lost when the stone dries.

Dolomite is said to be best suited for a building-stone, when it has a crystalline structure.

Name. After Dolomieu, the geologist.

For varieties of Dolomite, see Pearl Spar, Brown Spar, Ankerite, Miemite, Gurhofite, and Brossite.

Brit. Mus., Case 47.

M.P.G. Horse-shoe Case, No. 438 (crystals); No. 215 (granular).

DOLOMITE SINTER, *v. Kobel.* See HYDRO-DOLOMITE. A variety of Hydromagnesite, with part of the magnesia replaced by lime. It occurs on Somma, in isolated globular or stalactitic earthy masses, resembling Sinter, and of a white or yellowish colour.

Comp. According to Rammelsberg 3[(Ṁg, Ċa) C̈ + Ḣ] + Ṁg Ḣ.

Analysis by *v. Kobell:*

Carbonic acid	.	.	.	33·10
Lime	.	.	.	25·22
Magnesia	.	.	.	24·28
Water .	.	.	.	17·40
				100·00

DOLOMITE SPAR, *Jameson.* See BITTER SPAR.

DOLOMITIC OPHIOLITE. The name given by T. Sterry Hunt to the varieties of Serpentine which contain intimate admixtures of Dolomite.

DOMEYKITE, *Haidinger.* Occurs reniform and botryoidal; massive and disseminated. Colour tin-white; often with a slightly yellowish or iridescent tarnish. Lustre metallic. Fracture uneven. Also black and soft, soiling the fingers, when impure or decomposed. See CONDURRITE. H. 3 to 3·5. S.G. 4·5.

Fig. 170.

Comp. Arsenide of copper or C̵u⁵ As² = copper 71·63, arsenic 28·37 = 100·00.

Analysis, from Calabazo in Chili, by *Domeyko :*

Arsenic	.	.	.	. 28·36
Copper	.	.	.	. 71·64

$$100·00$$

BB fuses easily, with the odour of arsenic. Not soluble in muriatic acid.

Localities. The Calabazo Mine near Coquimbo ; Antonio Mine, Copiapo, Chili.

Name. After M. Domeyko, Professor of Chemistry at Coquimbo.

DONACARGYRITE. A scarce mineral consisting probably of a mixture of several sulph-antimonides of silver and lead. Brit. Mus., Case 10.

DOPPLESPATH. See CALCITE.

DOPPLÉRITE, *Dufrénoy.* An organic compound, occurring in thin plates or massive, in peat, near Aussee, in Styria. It has a brownish-black colour, with a dull brown streak and greasy subvitreous lustre, when fresh ; and a reddish-brown colour by transmitted light when in thin plates.

Comp. $C^8 H^5 O^5$, or, according to Schrötter, it is a homogeneous peaty substance, from whose cellulose two parts of water have been removed.

Analysis by *Schrütter :*

Carbon	.	.	.	. 51·63
Hydrogen	.	.	.	. 5·34
Oxygen	.	.	.	. 43·03

$$100·00$$

Name. After Mr. Doppler.

DORANITE, *Thomson, Greg & Lettsom.* A zeolitic mineral, probably allied to Analcime, in which the soda is replaced by magnesia. Occurs in aggregated translucent crystals of a yellowish-white colour. S.G. 2·15.

Analysis by *Thomson :*

Silica	.	.	.	. 48·00
Alumina	.	.	.	. 22·00
Protoxide of iron	.	.	.	. 2·75
Lime	.	.	.	. 6·00
Magnesia	.	.	.	. 13·00
Water	.	.	.	. 7·70

$$99·45$$

Locality. Two miles W. of Carrickfergus, co. Antrim, Ireland ; in basalt.

Name. After Pat. Doran, late fossil collector to the Geological Survey of Ireland.

DOUBLE FLUATE OF CERIUM AND YTTRIA, *Phillips.* DOUBLE REFRACTING SPAR. See CALCITE.

DOUBLE REFRACTING SPAR. GELF, *Kirwan.* The name given in Hungary to "a particular sort of Argentiferous Copper Pyrites."

DRAGÉES DE TIVOLI. Pisolite, which, when broken, exhibits calcareous matter covering a nucleus composed of some other substance, and thus acquiring the appearance of confectionary comfits.

DREELITE, *Dufrénoy.* Hexagonal : occurs in small truncated rhombohedrons. Colour and streak white. Lustre pearly ; externally dull, splendent on surfaces of fracture. H. 3·5. S.G. 3·3.

Comp. Sulphate of lime and baryta, or $\dot{C}a \ddot{S} + 2\dot{B}a \ddot{S}$.

Analysis, by *Dufrénoy :*

Sulphate of baryta	.	. 61·730
Sulphate of lime	.	. 14·275
Carbonate of lime	.	. 8·050
Silica	.	. . 9·710
Alumina	.	. . 2·405
Lime	.	. . 1·520
Water	.	. . 2·310

$$100·000$$

BB fuses to a white blistered glass, which is coloured blue by nitrate of potash.

Localities. In small rhombohedral crystals, disseminated over the surface, and in the cavities of a quartzose rock, near Beaujeu, Dep. of the Rhone, in France. Badenweiler, Baden.

Named after the Marquis de Dree.

DROP-STONES. Stalagmite. See also DRAGÉES DE TIVOLI.

DUCKTOWNITE. The name proposed by Prof. C. U. Shepard for a substance which is stated by Prof. G. J. Brush, by whom it has been examined. to be "a mixture of Iron Pyrites, and a rich sulphide of copper, which, if obtained pure, would probably prove to be Copper Glance." It is found at the Ducktown Copper mine, in Eastern Tennessee, U.S.

DUFRÉNITE, *Brongniart.* Rhombic : dull leek-green, or blackish-green, in needles, arranged in small radiated masses, with a weak silky lustre. The colour changes on exposure to yellow and brown. Streak olive-green. Slightly translucent. H. 3·5 to 4. S.G. 3·2 to 3·4.

Comp. Phosphate of peroxide of iron, or $\ddot{Fe}^2 \ddot{P} + 3\dot{H}$ = peroxide of iron 61·32, phosphoric acid 28·07, water 100·00.

Analysis, from Haute Vienne, by *Vauquelin :*

Peroxide of iron	.	. 56·20
Protoxide of manganese	.	6·76
Phosphoric acid	.	. 27·84
Water	.	. . 9·20

$$100·00$$

Extremely fusible, melting even in the flame of a candle.

BB fuses easily to a black opaque glass.

Localities. Department of la Haute Vienne, in France; at Anglar, near Limoges. Siegen, in Prussia. (See GREEN IRON ORE.)

Name. Named after Dufrénoy, Professor of Mineralogy.

DUFRÉNOYSITE, *Damour.* Cubical. Colour steel-grey. Lustre metallic. Streak reddish-brown. Brittle. Fracture uneven. S.G. 5·074 to 5 55.

Comp. 2PbS + AsS³ = lead 57·2, sulphur 22·1, arsenic 20·7 = 100.

Analysis, by *Damour :*

Lead	.	.	.	.	56·61
Sulphur	.	.	.	22·30
Arsenic	.	.	.	20 87
Iron	.	.	.	.	0·32
Copper	.	.	.	0·22
Silver	.	.	.	.	0·17

        100·49

BB fuses easily, yielding sulphurous and arsenical fumes and a globule of lead.

Dissolves in acids.

Localities St. Gotthard in small veins in Dolomite, with Realgar, Orpiment, Blende and Pyrites. Valley of Binnen in the canton of Valais, in Dolomite, with Realgar.

Name. After Dufrénoy, late Professor of Mineralogy at the Museum of Natural History, Paris.

Brit. Mus., Case 11.

DUNGIVEN CRYSTALS. Yellow or smoky Rock Crystal, found in large, and sometimes very perfect, detached crystals, imbedded in the soil at Finglen Mountain, close to Dungiven, in the parish of Banagher, in Ireland.

DUSODILE. See DYSODILE.

DYOXYLITE, *Shepard.* See LANARKITE.

DYSCLASITE, *Connel.* This mineral was formerly supposed to be a variety of Mesotype, but was subsequently described as a distinct species by Connel. It is now regarded as a kind of Okenite. S.G. 2·362.

Analysis by *Connel :*

Silica	.	.	.	57·69
Lime	.	.	.	26·83
Protoxide of manganese	.	0·22
Potash	.	.	.	0·23
Soda	.	.	.	0·44
Peroxide of iron	.	.	0·32

        100·44

Locality. The Faröe Isles.

Name. From δυς, *difficultly,* and κλαίω, *to break,* in allusion to the time and labour required to break a mass into smaller fragments, in consequence of its extreme toughness.

DYSKOLITE. See SAUSSURITE.

DYSLUITE. A Zinc-Manganese-and-Iron-Spinel of a yellowish-brown or greyish-brown colour, occurring at Sterling, in New Jersey, U. S., with Franklinite and Willemite. S.G. 4·55.

Comp. (Żn Mn) (Äl Fe).

DYSLYTITE, *Shepard.* Occurs as a blackish-brown powder in many meteorites, of which it generally constitutes from 0·25 to 2·25 per cent. It is supposed to be a phosphide of iron, nickel, and magnesium.

Name. From δυσλύτος, *insoluble.*

DYSODILE, *Cordier, Phillips.* A combustible mineral, found in secondary limestone, at Melili, near Syracuse, in Sicily, of a yellowish or greenish-grey colour, either compact or in foliated masses, composed of thin paper-like thin and flexible leaves, containing impressions of fish and dicotyledonous plants. It is extremely fragile, and emits an argillaceous odour when breathed on. It burns with a crackling noise, and considerable flame and smoke, and gives out a very fetid smell; whence it has acquired the name of *Stercus Diaboli* or *Merda del Diavolo* in Sicily. Macerated in water, it becomes translucent, and its laminæ acquire flexibility. S.G. 1·146.

It is also found in France, at Château Neuf, near Viviers, Dept. du Rhone; Saint-Amand, in Auvergne, and in the neighbourhood of Narbonne.

DYSTOMIC AUGITE SPAR, *Haidinger.* See BUCKLANDITE.

DYSTOMIC HABRONEM MALACHIT, *Mohs.* See ERINITE.

DYSSNITE, *v. Kobell.* A kind of Fowlerite, resembling Marceline, but less hard. It is an aluminate of iron and manganese, occurring in granular metallic masses, at Franklin, New Jersey, U. S.

DYSYNTRIBITE, *Shepard.* A massive, granular, or slaty and tough variety of Agalmatolite, somewhat resembling Serpentine in appearance, but of very variable composition. Colour dark green, greyish, or yellowish, sometimes mottled with red and black. Almost dull. Tough. Fracture even, splintery. H. 3 to 3·5. S.G. 2·76 to 2·81.

Analysis, by *Smith & Brush :*

Silica	.	.	.	44·80
Alumina	.	.	.	34·90
Peroxide of iron	.	.	3·01
Lime	.	.	.	0·66
Magnesia	.	.	.	0·42
Potash	.	.	.	6·87
Soda	.	.	.	3·60

Protoxide of manganese   . 0·30
Water . . . . . 5·38
                              ——
                            99·94

BB fuses in thin fragments to a white porcellaneous mass.

Localities. Rossie and Natural Bridge in Diana, St. Lawrence co., New York; generally with Specular Iron.

E.

EAGLE STONE. *Pliny.* According to Kirwan a kind of iron ore, consisting of a reniform crust of the oxide investing an ochreous kernel, which is sometimes loose.

EARTH FLAX, *Woodward.* See AMIANTHUS and ASBESTOS.

EARTH-FOAM, *Phillips.* See APHRITE.

EARTHY BITUMEN. Occurs massive, of a dull, blackish-brown colour, and an earthy and uneven fracture. It has a shining streak, and is so soft as to receive an impression from the nail. Smell strongly bituminous. Feel greasy. Burns with a clear and brisk flame, emits an agreeable bituminous smell, and deposits much soot. H. 2. S.G. 1·15.

Localities.— Scotch. Hurlet, near Glasgow, with Calcite; and in freestone at Binney quarries, near Edinburgh, where it is so abundant that the workmen make candles of it, and use it for domestic purposes; also in East Lothian, Caithness, the Orkneys, &c. — *Foreign.* Persia, between Schiraz and Bender Congo. The valley of Travers, in Switzerland. The Harz; and near Prague, in Bohemia.

Analysis of a specimen from Auvergne, by *Ebelmen :*

Carbon .   .   .   . 76·13
Hydrogen .   .   . 9·41
Oxygen   .   .   . 10·34
Nitrogen .   .   . 2·32
Ash .   .   .   . 1·80
                        ——
                      100·00

EARTHY CARBONATE of MAGNESIA, *Phillips.* See MEERSCHAUM.

EARTHY COBALT, *Phillips,* or ASBOLAN. A Wad, of which oxide of cobalt forms a large proportion. Colour various shades of brown, ash, and bluish-black. Amorphous, massive, mammillary, botryoidal, disseminated as a coating, and pulverulent. The fracture of the massive varieties is earthy and dull, but the streak is black, shining, and resinous. Soils somewhat. Yields easily to the knife. H. 1 to 1·5. S.G. 2·22.

Comp. Protoxide of cobalt with Oxide of manganese.

Analysis of ore from Saalfeld, by *Rammelsberg :*

Potash .   .   .   . 0·37
Baryta .   .   .   . 0·50
Protoxide of cobalt   . 19·45
Lime .   .   .   . 4·35
Protoxide of manganese . 40·05
Oxygen   .   .   . 9·47
Peroxide of iron   . . 4·56
Water .   .   .   . 21·24
                          ——
                        99·99

According to Rammelsberg, the foregoing analysis would give the formula $(\dot{C}o, \dot{C}u)2\,\overline{\overline{M}}n$ $+ 4\,\dot{H}$ for the ore from Saalfeld.

BB on charcoal does not fuse: with borax forms a deep cobalt-blue coloured globule. Dissolves in cold, strong, muriatic acid, with copious evolution of chlorine, forming a brown solution, which turns blue when heated, and becomes red on cooling.

Localities.—English. Cornwall, at Huel Unity, Huel Gorland. Alderley Edge, in Cheshire, in red sandstone.—*Scotch.* Leadhills and Preston, in Stirlingshire.—*Irish.* Roscommon Cliffs, in the peninsula of Howth, near Dublin, in clay-slate.—*Foreign.* It also occurs at Nertschinsk, in Siberia; at Riechelsdorf, in Hessia; at Schneeberg and Saalfeld, in Saxony; in Bohemia; Swabia; Kitzbüchl. in the Tyrol; Allemont, in Dauphiné; the valley of Gistain, in Spain, &c. The brilliancy of the streak afforded by this mineral, or which its surface attains when rubbed against a hard body, is very characteristic.

Brit. Mus., Case 17.

M. P. G. Principal Floor, Wall-case 20.

EARTHY MANGANESE, *Phillips.* See WAD.

EARTHY MINERAL PITCH, *Jameson.* See EARTHY BITUMEN.

ÉCUME DE MER, *Brochant.* See MEERSCHAUM.

ÉCUME DE TERRE, *Brochant.* See APHRITE.

EDELFORSITE. See ÆDELFORSITE.

EDELITE or EDELITH. A variety of Prehnite, from Edelfors.

Analysis by *Walmstedt :*

Silica .   .   .   . 43·03
Alumina .   .   .   . 19·30
Peroxide of iron .   . 6·81
Peroxide of manganese   . 0·15
Lime .   .   .   . 26·28
Water .   .   .   . 4·43
                          ——
                        100·20

EDENITE, *Breithaupt.* A whitish aluminous Hornblende, from Edenville, in the United States. S.G. 3·059.

Analysis by Rammelsberg:

Silica . . . . . 51·67
Alumina . . . . . 5·75
Peroxide of iron . . : 2·86
Lime . . . . . 12·42
Magnesia . . . . 23·37
Soda . . . . . 0·75
Potash . . . . . 0·84
Loss by ignition . . 0·46

98·12

EDINGTONIT, *Haidinger, Hausmann, Naumann*; EDINGTONITE, *Dana, Phillips, Greg & Lettsom.* Pyramidal, hemihedral : primary form an octahedron, with a square base. Occurs in extremely distinct, greyish-white, translucent crystals, none of which are known to exceed ⅜ths of an inch across. Lustre vitreous. Streak white. Brittle. Fracture imperfect-conchoidal, uneven. H. 4 to 4·5. S.G. 2·69 to 2·71.

 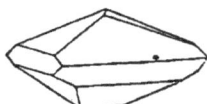

Fig. 171.   Fig. 172.

Comp. 3 $\ddot{B}a\ \ddot{S}i + 4\ddot{A}l\ \ddot{S}i + 12\ \ddot{H}$ = silica 37·263, alumina 23·751, baryta 26·524, water 12·462 = 100.

Analysis by Heddle :

Silica . . . . . 36·98
Alumina . . . . 22·63
Baryta . . . . . 26·54
Lime 0.22
Strontia 0 08
Soda . . . . . trace
Water . . . . . 12·46

98·91

BB fuses with difficulty to a colourless glass, after having given off water, and become white and opaque.

Locality. This rare mineral is met with near Old Kilpatrick, in Dumbartonshire, and is named after Mr. Edington, by whom it was first discovered in 1823.

Brit. Mus., Case 28.

EDLER OPAL, *Werner.* See PRECIOUS OPAL.

EDWARDSITE, *Shepard.* A variety of Monazite. Occurs in oblique rhombic prisms. Colour hyacinth-red. Transparent to translucent. Lustre vitreous to adamantine. Streak white. H. 4·5. S.G. 4·2 to 4·6.

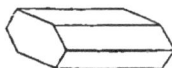

Fig. 173.

Comp. Sesquiphosphate of cerium.
Analysis :

Protoxide of cerium . . 56·53
Phosphoric acid . . . 26·66
Zirconia . . . . 7·77
Alumina . . . . 4·44
Silica . . . . . 3·33
Glucina, magnesia, protoxide
of iron . . . . traces

98·73

BB in minute fragments, loses its red colour, and becomes pearl-grey, with a tinge of yellow, and fuses with difficulty at the edges to a transparent glass.

In a powdered state slowly soluble in aquaregia.

Locality. Disseminated through Bucholzite, in gneiss, at the falls of the Yantic, in Norwich, Connecticut, U. S.

Name. After Henry W. Edwards, governor of the State.

Brit. Mus., Case 57.

EFFLORESCENT ZEOLITE. A name formerly given to Laumontite, in consequence of its efflorescing, and becoming opaque and crumbling on exposure to the air, probably owing to the loss of water.

EGERAN. A variety of Idocrase, of a liver-brown colour, occurring in diverging groups of crystals, whose form is that of a right rectangular prism, having its lateral edges replaced.

Analysis, by *Karsten :*

Silica . . . . . 39·70
Alumina . . . . 18·95
Protoxide of iron . . . 2·90
Lime . . . . . 34·88
Protoxide of manganese . 0·96
Soda . . . . . 2·10

99·49

BB fuses with intumescence to a greenish blebby glass.

Localities. Haslau, near Eger (whence the name Egeran), in Bohemia ; sometimes accompanied by Quartz and Tremolite.

Brit. Mus., Case 35.

EGYPTIAN JASPER ; EGYPTIAN PEBBLE. A variety of Jasper occurring in roundish pieces scattered over the surface of the desert, chiefly between Cairo and the Red Sea. The surface of these masses is rough, and of a yellowish or chestnut-brown colour, but internally the brown colour forms irregular concentric zones, between which are black spots, and small black dendritic markings in a base of a pale yellowish-brown colour. Towards the centre the colour becomes yellowish-grey, often passing into cream-yellow. S.G. 2·56 to 2·6.

Egyptian Jasper, when cut and polished, is used as a brooch-stone and for other ornaments. A specimen in the British Museum (Case 24) is remarkable for the resemblance which the markings on its fractured surface bear to the portraits of the poet Chaucer, the effect being similar to a drawing done in sepia. *M. P. G.* Horse-shoe Case, Nos.565 to 567. See foot-note to Agate.

EHLITE, *Breithaupt, Hermann.* A mineral nearly allied to Phosphorochalcite and to Libethenite. It occurs amorphous; also in reniform or botryoidal masses, with a radiating foliated structure. Colour verdigris-to emerald-green. Lustre pearly. Streak paler than the colour. Fracture conchoidal. H. 1·5 to 2. S.G. 3·8 to 4·27.

Comp. $\ddot{C}u^5 \overset{..}{P} + 3 \overset{.}{H}$ = oxide of copper 66·9, phosphoric acid 24·0, water 9·1 = 100·0.

Analysis from Tagilsk, by *Hermann*:

Phosphoric acid	23·14
Oxide of copper	66·86
Water	10·00
	100·00

BB in the matrass gives off water, and flies into powder with great vivacity.

Locality. Ehl, in Prussia (whence the name). Nischne Tagilsk in concretionary masses, with a radiating concentric structure.

EHRENBERGITE, *Nöggenrath.* An amorphous variety of Epistilbite, of a rose-red colour. Fracture granular.

Analysis by *Schnabel*:

Silica	56·77
Alumina	15·77
Peroxide of iron	1·65
Protoxide of manganese	0·80
Lime	2·76
Magnesia	1·30
Potash and soda	3·78
Water and organic matter	17·11
	100·00

Locality. Steinbruch, in Hungary, forming nodules in trachyte. The Siebengebirge, near Bonn.

Name. After Professor Ch. G. Ehrenberg, of Berlin.

EISENALAUN. See HALOTRICHITE.

EISENAPATIT, *Fuchs.* See ZWIESELITE.

EISENBLAU. See VIVIANITE.

EISENANATAS. The name given by Volger to Martite, on the supposition that it is a pseudomorphous form of the deutoxide of iron, which he supposes to be isomorphous with Anatase.

EISENCHLORITE. See DELESSITE.

EISENCHROM. See CHROMIC IRON.

EISENGLANZ.   } See HEMA-
EISENGLIMMER. *Werner.* } TITE,
EISENGYMNITE. See HYDROPHITE.

EISENKIES, *v. Leonhard.* See IRON PYRITES.

EISENKIESEL, *Werner.* A variety of Ferruginous Quartz. found in Bohemia, in iron-stone veins in the Harz, and at Altenberg in Upper Saxony.

EISENKOBALTERZ, EISENKOBALTKIES. See SAFFLORITE. It is identical in composition with Chathamite.

EISENMULM. An earthy variety of Magnetite, occurring at the Alte Birke Mine, in the neighbourhood of Siegen, in Prussia, where a vein of Spathic Iron is broken through by basalt and partially converted into Magnetic Iron-ore. It is a black, pulverulent mass, which attaches itself closely to anything on which it is rubbed, and is strongly attracted by the magnet. S.G. 3·76.

Comp. $\ddot{F}e$ ($\dot{F}e$ $\dot{M}n$) or Magnetite, in which about half the protoxide of iron is replaced by protoxide of manganese, which is isomorphous with it.

Analysis, by *Genth*:

Peroxide of iron	66·20
Protoxide of iron	13·87
Protoxide of manganese	17·00
Oxide of copper	0·09
Sand, &c.	1·75
	98·91

EISENNATROLITH. An Iron-Natrolite occurring in dull green, opaque prismatic crystals, and semicrystalline plates, with the Brevicite of Brevig in Norway. It has one-fourth of the alumina replaced by peroxide of iron. H. 5. S.G 2·35.

Analysis, by *C. Bergemann*:

Silica	46·54
Alumina	18·94
Peroxide of iron	7·49
Soda (and a little potash)	14·04
Protoxide of iron	2·40
Protoxide of manganese	0·55
Water	9·37
	99·33

EISENNICKELKIES, *Scheerer.* See Iron-nickel Pyrites.

EISENNIERE, *Werner.* Clay Ironstone from Coal-measures.

EISENOPAL. *Hausmann.* A ferruginous variety of Opal.

EISENOXYD, *Leonhard.* See HEMATITE.

EISENOXYDHYDRAT. See LIMONITE

EISENPECHERZ, *Werner.* See TRIPLITE and PITTICITE.

EISENPERIDOT. See FAYALITE.

EISENPHYLLIT. See VIVIANITE.

EISENRESIN, *Breithaupt.* See OXALITE.

EISENSINTER. See IRONSINTER.

EISENSPATH. See CHALYBITE.

EISENRAHM. See RED OCHRE.

EISENROSEN, or IRON-ROSES. See BASANOMELANE.

EISENRUTIL. See GÖTHITE.

EISENCHÜSSIG KUPFERGRÜN, *Werner.* See CHRYSOCOLLA.

EISENSTEINMARK. See TERATOLITE.

EISENTITAN, *Hausmann.* See RUTILE.

EISEN VITRIOL, *Werner.* See COPPERAS.

EIS-SPATH, *Werner.* See ICE-SPAR.

EIS-STEIN. (Ice-stone.) See CRYOLITE.

EKEBERGITE. *Berzelius.* A massive and subfibrous variety of Scapolite of a greenish, greyish or brownish colour. Transparent. Lustre vitreous or resinous. Harder than Scapolite. S.G. 2·746.

Analysis by Hermann :

Silica . . . . . 53·11
Alumina . . . . 27·97
Peroxide of iron . . . 2·84
Potash . . . . 0·86
Soda . . . . . 4·83
Lime . . . . . 9·73
Magnesia . . . 0·39
Protoxide of manganese . 0·27

100·00

BB whitens and fuses to a blistered glass like Wernerite.

Localities. Arendal in Norway. Hesselkula in Finland.

Name. After Ekeberg, the Swedish voyager.

ELÆOLITE. A variety of Nepheline, comprising the coarse massive kinds which have a greasy lustre. Primary form a right rhombic prism. Colour dark-green, bluish-grey, or brick-red. Translucent. Fracture conchoidal. Frequently opalescent when cut. H. 5·5 to 6. S.G. 2·5 to 2·6.

Comp. K̇, 2S̈i + 4(Ṅa, S̈i) + 5(A̅l S̈i) = potash 6·13, soda 16·21, alumina 33·37, silica 44·29 = 100·00.

Analysis of a brown specimen from Brevig, by *Scheerer :*

Silica . . . . . 44·59
Alumina . . . . 32·14
Peroxide of iron . . . 0·86
Lime . . . . . 0·28
Soda . . . . . 15·67
Potash . . . . 5·10
Water . . . . . 2·05

100·69

BB fuses easily to a white enamel.

When reduced to powder, completely decomposed by muriatic acid, and converted to a gelatinous mass.

Localities. Brevig, Stavern and Fredericksvärn in Norway, imbedded in Zircon-syenite. Ilmengebirge in Siberia. United States, at Lichfield, Maine; Salem, Mass.; and the Ozark Mountains, Arkansas.

Name. From ἔλαιον, oil, and λίθος, stone ; in allusion to its peculiar oily lustre.

The pale blue varieties of Elæolite possess a slight opalescence like Cat's-eye, and are sometimes used for ornamental purposes.

Brit. Mus., Case 31.

ELASMOSE, *Beudant* (from ἔλασμος, a *tear*). See NAGYAGITE.

ELASTIC BITUMEN, *Hatchett, Phillips;* ELASTIC MINERAL PITCH, *Jameson;* ELASTICHES BERGPECH, *Reuss;* ELASTICHES ERDPECH, *Werner;* or ELATERITE, *Beudant, Hausmann.* Occurs in soft reniform or fungoid masses, which sometimes become harder on exposure. Colour various shades of blackish-brown, with a resinous lustre. Translucent at the edges. Flexible, and elastic. Effaces lead-pencil markings like India-rubber, whence it has obtained the name of mineral Caoutchouc. S.G. 0·9 to 1·23.

Analysis of a specimen from Derbyshire, by *Johnston :*

Carbon . . . . 85·474
Hydrogen . . . 13·283

98·757

Burns readily with a lively yellow flame, and much smoke, giving out a bituminous odour.

Localities. British. — The Odin Lead-mine, at Castleton in Derbyshire. St. Bernard's Well near Edinburgh. *Foreign.* — In a coal-mine at Montrelais, in France. Neufchatel. The island of Zante.

Brit. Mus., Case 60.

ELASTIC QUARTZ, *Kirwan.* See FLEXIBLE SANDSTONE.

ELECTRIC CALAMINE. A name which

has been applied to Smithsonite, or the siliceous oxide of zinc, in consequence of its becoming electric by heat, and sometimes by friction.

ELECTRUM, *Klaproth.* A natural alloy of gold and silver in the proportion of two of gold to one of silver, or Gold 65, and Silver 36 = 100. It is distinguished by its silver-white colour. S.G. 14 to 17.

BB fuses to a more or less pale-yellow globule.

Localities. It occurs in tabular crystals and imperfect cubes at Schlangenberg, in Siberia; also at Kongsberg, in Norway; in Transylvania; near Mariposa in California, and in other mining districts.

Brit. Mus., Case 3.

ELHUYAZITE, *Fuchs.* A variety of Allophane.

ELIASITE. A mineral near to Pitchblende, but differing widely from it in its lower specific gravity and large proportion of water. It occurs in large flattened pieces, sometimes half an inch thick, of a dull reddish-brown colour, approaching to hyacinth-red at the edges. Lustre greasy to subvitreous. Subtranslucent. Streak dull. wax-yellow to orange. H. 3·5. S.G. 4·086 to 4·237.

Analysis, by *F. Ragsky*:

Peroxide of uranium	61·33
Peroxide of iron	6·63
Alumina	1·17
Protoxide of iron	1·09
Silica	5·13
Lime	3·09
Magnesia	2·20
Oxide of lead	4·62
Carbonic acid	2·52
Phosphoric acid	0·84
Water	10·68
Arsenic	trace
	99·30

BB like Pitchblende.

Decomposed by muriatic acid.

Locality. The Elias Mine, Joachimstahl; with Fluor, Dolomite, Quartz, &c.

ELIE RUBY. A variety of Pyrope found in trap-tufa at Elie in Fife.

Analysis by *Connell*:

Silica	42·80
Alumina	28·65
Peroxide of iron	9·3
Protoxide of manganese	0·25
Magnesia	10·67
Lime	4·78
Chromic acid	trace
	96·46

ELLAGITE, *Nordenskiöld.* Colour yellow, yellowish-brown, to yellowish-red. Opaque or feebly translucent. Lustre of cleavage-surface pearly, shining. Streak white.

Comp. $\dot{C}a^3 \ddot{S}i^4 + \ddot{A}l \ddot{S}i + 12 \dot{H}$.

Locality. Aoland, in Finland.

EMBOLITE, *Breithaupt.* Cubical: in cubes, and cubo-octahedrons. Colour varying from asparagus- to greyish-green. Lustre resinous. H. 1 to 1·5. S.G. 5·31 to 5·81.

Comp. Chlorobromide of silver, or 3 Ag Cl + 2 Ag Br = chlorine 13·2, bromine 19·8, silver 67·0 = 100·0.

Analysis, mean of three, by *Domeyko*:

Chloride of silver	51·6
Bromide of silver	48·4
	100·0

Localities. Abundant in Chili, at Quillota and Chañarcillo; found also at Eulalia, in Chihuahua, Mexico; and at Colula, in Honduras.

It is stated by Domeyko, that "the chlorobromides vary in colour from greyish-green or yellow to asparagus- and pistachio-green. In general the specimens that have a yellow colour have more bromine, and consequently less silver, than those of a grey or pearly-green colour."

EMBRITHITE, *Brochant.* See BOULANGERITE.

EMERALD. Hexagonal. Colour green, passing into light blue, impure yellow, and white for the Beryl. Lustre vitreous, sometimes resinous. Transparent to subtranslucent. Streak white. Brittle. Fracture conchoidal, uneven. H. 7·5 to 8 0. S.G. 2·67 to 2·732.

Fig. 174.

Fig. 175.

Comp. $\ddot{B} + \ddot{A}l + 4 \ddot{S}i = (\ddot{B} + \ddot{A}l) \ddot{S}i^3$ = glucina 14·1, alumina 19·0, silica 66·9 = 100·0.

Analysis of Emerald of Muzo:

Silica	68·0
Alumina	18·1
Glucina	12·2
Magnesia	0·9
Soda	0·6
Tantalic acid	trace
	99·8

In the above analysis, by M. Lewy, traces of chromium are reckoned with the magnesia, and perhaps there is a little Titanic acid with the alumina. In previous trials, he had found 1·65 to 2·15 of water, and 0·3 to 0·35 carbonic acid, corresponding to some organic matter present.

BB alone, unchanged or becomes clouded : at a high temperature, becomes rounded at the edges, and ultimately a vesicular scoria is formed. With borax forms a fine green glass, which is colourless for Beryl. Slowly dissolves with salt of phosphorus, leaving a siliceous skeleton.

Not acted on by acids.

Emerald and Beryl are varieties of the same mineral, under the former name being comprehended the rich green transparent specimens, and those of other colours under the latter.

Until very lately, the colouring matter of the Emerald was supposed to be due to the presence of 1 or 2 per cent. of oxide of chromium. This has, however, been proved to be incorrect by M. Lewy's recent chemical investigations into the formation and composition of the Emerald of Muzo. The quantity of chromic oxide obtained by analysis was so small as to be inappreciable, in fact, too minute to be weighed separately, and the beautiful tint of the Emerald is shown by M. Lewy to be produced by an organic substance, which he considers to be a carburet of Hydrogen, similar to that called *chlorophylle*, which constitutes the colouring matter of the leaves of plants.

Those Emeralds are of the darkest tint which contain the greatest amount of organic matter, and the colour is completely destroyed at a low red heat, which renders the stone white and opaque; while, on the other hand, heat produces no loss of colour on those minerals which are coloured by oxide of Chrome. (See OUWAROVITE.) The organic colouring matter of the Emerald is probably derived from the decomposition of the animals whose remains are now found fossilized in the rock which forms the matrix of the stone. This rock, which is a black limestone, with white veins, contains ammonites; and specimens of Emerald in fragments of the rock, shewing ammonites, are exhibited in the mineralogical gallery of the Jardin des Plantes, in Paris.

Besides the organic colouring matter, M. Lewy obtained from 1·65 to 2·15 of water; from which, in conjunction with the presence of fossil shells in the limestone in which they occur, he has arrived at the conclusion that Emeralds have been formed in the wet way, that is to say, that they have been deposited from a chemical solution.

According to the account of M. Lewy, who personally visited the mine at Muzo, the Emeralds, when first extracted, are so soft and fragile that the largest and finest specimens can be reduced to powder merely by rubbing them between the fingers, and the crystals often crack and fall to pieces after being removed from the mine, apparently from the loss of water.

When they are first found, it is necessary to place them aside carefully for a few days, until the water has evaporated from them. M. Kuhlmann has endeavoured to prove that the hardening of rocks and minerals is not owing solely to the evaporation of quarry-water, but that it depends upon the tendency which all earthy matters possess to undergo a spontaneous crystallization, by slow desiccation, which commences from the moment the rock is exposed to the air.

The hardening of the Emerald by exposure to the air does not appear to have been known to the ancient inhabitants of the portion of America more immediately under consideration ; for their mode of testing the value of a stone was by striking it a smart blow with a hammer, when it was first taken from the mine. If it bore the blow without injury, it was considered a perfect stone, but if it broke, it was deemed worthless. Under this rude mode of experimenting many valuable stones must necessarily have been destroyed.

As a precious stone, the Emerald ranks next to the Ruby in value. It may be distinguished from all the other gems by its colour, a pure green, without any admixture of blue or yellow.

It appears to the greatest advantage when table-cut, and surrounded by brilliants, the lustre of which contrasts agreeably with the quiet tint of the Emerald. Imitations are made with great success, both with respect to colour and the flaws from which real stones are seldom free. The last are produced by means of a sharp tool, after the paste imitation has been polished.

The Emerald is more valued in India than in many other parts of the world, on account of its foreign origin.

In the East, advantage is taken of the facility with which it may be broken at right angles to its axis ; and slices of prisms, sometimes polished, but frequently with the natural planes of cleavage preserved, are mounted, surrounded with diamonds. This was the usual mode of mounting them prior to 1456.

The Emerald was believed by the ancients to be "excellent in its virtues." Amongst other good qualities attributed to it, it was supposed to be good for the eyes, on which account they were in the habit of wearing it about their persons engraved as a seal, that they might have it to look at. It is doubtful, however, whether the eyes of the ancients derived any other benefit from its use in this way beyond the pleasure they experienced in beholding such a beautiful object, and the assurance they conveyed of the possession of an ornament of such rarity and value as we are told the Emerald was in those days.

It was, also, said to possess the peculiar property of causing water to appear of its own colour. "A stone of a middling size will do this to a small quantity only of the water into which it is put, a large one to the whole; but a bad one to no more than a little of it, which lies just about it." ('Theophrastus.)

Reduced to powder, and taken internally, in a dose of from 4 to 10 grains, it was accounted a certain antidote for poisons, and the bites of venomous animals, as well as a remedy for fluxes, the plague, infectious fevers, hæmorrhages, and dysentery.

Worn externally, as an amulet, it was also regarded by the ancients as a cure for epilepsy, to possess the power of assuaging terror, and driving away evil spirits; and when tied to the belly or thigh of pregnant women, of delaying or hastening delivery; they also thought it an infallible preservative of chastity, to the violation of which it possessed such an innate antipathy as to fly to pieces if worn in a ring on the finger of any person transgressing.

Whether the Emerald has lost its virtues, or more powerful remedies have superseded it, at all events, amongst the more civilised nations of the world, it has long since ceased to be used as a medicine. By the more imaginative people of the East, it is still believed to be endowed with certain medical and talismanic properties, to avert bad dreams, cure palsy, and the cold and bloody flux, and to impart courage to the wearer.

In the 'commentaries of the kings of Egypt, according to Theophrastus, it is recorded that an Emerald four cubits in length and three in breadth was sent as a present from a king of Babylon: and that in their temple of Jupiter there was an Obelisk, composed of four Emeralds, which was forty cubits long, and in some places four and in others two cubits wide. As, however, the author describes the Emerald to be a stone both scarce and small, and speaks, elsewhere, of Bastard Emeralds or the pseudo-Smaragdus, most likely the stones mentioned above were only Beryl,

and not true Emerald. At all events there can be no doubt many stones (of a green tint) were confounded under the term Σμάραγδ or Emerald, by Theophrastus and other old writers on minerals.

Necklaces of Emerald have been found at Herculaneum and in the Etruscan tombs.

The largest known Emerald is the property of the Duke of Devonshire. This magnificent stone, which was brought to England by Dom Pedro, measures two inches in length, and $2\frac{1}{4}$, $2\frac{1}{3}$, and $1\frac{1}{2}$ inches across the three diameters. It is a six-sided prism, weighing 8 oz. 18 dwts, but there is a small piece of quartz attached to it, which would diminish that weight by 3 or 4 dwts. Owing to flaws it is but partially fit for the purposes of the jeweller. It was obtained from the mines at Muzo. A smaller but more splendid specimen is in the possession of Mr. Hope. It cost £500, and weighs 6 ounces. Emeralds of less beauty but of larger size are found in Siberia. A specimen in the Royal collection measures $14\frac{1}{2}$ inches in length and 12 in breadth, and weighs $16\frac{3}{4}$ lbs. troy.

Mount Zabarah in Upper Egypt affords a less distinct variety, and was largely worked by the ancient Egyptians. Theophrastus states that the ancient locality of the true Emerald was the copper mines of Cyprus, and an island over against Carthage. It was believed to be produced from the Jasper, for it was said there had been found in Cyprus a stone, one half of which was Emerald, and the other Jasper, as yet not changed.

In Ezekiel, chap. xxvii. 16, it is written : "Syria was thy merchant by reason of the multitude of the wares of thy making : they occupied in thy fairs with Emeralds, purple, and broidered work, and fine linen, and coral, and agate." (See also chap. xxviii. 13.) In Exodus, chap. xxviii. 18, the Emerald is mentioned as occupying the fourth place amongst the twelve stones representing the twelve tribes of Israel, which formed the pectorate of the Jewish high-priest, and was symbolical of the tribe of Judah, the name of which was engraved upon it.

Localities. The most celebrated modern locality is the famous mine of Muzo in New Grenada. This mine is situated 4 miles west of Muzo (in lat. 5° 39′ 50″ N. and 76° 45′ west of Paris), in the eastern Cordillera of the Andes, about 75 miles N.N.E. of Santa-Fé-de-Bogotá. The matrix in which the Emeralds occur is a limestone containing ammonites, and is composed of:

Carbonate of lime	47·8
Carbonate of magnesia	16·7
Carbonate of manganese	0·5
Silica	24·4
Alumina	5·5
Glucina	0·5
Peroxide of iron	2·6
Pyrites	0·6
Alkali	2·7

101·2

Other localities are Columbia in a black bituminous limestone of comparatively recent age. Cundina-Marca, N.E. of Santa-Fé in Old Columbia. Peru*, in the valley of Tunca, between the mountains of New Grenada and Popayan. Norway. The hill of Barat near Limoges. Canjargum in Hindostan. Salzburg, imbedded in mica-slate.

Brit. Mus., Case 37.

M.P.G. Horse-shoe Case, Nos. 818, 825 to 835.

EMERALD NICKEL, *Silliman, Jr.* Occurs in the form of small stalactitic or mammillary crusts; sometimes appearing prismatic, with rounded summits; also massive and compact. Colour emerald-green. Lustre vitreous. Transparent to translucent. Streak yellowish-green. Brittle, with an uneven, somewhat scaly fracture. H. 3 to 3·25. S.G. 2·57 to 2·69.

Comp. $\dot{N}i^5\ddot{C}+6\dot{H}$, or $\dot{N}i\ddot{C}+2(\dot{N}i, 3\dot{H})$ =oxide of nickel 59·72, carbonic acid 11·66, water 28·62=100·00.

Analysis from Texas, by *Silliman, Jr.*:

Oxide of nickel	58·82
Carbonic acid	11·69
Water	29·49

100·00

Heated in a flask gives of water, and turns blackish-grey.

BB with borax yields a transparent globule of a dark yellow or reddish colour when hot, but nearly colourless when cold.

Readily soluble in muriatic acid, leaving a residue of chrome iron.

Localities. This rare mineral is found forming a crust on Chromic Iron at Texas, Lancaster co., Pennsylvania, U. S.; and at Swinaness, in Unst, one of the Shetlands. Brit. Mus., Case 49.

---

* In the collections of the Museum of Natural History in Paris, there are Emeralds known to have formerly adorned the Tiara of Pope Julius II. (1503 to 1513), who died thirty-two years before the conquest of Peru by Pizarro.

EMERAUDE VERT, *Haüy.* See EMERALD.

EMERAUDE DU PEROU, *Romé de Lisle.* See EMERALD.

EMERALD COPPER, *Phillips;* EMERALD MALACHITE, *Mohs.* See DIOPTASE.

EMERIL, *Haüy.* EMERY. An amorphous form of Corundum. Occurs massive, granular, or compact. More or less impure. When compact, exceedingly tough. Fracture conchoidal to uneven. Streak white. H. 4·0 to 5·7. S.G. 3·89 to 4·28.

Comp. Pure alumina, or $\ddot{A}l$.

Analysis: *a* from Naxos; *b* from Gumush-dagh, by *J. Lawrence Smith:*

	a	b
H.	46	47
S.G.	3·75	3·82
Alumina	68·53	77·82
Peroxide of iron	24·10	8·62
Silica	3·10	8·13
Lime	0·86	1·80
Water	4·72	3·11
	101·31	99·48

The column of hardness gives the effective abrasive power of the powdered mineral, that of Sapphire being 100.

BB unaltered both alone and with soda; fuses entirely with borax, though with great difficulty; and also, if powdered, with salt of phosphorus.

Not affected by acids.

Localities. Emery-stone is said to occur in Jersey; at Madron, in Cornwall; and at the base of one of the Mourne mountains, co. Down.—*Foreign.* In large boulders at Naxos, Nicaria, and Samos, in the Grecian Archipelago. In granular limestone in Asia Minor, near Gumush-dagh, 12 miles E. of Ephesus, associated with Margarite, Chloro-toid, Pyrites, Calc-spar, &c.; also at Kulah, Adula, and Mauser, 24 miles north of Smyrna. With talcose-slate at Ochseukopf in Saxony, of a dark blue or black colour, much resembling fine-grained basalt. Italy. Spain, &c.

The Emery generally used in this country is found in the Island of Naxos, in the Grecian Archipelago, where it occurs in large blocks imbedded in a red soil, and sometimes in white marble. These blocks are so abundant that, notwithstanding the immense quantities carried off, it is not yet requisite to quarry the rock itself. This substance is of so much value in the arts, that an English merchant found it advantageous to obtain a monopoly of it from the Greek government, in consequence of which its price in this country has been greatly enhanced, and at one time was as high as 30*l.* per ton.

The largest quantity is used in grinding and polishing plate-glass, but it is also very extensively employed in the metal-trades, and for various other purposes. Its preparation from the original blocks, as imported into this country, is effected by first breaking with large hammers, and then reducing to grains with steel-headed stamps driven by steam power. It is afterwards passed through various sieves, which assort it into the different sizes required and known as "flour," "corn," and "grinding emery," &c. &c. Much of it is used in the manufacture of emery-cloth and paper, in both of which articles it is frequently largely adulterated with iron slag, and other hard substances.

Name. The name emery is derived from Cape Emeri, in the island of Naxos, where it is found.

Brit. Mus., Case 19.

M. P. G. Horse-shoe Case, No. 782.

EMERYLITE, *Smith.* See MARGARITE.

EMMONITE, *Thomson.* A snow-white variety of Strontianite, with an obscurely foliated structure, and a scaly appearance, not unlike some varieties of Gypsum. Translucent at the edges. Very easily reduced to powder. Fracture flat, and smooth in the direction of the cleavage-planes. H. 2·75. S.G. 2·94.

It contains 82·7 per cent. of carbonate of strontia, and 12·5 per cent. of carbonate of lime.

Name. After Prof. Emmons, of William's College, Massachusetts, U. S.

ENARGITE, *Breithaupt.* Rhombic. Colour iron-black, with a metallic lustre. Streak black. Brittle. Fracture uneven. H. 3. S.G. 4·36 to 4·45.

Comp. ($\dot{C}u$, Fe, Zn) S + $\frac{1}{3}$(As, Sb)² S⁵ = sulphur 32·5, arsenic 19·1, copper 48·4 = 100·0.

Analysis by *Plattner* :

Sulphur	. . .	32·22
Arsenic	. . .	17·59
Antimony	. . .	1·61
Copper .	. . .	47·20
Iron	. . .	0·56
Zinc	. . .	0·22
Silver	. . .	0·01
		99·44

BB with borax, in the reducing flame, affords a globule of copper.

Locality. In large masses, in limestone, associated with Tennantite, at Morococha,

at an elevation of 15,000 feet in the Cordilleras of Peru.

ENCELADITE, *T. Sterry Hunt.* See WARWICKITE.

Named after Enceladus, one of the Titans of ancient mythology.

ENDELLIONE, *Bournon* ; ENDELLIONITE. This mineral was originally described by Count Bournon, and named by him after the locality, Endellion, in Cornwall, where it was first discovered. It was subsequently called Bournonite : which see.

M. P. G. Principal Floor, Wall-case 14, No. 647.

ENHYDROS, *J. Woodward.* ENHYDRITE, (From ἐν, *within*, and ὕδωε, *water*), the name given to crystals or nodules containing water.

Brit. Mus., Case 22.

ENTOMOUS COBALT PYRITES, *Mohs.* Ullmannite (in part).

EPHESITE, *J. L. Smith.* A mineral allied to Margarite. It has a pearly-white colour, and a lamellar structure, and resembles white Kyanite. Scratches glass. S.G. 3·15 to 3·2.

Analysis (mean of two), by *Smith* :

Silica	. . .	30·79
Alumina	. . .	57·17
Lime	. . .	2·00
Protoxide of iron .	.	1·17
Soda and a little potash	.	4·41
Water .	. . .	3·10
		98·63

Locality. The emery locality of Gumushdagh, near Ephesus, on Magnetite.

EPICHLORITE, *Rammelsberg.* A fibrous or columnar mineral between Schiller Spar and Chlorite. Colour dull leek-green ; bottle-green and translucent when in thin columns. Lustre greasy. Streak white to greenish. H. 2 to 2·5. S.G. 2·76.

Comp. $3\ddot{R}^3 \ddot{S}i + \ddot{R}^2 \ddot{S}i^3 + 9\dot{H}$.

Analysis by *Rammelsberg* :

Silica	. . .	40·88
Alumina	. . .	10·96
Peroxide of iron .	.	8·72
Protoxide of iron .	.	8·96
Magnesia	. . .	20·00
Lime	. . .	0·68
Water .	. . .	10·18
		100·38

BB fuses with difficulty in thin fibres.

Locality. Radauthal. Harzbugh in Brunswick .

EPIDOTE, *Haüy, Phillips.* Comprises

four groups: 1. Lime-and-iron-Epidote; Arendalite; Bucklandite; Pistacite or Epi-

Fig. 176.   Fig. 177.

dote proper; Puschkinite. 2. Lime Epidote; Zoisite. 3. Manganesian Epidote. 4. Cerium Epidote; Allanite; Thulite, Withamite.

These are described under their various names.

The general formula for Epidote, according to Hermann, is $(\dot{R}^3\ \ddot{\bar{R}})\ \ddot{Si} + n\,\dot{R}\,\dot{H}$, as translated by Dana.

BB fuses more or less easily, according to the amount of iron or manganese. In powder, after fusion or ignition dissolves in muriatic acid, and forms a jelly of silica.

Name. From ἐπίδοσις, *increase;* because the base of the primary form undergoes an increase in some of the secondary forms.

Epidote occurs in granite and other igneous rocks, and in various crystalline slates in attached crystals, generally grouped in druses, and in granular or columnar masses. Colour generally green, yellow and grey; sometimes red and black. Semi-transparent to transparent at the edges. Lustre vitreous; pearly on cleavage planes. Streak grey; except in the manganese variety from St. Marcel, which is red. Brittle. Fracture uneven—splintery. H. 6 to 7. S.G. 3 to 3·5.

Brit. Mus., Case 35.

M.P.G. Horse-shoe Case, Nos. 1030 to 1032.

EPISTILBIT, *Rose;* EPISTILBITE, *Phillips.* Rhombic: primary form a right rhombic prism. Commonly occurs in macled crystals. Colour white, bluish or yellowish-white; varying from transparent to translucent only at the edges. Lustre vitreous: on the faces of cleavage pearly. Fracture uneven. H. 3·5 to 4. S.G. 2·249 to 2·363.

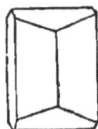

Fig. 178.   Fig. 179.

Comp. The same as that of Stilbite, with

one atom less of water; or, $(\dot{C}a, \dot{N}a)\ \ddot{Si}^3 +$ $\ddot{\bar{Al}}\ddot{Si}^3 + 5\dot{H} =$ silica 59·3, alumina 16·8, lime 9·2, water 14·7 = 100·0.

Analysis, from Berufiord, by *Rose:*

Silica	58·59
Alumina	17·52
Lime	7·56
Soda	1·78
Water	14·48
	99·93

When heated swells up strongly and evolves water.

BB alone, becomes white, intumesces and yields a highly blistered enamel, which does not run into a globule: with soda fuses to a transparent blistered glass.

Dissolves in concentrated muriatic acid, with separation of silica in the form of a granular powder.

Localities. The Isle of Skye, in small flesh-coloured crystals, in cavities in amygdaloid. In large distinct crystals in the trap rocks of Iceland (Berufiord), and the Farö Islands. Poonah in India. Bergen Hill, New Jersey, &c.

Brit. Mus., Case 38.

EPSOMITE, *Beudant;* EPSOM SALT, *Kirwan.* Rhombic: primary form a rhombic prism of 90° 30′ and 89° 30′. Occurs in botryoidal masses, and capillary efflorescences. Colour and streak greyish-white. Transparent to translucent. Taste bitter and saline. Very brittle. H. 2·25. S.G. 1·751.

Comp. When pure, $\dot{M}g\ \ddot{S} + 7\dot{H} =$ magnesia 16·26, sulphuric acid 32·52, water 51·22 = 100·00.

BB dissolves very easily by the assistance of its water of crystallization, but is difficultly fusible. Soluble in less than double its weight of cold water.

Localities. British.—Is a common ingredient in many mineral waters, as in those of Epsom, in Surrey; and appears as an efflorescence on the surface of certain rocks, as at the old coal-wastes and alum mines at Hurlet near Paisley, where it forms white capillary crystals. *Foreign.*—The quicksilver mines of Idria in Carniola. The gypsum quarries of Montmartre, near Paris. Aragon and Catalonia, in Spain. The mines at Clausthal in the Harz. The Cordillera of St. Juan, in Chili. Mammoth Cave of Kentucky, adhering to the roof in loose masses like snowballs.

Brit. Mus., Case 55.

When purified, the salt is used as a purgative medicine: the greater part of the Epsom salts of commerce, however, is manufactured from the Magnesian Limestone of Yorkshire.

ERCINITE. See HARMOTOME.

ERDIGER TALC, *Werner.* See NACRITE.

ERDIGES ERDPECH, *Werner.* ERDIGES BERGPECH, *Reuss.* See EARTHY BITUMEN.

ERDKOBOLD, *Werner.* See EARTHY COBALT.

ERDMANNITE. A name which has been given to Zircon found near Brevig in Norway. It is composed of Silica 33·43, Zirconia with some iron and manganese 65·97, loss by ignition, &c., 0·70 = 100·10.

ERDÖL, *Werner.* See NAPHTHA AND PETROLEUM.

ERDPECH, *Werner.* See BITUMEN.

ERDWACHS, *Rammelsberg.* See OZOCERITE.

EREMITE. *Shepard.* A variety of Monazite, found in minute crystals in a boulder of albitic granite, in the north-eastern part of Watertown, Connecticut, U.S. Colour between clove- and yellowish-brown. Semitransparent. Lustre resinous to vitreous. Streak paler than the colour. Brittle. Fracture conchoidal to uneven. H. 5 to 5·55. S.G. 3·714.

Fig. 180.

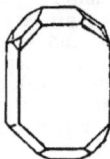

Name. From ἐρημία, *solitude,* in allusion to the isolated manner of its occurrence with respect to other individuals of the same species.

This name has been applied by Haidinger and Thomson to two minerals of very different composition.

ERINITE, *Haidinger.* Occurs in mammillated crystalline groups, consisting of concentric coats, with a fibrous structure, and rough surfaces formed by the ends of very minute crystals. Colour brilliant emerald-green, inclining to apple-green. Dull. Faintly translucent at the edges. Streak same as the colour, but paler. Brittle. Fracture uneven, or imperfect conchoidal. H. 4·5 to 5. S.G. 4·043.

Comp. $\ddot{C}u^5 \ddot{A}s + 2 \ddot{H}$ = arsenic acid 34·7, oxide of copper 59·9, water 5·4 = 100·0.

Analysis, by *Turner* :

Oxide of copper	.	. 59·44
Arsenic acid.	.	. 33·78

Alumina	. .	.	. 1·77
Water .	. .	.	. 5·01
			100·00

BB emits fumes of arsenic and melts. Soluble in nitric acid.

Locality. County of Limerick, in Ireland.

Name. The name bears reference both to the locality as well as to the characteristic emerald-green colour.

Only two specimens of this mineral have been preserved, one of which is in the collection of Mr. Greg.

ERINITE, *Thomson.* A compact, fine-grained variety of Bole, of a yellowish-red, or sometimes greenish colour. Lustre slightly resinous. Opaque. Feel soapy. Fracture small-conchoidal. H. 1·75. S.G. 2·04.

Analysis, by *Thomson* :

Silica	. . .	. 47·0
Alumina	. .	. 18·0
Protoxide of iron	.	. 6·4
Water .	. . .	. 25·0
		96·4

BB whitens, but does not melt.

Localities.—Irish. In Co. Antrim, four miles east of the Giant's Causeway, in amygdaloid ; Magee Island, at Dunluce Castle.

Name. After Erin, the name for Ireland in the native language.

ERLAMITE, *Breithaupt ;* ERLAN. Generally occurs in small and fine granular concretions of a pale greenish-grey colour, with a dull or feebly shining lustre. Streak white and shining, with a resinous lustre. Fracture foliated, sometimes splintery. H. 5. S.G. 3·0 to 3·1.

Analysis, by *Gmelin* :

Silica	. . .	. 53·16
Alumina	. .	. 14·03
Lime	. . .	. 14·39
Soda	. . .	. 2·61
Magnesia	. .	. 5·42
Oxide of iron	. .	. 7·14
Oxide of manganese	.	0·64
		97·39

BB fuses readily to a slightly coloured, transparent globule ; with borax yields a clear greenish glass.

Locality. The Saxon Erzgebirge, in gneiss.

Erlamite strongly resembles Gehlenite in appearance. It is probably only a mechanical mixture.

ERSBYITE. The name given by A. E. Nordenskiöld to the anhydrous Scolecite of Nordenskiöld, the father, from Ersby, in Finland.

ERUBESCITE, *Dana.* Purple Copper. Cubical. The crystals are generally cubes, of which the solid angles are replaced, and the faces are mostly curvilinear. Occurs both crystallized and massive. Colour of the latter, when recently fractured, between copper-red and tombac-brown, but it soon acquires an iridescent tarnish. Lustre metallic. Streak greyish-black, and somewhat shining. Slightly sectile. Easily frangible. Fracture imperfect conchoidal. H. 3. S.G. 4·4 to 5.

 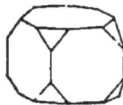

Fig. 181.   Fig. 182.

Comp. FeS + 2CuS, or (Fe,Cu)S, (Berzelius)=iron 13·8, sulphur 23·7, copper 62·5 =100·0.

Analysis of a crystallized specimen from the Condurro Mine, in Cornwall, by *Plattner:*

Sulphur	.	.	.	28·24
Copper	.	.	.	56·76
Iron	.	.	.	14·84

99·84

BB on charcoal acquires a dark tarnish, then becomes black, and, on cooling, red; at a higher temperature, fuses easily to a brittle globule, which is magnetic, and appears greyish-red on the fractured surface. When roasted for a considerable time, and then treated with a small quantity of borax, affords a globule of metallic copper.

Soluble in nitric acid.

Localities.—English. Cornwall, crystallized at Carn Brea, Tincroft, Cook's Kitchen, Dolcoath, Huel Jewel, Huel Falmouth, South Tolgus; Somersetshire, massive at Broomfield Consols.—*Irish.* The copper mines of Kerry and Cork.—*Foreign.* Massive and compact varieties occur at Arendal in Norway, Monte Catini in Tuscany, Siberia, Hesse, Silesia, Hungary, and the Bannat.

Name. From "erubesco," *to turn red;* given by Dana in allusion to its tendency to become tarnished, and acquire a reddish hue.

Brit Mus., Case 7.

M. P. G. A. 51 in Hall; mass from near Disco. Greenland. Principal Floor, Wall-cases 7 (British); 16 and 17 (Foreign).

ERUSIBITE. The name proposed by Prof. C. U. Shepard for a rusty, insoluble, ferric sulphate, met with at the Ducktown Copper Mine, in Eastern Tennessee.

ERYTHRINE, *Beudant.* Cobalt Bloom. Oblique. Is found in small botryoidal masses,

and acicular diverging crystals, modified at the edges, and whose form is a right oblique-angled prism. Colour carmine and peach-blossom red, sometimes whitish, or greyish-white, or greenish-grey. Lustre pearly, on some faces inclining to vitreous. Varies from translucent to transparent. Streak the same as the colour, but paler. The dry powder deep lavender blue. Flexible. Sectile. H. 1·5 to 2·5. S.G. 2·948.

Fig. 183.   Fig. 184.

Comp. $\ddot{C}o^3 \ddot{A}s + 8\ddot{H}$ =arsenic acid 38·43, oxide of cobalt 37·55, water 24·02=100 00.

Analysis, from Joachimsthal, by *Lindaker:*

Arsenic acid	.	.	.	36·42
Sulphuric acid	.	.	.	0·66
Oxide of cobalt	.	.	.	23·75
Oxide of nickel	.	.	.	11·26
Protoxide of iron	.	.	.	3·51
Lime	.	.	.	0·42
Water	.	.	.	23·52

99·74

BB on charcoal emits fumes of arsenic, and melts in the inner flame to a green globule of arsenide of cobalt; with fluxes yields a fine blue-coloured glass.

Soluble in muriatic or nitric acid, forming a red solution.

Localities. — *English.* Several Cornish mines; at Botallack, Polgooth, Huel Unity, Dolcoath, Huel Sparnon, Huel Trenwyth, &c.; Wilsworthy Mine, Devonshire; Tyne-bottom Mine, near Alston, in Cumberland. —*Foreign.* The principal foreign localities are Schneeberg, in Saxony (in micaceous radiating scales). Saalfeld in Thuringia, and Riegelsdorf in Hessia (in minute aggregated crystals). Dopschau, in Hungary.

The earthy peach blossom varieties are met with in Cornwall, Alston, Dauphiné, and Allemont; and a perfectly green variety occurs at Platten, in Bohemia; sometimes tinges both of red and green may be observed on the same crystal.

Name. From ἐρυθρός, *red.*

Cobalt-bloom is used for the manufacture of smalt.

Brit. Mus., Case 56.

M. P. G. Principal Floor, Wall-cases 9 (British); 20 and 40.

ERYTHRITE, *Thomson.* A flesh-coloured Felspar, found in amygdaloid, near Kilpatrick, in Dumbartonshire. S.G. 2·541.

Analysis, by *Thomson* :

Silica	. . .	67·90
Alumina	. . .	18·00
Peroxide of iron	. .	2·70
Potash	. . .	7·50
Lime	. . .	1·00
Magnesia	. . .	3·25
		100·35

Name. From ἐρυθρὸς, *red.*
ERZ. *German for Ore.*
ESCARBOUCLE, *French.* See CARBUNCLE.
ESCHENITE. See ÆSCHYNITE.
ESCHWEGITE, *Dufrénoy.* A variety of Anthosiderite, occurring in brownish filaments, associated with Specular Iron.
ESMARKITE, *Erdmann.* A hydrated Iolite from Bräkke, near Brevig, in Norway, corresponding in composition to IOLITE + 3 Ḣ. S.G. 2·709.
It occurs in large rounded prisms, with a cleavage parallel to the terminal face. H. between Calc-spar and Fluor.
BB fuses at the edges to a grey glass.
Name. After M. Esmark.
ESMARKITE, *Hausmann.* See DATHOLITE.
ESSONITE, *Haüy.* See CINNAMON STONE.
ETAIN OXYDÉ, *Haüy.* See CASSITERITE.
ETAIN PYRITEUX, *Brochant.*
ETAIN SULFURÉ, *Haüy.* } See TIN PYRITES.
ETAIN VITREUX, *De Born.* See CASSITERITE.
ETITES. Kidney-form hydrous peroxide of iron.
EUCAIRITE, *Berzelius.* Massive; in thin superficial black films, staining the calcareous spar in which it is contained. Colour between silver-white and lead-grey. Lustre metallic. Texture granular. Streak grey and shining. Soft; easily cut with the knife. Fracture fine-grained.
Comp. Selenide of silver and copper, or Cu Se + Ag Se = (Cu, Ag) Se = copper 25·3, silver 43·1, selenium 31·6 = 100·0.

Analysis, by *Berzelius* :

Selenium	. . .	26·00
Copper	. . .	23·05
Silver	. . .	38·93
Gangue	. . .	8·90
Carbonic acid and loss	.	3·12
		100·00

BB gives off a strong odour of selenium : on charcoal fuses readily to a grey metallic globule, which is not malleable.
Soluble in boiling nitric acid; on the addition of cold water to the solution a white precipitate is formed of selenite of silver.
Locality. This very rare mineral has only been met with in Norway, at the copper mine of Skrickerum in Smaoland.
It was discovered and analysed by Berzelius, who named it Eukairite (from εὖ, *well,* and καιρὸς, *opportune*) in allusion to its discovery soon after the completion of his examination of the metal selenium.
Brit. Mus., Case 4.
EUCHROITE, *Breithaupt.* Rhombic. Primary form a right rhombic prism. Colour bright emerald-green, with a vitreous lustre, and considerable double refraction. Transparent to translucent. Streak pale applegreen. Rather brittle. Fracture uneven to small conchoidal. H. 3·5 to 4. S.G. 3·389.

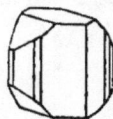

Fig. 185.

Comp. Cu^4 Äs + 7Ḣ = oxide of copper 47·15, arsenic acid 34·15, water 18·70 = 100.

Analysis, by *Turner* :

Oxide of copper	. .	47·85
Arsenic acid	. .	33·02
Water	. . .	18·80
		99·67

BB on charcoal fuses readily, giving off arsenical odours and deflagrating immediately; after long continued blowing, it yields a globule of malleable copper, with white metallic particles disposed through it.
Easily soluble in nitric acid.
Locality. This rare mineral is found in large crystals at Libethen, in Hungary, in quartzose mica-slate. It bears considerable resemblance to Dioptase.
Name. From εὔχροια, *beautiful colour.*
Brit. Mus., Case 56.
EUCHYSIDERITE. See PYROXENE.
EUCLASE. *Haüy, Phillips, Dana.* Oblique. Primary form a right oblique-angled prism. Occurs in oblique four-sided prisms with each of the lateral edges bevelled, and variously modified and terminated. Colourless and nearly transparent, or various shades of pale or bluish-green. Lustre vitreous.

Possesses double refraction. Rendered electric by pressure, a property which it retains for many hours. Very brittle. Fracture conchoidal. H. 7·5. S.G. 3·03 to 3·09.

Comp. $2\ddot{B}e^3 \ddot{S}i + \ddot{A}l \ddot{S}i^2 =$ silica 43·68, alumina 32·40, glucina 23·92 = 100.

Fig. 186.

Analysis, by *Berzelius*:

Silica	43·22
Alumina	30·56
Peroxide of iron	2·22
Glucina	21·78
Oxide of tin	0·70
	98·40

BB becomes opaque, swells up into a cauliflower-like mass, and then melts to a white enamel at the edges.

Not acted on by acids.

Localities. Euclase was originally brought from Peru by Dombey; it has since been procured from Boa Vista and from Capao in the mining district of Villa Rica, in Brazil, where it occurs in chloritic slate resting on sandstone. It is also found in the gold-stream-works of the S. Ural, near the river Sanarka, associated with Emerald, red Corundum, Disthene, &c. Peru.

Name. From ῦ, easily, and κλαίω, to break, in allusion to its easy frangibility. On that account, and from its rarity, it is very seldom used in jewelry, for which it is otherwise well suited from its hardness (which exceeds that of Topaz) and the high polish of which it is susceptible.

Brit. Mus., Case 37.

EUCLASTIC DISTHENE SPAR, *Haidinger.* See DIASPORE.

EUDIALITE. *Stromeyer;* EUDYALITE, *Phillips.* Hexagonal. Primary form an acute rhombohedron. Occurs in crystalline masses sometimes exhibiting a tolerably distinct double cleavage, and in crystals derived from a rhombohedron; but the crystals are *generally* small and irregular. Colour red or brownish-red, presenting tints like those of different varieties of Almandine Garnet. Lustre vitreous. Sometimes transparent, but usually cracked in every direction, and only transparent at thin edges. Streak white. Fracture subconchoidal or splintery. H. 6. S.G. 2·9.

Comp. $2\ddot{R}^3 \ddot{S}i^2 + \ddot{Z}r \ddot{S}i^2$

Analysis, by *Damour* :

Silica	50·38
Tantalic acid	0·35
Zirconia	15·60
Protoxide of iron	0·37
Protoxide of manganese	1·61
Lime	9·23
Soda	13·10
Chlorine	1·48
Volatile matters	1·25
	99·37

BB fuses tolerably easily to a greyish-green enamel.

When pulverized, soluble in muriatic acid with the formation of a thick jelly of silica.

Locality. Kangardluarsuk on the west coast of Greenland, associated with Arfvedsonite and Sodalite, or imbedded in white Felspar.

Name. From ῦ, easily, and διαλύω, to dissolve; in allusion to its easy solubility in acids.

Brit. Mus., Case 31.

EUDNOPHITE, *Weibye.* A variety of Analcime, found in white and greyish crystals on the island Lamö, in Norway. It occurs in syenite, associated with Leucophane and Mosandrite. H. 5·5. S.G. 2·27.

Analysis (mean of two), by *v. Borck & Berlin :*

Silica	55·00
Alumina	24·36
Soda	14 06
Water	8·23
	101·65.

Name. From ῦ, well, and γνόφος, a cloud, or darkness.

Brit. Mus., Case 28.

EUGENESITE. See SELENPALLADITE.

EUGENGLANZ. See POLYBASITE.

EUKLAS, *Werner.* See EUCLASE.

EUKLASTIC DISTHENE SPAR, *Haidinger.* See DIASPORE.

EUKOLITE, *Scheerer.* Is found in reniform masses of a brown colour at Brevig, and at Rödkindholm, near Fredericksvärn, in Norway. S.G. 3·01.

Comp. $6\ddot{R} + \ddot{R} + 6\ddot{S}i.$

Analysis, by *Damour :*

Silica	45·70
Tantalic acid	2·35
Zirconia	14·22
Protoxide of iron	6·63
Lime	9·16
Oxide of cerium	2·49
Oxide of lanthanium	1·11
Soda	11·59

Protoxide of manganese	.	2·35
Chlorine	. . .	1·11
Volatile matters	. .	1·83

$$\overline{99·24}$$

Eukolite is a variety of Eudialite, but differing from it in containing small quantities of oxides of Cerium and Lanthanium. From its crystallographic and optical properties Descloiseaux regards it as hexagonal, and near Eudialite, the axis being *negative*, instead of, as in the latter mineral, *positive*.

EULYTINE. *Breithaupt.* Cubical; tetrahedral. Usually occurs in minute trigonal dodecahedrons, or in implanted globular masses rarely exceeding a pin's-head in size. Colour dark hair-brown, yellowish-grey, greyish-white or wax-yellow. Lustre resinous or adamantine. Semitransparent or opaque. Streak yellowish-grey. Rather brittle. Fracture uneven. H. 4·5. S.G. 5·9 to 6.

Comp. $\ddot{B}i^2 \ddot{S}i^5$, with fluoride and phosphate of iron.

Analysis, from Schneeberg, by *Kersten* :

Oxide of bismuth	.	69·38
Silica . . .	.	22·23
Phosphoric acid .	.	3·31
Peroxide of iron .	.	2·40
Peroxide of manganese		0·30
Hydrofluoric acid and water		1·01

$$\overline{98·60}$$

BB decrepitates, gives off arsenical fumes, and fuses to a dark yellow mass.
Localities. Bräunsdorf, near Freiberg; and the neighbourhood of Schneeberg in Saxony, in Quartz, accompanied by Cobalt and Native Bismuth. Schemnitz in Hungary, of a yellowish-green colour; disseminated in oxide of iron.
Brit. Mus., Case 26.

EUMANITE, *Shepard.* A variety of Brookite found in the albite vein at Chesterfield, Massachusetts.

EUPHOTIDE-JADIEN. The term applied by Brongniart to a mixture of Saussurite (the Jade of De Saussure) with grass-green Smaragdite.

EUPHYLLITE, *Silliman, Jr.* A pearly-white mineral, forming apparently hexagonal laminæ, not so easily separated as in Mica. Laminæ rather brittle, inelastic, and transparent. Lustre pearly; of basal plane very brilliant, resembling Heulandite. Colour of cleavage-face pure white, of sides greyish, sea-green or whitish. H. 3. S.G. 2·963.

Comp. $\dot{R} \ddot{S}i + 2\ddot{A}l^3 \ddot{S}i^2 + 3\dot{H}.$

Analysis, by *J. J. Crooke :*

Silica .	. . .	39·04
Alumina	. . .	57·38
Lime .	. . .	3·19
Magnesia	. . .	1·09
Soda .	. . .	0·87
Water .	. . .	4·56

$$\overline{100·10}$$

BB exfoliates; fuses at the edges of thin laminæ, and emits a strong light.
Localities. Unionville, Pennsylvania, associated with black Tourmaline and Corundum.
Name. From ἐΰ. *beautiful,* and φύλλον, a *leaf;* in allusion to its beautiful foliæ.
Brit. Mus., Case 19.

EUPYRCHROITE, *Emmons.* A compact, concretionary, and subfibrous variety of Apatite, found at Crown Point, Essex co., U. S. S.G. 3·053.

EUTOMOUS COBALT PYRITES, *Mohs.* See BREITHAUPTITE.

EUXENITE, *Scheerer, Dufrénoy.* Rhombic? Occurs in rectangular prisms, with the lateral edges replaced, but commonly massive, without any traces of cleavage. Colour brownish-black, with a metallic, waxy lustre. Streak reddish-brown. Translucent in thin splinters, showing a reddish-brown colour, paler than the streak. Fracture conchoidal. H. 6·5. S.G. 4·6 to 4·76.

Comp. About $4(\dot{C}a, \ddot{M}g, \dot{C}e, \dot{L}a, \dot{Y}, \dot{U})$ $\ddot{T}i, \ddot{T}a.$ (Gmelin.)

Analysis, by *Scheerer :*

Titanic and columbic acid	.	57·60
Yttria . . .	.	25·09
Protoxide of uranium	.	6·34
Protoxide of cerium	.	2·18
Oxide of lanthanum	.	0·96
Lime	.	2·47
Magnesia . . .	.	0·29
Water . . .	.	3·97

$$\overline{98·90}$$

BB infusible: with borax, in the outer flame, yields a brownish-yellow glass, which, if a sufficient quantity of the mineral is dissolved, retains its colour on cooling, and also in the inner flame; by flaming it is converted into a yellowish enamel.
Localities. Norway, at Jölster, and near Tvedenstrand.
Name. The name Euxenite, from ἐΰ, *welcome,* and ξένος, *guest,* was given by Scheerer, in allusion to its rarity.
Brit. Mus., Case 38.

EUZEOLITH. See HEULANDITE.

EXANTHALOSE, *Beudant.* A variety of

Glauber Salt from Vesuvius, containing only two atoms of water instead of ten.

Comp. $\overset{.}{N}a \overset{..}{S} + 2\overset{.}{H}$.

Localities. Important deposits of this salt occur near Lodosa in Navarre, and other parts of Spain, especially at Calatayud, in Catalonia; it also forms veins at the salt mines of Villafranca (Basses Pyrenees).

Name. From ἐξανθέω, *to effloresce*, and ἅλας, *salt*.

 EXITÈLE, *Beudant.* From ἐξίτηλος, *vaporisable.* See VALENTINITE.

EYE-AGATE, or EYESTONE. The name given to those kinds of circle-Agate in which the central part shows spots more highly coloured than the other portions of the mass. The name Eyestone is also applied to stalactitic carbonate of lime, where slices, cut at right angles to the axis, display a darker coloured spot in the centre, presenting a fanciful resemblance to the pupil of the eye.

M. P. G. Horse-shoe Case, No. 387, from the Roman states.

F.

FAHL-ORE, *Jameson;* FAHLERZ, *Werner.* See TETRAHEDRITE.

FAHLES ROTHGILTIGERZ, *Hausmann.* A variety of Miargyrite, from Andreasberg, in the Harz, in which part of the antimony is replaced by arsenic.

FAHLUNITE. A hydrated variety of Iolite, occurring massive and in six-sided prisms. Colour dark reddish-brown, sometimes green or black, and opaque, but yellowish-brown by transmitted light, and translucent in thin fragments. H. 3. S.G. 2·74.

Comp. $2(\overset{.}{K}, \overset{.}{C}a, \overset{.}{M}g, \overset{.}{M}n, \overset{.}{F}e), 2 \overset{...}{A}l, 5 \overset{..}{S}i,$ $3 \overset{.}{H}$. (Gmelin.) According to Dana, Fahlunite is equivalent to (Iolite + 6 $\overset{.}{H}$), but the water is not a constant quantity.

Analysis, from Terra Nova Mine, by *Wachtmeister* :

Silica	. 44·60
Alumina . . .	. 30·10
Protoxide of iron . .	. 3·86
Potash	. 1·98
Magnesia . . .	. 6·75
Protoxide of manganese	. 2·24
Lime	. 1·35
Soda, hydrofluoric acid	. trace

100·23

BB becomes colourless, cracks and swells up slightly, fusing at the edges to a glass; with borax or salt of phosphorus melts slowly to a glass, which is slightly coloured by iron.

Locality. Fahlun, in Sweden (whence the name, Fahlunite), with Iolite, in Chlorite Slate.

Brit. Mus., Case 32.

FALLOW COPPER ORE, *Kirwan.* See TETRAHEDRITE.

FALSE TOPAZ. A name given by lapidaries to a light yellow pellucid variety of Quartz-crystal, ranking next to Amethyst in value. It may be distinguished from yellow Topaz (for which, when cut, it is frequently substituted), by the difference of its crystalline form, the absence of cleavage, inferior hardness, and lower specific gravity. The colour is of different degrees of intensity, and is frequently combined with a smoky brown, forming a tint of much warmth and richness when not in excess. In this respect it is equal to the Saxon Topaz, though inferior to the Brazilian. It is generally made into seals and brooches, and appears to the greatest advantage when cut in steps. The breadth of the table should be in porportion to the fulness of the colour, and, if deficient in the latter respect, it should be carefully set with a proper foil. (Mawe.)

It is found in the Brazils, and is sometimes called False Cairngorm of Brazil.

M. P. G. Horse-shoe Case, No. 509.

FARÖELITE, *Heddle, Greg & Lettsom.* A mineral intermediate in composition between Soda-Thomsonite and Mesolite. Rhombic: primary form a right rhombic prism. Colour white, bluish, yellowish, greyish. Lustre pearly or vitreous. Cleavage perfect.

Comp. Mesolite with one equivalent less of silica; or $(\overset{.}{N}a, 2\overset{.}{C}a) 2\overset{..}{S}i + 3(\overset{...}{A}l \overset{..}{S}i) + 8\overset{.}{H}$ =silica 42·45, alumina 28·27, lime 10·29, soda 5·75, water 13·24=100·00.

Fig. 186*.

Localities.—Scotch. Isle of Skye (*fig.* 186*.) at Portree in confused white globules; Storr in bluish-white implanted spheres with Mesolite; near Talisker in white radiated and implanted globules, with Laumonite and Tesselite ; at Uig, in white radiated globules, lining cavities in trap.

Irish. Antrim ; at Agnew's Hill at Portrush in greenstone. Black cave near Larne, at the N.W. of Rathlin Island.

Farȫe in stalactites, sometimes 3 inches long.

Name. From the locality where the finest specimens are found : *Farȫe*, and λιθος, *stone.*

FASERZEOLITH, *Werner.* See NATROLITE.

FASSAITE. A variety of Pyroxene of a beautiful grass-green colour, with a high lustre. It is found in the Valley of Fassa, in the Tyrol, whence the name *Fassaite.*

Brit. Mus.. Case 34.

M. P. G. Horse-shoe Case, No. 1042.

FAT QUARTZ, *Kirwan.* See GREASY QUARTZ.

FAUJASITE, *Damour*; FAUJASSITE, *Dufrénoy.* Dimetric. Occurs in octahedrons. Colourless to brown, with a vitreous and uneven fracture. H. 5. S.G. 1·923.

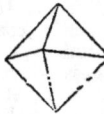

Fig. 187.

Comp. K̈ S̈i + A̅l S̈i² + 9 Ḣ = silica 46, alumina 17, lime 5, soda 5, water 27 = 100.

Analysis, by *Damour :*

Silica	46·12
Alumina . . .	16·81
Lime	4·90
Soda	5·09
Water	27·02
	99·83

BB intumesces and fuses to a white blebby enamel.

Soluble in muriatic acid.

Locality. Kaiserstuhl, in Baden, with black Augite.

Name, by Damour, in honour of Faujas de Saint-Fond, a celebrated naturalist.

Brit. Mus., Case 29.

FAYALITE, is a pure Iron-Chrysolite, or an anhydrous silicide of iron, in which a large quantity of the protoxide of iron is replaced by magnesia and other bases. It is sometimes fused and blistered, sometimes with a crystalline structure. Colour greenish or brownish-black. Sometimes iridescent. Opaque. Lustre semi-metallic in places. Strongly attracted by the magnet. H. 6·5. S.G. 4·138.

Comp. (Of the soluble portion) Ḟe² S̈i = protoxide of iron 70·45, silica 29·55 = 100·00.

Analysis, by *Fellenberg :*

Silica	31·04
Protoxide of iron . .	62·57
Lime	0·43

Protoxide of manganese .	0·79
Oxide of copper . . .	0·32
Oxide of lead . . .	1·71
Alumina	3·27
Sulphur and chlorine . .	traces
	100·13

BB fuses very easily and quietly, with evolution of sulphurous acid, to a black metallic globule, which is magnetic.

Strong-fuming nitric acid converts it into a jelly.

Localities. — Irish. In small detached masses at Slievecarrach, one of the Mourne mountains. Tullybrick, Ballinascreen. The foot of Slieve Gaillion, in Londonderry. It is also met with in volcanic rocks at Fayal, whence the name *Fayalite.*

Brit. Mus., Case 26.

FEATHER-ALUM, or FEDERALAUN. See ALUNOGEN and HALOTRICHITE.

FEATHER-ORE, or FEDERERZ. See HETEROMORPHITE.

FEATHER ZEOLITE. See NATROLITE.

FELDSPATH, *Haüy*; FELDSPAR; FELDSTEIN, *Hausmann*; FELSPAR, *Phillips.* Under this head are comprised several minerals, varying much in appearance, and presenting numerous and complicated crystalline forms. It has been divided into several species and varieties, the principal of which are described under the following names:— Adularia, Albite, Amazon-stone, Andalusite, Andesine, Anorthite, Cancrinite, Erythrite, Haüyne, Labradorite, Lapis-lazuli, Leucite, Moonstone, Murchisonite, Nosean, Oligoclase, Orthoclase, Petalite, Ryacolite, Soda-lite, and Variolite. The word Felspar is derived from the German name Feldspath, or field-spar, in allusion probably to the crystals being found loose on the surface of some parts of the country.* Several varieties of Felspar are used in jewelry; but all of them are indebted for this distinction, not on account of their possessing any transparency, but for their mutable reflection of light, or to their being chatoyant.

Brit. Mus., Case 29.

M. P. G. Horse-shoe Case, Nos. 944, 955 to 959, 965, 972, 973, 1039. Upper Gallery, Wall-case 6, Nos. 3 & 3a.

FELDSPATH APYRE, *Haüy.* See ANDALUSITE.

FELDSPATH ARGILLIFORME, *Haüy.* See KAOLIN.

FELDSPATH BLEU, *Haüy.* See LAZULITE.

---

* Kirwan states that the word Felspar is derived from *fels* (a rock), from the common occurrence of the mineral in granite.

FELDSPÀTH OPALIN, *Haüy*. See LABRA-DORITE.

FELDSPATH TENACE, *Haüy*. See SAUS-SURITE.

FELSOBANYITE. See GIBBSITE.

FEMININE. See GEM.

FER, French for IRON.

FER ARSÉNIATÉ, *Haüy*. See PHARMA-COSIDERITE.

FER ARSENICAL, *Haüy*. See MISPICKEL. (See also LEUCOPYRITE.)

FER ARSENICAL AXOTOME, *Dufrénoy*. See LEUCOPYRITE.

FER AZURÉ, *Haüy*; VIVIANITE. See BLUE IRON-EARTH.

FER CALCAREO-SILICEUX, *Haüy*. See LIEVRITE.

FER CARBONATÉ, *Dufrénoy, Levy*. See CHALYBITE.

FER CARBURÉ, *Haüy*. See GRAPHITE.

FER CHROMATÉ, *Haüy, brochant* See CHROMIC IRON.

FER HYDRO-OXIDÉ, *Bournon*. See LIMO-NITE.

FER MAGNETIQUE, *Brochant*. See MAG-NETITE.

FER MURIATÉ, *Haüy*. See PYROSMALITE.

FER NATIF, *Haüy*. See NATIVE IRON.

FER OLIGISTE, *Haüy*. See SPECULAR IRON.

FER OXALATÉ, *Levy*. See OXALITE.

FER OXIDÉ, *Berzelius*. See SPECULAR IRON.

FER OXIDÉ CARBONATÉ, *Haüy*. See CHALYBITE.

FER OXIDÉ HÆMATITE, *Haüy*. See BROWN HEMATITE (LIMONITE).

FER OXIDÉ HYDRATÉ, *Haüy*. See GOETHITE and LIMONITE.

FER OXIDÉ RESINITE, *Haüy*. See PITTI-CITE.

FER OXIDÉ RUBIGINEUX MASSIVE, *Haüy*; MORASS-ORE. See BOG IRON-ORE.

FER OXIDULÉ TITANÉ, *Haüy*. See CRICH-TONITE.

FER OXYDULÉ, *Haüy*. See MAGNETITE.

FER OXYDULÉ TITANIFÈRE, *Haüy*. See ISERINE.

FER PHOSPHATÉ, *Haüy*. See VIVIANITE.

FER SPATHIQUE, *Brochant*. See CHALY-BITE.

FER SPECULAIRE, *Brochant*. See SPE-CULAR IRON.

FER SULFURÉ, *Haüy*. See PYRITES.

FER SULFURÉ ACICULAIRE RADIÉ, *Haüy*. See MARCASITE.

FER SULFURÉ ARSENICALE, *Haüy*. See ARSENICAL PYRITES.

·FER SULFURÉ AURIFÈRE, *Haüy*. See AURIFEROUS PYRITES.

FER SULFURÉ BLANC, *Haüy*. See MAR-CASITE.

FER SULFURÉ CAPILLAIRE, *Haüy*. See MILLERITE.

FER SULFURÉ EPIGÈNE. See HEPATIC PYRITES.

FER SULFURÉ FERRIFÈRE, *Haüy*. See PYRRHOTINE.

FER SULFURÉ JAUNE, *Dufrénoy*. See PYRITES.

FER SULFURÉ MAGNETIQUE, *Haüy*. See PYRRHOTINE.

FER SULPHATÉ, *Haüy*. See COPPERAS.

FER SULPHATÉ ROUGE, *Dufrénoy*. See BOTRYOGENE.

FER TITANÉ, *Cordier*. See ILMENITE.

FERGUSONITE, *Haidinger*. Pyramidal : he-mihedral. Occurs in pyramidal crystals of a brownish-black colour. Opaque, but in thin laminæ translucent, and of a pale liver-brown by transmitted light. Lustre dull externally; of fractured surfaces bril-liantly vitreous and submetallic. Streak pale brown. Fracture imperfect-conchoidal. H. 5·5 to 6. S.G. 5·8 to 5·86.

Fig. 18ᵃ.

Comp. 6(Ẏ, Ċe) T̈a.

Analysis, by *Hartwall*:

Tantalic acid	. 47·75
Yttria	. 41·91
Oxide of cerium	. 4·68
Zirconia	. 3·02
Oxide of tin	. 1·00
Oxide of uranium	. 0·95
Peroxide of iron	. 0·84
	99·65

BB alone infusible, but becomes deep yellow, and subsequently pale yellow. Dis-solves slowly in borax, forming a glass which is yellow while hot; but if saturated, is rendered turbid by flaming, and acquires a dingy yellowish-red colour.

Locality. This rare mineral was dis-covered by Giesècké, disseminated in Quartz at Kikertaursak, near Cape Fare-well, in Greenland.

Name. In honour of Robert Ferguson of Raith.

FERROCOBALTINE. A variety of Cobaltine in which three-fourths of the cobalt is re-placed by iron. It is met with at the Ham-burg Mine, Siegen, in Westphalia.

Analysis of a plumose specimen, by *Schnabel*:

Sulphur	. . . . 19·98
Arsenic	. . . . 42·53
Cobalt .	. . . . 8·67
Iron	. . . . 25·98
Antimony	. . . 2 84

100·00

FERROTANTALITE. The name given to a variety of Tantalite, in consequence of the large quantity of iron which it contains.

FERRUGINOUS PHOSPHATE OF MANGANESE. See TRIPLITE.

FERRUGINOUS QUARTZ, OR IRON FLINT. A variety of Quartz forming the transition to Jasper. It occurs both massive and in distinct crystals, which are sometimes minute and aggregated into masses like the grains of sand in sandstone, and contains an admixture of about 5 per cent. of iron as red or yellow ochre, or Göthite It is opaque, and of various shades of red, yellow, or blackish-brown. Gives sparks with steel.

Localities. St. Just and Marazion in Cornwall. Clifton, near Bristol. Stocking Moor, near Glasgow. Dunbar in Haddingtonshire, in trap. Rathlin Island, N.Antrim. Massive and in minute yellow crystals at Benbradagh Hill, Londonderry. (See EISENKIESEL.)

Brit. Mus., Case 21.

M. P. G. Horse-shoe Case, Nos. 525, 526.

FERRUGINOUS SILICATE OF MANGANESE, *Thomson.* See TROOSTITE.

FERRUGINOUS ZINC-SPAR. The name proposed by Monheim for the light-green varieties of Zinc-spar, rich in zinc. See KAPNITE.

FETID CARBONATE OF LIME, *Cleaveland.* See SWINESTONE.

FETID SULPHATE OF BARYTES, *Cleaveland.* See HEPATITE.

FETTSTEIN, *Werner.* See ELÆOLITE.

FEUERBLENDE, *Breithaupt.* See FIRE-BLENDE.

FEUERSTEIN, *Werner.* See FLINT.

FIBROFERRITE, *Prideaux.* A variety of Copiapite, found investing Coquimbite. It is warty, separates in scales, and is fibrous in a direction perpendicular to the plane of separation. Colour pale greenish grey, affording a yellowish powder. Fibres translucent. Taste rough and somewhat sour. S.G. 2·5 about.

Comp. Sesquisulphate of iron or $\overset{...}{Fe}{}^2\overset{...}{S}{}^3$ +18$\overset{.}{H}$.

Analysis, by *Prideaux*:

Peroxide of iron .	. . 34·44
Sulphuric acid	. . . 28·89
Water .	. . . . 36·67

100·00

BB on charcoal, decrepitates violently; emits an odour of sulphur, and leaves peroxide of iron.

Locality. Chili, South America.

FIBROLITE, *Bournon.* A fibrous, massive variety of Sillimanite. Colour whitish or greenish-grey, with a lustre approaching to adamantine. The fibres are obliquely traversed by cracks, and sometimes approach to distinct prisms. Acquires resinous electricity by friction, and emits a reddish phosphorescent light when two pieces are rubbed together. Rather harder than Quartz, giving sparks with steel. S.G. 3·214.

Analysis, from the Carnatic, by *Chenevix*:

Alumina	. . . . 58·25
Silica .	. . . . 38·00
Iron	. . . . 0·75

97·00

BB infusible.

Locality. The Carnatic, accompanying Corundum, and as a component part of the granite which is the matrix of the Corundum.

Name. From φιβερν. *a fibre*, and λίθος, *stone*; in allusion to its fibrous structure.

Brit. Mus.. Case 26.

FIBROUS BROWN IRON ORE. A variety of Brown Hematite.

FIBROUS GYPSUM. See SATIN-SPAR.

FIBROUS QUARTZ. The name given to Quartz possessing a fibrous structure. It is found in Cornwall at Huel Virgin, near Scorrier, and at Tolcarn, near Truro; at the slate quarries at Bangor, in North Wales; in South Stirlingshire at the Campsie Hills, in small fibrous tufts on Heulandite; and in Ireland at Holy Park, near Rathfarnham, S. Dublin. A delicate variety occurs at Orange River, near the Cape of Good Hope.

FIBROUS RED COPPER-ORE, *Kirwan.* See CHALCOTRICHITE.

FIBROUS TIN: FIBROUS TIN STONE, *Kirwan.* A fibrous and radiated variety of Cassiterite. See WOOD-TIN.

FICHTELITE, *Bromeis.* A fossil resin, occurring chiefly in the form of shining transparent scales between the annual rings of growth of a species of pine-tree (*Pinites sylvestris*), which have separated from one another, or are still loosely united. The scales form layers (often $\frac{1}{10}$ of an inch thick) of a yellowish tinge, and lapping one over the other. If the wood is split in any direction, numerous shining points appear, showing that it is completely saturated with the mineral. Distils without being decomposed. Boiling point above 320°C. (608°F.)

Comp. $C_8 H_7$, or carbon 87·27, hydrogen 12 73 = 100.

Localities. The turf beds of Redwitz. The Fichtelgebirge of North Bavaria.

FIGURE STONE. A name given to Agalmatolite, from its being frequently carved into figures by the Chinese.

FIORITE, or PEARL SINTER. A hydrated form of silica (variety of Silicious Sinter), occurring in smooth and shining, globular or botryoidal masses with a pearly lustre. Colour white, yellowish-white, or greyish. Translucent at the edges. Fracture flat conchoidal. H. not so hard as Quartz.

Analysis, from the Geyser of Iceland, by *Damour:*

Silica	87·67·
Alumina and peroxide of iron	0·71
Lime	0·40
Soda	0·82
Potash	trace
	100·00

Localities. Santa Fiora (whence the name *Fiorite*), in Tuscany, incrusting volcanic tufa. The volcanic districts of Italy. Auvergne. Iceland.

FIREBLENDE, *Dana.* Oblique. Occurs in delicate crystals which are grouped like those of Stilbite. Colour hyacinth-red, with a pearly adamantine lustre. Translucent. Sectile and somewhat flexible. H. 2. S.G. 4·2 to 4·3.

Comp. Sulphur, antimony, and 62·3 per cent. of silver.

BB like Pyrargyrite.

Localities. Andreasberg, in the Harz. The Kurprinz mine, near Freiberg. Brit. Mus., Case 11.

FIRE GARNET. See PYROPE: also GARNET.

FIRE MARBLE. See LUMACHELLO.

FIRE OPAL. A variety of Opal presenting hyacinth-red and yellow reflexions.

Analysis, from Faröe, by *Forchammer:*

Silica · . . .	88·73
Alumina	0·99
Soda and potash · . .	0·34
Lime	0·49
Magnesia	1·48
Water	7·97
	99·96

Localities.—English. Cornwall at Huel

Spinster, Rosewarne Mine, and near St. Just.—*Foreign.* Zimapan in Mexico. Guatemala. Faröe Islands. Washington co., Georgia, U.S.

Brit. Mus., Case 24.

FISCHAUGENSTEIN, *Werner.*
FISH-EYE-STONE, *Jameson.* } See ICHTHYOPHTHALMITE. From ἰχθύς, *a fish,* and ὀφθαλμός, *an eye.*

FISCHERITE, *Hermann.* Rhombic. Occurs both crystalline and massive. Colourless, and translucent; dull green when massive. S.G. 2·46.

Comp. $\ddot{Al}^2 \ddot{P} + 8H$ = alumina 41·82, phosphoric acid 28·88, water 29·29 = 100.

Analysis, by *Hermann* :

Alumina	38·47
Phosphoric acid . . .	29·03
Peroxide of iron and manganese	1·20
Oxide of copper . . .	0·80
Phosphate of lime and gangue	3·00
Water	27·50
	100·00

BB turns white, with blackish spots; and gives off much water.

Locality. Nischne Tagilsk, in veins in ferruginous sandstone and clay-slate.

Name. By Prof. Tschuroffsky, after Mons. Fischer of Waldheim, V. P. of the Imperial Society of Naturalists of Moscow.

FLABELLIFORM KOUPHONE SPAR, *Haidinger.* See MESOLE.

FLECHES D'AMOUR. See VENUS' HAIRSTONE.

FLEURS DE COBALT, *Brochant.* See ERYTHRINE.

FLEW COAL. A kind of Coal resembling Flint-coal, found at Wedgebury in Staffordshire.

FLEXIBLE SANDSTONE. A fissile variety of Sandstone, thin slabs of which are somewhat flexible. The flexibility of the Sandstone occurring in thin layers at Villa Rica, in Brazil, is owing apparently to the dissemination of small scales of Mica through the mass; a similar flexible Sandstone occurs in the gold region of North Carolina. It is found also at Jujjur, about 120 miles N.W. of Delhi in India.

M.P.G. Horse-shoe Case, No. 731.

FLEXIBLE SILVER ORE, or FLEXIBLE SULPHURET OF SILVER, *Phillips.* A variety of Sternbergite, occurring both massive and in small tabular crystals, which appear to be right oblique angled prisms. Colour dark externally, with a metallic lustre, which is less brilliant than that of Silver Glance.

Very soft, yielding readily to the knife, and easily separable into thin laminæ, in which state it is flexible.

It consists of silver, sulphur, and a little iron. (Wollaston.)

This rare ore has only been found in Hungary and Saxony.

The crystal figured by Phillips from the Himmelsfürst mine at Freyberg is, according to Brooke and Miller, a distorted crystal of Silver Glance.

Brit. Mus., Case 10.

M. P. G. Wall-case 22.

FLINT. *Kirwan, Phillips.* A variety of Quartz somewhat allied to Chalcedony, but more opaque and of dull colours, which are of various shades of grey, yellow, and black. Translucent, the blackish varieties seldom more than translucent at the edges. Brittle when first extracted, but becomes tougher by exposure. Fracture perfect conchoidal, with sharp cutting edges and a feeble lustre. Slightly harder than common Quartz, which it scratches. It is often coated to a slight depth with a whitish crust, which in some instances appears to be the effect of weathering. S.G. 2·59:

Analysis, by *Klaproth :*

Silica	.	.	.	.	98·0
Lime	.	.	.	.	0·50
Alumina	.	.	.	0·25
Oxide of iron	.	.	0·25
Loss	.	.	.	.	1·00
					100·00

BB alone infusible ; but whitens and becomes opaque when exposed to heat.

Localities.—British. Flint occurs in the Chalk formation of England, and the north of Ireland, mostly in layers which are parallel with the stratification, and consist of irregularly shaped nodules, or flat tabular bands. The former is the most usual mode of occurrence, and the flints are in general most numerous in the Upper Chalk, where they contain the remains of sponges, alcyonia, echini, and other fossils, sometimes in a silicified state, sometimes in the form of casts.

"We find numerous flints in the Chalk, and indeed in the gravels above it, which, when cut and polished, have a good appearance if worked into snuff-boxes and articles of the like kind, particularly when the spongiform bodies included in them are marked by any varieties of colour. In the Greensand the Chalcedony is often extremely beautiful, and pieces sufficiently large to form small cups or vases might be sometimes obtained. Portions of this mineral when worked into seals cannot be distinguished from the finest white Carnelian, which, in fact, they then are. Both such flints and Chalcedony are found on the coast between Lyme Regis and Sidmouth, where also are discovered some varieties of Jasper (from the Greensand), many species of which closely approach to those known as Egyptian Pebbles, and, indeed, are quite as beautiful. Some of the silicified fossil wood is extremely handsome when worked into ornaments."—Report on the Geology of Cornwall, Devon, and W. Somerset, by Sir Henry T. De la Beche, p. 496.

Flints are also found forming tabular bands and irregular masses in the Purbeck strata, and in Portland Stone : in the former case inclosing remarkably perfect casts of freshwater, and in the latter of marine shells. The lower part of the Portland Stone of Dorsetshire consists in a great degree of Flint. Flint is also found (but rarely) in Scotland, on the shore by Burnt-island, S.W. of Fife. — *Foreign.* France. The Danish Islands of Rugen and Zeeland. Spain ; and elsewhere.

Flint, after having been calcined and ground, is often employed as a substitute for sand in the manufacture of glass, porcelain, and smalt. Formerly it was used in large quantities for making gun-flints ; and before the invention of lucifer matches had superseded the old-fashioned *tinder-boxes*, it was in universal use for obtaining a light, by means of the sparks given off when it was struck against steel ; hence the French name of *pierre à feu.* In Chalk districts it is employed as a building material, either in its natural rough state or squared and dressed, good examples of which latter application are afforded by houses at Lewes in Sussex, and elsewhere. Flints also furnish an excellent road material ; when employed for this purpose they should not be used immediately on being extracted from the quarry, as they acquire additional toughness by the evaporation of the water contained in them.

Brit. Mus., Case 22.

M.P.G. Horse-shoe Case, Nos. 703 to 730, 736, 739 to 748. Upper Gallery, Wall-case 42, Nos. 1 to 16.

FLINT COAL. A kind of Coal resembling Anthracite. It contains Bitumen, though not to so great an extent as is the case with Cannel Coal.

FLOATSTONE, *Jameson.* A variety of Quartz, of a spongy or porous description, which possesses the property of floating in water, until the air contained in its numerous cavities is displaced.

Localities. It is found at Huel Alfred, in Cornwall; and in beds of Flint, in chalk, at St. Omer, St. Ouen, and Menil Montant, near Paris.

Comp. According to Vauquelin it consists of carbonate of lime 2, silica 98=100.

FLORID or COCHINEAL RED COPPER, *Kirwan.* See RED COPPER ORE and CHALCOTRICHITE.

FLOS FERRI, or "FLOWER OF IRON." The name given to the branching or coralloid forms of Aragonite by the older mineralogists, by whom it was considered to be an ore of iron. It occurs in beds of iron-ore, and very beautiful specimens are found associated with Spathic Iron, in the Styrian mines of Eisenerz, and at Hüttenberg in Carinthia, coating the roofs and sides of considerable cavities. It is also found at Dufton, in Cumberland, and at Halwell Cavern, Broomfield, near Taunton in Somersetshire.

Brit. Mus., Case 42.

M.P.G. Horse-shoe Case, Nos. 429a to 432.

FLUATE OF CERIUM. See FLUOCERITE.

FLUATE OF LIME, *Phillips.* See FLUOR.

FLUATE OF YTTRIA AND CERIUM, *Berzelius.* See YTTRO-CERITE.

FLUCKRINE, *Beudant.* See FLUOCERITE.

FLUELLITE, *Levy, Wollaston.* Rhombic: primary form a right rhombic prism, whose base is to its height in the proportion of 1 to 3. Occurs in small acute rhombic octa-

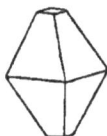

Fig. 189.

hedrons, with the solid angles generally replaced. White, and transparent or translucent, with a vitreous lustre. H. 3.

Localities. On a grey quartz-rock, associated with acicular Wavellite and Uranite, at Stenna Gwyn, near St. Austell in Cornwall.

This is a very scarce mineral. It was discovered by Levy, but examined and named by Wollaston, according to whom it is composed of fluorine and aluminium.

Brit. Mus., Case 58.

FLUOCERINE, *Hausmann.* Generally found massive, but is supposed to show traces of a rhombic dodecahedron. Colour a fine yellow, with a tinge of red; brownish-yellow when impure. Lustre vitreous or resinous. Streak yellow, brownish. Subtranslucent to opaque. H. 4·5 to 5.

Comp. $Ce^2 F^3 + 3\ddot{C}e$, $\dot{H}$.=cerium 17·56, fluorine 10·88, peroxide of cerium 66·41, water 5·15=100·00.

Locality. Finbo in Sweden.

FLUOCERITE, *Haidinger.* Hexagonal. Occurs in hexagonal prisms and plates: also massive. Colour dark tile-red, or nearly yellow, with a feeble lustre. Subtranslucent to opaque. Streak white or slightly yellowish. H. 4 to 5. S.G. 4·7.

Comp. Peroxide of cerium 82·64, yttria 1·12, hydrofluoric acid 16·24 = 100·00. (Berzelius.)

BB alone, infusible; but darkens. Fuses slowly but completely in borax and salt of phosphorus, affording a globule which is blood-red in the exterior flame, but becomes colourless on cooling.

Localities. Finbo and Broddbo, near Fahlun, in Sweden; imbedded in Quartz and Albite.

FLUOCERIUM BASISCHES. See FLUOCERINE.

FLUOCERIUM NEUTRALES. See FLUOCERITE.

FLUOCHLORE, *Hermann.* See PYROCHLORE.

FLUOPHOSPHATE OF MAGNESIA, *Thomson.* See WAGNERITE.

FLUOR, *Dana;* FLUORID OF CALCIUM; FLUORINE, *Beudant;* FLUOR SPAR; FLUORID OF CALCIUM; FLUSS, *Haidinger;* *Hausmann, Werner;* FLUSSAURER-KALK; FLUSS SPATH, *Werner, Naumann.* Cubical: primary form the regular octahedron. Occurs crystallized in cubes, octahedrons, rhombic dodecahedrons and their modifications; also nodular, compact and earthy. Colour white, grey, and various tints of blue,

Fig. 190.

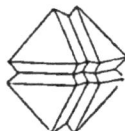

Fig. 191.

Fig. 192.

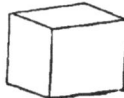

Fig. 193.

green, yellow, purple, and red. Perfectly limpid and transparent to subtranslucent. Lustre vitreous; sometimes splendent;

usually glimmering in massive varieties. Streak white. Brittle; fracture more or less perfectly foliated. Easily cleaved into the tetrahedron, acute rhombohedron, and octahedron. H. 4. S.G. 3·14 to 3·2. Mean of 60 experiments by Kengott, 3·183.

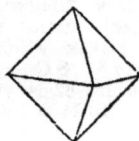

Fig. 194.

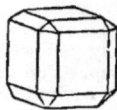

Fig. 195.

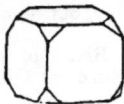

Fig. 196.

Fig. 197.

Comp. Fluoride of calcium or CaF= calcium 51·3, fluorine 48·7=100.

When pounded and placed on ignited coal it exhibits a phosphorescent light, which ceases at a high temperature, but may be partially restored by an electric discharge. Fragments rubbed against each other in the dark become luminous.

BB decrepitates and ultimately melts without addition to an opaque greyish-white enamel.

Localities.—English. Cornwall at several mines; at Huel Cupid and North Grambler, near Redruth; Huel Mary Ann, Menhenniot, in fine blue beveled cubes; near St. Agnes in translucent crystals of a rich lilac colour, *figs.* 190 and 197. Other Cornish forms are represented in *figs.* 194 and 195. Cumberland: at Cleator Moor, in fine, yellow, transparent crystals, the prevailing colours of which are lilac and green: at Alston in the cube and of the forms shown in *figs.* 196 and 192. A variety occurs at this locality which appears green by transmitted light and blue by reflected light. Crystals possessing a similar peculiarity also occur at Weardale, in Durham, but the colours exhibited by the latter are grey by transmitted and purple by reflected light. According to Professor Stokes this effect, termed by him *Fluorescence,* is due to a peculiar refracting power of the first surface on which the light falls. Cromford near Matlock Baths, Derbyshire. In Derbyshire compact and granular varieties of Fluor are abundant: the finest specimens for ornamental purposes come from Tray Cliff, and

are called *Blue John.* Beeralston in Devonshire, in cubic and octahedral forms, 193, 195, 197, 194, and 191; also fibrous and compact. *—N. Welsh.* Moel-y-Cria, and Halkin Mountain, near Holywell.*—Scotch.* Balater House, Glenmuick, Aberdeenshire. Dumbarton; Gourock near Greenock in Renfrewshire. — *Irish.* Several mines in Clare county. The Glendalough lead-mines, both crystallized and massive, of a pale violet-blue colour. — *Foreign.* Mont Blanc and St. Gotthard; on the latter in beautiful rose-coloured octahedrons in Dolomite. Saxony. The Bannat. Munsterthal in Baden, in hexakisocta-hedrons. Zinnwald in Bohemia, also at Schlackenwald in green octahedrons and violet-blue rhombic dodecahedrons — the latter with white stripes in the position of the longer diagonal. The Lombardian Alps at Monte Presolana, in the Val di Scalve, N.W. of Lago Palzone, in a vein 21 inches wide imbedded in the New Red Sandstone of Val Torgola, a branch of Val Trompia.

Besides the use of Blue John in the manufacture of ornamental articles, as tazzas, vases, obelisks, &c., Fluor-spar is employed for etching on glass. This is effected by exposing a plate of glass coated with wax (on which the required design has been previously drawn with an etching point, as in the ordinary process) to the action of the gaseous hydrofluoric acid obtained by treating Fluor-spar with sulphuric acid. Those parts of the plate which are covered with wax will remain unaffected, but wherever the wax has been removed the glass will be corroded, and in this manner drawings on glass may be produced without much difficulty.

Fluor-spar is also used in considerable quantities as a flux for metallic ores: hence its name from the Latin *fluo,* to flow, or probably the name may have originated in a belief that it was formed *ex fluido,* or out of water.

Ozone has lately been discovered by Prof. Schrötter, in the darkish blue variety of Fluor, which is found at Wulsendorf. The quantity was found to amount to 0·02 per cent.

Brit. Mus., Case 58.

M. P. G. Vase on pedestal 35, in Hall, from Derbyshire. Horse-shoe Case, Nos. 331 to 364. Wall-cases 27 and 30.

FLUSS-SAURES CERIUM, *German.* See FLUOCERITE.

FOAMING EARTH, *Jameson.* See APIIRITE.

FŒTID QUARTZ, *Bakewell.* A kind of Quartz yielding a peculiar odour of sulphuretted hydrogen when struck with a hammer on the angles or edges. This property is destroyed by exposure to a red heat. In all other respects this variety resembles common Quartz. It is found near Nantes in France, and in various parts of the United States.

FOLIATED ARSENIATE OF COPPER. *Cleaveland.* See CHALCOPHYLLITE.

FOLIATED BLACK MANGANESE ORE, *Jameson.* See HAUSMANNITE.

FOLIATED TELLURIUM, *Allan.* See NAGYAGITE.

FOLIATED ZEOLITE, *Jameson, Werner.* See HEULANDITE.

FOLIATED ZEOLITE, *Jameson.* See FOLIATED STILBITE.

FONTAINEBLEAU LIMESTONE. Aggregations of secondary rhombohedrons of Calcite, which contain a large amount of sand, mechanically mixed with them. The similar variety of Calcite which occurs in great quantities in the sands on the African coast, between Sandanha Bay and Ichaboe Island contain as much as 15 or 20 per cent. of sand.

FORSTERITE, *Levy.* A variety of Chrysolite, occurring in small, brilliant, white or colourless, translucent crystals at Vesuvius, where it is associated with Pleonaste and olive-green Pyroxene. H. about 7.

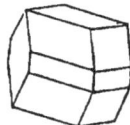

Fig. 198.

FOSSIL COPAL, *Phillips.* See COPALINE.

FOSSIL LIGHTNING. See FULGURITE.

FOSSIL OIL, *Jameson.* See NAPHTHA and PETROLEUM.

FOWLERITE. The variety of Rhodonite which occurs in large crystals, with Franklinite, at the Franklin Furnace, at Stirling, in New Jersey. It is often black externally from alteration, the action of the air converting the protoxide of manganese into peroxide.

Analysis, by *W. Camac :*

Silica	42·20
Protoxide of manganese	25·37
Protoxide of iron . .	11·00
Oxide of zinc . .	4·15
Lime	9·66
Magnesia . . .	5·27
Felspar . . .	3·56
	101·20

Name. After Mr. S. Fowler.

Brit. Mus., Case 26.

FRANCOLITE, *Henry.* A variety of Apatite, occurring in small compound crystalline masses. At Fowey Consols in Cornwall it is met with in minute, white, and transparent crystals, and in thin plates, associated with Quartz and Chalcopyrite: also, in thin hollow cubes above an inch square, which, when discovered, are half filled with a transparent fluid. The colours of the specimens from Huel Franco, near Tavistock, were greyish-green to brown.

Comp. $3\dot{C}a \ddot{P} + Ca \ddot{F}e = $ lime 49·48, phosphoric acid 41·34, calcium 3·96, fluorine 1·80, chlorine 3·42 = 100.

Mean of two analyses by *Henry :*

Phosphoric acid . . .	41·57
Lime	53·09
Protoxide of iron and protoxide of manganese	3·09
Fluorine and loss . .	2·25
Chlorine . . .	trace
	100

Name. After that of the locality where it was first discovered, Huel Franco.

M. P. G. Horse-shoe Case, No. 313.

FRANKENBURG CORN-EARS, *Nicol.* See CUIVRE SPICIFORME.

FRANKLINITE. Cubical. Occurs in grains or in granular masses, composed of imperfect crystals, occasionally exhibiting the planes of the octahedron. The structure is lamellar, parallel to the face of the regular octahedron. Colour iron–black, with a metallic lustre. Opaque. Brittle. Fracture conchoidal. Acts slightly on the magnet. H. 6 to 6·5. S.G. 5. to 5·3.

Fig. 199.

Comp. $(\dot{F}e, \dot{Z}n)^3 (\ddot{F}e, \ddot{M}n) = $ iron 45·16, manganese 9·38, zinc 20·30, oxygen 25·16, = 100.

Analysis (mean of three), by *Rammelsberg :*

Peroxide of iron . .	64·51
Peroxide of manganese	13·51
Oxide of zinc . .	25·30
	103·52

BB infusible: with borax forms a green glass, which, when completely saturated, becomes red, and on cooling assumes a greenish-brown colour, and remains transparent.

Soluble, without effervescence, in heated muriatic acid.

Localities. Extensive veins of Franklinite Ore are found in Sussex county, New Jersey, about seventy miles from New York. It is also said to occur, in amorphous masses, accompanying ores of zinc, at the mines of Altenberg, near Aix-la-Chapelle, and in the mines of Breitbek and Victoria, in Nassau.

Franklinite strongly resembles Oxidulated Iron, but may be distinguished from it by yielding a dark reddish-brown streak, that of the latter mineral being black. Chemically Franklinite differs from it by containing the oxides of zinc and manganese. The per centage of zinc is very variable, ranging from 21 per cent., in the crystals, to as much as 26 per cent. in the massive ore. The per centage of iron varies from 55 to 65, that of manganese from 12 to 16.

The oxides of zinc and manganese appear to exercise a very favourable influence upon the iron manufactured from this ore. Its tenacity is found to be very great, and it is stated to resist the attacks of oxygen (rusting) in a remarkable degree. It is also readily converted into steel, suited for the finest cutlery and razors, a result which is probably facilitated by the presence of manganese. In fact, the metal made from this ore is a coarse steel, and differs very greatly from ordinary pig-iron. It is also said that Franklinite smelted with Anthracite or Coal affords as good iron as can be made with charcoal, which is supposed to be caused by the zinc, when volatilized, carrying off with it any sulphur or phosphorus that the coal may contain. Franklinite pig-iron is represented as capable of bearing a tensile strain of 40,000 lbs. per square inch, or to be nearly double the average strength of the iron used by the British Government for casting heavy guns.

Name. After the celebrated Benjamin Franklin.

Brit. Mus., Case 26.

FRAUENEIS, *Werner.* See SELENITE.

FREIBERGITE. Argentiferous Tetrahedrite; the Polytelite of Glocker.

Analysis, from Freiberg, by *Rose* :

Sulphur	.	.	. 21·17
Antimony	.	.	. 24·63
Copper	.	.	. 14·81
Iron	.	.	. 5·98
Zinc	.	.	. 0·99
Silver	.	.	. 31·29

98·87

FREIESLEBENITE, *Haidinger.* Oblique. Occurs in small deeply striated crystals, which are irregularly associated, but more often separate. Colour and streak pale steel-grey, inclining to silver-white; also blackish lead-grey. Lustre metallic, externally shining and splendent. Yields readily to the knife, and is easily susceptible of mechanical division parallel to the planes of a right rhombic prism. Extremely brittle. Fracture conchoidal, uneven. H. 2 to 2·5. S.G. 6 to 6·4.

Comp. Sulphantimonide of silver and lead, or $(Pb, Ag) S + Sb^2 S^3$.

Analysis by *Wöhler* :

Sulphur	.	.	. 18·77
Antimony	.	.	. 27·72
Lead	.	.	. 30·00
Silver	.	.	. 22·18
Iron	.	.	. 0·11
Copper	.	.	. 1·62

100·00

BB emits copious white vapours, and a slight sulphurous odour; deposits oxides of antimony and lead round the assay, and finally a small white globule of silver remains.

Localities. The Himmelsfürst Mine, at Freiberg, in Saxony. Kapnik, in Transylvania. Ratieborzitz. Abundant at Hiendelaencina in Spain.

M. P. G. Principal Floor, Wall-case 14 (British).

Name. After Freiesleben.

FRENCH CHALK. A white or greyish kind of Steatite, used for taking grease out of silk, and also for slate-pencils, which are made in a similar manner to ordinary lead-pencils. It is also used, in a state of powder, to make new gloves and boots slip on easily

M. P. G. Horse-shoe Case, Nos. 1055, 1056.

FRIABLE LITHOMARGE. Usually massive, also as a crust, and composed of fine shaly particles. Colour snow-white or yellowish-white. Lustre glimmering. Adheres to the tongue and feels greasy.

Locality. Saxony, in tin-veins.

FRUGARDIT or FRUGARDITE. A variety of Idocrase, from Frugard, in Finland.

Analysis, by *Nordenskiöld* :

Silica	.	.	. 38·53
Alumina	.	.	. 17·40
Protoxide of iron	.	.	. 3·90
Lime	.	.	. 27·70
Magnesia	.	.	. 10·60
Protoxide of manganese		.	0·33

98·46

Brit. Mus., Case 35.

FUCHSITE. A variety of Mica, in which a portion of the alumina is replaced by sesquioxide of chromium. It is found in compact, scaly, and likewise regular slaty masses, frequently accompanied by pure Quartz. Colour emerald-green, passing into dull yellow. Hardness between Gypsum and Rock Salt. S.G. 2·86.

Comp. 38(3 K̈, S̈i) + 2(3 N̈a, S̈i) + 360(Äl,

S̈i) + 24(Ör, 3 S̈i) + 18(M̈g, S̈i) + 12(F̈e, 3 S̈i)

+ 9 Ċa F̈ (Schaffhäutl).

Analysis, by *Schaffäutl:*

Silica .	.	.	.	. 47·95
Alumina	.	.	.	. 34·45
Peroxide of iron	.	.	. 1·80
Oxide of chromium	.	. 3·95
Lime .	.	.	.	. 0·42
Potash .	.	.	.	. 10·75
Soda .	.	.	.	. 0·37
Magnesia	.	.	.	. 0·71
Fluoric acid .	.	.	. 0·35

100·75

BB with soda, swells up and fuses to a yellowish-brown globular slag, which, after continued exposure to the flame, acquires a dull green colour, and is slightly affected by the magnet.

Dissolves slowly in borax, forming a clear globule, which is yellow while hot (from the presence of peroxide of iron), but a fine yellowish-green when cold, owing to the presence of chromium.

Locality. Schwarzenstein, in the Tyrol.

Name. After Professor Fuchs, of Gottingen.

Brit. Mus., Case 32.

FULGURITES. (From *fulgur, lightning.*) Vitrified tubes, produced by the action of lightning on sand. They are found sometimes in the sand and sand-hills on the coasts of Cumberland and Lancashire and elsewhere.

Brit. Mus., Case 21.

M. P. G. Principal Floor, Wall-case 42.

FULLER'S EARTH, *Kirwan.* Massive. Colour usually greenish-brown, or greenish-grey, sometimes blue. It is opaque, soft, dull, with a greasy feel and an earthy fracture. Yields to the nail, and affords a shining streak. Scarcely adheres to the tongue. Becomes translucent when placed in water, and falls into a pulpy impalpable powder, without forming a paste with it. S.G. 1·7 to 2·4.

Comp. Earthy hydrous silicate of alumina, or Äl S̈i + Ḧ; consisting, when pure, of silica 45, alumina 20, water 25 = 100·00.

Analysis, from Reigate, by *Klaproth:*

Silica .	.	.	.	. 53·00
Alumina	.	.	.	. 10·00
Peroxide of iron	.	.	. 9·75
Magnesia	.	.	.	. 1·25
Lime .	.	.	.	. 0·50
Potash .	.	.	.	. trace
Muriate of soda	.	.	. 0·10
Water .	.	.	.	. 24·00

98·60

BB fuses to a porous slag, and ultimately forms a white blebby glass.

Localities. — English. Fuller's earth is found in several places in the United Kingdom; at Nutfield, near Reigate, and at Bletchingly, in Surrey, in Lower Greensand; Debtling, near Maidstone, in Kent; Tillington and Petworth, in Sussex; Apsley and Wavendon, near Woburn, in Bedfordshire; Catsgrove, near Reading, in Berkshire; the Downs, south of Bath, in Somersetshire, at the base of the Great Oolite.—*Scotch.* Quarry Wood, in Morayshire; Bridgehouse, in Peebles-shire. — *Foreign.* It is also found at Rosswein, in Upper Saxony; at Rittenau, in Alsace; Osmundburg, in Sweden; Vahls, near Aix-la-Chapelle; Zwikowetz, in Bohemia, &c. &c.

This substance was formerly used in large quantities by cloth manufacturers for cleansing woollen cloth, on account of its great capacity for absorbing oil and grease. The operation is called "fulling," hence the name, *Fuller's Earth,* was given to the substance employed. At the present day, however, the consumption of Fuller's Earth has very much fallen off, in consequence of the adoption of other substances for effecting the object.

Brit. Mus., Case 26.

FULLONITE. See ONEGITE.

FUNKITE. A variety of green Coccolite, found in lamellar limestone at Bodksater, in Gothland. It occurs in rounded grains of a clear olive-green colour, with a glassy lustre. H. scratches glass.

BB fuses with difficulty.

FUSCITE. Crystallized Pyrargillite, from Arendal, in Norway.

FUSIBLE QUARTZ, *Jameson.* See OBSIDIAN.

L

G.

GABRONITE, *Beudant, Dufrénoy.* A variety of Scapolite, found only at Arendal, in amorphous masses, with a compact or slightly lamellar texture. Colour stone-yellow. Lustre greasy. S.G. 2·74.

Name. From its resemblance in colour to the rock called *Gabbro.*

GADOLINITE, *Jameson, Phillips, Haüy, Mohs.* Oblique: when crystallized, usually in imperfect, oblique rhombic prisms, the primary form. Colour iron-black; dull externally, internally black and shining. Lustre vitreous, inclining to resinous. Opaque or feebly translucent at the edges, when it appears blackish-green. Streak greyish-green. Brittle. Fracture conchoidal. No distinct cleavage. H. 6·5 to 7. S.G. 4·097 to 4·226.

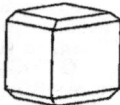

, Fig. 200.

Comp. $\dot{Y}^3 \ddot{S}i$, but in all varieties of Gadolinite, a portion of the yttria is replaced by several other bases.

Analysis, from Ytterby, by *Berlin :*

Silica .	. . .	24·85
Glucina	. . .	4·80
Yttria .	. . .	51·46
Oxide of cerium, with oxide of lanthanum	. .	5·24
Protoxide of iron .	. .	13·01
Lime .	. . .	0·50
Magnesia and protoxide of manganese	. .	1·11
		100·97

BB the Karafvet variety decrepitates and fuses, when strongly heated, to an opaque pearl-grey or reddish glass; that from Ytterby exhibits a vivid glow, and loses its colour, but does not fuse. With borax all the varieties melt readily to a globule, more or less tinged with iron.

Gelatinises in muriatic acid.

Localities.—British. In one single instance only, in the county of Galway, in trap.— *Foreign.* It occurs principally in Sweden, at the quarries of Karafvet and Finbo, near Fahlun, where, as well as at Ytterby, near Stockholm, it is found indistinctly crystallized,

and in amorphous masses, which are often encircled with a yellow crust, and are imbedded in coarse-grained granite. It has also been been met with at Disko, in Greenland; in granite, in Ceylon; at Finbo and Broddbo; and at Krageröe and Hitteröe, in the southern part of Norway.

Name. After the Russian chemist, Gadolin, by whom it was first noticed in 1794. He discovered in it the new earth Yttria.

Brit. Mus., Case 38.

GAGATES, *Dioscorides.* The name by which Jet was known to the ancients. It was so called from Gagis, a town in Lycia, where it was said to have been originally found.

GAHNITE, *Beudant, Hausmann.* A name for Automalite, after the discoverer Gahn. See AUTOMALITE.

GALACTITE, *Haidinger.* Occurs radiating and compact at the Campsie Hills, Stirlingshire, and in long acicular crystals, with Prehnite, at Bishoptown, Renfrewshire. Recent analyses, by Heddle and Kenngott, have proved it to be Natrolite.

Name. From γάλα, γάλακτος, *milk,* because when immersed or triturated in water, it gives the colour of milk.

GALAPECTITE, *Dufrénoy.* A variety of Halloysite occurring in greenish-white masses which are opaline in places, and analogous in that respect to certain kinds of opaline Quartz. Slightly hard. May be cut with a knife. Fracture conchoidal.

GALENA, *Kirwan, Brooke & Miller, Phillips, Greg & Lettsom ;* GALÈNE, *Beudant ;* GALENIT, *v. Kobell ;* LA GALÈNE COMMUNE, *Brochant.* Cubical. Occurs crystallized in the cube, octahedron, and in

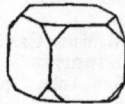

Fig. 201.   Fig. 202.

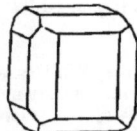
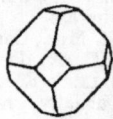

Fig. 203.   Fig. 204.

numerous combinations of these with planes of other figures : also in amorphous masses with a lamellar structure; frequently granular; sometimes almost compact, yielding a flat-conchoidal fracture, and presenting little lustre. Colour lead-grey, which in some varieties inclines to blackish lead-grey. On the surface sometimes shows an iridescent tarnish. Lustre metallic. Opaque. Structure lamellar. Cleavage parallel with the planes of the cube, highly perfect and easily obtained. Streak rather more shining than the surface of fracture. Sectile. Easily pulverised, and externally easily frangible. H. 2·5 to 2·75. S.G. 7·25 to 7·7.

Comp. Protosulphide of lead, or Pb S = lead 86·6, sulphur 13·4 = 100.

Silver and other metals are frequently present, as will be perceived by the following *analysis* of a specimen from Bottino, by C. Bechi:

Sulphur	12·840
Lead	80·700
Antimony	3·307
Iron	1·377
Copper	0·440
Zinc	0·024
Silver	0·325
	99·013

BB decrepitates, then melts and emits a sulphurous odour, and, when the sulphur has been driven off, affords a globule of pure lead, from which a grain of silver may frequently be obtained by cupellation. The proportion of silver varies considerably, and those varieties, the fractured surfaces of which exhibit a granular structure, often contain more silver than the more compact lamellar varieties. Formerly it was not considered profitable, in the north of England, to separate the silver from the lead, unless the former amounted to 6 ounces in the ton, and in Wales unless it amounted to 12 ounces to the ton. By the improved process, introduced by Mr. Pattinson, it is now, however, found profitable to extract the silver when the lead does not contain more than 3 ounces to the ton, at the same time that the cost of refining is reduced from 60s. to 30s. per ton, and the lead, after the separation of the silver, is rendered much more valuable, being less hard and brittle than before. Galena occurs in irregular deposits and in veins in igneous and sedimentary rocks.

Localities.—English. The largest crystals of Galena ever met with have been found at the Laxey and Foxdale Mines in the Isle of Man, some of which measure as much as 10 inches across. *Fig.* 202 represents the prevailing form, but combinations of the cube, octahedron, and dodecahedron also occur. Octahedral crystals, of very large dimensions, have also been found at Dufton

and Alston, in Cumberland, and large cubic crystals at Brownly Hill, in the same county; Cornwall and Devonshire, in veins traversing clay-slate (Killas), Cumberland, Derbyshire, Durham, Northumberland, Yorkshire and Flintshire, in limestone.—*Scotch.* Lead-hills, in Lanarkshire; Wanlock Head; in Dumfriesshire; and Monaltrie, in Aberdeenshire, in granite; Strontian, in Argyleshire, in gneiss; Isla, in limestone; Coll, in gneiss. —*Foreign.* Freyberg, in Saxony. Spain, in the granite hills of Linares; also in Catalonia, Grenada, and elsewhere. Rosmininhal, in Portuguese Estremadura. Sala, in Sweden. Clausthal, Neudorf, and Pfaffenberg, in the Harz. Przibram, Miess and Joachimsthal, in Bohemia. Schemnitz in Hungary. Bleiberg, in Carinthia. The Daouria mountains of Siberia. Algeria. Cape of Good Hope. Australia. In the United States extensive deposits of this ore exist in Missouri, Illinois, Iowa, and Wisconsin. The lead region of Wisconsin is stated by D. D. Owen to extend 87 miles from east to west, and 54 miles from north to south. Within this area there is scarcely a square mile in which traces of lead may not be found. Although the diggings are seldom more than 25 or 30 feet deep, as much as 1835 tons of ore have been raised from a single spot not more than 5 yards square.

Galena is the most abundant ore of lead, and that from which the greatest amount of the metal is obtained. In Hunt's Mineral Statistics for 1859, a list of all the lead mines in the United Kingdom will be found, together with the quantities of ore raised from each, and lead produced. The total produce of the United Kingdom during the year 1859 appears to be 91,735 tons of ore, the value of which was £1,268,677.

" Galena is distinguished from Plumbago by its weight, and by its not affording distinct traces on paper; from Sulphuret of Molybdena also by its structure, which is never foliated; and from the brilliant metallic varieties of Blende, by the surfaces of its crystals resuming their lustre instantly when breathed upon, while those of Blende remain dull for some time."—(*Allan.*) See also BLUE LEAD and SPECULAR GALENA.

Name. From γαλήνη, *tranquillity*, from its supposed effects in mitigating the violence of disease.

Brit. Mus., Case 8.

M. P. G. From the Grassington Mines, in the Hall. Principal Floor, Case 15 (Isle of Man and Ireland); Wall-cases 14, 25

L 2

to 33, and 43 to 45 (British); 41 (Newfound-and); 21 (Foreign).

GALENA DE BISMUTH, *Brochant.* See BISMUTHINE.

GALLICINITE ; GALLITZENSTEIN. Rutile. See GALLIZINITE.

GALLITZINITE, *Leymerie* ; GALLIZENSTEIN; GALLIZINITE, *Beudant.* See GOSLARITE, or SULPHATE OF ZINC. Named after Prince Gallitzin.

GALLIZINITE. A variety of Nigrine from Spessart, near Aschaffenburg in Franconia.

Analysis, by *Klaproth :*

Oxide of titanium	.	.	.	22
Oxide of iron	.	.	.	78
				100

GALMEI, *Hausmann.* See CALAMINE.

GALMEI, *Naumann.* See SMITHSONITE.

GALMEY, *Werner.* Refers both to Calamine and Smithsonite, or to the Carbonate and the siliceous oxide of Zinc.

GANOMATITE ; GÄNSE-KÖTHIG-ERZ. From γάνος, *brightness.* See CHENOCOPROLITE.

GARBENSTILBIT. See STILBITE.

GARNET. Cubical. Occurs in rhombic dodecahedrons and icositetrahedrons; also massive, granular, and lamellar. Cleavage dodecahedral ; sometimes distinct. Lustre vitreous, inclining to resinous. Colour black, red, brown, yellow, green, white. Transparent to opaque. Streak white-grey. Fracture subconchoidal, uneven. H. 6·5 to 7·5. S.G. 3·1 to 4·3.

Comp. A silicate of different bases, repre-

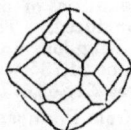 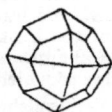 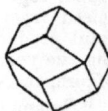

Fig. 205.   Fig. 206.   Fig. 207.

sented by the formula $\dot{R}^3 \ddot{\ddot{S}}i + \ddot{\ddot{\ddddot{H}}} \ddot{\ddot{S}}i = (\dot{R}^3 + \ddot{\ddddot{H}}) \ddot{\ddot{S}}i$, where $\dot{R}$ may be lime, magnesia, oxide of iron, and $\ddot{\ddddot{H}}$ is alumina.

Garnet has been divided into six sub-species, viz. :—

I. Alumina-lime Garnet, consisting of silicates of alumina and lime.

II. Alumina-magnesia Garnet, consisting of silicates of alumina and magnesia.

III. Alumina-iron Garnet, consisting of silicates of alumina and iron.

IV. Alumina-manganese Garnet, consisting of silicates of alumina and manganese.

V. Iron-lime Garnet, consisting of silicates of iron and lime.

VI. Lime-chrome Garnet, containing lime and oxide of Chromium.

I. *Lime-garnet* or *Grossular,* consists of

$\dot{C}a^3 \ddot{\ddot{S}}i + \ddddot{A}l \ddot{\ddot{S}}i = (\dot{C}a^3 + \ddddot{A}l) \ddot{\ddot{S}}i =$ silica 40·1, alumina 22·7, lime 37·2 = 100·0.

Colour pale greenish, clear red, and reddish orange; also cinnamon colour. H. 6·5 to 7. S.G. 3·43 to 3·73.

BB fuses to a slightly greenish glass or enamel.

Soluble, when powdered, in concentrated muriatic acid.

This section comprises Cinnamon-stone or Essonite, Grossular or Wiluite, Romanzovite, Topazolite, and Succinite.

II. *Magnesia-garnet.*

Comp. $(\dot{M}g \; \ddot{F}e^3) \ddot{\ddot{S}}i + \ddddot{A}l \ddot{\ddot{S}}i = (\dot{M}g \ddot{F}e^3 + \ddddot{A}l) \ddot{\ddot{S}}i.$

Colour deep coal-black. Lustre slightly resinous. H. 6·5 to 7. S.G. 3·157.

BB easily fusible, forming, with intumescence a dark greyish-green globule, which is non-magnetic.

III. *Iron-garnet.*

Comp. $\ddot{F}e^3 \ddot{\ddot{S}}i + \ddddot{A}l \; \ddot{\ddot{S}}i = (\ddot{F}e^3 + \ddddot{A}l) \; \ddot{\ddot{S}}i =$ silica 36·3, alumina 20·5, protoxide of iron 43·2 = 100.

S.G. 3·7 to 4·21.

BB fuses rather easily, with an iron reaction.

This section comprises Allochroite, Almandine or Precious Garnet, and Common Garnet.

IV. *Manganese-garnet* or *Spessartine.*

Comp. $(\dot{M}n^3 + \ddddot{A}l) \ddot{\ddot{S}}i.$

Colour brownish-red. H. 7 to 7·5. S.G. 3·7 to 4·2.

BB gives a manganese reaction.

See SPESSARTINE.

V. *Iron-lime Garnet.*

Comp. $\dot{C}a^3 \ddot{\ddot{S}}i + \ddot{F}e \ddot{\ddot{S}}i = (\dot{C}a^3 + \ddot{F}e) \ddot{\ddot{S}}i.$

Colour dark red, brownish-black, black. Lustre dull or shining, sometimes resinous (Colophonite). H. 7. S.G. 3·6 to 4·0.

This section includes Aplome (S.G. 3·45 to 3·85), Colophonite (S.G. 3·896), Melanite, and Pyreneite.

VI. *Lime-chrome Garnet* or *Ouvarovite.*

Colour emerald-green.

Comp. $\dot{C}a^3 \; \ddot{\ddot{S}}i + (\ddot{C}r, \; \ddddot{A}l) \; \ddot{\ddot{S}}i = (\dot{C}a^3 + \ddot{C}r$

Äl) S̈i, part of the lime being replaced by Fe, M̈g, and part of the Ör by Äl.

H. 7·5 to 8·0.   S.G. 3·4184.

BB infusible alone: with borax yields a fine chrome-green glass.

Pyrope, also, comes under this head, according to Rammelsberg.

BB many of the Garnets are easily fusible.

Localities. Cornwall, in perfect detached dodecahedrons in the Crown's Rock (greenstone), at Botallack, in St. Just; and near Camborne, *fig.* 206. On Dartmoor, in Devonshire. Cumberland at Saddleback, and near Keswick. Also in Ireland, Scotland, and various other countries, generally in granite, dolomite, or mica-slate.

The Garnet varies greatly in transparency, fracture, and colour, but when the colours are rich, and the stone is free from flaws, it constitutes a valuable gem, which may be distinguished by the following properties.

The colour should be blood- or cherry-red, on the one hand, often mixed more or less with blue, so as to present various shades of crimson, purple, and reddish violet; and, on the other hand, with yellow, so as to form orange-red and hyacinth-brown.

In size the stones vary from the smallest pieces that can be worked to the size of a nut. When above that size, they are scarcely ever free from flaws, or sufficiently transparent for the purposes of the Jeweller.

The Garnets of commerce are procured from Bohemia, Ceylon, Pegu, and Brazil. By Jewellers they are classed as Syrian, Bohemian, or Cingalese, rather from their relative value and fineness than with any reference to the country from which they are supposed to have been brought.

The most esteemed kinds are called Syrian Garnets, not because they come from Syria, but after Syrian, the capital of Pegu, and formerly the chief mart for the finest Garnets. The colour of the Syrian Garnet is violet-purple, in some rare instances rivalling that of the finest Oriental Amethyst, from which it may be distinguished, however, by acquiring an orange tint by candle-light. The Syrian Garnet may be also distinguished from all the other varieties of Garnet in preserving its colour (even when of considerable thickness, and unassisted by foil), unmixed with the black tint which usually obscures this gem. The Bohemian Garnet is generally of a dull poppy-red

colour, with a very perceptible hyacinth-orange tint, when held between the eye and the light. When the colour is a full crimson, it is called Pyrope or Fire-Garnet, a stone of considerable value, when perfect, and of large size.

The best manner of cutting Pyrope is *en cabochon*, with one or two rows of small facets round the girdle of the stone. The colour appears more or less black when the stone is cut in steps, but when cut *en cabochon* the point on which the light falls displays a brilliant fire-red.

Garnet is easily worked, and, when facet-cut, is nearly always (on account of the depth of its colour) formed into thin tables, which are sometimes concave or hollowed out on the under side. Cut stones of this latter description, when skilfully set with bright silver foil, have often been sold for rubies.

The Garnet, after having long been out of fashion, appears to be coming into favour again. About a century and a half ago, a fine set of Garnets was considered a magnificent ornament for ladies of the highest rank.

The Garnet may be distinguished from the Corundum or Spinel by its duller colour.

Coarse Garnets, though of inferior hardness to emery, are sometimes used as a substitute for it. When reduced to powder, they afford a material superior to sand for giving a smooth surface to metal and stone-work, preparatory to polishing, and for cutting gems.

The Carbunculus Garamanticus, or Garamantine Carbuncle of the ancients (the ἄνθραξ, of Theophrastus) was the true Garnet of the moderns.

Name. The word Garnet is derived from the Low Latin name Garanatus, which was given to the mineral from its red colour, resembling that of the seed of the pomegranate.

Brit. Mus., Case 36.

M. P. G. Horse-shoe Case, Nos. 880 to 904. Upper Gallery, Wall-case 1, No. 93.

GARNSDORFFITE. A name for Pissophane, from its occurrence at Garnsdorff, near Saalfeld.

GAY - LUSSITE, *Boussingault.* Oblique: primary form an oblique rhombic prism. Occurs in detached prisms, and aggregated crystals disseminated in clay. The less perfect of these bear a strong resemblance to Selenite; but the more perfect and smooth have rather the aspect of Calcareous Spar,

L 3

being yellowish-white and translucent and doubly refractive in a high degree. Lustre of fractured surfaces vitreous. Streak grey-ish. Extremely brittle. Fracture conchoidal. H. 2 to 3. S.G. 1·92 to 1·99.

Comp. Hydrated carbonate of lime and

soda, or $\ddot{N}a \; \ddot{C} + \dot{C}a \; \ddot{C} + 5 \; \dot{H}$ = carbonate of soda 35·9, carbonate of lime 33·8, water 30·3 = 100.

Analysis, by *J. B. Boussingault*:

Carbonate of soda	.	34·5
Carbonate of lime	.	33·6
Water . . .	.	30·4
Clay . . .	.	1·5
		100·0

Decrepitates slightly when heated, and becomes opaque from loss of water.

BB fuses rapidly to an opaque globule, (which when once formed, is no longer fusible, on account of the escape of carbonic acid,) and has a strong alkaline taste.

Readily soluble in nitric acid with effervescence. Soluble in water, to a trifling extent, when reduced to powder; yielding a solution which reddens turmeric paper, and is precipitated by oxalic acid.

Localities. This mineral is found abundantly at Lagunilla, near Merida, in Maracaibo, in crystals disseminated in a bed of clay, covering Trona at the bottom of a small lake. The natives call the crystals of Gay-Lussite *clavos* or *nails*, in allusion to their elongated forms; and in contradistinction to the Trona, which they term *urao*. It is also met with at Sangerhausen in Thuringia.

Name. The name was conferred upon it by Boussingault, in honour of the French chemist Gay-Lussac.

Brit. Mus. Case 46.

GEDIEGEN ARSENIK. See NATIVE ARSENIC.

GEDIEGEN ANTIMON. See NATIVE ANTIMONY.

GEDIEGEN BLEI. See NATIVE LEAD.

GEDIEGEN EISEN. See NATIVE IRON.

GEDIEGEN GOLD. See NATIVE GOLD.

GEDIEGEN KUPFER. See NATIVE COPPER.

GEDIEGEN PLATIN. See NATIVE PLATINUM.

GEDIEGEN QUECKSILBER. See NATIVE QUICKSILVER.

GEDIEGEN SPIESSGLANZ. See NATIVE ANTIMONY.

GEDIEGEN SILBER. See NATIVE SILVER.

GEDIEGEN SILVAN, *Werner.* See NATIVE TELLURIUM.

GEDIEGEN TELLUR, *Hausmann.* See NATIVE TELLURIUM.

GEDIEGEN WISMUTH. See NATIVE BISMUTH.

GEDRITE. A variety of Hornblende resembling Anthophyllite. It is fibrous and somewhat laminar. Colour violet-brown, with a semi-metallic lustre. S.G. 3·26.

Comp. $8\ddot{F}e, \; 6\ddot{S}i + \ddot{A}l, \; \ddot{S}i + \dot{H}.$?

Analysis, by *Dufrénoy*:

Silica . .	.	38·81
Protoxide of iron	.	45·83
Magnesia . .	.	4·13
Lime . . .	.	0·67
Alumina . .	.	9·31
Water . .	.	2·30
		101·05

Locality. Valley of Héas, near Gedré in the Pyrenees; whence the name *Gedrite*.

Brit. Mus , Case 34.

GEHLENITE, *Fuchs.* Pyramidal. Usually occurs in rectangular four-sided prisms, which are sometimes tabular, or nearly approach the form of the cube. The surfaces of crystals commonly rough and dull. Colour grey, frequently with a greenish or yellowish tinge. Lustre resinous, inclining to vitreous. Opaque; fragments feebly translucent at the edges. Streak white to greenish white. Fracture uneven and splintery. H. 5·5 to 6. S.G. 2·9 to 3·06.

Comp. $3\ddot{R}^3 \; \ddot{S}i + \ddot{R}^5 \; \ddot{S}i$, or $(\dot{C}a, \; \dot{M}g)^3 \; (\ddot{F}e \; \ddot{A}l) \; 2\ddot{S}i.$

Analysis, from Fassa by *Rammelsberg*:

Silica . . .	.	29·78
Alumina . .	.	22·02
Peroxide of iron .	.	3·22
Protoxide of iron .	.	1·73
Lime . . .	.	37·90
Magnesia . .	.	3·88
Protoxide of manganese	.	0·19
Water and loss .	.	1·28
		100·00

BB with difficulty fusible: with borax or microcosmic salt melts slowly to a glass coloured by iron.

Completely decomposed by muriatic acid, with separation of gelatinous silica.

Localities. Principally on Mount Monzoni, in the Valley of Fassa in the Tyrol, in crystals which are either isolated and invested by Calc Spar, or aggregated irregularly in groups. It also occurs massive, forming an extremely tough, difficultly frangible rock in the same locality.

Name. In honour of the chemist Gehlen.

Brit. Mus., Case 36.

GEKRÖSSTEIN. A contorted variety of

Anhydrite, found principally at Bochnia and Wieliczka in Poland.

GELB·BLEIERZ; GELBES BLEIERZ, *Werner*. See WULFENITE.

GELBEISENERZ. A potash-Copperas related to Jarosite, met with in reniform and in compact earthy masses in Bohemia, and at Modum in Norway. Colour ochre-yellow. Opaque. Lustre weak. H. 2·5 to 3. S.G. 2·7 to 2·9.

Analysis, from Brown Coal of Kolosoruk in Bohemia, by *Rammelsberg:*

Silica	32·11
Peroxide of iron . . .	46·74
Lime	0·64
Potash	7·88
Water	13·56
	100·93

GELBEISENSTEIN. See YELLOW OCHRE.

GELBERDE. See LIMONITE.

GELBERZ. See SYLVANITE.

Analysis, by *Klaproth:*

Tellurium	47·75
Gold	26·75
Silver	8·50
Lead	19·50
Sulphur . . .	0·5
	100·0

GELBES RAUSCHGELB, *Werner*. See ORPIMENT.

GELF, *Kirwan*. The name given in Hungary to "a particular sort of Argentiferous Copper Pyrites."

GELFERZ. See CHALCOPYRITE.

GEM. According to Pliny the ancients included under the term Gem all stones of beautiful colour, which were found in small quantity, and of a sufficient degree of hardness to be engraved as seals. By Gems the moderns understand those stones which, in a small compass, combine hardness and fire or lustre, with vivid, soft, or agreeable colours, and divide them into two kinds, real gems or jewels and precious stones. The real Gems comprise Diamond, Sapphire, Ruby, Spinelle, Emerald, Beryl, Topaz, Zircon, Garnet, Chrysoberyl, Tourmaline, Rubellite, Essonite, Cordierite, Iolite, Cyanite (Sappare), Chrysolite, and the varieties of Rock Crystal.

Precious stones are supposed to possess the same characters as the Gems, only in a minor degree. They are also generally only translucent or semitransparent, and occur in larger amorphous masses. Lapidaries and jewellers name Gems according to their colours, rather than with reference to their chemical composition, or their relative de-

grees of hardness and density. Thus the Corundum-ruby (Oriental Ruby), Spinelle or Topaz, are all, when red, called *Ruby*; if green, *Emerald*; if blue, *Sapphire*; and if yellow, *Topaz*.

The term Oriental is applied in the same way to the finest stones, whether found in the East or not; having been used, perhaps, originally to denote those stones which were really brought from the East, and were more highly valued in consequence, than the produce of other countries. In the same way the ancients called the most highly coloured stones *masculine*, and those of more subdued tints *feminine*.

GEMMA PELLUCIDISSIMA, *Wallerius*. See EMERALD.

GENESEE OIL. A kind of Petroleum. See SENECA OIL.

GEOCRONITE, *Dana*, *Greg & Lettsom*. GEOKRONITE, *Svanberg*, *Nicol*. Rhombic. Usually occurs massive; also granular or earthy. Colour and streak pale lead-grey. Lustre metallic. Brittle: fracture uneven. H. 2 to 3. S.G. 6·4 to 6·6.

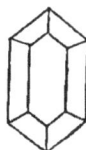

Fig. 208.

Comp. Sulphantimonite of lead, or 5 Pb S + (Sb, As) S³ = sulphur 16·5, antimony 16·7, lead 66·8 = 100.

Analysis, from Merido, by *Sauvage:*

Sulphur . . .	16·90
Antimony . . .	16·00
Lead	64·89
Copper . . .	1·60
	99·39

BB fuses readily, giving off fumes of antimony and sulphur, and colouring the charcoal around yellow.

Localities.—Irish. Kilbricken, co. Clare. See KILBRICKENITE.—*Foreign*. The silver mines of Sala in Sweden, at which locality a portion of the antimony is replaced by arsenic. In Spain, at Meredo in Gallicia; and in the valley di Castello, near Pietro Santo in Tuscany.

Name. The name Geocronite is derived from γῆ, *earth*, and Κρόνος, *Saturn*, the alchemistic name for lead.

Brit. Mus., Case 11.

GEODES. Are not, strictly speaking, distinct minerals, but hollow nodules, fre-

quently containing crystals of Quartz, Calcite, &c., coating their interior. Of such a
kind are the geodes of common occurrence
in the New Red Marl of Somersetshire and
Gloucestershire, to which the name of "po-
tato-stones" has been locally given, from
their external resemblance to the root of
that name. Specimens of these from the
neighbourhood of Bristol will be found in
the Upper Gallery of the Museum of Practical Geology. See Wall-case 44, Nos. 35
to 37.

GERSDORFFITE, *Haidinger.* Cubical; pyri-
tohedral. Occurs in octahedrons, sometimes
with the faces of the pentagonal dodecahedron, and cubo-octahedron. Colour tin-
white inclining to lead-grey; often with a
grey or greyish-black tarnish. Lustre
metallic. Streak greyish-black. Fracture
uneven. H. 5·5. S.G. 6·7 to 6·9.

Comp. Ni, S^2 + Ni, As=nickel 35·54,
arsenic 45·18, sulphur 19·28=100.

Analysis, from Schladming, by *Pless :*

Arsenic	.	.	.	39·40
Sulphur	.	.	.	16·91
Nickel	.	.	.	28·62
Iron	.	.	.	12·19
Cobalt	.	.	.	2·88
				100·00

Decrepitates strongly when heated in a
flask. Heated to redness, yields a strong
sublimate of fused, yellowish-brown sulphide of arsenic, while a mass like copper-
nickel is left behind. . (Berzelius.)

Dissolves in nitric acid, depositing sulphur
and arsenious acid.

Localities. Loos, in Helsingland, Sweden.
Albertine mine, near Harzgerode in the
Harz. Schladming in Styria. Hamsdorf, near
Lobenstein in Thuringia. Near Ems, in
fine crystals. (See also AMOIBITE.)

Brit. Mus., Case 6.

GEYSERITE. A loose hydrated form of
silica. It is held in solution by the hot
water of the Geysers of Iceland, and deposited by them on the ground around in
light, porous, concretionary or cellular
masses, somewhat resembling cauliflowers
in appearance.

GIBBSITE, *Torrey, Cleveland, Phillips,
Nicol.* (See also HYDRARGILLITE.) Hexagonal. In small crystals with the lateral
edges replaced, and a perfect basal cleavage.
Generally occurs in aggregations of irregular
stalactites, or small mammillary incrustations, with smooth surfaces. Structure indistinctly fibrous, the fibres radiating from
the centre. Colour greyish-, greenish-, or
reddish-white. Translucent. Lustre faint.

When breathed on gives off a strong argillaceous odour. Tough, but easily reduced
to powder. H. 3 to 3·75. S.G. 2·3 to 2·4.

Comp. Terhydrate of alumina or $\ddot{Al}$, $\overset{...}{H}{}^3$
=alumina 65·56, water 34·44=100.

Analysis, from Richmond, U.S., by *Smith
& Brush :*

Alumina	.	.	.	64·24
Water	.	.	.	33·76
Silica	.	.	.	1·33
Phosphoric acid	.	.	.	0·57
Magnesia	.	.	.	0·10
Protoxide of iron	.	.	trace
			.	100·00

In a matrass yields much water.

BB alone infusible, but becomes white:
on charcoal decrepitates, becomes opaque,
crystals exfoliate; phosphoresces.

Entirely soluble in concentrated sulphuric
acid.

Localities. Stalactitic, at Richmond, Massachusetts, U.S., in a bed of Limonite; and at
the Clove Mine, Duchess co. New York. Crystallized (Hydrargillite) in the Schischimskian Mountains, near Slatoust in the Ural.
Gumush-dagh in Asia Minor, with Corundum. Unionville, Pennsylvania, U. S.
Brazil, resembling Wavellite.

Name. After Colonel George Gibbs.

Brit. Mus., Case 19.

GIBSONITE, *Haidinger.* A mineral crystallizing in right rhomboidal prisms, partly
aggregated in little kidneys, and bearing
some resemblance to Prehnite. Colour rose-
white or pale rose.

Locality. Hartfield in Renfrewshire. Fig.
209.

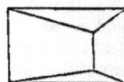

Fig. 209.

GIESECKITE ; GISECKITE, *Stromeyer.* A
pseudomorphus form of Elæolite, from which
it chiefly differs in containing 4·88 per cent.
of water. It occurs in regular six-sided
prisms of a brownish colour externally; internally greenish and blackish-green intermixed. The colour of the Diana specimens
varies from pea-green to leek-green. Lustre
greasy. Opaque, but translucent in small
fragments. Structure granular, sometimes
waxy; bearing a greater resemblance to a
pseudomorphous steatitic mineral than a
crystalline substance. Yields to the knife,
but scratches glass. Affords a white powder.
H. 3 to 3·35. S.G. 2·73 to 2·85.

Comp. $(\dot{R}^3 \ddot{H})^3 \ddot{S}i^4 + 3\dot{H}.$

Analysis (mean of three), from Diana, by Prof. *Brush* :

Silica	45·67
Alumina . . .	31·51
Peroxide of iron . .	0·27
Protoxide of iron . .	0·77
Lime	2·20
Magnesia . . .	3·48
Soda	0·88
Potash	8·21
Carbonate of lime .	0·32
Water	6·97
	100·28

BB becomes opaque and fuses to a white enamel.

Localites. Akulliarasiarsuk in Greenland, imbedded in compact Felspar. United States, at Diana, Lewis co., N. Y., in granular limestone with Pyroxene and Magnetic Pyrites.

Name. After Sir C. Giesècké, by whom it was first brought from Greenland.

GIFTKIES. See MISPICKEL.

GIGANTOLITE. The name given by Nordenskiöld to a hydrated Iolite (corresponding to Iolite+3H), found in gneissoid granite at Tamela in Finland. It is of a greenish-grey colour, with a vitreous and waxy lustre, approaching to submetallic. S.G. 2·862 to 2·878.

BB fuses with intumescence to a light greenish slag.

Analysis, from Tamela, by *Marignac* :

Silica	42·59
Alumina . . .	26·78
Peroxide of iron . .	14·21
Potash	5·44
Magnesia . . .	2·72
Protoxide of manganese .	1·07
Water	5·70
	98·51

Brit. Mus., Case 32.

GILBERTITE, *Thomson.* A hydrous Muscovite; a variety of Margarodite. H. 2·7. S.G. 2·6 to 2·8.

Analysis, from Cornwall, by *Lehunt* :

Silica	45·15
Alumina . . .	40·11
Magnesia . . .	1·90
Lime	4·17
Protoxide of iron . .	2·43
Water	4·25
	98·01

Locality. Stenna Gwynn, near St. Austell, in Cornwall, in considerable masses, of a yellowish-white colour, with granite and Fluor. *M.P.G.* Horse-shoe Case, No. 1001.

GILLINGITE. The name given by Hermann to the varieties of Hisingerite from Gillinge and Orijervi in Finland.

Analysis, from Gillinge, by *Rammelsberg* :

Silica	32·18
Peroxide of iron . .	30·10
Protoxide of iron . .	8·63
Lime	5·50
Magnesia . . .	4·22
Water	19·37
	100·00

Brit. Mus., Case 26.

GIOBERTITE, *Beudant.* A variety of Magnesite from Baumgarten, in Silesia; named after Giobert, who first pointed out the presence of carbonate of magnesia in the earthy varieties of Magnesite.

Analysis, by *Stromeyer* :

Magnesia . . .	48·36
Carbonic acid . .	50·32
Peroxide of manganese	0·21
Water . . .	1·39
	99·18

GIPSITE, *Beudant.* See GIBBSITE.

GIRASOL. The name given by the French to Fire-opal, and by *Wallerius & De Born* to milk-white translucent Opal. The name Girasol is derived from gyro, *to turn*, and Sol, *the sun*, because it constantly reflects a reddish colour when turned to the sun or any bright light. Sometimes it strongly resembles a translucent jelly.

GISMONDINE, *Beudant, Phillips.* Pyramidal. Occurs in octahedrons, either separate or clustered into mammillated forms with a drusy surface. Colour bluish-white, greyish, reddish. Lustre splendent. Transparent to translucent. H. 4·5. S.G. 2·265.

BB whitens, intumesces, and melts to a milky glass : at 100° C. (212° F.) loses one-third of its water.

Easily dissolves in acids and gelatinises.

Comp. $(\dot{C}a, \dot{K})^2 \ddot{S}i + 2 \ddot{A}l \ddot{S}i + 9\dot{H}.$

Analysis by *Marignac* :

Silica	35·88
Alumina . . .	27·23
Lime	13·12
Potash	2·85
Water	21·10
	100·18

Locality. Capo di Bove, near Rome; associated with Phillipsite.

The faces of the crystals never have the striæ of those of Phillipsite, and the mammillated specimens are not columnar within: moreover, Phillipsite does not lose any of its water below 100° C. (212° Fah.).

Name. After Charles-Joseph Gismondi, Professor of Mineralogy at Rome. Brit. Mus., Case 29.

GLACE DE MARIE. Selenite. See PIERRE à JESUS.

GLANCE-BLENDE, *Mohs.* See MANGAN-BLENDE.

GLANCE COAL, *Jameson.* See ANTHRACITE.

GLANCE COBALT, *Jameson.* See COBALTINE.

GLANCE COPPER. See COPPER GLANCE.

GLANZ, *Haidinger.* See GALENA.

GLANZARSENIKKIES. See LEUCOPYRITE.

GLANZBRAUNSTEIN, *Hausmann.* See HAUSMANNITE.

GLANZKOBALT; GLANZKOBOLD, *Werner.* See COBALTINE.

GLANZKOHLE, *Wenner.* See ANTHRACITE.

GLASERITE, *Hausmann.* Rhombic. Occurs in thin tables and in blades made up of aggregated crystals; also massive, or imperfectly mammillary, apparently formed in successive layers, and in crusts. Colour white or yellow, sometimes with a bluish or greenish stain. Lustre vitreous, inclining to resinous. Transparent to translucent or opaque. Taste saline and bitter. Cleavage and fracture indistinct.

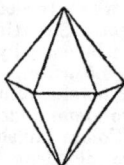

Fig. 210.

Comp. Sulphate of potash or $\overset{..}{K}\overset{...}{S}$=potash 54·1, sulphuric acid 45·9=100.

Analysis, from Vesuvius:
Sulphate of potash . . 71·4
Sulphate of soda . . 18·6
Chloride of sodium . . 4·6
Chloride of ammonium, copper and iron . . 5·4
————
100·0

BB fuses without intumescence.

Localities. In delicate white crystallizations, and in masses, often an inch or more in thickness, sublimed on lava round the fumaroles of Vesuvius and other volcanoes.

GLASERZ, *Hausmann, Werner.* Silver glass. See SILVER GLANCE.

GLASS-SCHORL or GLASTEIN, *Wiedenman.* See AXINITE.

GLASSY FELSPAR. See SANIDINE.

GLASSY QUARTZ, *Kirwan.* See GREASY QUARTZ.

GLÄTTE. See PLUMBIC OCHRE.

GLAUBER-SALT, *Kirwan;* GLAUBERSALZ, *Werner.* Oblique: primary form an oblique rhombic prism. Usually occurs in efflorescent crusts and in an earthy form, of a greyish or yellowish-white colour. Lustre vitreous on fresh fractures, dull at the surface. Translucent or opaque. Extremely efflorescent, falling spontaneously into powder. Brittle; easily frangible. Has a cooling, and then a bitter, saline taste. H. 1·5 to 2. S.G. 1·48.

Comp. Sulphate of soda, or $\overset{.}{Na}\overset{..}{S}+10\overset{...}{H}$ =soda 19·3, sulphuric acid 24·8, water 55·9 =100.

Analysis, from Nova Scotia, by *H. Haw:*
Sulphate of soda . . . 44·54
Water . . . . 55·46
————
100·00

In the matrass melts in its water of composition.

BB behaves like Epsomite, but its solution does not afford a precipitate with lime-water.

Localities. Eger, and in the hot springs of Carlsbad and Seidlitz, in Bohemia. Old salt mines at Ischl and Hallstadt, in Upper Austria. Altenberg, in Styria. Hungary. Switzerland. Italy. Near Aranjuez, in Spain; and in enormous quantities near Lodoso, on the borders of Navarre and Old Castile; also in the mountains at Santander, and Alcanadra. Egypt. On the banks of many Siberian salt lakes. A cavern on Hawaii, one of the Sandwich Islands. With Hayesine in cavities in the Gypsum of Nova Scotia, &c.

Name. After Glauber, a German chemist, who first discovered the artificial salt.

When purified, Glauber Salt is used as a purgative medicine.

GLAUBERITE, *Brongniart, Haüy, Jameson, Phillips.* Oblique: primary form an oblique rhombic prism. Occurs crystallized in the form of oblique and extremely flat rhombic prisms, of a pale yellow or grey colour. Lustre vitreous. Translucent, rarely transparent. Streak white. Brittle. Fracture conchoidal. Taste slightly saline. When immersed in water becomes opaque, and is partly dissolved.　H. 2·5 to 3.　S.G. 2·6 to 2·85.

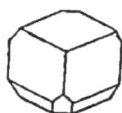

Fig. 211.

Comp.　Sulphate of soda and lime, or

$(\frac{1}{2}\overset{..}{Na} + \frac{1}{2}\overset{.}{Ca})\overset{..}{S}$=sulphate of soda 51·1, sulphate of lime 48·9=100.

Analysis, from Atacama, by *Hayes* :

Sulphuric acid	.	.	67·22
Soda	.	.	11·32
Lime	.	.	20·68
Iron	.	.	0·14

99·36

BB decrepitates and then melts to a clear glass.

Localities.　In crystals, imbedded in Rock Salt and clay, at the salt mines of Villa Rubia, near Ocana; and Aranjuez, near Madrid, in Spain.　Aussee and Ischl, in Upper Austria.　The salt mines of Vic, in France (see POLYHALITE DE VIC).　The province of Tarapaca, in Peru, with Hayesine, &c.

Name.　Glauberite is so called in consequence of its containing a very large amount of Glauber's salt.

Brit. Mus., Case 52.

GLAUCODOT or GLAUCODOTE, *Breithaupt.* A cobaltic variety of Mispickel, with which it nearly agrees in crystallization, and also in composition, except in the replacement of one-third of the cobalt by iron.　It is of a greyish, tin-white colour, with a metallic lustre.　Streak black.　H. 5.　S.G. 5·97 to 6.

Comp.　(Co, Fe) As + (Co, Fe) S² =sulphur 19·4, arsenic 45·5, cobalt 23·8, iron 11·3 =100.

Analysis, from Huasco, in Chili, by *Plattner* :

Sulphur	.	.	20·21
Arsenic	.	.	43·20
Cobalt	.	.	24·77
Nickel	.	.	trace
Iron	.	.	11·90
Silica	.	.	trace

100·08

BB gives the reaction of cobalt, iron, sulphur, and arsenic.

Gives only a trace of arsenic when heated in a glass closed at one end.

Localities.　In mica-schist, associated with Cobaltine, in the province of Huasco, in Chili; and at Orawitza, in the Bannat, with Calcite.

Name.　From γλαυκὸς, *grey.*

Brit. Mus., Case 12.

GLAUCOLITE, *Fischer.*　A massive variety of Scapolite of a lavender-blue or indigo-blue colour, occasionally passing into green, somewhat resembling blue Cancrinite.　Lustre vitreous.　Translucent at the edges.　Fracture splintery.　H. 5 to 6.　S.G. 2·65 to 2·67.

Comp.　$\overset{.}{R}^3 \overset{..}{Si}^2 + 2\overset{..}{Al} \overset{...}{Si}.$

Analysis, from Lake Baikal, by *Von Rath* :

Silica	.	.	46·01
Alumina	.	.	21·72
Peroxide of iron	.	.	1·49
Lime	.	.	15·68
Carbonate of lime	.	.	1·68
Magnesia	.	.	0·46
Potash	.	.	0·56
Soda	.	.	4·57
Water	.	.	0·47

97·64

BB whitens and fuses with difficulty. Dissolves slowly with effervescence in borax and salt of phosphorus.

Localities.　In veins in granite, in the vicinity of the river Sludianka, beyond Lake Baikal, in Siberia.　Laurvig, in Norway, accompanied by Elæolite.

Name.　From γλαυκὸς, *sea-green*, and λίθος, *stone.*

GLAUCONITE.　Occurs in green grains, or in small greenish masses, in the green sandstone of various countries, as in the Upper Greensand of the south of England and Havre; in the Greensand of Büderich, near Werl, in Westphalia; Gay Head, Massachusetts, U. S., &c.

Some of these varieties (as the first-mentioned) may be referred to Augite, others to Green Earth or Chlorite.

Analysis, from Gay Head, by *S. L. Dana* :

Silica	.	.	56·70
Alumina	.	.	13·32
Protoxide of iron	.	.	20·10
Magnesia	.	.	1·18
Lime	.	.	1·62

99·92

Name.　From γλαυκὸς, *sea-green.*

GLAUCOPHANE, *Hausmann.*　Probably the same as Wichtyne.　Occurs in indistinct, long, and thin six-sided prisms, longitudinally striated; also granular-massive. Colour blue, lavender-blue, bluish-black, greyish.　Lustre vitreous to pearly.　Translucent to opaque.　Streak greyish-blue. Powder slightly magnetic.　Brittle.　H. 5·5. S.G. 3·108.

Comp.　$(\frac{1}{2}\overset{.}{R}^3 + \frac{1}{2}\overset{...}{R}) \overset{..}{Si}^2.$

Analysis, by *Schnedermann*:

Silica	. . .	. 56·49
Alumina	. . .	. 12·23
Protoxide of iron .	.	. 10·91
Protoxide of manganese	.	0·50
Magnesia	. . .	7·97
Lime	. . . .	. 2·25
Soda, with traces of potash	.	9·28

                                     99·63

Locality.—The island of Syra, one of the Cyclades, in mica-slate.

Name. From γλαυχὸς, *bluish-green*, and φαίνω, *to appear*.

GLAUCOSIDERIT. See VIVIANITE.

The name is derived from γλαυχὸς, *bluish-green*, and σίδηϱος, *iron*.

GLIMMER, *Kirwan, Jameson, Werner.* See MICA. The name is confined by Haidinger and Hausmann to the variety called Muscovite.

GLINKITE, *Romanowski.* A greenish variety of Chrysolite, found in talcose slate at Perm, in Russia; and at Tunaberg, in gneiss, with Augite and Garnet.

Analysis, by *v. Beck*:

Silica	. . .	. 39·21
Magnesia	. . .	. 44·06
Protoxide of iron .	.	. 15·45

                                     100·72

GLOBULAR QUARTZ. A variety of common Quartz, found of a black colour, in chalk, at Dover; and at Knockmahon Copper Mines, near Bunmahon, S. Waterford.

GLOTTALITE, *Thomson.* A variety of Analcime, occurring in small aggregated and irregular, white or colourless crystals, somewhat like *fig.* 212; in greenstone at Port Glasgow in Scotland. Lustre vitreous. H. 3 to 4. S. G. 2·18.

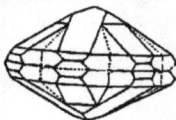

Fig. 212.

Comp. $3\overset{..}{Ca}^3 \ddot{S}i^2 + 3\overset{...}{Al} \ddot{S}i^2 + 24\overset{.}{H}$.

Analysis :

Silica	. . .	. 37·01
Alumina	. .	. 16·31
Peroxide of iron .	.	. 0·50
Lime	. .	. 23·93
Water	. . .	. 21·25

                                     99·00

Name. From Glotta, *the river Clyde*, and λίθος, *stone*.

GMELINITE, *Brooke.* Or Soda-Chabasite,

with which it is heteromorphous. Hexagonal: primary form an obtuse rhombohedron. Occurs in flat six-sided prisms, terminated at both extremities by truncated six-sided pyramids. *Fig.* 212*. Colour white or yellowish-white passing into flesh-red. Lustre vitreous. Translucent. Surface of the prisms striated horizontally. Streak white. Brittle. Fracture uneven. H. 4·5. S.G. 2·04 to 2·12.

 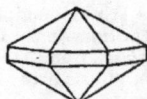

Fig. 212*.   Fig. 213.

Comp. Like that of Chabasite, but distinguished from it by having a portion of the lime replaced by a corresponding quantity of soda: $(\overset{.}{Na}^2, \overset{.}{Ca})^3 \ddot{S}i^2 + 3\overset{...}{Al} \ddot{S}i^2 +$ $18\overset{.}{H}$ = silica 47·57, alumina 19·85, lime 3·67, soda 8·05, water 20·86.

Analysis, from Glenarm, by *Connel:*

Silica	. . .	. 48·56
Alumina	. .	. 18·05
Peroxide of iron .	.	. 0·11
Lime	. . .	. 5·13
Soda	. . .	. 3·85
Potash	. . .	. 0·39
Water	. . .	. 21·66

                                     98·75

When held in the flame of a candle flies off in minute scales. In the matrass yields water and falls to powder.

BB shrinks up and fuses to a blistered, slightly transluceut enamel.

Forms a jelly of silica with muriatic acid.

Localities. Coating cavities in amygdaloidal rocks in the trap districts of the N. E. of Ireland, and at Talisker in Skye. Also in a similar manner at Montecchio Maggiore, and at Castel in the Vicentine.

Name. The name Gmelinite was proposed by Sir David Brewster in compliment to G. C. Gmelin, professor of chemistry in the University of Giessen.

Brit. Mus., Case 27.

GOETHITE, *Phillips.* GÖTHITE, *Beudant, Dana, Greg & Lettsom.* Rhombic: primary form a right rhombic prism: occurs in prisms longitudinally striated, and often flattened parallel to the shorter diagonal: also fibrous, reniform, and in minute laminæ or tables modified at their edges by oblique facets. Colour reddish and blackish-brown, yellowish by reflected light, and often blood-red by transmitted light. Lustre adamantine. Streak brownish-yellow. Brittle. H. 5 to 5·5. S.G. 4 to 4·4.

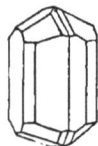

Fig. 214.

Fig. 215.

Comp. Hydrated peroxide of iron, or $\ddot{F}e\ \dot{H}$ = peroxide of iron 89·89, water 10·11 = 100.

Analysis, from Eisenfeld in Nassau, by *v. Kobell*:

Peroxide of iron	. . .	86·35
Silica	. . . .	0·85
Oxide of copper	. .	0·91
Lime	. . . .	trace
Peroxide of manganese	.	0·51
Water . , . .		11·38
		100·00

BB behaves like Limonite.

Localities.—English. The finest and most perfect crystals hitherto found occur in Quartz at Restormel iron-inine near Lostwithiel in Cornwall; it is also met with in the same county, at Botallack, near St. Just, and at Tincroft, Illogan, in fibro-crystalline specimens; at Carn Brea and Huel Beauchamp near Redruth, in translucent plates of a hyacinth-red colour. In Gloucestershire it is found in diverging tufts of needle-shaped crystals in the interior of geodes; in Somersetshire at the Providence iron-mines near Bristol, associated with very fine amethystine Quartz. — *Scotch.* Gourock in Renfrewshire, and at Burn of the Sail, Hoy, in the Orkneys.—*Foreign.* The principal foreign localities are Eiserfeld in Siegen, Prussia; Oberkirchen in Westerwald; Zwickau in Saxony; Przibram, &c.

Name. After the German poet and mineralogist, Goethe.

Brit. Mus., Case 16.

M.P.G. Principal floor, Wall-cases, 49, 27 and 43 (British).

For varieties of Goethite, see Lepidokrokite, Onegite, Przibramite, Rubinglimmer, Sammetblende, and Stilpnosiderite.

Gökumite. A variety of Idocrase from Gökum.

Gold. Primary form the octahedron. Often occurs in grains or scales (*Granos*), and in rolled masses (*Pepitas, Nuggets*) in alluvium and gravel. The crystals,

usually small and imperfect, are sometimes cubes or octahedrons (frequently with truncated edges or angles); dodecahedrons with rhombic faces, and solids with twenty-four trapezohedral faces. Colour and streak various shades of gold-yellow, sometimes inclining to silver-white. Lustre metallic. Opaque. Very ductile, flexible, and malleable. Fracture hackly, affording no trace of cleavage. H. 2·5 to 3. S.G. 15·6 to 19·5.

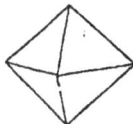

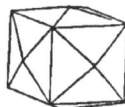

Fig. 216.　　　　　　Fig. 217.

Gold is almost always found native, but seldom perfectly pure, being alloyed with minute quantities of other metals, which sometimes considerably affect its colour. Sometimes it occurs in combination with silver, constituting Electrum; with tellurium, in Native Tellurium; with silver and tellurium, in Graphic and Yellow Tellurium; and with lead and tellurium, in Foliated Tellurium. A native amalgam of gold has been found in California, especially near Mariposa and in Columbia; and an alloy of gold and bismuth in Rutherford County, North America. It sometimes occurs in small quantities in metallic sulphides, as in Galena, Iron Pyrites, and Copper Pyrites, and is occasionally alloyed with Palladium (see Porpesite) and Rhodium.

Gold being one of the most widely diffused of minerals, a few only of the principal localities can be given here. It was probably discovered by the aboriginal inhabitants of the British Islands at a very early period, long prior to their invasion by the Romans, most of the fibulæ, torques, and other gold ornaments found in the barrows of this country and in the peat bogs of Ireland having been obtained from native sources. At a subsequent period, the Romans, always anxious to avail themselves of the natural resources of their colonies, carried on operations in a more systematic manner, and are supposed to have had works at North Molton in Devonshire, as well as at Gogofau, near Caio, in Caermarthenshire, in the neighbourhood of a place now called Pumpsant.* Since that time various attempts have been

---

* See " Note on the Gogofau, or Ogofau, Mine, by Warington W. Smyth, M.A.," in Memoirs of the Geological Survey of Great Britain, vol. i. p. 480.

made to work mines supposed to contain gold, but it has never been found in these islands in sufficient quantity to render such undertakings remunerative, and all these schemes have been attended by the loss of the capital employed. The most important of these explorations for gold were those carried on in the County Wicklow, in Ireland, to which attention was directed in 1795 by the discovery of lumps of gold in a valley situated on the flanks of the Crog-han Kinshela Mountain. Although these washings never proved permanently profit-able, considerable quantities of gold were obtained, the greater part of which was made into articles of jewelry. During the last occasion when the works were brought into active operation by the Government, gold to the value of £3675 was raised. Lumps of large dimensions were sometimes met with: one was found weighing 22 oz., a model of which is placed in the collection of Trinity College, Dublin: other specimens of two or three ounces weight were not unfrequently discovered, while several were procured exceeding an ounce—the latter occurring in sand covered with turf, adjacent to a rivulet. The gold from this locality is from $21\frac{3}{8}$ to $21\frac{7}{8}$ carats fine, the alloy being silver.

More recently the search for gold was resumed near North Molton, in lodes traversing the Devonian rocks. Gold is also found in veins of Quartz and Calc-spar, traversing Cambrian grits and talcose schists belonging to Lower Silurian Lingula flags, between Dolgelly and Barmouth in Merionethshire. The principal explorations have been made at Cwm-eisen, Tyddyn-gwladis, Dol-y-frwynog, the Prince of Wales, the Cambrian, and the Vigra and Clogau Mines. At the latter, within the last few months (Feb. 1861), above 200 ozs. have been extracted from about 10 fathoms of driving, where the better veinstuff yielded, in large lumps, at the rate of 150 ozs. of gold to the ton.

Gold has been occasionally met with in the tin-streams of Cornwall, at the Carnon stream-works, and at Crow Hill. It has also been found in the gossan at Nangiles and other Mines. The largest Cornish specimen yet found weighed 2 oz. 3 dwts. The Pyrites from the London Clay is said to contain a minute quantity of gold.*

Gold is found in the sediments of the Rhine, mostly in thin scales, lying among quartzite and other pebbles, often *beneath* but not *in* the loess. It is also found in Spain and Portugal. The Tagus, in the time of the Carthaginians, bore gold with its sands, derived from the reefs of Auriferous Quartz which traverse the Silurian rocks of Portuguese and Spanish Estremadura, where the traces of ancient workings of the Phenicians, the Carthaginians, the Romans, and subsequently of the Moors, still remain. Many of the Roman proconsuls are said to have obtained almost fabulous sums from the produce of the mines in Iberia (Spain and Portugal). In fact those countries, especially the former, were to the Carthaginians and Romans what Peru was to the subjects of Charles V. and Philip II. "Natura regionis circà se omnis aurifera, miniique, et chrysocollæ et aliorum colorum ferax. Itaque exerceri solum jussit. Sic Astures et latentes in profundo opes suas atque divitias, dùm aliis quærunt, nosse cœperunt."—*Florus,* lib. iv. cap. 12.

The principal sources of gold in Africa are those of Kordofan, between Darfour and Abyssinia; the desert of Zaara, in Western Africa, from the mouth of the Senegal to the Cape of Palms; and the south-east coast, between the twenty-second and twenty-fifth degrees of south latitude, in the country of Sofala, opposite to Madagascar. Large quantities of gold are procured by washing the alluvial deposits in Brazil, particularly near Villa Rica, in the neighbourhood of Cocães. The gold of Chili and Caracas, as well as that obtained at Choco, Antioquia, and elsewhere in New Grenada, is the product of the washings established in alluvial grounds. The gold of Mexico and Peru is mostly extracted from ores of other metals. Japan, Formosa, Ceylon, Java, Sumatra, Borneo, the Philippines, and some other islands of the Indian Archipelago are rich in gold streams.†

In India gold is found in two different localities, in grains, as stream-gold, and in lumps in alluvial deposits. It is also obtained from the washings of the sands of the Rivière du Loup, in Canada.

Gold was originally discovered in California by some of the Jesuits who accompanied the Spanish settlers to that colony; and there is in the Royal collection of Minerals in Madrid a large nugget, which was sent from that country as a present to the Emperor Charles V. Although it was stated by Jamieson, as early as the year 1816, that

---

* Specimens of British gold are contained in Wall-case 14, at the Museum of Practical Geology.

† See Ure's Dict. of Arts, Manufactures, and Mines (article, Gold), vol. ii.

"on the coast of California there is a plain, 14 leagues in extent, covered with an alluvial deposit, in which lumps of gold are dispersed," * it was only through the accidental discovery of gold in cutting a mill-race, on the river Americanos, that the attention of the world was drawn to the enormous quantities of the metal in question contained in that country.†

The gold produced in California in 1857 amounted to £13,110,000 ; in 1856 to £14,000,000.

Subsequently, however, to the re-discovery of gold in California, public attention was directed to Australia, where it had been foretold by Sir R. Murchison that the metal in question would, most probably, be found in as large quantities and under the same conditions as in Russia, California, and other great gold-producing countries, which assertion proved, on examination, to be correct. The Legislative Council of New South Wales voted a sum of £10,000 to Mr. Hargreaves for his discovery of the gold region.‡

The quantity of gold exported from Australia in 1857 amounted to £11,764,299.

More recently auriferous deposits have been discovered in Tasmania, and in British Columbia. In the latter country paying diggings have been found on the Fraser River, extending from Fort Hope almost to Fort Alexander, a continuous distance of nearly 400 miles.

Gold is stated, by Professor Hochstetter, to be found in beds of quartz-gravel in the rivers and creeks which flow down from both sides of the Coromandel range in New Zealand.

Gold to the annual value of nearly three millions sterling is obtained in Russia, chiefly "from local detritus or alluvia,

usually called 'gold-sand,' but for which (as far as Russia is concerned) the term shingle would be much more appropriate."— *Sir R. I. Murchison.*

Of the above produce about half a million sterling is obtained from the eastern flank of the Ural, and the remainder, amounting to considerably more than two millions and a quarter, from the governments of Tomsk and Yeniseisk in Siberia.§

The quantity of gold extracted from the gold mines of Eastern Siberia, in 1859, amounted to upwards of 1134 poods (of near 34 lbs each). This was 87 poods less than in 1858. The number of companies occupied in extracting gold was 160, and there were employed 26,112 men and 572 women belonging to the government of Siberia, and 5081 men and 29 women from Great Russia. The total number was nearly 5000 fewer than in the preceding year, and the falling off was caused by the dearness of provisions. The number of horses employed was 12,284.— *Irkutsk Gazette.*

The only work in the Ural Mountains at which subterranean mining for gold in the solid rock is still practised, is at Beresow, where (according to Murchison) the matrix is "a mass of apparently metamorphosed and crystalline rock, called ' *beresite*,' resembling a decomposed granite with veins of quartz, in which some gold is disseminated." At the Soimonofsk Mines, south of Miask, the gold is obtained from the vast deposits of ancient drift-gravel, or shingle, which cover and fill up inequalities in the eroded surface of highly inclined crystalline limestones, supposed to be of Silurian or Devonian age.

In Europe the gold mines of Salzburg, near Gastein, have been worked for centuries, as have also those of Hungary and Transylvania. In Hungary the principal mines are those of Schemnitz, Kremnitz, Felsobanya, Königsberg and Telkebanya to the south of Kaschau : in Transylvania those of Vöröspatak, Kapnik, Offenbanya, Zelatna and Nagy-ag.

Brit. Mus , Case 3.

M.P.G. In Hall, a large mass of gold-bearing Quartz from Grass Valley, Nevada co., California. Principal floor, Wall-cases 14 (British); 23 (Foreign); 37 (N. S. Wales) ; 40 (Queen Charlotte's Island, N. Pacific Ocean). Case 11 (Nuggets of Native Gold and models of remarkable nuggets from various diggings in Victoria and N. S. Wales).

---

* Jamieson's Mineralogy, vol. iii. p. 13, 1816.

† A large portion of a vein of Californian gold-bearing Quartz, together wi h some richer fragments of auriferous Quartz, from the Grass Valley, Nevada co., are contained in the entrance hall of the Museum of Practical Geology. The discovery of gold in New South Wales was originally made by Count Strzelecki, but the colonial government of that day kept the circumstance a secret, in the belief that the existence of a gold-seeking population would lead to the demoralisation of the colony.

‡ A model of the mines worked by the Clunes Mining Co., and of the machines of the Port Phillip Gold Mining Co., Victoria, as they appeared in December, 1858, will be found on the Principal Floor of the Museum of Practical Geology. This model, constructed on a scale of ¼ of an inch to a foot, shows in a very instructive manner the mode of occurrence of the gold-bearing Quartz veins (or reefs, as they are called by the miners), and the manner in which they are worked.

§ See Mus. Pract. Geol., Wall-case 23.

GOLD AMALGAM, *H. Schneider.* A Native Amalgam of gold has been found in the platinum district of Columbia, associated with a platinum-ore, in small white globules of the size of peas, and easily crushed by pressure.

Comp. $(Au, Ag)^2 Hg^5$.

Analysis, by *Schneider:*

Mercury	. . .	57·40
Gold	. . .	38·39
Silver	. . .	5·0
		100·79

The amalgam of gold is also reported to occur in California, especially in the neighbourhood of Mariposa.

GONGILYTE, *Thoreld.* An altered mineral. Occurs massive, with a cleavage in two directions. Colour yellow or yellowish-brown. Subtranslucent. Lustre greasy. Streak white. Fracture conchoidal. H. 4 to 5. S.G. 2·7.

Comp. $(\ddot{M}g \dot{K})^5 \ddot{S}i^2 + 3\ddot{A}l \ddot{S}i^2 + 4\frac{1}{2}\dot{H}$, or $2\dot{R} \ddot{S}i + 3\ddot{R} \ddot{S}i + 3\dot{H}$ (Nordenskiöld).

BB yields water, and fuses to a blebby glass.

Locality. Yli Kit Kajärvi, in Finland.

GOSHENITE, *Shepard.* A variety of Beryl. Occurs in large round transparent grains and in short six-sided prisms, with their alternate angles replaced by single planes. Colour bluish-white, rarely rose-red. S.G. 2·85 to 2·76.

Locality. Goshen, Massachusetts, U.S.

Goshenite, when cut and polished, forms a brilliant gem.

GOSLARITE, *Haidinger.* Rhombic. Primary form a right rhombic prism: crystals generally produced artificially. Usually occurs massive, stalactitic, botryoidal, reniform and investing. Slightly efflorescent on the surface. Colour greyish, reddish, bluish, and greenish-white. Lustre vitreous. Transparent or translucent. Taste astringent, metallic and nauseous. Streak white. Brittle. Fracture conchoidal. H. 2 to 2·5. S.G. 1·9 to 2·1.

Fig. 218.

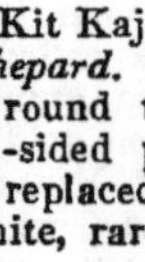

Comp. $\dot{Z}n \ddot{S} + 6\dot{H} =$ oxide of zinc 28·2, sulphuric acid 27·9, water 43·9 = 100.

Analysis, from Goslar, by *Klaproth:*

Sulphuric acid	. . .	22·0
Oxide of zinc	. . .	27·5
Oxide of iron	. . .	0·4
Oxide of manganese	. .	0·7
Water	. . . .	50·0
		100·6

In a matrass yields water.

BB fusible with intumescence, gives off sulphuric acid, and covers the charcoal with a white coating of oxide of zinc. Easily soluble in water.

This salt, supposed to result from the decomposition of Blende, with which it is frequently associated, is principally found in deserted galleries of old mines, in small crystalline tufts composed of minute interlaced needles, usually yellow, but sometimes coloured blue by sulphate of copper.

Localities.—British. Holywell in Flintshire, and occasionally in the Cornish mines: in acicular crystals at the Tresavean and Trethellan Mines, near St. Day.— *Foreign.* Rammelsberg Mine in the Harz, and particularly where much Blende occurs. Spitz in Austria. Schemnitz in Hungary. Salzburg. Fahlun and Sahlberg in Sweden, &c.

This salt, in its manufactured state, is extensively used in medicine and for dyeing. (See WHITE VITRIOL.)

Name. From one of its localities, Goslar, in the Harz.

Brit. Mus., Case 55.

GÖTHITE, *Dana, Beudant, Greg & Lettsom.* See GOETHITE.

GOTTHARDTITE, *Rammelsberg.* See DUFRENOYSITE.

GOUTTES D'EAU. A name sometimes given to pebbles of Topaz, in allusion to their limpidity. The Brazilian variety, when cut in facets like the diamond, closely resembles it in lustre and brilliance.

GOUTTE DE SANG. Fine cochineal-red or blood-red Spinelle.

GRAMENITE, *Krantz.* A mineral analogous to Pinguite and Nontronite, which has resulted from the decomposition of some felspathic rock, and by the substitution of peroxide of iron for alumina. It occurs in thin aggregated laminæ of a fine grass-green colour, like that of Pinguite. Lustre greasy. H. 1. S.G. of dried mass 1·87.

Comp. Silicate of peroxide of iron.

Analysis, by *Bergemann:*

Silica	. . .	38·39
Alumina	. . .	6·87
Peroxide of iron	. .	25·46
Protoxide of iron	. .	2·80

Protoxide of manganese	. 0·67
Magnesia . . .	. 0·75
Lime	. 0·56
Potash	. 1·14
Water . . .	. 23·36

100·00

In a tube becomes dull brown, giving off much water.

BB behaves like Pinguite; becomes magnetic.

Completely decomposes in acids, but with difficulty.

Locality. Menzenberg, in the Siebengebirge.

Name. From gramen, *grass*, because of its green colour.

GRAMMATITE (from γϱάμμη, *a line*). A variety of Tremolite, from Aker in Sweden.

GRAMMITE. See WOLLASTONITE.

GRANAT, *Werner, Mohs, Haidinger, Hausmann.* See GARNET.

GRANATIT, *Werner.* Staurotide. See GRENATITE.

GRANULAR CORUNDUM. See EMERY.

GRANULAR EPIDOTE, *Phillips.* See SCORZA.

GRANULAR HEAVY SPAR. The name given to fine-grained varieties of Barytes. It is found massive, in beds accompanying Galena, at Peggau, in Styria; also in the mining district of Freyberg, in Saxony, and at Schlangenberg, in Siberia, where it is associated with Copper-Green (Chrysocolla), and Native Copper. It may be distinguished from limestone, to which it bears a striking resemblance, in possessing less lustre and hardness, and in being much heavier.

GRANULAR IRON ORE, *Kirwan.* See BOHNERZ.

GRANULAR QUARTZ. Massive quartz-rock of a granular texture. Its colours are various, but always dull.

GRAPHIC GOLD, GRAPHIC TELLURIUM, *Phillips.* See SYLVANITE.

The name bears reference to the particular appearance produced by the aggregation of the capillary crystals, which are frequently disposed in rows more or less resembling graphic delineations.

GRAPHITE, *Dana, Greg & Lettsom, Jameson.* Hexagonal, primary form a regular six-sided prism. Occurs crystallized in flat six-sided tables, having the basal planes striated parallel to the alternate edges. Commonly in kidney-shaped concretions, or in imbedded, foliated, or granular masses. Colour iron- or dark steel-grey. Lustre me-

tallic. Opaque. Soils paper. Feels greasy. Sectile. Very flexible in thin laminæ. Streak black and shining. Not very brittle. Fracture granular and uneven. H. 1 to 2. S.G. 2·089.

Comp. C or carbon, with a variable quantity of iron, &c. mixed with it.

It always contains a small quantity of iron, often amounting to 5 per cent., but some specimens (as in those from Barreros in Brazil), scarcely contain a trace. The iron is, therefore, to be considered merely as an accidental admixture, and not as an essential constituent of the mineral.

Graphite, from Wunsiedel in Bavaria, yields only 0·33 per cent. of ash, consisting of potash, silica, and oxide of iron: it is therefore nearly pure carbon.—(*Fuchs.*) Graphite, from Germany (S.G. 2·273), contains 95·12 per cent. of carbon, and 5·78 per cent. of ash, chiefly consisting of grains of Quartz.—(*Regnault.*) Graphite, from Bustletown, in Pennsylvania, contains 95·4 per cent. of carbon, 0·6 of water, 2·6 of silica and alumina, and 1·4 of the oxides of iron and manganese.—(*Vanuxem.*) The purest Graphite, from Ceylon, yields only 1·2 per cent. of ash; other varieties 6 to 37·2 per cent., consisting of oxide of iron and earthy matters. Graphite, from the Himalaya Mountains, contains 71·6 per cent. of carbon, 5·0 of iron, 15 of silica, and 8·4 of alumina, &c.—(*J. Prinsep.*)

Analysis (*a*) from Borrowdale, (*b*) from Spain, by *Schräder*:

	(*a*)	(*b*)
Carbon . . .	85·25	88·7
Protoxide of iron .	5·80	7·1
Silica . . .	3·50	1·5
Alumina . . .	2·30	1·2
Oxide of copper .	0·00	1·0
Oxide of titanium .	3·15	1·5

100·00 100·00

At a high temperature, burns without flame or smoke, leaving usually some red oxide of iron.

BB becomes yellow or brown after long continued heat, but is infusible both alone and with reagents.

Unaltered by acids, which only affect the iron or other impurities.

Localities.—British. Graphite is found in nests of trap, occurring in clay-slate at Borrowdale, in Cumberland *; at a mine near

* "The *Plumbago*, from Borrowdale, in Cumberland, has long been celebrated for its fine quality; it is found in detached pieces, called, according to their size, *sops* or *bellies*, so that the supply is very irregular, the miners being fre-

M

Keswick, now nearly exhausted, a single mass of Graphite was found, about fifty years ago, which yielded about 70,000 lbs of the purer black-lead, worth about 30s. a lb. Graphite is also found at Bannerdale, near Keswick; in Cornwall, near Penryn, and at Grampound and Boscastle; at Beary, in the Isle of Man; in detached pieces, fit for common uses, at Killimore, in the Island of Mull. —*Irish.* Kilkenny.—*Foreign.* It also occurs in Greenland. At Pargas, in Finland. Arendal, in Norway. Passau, in Bohemia. Prussia. France; at Pontivy, in Brittany; in l'Aveyron, &c. Spain. Constantine, in Algeria. Ceylon. Travancore. Canada, at Grenville and Burgess. Mines are worked for this mineral in the United States, at Sturbridge, Massachusetts; Ticonderoga and Fishkill, N.Y., Brandon, Vt., and Wake, N.C. There is also a large deposit at St. John's, New Brunswick.

Name. The name Graphite is derived from γράφω, *to write*, in allusion to the purposes to which it is frequently applied.

Graphite is largely employed under the name of Plumbago, or Black-lead, for brightening iron, and protecting it from rust, and for diminishing friction in machinery. Crucibles are also made of it, which are capable of sustaining intense heat, and possess greater tenacity and expansibility than those made from ordinary clays. Its principal use, however, is in the manufacture of black-lead pencils.

Brit. Mus., Case 4.

M. P. G. Principal Floor, Wall-cases 39 (Ceylon and Travancore); 41 (Canada). Horse-shoe case, Nos. 17 to 54.

GRAUBRAUNSTEIN, *Haus-*⎫
mann. ⎬ Manganite.
GRAUBRAUNSTEINERZ, ⎪ See
Hausmann, Werner. ⎭ PYROLUSITE.

GRAUCOBALTERZ. See SYEPOORITE.

GRAUERZ. See GALENA.

GRAUGILTIGERZ. A dark grey copper (Tetrahedrite), rich in silver, from Wolfach, forming dodecahedrons with tetrahedral and cube-faces. S.G. 5·007.

ouently engaged for a long period in seeking for the graphite. Some years since a very large quantity of plumbago was obtained from Borrowdale; this has been stored by the proprietors, and sold in small parcels from time to time. The mine has not been worked for several years; it was examined by some skilled miners since the cessation of the work, and their opinions were not such as would lead us to believe that any large quantity of black lead would be discovered by any extension of the workings."—*R. Hunt's Descriptive Guide.* Workings have been again commenced, and, it is said, with some prospect of success.

Comp. (3Zn S, 4Fe S, 5Ag S) + 12 Cu² S + 6 Sb S⁵ = 4[($\frac{3}{12}$Zn, $\frac{4}{12}$Fe, $\frac{3}{12}$Ag) S] Sb S⁵ + Cu² S, Sb S⁵. (Gmelin.)

Analysis, by *H. Rose:*

Zinc	3·10
Iron	3·72
Silver	17·71
Copper	25·23
Antimony	26·63
Sulphur	23·52
	99·91

GRAUKUPFEREZ. See TENNANTITE.

GRAULITE. See TECTIZITE.

GRAUSILBER. See SELBITE.

GRAUSPIESSGLANZERZ,⎫
Hausmann. ⎬ Grey Antimony.
GRAUSPIESSGLASERZ, ⎪ See STIBNITE.
Werner. ⎭

GREASY QUARTZ. Those varieties of Milk-Quartz which display a greasy lustre.

GREEN CALAMINE, *Patrin.* Aurichalcite, found in cavities near Klopinski.

GREEN CARBONATE OF COPPER, *Phillips.* See MALACHITE.

GREEN DIALLAGE, *Haidinger.* Consists in some cases of laminæ of Amianthus, alternating with laminæ of Augite, both frequently of bright green colours, and forming a curious mixture in some of the rocks of Corsica, Monte Rosa, and the Bacher. In some specimens the passage from black crystallized Hornblende into white, silky Asbestos is distinctly visible. (Allan.)

GREEN EARTH, *Kirwan, Jameson, Phillips, Greg & Lettsom.* An altered form of Pyroxene, produced by the action of alkaline carbonates in solution; in which case alkalies take the place of the removed bases, and an alkaline silicate of alumina, or of iron and alumina, is formed. Green Earth is met with in small masses of an earthy or minutely crystalline appearance in, or lining cavities of, amygdaloid. Colour dark olive-green, with an unctuous feel. The Green Earth from Mount Baldo approaches to apple-green. Opaque. Soft: yields to the nail. Fracture generally earthy, glimmering, dull. S.G. 2·79 to 2·83.

Analysis, from Fassa, by *Rammelsberg:*

Silica	45·87
Alumina	11·18
Protoxide of iron	24·63
Magnesia	0·28
Lime	1·50
Potash and soda	6·72
Water	9·82
	100·00

Localities.—Scotch. Near Old Kilpatrick, S. Dumbarton. Kinnoul Hill near Perth. Little Cambray in the Isle of Arran.—*Irish.* In the trap and amygdaloidal rocks of Antrim.—*Foreign.* Faröe Isles. Saxony. Bohemia. Fassa in the Tyrol. Monte Baldo near Verona, &c. The Green Earth of Iceland occurs with Zeolites, and affords a trace of Vanadium. (S.G. 2·677.) Brit. Mus., Case 32.

GREEN IRON EARTH, *Phillips.* See HYPOCHLORITE.

GREEN IRON ORE; GREEN IRON STONE, *Karsten.* A mineral of similar nature to Dufrénite (which see).

Analysis, from Siegen in Prussia, by *Karsten:*

Peroxide of iron . . .	63·45
Phosphoric acid . . .	27·72
Water	8·56

99·73

GREEN LEAD ORE, *Jameson.* Mimetite. GREEN MALACOLITE. See PYROXENE. GREEN MARTIAL EARTH, *Kirwan.* See HYPOCHLORITE.

GREEN VITRIOL, *Allan.* See COPPERAS.

GREENLANDITE. The name given to the Precious Garnet of Greenland.

Analysis, by *Karsten:*

Silica	39·85
Alumina	20·60
Protoxide of iron . .	24·85
Protoxide of manganese .	0·46
Magnesia	9·93
Lime	3·51

99·20

GREENLANDITE. The name given by Breithaupt to Columbite crystals from the Cryolite vein of Greenland.

GREENOCKITE, *Brooke & Connel, Breithaupt, Greg & Lettsom, Dana.* Hexagonal; hemimorphous, that is to say, with the opposite extremities of the crystal dissimilar. Colour honey-yellow, orange-yellow, brown, veined parallel with the axes. Translucent, sometimes transparent or opaque. Lustre adamantine inclining to resinous. Streak between orange-yellow and brick-red. Strong double refraction: index of refraction 2·688. H. 3 to 3·5. S.G. 4·8 to 4·9.

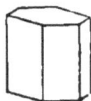
Fig. 219.

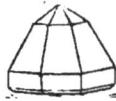
Fig. 220.

Comp. Sulphide of cadmium, or Cd S = cadmium 77·77, sulphur 22·23=100.

Analysis, by *Connel:*

Cadmium	77·30
Sulphur	22·56
Iron	trace

99·86

Decrepitates, when heated, somewhat strongly. Becomes carmine-red whenever it is heated, recovering its yellow colour on cooling.

BB on charcoal decomposed, and a yellowish-red ring of oxide of cadmium is deposited.

Soluble in strong muriatic acid, with violent evolution of sulphuretted hydrogen, and without separation of sulphur.

Localities.—Scotch. This rare mineral was first found in short hexagonal crystals in a railway cutting, at Bishoptown, near Paisley, in Renfrewshire. It occurred in small, but very perfect and brilliant, short hexagonal crystals, in a porphyritic greenstone, on Prehnite, and associated with Calcite and Natrolite. It has also been met with on the north of the Clyde, at Bowling quarry, near Old Kilpatrick, and elsewhere. It has also been obtained as a furnace product.

Name. In compliment to Lord Greenock, now Earl Cathcart, by whom it was first noticed.

Brit. Mus., Case 6.

M. P. G. Principal Floor, Wall-case 12, Nos. 543, 544 (British).

GREENOVITE, *Dufrénoy.* A dark rose-coloured variety of Sphene, from St. Marcel, in Piedmont, in which a portion of the lime is replaced by protoxide of manganese. S.G. 3·527.

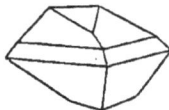
Fig. 221.

Analysis, by *Delesse:*

Silica	30·4
Titanic acid . . .	42·0
Protoxide of manganese .	3·6
Lime	24·3

100·3

Brit. Mus., Case 37.

GRENAT, *Brochant, Haüy.* See GARNET. The French word Grenat is in allusion to the resemblance of the stone in colour to the seeds of the pomegranate.

GRENAT BLANC, *Dufrénoy.* See LEUCITE.

GRENAT BRUN, &c., *Haüy.* Common Garnet.

GRENAT MANGANÈSE, *Brochant.* See MANGANESIAN GARNET.

GRENAT MELANITE, *Brochant.* See ME-LANITE.

GRENAT NOBLE, *Brochant.* See ALMAN-DINE, PRECIOUS GARNET.

GRENAT NOIR, *Haüy.* See MELANITE.

GRENAT RESINITE, *Haüy.* See COLOPHO-NITE.

GRENAT ROUGE DE FEU GRANULI-FORME, *Haüy.* See PYROPE.

GRENAT DU VESUVE, *Dufrénoy.* See LEUCITE.

GRENATITE, *Jameson.* A name given to Staurotide, in allusion to its (occasional) garnet colour.

GRENGESITE, *Hisinger.* A dark green variety of Delessite, occurring in hemi-spherical masses, with a radiated structure. Streak greyish-green. H. 2. S.G. 3·1.

Analysis, by *Hisinger:*

Silica . . . . 27·01
Alumina . . . 14·31
Peroxide of manganese . 2·18
Protoxide of iron . . 25·63
Magnesia . . . 14·31
Water . . . . 12·53
                         ——
                        95·97

Name. After the locality where it is found, Grengesberg, in Dalecarlia.

GREY ANTIMONY, *Jameson.* See STIBNITE.

GREY COBALT, *Allan.* See SMALTINE.

GREY COPPER, *Phillips.* } See
GREY COPPER-ORE, *Jameson,* } TETRA-
Kirwan. } HEDRITE.

GREY MANGANESE, *Allan.*}
GREY MANGANESE-ORE, }
Jameson. } See
GREY ORE OF MANGANESE, } MANGANITE.
Kirwan. }
GREY OXIDE OF MAN-}
GANESE, *Phillips.* }

GREY SILVER ORE, *Jameson.* See SEL-BITE.

GRINDING SPAR. A name applied in Madras to Corundum.

GROPPITE, *Svanberg.* A mineral sug-gested by L. Sæmann to be altered Parga-site. Colour rose-red to brownish red. Translucent in thin splinters. Streak paler than the mineral. Fracture splintery. H. 2·5. S.G. 2·73.

Comp. $\dot{R}^3 \ddot{S}i^2 + 2\ddot{A}l \ddot{S}i + 3\dot{H}$ (Svanberg)[*],

or $\dot{R}^2 \ddot{S}i + \ddot{H} \ddot{S}i + 2\dot{H}$ (Rammelsberg).

* See Ottrelite.

Analysis, by *Svanberg:*

Silica . . . . 45·01
Alumina . . . 22·55
Peroxide of iron . . 3·06
Lime . . . . 4·55
Magnesia . . . 12·28
Potash . . . . 5·23
Soda . . . . 0·22
Water . . . . 7·11
Undissolved . . . 0·13
                        ——
                       100·13

BB becomes white, and on thin edges shows only incipient fusion. Dissolves in borax, with intumescence.

Locality. In limestone, at Gropptorp, in Sweden, whence the name Groppite.

GROROILITE, *Berthier.* A variety of Wad, occurring in roundish masses, of a brownish-black colour, and with a reddish-brown streak. H. sometimes 6 to 6·5.

Analysis, by *Berthier:*

Protoxide of manganese . 62·4
Oxygen . . . . 12·8
Peroxide of iron . . 6·0
Water . . . . 15·8
Clay . . . . 3·0
                        ——
                       100·0

Localities. Vicdessos and Cautern, in France.

Name. After a locality in Groroi, in Mayenne.

GROSSULAR, *Phillips;* GROSSULARITE. A variety of calcareous Alumina-Garnet. Co-lour pale olive-green or greenish-white. Translucent. Brilliant. Hard. Fracture con-choidal, with a vitreous lustre. S.G. 3·42.

Comp. $\dot{C}a^5 \ddot{S}i + \ddot{A}l \ddot{S}i.$

Analysis, from the Sludianka River, by *N. v. Iwanow:*

Silica . . . . 49·99
Alumina . . . 14·90
Peroxide of iron . . 10·94
Protoxide of manganese . trace
Lime . . . . 32·94
Magnesia . . . 0·98
                        ——
                       100·15

BB like Almandine, but affords a brown-ish-coloured glass.

Localities. Near the river Wilui, in Si-beria, in a greenish-coloured serpentinous rock. (See Wiluite.) Tellemark, in Norway.

Name. From *grossula* (a gooseberry), in allusion to its colour, which is similar to that of a green gooseberry.

Brit. Mus., Case 36.
M. P. G. Horse-shoe Case, No. 901.
GRÜNAUITE, *Nicol, Dana.* Cubical. Occurs in very small crystals, also granular
and disseminated. Colour pale steel-grey,
inclining to silver-white, with a yellow or
greyish tarnish. Lustre metallic. Streak
dark grey. Brittle. H. 4·5. S.G. 5·13.
Comp. Ni S (Ni S³, Bi S³), or Bi S +
4Ni S³ = nickel 45·40, bismuth 15·76, sul·
phur 38·84 = 100. (v. Kobell.)
Analysis, (a) by *v. Kobell,* (b) by *Schnabel:*

	(a)	(b)
Nickel	40·65	22·78
Bismuth	14·11	10·41
Sulphur	38·46	33·10
Iron	8·48	6·06
Cobalt	0·28	11·43
Copper	1·68	11·56
Lead	1·58	4·36
	100·24	100·00

BB gives off sulphurous odours, and fuses
to a brittle, magnetic globule, colouring the
charcoal yellow; with borax gives a nickel-
reaction.
Forms a green solution in nitric acid,
the sulphur being precipitated.
Locality. Grünau, in Sayn-Altenkirchen,
in Prussia, usually mixed with Quartz and
Copper Pyrites.
Grünauite is distinguished from Arsenical
Iron, which it greatly resembles, by lower
specific gravity, and very easily by its be-
haviour with acids.
GRÜNBLEIERZ, *Hoffmann, Werner.* See
PYROMORPHITE, and MIMETITE.
GRÜNE EISENERDE, *Werner.* See HYPO-
CHLORITE.
GRÜNEISENSTEIN. See GREEN IRON-
STONE.
GRÜNERDE, *Werner.* See GREEN EARTH.
GRÜNERITE. A pure Iron-Augite. S.G.
3·713.

Comp. Fe³ Si² = protoxide of iron 54·8,
silica 57·1 = 100.

Analysis, from Collobrières, by *Grüner:*

Silica	43·9
Alumina	1·9
Magnesia	1·1
Lime	0·5
Protoxide of iron	52·2
	99·6

Locality. Collobrières, Dept. de l'Aude,
France.
Name. After Grüner, by whom it was
analysed.

GRÜNES URANERZ. See CHALCOLITE.
GUANITE, *E. F. Teschemacher.* See STRU-
VITE.
The name Guanite is in allusion to its
occurrence in guano.
GUARINITE, *G. Guiscardi.* A mineral
nearly allied in composition to the Sphene
of Piedmont (Greenovite). It occurs in
pyramidal crystals, with a difficult cleavage.
Colour honey-yellow. Translucent to trans-
parent. Lustre subadamantine : adamantine on cleavage faces. H. 6 to 6·5. S.G.
3·487.
Comp. Silica 33·64, titanic acid, 33·92,
lime 28·01, iron and peroxide of manganese
trace = 95·57.
Locality. Vesuvius.
Name. After Prof. G. Guarini, of Naples.
GUM-LEAD. A name given to Plumbo-
Resinite, because of its resemblance, in appearance, to gum-arabic.
GUMMI FUNEREUM, *Serapion.* See AS-
PHALT.
GUMMIERZ, *Breithaupt.* An amorphous
variety of Pitchblende, containing Vanadium and Selenium. Colour hyancith-red,
yellowish, and reddish-brown. Lustre resinous. Soft : breaks between the fingers.
Fracture conchoidal. H. 2·5 to 3. S.G.
3·9 to 4·18.

Comp. $\ddot{U} + 4\dot{H}$ (Dufrénoy); $\dot{C}a^3 \dddot{P} + 4\ddot{U}$
$\dot{H}$? (Kersten).

Analysis, by *Kersten:*

Peroxide of uranium	72·00
Peroxide of manganese	0·05
Silica	4·26
Phosphoric acid	2·30
Lime	6·00
Arsenic	trace
Hydrofluoric acid	trace
Water	14·75
	99·86

Locality. Johanngeorgenstadt, in Saxony.
Name. The name is in allusion to its
gum-like appearance.
GUMMISPATH. See GUM-LEAD.
GURHOFIAN. GURHOFITE. A snow-white
and subtranslucent compact variety of Dolomite, bearing, in some respects, a strong
remblance to Semi-opal. Fracture flat-conchoidal, with sharp edges.
Analysis, by *Klaproth:*

Carbonate of lime	70·50
Carbonate of magnesia	29·50
	100·00

Locality. Near Gurhof, in Lower Austria,

in veins traversing Serpentine; whence the name *Gurhofian.*

Brit. Mus., Case 47.

GURHOLITE, *Anderson.* See GYROLITE.

GUYACANITE, *F. Field..* A variety of Enargite, from the Cordilleras of Chili. H. 3·5 to 4. S.G. 4·39.

Name. The name Guyacanite was given to this variety in consequence of its having been first brought to the large copper-smelting works of Guyacana.

GUYAQUILLITE, *James, F. W. Johnston.* An acid-resin. Amorphous. Colour pale yellow, with a lustre not resinous, or imperfectly so. Opaque. Yields easily to the knife, and may be rubbed to powder. S.G. 1·092.

Comp. C^{20} H^{13} O^5 = carbon 76·665, hydrogen 8·174, oxygen 15·161 = 100.

Very slightly soluble in water, and largely in alcohol, giving a yellow solution, which has an *intensely bitter taste.*

Melts at 157° Fahr., but remains viscid, and does not flow easily until heated to nearly 212°. The action of liquid ammonia on this substance is very characteristic: the pale yellow solutions, by the addition of a few drops of ammonia, becoming gradually dark, and ultimately dark brownish-red.

Locality. Guyaquil, in S. America.

Guyaquillite, like Amber, is probably of vegetable origin; it occurs on the site of ancient forests of resiniferous trees.

GYMNITE. The name given by Thomson to Deweylite, from γυμνὸς, *naked,* in allusion to the locality, Bare Hills, Maryland, U.S.

Analysis, from Bare Hill, by *Thomson :*

Silica	.	.	.	40·16
Alumina	.	.	.	trace
Peroxide of iron	.	.	1·16
Magnesia	.	.	.	36·00
Lime	.	.	.	0·80
Water	.	.	.	21·60

99·72

GYPS, *Jameson, Haidinger, Hausmann.* GYPSUM, *Kirwan, Phillips.*

Comp. Bihydrated sulphate of lime, or

Ċa S̈ + 2Ḣ = lime 32·56, sulphuric acid 46·51, water 20·93 = 100.

There are several varieties of Gypsum, which are described under their respective names. The transparent crystals are called *Selenite,* the fibrous varieties *Satin Spar,* and the fine massive kinds *Alabaster.* See also SCHAUMKALK.

Satin Spar and Alabaster are manufactured largely into ornamental articles, and works of art. Gypsum is also used in the manufacture of glass and porcelain, and the coarser kinds are employed in agriculture as a top-dressing for grass-lands. Perhaps, however, the largest consumption of Gypsum is in the form of Plaster of Paris (or stucco), a name which is derived from the circumstance of its being found in large quantities in the Paris Basin.

Gypsum loses its water far below a red heat, splitting into layers, and crumbling to a white powder, which is Plaster of Paris. Moderately burned Gypsum, when ground up and mixed with water, forms a paste in the first instance, but this quickly hardens (into what is called *stucco*), heat being evolved, and the water passing into the solid condition of water of crystallization. The harder the Gypsum is before it is burnt, the more solid it becomes when subsequently mixed with water.

Localities.—*English.* Staffordshire; Nottinghamshire; Chellaston Hill, and elsewhere, in Derbyshire; on the coast of Glamorganshire, as well as in the cliffs between Pennarth and Lavernock; in the New Red Marl of those counties, and in the salt districts of Cheshire and Worcestershire. It occurs also in the New Red Marl of the vicinity of Watchet, in Somersetshire, where it is occasionally collected on the coast, and sent to Bristol, Swansea, and some other places in the Bristol Channel. The Isle of Purbeck, in Dorsetshire, forming large concretions in the Lower Purbeck Beds.—*Foreign.* France, in the lacustrine basins of Auvergne and Aix, in the latter containing an admixture of eight per cent. of carbonate of lime; in the fresh-water clays of the Paris basin, at Montmartre, Pantin, &c., with Sulphate of Strontia. Spain: near Madrid, in tertiary clays, accompanied by beds of Chert and of Magnesite; abundantly in the sandstones underlying Jurassic limestones both near Malaga and near the Sierra Nevada, in Andalusia. The Alps and Pyrenees, interstratified with crystalline schists. Switzerland, at Bex. The south foot of the Harz: Salzburg salt formations in Austria. Sicily with Sulphur. Italy, at Pomarance, Matarano, and Jano, in Tuscany, where Serpentine is found piercing limestones. Bologna, in miocene clays with flints, sulphates of baryta, and strontia, together with Pyrites and Sulphur. Algiers, associated with crystalline limestone, gneiss, Amphibolite, and Serpentine. Sweden, at Fahlun, associated with Dolomite and Serpentine in the chloritic bands of the oldest crystalline rocks of Scandinavia. Asia Minor. Nova Scotia, in rocks of the carboniferous series, with sulphate of soda and Boro-calcite. America: the oldest Gypsums in America occur near the base of the Palæozoic series in the so-called Calciferous Sand-rock of Canada ; it is occasionally met with in the Clinton and Niagara groups, and in the Onondaga salt-group in the Upper Silurian rocks of Canada and New York, sometimes accompanied by sulphur.*

Name. The word Gypsum is derived from γύψος, the name by which the substance, both in its burnt and native state, seems to have been known to the ancients, who obtained their supplies chiefly from Cyprus, Phœnicia and Syria, and applied it to the same purposes as the moderns. Theophrastus says, "The stone from which Gypsum is made, by burning, is like Alabaster ; it is not dug, however, in such large masses, but in separate lumps. Its viscidity and heat, when moistened, are very wonderful. They use this in buildings, casing them with it, or putting it on any particular place they would strengthen. They prepare it for use, by reducing it to powder, and then pouring water on it, and stirring and mixing the matter well together with wooden instruments : for they cannot do this with the hand because of the heat. They prepare it in this manner immediately before the time of using it ; for in a very little while after moistening, it dries and becomes hard, and not in a condition to be used.

"This cement is very strong, and often remains good, even after the walls it is laid on crack and decay, and the sand of the stone they are built with moulders away : for it is often seen, that even after some part of a wall has separated itself from the rest, and is fallen down, other parts of it shall yet hang together, and continue firm and in their place, by means of the strength of this matter which they are covered with.

"This Gypsum may also be taken off from buildings, and by burning, again and again, be made fit for use. It is used for the casing the outsides of edifices, principally in Cyprus and Phœnicia ; but in Italy, for whitening over the walls, and other kinds of ornaments within houses. Some kinds of it are also used by painters in their business ; and by the fullers, about cloths.

"It is also excellent, and superior to all other things for making images ; for which it is greatly used, and especially in Greece,

* See Memoir on the Formation of Gypsum and Magnesian Rocks, by T. Sterry Hunt. Am. Jour. Science and Arts, vol. xxviii.

because of its pliableness and smoothness." —*Theophrastus*, cxii. to cxvi. Brit. Mus., Case 54.

M. P. G. (See ALABASTER, and ARAGONITE), Case 10 in Hall. Horse-shoe Case, Nos. 216, 281 to 311, No. 286 specimen from Reinhardtsbrunn in Gotha, presented by H.R.H. Prince Albert. Upper Gallery, Wall-case 40, Nos. 33 to 42.

GYPSUM SELENITES, *Wallerius.* See SELENITE.

GYRASOLE of Kirwan. A variety of Oriental Sapphire. "Its colour is white with a slight tinge of red, and a still lighter of blue, which gives it some resemblance to Chalcedony."

GYROLITE, *Greg & Lettsom, Brooke & Miller.* GYROLITH, *v. Kobell, Naumann.* Occurs in spherical lamellar radiations, which are translucent when first found, but soon become opaque, or are only translucent in thin plates. Colour white, with a vitreous lustre when fresh, which turns to pearly on exposure to the air. Very tough. H. 3 to 4.

Comp. 3Ċa S̈i + 4Ḣ = silica 53·29, lime 32·86, water 13·85 = 100.

Analysis, by *Anderson :*

Silica . . . . . 50·70
Alumina . . . . 1·48
Lime . . . . . 33·24
Magnesia . . . . 0·18
Water . . . . . 14·18
                        ——
                        99·78

Localities.—British. The Storr, nine miles from Portree, in Skye, in the cavities of a very compact basalt; also Quirang and Lyndale; near Loch Screden, in Mull.— *Foreign.* Greenland, at Karartut; Disco Island, near Godhavn; and at Niakomak, Omensnaksfiord, Faröe.

Name. The name, derived from γύρος, a *circle,* and λίθος, *stone,* has reference to the spherical disposition of the mineral. Brit. Mus., Case 28.

H.

HAAR SALZ, *Werner.* MAGNESIA-ALUM. See ALUNOGEN. See also HAIR SALT.

HAARFÖRMIGES ROTHKUPFERERZ, *Werner.* See CHALCOTRICHITE.

HAARKIES, *Mohs, Werner.* See MILLERITE.

HABRONEME, from ἁβρός, *delicate,* and νῆμα, *thread* or *fibre.*

HACKED QUARTZ, *Bakewell.* A variety

of Quartz presenting incisions, as if produced by hacking it in various directions with a knife or other sharp instrument. These indentations are occasioned by laminæ or laminar crystals of other minerals once imbedded in the Quartz, the casts of which only are now left, the included minerals themselves having decomposed or been otherwise removed.

HÆMACHATES (from *αἶμα, blood,* and *"Αχατης, agate*), the name given by the ancient Greeks to Agate sprinkled with spots of red Jasper.

HEMATITE. See HEMATITE.

HAFNEFJORDITE. A variety of Oligoclase from Hafnefjord, in Iceland.

Analysis, by *Forchhammer :*

Silica	. . . .	61·22
Alumina	. . .	23·32
Peroxide of iron	. .	2·40
Lime	. . . .	8·82
Magnesia	. . .	0·36
Soda	. . . .	2·56
Potash	. . . .	trace
		98·68

HAIDINGERITE, *Berthier.* See BERTHIE-RITE.

HAIDINGERITE, *Turner.* Rhombic: primary form a rectangular four-sided prism. Usually occurs in minute crystals aggregated into botryoidal forms and drusy crusts. Colour and streak white, with a vitreous lustre. Transparent to translucent. Sectile. Slightly flexible in thin laminæ. H. 1·5 to 2·5. S.G. 2·848.

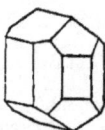

Fig. 222.

Comp. Di-arseniate of lime or $\ddot{C}a^2 \overset{...}{As} +$ $3\dot{H}=$ lime 28·28, arsenic acid 58·08, water 13·64=100.

Analysis, by *Turner :*

Arseniate of lime	.	85·68
Water	. . . .	14·32
		100·00

Dissolves readily in nitric acid.

BB it is almost entirely volatilized with a dense white arsenical vapour.

. *Locality.* Joachimsthal, where it occurs associated with Pharmacolite, from which it may be distinguished by its form and lustre: and by containing only half the quantity of water.

Name. After Herr W. Haidinger of Vienna, by whom it was first noticed. It is a very rare mineral.

HAIR PYRITES, *Jameson.* See MILLE-RITE.

HAIR SALT, *Jameson.* Magnesia Alum. See ALUNOGEN.

Comp. Tersulphate of alumina, or $\overset{..}{Al}$ $\overset{..}{S}^3 + 18\dot{H}.$

Analysis, from Bilin, by *Rammelsberg :*

Silica	. . . .	35·31
Alumina	. . .	15·86
Water	. . . .	48·83
		100·00

Brit. Mus., Case 55.

HAIR STONE. Rock Crystal inclosing capillary crystals of Rutile, crossing each other and traversing it in various directions.

HALBAZURBLEI, *Rammelsberg.* See CALE-DONITE.

HALBOPAL. See SEMIOPAL.

HALLITE. A variety of Websterite found with Gypsum, in Plastic Clay, at Halle in Prussia.

Comp. $\overset{..}{Al} \overset{..}{S} + 9\dot{H}.$

Analysis, by *Stromeyer :*

Alumina	. . .	20·26
Sulphuric acid	. .	23·36
Water	. . . .	46·38
		100·00

HALLOYLITE; HALLOYSITE, *Berthier.* HALLOYTE. A siliciferous hydrate of alumina or Kaolin, occurring in soft, smooth, compact amorphous masses, having the appearance of Steatite. Colour white, generally with a slight tint of blue, and a waxy lustre. Translucent at the edges or becomes so in water, which it imbibes, giving off numerous globules of air. Adheres to the tongue. Yields to the nail, and affords a shining streak. Fracture conchoidal, like that of wax. S.G. 1·8 to 2·1.

Comp. $\overset{..}{Al} \overset{..}{Si} + 3\dot{H}.$

Analysis, from Housscha, by *Berthier :*

Silica	. . . .	47·75
Alumina	. . .	35·49
Water	. . . .	16·76
		100·00

Loses weight when exposed to a high temperature, and becomes much harder, and of a milk-white colour.

Decomposed by sulphuric acid, with separation of gelatinous silica.

Locality. The neighbourhood of Liège and Namur; with ores of zinc, lead, and iron. Housscha near Bayonne, in graphic granite. Milo in a pumiceous tufa. Upper Silesia. Guateque in New Granada, &c.

Name. Named by Berthier after his uncle Omalius d'Halloy, by whom it was first noticed.

Brit. Mus., Case 26.

Halloysites are richer in alumina than Smectite, and contain like it 24 to 25 per cent. of water.

HALLOYSITE OF ST. JEAN-DE-COLE. A rose-coloured Nontronite, found at Thiviers.

HALOTRICHINE, *Scacchi.* A silky variety of Iron-alum from the Solfatara.

Comp. $3\ddot{F}e\ \ddot{S} + 2\ddot{A}l\ \ddot{S}^3 + 54\dot{H}.$

Analysis:

Alumina	. 9·76
Protoxide of iron .	. 10·20
Sulphuric acid	. 34·12
Water .	. 45·92
	100·00

HALOTRICHITE, *Brooke & Miller.* An Iron-alum.

Occurs in fibrous, silky masses of a yellowish-white colour. Taste sweet and astringent, somewhat resembling that of ink.

Comp. $\ddot{F}e\ \ddot{S} + \ddot{A}l\ \ddot{S}^3 + 24\dot{H} =$ sulphate of iron 16·4, sulphate of alumina 37·0, water 46·6 = 100.

Analysis, from Mörsfeld, by *Rammelsberg:*

Alumina . .	. 10·914
Protoxide of iron	. 9·867
Sulphuric acid .	. 36·025
Magnesia . .	. 0·235
Potash . .	. 0·434
Water . .	. 43·025
	100·000

Soluble in water.

Turns red, and parts with its water when heated.

Localities.—British. Abundantly in the shale of exhausted coal-beds at Hurlet and Campsie, near Paisley, probably mixed with Melanterite or sulphate of iron.—*Foreign.* Bodenmais and Mörsfeld in Rhenish Bavaria. Oroomiah in Persia, where it is used for making ink of a fine quality.

Name. From άλς, *salt,* and θρίξ, *hair.*

Brit. Mus., Case 55.

HÄMATIT, *Haidinger, Hausmann.* See HEMATITE.

HAMPSHIRITE, *Hermann.* The name given to the Steatite of certain steatitic

pseudomorphs (mostly after Quartz), described and analysed by Dewey.

Analysis:

Silica	. 50·60
Alumina . . .	. 0·15
Magnesia . . .	. 28·83
Protoxide of iron . .	. 2·59
Protoxide of manganese .	1·10
Water	. 15·00
	97·27

Locality. Middlefield, Hampshire co., U.S.,; in a great bed of Serpentine.

HARD COAL. Those kinds of Coal which burn without caking, and leave a white ash.

HARD FAHLUNITE, *Berzelius.* A brownish-yellow variety of Iolite, which owes its peculiar colour and opacity to accidental admixture.

Locality. Fahlun in Sweden.

HARD LITHOMARGE. See TERATOLITE.

HARD SPAR, *Jameson.* See ANDALUSITE.

HARMOTOME, *Dana, Greg & Lettsom, Haüy, Phillips.* Rhombic. Sometimes occurs in flattish rectangular prisms, terminated by rhombic planes, replacing the solid angles of the prism; these crystals often cross each other lengthwise and at right angles, so that their axes coincide; hence the name *Cross-stone,* applied to it by Jameson and others. Colour generally greyish-white, passing into grey, yellow, red, or brown. .Translucent. Lustre pearly. Streak white. Brittle. Fracture uneven, imperfectly conchoidal. H. 4·5. S.G. 2·39 to 2·498.

 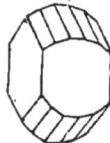 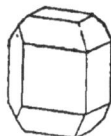

Fig. 223.　　　Fig. 224.　　　Fig. 225.

Comp. $\ddot{B}a\ \ddot{S}i + \ddot{A}l\ \ddot{S}i^2 + 5\dot{H} =$ silica, 44·0, alumina 16·6, baryta 24·8, water 14·6 = 100.

Analysis, from Strontian, by *Köhler:*

Silica . . .	. 46·10
Alumina . . .	. 16·41
Baryta . . .	. 20·81
Lime : . . .	. 0·63
Potash . . .	. 0·90
Water . . .	. 15·11
	99·96

BB on charcoal, melts easily, without intumescence, to a clear glass.

When finely pounded, perfectly decomposed by muriatic acid, though with difficulty, silica being separated in the pulverulent state. When powdered and thrown on charcoal emits a greenish-yellow phosphorescent light.

Localities. — Scotland. Abundantly at Strontian in Argyleshire, in fine white and translucent crystals, with Calcite and Barytes, in mineral veins in granite near its junction with gneiss. (See MORVENITE.) *Figs.* 223, 224, 225. Near Old Kilpatrick in Dumbartonshire, in small colourless crystals associated with Edingtonite and Cluthalite. Campsie Hills, Stirlingshire, *fig.* 223.—*Ireland.* The Giant's Causeway, in basalt, *fig.* 223.—*Foreign.* The cruciform varieties chiefly occur at Andreasberg in the Harz, in metalliferous veins, traversing clay-slate, generally in druses. Oberstein in Deux-ponts, in single crystals in the hollows of siliceous geodes. Kongsberg, in Norway, on gneiss.

Name. From ἁρμός, *a joint*, and τέμνω, *to cut;* in reference to the division of which the crystals are susceptible at the junction of the planes of the pyramid.

Brit. Mus., Case 29.

M. P. G. Horse-shoe Case, Nos. 1162, 1163.

HARRINGTONITE, *Thomson.* An amorphous variety of Mesolite. Occurs massive, of a chalky white colour. Opaque. Earthy. Very tough. H. 5·25. S.G. 2·21.

Comp. $(\dot{N}a, \dot{C}a^2) \, 3\ddot{S}i + 3\ddot{A}l \, \ddot{S}i + 6\dot{H}.$

Analysis, by *Thomson :*

Silica	44·84
Alumina . . .	28·48
Lime	10·68
Soda	5·56
Water . . .	10·28
	99·84

Localities.—Irish. In veins and layers traversing greenstone at Portrush, and at the Skerries, co. Antrim, Magee Island, and Agnew's Hill, west of Larne.

HARRISITE, *Genth* A Vitreous Copper with cubical cleavage, from the Canton mine in Georgia, U.S.

HARTBRAUNSTEIN, *Hausmann.* See BRAUNITE.

HARTINE, *Schrötter.* A resinous mineral resembling Hartite. It occurs massive, of a white colour, and is without taste or smell. Pulverises between the fingers. Melts at 210° C. (410° F.), and distills at 260° C. (500° F.).

Comp. $C^{20}, H^{17}, O^2.$

Analysis, by *Schrötter :*

Carbon	78·26
Hydrogen . . .	10·92
Oxygen . . .	10·82
	100·00

Locality. Oberhart, in Austria, in Brown Coal.

HARTITE, *Haidinger.* A fossil resin resembling wax in appearance. Colourless or greyish-white, with a somewhat greasy lustre. Translucent. Brittle. H. 1. S.G. 1·04 to 1·06.

Comp. $C^6, H^5 =$ carbon 87·473, hydrogen 12·048 = 100.

Fuses at 165° F. to a clear fluid, and at a high temperature distills.

Easily soluble in ether, less readily in alcohol, and crystallizes from each on evaporation.

Localities. Oberhart, near Gloggnitz, in Lower Austria, in small tables with six faces, in Brown Coal. Rozenthal, near Köflach, in Styria, in comparatively large, irregular, perfectly transparent, and cleavable pieces, showing, in the polarising apparatus, very distinct systems of elliptical coloured rings; and, still more frequently in the lignite, in small veins, incrustations or angular fragments.

Hartite is distinguished from Scheererite by its crystallization, and by fusing at a higher temperature.

Brit. Mus., Case 60.

HARTKOBALTERZ, }
HARTKOBALTKIES. } See SKUTTERUDITE.

HARTMANGAN, }
HARTMANGANERZ. } See PSILOMELANE.

HARTMANNITE. See ULLMANNITE.

HARZIGE STEIN-KOHLE, *Haidinger.* Bituminous Coal. See COAL.

HARZLOSE STEIN-KOHLE, *Mohs.* See ANTHRACITE.

HATCHETTINE, *Conybeare, Phillips.* A Mineral Tallow. Occurs either flaky like spermaceti, or subgranular like bees-wax. When flaky it has a slightly glistening and pearly lustre, and a considerable degree of translucency; when subgranular it is dull and opaque. Colour yellowish-white, to wax- and greenish-yellow, but becomes darker and more opaque on exposure. Feels greasy. About the consistency of soft tallow. S.G. at 60° F. 0·916.

Melts at 115° F. into a transparent colourless liquid, which becomes opaque and white on cooling. Slightly soluble in cold ether, more so in hot ether; on cooling the solution coagulates into a mass of minute pearly fibres. Sparingly soluble in boiling alcohol, from which it precipitates again on cooling. Heated cautiously, it distills over without change.

Comp. (C, H).

Analysis, from Merthyr-Tydvil, by *Johnston* :

Carbon . . . . 85·910
Hydrogen . . . . 14·624
               100·534

Localities. — British. Ebbw Vale, and neighbouring works, near Merthyr-Tydvil, in Glamorganshire; in masses, resembling wax or train-oil, in the crevices of coal-measure Clay Ironstone. Near Loch Fyne, in Argyleshire. Below the Hutton seam, at Pelton Colliery, Chester-le-Street. Urpeth Colliery, near Newcastle, in cavities near the side of a *fault*, and sometimes in the solid sandstone rock, at a depth of about 60 fathoms from the surface.—*Foreign.* Rossitz, in Moravia.

Name. In honour of the eminent chemist, Hatchett.

Brit. Mus., Case 60.

M. P. G. Horse-shoe Case, No. 103.

HAUERITE, *Haidinger.* Cubical; hemihedral like Pyrites; octahedral the most common form. Sometimes occurs in crystals clustered into spheroidal forms. Colour reddish-brown to brownish-black. Lustre metallic-adamantine. Streak brownish-red. H. 4. S.G. 3·463.

Comp. Mn S² = manganese 46·3, sulphur 53·7 = 100.

Analysis, by *Patera* :

Sulphur . . . . 53·64
Manganese . . . . 42·97
Iron . . . . . 1·30
Silica . . . . . 1·20
               99·11

BB is reduced to a simple sulphide (Mn S), with the evolution of much sulphur; with soda affords a manganese reaction.

Locality. The sulphur pits at Kalinka, near Neusohl, in Hungary, in clay, associated with Gypsum and Sulphur.

Name. After Privy Councillor Von Hauer, and because of the part which his son, F. v. Hauer, took in the determination of the species.

Brit. Mus., Case 5.

HAUSMANNITE, *Dana, Phillips.* Pyramidal. Occurs crystallized in acute, square-based pyramids ; also massive. Colour brownish- or iron-black. Lustre semi-metallic. Opaque. Yields a reddish- or chestnut-brown powder, which dissolves in cold concentrated sulphuric acid, forming a red solution. Very hard. Fracture uneven. H. 5 to 5·5. S.G. 4·72.

Comp. Mn M̈n, or Ṁn 31·03, M̈n 69·07 = manganese 72·1, oxygen 27·9 = 100.

Analysis, from Ihlefeld, by *Turner* :

Protoxide and peroxide of
  manganese . . . 98·09
Excess of oxygen . . 0·22
Baryta . . . . 0·11
Silica . . . . . 0·33
Metallic chloride . . . trace
Water . . . . . 0·44
               100·00

BB on charcoal fuses at the edges; with borax readily forms a deep violet-blue or nearly black globule, with soda a green slag.

Dissolves in heated muriatic acid, with the evolution of chlorine.

Localities. Æhrenstock, near Ilmenau, in Thuringia, in veins of porphyry, with other ores of manganese. Ihlefeld, in the Harz. Framont, in Alsace. Lebanon, Pennsylvania, U.S.

Name. After Professor Hausmann, of Göttingen.

See RANCIERITE.

Brit. Mus., Case 13.

M. P. G. Principal Floor, Wall-cases 13 (British).

HAÜYNA, *Karsten.* HAÜYNE, *Phillips.* Cubical. Occurs often in distinct rhombic dodecahedrons, but generally in crystalline grains, and massive. Colour indigo-blue and opaque, or blue or bluish–green and translucent. Lustre vitreous to greasy. Streak bluish-white. Very brittle. Fracture flat-conchoidal, and very splendent. H. 5·5. S.G. 2·4 to 3·0.

Comp. Na³ S̈i + 3Äl S̈i + 2Ċa S̈ = silica 32·1, alumina 27·3, lime 9·9, soda 16·5, sulphuric acid 14·21 = 100.

Analysis, from Monte Albano, by *Whitney* :

Silica . . . . . 32·44
Sulphuric acid . . . 12·98
Alumina . . . . 27·75
Lime . . . . . 9·96
Potash . . . . . 2·40
Soda . . . . . 14·24
               99·71

BB alone, on charcoal, decrepitates, and melts slowly to an opaque white or greenish-blue blebby glass; with borax effervesces and forms a transparent glass, which becomes yellow on cooling.

In heated muriatic acid forms a white transparent jelly.

Localities. The older lavas of Vesuvius, and the Papal States. Niedermendig, in basalt. Near Andernach, on the Rhine, in lava or pumice.

Name. In honour of the French mineralogist, René Just Haüy.

Brit. Mus., Case 55.

M. P. G. Horse-shoe Case, Nos. 1013, 1014. Upper Gallery, Table-case A, in recess 4, Nos. 75 to 78.

HAYDENITE, *Cleveland.* A yellowish variety of Chabazite, occurring in reddish or garnet-coloured scalenohedrons, which differ slightly from the rhombohedron. The crystals are often in twins, and incrusted with Chlorite. It is very liable to decomposition, becoming spongy or porous, but still retaining its form.

Analysis, by *Delesse :*

Silica . . . . . 49·5
Alumina and peroxide of iron 23·5
Lime . . . . . 2·7
Potash . . . . . 2·5
Magnesia . . . . trace
Water . . . . . 21·0
                        ———
                        99·2

BB fuses with some difficulty to a yellowish enamel.

Soluble in hot sulphuric acid : while dissolving, it produces a curdled mass, but afterwards the solution is clear.

Locality. Jones's Falls, Maryland, U.S., in fissures of gneiss.

Name. After the discoverer, Dr. Hayden, of Baltimore, U.S.

HAYESINE, *Dana.* Occurs in masses, having a globular or mammillated form, which, on being broken, present the appearance of a lustrous mass of fine interwoven silky fibres of a brilliant snow-white colour. Opaque. Tasteless, but with a peculiar odour. H. 1. S.G. 1·65.

Comp. $\dot{N}a \ddot{B}^2 + \dot{C}a^2 \ddot{B}^5 + 10\dot{H}$. Hayes states that the soda is an impurity, and that the composition of the pure mineral is represented by the formula $\dot{C}a \ddot{B}^2 + 6\dot{H}$ = boracic acid 45·95, lime 18·45, water 35·57=100.

Reichardt gives the formula $\dot{C}a \ddot{B}^4 + 10\dot{H}$.

Analysis, by *Reichardt :*

Boracic acid . . . . 52·05
Lime . . . . . 11·56
Soda . . . . . trace
Chlorine . . . . 0·94

Sulphuric acid . . . 0·53
Water . . . . . 34·91
                        ———
                        99·99

Localities. Nova Scotia, in narrow veins, in Gypsum, with Glauber Salt. At the Tuscan lagoons, as an incrustation. In white reniform masses, called *tiza,* on the dry plains near Iquique, in the province of Tarapaca, in Southern Peru, whence it has of late years been imported to Liverpool. (See TIZA.)

Named after Hayes.

Brit. Mus., Case 39.

M. P. G. Horse-shoe Case, No. 229.

HAYTORITE. Pseudomorphous Chalcedony in the form of Datholite, found at the Haytor Iron Mines in Devonshire; fig. 226.

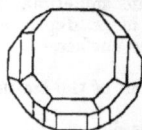

Fig. 226.

Also at N. Roskear Mine, Cornwall; and in cavities of compact radiating Prehnite in the Isle of May, Frith of Forth, *fig.* 226.

Brit. Mus., Case 22.

M. P. G. Horse-shoe Case, No. 534.

HEAVY SPAR, *Jameson.* A name given to Barytes in consequence of its great specific gravity.

HEBETINE. An impure variety of anhydrous silicate of Zinc or Willemite.

HEDENBERGITE. A black variety of Augite, containing a large proportion of iron, little or no magnesia, and no alumina. S.G. 3·5,

Comp. $(\dot{C}a, \dot{F}e) \ddot{S}i^2.$

Analysis, by *H. Rose :*

Silica . . . . . 49·01
Protoxide of iron . . . 26·08
Lime . . . . . 20·87
Magnesia . . . . 2·98
Protoxide of manganese . trace
                        ———
                        98·94

BB fuses readily to a shining black glass.

Locality. Tunaberg in Sweden.

Name. After L. Hedenberg, the Swedish Chemist.

HEDGEHOG-STONE. See STACHELSWEINSTEIN.

HEDIPHANE, *Dufrénoy.* HEDYPHANE, *Breithaupt.* A whitish variety of Mimetite, usually occurring in amorphous masses, with a subadamantine or resinous lustre inclining to greasy. H. 3 to 4. S.G. 5·3 to 5·5.

Analysis, by *Kersten:*

Arseniate of lead .	.	. 60·10
Chloride of lead .	.	. 10·29
Phosphate of lime	.	. 15·51
Arseniate of lime .	.	. 12·98

                   98·88

BB forms a white friable mass, but affords no arsenical odour.

Locality. Longbanshytta, in Sweden.

HELIOTROPE. See BLOODSTONE.

HELLEFLINTA of the Swedes. A compact and massive variety of Felspar, of a deep flesh-red colour, and with a peculiarly waxy texture, from Gryphyttan in Sweden.

HELMINTH, *G. H. Otto Volger.* A variety of Chlorite, occurring in Felspar and Quartz.

HELVIN, or HELVINE, *Haüy, Phillips, Werner.* Cubical. Primary form a regular tetrahedron. Occurs in small tetrahedrons, with their solid angles replaced. Colour wax-yellow, inclining to yellowish-brown or siskin-green. Subtranslucent. Lustre vitreous inclining to resinous. Streak white. Fracture uneven. H. 6 to 6·5. S.G. 3·1 to 3·3.

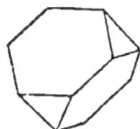 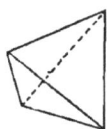

Fig. 227.   Fig. 228.

Comp. Silicate of glucina, and protoxide of manganese.

Analysis, by *C. Gmelin:*

Silica	. 33·25
Glucina and alumina .	. 12·03
Protoxide of manganese	. 31·82
Protoxide of iron .	. 5·56
Sulphide of manganese	· 14·00
Water	. 1·16

               97·82

BB in the inner flame fuses with ebullition, and forms a turbid yellow globule; in the outer flame fuses with greater difficulty, and acquires a deeper colour. Dissolves slowly in borax, forming a clear glass, which, till the whole of the substance is dissolved, has a yellowish tinge arising from the presence of sulphide of sodium, but after the solution is complete, it appears colourless in the inner flame, and amethyst-red in the outer. Dissolves in muriatic acid with evolution of sulphuretted hydrogen gas and separation of gelatinous silica.

Localities. Schwarzenberg in Saxony,

with Garnet, Quartz, Fluor and Calc-spar. Hortekulle, near Modum in Norway.

Name. The name was given by Werner, in allusion to the colour; from ήλιος, *the sun.*

Brit. Mus., Case 37.

M. P. G. Horse-shoe Case.

HEMATITE. *Dana, Brooke & Miller.* Hexagonal; primary form an acute rhombohedron: also occurs columnar; granular, botryoidal, and stalactitic: lamellar; friable or compact. Colour dark steel-grey or iron-black; of earthy varieties red.· Lustre metallic, sometimes splendent, or earthy. Opaque, but faintly translucent, and of a blood-red colour by transmitted light when in very thin laminæ, as it occurs in micaceous iron-ore. Streak cherry-red or reddish brown, which serves to distinguish it from Magnetite. Fracture subconchoidal, uneven. Sometimes feebly magnetic. H. 5·5 to 6·5. S.G. 4·5 to 5·3.

Distinguished from Magnetite by its cherry-red or reddish-brown streak.

Comp. Peroxide (sesquioxide) of iron, or

$$\ddot{F}e = iron\ 70,\ oxygen\ 30 = 100.$$

BB alone infusible; with soda on charcoal, it sinks together with the soda into the charcoal, and is easily reduced to a metallic powder, which may be separated from the charcoal·by pounding and levigation: with borax forms a green or yellow glass.

Readily soluble in hot muriatic acid, when reduced to powder.

Localities.—British. This ore is largely worked, and affords much of the iron manufactured in this and other countries. The Hematite of North Lancashire and West Cumberland produces not less than a million tons per annum. It is supposed that the Hematite which occurs in the Carboniferous· Limestone of the Mendip Hills in Somersetshire, and the so-called brown Hematite of the Forest of Dean in Gloucestershire were worked by the Romans during the period when they held possession of these islands. It is obtained also in Cornwall; Devonshire; in Glamorganshire, in the districts of Llantrissant and Llanhary, near Cowbridge, and at Newton Nottage, near Bridgend; in North Wales, and in the neighbourhood of Glasgow.—*Foreign.* Hematite is found in France, Spain, Germany, and Russia, where the mines of Goumeschefskoi contain much of it.

The mines of Elba have been worked from a very remote period, and the island is described by Virgil as being "Insula inexhaustis chalybdum generosa metallis."

The several varieties of iron-ore comprised in the species of Hematite, are described under their respective names. *Specular Iron* includes the specimens possessing a perfect metallic lustre, and is called *Micaceous Iron* when the structure is micaceous: *Red Hematite, Fibrous Red Iron-ore*, include the varieties with a sub-metallic or non-metallic lustre, which if soft and earthy are termed *Red Ochre, Reddle*, or *Red Chalk*, and when consisting of slightly coherent scales, *Scaly Red Iron-ore*, or *Red-Iron Froth*.

There are very remarkable deposits of Hematite in Missouri, ninety miles south of St. Louis, which are thus described by Dana: "The Iron Mountain is 300 feet in height, and consists wholly of massive peroxyd of iron lying in loose blocks, which are largest about the summit, many 10 to 20 tons in weight. The Pilot Knob is estimated by J. D. Whitney at 650 feet in height; it is made up of a quartzose rock of the azoic period, and is capped with specular iron, which has the appearance of stratification, and is micaceous in structure." *Dana's Mineralogy*, vol. ii. p. 114.

Hematite is sometimes hard enough to take a very fine polish, and is then used for polishing glass, gold, steel, and, in fact, nearly all metals: it also possesses the valuable property of laying on metals gold-and silver-leaf, without fraying, tearing, or detaching them. The highly-esteemed burnishers of gilders, goldsmiths, gunsmiths, and cutlers are made of Hematite, strongly fastened in wooden handles, guarded by a ring. The Hematite suited for this purpose is of a very dark red colour, and should have a fine grain, free from the slightest cracks, and above all should be susceptible of a high polish. Gallicia in Spain is the chief locality whence this description is obtained; and the people of Compostella, who specially devote themselves to the search for it, supply nearly the whole of Europe.

Reduced to powder Hematite is used for polishing tin, silver, and gold; and also as a colouring material.

Name. The name Hæmatite is derived from αἷμα, *blood*. "And the Hæmatites or Blood-stone, which is of a dense, solid texture, dry, or, according to its name, seeming as if formed of concreted blood."—*Theophrastus*, chap. lxvi. Five varieties of Hæmatite were known to the ancients, of which the most esteemed, and probably that referred to above, was obtained from Ethiopia.

Brit. Mus., Cases 14 and 16.

M. P. G. A. 50 in Hall; Boulder from New Red Sandstone, Porlock, Somersetshire.

Principal Floor, Wall-cases 18 and 19 (Foreign); 32 and 48 (British).

HEMIMORPHITE. Siliceous zinc ore.

HEMI-PRISMATIC AUGITE SPAR, *Mohs.* See HORNBLENDE.

HEMI-PRISMATIC BRYTHINE SALT, *Mohs.* See GLAUBERITE.

HEMI-PRISMATIC CHRYSOLITE, *Mohs.* See CHONDRODITE.

HEMI-PRISMATIC DYSTOME-MALACHITE, *Mohs.* See PHOSPHOCHALCITE.

HEMI-PRISMATIC EUCLAS HALOID, *Haidinger.* See PHARMACOLITE.

HEMI-PYRAMIDAL FELSPAR, *Haidinger.* See EDINGTONITE.

HEMI-PRISMATIC FLUOR-HALOID, *Haidinger.* See WAGNERITE.

HEMI-PRISMATIC GYPSUM-HALOID, *Haidinger.* See PHARMACOLITE.

HEMI-PRISMATIC HABRONEME-MALACHITE, *Mohs.* See MALACHITE.

HEMI-PRISMATIC HAL-BARYTE, *Mohs.* See HAYESINE.

HEMI-PRISMATIC KOUPHONE-SPAR,*Mohs.* See HEULANDITE.

HEMI-PRISMATIC LEAD-BARYTE, *Mohs.* See CROCOISITE.

HEMI-PRISMATIC NATRON-SALT, *Mohs.* See TRONA.

HEMI-PRISMATIC OLIVE-MALACHITE, *Mohs.* See VAUQUELINITE.

HEMI-PRISMATIC RUBY-BLENDE. *Mohs.* See MIARGYRITE.

HEMI-PRISMATIC SCHILLER-SPAR, *Mohs.* See BRONZITE.

HEMI-PRISMATIC SULPHUR, *Mohs.* See REALGAR.

HEMI-PRISMATIC TALC-MICA, *Mohs.* See MICA—(including LEPIDOLITE).

HEMI-PRISMATIC TITANIUM ORE, *Mohs.* See SPHENE.

HEMI-PRISMATIC VITRIOL-SALT, *Mohs.* See COPPERAS.

HEMI-PRISMATIC ZEOLITE. See HEULANDITE.

HENKELITE. See SILVER GLANCE.

HEPATIC BLENDE. See LEBER-BLENDE.

HEPATIC CINNABAR, *Phillips.* A mixture of Cinnabar, with Idrialite, carbon and earthy matter. It occurs both compact and slaty, of a dark red colour, sometimes almost iron-black. Opaque. Streak brownish-red. S.G. 6·8 to 7·3. See CORALLINERZ.

Locality. Idria in Carniola.

Brit. Mus., Case 9.

HEPATIC MERCURIAL ORE, *Kirwan.* See CINNABAR.

HEPATIC PYRITES, *Kirwan, Jameson.*

HEPATINERZ. The name applied to decomposed, liver-brown, tessular crystals of Iron Pyrites (Marcasite).

Localities. Cornwall. East Tulloch, S. of Loch Tay, in Perthshire.

Name.—From ἧπαϛ, *liver;* in allusion to the colour.

HEPATINERZ, *v. Kobell.* An amorphous mixture of Brown Iron-ore and Chrysocolla, from Touriusk in the Ural.

Analysis by v. Kobell :

Silica	9·66
Protoxide of iron .	59·00
Oxide of copper . .	13·00
Water	18·00
	99·66

HEPATITE. The name applied to such varieties of Barytes as emit a fetid, sulphurous, or hepatic odour on being rubbed or heated. They are generally of a yellow or brown colour. It occurs at Buxton, Matlock, and Eyam in Derbyshire; Andrarum and Kongsberg in Norway; Lublin in Gallicia; and Albemarle co., N. America. · Brit. Mus., Case 52.

HERCINITE, *Zippe.* A black Spinel found in rolled pebbles, in alluvium. Lustre vitreous. Streak deep greenish-grey. Fracture conchoidal. H. 7·5 to 8. S.G. 3·91 to 3·95.

Comp. Fe Äl, or an aluminite of iron, in which the protoxide is partly replaced by magnesia.

Analysis, by *Zippe:*

Alumina . . .	61·17
Protoxide of iron .	35·67
Magnesia . . .	2·92
	99·76

Localities. The vicinity of Natschetin and Horslau in Bohemia; where it is used instead of Emery for cutting glass.

BB infusible. The leek-green powder on ignition becomes brick-red, and increases 3·2 per cent. in weight, in consequence of the protoxide of iron becoming converted into peroxide.

HERDERITE, *Haidinger.* A very rare mineral, much resembling Asparagus-stone. Rhombic: primary form a right rhombic prism. Colour several shades of yellowish- and greenish-white. Very translucent. Lustre vitreous, inclining to resinous. Streak white. Very brittle. Fracture small conchoidal. H. 5. S.G. 2·9 to 3·1.

Fig. 229.

Comp. Probably an hydrous phosphate of alumina and lime with fluorine.

BB fuses with difficulty to a white enamel.

Dissolves in muriatic acid when finely powdered.

Locality. The tin mines of Ehrenfriedersdorf in Saxony, imbedded in Fluor.

Name. After the Baron von Herder, Director of the Saxon Mines at Freyberg.

HERMANNITE. See MANGAN-AMPHIBOLE.

HERRERITE, *Genth.* A carbonate of zinc, containing 3·4 per cent. of carbonate of copper. From the mines of Albarradon, Mexico.

HERSCHELITE, *Levy.* Occurs in colourless hexagonal prisms and tables, whose lateral faces are streaked horizontally. Colour white. Translucent or opaque. Fracture conchoidal. H. 4·5. S.G. 2·06.

Comp. $(\dot{N}a, \dot{K}) \ddot{S}i^2 + 3\ddot{A}l \ddot{S}i^2 + 15\dot{H}.$

Analysis, from Etna, by *Damour :*

Silica . . .	47·89
Alumina . . .	20·90
Lime	0·38
Soda	8·33
Potash	4·39
Water	17·84
	99·23

Localities. Aci Reale, near Catania in Sicily; associated with Phillipsite, in crystals which are generally closely aggregated like those of Prehnite, in cavities of trap.

Brit. Mus., Case 29.

HERVELECA. An ochre described by Forchammer.

HESSITE, *Fröbel.* Rhombic. Occurs in coarse-grained masses. Colour between steel-grey and lead-grey. Lustre metallic. Slightly malleable. H. 2 to 3·5. S.G. 8·3 to 8·9.

Comp. Ag, Te, or telluride of silver = silver 62·8, tellurium 37·2 = 100.

Analysis, from Sawodinski, by *G. Rose:*

Tellurium . . .	36·89
Silver	62·32
Iron	0·50
	99·71

BB on charcoal fuses to a black globule, which, when cold, exhibits on its surface numerous dendrites and globules of silver. Mixed with carbonate of soda, and subjected to a continued blast, yields pure silver.

Dissolves slowly in cold, quickly in hot nitric acid; the solution, after a while, deposits tellurite of silver-oxide.

Localities. The Altai Mountains of Siberia, at the silver mine of Sawodinski, in a talcose rock, associated with Iron Pyrites, Black Blende and Copper Pyrites. Nagyag in Transylvania, in right rhomboidal prisms on Quartz. California.

Brit. Mus., Case 3.

HESSONITE. See ESSONITE.

HETEPOSITE, *v. Kobell, Phillips, Naumann.* An altered form of Tryphiline. Only occurs in lamellar masses. Colour greenish-grey inclining to bluish-grey, with a waxy lustre; the faces which are exposed to the air exhibit a semi-metallic lustre and a violet colour. Streak sometimes grey, sometimes yellow; after weathering, violet. Scratches glass: easily scratched with a steel point. H. S.G. 3·524; after weathering, 3·39.

Comp. $3(\ddot{M}n\,\ddot{F}e)\,\overset{..}{P^2}+5\ddot{H}.$

Analysis, by *Dufrénoy:*

Phosphoric acid .	.	41·77
Protoxide of iron .	.	34·89
Protoxide of manganese	.	17·57
Silica . .	.	0·22
Water . . .	.	4·40
		98·85

BB fuses to a dark brown enamel with a semi-metallic lustre.

Soluble in muriatic acid, with the exception of a small quantity of silica.

Locality. Chiefly in the quarries at Hureaux in the Haute Vienne. In the pegmatite of the vicinity of Limoges, with Hureaulite.

Name. From ἕτερος, *different.*

Heteposite is distinguished from Triphyline by its colour; from Triplite, by the lustre of its fractured surface, which in the latter is vitreous.

HÉTÉROCLINE, *Dufrénoy.* HETEROKLINE, *Breithaupt.* Oblique. Occurs in oblique rhombic prisms, with the acute lateral edges generally replaced; also massive. Colour between iron-black and steel-grey. Lustre submetallic. Streak brownish-black. Fracture uneven to small conchoidal. H. 5. S.G. 4·562.

Comp. Trisilicate of peroxide of manganese, or $\overset{..}{S}i\,\overset{...}{M}n^3.$

Analysis, by *Ewreinow:*

Silica . . .	.	10·02
Peroxide of manganese	.	85·88
Peroxide of iron .	.	3·05
Lime . . .	.	0·60
Potash . . .	.	0·44
		99·99

BB like peroxide of manganese.

Locality. St. Marcel, in Piedmont.

Name. From ἱτεροκλίνης, in reference to its oblique form of crystallization.

HETEROMERITE, *Hermann.* A pale green mineral from Statoust; probably an altered Idocrase.

HETEROMORPHITE, *Rammelsberg.* Occurs in capillary forms resembling cobwebs; also massive. Colour between dark lead-grey and steel-grey; sometimes with an iridescent tarnish. Lustre dull metallic. H. 1 to 3. S.G. 5·67 to 5·9.

Comp. Pb S + ½Sb² S³ = lead 49·8, antimony 31·0, sulphur 19·2 = 100.

Analysis of massive form, from Wolfsberg, by *Poselger:*

Sulphur . .	.	20·32
Antimony . .	.	32·98
Lead . . .	.	48·48
		101·78

Fuses instantly in the flame of a candle, with the evolution of white fumes.

Localities. The Harz at Wolfsberg, Andreasberg and Clausthal. Freiberg, Schemnitz, near Neudorf in Anhalt. Near Bottino in Tuscany. Chonta in Peru.

Name. From ἕτερος, *another,* and μόρφη, *form.*

HÉTÉROSITE. *Beudant, Dana.* (From ἕτερος, *different.*) ⎫
HÉTÉROZITE, *Dufrénoy, Nicol.* ⎬ See HETEPOSITE.
  ⎭

HETEROTOMOUS FELSPAR, *Mohs.* See PERICLINE.

HEULANDITE, *Brooke, Phillips, Beudant.* Oblique; primary form a right rhombic prism. Occurs in attached crystals and in layers and granular masses, frequently in a globular form, in the cavities of amygdaloidal rocks and in certain metalliferous veins. Colourless or coloured yellowish, brownish, but chiefly flesh-red to tile-red. Lustre vitreous: pearly on planes of cleavage, and generally translucent, nearly transparent when colourless. Brittle. Fracture

subconchoidal, uneven. H. 3·5 to 4. S.G.
2·1 to 2·2.

Fig. 230.   Fig. 231.

Comp. Ċa S̈i + Ä̶l S̈i³ + 5Ḣ = silica 59·3,
alumina 16·8, lime 9·2, water 14·7 = 100.

Analysis, from Iceland, by *Damour* :

Silica	. . . .	. 59·64
Alumina	. . .	. 16·33
Lime	. . . .	. 7·44
Potash	. . . .	. 0·74
Soda	. . . .	. 1·16
Water	. . . .	. 14·33

99·64

BB melts with intumescence, and becomes
phosphorescent.

Readily decomposed by muriatic acid,
the silica being separated in the form of a
viscid powder.

Localities.—Scotch. Campsie Hills, Stirlingshire, in very fine brick-red crystals, associated with Quartz, Chlorite and Calcite.
Long Craig, Dumbarton Muir, in red crystals.
Ballygroggan, near the Mull of Cantyre, in
large red crystals. In small bright yellow
crystals in a vein of Calc Spar, traversing
Serpentine, at the south end of Balta Island,
one of the Shetlands. *Irish.*—The Giant's
Causeway. Portrush, co. Antrim. Sandy
Braes, in small olive-brown crystals, in
porphyry. *Foreign.*—The finest crystals are
brought from Iceland and the Faröe Isles,
and from the Vendayah Mountains in Hindostan. The red varieties are found in the
Fassa valley, Tyrol; in the Harz; at
Peter's Point, and at Cape Blomidon, in
Nova Scotia; in the amygdaloid of Abyssinia. (See BEAUMONTITE.)

Name. After Heuland, the English Mineralogist.

Brit. Mus., Case 28.

M. P. G. Horse shoe Case, No. 1165.

This is the Stilbite of Haüy and most
continental authors.

HEXAGONAL KOUPHONE SPAR, *Haidinger.* See GMELINITE.

HEXAGONAL PALLADIUM. See SELEN-
PALLADITE.

HEXAHEDRAL ARSENIATE, *Bournon.* See
CHALCOPHYLLITE.

HEXAHEDRAL COBALT-
KIES, *Mohs.*
HEXAHEDRAL COBALT-   } See COBALTINE.
PYRITES, *Mohs.*

HEXAHEDRAL COPPER-GLANCE, *Mohs.*
See TIN PYRITES.

HEXAHEDRAL CORNEOUS SILVER. See
KERARGYRITE.

HEXAHEDRAL GALENA, *Jameson.* See
GALENA.

HEXAHEDRAL GLANCE-BLENDE, *Mohs.*
See MANGANESE BLENDE.

HEXAHEDRAL GOLD, *Mohs.* Native
Gold. See GOLD.

HEXAHEDRAL IRON-PYRITES, *Mohs.* Iron
Pyrites. See PYRITES.

HEXAHEDRAL KOUPHONE-SPAR, *Mohs.*
See ANALCIME.

HEXAHEDRAL LEAD, *Haidinger.* See NA-
TIVE LEAD.

HEXAHEDRAL LEAD-GLANCE, *Mohs.* See
GALENA.

HEXAHEDRAL LIRO-
CONITE, *Jameson.*
HEXAHEDRAL LIRO-   } See PHARMACOSI-
CON-MALACHITE, *Mohs.* }   DERITE.
HEXAHEDRAL OLI-
VENITE, *Jameson.*

HEXAHEDRAL PEARL - KERATE, *Mohs.*
See KERARGYRITE.

HEXAHEDRAL PLATINA, *Mohs.* See NA-
TIVE PLATINA.

HEXAHEDRAL ROCK-SALT, *Mohs.* See
COMMON SALT.

HEXAHEDRAL SILVER, *Mohs.* See NA-
TIVE SILVER.

HEXAHEDRAL SILVER-GLANCE, *Mohs.*
See SILVER GLANCE.

HEXAHEDRAL TELLURIUM, *Mohs.* See
ALTAITE.

HEXYMURIATE OF COPPER, *Thomson.*
See ATACAMITE.

HIGHGATE RESIN. A name given to
Copaline, in consequence of its occurrence at
Highgate Hill.

Brit. Mus., Case 60.

M. P. G. Horse-shoe Case, No. 107.

HIMBEERSPATH. See DIALLOGITE.

HISINGERITE. *Berzelius, Allan, Phillips.*
Occurs in imperfectly crystallized masses,
which are cleavable in one direction only,
and possess a foliated structure. Colour
black. Dull. Streak greenish-grey or yellowish-brown. Opaque. Sectile. Fracture
earthy. Soft. S.G. 3·045.

Comp. Bisilicate of iron, or F̈e S̈i² + 4Ḣ =
peroxide of iron 44·32, silica 35·23, water
20·45 = 100.

N

Analysis, from Riddarhyttan, by *Rammelsberg*:

Silica	. 33·07
Peroxide of iron . .	. 34·78
Protoxide of iron .	. 17·59
Lime	. 2·56
Magnesia . . .	. 0·46
Water	. 11·54

100·00

From the above analysis, Rammelsberg deduces the formula $\ddot{F}e^2 \ddot{S}i + 2\ddot{F}e \ddot{S}i + 6\dot{H}$.

BB gives off water when heated: the blowpipe flame rounds it off at the edges, and renders it dull and magnetic. Decomposed by muriatic acid with the formation of gelatinous silica.

Locality. Sweden, Suarta in Suderman- land, in cavities of Calc Spar. The iron mines of Gillinge and Orijerfvi in Finland (see GILLINGITE). Bodenmais (THRAULITE, *v. Kobell*).

Name. After Hisinger.

Brit. Mus., Case 26.

HISLOPITE, *Haughton*. A Calc Spar of a brilliant grass-green colour. S.G. 2·64. It effervesces briskly with weak muriatic acid, which dissolves the calcareous portion, leaving a beautiful, green silicious skeleton, which seems to be Glauconite.

Comp. Hydrated tersilicate of protoxide of iron, or $\left.\begin{array}{c}\ddot{A}l \\ \ddot{R}_3\end{array}\right\}$ $3\ddot{S}i + 3\dot{H}$.

Locality. Brought from Tákli, near Nagpur in India, by Mr. Hislop, after whom it is named.

HOERNESITE, *Kenngott, Haidinger*. Occurs in spheroidal groups of crystals, developed within the free interstices into small rhom- boidal lamellæ, of 36°. White and flexible, with a single cleavage-plane of pearly lustre, parallel to the longitudinal surface. H.1. S.G. 2·474.

Comp. $3\dot{M}g \ddot{A}s + 8\dot{H}$.

Analysis, by *von Hauer*:

Arsenic acid. . .	. 46·33
Magnesia . . .	. 24·54
Water	. 29·07
Loss	. 0·06

100·00

Locality. The only known specimen is in the Vienna Imperial Museum; it is supposed to come from the Bannat, probably from the environs of Oravicza.

Name. After Dr. Hörnes, of the Imperial Museum at Vienna.

HOHLSPATH, *Werner.* } See CHIASTO-
HOLLOW-SPAR, *Jameson.* } LITE.

HOLMESITE, *Thomson.* A mineral iden- tical with Clintonite.

Comp. $2(\dot{M}g \ddot{A}l) + \dot{C}a \ddot{S}i + \dot{H}$.

Analysis, by *Richardson*:

Silica	. 19·35
Alumina . . .	. 44·75
Peroxide of iron . .	. 4·80
Zirconia . . .	. 2·05
Magnesia . . .	. 9·05
Lime	. 11·45
Protoxide of manganese	. 1·35
Fluoric acid . .	. 0·9
Water	. 4·55

98·25

HOLZ KUPFERERZ. WOOD-ARSENIATE OF COPPER.

HOLZOPAL. HOLSTEIN, *Werner, Bro- chant.* Woodstone. See WOOD-OPAL.

HOMICHLINE, *Breithaupt.* Probably a result of the decomposition of Chalcopyrite, or perhaps a mixture of it with some of the richer sulphides of Copper, as Erubescite or Copper-glance. Crystallization pyramidal, octahedral : generally compact - massive. Colour more bronzy than Chalcopyrite. Streak black. H. 4 to 5. S.G. 4·47 to 4·48.

Comp. $3Cu^2S$, Fe^2S^3 + 2FeS = copper 43·76, iron 25·81, sulphur 30·21 = 100.

Localities. Plauen in Voigtland, asso- ciated with Kupferpecherz and Malachite. Lauterbach in the Harz. Kupferberg in Silesia. Rheinbreitenbach on the Rhine. Friedensgrube and Lichtenberg in Bavaria. Near Viedendorf in Hesse. Oberlahnstein in Nassau. Johanngeorgenstadt. Quad- merget in Algeria. Remolinos and Tocopilla in Chili. Japan.

HONIGSTEIN, *Werner.* } See MELLITE.
HONEYSTONE, *Jameson.* }

HONEY-YELLOW QUARTZ, *Kirwan.* See CITRINE.

HOO-CANNEL. An earthy and impure kind of Cannel Coal, showing the lines of lamination, which are characteristic of other beds of coal.

HOPEITE, *Brewster.* Rhombic: primary form a right rhombic prism; also in reni- form masses and amorphous. Colour grey- ish-white, reddish-brown when compact. Lustre vitreous, inclining to pearly on the central terminal faces. Transparent or translucent. Streak white. Deeply striated longitudinally on the broad lateral face shown in *fig.* 232, other faces smooth. Sectile. Fracture uneven. H. 2·5 to 3. S.G. 2·85.

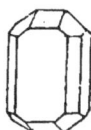

Fig. 232.

Comp. Supposed to be a hydrous compound of phosphoric acid and oxide of zinc, with a small quantity of cadmium.

Locality. The mines of Altenberg, near Aix-la-Chapelle, crystallized in small drusy cavities, with Smithsonite.

Name. In honour of Dr. Hope, Regius Professor of Chemistry in the University of Edinburgh.

HORNBLEI, *Karsten, Hausmann;* HORN-LEAD. See CROMFORDITE.

HORNBLENDE, *Kirwan, Jameson, Phillips, Werner.* Oblique: primary form an oblique rhombic prism. Occurs in prismatic crystals, which are sometimes isolated, but oftener confusedly aggregated, and frequently macled; also in imperfect crystallizations, fibrous or columnar, the fibres being sometimes like flax, sometimes lamellar, granular, friable. Colour passing through various shades of green to blackish-green on the one hand, and white on the other. Lustre vitreous to pearly on cleavage faces. Opaque to nearly transparent, generally subtranslucent. Streak white or paler than the colour. When massive tough, and difficultly frangible. Fracture sub-conchoidal, uneven. H. 5 to 6. S.G. 2·9 to 3·4.

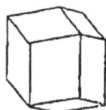

Fig. 233.

Under the term Hornblende are included a great number of minerals, the composition of which may be represented by the general formula ($\dot{R}^3 \ddot{R}$) $\ddot{S}i^2$. They are, therefore, bisilicates of various protoxides and peroxides. In the formula $\dot{R}$ represents variable proportions of lime, magnesia, protoxide of iron, and protoxide of manganese. Fluoride of calcium, also, is generally present in small and variable quantities, and therefore, most probably, in a state of mechanical mixture. Many varieties of Hornblende likewise contain alumina.

Originally the name Hornblende was restricted to the dark green and black varieties, whether crystallized or massive; now, however, it comprehends a great many minerals,

which will be found described in their proper places.

The principal varieties of Hornblende are Actinolite, Ægirine, Amianthus, Anthophyllite, Arfvedsonite, Asbestos, Calamite, Carinthine, Cummingtonite, Diastalite, Edenite, Grammatite, Mountain or Rock Cork, Mountain Leather, Pargasite, Raphilite, Tremolite.

Name. The name bears reference to its exceeding toughness. See HORNSTONE (*name*). Kirwan says, "The great weight of the stone called *hornblende* made the miners at first imagine it contained some metal, but finding none, except iron, they called it *blind,* in the same sense as the vulgar do nuts without a kernel. Hence the name *Hornblende.*"—Vol. i. p. 215.

Brit. Mus., Case 33.

M. P. G. Horse-shoe Case, Nos. 1047, 1048—1053.

HORNCOBALT. A mixture of earthy Cobalt and Quartz, found at Siegen, in Prussia.

HORNERZ, *Werner.* See KERARGYRITE.

HORN-LEAD. See CROMFORDITE.

HORNMANGAN. See RHODONITE.

HORN-ORE, *Jameson.* See KERARGYRITE.

HORN-QUECKSILBER, *Hausmann;* HORN-QUICKSILVER, *Phillips.* See CALOMEL.

HORN-SILBER, *Hausmann,* or HORN-SILVER. See KERARGYRITE.

HORNSTONE, *Phillips.* A variety of Quartz resembling flint, but more brittle, and breaking with a less conchoidal fracture. It is translucent or opaque, and is dull, or has a glimmering lustre. Generally grey, tinged blue, green, brown, or yellow. Scarcely as hard as Quartz. It is sometimes imbedded in limestone, as in the Tyrol; in veins in Hungary and Sweden, and in pseudomorphs in Saxony and Bohemia. It is distinguished from Compact Felspar, which it closely resembles in appearance, by being infusible, Felspar being fusible.

Hornstone is used for snuff-boxes, seals, mortars, &c., but chiefly for the handles of knives and forks. It is exported from Germany in large quantites for mounting butter- and dessert-knives.

"Hornstone differs from jaspers, often by its splintery fracture, always by its transparency, though imperfect, and want of lustre; from flints by its fracture, dulness, and hardness, but, when its fracture happens to be conchoidal, by its dulness, lesser transparency, and hardness; from quartz by its dulness and inferior hardness; from serpentine, generally in hardness, specific gravity, and fusibility; from heliotrope by the aggregate of its properties."—*Kirwan,* vol. i. p. 305.

Name. "This name took its rise from common working miners; they observed that a sort of stone, of a dusky colour, was cut through with great difficulty, by reason of a tenacity which resembled that of an horn or horse's hoof*; now, a horse's hoof, when in thin pieces, has also a slight degree of transparency, this sort of stone they therefore called *hornstone.* Mineralogical writers observing this combination of properties not to meet together in the same stone, distinguished two sorts of hornstone, both of a dusky colour, one that had the semitransparency, but not the tenacity, of a hoof or horn, and another which resembled that substance only in colour and tenacity. This distinction I find in Henckel, on the Origin of Stones.† Since time that the German writers in general have confined this name, with some modifications, to stones of the first kind; that is, to the stones that all writers had indicated by the name of *petrosilices,* and the English in particular by that of *chert.* But the Swedes and French still apply it in the latter sense."‡—*Kirwan,* vol. i. p. 215.

HORSE-FLESH ORE. The name by which Purple Copper (Erubescite) is known to Cornish miners.

HOUGHITE, *Shepard, S. W. Johnson.* A mineral resembling Völknerite, to which it is closely related, if not identical. Colour whitish externally, and bluish or reddish-white within, with a faint pearly lustre. H. 2·5. S.G. 2·02 to 2·03.

Comp. A hydrate of alumina and magnesia.

Analysis. by *S. W. Johnson :*

Alumina	23·847
Magnesia	43 839
Carbonic acid	5·833
Water	26·452
	99·995

BB decrepitates and gives off water, losing 33½ per cent. by ignition.

Localities. Near Oxbow, St. Lawrence co., New York. Rossie, associated with Spinel.

Name. After Dr. Franklin B. Hough, of Somerville, U. S.

This mineral is the material of pseudomorphous Spinel, and probably at times of Scapolite, according to S. W. Johnson. It occurs in crystals, which vary from pure Spinel to octahedrons, with rounded edges, and pitted or irregular surfaces. The last

---

are sometimes soft and altered, while the edges or angles have the hardness of Spinel. It also occurs in flattened kidney-form concretions, with botryoidal surfaces.

HOUILLE. *French* for Coal.

HOUILLE PAPYRACÉE, *Lucas.* See DYSODILE.

HOUILLE PICIFORME, *Brochant.* See JET.

HOWARDITE. An earthy mineral, abundant in meteoric stones.

Comp. Tersilicate of protoxide of iron and magnesia, or $\ddot{F}e\ \ddot{S}i^3 + \ddot{M}g\ \ddot{S}i^3$.

Named after Howard, meteorologist.

HUDSONITE, *Beck.* A black Pyroxene, identical with Polylite, and with a similar cleavage to Hedenbergite, from which it otherwise differs in having a considerable quantity of the silica replaced by alumina. It also contains manganese sometimes. It affords a green streak, and has often a brown tarnish. S.G. 3·43 to 3·5.

Comp. $(\ddot{C}a,\ \ddot{F}e)^3\ (\ddot{S}i,\ \ddot{A}l)^2$.

Analysis (mean), by *Smith & Brush :*

Silica	39·94
Alumina	10·41
Magnesia	3·00
Lime	10·36
Protoxide of iron	30·48
Protoxide of manganese	0·60
Potash	2·48
Soda	1·66
Loss by ignition	1·95
	97·92

BB fuses readily to a shining black glass.

Locality. Orange co., New York, U.S.; near the Hudson River; whence the name.

HUILE MINERALE COMMUNE, *Brochant.* See PETROLEUM.

HUMBOLDTILITE §, *Monticelli & Covelli; Phillips, Beudant.* HUMBOLDTILITH MELILITH, *Mohs.* A Mellilite found on Vesuvius in lava. It occurs in crystals derived from a rectangular prism with a square base; cleavage parallel to the base. Colour greyish-yellow or grey, with a vitreous lustre passing into resinous. Transparent to feebly

Fig. 234.

translucent. Fracture uneven and splintered. H. 5. S.G. 2·91 to 3·1.

---

* Vogel, Mineral. p. 130.

† P. 400 of the French translation.

‡ Wallerius.

§ Named after the Baron von Humboldt.

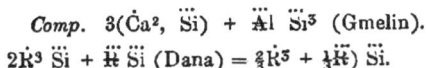

Comp. $3(\dot{C}a^2, \ddot{Si}) + \ddot{Al} \ddot{Si}^3$ (Gmelin).

$2\ddot{R}^3 \ddot{Si} + \ddot{H} \ddot{Si}$ (Dana) $= \frac{2}{3}\ddot{R}^5 + \frac{1}{3}\ddot{H}) \ddot{Si}$.

Analysis, from Somma, by *v. Kobell*:

Silica	43·96
Alumina	11·20
Lime	31·96
Magnesia	6·10
Soda	4·28
Potash	0·38
Protoxide of iron . .	2·32
	100·20

BB fuses readily with slight evolution of gas-bubbles, and forms a blistered, translucent glass, of a somewhat greyer or more greenish tint than the mineral. With borax melts slowly to a colourless glass. Easily decomposed by muriatic acid, with separation of gelatinous silica.

Brit. Mus., Case 60.

HUMBOLDTINE*, *Mariano de Rivero; Brooke & Miller.* } Oxalate of Iron. See OXALITE.
HUMBOLDTITE*, *Necker & Beudant.*

HUMBOLDTITE*, *Phillips.* The name given by Lévy to the Datholite found in Agate-balls at the Seisser Alp in the Tyrol. Brit. Mus., Case 39.

HUMITE, *Bournon.* A variety of Chondrodite found in ejected masses of a granular or crystalline rock, on Monte Somma, with brownish Mica, Olivine and Magnetite. Occurs in minute but very distinct crystals of a very variable colour, but generally yellowish or deep reddish-brown, with a shining lustre. Transparent or translucent. H. 6 to 6·5. S.G. 3·177 to 3·234.

Fig. 235.

Comp. $Mg^4 \ddot{Si}$, with part of the oxygen replaced by fluorine.

Analysis, by *Rammelsberg*:

Silica	33·26
Alumina	1·06
Magnesia	57·92
Protoxide of iron . .	2·30
Lime	0·74
Fluorine . . .	5·04
	100·32

BB becomes opaque, but does not melt; with borax affords a clear glass.

_____

* Named after the Baron von Humboldt.

Name. After Sir Abraham Hume.
Brit. Mus., Case 58A.

HUNTERITE, *Haughton.* A white felspathic mineral, with a fatty lustre. Softer than Felspar, but gritty under the agate pestle. S.G. 2·3.

Comp. Hydrated tersilicate of alumina, with hyaline silica, or $5\ddot{Al} \ddot{Si}^3 + \ddot{H} \ddot{Si}^3$.

Analysis, by *Haughton*:

Silica	65·93
Alumina	20·97
Lime	0·30
Magnesia	0·45
Loss by ignition . .	11·61
	99·26

Locality. Near Nagpur in Central India, in a vein of pegmatite in gneiss.

Name. After Mr. Hunter, by whom it was brought to England.

HUREAULITE, *Dufrénoy.* An altered form of Triplite, somewhat resembling Zircon in appearance. Oblique: primary form an oblique rhombic prism. In minute translucent crystals of a reddish-yellow colour, slightly paler than hyacinth-red; violet, brownish-orange, and rose-red. Lustre bright. Optically biaxial. No cleavage. Fracture conchoidal. H. 5. S.G. 2·27.

Fig. 236.   Fig. 237.

Comp. $(\ddot{M}n, \ddot{Fe})^5 \ddot{P}^2$.

Analysis, by *Damour*, of yellow variety from the quarry of Vilate near Chanteloube:

Phosphoric acid . .	37·96
Protoxide of manganese .	41·15
Protoxide of iron . .	8·10
Water	12·35
Mixed sand . . .	0·35
	99·91

BB gives off water when heated, and fuses very easily to a black globule, having a semi-metallic lustre.

Name. After the locality, the Commune of Hureaux, near Limoges, in Haute Vienne.

HURONITE, *Thomson; T. S. Hunt.* An altered mineral near Fahlunite. Forms spheroidal kidneys in rounded masses of black Hornblende. Colour greenish-yellow. Lustre resinous, passing into pearly. Translucent at the edges. Streak white. Fracture granular and imperfectly lamellar. Scratched easily with a steel point. H. 3·25. S.G. 2·862.

Analysis, by *Thomson*:

Silica	. . .	45·80
Alumina	. .	33·92
Protoxide of iron	.	4·32
Lime	. . .	8·04
Magnesia	. .	1·72
Water	. . .	4·16
		99·96

BB infusible; with fluxes yields a greenish glass.

Insoluble in acids.

Name. After the locality near Lake Huron, U.S.

HVERSALT, *Forchammer*. An alum allied to Halotrichite, in which part of the alumina is replaced by peroxide of iron, and part of the protoxide of iron by magnesia.

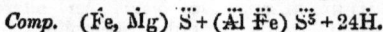

Comp. $(\ddot{F}e, \ddot{M}g) \ddot{S} + (\ddot{Al} \ddot{F}e) \ddot{S}^5 + 24H.$

Analysis:

Alumina	. .	11·22
Peroxide of iron	.	1·23
Protoxide of iron	.	4·57
Magnesia	. .	2·19
Sulphuric acid	.	35·16
Water	. . .	45·63
		100·00

Locality. Iceland.

Brit. Mus., Case 56.

HYACINTH (or JACINTH). The name under which are included the transparent bright coloured varieties of Zircon. Hyacinth differs from Jargoon merely in its colour, which is of various shades of red, passing into orange and poppy-red. Though not much worn at the present day, it is a valuable gem, and makes a very superb ring-stone when of a bright tint and free from flaws. The larger pieces are sometimes made into seals.

"Three various kinds the skilled as *Hyacinths* * name,
Varying in colour, and unlike in fame :
One, like pomegranate, flowers a fiery blaze,
And one, the yellow citron's hue displays ;
One charms with paley blue the gazer's eye,
Like the mild tint that decks the northern sky :
A strength'ning power the several kinds convey,
And grief and vain suspicions drive away."

Localities. Hyacinth occurs in the sands and alluvial deposits of certain rivers in

* From the Lapidarium (xiv.) of Abbot Marbodus (Marbœuf), master of the Cathedral School of Anjou, 1067 to 1081, when he became Bishop of Rennes. Extracted from "Antique Gems," by Rev. C. W. King, M.A.

Ceylon; also in the state of sand mingled with various other substances in the bed of a stream at Expailly (Haute Loire) in France, as well as in basalt near the same place; in volcanic tuff in Auvergne; at Bilin in Bohemia; Sebnitz in Saxony; Pfitsch in the Tyrol; Ohlapian in Transylvania; in Greenland; in the Zircon-syenite of Fredericks-värn in Norway; and in the iron mines of Arendal; at Miask in the Urals; at Vesuvius in white and blue octahedra in Ryacolite; in small colourless crystals at Santa Rosa in New Granada; in Scotland at Scalpay in Harris. Egypt, the East Indies, &c. The hyacinth-red varieties of Zircon are sold by the inhabitants of Ceylon as inferior rubies. (Prinsep.)

In speaking of the Hyacinth Pliny says, "Hunc colorem Indi *sacon* vocant et talem gemmam *sacodion*;" but it is doubtful whether the Hyacinth of the moderns is one of the stones known by the same name (*ύάζινθος*) to the ancients. Jamieson supposed that they applied this name to the Amethyst or Sapphire.

The name *ύάζινθος* is derived from the Persian and Arabian *yacut* (*ruby*).

Brit. Mus., Case 26.

M. P. G. Horse-shoe Case, Nos. 850, 853 to 858.

HYACINTH BLANCHE CRUCIFORME, *Romé de Lisle*. See HARMOTOME.

HYACINTH DE CEYLON. A French name for Essonite or Cinnamon-Stone.

HYACINTHE DE COMPOSTELLE. See COMPOSTELLA HYACINTH.

HYACINTH DE VESUVE, *Romé de Lisle*. Vesuvian. See IDOCRASE.

HYACINTHE LA BELLA. The name given by French lapidaries to Zircon, when of a decided red tint. Mons. Launoy states that it becomes of a much deeper tint on exposure to air, and that it reassumes its original colour when placed in the dark. The Italians apply the same name to orange-red Garnet or Vermeille.

HYACINTHINE. *La Metherie* ⎫
HYACINTH BLANCHE ⎬ See MEIONITE.
DE SOMMA, *Romé de Lisle.* ⎭

HYALITE, or MULLER'S GLASS. A transparent or semi-transparent variety of Opal, occurring in small reniform, botryoidal, and sometimes stalactitic forms, resembling colourless glass.

Analysis, from Walsch, by *Damour*:

Silica	. . .	96·94
Water	. . .	3·06
		100·00

Localities. — English. Whinstone quarries, south of Newcastle.—*Irish.* Donald's Hill, co. Down.— *Foreign.* Schemnitz in Hungary, in amygdaloid; Walsch in Bohemia, in clinkstone.

Name. From ὕαλος, *glass*, in allusion to its resemblance to that substance, and λίθος, *stone*.

Brit. Mus., Case 21.

M.P.G. Horse-shoe Case, Nos. 764, 765.

HYALOMELAN, *Hausmann.* A variety of Tachylite from Vogelsgebirge. S.G. 2·7144.

Comp. (K̇³ +A̅l) S̈i, or 2(K̇, Ṅa, Ċa, Ṁg, Ṁn, Ḟe) S̈i+(A̅l F̅e) S̈i.

Analysis, by *C. Gmelin :*

Silica	.	50·22
Titanic acid	.	1·42
Alumina	.	17·84
Protoxide of iron	.	10·27
Lime	.	8·25
Magnesia	.	3·37
Soda	.	5·18
Potash	.	8·87
Protoxide of manganese	.	0·40
Water and ammonia	.	0·50
		101·31

Name. From ὕαλος, *glass*, and μέλας, *black;* in allusion to the ease with which it melts *BB* to a blackish opaque glass.

HYALOPHANE, *v. Waltershausen.* A variety of Orthoclase containing baryta. Occurs in dolomite.

Analysis, by *Von Waltershausen :*

Silica	.	45·65
Sulphuric acid	.	4·12
Alumina	.	19·14
Baryta	.	21·32
Lime	.	0·77
Magnesia	.	0·73
Soda	.	0·49
Potash	.	8·23
Water	.	0·54
		100·00

S.G. (of transparent variety) 2·805 : (of translucent variety) 2·901.

Name. From ὕαλος, *glass*, and φαίνω, *to seem.*

HYALOSIDERITE, *Walchner.* A variety of Chrysolite, occurring in yellowish- and reddish-brown crystals, imbedded in brown basaltic amygdaloid, at the Kaiserstuhl in the Breisgau. Translucent at the edges, where it exhibits a hyacinth-red colour. Streak brown. H. 5·5. S.G. 3·287.

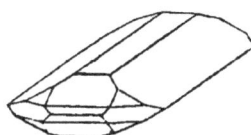

Fig. 238.

Comp. (½Ṁg + ½Ḟe)⁵ S̈i, with an excess of Ṁg S̈i, a large quantity of the protoxide of iron being replaced by magnesia and other bases.

Analysis, by *Walchner :*

Silica	.	31·63
Alumina	.	2·21
Protoxide of manganese	.	0·48
Magnesia	.	32·40
Protoxide of iron	.	28·49
Potash	.	2·69
Chromium	.	trace
		97·90

BB if not naturally magnetic, it becomes so when heated to redness, when it also turns black; at a higher temperature, it fuses to a black magnetic globule. With borax or microcosmic salt, gives the reactions of iron, and with microcosmic salt, immediately a skeleton of silica.

Dissolves with difficulty in cold, concentrated muriatic acid, and yields a jelly on evaporation.

Locality. The Kaiserstuhl in the Breisgau, in amygdaloid.

Name. From ὕαλος, *glass*, and σίδηρος, *iron.*

Brit. Mus., Case 25.

HYBLITE. A pseudomorph, after Augite.

Comp. R̈ S̈i + Ḧ S̈i) + 4Ḣ.

Analysis (mean of many analyses), by *Waltershausen :*

Silica	.	40·86
Alumina	.	10·22
Peroxide of iron	.	20·68
Lime	.	4·53
Magnesia	.	2·61
Soda	.	4·05
Potash	.	1·12
Water	.	15·93
		100·00

HYDRARGYLLITE, *G. Rose.* The name which has been given to crystallized Gibbsite. Occurs in regular six-sided prisms, or in prisms with twelve faces, resulting from the combination of two hexagonal prisms. Colour reddish-white. Translucent or transparent in thin laminæ. Lustre vitreous; on cleavage-faces pearly. H. 2·5. S.G. 2·87.

N 4

Comp. Hydrate of alumina, or $\ddot{A}l\ \dot{H}^3$ =alumina 65·56, water 34·44=100.

Analysis, from the Ural, by *Hermann:*

Alumina　.　.　.　64·03
Phosphoric acid　.　.　1·43
Water　.　.　.　.　34·54

100·00

BB whitens, becomes opaque, emits a brilliant light, but does not fuse.

In powder dissolves, but with difficulty, in muriatic acid.

Localities. The Schischimskian mountains, near Slatoust, in the Ural, where it was first discovered by *Lissensko.* Gumushdagh in Asia Minor, associated with Corundum. Unionville, Pennsylvania, U. S. Brazil, resembling Wavellite.

Name. From ὕδωρ, *water,* and ἄργιλλος, *clay.*

Hydrargyllite bears some resemblance in form to phosphate of lime; but is easily distinguished from it by inferior hardness.

Brit. Mus., Case 19.

HYDRATE OF ALUMINA. See DIASPORE.

HYDRATE OF MAGNESIA, *Allan, Phillips.* See BRUCITE.

HYDRATED DEUTOXIDE OF MANGANESE, *Turner.* See MANGANITE.

HYDRATED IOLITE, or BONSDORFFITE. See HYDROUS IOLITE.

HYDRO-ALUMINOUS LEAD. See PLUMBO-RESINITE.

HYDRO-APATITE. Occurs in semi-transparent mammillary concretions, somewhat resembling Chalcedony. H. 5·5. S.G. 3·1.

Comp. $\ddot{C}a^3\ \ddot{P}+Ca\ F+\dot{H}$.

Analysis:

Phosphoric acid　.　.　40·00
Lime　.　.　.　.　47·31
Calcium　.　.　.　3·60
Fluorine　.　.　.　3·33
Phosphate of iron　.　0·43
Water　.　.　.　.　5·30

100·00

Heated in a tube, decrepitates and disengages ammoniacal water.

Locality. The Pyrenees, in fissures of a ferruginous-brown argillaceous rock.

Name. From ὕδωρ, *water,* and *apatite.*

HYDROBOROCALCITE, or HAYESINE. The name (derived from ὕδωρ, *water,* boron, and calcium, *lime*), has reference to its chemical composition. See HAYESINE.

HYDROBORACITE, *Hess, Dufrénoy, Brooke & Miller.* Resembles in appearance a worm-eaten wood, and is riddled with small holes,

which are filled with a mixture of clay and salt.

Colour white, with red spots caused by the presence of iron. Structure radiating foliated, and resembling fibrous and foliated Gypsum. Transparent in thin plates. Л. 2. S.G. 1·9 to 2.

Comp. Hydrated borate of magnesia and lime, or $\dot{C}a^3\ \ddot{B}^4+\dot{M}g\ \ddot{B}^4+18\dot{H}$=lime 14·3, magnesia 10·3, boracic acid 47·7, water 27·7 =100·0

Analysis, by *Hess:*　·

Lime　.　.　.　.　13·30
Magnesia　.　.　.　10·45
Boracic acid　.　.　49·92
Water　.　.　.　.　26·33

100·00

BB fuses readily, with considerable loss of water, to a clear glass, imparting at the same time a greenish colour to the flame.

Yields borate of magnesia to boiling water, imparting to it an alkaline reaction.

Very soluble in warm muriatic acid.

Locality. The Caucasus.

Name. The name (from ὕδωρ, *water,* and *Boracite*), has reference to its chemical composition.

Hydroboracite may be distinguished from Gypsum, to which it bears a strong resemblance, by its fusibility.

HYDROBUCHOLZITE. Probably an altered or hydrous Kyanite, from Sardinia.

HYDROCALCITE. Occurs in small rhombohedral crystals, and forming an incrustation on wood under water.

Colour whitish, bluish, greyish. Translucent. Easily broken. Fracture splintery. S.G. 2·58.

Comp. $\dot{C}a\ddot{C}+5\dot{H}$=carbonate of lime 52·4, water 47·6=100.

Analysis, from the Giants' Causeway, by *Da Costa:*

Lime　.　.　.　.　47·0
Carbonic acid　.　.　36·0
Silica　.　.　.　.　3·0
Alumina　.　.　.　2·0
Water　.　.　.　.　12·0

100·0

The water passes off, and the mineral becomes anhydrous on exposure to the air.

Locality. The Giant's Causeway, on basalt.

Name. From ὕδωρ, *water,* and calcite, *Calc Spar.*

HYDROCARBONATE OF MAGNESIA, *Thomson.* See HYDROMAGNESITE.

HYDROCHLORE, *Hermann.* See PYRO-CHLORE.

HYDROHALITE, *Mitscherlich.* A hydrous chloride of sodium.

Comp. Na, Cl + 4H = chloride of sodium 62·0, water 38·0 = 100.

The name is derived from ὕδωρ, *water,* and ἅλς, *salt.*

HYDROLITE, *Beudant, De Dree.* HYDRO-LITH, *Leman.* Soda-Chabasite, or Gmelin-ite. See GMELINITE.

Fig. 239.

The name (from ὕδωρ, *water,* and λίθος, *stone*) has reference to the large amount of water contained in the mineral.

Brit. Mus., Case 27.

HYDROMAGNESITE, *v. Kobell.* Oblique; in small crystals, which are generally acicular, or bladed and tufted. Also amorphous or in chalk-like crusts. Colour and streak white. Lustre vitreous to subpearly; also earthy. Brittle. H. 3·5. S.G. 2·14 to 2·18.

Comp. 3(Mg C̈ + Ḣ) + Mg Ḣ = magnesia 43·9, carbonic acid 36·3, water 19·8 = 100.

Analysis, by *Wachtmeister:*

Magnesia	.	.	42·41
Carbonic acid	.	.	36·82
Silica, oxide of iron, &c.	.	2·24
Water	.	.	18·53
			100·00

BB infusible; gives off moisture, and is finally converted into pure magnesia.

Dissolves in acids with effervescence.

Localities. Swinaness, Isle of Unst, in the Shetlands, associated with Brucite. Hrubschitz in Moravia, in Serpentine. Negropont, near Kumi. United States, with Serpentine and Brucite, at Wood's and Low's Mines, near Texas, Pennsylvania. Hoboken, New Jersey, in acicular crystals like Natrolite, and in earthy crusts.

Name. From ὕδωρ, *water,* and *magnesite.*

Brit. Mus., Case 47.

HYDROMAGNOCALCIT, *Rammelsberg.* A kind of Hydromagnesite, in which the magnesia is partly replaced by lime. It is found in spherical masses on Vesuvius.

HYDRO-NICKEL-MAGNESITE, *Shepard.* See PENNITE.

HYDROPHANE. A variety of Opal which readily imbibes water and (though not naturally transparent) becomes so on being immersed in it. It is found in Hungary, and in Ireland. in small roundish masses in amygdaloid, of a brownish-white colour, near the Giants' Causeway, and at Crossreagh, parish of Ballywillin.

Name. The name is derived from ὕδωρ, *water,* and φαίνω, *to appear.*

It has also been called *oculus mundi.*

Brit. Mus., Case 24.

HYDROPHILITE, *Glocker.* A kind of Chloride of Calcium, found occasionally in Karstenite and Gypsum, and in the matrix containing Boracite at Lüneberg in Hanover, and also especially accompanying Rock Salt.

Comp. Ca Cl, or chlorine 63·79, calcium 36·21 = 100.

Name. From ὕδωρ, *water,* and φίλος, *a friend.*

HYDROPHITE, *Svanberg.* Massive, sometimes fibrous. Colour mountain-green to blackish-green, with a feeble subvitreous lustre. Translucent to opaque. Streak paler than the colour. H. 2·5. S.G. 2·4 to 2·66.

Comp. (Mg, Fe) S̈i + Mg Ḣ³.

Analysis, from Taberg, by *Svanberg:*

Silica	.	.	36·29
Alumina	.	.	2·90
Protoxide of iron	.	22·72
Protoxide of manganese	.	1·66
Magnesia	.	.	21·08
Vanadic acid	.	.	0·11
Water	.	.	16·08
			100·75

BB turns black and becomes magnetic, and finally melts to a black globule.

Locality. Taberg, in Smaoland, with Picrolite.

Name. From ὕδωρ, *water,* and *ophite.*

See also JENKINSITE.

Brit. Mus., Case 35.

HYDROSILICATE OF MANGANESE, *Phillips.* See OPSIMOSE.

HYDROSILICITE, *v. Waltershausen.* A calcareo-magnesian form of altered Augite, occurring as a very thin snow-white and amorphous crust (with Herschelite, Phillipsite, and Calcite), coating cavities and cracks in tufa at Palagonia, and Aci Castello in Sicily. Fracture dull and uneven. H. scarcely that of chalk. S.G. 2·2.

Comp. Hydrous Augite, or Ṙ³ S̈i² + 3Ḣ.

Analysis, by *Waltershausen:*

Silica	.	.	42·02
Alumina	.	.	4·95
Lime	.	.	27·19
Magnesia	.	.	8·41
Soda	.	.	2·57
Potash	.	.	2·67

Water and carbonic acid . 5·06
Insoluble .   .   .   . 2·19

                        ———
                        100·0

Name. From ὕδωρ, *water*, and *silex.*
The name Hydrosilicite has also been
given to Kerolite.

HYDROSTEATITE. A Steatite from Göpfersgrün, containing, according to Klaproth,
only 59·5 per cent. of silica. This variety
is remarkable for containing pseudomorphous crystals, probably after Quartz.

HYDROTALC, *Necker.* See PENNINE.

HYDROTALCITE, *Hochstetter.* A variety
of Völknerite, in which part of the alumina
is replaced by peroxide of iron. It is foliated pearly, with a greasy feel. Translucent, or transparent in thin folia. H. 2.

Comp. $\dot{M}g^6 (\ddot{A}l \ddot{F}e) + 16\dot{H}.$

Analysis, by *Hochstetter :*
Alumina   .   .   .   . 12·00
Peroxide of iron .   .   . 6·90
Magnesia .   .   . 36·30
Carbonic acid   .   .   . 10·54
Water .   .   .   . 32·06
Insoluble .   .   .   . 1·20

                        ———
                        99·60

Locality. Snarum, in Norway.
Name. From ὕδωρ, *water,* and *talcite.*
Brit. Mus., Case 19.

HYDROUS ALUMINATE OF LEAD, *Smithson.* See PLUMBO-RESINITE.

HYDROUS ANTHOPHYLLITE, *Thomson.*
This mineral has been re-examined by
Smith & Brush, who found it to contain
only 2·26 per cent. of water, instead of 11·45
per cent. as stated by Thomson. According
to Dana, it is altered asbestiform Actinolite.

Analysis, mean of two, by *Smith & Brush :*
Silica .   .   .   . 58·43
Magnesia   .   .   . 29·34
Protoxide of iron .   .   . 8·76
Soda .   .   .   .   . 0·88
Potash .   .   .   . trace
Alumina   .   .   .   . trace
Water .   .   .   . 2·26

                        ———
                        99·67

Localities. Girvan, in Argyleshire, in
fibro-columnar masses, of a greyish-brown
colour. New York Island.

HYDROUS APATITE. See HYDRO-APATITE.

HYDROUS BORATE OF LIME AND MAG-
NESIA. See HYDROBORACITE.

HYDROUS CARBONATE OF LIME, *Scheerer.*
See HYDROCALCITE.

HYDROUS DIPHOSPHATE OF ALUMINA
AND MAGNESIA, *Thomson.* See LAZULITE.

HYDROUS IOLITE, *Bonsdorff.* A variety

of altered Iolite, occurring in regular six-
sided and twelve-sided prisms, with a basal
cleavage, which is sometimes perfect. Colour greenish-brown, with a pearly lustre.
Translucent. Folia brittle. Rather harder
than Calc-spar.

Comp. Iolite + 6$\dot{H}$.

Analysis, by *Bonsdorff :*
Silica   .   .   .   . 45·03
Alumina   .   .   . 30·05
Magnesia   .   .   . 9·00
Protoxide of iron .   .   . 5·30
Water .   .   .   . 10·60

                        ———
                        100·00

BB becomes paler but does not fuse. It
is not completely decomposed by acids.
Locality. Abo.

HYDROUS MUSCOVITE. See MARGARO-
DITE.

HYDROUS OXIDE OF IRON, *Phillips.* See
LIMONITE.

HYDROUS PHOSPHATE OF COPPER, *Allan.*
See PHOSPHOCALCITE.

HYDROUS PYRITES. A variety of white
Iron Pyrites (Marcasite) containing water
in a state of chemical combination. H. 3 to
4. S.G. 4·925 to 5.
Locality. Moravia, Upper Silesia.

HYDROUS STEATITE. See SAPONITE.

HYDROZINCITE. See ZINC BLOOM.

HYPARGYRONBLENDE, *Breithaupt,* or
HYPARGYRITE. A variety of Miargyrite,
from Clausthal, in the Harz. According to
Plattner, it contains 35 per cent. of silver.

HYPERSTHENE, *Haüy, Phillips.* Occurs
massive or imbedded in rocks. Colour
greyish or greenish-black, with a lamellar
structure, and a bright metallic pearly lustre. Translucent in thin laminæ, with a
slight tinge of green, when viewed in one
direction, but opaque in the other. Streak
dark grey. Cleaves parallel with the diagonals and sides of a rhombic prism. Very
tough. Fracture uneven. Surface of fracture resinous. H. 6·0. S.G. 3·3 to 3·6.

Comp. $\dot{R} \ddot{S}i^2,$ in which $\dot{R}$ represents lime,
magnesia, and a large proportion of prot-
oxide of iron.

Analysis, from Florence, by *Köhler :*
Silica   .   .   .   . 53·20
Alumina   .   .   . 2·47
Magnesia   .   .   . 14·91
Lime   .   .   .   . 19·09
Protoxide of iron .   .   . 8·67
Protoxide of manganese . 0·38
Water .   .   .   . 1·77

                        ———
                        100·49

BB on charcoal, melts easily to a greyish-green opaque glass; with borax forms a greenish glass.

Localities. Coverack Cove, near the Lizard, Cornwall, in serpentine; the Cuchullin Hills, Isle of Skye; in crystalline concretions, of a dark-green or greyish-black colour, and having a strong metallic lustre, in the parish of Termonmaquirk, co. Tyrone, in Ireland. The Harz. Greenland. Island of St. Paul, on the coast of Labrador, as a constituent of a syenitic greenstone rock, but chiefly in rolled masses. Canada, with andesite rock, at Chateau Richer, and at St. Adèle, Mille Isles. United States, in Essex county, and near Wilmington, Delaware.

Name. From ὑπις, *exceeding,* and σθένος, *strength;* because it possesses greater lustre and hardness than Hornblende, with which it was formerly confounded.

Some varieties of Hypersthene have nearly the composition of Diallage, to which it bears the same relation that the dark varieties of Pyroxene bear to the paler ones. It is sometimes cut for ring-stones and brooches.

Brit. Mus., Case 34.

HYPOCHLORITE, *Schüler.* Occurs in reniform, botryoidal, and globular masses, with a minute crystalline structure. Colour feeble—green, passing into black and yellow. Lustre resinous and dull. Streak yellowish-grey. Brittle. Fracture even to flat conchoidal. H. 6. S.G. 2·9 to 3.

Comp. A mixture of a silicate of bismuth and iron, and a phosphate of alumina.

Analysis, by *Schüler:*

Silica	50·24
Alumina . . .	14·65
Oxide of bismuth .	13·03
Protoxide of iron .	10·54
Phosphoric acid . .	.9·62
Manganese . . .	trace
	98·08

BB becomes brown and black, but does not melt. Insoluble in acids.

Localities. County of Sayn, in Germany, and in minute crystals and grains, or massive and earthy, at Schneeberg, Johanngeorgenstadt, and Braunsdorf, in Saxony.

Brit. Mus., Case 57.

HYPOSCLERITE, *Breithaupt.* Has been shown by Rammelsberg to be probably Albite mixed with Augite. Occurs in crystals and lamellar masses, the latter distinguished by the fracture (which is conchoidal as well as lamellar) from the rose-coloured Orthose

with which it is associated. Colour greenish, very similar to that of Oligoclase. S.G. 2·6 to 2·60.

Analysis, by *Rammelsberg:*

Silica	67·62
Alumina . . .	16·59
Peroxide of iron . .	2·30
Soda	10·24
Lime . . ; .	0·85
Potash	0·51
Protoxide of manganese .	1·46
	99·80

Locality. Arendal, in Norway.

Name. From ὑπὸ, *under (less),* and σκληρός, *hard.*

HYPOSTILBITE, *Beudant.* According to Professor Haughton, should be regarded as an altered form of Stilbite. If considered a distinct mineral, it should be regarded as a hydrated lime-Oligoclase, represented by the formula $\ddot{\text{C}}\text{a}\,\dddot{\text{S}}\text{i}+\dddot{\ddot{\text{A}}}\text{l}\,\ddot{\text{S}}\text{i}^2+5\ddot{\text{H}}$.

Locality. Farôs.

HYSTATIQUE, *Breithaupt.* A variety of carbonate of lime, the angle of which is 107° 28' 30". H. 5·5 to 5·75. S.G. 3·089.

HYSTATISCHES EISENERZ, *Breithaupt;* or HYSTATITE. A variety of titaniferous iron, resembling Ilmenite in colour and cleavage. H. 6. S.G. 5.

Analysis, by *Mosander:*

Titanic acid . . .	24·19
Peroxide of iron . .	53·01
Protoxide of iron . .	19·91
Lime	0·33
Magnesia . . .	0·68
Silica	1·17
	99·29

Locality. Tvedestrand and Krageroe, near Arendal, in Norway, in gneiss.

I.

IBERITE, *Svanberg.* A variety of altered Iolite, occurring in large six-sided prisms with a basal cleavage. Lustre vitreous to pearly. H. 2·5. S.G. 2·89.

Analysis, by *Norlin:*

Silica	40·90
Alumina . . .	30·74
Protoxide of iron . .	15·47
Protoxide of manganese .	1·33
Lime	0·40
Magnesia . . .	0·81
Potash	4·57
Soda	0·04
Water	5·56
	99·82

BB melts to a dark pearl.

Locality. Montalban, near Toledo, in Spain.

Name. From *Iberia*, the ancient name of Spain.

ICE-SPAR. Is the name sometimes given to the transparent variety of Orthoclase (Glassy Felspar) found in Vesuvian lavas; and also to pellucid varieties of other species of Felspar.

It occurs on Monte Somma, near Naples, with Nepheline, Mica, Meionite and Hornblende. The name has reference to the resemblance of the mineral to ice, both in appearance and in brittleness.

Brit. Mus., Case 30.

ICELAND AGATE of many mineralogists. See OBSIDIAN.

ICELAND SPAR. The name applied to transparent Calc Spar, the finest specimens of which are found in Iceland.

Brit. Mus., Case 43.

M.P.G. Horse-shoe Case, No. 382.

ICHTHYOPHTHALME, *D'Andrada.* ICTHYOPHTHALMITE, or Fish-eye stone; (from *ἰχθὺς, a fish*, and *ὀφθαλμὸς an eye*), a name for Apophyllite, from its white pearly lustre, resembling that of a fish's eye.

Brit. Mus., Case 27.

IDOCRASE, *Haüy, Phillips.* Pyramidal: primary form a right prism with a square base. Occurs crystallized and massive. The general form of the crystals is that of a rectangular prism terminated by planes, and the edges of the prism are often replaced. Colour brownish and yellowish-green, sometimes sulphur-yellow, orange and also blue, rarely black; sometimes green when viewed in the direction of the axis, and pistachio-green in a transverse direction. Lustre vitreous, often inclining to resinous. Generally translucent, sometimes nearly transparent. Exhibits double refraction. Streak white. Fracture imperfect-conchoidal; small-grained, uneven. H. 6·5. S.G. 3·349 to 3·45.

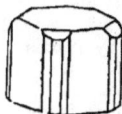

Fig. 240.

Comp. 3(Ċa, Ṁg, Ṁn, Ḟe), (F̈e Äl) 3S̈i = Ċa³ S̈i² + Äl S̈i (Gmelin). According to Hermann, its composition is represented by the general formula (Ṙ³, Ḧ) S̈i + n Ṙ Ḧ.

Analysis, from Vesuvius, by *Karsten:*

Silica	. . . . . 37·50
Alumina	. . . . 18·50
Peroxide of iron	. . . 6·25
Lime	. . . . . 33·71
Magnesia	. . . 3·10
Protoxide of manganese	. 0·10
	99·16

BB swells up and fuses readily, forming a yellowish-green or brownish glass. Dissolves easily in borax and microcosmic salt, forming a glass coloured by iron; the glass formed with microcosmic salt likewise contains a skeleton of silica, and becomes opalescent on cooling.

Partly decomposed by muriatic acid; but after it has undergone fusion, it is completely decomposed by that acid with the separation of gelatinous silica.

Localities. The limestone quarries at Glen Cairn in Aberdeenshire. Between Broadford and Killride in the Isle of Skye. *Irish.* Donegal; in prisms of a hair-brown colour at Derryloaghan, and at Bunbeg near Gweedore, &c.

The principal foreign localities are Vesuvius (*Vesuvian*), where crystals of a hair-brown or olive-green colour line the cavities of volcanic rocks, and are associated with Glassy Felspar, Garnet, Melanite, Mica and Nepheline. The finest specimens, however, come from Ala, in the Val di Brozzo, in Piedmont; these are in general semi-transparent, and of fine olive-green and hair-brown colours, and in some rare instances, perfectly black. Near Lake Baikal and on the banks of the Wiloui in Siberia (*Wiluite*). Egge near Christiansand in Norway. Cziklowa in the Bannat. Monzoni in the Fassa Valley, in sulphur-yellow crystals. Frugard in Finland (*Frugardite*), Gökum (*Gokumite* and *Loboite*). Haslau near Eger in Bohemia (*Egeran*). Near Tellemarken in Norway, (*Cyprine*), of a fine smalt-blue colour.

Name. From *εἴδω, to seem,* and *κράσις,* a *mixture,* in allusion to its crystalline forms being mixed figures, which have often been mistaken for those of other minerals.

Idocrase is cut into ring-stones and other ornaments at Naples and Turin, and sold under various names, as Chrysolite, Hyacinth, &c., according to the colour.

Brit. Mus., Case 35.

M.P.G. Horse-shoe Case, No. 882; Upper Gallery, Wall-case A, in recess 4, Nos. 112 to 118.

IDRIALINE, *Brooke & Miller, Dufrénoy.* IDRIALITE, *Schrötter.* A kind of Bitumen found mixed with Cinnabar at the quicksilver mines of Idria in Carniola. It occurs massive, of a greyish or brownish-black colour, with a greasy lustre. Opaque. Streak blackish inclining to red; shining. Unctuous. Sectile. H. 1 to 1·5. S.G. 1·4 to 1·6.

Comp. $C^{42} H^{14} + O$.

Analysis, by *Büdecker:*

Carbon	. . . . 91·828
Hydrogen	. . . . 5·299
Oxygen	. . . . 2·873

100·000

Brit. Mus., Case 60.

IDRIALINE CINNABAR. A compact and slaty mixture of Cinnabar with Idrialite and earthy particles. From the quicksilver mines of Idria in Carniola.

Brit. Mus., Case 9.

IGLESIASITE. See CERUSITE.

IGLITE, IGLOÏTE. A variety of Aragonite from Iglo in Hungary.

ILDEFONSITE, *Haidinger.* A variety of Columbite from Ildefonso in Spain, with a submetallic vitreo-adamantine lustre. S.G. 7·416.

ILLUDERITE, *Karsten.* See ZOISITE.

ILMENITE, *Brooke.* The Mengite of G. Rose.

ILMENITE, *Kupffer.* A variety of Titaniferous Iron, generally occurring massive, but sometimes in opaque crystals of a dark iron-black colour. Primary form an acute rhombohedron. Lustre sub-metallic. Slightly magnetic. Streak black. Fracture conchoidal. H. 6. S.G. 4·895.

Comp. Titanate of iron, or $\dot{F}e \ddot{T}i + \ddot{F}e$, in variable proportions.

Fig. 241.

Analysis, by *Mosander*, from the Ilmengebirg:

Titanic acid	. . 46·92
Protoxide of manganese	. 2·73
Magnesia	. . . 1·14
Protoxide of iron	. . 37·86
Peroxide of iron	. . 10·74

99·39

BB alone infusible; with fluxes behaves like oxide of iron.

Soluble in concentrated muriatic acid when finely pulverised.

Localities.—British. In crystalline lamellar masses at Glen Finnart, in Argyleshire, with Chlorite, in mica-slate. Ben Ima. and Hillswickness in Shetland —*Foreign.* Crystallized and massive at Lake Ilmen, near Miask, in Siberia. Krageroe, Arendal, &c.: in Norway.

Name. After the locality, Ilmen.

Brit. Mus., Case 37.

ILMENORUTILE, *Von Kokscharow.* A variety of Rutile occurring in the form of the fundamental pyramid, without any prismatic planes. It is iron-black and opaque, or in small crystals slightly red at the edges when held between the eye and the sun. H. above 6. S.G. 5·074 to 5·133.

Comp. According to R. Hermann: Titanic acid 89·3, peroxide of iron 10·7=100.

Locality. The Phenacite and Topaz mine of the Ilmen mountains.

ILVAITE. A name for Lievrite, after that of the Island of Elba, where it was first found.

IMPERFECT CORUNDUM, *Greville & Bournon.* See CORUNDUM.

IMPURE TOPAZ, *Kirwan.* See CITRINE.

INDIAN RED, *T. H. Rowney.* A kind of Ochre, imported from the Persian Gulf in small lumps, and partly as a coarse, hard, and gritty powder. Colour deep red with a shade of purple. S.G. 3·848.

Comp. Silicate of iron, or $\ddot{F}e \ddot{S}i$.

Analysis, by *T. H. Rowney:*

Silica	. . . . 30·17
Peroxide of iron	. . 56·59
Alumina	. . . 3·79
Lime	. . . . 2·65
Magnesia	. . . 1·43
Sulphuric acid	. . 2·28
Carbonic acid	. . 1·73
Water	. . . . 1·62

100·26

BB alone infusible, and, after cooling, is attracted by the magnet. On platinum wire, with borax and microcosmic salt, yields a transparent globule, with the usual reaction for iron.

By digestion with concentrated muriatic acid, a small portion is dissolved, and the remainder retains its red colour, and is not further altered by continued application of heat.

·Indian Red is the crude material which furnishes the well-known pigment of that name.

INDIAN TOPAZ. A name given by lapidaries to saffron-yellow Topaz.

INDIANITE, *Bournon.* A variety of Anorthite, occurring in masses which have a granular texture somewhat resembling that of statuary marble, and a glistening surface of fracture. Colour white or greyish, sometimes with a tinge of brown, from an admixture of Garnet. Scratches glass. S.G. 2·74.

Analysis, from India, by *G. J. Brush*:

Silica	.	.	. 42·09
Alumina	.	.	. 38·89
Lime	.	.	. 15·78
Soda	.	.	. 4·08
			100·84

BB infusible.

Readily gelatinises in acids.

This mineral forms the gangue of Corundum in the Carnatic (whence the name *Indianite*), and is accompanied by Garnet, Kyanite, Hornblende, &c.

Brit. Mus., Case 19.

INDICOLITE, the name which has been given to blue Tourmalines from their indigo-blue colour.

Brit. Mus., Case 40.

INDIGO COPPER. See COVELLINE.

INDURATED TALC. A hard, impure variety of slaty Talc. It occurs in nodules, with a compact texture, at Little Cambray in Arran; Portsoy in Banffshire; and Swinaness in Unst, one of the Shetlands.

INFLAMMABLE CINNABAR A name sometimes applied to Idrialite, in consequence of its combustibility.

INOLITE. A form of Calcite. See OSTREOCOLLA.

INTIRE METALS. The name applied by Kirwan both to "noble and perfect metals," as well as to the "base and imperfect metals," and including those which are in any degree malleable when cold.

IODIC MERCURY, *Phillips*. See COCCINITE.

IODITE, *Brooke & Miller, Haidinger*. IODSILBER, *Leonhard*. IODIC SILVER, *Phillips*. IODINSILBER, *Mohs*. IODURE D'ARGENT, *Beudant*. See IODYRITE.

IOD-QUECKSILBER, *Del Rio, Leonhard*. IODURE DE MERCURE, *Necker*. See COCCINITE.

IODOLITE, *Shepard*. A meteoric mineral found in small quantity diffused through Chladnite in the stone from Bishopville. Massive, in angular (somewhat rounded) grains, the largest of which are $\frac{1}{8}$ inch in diameter. Colour pale smalt-blue. Semi-transparent. Lustre vitreous. Brittle. H. 5·5 to 6.

BB fuses easily with ebullition to a blebby, coloured glass, which while warm retains a pale amethystine tinge.

Name. From ἰώδης, *violet coloured*.

IODYRITE. Hexagonal, with a highly perfect basal cleavage. Also occurs massive in thin plates of a greyish-white or silver-white colour, which changes to lavender-blue on exposure to the atmosphere; also citron- and sulphur-yellow, to yellowish-green.. Lustre resinous to adamantine. Transparent or translucent. Streak yellow. Flexible in thin laminæ. Sectile. H. about 1. S.G. 5·504.

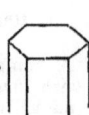 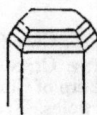

Fig. 242.   Fig. 243.

Comp. Iodide of silver, or Ag, I = silver 46, iodine 54 = 100.

Analysis, by *J. Lawrence Smith*:

Iodine	.	.	. 53·109
Silver	.	.	. 46·380
			99·489

BB on charcoal, melts instantly, giving off a vapour which tinges the flame of a beautiful violet colour, and yielding globules of silver.

Localities. Guadalajara in Spain; forming thin veins in Steatite at Albarradon, near Mazapil, in Zacatecas; and at Delirio mines of Chañarcillo, near Copiapo in Chili.

Iodyrite is homœomorphous with Greenockite.

IOLITE, *Phillips*. Rhombic; primary form a right rhombic prism. Occurs crystallised in stout prisms, which are often hexagonal. Colour various shades of pale and dark blue, sometimes with a tinge of grey or brown. Exhibits dichroism; often appearing of a deep blue colour along the vertical axis, but red, brownish-yellow, or yellowish-grey when viewed by transmitted light at right angles to the axis of the prism. Transparent or translucent. Lustre vitreous. Streak white. Fracture uneven or somewhat conchoidal. H. 7 to 7·5. S.G. 2·6 to 2·7.

Comp. $3\dot{M}g\ \ddot{S}i + \dot{F}e\ \ddot{S}i + 2\ddot{A}l^2\ \dddot{S}i^3$ (Gmelin), or if $\dot{R}$ represent $\dot{M}g$ and $\dot{F}e = \dot{R}^3\ \ddot{S}i^2 + 3\ddot{A}l\ \ddot{S}i$ = silica 49·6, alumina 33·8, magnesia 8·7, protoxide of iron 7·9 = 100.

Analysis, from Bodenmais, by *Stromeyer*:

Silica	.	.	. 48·33
Alumina	.	.	. 31·71
Magnesia	.	.	. 10·16

Protoxide of iron . . .	8·32	
Protoxide of manganese .	0·33	
Water	0·59	
	99·46	

BB alone fuses with difficulty at the edges to a transparent blue glass: with borax melts slowly to a clear globule. Only partially soluble in acids.

Localities.—Ireland. The Island of Rathlin; Dalkey, near the river Dodder, co. Dublin.—*Foreign.* Cape de Gata, in Spain, imbedded in granite. Ujordlersoak and Se mitok in Greenland in Quartz. Distinctly crystallized at Bodenmais in Bavaria (*Peliom*). Tunaberg in Sweden. Finland at Orijerfvi (*Steinheilite*), and Fahlun (*Hard Fahlunite*). Iolite is occasionally employed as an ornamental stone. The transparent variety found in small rolled masses in Ceylon, is the *Sapphire d'eau* of the jewellers. It is of a clear white mingled with celestial blue, forming a sort of mixed colour when viewed in different directions, in consequence of its property of dichroism.

Name. From *ἴον, violet*, and *λίθος, stone*, in allusion to its bluish-violet colour when viewed in one direction.

Brit. Mus., Case 36.

M. P. G. Horse-shoe Case, Nos. 1003, 1009.

IRIDESCENT COPPER PYRITES. See PEACOCK COPPER.

M. P. G. Principal Floor, Wall-case 6 (British).

IRIDESCENT QUARTZ. See IRIS. •

IRIDOSMINE, *Necker.* IRID-OSMIUM, *Hausmann.* IRIDIUM OSMIÉ, *Haüy.* Hexagonal; rarely found crystallized in hexagonal prisms with replaced basal edges; generally in small irregular flattened grains, which are harder, heavier, and of a somewhat paler steel-grey colour than Native Platinum. Lustre shining metallic. Opaque. Brittle and difficultly malleable. H. 7. S.G. 21·118. (G. Rose.)

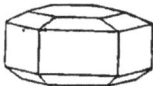

Fig. 244.

Comp. Osmide of iridium.

Analysis, from Australia, by *Deville & Debray :*

Iridium . . .	58·13	
Rhodium . . .	3·04	
Ruthenium . . .	5·22	

Osmium	33·46	
Copper	0·15	
	100·00	

BB infusible ; both alone and with fluxes. Insoluble in acids.

Localities. With platinum in the province of Choco in South America ; and in the Ural Mountains of Siberia. Rather abundant in the alluvial Gold of California, occurring in small bright lead-coloured scales, which are sometimes six-sided. Canada, in the gold washings on the rivers Du Loup and Des Plantes. Australia. Borneo.

For varieties, see NEWJANSKITE and SISSERSKITE.

Name. From Iris, *a rainbow :* the solutions of Iridium being of variegated colours. Iridium is used for the nibs of pens, and is worth £24 per ounce.

Brit. Mus., Case 3.

M. P. G. Principal Floor, Wall-case 28.

IRIS. The name applied by French jewellers to a very limpid and transparent variety of Rock Crystal, possessing the property of reflecting the prismatic colours by means of natural flaws in the interior of the stone. When cut in *cabochon* or *goutte de suif,* it imitates Opal to a certain extent, and the superb Iris ornaments worn by the Empress Josephine frequently deceived even persons skilled in such matters, by their brilliancy and play of colours. This stone is not made up at the present day. Rock Crystal may be easily made into Iris, either by a blow from a mallet, or by dropping it suddenly into boiling water, or by heating and suddenly dropping it into cold water; but in these cases the fissures produced are on the outer part of the stone instead of being in the interior, as is the case in true Iris. (Barbot.)

IRITE, *Hermann.* Cubical : occurs in octahedrons. Isomorphous with Spinel, Magnetic Iron, &c. Occurs in strongly lustrous black scales, which are attracted by the magnet. Soft. S.G. 6 506.

Comp. A compound of the peroxides of iron and chromium, with the protoxides of iridium and osmium, represented by the formula $\overset{...}{R}\overset{..}{R}$, or (Ir, Os, Fe) (Ir, Os, Cr)² Ö.

Analysis, by *Hermann :*

Peroxide of iridium .	62·86	
Protoxide of osmium .	10·30	
Protoxide of iron . .	12·50	
Peroxide of chromium .	13·70	
Peroxide of manganese	trace	
	99·36	

Not soluble in any acid.

Locality. The Ural, with Native Platinum, Titanic Iron, Iridosmine, and Hyacinth, often filling up interstices between the separate grains in large masses of platinum. Brit. Mus., Case 2.

IRON-ALUM. See HALOTRICHITE.

IRON-APATITE. See ZWIESELITE.

IRON-CHRYSOLITE. See FAYALITE.

IRON-EARTH. Occurs as a black pulverulent mass, which attaches itself closely to anything on which it is rubbed, and is strongly attracted by the magnet. S.G. about 3·8.

·*Comp.* (Fe Mn) F̈e, or Magnetic Iron-ore, in which about half the protoxide of iron is replaced by protoxide of manganese, with which it is amorphous.

Analysis, by *Genth:*

Peroxide of iron .	.	. 65·68
Protoxide of iron	.	. 14·09
Protoxide of manganese	.	16 25
Oxide of copper .	.	. 0·09
Oxides of cobalt .	.	. traces
Water .	.	. trace
Gold-sand, &c.	.	. 2·34
		98·45

Locality. The Alte Birke Mine, in the neighbourhood of Siegen, in Prussia, where a vein of Spathic Iron is broken through by basalt, and partly converted into Magnetic Iron-ore. (Gmelin.)

IRON-FLINT, *Jameson.* See FERRUGINOUS QUARTZ.

IRON-FOAM. See MICACEOUS IRON-ORE.

IRON-GLANCE, *Jameson.* See SPECULAR IRON.

IRON MICA, *Jameson.* Micaceous Iron-ore. Sometimes found in small and extremely thin six-sided plates, which are translucent and display a dark red colour by transmitted light. The principal locality is Cattas Altas, in the Brazils. It generally, however, occurs massive, and constitutes a valuable ore of iron. Brit. Mus., Case 15.

IRON NATROLITE. A variety of Natrolite in which one-fourth of the alumina is replaced by peroxide of iron. It occurs in dull green opaque prismatic crystals and semi-crystalline plates, with the Breviewite of Brevig, in Norway. H. 5. S.G. 2·353.

Analysis, by *C. Bergemann:*

Silica .	.	. 46·54
Alumina	.	. 18·94
Peroxide of iron .	.	. 7·49
Soda with a little potash	.	14·04

Protoxide of iron .	.	. 2·40
Protoxide of manganese	.	0·55
Water .	.	. 9·37
		99·33

IRON-NICKEL PYRITES. See SULPHIDE OF IRON and NICKEL.

IRON OCHRE, or OCHREOUS IRON-ORE. See HEMATITE and LIMONITE. *M. P. G.* Principal Floor, Wall-cases 38 (E. Indies) 49, No. 355.

IRON PYRITES, *Phillips.* See PYRITES.

IRON ROSES. (Eisenrosen.) See BASANOMELANE.

IRON RUTILE. See GÖTHITE.

IRONSHOT COPPER GREEN, *Jameson.* An impure Chrysocolla. When the colour inclines to brown the mineral is impure. ·

IRON SINTER, *Allan.* See PITTICITE.

IRON SPAR. An anhydrous carbonate of protoxide of iron. It occurs in rhombohedral forms, and is isomorphous with Calc-spar. See CHALYBITE.

IRON VITRIOL, *Jameson.* See COPPERAS.

ISERIN, *Werner;* ISERINE, *Jameson, Brochant, Phillips.* Cubical: in octahedrons, with the faces of the crystals uneven and rounded. Occurs in small obtuse angular grains, and in rolled pieces, with a somewhat rough surface, or in the form of black sand in alluvium or in the beds of rivers; also massive and disseminated in basalt. Colour iron-black. Lustre submetallic. Opaque. Streak black. Brittle. Some grains of this mineral are strongly magnetic, some slightly, others not at all. H. 6 to 6·5. S.G. 4·85 to 5·1.

Comp. 3Fe T̈i + F̈e.

Analysis, from Iserwiese, by *Rammelsberg* (small grains, S.G. 4·745):

Titanic acid	.	. 41·64
Oxide of iron	.	. 26 82
Protoxide of iron .	.	. 26·85
Do. of manganese	·	. 1·00
Magnesia	.	. 4·66
		100·97

BB alone infusible.

Localities. — British. The shore of the Mersey, nearly opposite Liverpool, and at Hunstanton, in Norfolk, mixed with Magnetite; near the mouth of the river Don, Aberdeenshire; in minute octahedrons among boulders at Ballygrogan, Mull of Cantyre. In the trap rocks of Arthur's Seat, near Edinburgh; on the shore of Loch Trista, one of the Shetlands.—*Foreign.* Unkel, on the Rhine, and on Etna, in basalt; also in

ISOMETRIC COBALT PYRITES.

Bohemia, Saxony, Calabria, and near Puy-de-Dome, in France.

This mineral was first found disseminated in granite-sand, in the Risengebirge of Silesia, near the source of the stream called the Iser, whence the name Iserine.

Brit. Mus., Case 37.

ISOMETRIC COBALT PYRITES, *Mohs.* See LINNÆITE.

ISOPHANE, *Berthier.* See FRANKLINITE.

ISOPYRE, *Turner, Phillips*; ISOPYRIC QUARTZ, *Haidinger.* Occurs in compact amorphous masses, of a greyish or velvet-black colour, and occasionally spotted red like Heliotrope. Lustre vitreous. Opaque, or faintly translucent at the thinnest edges. Streak pale greenish-grey. Brittle. Fracture flat-conchoidal. Slightly magnetic. H. 6 to 6·5. S.G. 2·9 to 3.

Comp. Ca S̈i+(Ä̈l, F̈e) S̈i=silica 49·66, alumina 13·78, peroxide of iron 21·51, lime 15·05=100.

Analysis, from Cornwall, by *Turner :*

Silica	47·09
Alumina	13·91
Peroxide of iron	20·07
Lime	15·43
Oxide of copper	1·94
	98·44

BB fuses readily to a magnetic globule. On platinum colours the flame green. Decomposed by the acids imperfectly and with difficulty, but easily and completely decomposed by alkaline carbonates.

Localities. Near St. Just and Penzance, in Cornwall, forming compact masses, sometimes two inches thick, in granite. It is associated with Tourmaline and Tin Stone.

Name. From ἴσος, *equal,* and πῦρ, *fire,* the effect produced on it *BB* being similar to that produced on several other minerals.

Isopyre bears a strong resemblance to Obsidian, but may be distinguished from it by a fainter and less vitreous lustre.

ISPADRAN. A name that has been given to Copper Pyrites, from the district of the Keradagh, in Persia, between Tabriz and the Caspian.

ITALIAN CHRYSOLITE. The name by which the Italian Idocrase, which is cut at Naples, is commonly called.

ITTNERITE, *Gmelin, Leonhard.* Cubical: primary form a rhombic dodecahedron. Occurs granularly massive, with an indistinct dodecahedral cleavage. Colour dark bluish- or ash-grey. Lustre resinous. Translucent. Fracture imperfect-conchoidal. H. 5·5. S.G. 2·3.

IXOLYT. 193

Comp. (N̈a, C̈a)⁵ S̈i + 3Ä̈l S̈i + 6Ḧ, with some Na Cl and Ca S̈.

Analysis, by *Gmelin :*

Silica	34·02
Sulphuric acid	2·86
Alumina	28·40
Peroxide of iron	0·62
Lime	7·27
Soda	12·15
Potash	1·56
Muriatic acid	0·75
Water and sulphuretted hydrogen	10·76
	98·36

BB when gently heated it becomes covered with blue spots like stars. Alone, on charcoal, swells up strongly, and fuses readily, with evolution of sulphurous acid, to a blistered enamel. With borax and microcosmic salt, it yields a transparent glass, in the latter case containing a skeleton of silica.

Dissolves quickly in muriatic acid, with evolution of sulphuretted hydrogen, and formation of a siliceous jelly. (*C. Gmelin.*)

Localities. The Kaiserstuhl, near Freiburg, in dolerites; also at Sasbach and Ihringen.

Name. After the discover, Von Ittner.

IWAARITE, *Nordenskiöld.* A mineral having apparently the characters of Schorlomite. It occurs either in cubical crystals or massive, and contains much titanium. Colour lustrous iron-black, like black or crystallized Melanite, with a grey streak.

Comp. C̈a³ S̈i + F̈e S̈i + ½T̈ T̈².

BB fuses to a black glass.

Locality. Iwaara, in the Kunsamo Kirchspiel, in Finland.

IXIOLITE. The name given by Nordenskiöld to the variety of Tantalite found only near Skogböle, in the diocese of Kimito in Finland. It usually occurs in rectangular prisms of a blackish-grey to steel-grey colour, with a weak metallic lustre. Streak brown. H. 6 to 6·5. S.G. 7 to 7·25.

It was formed into a separate species in consequence of the large quantity of tin and manganese it contains.

IXOLYT, *Haidinger.* IXOLYTE, *Dana.* A bituminous mineral closely resembling Hartite, but differing in the temperature at which it fuses, as well as in other respects. Amorphous. Colour hyacinth-red. Lustre greasy. Subtranslucent in thin fragments. Crumbles to powder between the fingers, becomes ochre yellow and yellowish-brown.

o

Fracture imperfect-conchoidal. H. 1. S.G. 1·008.

At 160° F. becomes soft, retains its tenacity at 212° F., whence the name ἴξός, *glue*, and λύω, *to dissolve*.

Locality. A bed of bituminous coal at Oberhart, near Gloggnitz, in Austria.

Brit. Mus., Case 60.

J.

JACINTH, or JACYNTH. See HYACINTH.

JADE, JADE ASCIEN, JADE DE LA CHINE, JADE NEPHRITIQUE, *Haüy.* See NEPHRITE.

JADE DE SAUSSURE.   } See
JADE TENACE, *Haüy.* } SAUSSURITE.

The French word Jade is supposed by Estner to be derived from the name *Iyida*, by which it is called in India.

JAIS, *French.* See JET.

JALPAITE, *Breithaupt.* Cubical. Colour blackish lead-grey. S.G. 6·877 to 6·89.

Comp. Cupriferous Silver Glance, represented by the formula ($\frac{3}{4}$Ag + $\frac{1}{4}$Cu) S.

Analysis, by *R. Richter*:

Sulphur	. . .	. 14·36
Silver .	. . .	. 71·51
Copper .	. . .	. 13·12
Iron .	. . .	. 0·79
		100·00

Name. From Jalpa, its locality in Mexico.

JAMESONITE, *Dufrénoy, Greg & Lettsom, Haidinger, Phillips.* Rhombic: primary form a right rhombic prism. Occurs in acicular crystals, or in fibrous masses, with a columnar structure, and composed of straight and parallel or divergent particles. Colour and streak steel-grey. Lustre metallic. Opaque. Sectile, H. 2 to 2·5. S.G. 5·5 to 5·8.

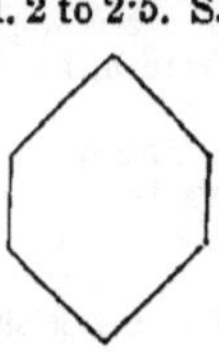

Fig. 245.

Comp. Sulphantimonite of lead, or 3Pb S, 2Sb ‴S, or Pb³, S̈b² = sulphur 20·2, antimony 36·2, lead 43·6 = 100.

Analysis, from Cornwall, by *H. Rose*:

Sulphur	. . .	. 22·15
Antimony	. . .	. 34·40
Lead .	. . .	. 40·75
Iron .	. . .	. 2·30
Copper .	. . .	. 0·13
		99·73

BB in an open tube affords dense white fumes of oxide of antimony. On charcoal, decrepitates, fuses readily, and almost entirely passes off in fumes, depositing a sublimate of the oxide of lead and antimony, and leaving a slag containing iron.

Soluble in warm muriatic acid.

Localities.—English. Cornwall; near Padstow; Huel Lee, near Calstock; Port Quin Cliffs and Trevinnock, near Endellion; Port Isaac, Pendogget.—*Foreign.* Siberia. Hungary, disseminated in Calc Spar. Spain. Brazil, &c.

Name. After Professor Jameson, of Edinburgh.

The perfect cleavage at right angles to the axis of the prism is very characteristic of Jamesonite, and is sufficient to distinguish it from those minerals which it may resemble in other respects.

Brit. Mus., Case 11.

M. P. G. Principal Floor, Wall-case 14 (British).

JANOLITE, *La Metherie.* See AXINITE.

JARGIONITE *, *C. Bechi.* A variety of Galena, from Tuscany, containing antimony and silver. It is near the Bleischweif of the Germans, and may be identical with Steinmannite, like which it occurs crystallized in octahedrons.

Analysis, from Argentiera, in the Val di Castello, by *Bechi*:

Sulphur	. . .	. 15·62
Lead .	. . .	. 72·90
Antimony	. . .	. 5·77
Iron .	. . .	. 1·77
Copper .	. . .	. 1·11
Zinc .	. . .	. 1·33
Silver .	. . .	. 0·72
		98·22

JARGON, or JARGOON. The name given

Fig. 246.

to a Cingalese variety of Zircon. It is seldom perfectly transparent, and is either colourless or grey, with tinges of green, blue, red,

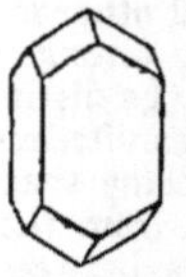

* The first notice of this mineral appeared in the American Journal of Science and Arts ([2] vol. xvi. p. 60), spelt as above. Most likely (as suggested by Mr. Warington Smyth), the name ought to be Targionite (after Targioni Tozzetti, the Italian geologist), in which case the error probably originated in a mistake on the part of the printer, in misreading J in the MS. for T.

and yellow of various shades, but generally smoky and ill-defined. It occurs in worn angular pieces, or in small detached crystals, rarely exceeding 6 or 8 carats in weight, chiefly in the sand of a river in Ceylon, accompanied by Sapphire, Spinelle, Tourmaline, &c.

The surfaces of the crystals are smooth, and possess a lustre approaching nearer to that of the Diamond than any other gem.

About the commencement of the last century, when the Jargoon was supposed to be an inferior variety of Diamond, it was in great request, especially for mourning ornaments, for which it was considered to be peculiarly appropriate, on account of its sombre tone, and almost adamantine lustre. At the present day, though out of fashion, and in no request, it is still occasionally sold for inferior diamonds.

Dr. J. Davy says, that the very light grey varieties of the Zircon are sold by the inhabitants of Ceylon as imperfect diamonds, the natives being altogether ignorant of the true nature of the mineral. It is most abundant in the district of Matura, whence it has its common name in Ceylon of *Matura diamond*. The colourless Zircon is also cut and sold as a false diamond in the bazaars of India. (Prinsep.)

M. P. G.   Horse-shoe Case, No. 846.

JAROSITE, *Breithaupt.* A potash copperas. Hexagonal. Cleavage basal. Colour yellowish.

Comp. $\dot{K}S + 4\ddot{F}e\ddot{S} + 6\dot{H}(+ \ddot{F}e\dot{H})$. Rammelsberg.

Analysis, by *Richter:*

Sulphuric acid	.	28·8
Peroxide of iron	.	52·5
Alumina	.	1·7
Potash with a little soda	.	6·7
Water	.	9·2
		98·9

Locality. Baranco Jaroso, in the Sierra Almagrera, in Spain.

JASP-OPAL. See OPAL-JASPER.

JASPACHATES. The name by which Jasper-agate was known to the ancients.

JASPE RUBANÉ, *Brochant.* See RIBBON JASPER.

JASPER. A compact variety of Quartz, usually of a dull red, yellow, brown, or green colour, sometimes blue or black, and distinguished from other varieties of Quartz by its complete opacity, even in very thin slices.

Jasper is frequently merely a form of silex rendered opaque either from alteration or

by the addition of a certain quantity of red oxide of iron, or the hydrate of that oxide.

When the colours are arranged in stripes, it is called *striped* or *ribbon-jasper.*

Egyptian Jasper occurs in the form of pebbles on the banks of the Nile, and is zoned with red and various shades of wood-brown fancifully intermixed with, and contrasted by, paler cream-coloured portions.

Porcelain Jasper is altered (or baked) clay, differing from true Jasper in being fusible at the edges *BB.*

Yellow Jasper is found at Vourla, in the Bay of Smyrna, and pebbles of *Red Jasper* on the plains of Argos.

Jasper is susceptible of a brilliant polish, and is manufactured into brooches, bracelets, snuff-boxes, vases, knife-handles, and other ornamental articles.

It occupied the twelfth place amongst the precious stones which were ordered to be placed on the breast-plate of the High Priest of the Jews, and bore the name of Benjamin engraved upon it. (Exodus xxviii. 20.) See also Ezekiel xxviii. 13; Rev. iv. 3; xxi. 11, 20.

Name. The word Jasper is derived from Ἴασπις, the name given by the ancients not only to the Jasper of the moderns, but to some other stones not of the true Jasper kind.

" Bright are the jasper's [*] tints, with clouds,
  And spots, and diverse stripes, and splendid veins
  Of green and various hues ; in mass opaque,
  But in thin fragments pervious to the light:
  With earthy fracture angularly sharp,
  Less hard than flint, but striking fire with steel.
  Jasper in large elliptic masses oft
  Occurs, or nodes detached, or rocks entire,
  To which Egyptian pebble's near allied."

Brit. Mus., Case 24.

M. P. G.   Horse-shoe Case, Nos. 563 to 568.

JASPERY IRON ORE, or JASPERY CLAY-IRON. An earthy variety of Hematite, having a firmer structure than Reddle or Red Chalk, and a large and flat conchoidal fracture.

JAULINGITE. A mineral resin, found between the layers of a kind of pine-tree at the lignite mine of Jauling, near Saint Veit in Austria.

JAY. A name given by the colliers in Derbyshire to Cannel Coal. See JET.

JAYET, *Haüy.* See JET.

JEAT, *Woodward.* See JET.

JEFFERSONITE, *Phillips.* A variety of Pyroxene, occurring in foliated or crystal-

* Werneria, or Short Characters of Earths, by Terræ Filius. 1805. Pp. 78-9.

line masses, of a dark olive-green colour, passing into brown, with a semimetallic lustre on the planes of cleavage, on the cross fracture resinous. Translucent at the edges. Yields to mechanical division in three directions. H. about 4·5. S.G. 3·6.

Comp. (Ċa, Ḟe, Ṁg, Żn)³ S̈i².
Analysis, by *Hermann :*

Silica	49·91
Alumina . . .	1·93
Lime	15·48
Protoxide of manganese	7·00
Oxide of zinc . .	4·39
Protoxide of iron .	10·53
Magnesia . . .	8·18
Loss by ignition . .	1·20
	98·62

BB fuses readily to a black globule. Partially soluble in heated muriatic acid.
Locality. Mine Hill, and Franklin ironworks, near Sparta, in Sussex County, New Jersey, associated with Franklinite and Garnet.
Name. In honour of Jefferson, President of the United States.
Brit. Mus., Case 34.
JEFREINOWITE. A variety of Idocrase, sometimes colourless, but generally of a yellowish-brown colour.
Analysis, by *Ivanow :*

Silica	37·41
Alumina . . .	20·00
Peroxide of iron . .	4·60
Lime	34·20
Potash	1·16
Soda	1·70
	99·07

Locality. Finland.
JELLELITE. The mineral to which this name was given by Apjohn is merely a Garnet. It occurs in Ireland, in rhombic prisms, as a yellowish, slightly greenish, incrustation, and is compact in texture.
It is composed of silica 38·09, peroxide of iron 33·41, lime 28·61 = 100. (Wright.)
JENITE. A name for Lievrite, bestowed by the French in commemoration of the battle of Jena.
JENKINSITE, *Shepard.* A variety of Hydrophite, occurring as a fibrous incrustation on Magnetite. Colour blackish-green, often with a tinge of olive. In powder pistachio-green. Translucent. Lustre vitreous. H. 2·6. S.G. 2·4 to 2·6.
Analysis, by *Smith & Brush :*

Silica	38·97
Alumina . . .	0·53

Protoxide of iron . . .	19·30
Protoxide of manganese .	4·36
Magnesia	22·87
Water	13·36
	99·39

Locality. O'Neil's mine, Orange co., U. S.
Name. After Mr. John Jenkins, of Monroe.
JET, *Kirwan.* A variety of Lignite. Colour velvet-black, or brownish-black, when passing into bituminous wood.
It occurs in elongated reniform masses, and sometimes in the shape of branches, which exhibit a regular woody internal structure, by transmitted light, when cut in extremely thin slices. Lustre brilliant and resinous. Sectile and brittle, breaking with a large and perfect conchoidal fracture ; and often showing a tendency to divide into prismatic or columnar masses. It feels remarkably smooth and does not stain the fingers. Slightly heavier than water. Burns with a greenish flame, and emits a very strong, sweetish bituminous smell, leaving a light yellowish-coloured ash.
Localities. Jet is found principally in marly, schistose, or sandy beds in France ; near Wittemberg in Prussia ; in the amber mines on the coast of the Baltic, where it is known by the name of Black Amber ; and in Alum shale in the neighbourhood of Whitby in Yorkshire, in hard and dark-coloured bituminous shale forming the lower part of the Upper Lias formation. Jet is made into various articles, and is especially used for mourning-ornaments. The value of the jet manufactured at Whitby in 1855, amounted to £20,000. In France the departments of Aude, of the Var, the Pyrenees, of Ariége, and of Ardennes are celebrated for this production. In the last century 1200 men were employed in the department of the Aude alone, in carving and turning the Jet of that neighbourhood into beads, rosaries, buttons, bracelets, earrings, necklaces, snuff-boxes, drinking vessels, and into pieces cut in facets, for mourning ornaments. 1000 cwts. were yearly consumed for these purposes, but the trade has now greatly fallen off. Considerable quantities are still, however, exported to Turkey, Senegal, but chiefly to Spain, to which latter country Jameson states that manufactured Jet to the value of 18,000 livres was sold in 1805.
This substance is the Gagates of the ancients, who gave it that name after the River Gaga, or the town of Gagis in Lycia, where it was originally found. The modern

words, Jayet, Jais, or Jet are doubtless derived from the ancient name Gagates or Gagat.

Artificial Jet is made of a kind of black glass, which is either cut into facets or blown into beads; and the blackness is produced by means of the black wax with which they are filled, or which fastens them to the iron backs on which they are mounted.

" Lycia her *jet* * in medicine commends ;
But chiefest, that which distant Britain sends :
Black, light, and polished, to itself it draws
If warmed by friction near adjacent straws.
Though quenched by oil, its smouldering embers raise
Sprinkled with water, a still fiercer blaze :
It cures the dropsy, shakey teeth are fixed,
Washed with the powder'd stone in water mixed.
The female womb its piercing fumes relieve,
Nor epilepsy can this test deceive :
From its deep hole it lures the viper fell,
And chases far away the powers of hell ;
It heals the swelling plagues that gnaw the heart,
And baffles spells and magic's noxious art.
This by the wise the surest test is styled
Of virgin purity by lust defiled.
Three days in water steeped, the draught bestows
Ease to the pregnant womb in travail's throes."

Brit. Mus., Case 60.
M.P.G. Horse-shoe Case, Nos. 89 and 90.

JEWREINOWITE.   See JEFREINOFFITE.
JEWS' PITCH. See ASPHALT.
JEWS' TIN. The name given in Cornwall to tin found near old smelting houses.

JOHANNITE, *Haidinger.* An ore of Uranium. Oblique ; primary form an oblique rhombic prism. Occurs in very minute flattened crystals, *fig.* 247, arranged in concentric druses or reniform masses. Colour beautiful, deep grass-green. Lustre vitreous. Transparent to opaque. Taste slightly bitter. Streak pale siskin-green. Fracture imperfect-conchoidal. H. 2 to 2·5. S. G. 3·19.

Fig. 247.

Comp. 2(U̇ Ü̈) S̈ + Ċu S̈ + 4Ḣ = sulphuric acid 19·37, oxides of uranium 68·40, oxide of copper 6·43, water 5·80=100.
Analysis (mean of two), by *Lindaker :*
   Sulphuric acid   .   .   20·02
   Oxide of uranium   .   67·72

* Lapidarium (xviii.) of Marbodus, from " Antique Gems, their Origin, Uses and Value," by Rev. C. W. King, M.A.

Oxide of copper	.	. 5·99
Protoxide of iron	.	. 0·20
Water	.	. 5·59

                   99·52

In a glass tube gives off water and sulphurous acid when highly heated, and becomes brown and finally black. *BB* on charcoal gives sulphur-fumes and a scoria of a black colour and dull green streak.

Locality. Near Joachimsthal, in Bohemia. Johanngeorgenstadt, in Saxony. The Middletown felspar quarry, in the United States.

Name. After the late Archduke Johann of Austria, a zealous mineralogist.

Brit. Mus., Case 55.

JOHNITE. A variety of Turquois, occurring in mammillary, stalactitic, and botryoidal masses, disseminated in siliceous schist. Colour bluish-green. H. 3.

Comp. Like Turquois, or a sub-phosphate of alumina, coloured by copper and iron.

Analysis, by *John :*
   Alumina   .   .   .   44·50
   Phosphoric acid   .   .   30·90
   Oxide of copper   .   .   3·75
   Protoxide of iron   .   .   1·80
   Water   .   .   .   19·00

                   99·05

Locality. Jordansmühle, in Silesia.

JOHNSTONITE, *Haidinger.* A finely granular Galena, mixed with more or less free sulphur. Massive. Opaque. Colour bluish. Lustre metallic. H. 3. S.G. 6·7.

Comp. Supersulphide of lead, or galena 90·38, sulphur 8·71=100. (*Johnston.*)

Localities. Dufton, in Westmoreland. Alston, in Cumberland. Cromford, in Derbyshire. Glen Malure, in Wicklow. — *Foreign.* The lead mines Neu-Sinka, near Fogaras, in Transylvania. (See SINKANITE.) In a vein in the Siegen mining district in the Rhine provinces, where it is known among the miners by the name of "burning galena," and is associated with unaltered Galena, some sulphate of lead, and a small quantity of sulphur.

Name. After Johnston, by whom it was first described.

Brit. Mus., Case 38.

JUDENPECH, *Wiedenman.* See ASPHALT.

JUNCKERITE, *Dufrénoy.* Occurs in yellowish-grey rhombic pyramids, with cleavage perpendicular to the axis, and parallel to two diagonals. It therefore exhibits, with regard to Spathic Iron, the same dimorphism that Aragonite exibits with regard to Calc Spar. Breithaupt, on the con-

198

trary, asserts that Junckerite has the same form as Spathic Iron, and that the so-called octahedron in which it occurs arises from the truncation of an acute rhombohedron. Lustre of rhombohedral planes somewhat lustrous and convex, the basal planes rough and dim. Transparent. S.G. 3·815.

Locality. Poullaouen, in Brittany.

Name. After Juncker, director of the mine of Poullaouen.

JURINITE, *Soret.* See BROOKITE.

K.

KAKOCHLOR, *Breithaupt.* A variety of Earthy Cobalt.

KALAIT. See TURQUOIS.

KALAMIT. See CALAMITE.

KALI ALAUN. See POTASH-ALUM.

KALI SALZSÄURES. See SYLVINE.

KALI-SULPHAT, *Naumann.* See GLASE-RITE.

KALIPHITE, *Ivanhow.* A mixture of brown iron-ore, oxide of manganese, and silicate of zinc with lime, from Hungary.

KALISALPETER. See NITRE.

KALK, German for lime.

KALK-MALACHIT, *Zincken.* A hydrous carbonate of copper, mixed with some carbonate and sulphate of lime and iron. It occurs massive, reniform, and botryoidal, with a fibrous and foliated structure. Colour verdigris-green. Lustre silky. H. 2·5.

Locality. Lauterberg, in the Harz.

KALK-MESOTYPE. See SCOLECITE.

KALKSALPETER, *Hausmann.* See NITRO-CALCITE.

KALK-SINTER, *Werner.* See CALC SINTER.

KALKSPATH, German. See CALC SPAR.

KALKSTEIN, *Werner.* LIMESTONE.

KALK-TUFF, *Werner.* CALCAREOUS TUFA.

KALKVOLBORTHITE. A variety of Volborthite, containing a large quantity of lime, found with Psilomelane, at Friedrichsrode. Colour siskin-green to greenish-grey. S.G. 3·495.

KALKURANITE, *G. Rose, Naumann.* AUTUNITE.

KALLAIT, *Hausmann.* See TURQUOIS.

KALLOCHROM, *Hausmann.* See CROCOISITE.

KALOMEL, *Haidinger.* See CALOMEL.

KALZEDON. CHALCEDONY; which see.

KÄMMERERIT, *Kenngott;* OR KÆMMERE-RITE, *Nordenskiöld.* A variety of Ripidolite, coloured red by chromic acid. It occurs foliated and massive, or granular; also in hexagonal prisms, of a reddish-violet colour. Lustre pearly. Translucent. Feels

greasy. Cleavage basal, perfect. Sectile. Flexible. H. 1·5 to 2·0. S.G. 2·76.

Analysis, by Smith & Brush:

Silica	33·30
Alumina	10·50
Oxide of chrome	4·67
Peroxide of iron	1·10
Magnesia	30·08
Potash, soda	0·35
Water	13·25
	99·75

BB exfoliates, and fuses at the edges only.

Localities.—British. Foliated and granular, also crystallized in small hexagonal plates, at Haroldswick, in Unst, one of the Shetlands, occasionally associated with chromate of iron and crystallized Talc.—*Foreign.* Bissersk, in Siberia, with chromic iron; at Texas, Lancaster co., Pennsylvania, with chromic iron, in Serpentine.

Name. After M. Kæmmerer, mineralogist. Brit. Mus., Case 25.

KAMMKIES. Cockscomb Pyrites; a variety of Marcasite.

KAMPYLITE, *Breithaupt.* A variety of Mimetite. It is found in large quantities crystallized, of various colours, yellowish to brown and brownish-red, at Drygill, in Cumberland. It also occurs at Badenweiler, and at Johanngeorgenstadt, in Saxony.

Analysis, from Cumberland, by Rammelsberg:

Chlorine	2·41
Lead	7·04
Oxide of lead	68·89
Lime	0·50
Arsenic acid	18·47
Phosphoric acid	3·34
	100·65

Name. Derived from καμπύλος, curved, in allusion to the barrel-shaped form of the crystals.

M. P. G. Wall-case 45, on Principal Floor (British).

KAND or CAND. A term applied by Cornish miners to Fluor.

KANEELSTEIN, *Werner.* See CINNAMON STONE.

KANEITF, *Haidinger.* Occurs in botryoidal masses with a foliated or granular structure. Colour greyish-white, with a black tarnish. Opaque. Lustre metallic-brilliant, like some varieties of Grey Copper. Very brittle. Fracture fine-grained, uneven. H. 5. S.G. 5·55.

KAOLIN. KAPNITE. 199

Comp. Arsenide of manganese, or Mn, As = manganese 42·4, arsenic 57·6 = 100.

Analysis, by *Kane*:

Manganese	. 45·5
Arsenic	. 51·8
Iron	. trace
	97·3

BB burns with a blue flame and falls to powder; at a greater heat the arsenic is given off, and redeposited upon the charcoal as a white powder.

Soluble without residue in aqua-regia.

Locality. Supposed to be Saxony.

Name. After Sir R. J. Kane of Dublin, by whom it was first observed, attached to a mass of Galena.

KAOLIN, or Porcelain Clay. Occurs massive and disseminated, and is composed of small particles which possess only a slight degree of coherence. Colour generally various shades of white or grey, inclining sometimes to blue, yellow, red or brown. Opaque, dull. Earthy, sectile. Friable. Adheres slightly to the tongue. Soft and meagre to the touch when dry, plastic when wet. H. 1 to 2. S.G. 2·25.

Comp. Hydrous silicate of alumina or $\ddot{A}l\ \ddot{S}i + 2\dot{H}$ = alumina 44·5, silica 40·0, water 15·5 = 100.

Analysis, from Plympton, Devonshire, by *Brongniart & Malaguti*:

Silica	. 44·26
Alumina	. 36·81
Lime, magnesia, potash	. 1·55
Iron and manganese	. trace
Non-argillaceous residue	. 4·30
Water	. 2·74
	99·66

BB infusible.

Decomposed by warm sulphuric acid, which dissolves the alumina, and leaves the silica.

Localities.—British. The best Kaolin, or Porcelain Clays, which are the result of the decomposition of felspar in granite, are procured from Cornwall and Devonshire. (*M.P.G.* Wall-case 7, in Upper Gallery). It is also found on the S. W. side of Fetlar, one of the Shetland Islands.—*Foreign.* The finest porcelain clay of Saxony is obtained from beds in gneiss at Aue, near Schneeberg; the Berlin porcelain is made from clay dug at Gömritz, below Halle, in the district of Magdeburg; also at Zotenburg and Giern in Lower Silesia. The Austrian porcelain is made of clay which is dug near Passau; that of Copenhagen from the produce of

Bornholm, an island in the Baltic; the French of Sèvres and Paris with clay dug at Saint-Yrieix, near Limoges, where it forms a Kaolin of great purity, derived from decomposed gneiss; and the English from the clays of Devon and Cornwall, Louhossoa, in the Basses Pyrenees. Zettlitz near Carlsbad, and many other places in Bohemia.

Kaolin is chiefly derived from the decomposition of Felspar, which may have been produced by the action of infiltrating waters containing carbonic acid in solution. The effect of such water would be to carry off the lime and the alkalies of the Felspar as carbonates, or as silicates in solution, and to leave the silica and the alumina behind in the form of a clay.

Name. The name, according to Dana, is a corruption of the Chinese word Kau-ling (meaning *high-ridge*), the name of a hill near Jauchau Fu, where this mineral is obtained.

KAPNICITE, *Kenngott.* In small radiated feathery rounded concretions, the needles apparently rhombic prisms, with acute edges replaced, and low pyramidal terminations. Colour yellowish or greenish-white. Lustre vitreous. H. 3·5 to 4.

Comp. Hydrous sulphate of alumina, $\ddot{A}l^3\ \ddot{S}^2 + 11\dot{H}$ = sulphuric acid 6·20, alumina 75·75, water (from the loss) 18·55 = 100. (*Von Hauer.*)

Name. After the locality, Kapnik, in Hungary, where it occurs, associated with Felsobanyite.

Fig. 248.

According to Städeler, Kapnicite only differs from Wavellite by containing two atoms less water.

KAPNITE, *Breithaupt.* A variety of Zincspar, containing more than 15 per cent. of protoxide of iron. S.G. 4 to 4·15.

Analysis, from Altenberg, by *Monheim*:

Carbonate of zinc	. 60·35
Carbonate of iron	. 32·21
Carbonate of manganese	. 4·02
Carbonate of lime	. 1·90
Carbonate of magnesia	. 0·14
Calamine	. 2·49
	101·11

o 4

Locality. Altenberg, near Aix-la-Chapelle. The proportion of iron being very variable, Monheim, who has analysed several specimens of this mineral, does not consider it to be a distinct species, and proposes the name *Ferruginous Zinc-spar* for the light-green varieties, which contain a large amount of zinc; and *Zinc-iron Spar* for the dark-green varieties, and those which become brown by the oxidation of the iron.

KARABÉ DE SODOME. See ASPHALT.

KARELINITE, *R. Hermann.* An oxisulphide of Bismuth, from the Sawodinsk Mine, in the Altai, where it occurs with Telluric Silver. Colour lead-grey. Lustre metallic. Fracture crystalline. H. 2. S.G. 6·6.

Comp. $\ddot{B}i + Bi \, S$.

Analysis, by *Hermann :*

Oxygen	5·21
Sulphur . . .	3·53
Bismuth . . .	91·26
	100·00

BB gives off fumes of sulphurous acid, and a grey slag, with a globule of bismuth.

Name. After Mr. Karelin, by whom it was brought from Siberia.

KARNEOL, *Werner.* See CARNELIAN.

KARPHOLITE, *Phillips;* OR KARPOLITH. See CARPHOLITE.

KARPHOSIDERIT, *Breithaupt.* See CARPHOSIDERITE.

KARSTENITE, *Hausmann.* See ANHYDRITE.

KASSITERIT, *Haidinger, v. Kobell.* See CASSITERITE.

KASSITEROTANTAL. See CASSITEROTANTALITE.

KATAPLEIIT, *Weibye & Sjögren;* KATAPLEIITE, *Brooke & Miller.* See CATAPLEIITE.

KAUSIMKIES. See LONCHIDITE.

KEFFEKILL, *Kirwan.* See MEERSCHAUM.

KEILHAUITE, *A. Erdmann.* Rhombic? also massive. Colour brownish - black, brownish-red, and translucent in splinters. Streak greyish-brown. H. 6·5. S.G. 3·69.

Comp. $3\dot{C}a^3 \ddot{S}i^2 + \ddot{H} \ddot{S}i + \dot{Y} \ddot{T}i^3$.

Analysis, by *Erdmann :*

Silica	29·45
Titanic acid . . .	28·14
Alumina . . .	5·90
Peroxide of iron . .	6·48
Peroxide of manganese .	0·86
Peroxide of cerium .	0·63
Lime	18·68
Yttria	9·64
	99·88

BB intumesces and fuses readily to a black shining slag. With borax yields an iron-coloured glass, which, in the inner flame, becomes blood-red.

Soluble in muriatic acid.

Locality. Buön, about 1½ mile from Arendal, in Norway, in a felspathic rock.

KÉMATINE, *Dufrénoy.* See CYMATINE.

KENNELL COAL, *Bakewell;* KENNELKOHLE, *Brochant, Werner.* See CANNEL COAL.

KENNGOTTITE. A mineral somewhat resembling Miargyrite, but containing a larger amount of silver. It is found in irregularly grouped crystals, of an iron-black, to a lead-grey colour, at Felsöbanya, in Hungary.

Name. After Kenngott, Professor of mineralogy at Zurich.

KERAMOHALITE, *J. Jurasky.* A mineral with the same composition as Alunogen, occurring in crystalline crusts, and also in six-sided tables, with Iron Vitriol, near Königsberg, in Hungary. Oblique. S.G. 1·6 to 1·7.

Analysis, by *Jurasky :*

Alumina . . .	14·30
Protoxide of iron . .	2·15
Sulphuric acid . .	36·75
Water	44·60
Insoluble . . .	2·01
	99·81

KERAPHYLLITE. See CARINTHINE.

KERARGYRE, *Beudant;* KERARGYRITE, *Dana.* Oblique: primary form the cube. Occurs crystallized in small cubes and acicular prisms, generally massive, and looking like wax; sometimes columnar; often in crusts, investing other substances. Colour most frequently pearl-grey, sometimes greenish or violet-blue. Acquires a brownish tarnish on exposure. Feebly translucent or opaque. Lustre resinous. Yields to the nail, and is malleable and sectile. Streak white and shining. No cleavage. Fracture imperfect flat-conchoidal. H. 1 to 1·5. S.G. 5·552.

Fig. 249.

Comp. Protochloride of silver, or Ag, Cl = silver 75·3, chlorine 24·7 = 100.

BB on charcoal yields metallic silver, with evolution of an odour of muriatic acid. Rubbed on a plate of moistened iron, the surface becomes covered with a thin film of metallic silver; on the addition of oxide of copper, the flame becomes blue.

Insoluble in nitric acid or water.

Localities. Cornwall (rarely), at Huel Duchy, Huel St. Vincent, Huel Mexico, Silver Valley, and Huel Brothers.—*Foreign.* The largest masses, especially those of a green colour, are brought from Chili, Peru, and Mexico, where it accompanies Native Silver. It also occurs at Huelgoet, in Brittany; Markirchen, in Alsace; Kongsberg, in Norway; Schemnitz, in Hungary; Schlangenberg, in the district of Koliwan, in Siberia, &c.

This mineral occurs in clay-slate, always in veins, and chiefly in their upper part. It is associated with other ores of silver, and sometimes with ochreous Brown Iron-ore, Quartz, Heavy Spar, ores of copper, &c.

The name Kerargyrite, or Horn Silver (derived from κἰρας, *horn*, and ἄργυρον, *silver*), appears to have reference to its property of cutting like horn.

This ore, especially the conchoidal subspecies, has an icy or glassy appearance, on which account it was called *vitreous* or *glassy silver-ore* by the older mineralogists. The vitreous silver-ore of Kirwan and others is Silver Glance.

Brit. Mus., Case 59.

M. P. G. Principal Floor, Wall-cases 14 (British); 22 (Foreign).

KERASIN. The name given by Von Kobell to Cromfordite, and by Beudant to Mendipite.

KERATE, *Haidinger, Nicol, Greg & Lettsom.* Hornsilver. See KERARGYRITE.

KÉRATOPHYLLITE, *Beudant.* See ACTINOTE.

KERMES, *Brooke & Miller*; KERMESITE, *Dana*; KERMESOME, *Chapman.* Oblique: primary form an oblique rhombic prism. Usually occurs in tufts of capillary crystals, consisting of elongated, slender, six-sided prisms, the surfaces of which are striated longitudinally. Colour cherry-red. Slightly translucent, appearing scarlet by transmitted light. Lustre adamantine. Streak brownish-red. Sectile. Slightly flexible in thin laminæ. H. 1 to 1·5. S.G. 4·5 to 4·6.

Comp. Oxy-sulphide of antimony, or $\ddot{\mathrm{Sb}}$ + 2Sb S^3 = oxide of antimony 69·82, sulphide of antimony 30·18 = antimony 76·33, sulphur 18·93, oxygen 4·74 = 100.

Analysis, by *H. Rose* :

Antimony	.	.	. 74·45
Sulphur	.	.	. 20·49
Oxygen	.	.	. 5·29

                         100·23

BB fuses very readily, sinking into the pores of the charcoal, and volatilizing in dense clouds. Becomes covered with a white coating when immersed in nitric acid.

Localities.—British. New Cumnock, Ayrshire, in capillary fibres, with Grey Antimony.—*Foreign.* Malaczka, near Posing, in Hungary, in veins with Quartz and Grey and White Antimony. Bräunsdorf, near Freyberg, in Saxony. Allemont, in Dauphiné.

Kermesite results from the decomposition of Grey Antimony.

Brit. Mus., Case 38.

KEROLITE, *Breithaupt.* Is found in kidney-shaped masses, which have a lamellar or compact structure, and a white, yellow, or green colour. Lustre vitreous or resinous. Transparent or translucent at the edges. Feels greasy, but does not adhere to the tongue. Streak white. Fracture conchoidal. H. 2 to 2·5. S.G. 2 to 2·4.

Comp. Sesquihydrate of silicate of magnesia, or 2Mg $\ddot{\mathrm{Si}}$ + 3$\dot{\mathrm{H}}$.

Analysis, from Zöblitz, by *Kühn* :

Silica	.	.	. 46·96
Magnesia	.	.	. 31·26
Water	.	.	. 21·22

                         99·44

BB becomes black, but does not fuse.

Localities. Zöblitz, in Saxony, and Frankenstein, in Silesia, associated with Serpentine.

Name. From κηρὸς, *wax*, and λίθος, *stone*.

Brit. Mus., Case 25.

KEVIL. A Derbyshire mining term for a sparry substance found in the vein and composed of Calc-spar, Fluor, and Barytes.

KIBDELOPHAN, *Beudant, Hausmann.* A titaniferous iron from Gastein. Occurs in crystals, having the form of Ilmenite and Iron Glance, but generally massive or in thin plates or laminæ. Slightly magnetic. H. 5 to 5·5. S.G. 4·66.

Analysis, by v. *Kobell* :

Titanic acid .	.	. 59·00
Protoxide of iron .	.	. 36·00
Peroxide of iron	.	. 4·25
Protoxide of manganese	. 1 65

                         100·90

Kibdelophane is the Axotomous Iron of v. Kobell.

See ILMENITE and TITANATE OF IRON.

Brit. Mus., Case 37.

KIDNEY-STONES. A local name for small hard nodules, not unlike septaria, composed of reddish-brown clay, with veins of Calc Spar, which are washed out of the cliffs on the north shore of Weymouth, in Dorsetshire.

KIESEL, *German* for silica or flint.

KIESELGALMEY. Siliceous oxide of Zinc. See SMITHSONITE.

KIESELKUPFER, *v. Leonhard.* } See CHRY-
KIESELMALACHIT, *Hausmann.* } SOCOLLA.

KIESELMANGAN. See RHODONITE.

KIESELSINTER, *Werner.* See SILICEOUS SINTER.

KIESELSPATH, *Hausmann.* See ALBITE.

KIESELWISMUTH, *Leonhard.* See EULYTINE.

KIESELZINKERZ, *G. Rose.* Siliceous oxide of Zinc. See SMITHSONITE.

KILBRICKENITE, *Apjohn.* A bluish-grey variety of Geocronite, from Kilbricken, Clare co., Ireland. H. 2 to 2·5. S.G. 6·407.

Analysis, by *Apjohn*:

Lead . . . . . 68·87
Antimony . . . 14·39
Iron . . . . . 0·38
Sulphur . . . 16·36
                    ———
                    100·00

Dissolves slowly in warm muriatic acid.

KILKENNY COAL, *Brochant.* See ANTHRACITE.

KILLINITE, *Thomson.* Occurs massive, with the occasional appearance of prisms. Colour pale green, sometimes stained brown or yellow. The coating which arises from decomposition yields an argillaceous odour when breathed on, and imparts a brownish-yellow stain to the granite. Structure lamellar. Lustre glimmering. Translucent. Yields to the knife. Brittle and easily frangible. Fracture fine-grained. H. 4. S.G. 2·65 to 2·75.

Comp. $(\dot{R}\,\ddot{S}i + \ddot{A}l^2\,\ddot{S}i^3) + 3\dot{H} =$ silica 51·12, alumina 28·37, potash 13·04, water 7·47 = 100.

Analysis, from Victoria Castle, near Killiney, by *Galbraith*:

Silica . . . . . 50·45
Alumina . . . 30·13
Protoxide of iron . . . 3·53
Magnesia . . . 1·09
Potash . . . . 4·81
Soda . . . . 0·95
Water . . . . 7·58
                    ———
                    98·54

BB loses colour and whitens, intumesces, and fuses to a white enamel.

Localities.—Irish. Killiney Hill, and near Dalkey and Scalp, near Dublin.

Killinite is considered by Dana to be an altered form of Spodumene, and by Blum and Haidinger an altered Iolite. The absence of a basal termination distinguishes it from Iolite, and the absence of lithia from Spodumene.

KILPATRICK QUARTZ, *Thomson.* Quartz found in the amygdaloid of the Kilpatrick hills, near Dumbarton. It occurs in small, white and translucent spherical masses, consisting of fibrous and radiated crystals, which are terminated at their outer extremities; also fibro-massive, and of a pale flesh-colour, accompanied by Stilbite, Natrolite, and other zeolitic minerals.

KIRWANITE, *Thomson.* Probably a variety of Green Earth. Occurs in small nodules of a dark olive-green colour, with a fibrous texture, and a somewhat radiated structure. Opaque. H. 2. S.G. 2·941.

Comp. $3\ddot{R}^2\,\ddot{S}i + \ddot{A}l\,\ddot{S}i + 2\dot{H}.$ *Rammelsberg.*

Analysis, by *Thomson*:

Silica . . . . . 40·5
Alumina . . . 11·4
Protoxide of iron . . . 24·0
Lime . . . . 19·8
Water . . . . 4·3
                    ———
                    100·0

BB blackens and partially fuses; with soda or borax forms a dark brown glass.

Localities.—Irish. Antrim, in basalt and amygdaloid; Glasdrumman, Kilkeel, and Dunmore Head, Co. Down.

Name. After Richard Kirwan, of Dublin, a distinguished mineralogist of the latter part of the last century.

KLAPROTHINE, *Brooke & Miller, Beudant.* See LAZULITE.

KLINOCLAS, *Breithaupt.* }
KLINOCLASE, *Brooke & Miller, Nicol.* } See CLINOCLASE.

KNAUFFITE. See VOLBORTHITE.

KNEBELITE, *Lenz.* Probably a ferruginous Tephroite. Massive, with an uneven and cellular surface. Colour grey, spotted with dirty white, brownish-red, brown, and green. Lustre glistening to dull. Opaque. Brittle, and difficultly frangible. Fracture subconchoidal. Hard. S.G. 3·714.

Comp. $(\dot{Fe}, \dot{Mn})^3\,\ddot{S}i =$ where Fe and Mn are in equal proportions.

Analysis, by *Döbereiner*:

Silica . . . . . 32·5
Protoxide of manganese . 35·0
Protoxide of iron . . 32·0
                    ———
                    99·5

BB alone unaltered; with borax fuses to a dark olive-green pearl.

Decomposed by muriatic acid, with separation of silica.

Locality. Unknown.

Name. After Major von Knebel, who gave the mineral to Döbereiner.

KNITS. A mining term in Derbyshire for small particles of lead ore.

KOBALDINE, KOBOLDINE, *Beudant.* See LINNÆITE.

KOBALT - BESCHLAG, *Kersten.* Cobalt Bloom, containing free arsenous acid. See COBALT COATING.

KOBALT-BLÜTHE, *Hausmann;* COBALT BLOOM. See ERYTHRINE.

KOBALTGLANZ, *Hausmann.* See COBALTINE.

KOBALTSULFURET, *Rammelsberg.* See SYEPOORITE.

KOBELLITE, *Sätterberg.* Colour dark lead-grey, like Grey Antimony, but with a brighter lustre. Streak black. Structure radiated. Soft. S.G. 6·29 to 6·32.

Comp. Sulphobismutbate of lead, or 2Pb³, S̈b+3P̈b³, B̈i (*Rammelsberg*).

Analysis, from Nerike, by *Sätterberg:*

Sulphur	17·86
Antimony	9·24
Bismuth	27·05
Lead	40·12
Iron	2·96
Copper	0·80
Matrix	1·45
	99·49

BB fuses with strong intumescence at first, but afterwards quietly, and becomes surrounded with a yellow glass. In the inner flame fumes strongly, and yields a white metallic globule.

Soluble in concentrated muriatic acid, with evolution of sulphuretted hydrogen.

Locality. The Cobalt mines of Sweden.

Name. After Von Kobell.

Brit. Mus., Case 11.

KOBOLDBLÜTHE, *Werner.* See ERYTHRINE.

KOCHSALZ, *Werner.* See ROCKSALT.

KOHLE, *German.* See COAL.

KOHLENBLENDE, *v. Leonhard.* See ANTHRACITE.

KOHLENSAURES BLEI, *v. Leonhard.* Carbonate of lead. See CERUSITE.

KOHLENSAURES MANGAN, *v. Leonhard.* Carbonate of manganese. See CALAMINE.

KORKOLITH, *Werner.* See COCCOLITE.

KOKSCHAROVITE, *N. Nordenskiöld.* A

mineral occurring in crystalline masses, with cleavage in two directions. Colourless to brown. Lustre approaching to adamantine, when colourless. H. 5 to 5·5.

Name. After Nicolai von Kokscharow, the crystallographer of St. Petersburg.

KOLLYRITE, *Friesleben.* See COLLYRITE.

KOLOPHONIT. See COLOPHONITE.

KONICHALCIT, *Breithaupt.* See CONICHALCITE.

KÖNIGINE, *Levy;* KÖNIGITE, *Beudant.* A variety of Brochantite. Colour emerald- or blackish-green. Transparent. Cleaves with facility parallel to the base of a rhomboidal prism, which is the primary form. H. 2 to 3.

Comp. Sulphuric acid, oxide of copper, and water.

Localities. Katherinenburg and Werchoturi, in Siberia.

Name. After König, late keeper of the Minerals in the British Museum.

Brit. Mus., Case 58.

KÖNLITE, *Schrötter;* KÖNLEINITE, *Kenngott.* A mineral resembling Scheererite, occurring in thin white plates and grains, composed of an aggregation of crystalline scales, in Brown Coal. Soft. S.G. 0·88.

Comp. C² H. ·

Analysis, by *Trommsdorff:*

Carbon	92·429
Hydrogen	7·571
	100·00

Localities. Near Redwitz, in Bavaria; and at Uznach, near St. Gallen, in Switzerland; in Brown Coal.

KOODILITE, *Dufrénoy.* Is merely Thomsonite mixed with silica. Occurs in isolated grains, cemented together, and of a reddish-grey colour.

KORÈITE, *Beudant, Dufrénoy;* KORITE. A hydrous Labradorite, occurring in dull brown grains. It has the same composition as Sideromelane, with which it is associated, except that it contains water.

Comp. R̈ S̈i + R̈ S̈i + 3Ḧ.

Analysis, by *v. Waltershausen:*

Silica	44·07
Alumina	12·00
Peroxide of iron	19·47
Lime	5·53
Magnesia	4·95
Soda	0·70
Potash	0·44
Water	12·84
	100·00

Localities. Nagyag. China.

KORUND, *Werner.* See CORUNDUM.

KÖTTIGITE, *Dana.* Oblique: occurs massive, or in fibrous crusts. Colour various shades of pale carmine and peach-blossom red. Lustre of surface of fracture silky. Translucent. Streak reddish-white. H. 2·5 to 3. S.G. 3·1.

Comp. Analogous to Cobalt Bloom, with which it is likewise isomorphous. $(\dot{Z}n, \dot{C}o, \dot{N}i)^3 \ddot{A}s + 8\dot{H}$.

Analysis, by *Köttig :*

Arsenic acid (by loss) .	.	37·17
Oxide of zinc	. .	30·52
Oxide of cobalt	. .	6·91
Oxide of nickel	. .	2·00
Lime .	. . .	trace
Water .	. . .	23·40·
		100·00

BB on charcoal in the outer flame changes colour and fuses to a pearl, gives off arsenical fumes, and leaves a slag of oxide of zinc. Readily soluble in dilute acids.

Locality. The Cobalt mine Daniel, near Schneeberg, in Saxony.

Name. After the discoverer, Otto Köttig.

KOUPHOLITE, *Vauquelin.* A variety of Prehnite, often containing dust or vegetable matter, which cause it to blacken and emit a burnt odour *BB.*

Analysis, by *Walmstedt ;*

Silica .	. . .	44·71
Alumina .	. .	23·99
Peroxide of manganese	.	0·19
Protoxide of iron .	.	1·25
Lime .	. . .	25·41
Water .	. . .	4·45
		100·00

Locality. Mont Blanc.

Name. From κοῦφος, *light,* and λίθος, *stone.* Brit. Mus., Case 28.

KRABLITE, *Forchammer.* A siliceo-felspathic mineral allied to Spherulite, and forming the basis of the trachyte, Pitchstone, and Obsidian of Iceland. H. 6. S.G. 2·57 to 2·65.

Comp. $(\dot{R} + \ddot{A}l) \ddot{S}i^8$.

Analysis, by *Forchammer* (S.G. 2·389):

Silica .	. . .	74·83
Alumina .	. .	13·49
Peroxide of iron .	.	4·40
Lime .	. . .	1·98
Magnesia .	. .	0·17
Soda .	. . .	5·56
Potash .	. . .	trace
		100·43

KRANTZITE, *C. Bergemann.* A fossil resin, occurring in grains and roundish pieces in the Brown Coal of Lattorf. Colour yellowish, but mostly brown to black, owing to the presence of earthy impurities. Elastic. Easily cut. S.G. 0·968; of the crust 1·002. Fuses at 225° C. (437° F.) without changing colour; becomes fluid at 288° C. (550·4° F.) and at 300° C. (572° F.), then distils over a brownish oil, having a very disagreeable and penetrating odour.

Name. After Dr. Krantz, of Bonn.

KRAURITE, *Brochant.* See DUFRENITE.

KREITTONITE. A black Spinel. S.G. 4·49.

Comp. $\dot{Z}n \ddot{A}l + \dot{F}e \ddot{F}e$, or $(\dot{Z}n, \dot{F}e) (\ddot{A}l \ddot{F}e)$.

Analysis, by *v. Kobell :*

Alumina .	. .	49·73
Peroxide of iron .	.	8·70
Oxide of zinc	. .	26·72
Protoxide of iron .	.	8·04
Protoxide of manganese	.	1·45
Magnesia .	. .	3·41
		98·05

Locality. Bodenmais, in Bavaria.

KREMERSITE. A mineral allied to Sylvine, occurring in ruby-red octahedrons on Vesuvius.

Comp. $2(K, Am, Na) Cl + Fe Cl^3 + 2\dot{H}$.

Analysis, by *Kremers :*

Chlorine .	. .	55·15
Iron .	. . .	16·89
Potassium	. . .	12·07
Sodium .	. .	0·16
Ammonium .	. .	6·17
Water .	. . .	9·56
		100·00

Name. After Kremers.

KREUZSTEIN, *Werner.* Cross-stone. See HARMOTOME.

KRISOBERIL, *Werner.* See CHRYSOBERYL.

KRISOLITH, *Werner.* See CHRYSOLITE.

KRISUVIGITE, *Forchammer.* A variety of Brochantite, occurring in small beds at Krisuvig, in Iceland.

Analysis, by *Forchammer :*

Sulphuric acid .	.	18·88
Oxide of copper .	.	67·75
Water .	. . .	12·81
		99·44

KROKOIT, *Breithaupt.* See CROCOISITE.

KROKYDOLITE, *Hausmann.* See CROCIDOLITE.

KRYOLIT, *Werner.* See CRYOLITE.

KUBIZIT, *Werner.* See ANALCIME.

KÜHNITE, *Brooke & Miller.* Massive, with cleavage in one direction. Colour dirty white or honey-yellow. Lustre waxy. Brittle. H. 5 to 6. S.G. 2·52.

Comp. (Ċa, Ṁg, Ṁn)³ Äs=arsenic acid 61·5, lime 22·5, magnesia 16·0=100.

Analysis, by *Kühn*:

Arsenic acid	. .	58·51
Lime	. . . .	23·22
Magnesia	. . .	15·68
Protoxide of manganese	.	2·13
Loss by ignition . .	,	0·30
		99·84

BB infusible, but turns grey. Soluble in nitric acid.

Locality. Longbanshyttan, in Sweden, with granular Bitter Spar and Iron Ore.

KUNKUR. The name commonly given in India to a more or less compact, tufaceous deposit of carbonate of lime with silica, found in the soil, in drift-sands covering other sands. This deposit, which is of comparatively recent age, occurs in the form of very irregularly shaped concretions, varying in size from that of a pea, in some places, to that of an egg in others, and bearing a resemblance sometimes to stalactites, and occasionally assuming moss-like and eccentric shapes.

The vast Kunkur deposits in the plains and valleys of India are sometimes seventy feet thick. Captain Newbold has brought forward evidence to prove that they have been produced from springs of water, the remains of which may, in some cases, be detected at the present day. It is also stated, on the same authority, that the siliceous deposits are apparently older than the calcareous, and that they were probably formed when the waters of the supposed springs had a somewhat higher temperature than is the case now.

All the lime of the Punjab is derived from Kunkur.

M. P. G. Wall-case, No. 39.

KUPAPHRITE, *Shepard.* Copper Froth. See TYROLITE. The name is derived from *cuprum, copper,* and ἀφϱὸς, *froth.*

KUPFER, *German* for Copper.

KUPFERANTIMONGLANZ, *Zincken.* See WOLFSBERGITE.

KUPFERBLEIGLANZ. See CUPROPLUMBITE.

KUPFERBLEISPATH. See LINARITE.

KUPFERBLENDE, *Breithaupt.* Tennantite, with part of the iron replaced by zinc. Colour of streak brownish, or dirty cherry-red. S.G. 4·2 to 4·4.

Analysis, by *Plattner*:

Sulphur	. . .	28·111
Arsenic	. . .	18·875
Copper	. . .	41·070
Iron .	. . .	2·219
Zinc .	. . .	8·894
Lead .	. . .	0·341
Silver	. . .	trace
Antimony .	. .	trace
		99·510

Locality. Near Freiberg in Saxony.

KUPFERBLÜTHE, *Hausmann.* See CHALCOTRICHITE.

KUPFERDIASPORE, *Kühn.* A variety of Phosphocalcite, with half an equivalent less water, the composition being represented by the formula Ċu⁵ P̈ + 2Ḧ.

Analysis by *Kühn*:

Phosphoric acid	.	24·13
Oxide of copper	.	69·61
Water or loss	. .	6·20
		100·00

KUPFERFAHLERZ. Tetrahedrite. The varieties belonging to the Fahlerz or Grey Ore of Werner have a steel-grey colour.

KUPFERGLAS, *Werner.* KUPFERGLANZ. *Haidinger, Naumann.* See COPPER-GLANCE.

KUPFERGLIMMER, *v. Kobell, Werner.* See CHALCOPHYLLITE.

KUPFERGRÜN, *Werner.* See CHRYSOCOLLA.

KUPFERINDIG, *Mohs.* See COVELLINE.

KUPFERKIES, *Werner, Naumann, Hausmann.* See CHALCOPYRITE.

KUPFERLASUR, *Werner.* See AZURITE.

KUPFER MANGAN, } See CUPREOUS
KUPFER MANGANERZ, } MANGANESE.

KUPFERNICKEL, *Werner.* See COPPER-NICKEL.

KUPFERPECHERZ. An impure variety of Chrysocolla, containing a large amount of Brown Iron-ore. The same specimen of this mineral presents very different appearance, in some parts being earthy like decomposed Felspar, and in others translucent and brittle.

Analysis, by *v. Kobell,* from Tourinsk:

Silica	. . . .	9·66
Oxide of copper .	.	13·00
Peroxide of iron .	.	59·00
Water .	. .	18·00
		99·66

Localities. Tourinsk in the Ural. The Basin of mines, in Nova Scotia.

KUPFERPHYLLIT. *Breithaupt*, See CHAL-COPHYLLITE.

KUPFERSAMMTERZ. See LETTSOMITE.

KUPFERSCHAUM, or COPPER FROTH, *Allan, Phillips.* See TYROLITE.

KUPFERSCHMARAGD, *Werner.* See COPPER-EMERALD, and DIOPTASE.

KUPFERSCHWÄRZE, *Werner.* BLACK COPPER. An impure, earthy black oxide of Copper, resulting from the decomposition of other ores, and mixed with impurities, sulphide of copper, pyrites, &c.

KUPFER-VITRIOL, *Werner, Hausmann, Naumann.* See CYANOSITE.

KUPFERURANGLIMMER, KUPFER-URANIT, *G. Rose.* See CHALCOLITE.

KUPFERWISMUTHERZ, *Klaproth.* See WITTICHITE.

KUPFERWISMUTHGLANZ, *R. Schneider.* See TANNENITE; also WITTICHITE.

KYANIT, *Werner.* KYANITE, *Jameson, Phillips.* Anorthic: primary form a doubly oblique prism, of which the terminations are nearly rhombs. Occurs massive, disseminated and crystallized in long and broad oblique four-sided prisms, which are irregularly terminated, and truncated on the lateral edges: they are either imbedded or intersect one another. Cleavage effected with difficulty transversely to the axis of the prism, but easily parallel to the lateral planes. Colour generally pale blue: also white (*Rhætizite*), grey, greenish and black; in some crystals the blue and grey are intermixed, and the blue is of a deeper tint along the middle of the prisms. Lustre pearly. Translucent; often transparent. Streak white. Brittle. Fracture foliated. Some crystals by friction become negatively electric, others positively. H. 5 on the lateral planes: 7 at the extremities. S.G. 3·54 to 3·61. Occurs chiefly in gneiss and mica-slate.

Comp. Anhydrous monosilicate of alumina; or $\ddot{A}l\ \ddot{S}i$=alumina 37·62, silica 62·38 =100.

Analysis, from St. Gotthard, by *Arfvedson:*

Silica	34·33
Alumina . . .	64·89
	99·22

BB infusible, but becomes colourless: with borax dissolves with difficulty, but completely, to a transparent glass. Not affected by acids.

Localities.— *Scotch.* Botriphinie, Banffshire, in blue crystals in gneiss. Near Banchory, in Aberdeenshire. Near the summit of Ben-y-Gloe in Perthshire, in Quartz. Hillswickness Point, in Zetland. —*Irish.* Erris in Mayo, in mica-slate.— *Foreign.* St. Gotthard in Switzerland in mica-slate, in transparent crystals, associated with Garnet, Staurolite, and Quartz. Greiner and Pfitsch (*Rhætizite*) in the Tyrol, with Quartz and Hornblende. The Sau-alp in Carinthia. Bohemia. Styria. Pontivy in France. Villa Rica in South America. Chesterfield, Worthington and Blandford, in Massachusetts, U. S. A black variety associated with Rutile is found in North Carolina.

Name. From ϰύανος, *dark blue.*

Brit. Mus., Case 26.

Kyanite, when transparent and of a fine blue colour, is sometimes cut and employed as a gem. It is generally imported from India cut and polished, as a variety of Sapphire. See SAPPARE, also RHÆTIZITE.

KYMATIN, *Breithaupt.* According to Rammelsberg a variety of Asbestos like that of Tarantaise, having the composition of Tremolite.

Comp. $\dot{C}a\ \ddot{S}i^3+(\dot{M}g\ \dot{F}e)^3\ \ddot{S}i^2$.

Analysis, by *Rammelsberg* :

Silica	57·98
Alumina . . .	0·58
Magnesia . . .	22·38
Lime	12·95
Protoxide of iron . .	6·32
	100·21

Locality. Kuhnsdorff, in Saxony.

KYPHOLITE, *Breithaupt.* A variety of Serpentine.

KYROSITE, *Breithaupt.* A variety of Marcasite, containing arsenic and copper. See WEISSKUPFERERZ.

Comp. Fe S² + Cu S.

Analysis (mean of 2), by *Scheidhauer* :

Sulphur . . .	52·63
Iron	45·63
Copper . . .	1·69
Arsenic . . .	0·93
	100·88

Localities. The mine Briccius, near Annaberg in Saxony. Chili.

M.P.G. Principal Floor, Wall-case 17.

L.

LABRADOR HORNBLENDE, *Jameson.*   } See HYPER-
LABRADORISCHE HORN-BLENDE, *Werner.*   } STHENE.

LABRADOR FELSPAR, *Phillips.* **LABRA-DORITE,** *La Metherie.* **LABRADORSTEIN,** *Werner.* **LABRADORESTONE,** *Kirwan.* A variety of Felspar sometimes used for ornamental purposes on account of its beautiful chatoyant reflections. Anorthic; frequently occurs in twin crystals like those of Albite. Colour smoke-grey, dark ash, brown, greenish, white, red and blue. Lustre vitreous, inclining to pearly on the faces of most perfect cleavage, to sub-resinous on the other surfaces. Streak white. Brittle. Fracture imperfectly conchoidal, uneven, splintery. H. 6. S.G. 2·67 to 2·76.

Fig. 250.

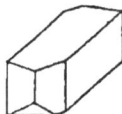

Comp. $\ddot{R}\ddot{S}i + \ddot{A}l \ddot{S}i = (\dot{R} + \ddot{A}l) \ddot{S}i$ where $\dot{R} = \dot{N}a$ and $\dot{C}a$: if $\dot{N}a$ be to $\dot{C}a$ in the proportion of 1 to 3, then the formula becomes $\dot{N}a \ddot{S}i + 3\dot{C}a \ddot{S}i + 4\ddot{A}l \ddot{S}i = $ silica 53·69, alumina 20·68, lime 12·13, soda 4·50 = 100.

Analyses, (a) from Labrador, by *Klaproth;* (b) from Campsie, by *Lehunt:*

	(a)	(b)
Silica	55·75	54·67
Alumina	26·50	27·89
Peroxide of iron	1·25	0·31
Lime	11·00	10·60
Soda	4·00	5·05
Potash	0·00	0·49
Magnesia	0·00	0·18
Water	0·50	,,
	99·00	99·19

BB on charcoal, behaves like Felspar, and fuses with rather less difficulty to a colourless glass. Yields a blue pearl with borax and oxide of nickel.

When powdered, entirely dissolved by heated muriatic acid, which does not act either on Felspar or Albite.

Labradorite occurs chiefly as a constituent of rocks; also in the lavas of Etna and Vesuvius, in the *Oriental verde antique* of Greece and other porphyries, as well as in certain hornblendic rocks, granites and syenites.

Localities.—Scotch. It is found in Stirlingshire in porphyritic greenstone, at Campsie, and at Milngavie in small crystals.— *Irish.* In Ireland it is met with in the basalt of Magee Island, co. Antrim: Mourne Mountains, co. Down, and in Galway finely crystallized and exhibiting a display of colours.—*Foreign.* Finland. Russia. Tyrol. The Harz. Corsica. Saxony. Sweden. Faröe. Norway. Canada at Granville, Cape Mahue, Abercrombie &c. United States. On the coast of Labrador, whence it was originally brought, it is associated with Hornblende, Hypersthene, and Magnetic Iron-ore.

Labradorite takes a fine polish, and on account of its beautiful chatoyant reflections it is valued for ornamental purposes, and sometimes used in jewelry. "Besides the fundamental colour, it presents a most beautiful play of vivid tints, varying according to the position in which it is viewed. Of blue, it exhibits all the varieties from violet to smalt-blue; of green, it displays the pure emerald-green, and various other tints approaching to blue on the one hand, and to yellow on the other. Of yellow, the most usual shades are golden and lemon-yellow, verging into deep orange, and thence into rich copper-red and tombac-brown. The parts exhibiting these beautiful colours are disposed in irregular spots and patches, and the same spot, if held in different positions, displays various tints: of these violet and red are the most rare." (*Mawe.*) The play of colour is supposed by some to be produced by microscopic crystals of Quartz imbedded in the stone; by others it is referred to the structure of the Felspar itself.

It is manufactured into brooches, pins, bracelets &c., also into snuff-boxes and similar articles. It looks best when cut in plain, very flat cabochon; a great deal of skill is required to divide the stone in such a manner, that the iridescent portions, on which its beauty depends, may be displayed to the utmost advantage.

Brit. Mus., Case 30.

M. P. G. Horse-shoe Case, Nos. 961 to 964; also on Floor at S.W. end of Case.

LABRADOR HORNBLENDE. See HYPERSTHENE.

LAGONITE. An earthy mineral of an ochreous-yellow colour, occurring as an incrustation at the lagoons of Tuscany.

Comp. $\ddot{F}e \ddot{B}^3 + 3\dot{H} = $ boracic acid 49·5, peroxide of iron 37·8, water 12·7 = 100.

Analysis, by *Bechi:*

Boracic acid	47·95
Protoxide of iron	36·26
Magnesia, lime, and loss	1·77
Water	14·02
	100·00

LAIT DE LUNE. Fibrous carbonate of lime, when the filaments have become flattened or broken by the action of infiltrating water, or by drying in the open air.

LAIT DE MONTAGNE, *Brochant.* See AGARIC MINERAL.

LAKE SALT, *Jameson.* See ROCK SALT.

LAMELLAR HEAVY SPAR, *Jameson.* See BARYTES.

LAMPADITE. A variety of Cupreous Manganese. Amorphous. Colour bluish-black. Lustre resinous. Structure sometimes reniform. H. above 2·5.

BB infusible.

Comp. Oxide of manganese 82, copper 13·5, silica 2·0=100.

Locality. Tin mines of Schlackenwald, in Bohemia.

Name. After Lampadius, the Saxon metallurgist.

LANARKITE, *Beudant*; LANARKIT, *Haidinger, v. Kobell.* Oblique: primary form a right rhombic prism. The crystals, which are aggregated lengthways, are minute and seldom distinct. Colour greenish - white, yellowish-white, or grey. Lustre adamantine, on the cleavage-face pearly. Transparent to translucent. Streak white. Sectile. Thin laminæ flexible, like Gypsum. H. 2 to 2·5. S.G. 6·8 to 7.

Fig. 251.

Comp. Sulphate and carbonate of lead-oxide. $\dot{P}b\ddot{S} + \dot{P}b\ddot{C}$ =sulphate of lead 53·15, carbonate of lead 46·85=100.

Analysis, by *Thomson :*

Carbonate of lead . . 46·04
Sulphate of lead . . 53·96
                          ————
                         100·00

BB on charcoal fuses to a globule, which is white when cold, and is nearly reduced to metallic lead.

Effervesces slightly with nitric acid, in which it is partially soluble, leaving a residue of sulphate of lead-oxide.

Localities.—Scotch. Leadhills in Lanarkshire, like *fig.* 251, in long slender crystals, associated with Susannite and Caledonite.— *Foreign.* Massive at Tanné in Brunswick, in the Harz, and in Siberia. Biberweier, in the Tyrol.

Brit. Mus., Case 55.

LANCASTERITE, *Silliman.* A mixture of Brucite and Hydromagnesite, from Lancaster co., Pennsylvania, U. S.

Brit. Mus., Case 47.

LANDSCAPE MARBLE. See COTHAM MARBLE.

LANTHANITE, *Haidinger.* Rhombic. Occurs in small, thin, four-sided, tabular crystals, with beveled edges. Generally fine granular or earthy. Colour greyish-white, yellowish, or pink. Lustre, dull or pearly. H. 2·5 to 3. S.G. 2·7.

Comp. La $\ddot{C}$ + 8$\dot{H}$ = lanthana 52·94, carbonic acid 21·11, water 25·95=100.

BB infusible; whitens, becomes opaque and brownish-yellow.

Effervesces in acids.

Localities. Bastnäs, in Sweden, coating Cerite. Lehigh co., Pennsylvania, in masses composed of minute aggregated tables. The Sandford Iron-ore bed, Moriah, Essex co., New York, in thin scales or plates, varying in colour from white to a delicate pink or rose-tint, with Allanite.

LAPIS AMPELITES of the ancients is the Cannel Coal of the moderns.

LAPIS ARMENIUS, *Kirwan.* "Is Chalk or Gypsum, impregnated with the blue calx (carbonate) of copper."

LAPIS LAZULI. Cubical. Occurs in dodecahedrons; commonly massive, compact. Cleavage dodecahedral, imperfect. Colour rich Berlin- or azure-blue. Lustre faintly glimmering. Usually translucent at the edges. Opaque. H. 5·5. S.G. 2·38 to 2·45.

Comp. Silicate of soda, lime, and alumina, with a sulphide probably of iron and sodium.

Analysis, by *Varrentrapp :*

Silica . . .	. 45·50
Sulphuric acid .	. 5·89
Alumina . .	. 31·76
Lime . . .	. 3·52
Soda . . .	. 9·09
Sulphur . .	. 0·95
Iron . . .	. 0·86
Chlorine . .	. 0·42
Water . . .	. 0·12
	————
	98·11

BB fuses with intense heat to a whitish enamel. Colour not affected by a low red heat ; effervesces and forms a colourless glass with borax.

Calcined, and reduced to powder, loses colour, and gelatinises in muriatic acid.

Lapis Lazuli is generally found in granite or crystalline limestone, mixed with Felspar, Quartz, and grains of Iron Pyrites. It is brought from near Lake Baikal, in Siberia ; also from Persia, China, and Bucharia. Notwithstanding its deficiency of lustre, and its not being susceptible of a very exquisite polish, the beauty of its colour has caused this stone to be used in jewelry, generally for brooches and shirt-studs. It is seldom employed for seals on account of its comparative softness. The more richly coloured varieties are used for mosaics, and are also made into vases and other costly ornaments.

When finely powered, and carefully washed, so as as to remove all foreign matters, the product is the pigment called *Ultramarine*, so celebrated for its permanency and the richness of its colour. The artificial Ultramarine prepared by carefully heating a mixture of clay, carbonate of soda and sulphur, is said to be as durable and as rich in tint as that manufactured from the native stone, and can be sold for 8s. per lb. while the latter costs five guineas an ounce. The composition of the artificial colour, which is now much used in the arts, according to Varrentrapp, is as follows:

Silica	45·60
Sulphuric acid . .	3·83
Alumina . . .	28·30
Lime	0·02
Soda	21·47
Potash	1·75
Sulphur . . .	1·68
Iron	1·63
Chlorine . . .	trace
	98·78

In the Oriental account of the precious minerals (*Prinsep*), it is said that "The country of Badakshan abounds in mountains, and contains several rivers. On the Jihún (Oxus) river, near where the Samarkand road crosses it, is the mine of *Lapis Lazuli*. This mineral has different shapes; one like the egg of a hen, which is covered with a thin, soft, and white stony coat, is reckoned the best when pounded,—it needs neither washing nor polishing; the others are without covering, and must be washed. The method of washing is this: first to pulverise it and afterwards to keep it wrapt in silk cloth, besmeared all over with gum-sandarach, which should be previously softened in very hot water, and then rubbed over or kneaded with the hands; it is kept in the water for three days, until all the foreign matter has been washed out."

Lapis Lazuli, or Azure Stone, is supposed to be the σάπφειρος of the ancients. Isidorus says, "Sapphirus cæruleus est cum purpurâ, habens pulveres aureos sparsos," the

spangles of Iron Pyrites disseminated through the stone bearing a great resemblance to gold.

Brit. Mus., Case 55.

M. P. G. Horse-shoe Case, Nos. 975 to 979.

LAPIS MUTABILIS. An ancient name for Hydrophane.

LAPIS OLLARIS. See POTSTONE.

LAPIS SPECULARIS, of the ancients, commonly signifies Mica, but sometimes Selenite. Pliny states that many persons had made beehives of Specular Stone that they might see the bees at work within.

LARDERELLITE, *Bechi*, *Dana*. A very light, white, and tasteless salt, which appears under the microscope to be composed of minute, oblique, rectangular tables.

Comp. Borate of ammonia, or $N\overset{...}{H^4}O$, $\overset{...}{B}^4$ + 4$\overset{.}{H}$.

Analysis, by *Bechi:*

Boracic acid . . .	68·56
Ammonia . . .	12·73
Water	18·32
	99·61

Soluble in hot water, and is transformed into a new crystallized salt, represented by the formula 4H^4 O $\overset{..}{B}^6$ + 9$\overset{.}{H}$.

Locality. The lagoons of Tuscany.

Name. After Count de Larderel, inventor of the successful method of obtaining Sassolin from the water of the *suffioni*.

M. P. G. Horse-shoe Case, No. 230.

LARDITE. A kind of Agalmatolite.

Analysis, from Voigtsberg, in Saxony, by *Kersten:*

Silica	66·02
Magnesia . . .	31·94
Protoxide of iron . .	0·81
Soda	0·75
Potash	trace
Water	0·20
	99·72

Name. After Mons. Charles Lardi, of Lausanne.

LASIONITE, *Fuchs.* A variety of Wavellite, found in very slender silky fibres in Jura limestone, at the mine of St. Jacques near Amberg, in Bavaria, on Brown Iron Ore.

Brit. Mus., Case 57.

LASUR, *Haidinger,* or LASURIT, *v. Kobell.* Blue carbonate of copper. See CHESSYLITE.

LASURITE, *Haidinger.* See AZURITE.

P

LASURSTEIN, *Werner.* See LAPIS LAZULI.

LATIALITE, *Haüy.* A name given to Haüyne, after *Latium* (one of its localities), in the neighbourhood of Rome.

LATROBITE, *Brooke, Gmelin.* A variety of Anorthite, occurring in crystalline masses, and in oblique rhombic prisms. Colour pale rose-red. Lustre vitreous. Opaque. Cleavage in three directions. Fracture uneven. H. 5 to 6. S.G. 2·72 to 2·8.

Analysis (mean of two), by *C. Gmelin :*

Silica	43·21
Alumina . . .	34·82
Peroxide of iron . .	3·16
Lime	9·03
Potash	6·57
Magnesia . . .	0·62
Water	2·04
	99·45

BB in the platinum forceps fuses with intumescence to a white enamel ; with borax yields a globule which is pale amethyst-red in the outer flame, and colourless in the inner one.

Locality. Amitok Island, on the coast of Labrador, with Felspar, Mica, and Calc Spar.

Name. After the Rev. C. J. Latrobe, by whom it was first brought to this country. Brit. Mus., Case 31.

LAUMONITE, *Phillips, Nicol ;* LAUMONTITE, *Haüy ;* LOMONIT, *Werner ;* LOMONITE, *Jameson.* Oblique : primary form an oblique rhombic prism. Occurs in aggregated columnar or radiating crystalline masses, or in separate crystals, related in form to Augite. Colour white or yellowish-white, sometimes with a slight tendency to reddish. Lustre vitreous, pearly on the cleavage plane. Transparent or translucent. Becomes opaque and pulverulent on exposure to the atmosphere. (See EFFLORESCENT ZEOLITE.) Streak white. Very brittle. H. 3·0 to 3·5. S.G. 2·29 to 2·36.

Fig. 252.   Fig. 253.

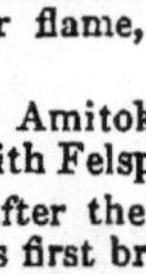

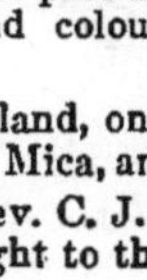

Comp. Ca³ S̈i² + 3 Äl S̈i² + 12 Ḣ = silica 51·1, alumina 21·8, lime 11·9, water 15·2 = 100.

Analysis, from Huelgoët, by *Malaguti & Durocher.* S.G. 2·29 :

Silica	52·47
Alumina . . .	22·56

Lime . . . . . 9·41
Water . . . . 15·56
           100·00

BB intumesces and fuses to a frothy mass ; with borax forms a colourless glass.

Forms a jelly with nitric or muriatic acid.

Found in greenstone and in cavities of amygdaloid.

Localities.—Scotch. Hartfield Moss, Renfrewshire, *fig.* 252, in translucent white crystals. Loch Screden, Isle of Mull, *fig.* 253. Long Craig, Dumbarton Muir ; near Old Kilpatrick, Dumbartonshire. Carbeth, Stirlingshire. Glen Farg, Fifeshire, of a deep red colour.— *Irish.* The Mourne Mountains, in granite. Ballintoy, with Stilbite. — *Foreign.* In trap in Iceland, the Faröe Islands, Disko in Greenland. St. Gotthard, in Switzerland. Eule, in Bohemia, in clayslate. Fassa-Thal, in the Tyrol, in large masses with a radiated structure. Nova Scotia, at Peter's Point, Port George, and coloured green by copper at Margaretville.

Name. After Gillet de Laumont, engineer and mineralogist, by whom it was discovered in 1785, at the lead mines of Huelgöet, in Lower Brittany.

Brit. Mus., Case 28.

LAVE VITREUSE DU CANTAL, *Beudant.* See CANTALITE.

LAVENDULAN, *Breithaupt.* Amorphous : occurs in thin reniform crusts, which are the result of the alteration of other ores. Colour lavender-blue. Lustre greasy, inclining to vitreous. Translucent. Streak paler than the colour. Fracture conchoidal. H. 2·5 to 3. S.G. 3·014.

Comp. Arsenous acid, the oxides of copper and cobalt, lime, sulphuric acid, and water.

BB fuses easily, colouring the flame of a deep blue, and affording a globule which becomes crystalline when cool.

Locality. Annaberg, in Saxony, with ores of cobalt, nickel, and copper.

LAVEZZO. See POTSTONE.

LAZIONITE. See LASIONITE.

LAZULITE, *Haüy, La Metherie ;* LAZURSTEIN, *Werner.* See LAPIS LAZULI.

LAZULITE, *Dana ;* LAZULITH, *Werner.* Oblique : primary form a right rhombic prism. Generally occurs granular or massive. Colour various shades of azure-blue, inclining to green or white. Lustre vitreous. Slightly translucent. Streak white. Brittle. Fracture uneven. H. 5 to 6. S.G. 3 to 3·122.

Comp. Phosphate of alumina and magnesia, or $2(\ddot{M}g, \ddot{F}e)^3 \ddot{P} + \ddot{A}l^5 \ddot{P}^3 + 5\ddot{H} = $ phos-

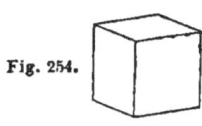

Fig. 254.

Fig. 255.

phoric acid 43·88, alumina 31·77, protoxide of iron 7·10, magnesia 11·87, water 7·12 = 100. (*Smith & Brush.*)

Analysis, from the Fischbach Alp in the circle of Gratz, by *Rammelsberg*. S.G. 3·11:

Phosphoric acid	. . .	43·84
Alumina	. . . .	33·09
Magnesia	. . . .	9·00
Protoxide of iron .	. .	6·69
Lime .	. . . .	1·44
Water .	. . . .	5·94
		100·00

BB swells up, becomes colourless, and falls to pieces, but does not fuse; colours the flame pale bluish-green.

Not affected by acids till after ignition, when it is almost wholly soluble.

Localities. In narrow veins traversing clay-slate, in the torrent beds of Schladming and Rädelgraben, near Werfen, in Salzburg, with Spathic Iron. Vorau (*Voraulite*), in Styria, with Quartz; also near Gratz and Krieglach. Tijuco, Minas Geraes, Brazil. Lincoln co., North Carolina, U.S., in beautiful sky-blue crystals.

Name. From an Arabic word *azul, heaven,* because of its blue colour.

Lazulite is distinguished from Lapis Lazuli by never being accompanied by Iron Pyrites. Brit. Mus., Case 57.

LEAD-EARTH. Earthy carbonate of lead.
LEAD-GLANCE, *Jameson.* Sulphide of lead. See GALENA.
LEAD-OCHRE. See PLUMBIC OCHRE.
LEAD-SPAR. See CERUSITE.
LEAD-VITRIOL, *Jameson.* See ANGLESITE.
LEADHILLITE, *Beudant.* LEADHILLIT, *Haidinger, v. Kobell.* Rhombic: primary form a right rhombic prism. Colour yellowish, or greenish-white, to grey, green, yellow, or brown. Lustre resinous, inclining to ada-

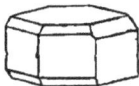

Fig. 256.

Fig. 257.

mantine; pearly on the cleavage-plane. Transparent to translucent. Streak white.

Rather brittle. Fracture obscure-conchoidal. H. 2·5. S.G. 6·2 to 6·5.

Comp. Sulphate and carbonate of lead-oxide, $\dot{P}b \ddot{S} + 3\dot{P}b \ddot{C} = $ sulphate of lead 27·44, carbonate of lead 72·56 = 100.

Analysis, by *Thomson*:

Sulphate of lead .	.	27·43
Carbonate of lead	.	72·57
		100·00

BB intumesces, and becomes yellow, but turns white again on cooling. On charcoal easily reduced to metallic lead.

Effervesces briskly in nitric acid, leaving a white residue of oxide of lead.

Localities.—British. Leadhills, in Lanarkshire, with other ores of lead. Red Gill, Cumberland, in Quartz. — *Foreign.* The Island of Serpho, in the Grecian Archipelago. Grenada, in Spain.

The pearly lustre of the cleavage face is very characteristic of Leadhillite. Brit. Mus., Case 55.

LEBER-BLENDE, *Breithaupt.* Is considered by Berzelius to be ordinary zinc-blende, rendered impure by a mineral resin, or some other mineral containing carbon.

LECERERZ, *Werner.* See HEPATIC CINNABAR.

LEBERKIES. Hepatic Pyrites (*Marcasite*).

LECONTITE, *W. J. Taylor.* Occurs in rhombic crystals (right rhombic prisms), varying much in size, some being an inch in length, and narrow prisms, while others are short, not exceeding the sixteenth of an inch in length, and quite broad. It is colourless and clear when free from the organic matter which covers it externally, and has a saline and rather bitter taste. H. 2 to 2·5.

Comp. Sulphate of soda and ammonia, or

$$(\dot{N}a + N\dot{H}N^4 O) \ddot{S} + 2\dot{H}.$$

Analysis, by *W. J. Taylor*:

Ammonia	. . .	12·94
Potash .	. . .	2·67
Soda .	. . .	17·56
Sulphuric acid	. .	44·97
Water .	. . .	19·45
Organic residue	. .	2·30
Inorganic do.	. .	0·11
Phosphoric acid .	.	trace
		100·00

It is named after Dr. John Le Conte, by whom it was discovered in the cave of Las Piedras, in the vicinity of Comayaga, in Honduras, imbedded in a black matrix resembling bitumen in appearance, which Dr. Le Conte considers to be the decomposed excrements of bats. These infest the cave in great numbers, and have most likely inhabited it for ages. The cave at the time of the doctor's visit was being worked for nitre, which was obtained "directly, by lixiviating the earth taken from near the entrance." "The matrix containing the crystals merely furnished a black, tar-like, semi-fluid mass, without nitre."

LEDERERITE, *C. T. Jackson, Dufrénoy.* A variety probably of Gmelinite, containing a certain quantity of phosphate of lime, as a mixture. Occurs in extremely brilliant, low, six-sided prisms, terminated at each extremity by six-sided pyramids, which are replaced at their summits by little hexahedral tables. Generally implanted in Analcime or Stilbite. Colour sometimes pale or salmon-red, and translucent only, but generally transparent and colourless. H. scratches Felspar with difficulty. S.G. 2·169.

Comp. According to Dana, the same as Chabazite, with one-third the amount of water, or $(\dot{C}a\,\dot{N}a)\,\ddot{S}i + 3\ddot{A}l\,\ddot{S}i^2 + 2\dot{H}$ = silica 55·75, alumina 23·10, soda 4·67, lime 8·39, water 8·09 = 100.

Analysis, by *Hayes:*

Silica	.	.	49·47
Alumina	.	.	21·48
Lime	.	.	11·48
Soda	.	.	3·94
Phosphoric acid	.	.	3·48
Oxide of iron	.	.	0·14
Foreign matter	.	.	0·03
Water	.	.	8·58
Loss	.	.	1·40
			100·00

BB becomes opaque, and yields a white enamel, which, by long exposure to the flame, becomes more glassy. With carbonate of soda effervesces, and yields a white enamel.

Entirely soluble in muriatic acid.

Locality. Cape Blomidon, Nova Scotia, in a basaltic rock, with Mesotype, Stilbite, and Analcime.

Name. After Baron Lewis von Lederer, formerly Austrian ambassador to the United States.

Brit. Mus., Case 37.

LEDERITE, *Shepard.* A variety of Sphene, occurring in masses and in amber-coloured crystals in a vein of Graphite. Colour also light clove- or chocolate-brown. Translucent. H. 5·5. S.G. 3·49 to 3·51.

Analysis, by *T. S. Hunt:*

Silica	.	.	31·83
Titanic acid	.	.	40·00

Lime	.	.	28·31
Loss by ignition	.	.	0·40
			100·54

Localities. Canada; at Grenville, Montreal, &c.

LEEDSITE, *Thomson.* A mechanical mixture of Gypsum and Barytes. Colour white. Lustre silky. Translucent at the edges. Brittle, and easily frangible. Texture foliated. H. 4. S.G. 3·87.

Comp. Sulphate of lime 71·9, sulphate of baryta 28·1 = 100.

Locality. Between Leeds and Harrowgate, in Yorkshire, in a carboniferous rock.

LEELITE, *Dr. Clarke.* The *Helleflinta* of the Swedes. It occurs compact and massive, with a peculiar wax-like texture, and a lustre and translucency like that of horn. Colour deep flesh-red. Fracture like that of flint. S.G. 2·71.

Analysis, by *Dr. Clarke:*

Silica	.	.	75·0
Alumina	.	.	22·0
Manganese	.	.	2·5
Water	.	.	0·5
			100·0

Locality. Gryphyttan, in Westmania, Sweden.

Name. After Dr. J. F. Lee, F.R.S. G.S. of St. John's College, Cambridge.

LEHMANNITE, *Brooke & Miller.* See CROCOISITE.

LEHRBACHITE, *Brooke & Miller.* Apparently a mixture of Clausthalite and Selenide of Mercury, having the structure and colour of Clausthalite. S.G. 7·3.

Analysis, by *Rose:*

Selenium	.	.	27·98
Lead	.	.	27·33
Mercury	.	.	44·69
			100·00

BB gives off the odour of Selenium; and with soda affords Mercury.

Localities. Lehrbach, and Tilkerode, in the Harz.

LEHUNTITE, *Thomson.* A compact variety of Natrolite with air-cavities, lined with minute crystals of Stilbite, which appear like minute scales. Colour flesh-red. Transparent at the edges. Lustre pearly. Fracture granular. H. 3·75. S.G. 1·953.

Comp. $\dot{N}a\,\ddot{S}i + \ddot{A}l\,\ddot{S}i + 3\dot{H}.$

Analysis, by *Thomson:*

Silica	.	.	47·33
Alumina	.	.	24·00

Soda	.	.	.	.	13·20
Lime	.	.	.	.	1·52
Water	.	.	.	13·60

99·65

BB fuses to a white enamel.
Locality. Glenarm, Antrim, Ireland.
Name. After Captain Lehunt.

LEIROCHROITE, or KUPFERSCHAUM. See TYROLITE.

LEMANITE, *Dufrénoy.* See SAUSSURITE.

LEMNIAN EARTH. A yellowish-grey or white earth, frequently speckled with ochreous spots. Dull. Feels meagre. Adheres slightly to the tongue. When placed in water gives out numerous air-bubbles and falls to pieces. Fracture earthy.

Comp. Hydrous silicate of alumina.

Analysis, by *Klaproth*:

Silica	.	.	.	.	66·00
Alumina	.	.	.	14·50
Oxide of iron	.	.	6·00
Soda	.	.	.	.	3·50
Lime and magnesia	.	.	traces
Water	.	.	.	.	8·50

98·50

Locality. Stalimene, the ancient Lemnos, in the Mediterranean, where it was formerly dug once a year, with great solemnity, on a certain holy day in July, in the presence of the clergy and magistrates of the island, after reading prayers. The pits are described by Woodward as situated in a great plain, and the earth as forming a horizontal stratum about four inches thick, the common sort of a paler complexion lying immediately beneath it. Two earths of Lemnos were known to the ancients, viz. Γῆ Λήμνια, *Terra Lemnia,* or Lemnian Earth, and Μίλτος Λήμνια, *Rubrica Lemnia,* or Lemnian Reddle.

We learn from Dioscorides that the Lemnian Earth was considered sacred, and that only the priests were allowed to meddle with it. They mixed it with goat's blood, and then made it into cakes, upon which the impression of a seal was added, with great ceremonies; from which circumstance it was called σφϱαγίς by the Greeks, and *Spragis* by the Latins, that is, *sealed earth.* In consequence of its being prepared by the priests it also got the name of Γῆ ἱεϱὰ, or *sacred earth,* which was the sealed earth very highly esteemed in medicine, and called Lemnian Earth by the physicians.

M.P.G. Horse-shoe Case, No. 1115.

LEMNIAN REDDLE. The Rubrica Lemnia,

or Lemnian Reddle, was a kind of Ochre of a firm consistence and a deep red colour, used by painters as a pigment. It was dug in the same place as the Lemnian Earth, but was not made into cakes or marked with the impression of a seal, being sold in the rough, as it was taken out of the pits.

LENTICULAR ARSENIATE OF COPPER, *Allan*; LENTICULAR ORE, *Jameson*; LENTIL-ORE, or LENTULITE. See LIROCONITE.

LENZINITE, *John.* An aluminous substance allied to Halloysite. It is divided by Phillips into two varieties, the opaline, S.G. 2·1; and the argillaceous, S.G. 1·8: both of a white colour, and occurring at Kall, in the Eifel.

The Lenzinite of Salvetat, which occurs in pegmatite at La Vilate, near Chanteloube (Haute Vienne) in France, is of a clear brown colour.

Comp. $\ddot{A}l\,\ddot{S}i + 3\dot{H}.$

Analysis of Opaline Lenzinite, by *John*:

Silica	.	.	.	.	37·5
Alumina	.	.	.	37·5
Lime	.	.	.	.	trace
Water	.	.	.	25·00

100·0

Analysis, from Chanteloube, by *Salvetat*:

Silica	.	.	.	.	36·36
Alumina	.	.	.	36·00
Peroxide of iron	.	.	1·95
Magnesia	.	.	.	0·18
Potash, Soda	.	.	0·50
Gelatinous silica	.	.	2·00
Quartz	.	.	.	1·64
Water	.	.	.	.	21·50

100·13

Name. After Lenz, a German mineralogist.

Brit. Mus., Case 26.

LEONHARDITE, *Blum.* Cubical. Occurs in prismatic crystals, grouped together in bundles; also columnar and granular. Cleavage parallel with the lateral edges, very perfect; basal cleavage imperfect. Colour white or yellowish-white; rarely brownish. Lustre vitreous; of cleavage-face pearly. Translucent at the edges. Very friable. Effloresces and whitens in the air. H. 3 to 3·5. S.G. 2·25.

Comp. $3\ddot{C}a\,\ddot{S}i + 4\,\ddot{A}l\,\ddot{S}i^3 + 12\,\dot{H}$ = silica 56·2, alumina 22·7, lime 9·2, water 11·9 = 100.

Analysis, by *Dellfs*:

| Silica | . | . | . | . | 56·13 |
| Alumina | . | . | . | 22·98 |

Lime . . . . . 9·25
Water . . . . . 11·64
———
100·00

BB swells up and fuses with intumescence to a white enamel. Forms a transparent glass with borax.
Dissolves readily in muriatic acid.
Localities. Schemnitz in Hungary, in a trachytic rock. Copper Falls, Lake Superior, U.S.: this variety does not become changed by exposure.
Name. After Professor von Leonhard of Heidelberg.
Brit. Mus., Case 28.
LEONINE (from *leoninus*, from *leo, a lion*). A brown kind of Agate, with spots like those of a panther, or with waved markings of a deeper tint than the ground.
LEOPARD STONE. A variety of compact Felspar, spotted with oxide of iron and manganese, from Charlotte, North Carolina, U.S.
LEPIDOCHLORE. The name proposed by Prof. C. U. Shepard for an impure Chlorite from Mount Pisgah.
LEPIDOKROKITE, *Ullman*. A variety of Göthite occurring in minute radiating crystals, or granular scales and feathery aggregations, imbedded in fibrous Red Oxide of Iron, in Quartz and in nodules of Chalcedony.
Analysis, from the Hollerterzug, by *v. Kobell*:

Peroxide of iron . . . 85·65
Peroxide of manganese . 2·50
Silica . . . . . 0·35
Lime . . . . . trace
Water . . . . . 11·38
———
99·88

In a specimen from Hamm, Breithaupt found 14·32 per cent. of water, and in one from Baden 13·49 per cent.
Localities. Oberkirchen; Hollerterzug in the Westerwald. Spring Mills, Montgomery co., Pennsylvania, U.S.
Name. From λεπίς, *a scale*, and κροκύς, *of a saffron or yellow colour*.
Brit. Mus., Case 16.

LEPIDOLITE, *Phillips.* LEPIDOLITH, *Hausmann, Werner.* LITHIA MICA. Rhombic. Frequently occurs in oblique rhombic, and hexagonal prisms; also in coarsely granular masses composed of an assemblage of small flexible scales, which are translucent and sometimes hexagonal. Colour peach-blossom red, verging on lilac-blue, and passing

into pearl-grey and yellowish-grey. Lustre silvery or pearly. Easily split into thin laminæ, which are flexible and highly elastic. Frequently silver-white by reflected light, rose-red by transmitted light. Biaxial. H. 2 to 3. S.G. 2·8 to 3.

Comp. $2\dot{L}i, \ddot{S}i + 3\,\ddot{A}l\,\ddot{S}i + (K\dot{F}, \ddot{S}i\,F^3)$.

Analysis, of grey variety, from Cornwall, by *Turner*:

Silica . . . . . 50·82
Alumina . . . . 21·83
Protoxide of iron . . . 9·08
Protoxide of manganese . trace
Potash . . . . . 9·86
Lithia . . . . . 4·05
Hydrofluoric acid . . 4·81
———
99·95

BB when heated gives off water and hydrofluoric acid. Fuses very readily, swelling up and forming a glass which is, for the most part, transparent and colourless, but brown or black if it contain a larger quantity of iron. Colours the flame *red*, especially on the addition of bisulphate of potash. Imperfectly decomposed by acids in its natural state; but after ignition, completely.
Localities.—*English.* St. Michael's Mount, Cornwall, in silvery hexagonal plates.—*Scotch.* East side of Loch Leven, in limestone.—*Irish.* Termonmaquirk, Tyrone.—*Foreign.* Mount Hradisko, near Rozena in Moravia, in granite with Rubellite. Isle of Utön in Sweden, with Petalite. Altenberg in Saxony. Zinnwald in Bohemia. Inschakowa, Mursinsk, &c., in the Ural. Chesterfield, Massachusetts; Paris, Maine; near Middletown, Connecticut, U.S.
Name. From λεπίδιον, *a small scale*, and λίθος, *stone*.
Brit. Mus., Cases 32 and 58A.
M.P.G. Horse-shoe Case, Nos. 1002, 1003.
Lithia is used in pyrotechny to produce a beautiful carmine colour.
LEPIDOMELANE, *Soltmann.* A variety of Uniaxial Mica, occurring in small six-sided tables, or an aggregation of minute opaque, micaceous, crystalline scales, united in granulo-laminar masses. Basal cleavage perfect. Opaque and raven-black, or translucent and leek-green. Lustre adamantine, inclining to vitreous. Streak mountaingreen. Rather brittle. H. 3. S.G. 3.

Comp. $4\ddot{K}, \ddot{S}i + 7\ddot{F}e\,\ddot{S}i + 7\ddot{F}e\,\ddot{S}i + 4\ddot{A}l\,\ddot{S}i$.

Analysis, by *Soltmann* :

Silica	. 37·40
Alumina	. 11·60
Peroxide of iron .	. 27·66
Protoxide of iron .	. 12·43
Lime, Magnesia .	. 0·26
Potash .	. 9·20
Water .	. 0·60
	——
	99·15

BB acquires a pinchbeck-brown colour, and fuses to a black magnetic globule; with borax forms a bottle-green glass.

Readily soluble in muriatic acid, with separation of silica in the form of the crystalline scales of the mineral.

Localities.—Irish. Three Rock Mountains, co. Dublin, in granite. — *Foreign.* Petersberg, Wermland, in Sweden.

Name. From λισις, *a scale*, and μίλας, *black*.

LEPOLITE. A variety of Amphodelite from Lojo and Orrijerfvi in Sweden. The crystals are sometimes two inches long.

Analysis, from Lojo, by *John Hermann* :

Silica .	. 42·80
Alumina	. 35·12
Peroxide of iron .	. 1·50
Lime .	. 14·94
Magnesia .	. 2·27
Potash .	. 1·50
Loss by ignition .	. 1·56
	——
	99·69

LETTSOMITE, *J. Percy.* Occurs in spherical globules, or in druses composed of short delicate fibres of a smalt-blue colour, with a velvet-like appearance. Lustre pearly.

Comp. $(\overset{..}{Cu}{}^6 \overset{...}{S} + 3\overset{.}{H}) + (\overset{...}{Al} \overset{...}{S} + 9\overset{.}{H}) =$ sulphuric acid 16·78, oxide of copper 49·85, alumina 10·76, water 22·75 = 100.

Analysis, by *Dr. John Percy* :

Sulphuric acid .	. 14·12
Alumina .	. 11·06
Peroxide of iron .	. 1·18
Oxide of copper .	. 46·59
Water .	. 23·06
Insoluble .	. 2·35
	——
	98·36

Locality. Sparingly at Moldawa in the Bannat, coating cavities in earthy hydrous oxide of iron.

Name. After W. G. Lettsom, Chargé d'affaires and Consul-General to Uruguay, and one of the authors of "The Mineralogy of Great Britain and Ireland."

Brit. Mus., Case 55.

LEUCACHATES. The name given by the ancients to white varieties of Agate.

From λιυχὸς, *white*, and 'Αχάτης, *Agate* (which see).

LEUCANTERITE. The name proposed by Professor C. U. Shepard for an efflorescence on the Copperasine found at Ducktown Copper Mine in Eastern Tennessee.

LEUCHTENBERGITE, *Kömonen.* A variety of Chlorite occuring crystallized in regular six-sided pyramids. Colour yellowish, internally greenish. Very translucent; transparent in thin laminæ. Soft like Gypsum. S G. 2·71.

Analysis, by *Hermann* :

Silica .	. 32·35
Alumina .	. 18·00
Peroxide of iron .	. 4·37
Magnesia .	. 32·29
Water .	. 12·50
	——
	99·51

Locality. Slatoust in the Ural. Brit. Mus., Case 32.

LEUCITE, *Werner.* Cubical: usual form the trapezohedron, *fig.* 258: often occurs disseminated in grains. Colour yellowish or greyish-white, passing into ash-grey, or smoke-grey; rarely reddish-white. Lustre vitreous. Translucent: opaque when decomposed. Streak white. Brittle. Fracture imperfect-conchoidal. H. 5·5 to 6. S.G. 2·483 to 2·49.

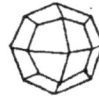

Fig. 258.

Comp. Anhydrous Analcime. $\overset{..}{K}{}^3 \overset{...}{S}i^2 +$ $3\overset{...}{Al} \overset{...}{S}i^2$ (Dana), or $\overset{..}{K} \overset{...}{S}i + Al \overset{...}{S}i^3 =$ silica 55·1, alumina 23·4, potash 21·5 = 100.

Analysis, from eruption of Vesuvius of 1845, by *Rammelsberg* :

Silica .	. 56·05
Alumina .	. 23·16
Soda .	. 0·30
Potash .	. 20·04
Loss by ignition .	. 0·52
	——
	100·07

Small quantities of lime and iron are also frequently present.

BB alone infusible: with borax or carbonate of lime melts with difficulty to a clear glass.

In a finely divided state, completely decomposed by muriatic acid, with separation of pulverulent silica.

Localities. The finest and most beautiful crystals are found in the older lavas of Vesuvius and Rocca Monfina, and in those of Borghetto, Albano, and Frascati in the neighbourhood of Rome, parts of which are almost entirely composed of it. The Leucitic lavas of these districts have been used for millstones for the last 2000 years. Between Lake Laach and Andernach on the Rhine, in trachyte.

From the circumstance of its occurrence in trapezohedrons similar to those of common Garnet, and from its white tint, Leucite was called "White Garnet" by Bergman, and "White Garnet of Vesuvius" by Kirwan. It is also known by the name of "White Garnet of Frascati" to the Italians.

Leucite is easily distinguished from Analcime by its infusibility, and by never showing faces of the cube.

It is found altered by decomposition to Kaolin or China-clay.

Name. From λευκὸς, *white;* in allusion to its colour.

Brit. Mus., Case 31.

M. P. G. Table-case A in recess 4, Nos. 79 to 83. Table-case B in recess 6, No. 83, &c. Horse-shoe Case, Nos. 1011, 1012.

Leuco-Garnet. A white variety of Garnet found at Tellemarken in Norway, and in Siberia.

Leucocyclite, *Dufrénoy.* (From λευκὸς, *white*, κύκλος, *a circle*, and λίθος, *stone.*) See Ichthyophthalmite.

Leucolite, *Dufrénoy.* (From λευκὸς, *white*, and λίθος, *stone*) See Leucite.

Leucolite d'Altenberg. See Pycnite.

Leucolite de Mauleon, *La Metherie.* See Dipyre.

Leucophane, *Esmark.* Rhombic. Rarely in crystals, usually massive and columnar. Cleavage in three directions. Colour wine-yellow to pale olive-green; in thin splinters transparent and nearly colourless. Lustre vitreous. Streak white. Strongly phosphorescent. Becomes electric when heated. H. 3·5 to 4. S.G. 2·964.

Fig. 259.

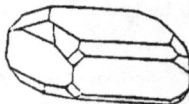

Comp. Silicate of Glucina and Lime, with Fluoride of Sodium, or $\ddot{C}a^3 \ddot{S}i^2 + \ddot{B}e \ddot{S}i + Na F =$ silica 45·3, lime 28·0, glucina 12·7, sodium 7·7, fluorine 6·3 = 100.

Analysis, by *Erdmann:*

Silica	47·82
Glucina . . .	11·51

Protoxide of manganese .	1·01
Lime	25·00
Sodium	7·59
Potassium	0·26
Fluorine	6·17
	99·36

BB fuses to a transparent, violet-coloured globule, which becomes opaque by flaming.

Locality. A rocky islet near the mouth of the Langesundfiord in Norway, in syenite with Albite, &c.

Name. From λευκὸς, *white,* and φαίνω, *to seem.*

Leucopyrite, *Shepard.* Arsenical Pyrites in part. Rhombic: primary form a right rhombic prism. Cleavage perfect at right angles to the axis. Generally occurs in masses of a colour between silver-white and steel-grey, with a yellowish tarnish. Lustre metallic. Streak greyish-black. Brittle. Fracture uneven. H. 5 to 5·5. S.G. 7 to 7·4.

Comp. Arsenide of iron, Fe As^2 = arsenic 72·8, iron 27·2, or (Fe, Ni, Co) As^2. Sometimes Fe^2 As^3.

Analysis, from Reichenstein, by *Karsten.* S.G. 7·09.

Arsenic	65·88
Sulphur . . .	1·77
Iron	32·35
	100·00

BB on charcoal fuses to a black magnetic mass, with the evolution of a strong odour of arsenic.

Soluble in nitric acid with separation of arsenious acid.

Localities. Cornwall and Devonshire. Schladming in Styria, with Copper Nickel. Reichenstein in Silesia with Serpentine. Löling near Hüttenberg in Carinthia, in Sparry Iron. Freiberg, and Ehrenfriedersdorf in Saxony.

Name. From λευκὸς *white*, and *Pyrites.*

This ore is employed for the production of white arsenic, and also of artificial Orpiment.

Leutrite, *Sartorius.* An indurated sandy marl, appearing to the naked eye like a lump of sugar. Colour greyish or yellowish. Becomes phosphorescent by friction, even with paper.

Locality. The Leutra, near Jena.

Leuzite, *Jameson.* See Leucite.

Levyne, *Brewster.* Hexagonal. Primary form a rhombohedron. Occurs in twin crystals. Crystals often striated. Colour white, yellowish, reddish. Lustre vitreous. Semi-transparent. Streak white. Brittle. Fracture imperfect-conchoidal. H. 4. S.G. 2 to 2·16.

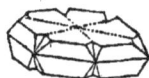

Fig. 260. Fig. 261.

Comp. $\dot{C}\,\ddot{S}i + \ddot{A}l\,\ddot{S}i + 4\dot{H} =$ silica 44·36, alumina 24·68, lime 13·68, water 17·28 $= 100$.

Analysis, from Iceland, by *Damour :*

Silica	.	.	.	.	44·48
Alumina		.	.	.	23·77
Lime	.	.	.	.	10·71
Soda	.	.	.	.	1·38
Potash		.	.	.	1·63
Water	.	.	.	.	17·41

99·36

BB on charcoal intumesces, and with microcosmic salt yields a transparent globule, which contains a skeleton of silica, and becomes opaque on cooling.

Soluble in acids when reduced to powder.

Localities. — *Scotch.* Storr in Skye: *fig.* 260. Hartfield Moss near Glasgow, of a flesh-red colour. — *Irish.* In trap with Mesotype at Little Deer Park, Glenarm, co. Antrim: *fig.* 261. — *Foreign.* Skagastrand in Iceland. Dalsnypen in Faröe. Godhaven, Disco Island, Greenland. The Vicentine.

Name. After Levy, the mineralogist, by whom its crystallographic properties were originally examined.

Brit. Mus., Case 27.

LHERZOLITE. An olive-green variety of Sahlite (Pyroxene), occurring both crystallized and lamellar at Lake Lherz in the Pyrenees.

LIBETHENITE, *Breithaupt.* Rhombic: primary form a right rhombic prism. Frequently crystallized in prisms, combined with the faces of the pyramid, and thus assuming an octahedral appearance. Cleavage imperfect. Occurs also in radiated masses. Colour olive-green, inclining to blackish-green. Lustre resinous. Translucent at the edges. Streak olive-green. Brittle. Fracture sub-conchoidal, uneven. H. 4. S.G. 3·6 to 3·8.

Comp. Phosphate of copper, or $\dot{C}u^4\,\ddot{P} +$

$\dot{H} =$ oxide of copper 66·5, phosphoric acid 29·7, water 3·8 = 100.

Fig. 262. Fig. 263.

Analysis, from Libethen, by *Hermann :*

Phosphoric acid	.	.	.	28·61
Oxide of copper	.	.	.	65·89
Water	.	.	.	.	5·50

100·00

BB on charcoal fuses to a brownish globule, which, by further action of the blowpipe, acquires a reddish-grey metallic lustre; in the centre is a small globule of metallic copper.

Soluble in nitric acid and ammonia, forming a sky-blue solution.

Localities. Cornwall; near Redruth, and at Gunnis Lake, near Callington, in gossan. —*Foreign.* Libethen, near Neusohl in Hungary, in cavities in Quartz, associated with Copper Pyrites. Rheinbreitenbach on the Rhine. Bolivia with Malachite. Mercedes Mine, about 20 miles E. of Coquimbo in Chili. Olive-green, sometimes approaching to black. Nischne-Taguilsk in the Ural. Congo, in Portuguese Africa.

Brit. Mus., Case 57.

M.P.G. Principal Floor, Wall-case 16 (Foreign).

LIEBENERITE, *Dana.* LIEBNERITE, *Brooke & Miller.* An altered form of Iolite. Occurs in greenish-grey six-sided prisms, which have no distinct cleavage. Lustre greasy. Fracture splintery. H. 3·5. S.G. 2·8.

Analysis, by *Marignac :*

Silica	.	.	.	44·66
Alumina	.	.	.	36·51
Peroxide of iron	.	.	1·75
Potash	.	.	.	9·90
Magnesia	.	.	.	1·40
Soda	.	.	.	.	0·92
Water, carbonic acid	.	4·49

99·68

BB intumesces and turns white, but does not fuse.

Locality. Mt. Viesena, Fleimser Valley, in the Tyrol; in porphyry.

Brit. Mus., Case 31.

LIEBENERITE. A pseudomorphous form of Elæolite.

LIEBIGITE, *J. L. Smith, Dufrénoy.* In mammillary concretions or thin crusts, having a distinct cleavage in one direction. Colour beautiful apple-green. Transparent. Lustre and fracture vitreous. H. 2 to 2·5.

Comp. Carbonate of Uranium and Lime.

$\ddot{U}\ddot{C} + \dot{C}a\ddot{C} + 20\dot{H}$ = oxide of uranium 36·3, carbonic acid 11·1, lime 7·1, water 45·5 = 100.

Analysis, by *J. L. Smith :*

Peroxide of uranium . .	38·0
Lime	8·0
Carbonic acid . . .	10·2
Water	45·2
	101·4

BB gently heated becomes greenish-grey. At a red heat, does not fuse but turns black, and acquires an orange-red colour on cooling. With borax forms a yellowish glass in the outer, and a green glass in the inner flame.

Dissolves readily in dilute muriatic acid, with violent effervescence, forming a yellow solution.

Locality. The neighbourhood of Adrianople in Turkey, with Medjidite, on Pitchblende. Johanngeorgenstadt, in Saxony, and Joachimstahl in Bohemia.

Name. After the Baron Liebig, Professor of Chemistry in the University of Giessen.

LIÈGE DE MONTAGNE. See MOUNTAIN CORK.

LIEVRITE, *Werner.* Rhombic : primary form a right rhombic prism, in which it occurs with the lateral faces striated longitudinally. Also compact, massive, and radiated. Cleavage indistinct, parallel to a plane passing through its longer diagonal. Colour brown or dark greyish-black. Lustre submetallic. Opaque. Streak black, inclining to green or brown. Brittle. Fracture uneven. H. 5·5 to 6. S.G. 3·8 to 4·2.

Fig. 264.　　Fig. 265.　　Fig. 266.

Comp. $3(\dot{F}e, \dot{C}a)^3 \ddot{S}i + \ddot{F}e^2 \ddot{S}i$ = silica 28·2, peroxide of iron 25·0, protoxide of iron 33·7, lime 13·1 = 100.

Analysis, from Elba, by *Rammelsberg :*

Silica	27·83
Peroxide of iron . .	24·58
Protoxide of iron . .	30·73

Lime	12·44
Protoxide of manganese .	1·51
	97·11

BB on charcoal fuses to a black globule, which attracts the magnet if it has not been heated to redness. With borax fuses readily to a dark green and almost opaque glass.

Soluble in muriatic acid, forming a jelly.

Localities. Cape Calamita and la Marina de Rio, Elba; in crystals and radiated masses in a dyke of Hornblende. Fossum and Skeen in Norway. Siberia. Near Andreasberg in the Harz. Schneeberg in Saxony. Near Predazzo in the Tyrol, in granite. Cumberland, Rhode Island, in the United States, in slender crystals traversing Quartz.

Name. After its discoverer, Le Lievre, mineralogist and engineer.

Brit. Mus., Case 34.

M.P.G. Principal Floor, Wall-case 19.

LIGHT PYRARGYRITE, or LIGHT RED SILVER ORE. See PROUSTITE, and PYRARGYRITE.

LIGNIFORM ASBESTOS, *Kirwan.* See MOUNTAIN WOOD.

LIGNITE, (from lignum, *wood.*) Brown Coal, in which the form and woody structure of the original tree is preserved.

According to the recently published researches of Mons. M. E. Fremy, Lignite may be divided into two classes; 1st. *Lignite xyloïde et fibreux,* or *bois fossile,* Lignite still displaying woody structure; and 2nd. *Lignite compacte et parfait,* or Lignite exhibiting the aspect and compactness of Coal.

The compact Lignites with the black and shining appearance of Coal are entirely soluble in alkaline hypochlorites, and are attacked by nitric acid with the greatest rapidity, producing a yellow resin. Lignite xyloïde and compact Lignite generally differ in the more combustible variety not being acted on by concentrated potash; and M. Fremy has invariably observed that those Lignites which resist the action of potash are those which are derived from beds whose stratigraphical position most nearly approaches the true Coal Measures.

Lignites may, therefore, be distinguished, on the one hand, from mere wood by their complete solubility in nitric acid and in hypochlorites, and by the above-mentioned characters from Coals, which last are insoluble in hypochlorites, and are only slowly attacked by nitric acid.

The following are, according to M. Fremy, the degrees of alteration of woody tissue :—

1. *Turf* and *Peat.* Characterised by the presence of Ulmic Acid, and also by the woody fibres or the cellules of the medullary rays, which may be purified and extracted in notable quantity by means of nitric acid or hypochlorites, in which they are insoluble.

2. *Fossil Wood,* or *Woody Lignite.* This, like the preceding, is partially soluble in alkalies, but its alteration is more advanced, for it is nearly wholly dissolved by nitric acid and hypochlorites.

3. *Compact,* or *Perfect Lignite.* This substance is characterised by its complete solubility in hypochlorites and in nitric acid. Alkaline solutions do not in general act on perfect Lignite. Reagents in this variety show a passage of the organic matter into Coal.

4. *Coal.* Insoluble in alkaline solutions and hypochlorites.

5. *Anthracite.* An approximation to Graphite, resists the reagents which act on the above-mentioned combustibles, and is only acted on by nitric acid with extreme slowness.

Analysis of Lignite, from Tasmania, by *C. Tookey:*

Carbon .	. 59·90
Hydrogen	. 4·66
Oxygen	. 15·99
Nitrogen	. 1·08
Sulphur	. 0·30
Ash	. 4·64
Water (hygroscopic) .	. 13·43
	100·00

Rolled masses of Lignite were formerly found on the shore at Brighton, in such abundance as to be used for fuel by the poorer classes, but its use was prohibited on account of the very offensive odour it gave out during combustion.

It was employed by Dr. Russell as a fumigation in certain glandular complaints, and it is said with decided benefit.

The provincial name (*Strombolo*) by which it was known is a corruption of *Strom-bollen,* stream or tide-balls, as they were called by the Flemings, who formerly settled in Brighton. (*Mantell.*)

LIGNITE JAYET. *French* for Jet.

LIGURE. The stone mentioned under this name in Exodus xxviii. 19 was probably the Jacinth or Hyacinth. It occupied the seventh place among the stones ordered to be set in the breast-plate of the Jewish high-priest, and was engraved with the name of the tribe of Gad. See HYACINTH.

LIGURITE, *Phillips.* A variety of Sphene (Dufrénoy), occurring in oblique rhombic prisms, which are sometimes modified and speckled externally. Colour apple-green. Lustre vitreous. Transparent or translucent. Streak greyish-white. Fracture uneven. H. 5 to 5·5. S.G. 3·49.

Analysis, by *Viviani:*

Silica .	. 57·45
Alumina	. 7·36
Lime	. 25·30
Magnesia	. 2·56
Oxide of iron	. 3·00
Oxide of manganese .	. 0·50
	96·17

Locality. The banks of the Stara in the Apennines, in a talcose rock.

Name. After Liguria, the country where it is found.

Ligurite is considered superior, as a gem, to Chrysolite, in colour, hardness and transparency.

LILAC STONE, ⎫
LILALITE,   ⎬ See LEPIDOLITE.

LILLITE, *Reuss.* A mineral resembling Glauconite in physical characters, and probably a product of the decomposition of Pyrites. Amorphous, earthy. Colour blackish-green. Lustreless. H. 2. S.G. 3·043.

Analysis, by *Payr:*

Silica .	. 32·48
Peroxide of iron .	. 54·95
Carbonate of lime .	. 1·96
Sulphide of iron (insol.)	. 0·63
Water	. 10·20
	100·22

Locality. Przibram in Bohemia.

LIMBELITE, *Saussure.* An altered form of Chrysolite, occurring in small, wax- or honey-yellow masses, in the basalt of Limbourg.

BB fuses with difficulty.

The name is derived from the locality, Limbourg.

LIME AND SODA MESOTYPE. See MESOLITE.

LIME CHABAZITE. See CHABAZITE.

LIME HARMOTOME, *Connel.* See PHILLIPSITE.

LIME MALACHITE. A hydrous carbonate of copper, with some carbonate and sulphate of lime and iron; from Lauterberg in the Harz. Massive, reniform, with a fibrous and foliated structure. Colour verdigris-green. Lustre silky. H. 2·5.

LIME MESOTYPE.   See SCOLEZITE.

LIME SALTPETRE.   See NITROCALCITE.

LIME URANITE. *Naumann.* See URANITE.

LIMNIT, *Glocker.* LIMNITE, *Brooke & Miller, Greg & Lettsom.* See LIMONITE. From λιμνὴ, *a salt-water marsh.*

LIMONITE, *Beudant.* Usually occurs in mammillated, botryoidal, and stalactitic aggregations, with a radiating fibrous structure; also compact and earthy, and pseudomorphous after Calcite and Pyrites. Colour various shades of brown, from yellowish-brown to clove- and blackish-brown. Lustre silky, sometimes dull and earthy. Opaque. Streak yellowish-brown. Brittle. H. 5 to 5·5. S.G. 3·4 to 3·95.

Comp. Hydrated peroxide of iron, or

$\ddot{F}e^2\dot{H}^3$ = peroxide of iron 85·6, water 14·4 = 100.

Analysis, from Perm, by *v. Kobell :*

Peroxide of iron	. .	83·38
Silica .	. .	1·61
Water .	. .	15·1
		100·0

BB blackens and becomes magnetic: in thin splinters fuses to a black magnetic glass.

Soluble in warm nitro-muriatic acid.

Localities.—British. Cornwall; at Botallack and other mines; Restormel, near Lostwithiel. Somerset, at Wrington Hill; near Clifton; also at the Brendon Hills in Devonian rocks. Weardale, Durham. Alston Moor and Carrock Fell, Cumberland. Isle of Man. Sandlodge in Zetland. — *Foreign.* Siberia. Carinthia. Thuringia. Styria. Nassau. The Harz. Siegen near Bonn. Pyrenees. Spain. Villa Rica in Brazil. United States.

Name. From λιμνὼν, *a meadow.* See MEADOW-ORE.

Limonite constitutes a valuable ore of iron. It is met with in secondary and more recent deposits, and is often associated with Siderite, Barytes, Calc Spar, Quartz, and frequently with ores of manganese. For varieties of Limonite, see BROWN HEMATITE. BOG-IRON ORE. OCHREY BROWN IRON-ORE. SCALY BROWN IRON-ORE. YELLOW IRON OCHRE. WOOD HEMATITE. BROWN OCHRE.

M. P. G. Principal Floor, Wall-cases 18 and 19 (Foreign); 33 and 49 (British).

LINARITE, *Beudant, Brooke.* Oblique: primary form an oblique rhombic prism. Often in twins. Colour deep azure-blue. Lustre vitreous or adamantine. Translucent. Streak

pale blue.   Brittle.   Fracture conchoidal. H. 2·5 to 3.   S.G. 5·3 to 5·5.

Fig. 267.

Comp. Cupreous sulphate of lead, $\dot{P}b$ $\ddot{S}+\dot{C}u\,\dot{H}$ = sulphate of lead 75·7, oxide of copper 19·8, water 4·5 = 100.

Analysis, from Wanlockhead, by *Thomson :*

Sulphate of lead	. .	74·8
Oxide of copper	. .	19·7
Water .	. . .	5·5
		100·0

BB on charcoal, in the inner flame, yields a metallic globule, which, on continuing the heat, deposits a coat of oxide of lead.

Localities.—British. Leadhills, Lanarkshire, with Cerusite. Mexico Mine, Red Gill, and Roughten Gill, Cumberland.— *Foreign.* Near Ems.

Name. After Linares, a reputed Spanish locality.

Brit. Mus., Case 55.

LINCOLNITE, *Hitchcock.* A variety of Heulandite, from Durfield, Massachusetts.

LINDACKERITE, *J. F. Vogl.* Occurs in oblong rhombohedral tables, grouped in rosettes and reniform masses. Colour verdigris- to apple-green. Lustre vitreous. Streak pale green to white. H. 2 to 2·5. S.G. 2 to 2·5.

Comp. $2\,\dot{C}u^3\,\ddot{A}s+\dot{N}i\,\ddot{S}+8\dot{H}.$

Analysis, by *Lindacker :*

Alumina	. . .	28·58
Sulphuric acid	. .	6·44
Oxide of copper	. .	36·34
Protoxide of nickel	.	16·15
Protoxide of iron .	.	2·90
Water .	. .	9·32
		99·73

BB on charcoal gives off arsenical fumes, and fuses to a black mass.

Soluble in muriatic acid after long heating.

Locality. Joachimsthal in Bohemia.

Name. After Lindacker, Austrian chemist.

LINDSAYITE, or LINSEITE, *Komonen, Dufrénoy.* A hydrated form of Amphodelite, the result probably of partial alteration. Colour black. Fracture granular.

LINNÆITE.

Analysis, by *Hermann :*

Silica	.	.	.	42·22
Alumina	.	.	.	27·55
Peroxide of iron	.	.		6·98
Protoxide of iron	.	.		2·00
Magnesia	.	.	.	8·85
Potash	.	.	.	3·00
Soda	.	.	.	2·53
Water	.	.	.	7·00

98·13

Locality. Orijerfvi, in Finland, associated with Copper Pyrites.

LINNÆITE, *Haidinger.* Cubical: occurs in regular octahedrons and cubo-octahedrons. Cleavage parallel to the faces of the cube, imperfect. Also massive and botryoidal. Colour steel-grey, tarnishing copper-red. Lustre metallic. Streak blackish-grey. Brittle. Fracture uneven, or sub-conchoidal. H. 5·5. S.G. 4·8 to 5.

Comp. Co S + Co² S⁵ = sulphur 42, cobalt 58 = 100. Sometimes the cobalt is partly replaced by nickel or copper.

Analysis, from Riddarhyttan, by *Hisinger :*

Sulphur	.	.	.	38·50
Cobalt	.	.	.	43·20
Copper	.	.	.	14·40
Iron	.	.	.	3·53
Matrix	.	.	.	0·33

99·96

BB gives off sulphurous odours, and fuses in the inner flame to a grey magnetic bead, of a bronze-yellow colour inside; after roasting, it imparts a blue colour to borax and microcosmic salt.

Dissolves in nitric acid, with separation of sulphur.

Localities. Bastnaes, near Riddarhyttan, in Sweden, in gneiss, with Copper Pyrites and Hornblende. Müsen, near Siegen, in Prussia, with Barytes and Spathic Iron. Mine la Motte, Missouri, U. S.

For varieties see CARROLLITE and SIEGENITE.

LINSENERZ, *Werner ;* LINSENKUPFER, *Hausmann.* See LIROCONITE.

LIPARITE, *Glocker.* See FLUOR.

LIROCONITE, *Beudant.* Rhombic. Occurs in obtuse rectangular pyramids. Cleavage imperfect, parallel to the planes of a flat octahedron. Colour sky-blue to verdigris-green. Lustre vitreous, inclining to resinous. Translucent. Streak paler than the colour. Sectile. Fracture imperfect-conchoidal, uneven. H. 2 to 2·5. S.G. 2·88 to 2·98.

Comp. Hydrated arseniate of copper,

$5\ddot{C}u^5 \ddot{A}s + \ddot{A}l \ddot{P} + 24\ddot{H}.$

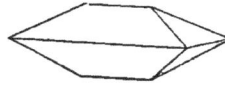 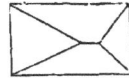

Fig. 268.   Fig. 269.

Analysis, from Cornwall, by *Hermann :*

Oxide of copper	.	.	.	36·38
Alumina	.	.	.	10·85
Peroxide of iron	.	.	.	0·98
Arsenic acid	.	.	.	23·05
Phosphoric acid	.	.	.	3·73
Water	.	.	.	25·01

100·00

BB in the forceps colours the flame bluish-green. On charcoal fuses imperfectly, and with slight intumescence, forming a brownish slag, which contains white granules of metal. With carbonate of soda yields a semi-malleable globule of copper containing arsenic.

Soluble in nitric acid.

Localities.—English. Huel Muttrell, Huel Gorland, and Huel Unity, in Cornwall, generally in attached crystals associated with other arseniates of copper.—*Foreign.* Herrengrund, in Hungary, in minute crystals. Voigtland.

Name. From λιερὸς, *pale,* and κονία, *dust,* in allusion to the paleness of the streak.

Brit. Mus., Case 56.

M. P. G. Principal Floor, Wall-case 2 (British).

LITHEOSPORE. See BARYTES.

LITHIA MICA; LITHIONGLIMMER, *Naumann.* LITHIONIT, *v. Kobell.* LITHION MICA. See LEPIDOLITE.

LITHOMARGA, *Kirwan ;* LITHOMARGE, *Jameson.* A form of Kaolin or China-clay. Amorphous. Colour generally white, yellowish or reddish, also grey or bluish, frequently spotted internally. Opaque. Dull. Adheres strongly to the tongue. Feels greasy. Very soft, and yields to the nail. Streak shining. Texture earthy. Fracture large-conchoidal. H. 2 to 2·5. S.G. 2·5.

Analysis, from Buchberge, by *Zellner :*

Silica	.	.	.	49·2
Alumina	.	.	.	36·2
Peroxide of iron	.	.		0·5
Water	.	.	.	14·0

99·9

BB infusible; hardens on exposure to a high temperature. Sometimes becomes phosphorescent when heated.

Localities. Cornwall, at Cook's Kitchen, and Tincroft, near Redruth, in veins traversing granite, also in St. Just. — *Foreign.* Saxony, at Ehrenfriedersdorf, Altenberg, Marienberg, Buchberge, near Rochlitz; the Harz. Planitz, near Zwickau; in Bohemia. Bavaria, &c.

Name. From λίθος, *stone*, and *marga, marl.*

For varieties of Lithomarge, see CARNAT, MELOPSITE, MYCLIN, FRIABLE LITHOMARGE, WONDER EARTH, or TERRA MIRACULOSA.

Brit. Mus., Case 25.

LITHOXYLON (from λίθος, *stone*, and ζυλὸν, *wood*). See WOOD OPAL.

LIVER-COLOURED COPPER ORE. See ERUBESCITE.

LIVER ORE OF MERCURY, or LIVER STONE. See HEPATIC CINNABAR.

LOBOITE. A variety of Idocrase, from Gökum, in Finland.

Brit. Mus., Case 35.

LODESTONE. The name given to Magnetic Iron-ore (*Magnetite*) when in a state of magnetic polarity. It is met with in masses in many beds of the ore in Siberia, Elba, the Harz, the United States, at Marshall's Island in Maine, and near Providence in Rhode Island. See MAGNETITE.

LŒWITE, *Beudant.* A reddish transparent mineral found associated with Blœdite, at Ischl, in Austria. See LÖVEITE.

LOGANITE, *T. S. Hunt.* A variety of Pyroselerite, occurring in short and thick (usually small) crystals; apparently oblique rhombic prisms, replaced on the acute and obtuse lateral edges, and on the acute solid angles. Colour clove-brown to chocolate-brown; sometimes pale. Lustre weak subresinous. Subtransparent. Streak greyish. Brittle. Fracture uneven. H. 3. S.G. 2·6.

Comp., Hydrated silicate of magnesia and lime, or $2(\ddot{Al}\ \ddot{Fe})\ \ddot{Si} + 4(\dot{Mg}^3\ \ddot{Si}) + 12\dot{H}$.

Analysis, by *T. S. Hunt:*

Silica	32·84
Alumina	13·37
Peroxide of iron	3·00
Magnesia	35·12
Lime	0·96
Water and carbonic acid	17·02
	101·31

BB loses colour and becomes greyish-white, but does not fuse.

Locality. Calumet Island, on the Ottawa, Canada, associated with Serpentine, Phlogopite, Apatite, and Pyrites, in crystalline limestone.

Name. After Sir William E. Logan, Director of the Geological Survey of Canada.

LÖLINGITE, *Haidinger.* See LEUCOPYRITE.

The name Lölingite is derived from that of one of its localities, Löling, near Hüttenberg, in Carinthia.

LOMONITE, *Jameson.* See LAUMONTITE.

LONCHIDITE, *Breithaupt.* A variety of Marcasite containing arsenic. Colour tin-white; sometimes with a greenish or greyish tarnish. Streak black. H. 6·5. S.G. 4·92 to 5.

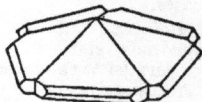

Fig. 270.

Comp. Fe S² + (Fe S² + Fe As)², or marcasite 88·79 + mispickel 9·57 = 100. (*Rammelsberg.*)

Analysis, from Cook's Kitchen, by *Plattner:*

Sulphur	49·61
Iron	44·23
Arsenic	4·40
Cobalt	0·35
Copper	0·75
Lead	0·20
	99·54

Localities. Cook's Kitchen, Cornwall, in small thin crystals, *fig.* 270, upon old specimens of Blistered Copper Ore. Freiberg, and Schneeberg, Saxony.

Name. From λόγχη, *a spear.*

Brit. Mus., Case 6.

LOPHOITE, *Breithaupt.* A variety of Ripidolite. S.G. 2·78 to 2·88.

Analysis (mean of two), by *v. Kobell:*

Silica	26·91
Alumina	21·20
Magnesia	23·86
Protoxide of iron	15·16
Protoxide of manganese	0·29
Water	12·00
	99·42

Locality. Zillerthal, in the Tyrol.

LOTALITE. A greenish-grey mineral, with a lamellar structure, and with deep parallel striæ, found at Peterlow, in Finland, associated with red Felspar.

LÖVEITE; LÖWEITE. A yellowish-white or reddish saline mineral, approaching Astrakanite. Lustre vitreous. Taste slightly saline. H. 2·5 to 3. S.G. 2·376.

Comp. $\dot{Mg}\ \ddot{S} + \dot{Na}\ \ddot{S} + 2\frac{1}{2}\dot{H}$.

Analysis, by *v. Hauer :*

Sulphuric acid	.	.	.	52·53
Magnesia	.	.	.	14·31
Soda	.	.	.	18·58
Peroxide of iron	.	.	.	trace
Chloride of sodium	.	.	.	trace
Water	.	.	.	14·80
				100·22

Locality. Ischl, in Austria.

LOWLAND IRON ORE, *Kirwan.* Comprises Morasterz or Morass Ore, Sumpferz or Swamp Ore, and Wiesenerz or Meadow Ore. See BOG-IRON ORE.

LOXOCLASE, *Breithaupt.* A variety of Orthoclase, containing a large proportion of soda. Colour yellowish-grey, sometimes bluish. Translucent. H. 7·5 to 7·75. S.G. 2·6 to 2·8.

Comp. R̈ S̈i + R̈ S̈i 2.

Analysis, by *Plattner :*

Silica	.	.	.	.	63·50
Alumina	.	.	.	20·29
Peroxide of iron	.	.	0·67
Lime	.	.	.	.	3·22
Potash	.	.	.	3·03
Soda	.	.	.	.	8·76
Magnesia	.	.	.	trace
Hydrofluoric acid	.	.	1·23
				100·70

Locality. Hammond, St. Lawrence co., New York, U. S.

Name. From λόξος, *oblique,* and κλάσις, *cleavage.*

LUCHS-SAPPHIRE. See LYNX SAPPHIRE.

LUCULLITE. A black marble, first brought to Rome by Lucullus; it is said from an island in the Nile.

LUDUS HELMONTII. From the account of Dr. Woodward, to whom the younger Van Helmont gave an authentic specimen, which had formerly belonged to his father, the Ludus would appear to be merely a kind of septaria. Prof. Ferber, writing from Bologna in 1771, also describes the Ludus Helmontii as "cubical marl-stone, ferruminated by calcareous spar-veins, from *rio delle maraviglie presso al Martignone sul Bolognese.*"
The Ludus of Paracelsus and Dr. Plot was tesselated Pyrites. "'Twas not a very wild name, *Ludus,* to be given to a *Dye* or *Talus lusorius,* considering how humorous a writer *Paracelsus* was." (*Dr. J. Woodward,* 1728.) See WAXEN-VEIN.

LUMACHELLA, *Cleaveland, Mohs.* LUMA-CHELLI, *Phillips ;* LUMACHELLO, *Nicol.* A compact limestone, with a dark grey or

brownish ground, in which are numerous fragments of Ammonites and other fossil shells. These last are sometimes iridescent and reflect green, blue, deep red, and orange tints, in which case it is called *Fire Marble.* A variety from Astrachan exhibits a beautiful golden yellow light in a reddish-brown base. The most common kind is found at Bleiberg, in Carinthia, where it forms the roof of the lead mines.

LUNAIRE. See PIERRE DE LUNE.

LUNNITE, *Bernhardi.* Hydrous phosphate of copper (Phosphochalite), usually in radiating fibrous masses, of a beautiful emerald-green colour.

LYDIAN STONE, *Jameson ;* LYDIENNE, *La Metherie ;* LYDITE. A compact variety of flinty slate of a velvet-black colour, and with a flat-conchoidal fracture.

Localities.—Scotch. Leadhills, in Lanarkshire; Pentland and Moorfoot Hills, near Edinburgh. — *Irish.* Near Carlow. Glasdumman in Downshire. — *Foreign.* The Harz. Saxony, at Haynichen, near Freyberg. Near Prague and Carlsbad, in Bohemia.

Name. After the province of Lydia, in Asia Minor, where it is said to have been first found, in the bed of the river Tmolus. This stone is used for testing the purity of gold and silver, which is effected by rubbing the metal to be tested upon a polished surface of the stone, the colour of the streak left upon which is sufficient to enable those experienced in its use to judge of the amount of alloy mixed with the gold. The ancients, who employed the stone for the same purpose, called it ἡ Λυδὴ (Lapis Lydius), or Lapis Basanites.

Brit. Mus., Case 21.

LYNCURION (Λυγκύριον), *Theophrastus;* LAPIS LYNCURIUS, *Pliny ;* λίθος λαγγούριος, *Epiphanius.* A stone used by the ancients for engraving seals on, and believed by them to be produced from the urine of the Lynx. By some authors, the Lyncurion is supposed to have been identical with the Amber of the moderns, but the description of the stone given by Theophrastus (l. li. lii.) does not at all favour this supposition. It is much more probable that the modern Hyacinth was the stone indicated (as was first suggested by Sir John Hill), the stone called ὑάκινθος, or the Hyacinthus, by the ancients being probably the same as our Amethyst.

LYNCURIUM, *Valerius.* See SCHORL.

LYNX SAPPHIRE, or LUCHS SAPPHIRE. A name given to dark greyish- or greenish-blue varieties of Sapphire, as well as to varieties of Iolite having the same colour, and also called when pale *Water Sapphire*, or *Sapphire d'eau*.

M.

MACLE, *Haüy, Brongniart, Cleaveland.* See CHIASTOLITE. The name, as that of a distinct species, is applied to the white prisms only. The black rhombs and lines are an argillaceous substance of the same nature as the gangue, with 'a few whitish particles of Macle intermixed.

M. P. G. Horse-shoe Case, No. 1005.

MACLUREITE, *Seybert.* A name given to Chondrodite, in honour of Mr. Maclure.

MACROTYPOUS KOUPHONE-SPAR, *Mohs.* See LEVYNE.

MACROTYPOUS LIME-HALOID, *Mohs.* See DOLOMITE.

MACROTYPOUS PARACHROSE - BARYTE, *Mohs.* See DIALLOGITE.

MAGNES. Pliny's name for the Lodestone, after that of the country (Magnesia, a province of ancient Lydia,) where it was found.

MAGNESIA-ALUM; MAGNESIA - ALAUN, *Rammelsberg.* Occurs in white fibrous masses, and efflorescences, which become opaque on exposure to the atmosphere. Lustre silky.

Comp. $Mg\ \ddot{S} + \ddot{A}l\ \ddot{S}^3 + 24H =$ sulphate of magnesia 13·4, sulphate of alumina 38·3, water 48·3 = 100.

Analysis, by A. A. Hayes:

Sulphuric acid	36·322
Alumina	12·130
Magnesia	4·682
Lime	0·126
Protoxides of iron and manganese	0·430
Muriatic acid	0·604
Water	45·450
	99·740

Locality. Near Iquique, in Peru. South Africa.

MAGNESIA-GLIMMER, *Naumann.* See BIOTITE.

MAGNESIA-HYDRAT. See BRUCITE.

MAGNESIA-MICA, *Nicol.* See BIOTITE.

MAGNESIAN CARBONATE OF LIME. See DOLOMITE.

MAGNESIAN PHARMACOLITE. See KUHNITE.

MAGNÉSIE BORATÉE, *Haüy.* See BORACITE.

MAGNÉSIE HYDRATÉE, *Haüy.* See BRUCITE.

MAGNÉSIE HYDRATÉE SILICEUSE, *Levy.* See MARMOLITE.

MAGNÉSIE NITRATÉE, *Dufrénoy.* See NITROMAGNESITE.

MAGNÉSIE PHOSPHATÉE, *Dufrénoy.* See WAGNERITE.

MAGNÉSIE SULFATÉE, *Haüy.* See EPSOMITE.

MAGNESITE, *Thomson.* See MEERSCHAUM.

MAGNESITE, *v. Leonhard.* Hexagonal. Cleavage rhombohedral, perfect. Also amorphous, massive, compact, and sometimes in radiating groups. Colour white, greyish-white, or yellowish, with blackish-brown markings. Lustre vitreous. Transparent to opaque. Somewhat meagre to the touch. Adheres to the tongue. Fracture flat-conchoidal. H. 3·5 to 4·5. S.G. 2·8 to 3·056.

Comp. Carbonate of magnesia, $Mg\ \ddot{C} =$ magnesia 47·62, carbonic acid 52·38 = 100.

Analysis, by *Stromeyer :*

Magnesia	47·64
Carbonic acid	50·75
Water and impurities	1·61
	100·00

BB infusible.

Dissolves slowly, with slight effervescence, in nitric or dilute sulphuric acid.

Localities. Gulsen Mountains in Upper Styria, in Serpentine, with Bronzite. Hrubschitz in Moravia. Baumgarten in Silesia. Baldissero and Castellamonte in Piedmont. Vallecas, near Madrid. Madras. United States. Canada, forming an immense bed at Bolton.

Brit. Mus., Case 47.

MAGNESITIC OPHIOLITE. The name proposed by T. Sterry Hunt for those varieties of Serpentine which contain Magnesite intimately mixed with the rock.

MAGNETEISENSTEIN, *Werner.* MAGNETIC· IRON, *Allan.* MAGNETIC IRON-ORE; MAGNETIC IRON-STONE, *Jameson, Kirwan.* See MAGNETITE.

MAGNETIC PYRITES, *Jameson, Kirwan, Phillips.* See PYRRHOTINE.

MAGNETITE, *Haidinger.* Cubical. Occurs in regular octahedrons; structure imperfectly

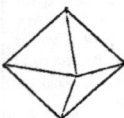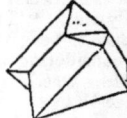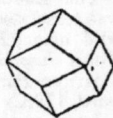

Fig. 271.　　　Fig. 272.　　　Fig. 273.

lamellar, parallel to the planes of the octahedron. Also earthy, compact, granular and

..utellar. Colour iron-black. Lustre metallic, or submetallic. Opaque. Streak black. Brittle. Fracture uneven or conchoidal, with a splendent lustre. Strongly magnetic, especially when massive, and sometimes exhibits polarity. H. 5·5 to 6·5. S.G. 4·9 to 5·2.

Comp. Fe $\ddot{\text{F}}$e = protoxide of iron 30·97, peroxide of iron 96·03, or iron 71·68, oxygen 28·32 = 100.

BB turns brown and loses its influence on the magnet, but fuses with difficulty.

Soluble in heated muriatic acid, but not in nitric acid.

Localities.—English. Cornwall: Treluswell, near Penryn; Roche and occasionally at St. Agnes, Huel Harmony and Fowey Consols. Haytor in Devonshire, with Felspar and Hornblende. — *Scotch.* Portsoy in Banffshire. Unst and other places in the Shetlands. East Rona, one of the Hebrides, in granite, *fig.* 272. Near Loch Long, &c. — *Irish.* Ballycoog, co. Wicklow. In amygdaloid at Muck and Magee Islands, co. Antrim, figs. 271, 273, containing 2·00 per cent. of magnesia and 0·23 oxide of manganese. (Dr. Andrews). — *Foreign.* The ore of Arendal in Norway, and of nearly all the celebrated iron mines of Sweden, consists of massive Magnetite. Dannemora, and the hill of Taberg in Smaoland, are almost entirely composed of it; and it is stated by Jameson that the loose masses found at the base of the latter hill have furnished materials for extensive iron-works for upwards of 150 years. Kurunavara and Gellivara in Lapland. Normark in Wermland in splendid dodecahedral crystals. Neudeck in Bohemia. Hungary. The Tyrol. Saxony. Silesia. The Harz. Traversella in Piedmont. St. Gotthardt, Switzerland. Puy in France. Vesuvius, in ejected masses. Elba. Corsica. The East Indies. Puchamanche in Chili. United States. The Canadas, &c. New Zealand, in the form of sand, derived from the decomposition of trachytic rocks.

The most powerful natural magnets are found in compact or earthy amorphous masses in Siberia, Sweden, Elba, and the Harz. See LODESTONE.

Brit. Mus., Case 14.

M. P. G. Principal floor, Wall-cases 47 (British); 18 (Foreign); 39 (E. Indies).

MAGNETKIES, *Werner.* See PYRRHOTINE.

MAGNOFERRITE. The name given by Rammelsberg to the octahedral iron which occurs interlaminated with Hematite, in the fumaroles formed at Vesuvius after the eruption of 1855. S.G. 4·56 to 4·838.

Comp. $\dot{\text{M}}$g^3 $\ddot{\text{F}}$e^4.

Analysis, by *Rammelsberg:*

Peroxide of iron	. .	. 82·91
Magnesia	. . .	. 13·60
Oxide of copper	. .	. 0·99
Insoluble	. . .	. 2·51

100·01

MALACHITE, *Jameson, Brochant, Kirwan, Beudant.* Oblique. Primary form a right rhombic prism, in twins, *fig.* 274. Rarely occurs crystallized, but generally massive, with a globular, reniform, botryoidal or stalactitic surface; frequently fibrous and banded in colour; often granular or earthy. Colour various shades of bright green, exhibiting all degrees of translucency down to complete opacity. Lustre of crystals adamantine, inclining to vitreous; of fibrous varieties, silky. Streak paler than the colour. Brittle. Fracture imperfect-conchoidal to uneven. H. 3·5 to 4. S.G. 3·7 to 4.

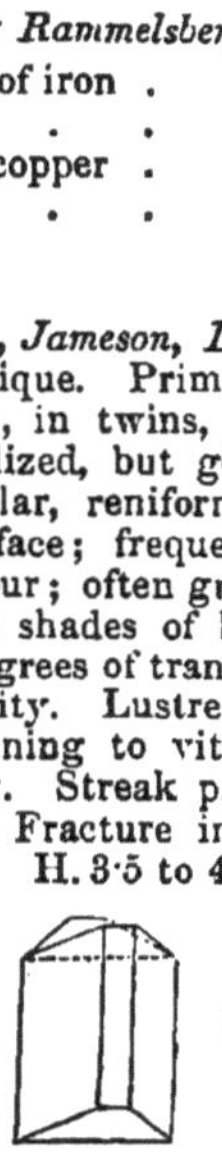

Fig. 274.

Comp. Carbonate of copper, $\dot{\text{C}}$u^2 $\ddot{\text{C}}$ = protoxide of copper 71·9, carbonic acid 19·9, water 8·2 = 100.

Analysis, by *Phillips:*

Carbonic acid	. .	. 18·5
Protoxide of copper	.	. 72·2
Water	. . .	. 9·3

100·0

BB alone infusible; decrepitates and turns black. With borax readily affords a globule of copper, and colours the flux green.

Soluble with effervescence in acids, and forms a blue solution with ammonia.

Localities.—English. Common in Cornwall, associated with Red Oxide of Copper. Cumberland; botryoidal at Huel Edward; crystallized (*fig.* 274), acicular, and fibrous, at Red Gill, Haygill, and Roughten Gill, near Hesket Newmarket, and at Mexico Mine. — *Scotch.* The old copper mine, Sandlodge, in Mainland, one of the Shetlands, in fine acicular crystals, &c. — *Irish.* Audley Mines, and Coosheen, near Skull, co. Cork. Limerick, &c. — *Foreign.* Compact at Schwatz in the Tyrol. Fibrous abundantly in Siberia. Chessy in France. Crystallized near Siegen in Prussia. Spain.

Q

United States. Cuba. Chili. S. Africa.
Mines at Bembe in Western Africa.

Name. From μαλάχη, *the marsh-mallow;*
on account of its resemblance in colour to
the leaves of that plant.

Malachite is a *copper-stalactite,* or *stalagmite.* Independently of its value as an ore
of copper, Malachite is used as a green pigment under the name of *emerald-green.* It
is also in great request for ornamental purposes, on account of the variety and beauty
of its markings, and the high degree of
polish of which it is susceptible. Its softness, however, renders it of less value than
it otherwise would be in jewelry. The compact specimens are worked into snuff-boxes,
vases, &c.; and at St. Petersburg large
tables are made by joining pieces of the
stone so as to render the concentric lines
continuous. Very fine specimens of Malachite ornaments were contained in the Russian department of the Great Exhibition of
1851.

The handsomest masses of Malachite are
procured from Siberia, about 100 miles south
of Bogoslofsk, and at Nijny-Taguilsk. At
the latter locality an enormous mass of solid
Malachite was met with, 18 feet long by 9
in'width, which was estimated to contain
500,000 lbs. of pure and solid Malachite.
Fine specimens are also found in Australia
at Burra Burra; and on the west coast of
Africa.

Sir Roderick Murchison, in his work on
the Geology of Russia, in noticing the above-
mentioned mass, states that it affords a
strong indication that Malachite has been
formed by a cupriferous solution, in the
manner of ordinary stalagmites, and adds
that "on the whole, we are disposed to view
it as having resulted from copper solutions
emanating from all the porous, loose, surrounding mass; and which, trickling through
it to the lowest cavity upon the subjacent
rock, have, in a series of ages, produced
this wonderful subterranean incrustation."—
Geology of Russia, p. 374.

Pliny, writing of the Malachite, or Molochites, says : — "Commended it is highly in
signets for to seale faire: and besides it is
supposed to be, by a naturall vertue that it
hath, a counthercharme to preserve little
babes and infants from all witchcrafts and
sorceries."—*Pliny,* book xxxviii. chap. 8.

Brit. Mus., Case 51.

M.P.G. Principal floor, Case 11 (Burra
Burra); Wall-cases 2 (British); 15 and 16
(Foreign); 37 and 38 (Burra Burra); 39
(W. Africa).

MALACOLITE.   MALACOLITHE,   *Haüy,*
Hausmann. A variety of Augite (*Sahlite*).

Analysis, from Orrijerfvi, by *H. Rose:*

Silica	54·64
Lime	24·94
Magnesia	18·00
Protoxide of manganese	2·00
Protoxide of iron	1·08
	100·66

Name. From μαλάχος, *soft,* and λίθος, *stone.*
Brit. Mus., Case 34.

MALACONE, *Scheerer.* MALAKON. Probably an altered Zircon, from which it
differs only in somewhat less density and
hardness, and in containing 8 per cent. of
water. Colour brown. Lustre vitreous to
subresinous. Streak white or reddish-brown.
H. 6·5. S.G. 8·9 to 4.

Comp. $\ddot{Z}r\overset{..}{S}i + \frac{1}{2}\dot{H}$.

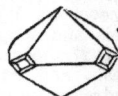

Fig. 275.

Analysis, from Hitteroe, by *Scheerer:*

Silica	31·31
Zirconia	63·40
Peroxide of iron	0·41
Yttria	0·34
Lime	0·39
Magnesia	0·11
Water	3·03
	98·99

BB gives off water and behaves like
Zircon.

Localities. Ilmen Mountains, in Siberia.
Hitteroe, in Norway. Chanteloube, Haute
Vienne, France.

Name. From μαλακὸς, *soft.*
Brit. Mus., Case 26.

MALTHA, *Kirwan.* Earthy mineral pitch.
See EARTHY BITUMEN.

MALTHACITE, *Breithaupt.* A clayey sub-
stance occurring massive and in thin plates.
Colour white or yellowish. Translucent.
Soft, like wax; or friable. S G. 1·99 to 2.

Comp. Hydrated octosilicate of alumina,
or $\overset{...}{Al}\overset{..}{Si}^8 + 20\dot{H}$.

Analysis, by *Meissner:*

Silica	50·2
Alumina	10·7
Peroxide of iron	8·1
Lime	0·2
Water	35·8
	100·0

Localities. Steindorfel, in basalt. Beraun in Bohemia, in greenstone.

Brit. Mus., Case 26.

MALTHE, *Beudant.* See EARTHY BITUMEN.

MANCINITE. A brown silicate of zinc from Mancino, near Leghorn.

MANGAN-AMPHIBOLE. The name given by Hermann to Manganese-spar from Cummington, Massachusetts, U. S. S.G. 3·42.

Analysis, by *Hermann :*

Silica	. 48·91
Protoxide of manganese	. 46·74
Lime	. 2·35
Magnesia	. 2·00
Protoxide of iron	. trace

                                100·00

MANGANBLENDE, *Breithaupt.* MANGANESE BLENDE, *Jameson.* Cubical. Occurs in cubes and octahedrons. Cleavage perfect, parallel to the faces of a cube. Generally occurs massive, sometimes botryoidal. Colour iron-black, acquiring a brown tarnish by exposure. Lustre submetallic. Streak dark green. Opaque. Fracture fine-grained. H. 3·5 to 4. S.G. 4.

Comp. Sulphide of manganese, or Mn S = manganese 63·3, sulphur 36·7 = 100.

Analysis, from Mexico, by *Del Rio :*

Manganese	. 54·5
Sulphur	. 39·0
Quartz	. 6·5

                                100·0

BB fuses with difficulty at the thinnest edges.

Soluble in acids with the evolution of abundance of sulphuretted hydrogen.

Localities. The gold mines of Nagyag in Transylvania, with Tellurium, &c. Preciosa Mine, Puebla, in Mexico; with Tetrahedrite.

Brit. Mus., Case 5.

M. P. G. Principal Floor, Wall-case 20.

MANGANESE ARSENICAL, *Dufrénoy.* See KANEITE.

MANGANÈSE HYDRATÉ CUPRIFÈRE. See MELACONITE, KUPFERSCHWÄRZE, and PELOKONITE.

MANGANÈSE NOIR, *Brochant.* See HAUSMANNITE.

MANGANÈSE OXIDÉ CARBONATÉ, *Haüy.* See DIALLOGITE.

MANGANÈSE OXIDÉ HYDRATÉ, *Haüy.* See HAUSMANNITE.

MANGANÈSE OXIDÉ HYDRATÉ CONCRÉTIONNÉ, *Haüy.* See PSILOMELANE.

MANGANÈSE OXYDÉ METALLOIDE, *Haüy.* See MANGANITE.

MANGANÈSE PHOSPHATÉ. See TRIPLITE.

MANGANÈSE SILICATÉ, *Rosr, Dufrénoy.* MANGANÈSE SILICIFÈRE, *Haüy.* } See RHODONITE.

MANGANESE SPAR, *Jameson.* See RHODONITE.

MANGANÈSE SULFURÉ, *Haüy.* MANGANGLANZ, *Leonhard.* } See MANGANBLENDE.

MANGANITE, *Haidinger, v. Kobell, Nicol.* Rhombic : primary form a right rhombic prism. Occasionally hemihedral. Occurs in columnar crystals striated vertically, and often grouped in bundles; also fibrous and massive, or radiating; granular. Colour dark steel-grey, passing into iron-black. Opaque; sometimes brown by transmitted light, in very thin fragments. Lustre submetallic. Streak reddish-brown; black in massive varieties. Rather brittle. Fracture uneven. H. 3·5 to 4. S.G. 4·2 to 4·4.

Fig. 276.

Comp. Hydrated peroxide of manganese, $\overset{...}{M}n, \overset{.}{H}$ = peroxide of manganese 89·79 (manganese 62·78, oxygen 27·22), water 10·21 = 100.

Analysis, from Ihlefeld, by *Turner :*

Manganese	. 62·77
Oxygen	. 27·13
Water	. 10·10

                                100·00

BB alone infusible : with borax affords a violet-blue globule.

Completely soluble in muriatic acid, with evolution of chlorine.

Localities.—English. Upton Pyne, Devonshire : *fig.* 276. Mendip Hills (at Churchill, &c.) Somerset. Cornwall ; Botallack Mine, St. Just ; Restormel Iron-mines, acicular ; massive at Trebartha ; Veryan and Indian Queen Mine. Hartshill, Warwickshire, lamellar and compact.— *Scotch.* Granam in Aberdeenshire, *fig.* 276.—*Irish.* Near Howth, co. Dublin. Cork ; Ross, Leap, Nobarval, Castleventry. Kilfaunabeg near Ross.— *Foreign.* Ihlefeld in the Harz, associated with Calc Spar and Barytes, in veins tra-

                                                        Q 2

versing porphyry. Thuringia. Bohemia.
Saxony. Undenaes in Sweden. Christiansand in Norway.

Manganite is the purest and most beautifully crystallized ore of manganese. It is
distinguished from Pyrolusite by its greater
hardness and brown streak, which sometimes appears black until a portion has been
abraded.

Brit. Mus., Case 13.

MANGANKIESEL. See RHODONITE.

MANGANKUPFERERZ, *Credner.* See CRED-
NERITE.

MANGANKUPFEROXYD, *Hausmann.* See
CREDNERITE.

MANGANOCALCITE, *Breithaupt.* A mineral
bearing the same relation to Diallogite
which Aragonite does to Calc Spar. Occurs
in rhombic prisms, like Aragonite, with a
lateral cleavage. Colour flesh-red to reddish-
white. Lustre vitreous. Translucent. H.
4 to 5. S.G. 3·037.

Comp. Like Diallogite or (Mn, Fe, Ċa,
Ṁg) Ċ.

Analysis, by *Rammelsberg* :

Carbonate of manganese	. 67·48
Carbonate of iron .	. 3·22
Carbonate of lime .	. 18·81
Carbonate of magnesia	. 9·97
	99·48

Locality. Schemnitz in Hungary.

MANGANSCHAUM, *Hausmann.* See WAD.

MANGANSPATH, *Werner.* See DIALLO-
GITE.

MANGAN-VITRIOL, *Glocker.* See SUL-
PHATE OF MANGANESE.

MARASMOLITE, *Shepard.* A partially
decomposed Marmatite, containing some
free sulphur; from Middletown, Connecticut, U.S.

MARCASITE, *Haidinger.* Iron Pyrites.
Rhombic : primary form a right rhombic
prism. Occurs crystallized in modified
rhombic prisms; also stalactitic, reniform,
and botryoidal. Colour pale bronze-yellow
or nearly tin-white, with a tinge of yellow
or grey. Lustre metallic. Streak dark
greenish-grey. Brittle. Emits a smell of
sulphur when triturated. Very liable to
decompose. Fracture uneven. H. 6 to 6·5.
S.G. 4·65 to 4·88.

Comp. Bisulphide of iron, or Fe S² = iron
46·7, sulphur 63·3 = 100.

BB behaves like Pyrites.

Localities. Often in the joints or "backs"

of coal. *English.* — Cornwall; Crowndale,
Cook's Kitchen, Huel Unity, Fowey Consols,

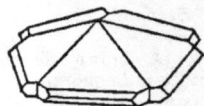

Fig 277.

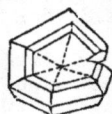　　

Fig. 278.　　　　　　Fig. 279.

East Huel Rose, stalactitic and radiated.
Devonshire : on crystallized Quartz at
Virtuous Lady Mine, *fig.* 279; Tamar Sil-
ver-lead Mines, near Tavistock; Combmar-
tin. Kent : in grey chalk marl near Folke-
stone and Dover, *fig.* 278; Isle of Sheppey.
Devizes, in Wiltshire. Near Castleton,
Derbyshire, *figs.* 277 and 279. On crystals
of Calc Spar at Garrigill in Cumberland,
fig. 278. — *Scotch.* Alva mine, Stirlingshire.
—*Irish.* Near Dublin : in lance-shaped crystals at Kilkee, co. Clare. — *Foreign.* In
the plastic clay of the Brown Coal formation at Littmitz and Alsatell, near Carlsbad
in Bohemia (*Spear and Radiated Pyrites*).
Joachimsthal and various parts of Saxony.

Name. The word Marcasite is stated by
Koch to be derived from an Arabic word,
mawr kjass idd, signifying "like a shining,
fire-giving stone."

Brit. Mus., Case 16.

M.P.G. Horse-shoe Case, No. 150.

Under the term Marcasite are included
several varieties, which have been named
after the forms they present : viz. Cellular
Pyrites, Cockscomb Pyrites, Hepatic Pyrites
or Leberkies, Lonchidite, Radiated Pyrites,
Spear Pyrites, &c. Marcasite is more liable
to decomposition than ordinary Pyrites, and
is of a much paler colour. It is used in the
manufacture of sulphur, sulphuric acid, and
sulphate of · iron, but not to so great an
extent as ordinary Pyrites. It is also employed for ornamental purposes. Formerly
it was made into shoe- and knee-buckles,
and set in pins, bracelets, watch-cases, &c.;
but the demand has very much diminished
of late years, owing probably to the mineral
being so common. The taste revived to
some extent in 1846, when a great quantity
of these stones, having reached Paris,
were mounted after the manner of old-
fashioned jewelry, and had a great run at

the time. Although less in request than formerly, large quantities of this stone are cut and polished in Geneva and the French Jura, and exported thence all over the world. It takes a good polish, and is cut in facets like rose-diamonds. In this state it possesses all the brightness of the polished steel, which is now so fashionable, without its tendency to become oxidised by exposure to the atmosphere. The Marcasite of commerce (which includes Pyrites proper) is generally small, rarely attaining the size of a stone of two carats. The stone which the ancient Peruvians polished and used for mirrors was a variety of Marcasite which occurred in large plates, none of which are found now. See PIERRE DES INCAS.

MARCELINE, *Beudant.* An impure variety of Braunite. S.G. 4·75.

Analysis, by *Damour :*

Peroxide of manganese	. 67·37
Protoxide of manganese	. 19·17
Peroxide of iron . .	. 1·45
Silica	. 7·71
Lime	. 1·22
Gangue . . .	. 2·72

99·54

Locality. St. Marcel in Piedmont. Brit. Mus., Case 13.

MAREKANITE. A variety of Pearlstone occurring in the form of pearly-white grains composed of thin concentric layers.

Locality. Marekan, in the Gulf of Kamtschatka. Brit. Mus., Case 30.

MARGARITE, *Fuchs, Phillips.* Rhombic; hemihedral, with an oblique aspect. Basal cleavage perfect. Occurs in thin crystalline laminæ, which intersect each other in all directions, and have the lateral planes striated horizontally. Colour pale pearlgrey, passing into reddish- and yellowish-white. Translucent. Lustre pearly on the terminal planes, vitreous on the others. Streak white. Laminæ rather brittle. In thin leaves slightly elastic. H. 3·5 to 4·5. S.G. 2·99.

Comp. $\dot{R}^3$ Si + 3$\ddot{A}l^2$ Si + 3$\dot{H}$ = silica 30·1, alumina 51·2, lime 11·6, soda 2·6, water 4·5 = 100.

Analysis, by *Smith & Brush :*

Silica	. 28·47
Alumina . . .	. 50·24
Peroxide of iron . .	. 1·65
Lime	. 11·50
Magnesia . . .	. 0·70
Soda, with a trace of potash	1·87

Water . . .	. 5·00

99·26

BB intumesces and fuses.
Is attacked by acids.

Localities. — Sterzing in the Tyrol, in foliated Chlorite. Greinerberg, Zillerthal, with Chlorite. With Corundum at Katherinenberg in the Ural. The emery localities in Asia Minor and the Grecian Archipelago. Pennsylvania, North Carolina, &c., U.S.

Name.—From Margarita, *a pearl;* because of its peculiar pearly lustre. Brit. Mus., Case 32.

MARGARODITE, *Dufrénoy, Schaffhäutl.* A hydrated Mica; rarely occurring in fine-grained laminæ, in which case it bears a great resemblance to Mica. Colour dull green, passing into bright green. Lustre sometimes opalescent, sometimes like mother-of-pearl. Slightly translucent at the edges. Easily pulverised. H. 2·5. S.G. 2·87.

Comp. $\dot{R}$ $\ddot{S}i$ + 2$\ddot{R}$ $\ddot{S}i$ + 2$\dot{H}$, or 12($\ddot{A}l^3$ $\dddot{S}i^2$) + 3(Mg, $\dddot{S}i^2$) + $\ddot{F}e$ $\dddot{S}i^3$ + 6$\dot{N}a$ $\ddot{S}i$ + 9$\dot{K}$ $\ddot{S}i$.

Analysis, from Pfitsch, by *Hlasiwitz :*

Silica	. 45·50
Alumina . . .	. 33·80
Peroxide of iron .	. 6·25
Potash	. 7·31
Soda	. 6·22
Lime	. 0·48
Loss by ignition .	. 0·36

99·90

BB in fine laminæ fuses, emitting a vivid light and yielding a white enamel. With borax yields a colourless glass.
Not affected by acids.

Localities. The S.E. of Ireland, in granite. The Zillerthal, forming the matrix of black Tourmaline. St. Etienne in France, in graphic granite. Poorhouse Quarry, Chester co., Pennsylvania, U.S.; Munroe, associated with Topaz and Fluor.

MARGODE. A bluish-grey stone resembling clay in external appearance, but so hard as to cut spars and zeolites. (*Nicholson*).

MARIALITE, *Ryllo.* See HAÜYNE.

MARIATITE. A variety of Blende, in which part of the zinc is replaced by iron and sometimes by cadmium. Occurs in tetrahedrons and massive.

Comp. 3Zn, S + Fe, S.

Analysis, by *Boussingault :*

Sulphide of zinc . .	. 76·8
Sulphide of iron . .	. 23·2

100·0

Localities. Marmato in Popayan. Bottino near Serravezza in Tuscany.

MARIONITE, *Elderhorst.* The variety of Zinc-bloom from Marion co., Arkansas.

MARMOLITE, *Nuttall, Beudant, Dufrénoy, Allan.* A thin foliated variety of Serpentine, occurring in translucent or opaque masses of a pale green colour: sometimes nearly white. Lustre pearly. Folia brittle and separable. S.G. 2·41.

Comp. $\overset{..}{Mg}{}^5$, $\overset{..}{Si}{}^2$, $\overset{.}{H}{}^4$.

Analysis, by *Lychnell:*

Silica	. . .	41·67
Magnesia	. .	41·25
Protoxide of iron	.	1·64
Carbonic acid	.	1·37
Water .	. .	13·80
		99·73

Localities. Hoboken in New Jersey, associated with Brucite, Magnesite, &c. Blandford, Massachusetts, U.S., with Schiller Spar.

Name. From μαρμαίρω, to shine.

When the laminæ are not separable it is sometimes miscalled Kerolite.

MARTIAL ARSENIATE OF COPPER. *Allan, Jameson.* See SCORODITE.

MARTIAL PYRITES. See PYRITES.

MARTINSITE, *Karsten.* A variety of Common Salt, from Stassfurth, containing 9·02 per cent. of sulphate of magnesia. It gives out a bituminous odour when rubbed, and dissolves in water with a very slight effervescence.

Analysis:

Chloride of sodium	.	90·30
Sulphate of magnesia .	.	9·02
Sulphate of lime .	.	0·50
Alumina and	. .	} 0·20
Peroxide of iron	.	}
		100·02

Name. After Captain Martin of Halle.

MARTITE, *Breithaupt.* Cubical. Occurs in regular octahedrons, which are often flattened, and have their faces striated parallel to the edges. Cleavage indistinct. Colour iron-black, sometimes with a bronze tarnish. Lustre submetallic. Streak reddish brown. Fracture conchoidal. H. 6. S.G. 4·6 to 5·33.

Comp. $\overset{...}{Fe}$=iron 70, oxygen 30 = 100.

Localities. Framont. Auvergne. Vesuvius. Peru. Brazil. Munroe. New York. See EISENANATAS.

MASCAGNIN, *Karsten, Reuss.* MASCAGNINE, *Dana.* Rhombic. Generally occurs stalactitic, pulverulent, or in mealy crusts. Colour greyish or yellow. Lustre of crystals vitreous. Translucent or opaque. Taste pungent and bitter. H. 2 to 2·5. S.G. 1·72 to 1·73.

Fig. 280.

Comp. Sulphate of ammonia, $\overset{..}{N}\overset{.}{H}{}^4$, $\overset{...}{S}$ + $2\overset{.}{H}$ = sulphuric acid 52·33, ammonia 34·67, water 12·00 = 100.

Readily soluble in water. Attracts moisture from the atmosphere, and is entirely volatile at a high temperature.

Localities. In fissures in the lavas of Etna and Vesuvius, and the Lipari Isles. The lagunes near Sienna in Tuscany.

Name. After Professor Mascagni, by whom it was discovered.

MASCULINE. See GEM.

MASONITE, *C. T. Jackson.* A variety of Chloritoid. Colour black. Lustre pearly. H. 6. S.G. 3·52.

Analysis, by *Whitney:*

Silica .	. .	28·27
Alumina	. .	32·16
Protoxide of iron .	.	33·72
Magnesia	. .	0·13
Water .	. .	5·00
		99·28

Locality. Near Natic Village, Rhode Island; in compact argillaceous states. Brit. Mus., Case 33.

MATLOCKITE, *R. P. Greg.* Pyramidal: primary form a right square prism. Occurs in tabular crystals with an imperfect basal cleavage. Colour yellowish, sometimes slightly greenish. Lustre adamantine, occasionally pearly on planes of cleavage. Transparent to translucent. Fracture un-

Fig. 281.   Fig. 282.

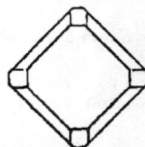

Fig. 283.

even and slightly conchoidal. H. 2·5 to 3. S.G. 7·21.

Comp. Pb Cl + $\dot{\text{P}}$b, = chloride of lead 55·5, oxide of lead 44·5 = 100.

Analysis, from Cromford, by *Dr. R. A. Smith :*

Chloride of lead .   .   . 55·177
Oxide of lead .   .   . 44·300
Water   .   .   .   . 0·072
                                    ———
                                    99·549

BB decrepitates, and on charcoal fuses easily to a greyish-yellow globule.
Readily soluble in nitric acid.
Locality. Near Cromford in Derbyshire, in one of the air-shafts of an old level.
Brit. Mus., Case 57B.
MAUILITE. A variety of Labradorite occurring in glassy colourless crystals, in Maui, one of the Sandwich Islands.

Analysis, by *Schlieper :*

Silica .   .   .   .   . 53·98
Alumina   .   .   .   . 27·56
Peroxide of iron .   .   . 1·14
Lime .   .   .   .   . 8·65
Soda .   .   .   .   . 6·06
Potash .   .   .   .   . 0·47
Magnesia   .   .   . 1·35
                                    ———
                                    99·21

MEADOW ORE, *Jameson.* MEADOW IRON-ORE, *Kirwan.* See BOG IRON-ORE.

MEALY ZEOLITE. The name sometimes given to the delicate interlacing crystals of Mesolite, when crushed.

MEDJIDITE, *J. L. Smith.* Massive, with an imperfectly crystalline texture. Colour dark copper-yellow. Lustre vitreous. Transparent. Often dull externally, owing to the loss of water. Fracture horny. H. 2·5.

Comp. Sulphate of uranium and lime, or $\ddot{\text{U}}$ $\ddot{\text{S}}$ + Ċa $\ddot{\text{S}}$ + 15$\dot{\text{H}}$.

Analysis ;

Sulphate of uranium .   . 37·21
Sulphuric acid   .   . 20·67
Lime .   .   .   .   . 7·24
Water .   .   .   . 34·88
                                    ———
                                    100·00

BB with borax behaves like Liebigite. At a gentle heat it loses water and assumes a lemon-yellow colour; blackens at a red heat, being converted into oxide of uranium and sulphate of lime.
Dissolves sparingly in dilute muriatic acid.
Localities. Near Adrianople In Turkey, accompanying an impure variety of Pitch-blende, and associated with Liebigite.

Joachimsthal in Bohemia, on Uranium Ore, with Liebigite.
Name. In honour of Abdul Medjid, Sultan of Turkey.

MEERSCHAUM, *Werner.* Compact. Colour white or yellowish. Dull and opaque. Adheres to the tongue. Yields to the nail. Feels smooth. Streak shining. Fracture earthy. H. 2 to 2·5. S.G. 1·3 to 1·6.
Comp. Hydrated silicate of magnesia, or $\ddot{\text{Mg}}$ $\ddot{\text{Si}}$ + 2$\dot{\text{H}}$ = silica 60·9, magnesia 26·1, water 12·0 = 100.

Analysis, from Asia Minor, by *Lychnell :*

Silica .   .   .   .   . 60·87
Magnesia   .   .   . 27·80
Peroxide of iron and alumina 0·09
Water .   .   .   .   . 11·29
                                    ———
                                    100·05

BB shrinks up, becomes hard and fuses at the edges to a white enamel.
Localities. In stratified earthy or alluvial deposits, at the plains of Eski-shehr in Asia Minor, and at Kiltschik, near Konieh, in Natolia. Islands of Samos and Negropont. Greece. Hungary. Hrubschitz in Moravia. Coulommiers, Dept. Seine-et-Marne, forming a bed in the upper green marls of the freshwater limestone of La Brie. Spain; at Valecas near Madrid, and near Toledo. Morocco.
Name. It is named Meerschaum, or *froth of the sea*, from its lightness and white colour.

Meerschaum when first dug up is soft and forms a lather like soap; on which account, and from its absorbing grease, it is used by the Turks for fuller's earth, for cleansing purposes, and in washing their linen. The Turks are also said to eat it as a medicine. but its principal use is in the manufacture of tobacco-pipes, for which it is peculiarly adapted from its porosity, which causes it to absorb the oily matter given out in smoking, and in doing so to acquire a beautiful warm-brown colour. The bowls of the pipes, when imported into Germany, are prepared for sale by soaking them first in tallow, then in wax, and finally by polishing them with shave-grass. Sometimes they are artificially stained by steeping them (before being soaked in wax) in a solution of copperas, either alone or tinged with dragon's blood.
Brit. Mus., Case 25.
M. P. G. Horse-shoe Case, Nos. 1188 to 1194.

MEGABROMITE, *Breithaupt.* A variety of Chloro-bromide of Silver, bearing a strong resemblance to Embolite in physical characters. Crystalline form cubic. Colour siskin- to pistachio-green, changing on exposure to the light to blackish-grey. Lustre adamantine. Streak pale green. Slightly malleable and sectile. Fracture conchoidal and uneven. H. 2·75 to 3. S.G. 6·23 to 6·234.

Comp. 4Ag Cl + 5Ag Br.

Analysis, by *T. Richter* :

Silver	.	.	.	. 64·19
Bromine	.	.	.	. 26·49
Chlorine	.	.	.	. 9·32
Iodine	.	.	.	. trace

100·00

Locality. Copiapo in Chili; in compact limestone.

MEÏONITE, *Haüy.* Pyramidal; primary form a right square prism. Generally occurs in small four- or eight-sided prisms terminated by tetrahedral pyramids, the edges or angles of which are sometimes replaced. Colour whitish or greyish-white. Lustre vitreous. Translucent to transparent. Often traversed by fissures internally. Scratches glass. H. 5·5 to 6. S.G. 2·5 to 2·74.

Comp. Ċa³ S̈i + 2Ä̶l S̈i = silica 42·1, alumina 31·9, lime 26 = 100.

Analysis, from Vesuvius, by *Stromeyer* :

Silica	.	.	. 40·53
Alumina	.	.	. 32·73
Lime	.	.	. 24·25
Soda and potash	.	.	1·81
Peroxide of iron	.	.	0·18

99·50

BB swells up strongly, and fuses to a blistered colourless glass.

Perfectly decomposed by muriatic acid, with the formation of a jelly.

Locality. Monte Somma, near Vesuvius, generally in geodes, or adhering to fragments of granular limestone.

Name. From μείων, *less*, in consequence of the pyramid with which the crystals are usually terminated being less acute than in Idocrase.

Brit. Mus. Case 31.

M.P.G. Upper Gallery, Table-case A in recess 4, Nos. 100 to 111.

MELACONISE, *Beudant.* MELACONITE, *Dana.* MELAKONITE, *Dufrénoy.* An earthy and impure black oxide of copper, resulting, probably, from the decomposition of Erubescite and other ores. Occurs in pseudomorphous cubic forms; also pulverulent and earthy, and massive. Colour dark steel-grey to black. Lustre sub-metallic. Opaque.

Streak shining. Commonly friable and soiling the fingers. S.G. 5·2.

Comp. Ċu = copper 79·85, oxygen 20·15 = 100. Often contains a large percentage of oxide of manganese and of water.

BB affords a globule of copper in the inner flame.

Localities. English.—Cornwall; at Huel Buller, Huel Trefusis, and other mines, in gossan. Hay Gill and Roughten Gill, Cumberland. Great Orme's Head, Caernarvonshire, in limestone. *Foreign.*—Chessy near Lyons. Siberia. Peru. Copper Harbour, Keweenaw Point, Lake Superior, forming a vein in conglomerate.

Name. From μίλας, *black*, and κόνις, *powder*. Brit. Mus., Case 17.

M.P.G. Principal Floor, Wall-cases 1 (British); 15 and 17 (Foreign).

MELANASPHALT, *Wetherill.* The name given to the Albert Coal of Nova Scotia, which has the appearance, but not the fusibility, of Asphaltum. It contains 58·8 to 61·67 per cent. of volatile matter, according to Dr. Jackson. Dr. Wetherill states that 4 parts are soluble in ether and 30 in turpentine.

Analysis, by *Dr. Wetherill* :

Carbon	.	.	. 82·670
Hydrogen	.	.	. 9·141
Oxygen, nitrogen	.	. 8·189

100·000

See ALBERT COAL.

MELANCHLOR, *Fuchs.* A blackish-green variety of phosphate of iron, from Rabenstein, stated by Sœmann to be a result of the alteration of Triphyline. It contains, besides impurities, about 3·87 per cent. of protoxide of iron, 38·9 peroxide of iron, 25·5 to 30·3 phosphoric acid, and 9 to 10 of water. S.G. 3·38.

BB fuses readily into a black magnetic globule.

Readily soluble in warm muriatic acid.

Name. From μίλας, *black*, and χλωρός, *green*, in allusion to its colour.

MELANGLANZ. See STEPHANITE.

MELANITE, *Jameson, Phillips.* A variety of Iron-lime Garnet, of a velvet-black colour. Opaque. Occurs in rhombic dodeca-

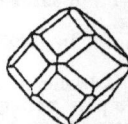

Fig. 284.

hedrons. whose edges are replaced. Streak grey. S.G. 3·7.

Analysis, from Frascati, by *Karsten*:

Silica . . . . . 34·60
Alumina . . . . 4·55
Peroxide of iron . . . 28·15
Magnesia . . . . 0·65
Lime . . . . . 31·80
                                  ———
                                  99·75

Comp. Ċa² S̈i + F̈e S̈i.
BB alone, fuses to a brilliant black globule; with borax, difficultly to an impure glass coloured green by iron.
Localities. Norway. The Pyrenees. The older lavas of Vesuvius, and the Papal States, chiefly at St. Albano and Frascati, near Rome. The latter are locally called Black Garnets of Frascati.
Name. From μίλας, black, in allusion to its colour.
Brit. Mus., Case 36.
M. P. G. Upper Gallery, Table-case B, in recess 6, No. 153.
MELANOCHROITE, *Hermann, Dufrénoy.* In rhombic prisms, with two faces enlarged, so as to impart to the crystal a tabular form; also massive. Colour between cochineal- and hyacinth-red. Lustre resinous. Translucent at the edges. Streak brick-red. H. 3 to 3·5. S.G. 5·75. ·

Comp. Chromate of lead, or Ṗb³ Ċr² = protoxide of lead 76·7, chromic acid 23·3 = 100.

Analysis, by *Hermann*:

Protoxide of lead . . . 76·69
Chromic acid . . . 23·31
                                  ———
                                  100·00

BB decrepitates slightly when heated, becoming for the time of a darker colour. On charcoal fuses to a dark coloured mass, which becomes crystalline on cooling. In the inner flame yields fumes of lead, lead globules, and oxide of chrome.
Locality. Beresow, in the Ural, in limestone, with Galena, Vauquelinite, Crocoisite, &c.
Name. From μίλας, black, and χεόα, colour.
Brit. Mus., Case 39.
M. P. G. Principal Floor, Wall-case 21.

MELANOLITE, *Wurtz.* Resembles Chlorite in appearance. Colour black. Opaque. Streak dark olive-green. Structure columnar, with a striated surface. H. 2. S.G. 2·69.

Analysis, by *Wurtz*:

Silica . . . . . 30·86
Alumina . . . . 3·92
Peroxide of iron . . . 21·97
Protoxide of iron . . . 21·97
Soda . . . . . 1·62

Carbonate of lime . . 12·77
Water . . . . . 8·94
                                  ———
                                  100·33

Locality. Milk Row Quarry, near Charlestown, Massachusetts, U.S., coating the sides of a fissure.
Name. From μίλας, black, and λίθος, stone.
MÉLANTÉRIE, *Leymerie.* MELANTERITE, *Haidinger, Greg & Lettsom.* See COPPERAS. The name is derived from Melanteria (from μίλας, black), the term used by Pliny for that mineral.

MELINOPHANE, *Th. Scheerer.* Pyramidal or hexagonal. Occurs massive, with a scaly and sometimes foliated structure. Cleavage in one direction. Colour sulphur-, lemon-, or honey-yellow. Lustre vitreous. Brittle. H. 5. S.G. 3·018.

Analysis, by *R. Richter*:

Silica . . . . . 44·8
Glucina . . . . 2·2
Alumina . . . . 12·4
Peroxide of manganese . . 1·4
Peroxide of iron . . . 1·1
Lime . . . . . 31·5
Magnesia . . . . 0·2
Soda . . . . . 2·6
Fluorine . . . . 2·3
Zirconia, oxide of chrome,
yttria, peroxide of nickel . 0·3
                                  ———
                                  98·8

Locality. Near Frederiksvärn, Norway, in zircon-syenite, with Elæolite, Magnetic Iron, Mica, &c.
MELINOSE, *Beudant*, (from μίλινος, pale yellow.) See WULFENITE.
MELLATE OF ALUMINA. See MELLITE.
MELLATE OF IRON. See HUMBOLDTINE. This name was given by Breithaupt to oxalate of iron, from its supposed composition.
MELLILITE, *Kirwan.* See MELLITE.
MELLILITE, *F. de Bellevue.* Pyramidal: Occurs in small square prisms, the lateral edges of which are mostly replaced. Colour yellowish-white, honey-yellow, or orange, but generally covered externally with a coating of oxide of iron. Lustre vitreous

Fig. 285.

or resinous. Translucent to opaque. Transparent in thin laminæ. Fracture uneven to conchoidal. H. 5. S.G. 2·9 to 3·1.

Comp. $\ddot{H}\ddot{S}i + 2\dot{R}^3\ddot{S}i^2$, or $(\ddot{A}l\,\ddot{F}e)\,\ddot{S}i + 2(\dot{C}a, \dot{M}g, \dot{N}a, \dot{K})\,\ddot{S}i^2$.

Analysis, from Capo di Bove, by *Damour* :

Silica	38·34
Alumina	8·61
Peroxide of iron	10·02
Lime	32·05
Magnesia	6·71
Soda	2·12
Potash	1·51
	99·36

BB fuses without effervescence to a greenish glass.

When reduced to powder gelatinises with nitric acid.

Localities. Capo di Bove, near Rome, in lava, with Nepheline, Pleonaste, &c.

Name. From *mel*, *honey*, and λίθος, *stone*, in allusion to its colour.

Brit. Mus., Case 36.

MELLITE, *Brochant, Haüy.* Pyramidal: primary form an octahedron with a square base, in which it also occurs with the terminal or lateral solid angles or edges replaced. Cleavage octahedral, indistinct. Colour honey- or wax - yellow, reddish, brownish. Lustre resinous, inclining to vitreous. Transparent to translucent. Sectile. Brittle. Fracture conchoidal. H. 2 to 2·5. S.G. 1·55 to 1·65.

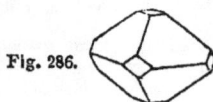

Fig. 286.

Comp. $\ddot{A}l\,\ddot{M}^3 + 18\ddot{H}$ = alumina 14·32, mellitic acid 40·53, water 45·15 = 100.

Analysis, by *Wöhler* :

Alumina	14·5
Mellitic acid	41·4
Water	44·1
	100·0

BB becomes opaque-white, with black spots, emits no vapour, and a scarcely perceptible odour, and is reduced to ashes without showing any flame.

Soluble in nitric acid.

Localities. Arten, in Thuringia, and Langenbogen, in Prussian Saxony; the mine of Dmitrizwsk, in the district of Nertschinsk, in Russia, in bituminous coal; Luschitz, near Bilin, in Bohemia; near Walchow, in Moravia. It occurs on bituminous wood and

earthy coal, and is generally accompanied by sulphur.

Name. From *mel*, *honey*, because of its honey-yellow colour.

Brit. Mus., Case 60.

M. P. G. Horse-shoe Case, No. 109.

MELOPSITE. A yellowish or greenish-white Lithomarge, from Neudeck, in Bohemia, H. 2 to 3. S.G. 2·5 to 2·6.

MENAC. See SPHENE.

MENACAN, *Werner;* MENACCANITE. A variety of Titaniferous Iron, occurring massive and in grains. Colour light iron-black to steel-grey. Streak black. Fracture uneven to flat-conchoidal. Magnetic. H. 5·5. S.G. 4·7 to 4·8.

Analysis, by v. *Kobell* :

Titanic acid	43·24
Peroxide of iron	28·66
Protoxide of iron	27·91
	100·00

Localities. Cornwall; in the bed of a rivulet, at Tregonwell Mill, near Menaccan, in grains and small angular fragments of an iron-black colour; also in a stream at Lanarth, St. Keverne; near Gwendra, on the south coast, in diallage rock.

Name. After the locality, Menaccan, where it was first observed.

Brit. Mus., Case 37.

M. P. G. Wall-case 13, on Principal Floor.

MENACHANITE, *Kirwan, Jameson.* MENAKANITE, *Brochant.* See MENACCANITE.

MENACHINE ORE, *Werner.* }   See
MENAKERZ, *Werner.*   } SPHENE.

MENDIPITE, *Breithaupt.* Anorthic: primary form a right rhombic prism. Occurs in crystalline masses, having a fibrous and radiated columnar structure. Colour white, sometimes with a yellow or reddish tinge. Feebly translucent to opaque. Lustre pearly on cleavage faces. Streak white. H. 2·5 to 3. S.G. 7·077.

Comp. Pb, Cl + 2Pb = chloride of lead 38·4, oxide of lead 61·6 = 100.

Analysis, from Churchill, by *Berzelius* :

Oxide of lead	60·18
Chloride of lead	39·82
	100·00

BB decrepitates slightly when heated, and appears yellower after cooling. Fuses very readily. On charcoal is reduced with evolution of acid vapours.

Easily soluble in nitric acid.

Localities. This rare mineral was principally found near Churchill, in the Mendip

Hills of Somersetshire, on earthy black manganese. It occurs also in opaque prismatic crystals at Tarnowitz, in Silesia, and at the Kunibert Mine, near Brilon, in Westphalia, with Calc Spar and Calamine. Brit. Mus., Case 57 B.

MENEGHINITE, *Bechi.* A kind of Heteromorphite or Feather - ore, occurring in compact fibrous forms. Very lustrous. H. 2·5.

Comp. 4Pb S + Sb S³.

Analysis, by *Bechi :*

Sulphur	17·52
Antimony	19·28
Lead	59·21
Copper	3·54
Iron	0·34
	99·90

Locality. Bottino, near Serravezza, in Tuscany.

Name. After Prof. Meneghini, of Pisa.

MENGITE, *G. Rose, Nicol, Dufrénoy.* Rhombic: occurs in small short prisms, which are often terminated by four-sided pyramids. Colour iron-black. Lustre submetallic; of fractured surface, sub-vitreous. Opaque. Streak chestnut-brown. Fracture uneven. H. 5 to 5·5. S.G. 5·48.

Fig. 287.

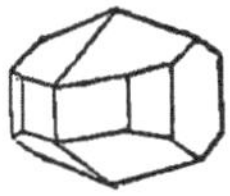

Comp. $\ddot{\text{F}}$e, $\ddot{\text{Z}}$r, $\ddot{\text{T}}$i.

BB infusible, but becomes magnetic. Almost wholly soluble in warm concentrated sulphuric acid.

Locality. Ilmen Mountains, in granite veins, imbedded in Albite.

Name. After Mons. Menge.

MENILITE, *Werner.* A brown and opaque variety of Opal, found in irregular, compact, reniform nodules, which are sometimes slaty, in tertiary strata in many localities in the neighbourhood of Paris. Translucent. Surface dull, and sometimes covered with a white crust. Brittle.

Analysis, by *Klaproth :*

Silica	85·50
Alumina	1·00
Peroxide of iron	0·50
Lime	0·50
Water and carbonaceous matter	11·00
	98·50

Localities. Principally at Saint-Ouen and

Menil-montant, near Paris, in beds of adhesive slate; and in the environs of Le Mans.

Name. After that of the locality.

Brit. Mus., Case 24.

M. P. G. Horse-shoe Case, No. 772.

MENNIGE, *Hausmann.* See MINIUM.

MERCURBLENDE. See CINNABAR.

MERCURE ARGENTAL, *Haüy.*
MERCURE ARGENTIF, *Haüy.* } See NATIVE AMALGAM.

MERCURE CHLORURÉ. See CALOMEL.

MERCURE CORNÉ, *Romé de Lisle.* See CALOMEL.

MERCURE IODURÉ, *Dufrénoy.* See COCCINITE.

MERCURE MURIATÉ, *Brochant, Haüy.* See CALOMEL.

MERCURE NATIF, *Haüy.* See QUICKSILVER.

MERCURE SULFURÉ, *Haüy.* See CINNABAR.

MERCURIAL HEPATIC-ORE, *Jameson.* See HEPATIC CINNABAR.

MERCURIAL HORN-ORE, *Jameson.* See CALOMEL.

MERCURIAL LIVER-ORE, *Jameson.* See HEPATIC CINNABAR.

MERDA DI DIAVOLO. Name for Dysodile, in Sicily.

MERKURGLANZ. See ONOFRITE.

MEROXENE, *Breithaupt.* The name given to the brilliant crystals of Biotite, from Vesuvius. Colour brownish-green. Unctuous to the touch. S.G. 2·8.

MESITINE SPAR, *Dana, Nicol.* MESITINSPATH, *Dufrénoy.* A variety of Breunnerite, occurring in lenticular forms at Traversella, in Piedmont.

Analysis, by *Gibbs :*

Carbonate of magnesia	56·14
Carbonate of iron	43·36
Carbonate of lime	0·29
	99·89

Name. From μέσος, in allusion to its composition, which is *intermediate* between Spathose Iron and Carbonate of Magnesia. Brit. Mus., Case 47.

MESOLE, *Haidinger, Rose.* Occurs in implanted globules, with a flat columnar or fibrous structure, radiating from the centre, or stalactitic. Colour greyish-white, yellowish, or reddish. Translucent. Lustre silky or pearly. Laminæ slightly elastic. Streak white. H. 3·5. S.G. 2·35 to 2·4.

Comp. ($\dot{\text{C}}$a², $\dot{\text{N}}$a) 2$\ddot{\text{S}}$i + 3$\ddot{\text{A}}$l $\ddot{\text{S}}$i + 8$\dot{\text{H}}$.

Analysis, from Skye, by *Thomson*:

Silica	. . . .	40·33
Alumina	. . .	29·00
Lime	. . . .	12·12
Soda	. . . .	5·33
Water	. . .	13·22

100·00

BB fuses with effervescence to a frothy enamel.

Forms a jelly with muriatic acid.

Localities. — Scotch. Isle of Skye, near Talisker, in white globules, with a radiated structure; at Storr, in bluish-white implanted spheres; Portree; Uig, lining cavities, in trap.— *Irish.* Antrim: Portrush, in greenstone; Black Cave, near Larne. Slieve Gallion Cairn, and Milligan, in Londonderry.— *Foreign.* Faröe Islands, sometimes in stalactites three inches long. Disco Island, Greenland, resembling crystallized spermaceti. Skagastrand, in the north of Iceland. Rostanga, in Scania, Sweden. Near the village of Fort George, in the Bay of Fundy.

Mesole is distinguished from Mesotype by its perfect single cleavage and pearly lustre; from Stilbite or Heulandite by its higher specific gravity; and from Apophyllite by its crest or fan-like aggregations, which never occur in that mineral. (*Allan's Manual.*)

In composition Mesole contains one equivalent less of soda than Mesolite, and stands intermediate between that mineral and Thomsonite.

Brit. Mus., Case 27.

MESOLIN, *Berzelius.* See LEVYNE.

MESOLITE, *Heddle.* A lime and soda Mesotype; occurs in long slender crystals, and massive. Colour dead-white or greyish. Lustre vitreous, never pearly as in Mesole. Pyroelectric. H. 5 to 5·5. S.G. 2·25.

Comp. $(\dot{N}a, \dot{C}a^2)\, 3\ddot{S}i + 3\ddot{A}l, \ddot{S}i + 8\dot{H}.$

Analysis, from Storr in Skye, by *Heddle*:

Silica	. . .	46·72
Alumina	. . .	26·70
Lime	. . .	8·90
Soda	. . .	5·40
Water	. . .	12·93

100·65

BB becomes opaque and curls up, and finally fuses to a porous and almost opaque globule.

Localities. — Scotch. Near Edinburgh. Near Kinross. Isle of Skye, at Talisker, Storr, Quirang and Kilmore.— *Irish.* Giant's Causeway, in fine acicular crystals. Down

Hill, Londonderry. — *Foreign.* Berufiord, Iceland, in diverging or interlacing crystals, often above two inches in length. Vindhya mountains of Hindostan. Greenland. Bohemia. Pargas, in Finland. Nova Scotia, in large masses with Mesole. North Mountains of Annapolis.

Name. From μέσος, *middle*, and λίθος, *stone*, because it is intermediate between Natrolite and Scolezite.

Brit. Mus., Case 27.

MESOTYPE, *Phillips.* See NATROLITE; SCOLEZITE, MESOLITE.

MESOTYPE, *Haüy.* See STILBITE.

The name is derived from μέσος, *middle*, and τύπος, *form;* because the primary form may be regarded as intermediate between those of Analcime and Stilbite.

MESOTYPE ÉPOINTÉE, *Haüy.* See APOPHYLLITE.

METACHLORITE, *K. List.* A Chlorite-like mineral occurring in aggregated crystals like Pennine. Colour dull leek-green. Lustre vitreous to pearly. Structure foliated-columnar. H. 2·5. S.G. 2·64.

Comp. $4\dot{R}^5\,\ddot{S}i + 3\ddot{H}\,\ddot{S}i + 14\dot{H}.$

Analysis, by *List*:

Silica	. . .	23·77
Alumina	. . .	16·43
Protoxide of iron	. .	40·36
Magnesia	. . .	3·10
Lime	. . .	0·74
Potash	. . .	1·37
Soda	. . .	0·08
Water	. . .	13·75

99·60

BB fuses at the edges to a dark enamel.

Forms a jelly with muriatic acid.

Locality.—Büchenberg, in the Harz.

METASTIQUE, *Haüy.* See DOG'S-TOOTH SPAR.

METAXITE, *Dufrénoy.* Asbestos mixed with Serpentine.

Brit. Mus., Case 25.

METAXITE, *Delesse.* See CHRYSOTILE.

Analysis, from Reichenstein in Silesia, by *Delesse*:

Silica	. . .	42·1
Magnesia	. . .	41·9
Protoxide of iron	.	3·0
Alumina	. . .	0·4
Water	. . .	13·6

100·00

METAXITE, *Breithaupt.* A fibrous variety of Serpentine, of a greenish-white colour, and a weak pearly lustre. Massive. H. 2 to 2·5. S.G. 2·52.

Comp. $2\dot{M}g\ddot{S} + Mg + 2\dot{H}$.
Analysis, by *Plattner* :

Silica	40·0
Alumina	10·7
Magnesia	32·8
Protoxide of iron . .	2·3
Lime	1·1
Water	12·6
	99·5

Localities. Schwartzenberg in Saxony. Windisch Matrei, in the Kalser Valley, Tyrol.
Name. From μιτάξα, silk.
Brit. Mus., Case 25.

METEORIC IRON is principally an alloy of iron and nickel. It generally contains from 1 to 20 per cent. of nickel, with small quantities of cobalt, chromium, copper, manganese, and tin ; also carbon, chlorine, phosphorus, sulphur, &c.
Analysis of the Pallas Meteoric Iron from Siberia, by *Berzelius* :

Iron	88·04
Nickel	10·73
Manganese . . .	0·13
Cobalt	0·46
Copper and tin . .	0·07
Magnesium . . .	0·05
Carbon	0·04
Sulphur . . .	trace
Insoluble . . .	0·48
	100·00

Analysing of the insoluble residue left on dissolving the Pallas iron in dilute muriatic acid :

Iron	48·67
Nickel	18·33
Phosphorus . . .	18·47
Magnesium . . .	9·66
Copper and tin . .	trace
Carbon and loss . .	4·87
	100·00

Analysis of Meteoric Iron from Zacatecas, in Mexico, by *Hugo Müller* :

Iron	90·91
Nickel	5·65
Cobalt	0·42
Phosphorus . . .	0·23
Sulphur . . .	0·07
Silica	0·50
Copper	trace
Magnesia . . .	trace
Insoluble residue . .	2·72
	100·50

The insoluble residue obtained in the foregoing analysis was magnetic. It consisted of a black flocculent substance, and a heavy shining body consisting of irregular flattened and pointed particles of the colour of pure nickel, which possessed all the characteristic properties of Schreibersite. On analysis it afforded —

Iron	75·02
Nickel	14·52
Phosphorus . . .	10·23
	99·77

The black substance was present only in very small quantity.

It was not Graphite, or any other form of carbon, but most likely some sulphide soluble only in concentrated muriatic acid. (*Hugo Müller*.)

Brit. Mus., Cases 1 and 1 A.: see also a large mass placed against the wall under the window.

M. P. G. Principal Floor, Wall-cases 18 : also 40 (Canada).

Meteoric Iron is perfectly malleable, and admits of being made into cutting instruments, and used for the same purposes as manufactured iron. It is also remarkable for exhibiting, when polished and etched with acids, linear and angular markings (termed Widmannstetten's figures), from which an impression may be printed on paper. (See *M.P.G.* Wall-case 18.) It generally occurs in irregular, frequently cellular, masses, or imbedded in meteoric stones — rarely crystallized in octahedrons. (See METEORIC STONES.)

METEORIC MINERALS. See APATOID, CHANTONNITE, CHLADNITE, DYSLYTITE, IODILITE, HOWARDITE, METEORIC IRON, OLIVINOID, PARTSCHITE, SCHREIBERSITE, or SHEPARDITE, SPHENOMITE.
Brit. Mus., Cases 1, 1A, 1*.

METEORIC STONES, or METEORITES, are not strictly simple minerals, but compound bodies, resembling greenstone and other rocks, which have fallen from the sky. The surface of these is generally covered with an exceedingly thin, black and shining crust, presenting an appearance of superficial fusion, or of a coating of pitch. S.G. 3·35 to 4·28.

Meteoric stones have been divided by Berzelius into two classes.—1st. Those containing Meteoric Iron, either in the form of disseminated grains, or as a continuous skeleton (see METEORIC IRON), together with other minerals (see METEORIC MINERALS). — 2nd. Those containing no iron, and possessing a more distinctly crystalline structure, and a less amount of magnesia in their composition than those of the first-mentioned class.

Prof. Lawrence Smith states that all the meteoric stones found in America contain *Schreibersite*, a mineral not known on the earth as a natural compound.

Various theories have been invented to account for the origin of these stones. By Laplace and others they were supposed to be thrown from the volcanos of the moon—by some they are believed to be formed in the atmosphere; while Chladni and others consider them to be cosmical bodies circulating in free space, and occasionally attracted to the surface of the earth when they come within the influence of its gravitation.

The fall of these stones, according to Prof. C. U. Shepard, is chiefly confined to two zones; one in America, lying between 33° and 44° N. lat. and about 25° in length; and the other in the eastern continent, bounded by the same degrees of latitude, but extending 10° further north, and with twice the length of the American zone. The direction of both these zones is more or less from north-east to south-west.

The most remarkable masses of Meteoric Iron are, that found in 1783 by Don Rubin de Celis, in Tucuman, in South America, weighing 15 tons; that discovered in 1784 on the Riacho de Bendego, in Brazil, estimated to measure 32 cubic feet and to weigh 17,300 lbs.; and that on the Red River, in Louisiana, weighing above 3000 lbs., and presenting distinct octahedral crystals.

A very interesting suite of meteorites will be found in Cases 1, 1 A, and 1* in the British Museum.

MIARGYRITE, *H. Rose.* Oblique: primary form an oblique rhombic prism. Occurs in thick tabular crystals with the lateral planes deeply striated. Colour varying from dark lead-grey to iron-black. Lustre between metallic and adamantine. Opaque: in thin fragments deep blood-red by transmitted light. Streak dark cherry-red. Soft and easily cut. Fracture subconchoidal. H. 2 to 2·5. S.G. 5·3.

Fig. 288.

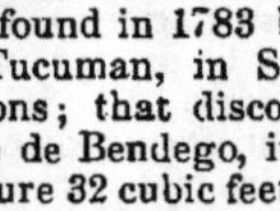

Comp. Ag,S + Sb²,S³ = silver 35·9, antimony 42·9, sulphur 21·2 = 100.

Analysis, by *H. Rose*:

Antimony	.	.	.	39·14
Silver .	.	.	.	36·40
Copper ·	.	.	.	1·06
Iron .	.	.	.	0·62
Sulphur	.	.	.	21·95
				99·17

BB fuses readily: on charcoal with carbonate of soda ultimately yields a globule of silver.

Locality. Braunsdorf, near Freiberg, in Saxony, associated with argentiferous Arsenical Pyrites.

Name. From μῖων, *less*, and ἄργυρος, *silver*; from its containing less silver than some of the other allied ores.

Brit. Mus., Case 11.

MIASCITE or MIASKITE. The mineral described by Dufrénoy under this name is, apparently, pseudomorphous Tremolite incrusted with carbonate of lime and magnesia. It is called Miaskite from its occurrence in the hills in the neighbourhood of Miask in Siberia.

MICA, *Haüy, Phillips, Allan.* Under this term are included several varieties of a mineral which possess in common a flaky structure and a glistening metallic lustre, characters with which most persons are familiar in the shining spangles which form one of the common constituents of granite.

The Micas are mostly biaxial, and, by the researches of Senarmont, Silliman, Blake, Dana and others, they have been divided into three groups, according to the variation between the apparent inclination of the optical axes; viz. 1. into *Muscovites*, in which the apparent inclination of the axes varies between 44° and 75°; 2. *Phlogopites*, between 5° and 20°; and 3. *Biotites*, in which it ranges below 5°. Lepidomelane is probably uniaxial.

According to Silliman Jr., the Muscovites are confined to granitic and other igneous rocks, and contain in general potash or lithia, and a small amount of magnesia; while the Phlogopites are only found in granular limestone and serpentine, and contain magnesia, and often only a small quantity of alkali.

From the researches of Schaffhäutl, it appears that the composition of the Micas

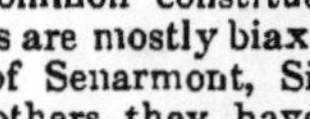

Fig. 289.

ranges between Ṁ 2S̈i and Ṁ⁵ 3S̈i, where Ṁ (which has a great range of variation) represents magnesia, potash, lithia and the other bases, including alumina.

See BIOTITE, LEPIDOLITE, MUSCOVITE, PHLOGOPITE, LEPIDOMELANE, &c.

Brit. Mus., Case 32.

M. P. G. Principal Floor, Wall-case 42. Horse-shoe Case, No. 1001. Upper Gallery, Table-case A in recess 4, Nos. 122 to 126. Wall-case 6, No. 4. Table-case B in recess 6, Nos. 140 to 149.

MICA NACRÉ. See MARGARITE.

MICACEOUS IRON. The name given to the varieties of Hematite which possess a micaceous structure.

M. P. G. Principal Floor, Wall-cases 48 (British); 18 (Foreign).

MICACEOUS URANITIC ORE, *Kirwan.* See CHALCOLITE and URANITE.

MICARELLE. The name given by Kirwan to Pinite, from its resemblance in external characters to Mica.

MICHAELITE. A white, fibrous, pearly variety of Opal, from the Island of St. Michael, in the Azores S.G. 1·88.

Analysis, by v. *Kobell :*

Silica . . . . . 83·65
Water . . . . 16·35
　　　　　　　　　———
　　　　　　　　　100·00

MICROCLINE, or MIKROKLINE, *Breithaupt.* A green and blue variety of Felspar (Orthoclase), exhibiting a play of colour, and containing nearly equal quantities of soda and potash. S.G. 2·582 to 2·56.

Analysis, from Greenland, by *Utendöffer :*

Silica . . . . . 66·9
Alumina . . . 17·8
Peroxide of iron . . 0·5
Lime . . . . . 0·6
Soda . . . . . 6·5
Potash . . . . 8·3
Magnesia . . . trace
　　　　　　　　　———
　　　　　　　　　100·6

Localities. Kangerdluarsuk, in Greenland, with Sodalite and Eudialyte. Norway, at Laurvig, Arendal, and Frederiksvarn, in Zircon-syenite, associated with Sodalite and Eukolite.

Name. From μικρὸς, *little,* and κλίνω, *to incline.*

MICROCOSMIC SALT, *Dana.* See STERCORITE.

MICROLITE, *Shepard.* A mineral proved by A. Hayes to be identical with Pyrochlore. Colour pale yellow to brown. H. 5·5. S.G. 5·4.

Analysis, by *Hayes :*

Columbic acid . . . 79·60

Peroxide of iron . . . . 0·99
Oxides of uranium and manganese . . . . 2·21
Lime . . . . . 10·87
Lead . . . . . 1·60
Tin . . . . . 0·70
　　　　　　　　———
　　　　　　　　95·97

The light coloured crystals seem to be nearly pure columbate of lime.

Locality. The Albite vein, Chesterfield, Massachusetts, U. S., associated with red and green Tourmaline.

Name. From μικρὸς, *small,* and λίθος, *stone.*

Brit. Mus., Case 38.

MIDDLETONITE, *J. F. W. Johnson.* A Mineral Resin, occurring in layers, or in rounded masses seldom larger than a pea. Colour reddish-brown ; by transmitted light deep red. Lustre resinous. Transparent in thin splinters. Streak light brown. Brittle, but easily cut with a knife. Blackens on exposure to air. No taste nor smell. S.G. 1·6.

Comp. $C^{20}H^{10} + HO$ = carbon 86·57, hydrogen 7·77, oxygen 5·66 = 100.

Analysis, by *Johnson :*

Carbon . . . . 86·43
Hydrogen . . . . 8·01
Oxygen . . . . 5·56
　　　　　　　　———
　　　　　　　　100·00

BB not altered at 400° F. (210° C.) ; on a red cider burns like resin. Softens and melts in boiling nitric acid, with the emission of red fumes ; affords a brown flocculent precipitate on cooling.

Localities. Middleton Collieries, near Leeds, between layers of coal, about the middle of the main coal, or Haigh Moor seam. Newcastle.

MIEMITE. A variety of Rhomb-spar, from Miemo, in Tuscany.

Brit. Mus., Case 47.

MIESITE, *Beudant.* A brown variety of Pyromorphite, from Mies, in Bohemia.

Analysis, by *Kersten :*

Phosphate of lead . . 89·27
Chloride of lead . . . 9·66
Phosphate of lime . . 0·85
Fluoride of calcium . . 0·22
　　　　　　　　　———
　　　　　　　　　100·00

MIKROBROMITE, *Breithaupt.* Crystalline form cubic. Colour between asparagus-green and greenish-grey, becoming ash-grey and opaque on exposure. Translucent. Lustre adamantine. Streak white. Very sectile and malleable. Fracture irregular. H. 2·5 to 3. S.G. 5·75 to 5·76.

Comp. Ag Br + 3Ag Cl.

Analysis, by *Richard Muller :*

Silver   .   .   .   .   . 70·28
Brumine .   .   .   . 12·35
Chlorine .   .   .   . 17·37
                        _____
                        100·00

Locality. Copiapo, in Chili, in a yellow-ish - red compact limestone, with Native Silver.

MIKROKLIN, *Breithaupt.* See MICRO-CLINE.

MILCH QUARZ, *Werner; MILK QUARTZ, Phillips, Jameson.* Is one of the vitreous varieties of Quartz. It occurs massive, of a milk-white colour, chiefly in Greenland. When, as is sometimes the case, it has a greasy lustre, it is called *Greasy Quartz.* When cut and polished it opalesces into wine-yellow.

Brit. Mus., Case 21.

MILLERITE, *Haidinger.* Hexagonal. In delicate, capillary, six-sided prisms, and sometimes in diverging filaments. Colour brass-yellow, inclining to bronze-yellow, with a grey or iridescent tarnish. Lustre metallic. Opaque. Streak bright. Brittle. H. 3 to 3·5. S.G. 5·278.

Comp. Sulphide of nickel, or Ni, S= nickel 64·9, sulphur 35·1 = 100.

Analysis, from Kamsdorf, by *Rammels-berg :*

Nickel .   .   .   .   . 61·84
Sulphur .   .   .   . 35·79
Iron   .   .   .   .   . 1·73
Copper .   .   .   . 1·14
                        _____
                        100·00

BB on charcoal gives off sulphurous acid, and fuses to a coagulated, ductile, mag-netic mass of nickel (*Berzelius*); a black bead (*Kobell*).

Dissolves with difficulty in nitric acid, easily in aqua-regia.

Localities. — *English.* Ebbw Vale, Nant-y-glo, and Merthyr-Tydvil, Glamorgan-shire, South Wales, in nodules of Clay Iron-stone. Devon; near Ilfracombe, and at Combe Martin. Cornwall; at Fowey Con-sols, Huel Chance and Pengelly Mine. — *Foreign.* Johanngeorgenstadt, in Saxony. Joachimsthal, in Bohemia. Andreasberg, in the Harz. Sterling Mine, Antwerp. New York, U. S.

Name. After W. H. Miller, Professor of Mineralogy in the University of Cambridge.

Brit. Mus., Case 6.

M. P. G. Principal Floor, Wall-case 9, Nos. 475, 476 (British).

MILOSCHINE, · *Herder.* A chromiferous

clay, of the same nature as Walchonskoite. Occurs in soft amorphous masses, of an indigo - blue to celandine - green colour. Translucent at the edges. Adheres to the tongue. Fracture conchoidal or earthy. H. 2. S.G. 2·031.

Comp. Hydrated silicate of alumina, or (Äl, Ġr) Si + 3H.

Analysis, by *Kersten :*

Alumina   .   .   .   . 45·01
Silica   .   .   .   .   . 27·50
Oxide of chrome .   . 3·61
Lime   .   .   .   .   . 0·30
Magnesia .   .   .   : 0·20
Water .   .   .   .   . 23·30
                        _____
                        99·92

BB infusible; decrepitates and falls to pieces in water.

Only partially soluble in muriatic acid.

Locality. Rudniak, in Servia, associated with Quartz and Brown Iron-ore.

Name. After Milosch Obrenowitsch, Prince of Servia.

MIMETENE, *Dana.* MIMÉTÈSE, *Beudant.* MIMETÉSITE, *Breithaupt, Nicol.* MIMETITE. Hexagonal: occurs in regular six - sided prisms, either perfect or with the terminal edges replaced; also fibrous and mammil-lary. Cleavage parallel to the planes of the prism, indistinct. Isomorphous with Pyro-morphite. Colour various tints of yellow, passing into brown. Lustre resinous. Trans-lucent. Streak white, or nearly so. Sectile. Brittle. Fracture imperfect-conchoidal, or uneven.   H. 3·5 to 4.   S.G. 7·19 to 7·25.

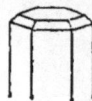

Fig. 290.

Comp. Pb Cl + 3Pb { Äs. | P̈

Analysis, from Johanngeorgenstadt, by *Wöhler :*

Arseniate of lead .   .   . 82·74
Chloride of lead .   .   . 9·60
Phosphate of lead   .   . 7·50
                        _____
                        99·84

BB on charcoal emits arsenical vapours, fuses with difficulty, and yields a globule of lead.

Dissolves readily in nitric acid, especially if heated. Gives a precipitate of lead from the solution on a zinc bar.

Localities. — *English.* Cornwall, Huel

Unity, in thick, light-brown, translucent crystals; North Downs Mine; Huel Gorland; Huel Alfred; Endellion. Beeralston, Devon. Cumberland, Roughten Gill, in wax-yellow crystals; Mexico Mine; Drygill (*Kampylite*); Brandygill; Carrock Fells; Saddleback. Allendale, Grasshill, Teesdale, Durham. Grassington, Yorkshire. —*Foreign.* Johanngeorgenstadt, in Saxony, in fine yellow crystals. St. Prix, Dept. of the Saone, in France, in capillary crystals. Zinnwald, Badenweiler. Nertschinsk, in Siberia.

Name. From μιμητής, *imitator*, from its resemblance to Pyromorphite, with which it also occurs, mixed in all proportions.

For varieties of Mimetite, see HEDYPHANE and KAMPYLITE.

M. P. G. Principal Floor, Wall-case 45, No. 191 (British).

This mineral was worked at Drygill, in Cumberland, as an ore of lead, and was used as an ingredient in the manufacture of flintglass, to which it imparted a peculiar brilliancy. (*Greg & Lettsom.*)

MINE CORNÉ, *Beudant.* See KERARGYRITE.

MINE D'ACIER, *Leymerie.* A name for Siderose, from its fitness for making steel.

MINE D'AMADOU. See TINDER ORE.

MINE D'ETAIN COMMUNE, *Brochant.* See CASSITERITE.

MINE DE CUIVRE COULEUR DE BRIQUE, *Brochant.* See TILE ORE.

MINE DE CUIVRE PANACHÉE OU VIOLETTE, *Brochant* See ERUBESCITE.

MINE DE FER BLANCHE, *von Born.* } See

MINE DE FER SPATHIQUE, *Brochant.* } CHALYBITE.

MINE DE MERCURE CORNÉE, *Brochant.* See CALOMEL.

MINE DE MERCURE HEPATIQUE, *Brochant.* See HEPATIC CINNABAR.

MINE DE PLOMB BLANCHE, *Brochant.* See CERUSITE.

MINE DE PLOMB BRUNE, *Brochant.* See PYROMORPHITE.

MINE DE PLOMB NOIRE. See GRAPHITE.

MINE DES LIEUX BOURBEUX, *Brochant.* Swamp-ore. } See BOG IRON-ORE.

MINE DES MARAIS, *Brochant.* Morass-ore. }

MINE DES PRAIRIES, *Brochant.* Meadowore. See BOG IRON-ORE.

MINERAL ALKALI, *Kirwan.* See NATRON.

MINERAL BLUE. The name given to Azurite when ground. to an impalpable powder. From its liability to turn green it is not of much value as a pigment.

MINERAL CAHOUTCHOU, *Kirwan.* See ELATERITE.

MINERAL CARBON, or CHARCOAL. The name given to the thin fibrous layers of a silky-black colour which occur in the Coalmeasures of this country, at Whitehaven in Cumberland; and at Vogtsberg in Styria, Disko Island, Greenland, and elsewhere. It is nearly pure carbon, and is called by colliers "*mother of coal.*"

MINERAL OIL, *Phillips.* See NAPHTHA, and PETROLEUM.

MINERAL PEA. See PISOPHALT.

MINERAL PITCH, *Jameson, Kirwan.* See ASPHALT and BITUMEN.

MINERAL RESIN. See AMBER.

MINERAL TALLOW. See HATCHETTINE.

MINERAL TAR. A more viscid variety of Mineral Pitch than Petroleum.

MINERAL TURQUOIS, *Jameson.* See TURQUOIS.

MINERAL WAX. See HATCHETTINE.

MINIUM, *Brooke & Miller, Dana.* Red Lead ore. Occurs amorphous and pulverulent, exhibiting a crystalline structure under the microscope. Colour bright red. Lustre feeble. Opaque. Streak orangeyellow. H. 2·5. S.G. 4·6.

Comp. Oxide of lead, or $Pb^3,O^4 = 2\dot{P}b, \ddot{P}b$ =lead 90·7, oxygen 9·3=100.

BB on charcoal it is first converted into litharge and becomes yellow, and then is reduced to metallic lead.

Localities. English.—The Parys Mine in Anglesea. Merionethshire. Snailbeach Mine, Shropshire. Alston, Cumberland. Grassington Moor, Yorkshire; and Weardale, Durham.— *Scotch.* Leadhills, Lanarkshire. — *Irish.* Lugganure, Wicklow co.—*Foreign.* Near Badenweiler, in Baden. Bleialf in the Eifel. Brilon, Westphalia. Austin's Mine, Virginia, U.S.

Brit. Mus., Case 18.

Minium is not a very common ore of lead. It is generally associated with Galena, of the decomposition of which it is probably a result.

MIRABILITE, *Haidinger, Brooke & Miller.* See GLAUBER SALT.

MIROIR D'ANE. See SELENITE.

MIROIR DES INCAS. See PIERRE DES INCAS.

MISENITE, *A. Scacchi.* A hydrous sulphate of alumina, occurring in white silky fibres, in a hot cavern, near Misene in the Campagna. Taste acid and bitter.

Comp. $\ddot{K}\dot{S} + \dot{H}\dot{S}$, or hydrated sulphate of potash.

R

Analysis, by *Scacchi:*

Sulphuric acid	.	.	.	56·93
Potash .	.	.	.	36·57
Alumina	.	.	.	0·38
Water .	.	.	.	6·12

$$100·00$$

MISPICKEL. Rhombic. Occurs crystal-lized in right rhombic prisms, parallel to whose planes it may be cleaved; also massive, acicular, and columnar. Colour tin-white. Lustre metallic. Streak black-ish-grey. Brittle. Fracture uneven. Gives a few sparks with steel, emitting an arseni-cal odour. H. 5·5 to 6. S.G. 6·13.

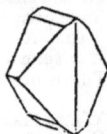

Fig. 291.

Comp. Arsenide with bisulphide of iron, or Fe As + Fe S² = iron 33·54, arsenic 46·58, sulphur 19·88 = 100.
Analysis, by *Stromeyer,* of crystals from Freiberg:

Iron	.	.	.	.	36·04
Arsenic	.	.	.	43·42
Sulphur	.	.	.	21·08

$$100·00$$

BB on charcoal emits strong arsenical fumes, and fuses to a globule which behaves like Magnetic Pyrites.

Dissolves in strong nitric acid or aqua-regia, with separation of sulphur and arseni-ous acid.

Localities. English.—Common in Corn-wall at Botallack, Levant, Cook's Kitchen, Huel Tolgus, Dolcoath, Carn Brea, Huel Vor, Calstock, United, Huel Martha, and other mines. Several mines near Tavistock, Devonshire, in very fine crystals. Brandy Gill, Carrock Fells, and Goldscope Mine, Cumberland.— *Scotch.* Near Loch Ness; Stonehaven, Aberdeenshire. — *Foreign.* Abundant at Freiberg and Munzig in Sax-ony. Andreasberg in the Harz. Joachims-thal in Bohemia. Tunaberg in Sweden. In gneiss at Franconia in New Hampshire, and at Tennessee, U.S.

Mispickel occurs chiefly in lodes in crystalline rocks, associated with Iron and Copper Pyrites, Blende, and ores of silver, lead and tin. It was formerly worked in Cornwall as an ore of arsenic, much of the white arsenic of commerce being obtained from it.

For varieties of Mispickel see DANAITE, and PLINIAN.

Brit. Mus., Case 12.

M. P. G. Principal Floor, Table-case 14; Wall-case 14 (British); 19 (Foreign).

MISY, *Hausmann.* An impure sulphate of peroxide of iron, mixed with other sul-phates, occurring in opaque, pulverulent masses of a sulphur- or lemon-yellow colour.

Comp. $4\ddot{\overline{Fe}}\,\ddot{S} + \ddot{KS} + 9\dot{H}$.
Analysis, by *List:*

Sulphuric acid	.	.	.	42·922
Peroxide of iron	.	.	30·066
Oxide of zinc	.	.	.	2·491
Magnesia	.	.	.	2·812
Potash	.	.	.	0·318
Water	.	.	.	21·391

$$100·000$$

Locality. Rammelsberg Mine, near Gos-lar in the Harz.

Name. Used by the miners.

Brit. Mus., Case 55.

Mysy is a stone or ore described by Pliny to be a kind of Pyrites.

"You shall know it by these signes: breake it (for crumble it will) there appeare within it certain sparkes shining like gold: and in the braying or stamping, it run-neth into Chalcitis. This Mysy is the mi-nerall that they put to gold ore, when it is to be tried and purified. . . The best is that which is found in the mines and forges of Cypresse."—*Pliny,* book xxxiv.

MIZZONITE, *Scacchi.* A variety of Meio-nite, from which it differs principally in not intumescing so much before the blowpipe, and in being acted on by acids in a less de-gree.

Locality. Monte Somma, near Naples.

MOCHA-STONE. MOCHO-STONE, MO-CHOS, *Kirwan.* A white translucent variety of Agate, containing brown markings re-sembling trees and vegetable filaments, occasioned probably by the infiltration of iron or manganese. It is chiefly brought from Arabia, whence the name Mocha-stone. "The variegated stones with landscapes, trees and water, beautifully delineated, are found at Cubberpunj (the five tombs), a place sixty miles distant" from Rajpipla in Guzerat.—*Forbes' Oriental Memoirs,* vol. ii. p. 20.

This stone is also met with in Wicklow.

Name. Perhaps the name Mocha-stone or Mochos-stone is a corruption of *Moschus-*(or *moss-*) stone.

Brit. Mus., Case 23.

M. P. G. Horse-shoe Case, No. 561.

MOCK LEAD. A name formerly given by Cornish miners to Blende.

MODUMITE, *Nicol.* See SKUTTERUDITE.

MOELLE DE PIERRE, *Brochant.* See LITHOMARGE.

MOFFRASITE, *Leymerie.* A kind of Bleineierite, composed of shelly masses forming alternating bands, some of which are coloured brownish-grey, others yellowish-brown. Fracture vitreous, with a somewhat brilliant lustre. H. 5·5, does not scratch glass. S.G. of yellow 4·25, of brown 5·46.

Comp. Antimonite of lead.

BB on charcoal fuses, giving off white fumes and yielding globules of lead.

Dissolves in nitric acid.

Locality. Zamora in Spain, forming a strong vein.

Name. After M. de Moffrah, attaché to the French embassy in Madrid.

MOHSINE. The name given to Leucopyrite by Chapman, in compliment to the late Professor Mohs, Aulic Councillor, of Vienna.

MOHSITE. *Levy.* A Titaniferous Iron from Dauphiné, named after the late Professor Mohs, Aulic Councillor, of Vienna.

Fig. 292.

MOLOCHITES, *Pliny.* See MALACHITE.

MOLYBDÄNGLANZ, *v. Leonhard.* See MOLYBDENITE.

MOLYBDÄNIT, *Haidinger.* See MOLYBDENITE.

MOLYBDÄNOCHER, *Karsten.* See MOLYBDINE.

MOLYBDÄNSILBER, *Mohs.* An argentiferous variety of Tetradymite (Telluric Bismuth) from Deutsch-Pilsen, in Hungary.

Analysis, by *Werhle :*

Tellurium	.	.	.	29·74
Bismuth	.	.	.	61·15
Silver .	.	.	.	2·07
Sulphur	.	.	.	2·33
				95·29

MOLYBDATE OF IRON. Occurs in subfibrous or in tufted crystals of a deep yellow colour; also pulverulent; near Nevada City, California.

MOLYBDATE OF LEAD, *Phillips.* See WULFENITE.

MOLYBDENA, *Jameson, Kirwan.* MOLYBDENA GLANCE. } See MOLYBDENITE.

MOLYBDENA OCHRE, *Nicol.* See MOLYBDINE.

MOLYBDÈNE SULFURÉ, *Brochant, Haüy.* See MOLYBDENITE.

MOLYBDENITE, *Haidinger, Beudant, Nicol.* Hexagonal. Occurs in flat hexagonal tables, with a cleavage parallel with their terminal planes : generally massive with a foliated structure, or in scales. Colour closely resembling that of fresh-cut metallic lead. Lustre metallic. Opaque. Laminæ highly flexible, but not elastic. Streak like colour, inclining to greenish. Leaves a metallic-grey trace on paper, a greenish streak on porcelain. Unctuous to the touch. Yields to the nail. H. 1 to 1·5. S.G. 4·44 to 4·8.

Comp. Bisulphide of Molybdenum, or Mo. S^2 = molybdenum 60, sulphur 40 = 100.

BB on charcoal infusible; gives off sulphurous acid, covering the charcoal with a yellowish-white incrustation. On platinum wire colours the outer flame green.

Dissolves in boiling sulphuric acid with evolution of sulphurous acid, and forms a blue solution.

Localities.—English. Cornwall : Gwinear and Gwennap, in Chlorite; in old heaps at Huel Gorland and Huel Unity; Huel Friendship, Huel Mary, Drakewalls Mine. Cumberland : near the source of the Caldew, in granite; Caldbeck Fell.—*Scotch.* Mount Coryby, at the head of Loch Creran, in Argyleshire. Perthshire. At Tomnadashan, on the S. side of Loch Tay, in abundance, with Copper-Glance and Molybdic Ochre in a dyke of syenite. — *Foreign.* Greenland. Arendal in Norway. Numedahl in Sweden, in hexagonal prisms. Saxony and Bohemia with tin. Silesia in granite. Chessy in France, in syenite. Near Mont Blanc, in grey granite. Haddam, Connecticut; Westmoreland, New Hampshire ; Chester, Pennsylvania, U.S. Peru. Brazil.

Name. From μολύβδαινα, a mass of lead.

Brit. Mus., Case 12.

M. P. G. Principal Floor, Wall-case 13 (British); 20 and 40 (Foreign).

Molybdenite is generally found imbedded in or disseminated through granite, gneiss, zircon-syenite, and other crystalline rocks. It is distinguished from Graphite by higher specific gravity, difference of streak, lustre and fracture, and behaviour before the blowpipe.

R 2

MOLYBDIC OCHRE, *Shepard.* See MOLYBDINE.

MOLYBDINE, *Greg & Lettsom.* Occurs as an incrustation or pulverulent. Colour various shades of yellow, to pale green. Dull. Earthy. Opaque.

Comp. Molybdic acid, or $\overset{...}{Mo}$=oxygen 33·3, molybdena 66·7=100.

BB on charcoal fuses to a slag; with salt of phosphorus affords a green glass.

Dissolves readily in muriatic acid, and the solution is turned blue by metallic iron.

Localities. — *English.* Caldbeck Fells, Cumberland, massive and disseminated on Molybdenite. — *Scotch.* Mount Coryby, Argyleshire. East Tulloch, Perthshire.— *Foreign.* See those of Molybdenite with which it occurs. At Altenberg in Saxony, it is found crystallized in rhombic prisms. (*Breithaupt.*)

Molybdine is only used in laboratories for extracting molybdenum, and for making molybdic acid.

Brit. Mus., Case 39.

MONAZITE, *Breithaupt.* Oblique. Occurs in oblique rhombic prisms, generally small and tabular, or very short, with an imperfect basal cleavage. Colour hyacinth-red, clove-brown, or brownish-yellow. Translucent at the edges. Lustre dull-resinous. Streak white. Brittle. H. 5 to 5·5. S.G. 4·9 to 5·02.

Fig. 293.

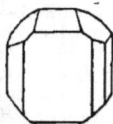

Comp. $(\overset{.}{Ce}, \overset{.}{La}, \overset{.}{Th})^3 \overset{..}{P}$.

Analysis, by *Kersten :*

Sesquioxide of cerium .	. 26 00
Oxide of lanthanum .	. 23·40
Thoria . . .	. 17·95
Protoxide of manganese	. 1·86
Binoxide of tin . .	2·10
Lime	1·68
Phosphoric acid . .	. 28·50
Potash and binoxide of titanium . . .	. traces

101·49

BB infusible, but turns grey, or greenish-yellow.

Dissolves in muriatic acid with evolution of chlorine, leaving a white powder undissolved.

Localities. Near Slatoust in the Ural, in granite, with flesh-red Felspar. Yorktown, Westchester county, New York, with Sillimanite. The gold-sand of Rio Chico in Antioquia. Halle, Norway.

Brit. Mus., Case 57.

Name. From μονάζω, to live alone.

MONAZITOÏDE, *Hermann.* Probably only a variety of Monazite, with which it is identical in crystallization and external characters. Colour brown. H. 5. S.G. 5·281.

MONHEIMITE. A name given to Kapnite, in honour of Von Monheim, by whom it has been analysed. See KAPNITE.

MONOPHANE, *Dufrénoy,* is Epistilbite : it occurs on Quartz in small white crystals, apparently derived from oblique rhombic prisms. Scratches phosphate of lime. S.G. 2·05.

BB fuses.

Locality. Unknown.

MONRADITE, *Erdmann.* Massive, granular; also foliated. Colour yellowish, with a tinge of red. Lustre vitreous. Translucent. H. 6. S.G. 3·267.

Comp. $(\overset{.}{Mg}, \overset{.}{Fe})^5 \overset{..}{Si}^2 + \overset{.}{H}$.

Analysis, by *Erdmann :*

Silica . . .	. 56·17
Magnesia . .	. 31·63
Protoxide of iron	. 8·56
Water . . .	. 4·04

100·40

BB alone infusible : with borax affords an iron reaction.

Locality. Bergen in Norway.

Name. After Mons. Monrad.

MONROLITE, *Silliman.* A variety of Kyanite from Monroe, Orange co., New York.

Analysis, by *Smith & Brush :*

Silica . . .	. 37·20
Alumina . .	. 59·02
Peroxide of iron .	. 2·08
Loss by ignition .	. 1·03

99·33

Brit. Mus., Case 32.

MONTICELLITE, *Brooke.* A variety of Chrysolite found in small imbedded crystals, having the general aspect of Quartz. Colour

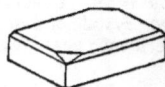

Fig. 294.

yellowish : sometimes colourless and nearly transparent. H. 5 to 6. S.G. 3·245 to 3·275.

Comp. $(\ddot{C}a^3 + \dot{M}g^3)\ \ddot{S}i^2$.

Locality. Vesuvius, imbedded in crystal-line carbonate of lime with black Mica and minute crystals of Pyroxene.

Name. After Monticelli, the Neapolitan mineralogist.

Brit. Mus., Case 25.

MONTMORILLONITE, *Salvetat.* A hydrous silicate of alumina, &c., of a rose-red colour. Fragile.

Analysis, by *Damour :*

Silica	50·04
Alumina . . .	20·16
Peroxide of iron . .	0·68
Lime	1·46
Magnesia . . .	0·23
Potash	1·27
Water	26·00
	99·84

Localities. Confolens in Charente. Near St. Jean de Colle, in Dordogne. Montmo-rillon, Dept. of La Vienne.

MOONSTONE. A transparent or translu-cent variety of Adularia. It contains blu-ish-white spots which, when held to the light, present a pearly or silvery play of colour not unlike that of the moon. It is held in considerable estimation as an orna-mental stone, but is more prized on the continent than in England. When set in rings and brooches surrounded by small rubies and emeralds, it forms an agreeable contrast to the latter. Fine stones are scarce; the most valued are those, which when cut in a very low oval, present the silvery spot in the centre. This (and the other varieties of Felspar) is so soft com-pared with other gems and precious stones, that few lapidaries know how to work it to the greatest advantage. (*Mawe.*) The finest stones are brought from Ceylon.

Brit. Mus., Case 29.

M. P. G. Horse-shoe Case, Nos. 955 to 957.

MOONTONS. A provincial name for Pea-cock coal.

MORASS-ORE, *Jameson.* MORASSY IRON-ORE, *Kirwan.* MORASTERZ, *Werner.* See BOG-IRON-ORE.

MORION. The name given by lapidaries to Rock Crystal of a brownish-black or char-coal-black tint.

Brit. Mus., Case 20.

M. P. G. Horse-shoe Case, No. 480.

MOROXITE. An opaque, greenish-blue variety of Apatite from Arendal in Norway,

and Pargas in Finland. The name is de-rived from μόροξος, an Egyptian stone used in the bleaching of linen.

Brit. Mus., Case 53.

MORVENITE, *Thomson.* A variety of Harmotome occurring in small transparent crystals in mineral veins in granite, near its junction with gneiss, at Strontian in Ar-gyleshire.

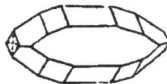

Fig. 295.

Analysis, by *Damour :*

Silica	47·60
Alumina . . .	16·39
Peroxide of iron . .	0·65
Baryta . . .	20·86
Soda	0·74
Potash	0·81
Water	14·16
	101·21

Brit. Mus., Case 29.

MOSANDRITE, *Erdmann.* In large flat prisms, with the lateral edges replaced by planes; also massive and fibrous. Colour dull greenish- or reddish-brown. Lustre resinous; of cleavage-face between vitreous and greasy. Translucent in thin splinters. deep-red by transmitted light. Streak grey-ish-brown. H. 4. S.G. 2·93 to 2·98.

Comp. $\dot{R}^3\ \ddot{S}i + 2\ddot{R}^3\ \ddot{S}i + 4\frac{1}{2}\dot{H}$.

Analysis, by *Berlin :*

Silica	29·93
Titanic acid . . .	9·90
Peroxide of cerium, Peroxide of lanthanum, Peroxide of didymium . . .	26·56
Peroxide of iron, with some Peroxide of manganese .	1·83
Magnesia	0·75
Lime	19·07
Potash	0·52
Soda	2·87
Water	8·90
	100·33

Locality. Brevig in Norway, with Albite and violet Fluor.

Name. After the Swedish chemist, Mo-sander.

Brit. Mus., Case 37.

MOSS AGATE. A variety of Chalcedony inclosing dendritic or moss-like markings of various shades, and occasionally traversed by irregular veins of red Jasper.

R 3

Brit. Mus., Case 23.

M. P. G. Horse-shoe Case, Nos. 658, 659.

MOSSOTTITE, *Luca.* A variety of Aragonite, occurring as prismatic fibrous radiated aggregations, of a pale green colour. S.G. 2·884.

Analysis :

Lime .	.	.	.	50·08
Strontia	.	.	.	4·69
Carbonic acid	.	.	41·43
Oxide of copper	.	.	0·95
Peroxide of iron	.	.	0·82
Fluorine	.	.	.	trace
Water .	.	.	.	1·36
				99·33

Localities. Gerfalco in Tuscany, in Lias: also in the province of Messina.

MOUNTAIN BLUE. Pulverized Blue Copper Ore. See AZURITE.

MOUNTAIN CORK. Asbestos in which the fibres are interlaced so intimately, as not to be perceptible, or capable of separation. Sectile. Somewhat elastic. So light, as to float on water. Opaque. Feels meagre, and resembles cork in feel and texture.

Localities. Norway, Saxony, Spain, &c.

MOUNTAIN CRYSTAL, *Jameson.* Rock Crystal (which see).

MOUNTAIN GREEN, *Kirwan.* See CHRYSOCOLLA.

MOUNTAIN LEATHER. A variety of Asbestos, from which it principally differs in the fibres of which it is composed being interlaced like those of felt, instead of being even and parallel. It occurs in flexible flat pieces, much resembling leather in appearance, of a whitish or yellowish-white colour, and is meagre to the touch.

Localities. Near the Lizard Point, Cornwall. Strontian, Argyleshire. Aghanloo and Slieve Gallion, Londonderry. Coagh and Curley Hill, Tyrone. (See MOUNTAIN PAPER.)

M. P. G. Horse-shoe Case, No. 1143.

MOUNTAIN MEAL, or BERGMEHL. An earthy mineral composed of silica 79, alumina 5, oxide of iron 3, water 12. (*Klaproth.*) It occurs at Santa Fiora, between Tuscany and the Papal States, and has been made into bricks, which are so light as to float in water.

MOUNTAIN PAPER. The name given to Mountain Leather, when in very thin laminæ.

M. P. G. Horse-shoe Case, No. 1143. Upper gallery, Wall case 41, No. 138a, from Seaton, Devon.

MOUNTAIN TALLOW. See HATCHETTINE.

MOUNTAIN TAR, *Hatchett.* See PETROLEUM.

MOUNTAIN WOOD. A harder variety of Asbestos than Mountain Leather or Mountain Cork, somewhat resembling wood in appearance. The fibres of which it is composed are slightly curved, and easily separated: they are not elastic. S.G. about 2.

Localities. — Scotch. Auchindoir, Aberdeenshire, in Serpentine. Portsoy, Banffshire. Glen Tilt, Perthshire. — *Foreign.* Schneeberg, near Sterzing in the Tyrol. Dauphiné. Styria. Maryland, U.S.

Brit. Mus., Case 34.

MUCKS. See SMUT.

MÜLLER'S GLASS. See HYALITE.

MÜLLERINE, *Beudant.* MÜLLERITE, *Haidinger.* Yellow Tellurium. See SYLVANITE.

Name. After Müller, the German chemist, discoverer of Tellurium.

MULLICITE, *Thomson.* A variety of Vivianite (phosphate of iron), occurring in cylindrical masses consisting of divergent fibres or acicular crystals, at Mullica* Hill, and Franklin, New Jersey.

Analysis, by *Thomson :*

Protoxide of iron .	.	.	42·65
Phosphoric acid .	.	.	24·00
Water .	.	.	.	25·00
Sand .	.	.	.	7·90
				99·55

Brit. Mus., Case 57.

MUNDIC. (? From *mun,* Celtic, for any fusible metal.) The name given by Cornish miners to Iron Pyrites.

MURCHISONITE, *Levy.* A yellowish-grey and flesh-red variety of Felspar, found in Arran, and in rolled pebbles at Dawlish and at Heavitree, near Exeter.

Analysis, from Dawlish, by *R. Phillips :*

Silica .	.	.	.	68·6
Alumina	.	.	.	16·6
Potash .	.	.	.	14·8
				100·0

Name. After Sir Roderick I. Murchison, the author of the "Silurian System."

Brit. Mus., Case 30.

MURIA FOSSILIS PURA, *Wallerius.* See COMMON SALT.

MURIACITE, or MURIAZIT, *Werner.* Anhydrite when in broad lamellar crystals.

Brit. Mus., Case 54.

MURIATE OF AMMONIA, *Phillips.* See SAL AMMONIAC.

MURIATE OF COPPER, *Phillips.* See ATACAMITE.

* Whence the name.

MURIATE OF LEAD, *Phillips*. See MEN-DIPITE.

MURIATE OF MERCURY, *Phillips*. See CALOMEL.

MURIATE OF POTASH. See SYLVINE.

MURIATE OF SILVER, *Phillips*. See KERARGYRITE.

MURIATE OF SODA, *Phillips*. See COMMON SALT.

MURIATED ANTIMONY, *Kirwan*. See VALENTINITE.

MURIATIC ACID. Is emitted in a gaseous form from the craters of active volcanoes, and is sometimes found in solution in crevices about their slopes.

MURIO-CARBONATE OF LEAD, *Phillips.* See CROMFORDITE.

MUROMONTITE, *Kerndt*. Probably a variety of Allanite, found in grains rarely exceeding half a pea in size. Colour black; slightly greenish by reflected light. Colour of powder greyish-white, with a tinge of grey. Lustre vitreous. H. nearly 9. S.G. 4·26.

Comp. $3\dot{R}\,\ddot{S}i+(\ddot{A}l\,\dddot{B}e)\,\ddot{S}i.$

Analysis, by *Kerndt*:

Silica	31·09
Alumina . . .	2·24
Glucina . . .	5·52
Yttria	37·14
Protoxide of cerium .	5·54
Protoxide of lanthanum .	3·54
Protoxide of iron . .	11·23
Magnesia . . .	0·42
Protoxide of manganese .	0·91
Lime	0·71
Soda	0·65
Potash	0·17
Water and loss . .	0·85
	100·00

BB glows like Gadolinite: fusible only at the edges after long heating.

Locality. Mauersberg and Boden, near Marienberg, in the Saxon Erzgebirge.

MURRHINA of the ancients, was probably a kind of Agate.

MUSCOVITE, *Dana*. MUSCOVY GLASS, *Woodward.* Rhombic. Chiefly occurs in rhombic or hexagonal tables, with a perfect basal cleavage; also in scales and scaly-massive. Colourless, or grey, pale green, and olive-green, red, brown, black and yellow. Lustre pearly. Transparent to translucent. Sectile : flexible and elastic in thin laminæ. Streak white to grey. Biaxial. Colours in direction of the axis and dia-

meter frequently different. Very tough. H. 2 to 2·5. S.G. 2·75 to 3·1.

Fig. 296. Fig. 297. Fig. 298.

Comp. $(\dot{R}^2\,\dddot{R}^3)\,\ddot{S}i$ or $3\ddot{A}l\,\ddot{S}i+\dot{K}\,\ddot{S}i.$

Analysis, from Utö, by *H. Rose:*

Silica	47·50
Alumina	37·30
Peroxide of iron . . .	3·20
Peroxide of manganese .	0·90
Potash	9·60
Hydrofluoric acid . .	0·56
Water	2·63
	101·59

BB fuses with difficulty to a greyish-yellow blebby glass.

Not decomposed by muriatic or sulphuric acid.

Localities.—English. Cornwall, St. Dennis. Saddleback and Brandygill, Cumberland.—*Scotch.* Rubislaw and Auchindoir, Aberdeenshire; of a pinkish-brown colour, in granite. Portsoy, Banffshire, plumose. In dark-brown hexagonal plates at Coiré Bhradan, Buteshire. — *Irish.* Killiney, Dublin, in fine plates in granite. Plumose at Three Rock Mountain. In perfect crystals in the granite of the Mourne Mountains, co. Down, *figs.* 296—298. — *Foreign.* Finbo, Sweden. Skutterud in Norway. Siberia. New Hampshire, U.S., in transparent plates. Crystallized at Vesuvius, St. Gotthard, Pargas, Arendal, Utö, Fahlun, &c. Schwartzenstein in the Tyrol. (See FUCHSITE.)

Brit. Mus., Case 32.

Muscovite is abundant in granite, of which it forms one of the constituents; also, in gneiss, syenite, mica-slate, and other rocks. In Siberia, and at Ackworth, Grafton, and Alstead in New Hampshire, U.S., it is met with in perfectly transparent plates, sometimes more than a yard across. The name Muscovy glass originated in the use of these plates in Russia for lanthorns and windows instead of glass. It has also been adopted in the Russian navy as a substitute for window-glass, in consequence of its not being liable to be broken by the concussion caused by the firing of heavy guns. It is likewise used as a substitute for window-glass in Siberia, Peru, Pennsylvania, &c. Advantage has been taken of its transpar-

R 4

ency and ability to withstand the effects of fire, to form the fronts of stoves with plates of Mica, by which means the peculiar advantage of the stove is in some degree combined with the cheerful appearance of an open fire.

Muscovite was used by the ancients for protecting plants against the cold; and in this way, it is stated by Columella, the table of Tiberius was supplied with cucumbers almost all the year round.

MÜSENITE. A name for Siegenite, given from the locality Müsen, where it occurs.

MUSHET STONE. See BLACK-BAND.

MUSSITE. A greyish-green variety of Diopside from the Mussa Alpe in Piedmont. Brit. Mus., Case 34.

MUSSONITE, *Dufrénoy.* A name for Parisite, after its locality, the Musso Valley.

MYELIN, *Breithaupt.* A variety of Kaolin of a yellowish or reddish colour, from Rochlitz in Saxony.

Analysis, by *Kersten:*

Silica	37·62
Alumina . . .	60·50
Magnesia . . .	0·82
Peroxide of manganese	0·63
Peroxide of iron . .	trace

99·57

MYSORINE, *Beudant.* Massive, with a pulverulent texture. Colour brownish-black, when pure, but generally tinged with green and red, from admixture with Malachite and oxide of iron. Fracture small-conchoidal. Soft. S.G. 2·62.

Comp. Anhydrous carbonate of copper.

Analysis, by *Thomson:*

Oxide of copper . .	60·75
Carbonic acid . . .	16·70
Peroxide of iron (mechanically mixed) . .	19·50
Silica	2·10

99·05

Locality. Mysore, in Hindostan, forming beds in the older rocks.

N.

NACRITE, *Thomson.* Consists of minute grains or scales, of a silvery-white or greenish colour, with a glimmering pearly lustre. Friable and unctuous to the touch, like a soft earthy Talc. Adheres to the fingers. Gives an argillaceous odour when breathed on. H. 0·5. S.G. 2·788.

Comp. Anhydrous silicate of alumina.

Analysis, from Brunswick, U. S., by *Thomson:*

Silica	64·44
Alumina . . .	28·84
Protoxide of iron .	4·43
Water	1 00

98·71

BB infusible.

Localities. Piedmont. Freyberg, in Saxony. Near Meronitz, in Bohemia.

Name. Sp. *nacar;* It. *nuxhera;* Fr. *nacre;* mother o' pearl.

See also TALCITE.

NADELEISENERZ, *Naumann.* See GÖTHITE.

NADELERZ, *Werner.* Acicular Bismuth. See AIKENITE.

NADELSTEIN, *Werner.* See SCOLECITE.

NAGYAGERERZ, *Werner.* NAGYAGITE, *Haidinger.* Pyramidal: primary form a right square prism. Occurs in small six-sided tables, with a basal cleavage; also massive-granular, but generally foliated. Colour and streak dark lead-grey. Lustre

Fig. 299.

metallic. Opaque. Soft and sectile. In thin laminæ highly flexible. H. 1 to 1·5. S.G. 6·68.

Comp. Telluride of lead and gold?

Analysis, by *Klaproth:*

Lead	54·0
Tellurium . . .	32·2
Gold	9·0
Copper . . .	1·3
Silver	0·5
Sulphur . . .	3·0

100·0

BB fuses very readily, emitting a dense vapour, colouring the flame blue, and depositing a yellow film on the charcoal, and yields a globule of gold, with a little silver.

Dissolves in nitric acid, leaving a residue of sulphur.

Localities. Nagyag and Offenbanya, in Transylvania, in foliated masses and crystalline plates.

Brit. Mus., Case 3.

NAIL-HEADED COPPER-ORE. The name given in Cornwall to certain crystals of Chalcosine, from their fanciful resemblance to the heads of nails. This resemblance is more striking when they form the termination to prismatic crystals, as is sometimes the case. This form of crystal has been found at Huel Abraham, Cook's Kitchen, St. Ives Consols, and at several of the Redruth and Camborne mines.

Fig. 300.

NAPHTHA, *Phillips, Beudant.* Νάφθα, *Dioscorides.* NAPHTE, *Beudant.* A fluid variety of Bitumen. Liquid and colourless when pure, but by exposure to the air becomes thick and solid. Smell bituminous and aromatic. Burns with a bituminous smell, and a white flame and much smoke, leaving no residue. Soluble in alcohol. Boils at a heat below 173° F. S.G. 0·7 to 0·84.

Comp. C^6, $H^5 = $ carbon 86·58, hydrogen 13·42 = 100.

Localities. — British. A mineral oil is found in the lower part of the Upper Lias of Whitby, in Yorkshire, in a stratum full of nodules of Lias limestone, which generally contain Ammonites. When first found it is a green liquid, which hardens into a kind of pitch on exposure to the air.— *Foreign.* Baku and Scamachia, on the western shore of the Caspian, especially in the peninsula of Abcheron, where it is collected by sinking pits several yards in depth. Near Amiano, in the Duchy of Parma. Tegern Lake, in Bavaria. Salies, in the Pyrenees. Rangoon. China. Persia. Little Kanawha, Virginia; Sewickly, Westmoreland co., Pennsylvania; Mahoning Valley, Ohio; Bourbon county, Kentucky; Parkersburg, Wood co. &c.; U.S. South America.

The Naphtha and Petroleum springs of Persia, India, Italy, and South America are considered by Reichenbach to have their origin in the slow distillation of large beds of coal by the ordinary heat of the earth. Brit. Mus., Case 60.

Springs of naphtha rise from nummulitic limestone, in the citadel on the summit of the rock of Vàn, in Armenia.

In Mesopotamia, and in the Persian Zágros, they rise from the gypsum deposits.

The most copious are in the Bákhtigáré Mountains, between the ancient temple called Mesjid í Súleïmán and the mountains Asmárí. They are situated in a wild and barren region of much contorted and highly elevated ridges of sandstones, marls, and gypsum. A small stream of cold water rises high up a narrow ravine, and is increased as it descends by streamlets from a multitude of sources, most of which furnish a supply of liquid black Bitumen and white Naphtha mixed together, some of them very abundantly. One spring yields yellow Naphtha only. The oily substances float on the surface of the stream, and are conveyed to an artificial dam. When the dam is nearly full, the water is drawn off at the bottom, and the bituminous mixture is left exposed to the heat of the sun, until reduced to the consistency of soft mud. It is then placed in a large cauldron, covered over, and submitted to a slight heat by keeping fire on the lid. After a gentle simmering for a short time, the fire is removed, and the substance when cold is Bitumen prepared for use.

About 12,000 lbs. of liquid Naphtha and prepared Bitumen are collected annually from these wells by the Seijids (or descendants of Mahomet), at Shuster, who enjoy the sole right and privilege of making Bitumen here. (*W. K. Loftus.*)

Naphtha is also obtained from the Pitch lake of Trinidad. It occurs associated and diluted with water, but, when concentrated, appears as a dense black fluid, with a powerful bituminous odour. If collected in an open vessel, the more volatile part evaporates after a few months, leaving a solid black substance, of similar appearance and analogous properties to Asphaltum Glance (which see).

The Trinidad Naphtha differs from the asphaltic oil of Ava and Pegu by not yielding paraffine. It furnishes, however, lamp and lubricating oils, the former of which is extensively used in the colony, and gives a rather intense light, combined with great economy of the fluid.

The lubricating oil is exported to the United States.

The Trinidad Naphtha, after it has been concentrated by evaporating the water which is always contained in it (by which process 32·12 per cent. of water is removed, and the specific gravity is raised from 1·298 to 1·439), is sent to France, under the name of "boiled pitch," and is used there chiefly in the formation of asphaltic pavements and as a mastic. In Trinidad it is used principally for flooring and paving, but only to a small extent. (*G. P. Wall.*)

NASTURAN, *v. Kobell.* See PITCHBLENDE.

NATIVE ALLOY. A name sometimes given to Iridosmine.

NATIVE ALUM. See POTASH ALUM.

NATIVE AMALGAM, *Phillips.* Cubical : primary form a rhombic dodecahedron. Also occurs massive, and in a semi-fluid state. Colour and streak silver-white. Lustre metallic. Opaque. Slightly brittle. Fracture flat-conchoidal. Gives a grating sound when cut with a knife. H. 3 to 3·5. S.G. 10·0 to 14 l.

Comp. Hg², Ag = quicksilver 64 93, silver 35·07 = 100 ; and Hg⁵, Ag = quicksilver 73·53, silver 26·47 = 100. ·

BB the quicksilver volatilizes, and a bead of silver is left.

Soluble in nitric acid.

Amalgam occasionally forms very perfect crystals, with numerous modifications of the rhombic dodecahedron, at Moschellandsberg, in Deux Ponts; also at Rosenau, in Hungary; Almaden, in Spain; Chili, &c. It is usually accompanied by Quicksilver and Cinnabar in ferruginous and argillaceous veins, and is said to occur at the intersection of veins of mercury and silver.

It may be distinguished from Native Silver by imparting a silvery lustre when rubbed warm upon it, and by colour, fracture, tenacity, specific gravity, and sound.

Name. From μαλάγμα (from μαλάσσω, *to soften*).

Brit. Mus., Case 2.

M. P. G. Principal Floor, Wall-case 23.

NATIVE ANTIMONY. Hexagonal: generally occurs reniform and amorphous, with a granular texture, and lamellar. Colour and streak tin-white, but acquires a yellow tarnish on exposure. Lustre splendent-metallic. Yields to the knife. Somewhat sectile. Rather brittle. H. 3 to 3·5. S.G. 6·6 to 6·72.

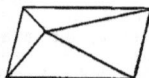

Fig. 301.

Comp. Antimony, sometimes with arsenic, iron, or silver.

Analysis, by *Klaproth* :

Antimony	98 00
Silver	1·00
Iron	0·25
	99·25

BB fuses readily, and continues to burn though the heat be removed; by continuing the heat, may be entirely volatilized in the form of a grey vapour; but if the fused mass be allowed to cool slowly, it becomes covered with brilliant white acicular crystals of oxide of antimony.

Localities. Sahlberg, in Sweden, in Calc Spar. Andreasberg, in the Harz. Allemont, in Dauphiné, in gneiss. Przibram, in Bohemia. Mexico.

Native Antimony may be distinguished from Antimonial Silver, with which it is frequently associated, by its behaviour before the blow-pipe.

Name. The name is derived, according to Furetieve, from *anti, against,* and *moine, monk,* from the circumstance of certain monks having been poisoned by it; Morin says it is from αντὶ, and μόνος, *alone,* because it is not found alone, but associated with ores of other metals.

Brit. Mus., Case 3.

NATIVE ARSENIC. The most common form is that· of reniform and stalactitic masses, often mammillated, and splitting off in thin successive layers like those of a shell. It possesses a somewhat metallic lustre, and a tin-white colour and streak, which soon tarnish to dark grey. Fracture uneven, and finely granular. Yields to the knife. Easily frangible. H. 3·5. S.G. 5·93.

Comp. Arsenic, often with antimony, and traces of gold, silver, iron, bismuth, or cobalt.

BB fuses readily, burns with a pale bluish flame, and dense white alliaceous fumes; and, when pure, is entirely volatilized.

Localities.— English. Dolcoath, and most tin mines in Cornwall. — *Foreign.* In the silver mines of Freiberg, in Saxony. The Harz. Bohemia. Transylvania. Norway. In large masses at Zimeoff, in Siberia. Alsace, at the Ste Marie-aux-Mines. Haverhill and Jackson, New Hampshire, U. S.

Name. From ἀρσενικόν, *musculine,* on account of its powerful properties.

Brit. Mus., Case 4.

This ore is one of the sources of the arsenic of commerce, but, owing to its scarcity, only to a small amount.

The principal sources of the arsenic used in the arts are arsenical ores of cobalt, iron, and nickel. (See ORPIMENT and REALGAR.)

NATIVE BISMUTH. Hexagonal: with a perfect basal cleavage. Occurs in rhombohedrons nearly approaching to a cube; also plumose, reticulated, foliated and granular. Colour whitish, with a faint reddish tinge ;

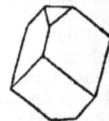

Fig. 302.

generally with an iridescent tarnish, especially in those varieties which contain cobalt. Lustre metallic. Opaque. Soft. Sectile. Brittle when cold; but somewhat malleable when heated. Fuses at 476° F. Crystallizes on slow cooling, after fusion, in rhombohedrons. See *M.P.G.* Principal Floor, Case 14. H. 2 to 2·5. S.G. 9·727.

Comp. Pure bismuth, frequently·with a slight admixture of arsenic.

B B fuses readily, and volatilizes in white fumes, which form a yellow coating on the charcoal. Crystallizes on slow cooling, after fusion, in rhombohedrons.

Dissolves in nitric acid, forming a solution which yields a white precipitate on being diluted.

Localities. — English. In Cornwall at Botallack; formerly at Huel Sparnon (*fig.* 302) with Smaltine and Erythrine; Trugoe Mine, St. Colomb; Consolidated Mines, St. Ives, lamellar. Caldbeck Fells, Cumberland. —*Foreign.* Modum in Norway. Fahlun in Sweden. Johanngeorgenstadt and Schneeberg in Saxony. Joachimsthal in Bohemia. Transylvania. Hanau. Brittany. Valley of Ossau (Busses-Pyrenees). Bolivia, on the sides of the mountain Illampu, in large masses, occasionally faced or incrusted on the sides with metallic gold sometimes in crystals. (*David Forbes.*)

Brit. Mus., Case 1.

M. P. G. Principal Floor, Wall-case 9. (British).

Native Bismuth, the only ore from which the metal is obtained in any quantity, occurs in veins in gneiss and clay-slate, and is usually accompanied by various ores of cobalt, lead, silver and zinc. Bismuth, in combination with other metals, forms a useful alloy, and is used in the manufacture of printers' type, pewter, solder, &c. It is also employed as an ingredient in a pomatum used for imparting a dark colour to the hair, and in the form of the oxide as a cosmetic under the name of *blanc de fard.* The reticulated varieties are distinguished from Native Silver by their colour and inferior maleability.

NATIVE BORACIC ACID, *Phillips.* See SASSOLIN.

NATIVE COPPER. Cubical. Occurs crystallized in numerous and often compound

Fig. 303.

forms: also capillary, dendritic, and in thin films filling crevices; generally massive.

Colour copper-red. Lustre metallic. Streak metallic-shining. Ductile and malleable. Tough. Fracture hackly. H. 2·5 to 3. S.G. 8·94.

Comp. Pure copper or Cu.

B B fuses readily to a globule of apparently pure copper, which on cooling is covered with a coating of black oxide.

Dissolves in nitric acid: forms a blue solution in ammonia.

Localities. Cornwall: in octahedrons at Carn Brea Mines; Huel Gorland in cubes and octahedrons; Relistian Mine; United Mines; Huel Buller; Ramose and mossy at Huel Cock, Tolcarne, and Botallack. Great Devon Consols, near Tavistock in Devonshire. Anglesea, in Serpentine.—*Scotch.* In trap near Stirling. The Shetlands. Mauchline, Ayrshire. Neilston, Renfrew.— *Irish.* Cronebane, and Tigroney, in Wicklow, crystallized and massive; also at Ballymurtagh. Knockmahon, in Waterford, crystallized and arborescent.—*Foreign.* Siberia, and the island of Nalsoe in Faröe, accompanying fibrous Mesotype in amygdaloid. Moldawa in the Banat. Chessy in France. Herrengrund in Hungary. Brazil. Chili, containing sometimes 7 to 8 per cent. of silver. Peru. New Jersey. Brunswick; Somerville; Schuyler's mines; and Flemington; &c. U.S.

Brit. Mus., Case 1.

M. P. G. Large mass in Hall from Trenance Mine, Cornwall.

Principal Floor, Wall-cases 1 and 26, No. 92 (British); 23 (Foreign); 40 (Jamaica); 42 on floor (Newfoundland).

The largest known supplies of Native Copper are those on the coast of Lake Superior in North America, near Keweenaw Point, where it occurs in veins near the junction of trap and sandstone, and disseminated in amygdaloid. "A large mass was thrown down July 8th, 1853, at the North American Mine; it was about 40 feet long, and its estimated weight was 200 tons. This copper contains intimately mixed with it about $\frac{3}{10}$ per cent. of silver; often this metal is in visible grains, lumps, or strings, and occasionally a mass of copper, when polished, appears sprinkled with large silver spots, resembling, as Dr. Jackson observes, a porphyry with its felspar crystals."—*Dana's Mineralogy*, p. 17.

Metallic copper occurs at the mines of Corocoro in Bolivia, both as small grains irregularly disseminated in beds of red sandstone, and also in nodules, irregular lumps, and plates or sheets interposed between the beds of sandstone, occasionally assuming crystalline and beautiful dendritic forms. These mines have been worked by the Indians from time immemorial, and were found in operation at the period of the Spanish conquest. Since then, up to the present date, they have gradually increased in importance. (*David Forbes.*)

Analysis of pseudomorphous crystals of Native Copper from the Veta Umacoia (main seam), in the Socabon de la Paz in Bolivia, by *M. Kroeber*:

Copper	. . .	98·605
Silica .	. . .	0·015
Silver .	. .	trace
Iron (as lost)	. . .	1·376
Metallic matter (insoluble in nitric acid)	. .	0·004
		100·000

NATIVE GLASS OF LEAD, *Kirwan.* Massive White-lead ore.

NATIVE GOLD. See GOLD.

NATIVE HYDRATE OF MAGNESIA. See BRUCITE.

NATIVE IRIDIUM. See IRIDOSMINE and PLATINIRIDIUM.

NATIVE IRON. Cubical: cleavage octahedral. Colour steel-grey. Lustre metallic. Opaque. Streak shining. Ductile and malleable. Fracture hackly. Acts strongly on the magnetic needle. H. 4·5. S·G. 7·8 to 7·8.

BB fuses with great difficulty.

Readily soluble in muriatic acid.

Localities.—Irish. In minute particles in the green basalt of Slieve Mish and in most of the basaltic rocks of Antrim.—*Foreign.* The mountain of Gravenoire in Auvergne, in lava. Thuringia, in the argillaceous Keuper Sandstone of Müllhausen. Hachenburg.

Brit. Mus., Case 1.

M.P.G. Principal Floor, Wall-case 18 (Siberia).

The iron found in the Pläner of Chotzen in Bohemia in driving a railway tunnel through a hill 120 feet below the surface, is considered by Naumann to be a Meteoric Iron which had fallen to the surface during the cretaceous period, and to be in every way similar to iron which has frequently fallen in modern times.

Pure Native Iron exists abundantly in the country back from the central part of the colony of Siberia. Early travellers state that the natives of Africa find iron *ore* so pure, that they heat and hammer it into form.

The *analysis* of Dr. Hayes shows the composition of this iron to be:

Pure iron	98·40
Quartz, magnetic oxide of iron and silicate of lime .	1·60
	100·00

Native Iron may be distinguished from manufactured iron by not containing carbon; and it is stated by Dr. Hayes and Professor Rogers, that the presence of carbon in iron is the best test of its having been artificially brought to the metallic state. See METEORIC IRON.

NATIVE LEAD. Cubical. Occurs in small globules. Colour lead-grey. Lustre metallic. Malleable and ductile. H. 1·5. S.G. 11·445.

Comp. Pure lead, or Pb.

BB fuses readily, covering the charcoal with a yellow oxide.

Localities. Madeira in lava. The mines near Carthagena in Spain. Guanaxuato in Mexico.

Brit. Mus., Case 1.

NATIVE MAGNESIA, *Bruce.* See BRUCITE.

NATIVE MAGNET. See LODESTONE and MAGNETITE.

NATIVE MERCURY, *Phillips.* See NATIVE QUICKSILVER.

NATIVE MINIUM, *Phillips.* See MINIUM.

NATIVE MURIATE OF IRON, *Jameson.* See PYROSMALITE.

NATIVE PALLADIUM. Cubical; primary form the octahedron. Occurs in grains, sometimes composed of diverging fibres. Colour steel-grey. Lustre metallic. Opaque. Ductile; very malleable. H. 4·5 to 5. S.G. 11·5 to 12·14. (*Lowry.*)

Comp. Palladium or Pd, alloyed with a little platinum and iridium.

BB alone infusible, but on the addition of sulphur fuses readily.

Forms a red solution in nitric acid.

Localities. With platinum ore in Brazil. Tilkerode, with gold and selenide of lead. Peru, forming $\frac{1}{200}$ in the platinum ore. Zacotinga and Condonga in Brazil in auriferous sand. Porpez in South America, with a large quantity of gold and a small quantity of silver in the ore called *Oro pudre.* The Ural.

Name. After the planet Pallas.

Brit. Mus., Case 2.

NATIVE PLATINUM. Cubical. Usually occurs in grains or irregular masses. Colour and streak pale steel-grey. Lustre metallic. Opaque. Ductile and malleable. Fracture hackly. H. 4 to 4·5. S.G. 16 to 19.

Comp. Platinum or Pt, with iron, iridium, rhodium and other metals.

Analysis, from the Pinto, by *Svanberg* :

Platinum	84·34
Palladium	1·66
Rhodium	3·33
Iridium	2·58
Osmium	0·19
Iron	7·52
Manganese	0·31
Osmium-iridium	1·56
Copper	trace
	101·29

BB infusible.

Soluble in heated nitro-muriatic acid only.

Localities. Irish. — The auriferous sands of some of the rivers in Wicklow.—*Foreign.* New Granada : in the province of Choco, at the *lavaderos*, or gold washings of Barbaços and in the weathered syenite near Sta. Rosa de Osos, in the province of Antioquia, in Colombia. In the provinces of Mato Grosso and Minas Geraes, in Brazil. Hayti. Borneo. The north of Ava. The gold-sand of the Rhine. Confolens, Aloué, Epénéde, Planveille, and Melle, in the Depts. Charente and Deux-Sèvres, in France. In silver-ore from Guadalcanal in Spain. Rutherford county, North Carolina. St. François Beauce, Canada East. California. Oregon. Australia. In drift or alluvium at Nijne Taguilsk, and Goroblagodat in the Ural.

Name. From *platina*, the Spanish diminutive for *plata* (silver).

Brit. Mus., Case 2.

M. P. G. Principal Floor, Wall-case 23.

Platinum is a useful metal on account of its hardness, infusibility, and the resistance which it offers to the action of air and moisture. It has been coined in Russia into pieces of eleven and twenty-two roubles each. Its principal use, however, is as a material for chemical vessels and crucibles, for which it possesses the advantages over other metals of withstanding oxidation at a red heat, of not being attacked by sulphur or mercury, and of not dissolving in any simple acid. It is the most ductile of the metals after gold and silver, and may be drawn out into wire $\frac{1}{1940}$ of an inch in diameter; and if enclosed within a silver wire it may be reduced to $\frac{1}{5000}$ and even to $\frac{1}{20000}$ of an inch in diameter. It may also be beaten out into very thin laminæ, like gold-leaf. It exceeds all metals in tenacity, except iron and copper. It may be welded at a white heat.

Platinum is also used for covering other metals, for painting on porcelain, &c.

NATIVE PRUSSIAN BLUE, or Blue Iron Earth. A variety of Vivianite.

NATIVE QUICKSILVER. Cubical. Occurs in small globules disseminated through its matrix. Colour silver-white. Lustre metallic. Opaque. Fluid. Freezes at —39·44°. Boils at 662° F. S.G. 13·568.

Comp. Pure Mercury or Hg ; sometimes with a little silver.

BB volatilizes entirely.

Readily dissolves in nitric acid.

Localities. Chiefly at Almaden in Spain, aud Idria in Carniola. Wölfstein and Mörsfield in the Palatinate. Carinthia. Hungary. France ; at Allemont in Dauphiné, and Peyrat le Chateau, Dept. of the Haute Vienne. Peru. California.

Brit. Mus., Case 2.

M. P. G. Principal Floor, Wall-case 23.

Cinnabar is a rare mineral, and most of the quicksilver of commerce is obtained from it. Quicksilver is used for a great variety of purposes, in the process of daguerreotyping, in pharmaceutical and chemical preparations, in the manufacture of fulminating powder for percussion caps, for thermometers and barometers, for silvering mirrors, in the amalgamation of gold and silver ores, &c. &c.

Name. The name Quicksilver, or *live silver* (Argentum vivum), has reference to its extreme mobility, and its resemblance in colour to silver.

NATIVE RED IRON VITRIOL OF FAHLUN, *Haidinger.* See BOTRYOGENE.

NATIVE SELENIUM has been observed by Del Rio, at Culebras, in Mexico, forming greyish- or brownish - black incrustations, which are translucent, and appear red, in thin splinters, by transmitted light. H. 2. S.G. 4·3.

According to Mons. Raphael Napoli, Professor of Chemistry at Naples, pure Selenium is deposited in the cavities and crevices of the lava of Vesuvius, as well as in the interior of the solidified mass.

NATIVE SILVER. Cubical. Occurs crystallized in cubes and octahedrons. Cleavage none ; also capillary, ramose, reticulated, in plates and superficial coatings, and massive. Colour and streak silver-white, but generally tarnished yellowish-brown or greyish-black. Lustre metallic. Opaque. Flexible. Ductile. Malleable. Fracture fine-hackly. H. 2·5 to 3. S.G. 10·0 to 11·1.

Comp. Silver, or Ag, with copper, gold, platinum, &c.

BB fuses, and crystallizes on cooling.

Soluble in nitric acid, and redeposited by copper.

Localities.— English. Cornwall: at Mount Mine, Dolcoath, and North Dolcoath, Fowey Consols, West Huel Darlington, Willsworthy Mine, with Arsenical Cobalt and Copper Pyrites; Huel Golden, in thick contorted threads; Huel Tremayne; Huel Brothers and other mines near Callington.— *Irish.* Ballycorus Mines, co. Dublin.— *Foreign.* In splendid crystals and large masses at the mines of Kongsberg, in Norway. Saxony, chiefly at Freiberg, Schneeberg, and Johanngeorgenstadt. Bohemia, principally at Przibram, Joachimsthal, and Ratiborzitz. Schemnitz, in Hungary. Transylvania. Silesia. Deux Ponts. Andreasberg, in the Harz. Alsace. Dauphiné. Kolywan and Nertschinsk, in Siberia. Java. Mexico. Peru. Chili. North America.

Brit. Mus., Case 2.

M. P. G. Principal Floor, Wall-cases 14 (British); 22 (Foreign).

Native Silver generally occurs in veins of Calcareous Spar or Quartz, traversing gneiss, slate, and others of the older rocks.

It is distinguished from Antimonial Silver and Native Antimony by its hackly fracture and malleability, the latter having a foliated fracture and being brittle.

The metal silver is the whitest of all the metals. It is harder than gold, but softer than copper, is elastic, gives a clear ringing sound, is very malleable and ductile, may be hammered into leaves 0·00001 of an inch in thickness, and one grain of silver may be drawn out into a wire 400 feet long. It admits of being welded.

Silver is used for a variety of useful and ornamental purposes. Its hardness renders it a useful medium of exchange, when coined into money. Its brilliancy and whiteness cause it to excel all other materials for plate and similar articles of luxury; and, in consequence of its sonorous properties, it is made into trumpets and other musical instruments. There is a great consumption of silver, at the present day, in the process of electrotyping. Certain preparations of silver are also used in medicine.

NATIVE SULPHATE OF COPPER AND IRON, *M. F. Pisani.* See VITRIOLITE.

NATIVE SULPHUR. Rhombic. Occurs in regular crystals, the prevailing form of which is an acute octahedron, composed of two four-sided pyramids, with rhombic bases, and sides composed of equal and similar scalene triangular planes. It most commonly occurs in amorphous compact masses, or in small fragments or grains disseminated in other minerals; sometimes pulverulent, in the state of a loose or slightly coherent dull powder, in the interior of other minerals, or coating their surface, especially that of lava.

NATIVE SULPHUR.

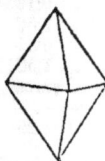 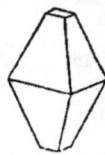 

Fig. 304. Fig. 305. Fig. 306.

Colour sulphur-yellow, sometimes red, grey, or brown, owing to the presence of impurities. Generally translucent, or very nearly transparent at the edges, sometimes opaque. Lustre usually more or less shining, and between resinous and adamantine. Streak sulphur-yellow, sometimes reddish or greenish. Sectile. Very brittle, and sometimes friable. Fracture conchoidal, or slightly splintery. Exhales a faint odour when rubbed, and has a scarcely perceptible taste. Does not conduct electricity, but becomes electrical when rubbed with other bodies. H. 1·5 to 2·5. S.G. 2·033 to 2·072.

Comp. S, or pure sulphur, often contaminated with other substances.

Burns readily with a blue lambent flame, giving off strong odours of sulphurous acid, and fusing to a brown liquid.

Insoluble in water. Not acted on by acids.

Sulphur is found in most places where salt mines or salt springs exist, and is very common in volcanic countries, where it is met with in the cavities and fissures of lava, into which it has been sublimed. It is found in a state of powder, or in crusts, or irregular masses, or in crystals, concretions, stalactites, &c.

Localities.—English. Cornwall, at Poldice and Nangiles Mines, in cavities in Iron Pyrites. Bole Hill, Derbyshire; and Dufton, Westmoreland, on Galena. Alston, Cumberland, with Gypsum.—*Irish.* Brooklodge, co. Galway, with Calc Spar. Castle Cara, co. Mayo, in limestone. — *Foreign.* The valleys of Noto and Mazzaro, in Sicily, in horizontal beds, from two feet to more than 30 feet thick, near large masses of Gypsum, and generally alternating with beds of limestone, marl, and clay, and accompanied by Sulphate of Strontian. The Sulphur is very irregularly distributed, partly in large holes in corroded limestone, where it generally forms small druses, incrustations, and nodules, an inch thick, and is partly disseminated in veins. Solfatara, near Naples. Crater of Vulcano. Bex, in Switzerland. Cracow, in Poland. Spain, three miles east of Conil, near Cape Trafalgar, in very fine crystals, in cavities in Gypsum and clay, and in limestone of comparatively recent age; also at Teruel, in Aragon, replacing the tests of shells which abound in certain bluish marls. Malvesi, near Narbonne, in France, in eocene gypsiferous marls. Pulverulent at Poligny, in the Jura, in silex. Saint-Boës, near Orthez in the Basses Pyrenees, near the junction of Chalk and Tertiary strata, and near Ophite. In Tertiary strata at Radoboj, in Croatia. Bagnères - de - Luchon, and Aix - la - Chapelle, forming incrustations on the walls of galleries from thermal waters. Iceland, deposited from hot springs. Guadaloupe. Martinique. Bourbon. Java. Upper Egypt. Quito, in a bed of Quartz, in mica-slate, and also in porphyry. Schwarzwald, in Suabia, in veins of Copper Pyrites, traversing granite. New York, Virginia, N. Carolina, U. S. Hawaii, at Kilauea, containing Selenium.

Brit. Mus., Case 5.

M. P. G. Horse-shoe Case, Nos. 118, to 147; Upper Gallery, Wall-case 1, No. 42 (Hawaii); 145 (Teneriffe); Table-case A, in Recess 4, Nos 6 and 7.

NATIVE SULPHURIC ACID, *Phillips.* Has been found in a diluted state in the neighbourhood of several volcanoes. It is a colourless liquid, with a pungent smell, and an intensely acid taste. S.G. 1·85.

It occurs in the cavities of Zocolino, a small volcanic mountain, near Sienna; in the caverns of Etna; and in a cavern near Aix, in Savoy; also in the United States, at Alabama; New York; at Tuscarora, Chippewa, and St. David's, Canada West.

Brit. Mus., Case 5.

NATIVE SYLVAN, *Jameson.* See NATIVE TELLURIUM.

NATIVE TALC EARTH, *Jameson.* Native carbonate of magnesia. See MAGNESITE.

NATIVE TELLURIUM. Hexagonal: primary form an acute rhombohedron. Occurs in six-sided prisms, with the terminal edges

Fig. 307.

replaced by single planes, generally massive and granular. Colour and streak tin-white,

passing into lead-grey. Lustre metallic, shining. Brittle. Yields to the knife. H. 2 to 2·5. S.G. 6·1 to 6·3.

Comp. Pure tellurium, or Te, containing small quantities of iron and gold.

BB fuses readily, burns with a greenish flame, and almost entirely volatilizes in dense white vapours.

Soluble in muriatic acid.

Localities. The Maria Loretto Mine, near Zalathna, in Transylvania, in veins traversing sandstone, and associated with Iron Pyrites, Quartz, and Gold.

Name. From Tellus, *the Earth.*

Brit. Mus., Case 3.

This is now a scarce mineral, but about fifty years ago it was found rather abundantly, and was smelted for the sake of the gold it contained, amounting to about 2·75 per cent.

NATIVE TIN. Is said to occur (mixed with some lead) in small greyish-white metallic grains with the gold of Siberia.

NATRO-BORO-CALCITE. See HAYESINE.

NATROCALCITE. A pseudomorphous variety of Calcite, after Gaylussite, from Sangerhausen, in Prussia.

Analysis, by *Marchand :*

Carbonate of lime	.	.	94·37
Alumina and peroxide of iron	.	.	1·15
Sulphate of lime	.	.	2·02
Water	.	.	1·34
Matrix	.	.	1·10
			99·98

NATROLITE, *Jameson.* NATROLITH, *Haidinger, v. Kobell, Naumann.* Rhombic: primary form a right rhombic prism. Generally in slender or acicular crystals; also in mammillary masses, with a radiating fibrous structure. Colour white, or yellowish, greyish, or reddish-brown. Lustre vitreous, inclining to pearly in fibrous varieties. Transparent to translucent. Streak white. Brittle. Fracture uneven, conchoidal. H. 5 to 5·5. S.G. 2·2.

Fig. 308.

Comp. $\overset{...}{Na}$ $\overset{...}{Si}$ + $\overset{...}{Al}$ $\overset{...}{Si}$ + 2$\overset{.}{H}$ = silica 47·4, alumina 26·9, soda 16·2, water 9·5 = 100.

Analysis, from Dumbarton Moor, by *Heddle :*

Silica . . . . . 46·96
Alumina . . . . 26·91
Soda . . . . . 12·83
Lime . . . . . 3·76
Water . . . . . 9·50

99·96

BB on charcoal fuses quickly to a transparent glass, full of small air-bubbles. ·
Dissolves in muriatic acid, with the formation of a jelly of silica.

Localities. — English. Cornwall: Huel Carne, near St. Just; between Botallack and Huel Cock; Stenna Gwynn, near St. Austell.—*Scotch.* Arbuthnott and St. Cyrus, Kincardineshire, in decomposed basalt. Stirlingshire; Campsie Hills, Carbeth, &c. Dumbartonshire; at Bowling, Cochnay, Duntocher, Dumbarton Moor, &c. Blin, near Burntisland, Fifeshire; also at Glen Farg, in flesh-red and colourless crystals (*fig.* 808). Bishoptown, Renfrewshire. — *Irish.* Cave Hill, Belfast, fibrous and compact. Londonderry, Portsteward, and Magilligan. Antrim; Craignashoke, Magee Island near Larne, in fine crystals, and radiating masses.—*Foreign.* Aussig, in Bohemia. Puy de Mouton, in Auvergne, in most brilliant crystals, in amygdaloid and in cavities in peperino. Nova Scotia. Copper Falls, Lake Superior, N. A.

Name. From *Natron, soda,* and λίθος, *stone.* It was so named by Klaproth, by whom it was first described, on account of the great quantity of soda he found it to contain.
For varieties of Natrolite, see BERGMANNITE, LEHUNTITE, RADIOLITE, BREVICITE, GALACTITE.

Brit. Mus., Case 27.
M. P. G. Horse-shoe Case, No. 1183.
NATROLITE DE HESSELKULA. See EKEBERGITE.
NATRON, *Kirwan, Beudant.* Oblique. Occurs crystallized, massive, fibrous, and sometimes radiated, in crusts and efflorescences. Colour grey or yellowish-white. Lustre glistening. Translucent, but becomes opaque by exposure. Taste alkaline. H. 1 to 1·5. S.G. 1·4.

Fig. 309.

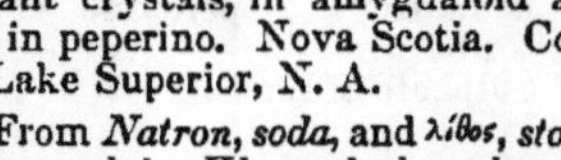

Comp. Ṅa C̈ + 10Ḣ, or hydrated carbonate of soda = carbonic acid 26·7, soda 18·8, water 54·5 = 100.

Localities. The soda lakes of Egypt. The hot springs of Carlsbad, in Bohemia; and Rykum, in Iceland. The plains of Debreczin, in Hungary. Vesuvius. Etna. Various parts of Asia, Africa, and America.

Name. From the name of the Desert *Natron,* whence it is supposed to have been procured in ancient times.
This salt, the nitre of the Bible, is used in bleaching, washing, dyeing, and in the manufacture of glass and soap. The ancient Egyptians are said to have prepared dead bodies for the process of embalming, by previously macerating them for several months in a solution of this salt.

Brit. Mus., Case 41.
NATRON ALAUN, *v. Kobell.* See SODA ALUM.
NATRONALAUN. See SODA ALUM.
NATRON-CHABAZIT. See GMELLNITE.
NATRON SALPETER, *Leonhard.* See NITRATINE.
NATRON-SPODUMENE, *Berzelius.* See OLIGOCLASE.
NATURAL SODA, *Jameson.* See TRONA.
NATÜRLICHES BITTERSALZ, *Werner.* See EPSOMITE.
NAUMANNITE, *Haidinger.* Cubical. Occurs in cubes, with a perfect cubic cleavage; also massive, in thin plates, and granular. Colour and streak iron-black. Lustre metallic. H. 2·5. S.G. 8.

Comp. Ag, Se, or selenide of silver = selenium 26·8, silver 73·2 = 100.
BB on charcoal, fuses easily; with soda and borax yields a globule of silver.
Locality. Tilkerode, in the Harz.
Name. After Dr. C. F. Naumann, the Saxon mineralogist.
NECRONITE. (From νεκρός, *a corpse.*) A variety of Orthoclase, which gives off a fetid smell when struck.
NECTIC QUARTZ. See FLOAT STONE. ·
NEEDLE ORE, *Jameson.* See AIKENITE.
NEEDLE SPAR. A name for Aragonite (which see).
NEEDLE STONE, NEEDLE ZEOLITE, *Jameson.* Names given to acicular varieties of Natrolite and Scolecite.
Brit. Mus., Case 27.
NEFELINA, *Monticelli.* See NEPHELINE.
NEMALITE (from νῆμα, *a wood,* and λίθος, *stone.*) A fibrous variety of Brucite (which see).
Brit. Mus., Case 47.
NEOCTESE, *Beudant.* A variety of Scorodite from St. Antonio Perreira, near Villa Rica, in Brazil, and near Edenville, New York. Colour green.

Comp. Hydrated arseniate of iron, or $\ddot{Fe}$ $\ddot{As} + 4\dot{H}$.

Analysis, from Brazil, by *Berzelius* :

Arsenic acid	. .	. 50·78
Peroxide of iron	. .	. 34·85
Phosphoric acid	. .	. 0·67
Oxide of copper	. .	. trace
Water	. .	. 15·55

101·85

BB gives off moisture when heated, and turns yellow. Imparts the colour of iron to the fluxes, and emits a strong odour of arsenic.

Name. From νέος, *new,* and κτῆσις, *acquisition.*

NEOLITE, *Scheerer.* A massive variety of Talc, in which a portion of the silica is replaced by alumina. Occurs either in small crystalline laminæ and silky fibres grouped, or in apparently an amorphous state. Colour brownish- and blackish-green, passing almost into black. Lustre silky or earthy. Unctuous to the touch, and may be cut like soap. H.: the crystalline variety is nearly as hard as Talc; the amorphous variety is softer. S.G. when perfectly dry 2·77.

Comp. $\ddot{R}\,\ddot{S}i$, or $(\ddot{Fe}\,\ddot{Mg})\,\ddot{S}i + \dot{H}$ nearly.

Analysis (mean of two), by *Scheerer* :

Silica	. 48·81
Alumina . . .	. 8·75
Magnesia . . .	. 27·99
Protoxide of iron . .	. 5·86
Lime	. 0·14
Protoxide of manganese	. 1·75
Water	. 5·10

99·52

Loses water and becomes nearly white at a temperature of 100°. When dried and immersed in water gives out bubbles of air, and reabsorbs water so rapidly as to fall in pieces soon after immersion.

Locality. Aslak Iron Mines, near Arendal in Norway.

Name. From νέος, *new,* and λίθος, *stone,* in allusion to the belief in its being newly formed by the infiltration of waters which have passed over rocks containing magnesia.

NEOPLASE, *Beudant.* From νέος, *new,* and πλάσις, *formation.* See BOTRYOGENE.

NEOTOKITE. Probably an altered form of Rhodonite, allied to Stratopeite. Amorphous. Colour black to brownish-black. Opaque or feebly translucent. Streak brown. H. 3·5 to 4. S.G. 2·7 to 2·8.

Comp. $\dot{M}g\,\ddot{S}i + (\ddot{Mn}\,\ddot{Fe})\,\ddot{S}i + 8\dot{H}$.
BB yields water, but is infusible.
Locality. Gaosböle in Finland.

Name. From νέος, *new,* and τόκος, *a birth.*

NEOTYPE, *Breithaupt.* A variety of Calcite containing Barytes. S.G. 2·82 to 2·83.

Name. From νέος, *new,* and τύπος, *a form* or *type.*

NEPHELINE, *Haüy.* Hexagonal. Occurs crystallized in regular six-sided prisms (the primary form), which have their terminal edges sometimes replaced; also compact, massive, and columnar. (See ELÆOLITE.) Colourless, or greyish-white: when massive greenish or bluish, brownish and brick-red. Lustre vitreous, shining. Transparent to opaque. Brittle. Fracture subconchoidal. H. 5·5 to 6. S.G. 2·5 to 2·6.

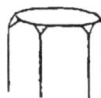 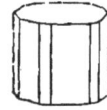 

Fig. 310. Fig. 311. Fig. 312.

Comp. $(\ddot{K}\,\ddot{Na})\,\ddot{S}i + \ddot{Al}\,\ddot{S}i$ or $\ddot{K}\,\ddot{S}i^2 + 4\ddot{Na}\,\ddot{S}i + 5\ddot{Al}\,\ddot{S}i$ (Scheerer).

Analysis, from Vesuvius, by *Scheerer* :

Silica	. 44·04
Alumina . . .	. 34·06
Peroxide of iron . .	. 0·44
Soda	. 15·91
Potash . . .	. 4·52
Lime	. 2·01
Magnesia . . .	. trace
Muriatic acid . .	. 0·14
Sulphuric acid . .	. 0·14
Water	. 0·21

101·38

BB fuses to a colourless blistered glass.

In fragments in nitric acid, the latter becomes turbid. In a powdered state, completely decomposed by muriatic acid, and converted into a gelatinous mass.

Localities. Monte Somma, in fine white crystals in cavities of the older lavas, with Idocrase, Mica, Hornblende, &c. Capo di Bove, near Rome, in lava. Katzenbüchel, near Heidelberg, in clinkstone.

Name. From νεφέλη, *a cloud;* in allusion to the clouded appearance assumed by a translucent fragment when immersed in nitric acid.

Brit. Mus., Case 31.

S

M. P. G. Upper gallery, Table-case A in recess 4, Nos. 84 to 88.

NEPHRITE, *Jameson.* JADE, or AXE-STONE. Occurs in compact masses of a leek-green colour, passing into grey and green-ish-white. Translucent. Very tough, break-ing with a coarse splintery fracture. H. 7. S.G. 2·9 to 3·1.

Analysis, by *Forchammer:*

Silica	58·88
Alumina . . .	1·56
Peroxide of iron . .	2·81
Peroxide of manganese .	0·82
Magnesia . . .	22·38
Potash . . .	0·80
Lime	12·15
Water . . .	0·26
	99·69

BB alone infusible (or with difficulty at the thinnest edges), but becomes white: with borax forms a transparent glass.

Localities. The Harz. Corsica. Egypt. Northwest America. New Zealand.

Name. From νεφρός, a *kidney ;* in allusion to the belief entertained in former times, of its influence in preventing and curing diseases of the kidneys.

Brit. Mus., Case 29.

M. P. G. Horse-shoe Case, Nos. 1017 to 1026.

The hardness of this stone renders it ex-ceedingly difficult to cut and polish. It is carved into handles of swords and daggers in Turkey, and the natives of New Zealand and other islands in the Pacific fashion it into clubs, hatchets, and other implements. In India it is sometimes worn as a talisman.

NEUKIRCHITE. A kind of Wad occurring in brilliant black needles forming a coating on red Hematite, at Neukirchen, in Alsace.

NEUROLITE, *Thomson.* Occurs massive and fine-columnar. Colour greenish-yellow. Translucent to opaque. H. 4·25. S.G. 2·47.

Comp. 2A̶l S̶i⁴ + C̶a S̶i + 3H̶.

Locality. Stamstead, Lower Canada.

Name. From νεῦρον, a *tendon,* and λίθος, *stone,* because of its fibrous structure.

NEUTRALES SCHWEFELSÄURES EISEN-OXYD. See COQUIMBITE.

NEWJANSKITE, *Haidinger.* A name for IRIDOSMINE (which see).

NICKEL ANTIMONGLANZ. See ULLMAN-NITE.

NICKEL ANTIMONIAL, *Dufrénoy.* See BREITHAUPTITE.

NICKEL ARSENIATÉ, *Haüy.* See NICKEL OCHRE.

NICKEL ARSENICAL, *Haüy.* See COPPER NICKEL.

NICKEL ARSENICAL ANTIMONIFÈRE. See NICKEL OCHRE.

NICKELARSENIC-GLANCE, ⎫
NICKELARSENIKGLANZ, ⎬ See GERS-
NICKELARSENKIES, *Nau-* ⎭ DORFFITE.
mann.

NICKEL-BISMUTH, *Dana,* ⎫ See GRÜ-
NICKEL-BISMUTH-GLANCE. ⎭ NAUITE.

NICKEL-BLOOM, ⎫ See NICKEL-
NICKEL-BLÜTHE, *Haus-* ⎬ OCHRE.
mann. ⎭

NICKEL-BOURNONITE, *Rammelsberg.* A variety of Bournonite, from Wolfsberg, having part of the lead replaced by cobalt and nickel.

NICKEL-GLANCE, *Dana,* ⎫ See GERSDORF-
NICKEL-GLANZ, *Haus-* ⎬ FITE, and
mann. ⎭ AMOIBITE.

NICKEL-GREEN, *Dana.* See NICKEL-OCHRE.

NICKEL-GYMNITE, *Genth.* Occurs amor-phous, reniform, or stalactitic. Colour pale apple-green or yellowish. Lustre resinous. Opaque to translucent. Streak greenish-white. H. 3 to 4. S.G. 2·4.

Comp. (N̈i, M̈g)² S̈i + 3Ḧ = silica 35·36, oxide of nickel 30·64, protoxide of iron 0·24, magnesia 14·60, lime 0·26, water 19·09 = 106·19.

Locality. Texas, Pennsylvania; Michi-picoten Island, Lake Superior, U. S.

NICKELIFEROUS GREY ANTIMONY, *Allan.* See ULLMANNITE.

NICKELINE, *Nicol.* See NICKEL-OCHRE.

NICKELKIES, *Hausmann.* See MILLERITE.

NICKEL NATIF, *Haüy.* See MILLERITE.

NICKEL OCHRE, *Kirwan, Phillips.* Occurs massive, earthy, friable, and in short capil-lary crystals of an apple-green colour. Streak greenish-white. Fracture uneven or earthy. H. 2 to 2·5. S.G. 3 to 3·1.

Comp. Arseniate of nickel, or N̈i³ Äs + 8Ḧ = nickel 37·6, arsenic 38·4, water 24 = 100.

Analysis, from Riechelsdorf, by *Stromeyer :*

Oxide of nickel . .	37·35
Peroxide of iron . .	1·13
Sulphuric acid . .	0·23
Arsenic acid . .	36·97
Water . . .	24·32
	100·00

BB on charcoal, gives off strong arsenical fumes, and fuses in the inner flame to a metallic globule containing arsenic.

NICKELOXYDE.

Readily soluble in muriatic or nitric acid. *Localities.* — *English.* Pengelly Mine, St. Austell Consols, and Huel Chance, in Cornwall. — *Foreign.* Allemont in Dauphiné, coating White Nickel. Annaberg, Kamsdorf, and Schneeberg, in Saxony. Michipicoten Island, Lake Superior, mixed with arsenide of copper.

Brit. Mus., Case 56.

NICKELOXYDÉ, *Brochant.* See PIMELITE.
NICKEL-SMARAGD. See EMERALD NICKEL.

NICKELSPIESGLASERZ, } See ULLMAN-
Hausmann. } NITE.
NICKEL-STIBINE, *Dana.* }

NICKEL-SULFURÉ, *Levy.* See MILLERITE.

NICKEL VITRIOL, *T. S. Hunt.* A hydrated sulphate of nickel, occurring generally as a greenish-white efflorescence, upon a sulphide of nickel and iron at Wallace Mine, Lake Huron.

NICKELWISMUTHGLANZ. See GRÜNAUITE.

NICOLO. See ONICOLO.

NIGRINE. A reddish-black variety of Titaniferous Iron, occurring at Ohlapian in Transylvania, in pebbles and in square translucent prisms exhibiting a blood-red colour at the edges. S.G. 4·45.

Analysis, by *Klaproth :*
Titanic acid 84
Protoxide and peroxide of iron 14
Protoxide of manganese . . 2
————
100

Name. From *niger, black.*
Brit. Mus., Case 37.

NIOBITE, *Haidinger.* See COLUMBITE.

NITRATE DE CHAUX, }
Beudant. } See NITROCAL-
NITRATE OF LIME, } CITE.
Phillips. }

NITRATE OF MAGNESIA, *Phillips.* See NITROMAGNESITE.

NITRATE OF POTASH, *Phillips.* See NITRE.

NITRATE OF SODA, *Phillips, Kenngott.*

NITRATINE, *Haidinger.* Hexagonal : primary form an obtuse rhombohedron ; cleavage rhombohedral, perfect. Occurs crystallized or efflorescent ; generally mixed with clay and sand. Colour white ôr greyish-

Fig. 313.

and yellowish-white. Lustre vitreous. Transparent or translucent : strongly double re-

NITRE. 259

fracting. Taste cool and bitter. Deliquescent. Melts and deflagrates on hot charcoal. Rather sectile. Fracture imperfect-conchoidal. H. 1·5 to 2. S.G. 2·1 to 2·2.

Comp. Nitrate of soda, or $\dot{N}a\ \ddot{N}i$ = soda 36·6, nitric acid 68·4 = 100.

BB fuses when heated, and on cooling solidifies in a white mass.

Locality. The pampa of Tarapaca on the borders of Chili and Peru. The dry plain is covered with a bed of this salt, to a depth of several feet, over an extent of forty leagues.

The deposits of nitrate of soda in Peru are described by David Forbes as being explored from the river of Pisagua, southward to Patillos, in Bolivia, a distance of about 110 miles ; but, latterly, new and extensive deposits have also been worked further south, inland from Tocopilla. These deposits, situated at about 2500 to 3500 feet above the present sea-level, appear to run from latitude 19° southward into the northern part of the Desert of Atacama, showing themselves, according to the configuration of the country, at distances varying from ten to forty miles inland.[*] (*David Forbes.*)

It is used in the arts as a substitute for nitre ; but in consequence of its deliquescence it has not been largely used for making gunpowder.

Brit. Mus., Case 55.

M. P. G. Horse-shoe Case, No. 201.

NITRE, *Kirwan.* NITRIT, *Kenngott.* Rhombic : primary form a rhombic prism. Occurs in thin crusts and acicular crystals. Colour greenish and yellowish-white. Lustre vitreous. Translucent or transparent. Streak white. Taste saline and cooling. Brittle. H. 2. S.G. 1·9.

Comp. Nitrate of potash, or $\dot{K}\ddot{N}$ = potash 46·64, nitric acid 53·36 = 100.

Deflagrates on hot coals, and detonates in the fire with charcoal and other combustible bodies. Readily soluble in water, producing great cold.

Localities. Spain, Egypt, Persia, Arabia, India, South America, and many places where organic matter has been decomposed, especially in hot climates. Also covering the bottoms of caverns in the United States.

Name. From Nitria, the name of a city in Upper Egypt, in the neighbourhood of which this salt is found in considerable quantities.

[*] Quarterly Journ. Geol. Soc. No. 65, part i. p. 16.

Brit. Mus., Case 52.

Nitre is employed in medicine, the arts, and in metallurgy.

Its principal use, however, is in the manufacture of gunpowder, lucifer matches, detonating powder, &c.

"In India, Spain, and, as some say, in Persia and China, it germinates in certain seasons out of the earth, and what is more singular, this earth, accumulated in large heaps, and thus exposing a larger surface to the atmosphere, is found to reproduce it annually." * * * "But the most celebrated discovery of native nitre was that made by Abbé Fortis, in Apulia, in the Pulo or cavity of Molfetta. In this hollow, which is about one hundred feet deep, there are several natural grottos, in the interior part of which, between strata of compact limestone, nitre is found irregularly crystallized. The stone itself is so richly impregnated with it, that it bursts it in many places, and forms white efflorescences and crusts resembling Canary Sugar, mixed with gypsum on its surface; when these efflorescences are scraped off, more is generated in the space of about a month, but more quickly in summer than in winter." (*Kirwan*, vol. ii. pp. 25, 26.) Similar efflorescences cover the surface of some beds of Portland stone, shooting out in the form of colourless acicular crystals, even after the stone has been painted for the purpose of preventing their appearance.

NITROCALCITE, *Shepard.* Occurs in efflorescent silky tufts and coatings of a white or grey colour. Taste sharp and bitter.

Comp. $\dot{C}a \ \ddot{\ddot{N}} + 4\dot{H}$ = lime 23·73, nitric acid 45·76, water 30·51=100.

On burning coals fuses slowly with slight detonation, and dries: deliquesces very rapidly in the air before being dried.

Dissolves in one-fourth its weight of water. This salt is found on old walls, in limestone caverns, and on calcareous rocks.

NITRO-MAGNESITE, *Shepard.* Occurs with Nitro-calcite, with which it agrees in colour and other characters.

Comp. $\dot{M}g \ \ddot{\ddot{N}} + \dot{H}$, or magnesia 24, nitric acid 65, water 11=100.

NOBLE HORNBLENDE. See PARGASITE.

NOBLE METALS. The name given to those metals which can be separated from oxygen by heat alone. They are Mercury, Gold, Silver, Platinum, Palladium, Rhodium, Iridium and Osmium.

NOBLE OPAL. See PRECIOUS OPAL.

NOBLE TOURMALINE. The name given to the finest transparent varieties of Tourmaline.

NONTRONITE, *Berthier.* Occurs massive, with an opal-like appearance, and earthy. Colour varying from siskin-green to straw-yellow. Lustre dull or glimmering. Opaque to translucent. Immersed in water, gives off bubbles and becomes transparent. Fracture splintery or earthy. Unctuous to the touch. Streak resinous. H. 2 to 3. S.G. 2 to 2·3.

Comp. Hydrated tersilicate of iron, or $\ddot{\text{F}}e \ \ddot{S}i^3 + 5\dot{H}$ = peroxide of iron 36·11, silica 43·06, water 20·83=100.

Analysis, from Montmort, by *Jacquelain*:

Silica	41·31
Peroxide of iron . .	35·69
Alumina . . .	3·31
Lime	0·19
Oxide of copper . .	0·90
Oxide of zinc . .	trace
Water	18·63
	100·00

BB decrepitates, turns yellow, then brown, then black, and becomes magnetic, but does not fuse.

Insoluble in cold acid, but dissolves in hot sulphuric, muriatic, or nitric acid, with separation of gelatinous silica.

Localities. France, at Nontron, Dept. of the Dordogne, in small kidney-shaped masses, among manganese. Montmort, Dept. du Marne. Andreasberg, in the Harz. In amorphous and kidney-formed masses, generally very small (rarely as large as a fist) in masses of manganese worked near the village of Saint-Pardoux, near Nontron.

Nontronite is known in commerce as Manganese de Périgueux.

Brit. Mus., Case 26.

NORMAL OPHIOLITE. The name adopted by T. Sterry Hunt for the purer Serpentine rocks, when free from foreign admixtures.

NOSEAN, NOSIANE, NOSIN, *Leonhard.* NOSINE, *Beudant.* Cubical. Occurs in rhombic dodecahedrons, with an indistinct cleavage parallel to the faces of that solid. Colour grey, brown, bluish; sometimes black. Lustre vitreous to resinous. Translucent to nearly opaque. Very brittle. H. 5·5. S.G. 2·25 to 2·28.

Comp. $\dot{N}a^3 \ \ddot{S}i + 3\ddot{A}l \ \ddot{S}i + \dot{N}a \ \ddot{S}$ = silica 36·3, alumina 30·9, soda 24·8, sulphuric acid 8·0=100.

Analysis, by *Bergemann*:

Silica	37·00
Alumina	27·50

Soda	.	.	.	.	12·24
Lime	.	.	.	.	8·14
Protoxide of iron	.	.	.	1·15
Protoxide of manganese	.	0·50
Sulphuric acid	.	.	11·56
Sulphur	.	.	.	1·41

99·50

BB becomes colourless when heated, and fuses to a blistered glass.

Decomposed by muriatic acid, with evolution of sulphuretted hydrogen and formation of gelatinous silica.

Localities. Lake Laach, near Andernach on the Rhine: also at Rieden and Volkersfield.

Name. After the discoverer, K. W. Nose. Brit. Mus., Case 37.

NOTITE. A variety of Palagonite from the Val di Noto, the composition of which is represented by the formula $\dot{R}^2 \overset{...}{Si} + 3\overset{..}{H} \overset{...}{Si} + 9\dot{H}$.

Analysis (mean of many), by *Von Waltershausen:*

Silica	.	.	.	.	36·96
Alumina	.	.	.	5.25
Peroxide of iron	.	.	21·66
Lime	.	.	.	.	3·26
Magnesia	.	.	.	11·64
Soda	.	.	.	.	0·97
Potash	.	.	.	0·99
Water	.	.	.	.	18·16

100·00

Name. From the locality, the Val di Noto.

NUSSIERITE, *Danhauser.* Occurs in very obtuse rhombohedrons. Colour yellowish, greenish or greyish, with a faint waxy lustre. H. 4 to 4·5. S.G. 5·041.

Comp. Phosphate of lead and lime with chloride of lead; containing chloride of lead 7·65, oxide of lead 46·50, lime 12·30, protoxide of iron 2·44, phosphoric acid 19·80, arsenic acid 4·06, quartz 7·20 = 99·95.

BB fuses and solidifies into a whitish angular enamel: with borax forms a yellowish glass.

Dissolves readily, without effervescence, in nitric acid.

Locality. Nussière, Dept. of the Rhone, in France.

Brit. Mus., Case 57B.

NUTTALITE, *Brooke.* A variety of Scapolite. Occurs in rectangular prisms. Colour white, in some parts yellowish, in others bluish or green. Lustre vitreous, with a

play of light on the faces of the prisms similar to that of Elæolite: on surface of fracture resinous. Streak white. H. 4 to 5. S.G. 2·7 to 2·8.

Analysis, from Bolton, by *v. Rath:*

Silica	.	.	.	.	44·40
Alumina	.	.	.	25·52
Peroxide of iron	.	.	3·79
Lime	.	.	.	.	20·18
Magnesia	.	.	.	1·01
Soda	.	.	.	.	2·09
Potash	.	.	.	.	0·51
Water	.	.	.	.	1·24

98·71

Localities. Bolton and Boxborough, Massachusetts, in coarse granular limestone, with Epidote and Titanium Ore; Lewis co., New York.

Name. After Mr. Nuttall, by whom the first specimens were brought to this country. Brit. Mus., Case 31.

O.

OBLIQUE MICA. See MUSCOVITE.

OBLIQUE PRISMATIC ARSENIATE OF COPPER, *Phillips.* See CLINOCLASE.

OBSIDIAN. A volcanic glass, produced by the fusion of felspathic rocks, or those containing or composed of alkaline silicates; hence the composition is very variable, and depends upon that of the rock which has been melted down. In fact, Obsidian, Pitchstone, and Pearlstone, are only different forms of the same mineral, produced by different rates of cooling from the melted state; and any lava or rock containing the necessary ingredients may become converted into all or either of these substances, according as it has cooled more or less quickly. Those portions of the fused mass which have been cooled the most rapidly will be converted into Obsidian; while the inner portions which have cooled more slowly will become Pitchstone, which, in its turn, passes gradually into the Pearlstone, forming the central part. This has been proved to be the case by experiments conducted on a large scale at the Eagle Foundry, at Birmingham, by Mr. Hawkes.

"A large mass of Rowley Rag, weighing about 31 cwt., having been melted in a large double reverberatory furnace, at the Eagle Foundry, Birmingham, was broken up, after cooling slowly for thirteen days. It was then found that the outer portions of the fused rock, that is, those portions which had cooled the most rapidly, owing to their contact with the air, had assumed the appearance and structure of Obsidian; while those from the middle and bottom, which had cooled more gradually, resembled Pitchstone. Some of the more glassy portions near the top were spherulitic and vesicular."* *Descriptive Catalogue of Rock Specimens, in the Museum of Practical Geology*, p. 306.

Obsidian is generally black, and opaque in mass, but appears ash-grey and translucent, or nearly transparent, at thin edges. It is remarkable for its perfect conchoidal fracture, and for its sharp cutting edges, advantage of which was taken by the ancient Peruvians and Mexicans, who made it into razors, knife-blades, and points of arrows and lances; uses to which it is still applied by the natives of the Azores, Ascension, and Guiana. The ancient inhabitants of Peru and Mexico, and also the Romans, made mirrors of Obsidian, and sometimes used it as a gem. Now-a-days it is converted into snuff-boxes, knife-handles, and into various articles of mourning jewelry.

Name. According to Sir John Hill, Obsidian was in great use among the ancients, because it took a good polish, and reflected the images of things as our looking-glasses do. "The finest kind was, for this reason, called ὀψιανὸς ἀπὸ τῆς ὀψεως, which was afterwards written by the Latins, *Opsianus, Opsidianus,* and *Obsidianus.* And the true origin of the name being forgotten from the false spelling of the word, after-ages thought it had received it from one *Obsidius,* whom they imagined the first finder of it."—Hill's *Theophrastus,* p. 39.

Localities. The principal localities are Iceland, Siberia, Hungary, New Zealand, Ascension, Teneriffe, the Lipari Islands, Mexico, Peru, Madagascar, South Sea Islands, and Melos and other islands in the Grecian Archipelago. S.G. 2·25 to 2·8.

Brit. Mus., Case 30.

M. P. G. Upper Gallery, Wall-case 1, Nos. 12 and 13; Wall-case 2, Nos. 28 to 31, 119, 126. Table-case B, Nos. 111 to 113. Horse-shoe Case, Nos. 1027 to 1029.

OBSIDIENNE DU CANTAL. See CANTALITE.

OCCIDENTAL CHALCEDONY. See ORIENTAL CHALCEDONY.

OCCIDENTAL DIAMOND. A name given

by lapidaries to limpid and colourless Rock-Crystal when cut and polished.

OCCIDENTAL TOPAZ. See CITRINE.

OCHRAN. A yellow variety of Bole, from Orawitza.

Analysis, by *Kersten :*

Silica	31·3
Alumina	43·0
Peroxide of iron	1·2
Water, and a trace of boracic acid	21·0
	96·5

OCHRE. Clay coloured yellow by hydrate of iron; but the term is applied to any combination of the earths with iron which can be used for pigments, such as *Reddle,* and the like. Ochres of good quality should contain at least 10 to 15 per cent. of hydrate; when that amount is exceeded the colour passes into brown. There are three mines worked for Ochre in France, 1st. at Vierzon, Dept. of Cher; 2nd. at Pourcain, near Auxerre, Dept. of the Yonne; and 3rd. at Saint Amand (Nièvre). Of these the Ochre of Vierzon is held in the greatest estimation on account of its beautiful yellow colour.

Name. The word Ochre is derived from ὤχρα, the Greek name for the same substance, and itself derived from ὤχρὸς, *pale.*

OCHREOUS IRON ORE. See HEMATITE and LIMONITE.

OCHREOUS WAD, or OCHRY WAD. A friable earthy substance; probably a mixture of hydrated sesquioxide, and anhydrous peroxide of manganese. Streak dark or blackish-brown. Very porous, and emits a copious stream of air-bubbles when placed in water. S.G. 4·506.

Comp. Anhydrous peroxide of manganese, with a casual admixture of a small quantity of some hydrated oxide, probably Manganite.

Dissolves in muriatic acid, with a free disengagement of chlorine, leaving merely traces of insoluble matter.

OCHROITE. The mineral to which this name was given by Hermann is probably a variety of Cerite, rendered impure by an admixture of Quartz. He deduced for it the formula, $2\dot{C}e\,\ddot{S}i + 3\dot{H}$ = silica 32·83, protoxide of cerium 57·58, water 9·59 = 100.

OCRE. See OCHRE.

OCTAEDRISCHES KUPFERERZ, *Mohs.* See RED COPPER.

OCTAEDRITE, *Werner;* OCTAHEDRITE, *Jameson.* A name for Anatase, from its occurrence in octahedrons.

OCTAHEDRAL ALUM SALT, *Mohs.* Native Alum. See POTASH ALUM.

OCTAHEDRAL AMMONIAC SALT, *Mohs.* See SAL AMMONIAC.

OCTAHEDRAL ARSENIATE OF COPPER, *Phillips.* See LIROCONITE.

OCTAHEDRAL ARSENIC ACID, *Mohs.* See ARSENOLITE.

OCTAHEDRAL BISMUTH, *Mohs.* See NATIVE BISMUTH.

OCTAHEDRAL CHROME ORE, *Mohs.* See CHROMIC IRON.

OCTAHEDRAL COBALT PYRITES, *Mohs.* See SMALTINE.

OCTAHEDRAL COPPER, *Mohs.* See NATIVE COPPER.

OCTAHEDRAL COPPER ORE, *Mohs.* See RED COPPER.

OCTAHEDRAL COPPER PYRITES, *Mohs.* See ERUBESCITE.

OCTAHEDRAL CORUNDUM, *Mohs.* See AUTOMALITE.

OCTAHEDRAL DIAMOND, *Mohs.* See DIAMOND.

OCTAHEDRAL FLUOR HALOID, *Mohs.* See FLUOR.

OCTAHEDRAL IRON, *Mohs.* See NATIVE IRON.

OCTAHEDRAL IRON ORE, *Mohs.* See MAGNETITE.

OCTAHEDRAL KOUPHONE SPAR, *Haidinger.* See SARCOLITE.

OCTAHEDRAL PALLADIUM, *Haidinger.* See NATIVE PALLADIUM.

OCTAHEDRAL TITANIUM ORE, *Mohs.* See PYROCHLORE.

OCULUS MUNDI, *Kirwan,* A hydrophanous variety of Chalcedony. See HYDROPHANE.

OCULUS PISCIS, or FISH-EYE STONE. See ICHTHYOPHTHALMITE.

ODONTOLITE, or BONE TURQUOIS. Fossil bones or teeth coloured by oxide of copper, found in Europe, in Bas Languedoc. The word is derived from ὀδὸς, *a tooth,* and λίθος, *a stone.* See TURQUOIS.

ŒRSTEDITE; ŒRSTEDTIT, *Kenngott.* Probably an altered Zircon. Colour reddish-brown Lustre adamantine-vitreous. Opaque, or subtranslucent. H. 5·5. S.G. 3·629.

Analysis, by *Forchammer :*

Zirconia and titanic acid	68·96
Silica	19·71
Lime	2·61
Magnesia . . .	2·05
Protoxide of iron .	1·14
Water	5·53
	100·00

BB infusible; with borax or microcosmic salt yields a colourless glass.

Locality. Arendal, in Norway, in brilliant crystals, generally on crystals of Pyroxene.

Name. After J. C. Œrsted, the Swedish chemist.

Brit. Mus., Case 37.

OGOÏTE, *Breithaupt.* A variety of Ripidolite, from Rauris, in Upper Austria. S.G. 2·9.

Analysis, by *v. Kobell :*

Silica	26·06
Alumina . . .	18·47
Magnesia . . .	14·69
Protoxide of iron .	26·87
Protoxide of manganese	0·62
Water	10·45
Gangue . . .	2·24
	99·40

Name. From ὀγκόω, *to increase in bulk;* in allusion to its behaviour before the blowpipe.

OIL COAL. A kind of Coal occurring under bituminous coal, and affording a large quantity of oil on distillation. It varies in colour from brown to black, and is dull when not exhibiting the polished appearance of "slickenside." Powder dark chocolate colour. Very tough. Fracture hackly. S.G. 1·103.

Analyses, by *Slessor :*

Volatile matters . .	66·56
Fixed carbon . .	25·33
Ash	8·21
	100·00

Carbon . . .	80·96
Hydrogen . . .	10·15
Nitrogen with oxygen and sulphur	0·68
Ash	8·21
	100·00

It takes fire very readily, and when removed from the lamp still burns for some time with a brilliant smoky flame, and while flaming melted fragments continue to drop from it in a highly characteristic manner.

Locality. This coal occurs in the Coal-measures of Nova Scotia, at Fraser Mine, near Pictou, in a bed from 14 inches to 20 inches thick, under bituminous coal. Throughout its entire thickness, it has a curly twisted structure, and many of its fractures look like the casts of shells, and the sharp edges have the polished character of slickensides.

Oil-coal yields from 40 to 77 gallons of crude oil per ton on distillation, and in picked samples as much as 179 gallons.

All the Oil Coals have a greater density than ordinary coals, and the volatile matters they contain are greatly in excess of the carbon; while in all the bituminous coals, and in a few cases in Cannel Coals, the volatile matters are considerably less in amount than the fixed carbon.

OISANITE. A name for Anatase, from its principal locality, Bourg d'Oisans, in Dauphiné.

OKENITE, *v. Kobell.* Generally occurs in delicately fibrous and sometimes in radiating masses. Colour snow-white, with a tinge of yellow or blue. Lustre glimmering or pearly, often opalescent. Translucent at the edges. Very tough. H. 5. S.G. 2·28.

Comp. Hydrated bisilicate of lime, or $\dot{C}a\ \ddot{S}i^2 + 2\dot{H} =$ lime 28, silica 62, water 18 = 100.

Analysis, by *v. Kobell :*

Silica . . . . . 55·64
Lime . . . . . 26·59
Alumina and peroxide of iron 0·53

                99·76

BB swells up, and fuses to a porcelain-like mass; with borax yields a colourless globule.

When pulverised, easily dissolved in cold muriatic acid (but not after ignition), with separation of gelatinous flakes of silica.

Localities. Disco Island and Tupaursak, in North Greenland, in amygdaloid. Faröe, Iceland.

Name. After Professor Oken, of Munich. Brit. Mus., Case 28.

OLIGISTE, *Haüy.* (From ὀλίγιστος, *least,* signifying that it is less rich in metal than Magnetite.) See SPECULAR IRON.

OLIGOCLASE. Anorthic: crystals rather rare, twins common, and resembling Albite. Cleavage perfect. Colour white, with a tinge of grey, green, yellow, or red. Lustre pearly or resinous on the cleavage planes; elsewhere vitreous. More or less translucent. Fracture conchoidal or uneven. H. 6. S.G. 2·58 to 2·7.

Comp. $3\dot{N}a\ \ddot{S}i + 4(\ddot{A}l\ \overset{...}{S}i^3)=$ silica 62·3, alumina 23·5, soda 14·2 = 100.

Analysis, from Teneriffe, by *Deville :*

Silica . . . . 62·97
Alumina . . . 22·29
Lime . . . . 2·06
Magnesia . . . 0·54

Soda . . . . . 8·45
Potash . . . . 3·69

               100·00

BB like Felspar, but fuses with much greater ease to a transparent, colourless glass. Not decomposed by acids.

Localities. Teneriffe, in trachyte. With Quartz and Mica forming granite at Kimito in Danvikszoll near Stockholm. Schaitansk and Lake Baikal, in Siberia. Iceland. Arendal, in Norway. Arriège. Morea. Haddam, Connecticut, &c. U. S.

Name. From ὀλιγός, *little,* and κλάω, *to break.*

Brit. Mus., Case 30.

For varieties of Oligoclase, see HAFNEFJORDITE, MOONSTONE, SUNSTONE, UNIONITE.

OLIGOCLASE-ALBITE. The name proposed by Scheerer, for an Albite from Snarum.

OLIGON SPAR, OLIGONSPATH, *Breithaupt.* A variety of Spathic Iron from Ehrenfriedersdorf, in Saxony, containing 25 per cent. of protoxide of manganese. Occurs in rhombohedrons. Colour reddish-yellow. H. 4. S.G. 3·74.

Comp. $2\dot{M}n\ \ddot{C} + 3\dot{F}e\ \ddot{C}.$

Analysis, by *Magnus :*

Carbonic acid . . . 38·35
Protoxide of iron . . 36·81
Protoxide of manganese . 25·31

               100·47

OLIVE COPPER ORE, *Kirwan.* See OLIVENITE.

OLIVE MALACHITE, *Mohs.* See OLIVENITE.

OLIVENCHALCIT. See LIBETHENITE.

OLIVENERZ, *Werner* OLIVÉNITE, *Beudant.* OLIVENIT, *Haidinger, Leonhard.* OLIVENITE, *Dana, Greg & Lettsom.* OLIVEN-ORE, *Jameson.* Rhombic: primary form a right rhombic prism. Occurs in prismatic crystals, which are usually attached to the matrix: also reniform, fibrous, and capillary, and granular. Colour olive-green, pistachio-green, and blackish-green,

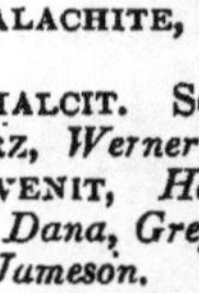

Fig. 314.

passing into liver-brown and wood-brown; the fibrous variety (*Wood-arseniate*) siskin-

OLIVIN.

or greenish-grey. Lustre vitreous to resinous. Translucent to opaque. Streak olive-green or brown. Brittle. Fracture conchoidal, uneven. H. 3. S.G. 4·1 to 4·4.

Comp. Hydrated arseniate of copper, or $\ddot{C}u^4 (\ddot{A}s, \ddot{P}) + \dot{H} =$ oxide of copper ,58·4, arsenic acid 31·7, phosphoric acid 6·6, water 3·3 = 100.

Analysis, from Cornwall, by *v. Kobell:*

Oxide of copper	. .	. 56·43
Arsenic acid	. .	. 36·71
Phosphoric acid	. .	. 3·36
Water	. .	. 3·50
		100·00

BB in the forceps fuses, imparts a pale blue colour to the flame, and on cooling, crystallizes to a blackish-brown, radiated mass, with an adamantine lustre and covered with a network of prismatic crystals. On charcoal, deflagrates, emits strong arsenical fumes, and yields a globule which is brownish on the outside, and white in the middle.

Soluble in nitric acid and in ammonia. *Localities.* The finest specimens of Olivenite have been found in Cornwall, principally at Huel Gorland, Ting Tang, Huel Unity, Carharrack, Tincroft, Huel Buller, and at Pednandrea. Bedford United Mines, near Tavistock, Devonshire. Tyne Head Mine, near Alston, Cumberland.— *Foreign.* Camsdorf and Saalfeld in Thuringia. The Tyrol. Siberia. Chili, &c.

Name. From its olive-green colour.

Brit. Mus., Case 56.

M. P. G. Wall-case 2 (British); Horse-shoe Case 922 to 924.

OLIVIN, *Werner.* OLIVINE, *Brooke & Miller.* Chrysolite of inferior colour and clearness, occurring in yellowish-green or olive-coloured, imbedded masses and grains. Lustre vitreous; sometimes when decomposing iridescent and somewhat metallic externally. Transparent. Fracture imperfect-conchoidal. Not so hard as Chrysolite. H. 6·5 to 7. S.G. 3·33 to 3·45.

Comp. Anhydrous silicate of magnesia, or $\dot{M}g^2 \ddot{S}i$, but a portion of the magnesia is frequently replaced by protoxide of iron, sometimes to the amount of 15 per cent.

Analysis, from Somma, by *Walmstedt:*

Silica	. . .	. 40·16
Alumina	. .	. 0·10
Magnesia	. .	. 44·87
Protoxide of iron	.	. 15·38

Protoxide of manganese	. 0·10
	100·61

BB alone infusible; with borax fuses slowly to a transparent glass, coloured by iron. In a powdered state readily decomposed by muriatic acid, yielding a jelly.

Localities. Near the Giant's Causeway in Ireland. In basalt and trap. In trap rock at Arthur's Seat near Edinburgh. Unkel, near Bonn on the Rhine. In trap-tuff at Kapferstein, in Styria. Vesuvius. In lava at Hawaii, and other islands in the Pacific. Thetford and Norwich, Vermont, U. S. in boulders of basalt.

Brit. Mus., Case 25.

M.P.G Horse-shoe Case, Nos. 922 to 924. Upper Gallery, Wall-case 1, Nos. 36 to 41. Table-case A in recess 4, Nos. 119 to 121.

OLIVINOID. The name given to a substance occurring in meteorites by Prof. C. U. Shepard, from its resemblance to Olivine. It is softer than Olivine. H. 5·5 to 6. It also differs from that mineral in turning black and fusing easily before the blowpipe; as well as in being more easily attacked by acids.

OLLITE. See POTSTONE.

OMPHAZITE, *Werner.* A foliated leek-green variety of Sahlite, usually containing some iron. It occurs at the Sau Alp, in Carinthia, with granular Garnet; and at Hof, in Bayreuth, accompanying the Smaragdite variety of Hornblende, to which it bears a close resemblance.

ONEGITE. A variety of Göthite, found at Lake Onega, in Siberia.

ONICOLO. A variety of Onyx with a deep brown ground, on which is a band of bluish-white. It differs from true Onyx in a certain blending of the two layers, the lowest of which is always the thinnest. It has often the constitution of a deep coloured Sard, but of an extraordinarily fine texture. It is used for cameos. (*Barbot.*) Sometimes the dark ground is covered with bluish spots, surrounded by milky zones. It is chiefly brought from Bohemia.

Name. The Nicolo or Onicolo is said to take its name from the Greek Νικόλαος.

ONKOSIN, *v. Kobell.* A kind of clay of an apple-green or brownish colour, passing into greyish and brownish, and occurring in roundish pieces. Lustre weak, slightly resinous. Translucent. Sectile. Fracture splintery or uneven. H. 2. S.G. 2·81.

Comp. $2\ddot{A}l \ddot{S}i + (\dot{K}, \dot{M}g) \ddot{S}i + 2\dot{H}.$
Analysis, by *v. Kobell:*

Silica	. . . .	. 52·52

Alumina	. 30·88
Magnesia	. 3·82
Potash	. 6·58
Protoxide of iron	. 0·80
Water	. 4·60
	101·90

BB swells up and fuses to a white blebby glass.

Soluble in sulphuric, but not in muriatic acid.

Locality. Posseggen, near Tamsweg in Salzburg, disseminated in slightly micaceous dolomite.

Brit. Mus., Case 26.

ONOFRITE, *Haidinger.* Occurs massive with a compact granular texture, and no cleavage. Colour steel grey to blackish-lead-grey, resembling that of Grey Copper. Lustre metallic. Streak shining. H. 2·5. S.G. 7·1 to 7·37.

Comp. Selenide of mercury, or Hg, Se = quicksilver 71·7, selenium 28·3 = 100.

Analysis, from Clausthal, by *Kerl:*

Selenium	. 24·05
Quicksilver	. 72·26
Quartz	. 2·86
Sulphur	. 0·12
	99·74

BB on charcoal gives off the odour of selenium; with soda yields metallic mercury.

Localities. Near San Onofre in Mexico, with other ores of mercury. Clausthal and Zorge in the Harz, with Copper Pyrites.

Brit. Mus., Case 4.

ONYX. A chalcedonic variety of Quartz, resembling Agate, and composed of alternate parallel layers of different colours—usually of a clear light brown, and an opaque white. Those with alternate bands of white and red and green and white are held in great esteem.

The Onyx is mentioned in Exodus, chap. xxviii. 17—20, amongst the twelve precious stones which were set on the breast-plate of the high-priest, each one of which was engraved with the name of one of the sons of Jacob. Being the eleventh stone, it bore, in consequence, the name of Joseph. The two stones, also, set in ouches of gold, and placed on the shoulders of the ephod or short sleeveless cloak of the high-priest, with the names of the children of Israel engraved upon them: six of their names on one stone and the other six names on the other stone, according to their birth, were likewise ordered to be Onyx.

See also Genesis ii. 12; Exodus xxxix. 6; and Job xxviii. 16.

The Onyx was highly prized by the ancients, who took advantage of the difference in colour to engrave it into what are called cameos. In these the figure in relief is carved out of one layer of the stone, generally the paler of the two, while the darker part forms the back ground. These fetch very high prices even at the present day, and are highly prized, not for their rarity only, but for their beauty as works of art. See ONICOLO, also SARD.

The tints of the Onyx may be heightened by boiling it for several days in honey and water, and then soaking it in sulphuric acid to bring out the black and white layers; or in nitric acid, to heighten the colours of the red and white layers.

Localities.—Onyx is found in Perthshire, in the Isle of Skye; in Antrim, at the Giant's Causeway, in amygdaloid; and in Rathlin Island, and on the shore of Lough Neagh.

Foreign. Oberstein in Saxony. The Deserts of the Nogaï Khirghiz in the S. of Russia. Yemen in Arabia. Guzerat.

Name. The word Onyx is derived from ὄνυξ, *a nail;* "because it hath a white in it resembling that in the nail of a man's finger." (*Pliny.*)

Brit. Mus., Case 22.

M. P. G. Horse-shoe Case, Nos. 580 to 582, 589.

OOSITE. A mineral related to Pinite, found near Baden.

Brit. Mus., Case 32.

OPAL. A kind of resinous or uncleavable Quartz. Occurs amorphous, massive, sometimes small-reniform, stalactitic, or large tuberose. Colour milk-white, red-brown, green, and pearl-grey; generally pale, but sometimes dark, owing to the admixture of other substances. Lustre vitreous, often inclining to resinous and sometimes to pearly. Some varieties exhibit a beautiful play of colours, or different colours by refracted and reflected light, which are the more beautiful owing to their not being the result of any particular tint in the stone itself, but from their being produced by reflected light. Semi-transparent or pellucid. Streak white. Very brittle. Fracture conchoidal. H. 5·5 to 6·5. S.G. 1·9 to 2·3.

The play of colours in the Opal is not satisfactorily accounted for. By Brewster it is attributed to the presence of internal fissures and cracks of a uniform shape.

Haüy ascribes it to thin films of air filling cavities in the interior of the stone, and reflecting the light agreeably with the law of Newton's coloured rings; Mohs, however, considers that these would produce iridescence only.

Comp. Amorphous silica or S̈i, frequently accompanied by small quantities of potash, soda, lime, magnesia, alumina, and peroxide of iron, together with between 5 and 10 per cent. of water. The water seems to be only mechanically mixed with the silica, and varies much in the different kinds of Opal.

BB infusible, but gives out water and becomes opaque: some varieties, containing iron, turn red.

Localities. Opal occurs in short irregular veins in porphyry, and in vesicular cavities of amygdaloid. The chief localities are Hungary, Mexico, the Faröe Islands, and Iceland. The Opals exported from Honduras are obtained at the mines of the department of Gracias, which lies between that of Comayagua and the Republic of Guatemala.

Name. From *opalus,* or *opalum,* the ancient Latin name for the stone.

For varieties of Opal, see PRECIOUS OPAL; FIRE-OPAL, or GIRASOL; COMMON OPAL; SEMI-OPAL; HYDROPHANE; CACHOLONG; HYALITE, or MULLER'S GLASS; MENILITE; OPAL JASPER; MICHAELITE; ALUMOCALCITE; RANDANITE; &c.

Brit. Mus., Case 24.

M.P.G. Horse-shoe Case, Nos. 767 to 771.

OPAL, or OPALINE ALLOPHANE. See SCHRÖTTERITE.

OPAL JASPER. A kind of Opal containing several per cent. of iron.

OPALE DE FEU. See FIRE-OPAL.

OPALE TERREUSE. See GEYSERITE.

OPERMENT, *Haidinger.* See ORPIMENT.

OPHIOLITE (from ὄφις, *a snake,* and λίθος, *stone*). A name given to include the various serpentine rocks. The purer Serpentines are called by T. Sterry Hunt *Normal Ophiolite,* and other varieties *Calcareous, Dolomitic,* or *Magnesitic,* according to the nature of the foreign admixtures which may be intimately mixed with them.

OPHITE (from ὄφις, *a snake,* because of its spotted appearance like the skin of a snake). See SERPENTINE.

OPSIMOSE, *Beudant.* Partially altered Fowlerite (crystallized Rhodonite), from Franklin, New Jersey, and Klaperude, Dalecarlia.

OR BLANC. Gold Amalgam. See ELECTRUM.

OR DE CHAT. A name sometimes given to the small spangles of lamellar Mica as they occur in granitic rocks.

OR NATIF. Native Gold. See GOLD.

ORANGITE, *Bergemann.* A name for the orange-yellow coloured varieties of Thorite. S.G. 5·34.

ORAVITZITE, *Dufrénoy.* ORAWITZITE. A variety of Halloysite from Oravicza in S.E. Hungary.

ORIENTAL. See GEM.

ORIENTAL ALABASTER (*Alabâtre calcaire oriental,* Fr.). The term Alabaster (*Albâtre*) is applied by the French both to the true mineral of that name and to the Oriental stone, although the two differ widely both in composition and relative hardness. True Alabaster is a *sulphate* of lime, but Oriental Alabaster is a stalagmitic *carbonate* of lime, which has been deposited from water holding that substance in solution. Such water, finding its way into the hollows and crevices of rocks, falls down, and on evaporation leaves a calcareous layer, which in time accumulates to such an extent as to entirely fill some caverns. Oriental Alabaster is generally clouded and zoned in a concentric manner; it effervesces with acids, and cannot be scratched with the nail; while ordinary Alabaster is more uniform in texture, is not acted on by acids, and is so soft as readily to yield to the nail. Very fine slabs of Oriental Alabaster are procured from the Pyrennees, Chili, and the mountain of Ourakan, E. of Benisouf in High Egypt. There are also old quarries in the province of Oran in Algeria. This stone was held in great estimation by the ancients, who procured it from the neighbourhood of Thebes, from quarries which are still unexhausted. By the Greeks it was called *Alabastrites,* and, also, sometimes *Onyx,* in allusion to its parallel undulating layers, sometimes of different colours, and supposed to bear a fanciful resemblance to the markings on the human nail; thus it is alluded to by Dioscorides, as λίθος ἀλαβαστρίτης ὁ καλούμενος ὄνυξ; by the Latins, *marmor onychites,* from its use in making boxes for preserving precious ointments, which boxes were commonly called Onyxes and Alabasters, after the material of which they were made. In Matt. xxxi. 7 we read: "There came unto him a woman having an alabaster-box of very precious ointment, and poured it on his head as he sat at meat." (See also Mark xiv. 3, and Luke

vii. 37.) In after times the boxes used for containing unguents were called Alabasters and Onyxes, without any reference to the materials out of which they were made. The name is said to be derived from Alabastron, an Egyptian village between the Nile and the Red Sea, which was the principal locality known in ancient times; but probably the village was called after the substance quarried there, and the ancient Greeks derived both the name and the stone itself from Arabia, which was for a long while the only country from which it was procured, and in whose language *al batstraton* signifies, the whitish stone.

The finest specimen of Oriental Alabaster in England is in the Soanean Museum. It consists of an Egyptian sarcophagus cut out of a single block of stone, and covered inside as well as outside with hieroglyphics carved in intaglio. This magnificent work of ancient Egyptian art was purchased by Sir John Soane for two thousand guineas. See ALABASTRITES.

Brit. Mus., Case 46.

M. P. G. Slabs A 14 and 21, in Hall. Horse-shoe Case, Nos. 406A, 409, 410.

ORIENTAL AMETHYST. A lilac-blue or violet variety of Sapphire, forming the passage between that gem and the Ruby.

ORIENTAL CHALCEDONY. A name sometimes applied by lapidaries to the finer kinds of Carnelian: Occidental Chalcedony, on the other hand, being used by them to denote the softer and less brilliant varieties of a yellowish-red colour.

ORIENTAL CHRYSOLITE. The name given by lapidaries to yellowish-green Sapphire.

ORIENTAL EMERALD. Sapphire of a greenish-yellow colour, tending more or less to olive.

ORIENTAL GARNET. Blood-red or dark crimson Garnet.

ORIENTAL HYACINTH. The name given by jewellers to rich reddish-brown varieties of Sapphire; and also to Hyacinth of a hyacinth-red or deep red colour with a tinge of brown, and sometimes of orange-yellow.

ORIENTAL OPAL. The name given by jewellers to the finest kinds of Precious Opal.

ORIENTAL PERIDOT. The name by which varieties of Sapphire of a greenish-yellow colour, verging on olive, are sometimes called.

ORIENTAL RUBY. The name sometimes given to fine red varieties of Sapphire. See RUBY.

ORIENTAL SAPPHIRE. The name given to blue transparent varieties of Corundum. When perfect, of a clear, bright, prussian-blue colour, and possessed of a high degree of transparency, this stone is valued next to the Oriental Ruby. It is, however, seldom found in this state, being more frequently pale blue, passing by degrees into entirely colourless. Pale varieties when exposed to a strong heat entirely lose their colour without undergoing any other alteration, and have often been sold for diamonds.

Sapphire is cut and polished on wheels of copper by means of emery-powder, and is generally cut in brilliant fashion, in steps, facets, and sometimes en cabochon, especially for eastern countries.

In the mineral collection at the Jardin des Plantes there is a Sapphire of an elongated oval shape, sapphire-blue at the two extremities and topaz-yellow in the middle. This stone is enumerated in the inventory of the French crown-jewels, taken in 1791, as weighing 19¼ carats, and was valued at 6000 francs (£240). Another stone, one of the finest in existence, is mentioned in the same inventory, where its weight is stated to be 132¼ carats, and its value 100,000 francs (£4000). This stone, which is without blemish or fault, was found in Bengal by a poor dealer in wooden spoons. After passing through many hands it eventually became the property of the house of Rospoli at Rome, from whom it was purchased by a German Prince, who resold it to Porret the French jeweller for the sum of 170,000 francs (£6800). It is now in the Museum of Mineralogy at the Jardin des Plantes. Two large Sapphires belonging to Miss Burdett Coutts, exhibited by the Messrs. Hancock at the French Exposition of 1855, were valued at 170,000 francs (£6800).

Brit. Mus., Case 19.

ORIENTAL TOPAZ. A variety of Sapphire of a yellow colour more or less mixed with red. The most esteemed colour is a bright jonquil-yellow, and next a pure lemon-yellow. It is a very beautiful stone, though inferior in value to Ruby or Sapphire.

M. P. G. Horse-shoe Case, Nos. 786—789.

OROBITES. See BEZOAR MINERALE, DRAGÉES DE TIVOLI.

OROPION, *Glocker*. Bergseife, or Rock Soap.

ORO PUDRE (or *impure gold*). An alloy of Gold, Silver, and Palladium, from Porpez in South America, composed of grains, with numerous edges, of an impure gold colour, which fuse *BB*, without imparting any colour to borax, and are malleable after cooling.

Analysis, by *Berzelius* :

Gold	.	.	.	. 85·98
Palladium	.	.	.	. 9·85
Silver	.	.	.	. 4·17

100·00

ORPIMENT. Rhombic: primary form a right rhombic prism with a perfect cleavage parallel to the longer axis. Occurs in small crystals, but rarely: also massive, foliated, or columnar, disseminated, and sometimes reniform. Colour bright lemon-yellow passing into golden-yellow. Lustre resinous; pearly on planes of perfect cleavage. Sub-transparent or translucent only at the edges. Sectile. Streak yellow, slightly paler than the colour. Thin laminæ obtained by cleavage. Flexible but not elastic. H. 1·5 to 2. S.G. 3·4 to 3·48.

Comp. Tersulphide of arsenic, or As S³ = arsenic 61, sulphur 39=100.

Analysis, by *Laugier* :

Arsenic	.	.	.	. 61·86
Sulphur	.	.	.	. 38·14

100·00

BB on charcoal, burns with a bluish flame, and gives off sulphurous and arsenical fumes.

Dissolves in nitro-muriatic acid or ammonia.

Localities. Tajowa, near Neusohl, in Lower Hungary, in small crystals, in stratified clay and limestone. It is generally found in foliated and fibrous masses. Kapnik, in Transylvania. Moldawa, in the Bannat. Felsobanya, in Upper Hungary. Hall, in the Tyrol, in Gypsum. St. Gotthard, in Dolomite. The Solfatara, near Naples. Julamerk, in Koordistan. Zimapan, in Mexico. The finest specimens of Orpiment are brought from Persia in brilliant yellow masses, with a lamellar texture, called Golden Orpiment.

Name. The word Orpiment is a corruption of the Latin name *Auripigmentum*, or golden paint (from *aurum, gold,* and *pigmentum, paint*), which was applied to it partly in consequence of its use as a pigment, and partly because it was believed to contain a small quantity of gold. The Orpiment employed as a pigment (*King's yellow* or *Orpin*) at the present day is prepared artificially by subliming arsenious acid with a small quantity of sulphur. It is also used by pyrotechnists and bookbinders, and

is an active ingredient in a kind of epilatory soap, as well as of a depilatory called *Poudre subtile,* in combination, according to Dr. Paris, with quicklime and a vegetable powder. Orpiment is the 'Αρρενιχὸν of the ancients, and 'Αρσενιχὸν of the later Greeks. (*Hill.*)

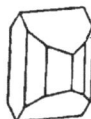

Fig. 315.

It is distinguished from Native Sulphur by its foliated structure.

Brit. Mus., Case 12.

M. P. G.   Wall-case 23.

ORTHITE, *Berzelius.* A variety of Allanite, occurring in long, thin, acicular crystals, and massive. Colour blackish-grey, inclining to black. Opaque; in very thin splinters subtranslucent. Lustre vitreous. Streak brownish-grey. Brittle. Fracture conchoidal, uneven. H. 5 to 5·75. S.G. 3·28 to 3·54.

Comp. R̈³ S̈i + R̈ S̈i + Ḧ.

Analysis, from Hitteröe, by *Rammelsberg* :

Silica	.	.	.	. 33·81
Alumina	.	.	.	. 13·04
Peroxide of iron	.	.	. 8·16
Protoxide of iron	.	.	. 8·30
Protoxide of cerium	.	.	. 20·50
Yttria	.	.	.	. 1·45
Lime	.	.	.	. 9·42
Magnesia	.	.	.	. 0·38
Potash	.	.	.	. 0·67
Water	.	.	.	. 3·38

99·11

BB swells up, boils, and fuses to a blackish blistered glass; with borax or microcosmic salt yields a glass coloured by iron.

Dissolves in muriatic acid (if not previously ignited), and is converted into a gelatinous mass.

Localities. Finbo, near Fahlun, in Sweden, in acicular, diverging prisms, of a dark brown colour, sometimes upwards of a foot long, imbedded in Quartz; also at Ytterby, in Sweden; Skeppsholm, an island near Stockholm, in black vitreous masses disseminated in gneiss; Krageröe, Hitteröe, Arendal, and Fille Fjeld, in Norway; Finland; Miask, in the Ural; Dresden, &c.

Name. From ὀρθὸς, *straight.*

Brit. Mus., Case 38.

ORTHOCLASE, *Dana.* ORTHOKLAS, *Breithaupt.* Potash Felspar. Oblique: primary form an oblique rhombic prism. Colour white, reddish-white, flesh-red, and greyish. Lustre vitreous, sometimes pearly on the cleavage-faces. Semi-transparent or translucent. Streak greyish-white. Fracture conchoidal to uneven and splintery. H. 6. S.G. 2·5 to 2·6, increasing as the potash is replaced by soda or lime.

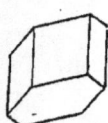

Fig. 316.

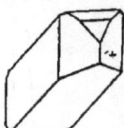

Fig. 317.

Fig. 318.

Fig. 319.

Comp. K̈ S̈i + A̎l S̈i³ = silica 64·8, alumina 18·4, potash 16·8 = 100; but a portion of the potash is frequently replaced by lime, soda, magnesia, &c.

Analysis, from Baveno, by *Abich* :

Silica	.	.	.	. 65·72
Alumina	.	.	.	. 18·57
Potash	.	.	.	. 14·02
Soda	.	.	.	. 1·25
Lime	.	.	.	. 0·34
Magnesia	.	.	.	. 0·10
				100·00

BB fuses with great difficulty to a blistered, turbid glass; in borax dissolves slowly, forming a transparent glass.
Not acted on by acids.

Localities. — English. Cornwall, in large opaque-white crystals, in the granite generally: in irregular crystalline mass, St. Stephens; near the old Lizard Head, in green Talc; St. Michael's Mount; Huel Coates, near St. Agnes, in twin crystals, converted into Cassiterite (*figs.* 317, 319) — *Scotch.* Rubislaw, Aberdeenshire; Drumidoon, or Drimadoon, in Arran, in claystone porphyry (*fig.* 318). — *Irish.* Slieve Corra, Mourne Mountains, in opaque-white crystals (*figs.* 316, 317), and in twins like those from St. Gotthard. — *Foreign.* Ekatherinenburg, in Siberia, and in many parts of the Ural; Arendal, in Norway; Carlsbad and Elnbogen, in Bohemia; Baveno, on Lago Maggiore, in Piedmont; Lomnitz, in Silesia; St. Gotthard (*figs.* 316, 317); United States, at Rossie, in New York; Brazil, &c.

Name. From ὀρθὸς, *straight*, and κλάω, to *cleave.*

Orthoclase, or Potash Felspar, enters into the composition of many rocks, and is one of the ordinary ingredients of granite, of which it commonly constitutes about 45 per cent.

This mineral is very liable to decomposition. In that process the potash enters into combination with a portion of the silica, and is carried off in a soluble form; while the residue, consisting of a white earth, composed of silicate of alumina, is the Kaolin or China-clay, which is used in the manufacture of porcelain and earthenware.

For varieties, see ADULARIA, AMAZON STONE, AVENTURINE FELSPAR, CHESTERLITE, ERYTHRITE, GLASSY FELSPAR, HELLEFLINTA or LEELITE, ICESPAR, LOXOCLASE, MICROCLINE, MOONSTONE, MURCHISONITE, PERTHITE, RHYACOLITE, SANIDINE, SUNSTONE, VALENCIANITE.

Brit. Mus., Case 29.

M.P.G. Horse-shoe Case, Nos. 944, 955—959, 965, 972, 973, 1039. Upper Gallery, Wall-case 6, No. 3, &c. &c.

ORTHOTOMOUS KOUPHONE SPAR, *Mohs.* See THOMSONITE.

OSERSKITE, *Breithaupt.* A variety of Aragonite, from Nertschinsk.

OSMELITE, *Breithaupt.* Occurs in thin prismatic concretions, radiated or stellar. Colour greyish-white, inclining to smoke-grey. Lustre between pearly and vitreous. Translucent. Feel greasy. Fracture fibrous and conchoidal. H. 4 to 5. S.G. 2·8 to 2·83.

Analysis; by *Adam* :

Silica	.	.	.	. 52·91
Lime	.	.	.	. 32·96
Soda	.	.	.	. 8·89
Potash	.	.	.	. 4·01
Oxide of iron	.	.	. 0·54
				100·75

Locality. In trachyte, at Niederkirchen, near Wolfstein, on the Rhine, on Calc Spar.

Name. From ὀσμὴ, *smell*, in allusion to the argillaceous smell given out by it when breathed upon.

OSMIDE OF IRIDIUM, } See IRIDOSMINE.
OSMIUM-IRIDIUM. }

OSTEOCOLLA. (From ὀστέον, *a bone*, and κόλλα, *glue.*) Calc Spar incrusted on sticks, stones, and other bodies. See OSTREOCOLLA.

OSTEOLITE, *Bromeis.* An earthy form of Apatite, occurring in altered dolomite, between Ostheim and Eichen, near Hanau; and at Amberg, in the Erzgebirge.

OSTRANITE, *Breithaupt.* A Zircon of a greyish- or clove-brown colour. Lustre vitreous. Very brittle.

Locality. Fredericksvärn, in Norway. Named after Ostera, the German goddess of spring and morning.

Brit. Mus., Case 26.

Fig. 320.

OSTREOCOLLA. (From *ὄστρεον, an oyster,* and *κόλλα, glue.*) The name given to calcareous incrustations deposited on roots, twigs, or small branches of trees, the vegetable matter of which being eventually destroyed, the lime is left in a tubular form, resembling small bones. Hence the name Osteocolla (which see), and the vulgar belief in their efficacy in uniting broken limbs.

OTTRELITE, *Haüy.* Occurs in small shining scales, disseminated through clay-slate. Colour greenish- or blackish-grey. Lustre vitreous. Translucent. Streak pale green. Scratches glass. S.G. 4·4.

Comp. $(\ddot{\mathrm{F}}\mathrm{e}, \ddot{\mathrm{M}}\mathrm{n})^3 \ddot{\mathrm{S}}\mathrm{i} + 2\ddot{\mathrm{A}}\mathrm{l} \ddot{\mathrm{S}}\mathrm{i} + 3\ddot{\mathrm{H}}.$

Analysis, by *Damour:*

Silica	43·34
Alumina	24·63
Protoxide of iron	16·72
Protoxide of manganese	8·18
Water	5·66
	98·53

BB fuses with difficulty at the edges to a black magnetic glass.

Decomposed only by heated sulphuric acid.

Localities. British. Ottrelite has been found by Mr. Warington Smyth on Snowdon and in the Isle of Man.

Name. After the locality, Ottrez, a village in Belgium, on the borders of Liège and Luxembourg.

OUTREMER, *Leymerie, Beudant.* A name for Lapis Lazuli, after that by which the finer pulverised portions used by painters are known in France.

OUVAROVITE. See UWAROWITE.

OWENITE, *Genth.* A mineral resembling Thuringite, named after Dr. David Dale Owen, U.S., geologist. Occurs massive, as an aggregation of minute scales. Colour olive-green. Lustre pearly. Streak paler

than the colour. Very tough. Fracture subconchoidal. Powder greasy to the touch. Odour argillaceous. H. 2·5. S.G. 3·197.

Comp. $2\ddot{\mathrm{R}}^3 \ddot{\mathrm{S}}\mathrm{i} + 3\ddot{\mathrm{R}} \ddot{\mathrm{S}}\mathrm{i} + 6\ddot{\mathrm{H}}.$

OXACALCITE, *C. U. Shepard.* See WHEWELLITE.

OXALATE OF IRON, *Phillips.* See OXALITE.

OXALATE OF LIME, *H. T. Brooke.* See WHEWELLITE and THIERSCHITE.

OXALITE, *Hausmann.* Occurs in capillary crystals; also botryoidal, fibrous, granular, or earthy. Colour yellow. Lustre dull. Opaque. Slightly sectile. Fracture uneven, earthy. H. 2. S.G. 2·13 to 2·5.

Comp. $2\ddot{\mathrm{F}}\mathrm{e}\, \ddot{\mathrm{C}} + 3\ddot{\mathrm{H}} =$ protoxide of iron 41·4, oxalic acid 42·7, water 16·1 = 100.

BB on charcoal, yields a vegetable odour, and becomes successively yellow, black, and red. Forms a yellow solution without effervescence in nitric aid.

Localities. Kolosoruk, near Bilin, in Bohemia, in Lignite. In Brown Coal, at Gross Almerode, and Duisburg, in Hesse. Potschappel, near Dresden. Cape Ipperwash, Canada, in shales.

OXHAVERITE, *Brewster.* A pale-green translucent variety of Apophyllite, found indistinctly crystallized on calcified wood, at Oxhaver springs, in Iceland.

OXIDE OF ANTIMONY, *Phillips.* See CERVANTITE.

OXIDE OF ANTIMONY, *Phillips.* See VALENTINITE.

OXIDE OF ARSENIC, *Phillips.* See ARSENOLITE.

OXIDE OF-BISMUTH, *Phillips.* See BISMUTH OCHRE.

OXIDE OF CHROME, *Phillips.* See CHROME OCHRE.

OXIDE OF COBALT. See EARTHY COBALT.

OXIDE OF COPPER. See CHALCOTRICHITE, MELACONITE, RED COPPER, TENORITE.

OXIDE OF IRON. See BOG-IRON ORE, GÖTHITE, HEMATITE, LEPIDOKROKITE, LIMONITE, MAGNETITE, SPECULAR IRON, STILPNOSIDERITE, TURGITE, YELLOW OCHRE.

OXIDE OF LEAD. See MENDIPITE, MINIUM, PLATTNERITE, PLUMBIC OCHRE.

OXIDE OF MANGANESE. See BRAUNITE, HAUSMANNITE, MANGANITE, PSILOMELANE, PYROLUSITE.

OXIDE OF MOLYBDENA, *Phillips.* See MOLYBDINE.

OXIDE OF NICKEL. See ANNABERGITE.

OXIDE OF TIN, *Phillips.* See CASSITERITE.

OXIDE OF TUNGSTEN, *Phillips.* See WOLFRAMINE.

OXIDE OF URANIUM. See PITCHBLENDE.

OXIDE OF ZINC. See ZINCITE.

OXIDE ROUGE DE TITANIUM, *La Metherie.*
See RUTILE.

OXYCHLORIDE OF COPPER. See ATACA-
MITE.

OXYCHLORIDE OF LEAD. See MENDIPITE
and MATLOCKITE.

OXYDE ZINCIQUE. See ZINCITE.

OXYDULATED COPPER. See RED COPPER.

OXYDULATED IRON, *Phillips.* See MAG-
NETITE.

OXYSULPHIDE OF ZINC. See VOLTZITE.

OZARKITE. An amorphous or fibrous-
radiated form of Thomsonite. It occurs associated with Elæolite and Apatite at the
Ozark mountains, Arkansas.

OZOCERITE, or OZOKERITE, *Glocker, Phillips, Dufrénoy.* A mineral resin, resembling
a resinous wax in consistence and translucence. Amorphous, sometimes fibrous or
foliated. Colour yellowish-brown by transmitted light, dark leek-green by reflected
light. Lustre glimmering, glistening on
principal fracture. Subtranslucent. Has
an agreeable aromatic odour. Softens by
the heat of the hand, and may be kneaded
like wax. Structure sometimes foliated.
Fracture flat-conchoidal in one direction, in
another splintery: can be reduced to powder
in a mortar. S.G. 0·955.

Comp. CH, or carbon 86, hydrogen 14
=100.

Fuses at 140° F., and boils at from 121° to
210° C. (249·8° to 410° F.), distilling to a
clear oily fluid, which becomes solid on
cooling. Burns with a bright clear flame,
without leaving any residue.

Forms a yellow solution readily in oil of
turpentine; with difficulty in ether or
alcohol.

Not acted on by acids.

Localities.—British. Urpeth Colliery, near
Newcastle-on-Tyne; Uphal, Linlithgow-
shire. — *Foreign.* Moldavia; at Slanik and
Zietrisika, in sandstone, in sufficient quan-
tity to be used for economical purposes; in
Austria, at Truskawiezi, in Galicia, and
Gresten, near Garning. Wettin in Prussia.

Name. From ὄζειν, *to smell,* and κηρός, *wax.*

M.P.G. Horse-shoe Case, Nos. 95 to 97.

Magnus, Schrötter, and Malaguti agree
in representing Ozocerite as a mixture of
several substances, differing in their physical
properties, yet possessing the same ultimate
chemical constitution.

P.

PACO, or PACOS. The Peruvian name for
an earthy-looking ore, composed of Brown
Oxide of Iron, with almost imperceptible
particles of Native Silver, or chloride of
silver, disseminated through it.

The greater part of the silver extracted
by mining in Peru is found in this species
of ore. This mineral is the *Argentiferous
Gossan* of the Cornish miners.

PAGODA STONE, *Muirhead.* The Chinese
name for a dark brown limestone containing
Orthoceratites. These when polished and
framed are held in great estimation in
China as ornaments for state apartments.
They are said to be common at Yunnan.
The Chinese name of "pagoda-stone" owes
its origin to the general belief that the
Orthoceratites (which show, in their al-
veoles and in the septa passing through
them, a certain resemblance to a Pagoda)
have been formed underground in places
where the towers of the buildings in question have cast their shadows on the surface
of the ground.

PAGODITE. See AGALMATOLITE.

PAISBERGIT, *Igelström.* A variety of
Rhodonite from Paisbergs Iron Mine, in
Phillipstadt, Sweden. S.G. 3·63.

Analysis, by *Igelström* :

Silica	46·46
Protoxide of manganese	41·88
Protoxide of iron . .	3·31
Lime	8·13
Magnesia . . .	0·91
	100·69

PALAGONITE, *v. Waltershausen.* A hydrous Scapolite. Amorphous, in grains and
fragments. Colour amber-yellow to yellowish-brown, and blackish. Lustre vitreous to resinous. Transparent to translucent.
Streak yellow. Easily frangible. Fracture
conchoidal, or uneven. H. 4 to 5. S.G.
2·4 to 2·7.

Comp. $2(\ddot{A}l, \ddot{F}e) \ddot{S}i + (\dot{C}a, \dot{M}g, \dot{N}a) \ddot{S}i^2$
$+ 6\dot{H}.$

Analysis, by *v. Waltershausen*

Silica	41·90
Alumina . . .	12·72
Peroxide of iron . .	16·74
Lime	6·71
Magnesia . . .	6·86
Soda	1·92

Potash . . . . . 0·99
Water . . . . . 12·16
                          ___
                          100·00

BB fuses readily to a shining magnetic globule.

Dissolves easily in acid.

Localities. Forms the basis of basaltic tufa and conglomerate in Iceland, France, Germany, the Azores, the Canary, Cape de Verde, Galapagos and Tortugas Islands.

Name. After one of the localities, Palagonia, in the Val di Noto, Sicily.

Palagonite is considered by Bunsen to have resulted from an alteration of pyroxene rocks, the iron in which has become converted into peroxide.

PALLADIUM. See NATIVE PALLADIUM.

PALLADIUM GOLD. See PORPEZITE.

PALLADIUM OCHRE, or PALLADIUM OXIDE. A brown ochreous substance associated with the Palladium-gold of Brazil.

PANABASE, *Beudant.* (From πᾶν, *all,* and βάσις, *base.*) See TETRAHEDRITE.

PANTHER-AGATE. See LEONINE.

PAPER-COAL, or PAPIER-KOHLE. The name given to certain layers of Lignite in consequence of their leaf-like structure.

PARACOLUMBITE, *C. U. Shepard.* A mineral occurring in grains and short irregular seams of an iron-black colour, very sparingly disseminated through a large boulder, near Taunton in Massachusetts. It consists probably of oxides of iron and uranium, combined with a metallic (not titanic) acid.

PARAGONITE, *Schafhäutl.* Allied to biaxial Mica (*Damourite*). Colour yellowish and greyish-white. Glittering. Translucent at the edges. Slightly unctuous to the touch. Somewhat harder than Rock Salt; easily scraped with a knife.

Comp. $24\ddot{A}l\ \ddot{S}i + 9\dot{N}a\ \ddot{S}i + \ddot{F}e\ \ddot{S}i^3$.

Analysis, by *Schafhäutl:*

Silica · . . . . 50·20
Alumina . . . . 35·90
Peroxide of iron . . . 2·86
Soda . . . . . 8·45
Water . . . . . 2·45
                          ___
                          99·36

BB alone, unchanged; with borax forms a clear glass.

Not acted on by acids.

Locality. St. Gotthard, in mica-slate.

PARALOGITE, *N. Nordenskiöld.* Occurs in four- and eight-sided prisms. Colour

white, blue, or reddish-blue. Lustre vitreous. H. 7·5. S.G. 2·6.

Analysis, by *Thoreld:*

Silica . . . . . 44·95
Alumina . . . . 26·89
Lime . . . . . 14·44
Magnesia . . . . 1·01
Soda . . . . . 10·86
Protoxide of manganese . trace
Loss by ignition . . 1·85
                          ___
                          100·00

BB fuses easily to a colourless blebby glass.

Locality. Bucharei in Siberia, associated with Lapis Lazuli and Felspar.

PARALUMINITE, *Steinberg.* Probably an impure Websterite.

Comp. $\ddot{A}l\ \ddot{S} + 15\dot{H} =$ Websterite $+ \ddot{A}l\ \dot{H}^6$.

Analysis, by *Märtens:*

Alumina . . . . 35·96
Sulphuric acid . . . 14·04
Water . . . . . 50·00
                          ___
                          100·00

Localities. Hallé and Morl in Prussia.

PARANTHINE, *Haüy.* A name for certain compact varieties and crystals of white and pale blue Scapolite.

Analysis, from Malsjö, by *v. Rath:*

Silica . . . . . 47·54
Alumina . . . . 24·69
Peroxide of iron . . . trace
Lime . . . . . 16·84
Soda . . . . . 3·55
Potash . . . . . 0·85
Magnesia . . . . 2·18
Water . . . . . 1·75
                          ___
                          97·06

Locality. The limestone quarries at Malsjö, in Wermland, Sweden.

Name. From παφάνθω, to glance on.

PARASTILBITE, *v. Waltershausen.* A mineral from Borgarfiord, resembling Stilbite, but differing from it in the measurement of its angles.

PARATOMOUS AUGITE SPAR, *Mohs.* See AUGITE and PYROXENE.

PARATOMOUS KOUPHONE SPAR, *Mohs.* See HARMOTOME.

PARATOMOUS LEAD BARYTE, *Haidinger.* See CALEDONITE.

PARATOMOUS LIME HALOID, *Mohs.* See ANKERITE.

PARGASITE, or NOBLE HORNBLENDE. Occurs disseminated in roundish semi-crystalline masses and in six-sided prisms

T

with dihedral summits.   Colour paler than
Hornblende; generally olive- or bottle-
green. Somewhat translucent. Lustre
vitreous or pearly. Harder than Fluor, but
softer than Quartz. S.G. 3·11.

Fig. 321.

Analysis, from Pargas, by Bonsdorff:

Silica	. . . .	45·69
Alumina	. . .	12·18
Magnesia	. . .	18·79
Lime	. . . .	13·83
Protoxide of iron	. .	7·32
Protoxide of manganese	.	0·22
Hydrofluoric acid	.	1·50

99·53

BB like Hornblende, but yields a paler
glass.
  Locality. Pargas (whence the name),
near Abo in Finland; in Calc Spar.
  Brit. Mus., Case 33.
  The name Pargasite is applied to certain
varieties of Hornblende of high lustre and
rather dark tints of green, but paler than
common Hornblende. . The crystals are
generally thick and short.
  PARISITE, L. di Medici-Spada. Hexagonal. Occurs in elongated double six-
sided pyramids, with truncated apex and
very perfect basal cleavage. Colour green-
ish- or browish-yellow with a tinge of red.
Lustre vitreous; pearly on cleavage planes.
Translucent at the edges; transparent in
thin laminæ.   Streak   yellowish-white.
Fracture slightly conchoidal. H. 4·5. S.G.
4·35.

Comp. $8(\dot{C}e, \dot{L}a, \dot{D}, \dot{C}a)\ \ddot{C} + (\dot{C}e, \dot{L}a, \dot{D})$

$\dot{H} + 2Ca\ F$.
  Analysis, by Bunsen (mean of two):

Protoxides of cerium, lan-		
thanum and didymium	.	59·85
Carbonic acid	. .	23·58
Lime	. . . .	3·16
Fluoride of calcium	.	11·02
Water	. . . .	2·40

100·01

BB infusible and incandescent; but turns
brown.
  Difficultly soluble in muriatic acid with
effervescence.
  Locality. Emerald mines of the Musso
Valley, New Granada.
  Name. In honour of the discoverer, J. J.
Paris.

Brit. Mus., Case 49.
  M.P.G. Horse-shoe Case, Nos. 839—843.
  PARROT-COAL. A Scotch term for Cannel Coal, from the loud crackling noise with
which it flies to pieces when placed upon
the fire. Chance Pit, Borrowstownness, Linlithgowshire. The Great Clyde Coal-field.
  PARTSCHIN, Haidinger. PARTSCHINE,
Dufrénoy. Found in reddish-brown grains
in small cubical crystals like Monazite, in
sand at Olahpian in Hungary. H. 6 to 6·5.
S.G. 4 to 4·1.

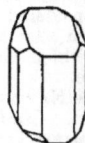

Fig. 322.

  Name. After the late Professor Paul
Partsch, of the Vienna Museum.
  PARTSCHITE, C. U. Shepard. A mineral
forming 1·05 per cent. of the meteorite of
Seneca River, Cayuga co., New York, U.S.
Occurs in four-sided oblique prisms with
dihedral summits. Colour silver-white or
with a tinge of reddish-grey. Streak dark
grey. Brittle. Magnetic. H. 5·6.
  Contains iron, nickel, magnesium and
phosphorus.
  Soluble, when powdered, in aqua-regia.
  Name. After Professor Paul Partsch, of
Vienna.
  PASSAUITE. A variety of Porcelain
Earth formed by the decomposition of
Porcelain Spar at Obernzell, near Passau, in
Bavaria.
  PATERAÏTE. Haidinger's name for a
sulphide of molybdena composed of Mo S³.
  PATRINITE. See AIKENITE.
  PAULITE, Werner. Hypersthene from the
island of St. Paul, on the coast of Labrador.
S.G. 3·389.
  Brit. Mus., Case 34.
  PEACOCK COPPER. The name given, in
Cornwall, to massive Copper Pyrites (Chal-
copyrite) when covered with an iridescent
tarnish. The finest specimens are obtained
at East Crinnis, and other mines in the
neighbourhood of St. Austell.
  PEACOCK-COAL. The name given to
Coals which display iridescent colours.
  PEA-IRON ORE. Bog Iron-ore when occurring in small globular concretions. This
variety is met with in Anglesea; at Tremadoc, Caernarvonshire; Galston, Ayrshire; Clonmore, Mayo, &c.
  Brit. Mus., Case 16.

PEA-MINERAL. See PISOPHALT.

PEACH. A name given by Cornish miners to Chlorite.

PEARL KERATE, *Mohs.* See CALOMEL and KERATE.

PEARL MICA, *Jameson.* See MARGARITE.

PEARL SINTER. See FIORITE.

PEARL SPAR. The most common variety of Bitter Spar. It comprises the rhombohedral crystallizations of Dolomite with curved faces and a shining, pearly lustre. Colour white, grey, or yellowish. Translucent. Yields to the knife. Harder than Calc Spar. S.G. 2·5.

Localities. — British. The lead mines of the north of England. Alston in Cumberland. Derbyshire. Beeralston, Devonshire. Cornwall. Leadhills and Charlestown, Scotland. — *Foreign.* Schemnitz in Hungary. Kapnik in Transylvania. Freyberg in Saxony. Traversella in Piedmont. Gap in France, &c.

Brit. Mus., Case 47.

PEARL-STONE, *Jameson.* See PERL-STEIN.

PEASTONE. Is, strictly speaking, a rock rather than a mineral. It resembles Oolite in structure, but differs from it in the larger size of the grains of which it is composed. These consist of concentric masses of a round or spherical shape, varying in size from a pea to a nut, and are imbedded in a calcareous cement.

Brit. Mus , Case 46.

PEAT. See LIGNITE.

PECH-BLENDE, *Werner.* See PITCHBLENDE.

PECHEISENERZ. See GÖTHITE.

PECHERZ, *Werner.* See PITCHBLENDE.

PECH-KOHLE, *Werner;* or PITCHCOAL. See JET.

PECHKUPFER, *Hausmann.* See KUPFERPECHERZ.

PECHSTEIN, *Werner.* See PITCHSTONE.

PECHSTEIN DE MÉNIL-MONTANT. A name for Menilite, after that of the locality.

PECHURAN, *Hausmann.* See PITCHBLENDE.

PECHURAN HYACINTHE, *Dufrénoy.* See GUMMIERZ.

PECTOLITE, *Beudant, Dana.* PECKTOLITE, *Dufrénoy.* PECTOLITH, *v. Kobell.* Oblique; primary form an oblique rhombic prism, and isomorphous with Wollastonite. Occurs in spheroidal masses composed of an aggregation of acicular crystals, or of delicate fibres arranged in a radiated or stellar form. Colour white or greyish. Lustre of crystals vitreous: of fibrous silky to dull. Transparent when crystallized: when fibrous translucent to opaque. Very tough.

Fracture splintery. H. 4 to 4·5. S.G. 2·65 to 2·88.

Fig. 323.

Comp. Silicate of lime and soda, or $(\overset{...}{KNa})^3 \overset{...}{Si}^4 + 4\overset{..}{Ca}^3 \overset{...}{Si}^2 + 3\overset{.}{H} = $ silica 54·22, lime 33·73, soda 9·30, water 2·74 = 100.

Analysis, from Ratho, by *Heddle :*

Silica	. 52·58
Lime	. 33·75
Soda	. 9·26
Alumina . . .	. 4·15
Water	. 2·80
	99·84

BB gives out a few bubbles of gas, and fuses readily to a white translucent glass. Small pieces placed in concentrated muriatic acid, after several days become disintegrated, and yield gelatinous silica.

Localities. — Scotch. Ayrshire: on the shore near Landelfoot in white, fibro-crystalline, translucent radiations; Knockdolian Hill. Ratho quarries near Edinburgh, in large orbicular masses (*Ratholite*), in greenstone. Castle Rock, Edinburgh. Prince Charles' Cave, and Taliskar, in Skye. Corstorphine Hills, in greenstone. Kilsyth, Stirlingshire (*Soda Table-Spar*). Kilpatrick (*Stellite*). — *Foreign.* Monte Baldo in the Southern Tyrol ; and Monte Monzoni in the Fassa-thal, in large masses. Isle Royal, Lake Superior, N. America.

Name. From σηκτὸς, *put together,* and λίθος, *stone.*

Brit. Mus., Case 28.

M. P. G. Horse-shoe Case, Nos. 1186, 1187.

PEGANITE, *Breithaupt.* Occurs in thin crusts or very small rhombic prisms, with the acute lateral edges truncated. Colour emerald-green to white. H. 3 to 4. S.G. 2·49 to 2·54.

Comp. Fischerite $-2\overset{.}{H}$, or $\overset{..}{Al}^2 \overset{...}{P} + 6\overset{.}{H}$.

Locality. Strigis, near Freiberg, and at Frankenberg in Saxony.

PEGMATOLITE, *Breithaupt.* Occurs in short thick (often macled) crystals, of much greater width than length, implanted in druses on Dolomite. Colour faint reddishor yellowish-white.

Analysis, by *Erni :*

Silica	. 65·58
Alumina . . .	. 18·45
Soda	. 10·41

T 2

Potash .	. .	2·84
Magnesia	. .	2·09
Lime .	. .	0·71

100·08

Locality. Poorhouse Quarry, Chester co., Pennsylvania.

PEKTOLITH, *v. Kobell.* See PECTOLITE.

PÉLÉ'S HAIR. Lava blown by the wind, when in a very fluid state, into hair-like fibres. It is called by the natives of Hawaii *Pélé's Hair,* after the principal goddess of the volcano of Kilauea. In chemical composition it closely resembles *Augite.* The following analysis is given by Dana:

Silica .	. .	39·74
Alumina	. .	10·55
Protoxide of iron	.	22·29
Lime .	. .	2·74
Magnesia	. .	2·40
Soda .	. .	21·62

99·34

Dana describes the mode of formation of this substance from actual observation, as follows:—" It covered thickly the surface to leeward, and lay like mown grass, its threads being parallel and pointing away from the pool (of melted lava). On watching the operation a moment, it was apparent that it proceeded from the jets of liquid lava thrown up by the process of boiling. The currents of air blowing across these jets bore off small points and drew out a glassy fibre, such as is produced in the common mode of working glass. The delicate fibre floated on till the heavier end brought it down, and then the wind carried over the lighter capillary extremity. Each fibre was usually ballasted with the small knob which was borne off from the lava-jet by the winds."— *Geology of the United States' Exploring Expedition,* 1828–42, p. 179.

Locality. Kilauea, Island of Hawaii. Also in Iceland.

The modern lava and volcanic glass of Kilauea are composed of silica, protoxide of iron, alumina, soda, potash, and lime, but these vary much in their relative proportions. They contain a large amount of oxide of iron. Professor Silliman, jun., asserts that soda is present to the exclusion of potash; but this is not borne out by Mr. Peabody's analysis of Pélé's Hair, in which both potash and soda are given.

M. P. G. Upper Gallery, Wall-case 1, Nos. 20, 20A.

PELICANITE, *Ouchakow.* A product of the decomposition of Felspar, and related to

Cimolite or Steiermark, and other minerals of the same kind. Colour pale greenish. Translucent at the edges. Amorphous. Fracture conchoidal. H. 3·5. S.G. 2·256.

Comp. $\ddot{A}l\ \ddot{S}i^3 + 2\dot{H}$, or Cimolite + $\dot{H}$.
Analysis, by *Ouchakow:*

Silica .	. .	58·90
Alumina	. .	20·49
Peroxide of iron	.	0·39
Lime .	. .	trace
Magnesia	. .	0·50
Potash .	. .	0·29
Phosphoric acid	.	0·16
Water .	. .	8·35
Quartz .	. .	10·33

99·41

In a matrass gives water.

BB burns white, but does not fuse even at the edges. With cobalt turns dark blue. Insoluble in muriatic acid.

Locality. The government of Kiew in Russia, as the base of a granitic rock.

PELIOM. The name sometimes given to Iolite from Bodenmais in Bavaria; from πελιός, *smoky-blue,* in allusion to its colour.

Analysis, by *Stromeyer:*

Silica .	. .	48·35
Alumina	. .	31·71
Magnesia	. .	10·16
Protoxide of manganese	.	0·33
Protoxide of iron .	.	8·32
Water .	. .	0·59

99·46

Brit. Mus., Case 36.

M. P. G. Upper Gallery, Wall-case 1, No. 20.

PELOKONITE (from πελός, *ash-coloured,* and κόνις, *powder*). A variety of Cupreous Manganese, found associated with Chrysocolla, in Chili. H. 3. S.G. 2·5 to 2·6.

PENCATITE. The name given by Roth to a variety of Predazzite. It is, however, a doubtful species.

Comp. $\dot{C}a\ \ddot{C} + \dot{M}g\ \dot{H}$.
Analysis, by *Roth:*

Carbonic acid	. .	27·45
Lime .	. .	33·53
Magnesia	. .	23·27
Alumina and peroxide of iron		2·88
Silica .	. .	3·28
Water .	. .	10·26

100·67

Locality. Predazzo, in the Southern Tyrol.

PENNINE. A species of Chlorite, occurring in acute rhombohedrons, truncated at the extremities, and often tabular. Colour bluish,and bluish-green by reflected light; by transmitted light, emerald-green in the direction of the axis, and brown at right angles to it. Transparent to translucent. S.G. 2·67.

Comp. $5(Mg^2, \dot{F}e) \ddot{S}i + \ddot{A}l \ddot{S}i + 7\dot{H}$.
Analysis, from Monte Rosa, by *Schweizer*:

Silica	.	.	.	33·07
Alumina	.	.	.	9·69
Magnesia	.	.	.	32·34
Protoxide of iron	.	·.	11·36
Water	.	.	.	12·58

                 99·04

BB swells up and fuses at the edges to a yellowish-white enamel.

Dissolves in muriatic acid, with separation of silica in a flocculent state, and with still greater facility in sulphuric acid.

Localities. Ala, in Piedmont. Zermatt, in Valais. The Tyrol.

Name. After the Pennine Alps.

Brit. Mus., Case 32.

M. P. G. Horse-shoe Case, No. 1170.

PENNITE, *Hermann.* Occurs in whitish or pale green incrustations, having a surface of minute spherules. Lustre weak. H. 3. S.G. 2·86.

Comp. $\dot{C}a \ddot{C} + 2\dot{M}g \ddot{C} + \dot{H}$.
Analysis, from Texas, by *Hermann*:

Carbonic acid	.	.	44·54
Magnesia	.	.	.	27·02
Lime	.	.	.	20·10
Oxide of nickel	.	.	1·25
Protoxide of iron	.	.	0·70
Protoxide of manganese	.	0·40
Alumina	.	.	.	0·15
Water	.	.	.	5·84

                 100·00

BB alone, infusible.

Localities. — *British.* The Shetlands: Swinaness, on chromate of iron with Emerald Nickel; Haroldswick, in Unst, massive-foliated. — *Foreign.* Texas, Lancaster co., Pennsylvania, U.S.

PENTAKLASIT, *Hausmann.* See PYROXENE.

PENTLANDITE. A variety of Eisen-nickelkies, from Craignure.

Name. After J. B. Pentland.

PEPLOLITE. A pseudomorph, after Iolite, from Ramsberg, in Sweden. H. 3 to 3·5. S.G. 2·68 to 2·75.

Analysis, (mean of three):

Silica	.	.	.	45·95
Alumina	.	.	.	30·51
Protoxide of iron	.	.	6·77

Magnesia	. . . . 7·99
Lime	. . . . 0·50
Protoxide of manganese	. trace
Water	. . . . 8·30

                 100·02

Name. From πίπλος, *a cover*, and λίθος, *stone.*

PEPONITE. *Dufrénoy.* A variety of fibrous, acicular and radiated Tremolite, forming kidneys in a serpentinous rock, mixed with oxydulated iron, at Berggies-Shübel in Saxony. It has a more decided green tint than Calamite, the result, doubtless, of its association with Serpentine; and its lustre is, also, very slight.

PERCYLITE, *H. J. Brooke.* A Chloride (perhaps oxychloride) of lead and copper. Occurs in minute cubes. Colour and streak sky-blue. Lustre vitreous. H. 2·5.

Comp. $(Pb, Cl + \dot{P}b) + (Cu, Cl + \dot{C}u) + \dot{H}$.

BB fuses readily; on charcoal, in the inner flame, affords metallic globules, which dissolve without residue in dilute nitric acid.

Locality. La Sonora, in Mexico, accompanying Gold, in a matrix of Quartz and Red Oxide of Iron.

Name. After John Percy, M.D., Professor of Metallurgical Chemistry in the Government School of Mines.

Brit. Mus., Case 57 B.

PERICLASE; PERICLASIA, *Scacchi.* PERIKLASE. Cubical. Occurs in octahedrons, with a perfect cubic cleavage, and in grains. Colour dark-green. Lustre vitreous. Transparent to translucent. H. 6. S.G. 3·75.

Comp. $\dot{M}g$, or magnesia with 5 to 8 per cent. of protoxide of iron.

Analysis, by *Damour*:

Magnesia	.	.	.	93·86
Protoxide of iron	.	.	5·97

                 99·83

BB infusible.

Slowly soluble in nitric acid when reduced to powder.

Locality. Monte Somma, in ejected masses of white limestone.

Name. From περί, *around*, and κλάσις, *cleavage*, in allusion to the cleavages at the angles.

Periclase is most surely distinguished by cubical cleavage from the white Peridotolivine with which it is associated. It is distinguished from Fluor and Scheelite (*Tungsten*), which it resembles in external characters, by cleavage and hardness.

                 T 3

PERICLINE, *Phillips.* PERIKLIN, *Breit-haupt.* A variety of Albite, in which a portion of the soda is replaced by potash. In twins like those of Albite. Generally more opaque, and of less specific gravity, than ordinary Albite or Felspar. H. 6. S.G. 2·64.

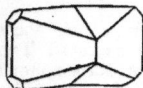

Fig. 324.   Fig. 325.

Comp. $(\dot{N}a, \dot{K} + \ddot{A}l) \ddot{S}i^6$.

Analysis, from Pantellaria, by *Abich :*

Silica	68·23
Alumina	18·30
Peroxide of iron	1·01
Soda	7·99
Potash	2·53
Lime	1·26
Magnesia	0·51
	99·83

BB fuses more readily than Albite.

Localities. St. Gotthard, in Switzerland, in large distinct crystals. Zöblitz, in Saxony. The Pfundersthal and Schmiernerthal, in the Tyrol. The Sau-alpe, in Carinthia.

Name. From σιριχλίνης, *inclined about* (the end).

Brit. Mus., Case 30.

PERIDOT, *Haüy;* PERIDOT-OLIVINE. See CHRYSOLITE. The name Peridot is derived from the Arabic *feridet,* a precious stone.

PERIDOT BLANC, *Scacchi.* Translucent, white, or colourless Chrysolite, from Vesuvius. See MONTICELLITE.

PERIDOT GRANULIFORME, *Haüy.* See OLIVINE.

PERISTERITE, *T. S. Hunt.* A variety of Albite containing disseminated grains of Quartz, or in fine cleaveable masses free from Quartz. Lustre vitreous. Exhibits a fine play of colours analogous to that of Labradorite. H. 6. S.G. 2·625 to 2·627.

Analysis, by *T. S. Hunt:*

Silica	66·80
Alumina	21·80
Peroxide of iron	0·30
Soda	7·00
Potash	0·58
Lime	2·52
Magnesia	0·20
Loss by ignition	0·60
	99·80

Locality. Bathurst, in Canada.

Name. From πιριστιρὰ, *a pigeon,* from the resemblance of its colours to those on a pigeon's neck.

When cut in a proper direction, Peristerite exhibits a delicate celestial-blue opalescence, which is very beautiful.

PERITOMOUS ANTIMONY GLANCE, *Mohs.* See FREIESLEBENITE.

PERITOMOUS AUGITE SPAR, *Mohs.* See ARFVEDSONITE.

PERITOMOUS HAL-BARYTE, *Mohs.* See STRONTIANITE.

PERITOMOUS KOUPHONE SPAR, *Mohs.* See MESOTYPE.

PERITOMOUS LEAD BARYTE, *Mohs.* See MENDIPITE.

PERITOMOUS RUBY BLENDE, *Mohs.* See CINNABAR.

PERITOMOUS TITANIUM ORE, *Mohs.* See RUTILE.

PERLAIRE, *Haüy.* PERLIT, or PERLSTEIN, *Werner.* See PEARLSTONE.

PERLGLIMMER, *Leonhard.* See MARGARITE.

PERL-STEIN, *Werner;* or PEARL-STONE, *Jameson.* When felspathic rocks have undergone perfect fusion, those portions of the mass which have cooled the least rapidly assume the form of Pearlstone. This has a pearly lustre, inclining to waxy, and is of various tints of grey, yellow, brown or red. It is translucent at the edges or opaque, and has a small-conchoidal fracture. H. 6. S.G. 2·25, to 2·38. The material (*Pitchstone*) forming the paste or main mass of the rock, contains rounded or completely spherical nodules of a clear grey colour, and easily detached from the matrix. These have been compared to pearls, and have given the name of Pearlstone to the rock, while the kernels in question have received the name of Spherulite, from their spherical shape.

BB swells up violently, and forms a white, spongy slag. See OBSIDIAN.

Brit. Mus., Case 31.

M. P. G. Upper Gallery, Wall-case 1, Nos. 48 to 55; Wall-case 2, Nos. 14 to 25.

PEROFSKITE, *G. Rose.* See PEROWSKITE.

PEROWSKINE. See TETRAPHYLINE.

PEROWSKITE, *Kenngot.* First discovered by Butzengeiger in the granular limestone of Vogtzburg, on the Kaiserstuhl, and described by Walchner in 1825. Crystallizes in cubes and individual crystals, made up of an aggregation of smaller cubes, between which there are sometimes delicate films of Calc Spar, as may be ascertained by treatment with acids. Cleavage very distinct, parallel to the faces of the cube. Colour iron-black. Lustre brilliant-metallic ; glassy on cleavage face. Streak white or greyish. H. 5·5. S.G. 4·02.

Comp. Titanate of lime, or Ċa T̈i = titanic acid 59, lime 41 = 100.

Analysis (mean of two), from Schelingen, by *Seneca :*

Titanic acid .	. . . 59·12
Lime .	. . . . 36·81
Water .	. . . . 6·11
	101·04

BB alone, infusible.

Localities. Achmatovsk, near Slatoust, in the Ural, in crystals, or druses of crystals, the largest of which do not exceed 6 lines in length, associated with crystallized Chlorite and Magnetic Iron, in Chlorite Slate. Schelingen, in the Kaiserstuhl, in small black cubes, with Mica, Magnetite, &c.

Name. After Count L. A. von Perowski, of St. Petersburg.

Brit. Mus., Case 37.

PEROXIDE OF IRON. See MAGNETITE, MARTITE, HEMATITE (*Red Iron Ore, Specular Iron*).

PEROXIDE OF TIN, *Thomson.* See CASSITERITE.

PERTHITE, *Thomson.* A flesh-red variety of Orthoclase from Perth, in Upper Canada. S.G. 2·576 to 2·579.

Analysis, by *T. S. Hunt :*

Silica .	. . . 66·44
Alumina .	. . . 18·35
Peroxide of iron .	. . 1·00
Lime .	. . . . 0·67
Potash .	. . . . 6·37
Soda .	. . . . 5·56
Magnesia .	. . . 0·24
Loss by ignition .	. . 0·40
	99·01

Brit. Mus., Case 29.

PETALIT, *Haidinger, Hausmann.* PETALITE, *Phillips, Dana, Brooke & Miller.* Massive : three cleavages ; structure perfectly lamellar in *one* direction. Colour white, greyish or greenish ; frequently with a tinge of red. Lustre glistening ; pearly on the face of perfect cleavage. Translucent. Streak white. Fracture imperfect-conchoidal. H. 6. S.G. 2·4 to 2·45.

Comp. N̈aS̈i² + 2L̈iS̈i² + 4(Ä̈lS̈i⁶), or (N̈a + 2L̈i) S̈i⁴ + 4Ä̈l S̈i⁶.

Analysis, from Utö, by *Hagen :*

Silica .	. . . . 77·81
Alumina	. . . 17·20

Soda .	. . . . . 2·30
Lithia .	. . . . 2·69
	100·00

BB fuses readily and quietly to a turbid and rather blistered glass, colouring the flame red, especially when powdered and mixed with fluor-spar and bisulphate of potash.

Not affected by muriatic or sulphuric acid.

Localities. The iron mine of Utö, S. E. of Stockholm, accompanied by Lepidolite, Tourmaline, Spodumene and Quartz. Near York, on Lake Ontario. Bolton, Massachusetts, U. S. Elba (var. *Castor*).

Name. From πέταλον, *a leaf,* in allusion to its lamellar structure in one direction.

PETRE SALT. Nitre in its native state (see NITRE). When refined, it is called *salt-petre.*

Brit. Mus., Case 31.

PETROL, *Hatchett, Brochant.* PETROLE, PETROLEUM. A blackish or reddish-brown viscid variety of Asphaltum, containing much Naphtha. Rather thicker than common tar. Generally translucent. Odour strongly bituminous. Easily inflames, and burns with a bluish flame, giving off a thick black smoke, and leaving a very small earthy residue. Soluble in ether and alcohol. S.G. 0·7 to 0·85.

Comp. C H².

Analysis, from Alsace, by *Boussingault :*

Carbon .	. . . . 88·7
Hydrogen	. . . 12·6
	101·3

Localities.—British. Cornwall ; at Huels Unity and Jewel, and Carharrack. Chudleigh, Devonshire. Shropshire : Coal Port, near Colebrook Dale, Madeley, Pitchford, Peualley lead mine. Ormskirk, Lancashire. St. Catherine's Well, near Edinburgh.—*Foreign.* Tegernsee in Bavaria. Near Neufchatel in Switzerland. Amiano in Italy, and Pietra Bianca, on the southern foot of Vesuvius. Sicily. Near the volcanic isles of Cape de Verde, the sea is sometimes covered with it. Parma. Alsace in France, and at Beziers (Dep. Herault), and Clermont (Puy-de-Dôme). Oil Creek, Venango co., Pennsylvania ; and in Kentucky, Ohio, Virginia, &c., in the United States. Inniskillen, Canada West, where there is a deposit of Mineral Pitch, or Mineral Caoutchouc, extending over several acres, and also springs. The Ionian Islands ; Zante, &c. Trujillo and Cumana (Gulf of Cariaco). Antilles. In the provinces of Merida and Coro, and especially in that of Maracaybo, where it is used for paying the ships which navigate the lake. Mexico: in the interior, bubbling up to the surface of freshwater-lakes. In Texas, within 100 miles of Houston, there are springs of Petroleum, which in the summer months continually boil up from the bottom, near the centre of a small lake about a quarter of a mile in circumference. The Petroleum hardens on exposure, and becomes converted into Bitumen or Asphaltum.

In Canada there are springs on the River Thames, near its right bank. The Petroleum is frequently collected on cloths from off the surface of the water, and is very generally used in the neighbourhood as a remedy for cuts and cutaneous diseases in horses.

There are numerous Petroleum-wells in Burmah.

The principal wells are situated about three miles from the town of Ye-nan-gyoung (*Fetid-water-rivulet*, from the Petroleum which is so called in Burmese), upon a plateau or irregular table-land, with a gently rising surface, forming a sort of peninsula among the ravines. The wells are frequent along its upper surface, and on the sides and spurs of the ravines which bound it on the north and south-east. They are said to be about 100 in number, but of these some are exhausted or not worked. The depth of the wells appears to vary in tolerable proportion with the height of the mouth of the well above the river-level. Those measured by Prof. Oldham were 180, 190, and 270 feet in depth to the oil, and one was said to be 306 feet deep. The area in which the wells stand, does not seem to exceed half a square mile. They are in some places pretty close together; less, that is, than a hundred feet apart. They are all exactly alike; rectangular orifices about 4½ × 3½ feet, lined with horizontal timbers the whole way down. The oil appears to be found in a stratum of impure Lignite, with a good deal of sulphur. In one of the valleys, a stratum of this was seen cropping out, with the oil oozing out between the laminæ. There is another group of oil wells about a mile to the south of those just described.

The northern group contains about eighty wells now yielding oil: the southern group about fifty, which yield an inferior kind of oil mixed with water. The yield of the wells varies greatly. Some afford no more than five or six viss, while others give 700, 1000, and even it is said 1500 daily. The average in the northern group seems to be about 220 viss — in the southern 40 viss (viss = 3·6516 lbs. avoirdupois) daily: or 6,424,000 viss annually in the north group, and 730,000 in the south: making a total quantity of 7,154,000 viss, equal to about 11,690 tons.

Generally the supply from a well deteriorates the longer it is worked, and, if it be allowed to lie fallow for a time, it is said that the yield is found to be diminished on the recommencement of work. The oil is described by the people as gushing like a fountain from openings in the earth. It accumulates in the well during the afternoon and night, and is drawn off in the morning. The oil is conveyed to the river-side in carts loaded with earthen pots, containing ten viss each. Purchasers generally buy at the river side. The ordinary price used to be one takal the 100lbs. or about 16s. a ton. Lately, in consequence of the demand from Rangoon, it has risen to about 35s. per ton.

The oil looks like thin treacle of a greenish colour, and the smell is not unpleasant in the open air and in moderate strength. The Petroleum from the pits is very generally used as a lamp-oil all over Burmah. It is also used largely on the woodwork and planking of houses, as a preservative from insects, and for several minor purposes; as a liniment, and even as a medicine taken internally. The Chinese geography, translated in Thévenot's "*Voyages curieux*," says that it is a sovereign remedy for the itch, which its sulphureous affinities render highly probable. There is now a considerable export of the article from Rangoon to England. Paraffine is obtained from it, which is used in the manufacture of candles; also Belmontine and Sherwodole, which are used for burning—and a heavier fluid employed as a lubricating oil. It has been sold in the London markets at from £40 to £45 a ton.

(See "Narrative of Mission to Court of Ava, in 1855, by Captain Henry Yule," p. 23.) See NAPHTHA.

Name. From πίτρον, *a rock*, and *oleum*, *oil*. Brit. Mus., Case 60.

PETROSILEX. Compact impure Felspar, often resembling Jasper in appearance, but distinguishable from it by being fusible *BB*. S.G. 2·6 to 2·66.

PETROSILEX RESINITE, *Haüy*. See PITCHSTONE.

PETUNTZE or PEH-TUN-TSZ. A quartzose felspathic rock, consisting largely of Quartz. It is used in China, when mixed with Kaolin, in the manufacture of porcelain.

"Grind with strong arms, the pond'rous quartz betwixt,
The soft kaolin with petuntze mix'd."

PETZITE, *Haidinger;* or TELLURGOLD-SILBER. A variety of Telluric Silver (*Hessite*), in which part of the silver is replaced by gold. S.G. 8·72 to 8·83.

Analysis, from Nagyag, by *Petz :*

Silver .	.	.	. 46·76
Tellurium	.	.	. 34·98
Gold .	.	.	. 18·26
Iron, lead, sulphur		.	. traces

100·00

Brit. Mus., Case 3.

PFEIFENSTEIN. See PIPESTONE.

PHACOLITE, *Breithaupt.* A variety of Chabasite.

Comp. $Ca^3 \ddot{S}i^2 + 2\ddot{A}l \ddot{S}i^3 + 10\dot{H}$

Analysis, from Leipa, by *Anderson :*

Silica .	.	.	. 45·63
Alumina	.	.	. 19·48
Peroxide of iron .	.	.	0·43
Lime .	.	.	. 13·30
Soda .	.	.	. 1·68
Potash .	.	.	. 1·31
Magnesia	.	.	. 0·14
Water .	.	.	. 17·98

99·95

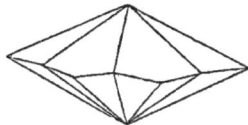

Fig. 326.

Localities. — *Irish.* Giant's Causeway, and Castle Rocks, Magilligan, Derry, *fig.* 326, in translucent to opaque, greyish-white or pinkish crystals, in cavities of amygdaloidal greenstone.—*Foreign.* Leipa in Bohemia. New York Island.

Name. From φακὸς, a bean, and λίθος, *stone.*

Brit. Mus., Case 37.

M. P. G. Horse-shoe Case, No. 1181.

PHARMACOCHALZIT, *Hausmann.* See OLIVINITE.

PHARMACOLITE, *Phillips, Nicol, Hausmann.* Oblique. Generally occurs in delicate silky fibres or acicular crystals forming stellated groups: also botryoidal, or globular and stalactitic. Rarely in distinct crystals. Colour white or greyish : often superficially tinged red or violet by arsenate of cobalt. Lustre vitreous. Translucent to opaque. Streak white. Fracture uneven. H. 2 to 2·5. S.G. 2·64 to 2·73.

Comp. Arseniate of lime, or $Ca^2 \ddot{A}s + 6\dot{H} =$ arsenic acid 51·11, lime 24·89, water 24·00 = 100.

Analysis, from Wittichen, by *Klaproth :*

Arsenic acid .	.	.	. 50·54
Lime .	.	.	. 25·00
Water .	.	.	. 24·46

100·00

BB is almost wholly volatilized, with dense white arsenical fumes.
Readily soluble, with effervescence, in nitric acid.

Localities. Andreasberg in the Harz. Riegelsdorf and Glücksbrunn, in Thuringia. St. Marie-aux-Mines, in the Vosges. Wittichen in Baden. Joachimsthal in Bohemia. Hesse.

Name. From φάρμακον, poison, and λίθος, *stone ;* in allusion to its containing arsenic.

Brit. Mus., Case 56.

PHARMACOSIDERITE, *Hausmann,* or arseniate of iron. Cubical : primary form the cube. Cleavage cubic, imperfect. Generally occurs crystallized in cubes : rarely massive. Colour various shades of green, inclining to yellowish-, and brownish green. Lustre vitreous. Semi-transparent to opaque. Streak pale olive-green or yellow. Pyro-electric. Fracture uneven or imperfect-conchoidal. H. 2·5. S.G. 2·9 to 3.

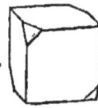
Fig. 327.

Fig. 328.

Comp. $\ddot{F}e^3\ddot{A}s + \ddot{F}e^3\ddot{A}s^2 + 18\dot{H}$ (Berzelius): or $\ddot{F}e, \ddot{F}e \ddot{A}s + 6\dot{H}$ (*Gmelin*).

Analysis, from Cornwall, by *Berzelius :*

Arsenic acid	.	.	. 38·00
Phosphoric acid .	.	.	0·70
Peroxide of iron .	.	.	40·56
Oxide of copper .	.	.	0·60
Water .	.	.	. 19·57
Matrix .	.	.	. 0·35

99·78

BB on charcoal, gives off strong arsenical odours, and fuses to a metallic, grey magnetic slag, which dissolves in borax or microcosmic salt, emitting an arsenical odour, and exhibiting an iron reaction.
Readily soluble in muriatic or nitric acid.

Localities.—English. Cornwall, *figs.* 327, 328, in tetrahedral crystals at Huel Jane; Huel Gorland; Huel Unity; Carharrack Mine; Carn Brea; Botallack. In cubes at Burdle Gill in Cumberland, on Quartz.— *Foreign.* St. Leonard in France. Schneeberg and Schwartzenberg in Saxony. Australia.

Name. From φάρμακον, *poison,* and σίδηρος, *iron.*

Brit. Mus., Case 56.

PHENACITE, *Dana.* PHENAKITE, *Nordenskiöld.* Hexagonal, often hemihedral. Primary form a rhombohedron. Colourless or bright wine-yellow, inclining to red. Lustre vitreous. Transparent to opaque. Refracts doubly. Fracture conchoidal, like that of Quartz. H.7·5. S.G.2·966 to 2·99.

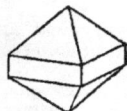 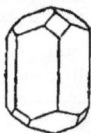

Fig. 329.   Fig. 330.

Comp. Silicate of glucina, or $\ddot{\mathrm{Be}}\ddot{\mathrm{Si}}=$ silica 55, glucina 45=100.

Analysis, from Perm, by *Hartwall:*
Silica . . . . . 55·44
Glucina . . . . 44·47
Magnesia and peroxide of
iron . . . . . traces

—
99·61

BB alone infusible: with borax slowly forms a clear glass; with carbonate of soda affords a white enamel. Ignited with solution of cobalt assumes a dull bluish colour. *Localities.* Siberia: in mica-slate at the emerald- and chrysoberyl-mine of Katharinenburg, in crystals sometimes nearly four inches across; in small crystals, on the east side of the Ilmen mountains, north of Miask, with Topaz, &c. In brown Iron Ore at Framont in Alsace. Durango in Mexico.

Name. From φέναξ, *a deceiver;* from its resemblance to Quartz, for which it may be mistaken.

Brit. Mus., Case 26.

PHENGITE, *v. Kobell.* See MUSCOVITE.

PHILLIPSITE, *Beudant, Dufrénoy.* Purple Copper. See ERUBESCITE.

PHILLIPSITE, *Levy.* Rhombic: primary form a right rectangular prism. Occurs in twin or compound crystals resembling those of Harmotome. Colour white, inclining to grey and sometimes pink. Lustre vitreous. Translucent to opaque. Streak white. Brittle. Fracture uneven, conchoidal. H. 4·5. S.G. 2·16 to 2·21.

Fig. 331.

Comp. $\ddot{\mathrm{K}}\ddot{\mathrm{Si}}+2\ddot{\mathrm{Ca}}\ddot{\mathrm{Si}}+4\ddot{\mathrm{Al}}\ddot{\mathrm{Si}}^3+18\dot{\mathrm{H}}.$
Analysis, from Marburg, by *L. Gmelin:*
Silica . . . . . 48·51
Alumina . . . . 21·76
Peroxide of iron . . . 0·99
Potash . . . . . 6·33
Lime . . . . . 6·26
Water . . . . . 17·23

—
101·08

BB gives off water, swells slightly, and fuses to a translucent glass. Readily and completely decomposed by muriatic acid, with the formation of a jelly of silica.

Localities.—Irish. Plaiskins, a headland near the Giant's Causeway, in white translucent crystals, in cellular trap rock, *fig.* 331. Magee Island, Londonderry, in minute flesh-coloured crystals, in amygdaloid.—*Foreign.* Capo di Bove, near Rome, in groups or sheaf-like aggregations. Aci Reale. Among the lavas of Vesuvius. Stempel near Marburg. Cassel. Giessen. Saint-Pancrace, Dept. de l'Aude, in France. Iceland.

Name. After the late William Phillips, author of " An Elementary Introduction to Mineralogy."

Brit. Mus., Case 29.

PHLOGOLITE, or PHLOGOPITE, *Breithaupt.* A uniaxial magnesian Mica belonging to the Biotite group. Rhombic. Occurs in rhombic or hexagonal prisms. Cleavage basal. Colour yellow or copper-red; also colourless, white or brown.

Comp. $2\ddot{\mathrm{Al}}\ddot{\mathrm{Si}}+3(\dot{\mathrm{Mg}},\dot{\mathrm{K}},\dot{\mathrm{Na}})\ddot{\mathrm{Si}}.$
Analysis, from the Vosges, by *Delesse:*
Silica . . . . . 37·54
Alumina . . . . 19·80
Protoxide of iron . . . 1·61
Protoxide of manganese . 0·10
Magnesia . . . . 30·32
Potash . . . . . 7·17
Soda . . . . . 1·00
Fluorine . . . . 0·22
Loss, ignition, &c. . . 1·51

—
99·97

BB like common Mica; fuses to a white enamel.

Localities. Found in limestone. Alt-Kemnitz, near Hirschberg, in Prussian Silesia, with Garnet and Idocrase. The Vosges Mountains. Sala, in Sweden. Edwards and Rossie, New York, St. Lawrence co., and other places in the United States.

Name. From φλογωπὸς (*of a fiery appearance*), on account of its colour.

Brit. Mus., Case 32.

PHŒNICITE, or PHŒNIKOCHROITE, *Glocker.* See MELANOCHROITE.

PHOLERITE. A hydrated silicate of alumina, resembling Kaolin in composition. Colour pure white. Formed of small convex scales of a pearly lustre. Soft to the touch. Friable between the fingers. Plunged in water gives out air-bubbles and adheres to the tongue; produces a doughy mass. S.G. 2·35 to 2·57.

Comp. $\ddot{A}l \ddot{S}i + 2\ddot{H}$.

Analysis, from Fins, by *Guillemin*:

Silica	42·93
Alumina	42·07
Water	15·00
	100·00

BB infusible.

Insoluble in nitric acid.

Localities. — English. Coalbrook Dale: of frequent occurrence in crevices of Ironstone nodules, especially in the Penneystone band; in the casts of plants in Ironstone, &c.—*Foreign.* France: Fins, Dept. of Allier; and Rive de Gier, Dept. of the Loire, in crevices in nodules of Coal-measure Ironstone. Belgium; Cache-Après and Mons. Naxos, with Emery. Schemnitz, with Diaspore. From the circumstance of its forming white spots or specks on various rocks, it is called by the workmen "*terrain fleuri.*" It is found abundantly, but not in large pieces, often associated with lamellar carbonate of lime. The coal-mines of Schuylkill co., Pennsylvania, U.S.

Name. From φολίς, *a scale.*

PHÖNICIT, *Kengott* (from φοινίκεος, *purple*). See MELANOCHROITE.

PHOSGENITE, *Breithaupt, Nicol.* See CROMFORDITE.

PHOSPHATE DE FER MANGANESIEN VERT, *Beudant.* See DUFRÉNITE.

PHOSPHATE OF CERIUM. See CRYPTOLITE.

PHOSPHATE OF COPPER, *Phillips.* See LIBETHENITE; also THROMBOLITE, and PHOSPHOCALCITE.

PHOSPHATE OF IRON, *Phillips.* See

VIVIANITE. See also CACOXENE, CARPHOSIDERITE, DELVAUXENE, DUFRÉNITE, and TRYPHILINE.

PHOSPHATE OF IRON AND MANGANESE, *Allan.* See TRIPLITE.

PHOSPHATE OF LEAD, *Phillips.* See PYROMORPHITE.

PHOSPHATE OF LIME. See APATITE.

PHOSPHATE OF MANGANESE, *Phillips.* See TRIPLITE.

PHOSPHATE OF URANIUM. See URANITE.

PHOSPHATE OF YTTRIA, *Phillips.* See XENOTIME.

PHOSPHATE OF ZINC. See HOPEITE.

PHOSPHOCERITE, *H. Watts.* Forms about one-thousandth part of the cobalt ore of Johannisberg, in Sweden. It remains as a residual product, in the form of a greyish-yellow crystalline powder, mixed with a few minute dark-purple crystals, which are strongly attracted by the magnet, and apparently consist of Magnetic Iron Ore and oxide of cobalt. The crystals of Phosphocerite are an octahedron and a four-sided prism, with quadrilateral terminations. Colourless, or of a pale sulphur-yellow. Lustre adamantine. H. 5 to 5·3. S.G. 4·78.

Comp. $(\dot{C}e, \dot{L}a, \dot{D})^3 \ddot{P}$, or identical in composition (though not in crystalline form) with Cryptolite.

Analysis, by *Watts*:

Protoxides of cerium, lanthanum, and didymium	64·68
Oxide of copper	2·83
Oxide of cobalt, silica, &c.	3·41
Phosphoric acid	28·46
	99·38

BB vitrifies partially at the edges and surface, and colours the flame slightly green.

PHOSPHOCHALCITE; PHOSPHOROCHALCITE, *v. Kobell.* Rhombic. Occurs crystallized in extremely minute individuals, and in fibrous and earthy masses. Colour emerald- or verdigris-green, often externally blackish-green at the surface, and dull. Lustre vitreous or adamantine. Translucent generally at the edges only. Streak slightly paler than the colour. Brittle. Fracture small-conchoidal to uneven. H. 5. S.G. 4 to 4·4.

Fig. 332.

Comp. Phosphate, of copper, or $\dot{C}u^5 \ddot{P} +$

$2\frac{1}{2}$H = oxide of copper $68\cdot0$, phosphoric acid $20\cdot3$, water $7\cdot07 = 100$.

According to Hermann, Phosphochalcite is a compound of Dihydrite ($\overset{..}{C}u^5\ \overset{...}{P} + 2\overset{.}{H}$),

and Ehlite ($\overset{..}{C}u^5\ \overset{...}{P} + 3\overset{.}{H}$); Nordenskiöld, on the contrary, concludes that Ehlite and Phosphochalcite are identical, and represented by the formula $\overset{..}{C}u^5\ \overset{...}{P} + 2\overset{.}{H}$.

Analysis, from Rheinbreitenbach, by *Hermann.* S.G. $4\cdot4$:

Oxide of copper	$67\cdot25$
Phosphoric acid	$24\cdot55$
Water	$8\cdot20$
	$100\cdot00$

BB alone when suddenly heated falls to powder; heated slowly on charcoal, turns black and fuses to a black globule, containing a small granule of copper.

Easily soluble in nitric acid and ammonia.

Localities. Rheinbreitenbach, Virneberg, and Linz, on the Rhine. Nischne Taguilsk, in the Ural. Hungary.

The Phosphochalcite from Taguilsk and Hungary contains a small quantity of arsenic, and Bergemann has found arsenic in all the native phosphates of copper.

For varieties, see DIHYDRITE, EHLITE, COPPER-DIASPORE, TAGILITE, PRASIN.

PHOSPHORBLEI. See PYROMORPHITE.

PHOSPHOREISENSINTER, *Rammelsberg.* See DIADOCHITE.

PHOSPHORITE, *Werner.* See APATITE.

PHOSPHORSAURE YTTERERDE. See XENOTIME.

PHOSPHYTTRIA, *Berzelius.* See XENOTIME.

PHOTICITE, or PHOTIZITE, *Dumenil.* A mixture of Rhodonite (silicate of manganese) and carbonate of manganese, from the neighbourhood of Rübeland, in the Harz. It has frequently a fibrous texture, and presents various tints of red, green, and grey, which become darker on exposure to the air.

Analysis, by *Dumenil:*

Silica	$39\cdot00$
Oxide of manganese	$49\cdot87$
Carbonic acid	$4\cdot00$
Alumina	$0\cdot12$
Oxide of iron	$0\cdot25$
Water	$6\cdot00$
	$99\cdot24$

PHOTOLITH, *Breithaupt.* See PECTOLITE.

PHYLLITE, *Thomson.* A variety of Ottrelite, met with in oblong or nearly elliptical scales, disseminated in argillaceous schist over a large area about Sterling, Gorham, and other places in the United States.

Analysis, from Leeds, by *T. Sterry Hunt:*

Silica	$26\cdot30$
Alumina	$37\cdot10$
Protoxide of iron	$25\cdot92$
Protoxide of manganese	$0\cdot93$
Magnesia	$3\cdot66$
Water	$6\cdot10$
	$100\cdot01$

Name. From φύλλον, *a leaf.*

PHYLLORETIN, *Forchammer.* A mineral resin, found in the pine stems in the marshes of Hottegard, in Denmark. It dissolves readily in alcohol, and melts at 87° C. ($124\cdot6^\circ$ F.).

Comp. C^3H^2 = carbon $88\cdot88$, hydrogen $9\cdot22 = 100$.

PHYSALITE, *Hisinger.* A coarse, almost opaque, variety of Topaz, found in yellowish-white crystals, occasionally of considerable dimensions, in Sweden, at Broddbo, and in a granite quarry at Finbo, near Fahlun. This variety intumesces when heated, whence the names Physalite, from φυσάω, *to blow,* and Pyrophysalite from πῦρ, *fire,* and φυσάω.

PIAUZITE, *Haidinger.* An earthy Mineral Resin of a brownish-black colour, much resembling slaty and lamellar black Coal. Texture never crystalline. Lustre resinous. Feebly translucent at the thinnest edges. Streak yellowish-brown. Sectile. Fracture imperfect-conchoidal. Fuses to a black mass like pitch at 600° F., and burns with a lively yellow flame, giving out an aromatic odour and a dense smoke. Soluble in ether, alcohol, and caustic potash. H. $1\cdot5$. S.G. $1\cdot22$.

Localities. Piauze, near Neustadt, in Carniola; the lignite mine of Mount Chum, near Markt Tüffer, in Styria. It is met with in small lumps, and very thin layers, in nearly all the mines in which the carboniferous strata are worked from Tüffer to Trifail and Sagor.

PICKERINGITE, *Hayes.* A variety of Magnesia Alum, occurring in masses, composed of long parallel fibres, generally affording rhombic forms. Colour white; pale rosered or delicate green in the direction of the fibres. Lustre like that of the finest Satinspar, which it much resembles. Transparent to translucent. Tastes like alum. S.G. $1\cdot78$ to $1\cdot8$.

Comp. $\overset{.}{M}g\ \overset{..}{S} + \overset{..}{A}l\ \overset{..}{S}^3 + 22\overset{.}{H}$.

PICRANALCIME.

Analysis:

Water of crystallization	. 45·45
Sulphuric acid . .	. 36·32
Alumina . . .	. 12·13
Magnesia . . .	. 4·68
Protoxide of iron and man-	
ganese	0·43
Lime	. 0·13
Muriatic acid . .	. 0·61
Loss	. 0·25
	100·00

Entirely soluble in cold water, forming a solution which has an acid reaction.
Locality. Near the port of Iquique, S. Peru.
Name. After John Pickering, President of the American Academy of Sciences.
Brit. Mus., Case 55.

PICRANALCIME, *Meneghini. Bechi.* An altered form of Analcime. Occurs in trapezohedral and cubo-trapezohedral crystals. Colourless to flesh-red and colophonite-red. Lustre vitreous. H. 5. S.G. 2·257.

Comp. (Ṁg Ṅa K̇)³ S̈i² + 3Äl S̈i² + 6Ḣ.
Analysis, by Meneghini:

Silica . . .	. 59·35
Alumina . . .	. 22·08
Magnesia . . .	. 10·25
Soda	. 0·45
Potash . . . ⌐	. 0·15
Water	. 7·65
	99·93

BB fuses with difficulty.
Soluble in acids.
Locality. Tuscany, covering the interior of geodes in Gabbro-rosso, or the surfaces of contact of Gabbro and Ophiolite; often accompanied by Calcite, Caporcianite, and Picro-Thomsonite.

PICROLITE, *Hausmann.* A fibrous variety of Serpentine, somewhat resembling Asbestos. Massive. Structure radiated. Colour leek-green, passing into yellow. Translucent at the edges. Streak somewhat shining. H. 3·5 to 4·0.

Analysis, from Wermeland, *by Stromeyer:*

Silica . . .	. 41·66
Peroxide of manganese	. 2·25
Magnesia . . .	. 37·16
Protoxide of iron . .	. 4·05
Water	. 14·72
	99·84

BB with borax, affords a green glass, which loses its colour on cooling.
Localities. The Taberg of Smaoland, in Sweden, in irregular veins traversing beds of Magnetic Iron Ore. Wermeland ; Silesia.
Name. From πικρὸς, *bitter,* and λίθος, *stone.*
Brit. Mus., Case 25.

PICROPHARMACOLITE, *Stromeyer.* A hydrated arseniate of lime and magnesia, with a large excess of magnesia: probably an impure Pharmacolite.

Comp. (Ċa Ṁg)⁵ Äs² + 12Ḣ.
Analysis:

Arsenic acid . .	. 46·97
Lime	. 24·65
Magnesia . . .	. 3·23
Oxide of cobalt . .	. 0·99
Water	. 23·97
	99·81

Locality. Riechelsdorf in Hesse.
Name. From πικρὸς, *bitter,* φάρμακον, *poison,* and λίθος, *stone.*

PICROPHYLL, or PIKROPHYLL, *Svanberg.* According to Breithaupt is an altered Augite. ·It occurs massive and foliated-fibrous, resembling Serpentine in appearance. Colour dark greyish-green. H. 2·5. S.G. 2·75.

Comp. (Ṁg Ḟe)⁵ S̈i² + 2Ḣ.
Analysis, by Svanberg:

Silica	. 49·80
Alumina . . .	. 1·11
Magnesia . . .	. 30·10
Lime	. 0·78
Protoxide of iron .	. 6·86
Protoxide of manganese	. trace
Water	. 9·85
	98·50

BB infusible but becomes white; ignited with cobalt solution, assumes a dingy red tint.
Locality. Sala, in Sweden.
Name. From πικρὸς, *bitter,* and φύλλον, *a leaf.*

PICROSMINE. Rhombic: primary form a right rectangular prism. Not found in crystals, but only massive, in granular or fine columnar aggregates. Colour greenish-white, or greenish-grey ; sometimes dark green. Translucent at the edges, or opaque.

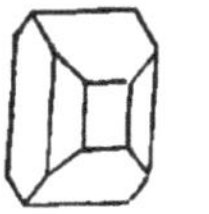

Fig. 333.

Lustre vitreous; on cleavage - surfaces pearly. Streak white and dull; very sectile. H. 2·5 to 3. S.G. 2·66.

Comp. Hydrated silicate of magnesia, or $\dot{M}g^5 \ddot{Si}^2 + \dot{H}$ = silica 55·9, magnesia 36, water 8·1.

Analysis, from Presnitz, by *Magnus*:

Silica	54·89
Alumina	0·79
Peroxide of iron	1·40
Magnesia	33·35
Protoxide of manganese	0·42
Water	7·30
	98·15

BB does not fuse, but increases in density, becomes black and afterwards white and opaque. Dissolves in borax and microcosmic salt, in the latter case leaving a skeleton of silica. Assumes a pale red colour when ignited with a solution of cobalt.

Localities. In the iron mine of Engelsberg, near Presnitz in Bohemia, in a bed in gneiss, associated with Magnetic Iron Ore. Greiner in Tyrol. Waldheim in Saxony.

Name. From πικρός, *bitter,* and ὀσμή, *smell;* in allusion to the bitter argillaceous odour it gives out when breathed on.

PICROTHOMSONITE. A mineral resembling Thomsonite in form, but differing from it in having the soda replaced by magnesia. Occurs in radiated masses with a laminated structure. Colour white. Lustre pearly. Transparent in thin fragments. Very fragile. H. 5. S.G. 2·278

Comp. $(\dot{C}a, \dot{M}g)^3 \ddot{Si} + 2\frac{1}{4}\ddot{Si} \ddot{A}l + 4\frac{1}{2}\dot{H}.$

Analysis:

Silica	40·36
Alumina	31·25
Lime	10·99
Magnesia	6·26
Soda and potash	0·29
Water	10·79
	99·94

BB intumesces and fuses to a white enamel.

Dissolves in cold acid with the formation of a jelly of silica.

Locality. Tuscany, associated with Caporcianite, in gabbro rosso.

Name. From πικρός, *bitter,* and *Thomsonite;* in allusion to the presence of magnesia.

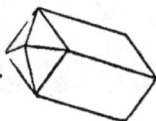

Fig. 334.

PICTITE. A name under which Turnerite (*Fig.* 334) has been occasionally brought to this country.

PIDDINGTONITE, *Haidinger.* A mineral substance composing nearly the whole of a large meteorite of a breccia-like aspect, which fell at Shalka in the East Indies, with the usual phenomena of light and detonations, on the 30th of November 1850. The Piddingtonite is of an ash-grey colour, more or less fine-grained, very fragile, (though of considerable hardness), more or less translucent, of oil-like brightness, imperfectly cleavable in two directions intersecting at angles of about 80° and 100°, and without magnetic action. H. 6·5.

Name. In honour of the late Mr. Piddington, Curator of the Calcutta Museum of Practical Geology.

PIEDMONTITE. A name for Manganesian Epidote from Piedmont.

PIERRE ALUMINEUSE, *Brochant.* See ALUM-STONE.

PIERRE À BRIQUET, } Names given in
PIERRE À FEU, } France to ordi-
PIERRE À FUSIL. } nary Chalk-flints,
and having reference to the purposes to which they were applied before the introduction of percussion locks to fire-arms, and the invention of more ready ways of obtaining a light than by means of the old-fashioned tinder-box.

PIERRE À JÉSUS. According to Beudant, a name given to transparent lamellar varieties of Gypsum (*Selenite*), in consequence of their being sometimes used, when divided into thin laminæ, instead of glass, for covering small images.

Most likely, as suggested by Mr. Warrington Smyth, the term is merely a corruption of the Italian *Gesso,* or Spanish *Yeso;* words themselves derived from γυψός, the Greek name for Gypsum.

PIERRE À LANCETTE. A name given to green Jasper on account of its being used for sharpening lancets in Java. It is, also, found in France, in the Dept. of Isère, and in Sicily.

PIERRE À MAGOT. See AGALMATOLITE.
PIERRE À NOYAUX. See COCCOLITE.
PIERRE À PLATRE, or Plaster-stone. See GYPSUM.
PIERRE À POT. See POTSTONE.
PIERRE CALAMINAIRE. See CALAMINE.
PIERRE CALCAIRE D'EDELFORS. See ÆDELFORSITE.
PIERRE CALCAIRE PUANTE, *La Metherie.* See STINKSTONE.

PIERRE CRUCIFORME, *Brochant.* Cross-stone. See HARMOTOME.

PIERRE D'ALUN. See ALUMSTONE.

PIERRE D'AMADOU. See TINDER-ORE.

PIERRE D'ARMENIE, *Beudant.* Compact earthy Augite, mixed with foreign matters.

PIERRE D'ARQUEBUSE. Iron Pyrites, (*Marcasite*). In the earlier times of the invention of fire-arms, Pyrites was used instead of Flint (see PIERRE À FUSIL), by which it was subsequently superseded. Hence it obtained the name of *Pierre d'arquebuse,* by which it was sometimes called.

PIERRE D'ASPERGE, *Brochant.* See AS-PARAGUS STONE.

PIERRE D'AZUR, *Brochant.* See LAPIS LAZULI.

PIERRE DE BARAM. A name for Pot-stone, which is made into culinary vessels in Upper Egypt.

PIERRE DE BOLOGNE. See BOLOGNESE STONE.

PIERRE DE CARABINE. Marcasite. See PIERRE D'ARQUEBUSE.

PIERRE DE CASSE-TÊTE. Jade. See NE-PHRITE.

PIERRE DE CÔME. A name for Potstone, after the quarries at Como in Italy, which have been worked from time immemorial.

PIERRE DE COSNE. Potstones from the Grisons.

PIERRE DE CORNE. See HORNSTONE.

PIERRE DE CROIX. See STAUROTIDE.

PIERRE DE FOUDRE. See METEORITE.

PIERRE D'ÉTAIN, *Brochant.* Tin-stone. See CASSITERITE.

PIERRE DE GALLINACE. A name ap-plied in Peru to greenish- or greyish-black Obsidian.

PIERRE DE HACHE, Axe-stone.
PIERRE DE IU of the Chinese. Jade.   } See NE-PHRITE.
PIERRE DE LA CIRCONCISION. Jade.

PIERRE DE LABRADOR, *Brochant.* See LABRADORITE.

PIERRE DE LARD. Lardite. See AGAL-MATOLITE.

PIERRE DE LUNE. See MOONSTONE.

PIERRE DE LUNE ARGENTINE. A name given by French lapidaries to Adularia (*Moonstone*), from Mt. Stella, St. Gotthard, where the finest stones are obtained.

PIERRE DE LYDIE. See LYDIAN STONE.

PIERRE DE MARMAROSCH. A pulverulent phosphate of lime from Marmaros, in Eastern Hungary, in which Klaproth detected the presence of fluoric acid.

PIERRE DE MIEL, *Brochant.* See MEL-LITE.

PIERRE DE PAILLE. See CARPHOLITE.

PIERRE DE POIX. The named used by Daubenton, to comprehend all the varieties of resinous Quartz.

PIERRE DE PORC. Lardite. See AGAL-MATOLITE.

PIERRE DE SAVON, *Haüy.* See SAPO-NITE.

PIERRE DE SERIN, *Haüy.* Epidote from Arendal. See ARENDALITE and ACANTI-CONITE.

PIERRE DE SOLEIL. See SUNSTONE.

PIERRE DE THUM, *Brochant.* Thumer-stone. See AXINITE.

PIERRE DE TRIPES, *Beudant.* A concre-tionary variety of Anhydrite, assuming the appearance of an intestine several times folded on itself. It is found at Wielickza in Poland, imbedded in Rock Salt.

PIERRE DE TOUCHE. See TOUCHSTONE.

PIERRE DES AMAZONES. See AMAZON STONE.

PIERRE DES INCAS. A kind of Marcasite, having a brilliant lustre, and a colour some-what approaching to tin-white, when first found, and bearing the same relation to European Marcasite, which is generally of a bronze colour, that white gold does to ordinary gold.

The Incas, or ancient kings of Peru, at-tributed many virtues to this stone, and wore it in rings and as amulets, which were buried with them after death. Some of these are said to have been taken from the tombs of princes who had been buried 400 years, without appearing to have undergone any alteration. It is said that the only mirrors in use amongst the ancient Peru-vians were formed of this stone, until the reign of the Inca Huaynacapac, who was defeated by Pizarro in 1532.

PIERRE DU LEVANT. See DOLOMITE.

PIERRE EN TIGE. See SCAPOLITE.

PIERRE GRANULAIRE. See SUGARSTONE.

PIERRE GRASSE, *Levy.* See ELÆOLITE.

PIERRE OLLAIRE. See POTSTONE.

PIERRE PONCE. See PUMICE.

PIERRE PUANTE, *Brochant, La Metherie.* See STINKSTONE.

PIERRE SANGUINE. A name given by the French to Hematite, because of its blood-red streak.

PIGOTITE, *Johnston.* A mineral compound of alumina and mudeseous* acid, forming an

---

* From μύδησις, *decay through excess of moisture.*

incrustation on the sides of certain caves, in the granite cliffs on the coast of Cornwall. It is of a brown colour in mass, and in powder of a yellow colour. Insoluble in water and alcohol. In the air, at a bright red heat, this mass burns very slowly, and leaves a grey or white ash, consisting of alumina with some slight foreign admixtures.

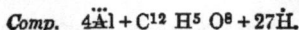

Comp. $4\ddot{A}l + C^{12} H^5 O^8 + 27\dot{H}$.

Name. After the Rev. M. Pigot.

The organic constituent of Pigotite is considered by James F. Johnston to be derived from the decay of the various plants which grow on the moist moorlands above, and which being carried by the waters into fissures in the granite beneath, combines with the alumina of the decomposed Felspar, and when it reaches the air, deposits itself over the roof and sides of the caverns in the form of layers varying from two to three inches in thickness.

Brit. Mus., Case 60.

PIHLITE, *Seftstrom.* A doubtful mineral species between Talc and Mica, from Fahlun in Sweden. Colour green. Lustre dull. Structure lamellar.

PIKROSMIN, *Haidinger.*

PIMELITE, *Karsten.* Massive or earthy. Colour apple-green or yellowish green. Translucent, with a dull greasy lustre. Feels greasy. Does not adhere to the tongue. Streak greenish-white. H. 2·5. S.G. 2·23 to 2·3.

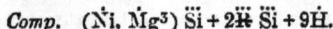

Comp. $(\dot{N}i, \dot{M}g^3) \ddot{S}i + 2\dot{H} \ddot{S}i + 9\dot{H}$.

Analysis, by *Baer* :

Silica	. 35·80
Alumina . . .	. 23·04
Peroxide of iron . .	. 2·69
Oxide of nickel . .	. 2·78
Magnesia . . .	. 14·66
Water	. 31·03

100·00

BB fuses to a slag only at thin edges: with borax gives a reaction of nickel.

Locality. Frankenstein, &c., in Silesia.

Name. From πιμελή, *fat,* and λίθος, *stone.* Brit. Mus., Case 25.

PINGUITE, *Berthier, Breithaupt.* A variety of Chloropal, resembling Bole. Occurs in masses of a siskin- or dark oil-green colour. Opaque or semitranslucent. Lustre slightly resinous. Streak paler than the colour. Feels greasy. Does not adhere to the tongue. Gives off a slight argillaceous odour when struck. Very soft, like newly made soap; does not become softer by immersion in water. Very sectile. Fracture flat-conchoidal or uneven-splintery. H. 1. S.G. 2·315.

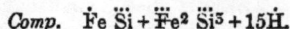

Comp. $\dot{Fe} \ddot{Si} + \ddot{Fe}^2 \ddot{Si}^5 + 15\dot{H}$.

Analysis, from Wolkenstein, by *Kersten* :

Silica	. 36·90
Alumina . . .	. 1·80
Peroxide of manganese	. 0·15
Peroxide of iron . .	. 29·50
Protoxide of iron .	. 6·10
Magnesia . . .	. 0·45
Water	. 25·10

100·00

BB becomes black, and fuses at the edges only; with carbonate of soda fuses to a black slag; dissolves in borax, exhibiting the reaction of iron.

Readily decomposed by warm muriatic acid, with separation of pulverulent silica, which retains the greenish colour of the mineral till it has been digested a considerable time.

Localities. Wolkenstein and Geilsdorf, in Saxony, in veins of Heavy Spar in gneiss. Tannhof, near Zwickau. Suhl, in the Thüringer Wald.

Name. From *pinguis, fat,* or *grease.* Brit. Mus., Case 26.

PINITE, *Werner.* PINITE, *Haüy.* An alkaline variety of altered Iolite. Occurs in six-sided or twelve-sided prisms, of which the lateral, and sometimes the terminal, edges are replaced. Cleavage sometimes basal, but often indistinct. Colour dirty grey, greyish-green, or brown. Slightly translucent or opaque. Lustre feeble. Yields easily to the knife. Streak white. Fracture uneven and splintery. H. 2·5. S.G. 2·78.

Fig. 335.

Analysis, from Auvergne, by *C. Gmelin* :

Silica	. 55·96
Alumina . . .	. 25·48
Protoxide of iron .	. 5·51
Magnesia . . .	. 3·76
Potash	. 7·89
Soda	. 0·39
Water	. 1·41

100·40

BB becomes colourless, and fuses at the edges to a blistered glass, which is either

PIOTINE.

colourless or black when a large proportion of iron is present.

Only imperfectly decomposed by muriatic acid.

Localities.—English. Cornwall: Lamorna Cove, in small dark brown crystals, *fig.* 335; in granite, near Breage, and at Tol Pedn Penwith, near the Land's End; near St. Just; Mulvra Hill, near Sancreed.—*Scotch.* Aberdeenshire. — *Foreign.* Auvergne, at the Puy-de-Dôme, in a felspathic porphyry. Penig, in Saxony. The Harz. United States.

Name. After *Pini*, the name of the mine near Schneeberg, in Saxony, where it was first discovered in granite.

Brit. Mus., Case 32.

PIOTINE. From πιότης, *fat.* See SAPO-NITE.

PIPESTONE, *Thomson.* A variety of clay-slate, or Argillite, of a dull greyish-blue or black colour, found in Northern Oregon, and carved by the Indians into the bowls of tobacco-pipes. Tender and soft to the touch. Easily moulded and cut. H. 1·5. S.G. 2·6.

Comp. $5\ddot{A}l\ \ddot{S}i^2 + 2\dot{C}a\ \ddot{S}i + 2\dot{H}$, or $2\ddot{A}l\ \ddot{S}i^5$ $+ (\dot{N}a\ \dot{C}a\ \dot{M}g)\ \ddot{S}i + \dot{H}.$

Analysis, by *Thomson :*

Silica	. 56·11
Alumina . . .	. 17·31
Peroxide of iron . .	. 6·96
Soda	. 12·48
Lime	. 2·17
Magnesia . . .	. 0·20
Water	. 4·58
	99·81

PIRENËITE. See PYRENEITE.

PIROP. See PYROPE.

PISOPHALT. (From πίσον, *a pea*, and *asphalt.*) A soft Bitumen, forming a passage between Petroleum and Asphalt.

PISSASPHALT. Πισσάσφαλτος, *Dioscorides.* (From πίσσα, *pitch*, and ἄσφαλτος, *asphalt.*) See EARTHY BITUMEN. The ancient Greeks gave the name to the liquid as well as the solid Bitumen, both of which, according to Dioscorides, they obtained from the Ceraunian mountains, near Apollonia.

PISSOPHANE, *Breithaupt.* Stalactitic, or amorphous. Colour olive-green to liver-brown. Lustre vitreous. Transparent. Streak greenish-white to pale yellow. Rather sectile. Easily frangible. Fracture conchoidal. H. 1·5. S.G. 1·93 to 1·98.

PISTACITE. 289

Comp. Sulphate of alumina, and per-oxide of iron, or $\left.\begin{matrix}\ddot{A}l \\ \ddot{F}e\end{matrix}\right\}^2 \ddot{S} + 15\dot{H}.$

Analysis, of green variety, by *Erdmann :*

Alumina . . .	. 35·301
Peroxide of iron . .	. 9·799
Sulphuric acid . .	. 12·487
Water	. 41·700
Gangue and loss .	. 0·709
	99·996

BB blackens, and with the fluxes gives a reaction for iron.

Dissolves readily in muriatic acid.

Localities. Garnsdorf, near Saalfeld, and at Reichenbach, in Saxony, on alum-slate.

Name. From πίσσα, pitch, and φαίνω, to seem.

Probably Pissophane is not a simple mineral, but a mixture of various salts, formed by the decomposition of alum-slate.

PISTACITE. PISTAZITE, *Werner.* Occurs in prismatic crystals, also granular, earthy, and in crusts. Colour pistachio-green, passing to olive- and blackish-green, also brown or yellow. Transparent. Easily frangible. S.G. 3·35 to 3·5.

Fig. 336.

Comp. Iron-and-lime Epidote, in which a large quantity of the lime is replaced by protoxide of iron, and a large proportion of the alumina by peroxide of iron.

Analysis, from Dauphiny, by *Descotils :*

Silica	. 37·0
Alumina . . .	. 27·0
Peroxide of iron . .	. 17·0
Peroxide of manganese .	. 1·5
Lime	. 14·0
	96·5

BB fuses at the edges, and subsequently swells up, forming a dark brown mass, which, by exposure to a more powerful blast, becomes black and somewhat rounded.

Localities.—Scotch. Shetland, in syenite. Rona, in Quartz. Mull and Skye, in trap rock. Arran.—*Foreign.* Arendal, in Magnetic Iron (*Arendalite*), in very fine crystals. The Ural. Finland. Greenland. Mont Blanc, and other parts of the Alps. The Pyrenees. Bourg d'Oisans, in Dauphiny. Grossarl, in Austria. The Fichtelgebirge. The Harz. North America.

U

Name. From its pistachio-green colour.
Brit. Mus., Case 35.

M. P. G. Horse-shoe Case, Nos. 1030 to 1032.

PISTOMESITE, *Breithaupt.* A variety of Breunnerite, composed of one atom of each of the carbonates of magnesia and iron. S.G. 3·415.

Comp. $\dot{M}g\ \ddot{C} + \dot{F}e\ \ddot{C}.$

Analysis, by *Fritzsche* :

Carbonate of magnesia	. 44·96
Carbonate of iron . .	55·27
	100·23

Locality. Thurnberg, near Flachau in Salzburg.

PITCH COAL, *Jameson.* A name for Jet, having reference to its pitch-like aspect.

PITCH OPAL. An inferior variety of Common Opal.

PITCHBLENDE, *Phillips.* PITCH ORE, *Jameson.* Amorphous: generally occurs massive and disseminated, also botryoidal and reniform, with a columnar or curved lamellar structure. Colour greyish-, greenish- or brownish-black. Opaque. Lustre dull or submetallic. Streak greenish-black. Very brittle. Fracture uneven or small-conchoidal. H. 5·5. S.G. 6·468 to 8.

Comp. Proto-peroxide of uranium, or

$\dot{U}\ddot{U}$=uranium 84·78, oxygen 15·22=100.

Analysis, from the Tanne Mine, Joachimsthal, by *Rammelsberg* :

Proto-peroxide of uranium .	79·30
Silica	5 30
Protoxide of iron . . .	3·03
Lime	2·81
Magnesia . . .	0·46
Lead	6·20
Arsenic	1·13
Bismuth, with lead and copper	0·65
Water	0·36
	99·09

BB alone, infusible: with borax and salt of phosphorus forms a yellow glass in the outer flame; a green glass in the inner flame.

Easily soluble in warm nitric and nitro-muriatic acid.

Localities.—*English.* Cornwall: St. Austell Consols; Huel Basset and Huel Buller; Ting Tang Mine; Tolcarne; Tin Croft Mine, in reniform masses; Huel Trenwith; Huel Providence.—*Foreign.* Kongsberg, in Norway. Marienberg, Schneeberg, Johanngeorgenstadt, and Wiesenthal, in Saxony, in botryoidal masses accompanying various ores of silver and lead. Joachimsthal and Przibram, in Bohemia. Retzbanya, in Hungary. Adrianople, in Turkey.

Pitchblende is distinguished from brown Blende by colour, specific gravity, fracture and streak; from Wolfram, by streak and fracture. Oxide of Uranium (prepared from an acid solution of Pitchblende) is used under the name of Uranium yellow, for colouring glass, to which it imparts a pale opalescent sea-green colour, much admired in Turkey, and used by the Turks and Egyptians for mouth-pieces to pipes. It is also very valuable in porcelain painting, affording an orange tint in the enamelling furnace, and a black colour in that in which it is baked.

Brit. Mus., Case 17.

M. P. G. Principal Floor, Wall-cases 13 (British), 20 (Foreign).

PITCHSTONE. A form of Obsidian or volcanic glass, having the lustre of pitch rather than glass. It presents various tints of yellow, green, grey, red, brown and black, and has a resinous lustre inclining to vitreous. Feebly translucent to opaque. Fracture conchoidal, splintery-uneven. H. 5 to 6. S.G. 2·2 to 2·3.

BB fuses with intumescence, and forms a blebby glass.

Localities.—*Scotch.* Arran, Rum, Canna, Mull, Lamlach. Argyleshire. Skuir of Eigg, Hebrides.— *Irish.* Newry. — *Foreign.* Siberia. Iceland. Auvergne. Saxony. Mexico. Peru, &c.

M. P. G. Upper Gallery, Wall-case 1, Nos. 10, 11, 144. Wall-case 2, Nos. 27, 28.

PITCHSTONE OF MENIL-MONTANT. A name given to the darker varieties of Menilite, on account of their resemblance to pitch.

PITCHY IRON ORE, *Phillips.* A name for Pitticite, from its more or less perfect resemblance to pitch.

PITCHY IRON ORE, *Jameson.* See TRIPLITE.

PITTICITE, *Beudant.* See VITRIOL OCHRE.

PITTICITE, *Hausmann.* PITTIZITE, *Levy.* Occurs in small masses, reniform and stalactitic, resembling pitch in appearance. Colour yellowish, reddish, or blackish-brown. Translucent at the edges. Lustre vitreous. Streak pale yellow. Yields to the knife. Brittle. Fracture flat-conchoidal. H. 2 to 3. S.G. 2·3 to 2·4.

Comp. Arsenio-sulphate of peroxide of iron. $\ddot{F}e^2\ \ddot{S}^3 + 2\ddot{F}e\ \ddot{A}s + 24\dot{H}.$ (Rammelsberg).

Analysis, from Schwarzenberg, by *Rammelsberg*:

Arsenic acid	.	.	. 26·70
Sulphuric acid	.	.	. 13·91
Peroxide of iron	.	.	. 34·85
Water	.	.	. 24·54

100·00

BB on charcoal, swells up, gives off strong arsenical odours, and fuses into a porous, dark reddish-brown slag, and ultimately to a blackish magnetic globule. Dissolves readily in warm muriatic acid, less easily in nitric acid.

Localities. In several old mines near Freiberg and Schneeberg, in Saxony. Pless, in Upper Silesia. Bleistadt, in Bohemia. Brittany. Chili.

Pitticite is supposed to result from the decomposition of Iron Pyrites, and is a recent product.

Name. From its pitch-like appearance (from πίσσα, or πίττα, pitch).

Brit. Mus., Case 56.

M. P. G. Principal Floor, Wall-case 19.

PITTINERZ. PITTINITE, *Breithaupt.* A variety of Pitchblende (probably the result of alteration) occurring in amorphous, opaque masses of a pitch-black hue. Lustre highly resinous. Streak greenish-brown. Fracture uneven and slightly conchoidal. H. 4. S.G. 5·16.

Locality. Joachimsthal, in Bohemia.

PLAGIONITE, *G. Rose.* Oblique. Occurs in thick, tabular, oblique four-sided prisms: also massive and granular. Colour dark lead-grey. Opaque. Lustre metallic. Brittle. H. 2·5. S.G. 5·4.

Comp. Sulphantimonite of lead, or 4Pb S + Sb S³ = lead 41·15, antimony 38·28, sulphur 20·57 = 100.

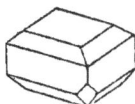

Fig. 337.

Analysis, from Wolfsberger Mine, by *Kudernatsch*:

Lead	.	.	. 40·98
Antimony	.	.	. 37·53
Sulphur	.	.	. 21·49

100 00

BB decrepitates violently, and fuses easily, giving off fumes of sulphur and oxide of antimony.

Localities. Wolfsberg in the Harz, on Quartz or in drusy cavities in massive Plagionite.

Name. From πλάγιος, *oblique;* in allusion to the very oblique form of the crystals.

Brit. Mus., Case 11.

PLAKODINE, *Breithaupt, Dufrénoy.* Oblique. Occurs in tabular, attached and sometimes intersecting crystals. Colour bronze-yellow, somewhat paler than Magnetic Pyrites. Streak black. Very brittle. H. 5 to 5·5. S.G. 7·98 to 8·06.

Fig. 338.

Comp. Sub-arsenide of nickel, or Ni² As = nickel 60·94, arsenic 39·06 = 100.

Analysis, by *Plattner*:

Arsenic	.	.	. 39·71
Nickel	.	.	. 57·05
Cobalt	.	.	. 0·92
Iron	.	.	. trace
Copper	.	.	. 0·86
Sulphur	.	.	. 0·62

99·16

BB on charcoal, fuses readily, and emits arsenical fumes: after roasting, yields a blue glass with borax.

Forms a green solution in nitric acid.

Locality. The Jungfer Mine, near Müsen in Siegen, Prussia, with Siderite and Gersdorffite.

Name. From πλακώδης, *a table.*

PLASMA. A faintly translucent Chalcedony, in which many ancient gems are engraved. Colour grass-green or leek-green, sprinkled with yellow and whitish specks, and possessing a glistening or waxy lustre.

Localities. India and China. Among the ruins of Rome. Olympus. Schwarzwald, near Baden. Hauskopf, near Oppenau.

Name. From πλάσμα, *an image.*

Brit. Mus., Case 23.

M. P. G. Horse-shoe Case, No. 675.

PLASTER OF PARIS. See GYPSUM.

PLATA AZUL. The name by which a rich ore of silver, found in great abundance at Real de Catorce in Mexico, is known to the miners of that country. It is considered by Hausmann to be identical with Selbite.

PLATA VERDE. Bromic Silver. See BROMYRITE.

PLATINA. See NATIVE PLATINUM.

PLATINIFEROUS GREY COPPER, *Phillips.*
A grey variety of Tetrahedrite, consisting of copper, lead, antimony, iron, silver, platinum, and sulphur, found in Spain, with ores of silver and arsenic, at Guadalcanal in Estremadura.

PLATINIRIDIUM, *Svanberg.* A mixture of platinum and iridium in different proportions, found in small rounded grains of a silver-white colour with Platinum, in the Ural, Brazil, Ava, &c. H. 6 to 7. S.G. 22·6 to 23.

Analysis, from N. Taguilsk, by *Svanberg* :

Iridium	.	.	. 76·80
Platinum	.	.	. 19·64
Palladium	.	.	. 0·89
Copper	.	.	. 1·78

99·11

An 'alloy of platinum and iridium, in the proportion of 5, 10, or 15 per cent. of the latter, possesses some excellent qualities, being highly ductile and easily coined.

PLATINUM. See NATIVE PLATINUM.

PLATTNERITE, *Haidinger.* In hexagonal prisms with the edges truncated : possibly pseudomorphous after Pyromorphite (*Greg & Lettsom*). Colour iron-black. Opaque. Lustre metallic-adamantine. Streak brown. Brittle. Fracture uneven. S.G. 9·4.

Comp. Binoxide of lead, or $\ddot{P}b$ =lead 86·6, oxygen 13·4=100.

BB on charcoal, easily reduced.

Locality. It is said to have been brought from Leadhills in Scotland; but it is a somewhat doubtful species.

Name. After Plattner, the Saxon chemist and metallurgist.

PLATYOPHTHALMON, or πλατυόφθαλμον, (from πλατύς, *broad,* and ὀφθαλμὸς, *eye.*) The name by which Grey Antimony was known to the ancients (see STIBNITE), by whom it was used for colouring the hair and eyebrows, but principally for staining the eyelids.

PLEONASTE, *Haüy, Phillips.* A dark or pearly black variety of Iron-and magnesia Spinel. Occurs in octahedrons and dodecahedrons. Opaque. Lustre splendent. Fracture flat-conchoidal. S.G. 3·64.

Fig. 339.

Comp. $(\ddot{M}g, \ddot{F}e) \ddot{A}l$.

PLOMB ARSENIATE.

Analysis, from Monzoni, by *Abich* :

Alumina	.	.	. 66·89
Silica	.	.	. 1·23
Magnesia	.	.	. 23·61
Protoxide of iron	.	.	8·07

99·80

Localities. Candy in Ceylon (see CANDITE). Monte Somma, in Dolomite. Near Kyschtimsk, in the Ural. Arendal, in Norway, in Calc Spar on iron ore. Monzoni, in the Tyrol. Bohemia. Montpellier. Warwick, in New York; and Amity, Orange co., U.S.

Name. From πλιονάστος, *abundant;* from its four facets, which are sometimes found on each solid angle of the octahedron.

When cut and polished Pleonaste is a stone of considerable brilliancy.

Brit. Mus., Case 19.

M.P.G. Upper Gallery, Table-case B, in recess 6, No. 154.

PLEUROCLASE, or PLEUROKLAS, *Breithaupt.* See WAGNERITE.

PLINIAN, *Breithaupt.* A variety of Mispickel occurring in monoclinohedric crystals at St. Gotthard, Ehrenfriedersdorf, and Zinnwald. S.G. 6·27 to 6·46.

Analysis, by *Plattner* :

Iron	.	.	. 34·46
Arsenic	.	.	. 45·46
Sulphur	.	.	. 20·07

99·99

PLINTHITE, *Thomson.* Compact. Earthy. Colour brick-red. Opaque. Lustre glimmering or dull. Fracture flat-conchoidal. H. 2·75. S.G. 2·35.

Comp. $2\ddot{F}e \ddot{S}i + 3\ddot{A}l \ddot{S}i + 16\dot{H}$.

Analysis, by *Thomson* :

Silica	.	.	. 30·88
Alumina	.	.	. 20·76
Protoxide of iron	.	.	26·16
Lime	.	.	. 2·60
Water	.	.	. 19·60

100·00

BB alone, infusible, but turns black.

Localities.—Irish. Down Hill, co. Antrim, and at the Little Deer Park near Glenarm, in reddish trap-rock.

Name. From πλίνθος, *a brick* or *tile;* in allusion to the colour.

PLOMB ANTIMONIÉ SULFURÉ. See BOULANGERITE.

PLOMB ARSENIATÉ, *Haüy.* See MIMETITE.

PLOMB BLANC. See CERUSITE.

PLOMB BLEU, *Brochant.* See BLUE LEAD.

PLOMB BRUN. Ser PYROMORPHITE.

PLOMB CARBONATÉ, *Dufrénoy.* See CERUSITE.

PLOMB CARBONATÉ MURIATIFÈRE, *Haüy.* See CROMFORDITE.

PLOMB CHLORO-CARBONATÉ, *Dufrénoy.* See CERASINE.

PLOMB CHLORURÉ, *Dufrénoy.* See MENDIPITE.

PLOMB CHROMATÉ *Haüy,*
PLOMB CHROMATÉ } See CROCOISITE.
ROUGE, *Haüy.*

PLOMB CORNÉ, *Brochant.* See CERASINE.

PLOMB GOMME, *Laumont.*
PLOMB HYDRO-ALUMI- } See PLUMBO-RESINITE.
NEUX, *Haüy.*

PLOMB JAUNE, *Brochant.*
PLOMB MOLYBDATÉ, } See WULFENITE.
Haüy.

PLOMB MURIATÉ, *Brochant.* See MENDIPITE.

PLOMB MURIO-CARBONATÉ, *Levy.* See CROMFORDITE.

PLOMB NATIF, *Haüy.* See NATIVE LEAD.

PLOMB NOIR. Black Lead. See GRAPHITE.

PLOMB OXIDÉ. See PLUMBIC OCHRE.

PLOMB OXIDÉ ROUGE, *Haüy.* See MINIUM.

PLOMB PHOSPHATÉ, *Haüy.* See PYROMORPHITE.

PLOMB ROUGE, *Brochant.* See MINIUM.

PLOMB SELENIURÉ, *Levy.* See CLAUSTHALITE.

PLOMB SPATHIQUE BLANC, *De Born.* See CERUSITE.

PLOMB SULFATÉ, *Haüy.* See ANGLESITE.

PLOMB SULFURÉ, *Haüy.* See GALENA.

PLOMB SULFURÉ ANTIMONIFÈRE, *Haüy.* See BOURNONITE.

PLOMB SULFURÉ PRISMATIQUE EPIGÈNE. *Haüy.* See BLUE LEAD.

PLOMB TUNGSTATÉ, *Dufrénoy.* See SCHEELETINE.

PLOMB VERTE, *Brochant.* See PYROMORPHITE.

PLOMBAGINE, or PLOMBAGINE VULGAIRE. See GRAPHITE.

PLOMBIERITE, *Daubrée.* A gelatinous substance precipitated by the thermal waters at Plombières in certain fissures and cavities where the Roman cement is exposed to a direct stream of warm water. In the open air it becomes hard, opaque, and white as snow.

Comp. Hydrated silicate of lime, or $\dot{C}a^3$ $\ddot{S}i^2 + 2\dot{H}$.

PLOMGOMME, *Beudant.* See PLUMBO-RESINITE.

PLUMBAGO, *Kirwan, Phillips* (from *plumbum, lead*). A name for Graphite, from its leaving a mark, when drawn across paper, similar in colour to that produced in the same way by lead. See GRAPHITE.

PLUMBIC OCHRE, *Dana.* Massive. Colour sulphur- or orpiment-yellow. Opaque. Lustre dull. Streak paler than the colour. S.G. 8.

Comp. Protoxide of lead, or Pb=lead 92·8, oxygen 7·2=100.

Analysis, from Eschweiler, by *John:*

Protoxide of lead . . .	93·27
Silica	2·40
Peroxide of iron and lime .	0·48
Carbonic acid . . .	3·84
Protoxide of copper . .	trace
	99·99

BB on charcoal, fuses readily and is reduced to metallic lead.

Localities. Badenweiler, in Baden. Popocatapetl and Jztaccituall, in Mexico, among volcanic products.

PLUMBOCALCITE, *Johnston.* A variety of Calcite, containing a variable quantity of carbonate of lead. Occurs in obtuse rhombohedrons. Colour white, yellowish, grey or occasionally pinkish. Transparent. Lustre pearly. S.G. 2·82.

Analysis, from Wanlockhead, by *Johnston:*

Carbonate of lime . .	92·2
Carbonate of lead . .	7·8
	100·0

BB decrepitates on charcoal; with carbonate of soda, yields a white enamel, but no globules of lead.

Localities.—Scotch. Lanarkshire: Leadhills; High Pern Mine, Wanlockhead, Dumfriesshire.

M. P. G. Horse-shoe Case, Nos. 442 and 443.

PLUMBO-CUPRIFEROUS SULPHURET OF BISMUTH, *Phillips.* See AIKENITE.

PLUMBO-RESINITE, *Framont.* Amorphous, or in reniform, globular or stalactitic masses, with a columnar structure. Colour yellowish- or reddish-brown. Translucent. Lustre resinous. Streak white. Fracture conchoidal, and splintery. H. 4 to 4·5. S.G. 6·3 to 6·4.

Comp. $6\ddot{A}l\ \dot{H} + \dot{P}b^3\ \ddot{P}$ (Damour).

Analysis, from Nussière, by *Dufrénoy*:

Oxide of lead	. .	43·42
Chloride of lead	. .	2·11
Alumina	. . .	34·23
Phosphoric acid	. .	1·89
Water	. . .	16·14

—————

97·79

BB decrepitates strongly, turns white, swells up, and fuses partially under a strong blast; on charcoal, with carbonate of soda, yields globules of lead. Soluble in nitric acid.

Localities. — Foreign. Huelgoet, in Brittany, in clay-slate. Nussière, near Beaujeu, in France. Mine La Motte, Missouri, U.S.

Name. From its composition, and its resemblance to gum-arabic.

Brit. Mus., Case 19.

PLUMBOSTIB, *Breithaupt.* Boulangerite from Nertschinsk, in Siberia.

PLUMOSE MICA. The name given to the variety of Mica composed of scales arranged in a plumose form.

PLUMOSE ORE OF ANTIMONY, or PLUMOSIT, *Haidinger, Nicol.* Capillary forms of Heteromorphite.

PLUSH COPPER. The name given in Cornwall to Chalcotrichite.

POCUAMU. The name given to Axe-stone by the natives of New Zealand.

PODAR. Mundic. Also an old Cornish name for Copper Ore.

POIX MINERALE ELASTIQUE, *Brochant.* See ELATERITE.

POIX MINERALE SCORIACÉE, *Brochant.* See ASPHALT.

POIX MINERALE TERREUSE, *Brochant.* See EARTHY BITUMEN.

POLIANITE, *Breithaupt.* A variety of Pyrolusite. Rhombic. Occurs in short, vertically striated, right rhomboidal prisms: also in granular masses. Colour pale steel-grey. Opaque. Lustre sub-metallic. H. 6·5 to 7. S.G. 4·84 to 4·88.

Analysis, by *Plattner* :

Proto-peroxide of manganese		87·27
Alumina and peroxide of		
iron .	. . .	0·17
Oxygen	. . .	12·11
Quartz .	. . .	0·13
Water	. . .	0·32

—————

100·00

Localities. Maria Theresa Zeche, near Platten, in Bohemia. Schneeberg, Geyer, and Johanngeorgenstadt, in Saxony. Prussia, at Eiserne Haardt, in Siegen. Ilmenau, in Thuringia.

Name. From πολιάνος, *grey*; because of its colour.

Brit. Mus., Case 13.

POLLUX, *Breithaupt, Plattner.* Massive. Resembles Quartz in appearance. Colourless. Transparent. Lustre splendent-vitreous. Cleavage none, or scarcely perceptible. Fracture conchoidal. H. 6 to 6·5. S.G. 2·87 to 2·89.

Comp. $3\dot{K} \ddot{S}i + 3\dot{N}a \ddot{S}i + 3\ddot{A}l \ddot{S}i + 2\dot{H}.$

Analysis, by *Plattner* :

Silica .	. .	46·20
Alumina	. .	16·39
Peroxide of iron	. .	0·86
Potash .	. .	16·51
Soda .	. .	10·47
Water	. .	2·32

—————

92·75

BB turns white, and when in thin laminæ becomes rounded at the edges, the fused portions resembling a blistered enamel. Colours the outer flame reddish-yellow. Entirely soluble in muriatic acid, with the aid of heat, with separation of gelatinous silica.

Locality. Elba, associated with Castor in granite.

Pollux appears to contain a larger quantity of alkali than any other known *silicate* mineral. (*L. Gmelin.*)

POLYADELPHITE, *Thomson.* A brownish-yellow Garnet, from the Franklin Furnace, New Jersey, U. S.

Analysis, by *Baumann* :

Silica .	. .	35·47
Alumina	. .	3·10
Peroxide of iron	. .	28·55
Protoxide of manganese	.	5·41
Magnesia	. .	2·13
Lime .	. .	26·74

—————

101·40

Name. From πολὺς, *many*, and ἀδελφὸς, *a brother*, because it consists of a union of five different silicates.

Brit. Mus., Case 36.

POLYARGITE, *Svanberg.* An altered form of Anorthite. Granular-massive, the form of the grains somewhat similar to those of granular Quartz. Colour garnet-red, passing into violet. Fracture vitreous, more shining that that of Garnet, and like that of Quartz. Scratches glass easily. S.G. 2·76.

Brit. Mus., Case 28.

POLYBASITE, *H. Rose.* Hexagonal. Occurs in short tabular, six-sided prisms striated parallel to their bases. Colour and streak iron-black. Opaque; cherry - red in thin crystals by transmitted light. Lustre metallic. Yields to the knife. Fracture uneven. H. 2 to 3. S.G. 6·214.

Comp. Sulphantimonite of silver, in which part of the silver is replaced by copper, and part of the antimony by arsenic, or

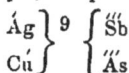

$$\left.\begin{matrix}\overset{'}{Ag}\\\overset{'}{Cu}\end{matrix}\right\}9\quad\left\{\begin{matrix}\overset{'''}{Sb}\\\overset{'}{As}\end{matrix}\right.$$

Analysis, from Durango, by *H. Rose* :

Silver	.	.	.	.	64·29
Sulphur	.	.	.	.	17·04
Copper	.	.	.	.	9·93
Antimony	.	.	.	.	5·09
Arsenic	.	.	.	.	3·74
Iron	.	.	.	.	0·06
					100·15

BB decrepitates slightly, fuses easily, yielding sulphurous acid and a film of antimony; with soda, fumes of arsenic; with fluxes gives a copper reaction.

Localities. Mexico, in the mines of Guanaxuato, and Guadalupe e Calvo, and Guarisame, in Durango. Mine of Morgenstern, near Freiberg, in Saxony. Schemnitz, in Hungary.

Name. From πολὺς, *much,* and βάσις, *base,* in allusion to the large proportion of silver present compared with the other sulphides of that metal.

Brit. Mus., Case 11.

Polybasite is distinguished from Brittle Sulphide of Silver by the arsenical odour which it gives off *BB* ; and from Bournonite, by yielding a button of silver instead of copper.

POLYCHROILITE, *Weibye.* Occurs in six-sided prisms, with flat summits; also reniform and massive. Colour blue, green, brown, red, or white. Lustre greasy. Fracture subconchoidal to even.

Fig. 340.

Analysis, by *Dahl* :

Silica	.	.	.	.	52
Alumina	.	.	.	.	37
Peroxide of iron	.	.	.	3
Magnesia	.	.	.	.	7
Lime and water	.	.	.	,,
					99

Locality. Krageröe, in Norway, in gneiss.

Name. From πολὺς, *many,* χροία, *colour,* and λίθος, *stone.*

POLYCHROMATIC FELSPAR, *Mohs.* See LABRADORITE.

POLYCRASE, *Dana.* Rhombic. Occurs in six-sided tables. Colour black; in thin splinters brownish. Opaque. Lustre bright. Streak greyish-brown. Fracture conchoidal. H. 5·5. S.G. 5·09 to 5·15.

Comp. Near Polymignite, with the addition of columbic acid and protoxide of uranium, but no manganese, and only a small quantity of lime.

Locality. Hitteröe, in Norway.

Name. From πολὺς, *many,* and κρᾶσις, *mixture,* in allusion to the numerous substances entering into its composition, viz. Titanic and columbic acids, zirconia, yttria, peroxide of iron, protoxide of uranium, protoxide of cerium, with a small quantity of alumina, and traces of lime and magnesia.

Brit. Mus., Case 37.

POLYHALITE, *Stromeyer.* POLYHALLITE, *Phillips.* Generally occurs in compact fibrous masses, with the fibres parallel, and mostly curved. Colourless, but usually brick-red or flesh-coloured. Slightly translucent. Lustre resinous or pearly. Taste faintly bitter and astringent. Streak white. Brittle. Fracture uneven. H. 2·5 to 3. S.G. 2·77.

Comp. $(\overset{'}{K},\ \overset{'}{Mg},\ \overset{'}{Ca})\ \overset{..}{S}+\tfrac{1}{2}\overset{.}{H}.$

Analysis, from Aussee, by *Rammelsberg* :

Sulphate of lime	.	.	.	45·43
Sulphate of magnesia	.	.	20·59
Sulphate of potash	.	.	28·10
Chloride of soda	.	.	.	0·11
Peroxide of iron	.	.	.	0·33
Silica	.	.	.	.	0·20
Water	.	.	.	.	5·24
					100·00

BB fuses instantaneously; in the flame of a candle forms an opaque brownish mass.

Localities. The mines of Ischel, Aussee, Hallstatt, and Ebensee, in Upper Austria.

Name. From πολὺς, *many,* and ἅλς, *salt,* in allusion to the number of salts which enter into its composition.

Brit. Mus., Case 55.

POLYHALITE DE VIC. Glauberite from Vic, Dept. de la Meurthe, in France, where it occurs in whitish or greyish crystals disseminated in Common Salt, or saliferous clays, or in compact and reddish kidneyform masses in saliferous clays; also at Villa Rubia, near Ocana, in Spain. See GLAUBERITE.

POLYHYDRITE, *Breithaupt.* See HISIN-GERITE.

POLYKRASE, *Scheerer.* See POLYCRASE.

POLYLITE, *Thomson.* A variety of Pyroxene, nearly related to Hedenbergite, occurring in plates with a lamellar structure and a cleavage in one direction. Colour black. Opaque. Lustre vitreous. Brittle. H. 6 to 6·5. S.G. 3·23.

Comp. (Fe, Ċa, Ṁn)³ (2S̈i Ä̈l).

Analysis, by *Thomson :*

Silica	40·04
Alumina . . .	9·43
Protoxide of iron . .	34·08
Protoxide of manganese .	6·60
Lime	11·54
Water	0·40
	102·08

BB alone, infusible ; with borax fuses to a black glass.

Locality. Hoboken, in New Jersey, forming a bed about a ¼ inch thick in Magnetic Iron Ore.

Name. From πολὺς, *many,* and λίθος, *stone,* in allusion to the numerous constituents of which it is composed.

POLYMIGNITE, *Berzelius.* Rhombic. Occurs in long thin prisms, generally striated longitudinally, and with the edges replaced. Colour black. Opaque. Lustre submetallic, but brilliant. Streak dark brown. Fracture conchoidal. H. 6·5. S.G. 4·77 to 4·85.

Comp. Titanate of Zirconia.

Analysis, by *Berzelius :*

Titanic acid . . .	46·30
Zirconia . . .	14·14
Yttria . . .	11·50
Peroxide of iron . .	12·20
Peroxide of cerium .	5·00
Lime	4·20
Peroxide of manganese .	2·70
Potash, magnesia, silica, and oxide of tin . .	traces
	96·04

BB alone, infusible and unchanged ; with borax fuses readily to a glass coloured by iron ; with tin to a yellowish-red globule. Soluble in sulphuric acid.

Locality. Fredericksvärn, in Norway, in zircon-syenite, in crystals sometimes upwards of an inch long.

Name. From πολὺς, *much,* and μίγνυμι, *to mix,* in allusion to the number of its components.

Brit. Mus., Case 37.

POLYSPHÆRITE, *Breithaupt.* A botryoidal variety of Brown Lead Ore (see PYROMORPHITE), containing phosphate of lime, as well as a certain quantity of. fluoride of calcium. Structure radiated internally. Colour brown or yellow; slightly darker than Pyromorphite. Lustre greasy. Fracture conchoidal. S.G. 5·9 to 6·1.

Analysis, by *Kersten :*

Phosphate of lead .	77·02
Phosphate of lime .	11·05
Chloride of lead .	10·84
Fluoride of calcium .	1·09
	100·00

Localities. The mines of Sonnenwirbel and St. Nicholas, near Freiberg, in Saxony.

Name. From πολὺς, *many,* and σφαίρος, *sphere,* in allusion to its occurrence in round-ish masses.

Brit. Mus., Case 54.

POLYSTOMOUS AUGITE SPAR, *Keating.* See JEFFERSONITE.

POLYTELITE. The name given by Glocker to varieties of Grey Copper (*Tetrahedrite*), containing silver and quicksilver.

Name. From πολιτελὴς, *valuable,* because of the large amount of silver it contains.

POLYXENE, *Hausmann.* See NATIVE PLATINUM.

PONCE, *Beudant.* See PUMICE.

POONAHLITE, *Brooke.* A variety of Scolecite, occurring in slender rhombic prisms and radiated fibrous masses, resembling Needlestone.. Colour white. Lustre pearly. H. 5 to 5·5.

Analysis, by *Gmelin :*

Silica	45·12
Alumina . . .	30·44
Lime	10·20
Soda, with a trace of potash .	0·66
Water	13·39
	99·81

Locality. Poonah, in Hindostan, associated with Apophyllite, and forming with it large kidney-form masses, in amygdaloid. Brit. Mus., Case 28.

M. P. G. Horse-shoe Case, No. 1174, from the Railway Tunnel, Bhore Ghaut, between Bombay and Poonah.

PORCELAIN CLAY, *Kirwan.* } See
PORCELAIN EARTH, *Jameson.* } KAOLIN.

PORCELAIN JASPER, or PORCELLANITE. Clay altered by heat, and often having the aspect of certain kinds of porcelain.

PORCELAIN SPAR. PORCELAN-SPATH, *Dufrénoy.* PORCELLAN-SPATH, *Fuchs.* Occurs in rhombic prisms ; also massive and coarsely granular. Colourless or pale-grey.

Transparent at the edges, or translucent. Lustre vitreous; on cleavage planes pearly. Fracture uneven. H. 5·5. S.G. 2·65 to 2·68.

Comp. 4A̶l S̈i + 2C̶a S̈i + N̶a S̈i + ⅓KCl (Schafhäutl).

Analysis, by *Schafhäutl:*

Silica	. 49·2
Alumina	. 27·3
Lime	. 15·4
Soda	. 6·5
Chloride of potassium .	. 1·2
Water	. 1·2
	100·8

BB fuses with tolerable facility, swelling up and forming a colourless blistered glass.

Decomposed by strong acids, without the formation of a jelly.

Locality. Obernzell, in Bavaria.

Brit. Mus., Case 30.

PORPEZITE. See ORO PUDRE.

PORRICIN. See PYROXENE.

PORTITE, *Meneghini, Bechi.* In radiated masses, with a very distinct rhombic cleavage. Colour opaque-white. Lustre vitreous. H. 5. S.G. 2·4.

Comp. (M̶g C̶a)³ S̈i² + 4A̶l S̈i² + 7H̶, or A̶l S̈i² + 2H̶ = if the protoxides are not taken into consideration.

Analysis, by *Bechi:*

Silica	. 58·12
Alumina . . .	. 27·50
Magnesia . . .	. 4·87
Lime	. 1·76
Soda	. 0·16
Potash	. 0·10
Water	. 7·92
	100·43

BB fuses with much intumescence to a milk-white enamel.

Soluble in acids, forming a jelly.

Locality. Tuscany, in gabbro rosso.

Name. After Mons. Porte, of Tuscany.

PORZELLANERDE, *Werner.* See KAOLIN.

POTASH ALUM. Found native in a few minerals, but generally as an efflorescence. Colour white. Transparent to opaque. Lustre vitreous; of fibrous varieties somewhat pearly. Taste astringent and sweetish. H. 2 to 2·5. S.G. 1·75.

Comp. Sulphate of alumina and potash, or (K̶ S̈ + 6H̶) + (A̶l S̈³ + 18H̶) Kane = sulphate of potash 18·4, sulphate of alumina 36·2, water 45·4 = 100.

Soluble in from 16 to 20 times its weight of cold water, and in slightly more than its own weight of boiling water. When gradually heated to a temperature just below redness, it loses water, swells up very much, and leaves a residue of anhydrous alum (*burnt alum*), which forms a loose, friable, porous mass.

Localities. — English. Near Whitby in Yorkshire, in Lias (alum-shale). Chudleigh in Devon, in clay, and in the Lower Bagshot clays of Branksea Island, and Isle of Purbeck, Dorsetshire. — *Scotch.* Hurlet, near Paisley; in shale. — *Irish.* Along the coasts of Clare and Kerry. Most of the caves at Ballybunnion in Kerry are coated with crystals of Alum of a whitish or pale yellowish-white colour. (F. J. Foot.) — *Foreign.* The volcanoes of the Lipari Islands, Sicily, and the Azores. Hesse and the Rhine, in the Brown Coal formation. Silurian alum-slate of Sweden and Christiana in Norway. Cape Sable, Maryland, U. S.

Brit. Mus., Case 55.

The alum of commerce is manufactured from the aluminous earth of volcanic regions, or from alum-shale, by disintegrating them by exposure to the air for a considerable time, or by roasting, during which process the sulphur becomes converted into sulphuric acid. The sulphate of alumina thus formed, together with the sulphates of iron, is extracted by digestion in water, and the latter being removed, potash is added to the purified sulphate of alumina.

Alum is made from the Dorsetshire and other clays, by treating them with sulphuric acid. The solution of sulphate of alumina thus obtained is evaporated to a certain point, and then mixed with ley from wood ashes, crude potash, or other substances containing potash. The potash-alum which then crystallizes out may be afterwards purified by repeated crystallization.

Alum is used in medicine as an astringent, and to prevent putrefaction: as a mordaunt in dyeing and calico printing; in the manufacture of paper and leather, and for rendering wood incombustible.

POTASH COPPERAS. See GELBEISENERZ.

POTASH HARMOTOME. See PHILLIPSITE.

POTASH MICA, *Nicol.* See MUSCOVITE.

POTASSE NITRATÉE, *Haüy.* See NITRE.

POTASSE SULPHATÉE, *Haüy.* See GLASERITE.

POTSTONE. A coarse granular variety of Steatite, or Soapstone, with a greenish-grey or leek-green colour, and a feeble or pearly lustre. Unctuous to the touch. Tough.

Analysis, from Sweden, by *Thomson :*

Silica	ʻ. 49·01
Magnesia . . .	. 30·20
Alumina . . .	. 6·08
Protoxide of iron .	. 11·40
Water	. 4·20
	100·89

Localities. — British. Polyphant, near Launceston, Cornwall. Loch Fyne, Argyleshire. Near Havre Gosslin, in Sark, where it is made into vessels for domestic use. — *Foreign.* Norway. Sweden. Finland. Greenland. Chiavenna, in the Valteline. Como, in Lombardy. (*Pierre de Côme.*) The Vallais and Grisons. Wald, in Styria. Corsica. Upper Egypt. (See PIERRE DE BARAM.) Brit. Mus., Case 32.

Potstone, from its infusibility, tenacity, and softness, which admits of its being turned in the lathe, has been used from very early times for culinary vessels, and a variety of other purposes. Vessels made from Potstone are called in Italy and the Grisons *lavezzi*, and possess the advantages of heating quickly, and of not communicating any taste to the substances cooked in them. In Italy, where it is called "*pierre à pot*," it is an object of considerable trade. That from Como is brownish-black, hard, and quite opaque, and withstands the action of fire. It is also quarried at. Val Sesia, near the village of Allagne, not far from Monte Rosa. Another kind, found at Quéiras, near Briançon, of an iron-grey colour, possesses similar qualities.

The Corsican Potstone is far superior to that from Germany, and its manufacture into a variety of ornaments and works of art affords employment to many persons in France, by whom it is made into candlesticks, taper-stands, snuff-boxes, &c. It polishes with difficulty, but acquires considerable translucency when cut thin.

Potstone is but little employed in jewelry, but it is sometimes made into pretty breloques, although it will not take a high degree of polish.

" Potstone *, by calcination white, acquires
    Its name by turning on the lathe to most
    Domestic uses."

POTTER'S ORE. An old miner's name for largely foliated pure Galena, or sulphide of lead. In some countries such ores are styled *blue ores.*

POUDRE D'OR or D'ARGENT. Names given to the pounded Mica used on the

* Werneria, or Short Characters of Earths, by Terræ Filius, page 28.

---

continent, instead of sand, for drying writing.

POUNXA. See BORAX.

POZZUOLANA. Volcanic ashes from Vesuvius, which, when mixed with lime, form a cement of the same name.

PRASE (from πρασον, *a leek*), a dark leek-green variety of vitreous Quartz, the colour of which is caused by an admixture of Amphibole.

Localities. The iron mines of Breitenbrunn, near Schwartzenberg, in Saxony. The Harz. The Cedar Mountain, S. Africa, in fine crystals.

Brit. Mus., Case 23.

PRASEOLITE, *Erdmann.* An altered form of Iolite, occurring in rounded rhombic prisms with four, six, eight or twelve sides, having a basal cleavage and a lamellar structure. Colour green. Opaque or subtranslucent. Lustre greasy. Fracture flat-conchoidal or splintery. H. 3·5. S.G. 2·754.

Comp. Iolite + 3Ḧ (Rammelsberg), or S̈i

$(\dot{M}g + \ddot{A}l) + \dot{H} (\dot{M}g, \dot{F}e, Mn) \ddot{S}i + 2\ddot{A}l\ddot{S}i + \dot{H}.$ (Erdmann.)

Analysis, from Bräkke, by *Erdmann :*

Silica	. 40·94
Alumina . . .	. 28·79
Protoxide of iron .	. 6·96
Magnesia . . .	. 13·73
Protoxide of manganese	. 0·32
Oxides of lead, copper, lime, cobalt	. 0·50
Titanic acid . . .	. 0·40
Water	. 7·38
	99·02

BB fuses with difficulty at the edges to a bluish-green glass.

Locality. Bräkke, near Brevig, in Norway; in quartz-veins traversing gneiss.

Name. From πρασον, *a leek,* and λιθος, *stone,* in allusion to its leek-green colour.

Brit. Mus., Case 32.

PRASOCHROME, *Landerer.* Carbonate of lime coloured by oxide of chrome, resulting from the alteration of Chromic Iron, and forming a dull green incrustation, on the Island Scyro, in the Grecian Archipelago.

PRECIOUS BERYLL, *Jameson.* See BERYL and AQUAMARINE.

PRECIOUS GARNET. See PYROPE, also GARNET.

M.P.G. Horse-shoe Case, Nos. 890 to 898.

PRECIOUS OPAL. Includes those varieties of Opal which exhibit a rich play of prismatic colours : it is always cut with a convex surface, and when large and exhibiting its peculiar play of colours in profection, is a gem held in high estimation. Fine stones are, however, extremely rare, and can seldom be obtained the size of a nut. When held between the eye and the light, it appears of a pale red and wine-yellow tint, with a milky transpareucy. By reflected light, as its position is altered, it displays the most beautiful iridescent colours, particularly verdigris-green, and emerald-green, golden yellow, fire-red, bright blue, rich violet, purple and pearl-grey. All these colours are generally displayed in the same specimen, being arranged in small spangles, in which case it is called *Harlequin Opal,* or in broader plates or in waved delineations. Sometimes only one colour is present, in which case the rich orange-yellow (called *Golden Opal*) or vivid emerald-green are the most beautiful.

An *analysis* of a Hungarian specimen (S.G. 2·07) afforded *Damour :*

Silica	93·90
Water	6·10
	100·00

while another yielded to Von Kobell 10·94 per cent. of water.

Precious Opal is found in irregular nests and veins, disseminated in trachyte at Czervenitza, near Kashau, in Hungary; at Frankfort; Gracias à Dios, in Honduras; also in Mexico; and in small rounded pieces in sand in Ceylon; and in Iceland.

The Opal has of late years become much worn as a gem, frequently set surrounded with brilliants. To be fully appreciated, the Opal requires a close inspection, and it is for that reason, probably, that the great admiration in which it is held in eastern countries may be partly accounted for. By the people of most nations gems are admired, to a great extent, in proportion to the brilliancy of their reflections, and the admiration they excite in others rather than for the pleasure they afford to those who wear them; whereas among eastern nations, where women of rank lead very secluded lives, it is the intrinsic beauty of the stone and the pleasure the wearers derive from beholding it, which chiefly constitute its value. The finest varieties are termed *Oriental Opal.*

Beautiful snuff-boxes and other ornaments can be made of the porphyry which forms the matrix of the Opal, when the veins are sufficiently rich in play of colours. In consequence of its softness, coupled with its extreme brittleness, Opal requires the greatest care in working, a moment of inattention on the part of the lapidary being sufficient to destroy its beauty.

It is related by Pliny that Marcus Antonius proscribed and outlawed Nonius (a Roman senator), on account of an Opal. Rather than part with it Nonius fled, carrying with him no other property than a ring, in which this Opal was set, which had been valued at 20,000 sesterces (£177,083). The largest known Opal is in the Imperial Museum in Vienna. It is 4¼ inches long, 2½ inches thick, and weighs 17 ounces. It has been valued at £70,000. Fine Opals of moderate size have been frequently sold at the price of diamonds of the same size. See OPAL.

Brit. Mus., Case 24.

M.P.G. Horse-shoe Case, Nos. 767, 770, 771.

PRECIOUS STONE. See GEM.

PREDAZZITE, *Petzholdt.* A variety of Bitter Spar mixed with Brucite, with a granular structure, a white colour, and a vitreous lustre on the planes of cleavage. H. 3·5. S.G. 2·634.

Comp. $\dot{C}a \ddot{C} + \dot{M}g \ddot{H}.$

Analysis, by *Roth :*

Lime	33·53
Magnesia . . .	23·27
Carbonic acid . .	27·45
Alumina and peroxide of iron . . .	2·88
Silica	3·28
Water	10·26
	100·67

Locality. Forms mountain masses at Predazzo, in the Southern Tyrol.

PREHNITE, *Werner, Haüy.* Rhombic: primary form a right rhombic prism. Occurs

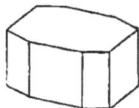 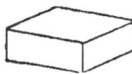 

Fig. 341.   Fig. 342.   Fig. 343.

in crystals which are generally closely aggregated; also massive. Colour greenish-white, also yellowish-grey or yellowish-green. Translucent to transparent. Lustre vitreous or pearly. Streak white. Brittle. Fracture uneven. Pyroelectric. H. 6 to 6·5. S.G. 2·926.

Comp. $\ddot{C}a^2 \ddot{S}i + \ddot{S}i \ddot{A}l + \dot{H}$ = silica 44·41, alumina 24·55, lime 26·74, water 4·30 = 100·00.

Analysis, from Dumbarton, by *Walmstedt*:

Silica	44·10
Alumina	24·26
Lime	26·43
Protoxides of iron, manganese, &c.	0 74
Water	4·18
	99·71

BB fuses to a blistered glass, with rapid evolution of gas bubbles.

Imperfectly acted on by acids; but after strong ignition or fusion, it is completely decomposed by acids, with the formation of a jelly.

Localities. — *English.* Botallack Mine and Huel Cock, Cornwall, in small, pale green groups, in clay-slate, Ponck Hill, Staffordshire. — *Scotch.* Bolan Quarry near Old Kilpatrick, Dumbartonshire, in pale greenish, mammillated concretions. Edinburghshire, at Samson's Ribs, Arthur's Seat, in porphyritic greenstone; at the Castle Rock, in basalt; Costorphine Hill, in greenstone. Leith, on the sea-shore. Campsie Hills, Stirlingshire. Friskie Hall, near Glasgow, of a fine sulphur-yellow colour, in porphyritic greenstone. Hartfield Moss, near Paisley, in Renfrewshire. Island of Mull. Isle of Skye. — *Irish.* Mourne Mountains, in white radiating concretions in granite. — *Foreign.* St. Christophe, in Dauphiné, with Axinite and Epidote. Fassa Valley, in the Tyrol, of a peculiar bluish-green tint. The copper region of Lake Superior, and in various parts of the United States. China. Cape of Good Hope.

Name. Named by Werner after Colonel Prehn, a Dutch officer, by whom it was first brought to Europe from the Cape of Good Hope.

·Brit. Mus., Case 29.

M. P. G. Horse-shoe Case, No. 1114.

PRISMATIC AMBLYGON SPAR, *Mohs.* See AMBLYGONITE.

PRISMATIC AMMONIAC SALT, *Mohs.* See MASCAGNINE.

PRISMATIC ANDALUSITE, *Mohs.* See ANDALUSITE.

PRISMATIC ANTIMONY, *Mohs.* See DISCRASITE.

PRISMATIC ANTIMONY BARYTE, *Mohs.* See VALENTINITE.

PRISMATIC ANTIMONY GLANCE, *Mohs.* See SYLVANITE.

PRISMATIC ARSENIATE OF COPPER, *Bournon.* See OLIVENITE.

PRISMATIC ARSENICAL PYRITES, *Mohs.* See MISPICKEL.

PRISMATIC AUGITE SPAR, *Mohs.* See WOLLASTONITE.

PRISMATIC AXINITE, *Mohs.* See AXINITE.

PRISMATIC AZURE MALACHITE, *Mohs.* See AZURITE.

PRISMATIC AZURE SPAR, *Mohs.* See LAZULITE.

PRISMATIC BISMUTH GLANCE, *Mohs.* See BISMUTHINE.

PRISMATIC BORACIC ACID, *Mohs.* See SASSOLIN.

PRISMATIC BORAX SALT, *Mohs.* See BORAX.

PRISMATIC CALAMINE, *Jameson.* See SMITHSONITE.

PRISMATIC CERIUM ORE, *Jameson.* See ALLANITE.

PRISMATIC CHRYSOLITE, *Mohs.* See CHRYSOLITE.

PRISMATIC COBALT MICA, *Mohs.* See ERYTHRINE.

PRISMATIC COPPER GLANCE, *Mohs.* See COPPER-GLANCE.

PRISMATIC COPPER MICA, *Jameson.* See CHALCOPHYLLITE.

PRISMATIC CORUNDUM, *Mohs.* See CHRYSOBERYL.

PRISMATIC CRYONE HALOID, *Mohs.* See CRYOLITE.

PRISMATIC DISTHENE SPAR, *Mohs.* See CYANITE.

PRISMATIC DYSTOME SPAR, *Mohs.* See DATHOLITE.

PRISMATIC EMERALD, *Mohs.* See EUCLASE.

PRISMATIC EMERALD MALACHITE, *Mohs.* See EUCHROITE.

PRISMATIC EPSOM SALT, *Mohs.* See EPSOMITE.

PRISMATIC EUCHLORE MICA, *Mohs.* See TYROLITE.

PRISMATIC EUTOME GLANCE, *Mohs.* See STERNBERGITE.

PRISMATIC FLUOR HALOID, *Mohs, Haidinger.* See HERDERITE.

PRISMATIC GADOLINITE, *Mohs.* See GADOLINITE.

PRISMATIC GARNET, *Jameson.* See STAUROLITE.

PRISMATIC GLAUBER SALT, *Mohs.* See GLAUBER SALT.

PRISMATIC GYPSUM HALOID, *Mohs.* See ANHYDRITE.

PRISMATIC HABRONEME MALACHITE, *Mohs.* See PHOSPHOCHALCITE.

PRISMATIC HALBARYTE, *Mohs.* See BARYTES.

PRISMATIC IRON MICA, *Mohs.* See VIVIANITE.

PRISMATIC IRON ORE, *Mohs.* (In part) Limonite.

PRISMATIC IRON PYRITES, *Mohs.* See MARCASITE.

PRISMATIC KOUPHONE SPAR, *Mohs.* See NATROLITE.

PRISMATIC LIME HALOID, *Mohs.* See ARAGONITE.

PRISMATIC LIROCONE MALACHITE, *Mohs.* See LIROCONITE.

PRISMATIC MANGANESE BLENDE, *Jameson.* See MANGANESE BLENDE.

PRISMATIC MANGANESE ORE, *Jameson.* See PYROLUSITE.

PRISMATIC MELANE GLANCE, *Mohs,* Brittle silver ore. See STEPHANITE.

PRISMATIC MICA. The name given to the variety of Mica having a diagonal cleavage.

PRISMATIC MONOCLASE HALOID, *Mohs.* See HOPEITE.

PRISMATIC NATRON SALT, *Mohs.* See NATRON.

PRISMATIC NEPHRITE SPAR, *Haidinger.* See SAUSSURITE.

PRISMATIC NICKEL PYRITES, *Mohs.* See COPPER-NICKEL.

PRISMATIC NITRE SALT, *Mohs.* See NITRE.

PRISMATIC OLIVE MALACHITE, *Mohs.* See OLIVENITE.

PRISMATIC ORTHOCLASE HALOID, *Mohs.* See ANHYDRITE.

PRISMATIC PETALINE SPAR, *Mohs.* See PETALITE.

PRISMATIC PURPLE BLENDE, *Mohs.* See KERMESITE.

PRISMATIC PYRAMIDAL GARNET, *Mohs.* See IDOCRASE.

PRISMATIC QUARTZ, *Mohs.* See IOLITE.

PRISMATIC RETIN BARYTE, *Mohs.* See TRIPLITE.

PRISMATIC SCHEELERZ, or SCHEELE ORE, *Mohs.* See WOLFRAM.

PRISMATIC SCHILLER SPAR, *Mohs.* See ANTHOPHYLLITE.

PRISMATIC SULPHUR, *Mohs.* See NATIVE SULPHUR.

PRISMATIC TALC MICA, *Mohs.* See CHLORITE.

PRISMATIC TANTALUM ORE, *Mohs.* See TANTALITE.

PRISMATIC TITANIUM ORE, *Mohs.* See SPHENE.

PRISMATIC TOPAZ, *Mohs.* See TOPAZ.

PRISMATIC TRIPHANE SPAR, *Mohs.* See SPODUMENE.

PRISMATIC VITRIOL SALT, *Mohs.* See GOSLARITE.

PRISMATIC WHITE ANTIMONY, *Jameson.* See CERVANTITE & VALENTINITE.

PRISMATIC ZINC BARYTE, *Mohs.* See SMITHSONITE.

PRISMATIC ZINC-ORE, *Mohs.* See ZINCITE.

PRISMATOIDAL ANTIMONY GLANCE,*Mohs.* See STIBNITE.

PRISMATOIDAL GARNET, *Mohs.* See STAUROLITE.

PRISMATOIDAL HAL BARYTE, *Mohs.* See CELESTINE.

PRISMATOIDAL KOUPHONE SPAR, *Mohs.* See STILBITE.

PRISMATOIDAL LEAD BARYTE, *Mohs.* See LANARKITE.

PRISMATOIDAL MANGANESE ORE, *Mohs.* See MANGANITE.

PRISMATOIDAL SCHILLER SPAR, *Mohs.* See HYPERSTHENE.

PRISMATOIDAL SULPHUR, *Mohs.* See ORPIMENT.

PROSOPITE, *Scheerer.* Colourless to white. Lustre vitreous. Subtransparent. Occurs in pseudomorphous crystals, some of which are converted into Kaolin, while others consist of violet Fluor, and others of Fluor only partially kaolinised. H. 4·5. S.G. 2·89 to 2·898.

This mineral has been supposed by Scheerer to be a Kaolin pseudomorph homœomorphous with Heavy Spar; and more recently, by Dana, an altered form of Datholite, in which fluorine has been introduced through the process of alteration.

The following formula and analysis by Scheerer explain its composition:

Formula. $\left. \begin{array}{c} \text{CaF,SiF}^3 \\ \text{CaF,AlF}^3 \end{array} \right\}$ $+ 4\,\ddot{\text{C}}\text{a}\,\ddot{\text{A}}\text{l} + (\dot{\text{H}})\,\text{Al}$

$+ 9\dot{\text{H}}.$

Analysis:

Alumina	. 42·68
Lime	. 22·98
Fluoride of silicon	. 10·71
Protoxide of manganese	. 0·31
Magnesia	. 0·25
Potash	. 0·15
Water	. 15·50
	92·58

Locality. The tin mines of Altenberg.

Name. from πρισωπίον, *a mask;* in allusion to its deceptive or masked condition.

M. P. G. Horse-shoe Case, No. 366.

PROTHEITE, *Dufrénoy,* or PROTHERITE, *Ure.* A variety of Idocrase from Zillerthal, in the Tyrol. Occurs in rectangular prisms, with the faces striated longitudinally. Colour olive-green or white. The smaller specimens translucent, the larger nearly opaque.

PROTOXIDE OF URANIUM. See PITCH-BLENDE.

PROUSTITE, *Beudant, Dufrénoy;* or LIGHT-RED SILVER ORE. Hexagonal: primary form an obtuse rhombohedron. Colour cochineal- to crimson-red. Subtransparent to translucent at the edges. Lustre adamantine. Streak cochineal-red. Sectile. Fracture conchoidal to uneven. H. 2 to 2·5. S.G. 5·42 to 5·56.

Comp. Sulphide of silver and arsenic, or $Ag^3 S + As S^3 =$ sulphur 19·4, arsenic 15·2, silver 65·4=100.

Analysis, from Joachimsthal, by *H. Rose:*

Sulphur	. . .	19·51
Arsenic	. . .	15·09
Silver .	. . .	64·67
Antimony	. . .	0·69
		99·96

BB fuses, giving off arsenical fumes; ultimately on charcoal yields a globule of silver.

Localities. Johanngeorgenstadt, Marienberg, and Annaberg, in Saxony. Joachimsthal, in Bohemia. Baden. Alsace. Guadalcanal, in Spain. Mexico. Peru.

Name. After J. L. Proust, the French chemist.

This is a valuable ore of silver. See PYRARGYRITE.

M. P. G. Principal Floor, Wall-case 22.

PRUNNERITE. A greyish-violet coloured calcareous tufa, found in Faröe.

PRYAN (from *Pryi,* clay, *Cornish*), PRYAN ORE, PRYAN TIN, PRYAN LODE. That which is productive of Copper Ore or Tin, but does not break in large solid stones, only in gross pebbles, or sandy with a mixture of clay. (*Pryce.*)

The word *Pryan* is now generally given to a white, fine, somewhat friable clay.

PRZIBRAMITE, *Huot.* Cadmiferous Blende, from Przibram in Bohemia. The same name has also been given to the capillary variety of Göthite (*Sammetblende*), which occurs at that locality.

PSATHYRIN, *Glocker.* See HARTINE.

PSATUROSE, *Beudant.* Colour dark lead-

grey, inclining to iron-black. Streak black. H. 2. S.G. 6·275.

Comp. Sulphantimonite of silver, or 6Ag, $S + Sb S^3 =$ silver 70·36, antimony 14·01, sulphur 15·63=100.

Analysis, from Schemnitz, by *H. Rose:*

Silver .	. . .	68·54
Antimony	. . .	14·68
Copper .	. . .	0·64
Sulphur	. . .	16·42
		100·28

BB on charcoal fuses readily, forming a white film, sometimes also giving out an odour of arsenic: yields a globule of silver in the outer flame.

Easily soluble in hot nitric acid, with separation of sulphur and antimonic nitrate.

Localities. Schemnitz, in Hungary. Freiberg, in Saxony. Zacatecas, in Mexico.

Name. From ψαθυρός, *fragile.*

PSEUDO-ADAMANTES, or MOCK DIAMONDS. A name for Cornish Diamonds, and similar limpid Rock Crystal from other localities.

PSEUDO-ALBITE. See ANDESINE.

PSEUDO-APATITE, *Breithaupt.* An impure Apatite, affected by decomposition; from the Kurprinz mines at Freiberg, in Saxony.

PSEUDO-DIAMOND. Transparent and colourless Rock Crystals, cut and polished.

PSEUDO-MALACHITE, *Hausmann.* See PHOSPHOCHALCITE.

PSEUDOMORPHOUS PYRITES. Is found at Alston, in Cumberland, in cubes after Fluor; near Tavistock, in Devonshire, in flat hexagonal crystals after Calcite; also at Herodsfoot Mine and Huel Mary, in Cornwall.

PSEUDO-NEPHELINE. See NEPHELINE.

PSEUDO-SAPHIR. See CORDIERITE.

PSEUDO-SOMMITE. Leucite changed by alteration to Glassy Felspar, has been observed by Scacchi on Somma.

PSEUDO-TRIPLITE. A form of Triplite which has undergone alteration by taking up water, and the protoxides passing to peroxides.

Comp. $(\ddot{F}e, \ddot{M}n)^3 \ddot{P}^2 + 2\dot{H}$.

Analysis, from Bodenmais, by *Delffs:*

Phosphoric acid	. .	35·71
Peroxide of iron	. .	51·00
Peroxide of manganese	.	8·07
Water .	. . .	4·52
Insoluble	. . .	0·70
		100·00

Locality. Bodenmais, in Bavaria.

PSILOMELANE, *Phillips, Nicol.* PSILO-MELANITE, *Thomson.* Amorphous. Massive, botryoidal, and stalactitic. Colour iron-black, passing into dark steel-grey. Opaque. Lustre submetallic. Streak brownish-black and shining. Brittle. Fracture flat-conchoidal. H. 5 to 6. S.G. 4·08 to 4·36.

Comp. Mn M̈n² + Ḣ mixed with M̈n, part of which may be an accidental admixture. The M̈n is often partly replaced by K̇, Ḃa, Ċa, Ċu, &c.

Analysis, from Romanèche, by *Turner :*

Proto-peroxide of manganese 70·97
Oxygen . . . . 7·26
Baryta . . . . . 16·69
Silica . . . . . 0·95
Water . . . . . 4·13

100·00

BB gives a violet colour to borax.
Soluble in muriatic acid (except a small quantity of silica), with evolution of chlorine.

Localities. — English. Restormel Royal Iron-mine, Cornwall, in fine velvet-black stalactitic masses. Devonshire: Upton Pyne, near Exeter; near Bideford; Black Down, near Tavistock; botryoidal and stalactitic. Ashton, near Chudleigh. Brendon Hill Mine, Somersetshire. Drygill, in Cumberland. Hartshill, in Warwickshire. — *Scotch.* Leadhills. Old Kilpatrick, Dumbartonshire. Orkneys; in old red sandstone at Braeborough (*coralloidal*). — *Irish.* Glendore, co. Cork. — *Foreign.* Ihlefeld, in the Harz. Siegen, in Hesse. Ilmenau. Schneeberg. Horhausen. Heidelberg. Romanèche. Haute Saone. Vermont, United States.

Name. From ψιλὸς, smooth, and μέλας, black : in allusion to its smooth or botryoidal form and black colour.

Brit. Mus., Case 13.
M.P.G. Principal Floor, Wall-case 13 (British).

This is a common ore of Manganese, and is frequently associated with Pyrolusite, with which it sometimes forms alternating layers of varying thickness. The beautiful dendritic or moss-like delineations often met with in the crevices of rocks are frequently produced by the infiltration of Psilomelane.

PUFFLÉRITE, *Dufrénoy.* The name given to the globular Prehnite of the Seisseralp in the Tyrol, where it occurs in the form of kernels in amygdaloidal trap, associated with Chabasie.

PUMICE, PUMITE (*French*). Vesicular or porous, so as to swim in water. Colours pale yellowish-grey, passing into grey, brown,

and black. Very brittle. Fracture uneven and conchoidal. H. 5. S.G. 2·2 to 2·4.

Analysis, from Lipari, by *Klaproth :*
Silica . . . . . 77·50
Alumina . . . . 17·50
Peroxide of iron . . . 1·75
Water . . . . . 3·00

99·75

BB fuses to a whitish glass.
Localities. Lipari Islands. Hungary. Banks of the Rhine, between Andernach and Coblentz. The summit of Puy Clerzoux, in Auvergne. Iceland. Island of Santorin, in the Grecian Archipelago. Ponza Islands. Ascension. Teneriffe. Aden. Ischia.

Pumice is a porous felspathic scoria, thrown out by volcanoes during the periodical explosions which take place simultaneously with their more quiet action, when ashes, cinders, masses of rock, and melted lava are hurled into the air by the action of pent-up steam and gases. Pumice, one of the ejected substances in question, becoming cooled in its passage through the air, retains the porous spongy structure it originally possessed, owing to the presence of the vapours or gases with which it was permeated at the time it was shot forth in a melted state.

Pumice is used at Andernach as a building stone.—It is also employed for polishing stones, metal, glass, and ivory; also, in a powdered state (under the name of pounce), for preparing parchment.

M. P. G. Upper Gallery, Wall-case 1, Nos. 14 to 16, 143; Wall-case 2, No. 63.

PURPLE COPPER, *Kirwan, Phillips.* See ERUBESCITE.

PUSCHKINITE, *Wagner.* A green, yellow, or red variety of Epidote, from Werchneudinsk and Katherinenburg, in the Ural, with a composition similar to that of the Pistacite of Burawa, or 2(R̈ S̈i + R̈ S̈i) + (2R̈ S̈i + 3R̈ S̈i). S.G. 3·066.

PYCNITE, *Haüy.* A massive variety of Topaz, with a parallel columnar structure, and oblique transverse divisions, along which it may be easily broken. Colour dull yellowish- or reddish-white. Translucent. Lustre vitreous. Brittle. Fracture imperfect-conchoidal. H. 7·5. S.G. 3·51.

Comp. Äl S̈i, with ¼th of the oxygen replaced by fluorine.

Analysis, from Altenberg, by *Berzelius :*
Alumina . . . . 51·00
Silica . . . . . 38·43

Fluoric acid . . . . 8·84
—
98·27

BB infusible; with borax fuses slowly to a transparent glass.

Localities. Altenberg, in Saxony. Schlackenwald and Zinnwald, in Bohemia.

Name. From πύκνος, *dense.*

Brit. Mus., Case 58.

M. P. G. Horse-shoe Case, No. 996.

PYKNOTROP (from πυκνοτρόπος, *compact*). A kind of Serpentine.

PYRALLOLIT, *Nordenskiöld.* PYRALLOLITE, *Phillips.* An altered form of Augite, in which magnesia takes the place of lime. Usually occurs massive, with a cleavage parallel to the planes of a rhombic prism; also crystallized in flat rhombic prisms. Colour greenish-white to yellowish-grey. Opaque, or subtranslucent in thin laminæ. Lustre resinous; on cleavage-planes pearly. Somewhat brittle. Fracture uneven, splintery. H. 3·5. S.G. 2·55 to 2·6.

Comp. $\ddot{M}g^3 \ddot{S}i^2 + \dot{H}$.

Analysis, by *Nordenskiöld :*

Silica	56·62
Alumina . . .	3·38
Peroxide of iron . .	0·99
Magnesia . . .	23·38
Lime	5·58
Protoxide of manganese	0·99
Water	3·58
Bituminous matter and loss .	6·38
	100·00

BB turns blackish, then becomes white and fuses at the edges to a white enamel; with borax fuses readily to a diaphanous glass.

Localities. Finland, at Storgard, in Pargas; in limestone, with Pyroxene, Felspar, and Scapolite.

Name. From πῦρ, *fire,* ἄλλος, *another,* and λίθος, *stone;* in allusion to its change of colour *BB.*

PYRAMIDAL ADIAPHANE. SPAR, *Mohs.* See GEHLENITE.

PYRAMIDAL CERIUM BARYTE, *Mohs.* See YTTROCERITE.

PYRAMIDAL COPPER PYRITES, *Mohs.* See CHALCOPYRITE.

PYRAMIDAL EUCHLORE MALACHITE MICA, *Mohs.* See URANITE.

PYRAMIDAL FELSPAR, *Mohs.* See SCAPOLITE.

PYRAMIDAL GARNET, *Mohs.* See IDOCRASE.

PYRAMIDAL KOUPHONE SPAR, *Mohs.* See APOPHYLLITE.

PYRAMIDAL LEAD BARYTE, *Mohs.* See WULFENITE.

PYRAMIDAL MANGANESE ORE, *Mohs.* See HAUSMANNITE.

PYRAMIDAL MELLICHROME RESIN, *Mohs.* See MELLITE.

PYRAMIDAL PEARL KERATE, *Mohs.* See CALOMEL.

PYRAMIDAL SCHEELIUM BARYTE, *Mohs.* See SCHEELITE.

PYRAMIDAL TELLURIUM GLANCE, *Mohs.* Black Tellurium. See NAGYAGITE.

PYRAMIDAL TIN ORE, *Mohs.* See CASSITERITE.

PYRAMIDAL TITANIUM ORE, *Mohs.* See ANATASE.

PYRAMIDAL ZEOLITE. See APOPHYLLITE; also ICHTHYOPHTHALMITE, OXHAVERITE, TESSELITE.

PYRAMIDAL ZIRCON, *Mohs.* See ZIRCON.

PYRANTIMONITE, *Brochant.* Red Antimony Ore. See KERMESITE.

PYRARGILLITE, *Dana, Nicol;* or PYRARGYLLITE, *Nordenskiöld, Phillips.* According to Bischof, an altered form of Iolite. Occurs massive and in prismatic forms with an indistinct cleavage. Colour partly black and shining, or partly bluish and without lustre; also liver-brown or dull red. Opaque or translucent at the edges. Lustre dull resinous. Fracture uneven. H. 3·5. S.G. 2·5.

Comp. $\dot{R} \ddot{S}i + \ddot{Al} \ddot{S}i + 6\dot{H}$.

Analysis, by *Nordenskiöld :*

Silica	43·93
Alumina . . .	28·93
Protoxide of iron . .	5·80
Magnesia . . .	2·90
Soda	1·85
Potash	1·05
Water	15·47
	99·43

BB alone infusible.

Entirely soluble in nitric acid.

Locality. Near Helsingfors, Finland; in granite.

Name. From πῦρ, *fire,* and ἄργιλλος, *clay;* in allusion to the argillaceous odour given out by it when heated.

Brit. Mus., Case 31.

PYRARGYRITE, *Glocker.* Hexagonal. Generally occurs in prismatic crystals. Twins. Is also found dendritic, massive, and micaceous. Colour lead-grey to iron-black; sometimes approaching to cochineal-red. Opaque to translucent at the edges. Lustre in dark varieties submetallic; in lighter varieties adamantine. Sectile; yields readily to the knife. Streak cochineal-red. Fracture shining-conchoidal.   H. 2 to 2·5.   S.G. 2·7 to 2·9.

Fig. 344.

Comp. Ag³ S + Sb S.
Analysis, from Mexico, by *Wöhler* :

Silver . . . . . 60·2
Antimony . . . . 21·8
Sulphur . . . 18·0
——
100·0

BB on charcoal, decrepitates slightly; then fuses, giving off an odour of sulphurous acid and antimonial fumes: and after long blowing in the outer flame yields a globule of pure silver.

Soluble without effervescence in nitric acid.

Localities. — *English.* Cornwall; at Huel Brothers, Huel Duchy near Callington, Herland Mine, Perran Mine, &c. — *Foreign.* Chiefly at Andreasberg, in the Harz, with Calc Spar, Native Arsenic, and Galena. Kongsberg, in Norway. Freiberg, in Saxony. Schemnitz, Kremnitz, Nagy- and Felsö-banya, in Hungary.   Guadalcanal, in Spain. Allemont, in Dauphiny. Ste. Marie-aux-Mines, in the Vosges. The Pyrenees. In S. America it is the source of immense produce, the mine of Veta-Negra near Som-brerete having yielded 700,000 marcs of silver in the course of a very few months.

Name. From πῦϱ, *fire*, and ἄϱγυϱος, *silver*. Brit. Mus., Case 11.

M.P.G. Principal Floor, Wall-cases 14 (British), 22 (Foreign).

Pyrargyrite has been subdivided into two varieties : *Dark red Silver-ore*, and *Light red Silver-ore* (see PROUSTITE), which may be distinguished from each other by the colour of the streak; the dark red affording a co-chineal-, or brick-red coloured streak, but the light red ore an aurora coloured streak. Jameson and Phillips disagree.

Both varieties constitute valuable ores of silver, and are occasionally found in masses of considerable magnitude.

Pyrargyrite may be distinguished from Cinnabar by inferior specific gravity, and by yielding a globule of silver before the blow-pipe, instead of volatilizing. Red Copper Ore, for which it may sometimes be mis-taken, has a lower specific gravity, and is usually accompanied by Native Copper,. Malachite, and Brown Iron-Ochre; while

Red Orpiment and Copper Glance, to which it bears a slight resemblance, have both a lower specific gravity, and afford a different streak, that of the former being yellow, and of the latter blackish.

PYRENEITE, *Jameson.* PYRENIT, *Werner.* A black or greyish-black variety of *Iron-lime* Garnet, occurring in small but very symmetrical rhombic dodecahedrons, which glisten externally.   Opaque.   Fracture uneven.   Hard.   S.G. 3·6 to 4:

Locality. In limestone in the Pic d'Eres-lids, near Barèges in the Pyrenees (whence the name Pyreneite.)

PYRGOM (from πύϱγωμα, *furnished with towers*). A dingy green variety of Sahlite, found in the Valley of Fassa, in the Tyrol.

PYRITE, *Haidinger*, *Nicol.*   PYRITES, *Dana*, *Greg & Lettsom.*   Cubical.   Commonly occurs in cubes, either imbedded singly or united into groups: often forming spheroidal, botryoidal or other aggregations, with a crystalline surface. Frequently in macles. Also radiated-fibrous and massive. Colour a peculiar brass-yellow.   Lustre metallic-splendent.   Opaque.   Streak brownish-black.   Strikes fire with steel.   Brittle. Fracture conchoidal, uneven.   When broken emits a sulphurous smell.   H. 6 to 6·5.   S.G. 4·83 to 5·03.

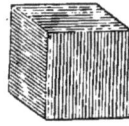 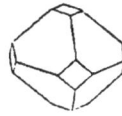 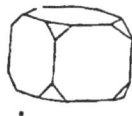

Fig. 345.   Fig. 346.   Fig. 347.

Fig. 348.   Fig. 349.

Comp. Bisulphide of iron, or Fe S²=iron 45·77, sulphur 54,23=100.

BB burns with a bluish flame and a strong smell of sulphur. In the reducing flame fuses readily to a black magnetic globule, which is crystalline on the surface.

Dissolves in concentrated nitric acid, leaving a residue of sulphur. Scarcely acted on by muriatic acid.

Localities. — *English.* Common in nearly all metallic mines. Well crystallized in Fowey Consols, Huel Maudlin, Huel Maria, and Herodsfoot Mines, Cornwall. Virtuous Lady Mine, Devonshire. Aust Passage, on the Severn, in sandstone. Alston Moor

x

Cumberland. Sussex: on the range of Downs between Sullington and Amberley Mount, in Upper Chalk.— *Welsh.* Pary's Mine, Anglesea.— *Scotch.* Leadhills, Lanarkshire. Perthshire.— *Irish.* Prehen and Hollywell Hill, near Derry, in hornblende-slate. Ballygahan and neighbouring mines, Wicklow. — *Foreign.* Elba, in pentagonal dodecahedrons, &c. Traversella, in Piedmont. Persberg and Fahlun, in Sweden. Kongsberg, in Norway. Münden, in Hanover. Peru. Huelva mines in Spain, containing from 1 to 10 per cent. of copper (on an average 3 to 4 per cent.).

Name. From πυρίτης, *full of fire* ; in allusion to its striking fire with steel. See PIERRE D'ARQUEBUSE.

Brit. Mus., Case 6.

M.P.G. Principal Floor, Wall-case 36, Nos. 95, 35, and 46 (British) ; 19 (Foreign). Horse-shoe Case, Nos. 149 to 154.

The greater part of the copperas and sulphuric acid of commerce is manufactured from Iron Pyrites, as well as much of the sulphur and alum.

The term Pyrites was restricted to *nodules* of sulphide of iron by Dr. Woodward and some of the older mineralogists ; the word Marcasite being applied by them to *veins* or perpendicular fissures of Iron Pyrites.

PYRITE DE BOOM. Speerkies, or Marcasite, from the tertiary clays of Boom, on the river Rappel in Belgium. It is used instead of sulphur in the manufactory at Brussels, for making sulphuric acid.

PYRITE CUIVREUSE, *Brochant.* See CHALCOPYRITE.

PYRITE D'ETAIN, *Brochant.* See TIN PYRITES.

PYRITE MAGNETIQUE, *Brochant.* See PYRRHOTINE.

PYRITE MARTIALE, *Brochant.* See PYRITES.

PYRITOUS COPPER. See CHALCOPYRITE.

PYROCHLORE, *Wöhler.* Cubical. Occurs in regular octahedrons, with indistinct octahedral cleavage. Colour pale honey-yellow, reddish- or blackish-brown. Opaque or translucent at the edges, exhibiting a brown colour by transmitted light. Lustre vitreous or resinous. Streak light-brown to

Fig. 350.

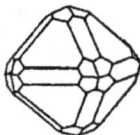

yellow. Brittle. Fracture conchoidal. H. 5 to 5·5. S.G. 4·206 to 4·326.

Comp. About 4($\dot{C}$a, $\dot{M}$g, $\dot{C}$e, $\dot{L}$a, $\dot{Y}$, $\dot{U}$) $\ddot{T}$i $\ddot{T}$a (*L. Gmelin*).

Analysis, from Miask, by *Hermann* :

Columbic acid	. . . 62·25
Titanic acid .	. . . 2·23
Zirconia	. . . 5·57
Protoxide of iron .	. . 5·11
Lime	. . . . 13·54
Yttria .	. . . . 3·09
Protoxide of lanthanum	. 20·00
Potash, soda, and lithia	. 8·72
Protoxide of manganese	. trace
Fluorine	. . . . 3·00
	101·71

BB becomes of a pale brownish-yellow colour, and fuses with great difficulty, yielding a black slag. With borax, in the inner flame, forms a clear reddish-yellow glass. Decomposed by long digestion with oil of vitriol at high temperatures.

Localities. Norway : Frederiksvärn and Laurvig, in syenite, and associated, with Zircon, Polymignite, &c. ; Brevig, with Thorite. Ilmengebirge, near Miask, in Siberia.

Name. From πῦρ, *fire,* and χλωρὸς, *green ;* in allusion to its forming a glass with microcosmic salt, which, in the outer flame, is yellow while hot, but becomes grass-green on cooling.

Brit. Mus., Case 37.

PYRODMALIT, *Leonhard,* } See PYRO-
PYRODMALITE, *Beudant.* } SMALITE.

From πῦρ, *fire,* ὀδμὴ, *odour,* and λίθος, *stone ;* from the odour it gives off when heated.

PYROELECTRIC WAVELLITE. Occurs in small emerald-green crystals mingled with white crystals, forming mammillated concretions cementing fragments of a quartzose grit, or forming the cement of a conglomerate composed of a black chertlike variety of Jasper.

Comp. 5($\ddot{A}$l $\ddot{F}$e) 3$\ddot{P}$ + 18$\dot{H}$.

Analysis, by *Alphonse Gages* :

Alumina	. . . 36·16
Silica	. . . . 3·61
Phosphoric acid	. . 30·88
Peroxide of iron .	. . 1·81
Phosphate of lime	. . 1·58
Iron	. . . . trace
Quartz	. . . . 1·00
Oxide of nickel	. . 0·32
Water	. . . . 23·56
	98·92

Locality. Found by Messrs. Jukes and

Kinahan, of the Geological Survey of Ireland, in the lower bed of the Coal Measures, just above the limestone, about three miles N.W. of Cahermoyle, in Limerick.

PYROLUSITE, *Allan, Haidinger, Dufrénoy.* Rhombic: primary form a right rhombic prism. Occurs crystallized, but generally in botryoidal and reniform masses, with a radiating fibrous or columnar structure; or in granular masses. Colour steel-grey inclining to iron-black; often bluish. Opaque. Lustre metallic. Streak black and soiling. Rather brittle, or friable. H. 2 to 2·5. S.G. 4·7 to 4·97.

Fig. 351.

Comp. Mn = manganese 63·64, oxygen 36·36 = 100.

Analysis, from Elgersburg, by *Turner:*

Protoperoxide of manganese	84·06
Oxygen	11·78
Barytes	0·53
Silica	0·51
Water	1·12
	98·00

BB in the inner flame, under a strong heat, becomes brownish-red, but does not fuse: with borax, effervesces strongly, and forms an amethyst-coloured globule, in the outer flame.

Soluble in muriatic acid, with evolution of chlorine.

Localities.—English. Cornwall, at some of the mines near Launceston and St. Minver. Creva Wood, Callington. Hartshill, Warwickshire; crystallized, *fig.* 351.— *Foreign.* Elgersburg, in Saxe-Coburg-Gotha. Ilmenau, in Thuringia. Vorderehrensdorf, near Mährisch-Trübau in Moravia. Hirschberg, in Westphalia. Near Giessen, in dolomite. Crystallized at Ihlefeld, and near Goslar in the Harz, and at Johanngeorgenstadt in Saxony. Bohemia. Hungary. France. Villa Rica, in Brazil.

Brit. Mus., Case 13.

M.P.G. Principal Floor, Wall-case 13 (British).

Name. From πῦρ, *fire,* and λύσις, *decomposition;* in allusion to its being extensively employed in glass manufactories.

Pyrolusite is the most valuable of the ores of manganese, in consequence of the large amount of oxygen it contains, which renders it of great value in the preparation of chloride of lime and in bleaching. It is also employed in the manufacture of glass, for discharging the brown and green tints and other colouring matters (on which account it is termed by the French, *le savon des verriers*); in enamel and glass painting, and in colouring pottery.

It may always be distinguished from Psilomelane, with which it is associated, by its inferior degree of hardness, being so soft as to soil the fingers when handled. From Manganite, Limonite, Hematite, and Specular Iron it differs in having a blackish streak or powder; and from certain ores of antimony it is distinguished by its infusibility at the blowpipe, while the latter may be melted in the flame of a candle.

PYROMELINE, *T. S. Hunt, v. Kobell.* A hydrated sulphate of nickel, occurring in interlacing capillary crystals, but chiefly as a greenish-white efflorescence, at Wallace Mine, Lake Huron, on sulphide of iron and nickel. It is also met with, forming a pale yellow earthy crust, at the Friederichs Mine, near Bayreuth, with Native Bismuth and Arsenical Nickel.

Name. It derives its name from πῦρ, *fire,* and μηλίνος, *bright yellow;* because the green mineral becomes bright yellow when first heated *BB.*

PYROMORPHITE, *Beudant, Greg & Lettsom.* Hexagonal. Primary form the regular six-sided prism, in which it also occurs crystallized, generally, however, modified on the edges. Commonly striated horizontally. Cleavage parallel to the planes of a six-sided pyramid. Also occurs globular, botryoidal, reniform, and massive. Colour green, yellow, grey and brown of various shades. Subtransparent to translucent at the edges. Lustre resinous. Streak white or yellow. Brittle. Fracture imperfect-conchoidal and dull. H. 3·5 to 4. S.G. 6·58 to 7.

Fig. 352.

Comp. Chlorophosphate of lead, or 3Ṗb³ P̈ + PbCl, but sometimes the chloride of lead is partly replaced by fluoride of calcium, and the triphosphate of lead by triphosphate of lime, or triarseniate of lead.

x 2

Analysis, from Zschopau, by *Wöhler* :

Oxide of lead . . .	82·29
Phosphoric acid . .	15·73
Chlorine	1·98
Peroxide of iron . .	trace
	100·00

BB fuses easily; on cooling, solidifies with vivid incandescence to an angular crystalline mass. On charcoal, with carbonate of soda, yields metallic lead. The arsenical ores also fuse on charcoal, and yield metallic lead.

Soluble in nitric acid, giving a turbidity with nitrate of silver.

Localities.— English. Cornwall ; at Huel Penrose, Huel Golden, Huel Alfred, Penberthy Croft Mine. Beeralston, Devonshire. Derbyshire; Bonsall Moor, Brassington, and near Wirksworth. Cumberland ; Mexico Mine, Driggeth Mines, Brandygill.— *Scotch.* Strontian Mine, Argyleshire. Leadhills, coloured red and orange by oxide of chrome. — *Irish.* Glenmalure, co. Wicklow. Lord Londonderry's Park, co. Derry, on ochreous sandstone.— *Foreign.* Zschopau and other places in Saxony. Przibram, Mies, and Bleistadt, in Bohemia. Szaszka, in the Bannat. Clausthal, in the Harz. Poullaouen, in Brittany. Beresowsk, in Siberia. Mexico.

Name. From πῦρ, *fire,* and μορφὴ, *form ;* in allusion to the crystalline form assumed in cooling by the fused globule *BB.*

Brit. Mus., Case 57A.

M.P.G. Principal Floor, Wall-cases 45 (British); 21 (Foreign). For varieties, see MIESITE, NUSSIERITE, POLYSPHÆRITE.

Pyromorphite is now utilised as an ore of lead, by careful roasting with charcoal.

PYROPE, *Karsten, Phillips.* A dark-red variety of Iron-Garnet, rarely found crystallized, but generally in rounded or angular grains, loose or imbedded. Transparent or translucent. Lustre vitreous. Fracture conchoidal. H. 7·5. S.G. 3·69 to 3·8.

Comp. $(\dot{R} + \ddot{R})$ $\ddot{S}i$.

Analysis, from Bohemia, by *Klaproth* :

Silica	40·00
Alumina	28·50
Peroxide of iron . .	16·50
Peroxide of manganese .	0·25
Chromic acid . . .	2·00
Magnesia . . .	10·00
Lime	3·50
	100·75

BB fuses with difficulty to a black glass : with borax gives an emerald-green globule. Brit. Mus., Case 36.

This variety of Precious Garnet, which is of a full crimson-red colour, approaching to that of a ripe mulberry, is sometimes also called Fire-Garnet, from the resemblance of its hue, when held between the eye and the sun, to that of a burning coal; hence the name, derived from πῦρ, *fire,* and ὄψις, *appearance.* For the same reason, the ancients called it ἄνθραξ, and also Carbuncle. The Carbunculus Garamanticus, or Garamantine Carbuncle, possessed this property in the greatest degree, and is the true Garnet of the moderns.

When perfect and of large size, this stone constitutes a valuable gem. The best way of cutting it is *en cabochon,* with one or two rows of small facets round the girdle of: the stone. When cut in steps, the colour is apt to appear more or less black ; but when cut *en cabochon,* the point on which the light falls displays a brilliant fire-red.

The ancients used the carbuncle for engraving seals on, and prized it so highly, that a very small stone was valued at 40 Aurei (£42 5s.) They obtained it from Carthage and Massilia. At the present day Pyrope is found in Ceylon in alluvial deposits, accompanied by Hyacinth and Sapphire; in serpentine at Zöblitz in Saxony, and on the mountains on the south side of Bohemia.

Pyrope may be distinguished from Corundum or Spinel by the greater dulness of its colour, and by inferior hardness.

PYROPHANE, *Von Born.* Hydrophane immersed in melted wax, by absorbing which it is rendered transparent. Opal impregnated with wax in a similar manner becomes opaque on cooling.

PYROPHANE. A variety of Semi-Opal, so called (from πῦρ, *fire,* and φαίνω, *to appear*) because when heated in a spoon it becomes transparent, but returns to its opaque state when cold. It is said that some Pyrophanes are found in Armenia, which are transparent while exposed to the sun, and opaque at night.—*Kirwan, Min.* vol. i. p. 291.

PYROPHYLLITE, *Hermann.* Foliated like Talc ; often in fibrous radiated masses, and small elongated prisms. Colour white or pale green. Subtransparent, or transparent and flexible in thin laminæ. Lustre pearly. Sectile. H. 1. S.G. 2·7 to 2·8.

Comp. $\ddot{Al}^2$ $\ddot{Si}^5 + 2\dot{H}$ = silica 65·2, alumina 29·6, water 5·2 = 100.

Analysis, from Siberia, by *Hermann*:

Silica	59·79
Alumina	29·46
Peroxide of iron . . .	1·80
Magnesia	4·00
Silver	trace
Water	5·62
	100·67

BB infusible, but exfoliates into white leaves, and increases to about twenty times its original size.

Partly soluble in sulphuric acid.

Localities. Between Pyschminsk and Beresow, in the Ural. Westana, Sweden. Cottonstone Mountain, New Carolina, U.S.

Name. From πῦρ, *fire,* and φύλλον, *a leaf;* in allusion to its behaviour before the blowpipe. Brit. Mus., Case 32.

PYROPHYSALITE, *Hisinger.* A coarse and nearly opaque variety of Topaz, found occasionally in yellowish-white crystals of considerable dimensions, at Finbo and Broddbo, in Sweden. A single crystal in the College of Mines at Stockholm weighs 80lbs.

Name. Derived from πῦρ, *fire,* and φυσάω, *to blow:* has reference to the manner in which it swells up when heated.

Brit. Mus., Case 58.

PYROPISSITE, *Kengott.* A Mineral Resin, resembling earthy Brown Coal in appearance, forming a layer six to eight inches thick in Brown Coal at Weissenfels, in Prussia. It is of an opaque, dull yellowish-brown colour, with a shining and greasy streak, and an earthy fracture. S.G. 0·49 to 0·52.

Burns like Bitumen, with a brownish-yellow flame and a weak aromatic odour. Largely soluble in sulphuric acid. Affords on distillation 62 per cent. of paraffine.

PYRORTHITE, *Berzelius.* Probably a decomposed Orthite, containing bituminous matter. H. 2·5. S.G. 2·19.

Locality. Kararfvet, near Fahlun, in Sweden, associated with Gadolinite, in granite.

Name. From πῦρ, *fire,* and *Orthite:* because if gently heated on one side it takes fire and burns (without either flame or smoke).

Brit. Mus., Case 38.

PYROSCLERITE, or PYROSKLERITE, *v. Kobell.* Massive; foliated and fibrous. Perfect basal cleavage. Colour apple-green, pale greenish - grey, or reddish. Translucent. Lustre dull; pearly on cleavage planes. Sectile. Fracture uneven and splintery. H. 2·5 to 3. S.G. 2·74.

Comp. $2\ddot{\text{Mg}}\,\ddot{\text{Si}} + \ddot{\text{Al}}\,\dddot{\text{Si}} + 4\dot{\text{H}}$ = silica 37·6, alumina 14·2, magnesia 33·2, water 14·9 = 100.

Analysis, from Elba, by *v. Kobell:*

Silica	37·03
Alumina	13·50
Oxide of chrome . . .	1·43
Protoxide of iron . . .	3·52
Magnesia	31·62
Water	11·00
	98·10

BB fuses with difficulty to a grey glass: with borax yields a glass-coloured green by chromium; and with solution of cobalt, a greyish mass.

Decomposed, in the state of fine powder, by concentrated muriatic acid, with separation of silica, though not in a gelatinous state.

Localities. Elba, with Chonikrite. Aker, in Südermanland: S.G. 2·605.

Name. From πῦρ, *fire,* and σκληρός, *hard;* in allusion to its refractory comportment before the blowpipe.

Descloiseaux considers Pyrosclerite to be a mixed mineral. Scheerer joins Pyrosclerite with Chonikrite.

PYROSIDERITE (from πῦρ, *fire,* and σίδηρος, *iron*). A variety of Göthite from Eiserfeld, in Nassau.

Comp. $\ddot{\text{F}}\text{e}\,\dot{\text{H}}$.

Analysis, by *v. Kobell:*

Peroxide of iron . .	86·35
Peroxide of manganese .	0·51
Silica	0·85
Oxide of copper . .	0·91
Lime	trace
Water . . .	11·38
	100·00

PYROSMALITE, *Hausmann.* PYROSMALITH, *Karsten.* Hexagonal. Occurs in six-sided prisms, of which the terminal edges are sometimes replaced; with a perfect basal cleavage; also massive. Colour liver-brown or pistachio-green: generally yellowish - brown without, greenish - yellow within. Translucent at the edges. Lustre of the terminal planes pearly; of other planes shining. Structure lamellar. Streak green, paler than the colour. Rather brittle. Fracture uneven and somewhat splintery. H. 4 to 4·5. S.G. 3·081.

Comp. $(\dot{\text{Fe}}, \dot{\text{Mn}})^3\,\ddot{\text{Si}}^2 + (\text{Fe}^2\,\text{Cl}^3 + \ddot{\text{F}}\text{e}\,6\dot{\text{H}})$.

Analysis, by *Hisinger:*

Silica	35·85
Peroxide of iron . .	35·48

x 3

Peroxide of manganese	. 24·26
Lime	. 1·21
Chlorine . . .	. 3·77
Water	. undetermined

——————
100·57

BB assumes a blackish-brown colour, gives off vapours of water, muriatic acid, and sesquichloride of iron, and fuses to a black magnetic globule.

Dissolves in nitric acid, with separation of silica.

Localities. Sweden: at Nya Kopparberg in Westmannland, and Bjelkeygrube, one of the iron mines of Nordmark, near Phillipstadt, in Wermland.

Name. From πῦϱ, *fire,* and ὀσμὴ, *odour;* in allusion to the smell given off when heated.

Brit. Mus., Case 57B.

PYROSTIBITE, *Glocker.* See KERMESITE.

PYROXENE, *Haüy.* Oblique; primary form an oblique rhombic prism. Generally occurs in short, thick crystals, and often in twins: also amorphous, coarsely laminar, granular and fibrous. Colour various shades of green, grey and black; but sometimes colourless or even white. Transparent to opaque. Lustre vitreous or inclining to resinous. Streak white to grey. Brittle. Fracture conchoidal to uneven. H. 5 to 6. S.G. 3·23 to 3·5.

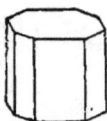 

Fig 353.   Fig. 354.

Comp. Bisilicate of various bases, represented by the general formula $(\dot{R}\ \ddot{R})\ \dddot{S}i^2$ (*Dana*), in which $\dot{R}$ may be $\dot{C}a$, $\dot{M}g$, $\dot{F}e$, $\dot{M}n$. When $\dot{R}=(\dot{C}a\ \dot{M}g)$ the colour is white or pale green; when $\dot{R}=(\dot{C}a, \dot{F}e)$ the colour varies from green to black; and when iron forms an abundant ingredient the colour becomes very dark green or black. In the aluminous species, *which all contain alkalies,* a portion of the silica is replaced by alumina (*Dana*).

BB the dark varieties, containing iron, afford an iron reaction. The paler varieties fuse with effervescence to a colourless glass, and with borax yield a clear glass.

Localities. — *English.* Teesdale, Durham, in basalt. — *Welsh.* Anglesea, in trap dykes. Caernarvon: near Bangor, in trap rock. Moel

Siabod. Summit of Penmaen Mawr.—*Scotch.* Islands of Canna, Mull, and Rum, Argyleshire; in basaltic rocks. Isle of Arran. Isle of Skye. Long Row and Lion's Haunch, Arthur's Seat, Edinburgh, in basalt. Island of Tiree, in Limestone. Fulford lime-quarry, near Raith, in Fifeshire. Blaikie Heugh, five miles east of Haddington, in felstone porphyry. North Berwick. — *Irish.* Antrim co., Portrush. Fairhead. Culfeightown, Tor Head. Near Clogher, Tyrone. Tullyreagh, in Derry.— *Foreign.* Aussig and Töplitz, in Bohemia; also at Oberrochlitz (compact white). Greenland. Arendal, in Norway. Hungary. Transylvania. Hesse. Auvergne. Monte Rossi, on Etna. Vesuvius. Stromboli. Teneriffe. Bourbon. Hawaii, in basaltic lava. Laachersee, &c., on the Lower Rhine, in basaltic lava of the extinct volcanos of the Eifel. Ascension, in basaltic lava. White Island, New Zealand.

Name. From πῦϱ, *fire,* and ξίνος, *a guest;* meaning a guest in the domain of fire; in allusion to its mode of occurrence, as though it had formed an original part of the lava in which it is found, which had escaped fusion, and was not, therefore, a result of crystallization consequent on the cooling of the mass.

Pyroxene is, according to Dana, isomorphous with Hornblende; and this opinion has been confirmed by the late researches of Rammelsberg, who also states that both are bisilicates. It differs from Hornblende, however, in containing a smaller quantity of silica, in being less fusible, and in having a higher specific gravity.

For varieties of Pyroxene, see ALGERINE, AUGITE, BAIKALITE, COCCOLITE, DIOPSIDE, FASSAITE, HEDENBERGITE, JEFFERSONITE, MALACOLITE, SAHLITE.

Brit. Mus., Case 34.

M.P.G. Horse-shoe Case, Nos. 1035, 1042.

PYROXÈNE FERRO-MANGANESIEN, *Beudant.* See PYROSMALITE.

PYROXÈNE GRANULIFORME, *Haüy.* See COCCOLITE.

PYRRHITE, *G. Rose.* Cubical. Occurs in minute octahedrons. Colour orange-yellow. Subtranslucent. Lustre vitreous. H. 6.

Comp. Probably Columbate of zirconia, coloured with oxides of iron, uranium and manganese.

BB infusible. In small splinters blackens, and colours the flame deep yellow.

Locality. Alabaschka, near Mursinsk, lining drusy felspar-cavities. The Azores.

Name. From πυϱϱὸς, *yellow.*

PYRRHOSIDERITE, *Hausmann.*   From

πυςϱὸς, *yellow*, and σίδηϱος, *iron*. See PYROSI-
DERITE.

PYRRHOTINE, *Breithaupt*. Hexagonal.
Rarely crystallized, in irregular six-sided
prisms, variously modified. Perfect basal
cleavage. Generally occurs massive and
amorphous. Structure granular. Colour
bronze-yellow, reddish, or brownish : liable
to speedy tarnish on exposure to the air,
Opaque. Lustre metallic. Streak greyish-
black. Brittle. Fracture uneven, passing into
small imperfect-conchoidal. Acts slightly on
the magnet. H. 3·5 to 4·5. S.G. 4·4 to 4·7.

Comp. Sulphide of iron, or Fe^7 S^8=iron
60·5, sulphur 39·5=100.

Analysis, from Bodenmais, by *H. Rose :*

Iron . . . . . . 60·95
Sulphur . . . . 39·05
—————
100·00

BB on charcoal, fuses, forming a greyish-
black magnetic globule. Roasted in the
state of fine powder, it is converted into
pure peroxide of iron.

Soluble in muriatic acid, leaving a residue
of sulphur.

Localities. — English. Cornwall : Botal-
lack, near St. Just ; Huel Maudlin (cleav-
able). Beeralston, Devonshire. Several
mines near Aldstone, Cumberland.— *Welsh.*
Near the base of Moel Elion, and Llanrwst,
Caernarvonshire. With Copper Pyrites,
Clogau Mine, near Dolgelly, Merionethshire.
— *Scotch.* Appin, Argyleshire, massive.
Near Inverary. Galloway Hills. — *Irish.*
Near Leahtown, Donegal, of a bronze colour.
—*Foreign.* Kongsberg, Norway ; and An-
dreasberg, in the Harz, in crystalline plates.
Bodenmais, in Bavaria (cleavable). Kupfer-
berg, in Bohemia. Bernkastel, on the Mo-
selle. Saxony. Silesia. Salzburg. Siberia.
St. Jerome, Canada, in large veins. United
States. Minas Geraes, Brazil, in very large
crystals,

Name. From πυςϱοτὴς, *reddish*, in allusion
to its colour.

Brit. Mus., Case 14.

M.P.G. Principal Floor, Wall-case 19
(Foreign).

Pyrrhotine may be distinguished from
common Iron Pyrites by inferior hardness.

Q.

QUARTZ, *Haüy.* See ROCK CRYSTAL.
QUARTZ, *Kirwan.* Common Quartz.
QUARTZ. Hexagonal. Occurs in hexa-
gonal prisms, sometimes terminated at both

ends by six-sided pyramids. (See ROCK
CRYSTAL.) Colourless, when pure ; various
shades of yellow, red, brown, green, blue,
violet and black. Transparent to opaque.
Lustre vitreous, sometimes inclining to
resinous. Streak white ; of impure varieties the same as the colour, but paler.
Tough, brittle, or friable. Uncleavable.
Fracture conchoidal. H. 7. S.G. 2·5 to 2 8.

Fig. 355.

Comp. S̈i ; pure silica in the insoluble
state, or that cannot be taken up by a
potash solution.

BB alone, undergoes no change ; with
soda fuses readily with efflorescence to a
transparent glass.

Insoluble in all acids except hydrofluoric
acid.

Name. Probably a German word, signifying the grating sound made by clay in
kneading it.

The Quartz family is divided into three
groups, viz. :

I. The *Vitreous*, comprising those varieties
which present the bright, glassy lustre of
broken Rock Crystal ; and including *Amethyst, Aventurine, False Topaz, Ferruginous
Quartz, Milky* (and *greasy*) *Quartz, Rock
Crystal, Rose Quartz, Siderite, Smoky
Quartz*, or *Cairngorum.*

II. The *Chalcedonic*, including those varieties which display the glistening subvitreous or waxy lustre, and the translucency
or transparency of Chalcedony ; as *Agate,
Carnelian, Cat's Eye, Chalcedony, Chrysoprase,
Flint, Hornstone, Mocha Stone, Onyx, Sard,
Sardonyx*, &c.

III. The *Jaspery*, or the varieties presenting the dull colours, lustre, and opacity
of Jasper ; as *Bloodstone* or *Heliotrope, Jasper,
Lydian Stone, Touchstone*, or *Basanite ;*
also *Fibrous Quartz, Floatstone, Granular
Quartz, Haytorite, Phthanite (Kieselschiefer),
Sandstone, Siliceous Sinter, Silicified Wood,*
&c.

Brit. Mus., Cases 21 and 22.

M.P.G. In Hall—Auriferous Quartz from
the Grass Valley, Nevada county, California.
Mass of crystallized Quartz from a mine in
Weardale, Durham. Large crystal from
Brazil, under Case III., in Entrance Hall.

x 4

QUARTZ AËROHYDRE, *Dufrénoy.* Quartz containing drops of liquid, because they were originally supposed to be water.

QUARTZ AVENTURINÉ. See AVENTURINE.

QUARTZ EN CHEMISE. Crystallized Quartz, opaque and white on the surface, but transparent within.

QUARTZ ENFUMÉE, or *Diamant d'Alençon.* Smoky Quartz. See CAIRNGORM.

QUARTZ HÉMATOÏDE. See COMPOSTELLA HYACINTH.

QUARZ-HYALIN AMORPHE, *Haüy.* Common Quartz.

QUARTZ HYALIN ENFUMÉE. Smoky Quartz. See CAIRNGORM.

QUARTZ HYALIN JAUNE. See CITRINE, FALSE TOPAZ, &c.

QUARTZ HYALIN LAITEUX, *Haüy.* See MILK QUARTZ.

QUARTZ HYALIN VERTE OBSCURE. See PRASE.

QUARTZ HYALIN VIOLET. See AMETHYST.

QUARTZ JASPE, *Haüy.* See JASPER.

QUARTZ LAITEUX, *Brochant.* See MILK QUARTZ.

QUARTZ LIMPIDE AÉROHYDRE. Limpid Rock Crystal, with internal cavities containing air and water. See ROCK CRYSTAL.

QUARTZ NECTIQUE, *Haüy.* See FLOATSTONE.

QUARTZ OPAQUE NOIR. See LYDIAN STONE.

QUARTZ RÉSINITE, *Haüy.* See OPAL.

QUARTZ RÉSINITE COMMUNE, *Haüy.* See SEMI-OPAL.

QUARTZ RÉSINITE GIRASOL, *Haüy.* See FIRE OPAL.

QUARTZ RÉSINITE HYDROPHANE, *Haüy.* See HYDROPHANE.

QUARTZ RÉSINITE MENILITE, *Haüy.* See MENILITE.

QUARTZ RÉSINITE OPALIN, *Haüy.* See PRECIOUS OPAL.

QUARTZ RÉSINITE SUBLUISANT, BRUNÂTRE, *Haüy.* See MENILITE.

QUARTZ ROSE, *Brochant.* See ROSE QUARTZ.

QUARTZ THERMOGÈNE. See GEYSERITE.

QUARZ-AGATHE-CALCEDOINE, *Haüy.* See CHALCEDONY.

QUARZ-AGATHE-CORNALINE, *Haüy.* See CARNELIAN.

QUARZ-AGATHE GROSSEUR, *Haüy.* See HORNSTONE.

QUARZ-AGATHE PYROMAQUE. *Haüy.* See FLINT.

QUARZ-AGATHE XYLOIDE, *Haüy.* See WOOD OPAL.

QUARZ ALUMINIFÈRE TRIPOLIEN, *Haüy.* See TRIPOLI.

QUEBEC DIAMONDS. Rock Crystal from Quebec, in Lower Canada.

QUECKSILBER. *German* for Quicksilver.

QUECKSILBERBRANDERZ, or *Inflammable Cinnabar.* See IDRIALITE.

QUECKSILBERFAHLERZ. See SPANIOLITE.

QUECKSILBER HORNERZ, *Werner.* See CALOMEL.

QUECKSILBER LEBERERZ, *Werner.* See HEPATIC CINNABAR.

QUELLERZ, *Hermann.* A variety of Limonite, from Novgorod in Russia, represented by the formula, $\ddot{\text{F}}\text{e}\ \ddot{\text{H}}^3$ (instead of $\overset{\cdots}{\text{F}}\text{e}^2$ H^3). It is composed of peroxide of iron 74·8, water 25·2 = 100.

QUICKSILVER. See NATIVE QUICKSILVER.

QUICKSILVER-LIVER-ORE. See HEPATIC CINNABAR.

QUINCITE, *Berthier.* Aphrodite, in pale carmine coloured particles disseminated through limestone, near the village of Quincey, Dept. du Cher, in France. It is composed of silica 54, magnesia 19, protoxide of iron 8, water 17 = 98.

Brit. Mus., Case 24.

R.

RABEN-GLIMMER, *Breithaupt.* See LEPIDOMELANE.

RADDLE. A provincial pronounciation of Reddle: (which see).

RADELERZ, or *Cog-wheel Ore.* A macled variety of Bournonite, from Kapnik, in Transylvania. It is also found at Herodsfoot Mine, near Liskeard, in Cornwall. See WHEEL-ORE.

RADIATED ACICULAR OLIVENITE, *Jameson.* See APHANESITE.

RADIATED BARYTES. See BOLOGNESE STONE.

RADIATED NATRON, *Jameson.* See TRONA.

RADIATED PYRITES. Radiated forms of Iron Pyrites. Under this term were formerly included the radiated masses and the more simple crystals of Marcasite or White Iron Pyrites. It is found at Joachimsthal, and near Carlsbad in Bohemia, and in several parts of Saxony.

M. P. G. Horse-shoe Case, No. 149.

RADIATED ZEOLITE, *Jameson.* See STILBITE.

RADIOLITE. A variety of Natrolite, from Brevig, in Norway.

Analysis, by *Scheerer* :

Silica	48·38
Alumina . . .	26·42
Peroxide of iron . .	0·24
Soda	13·87
Potash . . .	1·54
Lime	0·44
Water	9·42
	100·31

RAINBOW CHALCEDONY. Chalcedony consisting of thin concentric layers, which when cut across and held towards the light displays an iridescence, more especially if the stone is cut in thin slices.

RAMMELSBERGITE, *Haidinger*. See CHLOANTHITE, or Tesseral White Nickel.

RAMMELSBERGITE, *Breithaupt, Dana*. An arsenide of Nickel, with the same composition as Chloanthite, or Ni As^2 = Nickel 28·3, arsenic 71·7 = 100. In appearance and physical characters it resembles Marcasite, or White Iron Pyrites, but differs from it, according to Dana, in being slightly ductile. H. 5·25 to 5·75. S.G. 7 to 7·19.

Localities. Schneeberg in Saxony, and Riechelsdorf in Hesse.

Name. Named by Breithaupt after the chemist, C. F. Rammelsberg, of Berlin.

Brit. Mus., Case 4.

RANCIERITE, *Leymerie*. A variety of Hausmannite, resembling Pyrolusite, and like it giving off chlorine when treated with muriatic acid. Occurs in earthy masses of a deep brown colour. Soils the fingers. Streak chocolate-brown.

Analysis, from Groroi (Mayenne), by *Berthier* :

Oxygen . . .	26·79
Manganese . . .	48·41
Water	15·80
Ferruginous clay .	9·00
	100·00

RANCIERITE ARGENTINE, or RANCIERITE METALLOIDE. The purest and, in the absence of crystals, the typical form of the above mineral. Found in small spongy, prismatic, or filamentary masses, or in beds, with a metallic aspect, and a silvery colour, sometimes tinged with violet, in cavities of massive Limonite or Brown Hematite. Very soft and light.

Localities. The mountain Rancié or

Rancier (Ariège). In the mines of the same kind around Le Canigou, in the valley of Baigorry. Also in the Dept. of Isère, and at Saint-Jean de Gardonnenque, in the Cévennes.

RANDANITE, *Salvetat*. A soluble silica, principally composed of infusorial remains. It occurs as a fine earth, or in compact earthy masses near Algiers, and in France at Ceyssat, near Randan (whence the name *Randanite*), in the Puy-de-Dôme.

Analysis, from Ceyssat, by *Fournet* :

Soluble silica . . .	87·20
Alumina and peroxide of iron	2·00
Sand	0·80
Water, carbonic acid, and organic matter . . .	10·00
	100·00

RAPHANOSMITE. The name given by Von Kobell to varieties of Clausthalite, in which a part of the lead is replaced by copper. By Brooke & Miller they are comprised under the term *Zorgite*. Found in small fragments of a lead-grey and violet colour, or of a perfect violet colour when newly broken. Very soft and slightly malleable. H. 2·5 to 3. S.G. 5·6.

Comp. Pb Se + Cu Se.

Analysis, from Tilkerode, in the Harz, by *H. Rose* :

Selenium	34·26
Lead	47·43
Copper	15·45
Silver	1·29
Lead and peroxide of iron .	2·08
	100·51

RAPHILITE, *Thomson*. A variety of Asbestiform Tremolite, occurring in groups of delicate acicular crystals (whence the name, from ραφίς, a needle). Colour white or bluish-green. Translucent. Lustre vitreous or resinous. H. 3·5. S.G. 2·85.

Comp. Ċa S̈i + M̈g^3 S̈i^2 = silica 60·7, magnesia 26·8, lime 12·5 = 100.

Analysis, by *T. S. Hunt* :

Silica	55·30
Alumina . . .	0·40
Magnesia . . .	22·50
Lime	13·36 ·
Protoxide of iron . .	6·30
Protoxide of manganese	trace
Soda	0·80
Potash . . .	0·25
Loss by ignition . .	0·30
	99·31

BB whitens, becomes opaque, and fuses at the edges.

Locality. Perth, Upper Canada.
Brit. Mus., Case 33.

RASENEISENSTEIN. See BOG IRON-ORE.

RATOFFKIT, *John.* A granular or earthy blue variety of Fluor, rendered impure by an admixture of clay from Ratoffka, in Russia.

RAUCHKALK. A variety of Dolomite, occurring in the Zechstein of North Germany.

Comp. $\ddot{C}a \ddot{U} + \dot{M}g \ddot{C}$.

Analysis, by *Rammelsberg.*

Carbonate of lime	.	. 55·62
Carbonate of magnesia	.	42·40
Carbonate of iron	.	. 0·56

98·58

RAUSCHGELB, *Hausmann, Werner.* See ORPIMENT.

RAUTENSPATH. See RHOMB-SPAR.

RAZOUMOFFSKIN, *John.* A clayey mineral from Kosemutz, in Silesia.

Comp. $\ddot{A}l \ddot{S}i^2 + 3\dot{H}$.

Analysis, by *Zellner:*

Silica	.	.	.	. 54·50
Alumina	.	.	.	. 27·25
Lime	.	.	.	. 2·00
Magnesia	.	.	.	0·37
Protoxide of iron	.	.	0·25
Water	.	.	.	. 14·25

98·62

REALGAR, *Kirwan, Phillips;* or REALGAR ROUGE, *Brochant.* Oblique. Occurs in prismatic crystals, streaked longitudinally and shining; also massive, disseminated, investing. Colour aurora-red, of various degrees of intensity. Translucent to opaque; semi-transparent in crystals. Lustre resinous. Steak lemon- or orange-yellow. Sectile. Yields to the pressure of the nail. Fracture conchoidal to uneven. Becomes negatively electrical by friction. H. 1·5 to 2. S.G. 3·4 to 3·6.

Fig. 356.

Comp. Bisulphide of arsenic, As S^2 = arsenic 70·07, sulphur 29·93 = 100.

Analysis, from Pola de Lena, in Asturia, Spain, by *Dr. Hugo Müller:*

Sulphur	.	.	.	. 30·00
Arsenic	.	.	.	. 70·25

100·25

BB easily fusible. Burns in the air with a blue flame, forming sulphurous and arsenious acid, and usually leaving an earthy residue.

Localities. The most noted localities are Felsobanya, in Upper Hungary, and Kapnik and Nagyag, in Transylvania. It is also found at Andreasberg, in the Harz; Joachimsthal, in Bohemia; Schneeberg, in Saxony; Suabia; St. Gotthard, in Switzerland, in Dolomite; Guadaloupe; Vesuvius, and the Solfatara, in minute crystals.

Artistically prepared Realgar is used as a pigment, and was also employed by the ancients for the same purpose, under the name of Sandarach, or Σανδαράχη. The Chinese are said to form cups from Realgar, in which they let stand lemon-juice, which they afterwards drink as a purgative. See *M. P. G.* Case 23.

It is distinguished from Red Silver-ore by its lower specific gravity and orange-coloured streak, and from Red Lead-ore by its lower specific gravity.

Name. Used by the Alchemists.

Brit. Mus., Case 12.

M. P. G. Principal Floor, Wall-case 23 (Foreign).

REALGAR-JAUNE, *Brochant.* See ORPIMENT.

RED ANTIMONY, *Phillips.*
RED ANTIMONIAL ORE, *Kirwan.*
RED ANTIMONY-ORE, *Jameson.*
} See KERMESITE.

RED CHALK. An earthy kind of Hematite. See REDDLE.

RED COBALT OCHRE, *Jameson.* See ERYTHRINE.

RED COPPER, *Dana;* or RED COPPER

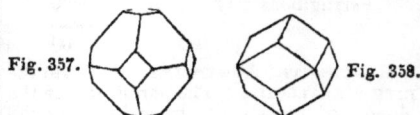

Fig. 357.   Fig. 358.

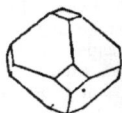

Fig. 359.

ORE, *Jameson.* Cubical. Occurs crystallized in the form of the octahedron and its modifications. Cleavage octahedral. Also in granular, compact, or earthy masses. Colour various shades of red, particularly cochineal-red; sometimes crimson-red by transmitted light. Semi-transparent to sub-translucent. Lustre submetallic, or adamantine. Streak brownish-red and shining. Yields easily to the knife. Brittle. Fracture conchoidal, or uneven. H. 3·5 to 4. S.G. 5·6 to 6·15.

Comp. Dioxide of copper, $\dot{\text{C}}\text{u} = $ copper 88·9, oxygen 11·1 = 100.

BB on charcoal, in the inner flame, affords a globule of pure copper; with borax fuses readily to a fine-green glass.

Dissolves, with effervescence, in nitric acid.

Localities.—*English.* Cornwall, in several mines, South Francis, Huels Gorland, Prosper, Unity, Muttrell, Basset, Carnbrea, Phœnix, Huel Crebor, Devonshire. Ecton Mine, Staffordshire.—*Foreign.* Chessy, near Lyons, in France, in isolated crystals, imbedded in Lithomarge. Linares, in Spain. Moldawa, in the Bannat. Siberia, at Katherinenburg, &c. Thuringia. Tuscany. Cuba. New Jersey, Lake Superior Copper region, and in many localities in North and South America. South Australia.

Brit. Mus., Case 17.

M. P. G. A 56, in Hall; mass of ore from Burra Burra mines, South Australia. Principal Floor, Case 11 (Burra Burra). Wall-cases 1, 30, and 32 (British); 15 (Foreign); 37 (Burra Burra).

See also ZIGUELINE or TILE-ORE, CHALCOTRICHITE, and PLUSH COPPER.

RED   HEMATITE,⎫   Under these terms
Phillips.   ⎪   are included those
RED IRON-ORE.   ⎬varieties of Hema-
RED IRON-STONE, ⎪tite which have a
Jameson.   ⎭non-metallic or
sub-metallic lustre; under the latter are comprised the *Red Iron Froth, Ochrey Red Ironstone, Compact Red Ironstone,* and *Red Hematite,* of Jameson.

RED IRON CHALK. An impure peroxide of iron, used as a drawing material. It has an earthy appearance and texture, and breaks with a conchoidal fracture. See REDDLE.

RED IRON FROTH, *Jameson.* A variety of Red Hematite, composed of friable or slightly coherent scaly particles. It is smelted at Sahl, in the Duchy of Henneberg, and yields good iron.

RED IRON OCHRE. See RED OCHRE.

RED IRON VITRIOL. See BOTRYOGENE.

RED LEAD SPAR, *Kirwan.*⎫   See
RED LEAD ORE, *Jameson.*⎭ CROCOISITE.

RED MANGANESE, *Allan.*⎫   See
RED MANGANESE ORE,⎬DIALLOGITE.
Jameson.   ⎭

RED OCHRE. A soft and earthy form of Hematite, or Peroxide of Iron. It occurs abundantly at Davidstow, near Camelford, in Cornwall; Chew Magna, near Wrington, in Somersetshire; at Ulverstone, in Lancashire, &c.

RED ORE OF MANGANESE, *Kirwan.* See DIALLOGITE.

RED ORPIMENT, *Jameson.* See REALGAR

RED OXIDE OF COPPER, *Phillips.* See RED COPPER.

RED OXIDE OF ZINC, *Phillips.* See ZINCITE.

RED SCALY IRON ORE, *Kirwan.* See RED IRON-FROTH.

RED   SILVER   ORE,⎫   See
Jameson.   ⎬PYRARGYRITE.
RED SILVER, *Phillips.*⎭

RED SULPHURET OF ARSENIC. See REALGAR.

RED VITRIOL, *Jameson.* See BIEBRITE.

RED ZEOLITE OF ÆDELFORS. See RETZITE.

RED ZINC ORE, *Jameson.* See ZINCITE.

REDDLE, *Jameson;* or RED IRON-CHALK. An impure peroxide of iron, occurring in opaque compact masses of various shades of light brownish-red, which sometimes passes into nearly brick-red. Soils the fingers, and, when rubbed on paper, leaves a red trace. Streak paler, more shining, and brighter than the fractured surface. Easily frangible. Fracture earthy and dull. Usually dry and meagre to the touch. Adheres strongly to the tongue. Gives off an argillaceous odour when breathed on. In water falls to powder, and does not form a paste. S.G. 3·14 to 3·93.

Exposed to a red heat it decrepitates, and becomes of a deeper red or blackish colour.

Reddle is found abundantly in England, France, and Germany.

The term Reddle is generally applied in this country to the kind which is used for marking sheep, for which purpose it is procured in considerable quantities from the Carboniferous Limestone of the Mendip Hills, in Somersetshire, and the Forest of Dean, in Gloucestershire; also at Wastwater, in Cumberland (*Red Iron Chalk*). It is prepared at Brixham and other places in Devonshire, from the iron ores which occur in the Devonian limestone of the west of England, and is used for the coarser kinds of paint, experience having proved it to be admirably adapted for painting the bottoms of ships. The coarser varieties are made into pencils, which are used by carpenters, and the finer kinds into crayons for artists' but to a less extent now than was the case a few years ago, when drawing in red chalk was more practised than it is at the present day. For these purposes it is either used in its natural, state, or it is ground, washed, and mixed with gum, to give it the necessary hardness, and then cast in moulds.

A Reddle is found about twelve miles from Rotheram, in Yorkshire, which is the best material known for polishing optical glasses.

REDRUTHITE. A name proposed, by Brooke & Miller, for Copper Glance, on the erroneous supposition that the best specimens of that mineral are obtained from the mines in the neighbourhood of Redruth, in Cornwall.

REFIKITE. Forms tubercles and small veins in Lignite. Structure fibrous-radiated. Colour wax-white. Lustre between resinous and greasy. Soft; scratched by Gypsum. Breaks between the fingers, and is easily reduced to powder. Fracture amorphous.

Comp. Carbon 78, hydrogen 11, oxygen 11 = 100.

Melts at 180° F. Soluble in boiling alcohol, and disappears altogether in a weak and boiling solution of potash.

Locality. The Abruzzi, in Naples, in macigno.

Name. After Refik Bey.

REMINGTONITE, *J. C. Booth.* A hydrocarbonate of cobalt, occurring as a rose-coloured coating, one hundredth of an inch in thickness. Very soft and earthy. Opaque, with a pale rose-coloured streak.

It is met with at the copper mine near Finksburg, Carroll County, Maryland, coating thin veins of Serpentine, which traverse Hornblende and Epidote, and is associated with Serpentine, Hornblende, Epidote, Carbonate of lime, and Carrollite.

It is named after Mr. Edward Remington, under whose immediate supervision the mines are where it is found.

REMOLINITE, *Brooke & Miller.* Atacamite, so named from its occurrence at Los Remolinos, in Chili.

RENSSELAERITE, *Emmons.* A steatitic mineral with a fine compact texture, and an unctuous feel. Colour grey, whitish, greenish, and sometimes brownish or black.

Translucent. H. 2·5 to 3. S.G. 2·75 to 2·87.

Comp. Like that of Talc.

Analysis, from Grenville, by *T. S. Hunt:*

Silica	. 61·60
Magnesia . .	. 31·06
Protoxide of iron .	. 1·53
Water	. 5·60
	99·79

Localities. Over large areas in Northern New York, U. S.; Grenville, Upper Canada; also at the rapids of the Peribanka, associated with Labradorite rock.

According to Beck, the crystals are pseudomorphs of Pyroxene.

It is worked in the lathe into inkstands and other articles.

Name. After Stephen Van Rensselaer.

RESINITE, *Haüy.*
RETINASPHALT, *Mohs.*
Phillips.
RETINASPHALTUM, *Hatchett.*

See RETINITE. The name Retin-asphaltum was given by Hatchett, in the belief that the mineral from Bovey Tracey was composed of a resinous substance, and a substance resembling Asphalt.

RETINALITE, *Thomson.* A massive variety of Serpentine, with a·resinous appearance. Colour honey-yellow to oil-green. Translucent. Lustre resinous. Fracture splintery. H. 3·5. S.G. 2·49. to 2·53.

Analysis, from Grenville, by *T. S. Hunt:*

Silica	. 40·10
Peroxide of iron .	. 1·90
Magnesia . . .	. 41·65
Lime	. 0·90
Water	. 15·00
	99·55

BB infusible, but whitens and becomes friable.

Localities. Grand Calumet Island, on the Ottawa; and Grenville, Upper Canada.

Name. From ριτίνη, *resin,* from its resemblance to that substance.

RETIN-ALLOPHANE, *Mohs.* See PITTICITE.

RETIN-BARYTE, *Mohs.* See TRIPLITE.

RETINITE, *Beudant.* See PITCHSTONE.

RETINITE, *Haidinger, v. Leonhard.* A mineral resin, found in roundish or irregular lumps. Colour yellowish to pale brownish-yellow. Opaque. Lustre glistening or resinous; often earthy externally. Soft, and very easily frangible. Fracture uneven or imperfect-conchoidal. H. 1 to 2·5. S.G. 1·1 to 1·2.

Analysis, by *Hutchett* ;

Resin, soluble in alcohol .	. 55
Insoluble bituminous matter	. 41
Earthy matter . . .	. 5
	—
	99

Melts when placed on red hot iron, smokes, and burns with a bright flame, and a fragrant odour.

Soluble in alcohol, leaving an unctuous residue.

Localities. Bovey Tracey, in Devonshire, with Lignite. Halle. Osnabrück, in Hanover, forming a layer in peat. Cape Sable. Brit. Mus., Case 60.

M.P.G. Horse-shoe Case, Nos. 107 and 115.

RÉTINITE DU CANTAL. See CANTALITE.

RÉTINITE PERLÉ. The name given by Cordier to the paste of those kinds of Pitchstone which, instead of presenting crystals like that of Cantal (see CANTALITE), contain rounded nodules, or Spherùlite (see PEARLSTONE).

RETZITE. A red zeolite, from Ædelfors, in Sweden, considered by N. J. Berlin to be a variety of Laumontite (allied to the red zeolite from Upsala), more or less disintegrated, and rendered impure by an admixture of Quartz. It is named after Retzius, by whom it was analysed, with the following results :

Silica	. 60·28
Alumina . . .	. 15·42
Peroxide of iron . .	. 4·16
Lime	8·18
Magnesia and peroxide of manganese . .	. 0·42
Water	. 11·07
	———
	99·53

It is of a white, light grey, or reddish colour, and translucent at the edges. H. 6. S.G. 2·5.

BB fuses with intumescence.

Dissolves in acids, forming a jelly.

REUSSIN, *Karsten* ; or REUSSITE, *Phillips.* Anhydrous sulphate of soda and magnesia, occurring in white, flat, six-sided crystals, and in acicular crystals, forming radiating groups, near Seidlitz and Saidschutz, in Bohemia ; also in mealy efflorescences. Taste saline and bitter. Shining. Fracture conchoidal.

Analysis, by *Reuss* :

Sulphate of soda . .	. 66·04
Sulphate of magnesia .	. 31·35
Chloride of calcium .	. 2·19
Sulphate of lime . .	. 0·42
	———
	100·00

Name. After Reuss, the Austrian mineralogist.

RHODALOSE, or RHODHALOSE, *Beudant.* (From ῥοδόεις, *rose,* and ἅλος, *salt.*) Red or cobalt vitriol. See BIEBRITE.

RHODIUM GOLD. Gold containing from 34 to 43 per cent. of rhodium.

RHODIZITE, *G. Rose.* A lime-boracite found in minute, translucent, and shining crystals, on red Tourmaline and Quartz, near Mursinsk, in the Ural. Colour white, inclining to yellow or grey. H. 8. S.G. 3·3 to 3 42.

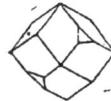

Fig. 360.

BB fuses with difficulty at the edges to a white opaque glass, tinging the flame green, then green above and red below, and finally altogether red ; hence the name from ῥοδίζειν, *to make red.*

Brit. Mus., Case 39.

RHODOCHROME, *G. Rose, Fiedler.* A massive or fine scaly variety of Kämmererite, of a greenish-black colour, but peach-blossom-red in fine splinters. Fracture splintery. H. 2·5 to 3. S.G. 2·668. ,

Analysis, by *Hermann* :

Silica	. 34·64
Alumina . . .	. 10·50
Peroxide of iron . .	. 2·00
Oxide of chrome . .	. 5·50
Magnesia . . .	. 35·47
Water	. 12·03
	———
	100·14

BB fuses at thin edges to a yellow enamel ; with borax yields a green glass.

Soluble with difficulty in muriatic acid.

Localities. Island Tino, in Greece. Bissersk and Kyschtimsk, in the Ural. Kraul, in Styria.

Name. From ῥόδος, *a rose,* and χρῶμα, *colour.*

Brit. Mus., Case 25.

RHODOCHROSITE, (from ῥοδοχρόος, *rose-coloured.*) See DIALLOGITE.

RHODOISE, *Beudant.* RHODONITE, *Dana, Nicol.* Oblique, and, like Pyroxene, with a cleavage in three directions, two of which are perpendicular to each other. Generally found massive and crystalline or granular. Colour rose-red or reddish-brown. Translucent. Lustre vitreous. Very hard. Streak white. Brittle. Fracture flat-conchoidal or uneven. H. 5·5 to 6. S.G. 3·4 to 3·68.

Comp. Manganese-Augite, or $Mn^3 \ddot{S}i^2 =$ protoxide of manganese 54·1, silica 45·9 = 100.

Analysis, from Langbanshytta, by *Berzelius :*

Silica . . . . . 48·00 ·
Protoxide of manganese . 49·04
Lime . . . . . 3·12
Magnesia . . . 0·22
                              _____
                              100·38

BB alone, on charcoal becomes dark brown, and fuses to a reddish-brown or black globule. With borax forms a violet-coloured glass.

Partially soluble in muriatic acid, when reduced to powder, and the insoluble residue becomes white.

Localities.—English. A manganese quarry, S. E. of Callington in Cornwall. Upton Pyne and Black Down, Devonshire.— *Foreign.* Langbanshytta in Sweden, in beds of iron ore. Katharinenburg in Siberia, in clay-slate. Elbingerode, in the Harz. New Jersey.

Name. From ῥόδον, *a rose,* in allusion to its colour.

Rhodonite is used, when cut and polished, for inlaid work.

Brit. Mus., Case 13.

M. P. G. Wall-cases 13 (British); 20 (Foreign). Horse-shoe Case, No. 1015.

For varieties, see ALLAGITE, BUSTAMITE, DYSSNITE, FOWLERITE, MARCELINE, OPSIMOSE, or HYDRO-SILICATE OF MANGANESE, PAISBERGITE, PHOTIZITE.

RHODOPHYLLITE, *Genth.* See PYROSCLERITE.

RHŒTIZITE. A nearly white or somewhat reddish variety of Kyanite, occurring in aggregated masses at the Pfitsch-thal, in the Tyrol. The name Rhœtizite has reference to the Rhœtian Alps, where this mineral is found.

RHOMB SPAR, *Jameson.* See BITTER SPAR.

RHOMBENGLIMMER, *Kengott.* A variety of Biotite, found in large and very regular rhombic prisms. and in tetrahedral pyramids, at Greenwood Furnace. Monroe, New York.

RHOMBIC MICA. See PHLOGOPITE.

RHOMBOHEDRAL ALUM HALOID, *Mohs.* See ALUMSTONE.

RHOMBOHEDRAL ANTIMONY, *Mohs.* See NATIVE ANTIMONY.

RHOMBOHEDRIC EUTOME GLANCE, *Mohs.* See TETRADYMITE.

RHOMBOHEDRAL ARSENIC, *Mohs.* See NATIVE ARSENIC.

RHOMBOHEDRAL CALAMINE, *Jameson.* See CALAMINE.

RHOMBOHEDRAL CERIUM ORE, *Mohs.* See CERITE.

RHOMBOHEDRAL CORUNDUM, *Mohs.* See CORUNDUM.

RHOMBOHEDRAL EMERALD, *Mohs.* See EMERALD.

RHOMBOHEDRAL EMERALD MALACHITE, *Mohs.* See DIOPTASE.

RHOMBOHEDRAL EUCHLORE - MALACHITE, *Mohs.* See CHALCOPHYLLITE.

RHOMBOHEDRAL FELSPAR, *Mohs.* See NEPHELINE.

RHOMBOHEDRAL FLUOR HALOID, *Mohs.* See APATITE.

RHOMBOHEDRAL GRAPHITE MICA, *Mohs.* See GRAPHITE.

RHOMBOHEDRAL IRIDIUM, *Mohs.* See IRIDOSMINE.

RHOMBOHEDRAL IRON ORE, *Mohs.* See HEMATITE.

RHOMBOHEDRAL IRON PYRITES, *Mohs.* See PYRRHOTINE.

RHOMBOHEDRAL KOUPHONE SPAR, *Mohs.* See CHABAZITE.

RHOMBOHEDRAL LEAD BARYTE, *Mohs.* See MIMETITE.

RHOMBOHEDRAL KUPHON-MICA, *Mohs.* See BRUCITE.

RHOMBOHEDRAL MELAN MICA, *Mohs.* See CRONSTEDTITE.

RHOMBOHEDRAL MOLYBDENA GLANCE. *Mohs.* See SULPHIDE OF MOLYBDENUM.

RHOMBOHEDRAL PEARL MICA, *Mohs.* See CLINTONITE.

RHOMBOHEDRAL QUARTZ, *Mohs.* See QUARTZ.

RHOMBOHEDRAL RUBY BLENDE, *Mohs.* See PYRARGYRITE.

RHOMBOHEDRAL TALC MICA, *Mohs.* See MICA.

RHOMBOHEDRAL TOURMALINE, *Mohs.* See TOURMALINE.

RHOMBOHEDRAL ZINC BARYTE, *Mohs.* See CALAMINE.

RHOMBOIDAL ARSENIATE OF COPPER, *Phillips.* See CHALCOPHYLLITE.

RHOMBOIDAL BARYTE, *Jameson.* See WITHERITE.

RHOMBOIDAL GRAPHITE, *Jameson.* See GRAPHITE.

RHOMBOIDAL PEARL MICA, *Jameson.* See MARGARITE.

RHYACOLITE, *Rose.* See RYACOLITE.

RIBBON JASPER. A variety of Jasper exhibiting green, red, and yellow colours, of various shades, arranged in stripes or parallel layers; whence the name *Ribbon* or *Striped Jasper*. It is found at Dressing Green, near Tortworth, in Gloucestershire, at Ballygroggan in the Mull of Cantyre, and is common in Scotland; amongst other localities, at Habbies Howe in the Pentland Hills; at Arthur's Seat, Edinburgh; Stirlingshire, at Campsie, &c.; in the Isles of Islay and Rum, &c. The principal foreign localities are Saxony, and the Ural Mountains of Siberia.

Brit. Mus., Case 24.

RIEMANNITE. A name for Allophane, after Riemann, by whom it was first observed.

RIOLITE, *Fröbel.* A selenide of silver, occurring in small hexagonal tables of a lead-grey colour, at Tasco in Mexico, and named after Del Rio, according to whom its composition is Ag Se², or silver 57·66, selenium 42·34=100.

RIPIDOLITE, *Hausmann, Nicol.* See CHLORITE.

RIPIDOLITE, *Rammelsberg, Dana, G. Rose.* Hexagonal. Occurs in tabular crystals, with perfect basal cleavage. Colour olive-green; by transmitted light often red across the chief axis. Translucent or nearly transparent. Lustre pearly. Streak white or greenish. Laminæ flexible, but not elastic. H. 1 to 2. S.G. 2·78 to 2·96.

Comp. R³ S̈i + Äl S̈i + 3Ḧ.

Analysis, from St. Gotthard, by *Varrentrapp :*

Silica .	. . .	. 25·37
Alumina	. . .	. 18·50
Magnesia	. . .	. 17·09
Protoxide of iron	.	. 28·79
Water .	. . .	. 8·96
		98·71

BB fuses with difficulty at thin edges. Soluble in concentrated sulphuric acid.

Localities. Penrhyn, Caernarvonshire. Argyleshire, in Scotland. Dauphiny. St. Gotthard, in Switzerland. Zillerthal, in the Tyrol. Miask, in the Ural. The Harz. The Alps. Gumush-dagh, in Asia Minor, with Emery.

Name. From ριπἰς, *a fan*; in allusion to the crystals being often united in comb-like or fan-like groups. For varieties, see APHROSIDERITE. LOPHOITE, OGCOITE.

Brit. Mus., Case 32.

Ripidolite is in part Chlorite, and is described under the latter name by Nicol, Phillips, and others. The name was also given by Von Kobell to a green Chlorite in grouped folia, found at St. Gotthard, at Rauris in

Salzburg, and in the Zillerthal, with Quartz and crystals of Adularia.

RISIGALLUM. A name for Realgar, used by the Alchemists.

RITTINGERITE, *Zippe*. Probably a compound of sulphide of silver and antimony, and considered by Breithaupt to be identical with Xanthocone. It occurs at Joachimsthal in Bohemia, in small rhombic tables with replaced basal edges. Colour iron-black: of crystals brownish-black. Translucent, and varying from dull honey-yellow to hyacinth-red when viewed by transmitted light, in the direction of the axis. Lustre metallic-adamantine. Streak orange-yellow. Brittle. H. 1·5 to 3.

Name. After Rittinger, an Austrian officer of mines.

ROCHLAUDITE. See SERPENTINE.

ROCK BUTTER, *Jameson.* See PETROLEUM.

ROCK CORK, *Jameson.* See MOUNTAIN CORK.

ROCK CRYSTAL (from κρύσταλλος, *ice*). The common name for the transparent crystals of Quartz, of which it is the purest form, being composed (according to an analysis by Bucholz) of 99·37 per cent. of silica, with a trace of alumina.

The following are some of the localities where fine specimens of Rock Crystal are found. — *English.* Cornwall; at the Tin-

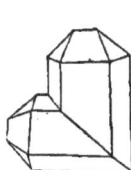  

Fig. 361.   Fig. 362.   Fig. 363.

 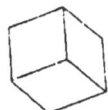

Fig. 364.   Fig. 365.

tagel cliffs and Delabole slate quarries, (*figs.* 363 to 365), near Camelford; Huel Mary Ann; Mainporth, near Falmouth, *fig.* 365; Carnbrea Mines, yellow; East Crinnis Mines. Devonshire; Huel Friendship, near Tavistock; North Bovey, in large opaque reddish twins, *fig.* 362. Gloucestershire, *figs.* 363, 365, at Clifton; known as "*Bristol*" or "*British diamonds.*" Ulverstone Iron Mines. Lancashire, *fig.* 364. Derbyshire, at Castleton and Masson Low.

Cumberland: Carrock Fells. Caldbeck Fells, Alston, Cleator Moor Iron Mines, on Hematite.— *Welsh*. Snowdon, Caernarvonshire. — *Scotch*. Leadhills, in Lanarkshire. In the neighbourhood of Cairngorm (which see). Argyleshire. Ballygroggan, Mull of Cantyre, in cavities of trap rock. — *Irish*. Divis Hill, near Belfast. Donegal. Downshire, in clefts and cavities of the Mourne Mountain-granite, with Topaz and Beryl. Palmerston, yellow. Killarney, in yellow detached crystals. Castle Comer, Kilkenny. Dungiven, Banagher. Finglen Mountain, close to Dungiven (*Dungiven crystals*). Donaghmore and Tullyniskan, in Tyrone. Glen Malur, in Wicklow, yellow.— *Foreign*. The finest specimens occur in Savoy, Dauphiné, and St. Etienne-la-Varenne in France. In the Carrara quarries of the N.W. part of the Apuanian Alp. Hungary. The Alps. East Indies. Ceylon. Hayti. Florida. Quito. Brazil. Madagascar. Cape Diamond, near Quebec. The northern part of the Desert of Atacama, in Bolivia. Tasmania, on the Islands in Bass Straits.

Brit. Mus., Case 20.

M. P. G. Horse-shoe Case, Principal Floor.

Rock Crystal sometimes contains included capillary crystals of Amphibole, Rutile, Epidote, scales of Mica, Chlorite, Bitumen, and other foreign matters. More rarely it contains cavities filled with liquids and gases. (See ENHYDROS.) The liquid was found, by Sir Humphrey Davy, to be water with saline matter; by Mr. Fox, water with chloride of sodium (Common Salt); by others, water has been discovered with various earthy and metallic sulphates and chlorides. Other liquids occur besides water. See BREWSTOLINE, AMETHYSTOLINE, CRYPTOLINE.

"The cavities are seldom full of the liquid — there is usually a bubble of air, which, except when the cavity is very small, changes place when the position of the crystal is altered. We may suppose with Mr. Sorby that the cavity was originally filled with the liquid, when the consolidation of the crystal happened, at a temperature more or less elevated above the actual temperature; that it has since contracted during the cooling, and now occupies a space which, as compared to the whole cavity in the crystal, is determined by the actual temperature as compared to the original temperature of consolidation — nearly in this proportion, not strictly, because pressure alters the bulk of a liquid,

and the pressure during the formation of the crystal is unknown. * * * · * In one case of Amethyst, the cavity being three-fourths full of liquid at ordinary temperature, becomes full of liquid at 83°F.; on being cooled again the vacuity reappears in the crystal, with signs of ebullition." * — *Anniversary Address of the President* (Professor John Phillips) *of the Geological Society* — 1859.

It is employed for ornamental purposes, and when perfectly clear and colourless, is made into lenses for spectacles, which are sold under the name of pebbles, and are better suited for the purpose than glass, owing to their superior hardness, and less liability in consequence to get scratched. The lenses should be cut at right angles to the axis of the crystals, in order to avoid the effects produced by double refraction, and the consequent production of a second more or less distinct image, which is not only unpleasant, but injurious to the eyesight. When cut for jewelry, it is called by lapidaries, "*white stone*." An asteriated variety contains whitish impurities or opacity, arranged along the diametral planes. Groups of crystals are highly valued in China as ornaments for the apartments of the rich, and fetch extravagant prices. Dr. Hochstetter states that a group of common Quartz crystals of very common appearance was offered to him for 20 Mexican dollars (about four guineas.)

ROCK LEATHER. See MOUNTAIN LEATHER.

ROCK MARROW, *Jameson*. See LITHOMARGE.

ROCK MILK, *Jameson*. See AGARIC MINERAL.

ROCK OIL. See PETROLEUM, SENECA OIL.

ROCK SALT. Cubical. Occurs in cubical crystals: the primary form being the cube, into which, when pure, it may readily be cleaved. Also in large beds and masses, and in the waters of the sea, as well as in those of certain springs and lakes. Colourless or white when pure, but frequently stained reddish-brown, brick-red, violet-blue or green, by iron or other foreign admixtures. Lustre vitreous. Translucent to transparent. Yields readily to the knife and may be scratched with the nail, receiving an impression but not affording a powder. Rather brittle. Fracture conchoidal. Taste purely saline. Attracts moisture, but remains unaltered in a dry atmosphere. One

* See Dr. Brewster, Ed. Roy. Soc. Trans., and Ed. Phil. Journ. ix.

of the most diathermanous of known substances. H. 2. S.G. 2·03 to 2·15.

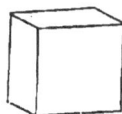

Fig. 366.

Comp. Chloride of sodium; or Na Cl = sodium 39·6, chlorine 60·4 = 100.

Analysis, from Cheshire, by *Henry:*

Chloride of sodium	. . 98·32
Sulphate of lime .	. . 0·65
Chloride of magnesium	. 0·02
Chloride of calcium	. . 0·01
Insoluble matter .	. . 1·00
	100·00

Fuses at a red heat, and forms a crystalline mass on cooling. Volatilizes at a white heat.

This mineral is the source of the common salt of commerce.

Salt is one of the principal articles of commerce mentioned in Domesday, and brought a considerable revenue to the crown before the Norman conquest. Half a million tons of salt are annually produced in this country at the present day, chiefly in the Valley of the Weaver in Cheshire, from immense beds belonging to the New Red Sandstone. One-fifth only of the above quantity is raised in the form of Rock Salt, the remaining four-fifths being obtained from brine-springs.

The principal salt-works in England are at Northwich, Winsford, Middlewich and Nantwich in Cheshire; at Droitwich in Gloucestershire; at Shirleywich in Staffordshire; in Durham; and at Carrickfergus, near Belfast. Formerly considerable quantities of salt were obtained by the evaporation of sea-water in salterns or shallow pits, on the coast of Hampshire and the Isle of Wight, as it is now practised on the shores of the Mediterranean, &c.; but this source of supply has very much diminished of late years.

There are immense deposits of Rock Salt in Spain, in Old and New Castile, and also at Cardona, in Catalonia, where it forms several hills, one of which is said to be between 400 and 500 feet high. It also forms hills in Moldavia. The other principal localities are Dieuze and Vic, in France; Bex, in Switzerland; Wieliczka,. in Poland; Hungary; Transylvania; Ischel, Berchtesgaden and

Hallein, in the North Eastern Alps, where the fibrous blue variety, which occasionally occurs at Hall in the Tyrol, is also sometimes found. Djebel Melah and Ouled Kebbah, in Algeria, and very extensively distributed in the north of Africa, on both sides of the Atlas Mountains. · Southern Russia, between the rivers Ural and Volga. At Ileksaia-Zachtchita, in the steppes of the Kirghiz, the Rock-Salt is crystalline, white without a stain, and so pure that the salt is at once pounded for use without undergoing any cleansing or recrystallization.

Large quantities of Rock Salt occur near Lake Oroomiah, in the N.W. of Persia. In the Desert of Caramania, according to Chardin, it is so abundant, and the atmosphere so dry, that houses are built of it. The salt of Lahore in the Punjab forms a hill as large as that of Cardona, and is cut into dishes, plates, and stands for lamps. Other localities are Cashmere, Abyssinia, China, Peru, the Cordilleras of New Granada, the United States (chiefly in Silurian sandstones in the middle and western states), forming brine springs at Salina in New York, in the Kenawha Valley (Virginia), Muskingum in Ohio, and in Kentucky; also forming beds with Gypsum in Virginia, Washington co., and in the Salmon River Mountains of Oregon. California. The salt found at the bottoms and sides of salt-lakes is the *lake-salt* of Jameson (*See-salz* of Reuss and Werner). It is collected in the islands of Cyprus and Milo, in the Mediterranean; in the neighbourhood of the Caspian, in the Crimea; and might be obtained, at a small cost, from many of the shallow lakes situated about 40 miles W. of Geelong, in Victoria. There are, also, salinas or natural salt-lakes on the eastern side of S. America, in the argillaceo-calcareous deposits of the Pampas; in the sandstone of the Rio Negro, about fifteen miles above the town of El Carmen; and in the pumiceous and other beds of the Patagonian tertiary formation, often several leagues in diameter, and generally very shallow. Victoria; in the Desert, towards the junction of the rivers Darling and Murrumbidgee with the river Murray.

Great quantities of fine white salt are afforded by two salt-lakes at Manzelack, near Alexandria; by salt-lakes in Caffraria; and from the lake of Dombu, in the great desert of Bilma in Bornu.

Salt is in all countries one of the necessaries of life, and is employed for a variety of purposes—chiefly as a seasoning for food, and in the preservation of meat, butter, &c. Formerly it was used more than is the case now, as a glaze for earthenware and pottery. The other principal uses to which it is applied are as a manure, in soap-making, as a flux in metallurgical operations, and in the manufacture of chlorine, carbonate of soda, muriate of ammonia, &c. The salt for commercial purposes is obtained: 1st. By mechanical extraction from salt-beds; 2nd. By dissolving impure Rock-Salt in fresh-water, in the water of saltsprings, or in sea-water, and then decanting and evaporating; 3rd. By boiling down the liquid from the salt-springs, after it has become concentrated either by exposure to the air in graduating works, or, more rarely, by partial congelation of the water; 4th. By the evaporation of sea-water either in the sun or by artificial heat.

Brit. Mus., Case 59.

M. P. G. Horse-shoe Case, Nos. 188 to 196. Wall-case 38. Upper Gallery, Wall-case 40.

ROCK SOAP, *Jameson.* Resembles Bole. Colour pitch- or brownish-black. Opaque. Dull. Feels slightly greasy. Streak shining and resinous. Sectile. Fracture fine, earthy, or conchoidal. Does not soil, but writes as well or better than drawing slate. Adheres strongly to the tongue. Falls to pieces in water. H. 1 to 2. S.G. 2·66 to 2·7.

Comp. Nearly $\ddot{A}l\,\dot{S}i^2 + 6\dot{H}$.
Analysis, from Plombières, by *Berthier:*

Silica	.	.	. 44·0
Alumina	.	.	. 22·0
Magnesia	.	.	. 2·0
Sand	.	.	. 6·0
Water	.	.	. 25·0
			99·0

Localities. Isle of Skye, in basalt, and in the trap rocks of Antrim, in nodules of a greenish-grey or brown colour (*Greg*). Artern, in Thuringia. Cassel. Bilin, in Bohemia. Olkuce, in Poland. Wehrau, in Upper Saxony.

Rock Soap is used for washing cloth, and for artists' crayons.

ROCK WOOD, *Jameson.* The name given to a ligniform variety of Asbestos, in which the fibres occur in long, curved, parallel masses, with a closer texture than in Rock Leather or Rock Cork. Its colour is various shades of wood-brown. It is chiefly found at Sterzing, in the Tyrol.

Brit. Mus., Case 34.

ROETHEL, *Werner.* See REDDLE.

ROHWAND. One of the names given to

Ankerite by the Styrian miners, who value it both as a flux and as an ore of iron.

ROMANZOVITE, or ROMANZOWITE, *Nordenskiöld.* A brown or brownish-black variety of Lime-Garnet, occurring in compact or crystalline plates, with a greasy lustre and a resinous fracture. Streak pale yellow.

Analysis, by *Nordenskiöld:*

Silica	.	.	. 41·24
Alumina	.	.	. 24·08
Peroxide of iron	.	.	7·02
Protoxide of manganese and magnesia	.	.	0·92
Lime	.	.	. ·24·76
Ignition and loss	.	.	1·98
			100·00

BB fuses without ebullition.
Locality. Kimito, in Finland.
Name. After Count Romanzow.
Brit. Mus., Case 36.
M. P. G. Horse-shoe Case, No. 899.

ROMEINE, *Damour, Dana, Dufrénoy.* ROMÉITE, *Nicol.* Pyramidal. Occurs in groups of minute octahedrons, or inclosed in the massive mineral. Colour hyacinth-red or honey-yellow. H. 5.

Comp. $\dot{R}^3$, $\ddot{S}b$ or $\dot{C}a\,\ddot{S}b$ (Rammelsberg).
Analysis, by *Damour:*

Antimonious acid	.		79·31
Lime	.	.	. 16·67
Protoxide of manganese	.	2·60
Protoxide of iron	.	.	1·20
Silica	.	.	. 0·64
			100·42

BB fuses to a blackish slag; with borax affords a colourless glass in the inner flame, and a violet glass in the outer flame.

Insoluble in acids.

Locality. The manganese mines of St. Marcel, in Piedmont.

Name. After Romé de Lisle, the celebrated crystallographer and mineralogist.

Brit. Mus., Case 38.

ROSE QUARTZ. A transparent, or nearly transparent, variety of Quartz, of a rose-red or pink colour. It usually occurs massive, and often much cracked. S.G. 2·659; after being heated 2·6578. Lustre vitreous, sometimes slightly greasy. Fuchs attributed the colour to oxide of Titanium, from the presence of 1 to 1·5 per cent. in specimens from Rabenstein, near Bodenmais. Berthier attributes the colour to organic matter. Probably it is produced by manganese, the colour resembling that of Manganese Spar.

Localities. — Scotch. On the hills of Kildrummy, Auchindoir, and Glenbucket, in Aberdeenshire. On the shores of Kirkaness, Shetlands. Island of Shiant, Hebrides, opalescent and pink. — *Irish.* Near Belfast. — *Foreign.* Rabenstein, in Bavaria, in a vein of manganese traversing granite. France; Misère, Dept. de l'Isère. Abo, in Finland. Near Connecticut, U.S. Kolyvan, in Siberia.

Rose Quartz is employed in jewelry. It takes a fine polish, and, when the colour is good, the ornaments made of it are beautiful. When cut and polished, and of a good colour, it is sometimes sold for Spinel, yet its deficiency in hardness, transparency, and fire is so great, that the deception may be easily detected. It is cut *en cabochon* or *en table*, and should be set with a coloured foil, as it fades if exposed for a long time to the light, or if kept in a warm place. The colour may, however, be restored by keeping it for some time in a damp place.

Brit. Mus., Case 21.

M. P. G. Horse-shoe Case, No. 472.

ROSELITE, *Levy.* A deep rose-red coloured variety of Cobalt Bloom, containing lime. Translucent. Lustre vitreous. Streak white. Fracture conchoidal. H. 3.

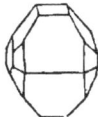
Fig. 367.

It occurs in small twin crystals at Schneeberg, in Saxony, and was named by Levy in honour of Gustave Rose, of Berlin.

Brit. Mus., Case 31.

ROSELLANE, *Svanberg.* According to G. Rose, is an altered Anorthite. Occurs in grains, rarely larger than hemp-seed. Colour varying from pale rose-red to deep red (whence the name). Translucent. Lustre on cleavage-planes splendent. Streak white. Perfect cleavage in one direction. Fracture crystalline. H. 2·5. S.G. 2·72.

Comp. $\dot{R}^3$ $\ddot{S}i + 2\ddot{A}l$ $\ddot{S}i + 2\dot{H}$, or $(\dot{K}, \dot{C}a, \dot{M}g)$ $\ddot{S}i + \ddot{A}l$ $\ddot{S}i + 2\dot{H}$.

Analysis, by Svanberg:

Silica	. 44·90
Alumina . . .	. 34·51
Peroxide of iron . .	. 0·69
Peroxide of manganese	. 0·19
Lime	. 3·59
Magnesia . . .	. 2·45
Potash . . .	. 6·63
Water	. 6·53
	———
	99·49

BB fuses with difficulty to a white slag.

Localities. Aker and Baldurstadt, in Sweden. Finland; at Abo, near Lake Manarou, in limestone.

ROSENITE. The name given by Zincken to Plagionite, in compliment to H. Rose, by whom it was analysed.

M. P. G. Principal Floor, Wall-case 28, No. 201.

ROSIN TIN. Tinstone of a pale colour, translucent and with a resinous lustre.

ROSITE, *Hausmann.* See ROSELLANE.

ROSSTREVORITE. A fibrous stellated variety of Epidote, met with near Rosstrevor, co. Down, Ireland.

ROSSZAHN. See ROHWAND.

ROSY RED QUARTZ, *Kirwan.* See ROSE QUARTZ.

ROTH BLEIRZ, *Werner.* See CROCOISITE.

ROTHBRAUNSTEINERZ, *Haidinger.* See DIALLOGITE.

ROTHEISENERZ, ROTHEISENSTEIN, *Werner.* See HEMATITE.

ROTHER-EISENSTEIN, *Werner.* See RED HEMATITE.

ROTHER-EISEN-VITRIOL, *v. Leonhard.* See BOTRYOGENE.

ROTHER ERDKOBALD, *Werner.* See COBALT-BLOOM.

ROTHER SCHORL, *Klaproth.* See RUBELLITE.

ROTHES BLEIERZ, *Werner.* ROTHES BLEYERZ, *Emerling.* See CROCOISITE.

ROTHES BRAUNSTEIN MANGANSPATH, *Werner.* See DIALLOGITE.

ROTHES RAUSCHGELB, *Werner.* See REALGAR.

ROTHGULDEN, ROTHGÜLTIGERZ. Names used by German and Hungarian miners for Dark and Light Red Silver Ore. See PYRARGYRITE.

ROTHKUPFERERZ, *Werner.* See RED COPPER ORE.

ROTHNICKELKIES. See COPPER NICKEL.

ROTHOFFITE. A variety of common Iron-Garnet from Längsbanshytta, in Sweden. It is remarkable for containing a large quantity of (protoxide of) manganese; sometimes as much as 7·14 per cent.

ROTHSPIESGLASERZ, *Werner.*⎫ See
ROTHSPIESGLANZERZ, *Haus-*⎬ KERME-
mann.⎭ SITE.

ROTHZINKERZ. See ZINCITE.

ROTTEN-STONE. A soft and earthy kind of stone, used in a state of powder, for polishing brass, silver, Britannia metal, glass, &c. Colour dirty-grey or reddish-brown, passing into black. Dull. Gives out a disagreeable odour when rubbed. Meagre to the touch.

Analysis, by *Richard Phillips*:

Alumina	86
Silica	4
Carbon	10
	100

Localities. Near Ashford and Bakewell, in Derbyshire. South Wales, in Caermarthenshire and Breconshire. Albany, near New York, U. S.

Rotten-stone is nearly peculiar to this country, and is supposed to be derived from the decomposition of shale or siliceous lime-stone.

RUBACE, or RUBASSE. Names given by French lapidaries and jewellers to a variety of Rock Crystal with rose-coloured cracks. These fissures, which characterise the stone as well as their colour, are artificially produced by heating the crystal red-hot, and then plunging it into a solution of purple of cassius or carmine. By these means it is made full of cracks, which become filled with the colouring matter. The great difficulty to be surmounted in the process is, that the stone should only be cracked in the interior, allowing a free passage to the colouring liquid from the outside, which it is difficult to understand.

The French jewellers also apply the name to cut and polished Quartz, slightly tinged with violet, and besprinkled internally with minute brown spangles of Specular Iron, which reflect a bright red light, equal to that of the most brilliant Ruby. These stones are very rare. They are brought from Brazil, but inferior kinds are found in the iron mines of Nassau Ussing.

RUBELLAN, *Breithaupt.* Probably an altered Biotite, occurs in small, reddish-brown, hexagonal tables, which are not flexible. Exfoliates in the flame of a candle. H. less than 3. S.G. 2·5 to 2·7.

Analysis, by *Klaproth*:

Silica	45
Alumina	10
Oxide of iron	20
Lime	10
Soda and potash	10
Volatile matter	5
	100

Localities. With Mica and Augite at Schima, in Bohemia; and also in Saxony. Brit. Mus., Case 32.

RUBELLITE, *Kirwan.* Red Tourmaline, containing a considerable proportion of manganese. It generally occurs in closely aggregated crystals, varying in colour from a slight tinge of red to a fine pink.

Analysis, from Sarapulsk, by *Hermann*:

Silica	39·70
Alumina	40·29
Peroxide of manganese	2·30
Boracic acid	6·65
Lithia	3·02
Magnesia	0·16
Soda	7·88
	100·00

BB alone on charcoal, turns milk-white, intumesces, splits, and vitrifies at the edges, but does not fuse: on platinum, with soda, exhibits in the outer flame the bluish-green colour indicative of manganese.

Localities. — *Irish.* Ox Mountain, near Sligo; of a red and green colour. — *Foreign.* Near Katherinenburg and Sarapulsk, near Mursinsk, in Siberia. Elba. Rozena, in Moravia. Very fine specimens have been found at Paris, Maine, U. S.: "some crystals over an inch in diameter, transparent, ruby-red within, surrounded by green, or red at one extremity, and green at the other." (*Dana.*) "Some of the Siberian specimens exhibit internally a brown or blue colour, surrounded with carmine-red, or some other lighter tinge, or internally a red hue bordered with pistachio-green." (*W. Phillips.*)

A specimen of uncommon form and dimensions, which was presented by the King of Ava to the late Colonel Symes, when ambassador to that country, and afterwards presented to the British Museum by the Hon. Mr. Greville, is stated by Jameson to have been valued at £1000. Brit. Mus., Case 40.

RUBICELLE. The name given to yellow or orange red varieties of Spinel.

RUBIE ÉTOILÉ. Star Ruby. See ASTERIA.

RUBIN. See RUBY.

RUBINBLENDE, *Hausmann.* See PROUSTITE.

RUBINE D'ARSENIC, *Von Born.* See REALGAR.

RUBINGLIMMER, *Hausmann.* A variety of Göthite, occurring in foliated crystallizations of a hyacinth-red colour, with Brown Hematite, at Eiserfeld, in the country of Nassau; and in the Hollerter Zug, in the Westerwald, in veins of Limonite. It is also met with in translucent scales at Kilpatrick in Dumbartonshire, with Zeolite.

RUBIS DE BOHÊME. Rose Quartz.

RUBY. Under the general term Ruby

lapidaries class several stones, of very different chemical composition, &c., which they distinguish chiefly by their colours. Thus, when of a full carmine-red, it is known by the name of *Spinel Ruby*; when the tinge verges upon rather pale rose-red, it is called *Balais* or *Balas Ruby*; when the red has a decided shade of orange, it is usually goes by the name of *Vermeil* or *Vermeille*; when of a yellowish-red, it is called *Rubicelle*. The Ruby is considered by jewellers to approach perfection the more closely it resembles the colour of pigeon's blood. The name Ruby should, however, be restricted to the oriental Ruby, or the red varieties of Sapphire. When perfect, both in colour and transparency, Rubies are much less common than good Diamonds, and are more valuable when of 3 or 4 carats. A perfect Ruby of 1 carat is worth 10 guineas, of 2 carats £42, of 3 carats 130 guineas, and of 6 carats above £1000. The Ruby very seldom exceeds 8 or 10 carats, but Tavernier mentions one of 50 carats, and Gustavus III., king of Sweden, had one the size of a small hen's egg, and of the finest water, which he gave to the Emperor of Russia when he visited St. Petersburgh.

The Ruby is generally set in rings and brooches, surrounded with brilliants. It is stated in Prinsep's "Oriental Accounts of the Precious Minerals," * that "not to be deceived in rubies is a work of difficulty, because there are spurious ones of polished crystal, which much resemble the true gem; these are called *áyn-ul-ruján*; but a skilful lapidary will easily recognise them. When placed in the fire, a true ruby becomes invisible, but when immersed in water it appears to glow with heat: it also shines like a coal in the dark."

The Ruby is imitated by Spinel, from which it is easily distinguished by superior hardness. The finest stones are found in the sand of rivers in Ceylon, in the sand of certain streams, and in the Capelan mountains near Syrian, the capital of Pegu, and in Ava.

The Ruby mines of the latter country are guarded most jealously from Europeans. Professor Oldham, who visited Ava in 1855 with the embassy from this country, could not hear of any well-authenticated instance of their ever having been visited by a British subject, except by one person who, having deserted into the King of Burmah's dominions, was sent by the king to super-

intend the intercepting of some drains and other appliances for regulating the supply of the mines.

In the Journal of the Asiatic Society of Bengal, vol. ii. p. 75, it is stated that the ruby mines of Burmah have long been known, and they are said to be situated about 60 to 70 miles from the capital, in a north-easterly direction. "The mode of seeking for them is described as consisting simply in sinking pits until the gem-bed or ruby-earth is met with. The gem-bed is met with at very various depths, sometimes not more than two or three feet from the surface, at other times more than forty feet, and occasionally not at all. When the layer of earthy sand containing the rubies is met with, lateral openings are driven in on it, and the bed followed up until it either becomes necessary to sink another pit on it, or it becomes exhausted. It varies in thickness from a few inches to two or three feet.

· The rubies are for the most part small, not averaging more than a quarter of a rutty, and when large, are generally full of flaws. Well marked crystals occasionally occur, but the vast majority of the stones are well rounded and ground down. It is a very rare case to find a large Ruby without flaws; and Mr. Spears states that he has never seen a perfect Ruby weighing more than ½ rupee.

The Sapphires are found in the same earth with the Rubies, but are much more rare, and generally of a larger size. "Stones of 10 to 15 rutties without a flaw are common, whereas a perfect Ruby of that size is hardly ever seen. The largest perfect Sapphire I ever saw weighed 1 tikal. It was polished, but I have seen a rough one weighing 25 tikals." "For every 500 rubies, I do not think they get one sapphire. You see very few small sapphires in the market, while small rubies are abundant and cheap." The value of Gems, Rubies, and Sapphires obtained in a year, may be from 1¼ to 1½ lac, from £12,500, to £15,000. They are considered solely the property of the king, and strictly monopolized; but notwithstanding the care that is taken, considerable quantities are smuggled.

There are about twenty lapidaries or polishers of these stones in Amarapoora. They are not allowed to carry on their trade at the mines. In polishing, "small rubies and worthless pebbles brought from the mines, pounded fine, and mixed up with an adhesive substance, and then made into cakes, some 10 inches long by 4 inches broad, are used to rub down the gem on; after it has been

* Journal of Asiatic Soc. Bengal, vol. i. p. 353.

brought to the form and size required, another stone of fine grain is required."

The last process is performed by rubbing the Ruby on a plate of copper or brass, until it is thoroughly polished, when the gem is ready for market.

Rubies are imitated by Spinel, Garnet, Hyacinth, red Quartz, calcined Amethyst, red burnt Brazilian Topaz, and by red Tourmaline.

The Ruby has been valued as a gem from the earliest times of which we have any record. The Sardius, mentioned in Exod. xxviii. 17, and supposed to mean the Ruby, held the first place amongst the twelve stones which were ordered to be placed on the ephod of the Jewish high-priest, and was engraved with the name of Reuben.

In Proverbs iii. 13, 15, Solomon says, "Happy is the man that findeth wisdom . . . . She is more precious than rubies, and all the things thou canst desire are not to be compared unto her." See also Job xxviii. 18. Prov. viii. 11; xx. 15; xxxi. 10. Lam. iv. 7.

Brit. Mus., Case 19.

M. P. G. Horse-shoe Case, Nos. 786, 787, 797—804.

RUBY SILVER. See PYRARGYRITE.

RUBY SULPHUR, *Jameson.* See REAL-GAR.

RUDDLE. See REDDLE.

RUIN AGATE. See BRECCIATED AGATE.

RUIN MARBLE. See COTHAM MARBLE.

RUTHERFORDITE, *C. U. Shepard.* Oblique. No cleavage. Occurs in crystals and grains. Iron-black externally, and not at first sight distinguishable from Samarskite. Colour of fresh surface, blackish- or yellowish-brown. Earthy. Opaque or translucent in thin fragments, and transmitting a smoky orange-brown light. Lustre vitreo-resinous, shining. Yields to the knife with difficulty. Streak yellowish - brown, approaching to fawn-colour. Very brittle. Fracture perfectly conchoidal. H. 5·5. S.G. 5·5.

Comp. Titanic acid and lime.

BB alone infusible; with borax forms slowly a clear yellow glass.

Exposed to heat in a glass tube, it decrepitates slightly, and gives off a little water; the mineral on cooling is dark yellowish-brown, with a resinous adamantine lustre, in appearance resembling some varieties of Blende. Decomposed by prolonged boiling with concentrated sulphuric acid, and is then completely soluble in a very large volume of warm water.

Locality. The gold-washings of Rutherford co., North Carolina; with Samarskite, Rutile, Brookite, Zircon, and Monazite.

Rutherfordite is easily distinguished from Samarskite, which it otherwise closely resembles, by the streak and by its translucency.

RUTHILE, *Brochant.* RUTIL, *Werner.* RUTILE, *Dana, Nicol, Phillips.* Pyramidal. Occurs in four- or eight-sided prisms, terminated by pyramids, either single or geniculated, and often striated longitudinally: also in reticulated masses formed by acicular and capillary macled crystals: also massive and imbedded. Structure lamellar. Colour usually reddish - brown and opaque; or blood-red and translucent or transparent: sometimes yellowish or black. Lustre metallic-adamantine. Streak very pale brown. Brittle. Fracture imperfect-conchoidal or uneven. Acquires negative electricity by friction. H. 6 to 6·5. S.G. 4·18 to 4·25.

Fig 368.

Comp. Binoxide of titanium or titanic acid, $\ddot{T}i$ = titanium 60·98, oxygen 39·02 = 100.

Analysis, from St. Yrieix, by *H. Rose*:

Titanic acid . . .	98·5
Peroxide of iron . .	1·5
	100·0

BB alone infusible, with borax yields a transparent reddish - yellow glass in the outer flame, which assumes a dirty violet-colour in the inner flame.

Localities. — *Scotch.* Glen Finnart, Argyleshire. Perthshire. Crianlarich, in large striated prisms and in fibrous masses; Craig Cailleach, near Killin, Fifeshire. Hillswick, Shetlands. — *Irish.* Co. Donegal; near Dunfanaghy, and at Malin Beg, in white crystalline Quartz. — *Foreign.* St. Yrieix, near Limoges, in France, and in Castile, in geniculated twin crystals, which are often of large size. The Alps. St. Gotthard, in Switzerland, reticulated on crystals of Specular Iron. Rosenau, in Hungary. Brazil, in acicular crystals imbedded in limpid Quartz, which, when polished, exhibits hair-like crystals of Rutile, of a blood-red colour by transmitted light: (*Venus' Hair-stone.*) Oblapian, in Transylvania. Horcajuelo, near Buitrago, in Spain. Gängehänsel, near Petschau in Bohemia (massive). Near Brevig, in Norway, in gneiss. The Ural. Massachusetts, and other parts of North America. Canada.

Name. From *rutilus,* signifying *shining red.*

Brit. Mus., Case 37.

M. P. G. Principal Floor, Wall-cases 13 (British); 20 and 42 (Foreign).

For varieties of Rutile, see CRISPITE, GALLICINITE, ILMENORUTILE, NIGRINE, SAGENITE, TITANE OXYDÉ CHROMIFÈRE. See also DIANIUM.

RUTILITE, *Jameson.* See SPHENE.

RYACOLITE, *G. Rose.* Occurs in thick tabular, or short prismatic crystals, resembling Glassy Felspar, of which it may, possibly, be only a variety. Colour white or grey, with a vitreous lustre. Transparent or translucent. H. 6. S.G. 2·618 (*Rose*).

Comp. $(\dot{\text{K}}, \dot{\text{N}}, \dot{\text{Ca}})\ \ddot{\text{S}}\text{i} + \ddot{\ddot{\text{A}}}\text{l}\ \ddot{\text{S}}\text{i}.$

Analysis, by *G. Rose:*

Silica	50·31
Alumina	29·44
Peroxide of iron	0·28
Magnesia	0·23
Lime	1·07
Soda	10·56
Potash	5·92
	97·81

BB fuses rather more readily than Adularia, and colours the flame of a more intense yellow.

Decomposed imperfectly by muriatic acid, with separation of pulverulent silica.

Localities. Vesuvius, in ejected blocks, associated with Nepheline, Augite, and Mica. Lake Laach.

Name. From ῥύαξ, *a lava stream.*

·Brit. Mus., Case 31.

S.

SACCHARITE, *Glocker.* Occurs in finely granular masses, with traces of cleavage in one direction. Colour white or greenish. Lustre vitreous. Translucent at the edges. Very fragile. Fracture splintery, uneven. H. 6. S.G. 2·668.

Comp. A hydrated Andesine, or $\dot{\text{K}}\ \ddot{\text{S}}\text{i} + 3\ddot{\ddot{\text{A}}}\text{l}\ \ddot{\text{S}}\text{i}^2 + \dot{\text{H}}.$

Analysis, by *Schmidt:*

Silica	58·93
Alumina	23·50

Peroxide of iron	1·27
Oxide of nickel	0·39
Lime	5·67
Magnesia	0·56
Potash	0·05
Soda	7·42
Water	2·21
	100·00

BB becomes opaque, and fuses only at thin edges: with borax forms a clear glass.

Localities. The Serpentine mines near Frankenstein in Silesia, in veins in Serpentine. Chateau Richer in Canada, of a flesh-red colour, with Hypersthene and Ilmenite.

Name. From σάκχαρ, *sugar;* from its saccharine appearance, resembling that of loaf-sugar.

SAFFLORITE, *Brooke & Miller, Haidinger.* A variety of Smaltine, containing 11 to 19 per cent. of iron, from Schneeberg, in Saxony. (See CHATHAMITE and EISENKOBALTKIES.) H. 5·5. S.G. 6·92 to 7·3.

Analysis, by *v. Kobell:*

Arsenic	71·08
Cobalt	9·44
Iron	18·48
Bismuth	1·00
Copper and sulphur	traces
	100·00

SAGENITE, *Saussure.* (From σαγήνη, *a net.*) A reticulated variety of Rutile.

SAHLITE, *Werner.* SAHLITE, *Jameson, Phillips.* A greenish-grey variety of Pyroxene, resembling Diopside. Massive, with a lamellar structure; seldom crystallized (see BAIKALITE). Translucent at the edges. Lustre vitreous, inclining to pearly. Streak white. Brittle. Fracture foliated. H. 5 to 6. S. G. 3·236.

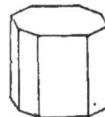

Fig. 369.

Analysis, from Sahla, by *H. Rose:*

Silica	54·86
Alumina	0·21
Peroxide of iron	4 44
Peroxide of manganese	0·42
Lime	23·57
Magnesia	16·49
	99·99

BB fuses, with a slight effervescence, to a translucent glass; with borax and soda forms a clear glass.

Localities. Sahlberg, in Westermann-
land, with Galena, and in many other parts
of Sweden. Arendal, in Norway. Harris,
in Scotland. The Tyrol. North America.
Name. From *Sahla*, and λίθος, *a stone.*
Brit. Mus., Case 34.

ST. STEPHEN'S STONES. White Chalcedony, containing blood-red spots.

SAL AMMONIAC, *Kirwan, Dana.* Cubical,
with an octahedral cleavage. Occurs in
minute octahedrons. Generally stalactitic,
in crusts, or as an efflorescence. Colour, when
pure, white; often greyish or yellowish.
Transparent to opaque Lustre internally
vitreous; externally dull. Streak white.
Fracture conchoidal. Taste pungent, cool,
and saline. H. 1·5 to 2. S.G. 1·52.
Comp. Muriate of ammonia, or NH⁴ Cl =
chlorine 66·3, ammonium 33·7=100.

Analysis, from Vesuvius, by *Klaproth :*
Muriate of ammonia	.	. 99·5
Sulphate of ammonia	.	. 0·5

100·0

BB sublimes at a high temperature, but
does not fuse.

Pulverised with soda or quicklime gives
out the odour of ammonia.

Soluble in 2·7 parts of water, at 66° F.,
and in about its own weight of boiling
water.

Very sparingly soluble in alcohol.

Localities.—English. Near Newcastle, in
Northumberland; and Bradley, Stafford-
shire. — *Scotch.* Hurlet, near Paisley. —
Foreign. · In the neighbourhood of volcanoes,
as at Etna; the Solfatara, near Naples;
Vesuvius; Kilauea, in Hawaii; Hecla, in
Iceland; Isle of Bourbon; Tuscany; St.
Etienne, in France; Duttweiler, in Saar-
brück; Thibet; Persia; Bucharia, in Tartary.

Name. From *sal* (*salt*), and *hama nijak*
(Arabic): i.e. *Salt from the dung of camels.*

Sal Ammoniac is found native near volcanoes, in the vicinity of ignited beds of
coal (as in Great Britain), and, in very
small quantity, in sea- and certain mineral
waters. It is supposed to have been one of
the salts included by the ancients under the
name of nitre (*nitrum*). The Sal Ammoniac (ἅλς ἀμμωνιακὸς), of Dioscorides and
Pliny, has been proved to be common salt,
dug near the temple of Ammon, in Egypt,
and the name to have been subsequently
transferred to the muriate of ammonia, prepared in that country by sublimation, from
the soot obtained by burning camel's dung.

Sal Ammoniac is easily recognised by its

urinous and pungent odour, and its complete volatility by the action of heat.

Both the natural and artificial salt are
used in medicine, dyeing, and in metallurgical operations.

Brit. Mus., Case 59.

M. P. G. Upper Gallery, Wall-case A,
in Recess 4, No. 146.

SAL GEM, *Kirwan.*
SAL GEMMÆ, *Wullerius.*   } See ROCK
SAL MARE, *Beudant.*   } SALT.

SAL MIRABILE, *Wallerius.* See GLAUBER
SALT.

SAL NEUTRUM ACIDULARE, *Wallerius.*
See ROCK SALT.

SALAMANDER'S HAIR, *Woodward.* Amianthus and Asbestos (which see).

SALAMSTEIN, or SALAMSTONE. The name
given by Werner to blue Sapphire from
Ceylon. It occurs in small transparent
crystals, generally six-sided prisms, of pale
reddish and bluish colours.

SALMIAK, *Reuss, Werner.* See SAL
AMMONIAC.

SALPETER, *Werner.* See NITRE.

SALPETER, *Leonhard.* Nitrate of Soda.
See NITRATINE.

SALT CLAY, *Humboldt.* A grey mass, interspersed with salt, separated mechanically
from the so-called *Haselgebirge* (which see),
occurring in certain salt formations.

It is a tersilicate of alumina, mixed with
carbonate of magnesia and other substances,
represented by the formula Äl S̈i³ + Mg C̈.

Analysis, by *Schafhaütl :*
Silica	.	. 45·5
Alumina	.	. 15·0
Carbonic acid	.	. 13·7
Magnesia	.	. 12·8
Iron	.	. 6·9
Manganese	.	. 0·3
Sulphur	.	. 2·2
Chloride of sodium	.	. 1·1
Bitumen	.	. 2·4

99·9

SALT OF PHOSPHORUS, *Dana.* See STER-
CORITE.

SALTPETRE. See NITRE.

SALZ, *Kenngott.* See ROCK SALT.

SALZSÄURES BLEI VON MENDIP. See
MENDIPITE.

SALZSÄURES QUECKSILBEROXYDUL. See
CALOMEL.

SALZSÄURESKUPFER.   } See
SALZKUPFERERZ, *Werner.* } ATACAMITE.

SALZTHON, *Humboldt.* See SALT CLAY.

SAMARSKITE, *H. Rose.* Rhombic. Usually

occurs in flattened and somewhat polygonal grains. Colour externally dull iron-black. Opaque even at the edges. Streak dark reddish- or clove - brown. Very brittle. Fracture subconchoidal, exhibiting a velvet-black colour, and a splendent vitreous lustre like Obsidian. H. 5·5. S.G. 5·614 to 5·746. *Comp.* A mixture of niobic and scheelic acids (H. Rose).

Analysis, from Siberia, by *Peretz* :

Metallic acid	. . 55·91
Peroxide of uranium	. . 16·77
Yttria	. . . 8·36
Protoxide of iron	. . 15·94
Protoxide of manganese and lime	. . . . 1·88
Magnesia	. . . 0·75
	99·61

BB decrepitates and loses density when heated ; exhibiting vivid incandescence, and is afterwards perfectly insoluble in muriatic acid.

When pulverised, readily and completely decomposed by boiling concentrated muriatic acid, forming a greyish and gelatinous mass, which yields with cold water an opalescent solution.

Localities. The Ilmen mountains, near Miask, in the Ural, in pieces not larger than a hazel-nut, imbedded in reddish-brown Felspar. Rutherford co., North Carolina, in auriferous gravel.

Name. After the Russian officer of mines, Von Samarski.

Brit. Mus., Case 49.

The metallic acid in Samarskite consists almost wholly of niobic acid, with small quantities of tungstic and pelopic acids: hence niobic acid may be obtained from it in a state of greater purity than from the Columbites of Bodenmais and North America. The large quantity of magnesia found in the Siberian Columbite distinguishes it from all other tantalites. (L. Gmelin.) See also Yttro-Ilmenite.

SAMMETBLENDE. A capillary variety of Göthite, found in veins at Przibram in Bohemia, at Hüttenberg in Carinthia, and near Ulefoss in Norway.

SAMOITE. A mineral occuring in thin and broad colourless tables, with a glassy lustre, thickly disseminated through a dark coloured, cellular, porphyritic basalt, on Upolu, one of the Samoan, or Navigator Islands. H. 5·5 to 6. S.G. 2·8 to 2·85.

Comp. 2 (Ċa, Ṁg, Ṅa) S̈i + (Ạ̈l, Ḟe) S̈i.
Analysis, by *Silliman, Jr.* :

Silica . . . . . 53·79

Alumina	. . . 18·79
Peroxide of iron	. . . 4·23
Magnesia	. . . . 8·87
Lime	. . . . . 9·86
Soda	. . . . . 3·11
Water and loss	. . . 1·35
	100·00

SANDARACA, *Pliny, Strabo*. SANDARACH, Σανδαράχη, *Theophrastus*. See REALGAR. Probably the name may be a corruption of the Arabic, *Zarnich-Ahmer*.

SANDASTROS. A kind of Aventurine, described by Jean de Saët, of a rufous red colour, and containing in the interior small brilliant grains. The Sandastrum of Pliny is a gem now wholly lost.

SANIDINE. A name for Glassy Felspar (from σανις, *a board*), on account of the tabular form of the crystals.

SAPHIR. *French* for Sapphire.

SAPHIR ASTERIÉ. See ASTERIA.

SAPHIR D'EAU. A name given by jewellers to a transparent variety of Iolite, of an intense blue colour, found in small rolled masses in Ceylon. Sometimes they are of a clear white, mingled with celestial blue, forming a mixed colour. This stone should be cut in the form of a brilliant.

SAPHIR DE CHAT, or *Cat Sapphire*. A name applied to Star Sapphire by French lapidaries. See ASTERIA.

SAPHIR DE FRANCE, or SAPHIR DE PUY-EN-VÉLAI. Names given to water-worn pebbles of Rock Crystal, of a beautiful blue colour, which are found, in France, in the stream Rioupezzouliou, near Expailly in Auvergne. They may be easily distinguished from true Sapphire by their greatly inferior hardness. S.G. 2·58.

SAPHIR DU BRÉSIL. Greenish-blue Tourmaline.

SAPHIR ÉTOILÉ. Star Sapphire. See ASTERIA.

SAPHIR FEMELLE. The name given by French lapidaries to clear blue Sapphire, the colour of which is so faint that it might almost be considered a limpid Sapphire, slightly tinged with blue. See GEM.

SAPHIR MÂLE. The name applied by French lapidaries to indigo-blue Sapphire. The tint of this stone is of a very agreeable kind, being neither too pale nor too dark.

SAPHIR OCCIDENTAL. See SAPHIR D'EAU.

SAPHIR PLOMBÉ. A name by which bluish-green varieties of Sapphire are known to French jewellers.

SAPHIRINE, *Phillips, Gisècké, Levy*. A variety of Spinel, occurring disseminated in pale blue or green translucent grains. Lustre vitreous. Streak white. Fracture imperfect-conchoidal. H. 7 to 8. S.G. 3·42.

Analysis, by *Stromeyer*:

Alumina	. 63·11
Silica	. 14·50
Magnesia . . .	. 16·85
Lime	. 0·38
Oxide of iron . .	. 3·92
Oxide of manganese .	. 0·53
Water	. 0·49
	99·78

BB unaltered either alone or with borax. *Localities.* Aker iron-works, Södermanland, in Sweden. Akudlek, in Greenland, associated with Mica and fibrous brown Anthophyllite.

The name Saphirine, or Sapphirine, is also applied by French lapidaries to the varieties of Chalcedony which approximate in colour to smalt-blue.

Brit. Mus., Case 19.

SAPONITE, (from *sapo, soap,*) or Soapstone. Amorphous, massive. Very soft and soapy, almost like butter when first dug, but hardens and becomes brittle on exposure. Colour various shades of white, grey, yellow, blue, and red; also mottled. Slightly translucent at the edges. Streak shining. Does not adhere to the tongue. Feels unctuous. Yields to the nail. Rather difficultly frangible. Fracture splintery. H. 1·5. S.G. 2·65.

Comp. $2\dot{M}g^3 \ddot{S}\cdot^2 + \ddot{A}l \ddot{S}i + 10\dot{H}$ = silica 45·56, alumina 10 84, magnesia 24·95, water 18·15 = 100.

Analysis, from the Lizard, by *Svanberg*:

Silica	. 45·00
Alumina . . .	. 9·25
Peroxide of iron . .	. 1·00
Magnesia . . .	. 24·75
Lime, soda, and potash	. 0·75
Water	. 18·00
	98·75

BB shows traces of incipient fusion and blistering, but is infusible (except at the edges) without addition. Dissolves in borax, forming a turbid glass, and also in microcosmic salt, with separation of a skeleton of silica. Soluble in sulphuric acid.

Localities. — *English.* Cornwall: near the Lizard Point, in a vein in Serpentine.— *Irish.* In the amygdaloids of Antrim, in greyish, yellowish, or brownish nodules. Magilligan, co. Derry. — *Foreign.* Svärdsjo, in Delarne, Sweden (*Piotine*). Northern shore of Lake Superior (*Thalite*).

SAPPARE. A name given to Kyanite, by De Saussure, owing to a mistake in reading a label on which it had been incorrectly called Sapphire. The name is used by French jewellers for the specimens of that mineral which are brought ready cut and polished from India, and sold as a variety of blue transparent Corundum (or *true Sapphire*). Although not held in any great estimation, and deficient in hardness, some of the crystals, owing · to their good colour and play of light, might vie in appearance with the Oriental or true (or Corundum-) Sapphire.

SAPPHIR CHATOYANT. A French lapidary's name for a kind of Sapphire, which displays very brilliant pearly reflections on a red or blue ground.

SAPPHIRE. The name given to brightly coloured varieties of Corundum. The blue are generally called *Oriental Sapphire*; the red, *Oriental Ruby*; the transparent or translucent yellow, or white, *Oriental Topaz*; the green, *Oriental Emerald*; the violet, *Oriental Amethyst*; the hair-brown, *Adamantine-spar*; the asteriated crystals, *Asteria*; when transparent, with a pale reddish or bluish reflection, *Girasol Sapphire*; with pearly reflection, *Chatoyant* or *Opalescent Sapphire*.

Fig. 370.

Fig. 371.

Sapphire is the hardest of all known substances, except the Diamond. It occurs crystallized in variously terminated six-sided prisms and in rolled masses, and is found in the beds of rivers or associated with crystalline rocks. It possesses double refraction, and becomes electric by friction. Is not acted on by acids, and remains unaltered by the fire; red and yellow varieties, if anything, being improved in colour by heating. With borax *BB* fuses slowly, but perfectly, to a colourless glass.

Localities. Sapphire is chiefly brought from Ceylon and Pegu, but it is also found in Bohemia; in France, in the brook Rioupezzouliou, near Expailly in Vélay, and in New South Wales. See RUBY.

In Prinsep's "Oriental Accounts of the Precious Minerals," it is stated, that under the name of Sapphire or Yaqút are comprised all those stones of the Sapphire and Ruby species which are distinguished (or rather connected, as being chemically one) by the epithet *Oriental*, in English books of mineralogy, and are now classed together under the general head of Corundum, because they are composed of the same earth, alumina, as the *Corundum*, or *Kúrún* of the Indians. The natives, like our own mineralogists, distinguish four principal species of *yaqút*; red (*Oriental Ruby*), blue (*Oriental Sapphire*), yellow, white, or colourless (*Oriental Topaz*), and green (*Oriental Emerald*).

The medical properties of the yaqút are remarkable: "it purifies the blood, strengthens, quenches thirst; it dispels melancholy reflections; and as a talisman averts dangers, and insures honours and competence."—*Prinsep, Jl. Asi. Soc. Bengal,* vol. i.

"From the earliest period of the Middle Ages, the symbol of investiture with the office of bishop, has been a ring set with a Sapphire or Ruby, and worn on the fore-finger. The reason for this choice was its violet colour, agreeing with the vestments appropriated to the episcopal office." *

Sapphire is cut by means of diamond-dust, and is polished on copper and lead wheels with emery powder.

Blue Sapphire is imitated with Iolite, Kyanite, &c.: hardness affords the best test of the genuineness of the stone. A good sapphire of 10 carats is valued at 50 guineas, and one of 20 carats at 200 guineas. Under 10 carats the price may be estimated by multiplying the square of its weight in carats into half a guinea; thus, one of 4 carats would be worth $4 \times 4 \times 10s. 6d. = £8. 8s.$

Name. The word sapphire is derived from σαπφειρος, the name of a blue stone amongst the ancients. Most probably the σαπφειρος of the ancients, however, was not our sapphire, but Lapis Lazuli.

See Lam. iv. 7. Isaiah liv. 11.

Brit. Mus., Case 19.

M. P. G. Horse-shoe Case, Nos. 786, 787, 792 — 794. Case 11 (W. Bathurst, N. S. Wales).

SARCOLITE, *Thomson.* SARCOLITHE DE THOMSON, *Haüy.* Pyramidal. Occurs in small, pale, flesh-red or brownish-white crystals. Semi-transparent. Lustre vitre-

* Antique Gems, their origin, uses, and value by Rev. C. W. King, M.A. p. 296.

ous. Extremely brittle, and full of flaws; falling to pieces unless carefully handled. H. 6. S.G. 2·545.

Comp. (Na Ca)³ + Al Si.

Analysis, by *Scacchi:*

Silica	42·11
Alumina . . .	24·50
Lime	32·43
Soda	2·93
	101·97

BB fuses to a white enamel. Forms a jelly with acids.

Locality. Vesuvius, at Monte Somma, associated with Wollastonite, Hornblende, and other Zeolites.

Name. From σαρξ, *flesh,* and λιθος, *stone;* in allusion to its colour.

SARD. Σαρδιον, *Theophrastus.* A deep brownish-red Chalcedony, of a blood-red colour by transmitted light.

It is difficult to draw the line of distinction between Sard and Carnelian; the former, however, when in its greatest perfection, is of a full, rich brown colour, approaching more or less to orange or yellow, and when held between the eye and the light exhibits a deep ruby colour, approaching to cherry-red or blood-red. Sard, though found under the same circumstances, is extremely rare compared with Carnelian, and obtains a much higher price, especially when of a very dark tint.

It is procured from the shores of the Red Sea; and is found also in Perthshire.

The name Sardus, or Sarda, is believed by some to be derived from Sardinia (the ancient Sardis), where it is said to have been originally found (Hill's *Theophrastus,* p. 96); by others it is supposed to be derived from σαρξ, *flesh,* because of its colour. The Sard was the precious stone ordered to be placed first on the breast-plate worn by the high-priest of the Jews, and to be engraved with the name of Reuben, but probably the word *Odem* (redness), rendered Sarde in the Bible, may have meant Carneliau, or possibly Ruby, rather than the Sard of the moderns. The Sard of the ancient Greeks and Romans was certainly our Carnelian. See Exod. xxviii. 17. Ezek. xxviii. 13.

"The Sard and Onyx in one name unite,
And from their union spring three colours bright,
O'er jetty black the brilliant white is spread,
And o'er the white diffused a fiery red:
If clear the colours, if distinct the line,
Where still unmix'd the various layers join,
Such we for beauty and for value prize,
Rarest of all that teeming earth supplies:

Chief amongst signets, it will best convey
The stamp impress'd, nor tear the wax.away."*

The Sard is said by Marbodus to be good
to be worn, and makes the person beloved
by women. It should have engraved upon
it a vine, and ivy twining round it.

M. P. G. Horse-shoe Case, Nos. 592—
595.

SARDACHATES. The name given by the
ancients to varieties of Agate partaking of
the nature of Carnelian, or which contained
layers of Sard or Carnelian.

SARDONYX is the name applied to those
varieties of Onyx which are composed of
alternate layers of Sard and nearly opaque
white Chalcedony. It is the most beautiful, the rarest, and the most valued form of
Onyx, and was the most esteemed for engraving into cameos by the ancients.

" The man of humble heart, and modest face,
And purest soul, the *Sardonyx* should grace ;
A worthy gem, yet boasts no mystic powers :
'Tis sent from Indian and Arabian shores." *

Scipio was the first Roman who wore
Sardonyx, which he did in a ring. The
precious ring, also, thrown into the sea by
Polycrates, tyrant of Samos, to defy fortune,
was a Sardonyx. The fakirs of India still
wear at the present day, as they did in the
time of Pliny, long chaplets of Sardonyx
and other kinds of agate. The stones dril-
led for stringing like beads were called by
the ancients *Indian Sardonyx.*

A cameo of the unusual size of 7½ inches
by 6 inches, formed of Sardonyx, sold at
the sale of the Hertz collection, in 1859, for
£126. It was an admirably executed cinque-
cento work, the subject of which was
" Thetis entreating Jupiter to give weapons
to her son Achilles." Another cameo, 1⅞
by 1⅜ inches, representing a " Bacchanalian
Mask," crowned with ivy, was also sold at
the same sale for £31.

The Sardonyx is found in Perthshire.
The Sardonyx mountains of Ptolemy are,
doubtless, the Cupperwange, or Cubberpunj
hills, still famous for Carnelians, Agates,
and the sprig-stones generally called Mocha-
stones. — *Forbes's Orl. Memoirs,* vol. iii.
p. 68.

M. P. G. Horse-shoe Case, Nos. 588, 628.

SASSOLIN, *Jameson, Hausmann, Nicol.*
Anorthic. Generally occurs in small scales,
apparently six-sided tables, and in stalactitic forms, which are also made up of small
scales. Colour white, sometimes greyish-
white, sometimes yellowish-white from the

* Lapidarium viii. of Marbodus. From " Antique Gems,' &c." by Rev. C. W. King, M.A.

presence of sulphur. Translucent to transparent. Lustre pearly. Streak white. Feel
smooth and unctuous. Taste acidulous, and
slightly saline and bitter. Sectile and flexible. H. 1. S.G. 1·48.

Comp. Hydrated boracic acid, or $\ddot{B}\dot{H}^3 =$
boracic acid 56·4, water 43·6 = 100.

Sulphate of magnesia and iron, sulphate
and carbonate of lime, silica and alumina,
are, according to Klaproth, mechanically
mixed with the native stalactitic salt.

Erdmann states that Sassolin contains
3·18 per cent., by weight, of ammonia, and
that, instead of being pure boracic acid, it
is a borate of ammonia.

BB fuses in the flame of a candle, tinging the flame green, until the water of crystallization is evaporated. The cooled globule
is glassy, and opaque if gypsum be present.
Soluble in water and in alcohol. When
dissolved in alcohol colours the flame green.

Localities. Abundantly in the crater of
Vulcano, one of the Lipari Isles, mixed
with sulphur; and around the fumaroles (or
outlets of the sulphureous exhalations) of
Tuscany. The hot vapours at the lagoons
of Tuscany — small hot lakes, into which
vapours rise from the volcanic bottom —
consist largely of boracic acid, which crystallizes on the edges of these lakes in the
form of Sassolin. Also in South America,
in the Andes of Atacama.

It is used for manufacturing borax.

Name. After Sasso, near Sienna, the first
locality known, where it occurs in the hot
springs.

Brit. Mus., Case 39.

M. P. G. Horse-shoe Case, Nos. 221 and
222.

SATERSBERGITE, *Kenngott.* A variety of
Leucopyrite, from Fossum, in Norway.
S.G. 7·09 to 7·2.

Analysis, by *Scheerer :*

Arsenic	.	.	. 70·22
Iron	.	.	. 28·14
Sulphur	.	.	. 1·28

99·64

SATIN SPAR. The name usually applied
to the fibrous varieties of Gypsum, occurring
at Red Hill and Newark, in Nottinghamshire; at Chellaston, near Ashbourne,
in Derbyshire; and near Carrickfergus, co.
Antrim, in Ireland. It is also found in
Gloucestershire, of a pale blue colour. This
variety of Gypsum is much used for ornamental purposes, and when cut *en cabochon*
and polished, it bears a certain outward re-

semblance to Cat's Eye, but is of a much softer nature.

The name Satin Spar is also given to a fibrous variety of Aragonite, which, when polished, has a satiny lustre, and is on that account employed in the manufacture of ornaments. It is found at Dufton, in Cumberland, in thin veins, traversing shale, and generally accompanied by Iron Pyrites. The spar from this locality contains 4·25 per cent. of carbonate of manganese, which sometimes communicates to it a roseate tinge. It is also met with, of snowy whiteness, in Buckinghamshire; Devonshire; and at Leadhills, in Scotland; in Dirk Hatterick's Cave, in Galloway; and in the Orkueys; in the island of Pharay, and at Rackwick, in Hoy.

Brit. Mus., Case 45.

M. P. G. Horse-shoe Case, Nos. 295 to 300.

SAUALPITE A name proposed for the so-called Zoisite, from the Saualp, in Carinthia, which has been separated from Epidote, by Brooke, on crystallographic grounds, and formed into a separate species.

SAVITE, *Menegheni.* Pyramidal. Occurs in radiating, acicular, rectangular prisms, which are either truncated or with pyramidal terminations. Colourless, and transparent, with a vitreous lustre. H. 3. S.G. 2·45.

Comp. $(\ddot{M}g\ \dot{N}a)^5\ \ddot{S}i^2 + \overset{...}{\ddot{A}l}\ \ddot{S}i + 2\dot{H}.$

Analysis, by *Bechi :*

Silica	.	.	.	.	49·17
Alumina	.	.	.	.	19·66
Magnesia	.	.	.	.	13·50
Soda	.	.	.	.	10·52
Potash	.	.	.	.	1·23
Water	.	.	.	.	6·57

100·65

Locality. Tuscany, in gabbro rosso, associated with Picranalcime.

Name. After Mons. Savi.

Savite, according to Q. Sella, has the same angles and crystalline form as Natrolite, of which mineral it is, probably, only a variety.

SAVON DE MONTAGNE, *Brochant, Beudant.* See ROCK SOAP.

SAVON DE VERRIERS. A name given by the French to Pyrolusite, in consequence of its being largely used in the manufacture of glass, for the purpose of getting rid of the brown and green tints and the colouring matters contained in the materials employed.

SAUSSURITE. A compact Epidote, forming the Jade of the Swiss Alps. Occurs in greenish-white, mountain-green, or ash-grey coloured masses. Cleavage in two directions. Translucent at the edges. Lustre pearly, inclining to vitreous on faces of cleavage: sometimes resinous, especially in massive varieties. Streak white. Unctuous to the touch. Extremely tough. Fracture splintery to uneven. H. 7. S.G. 3·25 to 3·38.

Comp. $(\dot{R} + \overset{...}{\ddot{R}})\ \overset{...}{Si}.$

Analysis, from Monte Rosa, by *T. Sterry Hunt :*

Silica	.	.	.	43·59
Alumina	.	.	.	27·72
Peroxide of iron	.	.	.	2·61
Lime	.	.	.	19·71
Magnesia	.	.	.	2·98
Soda	.	.	.	3·08
Loss by ignition	.	.	.	0·35

100·04

BB fuses with difficulty to a greenish glass.

Not acted on by acids.

Localities. — *English.* Said to occur in Cornwall, at Kynance Cove, Coverack Cove, and the Lizard.— *Scotch.* Glen Tilt, Perthshire. Portsoy, Banffshire. — *Foreign.* Originally discovered by Saussure, in rounded masses on the borders of the lake of Geneva. Monte Rosa, and its vicinity. Corsica. Greenland Madras, &c.

With Augite and Hornblende, it constitutes the rocks called Gabbro and Euphotide.

Name. After H. B. De Saussure, the Swiss geologist.

Brit. Mus., Case 31.

Saussurite may be distinguished from Augite and Diallage, by greater toughness and less decided cleavage.

Analyses of the Saussurites of Mont Genèvre and Orezza by Boulanger give the composition of a compact Lime-alumina Epidote (or Zoisite), containing small portions of magnesia and soda; and the more recent analysis of a fragment from Monte Rosa, by T. Sterry Hunt, affords the same result.

Saussurite is nearly related to the massive White Garnet from the Green Mountains, in Canada, which, mixed with Serpentine and Hornblende, gives rise to varieties of rocks resembling certain Euphotides. (*T. Sterry Hunt.*)

Dana, Beudant, Bischoff, Delesse, and other modern mineralogists, have referred Saussurite to Labradorite or some other

Felspar, from which it is distinguished by greater hardness and by specific gravity, which is much above that of the Felspars.

SAXON TOPAZ. A pale wine-yellow Topaz from Schneckenstein, in the Valley of Damberg. See TOPAZ.

SAYNITE, v. Kobell. A name for Bismuth Nickel, after the locality, Sayn - Altenkirchen. See GRÜNAUITE.

SCACCHITE. A combination of lead and selenium, discovered by Mons. Palmiere, the meteorologist, in certain fumaroles of Vesuvius, and named by him after Prof. Scacchi of Naples.

SCALE-STONE, Bakewell. See LEPIDOLITE.

SCALY TALC. See NACRITE.

SCALY TRICLASITE. See WEISSITE.

SCARBROÏTE, Phillips. A clay - like mineral related to Collyrite. Amorphous. Colour pure white. Devoid of lustre. Highly adhesive to moist surfaces. Easily scratched with the knife. Can be polished with the nail. Gives off a strong argillaceous odour when breathed on. Immersed in water, gains considerably in weight, but neither becomes translucent, nor falls in pieces. Fracture conchoidal. H. 2. S.G. 1·48.

Comp. Hydrous silicate of alumina, or $\ddot{A}l^3 \, \ddot{S}i + 15H$.

Analysis, by Vernon:

Silica	.	.	.	10·50
Alumina	.	.	.	42·50
Peroxide of iron	.	.	0·25
Water	.	.	.	46·75

100·00

Locality. Near Scarborough*, in Yorkshire, between septa of ironstone, in a calcareous rock.

Brit. Mus., Case 26.

SCAPOLITE, Phillips, Nicol; or SCAPOLITH, Werner. Pyramidal. Occurs in four-sided and eight-sided prisms, which are sometimes terminated by tetrahedral pyramids, and often aggregated laterally into masses composed of parallel (or somewhat diverging) or intermingled groups. These when broken often display a broad fibrous structure. Cleavage parallel to the sides, terminal planes, and both diagonals of a square prism. Also massive, granular, or columnar. Colours, white, grey, yellowish, blue, green, or red; generally pale. Transparent or translucent. Lustre vitreous or somewhat

---

* Whence the name, Scarbroïte.

pearly, inclining to resinous; cleavage planes and fracture resinous. Streak white. Brittle. Fracture sub-conchoidal. H. 5 to 5·5. S.G. 2·61 to 2·75.

Comp. $\dot{C}a \, \ddot{S}i + \ddot{A}l \, \ddot{S}i$.

Analysis, from Pargas, by Nordenskiöld:

Silica	.	.	.	43·83
Alumina	.	.	.	35·43
Lime	.	.	.	18·96
Water	.	.	.	1 03

99·25

BB fuses and swells up to a translucent mass, which is no longer fusible. Dissolves in borax or microcosmic salt, with continued effervescence, forming a transparent glass.

Perfectly decomposed by muriatic acid, when finely pounded, without forming a siliceous jelly ; (which serves to distinguish it from Meionite.)

Localities. Norway: iron mines at Arendal, in gneiss. Wermland, in Sweden. Pargas, in Finland. Akudlek, in Greenland. Various parts of the United States. Grand Calumet Island, Canada.

Name. from σκαπός, a club, and λίθος, stone ; in allusion to the form of the crystals.

Brit. Mus., Case 31.

M. P. G. Horse-shoe Case, No. 967.

Under the term Scapolite or Wernerite are comprehended the common white and greyish varieties. The crystals are sometimes rendered opaque externally by a chalky deposit (the result of exposure), or even throughout in consequence of a partial alteration. The massive varieties bear some resemble to the Felspars.

For varieties of Scapolite, see EKEBERGITE, GLAUCOLITE, NUTTALITE, PARANTHINE, PORCELAIN SPAR.

SCHAALSTEIN, Werner. See WOLLASTONITE.

SCHABAZITE, Werner. See CHABAZITE.

SCHAPBACHITE. A name for Bismuth Silver, from the locality Schapbach, in Baden.

SCHAUM EARTH. Jameson. }
SCHAUMERDE, Werner. } See
SCHAUMKALK. } APHRITE.

The term Schaumkalk also includes a variety of Gypsum, composed of fine scales, with a pearly lustre.

SCHAUMARTIGER WAD-GRAPHIT, Mohs. Earthy Manganese. See WAD.

SCHEELATE OF IRON AND MANGANESE. See WOLFRAM.

SCHEELBLEIERZ, Naumann. SCHEELBLEISPATH. SCHEELSAURES BLEI. SCHÉE-

LETINE. SCHEELITINE, *Nicol, Beudant.* Pyramidal: primary form a rectangular four-sided prism, with a single distinct cleavage parallel to its base. Isomorphous with tungstate of lime and molybdate of lead. Occurs in four-sided prisms (often small and indistinctly aggregated), the terminal edges of which are replaced by octahedral planes. Colourless or yellowish-grey, brownish or green. Faintly translucent. Lustre resinous. Streak white. Fracture conchoidal and shining. H. 3. S.G. 7·8 to 8·1.

Comp. Tungstate of lead, or $\overset{..}{P}b\ \overset{...}{W}=$ oxide of lead 48·28, tungstic acid 51·72 = 100.

Analysis, from Zinnwald, by *Chapman:*

Tungstic acid　.　.　. 59·50
Oxide of lead　.　.　. 33·26
Lime .　.　.　.　.　6·37
　　　　　　　　　　———
　　　　　　　　　　99·13

BB fuses, covering the charcoal with a deposit of oxide of lead, and on cooling solidifies to a dark crystalline globule. With carbonate of soda, on charcoal, yields globules of lead.

Soluble in nitric acid, with separation of yellow tungstic acid.

Localities. The tin mines of Zinnwald in Bohemia, associated with Quartz and Mica. Bleiberg in Carinthia, with molybdate of lead. Near Coquimbo, in Chili.

Name. After Scheele, the celebrated Swedish chemist.

Brit. Mus., Case 38.

SCHEELIN FERRUGINÉ, *Haüy.* See WOL-FRAM.

SCHEELINE CALCAIRE, *Dufrénoy.* See SCHEELITE.

SCHEELIT, *Von Kobell, Haidinger, Hausmann.* SCHEELITE, *Leonhard, Beudant.* Pyramidal: primary form a right square prism. Occurs in attached and imbedded four-sided pyramids, approaching nearly to the octahedron. Twins. Also reniform, with a columnar structure, and amorphous-granular. Colourless or greyish, yellowish or brownish: sometimes orange - yellow.

Fig. 372.

Translucent. Lustre vitreous, inclining to resinous on surfaces of fracture, to adaman-

tine on cleavage-faces. Streak white. Brittle. Fracture conchoidal and uneven. H. 4 to 4·5. S.G. 6 to 6·07.

Comp. Tungstate of lime, or $\overset{.}{C}a\overset{...}{W}$ = lime 18·92, tungstic acid 81·08 = 100.

Analysis, from Framont, by *Delesse:*

Tungstic acid　.　.　. 80·35
Lime .　.　.　.　. 19·40
　　　　　　　　　　———
　　　　　　　　　　99·75

BB crackles, becomes opaque, and fuses at the edges to a translucent glass. In borax dissolves readily, yielding a transparent glass, which on cooling rapidly becomes milk-white and crystalline.

Decomposed, when reduced to powder, by muriatic or nitric acid, with the separation of yellow tungstic acid. The lime is removed from the powdered mineral by a boiling solution of potash.

Localities. — English. Cornwall: at Pengelley Croft Mine, Breage; Huel Maudlin, near Lostwithiel. Huel Friendship, near Tavistock, Devon, imbedded in Chlorite. Near Brandygill, Carrock Fells, Cumberland, in transparent wine-yellow, or opaque greyish-brown crystals, in quartz-rock, associated with Wolfram.— *Foreign.* Schlackenwald and Zinnwald, in Bohemia. The gold mines of Schellgaden, in Salzburg; and Posing in Hungary. Neudorf, in the Harz. Ehrenfriedersdorf, in Saxony. Dalecarlia, in Sweden. Framont, in the Vosges. Katherinenburg, in Siberia. Coquimbo, in Chili. Monroe and Huntington, in Connecticut, U. S.

Name. In compliment to the Swedish chemist Scheele, who discovered Tungstic acid (or, as it was, in the first instance, called, "Scheelic acid,") in this mineral.

Brit. Mus., Case 88.

SCHEELITINE, *Beudant, Nicol.* See SCHEELETINE.

SCHEEL-ORE, *Mohs.* See WOLFRAM.

SCHEELSÄURE, *Naumann.* Tungstic ochre. See WOLFRAMINE.

SCHEELSAURE,
Naumann.　　　} Tungstate of lead. See
SCHEELSAURES　} SCHEELETINE.
BLEI, *v. Leonhard.* }

SCHEERERIT, *Stromeyer.* SCHEERERITE, *Phillips, Nicol.* A mineral resin occurring in loosely aggregated, feebly shining, crystalline grains and folia, or in minute acicular crystals, in small cavities in Coal. Colour white, inclining to yellow or green. Opaque. Lustre pearly. Soft and very friable. Tasteless. Inodorous when cold.

At 111° F. melts to a colourless liquid, resembling a fatty oil, which, like it, penetrates paper, and may be removed by heat. On cooling from a melted state, crystallizes in four-sided acicular crystals. Distils at 194° F. without being decomposed. Inflames easily, and burns completely away, giving out much smoke and a feeble aromatic smell.

Comp. CH^2 = carbon 75, hydrogen 25 = 100.

Insoluble in water, but readily soluble in alcohol, ether, and sulphuric acid.

Locality. Utznach, near St. Gallen, in Switzerland, in beds of Brown Coal. Denmark, in peat-mosses.

Name. After the Swiss Colonel Von Scheerer, by whom it was discovered in 1822.

Brit. Mus., Case 60.

SCHIEFER KOHLE, *Brochant*, *Werner.* See SLATE COAL.

SCHIEFER SPATH, *La Metherie.* See SLATE SPAR.

SCHIEFERSPAR, *Phillips.* } See SLATE
SCHIEFERSPATH, *Werner.* } SPAR.

SCHIEFERTHON, *Werner.* See SLATE CLAY.

SCHILFGLASERZ, *Freiesleben.* Antimonial Sulphide of Silver. See FREIESLEBENITE.

SCHILLER-SPAR, *Phillips.* SCHILLER-SPATH, *Breithaupt.* SCHILLERSTEIN, *Werner.* SCHILLER STONE, *Jameson.* Occurs granular and massive, with cleavage in two directions, one very perfect, the other only appearing in traces. Colour olive-green or pinchbeck-brown. Opaque, but translucent at thin edges. Lustre shining semi-metallic. Yields to the knife. Streak greyish or greenish-white. Rather brittle. Fracture foliated. H. 3·5 to 4. S.G. 2·6 to 2·8.

Comp. Hydrated silicate of magnesia, or $Mg \overset{\cdots}{Si}^2 + 3\overset{\cdot}{H}$; but a large proportion of the magnesia is replaced by the protoxides of iron and manganese, and by lime.

Analysis, from Baste, by *Kühler* :

Silica	43·08
Alumina . .	1·73
Protoxide of iron . .	10·91
Magnesia . .	26·16
Lime	2·75
Protoxide of manganese	0·57
Oxide of chrome . .	2·37
Water . . .	12·43
	100·00

BB fuses at the thinnest edges.

Localities. Baste in the Harz, in compact Schillerstein, and in Euphotide (*Bastite*) ; also at Radauthal.

Name. From *schillernd, shining,* and *spath, spar.*

Schiller spar is considered by G. Rose to be an altered Augite.

Brit. Mus., Cases 25 and 35.

SCHILLERNDER ASBEST, *v. Kobell.* See CHRYSOTILE : also BALTIMORITE and METAXITE.

SCHISTE GRAPHIQUE, *Haüy.* See BLACK CHALK.

SCHIUMA DI MARE. See MEERSCHAUM.

SCHLACKIGES ERDPECH, *Werner.* See ASPHALT.

SCHMARAGD, *Werner.* See EMERALD.

SCHMELZSTEIN, *Werner.* See DIPYRE.

SCHMIERGEL, *Werner.* See EMERY.

SCHNEIDERITE, *Meneghini.* An opaque-white mineral, occurring in confused laminar radiations in gabbro rosso. H. 3.

Comp. $3(\overset{\cdot}{Ca}\overset{\cdot}{Mg})^3 \overset{\cdots}{Si}^2 + \overset{\cdots}{Al}^3 \overset{\cdots}{Si}^2 + 3\overset{\cdot}{H}$.

Analysis, by *Bechi* :

Silica	47·79
Alumina . . .	19·38
Lime	16·77
Magnesia . . .	11·03
Potash and soda . .	1·62
Water	3·41
	100·00

BB swells up and fuses to a blue enamel. Soluble in acids, with the formation of a jelly of silica.

Locality. Tuscany, with Sloanite, in gabbro rosso.

Name. In honour of Hen. Schneider, director of the mines of Monte Catini, in Tuscany.

SCHÖRL, *Werner.* SCHORL, *Kirwan.* SCHORL NOIRE, *Brochant.* The name given to black opaque varieties of Tourmaline.

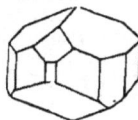 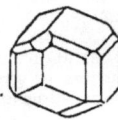 

Fig. 373.   Fig. 374.   Fig. 375.

Comp. $(\overset{3}{R} \text{ } \overset{\cdots}{\cancel{}} \overset{\cdots}{B}) \overset{\cdots}{Si}$.

Analysis, from Bovey Tracey, by *Rammelsberg* :

Silica	37·00
Alumina . . .	33·09
Boracic acid . .	7·66
Peroxide of iron . .	9·33

Protoxide of iron	.	.	6·19
Magnesia	.	.	2·58
Lime	.	.	0·50
Soda	.	.	1·89
Potash	.	.	0·65
Phosphoric acid	.	.	0·12
Fluorine	.	.	1·49

100·00

According to Gmelin, the Bovey Tourmaline consists of $2\ddot{N}a$, $\dot{C}a$, $\dot{M}g$, $14\dot{F}e + 2\ddot{F}e$, $22\ddot{A}l + 24\ddot{S}i + 4\ddot{B}$.

BB intumesces and forms a black scoriaceous mass. With borax fuses to a transparent glass, and gives the reaction of iron. With soda yields a manganese reaction. With Fluor colours the flame green.

Decomposed by concentrated sulphuric acid, after fusion.

Localities. — *English.* Cornwall: Boscawen Cliffs and Botallack mine, near St. Just (*figs.* 374 and 376), St. Michael's Mount, &c.; Devonshire, at Chudleigh, near Bovey Tracey (*fig.* 375), in granite, associated with fine translucent crystals of white Apatite. — *Scotch.* Portsoy, in Banffshire, in large curved crystallized prisms, imbedded in granite. — *Irish.* Stillorgen, co. Dublin. — *Foreign.* Karosulik, in Greenland. The Ural. Arendal, in Norway. Hörlberg, near Bodenmais, in Bavaria. Kärinbricka, in Sweden. The Harz. The Tyrol. The Pyrenees. Saxony. Haddam, Connecticut, U. S. Madagascar.

Name. After Schorlau, a village in Saxony, near which it was first found. According to v. Kobell, the name is derived from the old word *Schor*, meaning uncleanness (impurity); because Schorl appearing in a deposit of Stream Tin renders the Tin Stone impure. Kirwan, on the other hand, states the word Schorl to be derived from the Swedish *Shorl* (brittle), and to have been "first used by Cronstedt, to denote a class of stones of a columnar form, and considerable hardness and density," their specific gravity being from 3 to 3·4."

"It seems that the word Shorl has often been applied to stones of various species, not only by different writers, but often by the same author. Cronstedt, Wallerius, Bergman, Saussure, Romé de Lisle, and the older mineralogists, included several distinct minerals under the common name of Shorl. Cronstedt translated the word into Latin by *basaltes*, which increased the confusion; an instance of which is afforded by the mistake made by Wallerius, who, deceived by

the name (*basaltes crystallisatus*, by which Cronstedt translated *Shorl crystal*), comprehended also the columns of the Giant's Causeway under that species. Romé de Lisle constantly confounds Schorls, Actinolites, Tourmalines, and Basaltic Hornblendes." — *Kirwan's Min.* vol. i.

Schorl was confined by Rammelsberg to varieties of Iron Tourmaline. Hermann, however, divides Tourmaline into three groups, and only includes under the name Schorl those varieties which polarise light.

Brit. Mus., Case 40.

M. P. G. Horse-shoe Case, Nos. 844, 866—871.

SCHORL AIGUE - MARINE. The name given by Saussure to crystallized olive-green Epidote (*Delphinite*), from Dauphiny, on account of the very brilliant lustre reflected from its surface, and the high polish of which it is susceptible.

SCHORL BLANC, *Romé de Lisle.* See ALBITE.

SCHORL CRYSTALLISÉ OPAQUE ROUGE, *von Born.* See RUTILE.

SCHORL ELECTRIQUE, *Haüy.* See TOURMALINE.

SCHORL NOIRE, *Brochant.* See SCHORL.

SCHORL ROUGE, *Saussure.* See RUTILE.

SCHORL TRANSPARENT LENTICULAIRE, *Romé de Lisle.* See AXINITE.

SCHORL TRANSPARENT RHOMBOIDAL, *Romé de Lisle.* See TOURMALINE.

SCHORL VIOLET, *Dufrénoy.* See AXINITE.

SCHORLARTIGER BERIL, *Werner.* See TOPAZ.

SCHORLITE. A name that was given to Pycnite, in the belief that it was a white variety of Schorl.

SCHORLOMITE, *Shepard.* Massive, with indistinct cleavage; also in hexagonal prisms, the lateral edges of which are truncated by narrow and brilliant planes. Colour black, often with a blue tarnish and pavonine tints, causing a resemblance to Specular Iron, for which it has been sometimes mistaken. Lustre vitreous. Streak greyish-black, inclining to lavender. Fracture conchoidal. H. 7 to 7·5. S.G. 3·8.

Comp. $\dot{C}a^5 \ddot{S}i + \ddot{F}e \ddot{S}i + \dot{C}a \ddot{T}i^2$ = silica 24·9, oxide of iron 21·9, lime 30·7, titanic acid 22·5 = 100.

Analysis, by Rammelsberg:

Silica	.	.	.	.	25·24
Peroxide of iron	.	.	.	20·11
Titanic acid	.	.	.	22·34
Lime	.	.	.	.	29·38

z

Magnesia . . . . 1·36
Protoxide of iron . . 1·57

100·00

BB fuses, with difficulty, at the edges to
a black mass; with borax yields a pearl
which is yellow in the outer flame, and becomes colourless on cooling.

Locality. The Ozark Mountains, Magnet
Cove, Arkansas, U. S., in small masses, with
Elæolite and Brookite.

Name. From *Schorl,* and *ὅμοιος, like,* from
its resemblance to Schorl in colour, fracture,
and crystallization.

SCHORLOUS BERYL. See PYCNITE.

SCHREIBERSITE, *Haidinger.* A substance
common in meteorites, in the form of steel-
grey folia and grains, which are often mistaken for Iron Pyrites. Magnetic. Folia
flexible. H. 6·5. S.G. 7·1 to 7·22.

Comp. P, Ni², Fe⁴ = phosphorus 15·47,
nickel 29·17, iron 55·36 = 100. (Communicated by Dr. J. Lawrence Smith to Professor Dana.)

Analysis, by J. Lawrence Smith:

Phosphorus . . . . 13·92
Iron . . . . . 57·22
Nickel . . . . . 25·82
Cobalt . . . . . 0·32
Silica . . . . . 1·62
Alumina . . . . 1·63
Chlorine . . . . 0·13
Copper . . . . . trace
Lime . . . . . trace

100·66

Name. After Carl v. Schreibers, Director
of the Imperial Cabinet at Vienna, and an
author on Meteorites.

For further details, see METEORIC IRON.

SCHREIBERSITE, *C. U. Shepard.* See
SHEPARDITE.

SCHRIFTERZ, *Naumann.* } See
SCHRIFTELLUR, *Hausmann.* } SYLVANITE.

SCHRÖTTERITE, *Glocker.* Amorphous.
Colour greenish, yellowish, brownish, sometimes with brown spots. Lustre vitreous.
Fracture conchoidal. H. 3 to 3·5. S.G. 1·95
to 2·05.

Comp. Hydrated silicate of alumina, or
Al⁴ Si + 20H.

Analysis, from Alabama, by *J. W. Mallet:*

Silica . . . . . 10·53
Alumina . . . . 46·48
Oxide of zinc . . . 0·77
Protoxide of iron and mag-
nesia. . . . . trace

Sulphuric acid . . . 0·80
Water . . . . 41·09

99·67

BB infusible, but swells up and becomes
white.

Dissolves in warm muriatic acid, with
separation of gelatinous silica.

Localities. Dollinger Mountain, near
Freienstein, in Styria Falls of Little River,
on the Sand Mountain, Cherokee county,
Alabama, U. S., forming a faintly brownish
incrustation, above half an inch thick, and
partly stalactitic. It is translucent, and,
when broken, resembles gum-arabic.

Name. In compliment to Jean-Samuel
Schrötter, Superintendent of the Cabinets
of Natural History at Weimar and Buk-
stadt.

Brit. Mus., Case 26.

SCHULZITE, *Brooke & Miller.* A variety
of Geocronite found in Spain, in nodules in
Galena, at Meredo in Galicia. Colour and
streak lead-grey. Opaque. Lustre metallic.
Brittle. Fracture conchoidal, even. H. 2·5
to 3. S.G. 6·43.

Comp. Sulphantimonide of lead, or 5Pb S
+ Sb S³.

Analysis, by Sauvage:

Sulphur . . . . 16·90
Lead . . . . . 64·89
Antimony . . . . 16·00
Copper . . . . 1·60

99·39

SCHÜTZIT. See CELESTINE.

SCHWARZBLEIERZ, *Werner.* Black lead-
ore of Jameson. See CERUSITE.

SCHWARZBRAUNSTEIN, *Hausmann.* See
PSILOMELANE.

SCHWARZBRAUNSTEINERZ, *Werner.* See
HAUSMANNITE.

SCHWARZEISENSTEIN, *Werner.* See PSI-
LOMELANE.

SCHWARZER ERDKOBOLD, *Werner.* See
EARTHY COBALT.

SCHWARZER GLASKOPF, *Werner.* See
PSILOMELANE.

SCHWARZERZ, *Hausmann.* See MAN-
GANESE BLENDE.

SCHWARZ MANGAN-KIESEL. Hydro-
silicate of manganese. See ORSIMOSE.

SCHWARZERZ, *Werner.* An iron-black
variety of Spaniolite (see TETRAHEDRITE),
principally found at the old mine of Schwatz,
in the Tyrol, and at Kapnik, in Transylvania; also at Clausthal, in the Harz, imbedded in red manganese.

SCHWARZGILTIGERZ. Dark varieties of

Grey Copper (see TETRAHEDRITE), containing little or no arsenic. They occur at Clausthal, in the Harz; Kamsdorf and Freiberg, in Saxony; Angina, in Tuscany; Durango, in Mexico, &c.

SCHWARZGÜLTIGERZ, v. *Leonhard*. The name applied to the compact and massive variety of brittle sulphide of silver. See STEPHANITE.

SCHWARZKOHLE. Common Coal. See COAL.

SCHWARZMANGANERZ, v. *Leonhard*. See PSILOMELANE.

SCHWARZSPIESSGLASERZ, *Werner*. See BOURNONITE.

SCHWATZITE, *Kenngott*. See SCHWARTZ-ERZ.

SCHWEFEL. German for *Sulphur*. Probably derived from the Arabic *Schail*, i. e. *lightning*.

SCHWEFEL UND KOHLENSAURES BLEI. See LANARKITE.

SCHWEFEL UND KOHLENSAURES BLEI UND KUPFER. See CALEDONITE.

SCHWEFELANTIMONBLEI. See BOULANGERITE.

SCHWEFELKIES, *Werner*. See PYRITES.

SCHWEFELKOBALT, *Berzelius*. See LINNÆITE.

SCHWEFELKOHLE. Friable pulverulent Lignite, impregnated with Pyrites, found in Picardy. (See CENDRES NOIRES.) It has been used with success to preserve timber, more especially that employed in railway constructions.

SCHWEFELNICKEL, v. *Leonhard*. See MILLERITE.

SCHWEFELSÄURES BLEI UND KUPFER, v. *Leonhard*. See LINARITE.

SCHWEFELSILBER UND ANTIMON, v. *Leonhard*. See FREIESLEBENITE.

SCHWER SPATH, *Werner*. See BARYTES.

SCHWERBLEIERZ, *Breithaupt*. See PLATTNERITE.

SCHWERSTEIN, *Werner*. See SCHEELITE.

SCHWIMMKIESEL,   } See FLOAT-
SCHWIMMSTEIN, *Werner*. } STONE.

SCLERETINITE, *J. W. Mallet*. A mineral resin, occurring in small round and oviform drops, varying in size from a pea to a hazelnut. Colour black. Translucent in thin splinters; reddish-brown by transmitted light. Lustre brilliant, vitreo-resinous. Streak cinnamon-brown. Gives out a slightly resinous odour when pulverised. Brittle. Fracture conchoidal. H. 3. S.G. 1·136.

Comp. $C^{10} H^7 O$.

Analysis, by *J. W. Mallet*:

Carbon   .   .   .   . 77·15

Hydrogen   .   .   .   . 9·05
Oxygen   .   .   .   . 10·12
Ash   .   .   .   .   . 3·68
                —
           100·00

BB on platinum foil, swells up, burns (like pitch) with a disagreeable smell and smoky flame. leaving a coal rather difficult to burn, and finally a little grey ash.

Insoluble in water, ether, alcohol, caustic alkalies or dilute acids. Slowly acted on by strong nitric acid.

Locality. The coal-measures of Wigan, in Lancashire.

Name. From σκληρòς, hard, and ρητίνη, resin, because of its hardness, which exceeds considerably that of other minerals of the same class.

Scleretinite more nearly approaches Amber ($C^{40} H^{32} O^4$) in composition than any other fossil resin.

SCOLECITE, *Dana*. SCOLEZITE, *Fuchs*, *Beudant, Greg & Lettsom*. Oblique. Occurs in long or short prismatic or acicular crystals; very often in twins: also massive, with a fibrous and radiating structure. Colourless; snow-white, greyish, yellowish and reddish. Transparent to translucent at the edges. Lustre vitreous; of fibrous varieties silky. Brittle. Fracture uneven. Pyro-electric. H. 5 to 5·5. S.G. 2·2 to 2·7.

Fig. 376.

Comp. $\ddot{C}a \ddot{S}i + \ddot{A}l \ddot{S}i + 3\dot{H}$ = silica 46·64, alumina 25·78, lime 14·04, water 13·54 = 100·00.

Analysis, from Staffa, by *Fuchs & Gehlen* :

Silica   .   .   .   . 46·75
Alumina   .   .   . 24·82
Lime   .   .   .   . 14·20
Soda   .   .   .   . 0·39
Water   .   .   .   . 13·64
                —
           99·80

BB twists and curls up at first in a vermicular shape, and then fuses readily to a blistered glass.

With muriatic acid behaves like Sodalite: dissolves in oxalic acid, with separation of oxalate of lime.

Localities. — *Scotch*. Staffa, in Argyleshire, in delicate white fibrous tufts, in trap rock and basalt. Near Loch Screden, in the Isle of Mull. Talisker, in Skye.—*Foreign.* Burufiord, in Iceland. Greenland. The Faröe Islands. The Tyrol. Vindhyah mountains, in Central India.

Name. From σκώληξ, *a worm*, in reference to its behaviour before the blowpipe.

Brit. Mus., Case 27.

For varieties of Scolezite, see ANTRIMO-LITE, POONAHLITE, &c.

SCOLERITE, *Dufrénoy.* See SCORILITE.

SCOLEXEROSE, *Beudant*, or Anhydrous Scolezite A Lime Labradorite, from Pargas in Finland. It has been referred to Scapolite.

Analysis, by *Nordenskiöld:*

Silica . . . . . 54·13
Alumina . . . 29·23
Lime . . . . 15·45
Water . . . . 1·07
                  ————
                  99·88

SCORILITE, *Thomson.* Occurs in reddish-brown masses, full of cavities, like a scoria. Easily reduced to powder. Colour of powder white. S.G. 1·71.

Locality. Mexico.

Name. From *scoria*, *cinder*, and λίθος, *stone.*

SCORODITE, *Breithaupt*, *Dufrénoy*, *Phillips.* Rhombic: primary form a right rhombic prism. Generally occurs in druses or globular groups of small prismatic crystals, terminated by four-sided pyramids. Colour pale leek-green or liver-brown. Transparent or translucent. Lustre vitreous. Streak white or pale greenish-grey. Rather brittle. Fracture uneven. H. 3·5 to 4. S.G. 3·1 to 3·3.

Fig. 377.

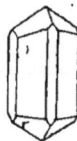

Comp. 2F̈e Äs + 2F̈e Äs + 12Ḧ (Berzelius), or F̈e Äs + 4Ḧ (Boussingault)=peroxide of iron 34·7, arsenic acid 49·8, water 15·5 = 100.

Analysis of bluish crystals, from Cornwall, by *Damour:*

Arsenic acid . . . 51·06
Peroxide of iron . . 32·74
Water . . . . 15·68
                  ————
                  99·48

BB behaves like Cube-ore: on charcoal fuses to a grey magnetic slag with metallic lustre, giving off arsenical fumes.

Caustic potash takes up the arsenic acid, and precipitates the peroxide of iron Readily soluble in muriatic acid.

Localities. — *English.* Formerly at Huel Gorland, Huel Unity, and several other mines near St. Day in Cornwall; on Ferruginous Quartz, and in pale bluish-green radiating groups, lining the interior of cavities.—*Foreign.* France: Vaulry; Chanteloube, near Limoges. Schwartzenberg, in Saxony (brown). Lölling, in Carinthia. Schlackenwald and Schönfeld, in Bohemia, in tin-ore. Antonio Pereira; Minas Geraes; in Brazil. Loaysa, near Marmato, in Popayan.

Name. From σκόροδον, *garlic*, in allusion to the smell of the arsenical fumes given off before the blowpipe.

Probably Scorodite is a result of the decomposition of Mispickel or other ores containing arsenic and iron, with which it is frequently associated. See NÉOCTÈSE.

Brit. Mus., Case 56.

SCORZA, or SKORZA. The name given by the people of Transylvania to the granular Epidote, which occurs in the form of sand near Muska, on the banks of the river Aranyos.

SCOTCH PEBBLE. Glandular concretions of Agate, displaying two or more colours, arranged in concentric laminæ. They are found abundantly in the amygdaloid of Dunbar, and the hill of Kinnoul, near Perth. See also AGATE, CAIRNGORM, CITRINE.

SCOTTISH MARBLE. A name given in Scotland to the Serpentine of Portsoy.

SCOULERITE, *Dana*, *Dufrénoy.* A bluish-grey kind of Pipestone, used by the North American Indians for making tobacco-pipes, and brought by Dr. Scouler from a locality which is unknown.

SCOULERITE, *Thomson.* A variety of Thomsonite, but containing less alumina and water, and as much as 6½ per cent. of soda. Occurs in small spherical concretions, composed of short fibres radiating from a centre, which are externally brownish-white, and reddish-brown internally, and pass into the compact variety Chalilite (which see).

Localities. — *Irish.* Portrush, Antrim co. Downhill, and Magilligan, Londonderry.

Name. After Dr. Scouler.

SEEERZ. See LIMONITE.

SEESALZ, *Werner.* See ROCK SALT.

SEIFENSTEIN, *Werner.* Soapstone. See SAPONITE.

SEL ADMIRABLE. See GLAUBER SALT.

SEL AMÈRE NATIF, *Brochant.* See EPSOMITE.

SEL AMMONIAC, *Romé de Lisle.*
SEL AMMONIAQUE, *Brochant.*
} See SAL AMMONIAC.

SEL CAPILLAIRE, *Brochant.* See HAIR SALT.

SEL D'ANGLETERRE, *Romé de Lisle.*
· SEL D'EPSOM, *Romé de Lisle.*
SEL D'EPSOM NATIF, *Brochant.*
} See EPSOMITE.

SEL DE GLAUBER, *Brochant, Romé de Lisle.* See GLAUBER SALT.

SEL DE SEDLITZ, *Romé de Lisle.* See EPSOMITE.

SEL MARIN, *Romé de Lisle.* See ROCK SALT.

SELADONITE. See GREEN EARTH.

SELBITE, *Haidinger.* A massive mineral, probably only a mechanical mixture, but considered by Hausmann to be identical with the Plata Azul of Mexican miners. It is of an ash-grey to a black colour, and very soft.

Analysis, by *Selb* :

Silver . . . . . 72·5
Carbonic acid . . . 12·0
Carbonate of antimony with oxide of copper . . . 15·5
_____
100·0

BB easily reduced.

Localities. Altwolfach, in Baden. Mexico.

Name. In compliment to Selb, by whom it was analysed.

M.P.G. Wall-case 14 on principal floor.

SELENBLEI, *H. Rose.* Selenide of lead. See CLAUSTHALITE.

SELENBLEIKUPFER. Selenide of lead and copper ; a variety of Clausthalite found in small fragments. Colour on a recent fracture between lead-grey and violet, or perfectly violet. Very soft. Somewhat malleable. S.G. 5·6.

Comp. Pb Se + Cu Se.

Analysis, from Tilkerode, by *H. Rose* :

Lead . . . . . 47·43
Selenium . . . 34·26
Copper . . . . 15·15
Silver . . . . 1·29
Peroxide of iron and lead . 2·08
_____
100·21

BB like Selenkupferblei, but fuses with greater facility. See SELENKUPFERBLEI.

SELENBLEISPATH, *Kersten.* See SELENATE OF LEAD.

SELENCOBALTLEAD, *Nicol.* See TILKERODITE.

SELENCOPPERLEAD, *Nicol.* See SELENKUPFERBLEI.

SELENCOPPERSILVER. See SELENKUPFERSILBER.

SELEN CUPRITE, *Shepard.* See BERZELIANITE.

SELENIC SILVER. See NAUMANNITE.

SELENIC SULPHUR. See SELENSULPHUR.

SELENIDE OF COPPER. See BERZELIANITE.

SELENIDE OF LEAD. See CLAUSTHALITE.

SELENIDE OF MERCURY. See ONOFRITE.

SELENIDE OF MERCURY AND LEAD. See LEHRBRACHITE.

SELENIET OF LEAD. See CLAUSTHALITE.

SELENITE, *Jameson, Brochant.* The name generally applied to the transparent varieties of Gypsum. Occurs generally in flattish crystals, the primary form of which is a right oblique angled prism. Cleaves with ease and brilliancy into thin laminæ, which are flexible but not elastic. Colour white, or various shades of yellow, grey, red, brown and violet. Lustre shining, sometimes pearly. More or less transparent. Yields to the nail. Streak white. H. 1·5 to 2. S.G. 2·28 to 2·33.

Fig. 378.

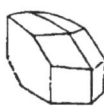
Fig. 379.

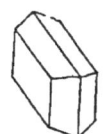
Fig. 380.

Fig. 381.

Comp. Hydrated sulphate of lime, or Ċa S̈ + 2Ḧ = lime 32·56, sulphuric acid 46·51, water 20·93 = 100.

BB becomes white and opaque, and fuses with difficulty to a white enamel.

Does not effervesce with acids, when pure.

Localities.—English. In the London Clay of London and Surrey ; the Isle of Sheppey ; of Walton-on-the Naze, in Essex. The Eocene clays of the Isle of Wight, at Alum Bay, and on the north coast between Newton and Cowes. Shotover Hill, Oxfordshire, in clay, in large transparent greyish-white crystals, *figs.* 379 to 381. Newhaven, in flattish crystals, 6 to 8 inches long. Telsford, Wilts.

Gloucestershire, in Lias. Aust Passage and Pyle Hill, near Bristol; and at Penarth and Cardiff, Glamorganshire. Cheshire. Alston Moor, Cumberland, *fig.* 878. Near Folkstone, in Kent, in gault. Epworth, in Lincolnshire. Somerset. Warwickshire, &c. &c.— *Scotch.* Banks of the Whitadder, Berwickshire, in red clay. Moffat, Dumfries shire. Hurlet, near Glasgow. — *Irish.* Kilroot, near Carrickfergus, co. Antrim. Ulster.—*Foreign.* Salt mines of Bex, in Switzerland. Hall, in the Tyrol. Sulphur mines of Sicily. Near Oçana, in Spain. Montmartre, near Paris. Near Lockport, in New York; Washington co., Virginia, and in other parts of the United States.

Name. From σελήνη, *the moon,* in allusion to the reflection it gives of the moon, as in a mirror; or rather from the vulgar belief formerly entertained in its being water congealed by the influence of the moon. See GYPSUM.

"The plates of this body were split, and anciently employed for the lights of windows, and when glass came afterwards to be more commonly made, and generally to obtain, they cut it into rhomboidal planes, in imitation of those plates, and framed them together with lead."—*J. Woodward*, 1729.

At Berenguela, in South America; some of the slabs of Alabaster quarried there are said by David Forbes[*] to be so transparent that tablets of it, until very lately, have been in general use in that part of Bolivia as a substitute for window - glass. He noticed that the windows of the church at Pisacoma were formed of this material, in slabs of about two inches thick.

See GYPSUM, ALABASTER, LAPIS SPECULARIS.

Brit. Mus., Case 54.

M. P. G. Horse-shoe Case, Nos. 286 — 299.

SELENIUM. See NATIVE SELENIUM.

SELENIUM SULPHUR. See SELENSULPHUR.

SELENIURE D'ARGENT, *Beudant.* See NAUMANNITE.

SELENIURE DE CUIVRE, *Berzelius.*
SELENIURET OF COPPER, *Phillips.* } See BERZELIANITE.

SELENIURET OF LEAD, *Phillips.* See CLAUSTHALITE.

SELENIURET OF LEAD AND COBALT, *Phillips.* See TILKERODITE.

SELENIURET OF LEAD AND COPPER, *Phillips.* See SELENBLEIKUPFER and SELENKUPFERBLEI.

SELENIURET OF LEAD AND MERCURY, *Phillips.* See LEHRBACHITE and SELENQUECKSILBERBLEI.

SELENIURET OF SILVER, *Phillips.* See NAUMANNITE.

SELENIURET OF SILVER AND COPPER, *Phillips.* See EUCAIRITE.

SELENKOBALTBLEI. Selencobalt lead. Clausthalite, in which cobalt replaces part of the lead. It is the Tilkerodite of Haidinger, and the Zorgite (in part) of Brooke & Miller.

SELENKUPFER. Selencopper. See BERZELIANITE.

SELENKUPFERBLEI. Selen-copper-lead. Occurs massive, of a paler lead-grey colour, and with a fainter lustre, than selenide of lead (*Clausthalite*). Often tarnished brassyellow or violet. H. 2 5. S.G. 6·96 to 7·04.

Comp. Selenide of copper and lead, or 2Pb Se + Cu Se.

Analysis, by *H. Rose* :

Lead	.	.	.	. 59·67
Copper	.	.	.	7·86
Selenium	.	.	.	29·96
Iron	.	.	.	0·83
Iron and lead	.	.	0·44
Undecomposed ore	.	1·00
				99·26

Localities. Tilkerode and Zorge, in the Harz, associated with Clausthalite. Glasbachgrund, in Thuringia.

Selenbleikupfer and Selenkupferblei are the names given to varieties of Clausthalite, in which a portion of the lead is replaced by copper. These have been called Raphanosmite by von Kobell, and Zorgite by Brooke & Miller.

SELENKUPFERSILBER, *v. Leonhard.* Selen-copper-silver. See EUCAIRITE.

SELENMERCUR. Selenide of Mercury. See ONOFRITE.

SELENPALLADITE, *Zinken.* Native Palladium, occurring in small, bright, hexagonal tables, of a pale steel-grey colour, at Tilkerode, in the Harz.

SELENQUECKSILBER. Selenide of Mercury. See ONOFRITE.

SELENQUECKSILBERBLEI. A mechanical mixture of Clausthalite and Selenide of Mercury, having the structure and colour of the former. S.G. 7·8.

Localities. Tilkerode and Lehrbach, in the Harz.

---

[*] Quarterly Journ. Geol. Soc. vol. xvii. p. 38.

SELENSCHWEFELQUECKSILBER. See ONO-
FRITE.

SELENSILBER, *Rose.* See NAUMANNITE.

SELENSULPHUR, *Dana, Stromeyer.* A
compound of selenium and sulphur, resembling the latter in appearance, but of an
orange or brownish colour. It occurs on
Vulcano, one of the Lipari Islands, and at
the volcano of Kilauea, in Hawaii.

Brit. Mus., Case 4.

M. P. G. Upper Gallery, Wall-case 1,
No. 20.

SELGEM, *Brochant.* SEL GEMME. SEL
GEMMERUM. Names for Common Salt,
"from its breaking frequently into Gemm-
like squares." (*Woodward.*) See ROCK
SALT.

SÉMÉLINE. An orange- and citron-yellow variety of Sphene, found in glassy trachyte, at the abbey of Laach, near Andernach, on *the left bank of the Rhine, by
Rose, who called it Spinelline.

Fig. 382.

Name. From *semen lini, linseed.*

SEMICARNELIAN. A name sometimes
given to yellow Carnelian.

SEMICOMPACT MINERAL PITCH, *Kirwan.*
See EARTHY BITUMEN.

SEMI-OPAL, *Kirwan, Jameson.* A dull
variety of Opal, which differs from common
Opal by its greater opacity, and the muddiness of its colours, its less perfect conchoidal fracture, and greater hardness and
weight. It is of various shades of white,
grey, yellow, brown and green, and is more
or less translucent, sometimes passing to
translucent at the edges. Very brittle.
When compact, the fracture is flat-conchoidal.

Analysis, from Hanau, by *Stucke :*

Silica	82·75
Peroxide of iron . . .	3·00
Alumina	3·50
Lime	0·25
Water	10·00
	99·50

Localities.—English. Cornwall: at Huel
Buller, near Redruth; near St. Ives and
St. Just. Oakhampton, in Devonshire. —
Foreign. Faröe Isles. Iceland. Steinheim,
near Hanau. Schiffenberg, near Giessen.

SENARMONTITE, *Dana.* Cubical. Occurs
in octahedrons, with an octahedral cleavage; also often in cavernous masses
composed of capillary filaments, parallel or
slightly divergent. Colourless or greyish.
Transparent to translucent. Lustre pearly;
resinous or adamantine on the natural faces,
and especially so in the fracture. Streak
white. Strongly refracting. Fracture uneven, often lamellar. H. 2 to 2·5. S.G. 5·22
to 5·3.

Comp. Teroxide of antimony, or Sb =
antimony 84·32, oxygen 15·68 = 100.

BB like Valentinite.

Insoluble in nitric acid; soluble in concentrated muriatic acid.

Localities. Sensa, near the sources of
Aïn-el-Belbouch, in the province of Con-
stantina, in Algeria; at another mine,
Mimina, in saccharoid masses, granular or
compact, covered with octahedral crystals.
Perneck, in Hungary.

Name. After H. de Senarmont, Professor
of Mineralogy at the Ecole des Mines, Paris.

SENECA OIL. The name given in some
parts of North America to a kind of Petroleum, which exudes from the rocks, or floats
on the surface of springs. It was named
after the Seneca Indians, a tribe famous in
the confederacy, known as the Six Nations,
by whom the oil in Pennsylvania was discovered and used.

A similar oil is found in abundance at
Amiano, in Italy; Burmah; on the borders
of the Caspian Sea; Trinidad. Along the
shore of the Kenawha, in Virginia; Kentucky, near Seneca Lake, New York; Duck
Creek, Ohio co.; and in great abundance
at Oil Creek, in Venango co., Pennsylvania.
In the north-western part of Pennsylvania
there is a subterranean spring of this oil, at
a depth of 71 feet from the surface, yielding
from 400 to 1600 gallons per day.

It is used as a medicine, both internally
and externally; and is an excellent stimu-
lating embrocation for chilblains, chronic
rheumatism, affections of the joints, para-
lysis, &c. It is also burned instead of oil
in lamps, and is one of the best lubricators
for machinery known. See PETROLEUM.

SEPIOLITE, *Glocker.* See MEERSCHAUM.

SEPTARIA. Rounded, and in most cases
somewhat flattened, nodular concretions of
argillaceous limestone, occurring at intervals in most clay formations, in layers
parallel with the stratification.

During the consolidation of the beds, the
calcareous matter contained in them appears to have separated from the muddy

sediment forming the clays in which the septaria are found, frequently collecting round shells, plants, or other organic substances. In the contraction undergone by these concretions during the process of solidification, they became traversed by cracks, which in many cases have subsequently become filled with an infiltration of carbonate of lime or Calc-spar, and it is from these *septa*, or divisions, that the concretions have derived their name of Septaria. The cracks generally form regular figures, all more or less partaking of a pentagonal shape, and the tendency of clayey matter to assume such figures in the contraction consequent on drying, may be observed on the surface of the mud of any shallow pool or puddle from which the water has dried off.

In consequence of the regularity of the patterns produced by the septa, Septaria are sometimes called "*Turtle-stones*," from their fancied resemblance to the plates forming the shell of a tortoise or turtle, the fossil remains of which they have been sometimes supposed to be by the ignorant. The turtle-stones from the Oxford Clay, of the neighbourhood of Weymouth, when cut and polished, form very handsome circular slabs for tables, examples of which may be seen in the entrance hall of the Museum of Practical Geology. (A 22, A 25.)

Septaria, when burned and ground, afford the best kind of Roman cement, and are in great request for that purpose. They are chiefly procured by dredging off the coasts of Essex, Hampshire, and Sussex, where they have accumulated at the bottom of the sea, after the softer materials forming the mainland have, by its destruction, been carried away. The septaria obtained from Harwich and Essex, as well as those from Chichester Harbour, on the coast of Sussex, have been derived from the London clay, while those found in Christchurch Bay belong to the Barton clay formation.

M. P. G. Table-case vi. in Hall: from Oxford clay, Upper Gallery, Wall-case 44.

Fig. 393.   Fig. 384.

SERBIAN, *Breithaupt.* See MILOSCHINE. The name is derived from that of the locality (*Serbia*) in which it is found.

SERICITE, *K. List.* A variety of Margarodite, allied to Damourite, occurring in undulating foliations. Colour greenish or yellowish-white, with a silky lustre. Found at Nerothal, near Wiesbaden, in slate, with Quartz and Albite. H. 1. S.G. 2·89.

SERIKOLITE. See SATIN SPAR.

SERPENTINE, *Jameson, Haüy, Phillips, Werner.* Usually occurs massive, granular, fibrous, or foliated; also as pseudomorphous crystals after Chrysolite, Augite, &c. Colour chiefly green; leek-green passing into greenish-black and blackish-green, sometimes oil- and olive-green, or yellow, rarely yellowish-brown. The colour is seldom uniform, but generally consists of several tints, arranged in dotted, striped, and clouded delineations. Faintly translucent at the edges to opaque. Lustre dull, or faintly glimmering. Streak white. Sectile. Tough. Fracture splintery, or conchoidal. Slightly unctuous to the touch. H. 3 to 4. S.G. 2·5 to 2·6.

Comp. Hydrated silicate of magnesia, or

$Mg^9 \ddot{S}i^4 \ddot{H}^6$ = magnesia 43·35, silica 43·64, water 13·01 = 100.

Analysis, from Ballinahinch in Galway:

Silica	40·12
Magnesia . . .	40·04
Alumina . .	2·00
Protoxide of iron . .	3·47
Water . . .	13·36
	98·99

BB on charcoal, fuses with difficulty at the edges: with borax dissolves readily, usually giving an iron reaction.

Soluble in muriatic and sulphuric acids.

Localities.—*English.* Kynance Cove, Goonhilly Downs, Cadgwith, and other places in the Lizard district. Anglesea; Pary's mine and Bullock's quarry.—*Scotch.* Alie Hills, Aberdeenshire. Portsoy, in Banffshire. Killin, Perthshire (*fibrous*). Swinaness, in the Shetlands. — *Irish.* Ballynahinch quarries, co. Galway. Co. Wicklow, near Westport. Co. Mayo. — *Foreign.* Zöblitz, in Upper Saxony. Bohemia. Silesia. Corsica. Italy. Siberia. Canada, at Gaspé Mount, &c.

Name. From its fancied resemblance to the markings on the skin of a serpent.

Serpentine has been divided into *Precious* or *Noble Serpentine*, comprising the purer translucent and massive varieties, with a rich oil-green colour. 2nd, *Common Serpentine*, or the opaque varieties forming extensive rock masses like those of the Lizard, Portsoy, Anglesea, and Zöblitz. 3rd, *Fibrous*

Serpentine, including Baltimorite, Chrysotile, Metaxite, Picrolite. 4th, *Foliated Serpentine*, comprising Antigorite, Marmolite, &c.

The purer forms of Serpentine are called by T. Sterry Hunt *Normal Serpentine*, and other varieties *Calcareous, Dolomitic*, and *Magnesitic Ophiolite*, according to the nature of the ingredient which may be present in the Serpentine.

Serpentine, though soft, takes a good polish, and forms a very beautiful ornamental stone. It has long been converted into various objects at Zöblitz; and, within the last few years, works have been established in Cornwall, where, by the aid of machinery, it is made into columns, chimney-pieces, vases, and other ornamental articles. Formerly it was sent to Bristol in considerable quantities, where it was used in the manufacture of carbonate of magnesia.

Brit. Mus., Case 25.

M. P. G. Irish Serpentine (Connemara marble) in Hall; Pilasters 2, 7; Pedestal 43; Columns 24, 37; Tazza on column of alabaster, 34; Cornish serpentine in Hall, Pedestals 28, 36; Columns 30, 57; Screen on eastern wall; Table-top *A* 24; Tazza on Pedestal 32; Inlaid Table-top A 11, under Case IV. Horse-shoe Case, Nos. 1066 to 1077, 1081 to 1084, 1092, 1093; Upper Gallery, Wall-case 5.

SESQUIARSENIET OF IRON, *Thomson*. See LEUCOPYRITE.

SESQUICARBONATE of SODA. See TRONA.

SEVERITE. A variety of Halloysite, occurring in small masses, and somewhat resembling Lithomarge. Colour white, without lustre, but slightly translucent. Soft, yielding easily to the knife, and receiving a high degree of polish by friction. Adheres strongly to the tongue. Fracture conchoidal.

The name is derived from the locality, St. Sever, in France, where it is found in the upper sandy deposits in tertiary Gypsum, in masses from two to five inches in diameter.

Comp. Äl S̈i + 2Ḧ.

Analysis, by *Pelletier*:

Silica	.	.	.	. 50
Alumina	.	.	.	. 22
Water	.	.	.	. 26
Loss	.	.	.	. 2

　　　　　　　　　　　　　100

SEXALUMINATE OF LEAD, *Thomson*. See PLOMBGOMME.

SEYBERTITE. The name given by Clem-son to Clintonite, occurring in beds of granular limestone, associated with Serpentine, at Amity, New York.

SHALE, *Kirwan*. Is rather a rock than a mineral, in the strict sense of the term, being an argillaceous deposit, generally of a grey or bluish colour, forming sometimes beds of considerable thickness in many formations, especially the Coal-measures. It is soft, earthy, and opaque, with a lamellar or slaty structure, yields to the knife readily, adheres to the tongue, and is meagre to the touch. S.G. about 2·6.

SHEPARDITE. A meteoric mineral called Schreibersite by Professor C. U. Shepard, in compliment to whom the present name was given by Haidinger.

SHORL, *Kirwan*. See SCHORL.

SHORL SPAR, *Kirwan*. Crystallized common Actinolite.

SIBERITE. A name for Rubellite, or red Tourmaline; after Siberia, one of its localities, *fig.* 385.

Fig. 385.

Brit. Mus., Case 38.

SIDERITE. A vitreous variety of Quartz, of an indigo or Berlin-blue colour, from Golling, near Salzburg.

SIDERITE, *Greg & Lettsom, Haidinger, Nicol*. (From σιδηρος, iron.) Sparry iron. See CHALYBITE.

SIDERITE. A name sometimes given to Cube Ore. See PHARMACOSIDERITE.

SIDERITE AIMANT, *Necker*. Magnetic Iron Ore. See MAGNETITE.

SIDERITE CHROMIFÈRE, *Necker*. Chromate of iron. See CHROMIC IRON.

SIDERITE TITANIQUE, *Necker*. Titanate of iron. See ILMENITE.

SIDERITE ZINCIFÈRE, *Necker*. See FRANKLINITE.

SIDERITINE, *Beudant*. (From σιδηρος, iron, and ρητίνη, resin.) See PITTICITE.

SIDEROCLEPTE, *Saussure*. A reddish crystalline mineral, with every appearance of an altered substance, and occuring under the same conditions as Chusite.

SIDEROMELANE. (From σιδηρος, iron, and μέλας, black.) An amorphous, ferruginous Labradorite.

SIDEROPLESITE. The name given by Breithaupt to a variety of Sparry Iron, the composition of which is represented by the formula, $\ddot{M}g \ddot{C} + 2\ddot{F}e \ddot{C}$=carbonate of magnesia 26·58, carbonate of iron 73·42=100. S.G. 3·616 to 3·66.

Analysis, by *Fritzsche* :

Carbonic acid	.	. 41·93
Protoxide of iron	.	. 45·06
Magnesia	.	. 12·16

99·15

Localities. — Pöhl, an island in the Baltic. Böhmsdorf, near Schleitz, in Upper Saxony. Traversella, in Piedmont.

Name. From σίδηρος, *iron*, and πλησίος, *a neighbour*.

SIDEROCHALCIT, *Breithaupt.* See APHANESITE.

SIDEROSCHISOLITE, *Wernekinck, Phillips.* Occurs in small, six-sided, black prisms, which are often grouped hemispherically. Basal cleavage perfect. Lustre brilliant. Opaque. Streak green, or greenish-grey. H. 2·5. S.G. 3.

Comp. $\dot{F}e^6 \ddot{S}i + \dot{H}$.

Analysis, by *Wernekinck* :

Silica	.	. 16·3
Protoperoxide of iron	.	. 75·5
Alumina	.	. 4·1
Water	.	. 7·3

103·2

BB fuses readily to a black magnetic glass.

Soluble in muriatic acid, with the formation of a jelly of silica.

Locality.—Conghonas do Campo, in Brazil, in cavities in iron ores.

Name. From σίδηρος, *iron*, σχιστός, *cleavable*, and λίθος, *stone.*

Brit. Mus., Case 26.

SIDEROSE, *Beudant.* (From σίδηρος, *iron.*) Sparry iron. See CHALYBITE.

SIDEROTANTAL. See TANTALITE.

SIEGELERDE. Seal Earth. See SPHRAGIDE.

SIEGENITE. A name for Cobalt Pyrites, after the locality, Siegen, where it occurs. See LINNÆITE.

SILBER-UND-ANTIMON. See FREIESLEBENITE.

SILBERBLENDE, *Breithaupt.* Red silver. See PYRARGYRITE.

SILBERFAHLERZ. Those varieties of Tetrahedrite in which part of the copper is replaced by silver.

SILBERGLANZ, *v. Leonhard.* See SILVER GLANCE.

SILBERHORNERZ. See KERARGYRITE.

SILBERKUPFERGLANZ, *Stromeyer.* Cu-

preous sulphide of Silver. See STROMEYERITE.

SILBERMULM. An earthy variety of Silver Glance, of a dark bluish-black colour, found in several of the mines in Saxony. See SILVER-BLACK.

SILBERPHYLLINGLANZ, *Breithaupt.* According to Plattner, it is a mixture of Selensilver and Selenmolybdena, containing a small quantity of gold. It occurs in dark grey foliated masses, with a perfect cleavage in one direction, at Deutsch - Pilsen, in Hungary, in gneiss. H. 1 to 2. S.G. 5·8 to 5·9.

SILBERSCHWARZ, *Estner, Reuss, Werner.* or SILBERSCHWÄRZE. Black Silver. See SILBERMULM and SILVER-BLACK.

SILBER-SPIESSGLANZ, *Hausmann.* See DISCRASITE.

SILBERWISMUTHGLANZ Silver-bismuthglance. See BISMUTH SILVER.

SILEX NECTIQUE. See FLOATSTONE.

SILICATE OF BISMUTH, *Thomson.* See EULYTINE.

SILICATE OF CERIUM, *Wollaston, Phillips.* See CERITE.

SILICATE OF IRON, *Thomson, Phillips.* See FAYALITE.

SILICATE OF MANGANESE, *Allan.* See RHODONITE.

SILICATE OF YTTRIA, of a brown colour, according to *Damour*, is found in the diamond-sands of Bahia in Brazil. H. 5 to 6. S.G. 4·391.

SILICATE OF ZINC. See MANCINITE, SMITHSONITE, WILLEMITE.

SILICE FLUATÉE ALUMINEUSE, *Haüy.* See TOPAZ.

SILICE GELATINEUSE. See RANDANITE.

SILICEOUS BORATE OF LIME. See DATHOLITE.

SILICEOUS CALAMINE, *L. Gmelin.* See SMITHSONITE.

SILICEOUS HYDRATE OF MAGNESIA, *Thomson.* See NEMALITE.

SILICEOUS OXIDE OF ZINC, *Phillips.* See SMITHSONITE. This name has also been applied by some authors to Willemite.

SILICEOUS SINTER. Amorphous silica deposited in the state of light cellular Quartz, or as opaline silica, by the waters of hot springs, whose solvent powers are due to their temperature and the presence of a small quantity of alkali. Silica is held in solution in the Geysers of Iceland and New Zealand, and traces of it are also present in ordinary waters as alkaline silicates. (See also PEARL SINTER or FIORITE.) The siliceous sinter deposited from the hot springs of the Geyser forms reniform, stalactitic, fibrous, porous, cauliflower-like, and sometimes even compact incrustations.

Brit. Mus., Case 21.

M. P. G. Upper Gallery, Wall-case 1, Nos. 95—99 (Ascension); 127, 128 (New Zealand); Table-case A in recess 4, No. 4 (Iceland).

SILICIFEROUS HYDRATE OF ALUMINA, *Phillips.* See COLLYRITE.

SILICIFEROUS OXIDE OF CERIUM. See CERITE.

SILICIFEROUS OXIDE OF MANGANESE, *Phillips.* See RHODONITE.

SILICIFIED WOOD. Wood petrified by silica or quartz, and sometimes converted into Chalcedony or Agate. It usually retains the structure of the original wood, and in the silicified palm-trees found in the Desert near Cairo, the arrangement of the cellular tissue is also preserved. Very fine examples of this conversion of wood into stone are also met with in the Island of Trinidad and other places.

Brit. Mus., Case 22.

M. P. G. Horse-shoe Case, Nos. 755, 758, 762. Case on model No. 29 (Antigua); Lower Gallery (west side), on floor near the stairs. Upper Gallery, Wall-case 42, Nos. 38 to 44 (British), 45.

SILICITE. The name given by Thomson to a yellowish-white Labradorite, from Antrim in Ireland. It has a vitreous lustre, and breaks with a conchoidal fracture. S.G. 2·66.

Analysis, by *Thomson:*

Silica :	. . . . 54·8
Alumina	. . . . 28·4
Peroxide of iron	. . . 4·0
Lime	. . . . . 12·4
Water	. . . . . 0·6
	100·2

SILLIMANITE, *Bowen.* Oblique: primary form an oblique rhombic prism. Cleavage perfect and brilliant. Occurs in slender prisms,often flattened and striated,imbedded in Quartz; also fibrous, columnar, and compact massive. Colour dark grey, passing into clove-brown. Translucent to transparent. Lustre vitreous, approaching subadamantine on the cleavage face. Streak white. Brittle, and easily reduced to powder. Fracture uneven, splintery. H. 6 to 7·25. S.G. 3·23 to 3·26.

Comp. Anhydrous silicate of alumina, or

$\ddot{A}l$ $\ddot{S}i$ = alumina 63, silica 37 = 100.

Analysis, from Chester County, by *Silliman:*

Silica	. . . . . 37·65
Alumina	. . . . 62·41
	100·06

BB alone unaltered: with borax fuses slowly to a transparent colourless glass.

Localities. Connecticut: at Chester, near Saybrook, in a vein of gneiss; Falls of the Yantic, near Norwich; Yorktown, New York.

Name. After Prof. Silliman.

Brit. Mus., Case 26.

Sillimanite may be readily distinguished from Anthophyllite, which it resembles, and for which it was formerly mistaken, by its superior hardness. For fibrous massive varieties, see BUCHOLZITE and FIBROLITE.

SILVANE BLANC, *Brochant.* Sylvanite of Nagyag, in Transylvania.

SILVANE GRAPHIQUE, *Brochant.* Graphic Tellurium. Sylvanite of Offenbanya.

SILVANE LAMELLEUX, *Brochant.* Foliated Tellurium. See NAGYAGITE.

SILVANE NATIF, *Brochant.* See NATIVE TELLURIUM.

SILVANITE, *Haidinger, Nicol.* See SYLVANITE.

SILVER-BLACK, *Jameson.* An earthy form of Silver Glance, of a dark bluish-black colour, found in several of the mines of Saxony and Hungary, associated with other ores of silver.

SILVER GLANCE, *Jameson.* Cubical; primary form the cube: also occurs in octahedrons and ♦hombic dodecahedrons, with traces of dodecahedral cleavage. Also reticulated, dendritic, stalactitic and amorphous. Colour blackish lead-grey; acquiring on exposure a superficial iridescent tarnish. Opaque. Lustre metallic. Malleable and sectile, yielding easily to the knife, and cutting like lead. Streak shining and like the colour. Flexible. Difficultly frangible. Fracture small-grained-uneven, sometimes inclining to imperfect-conchoidal. H. 2 to 2·5. S.G. 7·2 to 7·36.

Fig. 386.   Fig. 387,   Fig. 388.

Comp. Sulphide of silver,.or Ag S = silver 87·1, sulphur 12·9 = 100.

Analysis, from Joachimsthal, by *Lindaker:*

Silver	. . . . . 77·58
Sulphur	. . . . 14·46
Iron	. . . . . 2·02

Copper   .   .   .   1·53
Lead   .   .   .   .   3·68
——
99·27

BB or in the flame of a candle, the sulphur is driven off with intumescence, and the silver is reduced to its metallic state.

Soluble in tolerably strong sulphuric acid, with separation of sulphur.

Localities. — English. Cornwall: at Huel Herland, *fig.* 387. Huel Ann, Dolcoath Mine, Mexico Mine, Huel Duchy (*earthy*), Huel Vincent, Huel Basset. — *Foreign.* Siberia. Kongsberg, in Norway. Joachimsthal, in Bohemia. Schemnitz and Kremnitz, in Hungary. Schneeberg, Annaberg, Johanngeorgenstadt, Freiberg, in Saxony. Dauphiny. Mexico. Peru, Tenessee, and Northern Michigan, United States. Lake Superior.

Brit. Mus., Case 10.

M. P. G. Principal Floor, Wall-cases 14 (British); 22 (Foreign).

Silver Glance constitutes a valuable ore of silver. See also SILVER BLACK.

SILVER MULM. See SILVER BLACK.

SILVERPHYLLINGLANZ. See SILBERPHYLLINGLANZ.

SILVER-WHITE COBALT.   See COBALTINE.

SILVERY CHALK, *Kirwan.* See APHRITE.

SINKANITE, *Croerning.* A mechanical mixture of Galena, Anglesite, and Sulphur, from the lead mines of New Sinka, in Transylvania. It was first found at Dufton, and described by Johnston, and was subsequently named Johnstonite by Haidinger. See JOHNSTONITE.

SINOPITE, *Hausmann.* The Bole of Sinope.

SINOPLE, *Kirwan.* A dark red kind of Jasper, said to contain 18 per cent. of iron. S.G. 2·691. It occurs with auriferous ores at Schemnitz, in Hungary.

SISMONDINE, *Delesse.* A foliated variety of Chloritoid, of a dark greyish, or blackish-green colour, occurring at St. Marcel, in Piedmont, in chlorite-slate. Streak bright greyish-green. Brittle. H. 5·5. S.G. 5·36.

Comp. $\ddot{S}i^3 \dot{F}e^4 + 5\ddot{A}l \dot{H}$.

Name. After Mons. A. de Sismonda, Professor of Mineralogy at the University of Turin.

SISSERSKITE, *Haidinger.* A name for a variety of Iridosmine, derived from that of a locality, Sissersk, in the Ural. It occurs in six-sided scales of a steel-grey colour. H. 7. S.G. 21·11.

SKAPOLITH, *Werner.* See SCAPOLITE.

SKOGBÖLITE. The name proposed by Nordenskiöld for the varieties of Tantalit found at Skogböle, and Härkäsaari, in Finland. See TAMMELA-TANTALITE and TANTALITE.

SKOLECITE. See SCOLECITE.

SKOLOPSITE, *v. Kobell.* Occurs granular-massive, with no traces of cleavage. Colour greyish-white or reddish-grey. Translucent in thin splinters. Rather brittle. Fracture splintery. H. 5. S.G. 2·53.

Analysis, by *v. Kobell:*

Silica   .   .   .   .   41·13
Alumina   .   .   .   15·42
Protoperoxide of iron   .   2·49
Protoxide of manganese   .   0·86
Lime   .   .   .   .   15·48
Magnesia   .   .   .   2·23
Potash   .   .   .   1·30
Soda   .   .   .   10·06
Sulphuric acid   .   .   4·09
Sodalite   .   .   7·78
——
100·84

BB swells up and fuses to a shining, blebby, greenish-white glass. With borax forms a colourless glass.

Easily gelatinises in muriatic acid.

Locality. Kaiserstuhl, in Breisgau.

SKORODIT, *Breithaupt.* See SCORODITE.

SKORZA. See SCORZA.

SKUTTERUDITE, *Haidinger.* Cubical, with a distinct cubic cleavage. Occurs crystallized and massive granular. Colour between tin-white and lead-grey, with an iridescent tarnish sometimes. Lustre metallic. H. 6. S.G. 6·74 to 6·84.

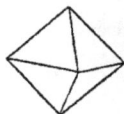

Fig. 389.

Comp. $CoAs^2$=cobalt 20·8, arsenic 79·2 = 100.

Analysis, of massive, from Skutterud:

Arsenic   .   .   .   .   79·0
Copper   .   .   .   .   19·5
Iron   .   .   .   .   1·4
——
99·9

BB like Smaltine nearly.

Locality.— Skutterud (whence the name Skutterudite), near Modum, in Norway.

SLAGGY MINERAL PITCH, *Jameson.* See ASPHALT.

SLATE COAL, *Jameson.* Coal with a slaty structure, and an uneven small-grained cross-fracture. The coal in the neighbourhood of Newcastle, and from Bolton to

Whitehaven, is of this description; as also much of that in the districts of the Forth and the Clyde, in Scotland, as well as of Dumfries-shire. See HARD COAL.

SLATE CLAY, *Jameson, Kirwan.* See SHALE.

SLATE SPAR, *Jameson.* A massive variety of carbonate of lime, occurring in very thin parallel laminæ, of a milk-greenish or reddish-white colour. It is friable, soft, and tender, and has a pearly lustre. Translucent. Yields easily to the knife, and often feels greasy. S.G. about 2·5.

Localities.—English. Cornwall : at Botallack, near St. Just; Delabole, near St.Teath; North Roskear; and Polgooth Mine, Beeraiston, in Devonshire. Coniston United Mine, Lancashire. — *Scotch.* Strontian, Argyllshire. Glen Tilt, Perthshire. Assynt, Sutherland .— *Irish.* Co. Wicklow; at Glendalough and Lugganure lead mines. Kilkenny. Carlow. Kildare.— *Foreign.* Königsberg, in Norway. Bergrun, near Schwarzenberg, in Saxony.

Brit. Mus., Case 45.

SLATY COAL. See SLATE COAL.

SLATY COPPER ORE, *Kirwan.* KUPFERSCHIEFFER.

SLOANITE, *Meneghini & Bechi.* Occurs in white and opaque radiated masses, with a pearly lustre, and frequently a fracture transverse to the radiations. H. 4·5. S.G. 2·44.

Comp. $(\dot{C}a\dot{M}g)^3 \ddot{S}i^2 + 5 \ddot{A}l \ddot{S}i + 9\dot{H}.$

Analysis, by *Bechi :*

Silica	42·19
Alumina . . .	35·00
Lime	8·12
Magnesia . . .	2·67
Soda	0·25
Potash	0·30
Water	12·50
	101·03

BB swells up and fuses to a white enamel. Soluble in acids, forming a jelly of silica.

Locality. Tuscany, in gabbro rosso.

Name. After Mr. Henry Sloane, proprietor of the mine of Monte Catini, in Tuscany.

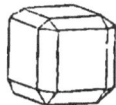  

Fig. 390.   Fig. 391.   Fig. 392.

SMALTINE, *Beudant, Haidinger, Nicol.*

Cubical, with a cleavage parallel to the faces both of the octahedron and cube. Occurs in octahedrons, cubes, and their modifications; also in reticulated, arborescent, botryoidal reniform and amorphous masses. Colour tin-white inclining to steel-grey when massive, and sometimes with a superficial greyish or iridescent tarnish. Opaque. Lustre metallic. Yields to the knife with difficulty. Streak greyish-black. Brittle. Fracture fine-grained and uneven. H. 5·5 to 6. S.G. 6·46 to 7·7.

Comp. Arsenide of cobalt, or (Co,Fe,Ni) $As =$ cobalt 9·4, iron 9·0, nickel 9·5, arsenic 72·1 = 100.

Analysis, from Joachimsthal, by *F. Marian :*

Arsenic	74·52
Cobalt	11·72
Iron	5·26
Nickel	1·81
Copper	1·00
Sulphur	1·81
	96·12

BB on charcoal gives off copious arsenical fumes, and fuses to a white, brittle, metallic globule, which after being roasted imparts a blue colour to glass. Soluble in hot nitric acid, with separation of arsenious acid.

Localities. — English. Cornwall, at Huel Sparnon, arborescent and reticulated on Quartz, and at the following mines : Dolcoath, St. Austell Consols, Huel Herland, Wherry, Botallack, &c. Force Craig, near Keswick, in Cumberland. — *Scotch.* Essochossan Glen, Argyllshire. Breeton, near Alva, in Stirlingshire. — *Foreign.* Tunaberg, in Sweden. Freiberg, Annaberg, and particularly at Schneeberg, in Saxony. Joachimsthal, in Bohemia. Andreasberg, in the Harz. Riechelsdorf, in Hesse. Allemont, in Dauphiny. Chatham, in Connecticut, U. S. (*Chathamite*).

Brit. Mus., Case 4.

M P. G. Principal Floor, Wall-case 9 (British).

Under the name Smaltine are, strictly speaking, included only the Cobaltic varieties represented by the formula CoAs= cobalt 28·2, arsenic 71·8 = 100. The nickel variety, represented by the formula NiAs, or nickel 28·3, arsenic 91·7, is called Chloanthite. These varieties merge into one another by gradual transitions.

Smaltine is one of the most important ores of Cobalt, being (with Cobaltine) that from which the greater part of the Smalts of commerce is manufactured. In this form it is used for painting and colouring glass and porcelain, and is the colour employed in printing the common blue willow-pattern earthenware, with which everybody is familiar. It is also employed for imparting a blue tint to paper and linen, and when ground and washed, forms a cheap and durable paint. The arsenic driven off in roasting the ore is also condensed and collected.

SMARAGD, *Estner.* } See EMERALD,
SMARAGDUS, *Wallerius.* } and BERYL.

SMARAGDIT, *Saussure.* SMARAGDITE, *Phillips, Leymerie.* A peculiar laminated form of Augite or Hornblende, with a cleavage parallel to the sides, and diagonals of a slightly rhombic prism. Colour bright or emerald-green. Transparent at the edges to opaque. Lustre silky or pearly. Yields to the knife. H. 5 to 6. S.G. 3.

Analysis, by *T. Sterry Hunt:*

Silica	54·30
Alumina	4·54
Lime	13·72
Magnesia	19·01
Soda	2·80
Protoxide of iron	3·87
Oxide of chrome	0·61
Oxide of nickel	traces
Loss by ignition	0·30
	99·15

BB fuses to a grey or greenish enamel.

Localities. Monte Rosa, and near Geneva, in Switzerland. Corsica, in Felspar.

Name. From σμάραγδος, *emerald*, in allusion to its colour.

Brit. Mus., Case 31.

According to Hisinger and De la Fosse, Smaragdite consists of laminæ of Pyroxene and Hornblende, united in a more or less regular manner.

The Smaragdite, which occurs in the Euphotide of the Swiss Alps, has been lately examined by T. Sterry Hunt, who pronounces it to be a Pyroxene containing chrome and nickel, with some admixture of Saussurite, and probably also of Talc. See analysis.

SMARAGDO-CHALCIT, *Breithaupt.* Emerald Copper. See DIOPTASE.

SMECTITE, *Salvetat.* A greenish kind of Halloysite from Condé, near Houdan, in France.

Comp. $\ddot{A}l^2 \ddot{S}i^3 + 7\frac{1}{2}\dot{H}$.

Analysis, by *Salvetat:*

Silica	43·00
Alumina	32·50
Gelatinous silica	1·50
Lime	1·02
Protoxide of iron	1·02
Magnesia	0·30
Potash and soda	0·40
Water	21·70
	101·44

SMECTITE, *Breithaupt.* An Halloysite-like substance from Cilly, in Lower Styria, and Zeng, in Croatia.

Analysis, by *L. A. Jordan:*

Silica	51·21
Alumina	12·25
Peroxide of iron	2·07
Lime	2·13
Magnesia	4·89
Water	27·89
	100·44

Name. From σμηκτός, *smeared*, on account of its greasy feel.

SMELITE. (From σμηλή, *soap*.) A greyish white or bluish kind of Kaolin, found in trachytic porphyry, near Telkebanya, in Hungary. Lustre dull. Opaque. Fracture conchoidal. May be worked in the lathe, and takes a polish when rubbed. Adheres slightly to the tongue, and feels unctuous to the touch. H. 2·5. S.G. 2·168.

Analysis, by *Oswald:*

Silica	50·0
Alumina	32·0
Peroxide of iron	2·0
Soda	2·1
Lime, magnesia and sulphuric acid	traces
Water	13·0
	99·1

BB infusible.

Scarcely acted on by boiling muriatic acid.

SMERALDO, *La Metherie, Brochant.* See EMERALD.

SMIRGEL. A name for Corundum mixed with Quartz and Magnetite; probably the σμύρις of the ancient Greeks.

SMITHSONITE. *Beudant, Dana, Haidinger, v. Kobell, Leymerie.* See CALAMINE.

SMITHSONITE, *Greg & Lettsom.* Rhombic: commonly with hemihedral terminations. Primary form a right rhombic prism. Occurs in attached crystals; also stalactitic, botryoidal, granular, and compact. Colourless; sometimes grey, blue, yellow, green or brown. Transparent to translucent or opaque. Lustre vitreous, inclining to adamantine. Streak white. Brittle. Fracture uneven. Becomes phosphorescent when rubbed, and electric by heat. H. 5. S.G. 3·16 to 3·38.

Fig. 393.

Fig. 394.

Comp. Silicate of zinc, or $2\ddot{Z}n^3 \overset{...}{S}i + \overset{..}{H} =$ oxide of zinc 67·4, silica 25·1, water 7·5.

Analysis, from Limburg, by *Berzelius*:

Oxide of zinc	. . . 66·37
Silica	26·23
Water . . .	7·40
	100·00

BB decrepitates; does not fuse, but swells up when strongly ignited; intumesces slightly with carbonate of soda, but does not dissolve in it, and gives, though not readily, a deposit of Zinc-oxide.

Dissolves readily in acids, with separation of a siliceous jelly; dissolves for the most part in caustic potash.

Localities. — *English.* Cumberland, at Roughten Gill, and Alston Moor. Derbyshire: at the Rutland Mine, *fig.* 394; near Matlock, at Masson Hill and Castleton. Mendip Hills, Somersetshire. — *Welsh.* Near Holywell, in Flintshire. — *Scotch.* Leadhills, in Lanarkshire. — *Foreign.* Nertschinsk, in Siberia. Aix-la-Chapelle. Raibel, in Carinthia. Tarnowitz, in Silesia. Olkucz, Miedziana-Gora, in Poland. Rezbanya, Schemnitz, in Hungary. Jefferson co., Missouri. Austin's Mines, Wythe co., Virginia.

Name. After the chemist, Smithson.

Brit. Mus., Case 26.

M.P.G. Principal Floor, Wall-case 12 (British).

SMOKE QUARTZ, *Bakewell*, or SMOKY QUARTZ. Has a brownish, smoke coloured tint, and comprises the wine-yellow and clove-brown crystals, which are the true Cairngorm. It is found in Scotland, Bohemia, Pennsylvania, Brazil, &c. See CAIRNGORM, FALSE TOPAZ, MORION, and TOPAZINE QUARTZ.

Brit. Mus., Case 20.

M. P. G. Horse-shoe Case, Nos 507, 508.

SMUT, or MUCKS. Names given by Derbyshire miners to bad, soft coal, containing much earthy matter, found in the immediate neighbourhood of faults, or decomposed near the surface by the influence of atmospheric causes.

SOAPSTONE, *Nicol, Phillips.* See SAPONITE. The name is also applied to Steatite (which see).

SODA ALUM, *Phillips, Thomson.* Occurs in white fibrous crusts or masses, exhibiting a glossy aspect internally. H. 2 to 3. S.G. 1·88.

Resembles potash-alum in taste, but is more soluble in water.

Comp. $\overset{..}{S} \overset{.}{N}a + \overset{..}{A}l \overset{..}{S}^3 24\overset{..}{H}$, or sulphate of soda 15·5, sulphate of alumina 37·4, water 47·1 = 100.

Analysis, from Mendoza, by *Thomson*:

Sulphuric acid .	. . 37·70
Alumina . . .	. . 12 00
Soda	. 7·96
Water . . .	. 41·96
	99·62

Localities. — St. Juan, near Mendoza, in S. America. Near the Solfatara, Naples. Island of Milo.

Brit. Mus., Case 55.

SODA CHABAZITE. See GMELINITE.

SODA COPPERAS. A mineral from Bohemia, related to Jarosite.

Analysis, by *Scheerer*:

Sulphuric acid .	. . 32·42
Protoxide of iron	. . 49·37
Soda	. 4·03
Water . . .	. 13·13
	98·95

SODA MESOTYPE. See NATROLITE.

SODA NITRE. See NITRATINE.

SODA SPODUMENE. See OLIGOCLASE.

SODA TABLE-SPAR, *Thomson.* A variety of Pectolite, met with at Kilsyth, in Stirlingshire.

SODA WALLASTONITE, *Thomson.* See PECTOLITE.

SODAÏTE. See EKEBERGITE.

SODALITE, *Phillips, Thomson, Haüy, Nicol.* Cubical. Generally occurs crystallized in

Fig. 395.

rhombic dodecahedrons, with a dodecahedral cleavage: also massive. Colour white, grey, vellowish, greenish, blue. Translucent. Lustre vitreous. Yields with difficulty to the knife. Fracture conchoidal. H. 5·5 to 6. S.G. 2·26 to 2·37.

Comp. $\dot{N}a^3 \ddot{S}i + 3\ddot{A}l \ddot{S}i + Na \, Cl$ = silica 37·2, alumina 31·7, soda 19·1, sodium 4·7, chlorine 7·3 = 100.

Analysis, from Greenland, by *Ekeberg*:

Silica	36·60
Alumina : . .	32·00
Soda	25·00
Peroxide of iron .	0·15
Muriatic acid . .	6·75
	99·90

BB fuses easily, sometimes tranquilly, sometimes swelling up and forming a blistered glass.

With muriatic acid, readily yields a siliceous jelly.

Localities.—The Kangerdluarsukfiord, W. Greenland, of a green colour. Ilmen Mountains, in the Ural. Near Brevig, in Norway. The Kaiserstuhl, in the Briesgau, massive, of a grey colour, in trap rock. Vesuvius, in large white dodecahedral crystals. Val di Nuto, in Sicily. Rüden, near Laach. United States: at Lichfield, Maine, in a granitic rock; Salem, Massachusetts, in a vein six feet wide, in syenitic porphyry.

Name. From *soda*, and λίθος, *stone*, in allusion to the soda it contains.

Brit. Mus., Case 31.

SOFT COAL. See CAKING COAL.

SOIMONITE. See CORUNDUM.

SOLFATARITE, *Shepard.* Soda alum. The name is in allusion to its occurrence at the Solfatara, near Naples.

SOMERVILLITE, *Brooke, Phillips.* A variety of Mellilite, of a dull yellow colour, occurring among the older scoria of Vesuvius, associated with black Mica, &c. It may be distinguished from Idocrase by decrepitating before the blowpipe, and by yielding alone, a *grey* globule. It was named by Brooke after Dr. Somerville, from whom he obtained his specimens.

Brit. Mus., Case 35.

SOMMIT, *Karsten.* ⎰ A name for Nephe-
SOMMITE, *Phillips.* ⎱ line, in allusion to its occurrence at Monte Somma, the ancient crater of Vesuvius.

SONNENSTEIN. See SUNSTONE.

SOOTY SILVER ORE, *Kirwan.* See SILVER BLACK.

SORDAWALITE, *Nordenskiöld.* A variety of Wichtyne, resembling Pit-coal in appearance, found in greyish or bluish-black

opaque masses, without any apparent cleavage. Lustre vitreous. Streak liver-brown. Brittle. Fracture conchoidal. H. 2·5. S.G. 2·53 to 2·58.

Comp. $(\dot{M}g \, \dot{F}e)^3 \ddot{S}i + \ddot{A}l \ddot{S}i$.

Analysis, by *Nordenskiöld*:

Silica	49·40
Alumina . . .	13·80
Protoxide of iron . .	18·17
Magnesia . . .	10·67
Phosphoric acid . .	2·68
Water	4·38
	99·10

BB alone fuses with difficulty to a blackish globule. With borax forms a green glass.

Partially soluble in muriatic acid, and turns red on exposure to the air.

Localities. Near Sordawala (whence the name) in Finland, forming thin layers in trap rock. Bodenmais, in Bavaria.

Brit. Mus., Case 31.

SOUDE BORATÉE, *Haüy.* See BORAX.

SOUDE CARBONATÉE, *Haüy.* See NATRON.

SOUDE CARBONATÉE PRISMATIQUE. *Dufrénoy.* See THERMONATRITE.

SOUDE MURIATÉE, *Haüy.* Common salt. See ROCK SALT.

SOUDE NITRATÉE, *Haüy.* See NITRATINE.

SOUDE SULFATÉE, *Haüy.* See GLAUBER SALT.

SOUFRE, *Haüy.* See SULPHUR.

SPADAITE, *v. Kobell.* Massive. Colour red, inclining to flesh-red. Translucent. Lustre resinous. Streak white. Sectile. Fracture imperfect-conchoidal. H. 2·5.

Comp. $\dot{M}g^5 \ddot{S}i^4 + 4\dot{H}$, or $4\dot{M}g \ddot{S}i + \dot{M}g \dot{H}$.

Analysis, by *v. Kobell*:

Silica	56·00
Magnesia . . .	30·67
Protoxide of iron . .	0·66
Alumina . . .	0·66
Water	11·34
	99·33

BB fuses to a glassy enamel.

Soluble in concentrated muriatic acid, the silica readily forming a jelly.

Locality. Capo di Bove, near Rome.

Name. After Signor de Medici Spada.

Brit. Mus., Case 26.

SPANIOLITE. The name given by v. Kobell to the varieties of Grey Copper containing quicksilver. S.G. 5·107.

Analysis, from Poratsch, in Hungary, by *v. Hauer* :

Copper .	30·58
Antimony	25·48
Sulphur	24·37
Quicksilver .	16·69
Iron	1·46
Silver .	0·09
Arsenic	trace
	98·58

Localities. Val di Castello and Angina, in Tuscany. Iglo and Poratsch, in Hungary. Schwatz, in the Tyrol.

SPAR. A term applied by Cornish miners to Quartz. In many parts of England the same name is used for Calc Spar, or crystalline carbonate of lime.

SPARABLE TIN. The name given in Cornwall to small crystals of Cassiterite (*figs.* 396, 397), from their fancied resemblance to the particular kind of nail called *a sparable.* This variety is found in the mines near Camborne, at Huel Harris, Huel Owles, and elsewhere.

Fig. 396.

Fig. 397.

M. P. G. Principal Floor, Wall-case 8, No. 396.

SPARGELSTEIN, *Werner.* SPARGEL STONE, *Jameson.* See ASPARAGUS-STONE.

SPARKIES. See SPEAR PYRITES.

SPARRY IRON, *Allan.*
SPARRY IRON-ORE, *Kirwan.*
SPARRY IRONSTONE, *Jameson.*   Carbonate of
SPATHEISENSTEIN,*Reuss,*   Iron. See
Werner.   CHALYBITE.
SPATHIGER EISENSTEIN, *Werner.*
SPATHOSE IRON, *Phillips.*

SPARTAITE. The name given by Breithaupt to the Calcite occurring at Sparta, in New Jersey, associated with Zincite. S.G. 2·808 to 2·818.

SPARTALITE, *Brooke & Miller.* See ZINCITE.

SPATH D'ISLANDE. See ICELAND SPAR.

SPATH EN TABLES, *Haüy.* Tabular Spar. See WOLLASTONITE.

SPATH FLUOR, ⎫ See FLUOR.
SPATH FUSIBLE. ⎭

SPATH MAGNESIEN, *Necker.* See BREUNNERITE.

SPATH PERLÉ, *Romé de Lisle.* See BROWN SPAR.

SPATH PESANT. See BARYTES.

SPATH SCHISTEUX, *Brochant.* See SLATE SPAR.

SPEAR PYRITES. Macled crystals of Marcasite, or White Iron Pyrites, presenting the appearance of dodecahedrons with triangular planes, but which are macles, consisting of similar portions of five crystals.

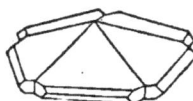

Fig. 398.

Localities. Near Castleton, Derbyshire, *fig.* 398 ; and in Ireland, at Kilkee, co. Clare. Freiberg, in Saxony. Schemnitz, in Hungary. Bohemia ; Teplitz, Przibram, and in the plastic clay of the Brown Coal formation, at Littmitz and Altsattel, where it is used for making sulphur and sulphate of iron.

Brit. Mus., Case 6.

SPECKSTEIN, *Werner.* See STEATITE.

SPECULAR IRON, *Phillips.* The name applied to those varieties of Hematite which possess a crystalline structure, and a high metallic lustre. Occurs crystallized in many forms (the primary being a slightly acute rhombohedron) ; also lamellar. Colour dark steel-grey, often with a brilliant iridescent tarnish. Opaque, but translucent in very thin laminæ, which show a blood-red colour by transmitted light. Streak cherry-red to reddish-brown. Structure lamellar. Brittle. Fracture uneven, passing into conchoidal. Occasionally feebly magnetic. H. 5·5 to 6·5. S.G. 5·19 to 5·23.

Fig. 399.

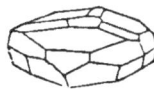

Fig. 400.

Comp. Sesquioxide of iron, or $\ddot{F}e$ = iron 69·23, oxygen 30·77 = 100.

BB alone infusible, but in the inner flame becomes black and magnetic ; with borax forms a green or yellow glass.

Localities.— English. Cornwall : at Botallack, *fig.* 399, implanted on crystals of Quartz ; Carnyorth, near St. Just. Near Ulverstone in Lancashire, *fig.* 400.—*Scotch.*

A A

Salisbury Craig, near Edinburgh. Dunkeld and Ben More, Perthshire. Hilleswick, in Mainland, one of the Shetlands. — *Irish.* Bennevenagh, in greenstone, associated with Stilbite. Kerry Head. — *Foreign.* Island of Elba, in very fine crystals, frequently presenting beautiful tarnish-colours, and occurring in druses of the massive variety. Arendal, in Norway. Katherinenburg and Nijni-Taguilsk, in the Ural. Langbanshyttan, in Sweden. St. Gotthard. Framont, in the Vosges. Tilkerode, in the Harz. Capas, in Brazil, associated with Quartz. Fowler, Hermon, Rossie Iron Mines, St. Lawrence co.; and at Antwerp, Jefferson co., in New York. Canada: in the Huronian series; also at the Bruce Mine, on the N. shore of Lake Huron, in Huronian Limestone. In the volcanic rocks of Auvergne, Vesuvius (especially on Monte Somma), Etna, the Lipari Islands (especially Stromboli), Island of Ascension, &c.

Brit. Mus., Case 14.

M. P. G. Principal Floor, Case 48 (British); Upper Gallery, Table-case A, in Recess 4, Nos. 72 to 74.

Specular Iron constitutes a highly valuable ore, which has been extensively worked in the Isle of Elba for upwards of 2000 years. It occurs in large beds or veins, chiefly in crystalline rocks, and is also met with among the ejected lavas of Vesuvius, and other volcanos.

It has lately been proved by Rammelsberg that some of the specimens from Elba contain titanic acid, and that all of them (as well as the Specular Iron from Vesuvius), invariably contain protoxide of iron, and an essential per centage of magnesia.

Brit. Mus., Case 15.

M. P. G. Principal Floor, Wall-cases 18 (Foreign); 41 (Ascension).

SPEERKIES. See SPEAR PYRITES.

SPEISKOBALT, *Werner.* See SMALTINE.

SPEISKOBOLD, *Werner;* or SPEISSKOBALT, *Hausmann.* Tin-white Cobalt. See SMALTINE.

SPELTER. A commercial name for Zinc.

SPESSARTINE, *Beudant.* A Manganese-alumina-Garnet, occuring in dodecahedral crystals and massive. Colour deep hyacinth or brownish-red. Slightly translucent at the edges. Fracture imperfect-conchoidal, and presenting a vitreous lustre. H. 7 to 7·5. S.G. 3·7 to 4·4.

Comp. $(\dot{M}n^3 + \ddot{A}l) \ddot{S}i$.

Analysis, from Miask, by *Lissenko.* S.G. 4·38.

Silica	.	.	.	36·30

SPHÆROSTILBITE.

Alumina	.	.	.	17·48
Protoxide of manganese	.	30·60
Protoxide of iron	.	.	14·32
Lime	.	.	.	0·51
				99·21

BB alone, fuses: with soda, on platinum foil, exhibits a decided green colour, indicative of the presence of manganese.

Localities. Aschaffenburg, in Franconia, in granite. Finbo and Brodbo, near Fahlun, in Sweden. Haddam, in Connecticut, in large brittle trapezohedrons, often two inches through, with Chrysoberyl.

Name. After that of the locality, *Spessart,* in Germany.

SPHÆROLITE. See SPHÆRULITE.

SPHÆROSIDERITE, or SPHÄROSIDERITE, *Hausmann.* A spheroidal and radiated variety of Sparry Iron (*Chalybite*), found in greenstone, at Hanau, in Western Germany, and in the circle of Jaslo, in Austrian Galicia.

Analysis, from Steinheim, near Hanau, by *Stromeyer:*

Carbonic acid	.	.	38·04
Protoxide of iron	.	.	59·63
Protoxide of manganese	.	1·89
Lime	.	.	.	0·20
				99·76

Many kinds of Brown Iron Ore appear to be formed by the deposition of hydrated peroxide of iron from water containing carbonate of iron in solution, as it issues out of the earth and evaporates in the air. If this water give off its carbonic acid out of contact of air, it deposits monocarbonate of protoxide of iron, in the form of Sphærosiderite. — (*Bischof,* quoted by L. Gmelin, vol. v. p. 196.)

Brit. Mus., Case 48.

SPHÆROSTILBITE, *Beudant.* A variety of Stilbite, occurring in minute crystals upon delicate radiated tufts of Mesolite, which cause it to assume a globular form. The crystals, which give it the appearance of having a radiated structure, are flexible, and the surfaces of the globules may be scratched with the nail. H. above 3. S.G. 2·31.

Analysis, from Skye, by *Heddle:*

Silica	.	.	.	56·54
Alumina	.	.	.	16·43
Lime	.	.	.	8·90
Soda	.	.	.	0·46
Water	.	.	.	17·05
				99·38

BB fuses, with exfoliation and intumescence.

Forms a jelly with acids, owing to the presence of the Mesolite.

Localities.   Iceland.   The Faröe Islands. Skye: at Storr, in minute spheroids on Faröelite; and at Quirang, in globules the size of a pea.

SPHÆRULITE, *Jameson, Phillips;* or SPHÆRULITH. A form of Pearlstone, occurring in small roundish or spherical concretions, of a brown, yellow, and grey colour; opaque, and without any regular cleavage. The composition of the concretions is felspathic, but they contain mixed Quartz, which is most abundant at the centre and in the outer layers.

Analysis, by *Delesse:*

Silica	88·09
Alumina . . .	6·03
Peroxide of iron . .	0·58
Lime	0·28
Magnesia . . .	1·65
Soda and potash . .	2·53
Water	0·84
	100·00

BB almost infusible, the edges becoming covered with a sort of enamel.

Localities.   The Shetlands, in soft friable clay.   Arran, with Pitchstone.   Tharand and Meissen, in Saxony, in Pitchstone. Brittany, in bright yellow, botryoidal masses.   Hungary; at Hlinik and Glasbütte, near Schemnitz, in ash-grey Pearlstone. Santorin in Obsidian.   Mexico.

Brit. Mus., Case 38.

M. P. G.   Upper Gallery, Wall-case 1, Nos. 52 and 53; Wall-case 2, Nos. 22 and 23.

SPHALERITE, *Glocker.* (From σφαλερὸς, *weak.*) Sulphide of zinc. See BLENDE.

SPHEN, *Karsten;* or SPHENE, *Phillips, Hausmann, Haüy.* Oblique: primary form an oblique rhombic prism. Occurs crystallized, and sometimes in granular or foliated masses. Colour brown, grey, yellow, green, and black. Opaque, or translucent at the edges to transparent. Lustre adamantine, often inclining to resinous. Streak greyish-white. Brittle. Fracture imperfect·conchoidal.   H. 5 to 5·5.   S.G. 3·49 to 3·56.

Fig. 401.

Fig. 402.

Comp.   Titanate and silicate of lime (or a silicate of titanium, in which a part of the latter is replaced by lime)$=Ca^3 \ddot{S}i + \ddot{T}i^5 \ddot{S}i$ = titanic acid 41·33, silica 30·45, lime 28·22 = 100.

Analysis, from Schwartzenstein, by *Fuchs :*

Silica	32·52
Titanic acid . . .	43·21
Lime	24·18
	99·91

BB swells up slightly, and fuses at the edges to a dark glass; in borax dissolves rather easily, forming a transparent yellow glass; with carbonate of soda yields a turbid glass.

Soluble in muriatic acid, which separates silica in a bulky form, and containing titanic acid—the lime, together with a portion of the titanic acid, being dissolved.

Localities.—English.   Virtuous Lady Mine, near Tavistock, in Devonshire, in Chlorite. — *Welsh.*   Fronolen, near Tremadoc. — *Scotch.*   Strontian, in syenite, *figs.* 401 and 402, in small hair-brown, or reddish-brown crystals.   King's House and Inverary, Argyleshire.   Criffel Hills, Galloway.   Craig Cailleach, Perthshire.   The Shetlands. — *Irish.* Co. Down, at Carriglinneen, and at Crow Hill, near Newry. — *Foreign.*   Arendal, in Norway, brown, and nearly opaque, in iron ore.   Malsjö, in Wermeland, Sweden.   Sarlut, in Greenland.   Near Slatoust, in the Ural.   Graubündten, in the Grisons.   St. Gotthard, in mica-slate.   Val Maggia, Piedmont, in brownish crystals on Chlorite.   Mont Blanc, and in many parts of the Alps.   Laacher See and Andernach, on the Rhine, in volcanic rocks.   (See SÉMÉLINE and SPINELLINE.)   Grenville, and other places in Canada.   Sanford and Thurston, in Maine; Lee, Massachusetts, U. S.   Brazil.

Name.   From σφὴν, a *wedge,* in allusion to the shape of the crystals.

Brit. Mus., Case 37.

Sphene occurs in the granites of Normandy, which are used for the Paris trottoirs. The Obelisk of Luxor, formed of red syenite, also contains numerous small yellowish crystals.   See also SÉMÉLINE.

SPHENOMITE, *C. U. Shepard.*   Occurs in brownish-grey (with a tinge of yellow) thin tabular crystals, implanted on crystals of black Pyroxene, and associated with Anorthite, in the Juvenas Meteorite.

SPHEROSTILBITE, *Phillips.* See SPHÆROSTILBITE.

SPHRAGIDE, *Hausmann.* } (From σφραγὶς, SPHRAGITE, *Dufrénoy.* } a *seal.*) See LEMNIAN EARTH.

A A 2

SPIESGLAS, *Werner.* Antimony. See NATIVE ANTIMONY.

SPIESGLAS-SILBER, *Werner.* Antimonial silver. See DISCRASITE.

SPIESSGLANZ-BLEIERZ, *Hausmann.* Cupreous sulphide of antimony and lead. See BOURNONITE.

SPIESSGLANZ - OCHER, *Hausman, Mohs.* Antimony-ochre. See STIBICONISE.

SPIESSGLANZ-WEISS, *Hausmann.* White Antimony. See VALENTINITE.

SPINEL, *Kirwan, Phillips.* SPINELL, *Werner, Haüy, Brochant;* or SPINELLE. Cubical : cleavage octahedral. Occurs in octahedrous, the edges of which are occasionally replaced, and sometimes in rhombic dodecahedrons, owing to the replacement of all the edges of the octahedron ; also in macles. Structure lamellar. Colour various tints of red, violet, and yellow, sometimes black, occasionally nearly white. Transparent to almost opaque. Lustre vitreous. Streak white. Fracture flat - conchoidal. H. 8. S.G. 3·5 to 4·9.

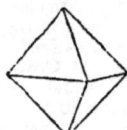  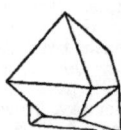

Fig. 403.   Fig. 404.   Fig. 405.

Comp. Anhydrous aluminate of magnesia, or $\overline{Mg} \ \overset{..}{Al}$ when pure = alumina 71·99, magnesia 28·01 = 100 ; but a portion of the magnesia is often replaced by lime and the protoxides of zinc, manganese and iron, and the alumina sometimes by peroxide of iron.

Analysis of Red Spinel, from Ceylon, by *Abich :*

Alumina	.	.	69·01
Magnesia	.	.	26·21
Silica	.	.	2·02
Oxide of chrome	.	.	1·10
Protoxide of iron	.	.	0·71
			99·05

BB infusible : the red variety from Ceylon, on cooling, becomes green, then nearly colourless, and lastly resumes its original red colour. When reduced to powder, turns blue on ignition with nitrate of cobalt. Very slightly soluble in muriatic acid ; when heated in oil of vitriol, till the latter begins to evaporate, about one-third of it dissolves.

Localities. — Irish. Wicklow, in small rounded grains, in the sands of mountain streams.—*Foreign.* Ceylon, Siam, Pegu, and other eastern countries, in rolled pebbles, in the beds of rivers. Amity, New York. Franklin, New Jersey. Burgess, Canada West.

Spinel may be readily distinguished from the Oriental (or Sapphire) Ruby, for which it is often sold, by inferior hardness and specific gravity, and also by its crystallization.

A fine stone, of 24 to 30 carats, is worth from £8 to £16.

There is considerable incertitude, according to Prinsep, concerning this gem amongst oriental authors. Jewellers in the east apply the term *lál* to all rubies of a fine red colour, but the *lál rumani* (scarlet or pomegranate ruby) is probably the true spinelle. The bright-red spinelle ruby, *lál rumani*, is called by modern jewellers *yaqút narm*, or simply in Hindostani, *narmah,* also *lábri;* it comes from Pegu and Ceylon, and less frequently from the north. Modern physicians ascribe the same medicinal properties to Spinelle as to the Oriental Ruby.

Persian authors are particular in their description of the locality and origin of Spinelle.

"The mine of this gem was not discovered until after a sudden shock of an earthquake, in Badakshan, had rent asunder a mountain in that country, which exhibited to the astonished spectators a number of sparkling pink gems of the size of eggs. The women of the neighbourhood thought them to possess a tingent quality, but finding they yielded no colouring matter, they threw them away. Some jewellers discovering their worth, delivered them to the lapidaries to be worked up, but, owing to their softness, the workmen could not at first polish them, until they found out the method of doing so with *mark-i-shésá* (marcasite). This gem was at first esteemed more than the ruby, but as its colour and hardness were found to be inferior to the latter, it became less prized."

In a MS. history of Cashmire, and the countries adjacent, by Abdúl Qádir Khan, Benares, 1830, is the following description of the manner of extracting Rubies from the Badakshan mines : it professes to be taken from an oral account by Mirza Nazar Báki Bég Khán, a native of Badakshan, settled at Benares. "Having collected a party of miners, a spot is pointed out by experienced workmen, where an adit is commenced. The aperture is cut in the rock large enough to admit a man upright ; the passage is lighted at intervals by cotton *maháls* placed in niches. As they proceed with the excavation, the rock is examined until a vein of reddish appearance is discovered, which is recognised as the matrix of the precious gem. This red coloured rock or vein is called *rag-i-lál*, or the vein of rubies; the miners set to work upon this with much art, following all its ramifications through the parent rock. The first rubies that present themselves are small, and of bad colour; these the miners call *piedehs* (foot-soldiers); further on, some larger and of better colour are found, which are called *sawars* (horse-soldiers); the next, as they still progress in improvement, are called *amirs, bakshis,* and *vazirs,* until at last they come to the *king jewell,* after finding which they give up working the vein, and this is always polished and presented to the king." The author proceeds to describe the finest Ruby of this kind that had ever fallen under his observation. It belonged to the Oude family, and was carried off by Vizir Ali, from whom the author was afterwards employed to recover it. It was of the size of a pigeon's egg, and the colour very brilliant. The weight was about two tolas. There was a flaw in it, and to hide it the name of *Julál-ud-din* was engraved over the part, hence the jewel was called *lál-i-jaláli.* A similar Ruby to this, but considerably larger, was in the possession of Runjit Sing, and has the names of five emperors engraved upon it.—*Prinsep.*

The scarlet Spinel is termed *Spinel Ruby* by lapidaries; the rose-red, *Balas Ruby;* the yellow or orange-red, *Rubicelle;* the violet-coloured, *Almandine Ruby.*

For varieties of Spinel, see AUTOMALITE, CANDITE, CEYLANITE, CHLOROSPINEL, DYSLUITE, GAHNITE, HERCINITE, KREITTONITE, PLEONASTE, SAPHIRINE, ZEILANDITE.

Brit. Mus., Case 19.

M. P. G. Horse-shoe Case, Nos. 929 to 934. Upper Gallery, Table-case A, in Recess 4, Nos. 66 to 71.

SPINEL RUBY. The name applied by lapidaries to the scarlet varieties of Spinel (which see).

M. P. G. Horse-shoe Case, Nos. 931 to 934.

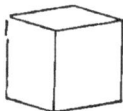

Fig. 406.

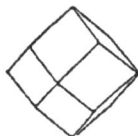

Fig. 407.

SPINELLANE, *Haüy, Dufrénoy, Phillips.*

See NOSEAN. This name was also given by Rose to the variety of Sphene (Séméline), from Lake Laach. See figs. 406 and 407.

SPINELLE, *Jameson.* See SPINEL.

SPINELLE PLEONASTE. The name given to a black variety of Spinel, which occurs in small octahedral crystals in some of the lavas of Etna and Vesuvius.

SPINELLE ZINCIFÈRE, *Haüy.* See AUTOMALITE.

SPINELLINE. See SPINELLANE.

SPINTHÈRE, *Haüy.* A greenish variety of Sphene, occurring crystallized in very irregular double four-sided pyramids, which are obliquely truncated. Slightly translucent at the edges. Lustre splendent. Fracture foliated.

Fig. 408.

BB fuses readily.

Locality. Dauphiné, in France, adhering to crystals of Calc Spar, in small crystals which, at first sight, strongly resemble green crystals of Axinite.

SPLENT COAL. See SLATE COAL.

SPLINT. A miner's name in Derbyshire for coarse, grey Coal.

SPLINT COAL. A variety of Bituminous (Cannel) Coal with a slaty structure, and of a harder and tougher nature than Cherry Coal.

SPLINTERY GARNET. See ALLOCHROITE.

SPODUMEN, *Haidinger, Werner.* SPODUMENE, *D'Andrada, Phillips.* Oblique. Primary form an oblique rhombic prism. Isomorphous with Augite. Also occurs massive with a lamellar structure. Colour pale greyish-green or greenish-white passing into apple-green. Translucent (often only at the edges) to opaque. Lustre vitreous; pearly on cleavage-planes. Streak white. Brittle. Cross-fracture fine-grained and uneven. H. 6·5 to 7. S.G. 3·1 to 3·2.

Comp. $4\ddot{A}l\,\ddot{S}i^2 + \dot{L}i^3\,\ddot{S}i^2 =$ silica 65·15, alumina 28·8, lithia 6·05 = 100. A portion o the lithia is replaced by soda.

Analysis, from Utö, by *Hagen:*

Silica	. 66·14
Alumina . . .	. 27·02
Peroxide of iron . .	. 0·32
Lithia	. 3·84
Soda	. 2·68
	100·00

BB swells up, imparting at the same time a slight and transient purple-red colour to the flame, and fusing with tolerable facility to a greyish-white glass, which is nearly transparent.

Is not acted on by acids.

Localities. — *Irish.* Killiney, co. Dublin, in long, bent prisms of a greenish-grey colour in white granite. — *Foreign.* Island of Utö, in Sweden, with Magnetic Iron Ore, red Felspar, Quartz and Tourmaline. Near Sterzing and Lisens, in the Tyrol. Sterling and Norwich, Massachusetts; and other places in the United States.

Name. From σποδιὸς, *ash-coloured.*

Brit. Mus., Case 31.

The Spodumene of Killiney is sometimes employed for obtaining lithia.

SPONGIFORM QUARTZ. Quartz presenting a porous spongiform appearance. See FLOAT-STONE.

SPREUSTEIN. See NATROLITE.

It has been shown by Scheerer that only the perfectly white specimens of this mineral are free from mechanical mixture; and the colour of the red and brown varieties is caused by the presence of mechanical impurities.

SPRÖDGLANZERZ, *Hausmann.* SPRÖDGLASERZ, *Werner.* Brittle Silver Ore. See STEPHANITE.

SPRUDELSTEIN. A stalactitic variety of Aragonite, deposited from the Carlsbad springs, and containing 0·69 per cent. of fluoride of calcium, and a trace of arsenic.

SPURIOUS COAL. The name used by Kirwan to denote those kinds of Coal which contain a notable quantity (more than 25 per cent.) of stony matter.

STACHELSCHWEINSTEIN, or *Hedgehogstone.* A variety of Brown Iron Ore, found inclosed in Rock Crystal, on the Nake, at Oberstein in Northern Germany.

STAHLCOBALT, or FERROCOBALTINE. A variety of Cobaltine from the Hamberg mine, Siegen, in Westphalia, which has three-fourths of the cobalt replaced by iron.

Analysis, by *Schnabel :*

Sulphur	.	.	.	19·98
Arsenic	.	.	.	42·53
Iron	.	.	.	25·98
Cobalt	.	.	.	8·67
Antimony	.	.	.	2·84
				100·00

STAHLSTEIN. See CHALYBITE.

STALACTITE (from σταλακτὶς, *that which drops*); or STALACTITIC CARBONATE OF LIME, *Phillips.* A form of Calcareous Spar, deposited in long mammillated and pendant masses resembling icicles, on the roofs of caverns and in fissures in limestone rocks. Water, charged with an excess of carbonic acid, in percolating through rocks containing carbonate of lime, dissolves a certain quantity of it, which it holds in solution, and carries away, until by the evaporation of the water, as it trickles from the roof of the cavern, a portion of the lime is redeposited in a solid form. The water which drops from the stalactite, or from the roof of the cavern, in a similar manner, leaves a deposit of Calc Spar, called Stalagmite, which sometimes forms a floor to the cavern, and sometimes a boss or protuberance, which gradually increases in height by repeated deposition of lime; and in this manner, by the increase in length of the Stalactite in a downward direction, and the growth of the Stalagmite upwards, the two frequently meet and become united into one mass. By the long continued operation of this slow process, in course of time, considerable masses of calcareous spar are accumulated, which frequently assume very fantastic and beautiful shapes, and sometimes fill up the entire cavity in the rock. In this manner the beautiful kind of Aragonite has been formed which is found in Egypt and Algeria, called Oriental Alabaster (which see).

M. P. G. Horse-shoe Case, Nos. 406a, 409, 410, 428. Upper Gallery, Wall-case 40, Nos. 1 to 5, and 9 to 11. Table-case B, in Recess 6, Nos. 215 to 219.

STALACTITES PANNIFORMES. A name sometimes used to denote those kinds of Stalactite which are attached to the sides of caves, and present the appearance of undulating folds of drapery.

STALAGMITE, from στάλαγμα, *a drop.* See STALACTITE.

STANGENSPATH, *Werner.* Columnar Heavy-spar, found in indistinct prismatic pearly crystals, of a white or greenish colour, near Freiberg in Saxony.

STANGENSTEIN. See PYCNITE.

STANNINE, *Beudant, Greg & Lettsom, Haidinger.* See TIN PYRITES.

STANNITE, *Breithaupt.* A mechanical mixture of Quartz and Oxide of Tin, found formerly at Huel Primrose, in Cornwall, both massive and in the form of Quartz crystals. It is of a greyish-white colour, with little lustre, and a conchoidal fracture. H. 6·5.   S.G. 3·5.

STANNOLITE (from *stannum*, tin, and λίθος, *stone*) The name given by Necker to Oxide of Tin or Tinstone. See CASSITE-RITE.

STANZAIT. See ANDALUSITE.

STAR RUBY. ⎫
STAR SAPPHIRE. ⎬ See ASTERIA.
STAR STONE. ⎭

STASSFURTHITE, *Rose.* Under the microscope appears to be formed of an aggregation of prismatic crystals, which have been shown by analyses of Karsten and Chapman to be identical in composition with Boracite. According to the following analysis by Heintz, by whom it has subsequently been examined, its composition is represented by the formula $2(\dot{Mg}^3 \ddot{B}^4) + Mg\ Cl\ \dot{H}$, or Boracite with one atom of water. S.G. 2·94.

Analysis :

Boracic acid	.	.	61·22
Magnesia	.	.	25·74
Magnesium	.	.	2·84
Chlorine	.	.	8·14
Peroxide of iron	.	.	0·43
Water	.	.	1·63
			100·00

BB more easily fusible than Boracite. Slightly soluble in hot water. Dissolves readily in warm concentrated muriatic acid.

Locality. Stassfurth, in Prussia. Lüneburg, in Brunswick.

STAUROLITE, *Kirwan*, (from σταυρὸς, a *cross*, and λίθος, stone.) See HARMOTOME.

STAUROLITE, *Karsten. Nicol, Phillips* STAUROLITH, *Werner.* STAUROTIDE, *Dana, Haüy.* Rhombic: primary form a right rhombic prism. Occurs sometimes in rhombic prisms, the acute edges of which are frequently replaced, converting them into six-sided prisms. The crystals are thick, and often intersect and cross each other at right angles, or at an angle of 120°; in which case they are often rough and of a dull brown colour; otherwise the colour varies from a reddish-brown to a brownish-black. Translucent to opaque. Lustre vitreo-resinous. Streak white or greyish. Fracture conchoidal. H. 7 to 7·5. S.G. 3·5 to 3·8.

Fig. 409.   Fig. 410.

Comp. $(\ddot{Al}\ \ddot{Fe})\ \ddot{Si}$, or silicate of alumina,

with about one-third of the alumina replaced by peroxide of iron=silica 29·3, alumina 53·5, peroxide of iron 17·2=100.

Analysis, from St. Gotthard, by *Jacobson :*

Silica	.	.	29·13
Alumina	.	.	52·01
Peroxide of iron	.	.	17·58
Magnesia	.	.	1·28
			100·00

BB in a finely powdered state, fuses to a black slag: in borax dissolves slowly, forming a clear, dark green glass: with carbonate of soda effervesces, and yields a yellow slag.

Not acted on by muriatic acid: partially decomposed by sulphuric acid.

Localities.—English. Cornwall and Devonshire, in clay-slate. — *Scotch.* Ardonald, Aberdeenshire. Unst, in the Shetlands.— *Irish.* Near Killiney, south of Dublin, at the junction of mica-slate and granite. Glen Malure, co. Wicklow.—*Foreign.* St. Gotthard, in Switzerland, in talc-slate, *fig.* 409. Greiner Mountain, in the Tyrol. The Ural. Bohemia. Brittany. St. Jago de Compostella, in Spain. Oporto, in Portugal. United States.

Name. From σταυρὸς, a *cross*, and λίθος, *stone.*

Staurolite generally occurs imbedded in mica-, talc-, and clay-slate, sometimes in gneiss.

Brit. Mus., Case 31.

M. P. G. Upper Gallery, Wall-case 45, Nos. 102 to 104, 138 to 140.

STAUROTYPOUS KOUPHONE SPAR, *Mohs.* See PHILLIPSITE.

STEATITE, *Phillips.* A massive variety of Talc, of various tints of white, grey, yellow, green and red. It has generally a soft and unctuous feel, like that of soap, and yields to the nail, but does not adhere to the tongue. Slightly translucent at the edges. Fracture splintery, but sometimes slaty. H. 1 to 1·5. S.G. 2·65 to 2·8.

Comp. Silicate of magnesia, or $\dot{Mg}^6\ \ddot{Si}^6$ + $2\dot{H}$=silica 62·14, magnesia 32·92, water 4·94=1·00.

Analysis, from Scotland, by *Lychnell :*

Silica	.	.	64·53
Magnesia	.	.	27·70
Protoxide of iron	.	.	6·85
			99·08

BB fuses at the edges to a white enamel: ignited with solution of cobalt, assumes a pale red colour.

Not decomposed by acids.

Localities. — English. Near the Lizard Point, Cornwall, with Serpentine. Caernarvonshire, at Glyder Rock, and Moel Siabod. Church Bay, Anglesea. Amlwch, Anglesea. Near Egremont, in Cumberland. Holybush Hill, Herefordshire. — *Scotch.* Portsoy, Banffshire, with Serpentine. Bogie Quarry, near Raith, Fifeshire. Chapel Quarry, near Kirkcaldy, in encrinital limestone. Hebrides. Shetlands. Skye. — *Irish.* Antrim, near the Causeway, and Dunluce Castle. Banagh, Donegal. Kilmacrenen Mountains, near Loch Swilly. — *Foreign.* Freiberg, in Saxony. Schlaggenwald, in Bohemia, pseudomorphous, after Quartz or Calc Spar. Göpfersgrün, in Bayreuth. New Jersey, Pennsylvania, Vermont, New Hampshire, Massachusetts, and other parts of the United States. Potton, Canada East.

Name. From στέαρ, *suet,* from its greasy feel.

Brit. Mus., Case 35.

M. P. G. Wall-case 40 (Canada). Horseshoe Case, Nos. 1056, 1057, 1071 to 1082, 1113.

Slabs of Steatite are used for lining furnaces and stoves. When ground, it is employed for diminishing the friction of machinery. It is also made, in Germany, into gas burners, which possess the advantage of not corroding, nor becoming stopped up. The white varieties, or those which become so by calcination, are employed in the manufacture of porcelains; others are used for fulling. The Arabs, according to Shaw, use Steatite in their baths instead of soap, to soften the skin; and Humboldt states that the Otomaques, a savage race, inhabiting the banks of the Oronoco, are almost entirely supported during three months of the year by eating a species of Steatite, which they first slightly bake, and then moisten with water.

The material generally used for ornamental carvings in China, is the well-known Chinese Steatite in its natural state, or artificially tinged with the most diversified colours. (See AGALMATOLITE.) At Hing-po (180 miles S. of Shanghai) and Tse-Kong-sa, where these objects are principally made, they are extremely cheap, but are held in very slight estimation compared with articles of crystalline limestone or marble. (*Hochstetter.*)

" If on a steatite you breathe, the smell
Is earthy, but to the tongue adheres not.
In many things like talc, and pot-stone, with

Less of silex and magnesia, and
Of iron still a smaller portion." *

STEINBUTTER, or STONEBUTTER. A fine clay, which is said to be spread on bread and eaten instead of butter, by the workmen employed at the sandstone quarries at Kiffhausen in Germany.

STEINHEILITE. A variety of Iolite, occurring with Copper Pyrites at Orijerfvi in Finland.

Analysis, by *Stromeyer*:

Silica	48·54
Alumina	31·37
Magnesia	11·31
Protoxide of iron	5·69
Protoxide of manganese	0·70
Loss by heat	1·69
	99·65

Name. After Count Steinheil, governor of Finland.

Brit. Mus., Case 36.

Steinheilite is used for stones of rings and breast-pins, and is considered by jewellers an inferior variety of Sapphire.

STEINKOHLE. Stone-Coal. See ANTHRACITE.

STEINMANNITE, *Phillips, Zippe, Nicol.* An impure variety of Galena. Occurs in octahedrons with a cubical cleavage; also massive, in botryoidal and reniform aggregations. Colour lead-grey. Lustre metallic. Fracture uneven. Sectile. H. 2·5. S.G. 6·83.

Comp. Sulphide of lead and antimony.

BB decrepitates violently: on charcoal fuses readily, giving off sulphurous acid and fumes of antimony, and yielding a metallic globule, which finally affords a bead of silver.

Locality. Przibram in Bohemia, with Native Silver, Quartz, Blende and Iron Pyrites.

Name. After the chemist, Steinmann.

Brit. Mus., Case 8.

STEINMARK, *Werner.* See LITHOMARGE.

STEINÖL, or Rock Oil, *Werner.* See BITUMEN, NAPHTHA, and SENECA OIL.

STEINSALZ, *Werner.* See ROCK SALT.

STELLITE, *Thomson.* A white, translucent and silky variety of Scolezite, occurring in concentric stellar groups of fine rhombic prisms, in greenstone, at Kilsyth in Scotland. H. 3 to 3·5. S.G. 2·6.

* Werneria, or Short Characters of Earths, by Terræ Filius, 1805, p. 29.

STEPHANITE.

Analysis, by *Thomson :*

Silica	48·47
Alumina	5·30
Lime	30·96
Protoxide of iron	3·53
Magnesia	5·58
Water	6·11
	99·95

The green variety of Natrolite, found at Bowling, in Dumbartonshire, is sometimes sold as Stellite.

Name. From *stella, a star ;* on account of the star-like form of the crystals.

STEPHANITE, *Dana, Haidinger, Nicol.* Rhombic : primary form a right rhombic prism. Occurs in short, prismatic, or in thick tabular crystals frequently in macles; also massive, disseminated, and compact. Colour dark lead-grey passing into iron-black. Lustre shining-metallic. Colour of powder dark grey or brownish. Structure lamellar. Soft. Sectile. Brittle. Fracture conchoidal. H. 2 to 2·5. S.G. 6·27.

Fig. 411.   Fig. 412.

Comp. Sulphide of silver and antimony, or AgS + Sb²S³ = silver 70·4, antimony 14·0, sulphur 15·6 = 100.

Analysis, from Schemnitz, by *H. Rose :*

Silver	68·54
Antimony	14·68
Sulphur	16·42
Copper	0·64
	100·28

BB gives off fumes of sulphur, antimony, and arsenic, and fuses to a dark metallic globule, which may be reduced on the addition of soda.

Soluble in heated dilute nitric acid, with deposition of sulphur and oxide of antimony.

Localities. Freiberg, Schneeberg, and Johanngeorgenstadt, in Saxony, associated with other ores of silver. Præibram and Ratieborzitz, in Bohemia. Kremnitz and Schemnitz, in Hungary. Andreasberg, in the Harz. Mexico. Peru. Siberia.

Name. After the Archduke Stephan, of Austria.

Brit. Mus., Case 11.

Stephanite is a valuable ore of silver. It occurs principally in veins in the older rocks. See also SCHWARZ-GÜLTIGERZ, and WEISS-GÜLTIGERZ.

STEPHENSONITE. The name proposed by Prof. C. U. Shepard for a "hydro-sulphato-carbonate of copper, of a chrysoprase-green colour," met with at the Ducktown Copper mine, in Eastern Tenessee.

STERCORITE, *Herapath.* Occurs in crystalline masses and nodules in guano. Colour white, with light yellowish-brown stains. Transparent. Lustre vitreous. Very fragile. Soluble in hot and cold water. S.G. 1·615.

Comp. NaAmP̈ + 9Ḧ

Analysis, by *T. J. Herapath :*

Crystallized ammonio-phosphate of soda	91·66
Phosphate of lime	2·10
Organic matters	1·96
Carbonate of lime	0·28
Carbonate of magnesia	traces
Phosphate of potash	traces
Chloride of sodium	0·52
Silica, sand, &c.	2·15
Water and loss	1·33
	100·00

BB swells up, blackens, gives off water and ammonia, and then fuses to a transparent colourless glass, which is readily dissolved in boiling water.

Easily soluble, both in hot and cold water.

Locality. Ichaboe, on the western coast of Africa.

Name. From *stercoro,* to dung or manure land.

STERCUS DIABOLI. A name for Dysodile, in allusion to the bad odour it gives off in burning.

STERNBERGITE, *Haidinger, Nicol, Phillips.* Rhombic, primary form a rhombic octahedron. Generally occurs in implanted crystals attached to the matrix laterally, so as to form rose-like or fan-like aggregations. Sometimes in macles. Perfect basal cleavage. Also massive. Colour pinchbeck-brown, with a violet-blue tarnish. Opaque. Lustre of broad faces bright metallic. Streak black. Flexible in thin laminæ, which after being bent may be smoothed down again with the nail, like tin-foil. Very sectile. Leaves marks on paper like black-lead, which may be removed by means of india-rubber. H. 1 to 1·5 S.G. 4·215.

Comp. Sulphide of silver and iron, or AgS + 2Fe²S³ = iron 35·44, silver 34·18, sulphur 30·38 = 100.

Analysis, from Joachimsthal, by *Zippe :*

Iron	36·0
Silver	33·2
Sulphur	30·0
	99·2

BB on charcoal, burns with a blue flame, giving off odours of sulphurous acid, and fuses to a magnetic (generally hollow) globule, having a crystalline surface covered with silver: with borax, (which becomes coloured by iron,) readily yields a globule of silver.

Decomposed even by cold aqua-regia, with evolution of heat and evaporation of sulphur and chloride of silver.

Localities. Joachimsthal, in Bohemia. Schneeberg and Johanngeorgenstadt, in Saxony.

Name. After Count Caspar Sternberg, of Prague.

Brit. Mus., Case 10.

STIBICONISE, *Beudant.* Occurs in amorphous earthy masses, of a yellow, grey, or brownish colour. Opaque, dull, soft and friable. Streak yellowish-white or grey. Fracture earthy, uneven. H. 5·5. S.G. 5·28.

Comp. S̈b,S̈b + 2Ḧ = oxide of antimony 45·01, antimonic acid 49·70, water 5·29, or antimony 75·89, oxygen 18·82, water 5·29 = 100.

Analysis, by *Blum & Delffs*:

Antimony	75·83
Oxygen	19·54
Arsenic	trace.
Water	4·63
	100·00

BB with borax or salt of phosphorus behaves like oxide of antimony.

Localities.—*English.* Trewinnick, near Endellion, Cornwall.— *Foreign.* Goldkronach, in Bavaria. Bruck, in Rhenish Prussia. Nassau. Erzgebirge, of Saxony. Felsobanya and Kremnitz in Hungary. Spain; at Losacio, in Gallicia. France: Mine of Malbosc (Ardèche); Ariège (La Vendée). Tuscany. Morocco. Mexico.

Name. From *stibium*, antimony, and χόνις, powder.

STIBINE, *Beudant, Nicols.* ⎫
STIBIUM, *Pliny.* ⎬ See STIBNITE.
Στίμμι, *Dioscorides.* ⎭

STIBLITE, *Blum, Greg & Lettsom.* See STIBICONISE.

STIBNITE, *Dana.* Rhombic: primary form a right rhombic prism. Occurs crystallized in variously modified and terminated rhombic prisms, which are sometimes closely aggregated laterally; also disseminated; massive, with a long columnar structure; and fibrous with a plumose, woolly, or felt-like appearance (*Federerz*). Colour and streak lead-grey, inclining to steel-grey; some-

times blackish and dull externally, and with an iridescent tarnish. Opaque. Lustre metallic. Sectile. Slightly flexible in thin laminæ. Very brittle. Fracture small- and imperfect-conchoidal. Yields to the pressure of the nail. Leaves a mark like black-lead when rubbed on paper. Gives off a sulphurous smell when rubbed. H.2. S.G.4·5 to 4·6.

Fig. 413.

Comp. Tersulphide of antimony, or SbS³ = antimony 72·88, sulphur 27·12 = 100.

Melts readily in the flame of a candle, colouring it greenish.

BB is absorbed by the charcoal, leaving a white slag, and emits a strong sulphurous odour and white fumes.

Perfectly soluble in muriatic acid.

Localities. — *English.* Cornwall: near Padstow and Tintagel, in veins; Huel Boys, in Endellion, *fig.* 413; also plumose at Old Trewetha, Port Isaac, and Pendogget in St. Kew. Cumberland; Robin Hood Mine, and Carrock Fells. — *Scotch.* Hare Hill, near New Cumnock, Ayrshire. Ben Lawes, Perthshire. Glendinning, Dumfriesshire. Keith, Banffshire.— *Foreign.* Felsobanya, Schemnitz and Kremnitz, in Hungary, in diverging prisms several inches long. Wolfsberg, in the Harz. Pösing, and Magurka, in Hungary. Borneo. France: Mine of Malbosc (Ardèche), and in those of Auvergne. Tuscany.

Brit. Mus., Case 10.

M. P. G. Principal floor, Wall-cases 14 (British); 20 (Foreign).

This ore of antimony usually occurs in very long prismatic or acicular crystals, or in a fibrous form. It may be distinguished from a similar ore of manganese by its easy fusibility, crude antimony being obtained from it by simple fusion. From the latter product the pure metal is extracted, and most of the pharmaceutical preparations are prepared. It is the source of most of the antimony of commerce.

This ore is the Stibium and Στίμμι of the ancients, by whom it was also called πλατυ-όφθαλμον (from πλατύς, broad, όφθαλμός, eye), because of the use to which it was applied in darkening the upper and under sides of the eyelids, for the purpose of increasing the apparent size of the eye. It was supposed not only to impart additional beauty and brilliancy to the eye, and to make it appear larger, but it was also considered to be beneficial to the sight. This practice of staining the eyelids was adopted among oriental nations from a very remote period, and is still followed by the women of Syria at the present day. In 2 Kings ix. 30 we read, "And when Jehu was come to Jezreel, Jezebel heard of it, and she painted her face" (literally, "put her eyes in painting"), "and tired her head, and looked out at a window." So also Ezekiel (xxiii. 40), in reproving the adulteries of Aholah and Aholibah, says, "For whom thou didst wash thyself, paintedst thine eyes, and deckedst thyself with ornaments." In this passage *Kachalt aineycha* is rendered by the LXX. ἐστιβίζου τοὺς ὀφθαλμοὺς σου, "Thou didst paint thine eyes with stibium;" and in the Vulgate, *Circumlinisti stibio oculos tuos*," "Thou didst paint round thine eyes with stibium." In carelessly using the antimonial powder, some of it frequently enters the eye itself; hence the expression in Jer. iv. 30, "Though thou rentest thy face (in Hebrew, "rentest thine eyes") with painting, in vain shalt thou make thyself fair."

It was also employed as a hair-dye, and to colour the eyebrows. Dioscorides states that the mode of preparing it for this purpose was to enclose it in a lump of dough, and burn it in the coals till it was reduced to a cinder. It was then extinguished with milk and wine, and again placed upon the coals and blown till ignition took place; after which the heat was discontinued, lest, as Pliny says, "*plumbum fiat*," it should become lead, *i.e.* be reduced to the metallic state.

Stibnite is the "Lupus Metallorum" of the Alchemysts.

STIGMITE. See ST. STEPHEN'S-STONE.

STILBIT, *Haidinger*; or STILBITE, *Beudant, Haüy, Phillips, Nicol.* Primary form a right rhombic prism. Generally occurs in prisms of which the edges are replaced, and with four-sided summits resting on the lateral edges; often in sheaf-like aggregations and in diverging groups; also massive, in radiating and broad columnar forms. Colour white;

Fig. 414.

Fig. 415.

sometimes yellow, grey, red or brown. Lustre vitreous. Translucent to transparent at the edges. Streak white. Brittle. Fracture uneven. H.3·5 to 4. S.G. 2 to 2·2.

Comp. Anhydrous Lime-Oligoclase, or $\ddot{C}a\ddot{S}i + \dddot{A}l\ddot{S}i^3 + 6\ddot{H}$ = silica 58·2, alumina 16·1, lime 8·8, water 16·9 = 100.

Analysis, from Iceland, by *Hisinger:*

Silica	.	.	.	. 58·00
Alumina	.	.	.	. 16·10
Lime	.	.	.	. 9·20
Water	.	.	.	. 16·40
				99·70

BB swells up strongly and fuses with difficulty to a blistered glass.

Slowly but completely decomposed by concentrated muriatic acid, with separation of silica in the form of a viscid powder.

Localities.—English. Cornwall: between Botallack and Huel Cock.— *Scotch.* Garbh Corre Du, Isle of Arran, *fig.* 414, in granite. Long Craig, Dumbarton Muir, *fig.* 414. Skye: at Storr, Talisker, *fig.* 415; Quiraing, Snizort. Stirlingshire; Campsie and Fintry, in fine red crystals, *fig.* 415, in porphyritic amygdaloid. At Kilpatrick, Kilmalcolm, Kincardine, in sheaf-like aggregations. Call Hill, near Aberdeen, plumose.— *Irish.* Giant's Causeway, in geodes. Mourne Mountains, in sheaf-like aggregations, in granite. Ballintoy. Port Rush. Bruce's Castle, Rathlin Island, in greenstone. Bengore Head.— *Foreign.* Iceland. Farŏe Islands. Konigsberg and Arendal, in Norway. Gustafsberg, near Fahlun, in Sweden. Fassa Valley, in the Tyrol. Andreasberg, in the Harz. Dauphiny. Vindhya Mountains, in Hindostan. Partridge Islands, Nova Scotia, white and flesh-red. United States.

Name. From στίλβη, *lustre*, in allusion to the pearly lustre of some of the faces of the crystals.

Brit. Mus., Case 28.

M. P. G. Horseshoe-Case, No. 1166.

Stilbite occurs chiefly in cavities in amygdaloidal rocks; also in some metalliferous veins, and in granite, gneiss, and slate.

It should be remarked that German mineralogists call our Stilbite *Desmine*, and our Heulandite *Stilbite*.

STILBITE ANAMORPHIQUE, *Haüy.* See HEULANDITE.

STILLOLITE. See OPAL.

STILPNOMELAN, *Glocker, Nicol*; or STILPNOMELANE, *Dana.* Occurs massive and disseminated, with a granular or radiating and foliated structure. Colour blackish-green to greenish-black. Opaque. Lustre vitreous, inclining to pearly on the planes of cleavage. Streak greenish. Rather brittle. H. 3 to 4. S.G. 3 to 3·4.

Comp. $Fe^3\ddot{S}i^2 + \ddot{A}l\ddot{S}i^2 + 7\dot{H}$=silica 46·5, alumina 8·5, protoxide of iron 36·0, water 9=100.

Analysis, by *Rammelsberg :*

Silica	. 45·02
Alumina . . .	. 6·75
Protoxide of iron .	36·04
Magnesia . . .	. 2·39
Lime	. 0·52
Potash, with a trace of soda .	0·75
Water	. 7·96
	99·43

BB fuses with difficulty to a black shining globule: with borax dissolves completely, and gives an iron reaction; and with micro-cosmic salt, with separation of a siliceous jelly.

Only partially soluble in warm and concentrated muriatic acid.

Locality. Zuckmantel, in Austrian Silesia, in clay-slate, with Calc Spar and Quartz.

Name. From στιλπνος, *shining,* and μιλας, *black.*

Brit. Mus., Case 26.

STILPNOSIDERITE, *Ullmann.* A hydrated peroxide of iron, referred by Ullmann to Limonite, and by Von Kobell to Göthite. It occurs massive, or in stalactitic, botryoidal and dendritic forms. Colour pitch-black to blackish-brown. Opaque. Lustre splendent. Streak yellowish-brown. Brittle. Fracture conchoidal. H. 4·5 to 5. S.G. 3·6 to 3·8.

Analysis, from Amberg, by *v. Kobell :*

Peroxide of iron . .	86·24
Silica	. 2·00
Phosphoric acid . .	. 1·08
Water	. 10·68
	100·00

BB infusible, but turns black.

Localities. — English. Tincroft, in Cornwall.— *Foreign.* Scheibenberg and Rashau, in Saxony. Thuringia. The Harz. Nassau. Amberg, in Bavaria. Siegen, in Prussia.

Name. From στιλπνος, *shining,* and σιδηρος, *iron.*

STINKSTEIN, *Werner.* } The name given
STINKSTONE, *Jameson.* } to those varieties
} of limestone which give off a fetid odour when rubbed or struck with a hammer.

Amongst other localities it is met with at Matlock, in Derbyshire ; near Clifton, in the mountain limestone on the banks of the Avon ; near Sunderland ; and in the isles of Purbeck and Portland, in limestones of the Purbeck and Portland beds. In the latter localities, where the limestones in question

are used as a road material, a very strong odour is frequently perceptible when the stones are crushed by a heavy vehicle passing over them.

" Swinestone, when scraped or pounded, offensive
Smells from rank petroleum's fossil oil,
And yet the smell is not the same, but more
Like bluejohn newly broke ; and in swinestone
Bitumen is not always found, that can
From distillation be obtain'd ; from whence
We safely may conclude the swinish smell,
Most fœtid, to some other cause is owed." [*]

Brit. Mus., Case 48.

M. P. G. Upper Gallery, Table-case B, in Recess 6, Nos. 197, 207.

STINKZINNOBER LEBERERZ, *Hausmann.* See CINNABAR.

STOLPENITE, *Kenngott.* The Bole of Stolpen, in Saxony.

STOLZITE, *Haidinger.* Tungstate of lead. Named after Dr. Stolz, of Teplitz.   See SCHEELETINE.

STONE. A miner's name in Derbyshire for Ironstone.

STONE-BUTTER. See STEINBUTTER.

STONE COAL. See ANTHRACITE.

STONE SALT, *Jameson.* See ROCK SALT.

STONY COAL. The name given by Berger to bituminous Kimmeridge Shale.

STONY COMFITS. See DRAGÉES DE TIVOLI.

STONY ICICLE, *Woodward.* Stalactite (which see).

STRAHL SCHORL, *Werner.* Crystallized common Actinolite.

STRAHLENKUPFER, STRAHLERZ, *Allan, Hoffmann, Werner.* Arseniate of Copper. See APHANESITE.

STRAHLKIES, *Werner.* See RADIATED PYRITES.

STRAHLSTEIN, *Werner.* See ACTINOLITE.

STRAHLZEOLITH, *Werner.* See STILBITE.

STRAKONITZITE, *v. Zepharovich.* A yellowish-green steatite-like mineral, found in pseudomorphous crystals, at Mutenitz, near Strakonitz, in Bohemia. It is soft, feels greasy, and yields a pale yellowish powder, which becomes of a dull brown colour on being heated. S.G. 1·91.

Analysis, by *v. Zepharovich :*

Silica	. 53·42
Alumina . . .	. 7·00
Protoxide of iron .	. 15·41
Lime	. 1·37
Magnesia . . .	. 2·94
Water	. 19·86
	100·00

* Werneria, by Terræ Filius.

STRATOPEITE, *Igelström*. Probably an altered form of Rhodonite (*Manganese Spar*). Occurs amorphous-massive, of a pitch-black colour, or brown, or brownish-red, in thin splinters. Yields to the knife, and affords a brown streak. Fracture flat-conchoidal. S.G. 2·64.

Comp. $\dot{M}g^3 \ddot{S}i^2 + 4(\ddot{M}n, \ddot{F}e) \ddot{S}i + 12\dot{H}$.
Analysis, by *Igelström*:

Silica	35·43
Peroxide of manganese .	32·41
Peroxide of iron . .	10·27
Magnesia	8·04
Water	13·75
	100·00

BB fuses to a black transparent globule.
Locality.—Pajsberg's iron mine, Philipstadt, Sweden.

STREAM TIN. Rounded fragments of Oxide of Tin (*Cassiterite*). They are so called from the circumstance of their being obtained by washing the deposits formed, in the valleys, by the disintegration of the rocks constituting the neighbouring hills.

M.P.G. Principal floor, Wall-case 8, Nos. 413 to 435 (British); 39 (East Indies); 37 (Victoria and Australia).

STRIEGESAN, *Breithaupt.* A variety of Wavellite, from Striegis, in the Erzgebirge.

STRIPED JASPER, *Kirwan.* See RIBBON JASPER.

STROGANOWITE, *Hermann.* An altered form of Scapolite, which it much resembles both in form and appearance. Colour clear, pale oil-green, or yellowish green. Lustre subvitreous, inclining to greasy. Cleaves in two directions, nearly at right angles to each other. H. 5·5. S.G. 2·79.

Analysis, by *Hermann*:

Silica	40·58
Alumina	28·57
Lime	11·05
Chloride of lime . . .	14·55
Soda	3·50
Protoxides of iron and manganese · · ·	0·89
	100·14

Locality. Found in loose blocks near the river Sljudenkä, in Dauria.
Name. After Count Stroganow.

Stroganowite agrees with Cancrinite, except that a considerable proportion of lime replaces a corresponding proportion of soda. It was subsequently united by Dufrénoy to Wernerite, in consequence of its rectangular cleavage.

STROHSTEIN, *Werner.* See CARPHOLITE.

STROMBOLO. See LIGNITE.

STROMEYERINE, *Beudant*, or STROMEYERITE, *Haidinger.* Rhombic: isomorphous with Copper Glance. Occurs also compact. Colour dark steel-grey. Lustre strong metallic. Streak shining. Sectile. Very brittle. Fracture brilliant, granular and imperfect-conchoidal. H. 2·5 to 3. S.G. 6·25.

Comp. Sulphide of silver and copper, or $Cu^2 S + Ag S = $ sulphur 15·7, silver 52·9, copper 31·4 = 100.

Analysis, from Rudolstadt, by *Sander*:

Sulphur	15·92
Silver	52·71
Copper	30·95
Iron	0·24
	99·82

BB gives off an odour of sulphurous acid, and fuses readily to a grey semi-malleable globule, having a metallic lustre. Colours fluxes green by the copper it contains. Cupelled with lead, yields silver.
Dissolves in nitric acid, with separation of sulphur.

Locality. Schlangenberg, or Zmeinogorsk, south of Barnaoul, in Siberia, associated with Copper Pyrites, Calc Spar, and Hornblende. Rudolstadt, in Silesia. Copiapo, in Chili. Combarvalla, in Peru.
Name. After Stromeyer, by whom it was first distinguished and described as a new species.

Brit. Mus., Case 10.

STROMITE. A variety of Diallogite, named after the Director of Mines, Strom.

STROMNITE. A name given by Traill to the Strontianite from Stromness, in the Orkneys. See BARYSTRONTIANITE.

STRONTHIAN, *Werner.* STRONTHIANITE, *Kirwan.* STRONTIANE, *Jameson.* STRONTIANE CARBONATÉE, *Haüy.* See STRONTIANITE.

STRONTIANE SULFATÉE, *Haüy.* See CELESTINE.

STRONTIANIT, *Hausmann, v. Kobell, Naumann.* STRONTIANITE, *Nicol, Dana, Greg & Lettsom.* Rhombic: primary form a right rhombic prism. Occurs crystallized in hexahedral prisms, which are modified on the

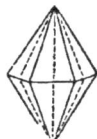 Fig. 416.　　　　Fig. 417.

edges, or terminated by pyramids: also in fibrous, stellated, columnar-globular, and granular masses. Colour pale asparagus-green, or apple-green; also white, yellow, grey, or brown. Transparent to translucent. Lustre shining, pearly. Yields easily to the knife. Streak white. Brittle. Fracture uneven. H. 3·5 to 4. S.G. 3·6 to 3·71.

Comp. Carbonate of strontia, or $\ddot{S}r\,\ddot{C}=$ strontia 70·27, carbonic acid 29·73=100.

Analysis from Strontian, by *Thomson* :
Carbonate of strontia . . 93·43
Carbonate of lime . . 6·28
Protoxide of iron . . 0·01
———
99·72

BB fuses at the edges, then rapidly swells up and forms a cauliflower-like mass, which becomes highly incandescent, imparting a reddish colour to the flame, and giving an alkaline reaction.

Effervesces in nitric and muriatic acids.

Soluble in 18,045 parts of pure water at ordinary temperatures, and in 1536 parts of boiling water.

Localities. — *English.* Yorkshire; Pately Bridge and Nidderdale, in snow-white translucent crystals, *fig.* 416.—*Scotch.* Strontian, in Argyleshire, sometimes as in *fig.* 417, but generally in acicular, diverging groups. —*Foreign.* Bräunsdorf, in Saxony. Hamm, Westphalia. The Harz. Leogang, in Salzburg. United States, at Schoharie, &c.

Name. After the locality, Strontian, where it was first found.

Brit. Mus., Case 41.

M. P. G. Horse-shoe Case, Nos. 275 to 278.

Dr. Hope first discovered the earth Strontian in this mineral, and named it after the locality where the specimens had been obtained.

STRONTIANOCALCITE, *Genth.* A variety of Calcite containing strontia.

STRONTITES, *Allan, Hope, Phillips:* See STRONTIANITE.

STRUVÉITE, *Dufrénoy.* STRUVITE, *Ulex.* Occurs in regular six-sided prisms, with dihedral terminations. Primary form a right rhombic prism. Colour pale yellow, and

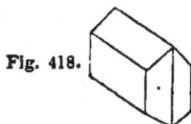

Fig. 418.

sometimes transparent, but generally rendered black and opaque by the interposition of organic matter. Lustre vitreous. Brittle. Tasteless, and very slightly soluble in water. H. 2. S.G. 1·7.

Comp. Phosphate of magnesia and ammonia, or $\ddot{M}g\,\ddot{P}+NH^4O+13\ddot{H}=$ phosphoric acid 29·9, magnesia 16·3, ammonia 10·6, water 44·0=100.

Analysis, by *Ulex :*
Phosphoric acid . . . 28·56
Magnesia . . . . 13·46
Protoxide of iron . . . 3·06
Protoxide of manganese . 1·12
Ammonia and water . . 53·76
———
99·96

BB falls to powder, giving off water and ammonia, and fuses to a colourless glass which, when cool, forms a white enamel.

Readily soluble in acids.

Locality. Saldanha Bay, on the coast of Africa, in guano.

Numerous crystals, some of which were from an inch to an inch and a quarter long, and a quarter of an inch thick, were found, in 1845, in digging the foundations of the church of St. Nicholas, at Hamburg. The soil in which they occurred was a bed of peat or turf, formed by the putrefaction of organic matter (stable litter), and the rubbish from an old chateau, which was destroyed by fire in 1072. The same salt exists in certain animal secretions, and is deposited from decomposing urine.

Name. After the Russian Councillor of State, von Struve.

Brit. Mus., Case 60 A.

STYGMITE. A beautiful variegated variety of Carnelian, of a reddish-yellow or yellowish-red colour, traversed by numerous white lines.

STYLOBATE. (From στυλοβάτης, *the foot of a column.*) See GEHLENITE.

STYPTICITE. The fibrous form of yellow copperas (*Copiapite*).

Comp. $2\ddot{F}e\,\ddot{S}^2+21\ddot{H}$.

Analysis, by *H. Rose :*
Sulphuric acid . . . 31·73
Peroxide of iron . . . 28·11
Silica . . . . 1·43
Magnesia . . . . 0·59
Lime . . . . 1·91
Water . . . . 36·56
———
100·53

SUBFLUATE OF CERIUM, *Phillips.* See FLUOCERINE.

SUBPHOSPHATE OF ALUMINA. See WAVELLITE.

SUBSESQUICHROMATE OF LEAD, *Thomson.* See MELANOCHROITE.

SUBSULPHATE OF ALUMINA, *Phillips.* See WEBSTERITE.

SUCCIN, *Haüy.*
SUCCINITE, *Breithaupt.* } See AMBER.

SUCCINITE, *Bonvoisin.* An amber-coloured variety of Topazolite (*Lime-Garnet*), found in small, rounded, translucent masses, in a serpentine rock in the Vin valley, which forms part of the great valley of Lans, in Piedmont.

SULFATE VERT D'URANE, *Beudant.* See JOHANNITE.

SULPHATE DE PLOMB CUIVREUX, *Beudant.* See LINARITE.

SULPHATE OF ALUMINA, *Phillips.* See ALUNOGENE.

SULPHATE OF ALUMINA (ANHYDROUS). See THENARDITE.

SULPHATE OF ALUMINA AND AMMONIA, *Phillips.* See AMMONIA-ALUM.

SULPHATE OF BARYTES, *Phillips.* See BARYTES.

SULPHATE OF COBALT. See BIEBERITE.

SULPHATE OF COPPER, *Phillips.* See CYANOSITE.

SULPHATE OF IRON, *Phillips.* See COPPERAS.

SULPHATE OF LEAD, *Phillips.* See ANGLESITE.

SULPHATE OF LIME. See ALABASTER, ANHYDRITE, GYPSUM, SATIN-SPAR, SCHAUMKALK, SELENITE.

SULPHATE OF MAGNESIA, *Phillips.* See EPSOMITE.

SULPHATE OF POTASH, *Phillips.* See GLASERITE.

SULPHATE OF SODA, *Phillips.* See GLAUBER SALT.

SULPHATE OF STRONTIA. See CELESTINE.

SULPHATE OF URANIUM. See JOHANNITE.

SULPHATE OF URANIUM AND LIME. See MEDJIDITE.

SULPHATE OF ZINC, *Phillips.* See GOSLARITE.

SULPHATO - CARBONATE OF BARYTA, *Thomson.* Carbonate of baryta (*Witherite*),

Fig. 419.

incrusted more or less with minute crystals of Barytes, and found at Brownley Hill, near Alston in Cumberland, *fig.* 419.

SULPHATO-CARBONATE OF LEAD,*Phillips.* See LANARKITE.

SULPHATO-CHLORID OF COPPER, *Connel.* See CONNELLITE.

SULPHATO - TRICARBONATE OF LEAD, *Brooke, Phillips.* See LEADHILLITE.

SULPHIDE, *Syn.* Sulphuret.

SULPHIDE OF ANTIMONY AND LEAD, *Boulanger.* See BOULANGERITE.

SULPHIDE OF COPPER AND ANTIMONY. See WOLFSBERGITE.

SULPHURATED BISMUTH, *Kirwan.* See BISMUTHINE.

SULPHURATED NICKEL, *Kirwan.* See COPPER NICKEL.

SULPHURATED SILVER-ORE, *Kirwan.* See SILVER GLANCE.

SULPHURET, *Syn.* Sulphide.

SULPHURET OF ANTIMONY, *Phillips.* See STIBNITE.

SULPHURET OF ARSENIC, *Phillips.* See ORPIMENT AND REALGAR.

SULPHURET OF BISMUTH, *Phillips.* See BISMUTHINE.

SULPHURET OF CADMIUM. See GREENOCKITE.

SULPHURET OF COBALT, *Phillips.* See LINNÆITE.

SULPHURET OF COPPER, *Allan, Phillips.* See COPPER GLANCE.

SULPHURET OF LEAD, *Phillips.* See GALENA.

SULPHURET OF LEAD AND ANTIMONY, *Phillips.* A variety of Galena, containing antimony.

SULPHURET OF MANGANESE, *Phillips.* See MANGANESE BLENDE.

SULPHURET OF MERCURY, *Phillips.* See CINNABAR.

SULPHURET OF MOLYBDENA, *Phillips.* See MOLYBDENITE.

SULPHURET OF NICKEL, *Phillips.* See MILLERITE.

SULPHURET OF SILVER, *Phillips.* See SILVER GLANCE.

SULPHURET OF SILVER and ANTIMONY, *Phillips.* See FREIESLEBENITE.

SULPHURET OF SILVER AND COPPER, *Phillips.* See STROMEYERITE.

SULPHURET OF TIN, *Phillips.* See TIN PYRITES.

SULPHURET OF ZINC, *Phillips.* See BLENDE.

SUMPFERZ, *Brochant, Werner.* Swamp-ore. See BOG IRON-ORE.

SUNDOIKITE, *A. E. Nordenskiöld.* An altered Anorthite.

SUN-OPAL. See FIRE-OPAL.

SUNSTONE. A variety of Adularia, of a very pale yellowish colour. It is almost perfectly transparent when viewed in one direction, but by reflected light it appears full of minute golden spangles, owing to the presence of scales (or, according to Scheerer, crystals), of oxide of iron, or Göthite, disseminated through the mass. The principal localities are, Lake Baikal, in Siberia; Archangel; Tvedestrand, on the Christiana-fiord, in Norway; and Ceylon.

Brit. Mus., Case 29.

SUPEROXIDE OF LEAD, *Dana*. See PLATTNERITE.

SUPERSULPHIDE OF LEAD, } See JOHN-
SUPERSULPHURETTED LEAD. } STONITE.

SURTURBRAND. The name given in Iceland to the fibrous Brown Coal, or bituminous wood which is found in that country. See LIGNITE and BROWN COAL.

SUSANNITE, *Dana*, *Greg & Lettsom*. SUZANNIT, *Haidinger*. Hexagonal. Colour pale green, yellow, grey, dark brown. Transparent to opaque. Lustre resinous, or pearly-adamantine. Streak white. H. 2·5. S.G. 6·55.

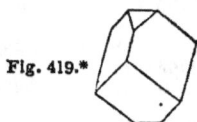

Fig. 419.*

Comp. Similar to Leadhillite, or $\dot{P}b\ddot{S}$ + $3\dot{P}b\ddot{C}$.

Analysis, by *Brooke*:

Sulphate of lead . .	. 27·5
Carbonate of lead . .	. 72·5
	100·0

Localities.—Scotch. In attached crystals on the Susanna lode at Leadhills, in Lanarkshire, associated with Lanarkite, Leadhillite, and Cerussite. — *Foreign.* Moldawa, in the Bannat, on Brown Iron-ore and Galena.

Brit. Mus., Case 55.

Susannite may be distinguished from Leadhillite, to which it otherwise bears a close resemblance, by the rhombohedral form of its crystals, and its higher specific gravity.

SVANBERGITE, *Igelström.* Occurs massive. Colour pale red. H. 5. S.G. 3·3.

Analysis:

Sulphuric acid . .	. 17·52
Phosphoric acid . .	. 17·80

Alumina . . .	. 37·84
Lime	. 6·00
Protoxide of iron . .	. 1·40
Soda	. 12·84
Water	. 6·80
Chlorine . . .	. trace
	100·00

Locality. Wermland, in Sweden, with Cyanite, Mica, Quartz, and Hematite.

The name Svanbergite has also been applied by Shepard to Platiniridium.

SWAGA. See BORAX.

SWAMP-ORE, *Jameson.* } See BOG
SWAMPY IRON-ORE, *Kirwan.* } IRON-ORE.

SWIMMING QUARTZ, *Bakewell.* See FLOAT-STONE.

SWINESTONE, *Kirwan.* See STINKSTONE.

SYEPOORITE, *Nicol, Brooke & Miller.* A Sulphide of Cobalt, occurring in considerable quantities in grains or veins, in primary schist, mechanically mixed with Magnetic Pyrites, at Saipoor, near Rajpootanah, in North Western India. It is of a steel-grey colour, inclining to yellow. S.G. 5·45.

Comp. $Co^2 S$.

Analysis, by *Middleton:*

Sulphur . . .	. 35·36
Cobalt	. 64·64
	100·00

It is used by Indian jewellers for imparting a delicate rose colour to gold.

SYLVAN, *Werner.* Tellurium.

SYLVANITE, *Kirwan.* The name originally given to Native Tellurium, from its being first found in Transylvania.

SYLVANITE, *Dana.* Rhombic: primary form a right rhombic prism. Generally occurs in indistinct and minute circular crystals, modified at the edges and angles, and often grouped in rows, forming triangular figures like letters. Cleavage in two directions, nearly at right angles; one very

Fig. 420·   Fig. 421.

perfect. Colour steel-grey to tin-white, and brass-yellow. Opaque. Lustre metallic; sometimes with a slight tarnish. Streak like the colour. Yields easily to the knife. Soft

SYLVIN.

and very sectile. Brittle. Fracture semi-conchoidal. H. 1·5 to 2. S.G. 7·99 to 8·28.

Comp. Telluride of gold and silver, or Ag Te⁴ + Au Te⁵ = silver 13·8, gold 20·5, tellurium 59·7 = 100.

Comp. $Telluride$ of gold and silver, or $\text{Ag Te}^4 + \text{Au Te}^5 = $ silver 13·8, gold 20·5, tellurium 59·7 = 100.

Analysis, from Offenbanya, by *Petz* :

Silver .	.	.	.	. 11·47
Gold .	.	.	.	. 21·97
Tellurium	.	.	.	. 39·97
Lead .	.	.	.	. 0·25
Copper .	.	.	.	. 0·76
Antimony	.	.	.	. 0·58

100·00

BB on charcoal fuses, emitting a slightly acid odour, covers the charcoal with a white deposit, and is reduced to a dark grey me-tallic globule, which is converted, by long blowing, into a pale yellow alloy of gold and silver, exhibiting incandescence at the moment of solidification.—(*Berzelius.*)

Dissolves in aqua-regia, with separation of chloride of silver, and forms a solution which gives a white precipitate on dilution with water.

Localities. Offenbanya, in Transylvania (*Graphic Tellurium* of Phillips), associated with Gold, in narrow veins traversing por-phyry. Nagyag, in Transylvania (*Yellow Tellurium* of Phillips). Gold Hill, North Carolina, U. S.

Brit. Mus., Case 3.

Sylvanite constitutes a valuable ore of gold and silver.

SYLVIN, *Nicol, Vogel.* SYLVINE, *Dana.* SYLVYNE, *Beudant, Phillips.* Cubical. Oc-curs crystallized in cubes, with a cleavage parallel to the faces of the cube. Colourless, or white. Lustre vitreous. Soluble. Tastes like Common Salt. S.G. 1·91 to 1·95.

Comp. Chloride of potassium, or K Cl = potash 52·6, chlorine 47·4 = 100.

Decrepitates when heated, fuses at a low red heat, volatilizes at a higher temperature unchanged. It is somewhat more volatile than Common Salt; in a covered crucible, it may be kept in a state of fusion without loss; in open vessels, it volatilizes gra-dually in the constantly renewed current of air.—(*H. Rose.*)

Localities. The mines of Hallein in Salzburg, and Berchtesgaden in Bavaria, with Common Salt (*Vogel*). Vesuvius, in a state of sublimation about the fumaroles.—(*Smithson*).

Name. The name Sylvine was given to this mineral in consequence of its being the digestive salt of Sylvius de la Boë.

SYMPLESITE, *Breithaupt.* Oblique. Oc-

TABERGITE. 369

curs in very minute prismatic crystals, and also in acicular radiations. Colour pale indigo, inclining to celandine-green. Trans-parent to translucent. Lustre vitreous; of cleavage-planes pearly. Streak bluish-white. Rather sectile. H. 2·5. S.G. 2·957.

Comp. Hydrated arseniate of protoxide of iron, or 3Fe As² + 8H.

Comp. $Hydrated$ arseniate of protoxide of iron, or $3\dot{\text{Fe}}\,\ddot{\text{As}}^2 + 8\dot{\text{H}}$.

BB gives off strong arsenical odours, be-comes black and magnetic, but does not fuse.

Locality. Klein-Friesa, near Lobenstein, in Reuss, with Sparry Iron and Cobaltic Pyrites.

Name. From συμπλησιάζω, *to draw close together.*

T.

TABASHEER. A siliceous concretion, bearing some resemblance to Hydrophane, found in the interior of the stem of the large Indian bamboo. It is imperfectly trans-parent, and sometimes altogether opaque, but, when immersed in water, it gives out a quantity of air-bubbles, and becomes more transparent, returning to its original opacity on exposure to the air. S.G. 2·059 to 2·412 (Brewster) when completely saturated with water, when its weight is more than doubled.

Analysis :

Silica .	.	.	.	. 96·94
Potash and lime .		.	.	0·13
Water .	.	.	.	. 2·93
Organic matter	.	.	.	. trace

100·00

Silica enters into the composition of the stem of the Indian bamboo, in the same way that it does into that of ordinary wheat-straw. In the former case, the silica is found to occur in different quantities in the different parts of the cane. Thus, the pith contains 0·448 per cent., the inner wood much less, and the greater proportion is found in the external wood. Reasoning on this fact, the formation of Tabasheer is explained by Mons. Guibourt in the following manner: " At the time when the straw is developed, the outer wood has no longer any necessity for silica, which is carried inwards and de-posited in the cavity of the straw."

The Orientals regard Tabasheer as one of the most valuable of medicines. In India it is called *Vedroo - paloo* (bamboo - milk), *Vedroo-carpooram* (bamboo - camphor), and *Manzil-upoo* (bamboo-salt).

TABERGITE, *Rose.* The name given to the Pyrosclerite of Taberg, in Wermland.

B B

Analysis, by *Svanberg:*

Silica		35·76
Alumina		13·03
Magnesia		29·27
Protoxide of iron		6·34
Protoxide of manganese		1·64
Potash		2·07
Fluoride of magnesium		1·10
Water		11·76
		100·97

TABLE SPAR,   } See WOLLAS-
TABULAR SPAR, *Phillips.* }   TONITE.

TABULAR QUARTZ. Thin plates of Quartz, either arranged parallel to or crossing one another, so as to form open cells.

TACHYAPHALTITE, *Berlin.* Probably an altered Zircon. Occurs in short thick prisms of a dark reddish-brown colour, with a lustre varying from submetallic to vitreous. Subtranslucent. Streak dirty yellow. Fracture conchoidal. H. 5·5. S.G. 3·6.

Analysis, by *Berlin :*

Silica		34·58
Zirconia		38·96
Peroxide of iron		3·72
Alumina		1·85
Thoria?		12·32
Water		8·49
		99·92

BB infusible, but becomes dirty white: with borax dissolves with difficulty.

Locality. Krageroe in Norway, in granite veins traversing gneiss.

Name. From ταχὺς, *quick*, and ἄφαλτος, *springing off;* in allusion to the readiness with which the mineral flies from the gangue when struck.

TACHYDRITE, *Rammelsberg.* An extremely deliquescent salt, resembling Carnallite, occurring in round masses in compact Anhydrite. Colour yellow. Transparent or translucent. Cleavable in two directions.

Comp. $2Mg\ Cl + Ca\ Cl + 12\dot{H}$.

Analysis (mean of two):

Calcium		7·46
Magnesium		9·51
Chlorine		40·34
Water		42·69
		100·00

Locality. Stassfurt.

TACHYLITE, *Breithaupt, Mohs.* The name proposed by Breithaupt for a kind of Isopyre. Amorphous-massive or in plates. Colour velvet-brown or black. Opaque.

Lustre vitreous to greasy. Streak dark grey. Fracture conchoidal. H. 6·5. S.G. 2·5 to 2·7.

Comp. ($\ddot{R}^3 + \ddot{A}l$) $\ddot{S}i$, or $2(\dot{K}, \dot{N}a, \dot{C}a, \dot{M}g, \dot{M}n, \dot{F}e)$ $(\ddot{F}e, \ddot{A}i,)$ $\ddot{S}i^4$.

Analysis, from Säsebühl, by *Schnedermann :*

Silica		55·74
Alumina		12·40
Protoxide of iron		13·06
Lime		7·28
Magnesia		5·92
Soda		3·88
Potash		0·60
Protoxide of manganese		0·19
Water		2·73
		101·80

BB fuses very readily to an opaque glass. Decomposed completely by concentrated muriatic acid in the cold.

Localities. On the Säsebühl near Dransfeld, and at Höllengrund near Münden; forming small masses in basalt and wacke. The Vogelsgebirge in igneous rocks. See SIDEROMELAN.

Name. From ταχὺς, *quick*, and λύω, *to fuse*. Brit. Mus., Case 38.

Tachylite is stated by Naumann & Rammelsberg to be a basaltic glass, and, consequently, to have no definite composition.

TAFELSPATH, *Stutz.* Table-spar. See WOLLASTONITE.

TAGILITE, *Hermann.* Occurs in fungoid or botryoidal masses, with a rough and earthy surface. Structure radiating - fibrous and earthy. Colour emerald-green, or mountaingreen when weathered. H. 3. S.G. 4·35.

Comp. (Libethenite + $2\dot{H}$), or phosphate of copper: $= \dot{C}u^4 \ddot{P} + 3\dot{H}$, with a trace of arsenic.

Analysis, by *Hermann :*

Phosphoric acid		27·70
Oxide of copper		61·80
Water		10·50
		100·00

Locality. Nijni-Taguilsk, in the Ural; on Brown Iron Ore. The Mercedes Mine, about 20 miles E. of Coquimbo, in Chili, forming stellated and fibrous masses in Brown Iron Ore.
Brit. Mus., Case 57.

TALC, *Haüy.* Occurs rarely in rectangular prisms, and in thin hexagonal plates, with a perfect basal cleavage. Generally massive, foliated, and granular; also slaty and earthy. Colour apple-green to silver-white, grey, dark-green, brown, and red. Lustre pearly. Semi-transparent to sub-translucent. Highly sectile. In thin laminæ flexible, but not elastic. Yields to the nail. Streak white, or in dark-green varieties paler than the colour. More unctuous to the touch than Chlorite. H. 1 to 1·5. S.G. 2·65 to 2·74.

Comp. Silicate of magnesia, or $\dot{M}g^6 \overset{...}{S}i^5$

$+ 2\dot{H} =$ silica 62·14, magnesia 32·92 $= 100.$

Analysis, from Greiner, by *v. Kobell:*

Silica	62·8
Magnesia	32·4
Alumina	1·0
Protoxide of iron, with oxide of titanium . . .	1·6
Water	2·3
	100·1

BB splits up into laminæ, and hardens without fusing. With microcosmic salt yields a turbid glass, together with an insoluble skeleton of silica. Not acted on, to any perceptible degree, either before or after ignition, by muriatic acid or oil of vitriol.

Localities. Greiner, in the Tyrol. Sala, Fahlun, and other places in Sweden. Pyrenees. United States, &c.

Brit. Mus., Case 32.

Talc is a very generally diffused mineral, and not only enters into the composition of many crystalline rocks, but some of its varieties form extensive beds in districts occupied by crystalline rocks. The common variety forms the basis of the *rouge* used by ladies — the Talc being coloured by an extract from the *Carthamus tinctorius,* or *Safflower.* In a powdered state it is also employed to make new boots and gloves slip on easily, and to diminish friction in machinery. In its natural state it is used by tailors for drawing lines on cloth. For varieties of Talc and localities, &c., see INDURATED TALC, TALCOSE SLATE. SOAPSTONE or STEATITE (*Speckstein*), VENETIAN TALC.

Brit. Mus., Case 32.

M. P. G. Horse-shoe Case, No. 1170.

TALC-APATITE, *Hermann.* A variety of Apatite containing magnesia. It occurs in six-sided crystals in Chlorite-slate, on the Schischimskian mountains, near Slatoust, in the Ural.

Comp. $3\dot{C}u^3 \overset{...}{P} + \dot{M}g^3 \overset{...}{P}.$

Analysis, by *Hermann:*

Lime	37·50
Phosphoric acid . .	39·02

Magnesia	7·74
Sulphuric acid . . .	2·10
Chlorine	0·91
Oxide of iron . . .	1·00
Fluorine and loss . .	2·23
Insoluble	9·50
	100·00

Brit. Mus., Case 57 B.

TALC COMMUN, *Brochant.*
TALC ECAILLEUX, *La Metherie.* } See TALC.

TALC ENDURCI, *Brochant.* INDURATED TALC (which see).

TALC GRANULEUX, *Haüy.* See NACRITE.

TALC GRAPHIQUE, *Haüy.* See AGALMATOLITE.

TALC MICA, *Mohs.* Includes Potash-Mica, Lithia - Mica, Biotite or Magnesia-Mica, Talc and Chlorite.

TALC OLLAIRE, *Haüy.* See POTSTONE.

TALC PHOSPHORSÄURER. See WAGNERITE.

TALC STEATITE, *Haüy.* Soapstone. See STEATITE.

TALC ZOGRAPHIQUE, *Haüy.* See GREEN EARTH.

TALCITE, *Thomson.* See NACRITE. Talcite occurs in co. Wicklow, in Ireland, investing; and in the form of crystals of Andalusite at Glendalough, Glen Malure, and Lough Dan; also at Mount Leinster in Carlow, and Three Rock Mountain, co. Dublin.

Analysis, from Three Rock Mountain, by the *Rev. S. Haughton:*

Silica	43·47
Alumina . . .	31·42
Peroxide of iron . .	4·79
Magnesia . . .	1·13
Lime	1·38
Soda	1·44
Potash	10·71
Water	5·43
	99·77

TALKARTIGER DIALLAG, *Hausmann.* See DIALLAGE.

TALKERDE, *Werner.* Magnesia.

TALKERDE-ALAUN, *v. Kobell.* See MAGNESIA ALUM.

TALKHYDRAT, *v. Leonhard.* Native Magnesia. See BRUCITE.

TALKOID. The name given by Naumann to sparry crystalline Talc from Presnitz, where it occurs in snow-white, broad foliations, with Magnetite. S.G. 2·48.

Comp. $\overset{4}{\dot{M}}g^3\overset{...}{S}i^5 + \dot{H}.$

TALKSPATH, *Hartmann, Naumann.* Native Carbonate of Magnesia. See MAGNESITE. The name Talkspath is also used by G. Rose and others for carbonate of magnesia-and-iron (Bitter Spar and Brown Spar in part). See BREUNNERITE.

TALKSTEINMARK. See MYELIN. A variety of Lithomarge, from Rochlitz in Saxony.

TAMARITE, *Greg & Lettsom.* The name proposed by Brooke and Miller for Copper-Mica (Chalcophyllite), from its occurrence, amongst other localities, at Huel Tamar.

TAMMELA-TANTALITE. A variety of Tantalite, from Tammela, in Finland, containing only a small quantity of tin. Colour black. Lustre submetallic. Streak blackish-brown to cinnamon-brown. S.G. 7·811 to 7·943.

Analysis, by *Weber:*

Tantalic acid	. .	83·90
Oxide of tin	. .	0·66
Protoxide of iron	.	13·81
Protoxide of manganese	.	0·74
Oxide of copper .	. .	0·11
		99·22

See SKOGBÖLITE and TANTALITE.

TANKITE. See CHIASTOLITE.

TANNENITE, *Dana.* A sulphide of bismuth and copper, occurring in thin striated prisms, of a colour varying from greyish to tin-white, with a bright metallic lustre.

Comp. CuS + Bi²S⁵.

Analysis, by *R. Schneider:*

Sulphur	. . .	18·83
Bismuth	. . .	62·16
Copper	. . .	18·72
		99·71

BB on charcoal, swells up and fuses readily; with soda yields a globule of copper. With nitric acid forms a deep bluish-green solution, which becomes dark blue on the addition of ammonia.

Locality. Tannenbaum, near Johanngeorgenstadt in Saxony.

TANTALE OXIDÉ, *Haüy.* See COLUMBITE.

TANTALE OXIDÉ FERRO-MANGANESIFÈRE, *Haüy.* See COLUMBITE.

TANTALE OXIDÉ YTTRIFÈRE, *Haüy.* See YTTROTANTALITE.

TANTALATE OF IRON. See TANTALITE.

TANTALITE, *Eckeberg, Jameson, Phillips.* Rhombic: primary form a right rectangular prism. Occurs in single crystals and in small crystalline masses; the crystals are mostly incomplete, but possess the general form of quadrangular prisms, striated longitudinally, and variously modified. Opaque. Colour iron-black, with a nearly pure me-

tallic lustre. It scratches glass and gives sparks with steel. Streak reddish-brown, or

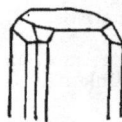

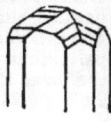

Fig. 422.   Fig. 423.   Fig. 424.

coffee-coloured. Brittle. Fracture uneven or cenchoidal. H. 6 to 6·5. S.G. 7·1 to 7·96.

Comp. (Fe Mn) (Ta Cb).

Analysis, from Kimito, by *Weber:*

Tantalic acid	. .	75·71
Oxide of tin	. .	9·67
Protoxide of iron	.	9·80
Protoxide of manganese	.	4·32
		99·50

BB alone, unchanged: with borax, the varieties containing large proportions of tantalum dissolve slowly but perfectly, imparting to it a faint green colour. Those with less tantalum fuse readily to a black or dark green glass, which is nearly opaque.

Partly soluble in heated sulphuric acid.

Localities.— Finland: at Skogböle, in the diocese of Kimito, and Härkäsaari in that of Tammela; also at Björtboda.

The metal Tantalum was discovered by Eckeberg, in specimens from Kimito.

The tantalites from Finbo and Broddbo, as well as some of those from Kimito contain a large quantity of oxide of tin (see CASSITEROTANTALITE), and in those from the latter locality, part of the iron is replaced by manganese. Tantalite was first found in America, at Haddam, in Connecticut: it also occurs at Bodenmais in Bavaria, associated with Beryl, and remarkable for containing niobic acid; likewise in France, at Chanteloube near Limoges.

The two first localities are properly for *Columbite* (which see). The following is an analysis by Jenzsch from Chanteloube, (S.G. 7·703) which is Tantalite proper.

Tantalic acid	. .	83·55
Oxide of tin	. .	1·02
Zirconia	. .	1·54
Protoxide of iron	.	14·48
Oxide of manganese .	.	trace
		100·59

The name Tantalite was restricted by Nordenskiöld to the varieties containing only a small quantity of oxide of tin, from Tammela, Björtboda and Kimito in Fin-

land. See also IXIOLITE, KIMITO-TANTA-
LITE, SKOGRÖLITE, TAMMELA-TANTALITE,
and COLUMBITE.

Brit. Mus. Case 38.

TARNOWITZITE. A variety of Aragonite,
from Tarnowitz in Upper Silesia, containing
carbonate of lead.

Analysis, by *Böttger* ;

Carbonate of lime	. 95·94
Carbonate of lead	. 3·86
Water .	. 0·16
	99 96

Brit. Mus., Case 41.

TAURISCITE, *Volger.* A mineral isomorphous with Epsomite. Occurs in acicular
right rhomboidal prisms, with the composition of ordinary sulphate of iron. H. 2·5.

Comp. $\dot{F}e\dot{H} + \ddot{H}^6\dddot{S}$, or $\dot{F}e\dddot{S} + 7\dot{H}$.

Locality. Windgälle, Canton of Uri (*pagus
Tauriscorum*), with crystals of Alum and
common Sulphate of Iron.

TAUTOLITE. *Breithaupt ;* or TAUTOLITH.
A mineral resembling Hyalosiderite, found
in volcanic rocks near Lake Laach, on the
Lower Rhine. Colour velvet-black. Opaque.
Lustre vitreous, Streak grey. Very brittle.
Fracture conchoidal to uneven. H. 6·5.
S.G. 3·865.

BB fuses to a black magnetic slag : with
borax yields a clear green glass.

Name. An abbreviation of Tautometro-
lite (from ταῦτο, *the same,* μέτρον, *measure,* and
λίθος, *stone*), because of the resemblance of
the measurements of the angles of its crystals with those of Chrysolite, and many
other analogous minerals.

TCHINGTCHANG. The Chinese name for
dark blue kinds of Lapis Lazuli, containing
disseminated spangles of Iron Pyrites. It
is made into buttons, snuff-boxes, cups,
vases, &c.

TECTIZITE, *Breithaupt.* Occurs in small
acicular and pyramidal crystals and massive.
Colour clove-brown. Lustre vitreous or
resinous. Soft and friable. H. 1·5 to 2.
S.G. nearly 2.

Comp. Unknown, but supposed to be a
hydrous sulphate of peroxide of iron.

BB fuses in its water of crystallization.
Readily soluble in water.

Localities. Graul, near Schwartzenberg,
in Saxony. Bräunsdorf, in the Erzgebirge.

TEKORETINE, *Forchammer.* A crystallized mineral resin, found in fossil wood in
Denmark. It resembles Fichtelite, except
in composition. It consists of C H, or carbon 85·89, hydrogen 12·81.

Soluble in ether ; in alcohol only slightly.
Fuses at 45° C. (113° F.) and distills at
nearly 336° C. (636° F.).

TÉLÉSIE, *Haüy.* The name given by
French lapidaries to crystallized and transparent kinds of Corundum, and to the varieties which are used for fine stones in
jewelry. See SAPPHIRE.

TELLUR AURIFÈRE ET PLOMBIFÈRE,
Haüy. See SYLVANITE.

TELLUR-BISMUTH, *v. Leonhard.* See TE-
TRADYMITE.

TELLURBLEI, *G. Rose.* Telluride of lead.
See ALTAITE.

TELLUR-SILBER, *Rose.* See HESSITE.

TELLUR-WISMUTH, *v. Leonhard.* See
TETRADYMITE.

TELLURE NATIF AURIFÈRE ET PLOMBI-
FÈRE, *Haüy.* Yellow Tellurium. See SYL-
VANITE.

TELLURE NATIF AURO - ARGENTIFÈRE,
Haüy. Graphic Tellurium. See SYL-
VANITE.

TELLURE NATIF AURO-FERRIFÈRE, *Haüy.*
See NATIVE TELLURIUM.

TELLURE NATIF AURO - PLOMBIFÈRE,
Haüy. Black Tellurium. See NAGYAGITE.

TELLURGOLDSILBER, *Hausmann.* See
PETZITE.

TELLURIC BISMUTH, *Phillips.* See TE-
TRADYMITE.

TELLURIC OCHRE, *Dana.* } See TELLU-
TELLURIC OXIDE. } RITE.

TELLURIC SILVER, *Allan, Phillips.* See
HESSITE.

TELLURIDE OF LEAD. See ALTAITE.

TELLURIGE SÄURE, *Petz.* See TELLU-
RITE.

TELLURITE, *Nicol.* Telluric Ochre, occurring in small white beads or spherical
masses, having a tinge of greyish-yellow,
and a fibrous radiated structure, at Face-
bay and Zalathna, in Transylvania, with
Native Tellurium.

Comp. Telluric oxide or Tellurous acid ;

$\ddot{Te}$ = tellurium 80, oxygen 20 = 100.

TELLURIUM-GLANCE. See NAGYAGITE.

TELLURIUM-OCHRE, *Petz.* See TELLU-
RITE.

TELLUROUS ACID. See TELLURITE.

TELLUR-SILBER, *G. Rose.* See HESSITE.

TELLUR-SILBERBLEI. See SYLVANITE.

TELLUR-WISMUTH. See TETRADYMITE.

TENASSERIME, *Rev. F. Mason.* See TRE-
MENHEERITE.

TENNANTIT, *Haidinger, Naumann*: or
TENNANTITE, *Dana, Phillips, Greg & Lettsom.* Cubical ; primary form the octahedron. Cleavage dodecahedral ; imperfect.

B B 3

Occurs crystallized in rhombic dodecahedrons, sometimes variously modified; also in cubes and octahedrons, of which the edges and angles are replaced. Twins. Rarely

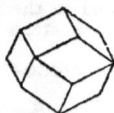 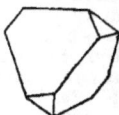

Fig. 425.   Fig. 426.

found massive. Colour lead-grey, inclining to iron-black. Opaque. Lustre metallic. Streak dark reddish-grey. Brittle. Fracture imperfectly lamellar and uneven. H. 5·3 to 4. S.G. 4·37 to 4·5.

Comp. (Cu Fe) S + As² S³ = copper 46·68, arsenic 19·90, iron 3·71, sulphur 29·71 = 100.

Analysis, from Cornwall, by *Phillips :*

Copper	. . .	47·70
Arsenic	. . .	12·46
Iron .	. . .	9·75
Sulphur	. . .	30·25

                     100·16

BB decrepitates, burns with a blue flame, giving off arsenical fumes, and fuses to a magnetic slag.

Soluble in nitric acid.

Localities. — English. Cornwall: Carn Brea; East Relistian Mine; Dolcoath; Roskear; Cook's Kitchen; Tincroft; Huel Jewel; Huel Unity; Trevascus, &c. — *Foreign.* Skutterud, in Norway. Algeria.

Name. After Smithson Tennant, chemist. Brit. Mus., Case 7.

M. P. G. Principal Floor, Wall-case 7, Nos. 543 to 547 (British).

TENORITE, *Semmola.* Occurs in small hexagonal and sometimes triangular laminæ, attached by their edges; sometimes obliquely—never flat: also earthy, and as a black powder. Colour dark steel-grey, inclining to black. Opaque; slightly translucent and brownish in thin folia. Lustre metallic. Streak black. Elastic.

Comp. Protoxide of copper, or Ċu = copper 79·85, oxygen 20·15 = 100.

BB on charcoal, fuses to a red globule (generally covered with a black scoriaceous crust), which dissolves with effervescence in nitric acid. With borax, yields an emerald-green glass. Colours the flame of a spirit lamp slightly green.

Locality. In the lava of Vesuvius; in the crater and the outlets of extinct or active eruptions. It is most frequently accompanied by Common Salt, and is evidently produced by sublimation, being always superimposed on other sublimed substances.

Name. After Tenore, a celebrated Italian botanist, and President of the Neapolitan Academy of Sciences.

Brit. Mus., Case 17.

TEPHROITE, *Breithaupt, Mohs, Dufrénoy.* Occurs in compact crystalline and granular masses, with a cleavage parallel to the sides of a square or rectangular prism. Colour ash-grey, turning black on exposure. Lustre adamantine. Streak paler then the colour. Fracture imperfect-conchoidal or uneven. H. 5·5 to 6. S.G. 4 to 4·116.

Comp. Silicate of protoxide of manganese,

or Mn⁵ S̈i = protoxide of manganese 70·2, silica 29·8 = 100.

Analysis, from Sparta, by *Rammelsberg :*

Silica .	. .	28·66
Protoxide of manganese	.	68·88
Protoxide of iron	. .	2·92

                     100·46

BB fuses readily to a black slag.

Soluble in muriatic acid (without evolution of chlorine), forming a jelly of silica.

Localities. Stirling, Sparta, and New Jersey, with Franklinite and Red Zinc.

Name. From τέφρος, *ash-grey.*

Brit. Mus., Case 26.

TERATOLITE, *Glocker.* Compact and earthy. Colour pale violet to bluish-grey; often with reddish-white veins and spots. Opaque. Dull. Rough and meagre to the touch. Fracture uneven, earthy to flat-conchoidal. H. 2·5 to 3. S.G. 2·5.

Analysis, by *Schüler :*

Silica .	. .	41·66
Alumina .	. .	22·85
Peroxide of iron	. .	12·98
Peroxide of manganese	.	1·68
Lime .	. .	3·04
Magnesia .	. .	2·56
Potash .	. .	0·93
Water	. . .	14·20

                     99·89

BB infusible. With borax gives an iron reaction.

Locality. Planitz, near Zwickau, in Saxony; in beds in the coal formation.

Brit. Mus., Case 25.

Teratolite is the *Terra Miraculosa Saxoniæ* of old authors; which was valued on account of its supposed medicinal properties.

TERENITE, *Emmons, Dufrénoy.* (From τέρην, *tender.*) An altered form of Scapolite.

TERNÄRBLEIERZ. See LEADHILLITE.

TERRA CIMOLITA. See CIMOLITE.

TERRA DI SIENNA.

TERRA DI SIENNA, *T. H. Rowney.* A kind of Ochre, of a brownish-yellow colour, which acquires a fine and rich chestnut colour by ignition, in which state it is used as a paint, under the name of *burnt Sienna.* Adheres to the tongue, and absorbs much water without appearing moist. Fracture earthy and conchoidal. Easily scratched with the nail. S.G. 3·46.

Comp. $4\ddot{R} \ddot{S}i + 6\ddot{H}$.
Analysis, by *T. H. Rowney*;

Silica	. 11·14
Alumina . . .	. 9·47
Peroxide of iron . .	. 65·35
Lime	. 0·53
Magnesia . . .	. 0·03
Water	. 13·00
	99·52

BB with borax and microcosmic salt gives a transparent globule, with an iron reaction.
Not in the least degree attacked by concentrated muriatic acid.
. *Locality.* The neighbourhood of Sienna, in Italy.

TERRA MIRACULOSA SAXONIÆ. See TE-RATOLITE.
TERRE À FOULON. See FULLER'S EARTH.
TERRE À PORCELAINE, *Brochant.* See KAOLIN.
TERRE DE LEMNOS. See LEMNIAN EARTH.
TERRE D'OMBRE, *Haüy.* See UMBER.
TERRE SIGILLÉE. See LEMNIAN EARTH.
TESSELITE, *Brewster.* A cube-like variety of Apophyllite which, when optically examined, exhibits a peculiar tesselated or mosaic-like structure.

Analysis, from Faröe, by *Berzelius :*

Silica	. 52·38
Lime	. 24·98
Potash	. 5·37
Hydrofluoric acid .	. 0·64
Water	. 16·20
	99·57

Localities. Near Talisker, in Skye, in fine white and nearly opaque crystals, associated with Scolezite. Naalsoe, in the Faröe Islands, with Mesole and Chabasie.
Brit. Mus., Case 27.

TESSERALKIES, *Breithaupt.* See SKUT-TERUDITE.
TETARTIN, *Breithaupt.* (From τίταρτος, the *fourth part,* because a fourth part only of a certain group of faces occurs in the crystals.) See ALBITE.

TETRAHEDRAL BORACITE. 375

TETARTO - PRISMATIC FELSPAR, *Mohs.* See ALBITE.
TETARTO - PRISMATIC VITRIOL SALT. *Mohs.* Sulphate of Copper. See CYANOSITE.
TETRADYMITE, *Brooke & Miller, Haidinger, Hausmann.* Rhombohedral : primary form an acute rhombohedron. Generally occurs massive, with a foliated structure; sometimes in tabular crystals, with a very perfect basal cleavage. Colour pale lead-grey, inclining to tin-white; internally splendent and shining. Lustre metallic. In thin laminæ, flexible and slightly elastic. Soils paper. Sectile. H. 1·5 to 2. S.G. 7·2 to 8·44.
Comp. Sulphotelluride of bismuth, or $2\text{Bi Te}^3 + \text{Bi S}^3$ = bismuth 59·66, tellurium 35·86, sulphur 4·48 = 100.

Analyses, (*a*) from Schubkau, by *Wehrle* ; (*b*) from Cumberland, by *Rammelsberg :*

	(*a*)	(*b*)
Bismuth . .	60·0′	84·33
Tellurium . .	34·6	6·73
Sulphur . .	4·8	6·43
Selenium . .	trace	—
	99·4	97·49

Analysis (*b*) gives the formula $\text{Bi}^4 + \text{Te} + \text{S}^4$.
Heated in a glass tube, yields metallic tellurium, which sublimes in drops.
BB fuses readily, exhaling odours of sulphur and selenium; burns with a bluish flame, forms a yellow film, with a white border on the charcoal, and leaves a shining metallic globule, which, on cooling, becomes covered with a reddish film. The reduced metal is brittle, and has a granular fracture.
Dissolves readily in nitric acid, depositing flakes of sulphur.
Localities. — *English.* Brandy Gill, Carrock Fells, Cumberland, in foliated masses in quartz rock. — *Foreign.* Hungary, at Schubkau, near Shemnitz, in trachytic conglomerate, and Deutsch-Pilsen (*Molybdan silver*). Tellemark, in Norway. Bastnaes, in Sweden. San José, in Brazil (*Bornite*). Tellurium Mine, Fluvanna co., Virginia, in mica-slate; near Pioneer Mills, Cabarras co., North Carolina, &c. U. S.
Name. From τιτράδυμος, *fourfold,* because of the occurrence of quadruple crystals.
Brit. Mus., Case 3.
M. P. G. Principal Floor, Wall-case 13 (British).
TETRAEDRIT, *Haidinger, v. Kobell.* ●Grey Copper. See TETRAHEDRITE.
TETRAHEDRAL BORACITE, *Mohs.* See BORACITE.

BB 4

TETRAHEDRAL COPPER GLANCE, *Mohs.*
See TETRAHEDRITE.

TETRAHEDRAL GARNET. See HELVINE.

TETRAHEDRITE, *Dana, Greg & Lettsom.*
Grey Copper or Fahlerz. Cubical. Occurs
crystallized in tetrahedrons; also massive
and disseminated. Cleavage imperfect, octahedral. Colour between steel-grey and

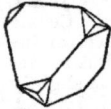 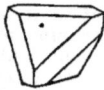 

Fig. 427.   Fig. 428.   Fig. 429.

iron-black. Opaque; in thin splinters
cherry-red by transmitted light. Lustre
metallic. Streak like the colour, or inclining to brown. Rather brittle. Fracture
fine-grained, uneven, or imperfect-conchoidal. H. 3 to 4. S.G. 4·5 to 5·2.

Comp. (Cu, Ag, Fe, Zn) $S + (Sb, As) S^3$.

Analysis, from Andreasberg, by *C. Kuhle-
mann;*

Sulphur	.	.	.	25·22
Copper .	.	.	.	37·18
Antimony	.	.	.	27·38
Zinc	.	.	.	5·00
Iron	.	.	.	3·94
Silver .	.	.	.	1·58
Arsenic	.	.	.	0·67
				100·97

BB gives off arsenical and antimonial
vapours; with borax affords the deep-green
reaction of iron; with soda, after much
roasting, yields a globule of metallic copper.
When reduced to powder, it is decomposed
by nitric acid, affording a green solution.

Localities. — *English.* Various Cornish
mines: Crinnis, Levant, Condurrow, Huel
Prosper (*figs.* 427 and 429), Herodsfoot, &c.
Combe Martin, Devonshire. — *Scotch.* Fass-
ney Burn, E. Lothian. Airthrie, in the
Ochil Hills. Mainland, Shetlands, at Sand-
lodge Mine. — *Irish.* Audley and Ardtulley,
and several other mines in Cork and Water-
ford. — *Foreign.* Andreasberg, in the Harz.
Kremnitz, in Hungary. Freiberg, in Saxony.
Kapnik, in Transylvania. Dillenburg, in
Nassau.

Name. The name Tetrahedrite alludes
to the tetrahedral form of the crystals, in
which it ordinarily occurs.

Brit. Mus., Case 12.

M.°P. G. A 19, in Hall; mass of ore
with Iron Pyrites and Quartz, from Toman-
dashan copper mine, Loch Tay, Perthshire.
Principal Floor, Case 7 ('Tuscany); Case 15

(Cornwall); Wall-cases 7 and 28 (British);
16 and 17 (Foreign); with antimony and
silver, 16 (Spain).

Some varieties of Tetrahedrite contain a
large proportion of silver, amounting sometimes to as much as 31 per cent. (*Weiss-
gültigerz*); others, especially those of North
Hungary and Schwatz, contain mercury,
up to 15 per cent. (*Schwarzerz.*)

A new variety of Tetrahedrite, from Ar-
dillats (Dept. du Rhône), in France, has
been described by Charles Mine, under the
name of *Fournelite.* It occurs with Galena
in a quartzose porphyry, and has a S.G. from
4·305 to 4 320. Its composition calculated
from the mean of three analyses is, copper
32·00, lead 12·00, sulphur 23·00, iron 3·00,
arsenic 8·00, antimony 22·00 = 100.

Tetrahedrite is distinguished from Magnetic and Specular Oxides of Iron by its
total want of action on the magnetic needle;
from Arsenical Iron by inferior hardness,
usually by its darker colour, and by not
yielding the odour of arsenic when struck.

For varieties of Tetrahedrite, see APH-
TONITE, FAHLERZ, POLYTELITE, SCHWARZ-
ERZ, SILBERSCHWARZERZ, SPANIOLITE.

TETRAKLASIT, *Hausmann.* See SCAPO-
LITE.

TETRAPHYLINE. A variety of Triphyline,
from Keiti, in Finland. Is is of a yellow
colour when fresh broken, but becomes black
on exposure; in other respects it resembles
Triphyline in outward aspect. It likewise
gives a stronger manganese reaction before
the blowpipe.

Comp. $3(Li, Mg, Mn, Fe) P$.

Analysis, by *Berzelius* and *Nordenskiöld:*

Phosphoric acid	.	.	42·6
Protoxide of iron	.	.	38·6
Protoxide of manganese	.	12·1
Lithia	.	.	.	8·2
Magnesia	.	.	.	1·7
			103·2

BB with carbonate of soda on platinum
colours the flame red; with boracic acid and
iron wire yields phosphide of iron.

TEXASITE, *Kenngott.* A variety of Emerald
Nickel found on Chrome-Iron, in Serpentine,
at Texas, Lancaster co., Pennsylvania.

THALITE, *Owen.* A kind of Saponite.
Does not occur crystallized, but diffused in
the amygdaloidal trap rocks of Lake Superior. Colour pale yellowish-green, of the
consistence and hardness of wax. S.G.
2·548.

BB tinges the outer flame slightly green;
in thin splinters fuses at the edges.

THALLITE.

When first noticed, this mineral, which is identical with Saponite, was supposed to contain a new metal, to which the name Thalium was given. The earth of this base was called Thalia, and the mineral from which it was extracted Thalite.

Locality. Between Pigeon Point and Fond du Lac, on the north shore of Lake Superior.

THALLITE, *Karsten.* (From θάλλω, *to grow green.*) Acicular crystals of Epidote, met with in the Department of Isère, in France; at Bourg d'Oisans, in Dauphiny; the Alps, &c. Beaudant also applies the name to the Epidote from Logrosan, on the slope of the Sierra de Toledo, in Spain.

Brit. Mus., Case 35.

THARANDITE, *Kühn.* A greenish macled variety of Pearl Spar, found at Tharand, in Saxony.

Fig. 430.

Comp. Ċa C̈ + M̈g Ċ.

Analysis, by *Kühn:*

Carbonate of lime	54·76
Carbonate of magnesia	42·10
Carbonate of iron	4·19
	101·05

Brit. Mus., Case 47.

THENARDITE, *Casaseca, Dufrénoy, Nicol, Phillips.* Rhombic. Cleavage basal. Primary form a right rhombic prism. Occurs in rhombic octahedrons, simple or modified on the summit, aggregated in crusts and druses. Colour white. Translucent, or pellucid. Lustre vitreous. Effloresces and becomes covered on the surface with a white powder on exposure to the air. Taste saline. Wholly soluble in distilled water. Refracts doubly. H. 2·5. S.G. 2 6 to 2·73.

Comp. Anhydrous sulphate of soda, or Ṅa S̈ = soda 56·3, sulphuric acid 43·7 = 100.

Analysis, from Tarapaca, by *Allan Dick:*

Sulphuric acid	55·11
Soda	42·37
Insoluble	2·19
	99·67

BB colours the flame deep yellow, fuses, and on charcoal is reduced to sulphide of sodium.

Localities. Les Salines d'Espartines, five

THERMOPHYLLITE.   377

leagues from Madrid, and 2½ from Aranjuez. In the winter, saline springs rise from the bottom of a basin, and in the summer, when the liquid has attained a certain degree of concentration in consequence of the evaporation, a portion of the salt, which was held in solution, is deposited in more or less regular crystals.

Locality. Tarapaca, in Peru; with Glauberite and Hayesine.

Name. After L. J. Thenard, French chemist.

Brit. Mus., Case 52.

Thenardite has been used by Mons. Rodas in the manufacture of soap.

THERMONATRITE, *Haidinger, Dana, Nicol.* Rhombic. Occurs in rectangular tables with bevelled sides; also as an efflorescence. Colourless. Lustre vitreous. H. 1 to 1·5. S.G. 1·5 to 1·6.

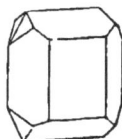

Fig. 431.

Comp. Hydrous carbonate of soda, or Ṅa C̈ + Ḧ = soda 50·0, carbonic acid 35·5, water 14·5 = 100.

Analysis, from Debreczin, by *Beudant:*

Carbonate of soda	73·6
Sulphate of soda	10·4
Chloride of sodium, &c.	10·4
Water	13·8
	108·2

BB like Natron, but does not melt in its water of crystallization.

Localities. The Steppes between the Ural and Altai Mountains. The Macarius desert, in Lower Egypt. The natron lakes at Lagunilla, in Colombia. The plains of Debreczin, in Hungary.

THERMOPHYLLITE, *Nordenskiöld.* A mineral resembling Chlorite, occurring in crystals and grains in an amorphous base resembling Steatite, which is probably amorphous Thermophyllite. Colour light brown to silver-white. Lustre pearly. Fracture uneven, except in the direction of the cleavage. H. 1·5 to 2. S.G. 2·66.

Comp. (R̊3 Ḧ) S̈i + 2Ḧ.

Analysis, by *Augustus B. Northcote:*

Silica	41·73
Alumina	5·52
Protoxide of iron	1·60

Magnesia	. 37·65
Soda	. 2·85
Water .	. 10·65

100·00

BB swells up more than Pyrophyllite and Vermiculite.

Scarcely acted on by muriatic acid.

Locality. Hoponsuo, near Pitkaranda, in Finland.

THIERSCHITE. Oxalate of lime, occurring in the form of a thin, greyish, opaline incrustation, on the marble of the Parthenon at Athens.

THIOSAURITE, *Genth.* A variety of Anorthite from Iceland, of a white to a greyish colour. H. 6. S.G. 2·688.

Analysis, by *Genth:*

Silica .	. 48·36
Alumina	. 30·59
Peroxide of iron .	. 1·37
Magnesia	. 0·97
Protoxide of manganese	. trace
Lime .	. 17·16
Soda .	. 1·13
Potash	. 0 62

100·20

The name is derived from that of the locality where the mineral is found — the Plain of Thiorsa.

THIOMAITE, *Dana.* A prismatic form of carbonate of iron, from the Siebengebirge, in Rhenish Prussia. S.G. 3·10.

It was named after Professor Thomä, of Wiesbaden.

THOMSONIT, *Haidinger, v. Kobell;* or THOMSONITE, *Brooke, Dana, Greg & Lettsom.* Rhombic: primary form a right rhombic prism, with cleavage parallel to its side. It generally occurs in masses with a columnar or radiated structure, in the occasional cavities of which indistinct crystals may be observed. Colourless or snow-white: impure varieties brown. Translucent; in small fragments transparent. Lustre vitreous, inclining to pearly. Streak white. Brittle. Fracture uneven. H. 5 to 5·5. S.G. 2 35 to 2·4.

Fig. 432.   Fig. 433.

Comp. $(\dot{C}a, \dot{N}a)^5 \ddot{S}i + 3\ddot{A}l \ddot{S}i + 7\dot{H} = $ silica 37·4, alumina 31·8, lime 13·0, soda 4·8, water 13·0 = 100.

Analysis, from the Kilpatrick Hills, by *Berzelius :*

Silica .	. 38·30
Alumina	. 30·70
Lime .	. 13·54
Soda .	. 4·53
Water .	. 13·10

100·17

BB swells up, becomes opaque, and fuses at the edges to a white enamel.

Yields a jelly with acids.

Localities. — Scotch. St. Cyrus and Arbuthnot, in Aberdeenshire, in basalt. In the neighbourhood of Kilpatrick and Dumbarton, Dumbartonshire (*figs.* 432, 433). Kilmalcolm and Port Glasgow, in Renfrewshire. — *Irish.* Near the Giant's Causeway. Magee Island.

Name. After Dr. Thomson, Professor of Chemistry in the University of Glasgow.

Brit. Mus., Case 27.

M. P. G. Horse-shoe Case, No. 1175.

THON, *Werner.* Clay.

THONEISENSTEIN, *Werner.* CLAY IRONSTONE.

THONERDE. Alumina.

THONERDE SCHWEFELSÄURE. See ALUNOGENE.

THORITE, *Berzelius, Dana.* In pyramidal prisms: generally massive and compact. Ismorphous with Zircon (*E. Zschau*). Colour black, reddish-brown, or orange-yellow (*Orangite*). Opaque; in thin splinters transparent. Lustre of fresh fracture vitreous. Streak dark brown, or pale orange. Easily frangible. Fracture conchoidal. H. 4·5 to 5. S.G. 4·63 to 4·8.

Comp. Silicate of thoria, or $\dot{T}h^3 \ddot{S}i +$ $3\dot{H} = $ thoria 73·7, silica 16·5, water 9·8 = 100.

Analysis, by *Berzelius :*

Thoria .	. 57·91
Silica .	. 18·98
Peroxide of iron .	. 3·40
Peroxide of manganese	. 2·39
Alumina	. 0·06
Peroxide of uranium .	. 1·61
Oxide of tin .	. 0 01
Oxide of lead .	. 0·80
Lime .	. 2·58
Magnesia .	. 0·36
Soda .	. 0·10
Potash .	. 0·24
Water .	. 9·50
Undecomposed mineral	. 1·70
Loss .	. 0·49

100·13

BB becomes of a reddish-brown colour, without fusing; with borax forms a glass coloured by iron.

Decomposed by muriatic acid, with formation of a jelly.

Locality. Lövön, near Brevig, in Norway, in syenite on compact Analcime.

Brit. Mus., Case 26.

The metal Thorium was first discovered in this mineral by Berzelius. See also ORANGITE.

THRAULITE, *v. Kobell.* (From θραυλὸς, *easily frangible*). A variety of Hisingerite, occurring with Magnetic Pyrites at Bodenmais, in Bavaria.

Analysis, by *v. Kobell :*

Peroxide of iron	.	.	. 50·86
Silica	.	.	. 31·28
Water	.	.	. 19·12

101·26

THROMBOLITE, *Dana, Breithaupt, Nicol.* Amorphous. Colour yellowish-green, inclining to emerald-, leek-, or dark-green; becoming black on exposure to the air. Opaque. Lustre vitreous. Rather brittle. Fracture conchoidal. H. 3 to 4. S.G. 3·38 to 3·4.

Comp. Phosphate of copper, or $\ddot{C}u^2\ddot{P} +$ 6$\ddot{H}$.

Analysis, by *Plattner :*

Phosphoric acid	.	.	. 41·0
Silica, alumina	.	.	. trace
Oxide of copper	.	.	. 39·2
Water	.	.	. 16·8

97·0

BB colours the flame blue and then green; on charcoal fuses readily to a black globule, and finally yields a globule of metallic copper.

Locality. Rezbanya, in Hungary, with Malachite on limestone.

Name. From θρομϐὸς, *numb* or *stiff*, and λίθος, *stone*.

THULITE, *Brooke.* Occurs in translucent, rose coloured, or peachblossom-red crystalline masses, or in small crystals more or less imperfect; with a composition analogous to that of Epidote, except that they contain a small per centage of protoxide of iron. Lustre vitreous. Streak greyish - white. H. 6·5. S.G. 3·1 to 3·4.

Analysis, from Souland, by *C. Gmelin :*

Silica	.	.	. 42·81
Alumina	.	.	. 31·14
Protoxide of iron	.	. 2·29
Lime	.	.	. 18·73

Magnesia	.	.	. 1·63
Soda	.	.	. 1·89
Water	.	.	. 0·64

99·13

BB froths, swells up to a white porous mass and fuses at the edges only.

Localities. Norway ; at Souland, in Tellemarken, associated with Quartz, Fluor, and Cyprine; and at the iron mine, near Klodeberg.

Name. From *Thule,* another name for Norway.

Thulite, instead of being classed with Epidote (as it was by Brooke), ought (according to Descloizeaux), on account of its optically biaxial properties, to be referred to a right prism, the angles and cleavage of which have nothing in common with those of Epidote.

THUMERSTEIN, *Werner.* ⎫ A name given
THUMERSTONE, *Jameson,* ⎬ to Axinite, af-
Kirwan. ⎭ ter that of the place in Saxony (Thum) where it was first found.

THURINGITE, *Breithaupt, Dana.* Massive, consisting of an aggregation of minute scales. Cleavage in one direction. Colour olive-green. Lustre pearly. Streak paler than the colour. Feel of powder greasy. Gives off an argillaceous odour. Very tough. Fracture subconchoidal. H. 2 to 2·5. S.G. 3·151 to 3·197.

Comp. $Fe^3\ddot{S}i + \ddot{R}(\ddot{S}i\ddot{A}l) + 3\ddot{H}$.

Analysis, by *Smith :*

Silica	.	.	. 22·05
Alumina	.	.	. 16·40
Peroxide of iron	.	. 17·66
Protoxide of iron	.	. 30·78
Protoxide of manganese	. 0·89
Potash and soda	.	. 0·14
Water	.	.	. 11·44

99·36

BB fuses easily to an iron-black globule; with borax affords an iron reaction.

Dissolves easily in dilute muriatic acid.

Localities. Schmiedfeld, near Saalfeld, in Thuringia, whence the name Thuringite. Near Harper's Ferry, on the Potomac, U. S., in metamorphic rocks.

TIEMANNIT, *Kenngott.* A name given to Onofrite (which see), in honour of the discoverer, Tiemann.

TILE-ORE, *Jameson, Kirwan.* A name applied to the earthy varieties of Red Copper from its colour, which is usually brick-red, or reddish-brown. It consists of Red Oxide of Copper, mixed with variable proportions of Hydrous Oxide of Iron or Limonite, and passes sometimes by the increase of the quantity of iron into Brown Ironstone. The red varieties contain the greatest amount of copper, and the brown the greatest amount of iron.

BB becomes black, but is infusible without addition; with borax yields a dirty-green glass.

Localities.— English. Cornwall, at Huel Edward, St. Just, and in several mines near Redruth.—*Foreign.* The Banat. Hungary. Thuringia. Saxony. Silesia. The Harz. Norway. Siberia. Chili, &c.

Brit. Mus., Case 17.

TILKERODITE. The name applied by Haidinger to those varieties of Clausthalite in which cobalt replaces part of the lead.

Analysis, from Clausthal, by *H. Rose :*

Selenium	.	.	.	.	31·42
Lead	.	.	.	.	63·92
Cobalt	.	.	.	.	3·14
Iron	.	.	.	.	6·45
					98·93

Name. It received the name Tilkerodite in consequence of its being found at Tilkerode, in the Harz.

Brit. Mus., Case 4.

TIN HEMATITES, *Kirwan.* Fibrous oxide of tin. See WOOD-TIN.

TIN-ORE, *Allan.* The name given by Cornish miners to the Tin Ore Cassiterite. The term *black tin* is specially given to the ore as prepared for the smelter, whilst the metal is called *white tin.* See CASSITERITE.

TIN PYRITES, *Allan, Dana, Jameson, Kirwan.* Occurs massive and disseminated. Colour steel-grey, when pure, but often inclining to brass-yellow, owing to an admixture of Copper Pyrites. Opaque. Lustre metallic. Streak black. Brittle. Fracture uneven, sometimes inclining to imperfect conchoidal. H. 4. S.G. 4·35 to 4·5.

Comp. Sulphostannate of iron and copper, or $2Fe,SnS^2 + 2CuS,SnS^2 = $ sulphur 29·77, copper 29·77, tin 27·44, iron 13·02 = 100.

Analysis, from St. Michael's Mount, by *Johnston :*

Sulphur	.	.	.	29·93
Tin	.	.	.	31·62
Copper	.	.	.	23·55
Zinc	.	.	.	10·11
Iron	.	.	.	4·79
				100·00

BB on charcoal, sulphurous odours are given off, and the charcoal is covered with white oxide of tin, after which it fuses

readily to a black scoria : after long roasting it yields a brittle metallic globule, which colours fluxes like iron and copper, and with a mixture of carbonate of soda and borax it yields a hard, pale red, somewhat brittle globule of metal.

Dissolves readily in nitric acid, forming a blue solution, and separating oxide of tin and sulphur.

Localities. — English. Cornwall, at Carn Brea Mines; also at Huel Rock, Stenna Gwynn. Huel Primrose, Botallack Mine, St. Michael's Mount, in small granite veins. &c. — *Foreign.* Zinnwald, in the Erzgebirge, with Blende and Galena.

Brit. Mus., Case 9.

M.P.G. Wall-case 9, on principal floor (British).

Tin Pyrites may be distinguished from either Copper Pyrites or Grey Copper, by its peculiar yellowish tinge, frequently resembling that of bell-metal, and by its black streak.

TIN SPAR, *Kirwan.* The name often given to the yellowish grey Weiss Scheelerz.

TIN STONE, *Jameson, Kirwan.* The name generally given to massive oxide of tin. See CASSITERITE.

TIN-WHITE COBALT, *Jameson, Phillips.* See SMALTINE.

TINCAL or TINKAL. · (The Oriental name for Borax.) Crude Borax is imported into this country, under the name of Tincal, chiefly from the East. Large quantities are, however, furnished by the lagoons near Monte Cerbole, in Tuscany, from which 10,000 to 12,000 lbs. were daily produced a few years ago. These lagoons occupy a large extent of surface, and consist of numerous low volcanoes and springs in a furious state of ebullition. The vapours constantly bursting forth from the boiling lagoons contain boracic acid, which is obtained by causing the vapours to pass through pans, and in so doing to impregnate the water in them with the acid. The water so impregnated with the acid is kept boiling by the heat of the lagoons, and the water being evaporated, the acid is obtained in crystals.

Brit. Mus., Case 41.

M.P.G. Horse-shoe Case, No. 204.

TINDER ORE. An impure arsenical sulphide of antimony and lead; apparently a mixture of Heteromorphite, Mispickel, and Pyrargyrite. It occurs in soft, flexible flakes resembling tinder of a dirty reddish colour, and with little lustre.

Analysis, from Andreasberg, by *Bornträger :*

Lead . . . . . 43·06
Antimony . . . . 16·88
Arsenic . . . . 12·60
Iron . . . . . 4·52
Silver . . . . . 2·56
Sulphur . . . 19·57

———
98·29

The principal localities are Andreasberg and Clausthal, in the Harz.

Brit. Mus., Case 38.

TINKAL, *Hausmann.*   See BORAX.

TIROLITE, *Haidinger, Nicol.* See TYROLITE.

TITAN SCHORL, *Reuss.*   See RUTILE.

TITANATE OF IRON. See ILMENITE.

TITANATE OF LIME. See PEROWSKITE.

TITANE ANATASE, *Haüy.* See ANATASE.

TITANE OXYDÉ, *Haüy.* See RUTILE.

TITANE OXYDÉ CHROMIFÈRE, *Haüy.* A variety of Rutile containing a small percentage of chrome, from Karingsbricka, in Sweden.

TITANE SILICEO-CALCAIRE, *Haüy.* See SPHENE.

TITANEISEN, *v. Leonhard.*   Titaniferous Magnetite.

TITANEISEN, or TITANEISENERZ, *Naumann.* See ILMENITE.

TITANEISENSTEIN, *Hausmann.* See ISERINE.

TITANIC ACID, *Thomson.* See RUTILE.

TITANIC IRON, *Allan.* See ILMENITE.

TITANIFEROUS CERITE, *Laugier.* A variety of Cerite, of a blackish-brown colour from the coast of Coromandel.

TITANIFEROUS IRON. See ILMENITE, and ISERINE.

TITANIFEROUS IRON SAND, *Breithaupt.* Iserine occurring in octahedrons and cubes in roundish grains. This kind of iron-sand is very abundant in the tertiary, fine basaltic and sedimentary formations of many localities in the colony of Victoria. A fine sand, containing 88·45 of peroxide of iron, 11·43 of oxide of titanium, with silica, and 12 per cent. of waste — is found in New Zealand, along the shores of New Plymouth, in Taranaki. "This sand has the appearance of fine steel filings, and if a magnet be dropped upon it and taken up again, the instrument will be found thickly coated with the iron granules. The place where the sand abounds, is along the base of Mount Egmont, an extinct volcano; and the deposit extends several miles along the coast to the depth of many feet, and having a corresponding breadth.

"The sand, as it is taken from the beach, has been found to produce sixty-one per cent. of iron of the very finest quality; and if the sand be subjected to the process of cementation, the result is a tough steel, the properties of which seem to surpass any other description of that metal at present known."—(*Australian Mail,* quoted in *The Geologist,* No. 40, April 1861, p. 162.)

TITANIT, *Reuss.* ⎫
TITANITE, *Kirwan,* ⎬ See SPHENE.
Klaproth. ⎭

TIZA. The name by which Borate of lime (*Hayesine*) is called in Southern Peru, where it occurs on the dry plains in the neighbourhood of Iquique, in white reniform masses, varying in size from a hazel-nut to a potato.

TOAD'S-EYE TIN. A light hair-brown variety of Wood-tin. It is found in minute spherical masses, with a fibrous structure imbedded in a quartzose rock, in several mines near Tregurthy Moor, in Cornwall.

M. P. G. Principal Floor, Wall-case 28, No. 198.

TOLFA DIAMONDS. Colourless Rock Crystals, found in a quartz-rock near Tolfa, in the Papal States.

M. P G. Upper Gallery, Table-case B, in Recess 6. No. 171.

TOMBAZITE, *Breithaupt.* A variety of Gersdorffite, occurring in bronze-yellow or pinchbeck-brown cubes, with a hexahedral cleavage, near Lobenstein, in Thuringia. It contains nickel, arsenic, a little sulphur, and traces of cobalt and iron (*Plattner*). H. 4 to 5. S.G. 6·637.

Brit. Mus., Case 6.

TOMOSITE, *Dufrénoy.* An amorphous compact silicate of manganese, from the Harz. See PHOTOZITE and DIAPHORITE.

TOPAZ. Is a fluo-silicate of alumina, or a silicate of alumina with one-seventh of the oxygen replaced by fluorine. Rhombic: primary form a right rhombic prism. Cleavage perfect at right angles to the principal axis. Colour white, yellow, blue, and green. Lustre vitreous. Transparent to subtranslucent. Streak white. Fracture uneven-con-

 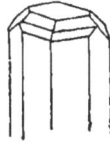

Fig. 434.   Fig. 435.

choidal. Pyroelectric. Cuts Quartz, but is cut by Ruby. H. 8. S.G. 3·4 to 3·6.

Comp. Silicate of alumina with fluoride of silicium, or fluoride of aluminium ; or $6\ddot{A}l^3$

$$\ddot{S}i^2 + (3Al\ F^3 + 2Si\ F^3).$$

Fig. 436.

Fig. 437.

Analyses, by *Forchammer;* (*a*) Saxon: (*b*) Brazilian.

			(*a*)	(*b*)
Silica	.	.	22·3	25·1
Alumina	.	.	54·3	53·8
Silicium	.	.	6·5	5·8
Fluor	.	.	17·3	15·7
			100·4	100·4

A sensible quantity of Vanadium has been found by Mons. Henri Sainte-Claire Deville in Topaz from Brazil.

Mons. Deville, also, states. that Topaz has been formed in the wet way (as was proved by Brewster's observations on the liquids it sometimes contains), probably from hydro-fluo-aluminous acids.

BB alone on charcoal infusible; exposed to a strong heat blisters rise on the surface, which burst as soon as formed, evolving hydrofluoric acid, or probably fluoride of silicium. Fuses slowly to a transparent glass with borax.

Not acted on by muriatic acid. Digested for some time in sulphuric acid, yields hydrofluoric acid.

The Topaz is divided by jewellers into two kinds, Oriental and Occidental. The first of these is, in fact, not Topaz, but a hyalin Corundum, which has been described already in its proper place. (See ORIENTAL TOPAZ.) Occidental Topaz may be divided into three varieties : viz. yellow, blue, and white.

I. *Yellow Topaz.* The colour is generally a beautiful wine-yellow of different degrees of intensity, but at the same time very limpid. The stone is valued in proportion to the fulness of its colour, provided it loses no portion of its brightness. Yellow Topaz occurs of large size compared with many other precious stones, and is universally esteemed on account of the rich warm tone of its colour, which it retains even by the side of the Diamond.

Considerable skill and taste are required

in cutting this stone. To display it to the greatest advantage, the table should be perfectly symmetrical, and not too large, the bizel should be of sufficient breadth, and the under side should be formed into delicate steps, not into pavilion facets. One of the most remarkable properties of the Brazilian Topaz is that of changing from yellow to pink or pale crimson on exposure to a gentle heat and of retaining this colour permanently. This process was discovered by Dumelle, a Parisian jeweller, in 1750. He used to heat Brazilian Topaz in a sand bath, but the process is much simplified now, and, consists in closely wrapping the stone to be operated on in amadou, and binding it round with a piece of tin wire. The amadou is lighted, and when consumed, the Topaz is found to be rose-coloured, without producing any injury to the polish of the stone, which has only to be cleaned to be restored to all its former brilliancy. The deeper the tint of the original colour, the deeper will be the rose colour — which sometimes becomes wine-coloured like that of the Balas Ruby, with which it is often confounded.

Many stones called Brazilian Rubies are only Topaz which have been successfully operated upon in this manner. It is, however, rather a hazardous experiment to perform, the Topaz being very apt to crack and flaw by the action of fire. The finest Brazilian yellow Topazes come from Villa Rica, where they are found in the form of loose crystals or rounded pebbles, or in veins or nests imbedded in Lithomarge.

The *Saxon Topaz* is generally of a pale yellow bordering on canary colour. It occurs in quadrangular prisms, terminated by a truncated pyramid with unequal faces. Sometimes (but rarely) it possesses brilliancy, but, unless of extraordinary size and beauty, this variety is of scarcely any value. The colour of this variety disappears in proportion as it is heated, and returns as gradually on cooling. It is found in the rock of Schneckenstein, in the valley of Damberg.

Mexican Topaz is nearly similar to the last in qualities and defects, only that it is more variable in its different tints.

That from Siberia is very limpid, of a beautiful jonquil-yellow when fine, but it more frequently resembles Aquamarine than Topaz, at least in colour. It is brought from the Uralian and Altai mountains ; Miask, in Siberia ; and from Kamschatka, of green and blue colours.

II. The *Blue* or *Brazilian Sapphire,* as it has been called by some authors, varies in size from 1 to 2 carats to 3 ounces and more. The utmost skill on the part of the lapidary is required to display this stone to the greatest advantage. Its proportions must be very exact; the table should be somewhat small, the bizel deep, and the under parts, from the girdle to the collet, graduated into fine and delicate steps, with equidistant ribs. Cut in this manner, it reflects a full celestial blue colour throughout the stone, especially round the girdle. Sometimes it requires a foil.

III. *White* or perfectly colourless varieties are much esteemed in the Brazils, where they are called *Minas Novas*, after the locality from which they are brought. They are generally of small size, and are used for circular ear-rings, or for setting round the yellow Topaz. In lustre they far surpass Rock Crystal. The most advantageous way of cutting them is like a brilliant with a small table, in which case the setting should be open. The purest varieties, called *Gouttes-d'eau* (Pingos d'agoa, or water-drops), from their peculiar limpidity, when cut in facets, like the Diamond, bear a close resemblance to it both in lustre and brilliancy. Coarse varieties of Topaz may be employed as a substitute for Emery.

Localities.—*English.* The Topaz is found in Cornwall, at St. Michael's Mount (*fig.* 437), at the granite quarries of Constantine and Mabe, at St. Austell Hill Mine, at Kea, and at Huel Kind and Huel Trevaunance, near St. Agnes.—*Scotch.* Fine specimens have been found in Scotland, in Aberdeenshire and Banffshire; near Cairngorm, they occur sometimes in transparent rolled crystals and masses, three or four inches in diameter. The colour of the Scotch Topaz is generally pale blue, with a tinge of reddish-brown along the acute edges of the prism. Good crystals also occur in the Hebrides, in the part of Lewis called Harris. — *Irish.* In the Mourne Mountain district of Ireland, Topazes are found on Slieve Carragh, generally in doubly terminated colourless crystals, or with faint tinges of blue, green, or pink. — *Foreign.* Brazil. Siberia. Alabaschka, near Mursinsk, the Ilmen mountains, Adon-Tschelon, and the mountains near Nertchinsk. A Topaz, weighing nearly 20 lbs., was lately found in the river of Uralga, in the province of Nevansk, in Russia, and was presented by the finder, a tradesman, to the Emperor Alexander. Kamschatka. Asia Minor. Pegu. Ceylon. New Holland. Victoria. Bohemia. Saxony. Peru. Trumbull and Middleton, Connecticut, U.S. Tasmania, of the finest water and

of brilliancy scarcely inferior to that of the Diamond.

Name. The name is derived from Τόπαζιος, an island in the Red Sea, whence the ancients procured their Topazes; but it is supposed that the stone called Topaz by them was that called Chrysolite now, and *vice versâ*.

Even at the present day, in the East, the name Zabarjad is applied indiscriminately to varieties of the Topaz, Chrysolite and Beryl. This confusion may be accounted for by the ignorance of the lapidaries of eastern countries, of chemistry, and of the mode of distinguishing between substances resembling one another in other respects, by determining their specific gravity. Beryl and Aquamarine pass from pale green into yellow, while the striated prisms of Topaz pass from a deep yellow to pale green; their hardness is nearly the same, and they occur in the same mines in Egypt and elsewhere; indeed, the term Beryl was applied to both by Werner.

Aquamarine and Chrysolite are sometimes substituted for Topaz, but may easily be distinguished by difference of hardness, specific gravity, and especially by not becoming electric by friction.

Brit. Mus., Case 58.

M. P. G. Horse-shoe Case, Nos. 905 to 920, 996.

TOPAZE BACCILLAIRE. See PYCNITE.

TOPAZE DE BOHÈME,   Yellow Rock
TOPAZE D'INDE,*   Crystal. See CITRINE and FALSE
TOPAZE DE SAXE.   TOPAZ.

TOPAZE ENFUMÉE. Smoky Quartz. See CAIRNGORM.

TOPAZE GRENUE, *Beudant.* Granular Topaz, forming veins in what is called the Topaz rock.

TOPAZE OCCIDENTALE. Yellow Rock Crystal. See FALSE TOPAZ.

TOPAZINE QUARTZ. See FALSE TOPAZ, also SMOKY QUARTZ.

TOPAZOLITE, *Bonvoisin.* A variety of Lime-

Fig. 438.

Garnet, occurring in translucent and well-

---

* This name is also applied by jewellers to the False Topaz brought from Brazil.

defined dodecahedrons of a honey-yellow, (sometimes of an olive-green) colour, at Mussa, in Piedmont.

Analysis, by *Bonvoisin :*

Silica	 37
Lime	 29
Iron	 25
Glucina	 4
Alumina	 2
Manganese	. . . 2
	—
	99

The name (from *Topaz,* and λίθος, *stone*) is in allusion to the resemblance of its colour to that of yellow Topaz.

TOPFSTEIN, *Werner.* See POTSTONE.

TORBANE-HILL COAL; TORBANE MINERAL, or TORBANITE, *Greg & Lettsom.* A kind of Brown Cannel Coal. Amorphous. Compact. Colour clove-brown, without lustre, becoming darker (deep brown or brownish-black) on exposure to air and moisture. Streak light brown or yellow. Brittle but very tough. Fracture subconchoidal. Comes out of the mine in cubical masses like ordinary coal. Takes fire easily, splits, and burns with an empyreumatic odour, giving out much smoke, and leaving a considerable quantity (about 20 per cent.) of white ash. H. 2·5. S.G. 1·2.

Analysis, by *O. Mather :*

Carbon .	. . . . 60·81
Hydrogen	. . . 9·18
Nitrogen	. . . 0·78
Oxygen	. . . 4·39
Silica .	. . . 13·19
Alumina	. . . 9·50
Peroxide of iron	. . 1·22
Water .	. . . 0·39
Sulphur	. . . 0·32
Lime .	. . . 0·27
	100·05

Localities. Torbane, Inchcross, Boghead, Capper's and Bathvale, near Bathgate, in Linlithgowshire; in the upper Coal Measures of Scotland, immediately above the Millstone Grit. The Torbanite occurs in a bed varying in thickness from 16 inches to 2 feet, in contact with shales and Clay Ironstone, and resting on a bed of underclay, after the manner of ordinary Coal. It occasionally contains casts and impressions of the stems of large sigillaria and other fossil plants, which are also found in the accompanying shales. The mass is also traversed by the roots of Sigillaria (*Stigmaria*), which penetrate the bed of " underclay " on which the coal is based.

The Torbane-Hill Coal sometimes passes into Black-band Ironstone and into ordinary Cannel Coal.

This remarkable mineral is the most valuable Coal hitherto discovered for making gas and oil (paraffine). Dr. Andrew Fyfe, from a ton of the Coal, obtained 760 lbs. of coke, and 14,880 cubic feet of gas, the illuminating power of which was equal to the light of 7·72 spermaceti candles. It also yields, on distillation, 125 gallons of crude oil per ton. — (See *Ure's Dict. of Arts, &c.*)

M. P. G. Horse-shoe Case, No. 78.

TORBERITE, *Brooke & Miller.* Copper-Uranite. See CHALCOLITE.

TORRELITE, *Thomson.* See COLUMBITE. Named after Dr. John Torrey.

TOUCHSTONE. See LYDIAN STONE.

TOURMALINE, *Werner.* Hexagonal. Occurs in crystals, which are usually terminated differently at the opposite extremities, and the prisms often assume triangular forms, owing to the absence of alternate faces. Sometimes occurs massive, compact; also columnar, coarse or fine, parallel or divergent; also in detached crystals. Colour black, brown, blue, green, red, and rarely white or colourless. Exhibits dichroism. Some specimens are red internally and green externally; others are red at one end, and green, blue, or black at the other. Of every variety of transparency, from perfect clearness to opacity. Differs in transparency across the prism, and in the line of its axis. Streak uncoloured. Brittle. Fracture subconchoidal, uneven. H. rather greater than Quartz, 7 to 7·5. S.G. 2·94 to 3·3.

Pyroelectric.

BB swells up and fuses to a slag.

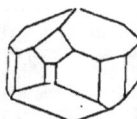 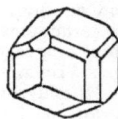 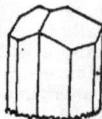

Fig. 439.   Fig. 440.   Fig. 441.

Comp. (R̶³ Ḧ B̶) S̶i.

Rammelsberg has divided Tourmaline into five sub-groups, viz. I. *Magnesia Tourmaline.* II. *Iron-magnesia Tourmaline.* III. *Iron Tourmaline,* black. IV. *Iron-manganese-lithia Tourmaline.* V. *Lithia Tourmaline.*

I. Magnesia Tourmaline.

Comp. $\ddot{R}^5\,\ddot{S}i$ + $3\ddot{R}\,\ddot{S}i + \ddot{B}\,\ddot{S}i$, or $(\ddot{R}^5\,\ddot{R}\,\ddot{B})\,\ddot{S}i$. S.G. 3 to 3·07; mean 3·05.

Analyses, by *Rammelsberg.* (a) *Brown,* from W. Kappel, Carinthia. S.G. 3·049. (b) *Black,* from Zillerthal. S.G. 3·054.

	(a)	(b)
Loss by ignition	3·19	3·54
Silica	38·85	37·94
Alumina	31·32	33·64
Boracic acid	8·25	8·58
Peroxide of iron	1·27	2·79
Protoxide of iron	—	0·37
Magnesia	14·89	10·46
Lime	1·60	0·98
Soda	1·28	2·13
Potash	0 26	0·87
Phosphoric acid	—	0·24
Fluorine	2·28	2·50
	103·19	103·54

II. Iron-magnesia Tourmaline.

S.G. 3·05 to 3·2; mean 3·11. *Black,* from Greenland. S.G. 3·072.

Silica	37·70
Alumina	34·43
Boracic acid	7·36
Peroxide of iron	4·63
Protoxide of iron	0·25
Magnesia	9·51
Lime	1·25
Soda	2·00
Potash	0·43
Phosphoric acid	0·11
	97·67

III. Iron Tourmaline.

S.G. 2·94 to 3·11. *Black,* from Bovey Tracey. S.G. 3·205.

Silica	37·00
Alumina	33·09
Boracic acid	7·06
Peroxide of iron	9·33
Protoxide of iron	6·19
Magnesia	2·58
Lime	0·50
Soda	1·39
Potash	0·65
Phosphoric acid	0·12
	98·51

IV. Iron - manganese - lithia Tourmaline.

S.G. 2·94 to 3·11. (a) *Bluish-black,* from Sarapulsk, in the Ural. S.G. 3·164. (b) *Green,* from Elba. S.G. 3·112.

	(a)	(b)
Silica	38·30	38·19
Alumina	36·17	39·16
Boracic acid	6·32	7·10
Peroxide of iron	6·35	3·14
Protoxide of iron	3·84	4·74
Protoxide of manganese	3 71	—
Magnesia	0·53	1·00
Lime	0·27	0·84
Soda	3·37	2·40
Potash	0·33	0·34
Phosphoric acid	0·06	Lithia, 0·74
	99·25	97·65

V. Lithia Tourmaline.

S.G. 3 to 3·1. *Red,* from Schaitansk, in the Ural. S.G. 3·082.

Silica	38·88
Alumina	43·97
Boracic acid	7·41
Protoxide of manganese	2·60
Magnesia	1·60
Lime	0·62
Soda	1·97
Potash	0·21
Lithia	0·48
Phosphoric acid	0·27
	97·51

Brit. Mus., Case 40.

M. P. G. Horse-shoe Case, Nos. 866 to 881.

The colours of the Tourmaline are generally dull, and so dark as to appear nearly black. It varies, too, very much in transparency, and consequently the stones which possess that quality in the highest degree are the best adapted for the use of the jeweller. On account of its deficiency of lustre, and its smoky or muddy tint, it is not held in any great estimation as a gem; nevertheless, when well selected, cut thin, and set with a proper foil, it possesses considerable beauty. Though classed amongst the least valuable of the precious stones in Europe, it is highly prized in Brazil, where it is worn in rings, chiefly by dignitaries of the church.

The Red Tourmaline, or *Rubellite,* also constitutes a fine stone when it is free from flaws. The finest known specimen of this gem is in the collection of minerals in the British Museum, Room III. Case 40. It is of uncommon form and dimensions, and was presented to Colonel Symes by the king of Ava, when on an embassy to that country. It has been valued at £1000 sterling.

This variety comes from Siberia, Ava, and Ceylon. The yellowish-grey and hyacinth-brown varieties are chiefly brought from Ceylon, and the smoky green and blue from Brazil, on which account they are often called Brazilian Emeralds and Sapphires.

Though the Tourmaline is occasionally used as a gem, it is chiefly interesting on account of its mineralogical characters, and certain curious physical properties which it possesses. The crystals are generally differently terminated, which is an exception to the law of crystallography, that all facets of the same kind should be similarly reproduced on all identically similar elements of a crystal. The electric properties of Tourmaline have relation to this crystallographical anomaly; and a prism heated in a particular way speedily manifests two kinds of electricity, becoming positively electrical at one end and negatively at the other. It becomes positively electrical when rubbed, and on being heated it becomes electrical while cooling, being positively electrical at the end of the crystal which has the greatest number of facets, and negatively at the opposite end. This state of polarity may be reversed by intense cold; and if a prism be broken while in an electric state by heat, the fragments present opposite poles, like artificial magnets. The crystals are also frequently particoloured, being of one colour at one end, and of another colour at the end opposite.

Cut in thin slices, and mounted in an instrument called a polariscope, the Tourmaline is used to analyse the optical properties of other minerals.

It is usually found in granite, gneiss, or mica-slate, also in Dolomite or granular limestone, and in sandstone near dykes of igneous rocks.

Black Tourmaline, or Schorl, is very abundant in almost all stanniferous granites, especially in Cornwall, in the neighbourhood of St. Austell; and in Devonshire, in the granite of Dartmoor, particularly near Bovey-Tracey. It also occurs in mica-schist at Karosulik, in Greenland; at Hörlberg, near Bodenmais, in Bavaria; at Käringbricka, in Sweden; with Emery, at Naxos; and in the U. S., at Haddam, Connecticut; Tasmania, imbedded in gravel, overlying granite, on Flinder's Island, in Bass Strait. The rare white variety is found on St. Gotthard, Siberia, and in Elba, in grey granite; the green variety (coloured by iron) near Katherinburg, in Siberia; Campo-longo, St. Gotthard, Canton of Tessin, and at Airolo, in Switzerland. Pale brownish crystals at Windisch Kappell, in Carinthia; also in Brazil, and elsewhere.

TOWANITE. The name given by Brooke & Miller to Chalcopyrite, after the Cornish locality (Huel Towan), where fine crystals have been found.

TRAPEZOIDAL KOUPHONE SPAR, *Mohs.* See LEUCITE.

TRAPPISCHES-EISENERZ, *Breithaupt.* See TITANIFEROUS IRON-SAND.

TRAUBENBLEI, *Hausmann.* See PYROMORPHITE.

TRAVERTINE. The name given to the harder and more compact kinds of Calcareous Tufa, formed by the evaporation of water holding lime in solution on the sides of rivers, waterfalls, &c. Large deposits of this nature are formed by some of the rivers and springs in Italy. " The calcareous waters of the Anio incrust the reeds which grow on its banks, and the foam of the cataract of Tivoli forms beautiful pendant stalactites. On the sides of the deep chasm into which the cascade throws itself, there is seen an extraordinary accumulation of horizontal beds of Tufa and Travertine, from four to five hundred feet in thickness."— Lyell's *Principles of Geology,* p. 241.

The name Travertine is derived from that of the River Tiber, and means Tiber-stone.

Brit. Mus., Case 46.

M. P. G. Table-case B, in Recess 6, Nos. 206 to 210, and 219 to 223.

TREMENHEERITE, *Piddington.* An impure Indian variety of Graphite.

Analysis, from New Jersey:

Carbon	85·7
Peroxide of iron . . .	2·5
Earthy matter . . .	7·8
Water and insoluble matter .	4·0
	100·0

Name. After Major-General Tremenheere, of the Bengal Engineers.

TREMOLITE, *Jameson ;* TREMOLITH, *Werner ;* TREMOLITHE, *Brochant.* A variety of Hornblende, differing from Actinolite principally in its pale green, grey, or white colour. It occurs both crystallized and in masses which have a columnar composition, and low degrees of transparency. The crystals are often in long slender blades, either distinct and traversing the gangues, or in columnar and radiated aggregations. The clear crystals are called *Glassy Actinolite* — the fibrous or thin capillary crystals *Asbestiform Tremolite.* The fibres are generally slightly elastic. S.G. 2·93.

Comp. Silicate of Magnesia and Lime.

Analysis, from Fahlun, by *Bonsdorff:*

Silica	60·10
Magnesia	24·31

TRICLASITE.

Lime	. . . .	. 12·73
Protoxide of iron	.,	. 1·00
Protoxide of manganese		. 0·47
Fluoric acid .	. .	. 0·83
Alumina	. . .	. 0·42
Water .	. . .	. 0·15

$$100·01$$

BB swells up and fuses with difficulty to a glass nearly transparent to milk-white; with borax, forms a transparent colourless glass.

Localities. Occurs most commonly in Dolomite and granular limestone — in the limestone of Glen Tilt, and in many parts of Scotland; at St. Gotthard, the Tyrol, the Bannat, Gulsjö in Sweden, the Pyrenees, Siberia, North America.

Name. From a locality, the valley of Tremola, in Switzerland, where it was first discovered.

Brit. Mus., Case 33.

M.P.G. Horse-shoe Case, Nos. 1007, 1052, 1053.

TRICLASITE, *Haüy.* } From τρὶς,
TRIKLASITE, *L. Gmelin,* } *triple,*and κλά-
Dufrénoy } σις, *cleavage,* in allusion to its threefold cleavage. See FAH-LUNITE.

TRIHEDRAL ARSENIATE OF COPPER, *Bournon.* See CLINOCLASE.

TRINACRITE, *v. Waltershausen.* A dull brown micaceous mineral, the composition of which is represented by the formula R̈³ S̈i + 3Ḧ S̈i + 9Ḧ.

Locality. Sicily.

Name. From Trinacria, an ancient name for Sicily.

TRIPEL, *Werner.* See TRIPOLI.

TRIPE-STONE. The name given to An-hydrite when composed of contorted plates, which bear a sort of resemblance to the convolutions of the intestines. It is found chiefly at Wieliczka and Bochnia, in Poland.

TRIPHANE, *Hausmann,* } See SPODU-
v. Kobell. } MENE. Derived
TRIPHANE, *Brochant,* } from τριφανὴς, ap-
Haüy. } *pearing three-fold.*

TRIPHYLINE, *Dana, Fuchs, Nicol.* Rhom-bic. Basal cleavage perfect. Commonly occurs in coarsely granular, crystalline masses. Colour greenish-grey; bluish in places, becoming brown and opaque when weathered. Slightly translucent, with a strong waxy lustre. Streak greyish-white. H. 5. S.G. 3·6.

Comp. 3(L̇i,Ṁn,Ḟe)P̈=lithia 3·42, prot-

TRIPLITE. 387

oxide of manganese 4·28, protoxide of iron 49·89, phosphoric acid 42·41 = 100.

Analysis, from Bodenmais, by *F. Oesten :*

Phosphoric acid .	. .	. 44·19
Protoxide of iron	.	. 38·21
Protoxide of manganese		. 5·63
Lithia .	. . .	. 7·69
Magnesia	. . .	. 2·39
Lime .	. . .	. 0·76
Soda .	. . .	. 0·74
Potash .	. . .	. 0·04
Silica	. . .	. 0·40

$$100·05$$

BB decrepitates and then fuses very easily and quietly to a dark steel grey, magnetic globule, at the same time colouring the flame pale bluish-green, reddish at intervals; and after moistening with sulphuric acid, a deeper bluish-green.

Easily soluble in muriatic acid; the solution evaporated to dryness and boiled with alcohol, imparts a purple-red colour to the flame of the alcohol.

Locality. Rabenstein, near Bodenmais, in Bavaria.

Name. From τρὶς, *three,* and φυλὴ, *family,* in allusion to its being composed of three phosphates.

Brit. Mus., Case 57.

TRIPLE SULPHURET, *Phillips.* See BOURNONITE.

TRIPLITE, *Dana, Hausmann, Nicol.* Rhom-bic: primary form a rectangular prism. Occurs in compact crystalline masses, with a lamellar structure and a cleavage in three directions perpendicular to each other. Colour from pitch-black to clove-brown. Opaque. Semi-transparent in thin fragments. Lustre resinous, adamantine. Streak yellowish-grey. Fracture flat-conchoidal. H. 5 to 5·5. S.G. 3·43 to 3·8.

Comp. Phosphate of protoxides of manganese and iron, or Ṁn4P̈ + Ḟe4P̈=4(Ṁn Ḟe)P̈.

Analysis, from Limoges, by *Berzelius :*

Phosphoric acid .	. .	. 32·78
Protoxide of manganese		. 32·60
Protoxide of iron	.	. 31·90
Phosphate of lime	.	. 3·20

$$100·48$$

BB on charcoal fuses readily. effervescing strongly, and yielding a black, metallic-shining, strongly magnetic globule, which, when heated with carbonate of soda in the

CC 2

inner flame, yields a large quantity of phosphide of iron.

Easily soluble in muriatic acid.

Localities. Near Limoges, in France, associated with Apatite, in a quartz-vein traversing large-grained granite. Peilau, in Silesia (H. 4. S. G. 3·617), frequently coated with Oxide of Manganese.

Name. From τριπλόος, *three-fold*, in allusion to its three component parts, and the cleavage in three different directions.

Brit. Mus., Case 57.

TRIPLOKLAS, *Breithaupt.* See THOMSONITE.

TRIPOLI, *Jameson, Kirwan, Phillips.* A variety of earthy silica, or a fine arenaceous variety of Quartz mixed with clay. It occurs massive with a coarse, dull, earthy fracture, is meagre and rough to the touch, and yields to the nail. Colour various shades of grey, yellow and red. Opaque. Soft and friable. S.G. 1·86 to 2·2.

It is found in veins in Tripoli, in Africa, (whence it was first brought and derived its name); at Arnberg, in Bohemia, near Prague; in Saxony, Thuringia, Tuscany, the Puy de Dôme in France, and near a stream seven leagues from Menat in Auvergne; Corfu, &c. Near Bakewell in Derbyshire, in upper Mountain Limestone.

Tripoli is used, when reduced to powder, for polishing metals, marbles, the glasses of optical instruments, and other hard substances. The Tripoli of Polinier, near Pontpean, four leagues from Rennes, in Brittany, is the most suited for lapidaries who polish gems of the first order. That approximating in colour to a yellowish-white should be preferred, because it is rarely sandy.

The Tripoli of Menat is produced from shale, by the spontaneous combustion of lignites.

TRIPPEL. See TRIPOLI.

TRITOMITE, *Dana, Weibye & Berlin.* A hydrous mineral related both in form and composition to Helvine and Garnet. Cubical. Tetrahedral. Cleavage indistinct. Colour dull brown. Subtranslucent. Lustre submetallic, vitreous. Streak dirty yellowishgrey.

Comp. $\ddot{R} \ddot{S}i + 2\dot{H}$.

Analysis, by *Berlin:*

Silica	20·13
Alumina . . .	2·24
Peroxide of cerium .	40·36
Peroxide of lanthanium	15·11
Yttria	0·46
Lime	5·15

Magnesia . . .	0·22
Protoxide of iron .	1·83
Soda	1·46
Manganese, copper, tin, wolframium	4·62
Loss by ignition . .	7·86
	99·44

BB yields water and affords a weak fluorine reaction : with borax a glass which is reddish-yellow when hot, but becomes colourless when cold.

In powder, gelatinises in muriatic acid, with evolution of chlorine.

Locality. The Island Lamö, near Brevig, in Norway, in coarse syenite.

TROMBOLITE, *Breithaupt.* See THROMBOLITE.

TRONA, *Dana, Dufrénoy, Hausmann, Nicol, Phillips.* Native Sesquicarbonate of Soda. Oblique: primary form an oblique rhombic prism. Seldom occurs distinctly crystallized, but generally in fibrous masses composed of a congeries of minute crystals. Colour white, inclining to yellowish-grey when impure. Lustre vitreous, glistening. Transparent when in minute crystals; in large masses translucent. Streak white. Taste pungent and alkaline. Rather brittle. Fracture uneven. H. 2·5 to 3. S.G. 2·112.

Fig. 442.

It dissolves in water more readily than the bicarbonate, but less so than the simple salt (Natron), from which it is also distinguished by crystalline form, superior hardness and specific gravity, and by not being deliquescent.

Comp. Sesquicarbonate of soda, or $\dot{N}a^2$ $\ddot{C}^3 + 3\dot{H}$ = soda 37·8, carbonic acid 40·2, water 22·0 = 100.

Analysis, by *Klaproth:*

Carbonic acid . .	38·0
Soda	37·0
Sulphate of soda . .	2·5
Water	22·5
	100·0

Localities. Suckena, two days' journey from Fezzan, in Africa. Barbary. Columbia. (See URAO.) Maracaibo, South America. Near the Sweetwater River, Rocky Mountains, N.A.

Brit. Mus., Case 41.

TROOSTITE, *Shepard, Mohs, Nicol.* A variety of Willemite containing 2·0 per cent. of oxide of manganese. Hexagonal. Also massive and granular. Colour asparagus-green, also yellow, grey, and reddish-brown. Transparent to opaque. Lustre vitreo-resinous. Brittle. Fracture conchoidal. H. 5·5. S.G. 4 to 4·1.

Comp. $2\ddot{M}n^3 \ddot{S}i + \ddot{F}e^3 \ddot{S}i^2$.

Analysis, by *Thomson*:

Protoxide of manganese	. 46·22
Silica	. 30·65
Protoxide of iron	. 15·45
Water and carbonic acid	. 7·30
	99·62

BB fuses at the edges; imparts a faint violet tinge to borax.

Locality. New Jersey.

Name. After Dr. G. Troost, Professor of Geology in Nashville College, Tennessee. Brit. Mus., Case 28.

TSCHEFFKINITE, *Dana.* See TSCHEW-KINITE.

TSCHERMIGIT, *Kenngott.* A kind of Ammonia-Alum.

It occurs compact and lamellar. Colourless or greyish-white. Lustre vitreous. Transparent to semitransparent. Brittle. Streak white. H. 2 to 2·5. S.G. 1·75.

Comp. $\dot{A}m \ddot{A}l + 4H^6\ddot{S}$ or $\dot{A}m \ddot{S} + \ddot{A}l \ddot{S} +$

$24\dot{H}$ = ammonia 5·7, alumina 11·4, sulphuric acid 35·3, water 47·6 = 100·0.

Localities. Tschermig, in Bohemia, in the Brown Coal formation. The crater of Etna.

TSCHEWKINITE, *Nicol, G. Rose.* Massive or amorphous. Colour velvet-black. Nearly opaque. Lustre vitreous. Streak dark brown. H. 5·5. S.G. 4·5 to 4·56.

Analysis, by *H. Rose*:

Silica	21·04
Titanic acid . . .	20·17
Lime	3·50
Magnesia . . .	0·22
Protoxide of manganese	0·83
Protoxide of iron	11·21
Peroxide of cerium, lanthanium, and didymium	47·29
Potash and soda . .	0·12
	104·38

BB intumesces much, becomes porous, and often incandesces; in the strongest heat fuses to a black glass.

Gelatinises readily in warm muriatic acid.

Locality. Near Miask, in the Ilmen. Mountains of Siberia, in granite.

Name. In honour of General Tschewkin, Chief of the Russian Mining Corps. Brit. Mus., Case 38.

TUESITE, *Thomson, Greg & Lettsom.* A mineral closely allied to Halloysite, Kaolin and Lithomarge. Amorphous. Colour bluish or milk-white. Opaque. Lustre resinous. Sectile. H. 2·3. S.G. 2·5.

Analysis, by *Thomson*:

Silica	. 44·3
Alumina	. 40·4
Iron, magnesia, and lime	. 1·5
Water	. 13·5
	99·7

BB becomes light blue and brittle: with soda fuses to an opaque mass.

Locality. The banks of the Tweed, in New Red Sandstone.

Name. From *Tuesa,* the Latin name for the River Tweed.

Tuesite makes excellent slate-pencils.

TUFA. See CALCAREOUS TUFA; also TRAVERTINE, OSTEOCOLLA.

TUNGSTATE OF COPPER is said by Dr. Genth to occur in large crystals at Cosby's mine, Cabarras co., N. Carolina.

TUNGSTATE OF IRON, *Phillips.* See WOLFRAM.

TUNGSTATE OF LEAD, *Phillips.* See SCHEELETINE.

TUNGSTATE OF LIME, *Phillips.* See SCHEELITE.

TUNGSTEIN BLANC. See SCHEELITE.

TUNGSTEN, *Scheele, Allan, Jameson.* See WOLFRAM.

TUNGSTEN OCHRE, *Nicol.* } See WOLFRAM-

TUNGSTIC OCHRE, *B. Silliman.* } INE.

TURGITE, *Hermann.* A reddish-brown mineral (possibly a Red Hematite) from the Turginsk Copper Mines in the Ural, and the Altai. Its composition may be represented by the formula $\ddot{F}e^2\dot{H}$ = peroxide of iron 94·7, water 15·3 = 100. S.G. 3·54 to 3·74.

Name. After the River Turga, in the Ural, because it is found in the copper mines of that district.

TÜRKIS, *v. Leonhard.* See TURQUOIS.

TURMALIN, *Werner.* See TOURMALINE.

TURNERITE, *Levy, Dana.* A mineral containing alumina, lime, magnesia and a little iron. Colour yellow or brown. Transparent to translucent. Lustre adamantine. Streak white or greyish. H. above 4.

Fig. 443.

Locality. France, at Mount Sorel, in Dauphiny.

Name. Named by Levy after Mr. Turner, in whose collection it was first noticed.

TURQUOIS, *Dana*, or TURQUOISE. There are two varieties of Turquois, the Oriental or Mineral Turquois (*Turquois de vieille roche*), and the Occidental or Bone-Turquois (Odontolite: *Turquois de nouvelle roche*).

The first, or true Turquois, occurs reniform, stalactitic or incrusting. Colour a peculiar bluish-green. Feebly translucent to opaque. Lustre somewhat waxy, internally dull. Streak white. Cleavage none. Fracture small-conchoidal. H. 6. S.G. 2·6 to 2·83.

Comp. Diphosphate of alumina, or $\ddot{A}l^2$ $\overset{..}{P} + 5\overset{.}{H}$ (coloured by oxide of copper)= alumina 46·9, phosphoric acid 32·6, water 20·5=100.

Analysis of blue Oriental Turquois, by *Hermann*:

Alumina	.	.	47·45
Phosphoric acid	.	.	27·84
Oxide of copper	.	.	2·02
Peroxide of iron	.	.	1·10
Peroxide of manganese	.	0·50
Phosphate of lime	.	3·41
Water	.	.	18·18

100·00

Berzelius obtained, by analysis, phosphate of alumina, phosphate of lime, silica, oxide of iron and copper.

In matrass decrepitates violently, and gives off water. *BB* in the reducing flame becomes brown, and colours it green, but is infusible; with borax or salt of phosphorus fuses readily to a transparent glass, which on cooling is faint copper-green in the outer flame, and cloudy-red in the inner, especially if tin be added.

Soluble in muriatic acid without effervescence: the solution affords a fine blue colour with ammonia, which is not the case with Odontolite. It may also be distinguished from Odontolite by its perfectly even and uniform texture, by its specific gravity, and by not effervescing with acids.

Odontolite is found with fossil bones and teeth (on which account it was called by

the ancients ἐλέφας ὀρυκτός), and appears to be bone or ivory coloured by phosphate of iron. It is of a sky-blue colour, passing into greenish-blue and apple-green; frequently with black dendritical markings, which greatly impair its beauty and value. Its texture, which is very compact and earthy, exhibits traces of animal structure, in slender fibres of a lighter tinge than the rest of the mass, either parallel with or crossing each other, so as to present a sort of net-work, according as the section has been made parallel with or at right angles to the tusk.

The distinction is made in commerce between Turquois and Odontolite; the terms oriental and occidental being employed by jewellers rather to distinguish the finer from inferior stones, than to denote any difference either of chemical composition, or of country. (*Mawe.*)

In the "Oriental accounts of the Precious Minerals," by Prinsep, it is stated, that "the *Abu-Is'haqi* (father of Isaac), or genuine turquois, is the produce of the mines of *Ansar*, near *Nishapúr*, in Khorasan (the same place mentioned as *Michebourg*, in Tavernier's Travels in India). All authorities concur that these are the only turquois mines in the world: the stones are said to vary from pale blue to green and white, but all except the azure are worthless. A curious fact is mentioned, also, which, from the nature of the mineral may readily be believed, though it has not been observed in Europe: the real blue turquois of Nishapúr changes in colour when kept near musk or camphor, also from the dampness of the ground, as well as from exposure to the fire (Pliny also remarks of the *Callais* 'quæ sunt earum pulchriores, oleo, unguento, et mero colorem deperdunt'); the inferior stones become discoloured even without this test 'by gradual decomposition or efflorescence.'[*] The *Khawas-ul hejar* makes the clearness or dulness of the Turquois vary according to the atmospheric changes. 'It brightens the eyes; is a remedy for ophthalmia, and bites of venomous animals; it is used in enamelling sword handles,' &c. 'The *Badakhshani* Turquois essentially differs from the *Nishapúri*, in being able to withstand the heat of a fire for ten days

* When the Oriental Turquois becomes discoloured, it is only necessary to pass it over the mill, so as to remove the external surface, to restore its former appearance and colour. Odontolite when discoloured by time may be revived by immersion in a solution of oxide of copper, but the effect only lasts for a few days.

without alteration: for this quality it is much esteemed, although in other respects not so good as the produce of *Ansar*.' Now, the *Caluite*, which contains 18 per cent. of water, would be entirely destroyed by such an operation, while the *Bone Turquois* is actually made in many places by exposure to the fire of fossil bones impregnated with iron; and the fossil bones brought from the north of the Himalayan range, when exposed to a red heat, are found to assume the very appearance of *Odontolite*; it is possible, therefore, that a supply of this artificial gem may find its way into Persia through Balkh, and take its name from that country as its known market. Arguments on the other hand to show that the *Badakshâni* Turquois is nothing more than *Lapis Lazuli*, or *lájnward*, and the descriptions of the two are mixed up together like those of the Emerald and Topaz."

As stated above, the best stones are obtained from Persia; but the largest and most beautifully tinted specimens rarely reach Europe, being retained by the Shah for his own use, or bought up by the grandees of that and the adjoining Mahometan states. An inferior Turquois (*Firozeh nakis*) is enumerated amongst the mineral products of Thibet. Less pure varieties are found in Silesia and Oelsnitz, in Saxony.

The Turquois cut in low cabochon is much employed in jewelry, on account of its beautiful tone of colour, which contrasts agreeably with diamonds, pearls and gold, and is not impaired by candlelight. It is frequently imitated, and with much success, so far as colour is concerned; but the artificial stone may be readily distinguished from the real by its greater vitreous lustre and gloss. In the real stone there are, generally, moreover, minute conchoidal fractures round the girdle, where it has been left rough, in order to receive the setting, which afford a certain mark of distinction. Turquois de nouvelle roche (Odontolite) is found in Bas Languedoc. The Turquois is frequently engraved in intaglio by the people of the East, and the hollows covered with gold, presenting to the eye a kind of damascening. It was also engraved by the Greeks and Romans, but, mostly in relief. Numbers of Turquois rings are still in existence with the *phallus* (which is believed to have been the distinguishing emblem of the Roman cavaliers) engraved in relief upon them.

Brit. Mus., Case 57.

M. P. G. Horse-shoe Case, Nos. 1126 to 1142.

In the Horse-shoe Case at the Museum of Practical Geology, there is a very fine collection of Turquoises, which obtained the prize medal at the Great Exhibition of 1851. (See Nos. 1126, 1127.)

They were brought by Major C. Macdonald from Arabia Petrea, from five or six localities, all included within a range of about forty miles, in the country of Sonalby, sixteen days' journey S.E. of Suez. Most of the specimens were found in the ravines on the further side of a chain of mountains having an east and west direction, and a mean elevation of five or six thousand feet: but some were met with *in situ*. These latter are still attached to the parent rock, which is a reddish sandstone composed of Quartz grains, and resembling in appearance the Old Red Sandstone of Brecon.

" The colour of the turquoises discovered by Major Macdonald, differs in the shade of blue from that of the turquoises of Persia, but agrees exactly with those brought from Abyssinia by M. Rochet d'Héricourt. Both exhibit small globular concretions, whose hardness is equal to that of agate. The nodules of turquoise form groups almost like currant-seeds in the sandstone. The intensity of the colour of adjacent lumps is different; and when the groups are of tolerably large dimensions, zones of different tints may be observed.

" This collection also, presents, besides the small concretions, veins of turquoise from a tenth to a twentieth of an inch thick, which cut across the bedding of the sandstone like small threads."—*Reports of the Juries.*

TYRITE, *David Forbes.* A mineral allied to, and perhaps identical with, Fergusonite. Colour varying from greyish-brown to rich clove-brown. Lustre resinous to semimetallic. Translucent in thin splinters. Streak yellowish-brown. Brittle. Fracture splintery and conchoidal. H. 6·5. S.G. 5·13 to 5·36.

Analysis, by *David Forbes:*

Columbic acid	44·48
Yttria	27·83
Alumina	3·55
Protoxide of cerium	5·63
Protoxide of uranium	5·99
Protoxide of lanthanium	1·47
Protoxide of iron	2·11
Lime	1·68
Zirconia (and glucina?)	2·78
Binoxide of tin	trace
Water	4·66
	100·18

BB in borax, dissolves to a glass which is brownish-yellow when hot, becomes green when cooling, and when cold greenish-yellow.

Localities. A large felspar quarry at Helle, at Næskül, 10 miles E. of Arendal, in Norway, where it occurs abundantly, and occasionally in crystals above two inches long. The crystals are always attached at their bases to plates of black Mica, and shoot out and imbed themselves in the red Ortho-clase.

TYROLITE, *Dana.* Rhombic: crystalline form unknown. Found in reniform masses, with a radiating foliated structure, and a drusy surface. Usually occurs in small aggregations, and diverging fibrous groups, of a pale green colour, and with a pearly lustre. Colour verdigris-green to sky-blue. Translucent. Lustre pearly. Streak paler than the colour. Very sectile. Thin laminæ flexible. H. 1·5 to 2. S.G. 3·02 to 3 1.

Comp. $\dot{C}u^5 \ddot{A}s + 10\dot{H} + \dot{C}a\ddot{C}$ = arsenic acid 25·4, oxide of copper 43·8, water 19 8, carbonate of lime 11·0 = 100.

Analysis, from Falkenstein, by *v. Kobell*:

Arsenic acid	25·01
Oxide of copper	43·88
Water	17·46
Carbonate of lime	13·65
	100·00

BB decrepitates violently, and fuses to a steel-grey globule.

Soluble in acids, with evolution of carbonic acid.

Localities. Falkenstein, and other parts of the Tyrol, whence the name *Tyrolite*. Posing and Libethen, in Hungary. Nertchinsk, in Siberia. Saalfeld, in Thuringia. Riechelsdorf, in Hesse. Schneeberg, in the Erzgebirge. Campiglia, in Italy. Asturia and Linares, in Spain.

U.

UIGITE, *Heddle.* Occurs in radiated sheafy plates, somewhat resembling the structure of a plumose Mica. Colourless, or slightly yellowish. Lustre tremulous and pearly. Brittle. H. 5·5. S.G. 2 284.

Comp. $\ddot{S}i^5 (\dot{C}a^4 \dot{N}a) + \ddot{S}i^2 \ddot{A}l + 9\dot{H}.$

Analysis, by *Heddle*:

Silica	45·98
Alumina	21·93
Lime	16·15

Soda	4·70
Water	11·25
	100·01

BB fuses readily and quietly, with a strong reaction of soda, to a white opaque enamel.

Locality. A quarry near Uig, in Skye, in small nests in amygdaloid.

ULEXITE. The name applied by Dana, in the 3rd edition of his Mineralogy, to Borate of Lime, from a supposed difference in composition from Hayesine.

Named after Ulex, by whom it has been analysed.

ULLMANNITE, *Fröbell, Dana, Haidinger, Nicol.* Cubical: cubic cleavage perfect. Generally occurs massive, with a granular structure, or disseminated. Colour grey, inclining to tin-white or steel-grey. Opaque. Lustre metallic. Brittle. Fracture uneven. H. 5 to 5·5. S.G. 6·2 to 6·5.

Comp. Ni (S, Sb, As)^3 = nickel 26·9, sulphur 14·5, antimony (often partly replaced by arsenic) 58·6 = 100.

Analysis, from Siegen, by *Ullmann*:

Antimony	47·56
Nickel	26·10
Arsenic	9·94
Sulphur	16·40
	100·00

BB on charcoal partly volatilizes, with fumes of sulphurous acid and antimony, and ultimately fuses to a metallic globule, which often gives a blue colour with borax.

Soluble in concentrated nitric acid, with a residue of sulphur, oxide of antimony, and arsenious acid.

Localities. The copper mines of Frensberg, Eisern, &c., in the Duchy of Nassau. Landskrone, in Siegen, Prussia. Harzgerode and Lobenstein, in Central Germany.

Name. After Ullmann, the Hessian chemist and mineralogist.

M. P. G. Principal Floor, Wall-case 20.

ULTRAMARINE. The name given to the colour prepared from pulverised Lapis Lazuli.

UMBER, *Jameson, Werner.* An earthy variety of Limonite, used as a brown pigment. It is found massive, in beds, in the island of Cyprus. Its colour is between liver-brown and dark yellowish-brown. It is very soft, feels meagre, adheres slightly to the tongue, and breaks with a large conchoidal fracture.

Analysis, by *Klaproth*:

Peroxide of iron	48
Peroxide of manganese	20

Silica　.　.　.　.　. 13
Alumina　.　.　.　.　5
Water　.　.　.　.　. 14
——
100

The principal British localities are near Castletown, in the Isle of Man. Fine pigments of various shades of brown and purple are also obtained from Umber found at the iron mines in the Forest of Dean.
Brit. Mus., Case 16.

UNCLEAVABLE ADIAPHANE SPAR, *Mohs.* See NEPHRITE.

UNCLEAVABLE AZURE SPAR, *Mohs.* See TURQUOISE.

UNCLEAVABLE IRON ORE, *Shepard.* See MOHSITE.

UNCLEAVABLE MANGANESE ORE, *Mohs.* See PSILOMELANE.

UNCLEAVABLE NEPHRITE SPAR, *Haidinger.* See NEPHRITE.

UNCLEAVABLE QUARTZ, *Mohs.* See OPAL.

UNCLEAVABLE RETIN-ALLOPHANE, *Mohs.* See PITTICITE.

UNCLEAVABLE STAPHYLINE MALACHITE, *Mohs* See CHRYSOCOLLA.

UNCLEAVABLE URANIUM ORE, *Mohs.* See PITCHBLENDE.

UNGWARITE, *Glocker.* A name given to Chloropal, after the locality, Unghwar, in Hungary.

UNIAXIAL MICA. See BIOTITE.

UNIONITE, *Sillimann, Jr.* A mineral resembling Soda-Spodumene in general appearance, and proved by the analyses of Smith & Brush to be a white Lime-Epidote. Colour white. Lustre vitreous. H. 6. S.G. 3·299. Very distinct cleavage in one direction.

Comp. R̈ S̈i + Äl S̈i².

Analysis, by *Smith & Brush:*
Silica　.　.　.　.　. 40·61
Alumina　.　.　. 33·44
Peroxide of iron　.　. 0·49
Lime　.　.　.　. 24·13
Magnesia　.　.　. trace
Loss by ignition　.　. 2·22
——
100·89

Named after the locality, Unionville, in Pennsylvania, where it occurs with Euphyllite, at the Corundum locality.

URACONISE, *Beudant.* See ZIPPEITE.

URALITE, *G. Rose.* A pseudomorphous mineral of a dark green or greenish-black colour, with the cleavage and composition of Hornblende, and the external form of Augite.

Analysis, from the shores of the Baltic Sea, by *Kudernatsch:*
Silica　.　.　.　.　. 53·05
Protoxide of iron.　.　. 16·37
Magnesia　.　.　.　. 12·90
Lime　.　.　.　.　. 12·47
Alumina　.　.　.　. 4·56
——
99·85

Localities. The Ural (where it was first observed), in augite-porphyry. In the augitic rocks of the Veltlin, of the East and West Indies, of America, and at Arendal.

Uralite is considered by Gustave Rose to be a pseudomorph of Hornblende, after Augite; by others it is regarded rather as an intimate admixture of those minerals in indefinite proportions.

URALORTHITE, *Hermann.* A variety of Orthite, found associated with small crystals of Zircon, in the flesh-coloured Felspar of Miask, in the Ural. S.G. 3·41 to 3·6.

Comp. R̈² S̈i + Ḧ S̈i + H.

Analysis, from the Ilmen Mountains, by *Hermann:*
Silica　.　.　.　.　. 35·49
Alumina　.　.　.　. 18·21
Protoxide of iron　.　. 13·03
Protoxide of cerium　.　. 10·85
Lime　.　.　.　.　. 9·25
Magnesia　.　.　.　. 2·06
Peroxide of manganese　. 2·37
Protoxide of lanthanium　. 6·54
Water　.　.　.　.　. 2·00
——
99·80

BB intumesces and fuses at the edges to a black blebby glass.

Dissolves in acids — somewhat gelatinising.
Brit. Mus., Case 38.

URANATE DE CHAUX. See URANITE.

URANBLOOM; URANBLÜTHE, *Zippe.* See ZIPPEITE.

URANCHALZIT. See URANGREEN.

URANE MICACÉ, *Brochant,* ⎱ See
URANE OXIDÉ, *Haüy.* ⎰ URANITE.

URANE OXIDÉ TERREUX, *Haüy.* Uran Ochre. See ZIPPEITE.

URANE OXYDULÉ, *Haüy.* See PITCHBLENDE.

URANE PHOSPHATÉ. See URANITE.

URANE SULFATÉ, *Necker.* See JOHANNITE.

URANERZ, *Karsten.* See JOHANNITE.

URANGLIMMER, *Werner.* See URANITE and CHALCOLITE.

URANGREEN, URANGRÜN, *Hartmann.* A basal sulphate of the oxides of copper and uranium, from Joachimsthal, in Bohemia. It occurs in acicular crystals, forming small nodular crusts and velvety druses. Colour grass-green to apple-green.

Comp. $\dot{U}\ddot{U} + \dot{C}u\overset{..}{S} + 2\dot{C}a\overset{..}{S} + 18\dot{H}.$

Analysis (mean of two), by *Lindaker* :

Sulphuric acid . . .	20·03
Proto-peroxide of uranium .	36·14
Oxide of copper . . .	6·55
Lime	10·10
Protoxide of iron . .	0·14
Water	27·16
	100·12

URANINE, *Haidinger.* See PITCHBLENDE.
URANITE, *Dana, Nicol, Phillips* (in part). Pyramidal; basal cleavage very perfect. Occurs almost always in tabular crystals, attached singly or united in small druses. Colour siskin-green to sulphur-yellow. Translucent. Lustre sub-adamantine; pearly on cleavage-plane. Sectile. Streak yellow. Laminæ brittle and not flexible. Fracture not observable. H. 2 to 2·5. S.G. 3 to 3·2.

Comp. Phosphate of uranium and lime, or $(\dot{C}a\ddot{U}^2)\overset{...}{P} + 8\dot{H}$ = peroxide of uranium 62·69, lime 6·10, phosphoric acid 15·54, water 15·67 = 100.

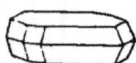 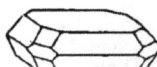

Fig 444.   Fig. 445.

Fig. 446.

Analysis, by *Peligot :*

Peroxide of uranium . .	63·91
Lime	6·20
Phosphoric acid . .	15·20
Water	15·30
	100·6

Becomes straw-coloured and opaque when heated.

BB on charcoal, increases slightly in bulk, and fuses to a black mass with a semi-crystalline surface. With carbonate of soda, forms a yellow infusible slag.

Soluble in nitric acid.

Localities.— *English.* Cornwall : South

Huel Basset; Tolcarne Mine and Huel Edwards (*Autunite*); also at Gunnis Lake, near Callington ; Stenna Gwynn, &c.

Foreign. France : at St. Yrieix near Limoges ; and in granite at St Symphorien, near Autun. Johanngeorgenstadt and Eibenstock, in Saxony. Wolf Island, Lake Onega, in Russia. Middletown and Chesterfield ; Massachusetts, U.S.

Uranite differs from Mica in being neither flexible nor elastic.

Name. After Uranium (from οὐρανὸς, *Uranus*), the name given to the planet Herschel by German astronomers.

Brit. Mus., Case 57.

M. P. G. Wall-case 13, Principal Floor (British).

URANIUM OCHRE, *Nicol.* See ZIPPEITE.
URANIUM ORE, *Allan.* See PITCHBLENDE.
URANIUM VITRIOL. See JOHANNITE.
URANKALK-CARBONAT, *Vogl.* An ore of Uranium, nearly allied to Liebigite, occurring in scaly aggregations on Pitchblende, at Elias Mine, near Joachimsthal, in Bohemia. Colour siskin-green. Subtransparent to translucent. Lustre pearly on cleavage-face. H. 2·5 to 3.

Comp. $\dot{U}\ddot{U} + \dot{C}u\overset{..}{S} + 2\dot{C}a\overset{..}{S} + 18\dot{H}.$

Analysis (mean of two), by *Lindaker :*

Sulphuric acid . . .	20·03
Protoperoxide of uranium .	36·14
Oxide of copper . . .	6·55
Lime	10·10
Protoxide of iron . .	0·14
Water	27·16
	99·12

BB on charcoal, infusible : with borax and salt of phosphorus affords the reaction of uranium.

Dissolves with effervescence in sulphuric acid, a white precipitate being thrown down.

URAN-KALK-KUPFER-CARBONAT, *Vogl.* See VOGLITE.

URANMICA, *Jameson.* See URANITE.
URANOCHALCITE. See URANGREEN.

The name Uranochalcite has also been given by Hermann to a mineral from Joachimsthal, occurring in reniform amorphous masses, with a metallic appearance. Colour between steel-grey and pinchbeckbrown. Opaque. Lustre feeble-metallic. Streak black. Brittle. Fracture compact and slightly conchoidal. H. 4. S.G. 5·04.

URANOCHRE, *Phillips, Werner.* See ZIPPEITE.

URANONIOBITE. The name given by Hermann to the crystallized Pitchblende from Stromshein, in Norway.

URANOTANTAL, *G. Rose.* See SAMARS-
KITE.
URANOXYD, *Hausmann.* See URANITE.
URANPECHERZ, *Werner.* See PITCH-
BLENDE.
URANPHYLLIT. See URANITE.
URANVITRIOL, *John.* See JOHANNITE.
URAO, *Beudant.* Native sesquicarbonate
of soda, found at the bottom of a lake in
Macaraibo, a day's journey from Merida, in
Columbia.
URDITE. See MONAZITE.
UWAROWITE, *Kenngott.* A lime-chrome
Garnet, of an emerald-green colpur. Lustre
vitreous. Translucent at the edges. Streak
greenish-white. H. 7·5. S.G. 3·4.

Comp. $\mathrm{\overset{.}{C}a\overset{..}{S}i + (\overset{..}{U}r\overset{..}{A}l)\overset{..}{S}i}$.

Analysis, from Bissersk, by *Komonen* :

Silica	37·11
Oxide of chrome.	22·54
Alumina	5·88
Lime	30·34
Protoxide of iron.	2·44
Magnesia	1·10
Water	1·01
	100·42

BB alone infusible; with borax yields a
clear chrome-green glass.
Localities. Kyschtimsk, and the mine of
Bissersk, in the Ural, in dodecahedral crys-
tals, with Chromic Iron.
Name. After Uwarow, President of the
Imperial Academy of St. Petersburg.
Brit. Mus., Case 36.
M. P. G. Horse-shoe Case, No. 900.

V.

VALENCIANITE, *Breithaupt.* A variety of
Adularia, found at the Valenciana Mine, in
Mexico.
Analysis, by *Plattner* :

Silica	66·82
Alumina	17·58
Peroxide of iron	0·09
Potash	14·80
	99·29

VALENTINITE, *Dana, Haidinger, Nicol.*
Rhombic: cleavage perfect and easily obtained. Occurs in acicular rhombic prisms,
and in rectangular plates with the lateral
edges bevelled, either attached singly or
arranged in fan-shaped, radiating or cellular
aggregations; also massive with a lamellar,
columnar and granular structure. Colour

snow-white and ash-grey to brownish, rarely
peach-blossom-red. Translucent to subtransparent. Lustre adamantine, often
pearly. Streak white. Sectile. H. 2·5 to 3.
S.G. 5·56.

Fig. 447.

Comp. Antimonic oxide, or $\overset{...}{\mathrm{Sb}}$ = antimony
84·31, oxygen 15·69 = 100.
Analysis, from Wolfach, by *Suckow* :

Oxide of antimony	91·7
Peroxide of iron	1·2
Silica	0·8
Antimony	6·3
	100·0

Turns yellow every time it is heated, and
fuses in the flame of a candle, forming a
yellowish or greyish liquid, which on cooling
solidifies to a white asbestos-like mass,
having a silky lustre.
BB volatilizes, covering the charcoal with
a white coating.
Localities. Przibram, in Bohemia, in
tabular crystals. Braunsdorf, in Saxony.
Wolfsberg, in the Harz. Horhausen, in
Nassau. Malaczka, in Hungary. Baden.
Nertchinsk, in Siberia. Allemont, in Dauphiny.
Name. In honour of Basilius Valentinus.
Valentinite occurs in veins traversing
primary rocks, with other ores of antimony
(of the alteration of which it is a result),
Galena and Blende.
Brit. Mus., Case 38.

VANADATE OF COPPER ($\overset{..}{\mathrm{Cu}}\overset{...}{\mathrm{V}}$). Of a
citron-yellow colour, and with a foliated
structure, is said to occur, either reniform or
pulverulent, at Wosskressensk, in the Ural.
VANADATE OF LEAD AND COPPER. Is
described by Domeyko as occurring in an
earthy state, in cavities in an arseno-phosphate of lead, at the Mina Grande silver
mine, or the Mina de la Marqueza, in Chili.
It is of a dark brown or brownish-black
colour, and resembles a ferruginous clay or
earth in appearance.

Comp. ($\overset{.}{\mathrm{Pb}}{}^{6}\overset{..}{\mathrm{V}} + \overset{.}{\mathrm{Cu}}{}^{6}\overset{...}{\mathrm{V}}$).
A similar ore is reported to be met with
at the Cliff Mine, in the copper region of
Lake Superior, in North America.
Brit. Mus., Case 38.
VANADATE OF LEAD, *Phillips.* VANA-
DINBLEIERZ, *Mohs.* VANADINITE, *Dana,
Nicol.* Hexagonal. Occurs in small and
indistinct hexagonal prisms; generally in

implanted globules or incrustations. Colour varying from straw - yellow to reddish-brown. Opaque. Dull. Lustre of fractured surface resinous. Streak white or yellowish. Brittle. Fracture uneven or flat-conchoidal. H. 2·75 to 3. S.G. 6·66 to 7·23.

 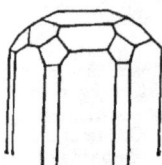

Fig. 448.   Fig. 449.

Comp. Vanadiate of lead, or $3\dot{P}b^{5}\,\ddot{V}$ + Pb Cl = vanadiate of lead 89·72, chloride of lead 9·78 = 100.

Analysis, from Wanlock Head, by *R. D. Thomson :*

Vanadic acid	.	.	. 23·44
Oxide of lead	.	.	. 66·33
Lead	.	.	. 7·06
Muriatic acid	.	.	. 2·45
			99·28

BB decrepitates strongly, and on charcoal fuses to a globule which yields metallic lead, with emission of sparks and the formation of a yellow film on the charcoal.

Dissolves easily in nitric acid, and nitrate of silver throws down a large quantity of chloride of silver from the solution.

The ore from *Wanlock Head* fuses readily on charcoal, exhaling odours of arsenic, yields globules of lead, and after fusion for some time in the inner flame, likewise yields a steel-grey, very fusible slag, which exhibits the reaction of chromium. With muriatic or sulphuric acid forms a green solution, with separation of chloride or sulphate of lead.

Localities.— *Scotch.* Wanlock Head, Dumfriesshire, on common and cupreous Calamine, at the Hegh-pirn of the Susannah Mine. — *Foreign.* Beresowsk, near Katherinenburg, in Siberia, associated with phosphate of lead. Zimapan, in Mexico. The Zanchen, in S.E. Carinthia.

Name. The name Vanadinite is derived from *Vanadis,* a cognomen of the Scandinavian goddess *Freia.*

The following will be found a ready test for this mineral. If nitric acid be dropped on the crystals, they become first deep red, owing to the separation of the vanadic acid, and afterwards (upon its solution) of a brilliant yellow. (*Heddle.*)

M. P. G. Principal Floor, Wall-cases 13 and 45 (British.)

VARIEGATED COPPER-ORE, *Jameson.* See ERUBESCITE.

VARIEGATED VITREOUS COPPER, *Phillips.* A mixture of Vitreous Copper (Copper-Glance) and Copper Pyrites, found in most of the Cornish mines in which the former ore occurs. The colour is that of tempered steel, violet-blue, greenish and yellow.

VARIOLITE. A dark green variety of Felspar, containing disseminated spherules or globular particles of a paler colour.

Variolite is an orbicular rock, generally of a deep green colour, speckled with different tints of grey. It takes a high polish (especially in those parts which are spotted) the brilliancy of which equals that of the finest oriental stones. The most remarkable circumstance attending this stone (whence probably it derives its name) is, that in weathered specimens the spots, which consist of a black point surrounded by a brown ring, stand out from the surface of the stone, showing that the influences which had produced the erosion of the base of the rock, had not been able to produce an equal effect on the harder portions of it.

Though most frequently of a dark green there are white, blue and red varieties, with others of intermediate tints. The spherules vary also in colour. In some the black points are surrounded with a white ring, while in others they have, in addition, a second whitish circle, which gives it exactly the appearance of a small Onyx. These singularities, coupled with the remarkable appearance of the stone, caused it to be believed by the vulgar, in times of greater ignorance than the present, to be an effectual remedy for small-pox, whence the name perhaps (from *variola,* small-pox, and λίθος, *stone*).

Anciently this stone was brought from the Indies, but it has since been discovered in various countries of Europe, especially in France (in the river Drac), Piedmont, and Switzerland. It is also found at Durance, in Savoy, where the spherules, which are white or greenish-white, are often changed into Kaolin or China-clay; and Antrim co., in Ireland.

Large masses are also procured from the High Alps. It is used to ornament cabinets, and for caskets, snuff-boxes, &c.

Analysis, by *Delesse,* of the rock. (S.G. 2·896 to 2·934) :

Silica	.	.	.	. 52·79
Alumina	.	.	.	. 11·16

Protoxide of iron	11·07
Lime	5·90
Magnesia	9·01
Soda	3·07
Potash	1·16
Water and carbonic acid	4·38
	98·54

Analysis, by *Delesse*, of the spherules (S.G. 2·923):

Silica	56·12
Alumina	17·40
Peroxide of iron	7·78
Oxide of chrome	0·51
Lime	8·74
Magnesia	3·41
Soda	3·72
Potash	0·24
Water	1·93
	99·85

VARISCITE, *Breithaupt*. An apple-green mineral with a weak resinous lustre, and a greasy feel, forming a reniform incrustation on flinty slate at Messbach, near Plauen, in the Voigtland It is considered by Plattner to consist of alumina and phosphoric acid, with ammonia, magnesia, protoxide of iron, oxide of chrome and water.

The word Variscite is derived from *Variscia*, the Latin name of Voigtland.

VARVACITE, *Thomson*. VARVICITE, *R. Phillips*. Probably a mixture of Pyrolusite and Psilomelane, or Manganite; the former of which it resembles in hardness and the colour of its powder, and the latter in appearance. It is found at Hartshill, in Warwickshire, in slightly radiating, fibro-lamellar masses, of a steel-grey colour. Lustre submetallic. H. 2·5 to 3. S.G. 4·3.

Analysis, by *R. Phillips*:

Manganese	63·3
Oxygen	31·7
Water	5·0
	100·0

Name. The name Varvicite was devised by the late Richard Phillips, to facilitate the pronunciation by foreigners of the word *Warwick* (*Varvic*), the locality after which the mineral was called.

VAUQUELINITE, *Dana, Nicol, Phillips, Steffens*. Oblique. Occurs in irregularly aggregated, minute and generally macled crystals, or in mammillated masses forming thin crusts, which are sometimes hollow and approaching to stalactitic. Colour black (occasionally with a tinge of green)

or brown. Faintly translucent or opaque. Lustre adamantine to resinous : faint in the brown varieties. Streak siskin-green or brownish. Rather brittle. Fracture uneven. H. 2·5 to 3. S.G. 5·5 to 5·8.

Fig 450. Fig. 451.

Comp. Chromate of copper and lead, or $\dot{C}u^3 \ddot{C}r^2 + 2\dot{P}b^3\ddot{C}r^2 = $ oxide of copper 10·9, oxide of lead 61·2, chromic acid 27·9=100.

Analysis, from Beresow, by *Berzelius*:

Oxide of lead	60 87
Oxide of copper	10·80
Chromic acid	28·33
	100·00

BB on charcoal swells up slightly, and then fuses with strong intumescence to a dark grey globule, with a metallic lustre, and surrounded with small granules of metal. With borax and microcosmic salt in small quantity, dissolves with intumescence, and forms a green glass which, if subjected to the action of the inner flame, and then left to cool, becomes red, opaque-red, or black according to the quantity of the mineral : a large quantity of the mineral forms a black globule with borax immediately.

With nitric acid forms a dark green solution, and leaves a yellow residue.

Localities. Beresow in Siberia, on Quartz, accompanied by Crocoisite (chromate of lead). Pont Gibaud, in the Puy de Dôme (Auvergne). Brazil, with Crocoisite, at Congonhas do Campo. The Sing-sing Lead mine in New York.

Name. In compliment to the French chemist, Vauquelin.

Brit. Mus., Case 39.

VELVET BLUE COPPER ORE, *Jameson*. See LETTSOMITE.

VENETIAN TALC, *Jameson, Kirwan*. A kind of indurated common Talc or Steatite, used, when reduced to powder, for making the coloured crayons called *pastels*. The same mineral powdered and coloured with a little safflower, constitutes the cosmetic called *Fard*.

VENUS' HAIR-STONE. A name for pure Rock Crystal, containing included hair-like filaments, or long acicular crystals of Titanium; found in Madagascar and Brazil. This is the *true* Venus' Hair-stone; but the same name is applied to Rock Crystal in-closing silky tufts of Amianthus of great fineness, and displaying a pearly lustre. Both varieties are employed in jewelry.

There is also another kind found at St. Gotthard, in which the red oxide of tita-nium occurs in needle - shaped crystals, crossing each other in all directions. In consequence of this reticulated appearance, this sub-variety has received the name of *Cupid's net,* or *Love's meshes,* and also of *Flèches d'Amour.*

VENUS' or CUPID'S PENCILS. Violet Quartz, enveloping small separate fibres of capillary oxide of iron, of a golden brown colour. They are found at Bristol; Troza-vodsk, in Russia; Oberstein, in Germany; Framont, in the Vosges; in Hungary, Bo-hemia, &c.

VERDE ANTIQUE. An aggregate of Ser-pentine and Limestone irregularly mingled, and constituting a very beautiful marble.

VERDE DI CORSICA DURO. A variety of Hornblende, admitting of a high polish. It is found in the island of Corsica. The name Verde di Corsica is restricted by Beudant to the included Smaragdite.

VERDE DI PRATO. A dark-green variety of Serpentine, with black or red and white veins. It is found at Prata, near Pistoja in Florence, and is much used for statuettes and sculptured ornaments.

VERDE DI SUSA. Green Serpentine, mar-ked with white veins.

VERMEIL, or VERMEILLE. The name given by jewellers to crimson-red Garnet, inclining slightly to orange (see PYROPE). It is cut like the Dutch rose, and is set side by side, either as a border for other stones, or in clustered masses.

VERMICULITE, *Webb.* A variety of Py-rosclerite, resembling Talc in appearance. It has a granular scaly structure and greasy feel. When heated to 500° or 600° F. the scales divide into worm-like threads made up of separated laminæ of cleavage, swelling out to nearly a hundred times the original length, with such force as to burst the glass tube in which they are confined, and scatter the fragments to a distance. S.G. 2·756.

BB in the forceps, a scale fuses readily to a yellowish green glass: with soda to an opaque brown globule.

Analysis, from Millbury, by *Crossley:*

Silica .   .   .   .   . 35·74
Alumina .   .   .   . 16·42
Magnesia .   .   . 27·44

Protoxide of iron .   .   . 10·02
Water .   .   .   .   . 10·30
                                  ————
                                  99·92

Localities. Millbury, Massachusetts, and Vermont, United States.

Name. From *vermes, a worm,* and λίθος, *stone.*

VERMONTITE. See MISPICKEL.

VERONITE, *Leymerie.* See TERRE DE VERONE.

VERT ANTIQUE. See VERDE ANTIQUE.

VERT DE CUIVRE, *Brochant.* See CHRY-SOCOLLA.

VESUVIAN. The name given by Werner to Idocrase, after the locality, Vesuvius, where it was originally observed in ejected calcareous blocks, in druses, associated with Glassy Felspar, Mica, Garnet, Hornblende, &c. The Vesuvian Idocrase is of a hair-brown or olive-green colour.

Brit. Mus., Case 35.

VESUVIAN GARNET, *Kirwan.* See LEU-CITE.

VESUVIAN SALT. See GLASERITE.

VIERZONITE. Yellow Ochre from Vier-zon, Dept. du Cher, in France. See OCHRE.

VIGNITE, *Dufrénoy.* It is considered by Rammelsberg to be a simple mixture of Magnetic Iron, Carbonate and Phosphate of Iron.

Analysis, by *Kersten:*

Peroxide of iron .   .   . 49·03
Protoxide of iron .   . 33·75
Carbonic acid .   .   . 11·19
Phosphoric acid .   .   . 4·03
                                  ————
                                  100·00

Locality. Vignes, in the Moselle, France.

VILLARSITE, *Dufrénoy, Nicol.* A pseudo-morphic mineral after Chrysolite, resembling Serpentine in hardness and translucence, and in texture and colour very like certain kinds of phosphate of lime, from Arendal. It occurs in small crystalline veins and in

Fig. 452.

rhombic octahedrons, with truncated sum-mits and brilliant faces; also massive and granular. Colour yellowish-green or grey-ish yellow. Translucent. Easily frangible. Fracture uneven. Easily scratched. H. 3. S.G. 2 9 to 3.

Comp. — Hydrated Olivine, or $\ddot{M}g^3\ddot{S}i$ + $\dot{H}$.

VIOLAN.

Analysis by Dufrénoy:

Silica	.	.	. 39·60
Magnesia	.	.	. 47·87
Protoxide of iron	.	.	3·59
Protoxide of manganese	.	2·42
Lime	.	.	. 0·53
Potash	.	.	0 46
Water	.	.	. 5·80

99·77

BB infusible; with 8 or 10 parts of borax fuses to a green enamel. Soluble in strong acids.

Locality. Traversella, in Piedmont, in veins of Magnetic Iron-ore, accompanied by lamellar Dolomite, Mica, Quartz, and dodecahedral crystals of Magnetic Iron-ore.

Name. After Mons. Villars, author of a Natural History of Dauphiny.

Brit. Mus., Case 25.

VIOLAN, *Breithaupt.* A mineral resembling Glaucophane. Occurs massive with the cleavage of a slightly oblique rhombic prism. Colour dark violet-blue. Opaque. Lustre waxy. Streak bluish-white. H. 6. S.G. 3·23.

BB fuses to a clear glass; with borax in the outer flame yields a brownish-yellow glass, which is violet-red when cold; in the inner flame a yellow glass, colourless when cold.

It is found with Manganese-Epidote, at St. Marcel, in Piedmont.

Name. In allusion to its *violet* colour.

Brit. Mus., Case 35.

VITREOUS COPPER, *Phillips.* } See
VITREOUS COPPER-ORE, } COPPER
Kirwan. } GLANCE.

VITREOUS SILVER, *Phillips;* or VITREOUS SILVER-ORE. See SILVER GLANCE.

VITRIOL. The name used for the sulphates of the oxides of the metals. Haidinger uses the term alone for Copper Vitriol, or Cyanosite (which see). It is derived from *vitrum* (glass), because of its glittering like that substance.

VITRIOL BLEIERZ, *Werner.* Lead Vitriol. See ANGLESITE.

VITRIOL BLEU, or Blue Vitriol. See CYANOSITE.

VITRIOL OF COPPER, *Kirwan.* See CYANOSITE.

VITRIOL GELB. Potash Copperas. See GELBEISENERZ.

VITRIOL DE GOSLAR. See GALLIZINITE.

VITRIOL OF IRON, *Kirwan.* See COPPERAS.

VITRIOL DE PLOMB NATIF, *Brochant.* See ANGLESITE.

VIVIANITE. 399

VITRIOL OCHRE. See PITTICITE.

VITRIOL OF ZINC, *Kirwan.* See GOSLARITE.

VITRIOLITE, *Phipson.* A variety of Green Vitriol, in which a certain quantity of iron is replaced by copper. Colour like sulphate of copper when freshly broken; but with a green ochraceous tint externally, by long exposure to the air, owing to the peroxidation of the iron. Crystalline form, that of sulphate of iron.

Comp. Sulphate of protoxide of iron, with a small amount of sulphate of copper, or

$(\overset{..}{Fe} \overset{..}{Cu}) \overset{...}{S^3} + 7\dot{H}.$

Analysis, by *Dr. T. L. Phipson*:

Oxide of copper	.	.	. 15·86
Protoxide of iron	.	.	11·00
Sulphuric acid	.	.	. 28·08
Water	.	.	. 45·06

100·00

Locality. The interior of Turkey, forming large stalactites and mammillary masses in a cave near a mine of Copper Pyrites.

VIVIANITE, *Allan, Dana, Dufrénoy, Nicol.* Oblique. Occurs in oblique prisms, sometimes exceedingly thin, and seldom terminated. The crystals are of considerable length, and often very small, aggregated, and divergent. Frequently reniform and globular. Structure divergent, fibrous, or earthy, also incrusting. Colour pale green to indigo-blue, darkening on exposure; generally pale green by transmitted light, when viewed at right angles to the axis, and pale blue parallel with it. Transparent to translucent. Lustre partly metallic, partly vitreous. Streak bluish-white, changing to indigo-blue on exposure to the air. The colour of the powdered mineral in a dry state is liver-brown. Flexible in thin laminæ. Sectile. Fracture not observable. H. 1·5 to 2. S.G. 2·66.

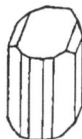

Fig. 453.

Comp. Phosphate of protoxide of iron, or

$\dot{Fe}^5 \overset{...}{P} + 8 \dot{H} =$ protoxide of iron 42·27, phosphoric acid 28·75, water, 28·98 = 100.

Analysis, from St. Agnes, by *Stromeyer:*

Protoxide of iron	.	.	41·22
Phosphoric acid	.	.	31·18
Water	.	.	. 27·48

99·88

BB fuses very readily with intumescence and loss of water, forming a grey, shining, magnetic bead, and imparting a bluish-green colour to the flame.
Readily soluble in muriatic or nitric acid.
Localities. English. — Cornwall: Huel Kind, near St. Agnes, in very fine crystals on Pyrrhotine, with small crystals of Siderite; Huel Falmouth, Kea; Parknoweth and Botallack, St. Just. Devonshire: at Huel Betsy, near Tavistock; Huel Jane. Odin mine, near Matlock, in Derbyshire. Isle of Dogs, in mud. *Foreign.* — Bodenmais, in Bavaria, in gneiss, with iron and Magnetic Pyrites. The gold mines of Vöröspatak, in Transylvania. Kertsch, in the Crimea, in the interior of shells. Isle of Bourbon. Brazil. Imleytown, New Jersey, in fine translucent dark blue crystals. Sicily. Auvergne.
See also MULLICITE, BLUE IRON EARTH, ANGLARITE.
Name. After J. G. Vivian, English mineralogist.
Brit. Mus., Case 57.
M. P. G. Horse-shoe Case, No. 361A.
Vivianite is much used as a colour by carriage-painters.
VIVIANITE TERREUSE. See BLUE IRON-EARTH.
VOGLITE, *Haidinger, Dana.* Occurs in aggregations of rhomboidal scales with a pearly lustre. Colour from emerald-green to bright grass-green.

Comp. $2\dot{U}\ddot{C} + \dot{C}a\ddot{C} + \dot{C}u^3\ddot{C}^2 + 14\dot{H}$.
Analysis, by *Lindaker :*

Carbonic acid . . . 26·41
Protoxide of uranium . 37·00
Lime . . . . 14·09
Oxide of copper . . 8·40
Water . . . 13·90

99·80

BB on charcoal, infusible alone. With borax in the outer flame affords a pearl which is brown when hot, and becomes brown and opaque when cool.
Easily soluble in dilute muriatic acid.
Locality. The Elias mine, near Joachimsthal, in Bohemia, on Pitchblende.
VOIGTITE, *Beudant.* A mineral replacing Mica in the granite of the western part of Ehrenberg, near Ilmenau. It is nearly almost always altered, and occurs in small long and narrow leaves, of a leek-green colour. Transparent in thin laminæ. Lustre pearly. Turns yellow or brown by decomposition. H. above 2. S.G. 2·91.

Comp. $3\dot{R}\ddot{S}i + \dddot{R}\ddot{S}i + 3\dot{H}$, or like Biotite all but the water.
BB fuses easily to a black glass, and gives an iron reaction.
Attacked by cold muriatic acid.
VOLBORTHITE, *Hess, Dana, Nicol.* Hexagonal. Occurs in small tabular crystals, which are often aggregated in spherical groups or foliated masses. Colour olive-green; grey. Translucent in thin splinters. Lustre pearly to vitreous. Streak yellowish-green, nearly yellow. H. 3. S.G. 3·46 to 3·86 (grey).

Comp. Vanadiate of copper.

Analysis, by *Credner :*

Vanadic acid . . . 36·58
Oxide of copper . . 44·15
Lime . . . . 12·28
Magnesia . . . 0·50
Protoxide of manganese 0·40
Water . . . . 4·62
Gangue . . . 0·10

98·63

BB on charcoal, fuses easily without fume or deposit, and, when more strongly heated, solidifies in the form of a graphitic slag, containing granules of metallic copper. With carbonate of soda, on charcoal, immediately yields copper. In borax or microcosmic salt dissolves, and produces a beautiful green colour.
Dissolves in muriatic acid, with evolution of chlorine.
Localities. Sissersk and Nijni-Taguilsk, in Siberia. Friederichsrode, in Thuringia.
Name. After Dr. V. Volborth, of St. Petersburg, by whom it was first recognised as a distinct species.
Brit. Mus., Case 38.
VOLCANIC GLASS. See OBSIDIAN.
VOLCANITE. See SELENSULPHUR.
VOLGERITE, *Dana.* A mineral occurring as a white powder or crust with Cervantite, of the alteration of which it is a result.

Comp. $\dddot{S}b + 5\dot{H}$ = antimony 60·3, oxygen 18·8, water 21·0 = 100.
Name. After Volger, by whom it was first analysed.
VÖLKNERITE, *Dana, Hermann.* Occurs in six-sided prisms with a perfect basal cleavage; also lamellar-massive. White. Lustre pearly. Feels greasy. S.G. 2·04.

Comp. $\dot{M}g^6\dddot{A}l + 16\dot{H}$.

VOLTAITE.

Analysis, by *Hermann* :

Magnesia	.	.	. 37·07
Alumina	.	.	. 16·95
Water	.	.	. 48·87

102·89

BB infusible, but exfoliates slightly and gives out light.

Locality. The mines of Schischimskaja Gora, in the Ural; on talcose schist.

Name. In honour of Völkner, Director of Mines at Katherinenburg.

VOLTAITE, *Scacchi, Dana.* Occurs in cubes, octahedrons, dodecahedrons, and their modifications. Colour dull oil-green to brown or black. Opaque. Lustre resinous. Streak greyish-green.

Comp. $\dot{F}e\ \ddot{S} + \ddot{F}e\ \ddot{S}^3 + 24\dot{H}$.

Dissolves in water, but with difficulty, and at the same time decomposes.

Localities. The Solfatara, near Naples. The Rammelsberg Mine, near Goslar, in Hanover.

Name. After the Italian physician, A. Volta.

VOLTZINE, *Fournet, Mohs, Nicol.* VOLTZITE, *Dana.* Occurs in small hemispherical incrustations, with a thin curved-lamellar structure. Colour dirty rose-red, inclining to yellowish or brown. Opaque or slightly translucent. Lustre vitreo-resinous; pearly on surfaces of cleavage. Fracture conchoidal. H. 4·5. S.G. 3·66.

Comp. Oxy-sulphide of zinc, or 4Zn S + $\dot{Z}$n=sulphide of zinc 82·7, oxide of zinc 17·3=100.

BB behaves like Blende.

Localities. Rozières, near Pont Gibaud, in Auvergne. Elias Mine, near Joachimsthal, in Bohemia.

Name. After Mons. Voltz, French mining engineer.

VORAULITE. A variety of Lazulite, found in a gangue of Quartz, at Waldbach Vorau, in Styria.

VORHAUSERITE. The name given by Kenngott to a mineral from the Fleims Valley, in the Tyrol, with the composition of Retinalite, but rendered impure by a slight admixture of the oxides of manganese and iron. It occurs amorphous. Colour brown to greenish-black, with a weak waxy lustre. Streak pale or brownish-yellow to brownish. H. 3·5. S.G. 2·45.

Name. In honour of the Tyrolese minister, Vorhauser.

VOSGITE. The name given by Delesse to

WAD. 401

a Labradorite, wihch has been rendered hydrous by partial alteration. It is of a whitish colour, sometimes with a shade of green or blue, and has a pearly or greasy lustre. S.G. 2·77.

Analysis, by *Delesse* :

Silica	.	.	. 49·32
Alumina	.	.	. 30·07
Peroxide of iron	.	.	. 0·70
Protoxide of manganese	.		0·60
Lime	.	.	. 4·25
Magnesia	.	.	. 1·96
Soda	.	.	. 4·85
Potash	.	.	. 4·45
Water	.	.	. 3·15

99·35

Locality and Name. It constitutes the porphyry of Ternuay, in the Vosges, whence the name Vosgite.

VULPINITE. A siliceous variety of Anhydrite, containing 8 per cent. of silica. H. 3·5.

The Vulpinite from Vulpino, near Bergamo, in Italy, takes a fine polish, and admits of being cut for ornamental purposes. It is known by artists as the *Marmo Bardiglio di Bergamo.*

W.

WAD. The local name by which Graphite (or Plumbago), is commonly known in the North of England. For Cumberland Wad, see GRAPHITE.

WAD, *Allan, Dana, Nicol, Phillips.* Occurs in reniform, botryoidal, and arborescent shapes, sometimes pulverulent or in froth-like coatings on other minerals; also massive, sometimes with curved laminar divisions. Colour and streak brown or black. Opaque. Lustre dull; glimmering in grey varieties. Very sectile. Yields to the nail and soils the fingers. Feels meagre. Very sectile. Fracture earthy. H. about 0·5 to 1·0. S.G. 3·7.

Analysis, from Upton Pyne, by *Turner* :

Protoxide of manganese		. 73·60
Oxygen	.	.	. 14·34
Water	.	.	. 10·66
Baryta	.	.	. 1·40

100·00

Gives off water abundantly on exposure to heat in the matrass.

BB behaves like Manganite; with borax affords a violet-blue globule.

D D

Almost wholly soluble in muriatic acid.

Localities. — *English.* Upton Pyne, Devonshire, in very light masses of a dark-brown colour. Near Redruth (Huel Buckets,&c.) in Cornwall. Near Middleton, at the Ball Eye Mine, near Bonsall, and elsewhere, in Derbyshire. — *Scotch.* Leadhills (pseudomorphous after Calcite). Hoy Head, Orkneys. — *Foreign.* The Harz, at Elbingerode, Iberg, &c. Franconia. Siegen, in Prussia. Nassau. Piedmont. France.

Brit. Mus., Case 13.

Wad is sometimes an abundant and valuable ore of manganese, though it seldom occurs in large masses, and forms the dendritic markings frequently seen on chalk, limestone, Steatite, &c. It is chiefly used in the manufacture of glass, for colouring and glazing pottery, and as a coarse pigment in oil-painting. Like Bog Iron-ore, it results from the decomposition of other ores. It consists chiefly of oxides of manganese and water, with oxide of iron, and frequently small proportions of alumina, baryta, lime, silica, &c.

Name. The name is in allusion to the light forms, like *wadding*, which this mineral assumes.

WAGNERITE, *Fuchs, Dana, Phillips.* Occurs in very complicated crystals, apparently short prisms with vertical striæ. Colour various tints of yellow, often greyish. Translucent. Lustre vitreous. Streak white. Fracture conchoidal or splintery. H. 5 to 5·5. S.G. 2·98, untransparent; 3·068 transparent.

Comp. Phosphate of magnesia with fluoride of magnesium, or $3\ddot{M}g\,\ddot{P} + Mg\,F$.

Analysis, by *Rammelsberg*:

Phosphoric acid . . .	40·61
Magnesia	46·27
Protoxide of iron . .	4·59
Lime	2·38
Fluorine . . .	9·36
	103·21

BB alone, fuses with difficulty to a dark greenish-grey glass.

In a powdered state dissolves slowly in warm nitric and sulphuric acid, with evolution of fumes of hydrofluoric acid.

Locality. Austria, in the valley of Hollengraben, near Werfen, in Salzburg, in veins of Quartz traversing clay-slate.

Name. After von Wagner, Director of Mines in Bavaria.

Brit. Mus., Case 57.

WALCHOWITE, *Haidinger, Dana.* A

mineral resin occurring in rounded translucent masses, often striped with brown. Lustre resinous. Streak yellowish-white. Fracture conchoidal. H. 1·5 to 2. S.G. 1 to 1·07.

Comp. $C^{12}\,H^9O =$ carbon 80·41, hydrogen 10·66, oxygen 8·93 = 100.

Fuses to a yellow oil at 482° F., and burns readily.

In sulphuric acid forms a dark brown solution.

Locality. Walchow, in Moravia; in Brown Coal.

WALKERDE, *Werner,*   ⎫ See FULLER'S
WALKTHON, *Hausmann.* ⎬   EARTH.

WALL SALTPETRE. See NITROCALCITE.

WALMSTEDTITE. A name given to Breunnerite (which see), in honour of Walmstedt, the Swedish chemist.

WANDSTEIN. See ROHE WAND.

WARWICKITE, *Shepard.* Borotitanate of magnesia and iron. Crystallizes in rhombic prisms, with their obtuse edges truncated, and the acute edges bevelled. Colour dark hair-brown to dull black. Appears translucent at the thin edges, and of a reddish brown colour. Lustre submetallic; on cleavage-surfaces pearly. Streak bluish-black. Brittle. Fracture uneven. H. 3 to 4. S.G. 3·188.

BB alone, infusible; but becomes paler.

Localities. S. W. of Edenville, New York, U. S.; in granular limestone.

WASHINGTONITE, *Shepard.* A titaniferous iron nearly allied in composition to Hystatite. Occurs in large hexagonal tables with the faces of the rhombohedron. H. 5·75. S.G. 4·96 to 5·01.

Analysis, from Connecticut, by *Marignac*:

Titanic acid . . .	22·21
Peroxide of iron . .	59·07
Protoxide of iron .	18·72
	100·00

Localities. Westerly and Litchfield, Connecticut, U. S.

A similar ore is said by Greg & Lettsom to occur, of a steel-grey colour, at Breaghy Head, co. Donegal; and in lamellar crystalline masses at Ballinascreen, co. Derry.

WASSERBLEI, *Werner.* See MOLYBDENITE.

WASSERGLIMMER, *Morin.* Mica containing or inclosing water.

WASSERKIES, *Glocker.* A variety of White Iron Pyrites from Moravia and Upper Silesia, containing water in chemical combination. H. 3 to 4. S.G. 3·3 to 3·5.

WATER SAPPHIRE. A name by which the very pale blue variety of Oriental Sapphire is sometimes called.

WATERDROPS. A name sometimes given to clear limpid pebbles of Topaz.

WAVELLIT, *Klaproth.* WAVELLITE, *Dana, Phillips, Dufrénoy.* Rhombic: primary form a right rhombic prism. Occurs in minute crystals, which generally form hemispherical or globular concretions, with a radiated structure. Colour yellowish-white, greyish, green or bluish; sometimes brown or black from decomposition. Translucent. Lustre vitreous or silky. Streak white. Brittle. H. 3·5 to 4. S.G. 2·33 to 2·36.

Fig. 454.

Comp. Phosphate of Alumina or $(\ddot{A}l^4\ddot{P}^3$

$+18\dot{H})+Al^2F^3=$ alumina 33·8, phosphoric acid 34·9, aluminium 1·5, fluorine 3 1, water 26·6 = 100.

Analysis, from Barnstaple, by *Berzelius:*

Alumina	35·85
Phosphoric acid	33·40
Peroxides of iron and manganese	1·25
Lime	0 50
Hydrofluoric acid.	2·06
Water	26·80
	99·36

BB infusible, but intumesces, becomes white and opaque, losing its crystalline form and imparting a slight bluish-green tint to the flame.

Soluble in acids, and in caustic potash. Heated with sulphuric acid it frequently evolves vapours of fluoric acid, which slightly corrode the glass.

Localities. — English. Cornwall: Stenna Gwynn, near St. Austell, on decomposing granite; Kit Hill, on elvan. Barnstaple in Devonshire, on clay-slate. Near Newcastle. — *Scotch.* Shiant Islands. — *Irish.* Clonmel, in dark apple-green mammillary masses. Traeton, Cork, in radiating crystalline aggregations of a bright green colour. Near Cahermoyle, in Limerick (see PYROELECTRIC WAVELLITE); also in the townland of Lisgordan, a mile to the north of Cahermoyle, forming two large veins in lower Coal-measure shales. — *Foreign.* Zbirow, in

Bohemia. Amberg, in Bavaria (see LASIONITE). Striegis in Frankenberg, Saxony (see STRIEGESAN). Weinbach near Weilberg, in Nassau. Near Giessen, Hesse-Darmstadt. Villa Rica, Brazil. Washington Mine, Davidson co., North Carolina, U. S.

Name. After Dr. Wavell, by whom it was discovered at Barnstaple.

See also PYROELECTRIC WAVELLITE.

Brit. Mus., Case 57.

M. P. G. Principal Floor, Nos, 1122 to 1124.

WAX OPAL. An inferior kind of Common Opal.

WAXEN VEIN. A name formerly given to septaria, from the resemblance of the spar of some of the veins or septa to the yellowish colour of melted wax.

WEBSTERITE, *Levy, Dufrénoy, Dana.* Occurs in reniform masses and botryoidal concretions. Colour white or yellowish-white. Opaque, occasionally translucent. Lustre dull. Yields to the nail. Meagre to the touch. Adheres to the tongue. Fracture earthy. Possesses considerable hardness, and is susceptible of a fine polish. H. 1 to 2. S.G 1·66.

Comp. Subsulphate of alumina, or $\ddot{A}l\ddot{S} +$

$9\dot{H}=$ alumina 29·8, sulphuric acid 23·2, water 47·0 = 100.

Analysis, from Newhaven, by *Stromeyer :*

Alumina	29·87
Sulphuric acid	23·37
Water	46·76
	100·00

BB parts with all its acid at a red heat, and fuses with difficulty.

Dissolves in muriatic acid, without effervescence.

Localities.— English. Newhaven, in Sussex, imbedded in a layer of ochreous clay, midway between the summit of the cliffs and the sea-shore ; but specimens may generally be picked up amongst the fallen masses of the cliffs, which lie scattered on the shore from half a mile to a mile westward of Newhaven Harbour. It occurs in veins and in tabular and tuberose masses, the former frequently several feet in length, and the latter exceeding 3 lbs. or 4 lbs. in weight. It also forms veins and tabular layers, in potholes, in the railway cutting through the chalk, between Brighton and Hove Station; with peroxide of iron. — *Foreign.* Hill of Bernon, near Epernay, and the environs of Lunel-Vieil, and Auteuil, in France. Hallé and Morl, in Prussia, in plastic clay.

Name. After Professor Thomas Webster. The Pyrites in the clay, on decomposition, *forms* sulphate of alumina; which again being decomposed by the underlying chalk, — aluminous earth, Selenite, and oxide of iron, are the results.

Brit. Mus., Case 55.

M. P. G. Horse-shoe Case, No. 1120.

WEHRLITE. The name given by Von Kobell to a massive granular mineral, which is probably a variety of Lievrite. Colour iron-black. Streak greenish-grey. Slightly magnetic. H. 6 to 6·5. S.G. 3·9.

Analysis by Wehrle:

Silica	34·60
Peroxide of iron . .	42·38
Peroxide of manganese	0·28
Alumina . . .	0·12
Protoxide of iron. .	15·78
Lime	5·84
Water	1·00
	100·00

BB fuses with difficulty, at the edges. Imperfectly soluble in muriatic acid.

Locality. Szurzaskö, in Hungary.

Name. After Adolph Wehrle, Austrian Councillor of Mines, by whom it was first analysed.

Brit. Mus., Case 34.

WEICHBRAUNSTEIN. See PYROLUSITE.

WEICHEISENKIES, *Breithaupt.* See WAS-SERKIES.

WEICHMANGAN. See PYROLUSITE.

WEISS-BLEIERZ, *Werner.* See CERUSITE.

WEISSER-SPEISKOBOLD, *Werner.* See SMALTINE.

WEISSGILTIGERZ, *Werner.* Silver Fahlore. See TETRAHEDRITE.

WEISSIAN. See SCOLECITE.

WEISSIGITE, *Jenzsch, Greg & Lettsom.* Occurs in small and indistinct crystals, sometimes in twins: also massive. Colour white to pale rose-red. Lustre vitreous. Streak white. H. 6·5. S.G. 2·538 to 2·546.

Analysis, by G. Jenzsch:

Silica	64·5
Alumina. . . .	17·0
Magnesia . . .	0·9
Potash	14·6
Soda and Lithia . .	2·2
Water	0·8
	100·0

BB fuses easily at the edges to a white and somewhat blebby enamel, tinging the outer flame slightly red, and yellow at the point. With borax forms a colourless glass

Insoluble in acids,

Localities. — *Scotch.* Calton Hill, Edinburgh, in pseudomorphous crystals of a dull brick-red colour, in trap-rock. Old Kilpatrick, and Long Craig; Dumbartonshire. Harfield Moss, Renfrewshire. Campsie Hills, Stirlingshire. — *Foreign.* Weissig, in Saxony, in porphyritic amygdaloid.

The Scotch and Saxon varieties bear a very close resemblance to each other, and occur under precisely similar conditions; the former, however, seems to be *Albite,* the latter *Felspar* (*Greg & Lettsom*).

WEISSITE, *Wachtmeister.* An altered form of Iolite, resembling Fahlunite. It occurs in oblique rhombic prisms, and in kidney-shaped masses of an ash-grey or brownish colour, showing only slight traces of cleavage. Translucent. Lustre pearly or waxy. Fracture even or coarsely granular. Scratches glass. S.G. 2·8.

Comp. $\ddot{R}^3 \ddot{S}i^2 + 2\ddot{R} \ddot{S}i^2$, or $3(\dot{K} \dot{N} \dot{M}g \dot{Z}n$ $\dot{M}n \dot{F}e) \ddot{S}i^2 + 2\ddot{A}l \ddot{S}i^2$ (*Wachtmeister*).

BB on charcoal, whitens, fuses at the edges and becomes surrounded with an areola of zinc-fumes.

Locality. The Copper mine of Eric Matts, at Fahlun, in Sweden.

Name. After Weiss, late Professor of Mineralogy in Berlin.

Brit. Mus., Case 32.

WEISSKUPFERERZ, *Hausmann, Werner.* See DOMEYKITE.

WEISSKUPFERERZ, *Breithaupt.* See KYROSITE.

WEISSNICKELKIES, *Breithaupt.* White Nickel-Pyrites. See RAMMELSBERGITE.

WEISSPIESSGLANZERZ, *Hoffmann, Werner.* White antimony. See VALENTINITE.

WEISSPIESSGLANZERZ, *Rammelsberg.* See CERVANTITE.

WEISSTELLUR. See WHITE TELLURIUM.

WEISSYLVANERZ, *Werner.* See YELLOW TELLURIUM.

WERNERITE, *Haüy.* A name given to Scapolite in honour of the German mineralogist, A. G. Werner.

WHEEL-ORE, or RADELERZ. A macled

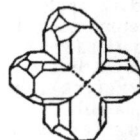

Fig. 455.

varietyof Bournonite,which occurs at Kapnik

in Transylvania. It is also found at Herodsfoot Mine, near Liskeard in Cornwall; *fig.* 455. See BOURNONITE.

WHEWELLITE, *Brooke & Miller, Dana.* An oxalate of lime. Oblique. Twins. Colourless. Lustre vitreous inclining to adamantine. Transparent to opaque. Streak white. Very brittle. Fracture conchoidal. H. 2·5 to 2·75. S.G. 1·833.

Comp. $\dot{C}a \, \ddot{C} + \dot{H}$.

Analysis, by *Sandall:*

Oxalic acid	. .	49·31
Lime	. . .	38·36
Water .	. . .	12·53

$\overline{100·00}$

Locality. Supposed to be Hungary.
Name. After Dr. Whewell, Master of Trinity College, Cambridge.

WHITE ANTIMONY, *Phillips.*
WHITE ANTIMONY-ORE, *Jameson.* } See VALENTINITE.

WHITE ARSENIC. See ARSENOLITE.

WHITE BISULPHURET OF IRON. See MARCASITE.

WHITE COBALT, *Allan.* See COBALTINE.

WHITE COBALT ORE, *Jameson.* See SMALTINE.

WHITE COPPER, or WHITE COPPER-ORE, *Kirwan, Jameson.* See DOMEYKITE.

WHITE COPPERAS. See COQUIMBITE.

WHITE GARNET OF VESUVIUS, *Kirwan.* See LEUCITE.

WHITE GOLD-ORE. A name applied to Native Tellurium in older works on Mineralogy.

WHITE HYACINTH OF SOMMA. See MEIONITE.

WHITE IRON PYRITES, *Phillips.* See MARCASITE.

WHITE LEAD-ORE, *Kirwan, Jameson,* or WHITE-LEAD SPAR. See CERUSITE.

WHITE MUNDIC. See MISPICKEL.

WHITE NICKEL-PYRITES. See RAMMELSBERGITE.

WHITE STONE. A name given by lapidaries to limpid and colourless Rock Crystal when cut for jewelry.

WHITE TELLURIUM. The name given to silver-white (inclining to yellow) varieties of Sylvanite. It occurs in needle-shaped crystals, is soft, and brittle. S.G. 7·99 to 8·33. In composition it is a telluride of gold and silver represented by the same formula (Ag Te³ + Au Te³), as Graphic Tellurium, with which it is probably identical.

Analysis, from Nagyag, by *Petz:*

Silver	. . . .	14·68
Gold	. . . .	24·89
Tellurium	. . .	55·39
Lead	. . . . .	2·54
Antimony	. . .	2·50

$\overline{100·00}$

BB behaves like Foliated Tellurium, except that it does not give off sulphurous acid.

Dissolves in nitric acid, leaving a residue of gold.

WHITE TOPAZ. The remarkably peculiar crystals found in the Ecklogite of the Sau-Alpe in Carinthia, which have been hitherto referred to Topaz, have been shown by Kenngott to be either imperfect or misformed crystals of Quartz.

WHITE VITRIOL, *Allan.* See GOSLARITE. This term, as used in the arts, is applied to sulphate of zinc in a granular state, produced by agitating the melted mass during the process of cooling.

" The salt is prepared on the large scale by roasting ores containing sulphide of zinc, afterwards exhausting them with water, and evaporating the solution to the crystallizing point. By fusion in its own water of crystallization, stirring in wooden troughs with wooden shovels till crystallization takes place, and subsequent pressing in boxes, commercial zinc-vitriol is made to assume the appearance of loaf - sugar."— *Gmelin.*

WHITNEYITE, *F. A. Genth.* Occurs massive, with a crystalline or finely granular structure. Colour reddish-white, or like that of an alloy of equal parts of copper and silver. Lustre metallic. Somewhat malleable. Takes a high polish, but soon tarnishes; sometimes iridescent. H. 3·5. S.G. 8·408.

Comp. Cu¹⁸As, or copper 88·37, arsenic 11·63=100.

Analysis, by *Genth:*

Copper	. . .	88·19
Arsenic	. .	11·41
Silver and insoluble	.	0·47

$\overline{100·07}$

BB fuses readily, and gives off the odour of arsenic.

Insoluble in muriatic acid. Soluble in nitric acid.

Localities. Occurs coated with Red Copper and a copper salt resulting from its oxidation. A boulder 40lb. in weight has been found at Pewabie Mine, Houghton co., Michigan. Also a mile from the Cliff Mine, at the Albion location, 3 to 4 inches wide.

Name. After Professor J. D. Whitney.

For variety, see DARWINITE.

WICHTISITE, *Hausmann.* WICHTYNE, *Laurent.* Massive, with traces of cleavage parallel to the sides of a nearly rectangular rhombic prism. Colour black. Lustre dull. Fracture angular or flat-conchoidal. H. scratches glass. S.G. 3·03.

Comp. ($\dot{R}^3 + \ddot{H}$) $\ddot{S}i^2$, or ($\dot{N}a$, $\dot{C}a$, $\dot{M}g$, $\dot{F}e$)^3 $\ddot{S}i^2 + (\ddot{A}l \; \ddot{F}e) \; \ddot{S}i^2$.

Analysis, by *Laurent :*

Silica	56·3
Alumina	13·3
Peroxide of iron	4·0
Protoxide of iron	13·0
Lime	6·0
Soda	3·5
Magnesia	3·0
	99·1

BB forms a black globule: with borax fuses to a bottle-green glass.

Not attacked by muriatic acid.

Locality. Wichtis*, in Finland.

Brit. Mus., Case 33.

WIESENERZ, *Werner.* Meadow ore. See BOG IRON-ORE.

WILD LEAD. A Cornish Miner's name for Blende.

WILHELMITE. WILLEMITE, *Levy, Dana.* WILLELMINE, *Phillips, Beudant.* WILLEMIT, *v. Leonhard.* WILLIAMITE, *Nicol.* WILLIAMSITE. Hexagonal: primary form an obtuse rhombohedron. Occurs in regular six-sided prisms. Also in grains or massive. Colour white, yellow, red or reddish-brown. Transparent to opaque. Lustre vitreoresinous. Streak white. Brittle. Fracture conchoidal. H. 5·5. S.G. 3·89 to 4·18.

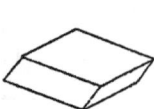
Fig. 456.

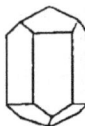
Fig. 457.

Comp. Anhydrous silicate of zinc, or $\dot{Z}n^3$ $\ddot{S}i$ = silica 27·15, oxide of zinc 72·85 = 100.

Analysis, from Stirling, by *Vanuxem & Keating :*

Oxide of zinc	68·06

* Whence the name Wichtisite.

Silica . . . . . 25·44

Peroxides of iron and manganese . . . . 6·50

               101·00

BB decrepitates and becomes opaque, but fuses only at the edges to a white enamel.

In a powdered state, easily forms a jelly in concentrated muriatic acid.

Localities. Vieille Montagne, near Aixla-Chapelle. Moresnet, near Liege. Raibel. Stirling Hill, New Jersey.

Name. After Wilhelm I. (Willem), King of the Netherlands.

Brit. Mus., Case 26.

WILLD LEAD. See WILD LEAD.

WILLIAMSITE, *Shepard.* A variety of Serpentine. Occurs in irregularly-shaped seams, sometimes above an inch thick between Chrome Iron-ore and Serpentine. Massive. Structure lamellar. Colour applegreen. Lustre feebly shining, pearly to resinous. Surface very dull. Translucent. Streak white. Fracture even. H. 4·5. S.G. 2·59 to 2·64.

Comp. $3\dot{M}g \; \ddot{S}i + \ddot{A}l \; \ddot{S}i + 3\dot{H}$.

Analysis, from Pennsylvania, by *Smith & Brush :*

Silica	41·60
Alumina	trace
Magnesia	41·11
Protoxide of iron	3·24
Protoxide of nickel	0·50
Water	12·70
	99·15

BB phosphoresces, turns white, and hardens so as to scratch glass, but does not fuse; dissolves with difficulty in borax.

In powder dissolves slowly in hot muriatic acid.

Localities. West Chester, Pennsylvania, U. S. Also of a pale green colour at Haroldswick, in Unst, one of the Shetlands, with chromate of iron.

Name. After the discoverer, L. White Williams, of West Chester, Pennsylvania.

Brit. Mus., Case 34.

WILSONITE, *T. S. Hunt.* A mineral bearing some resemblance to Scapolite. Occurs massive, with a cleavage in two directions, at right angles to each other. Colour rose-red to peach-blossom-red. Subtranslucent. Lustre vitreous; occasionally pearly on cleavage-surfaces. Fracture uneven. H. 3·5. S.G. 2·765 to 2·776.

Analysis, by *T. S. Hunt :*

Silica . . . . . 43·55

Alumina	.	.	.	.	27·94
Peroxides of iron and man-					
ganese	.	.	.	.	0·20
Lime	.	.	.	.	6·50
Magnesia	.	.	.	.	3·81
Potash	.	.	.	.	8·37
Soda	.	.	.	.	1·45
Water	.	.	.	.	8·61
					100·43

BB whitens and becomes opaque from loss of water. Fuses with intumescence to a white enamel.

Locality. Bathurst, Canada West.

Name. After the discoverer, Dr. Wilson, of Canada, mineralogist.

WILUITE. A name for Grossular, from its occurrence near the river Wilui, in Siberia. See GARNET.

WISERITE, *Haidinger.* A fibrous, silky, and yellowish (or reddish) hydrated variety of carbonate of manganese (*Diallogite*), occurring at Gonzen, near Sarganz, in Switzerland.

It is named in honour of D. F. Wiser, Swiss mineralogist.

WISMUTGLANZ, *Naumann,*⎫ Bismuth
WISMUTHGLANZ, *Werner,*⎬ Glance. See
Hausmann. ⎭ BISMUTHINE.

WISMUTH, German for Bismuth. According to Matthesius, Wismuth is a name used by the old miners, because it flowers like a beautiful meadow (Wiese-wiesmatt, Wiesmatte), upon which flowers of various colours are growing; alluding thereby to the iridescence of the metal. Koch considers the name to be derived from the Arabic *wiss majaht,* or that which melts as easily as Storax.

WISMUTHBLEIERZ, *Hausmann.* See BISMUTH SILVER.

WISMUTHOCHER, *Werner.* See BISMUTH OCHRE.

WISMUTHOXYD KOHLENSÄURES. See BISMUTITE.

WISMUTHSILBERERZ, *Selb.* See BISMUTH SILVER.

WISMUTHSPATH. See BISMUTITE.

WITHAMITE, *Phillips.* A variety of Manganesian-Epidote, occurring in transparent and minute but brilliant crystals, radiating from a centre, which appear of a carmine-

Fig. 458.

red colour in one direction, and of a pale straw-yellow colour when viewed at right

angles to the former direction and across the prism. Lustre vitreous. Streak white. H. 6 to 6·5. S.G. 3·1 to 3·3.

BB intumesces, and fuses with difficulty to a dark greenish-grey scoria.

Not acted on by acids.

Locality. — *Scotch.* Glencoe, in Argyleshire, both crystallized and massive, lining small cavities in trap-rock (*fig.* 458).

Name. Named by Sir David Brewster after the discoverer, Henry Witham.

Brit. Mus., Case 35.

WITHERIT, *Werner.* WITHERITE, *Dana,*

Fig. 459.

Fig. 460.

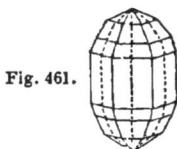
Fig. 461.

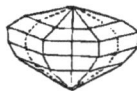
Fig. 462.

Phillips, Greg & Lettsom, Nicol. Rhombic: primary form a right rhombic prism. Occurs in crystals, which are nearly, if not always, compound, and resembling the common form of Quartz, viz. six-sided prisms, terminated by six-sided pyramids; also in globular, tuberose, botryoidal, stalactitic forms. Also amorphous. Colour generally white; sometimes greyish or greenish. Translucent, sometimes transparent. Lustre vitreous; of fracture resinous. Streak white. Brittle. Fracture uneven. Tasteless and poisonous. H. 3 to 3·5. S.G. 4·29 to 4·35.

Comp. Carbonate of baryta, or B̈a C̈ = baryta 77·7, carbonic acid 22·3 = 100.

BB fuses readily, forming a clear bead, which becomes white and opaque on cooling; on charcoal boils violently, becomes caustic, and is absorbed.

Soluble in 4304 parts of cold, and 2304 parts of boiling, water.

Dissolves slowly and with slight effervescence in dilute muriatic or nitric acid.

Localities. — *English.* Alston Moor, Cumberland (*fig.* 461). Wolhope, Durham. Arkendale, Yorkshire (*fig.* 459). Anglezarke, Lancashire. Snailbeach lead mines, Shropshire. Fallowfield, near Hexham, Northumberland, in large and very perfect crystals (*fig.* 462). Dufton Fells, Westmoreland (*fig.* 460). Foxdale lead mine, Isle of Man. — *Welsh.* Near St. Asaph, Flintshire. — *Foreign.* Tarnowitz, in Silesia. Szlana, in Hungary. Leogang, in Salzburg. Peggau, in Styria. The Altai Mountains, Siberia. Sicily. Near Coquimbo, Chili, &c.

Name. After Dr. Withering, by whom it was first discovered at Anglezarke, near Chorley in Lancashire.

Witherite is employed extensively in chemical works, and in the manufacture of plate-glass, porcelain, &c. It is also exported to France. where it is used in the manufacture of beet-root sugar.

Brit. Mus., Case 41.

M. P. G. Horse-shoe Case, Nos. 255 to 265.

WITTICHITE, *Dana, v. Kobel.* Occurs massive and disseminated; also coarsely columnar, or in aggregations of imperfect prisms. Colour steel-grey to tin-white, with a pale lead-grey tarnish. Streak black. H. 3·5. S.G. 5.

Comp. Cupreous bismuth, or $Cu S + Bi^2 S$.

Analysis, by *Klaproth :*

Bismuth   . . .   47·24
Copper .   . . . 34·66
Sulphur   . . . 12·58

              94·48

BB on charcoal, decrepitates, fuses, and yields a bismuth slag; and, after roasting with soda, a globule of copper.

Locality. Cobalt mines, near Wittichen (whence the name Wittichite), in Baden.

WITTINGITE. An altered form of Rhodonite (probably), and related to Stratopeite. S.G. 2·71 to 2·76.

Comp. $2(\overset{..}{Fe} \overset{..}{Mn}) \overset{..}{Si} + 3H.$

Locality. Wittinge, in Finland.

WODANKIES. A variety of Gersdorffite, from Topschau, in Hungary, in which Lampadius supposed he had discovered a new metal, which he named *Wodan*.

WŒRTHITE, *Dufrénoy,* or WÖRTHITE, *Hess.* See WÖRTHITE. A variety of Sillimanite, resembling Kyanite. Colourless. Lustre vitreous or pearly. Translucent to opaque. H. 7·25. S.G. 3.

Comp. $2\overset{..}{Al} \overset{..}{Si} + \overset{..}{H}.$

Analysis, by *Hess :*

Silica .   . . . 40·58
Alumina   . . . 53·50
Magnesia   . .   1·00
Water .   . . . 4·63

              99·71

BB infusible.

Locality. The neighbourhood of St. Petersburg, from loose blocks.

WOHAN. According to Kirwan, the Chinese name for the loose or friable varieties of Calamine.

WÖHLERITE. *Scheerer.* Rhombic. Occurs in indistinct tabular crystals, and in strongly striated six- or eight-sided prisms. Also massive, in angular grains. Colour various tints of yellow, inclining to red, brown, or grey. Translucent.. Lustre vitreous inclining to resinous. Streak yellowish-white. Fracture conchoidal. Splintery. H. 5·5. S.G. 3·41.

Comp. $\overset{..}{Zr}^5\overset{..}{Cb} + 5(\overset{..}{Na}\overset{..}{Si} + \overset{..}{Ca}^5\overset{..}{Si})($ *Scheerer* $).$

Analysis, by *Scheerer :*

Silica .   . . . . 30·62
Columbic acid   . . 14·47
Zirconia   . .   15·17
Peroxide of iron .   . 2·12
Protoxide of manganese . 1·55
Lime .   . . . 26·19
Soda .   . . . 7·78
Water .   . . . 0·24

              98·14

BB fuses to a yellowish glass. With fluxes affords reactions of iron, manganese, and silica.

Dissolves readily in warm concentrated muriatic acid, with separation of the silica and columbic acid.

Locality. Near Frederiksvärn and Brevig, in Norway, in Zircon-syenite. with Elæolite.

Name. In honour of the Hanoverian chemist, F. Wöhler, of Göttingen.

Brit. Mus., Case 38.

WÖLCHITE, *Haidinger.* Occurs in short rhombic prisms; also massive. Colour blackish lead-grey. Brittle. Fracture imperfectconchoidal. H. 3. S.G. 5·7 to 5·8.

Analysis, by *Schrütter :*

Sulphur   . . . 28·60
Lead .   . . . 29·90
Copper   . . . 17·35
Antimony   . .   16·65
Arsenic   . .   6·04
Iron   . . . . 1·40

              99·94

BB on charcoal, fuses with effervescence, to a lead-grey metallic globule, which, with soda, yields metallic copper.

Locality. Iron mines, at Wölch (whence the name Wölchite), or St. Gertraud, in the valley of Lavant, in Carinthia.

WOLCHONSKITE, *Berthier.* WOLCHONSKOITE, *Kenngott.* Massive. Colour bluish- or blackish-green, passing into grass-green.

Dull — shining. Streak bluish-green and shining. Adheres slightly to the tongue. Very fragile. Fracture sub-conchoidal. H. 2 to 2·5. S.G. 2·213 to 2·303.

Comp. Impure hydrated silicate of chrome, containing from 18 to 34 per cent. of chrome oxide.

Analysis, by *Ivanow* :

Silica	36·84
Oxide of chrome . .	18·85
Peroxide of iron . .	17·85
Alumina	3·50
Peroxide of manganese	trace
Lime	1·39
Water	22·46
	100·89

Gelatinises in hot concentrated muriatic acid.

Locality. Okhansk, in Siberia.

Name. In honour of the Russian Prince Wolchonsky.

Brit. Mus., Case 39.

WOLFRAM, *Werner, Allan, Dana, Nicol, Hausmann, Haidinger, v. Kobell, Naumann.* Rhombic : primary form a right rhombic prism. Occurs massive and crystallized. Colour dark greyish- or brownish-black. Opaque. Lustre brilliant ; often metallic. Streak dark reddish-brown. Sometimes feebly magnetic. Brittle. Structure lamellar. Fracture uneven. H. 5 to 5·5. S.G. 7·1 to 7·6.

Fig. 463.   Fig. 464.   Fig. 465.

Comp. Tungstate of iron-protoxide, or $\ddot{W}Fe$, with a greater or less proportion replaced by tungstate of manganese-protoxide.

Analysis, from Godolphin's Ball, by *Kerndt* :

Tungstic acid . .	75·92
Protoxide of iron .	19·35
Protoxide of manganese .	4·73
	100·00

BB on charcoal fuses to an iron-black magnetic globule, exhibiting externally an aggregation of laminar crystals. With carbonate of soda, is reduced to tungstide of iron, easily separated by levigation. With borax, dissolves with tolerable facility, and gives the reaction of iron.

Is decomposed by strong aqua-regia more quickly than by muriatic acid ; the small quantity of tungstic acid dissolved in the liquid is precipitated together with iron, on the addition of water.

Localities. — English. Cornwall : Huel Fanny, (*figs.* 464, 465), Poldice, Stenna Gwynn near St. Austell, Godolphin's Ball, Drake Walls Mine, Kit Hill, Huel Maudlin in pseudomorphs after Scheelite. Cumberland ; Brandygill, Carrock Fells, Lockfells. — *Scotch.* Island of Rona, in granite. — *Foreign.* Altenberg, Geyer, and Ehrenfriedersdorf, in Saxony, with tin-ore ; also at Schlackenwald and Zinnwald, in Bohemia, and in France. The Harz. Lane's Mine, Connecticut, U. S., in Quartz. Nertchinsk, in the Ural. Ceylon.

A variety of Wolfram with a composition represented by the formula $\ddot{F}e\ddot{W} + 4Mn\ddot{W}$ is said to occur about a mile and a half from St. Francis River, St. Francis co., Missouri, associated with Quartz and Mica. S.G. 6·67.

Name. From *wolfrig (eating)*, because the presence of the mineral diminishes the percentage of tin in smelting.

Brit. Mus., Case 38.

M. P. G. Principal Floor, Wall-cases 9 (British) ; 20 (Foreign).

Crystals of Wolfram are extremely rare in England, but are common in Bohemia and Saxony.

Wolfram is distinguished by its reddish-brown streak from Tinstone, which gives a grey streak. It is confined to primitive rocks, and is frequently associated with the tin-ores of Cornwall, Saxony, and other countries ; sometimes it occurs in such abundance as to render the dressing of the tin-ore difficult, in consequence of the little difference in the specific gravity of the two ores. The separation of the Wolfram is, however, now easily effected by the process discovered by Mr. Oxland, which is as follows : "After crushing or otherwise pounding the mixed substances, they are roasted, and, the Wolfram still remaining unaffected, after again washing, they are roasted with carbonate of soda, thus decomposing the Wolfram, and tungstate of soda being formed, the tin-ore is then fitted for further treatment in the smelting-house." * (*Sir H. T. De la Beche.*)

The tungstate of soda formed in this process is used for giving hardness to Plaster of

---

* In the modification of the above process, which is now generally adopted, sulphate of soda and carbon are substituted for the carbonate of soda.

Paris, as a mordant in dyeing, and is the best known substance for rendering ladies' dresses incombustible.

At Kaptenberg, in Styria, Tungsten is used for hardening steel. Knife-blades made with an alloy composed of from 2 to 5 per cent. of Tungsten added to the steel, are said to retain their edge four times longer than those made with common iron. An alloy formed of 80 per cent. of steel and 20 per cent. of tungsten possesses a degree of hardness which has never yet been obtained in the manufacture of steel. See also AIKENITE.

WOLFRAM BLANC. See SCHEELITE.

WOLFRAMBLEIERZ. See SCHEELETINE.

WOLFRAMINE, *Greg & Lettsom, Dana.* Cubical. Occurs in cubes; also pulverulent and earthy. Colour yellow or yellowish-green. Opaque. Dull.

Comp. Pure tungstic acid, or $\overset{...}{W}$ = tungsten 79·3, oxygen 20·7 = 100.

BB on charcoal, infusible; but becomes blackish-blue and then black in the inner flame.

Localities. — *English.* Cornwall; Drakewalls tin-mine, Huels Friendship and Poldice, investing Wolfram. Brandygill, Cumberland, with Wolfram and Scheelite. — *Foreign.* St. Leonard, near Limoges, in France. U. S.: Cabarras co., N. Carolina; Huntington, in a quartz vein with Wolfram.

WOLFRAMOCHER, *Hausmann.* See WOLFRAMINE.

WOLFSBERGITE, *Nicol.* Rhombic. Occurs in small aggregated tabular prisms, usually broken at the ends; also massive, and disseminated, and fine-granular. Colour lead-grey to iron-black, sometimes with an iridescent tarnish. Opaque. Lustre metallic. Streak black. Fracture conchoidal to uneven. H. 3·5. S.G. 4·748.

Comp. $Cu\,S + Sb^2\,S^3$ = copper 24·9, sulphur 24·9, antimony 50·2 = 100.

Analysis, by *H. Rose:*

Sulphur	.	.	.	26·34
Copper.	.	.	.	24·46
Antimony	.	.	.	46·81
Iron	.	.	.	1·39
Lead	.	.	.	0·56

99·56

BB decrepitates and fuses readily; on charcoal gives off fumes of antimony, and with soda, after long fusion, yields a globule of copper.

Locality. Wolfsberg*, in the Harz, imbedded in Quartz, and generally covered with a coating of Pyrites.

WOLLASTONITE, *Dana, Nicol, Haüy, Hausmann, Haidinger.* Chemically, Wollastonite is a Pyroxene with a lime base, but differing altogether from it in form, and optical properties.

Oblique: primary form a rhombic prism. Occurs rarely in distinct tabular prisms; mostly in broad prismatic or laminar masses. Colour white, inclining to yellow, green, red, or brown. Translucent. Lustre vitreous, inclining to pearly on cleavage-faces. Streak white. Rather brittle. Sometimes very tough. Fracture uneven. Becomes phosphorescent by heat or when scratched with a knife. H. 4·5 to 5. S.G. 2·78 to 2·9.

Fig. 466.

Comp. Silicate of lime, or $\overset{..}{Ca}^3\,\overset{...}{Si}^2$ = silica 52, lime 48 = 100.

Analysis, from Capo di Bove, by *v. Kobell:*

Silica	.	.	.	51·50
Lime	.	.	.	45·45
Magnesia	.	.	.	0·55
Water	.	.	.	2·00

99·50

BB fuses with difficulty to a semi-transparent glass.

Decomposed perfectly by muriatic acid, either before or after ignition, with separation of gelatinous silica.

Localities. — *Scotch.* Glengairn, Aberdeenshire, with Idocrase. — *Irish.* Dunmore Head, co. Down, massive, and with a confusedly fibrous texture. — *Foreign.* Capo di Bove, near Rome, of a greenish-white colour, in lava; also in ejected blocks from Vesuvius. Cziklowa and Dognatska, in the Bannat of Temeswar. Pargas, Porhoniesni, Skräbböle, in Finland. Kongsberg, in Norway. Ceylon. Grenville, Canada. Cliff Mine. Lake Superior. United States, at Willsborough, New York, and at Lewis, south of Keeseville.

Name. In compliment to Dr. Wollaston. Brit. Mus., Case 25.

WOLNYNE. The name by which a variety of Sulphate of Baryta, found at Muzsay, in Hungary, was once known on the continent.

---

* Whence the name Wolfsbergite.

The crystals, of a pale yellow colour, and nearly transparent, were disposed on vesi-

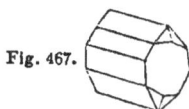

Fig. 467.

cular iron-ore. It has also been found in Cornwall (*fig.* 467).

Brit. Mus., Case 52.

WONDER-EARTH. See TERATOLITE.

WOOD-ARSENIATE OF COPPER. A fibrous kind of Olivenite, found investing or passing into the crystallized variety. It is found in Cornwall, at Huel Gorland, Huel Unity, Carharrack, Gunnis Lake, and amianthiform at Tin-Croft.

M. P. G. Principal Floor, Wall-case 2.

WOOD COAL, *Bakewell.* See CANNEL COAL.

The name is, also, sometimes given to fibrous Lignite.

WOOD IRON-ORE. A variety of Limonite with a fibrous structure, found at the Royal Restormel Iron Mines, Lostwithiel, in Cornwall.

M. P. G. Principal Floor, Wall-case 49, Nos. 337, 338, and 354.

WOOD-OPAL; WOODSTONE, *Jameson, Kirwan.* A variety of Opal, with a peculiar ligneous structure. It is somewhat harder than Semi-Opal, from which it does not materially differ in fracture, translucency. and lustre. It is found forming large trees in the pumiceous conglomerates of Saiba, near Neusohl and Kremnitz, in Hungary; in Faröe; near Hobart Town, in Tasmania, &c.

Portions of the silicified stems of coniferous trees which are met with lying prostrate in the dirt-beds, near the base of the Purbeck strata of Dorsetshire, are sometimes partially converted into this substance.

The whole of the Desert between Cairo and Suez (for about 86 miles) is covered with silicified trunks of trees, belonging, without exception, to the *Nicolia Ægyptiaca* (*Unger*), sometimes 40 or 50 feet long, and 1 or 2 feet in diameter, and lying in all directions.

The fragments are losely imbedded in the sands of the Desert, and may be seen in their original situation, in Tertiary sandstone, at the Gebel Akmar, a locality strikingly analogous to the sandstone containing woodstems near Gleischenberg, in Styria. Prof.

Unger is of opinion that the trees became silicified in consequence of their having drifted into a basin separated from the main sea, and filled with water saturated with silica.

There is another deposit of fossil wood near Assuan (Syene), on the frontiers of Ægypt and Nubia; and a third near Koum-Ombos, in the Desert west of the Nile.

The wood of these two latter localities belongs to an undescribed coniferous tree, of the Araucarian division, for which the name of *Dadoxylon Ægyptiacum* has been proposed by Prof. Unger.

In the Island of Unga, on the north coast of America, there are blocks of wood and whole trunks of trees, (some of which) distinctly show the marks of hatchets), converted into Opal.

Wood Opal is made into snuff-boxes and other ornamental articles, at Vienna, &c.

Brit. Mus., Case 24.

M. P. G. A 47, in Hall, from the Desert, near Cairo. Lower Gallery, west side, on floor near the stairs. Horse-shoe Case, No. 759.

WOOD-TIN, or fibrous oxide of tin, is a variety of Cassiterite, containing from 5 to 9 per cent. of oxide of iron, met with in a few mines and some of the principal stream works in Cornwall, frequently in masses of several pounds weight.

It occurs in reniform, globular, or in broken wedge-shaped pieces, the surfaces of which generally present a water-worn appearance. The structure is concentric-lamellar in one direction, and divergingly fibrous in the other, which, in connection with its brown and yellow colour, causes it to present a ligniform appearance.

Localities. Cornwall: Carnon Stream, Bodmin Moor, St. Austell, Roach, Pentuan, Polberrow Consols, Sancreed, and elsewhere.

Brit. Mus., Case 18.

M. P. G. Principal Floor, Wall-case 8, Nos. 406 and 407 (British).

WÖRTHITE, *Phillips.* A silicate of alumina, found in transparent and foliated, colourless crystalline masses in Sweden or Finland. It has a vitreous lustre, scratches Quartz. and, according to Hess, is composed of alumina 54·45, silica 40·79, water 4·76 = 100. H. 7·25. S.G. 3.

BB infusible.

· *Name.* After the discoverer, Fr. Von Wörth, secretary to the Mineralogical Society of St. Petersburgh.

Brit. Mus., Case 26.

Wörthite has been proved by the recent

examination of its optical properties, made by Des Cloiseaux with the polarising microscope, to belong to Sillimanite.

WULFENITE, *Dana, Haidinger, Nicol.* Pyramidal: primary form the octahedron with a square base. Occurs crystallized in flat and in acute four-sided pyramids, variously modified; and in tabular crystals. Also massive-granular. Colour generally orange- or wax-yellow, passing into grey, green or brown; rarely aurora-red. Translucent. Lustre waxy or adamantine. Streak white. Soft. Brittle. Fracture uneven or imperfect-conchoidal. H. 3. S.G. 6·3 to 6·9.

Fig. 468.

Comp. Molybdate of lead, or $\dot{P}b\ \ddot{M}o$ = oxide of lead 60·87, molybdic acid 39·13 = 100.

Decrepitates strongly when heated, and assumes a darker colour, which, however, disappears on cooling; fuses to a yellow mass.

BB sinks into the charcoal, leaving globules of lead, while the charcoal becomes impregnated with molybdenum and molybdide of lead. With carbonate of soda dissolves and sinks into the charcoal, leaving globules. With borax dissolves easily; the glass formed in the outer flame is slightly coloured; that formed in the inner flame is clear while hot, but in cooling, suddenly becomes dark and opaque.

Dissolves in heated nitric acid, with separation of yellowish-white nitrate of molybdic acid. Soluble in caustic potash, but insoluble in water.

Localities. — Foreign. Schwarzenbach, Bleiberg, Windisch-Kappel, in Carinthia. Rezbanya, in Hungary. Moldawa, in the Bannat (in red crystals resembling chromate of lead). Austria. Tyrol. Baden. Saxony. Dauphiny. Zimapan in Mexico. Massachusetts and Philadelphia, U.S.

Name. After the Austrian metallurgist, Wulfen.

Brit. Mus., Case 39.

WUNDERERDE. Wonder-earth. See TERATOLITE.

WUNDERSALZ. See GLAUBER SALT.

WÜRFELERZ, *Werner.* See PHARMACOSIDERITE.

WURFELSPATH, *Werner.* See ANHYDRITE.

X.

XANTHITE, *Mather, Thomson, Phillips.* A variety of Idocrase occurring in the form of small rounded grains easily separable from each other, and which appear under the microscope to be imperfect crystals, having a foliated texture. Colour light greyish or yellow. Translucent or transparent. Lustre splendent, inclining to resinous. H. easily crushed with the nail. S.G. 3·2.

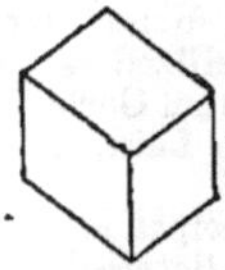

Fig. 469.

Locality. Amity, in New York, U. S.

Name. From ξανθὸς, *yellow*, in allusion to its colour.

Brit. Mus., Case 35.

XANTHOCONE, *Dana.* XANTHOKON, *Breithaupt, Nicol.* Hexagonal. Occurs in very thin six-sided tabular crystals, with alternating oblique side-faces. Generally in small reniform masses made up internally of minute crystals. Colour dull red to clove-brown. Orange-yellow at the edges by transmitted light. Lustre adamantine. Streak orange-yellow. Brittle. H. 2·25. S.G. 5 to 5·2.

Comp. Arsenio-sulphide of silver, or $(3Ag\ S + As^2\ S^5) + 2(3\dot{A}gS + As^2\ S^3)$ = silver 66·2, arsenic 15·3, sulphur 18·5 = 100.

BB on charcoal, gives off fumes of sulphur and arsenic, and leaves a grain of silver.

Locality. The Himmelsfürst Mine, at Freiberg, in Saxony.

Name. From ξανθὸς, *yellow*, and κόνις, *powder*, in allusion to its yellow powder.

XANTHOPHYLLITE, *G. Rose.* A variety of Clintonite found in implanted globules, and in columnar and lamellar individuals which sometimes contain within thin, tabular, six-sided crystals. H. 4·5 to 6·5. S.G. 3·01 to 3·1.

Comp. Combination·of a silicate with aluminate of magnesia, or $2\ddot{M}g\ \ddot{A}l + \dot{C}a\ \ddot{S}i.$

Locality. Schischimskian Mountains, near Slatoust. in the Ural.

Name. From ξανθὸς, *yellow*, and φύλλον, *a leaf*, in allusion to its colour and lamellar structure.

Brit. Mus., Case 25.

XANTHORTHITE. A yellowish variety of

Orthite containing much water. S.G. 2·78 to 2·9.

Locality. Eriksberg and Kullberg, in Sweden.

Name. From ξανθὸς, *yellow,* and *Orthite* (from ὀρθὸς, *straight*).

XANTHOSIDERITE, *E. Schmidt.* Occurs in stellate and concentric aggregations of fine needles or fibres, with a silky or greasy lustre. Colour golden yellowish-brown to brownish-red. H. 2·5.

Comp. F̈e Ḧ².

Analysis, of brown variety, by *E. Schmidt :*

Peroxide of iron . . .	75·00
Silica	5·02
Alumina	1·51
Peroxide of manganese	1·33
Water	14·10
	96·96

Locality. Ilmenau, in the Harz, with ores of manganése.

Name. From ξανθὸς, *yellow,* and σίδηρος, *iron.*

XENOLITE. A fibrous mineral resembling Kyanite, as well as Bucholzite. The recent investigations by Des Cloiseaux into the optical properties of Xenolite, made with the polarising microscope, prove it to be a Sillimanite. S.G. 3·58.

Comp. 2A̤l S̤i, or A̤l⁴ S̤i³ (Des Cloiseaux).

Analysis, from Finland, by *Komonen :*

Silica	52·54
Alumina	47·44
Potash	trace
	99·98

Locality. Peterhoff, Finland ; in loose blocks with Wörthite.

Name. From ξίνος, *a guest,* and λίθος, *stone.* Brit. Mus., Case 26.

XENOTIME, *Beudant.* Pyramidal : primary form a rectangular prism, with a square base. Colour yellowish - brown. Nearly opaque. Lustre resinous. Streak pale brown. Fracture uneven and splintery. H. 4·5 to 5. S.G. 4·4 to 4·55.

Fig. 470.

Comp. Phosphate of Yttria, or Ÿ³P̈= yttria 63, phosphoric acid 37 = 100.

Analysis, from Norway, by *Berzelius :*

Phosphoric acid, with trace of fluoric acid . .	33·49
Yttria	62·58
Sub-phosphate of iron .	3·93
	100·00

BB on charcoal, alone, infusible. With borax, yields a colourless globule, which becomes milky on cooling.

Insoluble in acids.

Localities. Ytterby, in Sweden. Lindesnaes, in Norway, in crystalline masses, imbedded in granite. Clarksville, Georgia, U. S.

Name. From ξένος, *vain,* and τιμή, *honour,* because phosphate of Yttria has been mistaken for a new metal, to which the name Thorium was given, which is now applied to the metal discovered in Thorite.

Brit. Mus., Case 57.

XYLITE, *Hermann.* A mineral allied to Xylotile, in composition, and resembling it also in its brown colour and asbestiform structure.

It is supposed to have been brought from the Ural.

Name. From ξύλον, *wood,* and λίθος, *stone.*

XYLOCHLORE, *v. Waltershausen.* A mineral bearing a close resemblance to Apophyllite, found in olive-green crystals in Iceland. H. 6. S.G. 2·29.

Name. ξύλον, *wood,* and χλωρός, *green.*

XYLOTILE, *Glocker.* A delicately fibrous mineral, considered by Kenngott to be altered Chrysotile. Colour various shades of wood-brown, also green. Opaque. Lustre glimmering. Streak shining. Soft. S.G. 2·4 to 3·56.

Locality. Sterzing, in the Tyrol.

Name. From ξύλον, *wood,* and τίλος, *fibre.*

Y.

YANOLITE. See AXINITE.

YELLOW COPPERAS. See COPIAPITE.

YELLOW COPPER ORE, *Kirwan.* ⎫
YELLOW COPPER PYRITES. ⎬ See CHALCO-PYRITE.

YELLOW EARTH, *Jameson, Nicol.* ⎫ An impure variety of Limonite, or perhaps a mixture of Limonite with hydrous silicate of alumina. It is found at Pary's Mine, in Anglesea ; in the Forest of Dean, Gloucestershire ; and in

YELLOW IRON OCHRE, *Greg & Lettsom.* ⎭

many other localities in the United Kingdom. Also at Amberg, in Bavaria, the Harz, France, &c. It is used as a yellow pigment.

YELLOW GOLD-GLANCE. See YELLOW TELLURIUM.

YELLOW LEAD ORE, or YELLOW LEAD SPAR. See WULFENITE.

YELLOW MINERAL RESIN, *Mohs.* See AMBER.

YELLOW MOLYBDENATED LEAD ORE, *Kirwan.* See WULFENITE.

YELLOW OCHRE. A variety of Ochre resulting from the decomposition of Limonite. Haussmann believes it to be a distinct species, composed of 81·6 peroxide of iron, and 18·4 water, in which case its chemical composition is represented by the formula

$$\ddot{F}e + 2\ddot{H}.$$

It is found in several localities, amongst others at Pary's Mine, Anglesea.

When prepared by grinding and washing, Yellow Ochre is used as a yellow pigment. Sometimes it is exposed to the action of fire, to increase the oxidation of the iron, and to deepen the colour, which then becomes reddish-brown. Yellow Ochre is stated by Bunsen to be a valuable antidote to the poison of arsenic.

YELLOW ORPIMENT, *Jameson.* See ORPIMENT.

YELLOW QUARTZ. See CITRINE. Limpid and transparent Rock Crystal of a lemon-, golden-, or wine-yellow colour; resembles Yellow Topaz in appearance, and is often sold for it, though neither of the same hardness, specific gravity, nor brilliancy. It is used chiefly for seal-stones; it is also sometimes used in jewelry for brooches, ear-rings, &c. Very good specimens are found at Olivet, near Orleans.

Brit. Mus., Case 20.

M. P. G. Horse-shoe Case, No. 509.

YELLOW SULPHURET OF ARSENIC. See ORPIMENT.

YELLOW TELLURIUM, *Allan, Phillips.* See SYLVANITE.

YENITE. A name given to Lievrite, in commemoration of the battle of Jena, fought in 1806.

M. P. G. Principal Floor, Wall-case 19.

YOU-STONE. Jade. See NEPHRITE.

YPOLEIME, *Beudant* (from ὑπολίμμα, *the balance of account, i. e.* the species of Haüy left after the separation of Apharèse.). See PHOSPHOCHALCITE.

YTTERBITE. A name given to Gadolinite, after that of one of its localities, Ytterby, in Sweden.

YTTERSPATH. See XENOTIME.

YTTERTANTAL, *Eckeberg.* ⎱ See YTTRO-
YTTERTANTALITE, *Jameson.* ⎰ TANTALITE.

YTTRIA FLUATÉE, *Dufrénoy.* See YTTROCERITE. YTTRIA PHOSPHATÉE, *Necker.* See XENOTIME.

YTTRIA SPAR. See XENOTIME. It occurs as a white incrustation on Gadolinite and other minerals from Ytterby, in Sweden, (*Nicol*).

YTTROCERITE, *Berzelius, Beudant, Dana, Nicol, Phillips.* Occurs in amorphous masses, with a crystalline-granular and earthy structure. Colour violet-blue, inclining to white and grey, or greyish-red. Opaque. Lustre glistening. Fracture uneven. H. 4 to 5. S.G. 3·4 to 3·5.

Comp. CaF,YF,CeF, or sesquifluoride of cerium, with fluoride of yttrium and fluoride of calcium (Fluor).

Analysis, from Finbo, by *Gahn & Berzelius:*

Lime	. 50·00
Peroxide of cerium	. 16·45
Yttria	. 8·10
Hydrofluoric acid.	. 25·45
	100·00

BB alone, loses colour and becomes white, but does not fuse. With Gypsum, fuses to an opaque globule.

Dissolves in boiling muriatic acid.

Localities. Finbo and Broddbo, near Fahlun, in Sweden; imbedded in Quartz, with Albite and Topaz. Amity, Orange co., New York, U.S.

Name. From its composition; chiefly Yttria and Cerium.

Brit. Mus., Case 58.

YTTRO-COLUMBITE, *Dana.* See YTTRO-TANTALITE.

YTTROILMENITE, *Hermann.* See SAMARSKITE.

YTTROTANTAL, *Kursten.* YTTROTANTALITE, *Dana, Eckeberg, Dufrénoy, Nicol, Phillips.* Three varieties of this mineral are described by Berzelius, viz. 1, *Dark* or *Brownish-black;* 2, *Yellow;* and 3, *Black.*

1. *The dark or brownish-black* is translucent, and of a pale yellow colour, when in thin laminæ. Lustre vitreo-resinous. Streak white. Occurs in amorphous masses, or in thin plates with the yellow variety. H. 4·5 to 5. S.G. 5·39 to 5·88.

Comp. 4 $(\dot{C}a, \dot{Y}, \dot{U}, \dot{F}e) \ddot{T}a.$

BB decrepitates slightly, and becomes light yellow, but does not fuse. With a large quantity of borax, forms a transparent, yellow glass; with a smaller quantity, a dark yellowish-brown glass. Does not dissolve in carbonate of soda.

2. *Black Variety.* Presents indistinct traces of four- or six-sided irregular prisms and plates. Colour black. Opaque. Lustre metallic. Streak grey. H. scratches glass. S.G. 5·395.

Comp. $3 (\dot{C}a, \dot{Y}, \dot{F}e) (\ddot{T}a, \ddot{W})$.

Analysis by *Nördenskiöld:*

Oxide of tantalum	.	56·56
Tungstic acid	. .	8·87
Yttria	. . .	19·56
Lime .	. . .	4·47
Protoxide of iron	. .	8·90
Protoxide of uranium	.	0·82
Oxide of copper	. .	traces
Water	. . .	6·68
		100·66

BB decrepitates slightly, and becomes dark brown, but does not fuse. With borax yields a transparent, colourless or yellowish glass, which when it contains a comparatively small proportion of the Yttro-Tantalite, is rendered opaque by flaming; but when it contains a larger quantity, becomes opaque without flaming. With carbonate of soda swells up, and remains in the form of a white mass after the soda has been absorbed by the charcoal.

3. *Yellow Variety.* Occurs in laminæ in fissures in Felspar. Colour brownish-yellow. Opaque. Streak white. Not crystalline. Softer than glass. S.G. 5·882.

Comp. The same as No. 2 or 3 $(\dot{C}a, \dot{Y}, \dot{F}e) (\ddot{T}a, \ddot{W})$.

BB decrepitates slightly, and becomes pale yellow, but does not fuse. With borax, in the inner flame, yields a transparent, yellow glass, which becomes darker yellow on cooling, and is rendered milk-white by flaming.

All three varieties are insoluble in aqueous acids, but are completely decomposed by fused bisulphate of potash.

Yttrotantalite has recently been stated by Nordenskiöld to be isomorphous with Polycrase and Polymignite.

Localities. — Sweden: Ytterby in flesh-red Felspar with Gadolinite; Broddbo, Finbo, and Kararfvet, near Fahlun, in granite veins; associated with Garnet, Mica, and Pyrophysalite. The Ilmen Mountains, near Miask in the Ural.

Name. From its composition: chiefly of Yttria and Tantalum.

Brit. Mus., Case 38.

YTTROTITANITE, *Scheerer.* See KEILHAULITE.

YU. The Chinese name for Jade.

Z.

ZALA. See BORAX.

ZAVALITE. Probably hydrated carbonate of Nickel, resembling Nickel-Emerald. Does not occur crystallized. Lustre waxy, inclining to vitreous. Streak apple-green. Yields to the knife.

Locality. Spain.

ZEAGONITE, *Gismondi.* A Vesuvian mineral occurring in rhombic crystals on Somma, and identical with Gismondine (which see).

ZEASITE. See OPAL.

ZEILANIT, *Werner,* or CANDITE. A variety of Pleonaste, in which part of the magnesia is replaced by protoxide of iron. It occurs in black octahedrons which are harder than Quartz. Translucent to opaque. Powder greyish-green. S.G. 3·6 to 3·8.

Comp. $(\dot{M}g^2 \dot{F}e) \ddot{A}l^5$.

Analysis, by *Gmelin:*

Alumina	. . .	67·28
Magnesia	. . .	17·45
Protoxide of iron	. .	15·27
		100·00

BB infusible. With borax, or microcosmic salt, dissolves, forming a glass coloured by iron.

Scarcely acted on by acids.

Locality. Near Candy, in Ceylon (whence the name).

ZELLKIES, *Werner.* See CELLULAR PYRITES.

ZEOLITE or ZEOLITH, *Hausmann.* A term under which are comprised several minerals, all of which possess, in common, the tendency to form a jelly with acids.

The different varieties of Zeolitic minerals may be divided into six groups, viz. :—

1. Efflorescing Zeolite, or Laumonite.
2. Feather Zeolite, or Natrolite, Scolecite.
3. Foliated Zeolite, or Heulandite and Stilbite.
4. Needle Zeolite. or Scolecite and Natrolite; including Mesolite.
5. Pyramidal Zeolite, or Apophyllite; including Ichthyophthalmite, Oxhaverite, Tesselite.
6. Radiated Zeolite, or Mesotype.

Name. From ζέω, *to boil,* because of their general character of intumescing when heated.

Brit. Mus., Cases 27, 28.

ZÉOLITE COMMUNE, *Nap.* See STILBITE.

ZÉOLITE DUR. See ANALCIME.

ZÉOLITE EFFLORESCENTE. See LAUMONITE.

ZÉOLITE FIBREUSE. See NATROLITE.

ZÉOLITE RAYONNÉE. See STILBITE and MESOTYPE.

ZÉOLITE TENACE. See DYSCLASITE.

ZEOLITHE LAMELLEUSE, *Brochant.* ⎫
ZEOLITHE NACRÉE, ⎬ See FOLIATED STILBITE.
Ladnelherie. ⎭

ZEOLITHE RAYONNÉE, *Brochant.* See STILBITE.

ZEUXITE, *Thomson.* The name given by Dr. Thomson to a variety of Iron-Tourmaline met with at Huel Unity, in Cornwall, in small translucent, acicular crystals, of a greenish-black colour. The crystals, apparently rectangular prisms, were much interlaced and collected into fibrous masses. H. 4 to 5. S.G. 3 to 3·1.

BB alone infusible; with borax, forms a dark-brown glass.

Name. From ζεῦξις, *a connexion;* because of its occurrence at the United Mines.

ZEYLANITE, or CEYLANITE, *Werner.* A variety of PLEONASTE. See ZEILANITE.

ZIANITE, *Werner.* See KYANITE.

ZIEGELERZ, *Werner.* ZIEGUELINE, *Beudant.* Earthy Red Oxide of Copper. See TILE ORE.

ZINC is stated by G. Ulrich to have been found in a metallic state near Victoria, in Australia. According to Becker it occurs, also, in the gold washings of the Mitta River.

ZINC-BLENDE, *Jameson.* See BLENDE.

ZINC BLOOM, *Smithson, Dana.* Occurs in reniform earthy masses, and incrustations, and is probably a result of the decomposition of Calamine. Colour white, greyish, or yellowish. Opaque. Lustre dull. Streak shining. H. 2 to 2·5. S.G. 3·58 to 6.

Comp. $\dot{Z}n^3 \ddot{C} + 3\dot{H}$ (*Smithson*), or $\dot{Z}n \ddot{C} + \dot{Z}n^2 \dot{H}$ (*Rammelsberg*).

Analysis, by *Smithson:*

Oxide of zinc	. .	71·4
Carbonic acid	. .	13·5
Water .	. . .	15·1
		100·0

Localities. Bleiberg and Raibel in Carinthia; associated with ores of zinc and lead.

Santander, Spain; of a pure white, and S.G. 2·25.

ZINC-CARBONATÉ, *Haüy, Dufrénoy.* See CALAMINE.

ZINCFAHLERZ. See KUPFERBLENDE.

ZINC-GLANCE. See SILICEOUS CALAMINE or SMITHSONITE.

ZINC HYDRATE CUPRIFÈRE, *Levy.* See TYROLITE.

ZINC HYDRO-CARBONATÉ, *Dufrénoy.* See ZINCITE.

ZINC-IRON SPAR. The name proposed by Monheim for the dark-green varieties of Zinc-spar (Calamine), and also to those which turn brown by oxidation of the iron.

ZINC-LEAD-SPAR, *Karsten.* Carbonate of lead, containing an admixture of 7 per cent. of carbonate of zinc.

ZINC OXIDÉ. See ZINCITE.

ZINC OXIDÉ FERRIFÈRE, *Haüy.* See FRANKLINITE.

ZINC OXIDÉ ROUGE, *Dufrénoy.* See SPARTALITE.

ZINC OXIDÉ SILICIFÈRE, *Haüy.* See SMITHSONITE.

ZINC OXYD, *v. Leonhard.* See ZINCITE.

ZINC SPAR. See CALAMINE.

ZINC SULFATÉ, *Haüy.* See GOSLARITE.

ZINC SULFURÉ, *Haüy.* See BLENDE.

ZINC VITRIOL, *Kirwan, Jameson.* See GOSLARITE.

ZINCITE, *Haidinger, Dana, Nicol.* ZINCONISE, *Beudant.* Hexagonal; with a perfect basal cleavage. Generally occurs disseminated in crystalline grains or coarse particles, and aggregates. Structure granular, also foliated. Colour blood-, or hyacinth-red, also inclining to yellow. Translucent at the edges. Lustre subadamantine. Streak orange-yellow. Brittle. Fracture subconchoidal. H. 4 to 4·5. S.G. 4·32 to 5·53.

Comp. Oxide of zinc, or $\dot{Z}n$=zinc 80·26, oxygen 19·74=100.

According to Leopold Gmelin, Zincite is a mixture of 88 parts of zinc-oxide and 12 parts protoperoxide of manganese.

Analysis, from Franklin, by *W. P. Blake.* S.G. 5·684 (at 60° F.):

Oxide of zinc	. .	99·47
Peroxide of manganese	.	0·68
Loss by ignition .	.	0·23
		100·38

BB alone, infusible, but emits a strong light. Volatilizes at a strong white heat. With borax yields a yellow transparent glass.

Dissolves without effervescence in nitric acid.

Localities. New Jersey, at Stirling Hill, Sussex co., with Franklinite and Calc Spar; also at Franklin. "At the zinc-smelting works at Filisur, in the Grisons, there are found sublimed in the upper part of the crucibles, in which the zinc is melted, amber-coloured, transparent, hard, shining, six-sided prisms, which have a density of 6·0, yield a white powder, becoming yellow when heated, and consist of zinc-oxide with a trace of sulphide."— (*L. Gmelin,* vol. v. p. 10.)

ZINCKENITE, *Nicol.* See ZINKENITE.

ZINKARSENIAT, *Otto Köttig.* See KÖTTIGITE.

ZINKBLENDE, *Hausmann.* See BLENDE.

ZINKBLÜTHE. See ZINC BLOOM.

ZINKENITE, *G. Rose, Dana, Phillips.* Rhombic. Occurs in regular six-sided prisms, terminated by low six-sided pyramids. The faces of the prisms are generally deeply striated longitudinally, while those of the pyramids are uneven, but not furrowed. Colour steel-grey. Opaque. Lustre bright-metallic. Streak same as the colour. Frac-

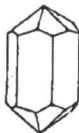

Fig. 471.

ture somewhat uneven. H. 3 to 3·5. S.G. 5·3 to 5·35.

Comp. Sulphantimonite of lead, or Pb S + Sb S³=antimony 43·43, lead 35·02, sulphur 21·55; or sulphide of lead 40·4, sulphide of antimony 59·6=100.

Analysis, from Wolfsberg Mine, by *H. Rose :*

Antimony	.	.	.	44·39
Lead	.	.	.	31·84
Sulphur	.	.	.	22·58
Copper	.	.	.	0·42
				99·23

BB decrepitates strongly. On charcoal melts as readily as Grey Antimony; small metallic globules are formed, which entirely volatilize, while the charcoal is covered with a white coating of oxide of lead. With carbonate of soda yields globules of metallic lead.

Locality. The antimony mine of Wolfsberg, near Stolberg, in the Harz.

The crystals, which are aggregated in groups, and present a columnar composition, occur on a massive variety of the same species in Quartz. Their length often exceeds half an inch, their breadth two or three lines; but frequently they are extremely thin, and form fibrous masses.— (*Allan.*)

Name. Named by Gustav Rose in honour of Zinken, director of the mines of Anhalt, in Hanover.

Brit. Mus., Case 11.

Zinkenite may be distinguished from Grey Antimony and Bournonite, to which it bears a strong resemblance both in colour and fracture, by its greater hardness and higher specific gravity.

ZINKGLAS, *Hausmann.* See SMITHSONITE.

ZINKIT, *Haidinger.* See ZINCITE.

ZINKKIESELERZ, *Berzelius.* See SMITHSONITE.

ZINKOXYD, *v. Leonhard.* See ZINCITE.

ZINKPHYLLIT, *Breithaupt.* See HOPEITE.

ZINKSPATH, *v. Leonhard.* See CALAMINE.

ZINKVITRIOL, *Hausmann.* See GOSLARITE.

ZINN, *German* for Tin.

ZINNERZ, *Naumann.* See CASSITERITE.

ZINNKIES, *Werner, Hausmann.* See TIN PYRITES.

ZINNOBER, *Werner.* See CINNABAR. The word Zinnober is derived from the ancient Greek name for the mineral κιννάβαρι, which, again, is derived from the Arabic, *Konou apar,* i. e. *very red stuff.*

ZINNSTEIN, *Werner.* Tin Stone. See CASSITERITE.

ZINNWALDITE, *Haidinger.* The name given to the variety of Lithia Mica (*Lepidolite*) from Zinnwald.

Comp. $2\dot{R} \ddot{S}i + 3\ddot{R} \ddot{S}i.$

Analysis, by *Rammelsberg :*

Silica	.	.	.	51·70
Alumina	.	.	.	26·76
Peroxide of manganese	.	1·29
Potash	.	.	.	10·29
Lithia	.	.	.	1·27
Fluorine	.	.	.	7·12·
Magnesia	.	.	.	0·24
Lime	.	.	.	0·40
Soda	.	.	.	1·15
Phosphoric acid	.	.	0·16
				100·88

ZIPPEITE, *Dana, Greg & Lettsom.* Occurs earthy and pulverulent. Amorphous. Opaque. Dull. Fracture earthy.

E E

There are two varieties, one (*a*) containing copper, and the other (*b*) without copper. The former is of a fine sulphur-yellow colour, and occurs in delicate needles, or acicular rosettes, or warty crusts; the latter lemon- to orange-yellow.

Comp. Of copper variety $\dot{C}u\ \ddot{S} + \dddot{U}^3\ \ddot{S}^2 +$ 12$\dot{H}$; of variety without copper $\dddot{U}^3\ \ddot{S}^2 +$ 12$\dot{H}$.

Analysis, from Joachimsthal, by *Vogl* :

	(*a*)	(*b*)
Sulphuric acid	17·36	13·06
Peroxide of uranium	62·04	67·85
Peroxide of iron	—	0·17
Oxide of copper	5·20	—
Lime	—	0·67
Water	15·23	17·70
	99·84	99·39

BB becomes orange-yellow when heated gently. In the reducing flame changes to green, but does not fuse.

Localities. — English. Cornwall: Callington; Carharrack; Withiel Iron-mine; Huel Edward; Huel Buller; near St. Michael's Mount, coating Mica, on a quartzose rock. — *Foreign.* Joachimsthal, in Bohemia. Symphorien, in France. The felspar quarry, near Middletown, Connecticut, U.S.

Name. In honour of Zippe, Professor of Mineralogy in Prague.

ZIRCON. *Werner. Dana, Phillips, Nicol, Brooke & Miller, Haüy, Hausmann, Greg & Lettsom.* Pyramidal: primary form an obtuse octahedron, with a square base. Occurs in crystals bearing a remarkable resemblance to those of oxide of tin (*Cassiterite*) with which it is isomorphous: also in rounded grains. Colour red, brown, yellow, green or grey; rarely white. Transparent to opaque. Doubly refractive. Lustre more or less adamantine. Streak white. Fracture conchoidal and brilliant. H. 7·5. S.G. 4 to 4·75.

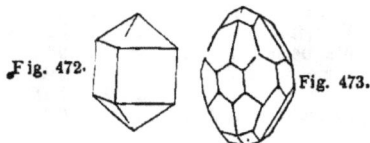

Fig. 472.   Fig. 473.

Comp. Silicate of zirconia, or $\ddot{Z}r\ \dddot{S}i =$ zirconia 66·23, silica 33·77 = 100.

Analysis, from Ceylon, by *Vauquelin* :

Zirconia	.	.	.	64·5
Silica	.	.	.	32·6
Peroxide of iron	.	.	.	2·0
				99·1

BB loses colour but does not fuse. In a large quantity of borax, dissolves with difficulty, and forms a transparent glass; with a smaller quantity forms a turbid glass. Does not dissolve to any perceptible extent in microcosmic salt or carbonate of soda. Zircon may be fused with potash, lime, or oxide of lead.

Not decomposed by acids — even by muriatic acid — hot oil of vitriol, however, acts slightly on it.

Localities. — Scotch. Strontian, Argyleshire; *fig.* 472. Isle of Harris, *fig.* 473. Sutherlandshire. — *Irish.* Croghan Kinshela mountain, in the auriferous streams. — *Foreign.* Kitiksut, in Greenland. Norway, along the Christianiafjord, between Stavärn and Hackedalen. Sweden. The Sau-Alp, in Carinthia. The Siebengebirge. Expailly, in Auvergne. Vicenza, in Italy. Vesuvius, in ejected blocks. Assuan, in Upper Egypt. Some stones of very fine colour and transparency," constituting veritable gems," have been obtained by Sir William E. Logan, in Canada; they occur in the crystalline limestone of the Laurentian series, at Grenville Township, Argenteuil co., C. E.

Name. From the Arabic word *Zerk,* signifying *a precious stone.*

Brit. Mus., Case 26.

M. P. G. Horse-shoe Case, Nos. 845, 846, 850 to 852.

Zircon is divided into three varieties; 1st, the colourless or slightly smoky or *Jargoon;* 2nd, the bright red or *Hyacinth;* and 3rd, the greyish or, brownish, called *Zirconite.* See also ERDMANNITE and OSTRANITE.

Zircons with the same crystalline form, the same external characters, and in every respect precisely identical with the Zircons of Somma (Vesuvius) have been recently obtained artificially by Mons. Henri Sainte-Claire Deville, by passing fluoride of silicium over Zirconia at a red heat. Mons. Deville believes that it may be inferred, with nearly absolute certainty, that the Zircon has been formed by igneous agency, from the small quantities of Fluor which are present in the metamorphic rocks in which it occurs.

ZIRCONITE. The name applied to the greyish or reddish-brown and nearly opaque varieties of Zircon.

Localities. — Foreign. Miask, in the Ural. Kitiksut, in Greenland. Frederiksvärn, in Norway, in syenite. Scalpay, in the Isle of Harris, one of the Hebrides. Buncombe co., North Carolina. New York co.

Fig. 474.

Fig. 475.

Brit. Mus., Case 26.

ZIRKON, *Werner.* See ZIRCON.

ZOISIT, *Karsten, Werner.* ZOISITE, *Phillips, Greg & Lettsom.* A variety of Lime-Epidote occurring in rhombic prisms which are usually deeply striated, and often columnar-massive. The crystals are seldom perfect, the obtuse lateral edges of the prisms being often rounded, and the terminations incomplete. Colour grey, yellowish-grey or brown. Translucent. Lustre pearly. H. 6 to 7. S.G. 3·28 to 3·35.

BB alone, fuses at the outer edges to a yellowish transparent glass, but finally to a vitreous scoria. With borax swells up and forms a pale yellow diaphanous glass which is colourless when cold.

Comp. $\dot{C}a^3 \ddot{S}i + 3\ddot{A}l \ddot{S}i$.

Analysis, by *Rammelsberg*:

Silica	. 41·51
Alumina . . .	. 28·90
Peroxide of iron . .	. 3·98
Lime	. 24·78
Magnesia . . .	. 0·58
	99·75

Localities. — Scotch. Glenelg, Inverness-shire. — *Irish.* Holly Hill, near Strabane, co. Tyrone. — *Foreign.* Bacher mountain, and Sau - Alp, in Carinthia. The Ural. Bayreuth, Conradsreuth; in Bavaria. Fern-leite, in Salzburg. Sterzing, in the Tyrol. The Valais. Various parts of the United States, as Willsboro', Vermont; Montpelier, Chester and other places in Massachusetts; Milford, Connecticut; Pennsylvania, &c.

Name. After the Austrian mineralogist, the Baron Von Zois.

Brit. Mus., Case 35.

This mineral was separated from Epidote, and named a distinct species by Brooke & Miller, on crystallographic grounds. Des Cloiseaux has, also, shown from the optical properties of Zoisite that it is distinct from

Epidote, the former belonging to the oblique system, while the latter has the rhombic form.

ZÖLESTIN, *Werner.* See CELESTINE.

ZOOTINSALZ, *Breithaupt.* See NITRATINE.

ZORGITE. The name applied by Brooke & Miller to the Tilkerodite of Haidinger, and the Raphanosmite of Von Kobell; *i.e.* to those varieties of Clausthalite in which a portion of the lead is replaced by cobalt or copper.

ZUISANG. The Chinese name for pure and sky-blue varieties of Lapis Lazuli.

ZUNDERERZ. Tinder Ore (which see).

ZURLITE, *Ramondini.* A variety of Mellilite. Occurs on Vesuvius, generally in large, distinct, rectangular, four-sided prisms, with their lateral edges occasionally replaced. The surface of the crystals is rough, and frequently covered with a white coating. Colour asparagus-green, inclining to grey. Opaque. Lustre resinous. Fracture conchoidal. H. about 6. S.G. 3·27.

BB infusible. With borax gives a black glass.

Dissolves with effervescence in nitric acid and the solution becomes yellow.

Name. After the Neapolitan minister, Signor Zurlo.

ZWIESELITE, *Breithaupt, Dana, Nicol.* ZWISELITE, *Brooke & Miller, Haidinger.* Occurs in crystalline masses, with an imperfect cleavage in three directions. Colour clove-brown. Translucent at the edges. Lustre greasy. Streak greyish-white. Fracture conchoidal or uneven. H. 5. S.G. 3·95 to 4.

Comp. $\ddot{F}e^3 \ddot{P} + Fe \, F$.

Analysis, by *Rammelsberg* .

Phosphoric acid .	. 30·33
Protoxide of iron .	. 41·42
Protoxide of manganese	. 23·25
Fluorine . . .	. 6·00
	101·00

BB decrepitates, and finally fuses to a bluish-black magnetic glass.

Easily soluble in warm sulphuric acid, affording traces of fluorine.

Locality. Zwisel, near Bodenmais, (whence the name Zwiselite), in Bavaria, in granite.

Zwiselite has been shown by Kenngott to be a variety of Triplite, with which it is identical in crystalline form, and other physical properties, and similar in chemical composition.

ZYGADITE, *Breithaupt.* Occurs in thin tabular right rhombic prisms, and in twins like Albite. Colour reddish or yellowish-white. Feebly transparent or slightly translucent. Lustre vitreous, inclining to pearly on the distinct cleavage-planes. H. below 6. S.G. 2·511.

Comp. Silica, alumina, and lithia, without water.

Locality. Katherina-Neufang Mine, near Zellerfeld, in the Harz, with Quartz and Stilbite.

Name. From ζύγαδην, *in pairs*, in allusion to the occurrence of the crystals in twins.

FINIS

LONDON
PRINTED BY SPOTTISWOODE AND CO.
NEW-STREET SQUARE

In Crown 8vo. Cloth, Price 12s. 6d.

A

MANUAL OF BOTANY

BEING

AN INTRODUCTION

TO THE

STUDY OF THE STRUCTURE, PHYSIOLOGY, AND CLASSIFICATION OF PLANTS

BY

JOHN HUTTON BALFOUR, A.M., M.D. EDIN.,

F.R.S., Sec. R.S.E., F.L.S.,

PROFESSOR OF MEDICINE AND BOTANY AND DEAN OF THE MEDICAL FACULTY IN THE UNIVERSITY OF EDINBURGH, HER MAJESTY'S BOTANIST FOR SCOTLAND, AND REGIUS KEEPER OF THE ROYAL BOTANIC GARDEN.

FIFTH EDITION

WITH UPWARDS OF NINE HUNDRED ILLUSTRATIONS

EDINBURGH

ADAM AND CHARLES BLACK

1875

GENERAL LIST OF WORKS

PUBLISHED BY

Messrs. LONGMANS, GREEN, and CO.

PATERNOSTER ROW, LONDON.

———o○}●{○o———

History, Politics, Historical Memoirs, &c.

JOURNAL of the REIGNS of KING GEORGE IV. and KING WILLIAM IV. By the late CHARLES C. F. GREVILLE, Esq. Clerk of the Council to those Sovereigns. Edited by HENRY REEVE, Registrar of the Privy Council. 3 vols. 8vo. 36s.

RECOLLECTIONS and SUGGESTIONS of PUBLIC LIFE, 1813– 1873. By JOHN Earl RUSSELL. 1 vol. 8vo. [*Nearly ready.*

The **HISTORY of ENGLAND** from the Fall of Wolsey to the Defeat of the Spanish Armada. By JAMES ANTHONY FROUDE, M.A. late Fellow of Exeter College, Oxford.

> LIBRARY EDITION, Twelve Volumes, 8vo. price £8. 18s.
> CABINET EDITION, Twelve Volumes, crown 8vo. price 72s.

The **ENGLISH in IRELAND** in the **EIGHTEENTH CENTURY.** By JAMES ANTHONY FROUDE, M.A. late Fellow of Exeter College, Oxford. 3 vols. 8vo. price 48s.

ESTIMATES of the ENGLISH KINGS from WILLIAM the CON- QUEROR to GEORGE III. By J. LANGTON SANFORD. Crown 8vo. 12s. 6d.

The **HISTORY of ENGLAND** from the Accession of James II. By Lord MACAULAY.

> STUDENT'S EDITION, 2 vols. crown 8vo. 12s.
> PEOPLE'S EDITION, 4 vols. crown 8vo. 16s.
> CABINET EDITION, 8 vols. post 8vo. 48s.
> LIBRARY EDITION, 5 vols. 8vo. £4.

LORD MACAULAY'S WORKS. Complete and Uniform Library Edition. Edited by his Sister, Lady TREVELYAN. 8 vols. 8vo. with Portrait price £5. 5s. cloth, or £8. 8s. bound in tree-calf by Rivière.

On **PARLIAMENTARY GOVERNMENT** in **ENGLAND;** its Origin, Development, and Practical Operation. By ALPHEUS TODD, Librarian of the Legislative Assembly of Canada. 2 vols. 8vo. price £1. 17s.

The **CONSTITUTIONAL HISTORY of ENGLAND,** since the Accession of George III. 1760–1860. By Sir THOMAS ERSKINE MAY, C.B. The Fourth Edition, thoroughly revised. 3 vols. crown 8vo. price 18s.

DEMOCRACY in **EUROPE;** a History. By Sir THOMAS ERSKINE MAY, K.C.B. 2 vols. 8vo. [*In the press.*

A

The ENGLISH GOVERNMENT and CONSTITUTION from Henry
VII. to the Present Time. By JOHN Earl RUSSELL, K.G. Fcp. 8vo. 3s. 6d.

The OXFORD REFORMERS — John Colet, Erasmus, and Thomas
More ; being a History of their Fellow-work. By FREDERIC SEEBOHM.
Second Edition, enlarged. 8vo. 14s.

LECTURES on the HISTORY of ENGLAND, from the Earliest Times
to the Death of King Edward II. By WILLIAM LONGMAN, F.S.A. With Maps
and Illustrations. 8vo. 15s.

The HISTORY of the LIFE and TIMES of EDWARD the THIRD.
By WILLIAM LONGMAN, F.S.A. With 9 Maps, 8 Plates, and 16 Woodcuts.
2 vols. 8vo. 28s.

INTRODUCTORY LECTURES on MODERN HISTORY. Delivered
in Lent Term, 1842 ; with the Inaugural Lecture delivered in December 1841.
By the Rev. THOMAS ARNOLD, D.D. 8vo. price 7s. 6d.

WATERLOO LECTURES ; a Study of the Campaign of 1815. By
Colonel CHARLES C. CHESNEY, R.E. Third Edition. 8vo. with Map, 10s. 6d.

HISTORY of ENGLAND under the DUKE of BUCKINGHAM and
CHARLES the FIRST, 1624–1628. By SAMUEL RAWSON GARDINER, late
Student of Ch. Ch. 2 vols. 8vo.   [In the press.

The SIXTH ORIENTAL MONARCHY; or, the Geography, History,
and Antiquities of Parthia. By GEORGE RAWLINSON, M.A. Professor of Ancient
History in the University of Oxford. Maps and Illustrations. 8vo. 16s.

The SEVENTH GREAT ORIENTAL MONARCHY; or, a History of
the Sassanians : with Notices, Geographical and Antiquarian. By G. RAWLINSON,
M.A. Professor of Ancient History in the University of Oxford. 8vo. with Maps
and Illustrations.   [In the press.

A HISTORY of GREECE. By the Rev. GEORGE W. COX, M.A. late
Scholar of Trinity College, Oxford. VOLS. I. & II. (to the Close of the Peloponnesian War) 8vo. with Maps and Plans, 36s.

The HISTORY of GREECE. By Rev. CONNOP THIRLWALL, D.D. late
Bishop of St. David's. 8 vols. fcp. 8vo. 28s.

GREEK HISTORY from Themistocles to Alexander, in a Series of
Lives from Plutarch. Revised and arranged by A. H. CLOUGH. New Edition.
Fcp. with 44 Woodcuts, 6s.

The TALE of the GREAT PERSIAN WAR, from the Histories of
Herodotus. By GEORGE W. COX, M.A. New Edition. Fcp. 3s. 6d.

The HISTORY of ROME. By WILLIAM IHNE. VOLS. I. and II.
8vo. price 30s. VOLS. III. and IV. preparing for publication.

HISTORY of the ROMANS under the EMPIRE. By the Very Rev.
C. MERIVALE, D.C.L. Dean of Ely. 8 vols. post 8vo. 48s.

The FALL of the ROMAN REPUBLIC ; a Short History of the Last
Century of the Commonwealth. By the same Author. 12mo. 7s. 6d.

The STUDENT'S MANUAL of the HISTORY of INDIA, from the
Earliest Period to the Present. By Colonel MEADOWS TAYLOR, M.R.A.S
M.R.I.A. Second Thousand. Crown 8vo. with Maps, 7s. 6d.

The HISTORY of INDIA, from the Earliest Period to the close of Lord
Dalhousie's Administration. By J. C. MARSHMAN. 3 vols. crown 8vo. 22s. 6d.

INDIAN POLITY; a View of the System of Administration in India. By Lieutenant-Colonel GEORGE CHESNEY, Fellow of the University of Calcutta. New Edition, revised; with Map. 8vo. price 21s.

The IMPERIAL and COLONIAL CONSTITUTIONS of the BRI- TANNIC EMPIRE, including INDIAN INSTITUTIONS. By Sir EDWARD CREASY, M.A. With 6 Maps. 8vo. price 15s.

The HISTORY of PERSIA and its PRESENT POLITICAL SITUA- TION; with Abstracts of all Treaties and Conventions between Persia and England, and of the Convention with Baron Reuter. By CLEMENTS R. MARKHAM, C.B. F.R.S. 8vo. with Map, 21s.

REALITIES of IRISH LIFE. By W. STEUART TRENCH, late Land Agent in Ireland to the Marquess of Lansdowne, the Marquess of Bath, and Lord Digby. Cheaper Edition. Crown 8vo. price 2s. 6d.

CRITICAL and HISTORICAL ESSAYS contributed to the *Edinburgh Review*. By the Right Hon. LORD MACAULAY.

CHEAP EDITION, authorised and complete. Crown 8vo. 3s. 6d.

CABINET EDITION, 4 vols. post 8vo. 24s.	LIBRARY EDITION, 3 vols. 8vo. 36s.
PEOPLE'S EDITION, 2 vols. crown 8vo. 8s.	STUDENT'S EDITION, 1 vol. cr. 8vo. 6s.

HISTORY of EUROPEAN MORALS, from Augustus to Charlemagne By W. E. H. LECKY, M.A. Second Edition. 2 vols. 8vo. price 28s.

HISTORY of the RISE and INFLUENCE of the SPIRIT of RATIONALISM in EUROPE. By W. E. H. LECKY, M.A. Cabinet Edition, being the Fourth. 2 vols. crown 8vo. price 16s.

The HISTORY of PHILOSOPHY, from Thales to Comte. By GEORGE HENRY LEWES. Fourth Edition. 2 vols. 8vo. 32s.

The HISTORY of the PELOPONNESIAN WAR. By THUCYDIDES. Translated by R. CRAWLEY, Fellow of Worcester College, Oxford. 8vo. 21s.

The MYTHOLOGY of the ARYAN NATIONS. By GEORGE W. COX, M.A. late Scholar of Trinity College, Oxford, 2 vols. 8vo. 28s.

HISTORY of CIVILISATION in England and France, Spain and Scotland. By HENRY THOMAS BUCKLE. New Edition of the entire Work, with a complete INDEX. 3 vols. crown 8vo. 24s.

SKETCH of the HISTORY of the CHURCH of ENGLAND to the Revolution of 1688. By the Right Rev. T. V. SHORT, D.D. Lord Bishop of St. Asaph. Eighth Edition. Crown 8vo. 7s. 6d.

HISTORY of the EARLY CHURCH, from the First Preaching of the Gospel to the Council of Nicæa, A.D. 325. By Miss SEWELL. Fcp. 8vo. 4s. 6d.

MAUNDER'S HISTORICAL TREASURY; General Introductory Outlines of Universal History, and a series of Separate Histories. Latest Edition, revised by the Rev. G. W. Cox, M.A. Fcp. 8vo. 6s. cloth, or 10s. calf.

CATES' and WOODWARD'S ENCYCLOPÆDIA of CHRONOLOGY, HISTORICAL and BIOGRAPHICAL; comprising the Dates of all the Great Events of History, including Treaties, Alliances, Wars, Battles, &c.; Incidents in the Lives of Eminent Men and their Works, Scientific and Geographical Discoveries, Mechanical Inventions, and Social Improvements. 8vo. price 42s.

The FRENCH REVOLUTION and FIRST EMPIRE; an Historical Sketch. By WILLIAM O'CONNOR MORRIS, sometime Scholar of Oriel College, Oxford. With 2 Coloured Maps. Post 8vo. 7s. 6d.

The HISTORICAL GEOGRAPHY of EUROPE. By E. A. FREEMAN, D.C.L. late Fellow of Trinity College, Oxford. 8vo. Maps. [*In the press.*

A 2

EPOCHS of HISTORY; a Series of Books treating of the History of England and Europe at successive Epochs subsequent to the Christian Era. Edited by EDWARD E. MORRIS, M.A. of Lincoln College, Oxford. The three following are now ready :—

The Era of the Protestant Revolution. By F. SEEBOHM. With 4 Maps and 12 Diagrams. Fcp. 8vo. 2s. 6d.

The Crusades. By the Rev. G. W. Cox, M.A. late Scholar of Trinity College, Oxford. With Coloured Map. Fcp. 8vo. 2s. 6d.

The Thirty Years' War, 1618–1648. By SAMUEL RAWSON GARDINER, late Student of Christ Church. With Coloured Map. Fcp. 8vo. 2s. 6d.

The Houses of Lancaster and York; with the Conquest and Loss of France. By JAMES GAIRDNER, of the Public Record Office. With Maps. Fcp. 8vo. 2s. 6d.

Edward the Third. By the Rev. W. WARBURTON, M.A. late Fellow of All Souls College, Oxford. With Maps. Fcp. 8vo. 2s. 6d.

Biographical Works.

AUTOBIOGRAPHY. By JOHN STUART MILL. 8vo. price 7s. 6d.

The LIFE of NAPOLEON III. derived from State Records, Unpublished Family Correspondence, and Personal Testimony. By BLANCHARD JERROLD. In Four Volumes. VOL. I. with 3 Portraits engraved on Steel and 9 Facsimiles. 8vo. price 18s. VOL. II. is in the press.

LIFE and CORRESPONDENCE of RICHARD WHATELY, D.D. Late Archbishop of Dublin. By E. JANE WHATELY. New Edition, in 1 vol. crown 8vo. [In the press.

LIFE and LETTERS of Sir GILBERT ELLIOT, First EARL of MINTO. Edited by the COUNTESS of MINTO. 3 vols. 8vo. 31s. 6d.

MEMOIR of THOMAS FIRST LORD DENMAN, formerly Lord Chief Justice of England. By Sir JOSEPH ARNOULD, B.A. K.B. late Judge of the High Court of Bombay. With 2 Portraits. 2 vols. 8vo. 32s.

ESSAYS in MODERN MILITARY BIOGRAPHY. By CHARLES CORNWALLIS CHESNEY, Lieutenant-Colonel in the Royal Engineers. 8vo. 12s. 6d.

ISAAC CASAUBON, 1559–1614. By MARK PATTISON, Rector of Lincoln College, Oxford. 8vo. [In the press.

BIOGRAPHICAL and CRITICAL ESSAYS, reprinted from Reviews, with Additions and Corrections. Second Edition of the Second Series. By A HAYWARD, Q.C. 2 vols. 8vo. price 28s. THIRD SERIES, in 1 vol. 8vo. price 14s.

The LIFE of LLOYD, FIRST LORD KENYON, LORD CHIEF JUSTICE of ENGLAND. By the Hon. GEORGE T. KENYON, M.A. of Ch. Ch. Oxford. With Portraits. 8vo. price 14s.

MEMOIR of GEORGE EDWARD LYNCH COTTON, D.D. Bishop of Calcutta and Metropolitan. With Selections from his Journals and Correspondence. Edited by Mrs. COTTON. Crown 8vo. 7s. 6d.

LIFE of ALEXANDER VON HUMBOLDT. Compiled in Commemoration of the Centenary of his Birth, and edited by Professor KARL BRUHNS; translated by JANE and CAROLINE LASSELL, with 3 Portraits. 2 vols. 8vo. 36s.

LORD GEORGE BENTINCK; a Political Biography. By the Right Hon. BENJAMIN DISRAELI, M.P. Crown 8vo. price 6s.

The **LIFE OF ISAMBARD KINGDOM BRUNEL, Civil Engineer.** By ISAMBARD BRUNEL, B.C.L. With Portrait, Plates, and Woodcuts. 8vo. 21s.

RECOLLECTIONS of PAST LIFE. By Sir HENRY HOLLAND, Bart. M.D. F.R.S. late Physician-in-Ordinary to the Queen. Third Edition. Post 8vo. price 10s. 6d.

The **LIFE and LETTERS of the Rev. SYDNEY SMITH.** Edited by his Daughter, Lady HOLLAND, and Mrs. AUSTIN. Crown 8vo. price 2s. 6d.

LEADERS of PUBLIC OPINION in IRELAND; Swift, Flood, Grattan, and O'Connell. By W. E. H. LECKY, M.A. New Edition, revised and enlarged. Crown 8vo. price 7s. 6d.

DICTIONARY of GENERAL BIOGRAPHY; containing Concise Memoirs and Notices of the most Eminent Persons of all Countries, from the Earliest Ages to the Present Time. Edited by W. L. R. CATES. 8vo. 21s.

LIFE of the DUKE of WELLINGTON. By the Rev. G. R. GLEIG, M.A. Popular Edition, carefully revised ; with copious Additions. Crown 8vo. with Portrait, 5s.

FELIX MENDELSSOHN'S LETTERS from *Italy and Switzerland,* and *Letters from* 1833 *to* 1847, translated by Lady WALLACE. New Edition, with Portrait. 2 vols. crown 8vo. 5s. each.

MEMOIRS of SIR HENRY HAVELOCK, K.C.B. By JOHN CLARK MARSHMAN. Cabinet Edition, with Portrait. Crown 8vo. price 3s. 6d.

VICISSITUDES of FAMILIES. By Sir J. BERNARD BURKE, C.B. Ulster King of Arms. New Edition, remodelled and enlarged. 2 vols. crown 8vo. 21s.

The **RISE of GREAT FAMILIES,** other Essays and Stories. By Sir J. BERNARD BURKE, C.B. Ulster King of Arms. Crown 8vo. price 12s. 6d.

ESSAYS in ECCLESIASTICAL BIOGRAPHY. By the Right Hon. Sir J. STEPHEN, LL.D. Cabinet Edition. Crown 8vo. 7s. 6d.

MAUNDER'S BIOGRAPHICAL TREASURY. Latest Edition, reconstructed, thoroughly revised, and in great part rewritten ; with 1,000 additional Memoirs and Notices, by W. L. R. CATES. Fcp. 8vo. 6s. cloth ; 10s. calf.

LETTERS and LIFE of FRANCIS BACON, including all his Occasional Works. Collected and edited, with a Commentary, by J. SPEDDING, Trin. Coll. Cantab. Complete in 7 vols. 8vo. £4. 4s.

Criticism, Philosophy, Polity, &c.

A SYSTEMATIC VIEW of the SCIENCE of JURISPRUDENCE. By SHELDON AMOS, M.A. Professor of Jurisprudence to the Inns of Court, London. 8vo. price 18s.

A PRIMER of the ENGLISH CONSTITUTION and GOVERNMENT. By SHELDON AMOS, M.A. Professor of Jurisprudence to the Inns of Court. New Edition, revised. Post 8vo. [*In the press.*

The INSTITUTES of JUSTINIAN; with English Introduction, Translation and Notes. By T. C. SANDARS, M.A. Sixth Edition. 8vo. 18s.

SOCRATES and the SOCRATIC SCHOOLS. Translated from the German of Dr. E. ZELLER, with the Author's approval, by the Rev. OSWALD J. REICHEL, M.A. Crown 8vo. 8s. 6d.

The STOICS, EPICUREANS, and SCEPTICS. Translated from the German of Dr. E. ZELLER, with the Author's approval, by OSWALD J. REICHEL, M.A. Crown 8vo. price 14s.

The ETHICS of ARISTOTLE, illustrated with Essays and Notes, By Sir A. GRANT, Bart. M.A. LL.D. Third Edition, revised and partly rewritten. [In the press.

The POLITICS of ARISTOTLE; Greek Text, with English Notes. By RICHARD CONGREVE, M.A. New Edition, revised. 8vo. 18s.

The NICOMACHEAN ETHICS of ARISTOTLE newly translated into English. By R. WILLIAMS, B.A. Fellow and late Lecturer of Merton College, and sometime Student of Christ Church, Oxford. 8vo. 12s.

ELEMENTS of LOGIC. By R. WHATELY, D.D. late Archbishop of Dublin. New Edition. 8vo. 10s. 6d. crown 8vo. 4s. 6d.

Elements of Rhetoric. By the same Author. New Edition. 8vo. 10s. 6d. crown 8vo. 4s. 6d.

English Synonymes. By E. JANE WHATELY. Edited by Archbishop WHATELY. Fifth Edition. Fcp. 8vo. price 3s.

DEMOCRACY in AMERICA. By ALEXIS DE TOCQUEVILLE. Translated by HENRY REEVE, C.B., D.C.L., Corresponding Member of the Institute of France. New Edition, in two vols. post 8vo. [In the press.

POLITICAL PROBLEMS. Reprinted chiefly from the *Fortnightly Review*, revised, and with New Essays. By FREDERIC HARRISON, of Lincoln's Inn. 1 vol. 8vo. [In the press.

THE SYSTEM of POSITIVE POLITY, or TREATISE upon SOCIOLOGY, of AUGUSTE COMTE, Author of the System of Positive Philosophy. Translated from the Paris Edition of 1851-1854, and furnished with Analytical Tables of Contents. In Four Volumes, 8vo. to be published separately:— [In the press.

VOL. I. The General View of Positive Polity and its Philosophical Basis. Translated by J. H. BRIDGES, M.B.

VOL. II. The Social Statics, or the Abstract Laws of Human Order. Translated by F. HARRISON, M.A.

VOL. III. The Social Dynamics, or the General Laws of Human Progress (the Philosophy of History). Translated by E. S. BEESLY, M.A.

VOL. IV. The Synthesis of the Future of Mankind. Translated by R. CONGREVE, M.A.

BACON'S ESSAYS with ANNOTATIONS. By R. WHATELY, D.D. late Archbishop of Dublin. New Edition, 8vo. price 10s. 6d.

LORD BACON'S WORKS, collected and edited by J. SPEDDING, M.A. R. L. ELLIS, M.A. and D. D. HEATH. 7 vols. 8vo. price £3. 13s. 6d.

ESSAYS CRITICAL and NARRATIVE. By WILLIAM FORSYTH, Q.C. LL.D. M.P. for Marylebone; Author of 'The Life of Cicero,' &c. 8vo. 16s.

The **SUBJECTION** of **WOMEN.** By JOHN STUART MILL. New Edition. Post 8vo. 5s.

On **REPRESENTATIVE GOVERNMENT.** By JOHN STUART MILL. Crown 8vo. price 2s.

On **LIBERTY.** By JOHN STUART MILL. New Edition. Post 8vo. 7s. 6d. Crown 8vo. price 1s. 4d.

PRINCIPLES of **POLITICAL ECONOMY.** By the same Author. Seventh Edition. 2 vols. 8vo. 30s. Or in 1 vol. crown 8vo. price 5s.

ESSAYS on **SOME UNSETTLED QUESTIONS** of **POLITICAL** ECONOMY. By JOHN STUART MILL. Second Edition. 8vo. 6s. 6d.

UTILITARIANISM. By JOHN STUART MILL. New Edition. 8vo. 5s,

DISSERTATIONS and **DISCUSSIONS, POLITICAL, PHILOSOPHI-** CAL, and HISTORICAL. By JOHN STUART MILL. 3 vols. 8vo. 36s.

EXAMINATION of Sir. **W. HAMILTON'S PHILOSOPHY,** and of the Principal Philosophical Questions discussed in his Writings. By JOHN STUART MILL. Fourth Edition. 8vo. 16s.

An **OUTLINE** of the **NECESSARY LAWS** of **THOUGHT**; a Treatise on Pure and Applied Logic. By the Most Rev. W. THOMSON, Lord Archbishop of York, D.D. F.R.S. Ninth Thousand. Crown 8vo. price 5s. 6d.

PRINCIPLES of **ECONOMICAL PHILOSOPHY.** By HENRY DUNNING MACLEOD, M.A. Barrister-at-Law. Second Edition. In Two Volumes. VOL. I. 8vo. price 15s.

A **SYSTEM** of **LOGIC, RATIOCINATIVE** and **INDUCTIVE.** By JOHN STUART MILL. Eighth Edition. Two vols. 8vo. 25s.

The **ELECTION** of **REPRESENTATIVES,** Parliamentary and Municipal; a Treatise. By THOMAS HARE, Barrister-at-Law. Crown 8vo. 7s.

SPEECHES of the **RIGHT HON. LORD MACAULAY,** corrected by Himself. People's Edition, crown 8vo. 3s. 6d.

Lord Macaulay's Speeches on Parliamentary Reform in 1831 and 1832. 16mo. 1s.

FAMILIES of **SPEECH:** Four Lectures delivered before the Royal Institution of Great Britain. By the Rev. F. W. FARRAR, D.D. F.R.S. New Edition. Crown 8vo. 3s. 6d.

CHAPTERS on **LANGUAGE.** By the Rev. F. W. FARRAR, D.D. F.R.S. New Edition. Crown 8vo. 5s.

A **DICTIONARY** of the **ENGLISH LANGUAGE.** By R. G. LATHAM, M.A. M.D. F.R.S. Founded on the Dictionary of Dr. SAMUEL JOHNSON, as edited by the Rev. H. J. TODD, with numerous Emendations and Additions. In Four Volumes, 4to. price £7.

A **PRACTICAL ENGLISH DICTIONARY,** on the Plan of White's English-Latin and Latin-English Dictionaries. By JOHN T. WHITE, D.D. Oxon. and T. C. DONKIN, M.A. Assistant-Master, King Edward's Grammar School, Birmingham. Post 8vo. [*In the press.*]

THESAURUS of **ENGLISH WORDS** and **PHRASES,** classified and arranged so as to facilitate the Expression of Ideas, and assist in Literary Composition. By P. M. ROGET, M.D. New Edition. Crown 8vo. 10s. 6d.

LECTURES on the SCIENCE of LANGUAGE. By F. MAX MÜLLER, M.A. &c.   Seventh Edition. 2 vols. crown 8vo. 16s.

MANUAL of ENGLISH LITERATURE, Historical and Critical. By THOMAS ARNOLD, M.A. New Edition. Crown 8vo. 7s. 6d.

SOUTHEY'S DOCTOR, complete in One Volume. Edited by the Rev. J. W. WARTER, B.D. Square crown 8vo. 12s. 6d.

HISTORICAL and CRITICAL COMMENTARY on the OLD TESTA- MENT; with a New Translation. By M. M. KALISCH, Ph.D. VOL. I. *Genesis*, 8vo. 18s. or adapted for the General Reader, 12s. VOL. II. *Exodus*, 15s. or adapted for the General Reader, 12s. VOL. III. *Leviticus*, PART I. 15s. or adapted for the General Reader, 8s. VOL. IV. *Leviticus*, PART II. 15s. or adapted for the General Reader, 8s.

A DICTIONARY of ROMAN and GREEK ANTIQUITIES, with about Two Thousand Engravings on Wood from Ancient Originals, illustrative of the Industrial Arts and Social Life of the Greeks and Romans. By A. RICH, B.A. Third Edition, revised and improved. Crown 8vo. price 7s. 6d.

A LATIN-ENGLISH DICTIONARY. By JOHN T. WHITE, D.D. Oxon. and J. E. RIDDLE, M.A. Oxon. Revised Edition. 2 vols. 4to. 42s.

WHITE'S COLLEGE LATIN-ENGLISH DICTIONARY (Intermediate Size), abridged for the use of University Students from the Parent Work (as above). Medium 8vo. 18s.

WHITE'S JUNIOR STUDENT'S COMPLETE LATIN-ENGLISH and ENGLISH-LATIN DICTIONARY. New Edition. Square 12mo. price 12s.

Separately { The ENGLISH-LATIN DICTIONARY, price 5s. 6d.
{ The LATIN-ENGLISH DICTIONARY, price 7s. 6d.

A LATIN-ENGLISH DICTIONARY, adapted for the Use of Middle-Class Schools. By JOHN T. WHITE, D.D. Oxon. Square fcp. 8vo. price 3s.

An ENGLISH-GREEK LEXICON, containing all the Greek Words used by Writers of good authority. By C. D. YONGE, B.A. New Edition. 4to. price 21s.

Mr. YONGE'S NEW LEXICON, English and Greek, abridged from his larger work (as above). Revised Edition. Square 12mo. price 8s. 6d.

A GREEK-ENGLISH LEXICON. Compiled by H. G. LIDDELL, D.D. Dean of Christ Church, and R. SCOTT, D.D. Dean of Rochester. Sixth Edition. Crown 4to. price 36s.

A Lexicon, Greek and English, abridged from LIDDELL and SCOTT'S *Greek-English Lexicon.* Fourteenth Edition. Square 12mo. 7s. 6d.

A SANSKRIT-ENGLISH DICTIONARY, the Sanskrit words printed b h in the original Devanagari and in Roman Letters. Compiled by T. B FEY, Prof. in the Univ. of Göttingen. 8vo. 52s. 6d.

A PRACTICAL DICTIONARY of the FRENCH and ENGLISH LAN- GUAGES. By L. CONTANSEAU. Revised Edition. Post 8vo. 10s. 6d.

Contanseau's Pocket Dictionary, French and English, abridged from the above by the Author. New Edition, revised. Square 18mo. 3s. 6d.

NEW PRACTICAL DICTIONARY of the GERMAN LANGUAGE; German-English and English-German. By the Rev. W. L. BLACKLEY, M.A and Dr. CARL MARTIN FRIEDLÄNDER. Post 8vo. 7s. 6d.

The **MASTERY of LANGUAGES;** or, the Art of Speaking Foreign Tongues Idiomatically. By THOMAS PRENDERGAST. 8vo. 6s.

Miscellaneous Works and *Popular Metaphysics.*

ESSAYS on FREETHINKING and PLAIN-SPEAKING. By LESLIE STEPHEN. Crown 8vo. 10s. 6d.

THE MISCELLANEOUS WORKS of THOMAS ARNOLD, D.D. Late Head Master of Rugby School and Regius Professor of Modern History in the University of Oxford, collected and republished. 8vo. 7s. 6d.

MISCELLANEOUS and POSTHUMOUS WORKS of the Late HENRY THOMAS BUCKLE. Edited, with a Biographical Notice, by HELEN TAYLOR. 3 vols. 8vo. price 52s. 6d.

MISCELLANEOUS WRITINGS of JOHN CONINGTON, M.A. late Corpus Professor of Latin in the University of Oxford. Edited by J. A. SYMONDS, M.A. With a Memoir by H. J. S. SMITH, M.A. 2 vols. 8vo. 28s.

ESSAYS, CRITICAL and BIOGRAPHICAL. Contributed to the *Edinburgh Review.* By HENRY ROGERS. New Edition, with Additions. 2 vols. crown 8vo. price 12s.

ESSAYS on some THEOLOGICAL CONTROVERSIES of the TIME. Contributed chiefly to the *Edinburgh Review.* By HENRY ROGERS. New Edition, with Additions. Crown 8vo. price 6s.

LANDSCAPES, CHURCHES, and MORALITIES. By A. K. H. B. Crown 8vo. price 3s. 6d.

Recreations of a Country Parson. By A. K. H. B. FIRST and SECOND SERIES, crown 8vo. 3s. 6d. each.

The Common-place Philosopher in Town and Country. By A. K. H. B. Crown 8vo. price 3s. 6d.

Leisure Hours in Town; Essays Consolatory, Æsthetical, Moral, Social, and Domestic. By A. K. H. B. Crown 8vo. 3s. 6d.

The Autumn Holidays of a Country Parson; Essays contributed to *Fraser's Magazine,* &c. By A. K. H. B. Crown 8vo. 3s. 6d.

Seaside Musings on Sundays and Week-Days. By A. K. H. B. Crown 8vo. price 3s. 6d.

The Graver Thoughts of a Country Parson. By A. K. H. B. FIRST and SECOND SERIES, crown 8vo. 3s. 6d. each.

Critical Essays of a Country Parson, selected from Essay contributed to *Fraser's Magazine.* By A. K. H. B. Crown 8vo. 3s. 6d.

Sunday Afternoons at the Parish Church of a Scottish University City. By A. K. H. B. Crown 8vo. 3s. 6d.

Lessons of Middle Age; with some Account of various Cities and Men. By A. K. H. B. Crown 8vo. 3s. 6d.

Counsel and Comfort spoken from a City Pulpit. By A. K. H. B. Crown 8vo. price 3s. 6d.

CHANGED ASPECTS of UNCHANGED TRUTHS; Memorials of St.
Andrews Sundays. By A. K. H. B. Crown 8vo. 3s. 6d.

Present-day Thoughts; Memorials of St. Andrews Sundays. By
A. K. H. B. Crown 8vo. 3s. 6d.

SHORT STUDIES on GREAT SUBJECTS. By JAMES ANTHONY
FROUDE, M.A. late Fellow of Exeter Coll. Oxford. 2 vols. crown 8vo. price 12s.

LORD MACAULAY'S MISCELLANEOUS WRITINGS :—
> LIBRARY EDITION. 2 vols. 8vo. Portrait, 21s.
> PEOPLE'S EDITION. 1 vol. crown 8vo. 4s. 6d.

LORD MACAULAY'S MISCELLANEOUS WRITINGS and SPEECHES.
> STUDENT'S EDITION, in crown 8vo. price 6s.

The Rev. SYDNEY SMITH'S ESSAYS contributed to the Edinburgh
Review. Authorised Edition, complete in 1 vol. Crown 8vo. price 2s. 6d.

The Rev. SYDNEY SMITH'S MISCELLANEOUS WORKS; including
his Contributions to the *Edinburgh Review.* Crown 8vo. 6s.

The Wit and Wisdom of the Rev. Sydney Smith; a Selection of
the most memorable Passages in his Writings and Conversation. 16mo. 3s. 6d.

The ECLIPSE of FAITH; or, a Visit to a Religious Sceptic. By
HENRY ROGERS. Latest Edition. Fcp. 8vo. price 5s.

Defence of the Eclipse of Faith, by its Author; a rejoinder to Dr.
Newman's *Reply.* Latest Edition. Fcp 8vo. price 3s. 6d.

CHIPS from a GERMAN WORKSHOP; Essays on the Science of
Religion, and on Mythology, Traditions, and Customs. By F. MAX MÜLLER,
M.A. &c. Second Edition. 3 vols. 8vo. £2.

ANALYSIS of the PHENOMENA of the HUMAN MIND. By
JAMES MILL. A New Edition, with Notes, Illustrative and Critical, by
ALEXANDER BAIN, ANDREW FINDLATER, and GEORGE GROTE. Edited, with
additional Notes, by JOHN STUART MILL. 2 vols. 8vo. price 28s.

An INTRODUCTION to MENTAL PHILOSOPHY, on the Inductive
Method. By J. D. MORELL, M.A. LL.D. 8vo. 12s.

ELEMENTS of PSYCHOLOGY, containing the Analysis of the
Intellectual Powers. By J. D. MORELL, M.A. LL.D. Post 8vo. 7s. 6d.

The SECRET of HEGEL; being the Hegelian System in Origin,
Principle, Form, and Matter. By J. H. STIRLING, LL.D. 2 vols. 8vo. 28s.

SIR WILLIAM HAMILTON; being the Philosophy of Perception: an
Analysis. By J. H. STIRLING, LL.D. 8vo. 5s.

The SENSES and the INTELLECT. By ALEXANDER BAIN, M.D.
Professor of Logic in the University of Aberdeen. Third Edition. 8vo. 15s.

MENTAL and MORAL SCIENCE: a Compendium of Psychology
and Ethics. By the same Author. Third Edition. Crown 8vo. 10s. 6d. Or
separately: PART I. *Mental Science*, 6s. 6d. PART II. *Moral Science*, 4s. 6d.

LOGIC, DEDUCTIVE and INDUCTIVE. By the same Author. In
TWO PARTS, crown 8vo. 10s. 6d. Each Part may be had separately :—
> PART I. *Deduction*, 4s. PART II. *Induction*, 6s. 6d.

The **PHILOSOPHY of NECESSITY**; or, Natural Law as applicable to Mental, Moral, and Social Science. By CHARLES BRAY. 8vo. 9s.

On **FORCE**, its **MENTAL** and **MORAL CORRELATES**. By the same Author. 8vo. 5s.

A **MANUAL of ANTHROPOLOGY**, or **SCIENCE of MAN**, based on Modern Research. By CHARLES BRAY. Crown 8vo. price 6s.

A **PHRENOLOGIST AMONGST the TODAS**, or the Study of a Primitive Tribe in South India; History, Character, Customs, Religion, Infanticide, Polyandry, Language. By W. E. MARSHALL, Lieutenant-Colonel B.S.C. With 26 Illustrations. 8vo 21s.

A **TREATISE of HUMAN NATURE**, being an Attempt to Introduce the Experimental Method of Reasoning into Moral Subjects; followed by Dialogues concerning Natural Religion. By DAVID HUME. Edited, with Notes, &c. by T. H. GREEN, Fellow and Tutor, Ball. Coll. and T. H. GROSE, Fellow and Tutor, Queen's Coll. Oxford. 2 vols. 8vo. 28s.

ESSAYS MORAL, POLITICAL, and LITERARY. By DAVID HUME. By the same Editors. 2 vols. 8vo. price 28s.

UEBERWEG'S SYSTEM of LOGIC and HISTORY of LOGICAL DOCTRINES. Translated, with Notes and Appendices, by T. M. LINDSAY, M.A. F.R.S.E. 8vo. price 16s.

A **BUDGET of PARADOXES.** By AUGUSTUS DE MORGAN, F.R.A.S. and C.P.S. 8vo. 15s.

Astronomy, Meteorology, Popular Geography, &c.

BRINKLEY'S ASTRONOMY. Revised and partly re-written, with Additional Chapters, and an Appendix of Questions for Examination. By J. W. STUBBS, D.D. Fellow and Tutor of Trinity College, Dublin, and F. BRUNNOW, Ph.D. Astronomer Royal of Ireland. Crown 8vo. price 6s.

OUTLINES of ASTRONOMY. By Sir J. F. W. HERSCHEL, Bart. M.A. Latest Edition, with Plates and Diagrams. Square crown 8vo. 12s.

ESSAYS on ASTRONOMY, a Series of Papers on Planets and Meteors, the Sun and Sun-surrounding Space, Stars and Star-Cloudlets; with a Dissertation on the approaching Transit of Venus. By RICHARD A. PROCTOR, B.A. With 10 Plates and 24 Woodcuts. 8vo. 12s.

THE TRANSITS of VENUS; a Popular Account of Past and Coming Transits, from the first observed by Horrocks A.D. 1639 to the Transit of A.D. 2112. By R. A. PROCTOR, B.A. Cantab. With 20 Plates and numerous Woodcuts. Crown 8vo. [Nearly ready.

The **UNIVERSE and the COMING TRANSITS**: Presenting Researches into and New Views respecting the Constitution of the Heavens; together with an Investigation of the Conditions of the Coming Transits of Venus. By R. A. PROCTOR, B.A. With 22 Charts and 22 Woodcuts. 8vo. 16s.

The **MOON; her Motions, Aspect, Scenery, and Physical Condition.** By R. A. PROCTOR, B.A. With Plates, Charts, Woodcuts, and Three Lunar Photographs. Crown 8vo. 15s.

The SUN; RULER, LIGHT, FIRE, and LIFE of the PLANETARY
SYSTEM. By R. A. PROCTOR, B.A. Second Edition, with 10 Plates (7 coloured) and 107 Figures on Wood. Crown 8vo. 14s.

OTHER WORLDS THAN OURS; the Plurality of Worlds Studied
under the Light of Recent Scientific Researches. By R. A. PROCTOR, B.A. Third Edition, with 14 Illustrations. Crown 8vo. 10s. 6d.

The ORBS AROUND US; a Series of Familiar Essays on the Moon
and Planets, Meteors and Comets, the Sun and Coloured Pairs of Stars. By R. A. PROCTOR, B.A. Crown 8vo. price 7s. 6d.

SATURN and its SYSTEM. By R. A. PROCTOR, B.A. 8vo. with 14
Plates, 14s.

SCHELLEN'S SPECTRUM ANALYSIS, in its application to Terrestrial Substances and the Physical Constitution of the Heavenly Bodies. Translated by JANE and C. LASSELL; edited, with Notes, by W. HUGGINS, LL.D. F.R.S. With 13 Plates (6 coloured) and 223 Woodcuts. 8vo. price 28s.

A NEW STAR ATLAS, for the Library, the School, and the Observatory,
in Twelve Circular Maps (with Two Index Plates). Intended as a Companion to 'Webb's Celestial Objects for Common Telescopes.' With a Letterpress Introduction on the Study of the Stars, illustrated by 9 Diagrams. By R. A. PROCTOR, B.A. Crown 8vo. 5s.

CELESTIAL OBJECTS for COMMON TELESCOPES. By the Rev.
T. W. WEBB, M.A. F.R.A.S. Third Edition, revised and enlarged; with Maps, Plate, and Woodcuts. Crown 8vo. price 7s. 6d.

AIR and RAIN; the Beginnings of a Chemical Climatology. By
ROBERT ANGUS SMITH, Ph.D. F.R.S. F.C.S. With 8 Illustrations. 8vo. 24s.

NAUTICAL SURVEYING, an INTRODUCTION to the PRACTICAL
and THEORETICAL STUDY of. By J. K. LAUGHTON, M.A. Small 8vo. 6s.

MAGNETISM and DEVIATION of the COMPASS. For the Use of
Students in Navigation and Science Schools. By J. MERRIFIELD, LL.D. 18mo. 1s. 6d.

DOVE'S LAW of STORMS, considered in connexion with the Ordinary
Movements of the Atmosphere. Translated by R. H. SCOTT, M.A. 8vo. 10s. 6d.

KEITH JOHNSTON'S GENERAL DICTIONARY of GEOGRAPHY,
Descriptive, Physical, Statistical, and Historical; forming a complete Gazetteer of the World. New Edition, revised and corrected to the Present Date by the Author's Son, KEITH JOHNSTON, F.R.G.S. 1 vol. 8vo. [Nearly ready.

The POST OFFICE GAZETTEER of the UNITED KINGDOM. Being
a Complete Dictionary of all Cities, Towns, Villages, and of the Principal Gentlemen's Seats, in Great Britain and Ireland; Referred to the nearest Post Town, Railway and Telegraph Station: with Natural Features and Objects of Note. By J. A. SHARP. 1 vol. 8vo. of about 1,500 pages. [In the press.

The PUBLIC SCHOOLS ATLAS of MODERN GEOGRAPHY. In
31 Maps, exhibiting clearly the more important Physical Features of the Countries delineated, and Noting all the Chief Places of Historical, Commercial, or Social Interest. Edited, with an Introduction, by the Rev. G. BUTLER, M.A. Imp. 4to. price 3s. 6d. sewed, or 5s. cloth.

The PUBLIC SCHOOLS MANUAL of MODERN GEOGRAPHY. By
the Rev. GEORGE BUTLER, M.A. Principal of Liverpool College; Editor of 'The Public Schools Atlas of Modern Geography.' [In preparation.

The PUBLIC SCHOOLS ATLAS of ANCIENT GEOGRAPHY Edited, with an Introduction on the Study of Ancient Geography, by the Rev. GEORGE BUTLER, M.A. Principal of Liverpool College. Imperial Quarto.
[In preparation.

A MANUAL of GEOGRAPHY, Physical, Industrial, and Political. By W. HUGHES, F.R.G.S. With 6 Maps. Fcp. 7s. 6d.

MAUNDER'S TREASURY of GEOGRAPHY, Physical, Historical, Descriptive, and Political. Edited by W. HUGHES, F.R.G.S. Revised Edition, with 7 Maps and 16 Plates. Fcp. 6s. cloth, or 10s. bound in calf.

Natural History and Popular Science.

TEXT-BOOKS of SCIENCE, MECHANICAL and PHYSICAL, adapted for the use of Artisans and of Students in Public and Science Schools. Edited by T. M. GOODEVE, M.A. and C. W. MERRIFIELD, F.R.S.

ANDERSON'S Strength of Materials, small 8vo. 3s. 6d.
ARMSTRONG'S Organic Chemistry, 3s. 6d.
BLOXAM'S Metals, 3s. 6d.
GOODEVE'S Elements of Mechanism, 3s. 6d.
———— Principles of Mechanics, 3s. 6d.
GRIFFIN'S Algebra and Trigonometry, 3s. 6d. Notes, 3s.6d.
JENKIN'S Electricity and Magnetism, 3s. 6d.
MAXWELL'S Theory of Heat, 3s. 6d.
MERRIFIELD'S Technical Arithmetic and Mensuration, 3s. 6d. Key, 3s. 6d.
MILLER'S Inorganic Chemistry, 3s. 6d.
SHELLEY'S Workshop Appliances, 3s. 6d.
THORPE'S Quantitative Chemical Analysis, 4s. 6d.
THORPE & MUIR'S Qualitative Analysis, 3s. 6d.
WATSON'S Plane and Solid Geometry, 3s. 6d.
₊ Other Text-Books in active preparation.

ELEMENTARY TREATISE on PHYSICS, Experimental and Applied. Translated and edited from GANOT'S *Éléments de Physique* by E. ATKINSON, Ph.D. F.C.S. New Edition, revised and enlarged; with a Coloured Plate and 726 Woodcuts. Post 8vo. 15s.

NATURAL PHILOSOPHY for GENERAL READERS and YOUNG PERSONS; being a Course of Physics divested of Mathematical Formulæ expressed in the language of daily life. Translated from GANOT'S *Cours de Physique* and by E. ATKINSON, Ph.D. F.C.S. Crown 8vo. with 404 Woodcuts, price 7s. 6d.

HELMHOLTZ'S POPULAR LECTURES on SCIENTIFIC SUBJECTS. Translated by E. ATKINSON, Ph.D. F.C.S. Professor of Experimental Science, Staff College. With an Introduction by Professor TYNDALL. 8vo. with numerous Woodcuts, price 12s. 6d.

SOUND: a Course of Eight Lectures delivered at the Royal Institution of Great Britain. By JOHN TYNDALL, LL.D. D.C.L. F.R.S. New Edition, with 169 Woodcuts. Crown 8vo. 9s.

HEAT a MODE of MOTION. By JOHN TYNDALL, LL.D. D.C.L. F.R.S. Fourth Edition. Crown 8vo. with Woodcuts, 10s. 6d.

CONTRIBUTIONS to MOLECULAR PHYSICS in the DOMAIN of RADIANT HEAT. By J. Tyndall, LL.D. D.C.L. F.R.S. With 2 Plates and 31 Woodcuts. 8vo. 16s.

RESEARCHES on DIAMAGNETISM and MAGNE-CRYSTALLIC ACTION; including the Question of Diamagnetic Polarity. By J. Tyndall, M.D. D.C.L. F.R.S. With 6 plates and many Woodcuts. 8vo. 14s.

NOTES of a COURSE of SEVEN LECTURES on ELECTRICAL PHENOMENA and THEORIES, delivered at the Royal Institution, A.D. 1870. By John Tyndall, LL.D., D.C.L., F.R.S. Crown 8vo. 1s. sewed ; 1s. 6d. cloth.

A TREATISE on MAGNETISM, General and Terrestrial. By Humphrey Lloyd, D.D., D.C.L., Provost of Trinity College, Dublin. 8vo. price 10s. 6d.

ELEMENTARY TREATISE on the WAVE-THEORY of LIGHT. By Humphrey Lloyd, D.D. D.C.L. Provost of Trinity College, Dublin. Third Edition, revised and enlarged. 8vo. price 10s. 6d.

LECTURES on LIGHT delivered in the United States of America in the Years 1872 and 1873. By John Tyndall, LL.D. D.C.L. F.R.S. With Frontispiece and Diagrams. Crown 8vo. price 7s. 6d.

NOTES of a COURSE of NINE LECTURES on LIGHT delivered at the Royal Institution, A.D. 1869. By John Tyndall, LL.D. D.C.L. F.R.S. Crown 8vo. price 1s. sewed, or 1s. 6d. cloth.

ADDRESS delivered before the British Association assembled at Belfast; with Additions and a Preface. By John Tyndall, F.R.S. President. 8vo. price 3s.

FRAGMENTS of SCIENCE. By John Tyndall, LL.D. D.C.L. F.R.S. Third Edition. 8vo. price 14s.

LIGHT SCIENCE for LEISURE HOURS; a Series of Familiar Essays on Scientific Subjects, Natural Phenomena, &c. By R. A. Proctor, B.A. First and Second Series. Crown 8vo. 7s. 6d. each.

The CORRELATION of PHYSICAL FORCES. By the Hon. Sir W. R. Grove, M.A. F.R.S. one of the Judges of the Court of Common Pleas. Sixth Edition, with other Contributions to Science. 8vo. price 15s.

Professor OWEN'S LECTURES on the COMPARATIVE ANATOMY and Physiology of the Invertebrate Animals. Second Edition, with 235 Woodcuts. 8vo. 21s.

The COMPARATIVE ANATOMY and PHYSIOLOGY of the VERTE-BRATE ANIMALS. By Richard Owen, F.R.S. D.C.L. With 1,472 Woodcuts. 3 vols. 8vo. £3. 13s. 6d.

PRINCIPLES of ANIMAL MECHANICS. By the Rev. S. Haughton, F.R.S. Fellow of Trin. Coll. Dubl. M.D. Dubl. and D.C.L. Oxon. Second Edition, with 111 Figures on Wood. 8vo. 21s.

ROCKS CLASSIFIED and DESCRIBED. By Bernhard Von Cotta. English Edition, by P. H. Lawrence; with English, German, and French Synonymes. Post 8vo. 14s.

The ANCIENT STONE IMPLEMENTS, WEAPONS, and ORNA-MENTS of GREAT BRITAIN. By John Evans, F.R.S. F.S.A. With 2 Plates and 476 Woodcuts. 8vo. price 28s.

PRIMÆVAL WORLD of SWITZERLAND. By Professor OSWALD HEER, of the University of Zurich. Translated by W. S. DALLAS. F.L.S., and edited by JAMES HEYWOOD, M.A., F.R.S. 2 vols. 8vo. with numerous Illustrations. [*In the press.*

The ORIGIN of CIVILISATION and the PRIMITIVE CONDITION of MAN ; Mental and Social Condition of Savages. By Sir JOHN LUBBOCK, Bart. M.P. F.R.S. Third Edition, revised, with Woodcuts. [*Nearly ready.*

BIBLE ANIMALS; being a Description of every Living Creature mentioned in the Scriptures, from the Ape to the Coral. By the Rev. J. G. WOOD, M.A. F.L.S. With about 100 Vignettes on Wood. 8vo. 21s.

HOMES WITHOUT HANDS; a Description of the Habitations of Animals, classed according to their Principle of Construction. By the Rev. J. G. WOOD, M.A. F.L.S. With about 140 Vignettes on Wood. 8vo. 21s.

INSECTS AT HOME; a Popular Account of British Insects, their Structure, Habits, and Transformations. By the Rev. J. G. WOOD, M.A. F.L.S. With upwards of 700 Illustrations. 8vo. price 21s.

INSECTS ABROAD; a Popular Account of Foreign Insects, their Structure, Habits, and Transformations. By J. G. WOOD, M.A. F.L.S. Printed and illustrated uniformly with ' Insects at Home.' 8vo. price 21s.

STRANGE DWELLINGS; a description of the Habitations of Animals, abridged from ' Homes without Hands.' By the Rev. J. G. WOOD, M.A. F.L.S. With about 60 Woodcut Illustrations. Crown 8vo. price 7s. 6d.

OUT of DOORS; a Selection of original Articles on Practical Natural History. By the Rev. J. G. WOOD, M.A. F.L.S. With Eleven Illustrations from Original Designs engraved on Wood by G. Pearson. Crown 8vo. price 7s. 6d.

A FAMILIAR HISTORY of BIRDS. By E. STANLEY, D.D. F.R.S. late Lord Bishop of Norwich. Seventh Edition, with Woodcuts. Fcp. 3s. 6d.

FROM JANUARY to DECEMBER; a Book for Children. Second Edition. 8vo. 3s. 6d.

The SEA and its LIVING WONDERS. By Dr. GEORGE HARTWIG. Latest revised Edition. 8vo. with many Illustrations, 10s. 6d.

The TROPICAL WORLD. By Dr. GEORGE HARTWIG. With above 160 Illustrations. Latest revised Edition. 8vo. price 10s. 6d.

The SUBTERRANEAN WORLD. By Dr. GEORGE HARTWIG. With 3 Maps and about 80 Woodcuts, including 8 full size of page. 8vo. price 21s.

THE AERIAL WORLD. By Dr. GEORGE HARTWIG. With 8 Chromoxylographs and 60 Illustrations engraved on Wood. 8vo. price 21s.

The POLAR WORLD, a Popular Description of Man and Nature in the Arctic and Antarctic Regions of the Globe. By Dr. GEORGE HARTWIG. With 8 Chromoxylographs, 3 Maps, and 85 Woodcuts. 8vo. 10s. 6d.

KIRBY and SPENCE'S INTRODUCTION to ENTOMOLOGY, or Elements of the Natural History of Insects. 7th Edition. Crown 8vo. 5s.

MAUNDER'S TREASURY of NATURAL HISTORY, or Popular Dictionary of Birds, Beasts, Fishes, Reptiles, Insects, and Creeping Things. With above 900 Woodcuts. Fcp. 8vo. price 6s. cloth, or 10s. bound in calf.

MAUNDER'S SCIENTIFIC and LITERARY TREASURY. New Edition, thoroughly revised and in great part rewritten, with above 1,000 new Articles, by J. Y. JOHNSON. Fcp. 8vo. 6s. cloth, or 10s. calf.

HANDBOOK of HARDY TREES, SHRUBS, and HERBACEOUS PLANTS, containing Descriptions, Native Countries, &c. of a Selection of the Best Species in Cultivation; togethér with Cultural Details, Comparative Hardiness, Suitability for Particular Positions, &c. By W. B. HEMSLEY. Based on DECAISNE and NAUDIN'S *Manuel de l'Amateur des Jardins*, and including the 264 Original Woodcuts. Medium 8vo. 21s.

A GENERAL SYSTEM of BOTANY DESCRIPTIVE and ANALYTICAL. I. Outlines of Organography, Anatomy, and Physiology; II. Descriptions and Illustrations of the Orders. By E. LE MAOUT, and J. DECAISNE, Members of the Institute of France. Translated by Mrs. HOOKER. The Orders arranged after the Method followed in the Universities and Schools of Great Britain, its Colonies, America, and India; with an Appendix on the Natural Method, and other Additions, by J. D. HOOKER, F.R.S. &c. Director of the Royal Botanical Gardens, Kew. With 5,500 Woodcuts. Imperial 8vo. price 52s. 6d.

The TREASURY of BOTANY, or Popular Dictionary of the Vegetable Kingdom; including a Glossary of Botanical Terms. Edited by J. LINDLEY, F.R.S. and T. MOORE, F.L.S. assisted by eminent Contributors. With 274 Woodcuts and 20 Steel Plates. Two Parts, fcp. 8vo. 12s. cloth, or 20s. calf.

The ELEMENTS of BOTANY for FAMILIES and SCHOOLS. Tenth Edition, revised by THOMAS MOORE, F.L.S. Fcp. with 154 Woodcuts, 2s. 6d.

The ROSE AMATEUR'S GUIDE. By THOMAS RIVERS. Fourteenth Edition. Fcp. 8vo. 4s.

LOUDON'S ENCYCLOPÆDIA of PLANTS; comprising the Specific Character, Description, Culture, History, &c. of all the Plants found in Great Britain. With upwards of 12,000 Woodcuts. 8vo. 42s.

A DICTIONARY of SCIENCE, LITERATURE, and ART. Fourth Edition, re-edited by W. T. BRANDE (the original Author), and GEORGE W. COX, M.A., assisted by contributors of eminent Scientific and Literary Acquirements. 3 vols. medium 8vo. price 63s. cloth.

Chemistry and *Physiology*.

A DICTIONARY of CHEMISTRY and the Allied Branches of other Sciences. By HENRY WATTS, F.R.S. assisted by eminent Contributors. 6 vols. medium 8vo. price £8. 14s. 6d. SECOND SUPPLEMENT *in the Press.*

ELEMENTS of CHEMISTRY, Theoretical and Practical. By W. ALLEN MILLER, M.D. late Prof. of Chemistry, King's Coll. London. New Edition. 3 vols. 8vo. £3. PART I. CHEMICAL PHYSICS, 15s. PART II. INORGANIC CHEMISTRY, 21s. PART III. ORGANIC CHEMISTRY, 24s.

A Course of Practical Chemistry, for the use of Medical Students. By W. ODLING, F.R.S. New Edition, with 70 Woodcuts. Crown 8vo. 7s. 6d.

A MANUAL of CHEMICAL PHYSIOLOGY, including its Points of Contact with Pathology. By J. L. W. THUDICHUM, M.D. With Woodcuts. 8vo. price 7s. 6d.

SELECT METHODS in CHEMICAL ANALYSIS, chiefly INORGANIC. By WILLIAM CROOKES, F.R.S. With 22 Woodcuts. Crown 8vo. price 12s. 6d.

A PRACTICAL HANDBOOK of DYEING and CALICO PRINTING.
By WILLIAM CROOKES, F.R.S. With 11 Page Plates, 49 Specimens of Dyed and Printed Fabrics, and 36 Woodcuts. 8vo. 42s.

OUTLINES of PHYSIOLOGY, Human and Comparative. By JOHN MARSHALL, F.R.C.S. Surgeon to the University College Hospital. 2 vols. crown 8vo. with 122 Woodcuts, 32s.

PHYSIOLOGICAL ANATOMY and PHYSIOLOGY of MAN. By the late R. B. TODD, M.D. F.R.S. and W. BOWMAN, F.R.S. of King's College. With numerous Illustrations. Vol. II. 8vo. 25s.

VOL. I. New Edition by Dr. LIONEL S. BEALE, F.R.S. in course of publication, with many Illustrations. PARTS I. and II. price 7s. 6d. each.

The Fine Arts, and Illustrated Editions.

A DICTIONARY of ARTISTS of the ENGLISH SCHOOL : Painters, Sculptors, Architects, Engravers, and Ornamentists ; with Notices of their Lives and Works. By S. REDGRAVE. 8vo. 16s.

The THREE CATHEDRALS DEDICATED to ST. PAUL, in LONDON ; their History from the Foundation of the First Building in the Sixth Century to the Proposals for the Adornment of the Present Cathedral. By WILLIAM LONGMAN, F.A.S. With numerous Illustrations. Square crown 8vo. 21s.

IN FAIRYLAND ; Pictures from the Elf-World. By RICHARD DOYLE. With a Poem by W. ALLINGHAM. With Sixteen Plates, containing Thirty-six Designs printed in Colours. Second Edition. Folio, price 15s.

ALBERT DURER, HIS LIFE and WORKS; including Auto-biographical Papers and Complete Catalogues. By WILLIAM B. SCOTT. With Six Etchings by the Author, and other Illustrations. 8vo. 16s.

The NEW TESTAMENT, illustrated with Wood Engravings after the Early Masters, chiefly of the Italian School. Crown 4to. 63s. cloth, gilt top; or £5 5s. elegantly bound in morocco.

LYRA GERMANICA ; the Christian Year and the Christian Life. Translated by CATHERINE WINKWORTH. With about 325 Woodcut Illustrations by J. LEIGHTON, F.S.A. and other Artists. 2 vols. 4to. price 42s.

The LIFE of MAN SYMBOLISED by the MONTHS of the YEAR. Text selected by R. PIGOT; Illustrations on Wood from Original Designs J. LEIGHTON, F.S.A. 4to. 42s.

SACRED and LEGENDARY ART. By MRS. JAMESON.

Legends of the Saints and Martyrs. New Edition, with 19 Etchings and 187 Woodcuts. 2 vols. square crown 8vo. 31s. 6d.

Legends of the Monastic Orders. New Edition, with 11 Etchings and 88 Woodcuts. 1 vol. square crown 8vo. 21s.

Legends of the Madonna. New Edition, with 27 Etchings and 165 Woodcuts. 1 vol. square crown 8vo. 21s.

The History of Our Lord, with that of his Types and Precursors. Completed by Lady EASTLAKE. Revised Edition, with 31 Etchings and 281 Woodcuts. 2 vols. square crown 8vo. 42s.

B

DAEDALUS; or, the Causes and Principles of the Excellence of Greek Sculpture. By EDWARD FALKENER, Member of the Academy of Bologna, and of the Archæological Institutes of Rome and Berlin. With Woodcuts, Photographs, and Chromolithographs. Royal 8vo. 42s. ;

FALKENER'S MUSEUM of CLASSICAL ANTIQUITIES; a Series of Essays on Ancient Art. New Edition, complete in One Volume, with many Illustrations. Royal 8vo. price 42s.

The Useful Arts, Manufactures, &c.

HISTORY of the GOTHIC REVIVAL; an Attempt to shew how far the taste for Mediæval Architecture was retained in England during the last two centuries, and has been re-developed in the present. By C. L. EASTLAKE, Architect. With 48 Illustrations Imperial 8vo. 31s. 6d.

GWILT'S ENCYCLOPÆDIA of ARCHITECTURE, with above 1,600 Engravings on Wood. Fifth Edition, revised and enlarged by WYATT PAPWORTH. 8vo. 52s. 6d.

A MANUAL of ARCHITECTURE: being a Concise History and Explanation of the principal Styles of European Architecture. Ancient, Mediæval, and Renaissance; with a Glossary of Technical Terms. By THOMAS MITCHELL. Crown 8vo. with 150 Woodcuts, 10s. 6d.

HINTS on HOUSEHOLD TASTE in FURNITURE, UPHOLSTERY, and other Details. By CHARLES L. EASTLAKE, Architect. New Edition, with about 90 Illustrations. Square crown 8vo. 14s.

PRINCIPLES of MECHANISM, designed for the Use of Students in the Universities, and for Engineering Students generally. By R. WILLIS, M.A. F.R.S. &c. Jacksonian Professor in the University of Cambridge. Second Edition, enlarged; with 374 Woodcuts. 8vo. 18s.

GEOMETRIC TURNING: comprising a Description of Plant's New Geometric Chuck, with directions for its use, and a series of Patterns cut by it, with Explanations. By H. S. SAVORY. With numerous Woodcuts. 8vo. 21s.

LATHES and TURNING, Simple, Mechanical, and Ornamental. By W. HENRY NORTHCOTT. With about 240 Illustrations. 8vo. 18s.

PERSPECTIVE; or, the Art of Drawing what One Sees. Explained and adapted to the use of those Sketching from Nature. By Lieut. W. H. COLLINS, R.E. F.R.A.S. With 37 Woodcuts. Crown 8vo. price 5s.

INDUSTRIAL CHEMISTRY; a Manual for Manufacturers and for use in Colleges or Technical Schools. Being a Translation of Professors Stohmann and Engler's German Edition of PAYEN'S *Précis de Chimie Industrielle*, by Dr. J. D. BARRY. Edited and supplemented by B. H. PAUL, Ph.D. 8vo. with Plates and Woodcuts.   [*In the press.*

URE'S DICTIONARY of ARTS, MANUFACTURES, and MINES. Sixth Edition, rewritten and enlarged by ROBERT HUNT, F.R.S. assisted by numerous Contributors eminent in Science and the Arts, and familiar with Manufactures. With above 2,000 Woodcuts. 3 vols. medium 8vo. £4 14s. 6d.

HANDBOOK of PRACTICAL TELEGRAPHY. By R. S. CULLEY Memb. Inst. C.E. Engineer-in-Chief of Telegraphs to the Post Office. Sixth Edition, with 144 Woodcuts and 5 Plates. 8vo. price 16s.

The ENGINEER'S HANDBOOK; explaining the Principles which should guide the Young Engineer in the Construction of Machinery, with the necessary Rules, Proportions, and Tables. By C. S. LOWNDES. Post 8vo. 5s.

ENCYCLOPÆDIA of CIVIL ENGINEERING, Historical, Theoretical, and Practical. By E. CRESY, C.E. With above 3,000 Woodcuts. 8vo. 42s.

The STRAINS IN TRUSSES computed by means of Diagrams ; with 20 Examples drawn to Scale. By F. A. RANKEN, M.A. C.E. With 35 Diagrams. Square crown 8vo. 6s. 6d.

TREATISE on MILLS and MILLWORK. By Sir W. FAIRBAIRN, Bart. F.R.S. New Edition, with 18 Plates and 322 Woodcuts, 2 vols. 8vo. 32s.

USEFUL INFORMATION for ENGINEERS. By Sir W. FAIRBAIRN, Bart. F.R.S. Revised Edition, with Illustrations. 3 vols. crown 8vo. price 31s. 6d.

The APPLICATION of CAST and WROUGHT IRON to Building Purposes. By Sir W. FAIRBAIRN, Bart. F.R.S. Fourth Edition, enlarged ; with 6 Plates and 118 Woodcuts. 8vo. price 16s.

GUNS and STEEL ; Miscellaneous Papers on Mechanical Subjects. By Sir JOSEPH WHITWORTH, Bart. C.E. Royal 8vo. with Illustrations, 7s. 6d.

A TREATISE on the STEAM ENGINE, in its various Applications to Mines, Mills, Steam Navigation, Railways, and Agriculture. By J. BOURNE, C.E. Eighth Edition ; with Portrait, 37 Plates, and 546 Woodcuts. 4to. 42s.

CATECHISM of the STEAM ENGINE, in its various Applications to Mines, Mills, Steam Navigation, Railways, and Agriculture. By the same Author. With 89 Woodcuts. Fcp. 8vo. 6s.

HANDBOOK of the STEAM ENGINE. By the same Author, forming a KEY to the Catechism of the Steam Engine, with 67 Woodcuts. Fcp. 9s.

BOURNE'S RECENT IMPROVEMENTS in the STEAM ENGINE in its various applications to Mines, Mills, Steam Navigation, Railways, and Agriculture. By JOHN BOURNE, C.E. New Edition, with 124 Woodcuts. Fcp. 8vo. 6s.

HANDBOOK to the MINERALOGY of CORNWALL and DEVON ; with Instructions for their Discrimination, and copious Tablets of Localities. By J. H. COLLINS, F.G.S. With 10 Plates. 8vo. 6s.

PRACTICAL TREATISE on METALLURGY, adapted from the last German Edition of Professor KERL'S *Metallurgy* by W. CROOKES, F.R.S. &c. and E. BÖHRIG, Ph.D. M.E. With 625 Woodcuts. 3 vols. 8vo. price £4 19s.

MITCHELL'S MANUAL of PRACTICAL ASSAYING. Fourth Edition, for the most part rewritten, with all the recent Discoveries incorporated, by W. CROOKES, F.R.S. With 199 Woodcuts. 8vo. 31s. 6d.

LOUDON'S ENCYCLOPÆDIA of AGRICULTURE: comprising the Laying-out, Improvement, and Management of Landed Property, and the Cultivation and Economy of Agricultural Produce. With 1,100 Woodcuts. 8vo. 21s.

Loudon's Encyclopædia of Gardening: comprising the Theory and Practice of Horticulture, Floriculture, Arboriculture, and Landscape Gardening. With 1,000 Woodcuts. 8vo. 21s.

Religious and *Moral Works.*

SERMONS; Including Two Sermons on the Interpretation of Prophecy, and an Essay on the Right Interpretation and Understanding of the Scriptures. By the late Rev. THOMAS ARNOLD, D.D. 3 vols. 8vo. price 24s.

CHRISTIAN LIFE, its COURSE, its HINDRANCES, and its HELPS; Sermons preached mostly in the Chapel of Rugby School. By the late Rev. THOMAS ARNOLD, D.D. 8vo. 7s. 6d.

CHRISTIAN LIFE, its HOPES, its FEARS, and its CLOSE; Sermons preached mostly in the Chapel of Rugby School. By the late Rev. THOMAS ARNOLD, D.D. 8vo. 7s. 6d.

SERMONS chiefly on the **INTERPRETATION** of **SCRIPTURE.** By the late Rev. THOMAS ARNOLD, D.D. 8vo. price 7s. 6d.

SERMONS preached in the Chapel of Rugby School; with an Address before Confirmation. By the late Rev. THOMAS ARNOLD, D.D. Fcp. 8vo. price 3s. 6d.

THREE ESSAYS on RELIGION: Nature; the Utility of Religion; Theism. By JOHN STUART MILL. 8vo. price 10s. 6d.

INTRODUCTION to the SCIENCE of RELIGION. Four Lectures delivered at the Royal Institution; with Two Essays on False Analogies and the Philosophy of Mythology. By F. MAX MÜLLER, M.A. Crown 8vo. 10s. 6d.

SUPERNATURAL RELIGION; an Inquiry into the Reality of Divine Revelation. Third Edition, revised. 2 vols. 8vo. 24s.

ESSAYS on the HISTORY of the CHRISTIAN RELIGION. By JOHN Earl RUSSELL. Cabinet Edition, revised. Fcp. 8vo. price 3s. 6d.

The **NEW BIBLE COMMENTARY,** by Bishops and other Clergy of the Anglican Church, critically examined by the Right Rev. J. W. COLENSO, D.D. Bishop of Natal. 8vo. price 25s.

REASONS of FAITH; or, the ORDER of the Christian Argument Developed and Explained. By the Rev. G. S. DREW, M.A. Second Edition, revised and enlarged. Fcp. 8vo. price 6s.

SYNONYMS of the OLD TESTAMENT, their BEARING on CHRIS-TIAN FAITH and PRACTICE. By the Rev. R. B. GIRDLESTONE, M.A. 8vo. 15s.

An **INTRODUCTION to the THEOLOGY of the CHURCH of** ENGLAND, in an Exposition of the Thirty-nine Articles. By the Rev. T. P. BOULTBEE, LL.D. New Edition, Fcp. 8vo. price 6s.

SERMONS for the TIMES preached in St. Paul's Cathedral and elsewhere. By the Rev. THOMAS GRIFFITH, M.A. Crown 8vo. 6s.

An **EXPOSITION of the 39 ARTICLES,** Historical and Doctrinal. By E. HAROLD BROWNE, D.D. Lord Bishop of Winchester. New Edit. 8vo. 16s.

The **LIFE and EPISTLES of ST. PAUL.** By the Rev. W. J. CONYBEARE, M.A., and the Very Rev. J. S. HOWSON, D.D. Dean of Chester :—
LIBRARY EDITION, with all the Original Illustrations, Maps, Landscapes on Steel, Woodcuts, &c. 2 vols. 4to. 48s.
INTERMEDIATE EDITION, with a Selection of Maps, Plates, and Woodcuts. 2 vols. square crown 8vo. 21s.
STUDENT'S EDITION, revised and condensed, with 46 Illustrations and Maps. 1 vol. crown 8vo. price 9s.

The **VOYAGE** and **SHIPWRECK** of **ST. PAUL**; with Dissertations on the Life and Writings of St. Luke and the Ships and Navigation of the Ancients. By JAMES SMITH, F.R.S. Third Edition. Crown 8vo. 10s. 6d.

COMMENTARY on the **EPISTLE** to the **ROMANS**. By the Rev. W. A. O'CONOR, B.A. Crown 8vo. price 3s. 6d.

The **EPISTLE** to the **HEBREWS**; with Analytical Introduction and Notes. By the Rev. W. A. O'CONOR, B.A. Crown 8vo. price 4s. 6d.

A **CRITICAL** and **GRAMMATICAL COMMENTARY** on **ST. PAUL'S** Epistles. By C. J. ELLICOTT, D.D. Lord Bishop of Gloucester and Bristol. 8vo.

Galatians, Fourth Edition, 8s. 6d.

Ephesians, Fourth Edition, 8s. 6d.

Pastoral Epistles, Fourth Edition, 10s. 6d.

Philippians, Colossians, and Philemon, Third Edition, 10s. 6d.

Thessalonians, Third Edition, 7s. 6d.

HISTORICAL LECTURES on the **LIFE** of **OUR LORD**. By C. J. ELLICOTT, D.D. Bishop of Gloucester and Bristol. Fifth Edition. 8vo. 12s.

EVIDENCE of the **TRUTH** of the **CHRISTIAN RELIGION** derived from the Literal Fulfilment of Prophecy. By ALEXANDER KEITH, D.D. 37th Edition, with Plates, in square 8vo. 12s. 6d.; 39th Edition, in post 8vo. 6s.

The **HISTORY** and **LITERATURE** of the **ISRAELITES**, according to the Old Testament and the Apocrypha. By C. DE ROTHSCHILD and A. DE ROTHSCHILD. Second Edition, revised. 2 vols. post 8vo. with Two Maps, price 12s. 6d. Abridged Edition, in 1 vol. fcp. 8vo. price 3s. 6d.

An **INTRODUCTION** to the **STUDY** of the **NEW TESTAMENT**, Critical, Exegetical, and Theological. By the Rev. S. DAVIDSON, D.D. LL.D. 2 vols. 8vo. 30s.

HISTORY of **ISRAEL**. By H. EWALD, Prof. of the Univ. of Göttingen. Translated by J. E. CARPENTER, M.A., with a Preface by RUSSELL MARTINEAU, M.A. 5 vols. 8vo. 63s.

The **TREASURY** of **BIBLE KNOWLEDGE**; being a Dictionary of the Books, Persons, Places, Events, and other matters of which mention is made in Holy Scripture. By Rev. J. AYRE, M.A. With Maps, 16 Plates, and numerous Woodcuts. Fcp. 8vo. price 6s. cloth, or 10s. neatly bound in calf.

LECTURES on the **PENTATEUCH** and the **MOABITE STONE**. By the Right Rev. J. W. COLENSO, D.D. Bishop of Natal. 8vo. 12s.

The **PENTATEUCH** and **BOOK** of **JOSHUA CRITICALLY EXAMINED**. By the Right Rev. J. W. COLENSO, D.D. Bishop of Natal. Crown 8vo. 6s.

THOUGHTS for the **AGE**. By ELIZABETH M. SEWELL, Author of 'Amy Herbert,' &c. New Edition, revised. Fcp. 8vo. price 3s. 6d.

PASSING THOUGHTS on **RELIGION**. By Miss SEWELL. Fcp. 8vo. 3s. 6d.

SELF-EXAMINATION before **CONFIRMATION**. By Miss SEWELL. 32mo. price 1s. 6d.

READINGS for a **MONTH** preparatory to **CONFIRMATION**, from Writers of the Early and English Church. By Miss SEWELL. Fcp. 4s.

READINGS for EVERY DAY in LENT, compiled from the Writings of Bishop JEREMY TAYLOR. By Miss SEWELL. Fcp. 5s.

PREPARATION for the HOLY COMMUNION ; the Devotions chiefly from the Works of JEREMY TAYLOR. By Miss SEWELL. 32mo. 3s.

THOUGHTS for the HOLY WEEK for Young Persons. By Miss SEWELL. New Edition. Fcp. 8vo. 2s.

PRINCIPLES of EDUCATION Drawn from Nature and Revelation, and applied to Female Education in the Upper Classes. By Miss SEWELL. 2 vols. fcp. 8vo. 12s. 6d.

LYRA GERMANICA, Hymns translated from the German by Miss C. WINKWORTH. FIRST and SECOND SERIES, price 3s. 6d. each.

SPIRITUAL SONGS for the SUNDAYS and HOLIDAYS throughout the Year. By J. S. B. MONSELL, LL.D. Fcp. 8vo. 4s. 6d.

ENDEAVOURS after the CHRISTIAN LIFE: Discourses. By the Rev. J. MARTINEAU, LL.D. Fifth Edition, carefully revised. Crown 8vo. 7s. 6d.

HYMNS of PRAISE and PRAYER, collected and edited by the Rev. J. MARTINEAU, LL.D. Crown 8vo. 4s. 6d.

WHATELY'S INTRODUCTORY LESSONS on the CHRISTIAN Evidences. 18mo. 6d.

BISHOP JEREMY TAYLOR'S ENTIRE WORKS. With Life by BISHOP HEBER. Revised and corrected by the Rev. C. P. EDEN. Complete in Ten Volumes, 8vo. cloth, price £5. 5s.

Travels, Voyages, &c.

EIGHT YEARS in CEYLON. By Sir SAMUEL W. BAKER, M.A. F.R.G.S. New Edition, with Illustrations engraved on Wood, by G. Pearson. Crown 8vo. 7s. 6d.

The RIFLE and the HOUND in CEYLON. By Sir SAMUEL W. BAKER, M.A. F.R.G.S. New Edition, with Illustrations engraved on Wood by G. Pearson. Crown 8vo. 7s. 6d.

MEETING the SUN; a Journey all round the World through Egypt, China, Japan, and California. By WILLIAM SIMPSON, F.R.G.S. With 48 Heliotypes and Wood Engravings from Drawings by the Author. Medium 8vo. 24s.

UNTRODDEN PEAKS and UNFREQUENTED VALLEYS; a Midsummer Ramble among the Dolomites. By AMELIA B. EDWARDS. With a Map and 27 Wood Engravings. Medium 8vo. 21s.

The DOLOMITE MOUNTAINS; Excursions through Tyrol, Carinthia, Carniola, and Friuli, 1861-1863. By J. GILBERT and G. C. CHURCHILL, F.R.G.S. With numerous Illustrations. Square crown 8vo. 21s.

The VALLEYS of TIROL; their Traditions and Customs, and how to Visit them. By Miss R. H. BUSK, Author of 'The Folk-Lore of Rome,' &c. With Maps and Frontispiece. Crown 8vo. 12s. 6d.

HOURS of EXERCISE in the ALPS. By JOHN TYNDALL, LL.D.
D.C.L. F.R.S. Third Edition, with 7 Woodcuts by E. Whymper. Crown 8vo.
price 12s. 6d.

The ALPINE CLUB MAP of SWITZERLAND, with parts of the
Neighbouring Countries, on the Scale of Four Miles to an Inch. Edited by R.
C. NICHOLS, F.S.A. F.R.G.S. In Four Sheets, price 42s. or mounted in a case,
52s. 6d. Each Sheet may be had separately, price 12s. or mounted in a case, 15s.

MAP of the CHAIN of MONT BLANC, from an Actual Survey in
1863–1864. By ADAMS-REILLY, F.R.G.S. M.A.C. Published under the Authority of the Alpine Club. In Chromolithography on extra stout drawing-
paper 28in. × 17in. price 10s. or mounted on canvas in a folding case, 12s. 6d.

TRAVELS in the CENTRAL CAUCASUS and BASHAN. Including
Visits to Ararat and Tabreez and Ascents of Kazbek and Elbruz. By D. W.
FRESHFIELD. Square crown 8vo. with Maps, &c. 18s.

PAU and the PYRENEES. By Count HENRY RUSSELL, Member of
the Alpine Club, &c. With 2 Maps. Fcp. 8vo. price 5s.

HOW to SEE NORWAY. By Captain J. R. CAMPBELL. With Map
and 5 Woodcuts. Fcp. 8vo. price 5s.

GUIDE to the PYRENEES, for the use of Mountaineers. By
CHARLES PACKE. With Map and Illustrations. Crown 8vo. 7s. 6d.

The ALPINE GUIDE. By JOHN BALL, M.R.I.A. late President of
the Alpine Club. 3 vols. post 8vo. Thoroughly Revised Editions, with Maps
and Illustrations:—I. *Western Alps,* 6s. 6d. II. *Central Alps,* 7s. 6d. III.
Eastern Alps, 10s. 6d.

Introduction on Alpine Travelling in General, and on the Geology
of the Alps, price 1s. Each of the Three Volumes or Parts of the *Alpine Guide*
may be had with this INTRODUCTION prefixed, price 1s. extra.

VISITS to REMARKABLE PLACES: Old Halls, Battle-Fields, and
Stones Illustrative of Striking Passages in English History and Poetry. By
WILLIAM HOWITT. 2 vols. square crown 8vo. with Woodcuts, 25s.

The RURAL LIFE of ENGLAND. By the same Author. With
Woodcuts by Bewick and Williams. Medium 8vo. 12s. 6d.

Works of *Fiction.*

WHISPERS from FAIRYLAND. By the Rt. Hon. E. H. KNATCH-
BULL-HUGESSEN, M.P. Author of 'Stories for my Children,' 'Moonshine,'
'Queer Folk,' &c. With Nine Illustrations from Original Designs engraved on
Wood by G. Pearson. Crown 8vo. price 6s.

ELENA, an Italian Tale. By L. N. COMYN, Author of 'Atherstone
Priory.' 2 vols. post 8vo. 14s.

CENTULLE, a Tale of Pau. By DENYS SHYNE LAWLOR, Author of
'Pilgrimages in the Pyrenees and Landes.' Post 8vo. 10s. 6d.

LADY WILLOUGHBY'S DIARY, 1635—1663; Charles the First, the
Protectorate, and the Restoration. Reproduced in the Style of the Period to
which the Diary relates. Crown 8vo. price 7s. 6d.

TALES of the TEUTONIC LANDS. By the Rev. G. W. Cox, M.A. and E. H. JONES. Crown 8vo. 10s. 6d.

The FOLK-LORE of ROME, collected by Word of Mouth from the People. By Miss R. H. BUSK, Author of 'Patrañas,' &c. Crown 8vo. 12s. 6d.

NOVELS and TALES. By the Right Hon. B. DISRAELI, M.P. Cabinet Edition, complete in Ten Volumes, crown 8vo. price £3.

LOTHAIR, 6s.	HENRIETTA TEMPLE, 6s.
CONINGSBY, 6s.	CONTARINI FLEMING, &c. 6s.
SYBIL, 6s.	ALROY, IXION, &c. 6s.
TANCRED, 6s.	The YOUNG DUKE, &c. 6s.
VENETIA, 6s.	VIVIAN GREY, 6s.

The MODERN NOVELIST'S LIBRARY. Each Work, in crown 8vo. complete in a Single Volume :—

ATHERSTONE PRIORY, 2s. boards ; 2s. 6d. cloth.
MELVILLE'S GLADIATORS, 2s boards ; 2s. 6d. cloth.
———— GOOD FOR NOTHING, 2s. boards ; 2s. 6d. cloth.
———— HOLMBY HOUSE, 2s. boards ; 2s. 6d. cloth.
———— INTERPRETER, 2s. boards ; 2s. 6d. cloth.
———— KATE COVENTRY, 2s. boards ; 2s. 6d. cloth.
———— QUEEN'S MARIES, 2s. boards ; 2s. 6d. cloth.
———— DIGBY GRAND, 2s. boards ; 2s. 6d. cloth.
———— GENERAL BOUNCE, 2s. boards ; 2s. 6d. cloth.
TROLLOPE'S WARDEN, 1s. 6d. boards ; 2s. cloth.
————BARCHESTER TOWERS, 2s. boards ; 2s. 6d. cloth.
BRAMLEY-MOORE'S SIX SISTERS of the VALLEYS, 2s. boards ; 2s. 6d. cloth.
The BURGOMASTER'S FAMILY, 2s. boards ; 2s. 6d. cloth.

CABINET EDITION of STORIES and TALES by Miss SEWELL :—

AMY HERBERT, 2s. 6d.	IVORS, 2s. 6d.
GERTRUDE, 2s. 6d.	KATHARINE ASHTON, 2s. 6d.
The EARL'S DAUGHTER, 2s. 6d.	MARGARET PERCIVAL, 3s. 6d.
EXPERIENCE of LIFE, 2s. 6d.	LANETON PARSONAGE, 3s. 6d.
CLEVE HALL, 2s. 6d.	URSULA, 3s. 6d.

CYLLENE ; or, the Fall of Paganism. By HENRY SNEYD, M.A. University College, Oxford. 2 vols. post 8vo. price 14s.

BECKER'S GALLUS ; or, Roman Scenes of the Time of Augustus : with Notes and Excursuses. New Edition. Post 8vo. 7s. 6d.

BECKER'S CHARICLES ; a Tale illustrative of Private Life among the Ancient Greeks : with Notes and Excursuses. New Edition. Post 8vo. 7s. 6d.

TALES of ANCIENT GREECE. By GEORGE W. COX, M.A. late Scholar of Trin. Coll. Oxon. Crown 8vo. price 6s. 6d.

Poetry and The Drama.

FAUST : a Dramatic Poem. By GOETHE. Translated into English Prose, with Notes, by A. HAYWARD. Ninth Edition. Fcp. 8vo. price 3s.

MOORE'S IRISH MELODIES, Maclise's Edition, with 161 Steel Plates from Original Drawings. Super-royal 8vo. 31s. 6d.

Miniature Edition of Moore's Irish Melodies, with Maclise's Designs (as above) reduced in Lithography. Imp. 16mo. 10s. 6d.

BALLADS and **LYRICS** of **OLD FRANCE**; with other Poems. By A. LANG, Fellow of Merton College, Oxford. Square fcp. 8vo. price 5s.

MOORE'S LALLA ROOKH. Tenniel's Edition, with 68 Wood Engravings from Original Drawings and other Illustrations. Fcp. 4to. 21s.

SOUTHEY'S POETICAL WORKS, with the Author's last Corrections and copyright Additions. Medium 8vo. with Portrait and Vignette, 14s.

LAYS of **ANCIENT ROME**; with **IVRY** and the **ARMADA.** By the Right Hon. Lord MACAULAY. 16mo. 3s. 6d.

LORD MACAULAY'S LAYS of **ANCIENT ROME.** With 90 Illustrations on Wood, from the Antique, from Drawings by G. SCHARF. Fcp. 4to. 21s.

Miniature Edition of Lord Macaulay's Lays of Ancient Rome, with the Illustrations (as above) reduced in Lithography. Imp. 16mo. 10s. 6d.

The ÆNEID of VIRGIL Translated into English Verse. By JOHN CONINGTON, M.A. New Edition. Crown 8vo. 9s.

HORATII OPERA. Library Edition, with Marginal References and English Notes. Edited by the Rev. J. E. YONGE. 8vo. 21s.

The LYCIDAS and **EPITAPHIUM DAMONIS of MILTON.** Edited, with Notes and Introduction (including a Reprint of the rare Latin Version of the Lycidas, by W. Hogg, 1694), by C. S. JERRAM, M.A. Crown 8vo. 3s. 6d.

BOWDLER'S FAMILY SHAKSPEARE, cheaper Genuine Editions. Medium 8vo. large type, with 36 WOODCUTS, price 14s. Cabinet Edition, with the same ILLUSTRATIONS, 6 vols. fcp. 8vo. price 21s.

POEMS. By JEAN INGELOW. 2 vols. fcp. 8vo. price 10s.
FIRST SERIES, containing ' DIVIDED,' ' The STAR'S MONUMENT,' &c. Sixteenth Thousand. Fcp. 8vo. price 5s.
SECOND SERIES, ' A STORY of DOOM,' ' GLADYS and her ISLAND,' &c. Fifth Thousand. Fcp. 8vo. price 5s.

POEMS by Jean Ingelow. FIRST SERIES, with nearly 100 Illustrations, engraved on Wood by Dalziel Brothers. Fcp. 4to. 21s.

Rural Sports, &c.

DOWN the **ROAD**; Or, Reminiscences of a Gentleman Coachman. By C. T. S. BIRCH REYNARDSON. With Twelve Chromolithographic Illustrations from Original Paintings by H. Alken. Medium 8vo. [*Nearly ready.*

The DEAD SHOT; or, Sportsman's Complete Guide: a Treatise on the Use of the Gun, Dog-breaking, Pigeon-shooting, &c. By MARKSMAN. Revised Edition. Fcp. 8vo. with Plates, 5s.

ENCYCLOPÆDIA of RURAL SPORTS; a complete Account, Historical, Practical, and Descriptive, of Hunting, Shooting, Fishing, Racing, and all other Rural and Athletic Sports and Pastimes. By D. P. BLAINE. With above 600 Woodcuts (20 from Designs by JOHN LEECH). 8vo. 21s.

The **FLY-FISHER'S ENTOMOLOGY.** By ALFRED RONALDS. With coloured Representations of the Natural and Artificial Insect. Sixth Edition, with 20 coloured Plates. 8vo. 14s.

A **BOOK on ANGLING**; a complete Treatise on the Art of Angling in every branch. By FRANCIS FRANCIS. New Edition, with Portrait and 15 other Plates, plain and coloured. Post 8vo. 15s.

WILCOCKS'S SEA-FISHERMAN; comprising the Chief Methods of Hook and Line Fishing, a Glance at Nets, and Remarks on Boats and Boating. New Edition, with 80 Woodcuts. Post 8vo. 12s. 6d.

HORSES and STABLES. By Colonel F. FITZWYGRAM, XV. the King's Hussars. With Twenty-four Plates of Illustrations, containing very numerous Figures engraved on Wood. 8vo. 10s. 6d.

The **HORSE'S FOOT, and HOW to KEEP it SOUND.** By W. MILES, Esq. Ninth Edition, with Illustrations. Imperial 8vo. 12s. 6d.

A **PLAIN TREATISE on HORSE-SHOEING.** By W. MILES, Esq. Sixth Edition. Post 8vo. with Illustrations, 2s. 6d.

STABLES and STABLE-FITTINGS. By W. MILES, ESQ. Imp. 8vo. with 13 Plates, 15s.

REMARKS on HORSES' TEETH, addressed to Purchasers. By W. MILES, Esq. Post 8vo. 1s. 6d.

A **TREATISE on HORSE-SHOEING and LAMENESS.** By JOSEPH GAMGEE, Veterinary Surgeon. 8vo. with 55 Woodcuts, price 10s. 6d.

The **HORSE**: with a Treatise on Draught. By WILLIAM YOUATT. New Edition, revised and enlarged. 8vo. with numerous Woodcuts, 12s. 6d.

The **DOG.** By WILLIAM YOUATT. 8vo. with numerous Woodcuts, 6s.

The **DOG in HEALTH and DISEASE.** By STONEHENGE. With 70 Wood Engravings. Square crown 8vo. 7s. 6d.

The **GREYHOUND.** By STONEHENGE. Revised Edition, with 24 Portraits of Greyhounds. Square crown 8vo. 10s. 6d.

The **OX**; his Diseases and their Treatment: with an Essay on Parturition in the Cow. By J. R. DOBSON. Crown 8vo. with Illustrations, 7s. 6d.

Works of Utility and General Information.

The **THEORY and PRACTICE of BANKING.** By H. D. MACLEOD, M.A. Barrister-at-Law. Second Edition, entirely remodelled. 2 vols. 8vo. 30s.

M'CULLOCH'S DICTIONARY, Practical, Theoretical, and Historical, of Commerce and Commercial Navigation. New and revised Edition. 8vo. 63s.

The **CABINET LAWYER**; a Popular Digest of the Laws of England, Civil, Criminal, and Constitutional: intended for Practical Use and General Information. Twenty-fourth Edition. Fcp. 8vo. price 9s.

BLACKSTONE ECONOMISED, a Compendium of the Laws of England to the Present time, in Four Books, each embracing the Legal Principles and Practical Information contained in their respective volumes of Blackstone, supplemented by Subsequent Statutory Enactments, Important Legal Decisions, &c. By D. M. AIRD, Barrister-at-Law. Revised Edition. Post 8vo. 7s. 6d.

PEWTNER'S COMPREHENSIVE SPECIFIER; a Guide to the Practical Specification of every kind of Building-Artificers' Work, with Forms of Conditions and Agreements. Edited by W. YOUNG. Crown 8vo. 6s.

COLLIERIES and COLLIERS; a Handbook of the Law and Leading Cases relating thereto. By J. C. FOWLER. Third Edition. Fcp. 8vo. 7s. 6d.

HINTS to MOTHERS on the MANAGEMENT of their HEALTH during the Period of Pregnancy and in the Lying-in Room. By the late THOMAS BULL, M.D. Fcp. 8vo. 5s.

The MATERNAL MANAGEMENT of CHILDREN in HEALTH and Disease. By the late THOMAS BULL, M.D. Fcp. 8vo. 5s.

The THEORY of the MODERN SCIENTIFIC GAME of WHIST. By WILLIAM POLE, F.R.S. Fifth Edition, enlarged. Fcp. 8vo. 2s. 6d.

CHESS OPENINGS. By F. W. LONGMAN, Balliol College, Oxford. Second Edition revised. Fcp. 8vo. 2s. 6d.

THREE HUNDRED ORIGINAL CHESS PROBLEMS and STUDIES. By JAMES PIERCE, M.A. and W. T. PIERCE. With numerous Diagrams. Square fcp. 8vo. 7s. 6d. SUPPLEMENT, price 2s. 6d.

A PRACTICAL TREATISE on BREWING; with Formulæ for Public Brewers, and Instructions for Private Families. By W. BLACK. 8vo. 10s. 6d.

MODERN COOKERY for PRIVATE FAMILIES, reduced to a System of Easy Practice in a Series of carefully-tested Receipts. By ELIZA ACTON. Newly revised and enlarged; with 8 Plates and 150 Woodcuts. Fcp. 8vo. 6s.

MAUNDER'S TREASURY of KNOWLEDGE and LIBRARY of Reference; comprising an English Dictionary and Grammar, Universal Gazetteer, Classical Dictionary, Chronology, Law Dictionary, a synopsis of the Peerage useful Tables, &c. Revised Edition. Fcp. 8vo. 6s. cloth, or 10s. calf.

Knowledge for the *Young.*

The STEPPING-STONE to KNOWLEDGE; or upwards of 700 Questions and Answers on Miscellaneous Subjects, adapted to the capacity of Infant minds. 18mo. 1s.

SECOND SERIES of the STEPPING-STONE to KNOWLEDGE: Containing upwards of 800 Questions and Answers on Miscellaneous Subjects not contained in the FIRST SERIES. 18mo. 1s.

The STEPPING-STONE to GEOGRAPHY: Containing several Hundred Questions and Answers on Geographical Subjects. 18mo. 1s

The **STEPPING-STONE to ENGLISH HISTORY**; Questions and Answers on the History of England. 18mo. 1s.

The **STEPPING-STONE to BIBLE KNOWLEDGE**; Questions and Answers on the Old and New Testaments. 18mo. 1s.

The **STEPPING-STONE to BIOGRAPHY**; Questions and Answers on the Lives of Eminent Men and Women. 18mo. 1s.

The **STEPPING-STONE to IRISH HISTORY**: Containing several Hundred Questions and Answers on the History of Ireland. 18mo. 1s.

The **STEPPING-STONE to FRENCH HISTORY**: Containing several Hundred Questions and Answers on the History of France. 18mo. 1s.

The **STEPPING-STONE to ROMAN HISTORY**: Containing several Hundred Questions and Answers on the History of Rome. 18mo. 1s.

The **STEPPING-STONE to GRECIAN HISTORY**: Containing several Hundred Questions and Answers on the History of Greece. 18mo. 1s.

The **STEPPING-STONE to ENGLISH GRAMMAR**: Containing several Hundred Questions and Answers on English Grammar. 18mo. 1s.

The **STEPPING-STONE to FRENCH PRONUNCIATION and CON**-VERSATION : Containing several Hundred Questions and Answers. 18mo. 1s.

The **STEPPING-STONE to ASTRONOMY**: Containing several Hundred familiar Questions and Answers on the Earth and the Solar and Stellar Systems. 18mo. 1s.

The **STEPPING-STONE to MUSIC**: Containing several Hundred Questions on the Science ; also a short History of Music. 18mo. 1s.

The **STEPPING-STONE to NATURAL HISTORY**: VERTEBRATE OR BACK-BONED ANIMALS. PART I. *Mammalia*; PART II. *Birds, Reptiles, Fishes.* 18mo. 1s. each Part.

THE **STEPPING-STONE to ARCHITECTURE**; Questions and Answers explaining the Principles and Progress of Architecture from the Earliest Times. With 100 Woodcuts. 18mo. 1s.

INDEX.

Spottiswoode & Co., Printers, New-street Square, London.

www.ingramcontent.com/pod-product-compliance
Lightning Source LLC
Chambersburg PA
CBHW020449270326
41926CB00008B/541